THI

Ge … Woudhuysen

TWELFTH NIGHT, OR WHAT YOU WILL

THE ARDEN SHAKESPEARE

ALL'S WELL THAT ENDS WELL	edited by G.K. Hunter*
ANTONY AND CLEOPATRA	edited by John Wilders
AS YOU LIKE IT	edited by Juliet Dusinberre
THE COMEDY OF ERRORS	edited by R.A. Foakes*
CORIOLANUS	edited by Philip Brockbank*
CYMBELINE	edited by J.M. Nosworthy*
DOUBLE FALSEHOOD	edited by Brean Hammond
HAMLET	edited by Ann Thompson and Neil Taylor
JULIUS CAESAR	edited by David Daniell
KING HENRY IV Part 1	edited by David Scott Kastan
KING HENRY IV Part 2	edited by A.R. Humphreys*
KING HENRY V	edited by T.W. Craik
KING HENRY VI Part 1	edited by Edward Burns
KING HENRY VI Part 2	edited by Ronald Knowles
KING HENRY VI Part 3	edited by John D. Cox and Eric Rasmussen
KING HENRY VIII	edited by Gordon McMullan
KING JOHN	edited by E.A.J. Honigmann*
KING LEAR	edited by R.A. Foakes
KING RICHARD II	edited by Charles Forker
KING RICHARD III	edited by James R. Siemon
LOVE'S LABOUR'S LOST	edited by H.R. Woudhuysen
MACBETH	edited by Kenneth Muir*
MEASURE FOR MEASURE	edited by J.W. Lever*
THE MERCHANT OF VENICE	edited by John Drakakis
THE MERRY WIVES OF WINDSOR	edited by Giorgio Melchiori
A MIDSUMMER NIGHT'S DREAM	edited by Harold F. Brooks*
MUCH ADO ABOUT NOTHING	edited by Claire McEachern
OTHELLO	edited by E.A.J. Honigmann
PERICLES	edited by Suzanne Gossett
SHAKESPEARE'S POEMS	edited by Katherine Duncan-Jones and H.R. Woudhuysen
ROMEO AND JULIET	edited by Brian Gibbons*
SHAKESPEARE'S SONNETS	edited by Katherine Duncan-Jones
THE TAMING OF THE SHREW	edited by Barbara Hodgdon
THE TEMPEST	edited by Virginia Mason Vaughan and Alden T. Vaughan
TIMON OF ATHENS	edited by Anthony B. Dawson and Gretchen E. Minton
TITUS ANDRONICUS	edited by Jonathan Bate
TROILUS AND CRESSIDA	edited by David Bevington
TWELFTH NIGHT	edited by Keir Elam
THE TWO GENTLEMEN OF VERONA	edited by William C. Carroll
THE TWO NOBLE KINSMEN	edited by Lois Potter
THE WINTER'S TALE	edited by John Pitcher

* Second series

THE ARDEN SHAKESPEARE

TWELFTH NIGHT, OR WHAT YOU WILL

Edited by

KEIR ELAM

BLOOMSBURY

LONDON • NEW DELHI • NEW YORK • SYDNEY

Bloomsbury Arden Shakespeare
An imprint of Bloomsbury Publishing Plc

50 Bedford Square
London
WC1B 3DP
UK

1385 Broadway
New York
NY 10018
USA

www.bloomsbury.com

This edition of *Twelfth Night* by Keir Elam,
first published 2008 by Bloomsbury Arden Shakespeare
Reprinted 2009, 2010, 2011 (twice), 2012, 2013 (three times)

British Library Cataloguing-in-Publication Data
A catalogue record for this book is available from the British Library.

ISBN: HB: 978-1-9034-3698-1
PB: 978-1-9034-3699-8

Library of Congress Cataloging-in-Publication Data
A catalog record for this book is available from the Library of Congress.

Printed and bound in the United States of America

The Editor

Keir Elam is Professor of English Literature at the University of Bologna, where he is Head of the Department of Modern Languages. His publications include *Semiotics of Theatre and Drama* and *Shakespeare's Universe of Discourse: Language-Games in the Comedies.* He is general editor of the BUR Shakespeare (Rizzoli, Milan). With Lilla Maria Crisafulli he has edited *Women's Romantic Theatre and Drama: History, Agency, Performativity* (Ashgate, forthcoming).

For Alice and Viola

CONTENTS

LIST OF ILLUSTRATIONS

GENERAL EDITORS' PREFACE

The earliest volume in the first Arden series, Edward Dowden's *Hamlet*, was published in 1899. Since then the Arden Shakespeare has been widely acknowledged as the pre-eminent Shakespeare edition, valued by scholars, students, actors and 'the great variety of readers' alike for its clearly presented and reliable texts, its full annotation and its richly informative introductions.

In the third Arden series we seek to maintain these well-established qualities and general characteristics, preserving our predecessors' commitment to presenting the play as it has been shaped in history. Each volume necessarily has its own particular emphasis which reflects the unique possibilities and problems posed by the work in question, and the series as a whole seeks to maintain the highest standards of scholarship, combined with attractive and accessible presentation.

Newly edited from the original Quarto and Folio editions, texts are presented in fully modernized form, with a textual apparatus that records all substantial divergences from those early printings. The notes and introductions focus on the conditions and possibilities of meaning that editors, critics and performers (on stage and screen) have discovered in the play. While building upon the rich history of scholarly activity that has long shaped our understanding of Shakespeare's works, this third series of the Arden Shakespeare is enlivened by a new generation's encounter with Shakespeare.

THE TEXT

On each page of the play itself, readers will find a passage of text supported by commentary and textual notes. Act and scene divisions (seldom present in the early editions and often the product of eighteenth-century or later scholarship) have been retained for ease of reference, but have been given less prominence than in previous series. Editorial indications of location of the action have been removed to the textual notes of commentary.

In the text itself, unfamiliar typographic conventions have been avoided in order to minimize obstacles to the reader. Elided forms in the early texts are spelt out in full in vese lines wherever they indicate a usual late twentieth-century pronunciation that requires no special indication and wherever they occur in prose (except where they indicate non-standard pronunciation). In verse speeches, marks of elision are retained where they are necessary guides to the scansion and pronunciation of the line. Final -ed in past tense and participial forms of verbs is always printed as -ed, without accent, never as -'d, but wherever the required pronunciation diverges from modern usage a note in the commentary draws attention to the fact. Where the final -ed should be given syllabic value contrary to modern usage, e.g.

> Doth Silvia know that I am banished?
> (*TGV 3.1.214*)

the note will take the form

> 214 **banished** banishèd

Conventional lineation of divided verse lines shared by two or more speakers has been reconsidered and sometimes rearranged. Except for the familiar *Exit* and *Exeunt*, Latin forms in stage directions and speech prefixes have been translated into English and the original Latin forms recorded in the textual notes.

COMMENTARY AND TEXTUAL NOTES

Notes in the commentary, for which a major source will be the *Oxford English Dictionary*, offer glossarial and other explication of verbal difficulties; they may also include discussion of points of interpretation and, in relevant cases, substantial extracts from Shakespeare's source material. Editors will not usually offer glossarial notes for words adequately defined in the latest edition of *The Concise Oxford Dictionary* or *Merriam-Webster's Collegiate Dictionary*, but in cases of doubt they will include notes. Attention, however, will be drawn to places where more than one likely interpretation can be proposed and to significant verbal and syntactic complexity. Notes preceded by * discuss editorial emendations or variant readings from the early edition(s) on which the text is based.

Headnotes to acts or scenes discuss, where appropriate, questions of scene location, Shakespeare's handling of his source materials, and major difficulties of staging. The list of roles (so headed to emphasize the play's status as a text for performance) is also considered in the commentary notes. These may include comment on plausible patterns of casting with the resources of an Elizabethan or Jacobean acting company and also on any variation in the description of roles in their speech prefixes in the early editions.

The textual notes are designed to let readers know when the edited text diverges from the early edition(s) or manuscript sources on which it is based. Wherever this happens the note will record the rejected reading of the early edition(s), in original spelling, and the source of the reading adopted in this edition. Other forms from the early edition(s) recorded in these notes will include some spellings of particular interest or significance and original forms of translated stage directions. Where two or more early editions are involved, for instance with *Othello*, the notes also record all important differences between them. The textual notes take a form that has been in use since the nineteenth century. This comprises, first: line reference, reading adopted in the text and closing square bracket; then: abbreviated reference, in italic, to the earliest edition to adopt the accepted reading, italic semicolon and noteworthy alternative reading(s), each with abbreviated italic reference to its source.

Conventions used in these textual notes include the following. The solidus / is used, in notes quoting verse or discussing verse lining, to indicate line endings. Distinctive spellings of the basic text (Q or F) follow the square bracket without indication of source and are enclosed in italic brackets. Names enclosed in italic brackets indicate originators of conjectural emendations when these did not originate in an edition of the text, or when the named edition records a conjecture not accepted into its text. Stage directions (SDs) are referred to by the number of the line within or immediately after which they are placed. Line numbers with a decimal point relate to centred SDs not falling within a verse line and to SDs more than one line long, with the number after the point indicating the line within the SD: e.g. 78.4 refers to the fourth line of the SD following line 78. Lines of SDs at the start of a scene are numbered 0.1, 0.2, etc. Where only a line number precedes a square bracket, e.g. 128], the note relates to the whole line; where SD is added to the number, it relates to the whole of a SD within or immediately following the line. Speech prefixes (SPs) follow similar conventions, 203 SP] referring to the speaker's name for line 203. Where a SP reference takes the form e.g. 38+SP, it relates to all subsequent speeches assigned to that speaker in the scene in question.

Where, as with *King Henry V*, one of the early editions is a so-called 'bad quarto' (that is, at text either heavily adapted, or reconstructed from memory, or both), the divergences from the present edition are too great to be recorded in full in the notes. In these cases the editions will include a reduced photographic facsimile of the 'bad quarto' in an appendix.

INTRODUCTION

Both the introduction and the commentary are designed to present the plays as texts for performance, and make appropriate reference to stage, film and television versions, as well as introducing the reader to the range of critical approaches to the plays. They discuss the history of the reception of the texts within the theatre and scholarship and beyond, investigating the interdependency of the literary text and the surrounding 'cultural text' both at the time of the original production of Shakespeare's works and during their long and rich afterlife.

PREFACE

Editing a play, like staging a play, is a collaborative enterprise. This edition is the result of the efforts not of the volume editor alone but of many members of the Arden Shakespeare team, some of whom left while others joined and still others stayed on the scene, as work on the play was caught up in the whirligig of time. Three of the general editors of the Arden Shakespeare played a substantial role during the production of this volume. Richard Proudfoot lent me his formidable knowledge and wisdom, on textual and other matters. David Kastan's acute critical judgement, expressed with his inimitable wit, was illuminating, particularly in the shaping of the Introduction. Ann Thompson offered me unsparingly her expertise, intelligence and friendship at every stage of the editing, from its conception onwards, and my gratitude to her is boundless.

Other members of the Arden team have also played a significant role. Jessica Hodge greatly encouraged me during and after her time as publisher. Her successor Margaret Bartley has been an exceptionally positive and supportive publisher, with unusual gifts of diplomacy; to her a special thank-you. I also owe a real debt of gratitude to Linden Stafford, the best copy-editor one could hope for: sharp, insightful, with a genuine understanding of language, grammar and style (Shakespeare's and even the editor's); among other things, I will always cherish her passionate and persuasive defence of the parenthetical comma. An earlier copy-editor, Nicola Bennett, went well beyond the call of duty in her searching questions and thoughtful suggestions, putting at my disposal her learning and her keen sense of dramaturgy. The edition also benefited from the tireless researches, especially in the visual field, of Philippa Gallagher and Charlotte Loveridge.

Thanks to Alissa Chappell for taking care of the edition in its final stages. I also wish to thank Jane Armstrong for her kindness when she was a leading player in the Arden team. To my fellow Arden editor Jonathan Bate my thanks for his early encouragement to join the team.

The collaborative effort extended beyond Arden, however. Of the many friends and colleagues from whose help and support I have benefited, I wish in particular to thank the following: Alessandro Serpieri for the many fruitful interchanges and collaborations on Shakespeare and company over the years; William Dodd for keeping me on my toes regarding new critical discourses; Nora Crook for intriguing leads regarding Mary Shelley and Illyrian same-sex marriages; Steve Sohmer for enlightenment on dates and calendars; George Walton Williams for stimulating suggestions on prosody and lineation; Tom Craik, my predecessor as editor of the Arden *Twelfth Night*, for his helpful advice in the early stages of the editing; Paola Pugliatti for her leads on beggars and vagrants; Fernando Cioni, our man at the Folger, for information on editions and sources; Fabio Liberto for timely bibliographical assistance with Plato. Liz Schafer brought her great knowledge of the field to her reading of the performance history sections of the introduction and commentary. I wish to thank especially our two leading scholars of Shakespeare's grammar: Jonathan Hope allowed me to see a draft of his book and commented helpfully on my own linguistic discourse, as did Norman Blake, who, with unparalleled generosity, corresponded with me over a long period of time about text, punctuation, discourse markers, meaning and spelling, opening up new interpretative vistas.

The following friends gave me the opportunity to explore different aspects of *Twelfth Night* by inviting me to give lectures or seminars on the play and by engaging me afterwards in thought-provoking discussion: William Carroll and James Siemon at Boston University and the Harvard Shakespeare seminar; Virginia Vaughan at Clark; Gary Taylor at Alabama; Gary Kelly at Edmonton; Michele Marrapodi at Palermo; Rosa Maria Colombo at Roma la Sapienza; Debs Callan at the Globe theatre, where I was a Sam Wanamaker fellow; Lynette Hunter and Ann Thompson at Gresham College, London; and Gail Kern Paster and Carol Neely at the 'Mediterranean Bodies' panel of the World Shakespeare Conference in Valencia. Other friends helped equally by inviting me to contribute articles or chapters on the play: Gail Kern Paster in *Shakespeare Quarterly*; Stanley Wells in *Shakespeare Survey*; Terry Hawkes in *Alternative Shakespeares 2*.

I have also had the good fortune to be able to discuss *Twelfth Night* with directors and actors involved in staging it. Tim Carroll, director of the celebrated Middle Temple production of 2002, generously shared information and illumination on his and the company's work. Paul Chahidi, an extraordinary Maria in the same production, volunteered enlightening insight into his character's infertility. Declan Donnellan, great director of *Twelfth Night* and countless other plays, shared his brilliant views on the comedy, Shakespeare and the world at large in various venues: in Taormina, in Pisa and, most memorably, over tea at the Middle Temple, of which he is a member.

Like every editor of a Shakespeare play, I am indebted to my distinguished predecessors, whose work has been an invaluable point of reference for my own, especially to the editors of the Oxford edition, Stanley Wells and Roger Warren; of the Arden second series edition, Tom Craik and Jim Lothian; and of the Penguin edition, Molly Mahood.

Last but certainly most, I wish to thank Lilla Maria Crisafulli for her tireless and loving support both moral and material, especially during the times when I was lost in the dark room of the editing process; to her I can no other answer make but thanks, and thanks, and ever thanks.

INTRODUCTION

'AY, THAT'S THE THEME': TOPICS IN *TWELFTH NIGHT*

Endings and beginnings

A play, like a cat, has several lives. It has a pre-theatrical life as an authorial manuscript, being read and perhaps modified by producers, actors and others. It later becomes a performance script, undergoing rehearsal and possible further revision. It then comes fully to life onstage, in the interplay between actors and audience. The performance takes on its own life, and may be described, debated and reviewed in other private or published texts. Each subsequent staging of the play is a new beginning, producing new responses. If the text of the play is printed or otherwise circulated, it may also enjoy various kinds of afterlife: revivals, successive printings or editions, adaptations, film versions, quotation in other works, critical analyses, even paintings of given scenes, etc. This introduction will give an account of some of the many lives of Shakespeare's *Twelfth Night, or What You Will* – the multiple factors that make up its rich textual, theatrical, critical and cultural history.

Twelfth Night continues to maintain its long-established place as one of the most popular and admired of Shakespeare's plays. The reasons for the enduring fortune of the comedy have to do with both production and reception. It is a play that demonstrably works onstage, even in relatively modest performances, a fact that secures its stable position in both professional and amateur repertories. There is probably no other Shakespeare comedy, moreover, that gives so many actors the chance to shine, and indeed the play's stage history suggests that the star performance may come not from Malvolio or Viola but from Feste, Sir Toby, Sir Andrew or even Maria (see p. 122). As a text for performance, *Twelfth Night* is also an open challenge to the director to come up with a strong reading. For example, the interpretation of 'Twelfth Night' and 'Illyria' – not only as seasonal and geographical settings but also as dominant symbolic time and space – creates an all-important frame for the understanding of the overall action. Over time this challenge has provoked actor-managers and directors – from Beerbohm Tree to Granville-Barker, and from John Barton to Sam Mendes – to produce some of their most innovative and characteristic work. As for reception, *Twelfth Night* has enjoyed, at least from the eighteenth century onwards, approval from audiences and critical judges alike, and is often considered Shakespeare's finest and maturest comedy. It has attracted over the decades an unusual degree of interpretative attention, and in recent years has returned to the centre of critical debate, thanks especially to its dramatization of currently fashionable issues such as gender and sexuality.

It is not, however, an easy play to place within the development of Shakespearean comedy. It is by no means the last of its kind – being followed by *Measure for Measure*, *All's Well That Ends Well* and other comedies – but it does in various ways represent a point of arrival within the genre. It is the last of the so-called 'romantic' comedies (see Frye). It is the last and arguably the most successful of the four cross-dressing comedies (after *The Two Gentlemen of Verona*, *The Merchant of Venice* and *As You Like It*). It is one of the last of the Elizabethan comedies, composed at the close of Elizabeth's reign and reflecting the anxieties and uncertainties of its historical moment. It has been seen as the last of Shakespeare's so-called 'happy comedies' (Wilson), or indeed as the dramatist's 'farewell to comedy' (Quiller-Couch, xi). Alternatively, it can be seen as a first. It is probably Shakespeare's first seventeenth-century comedy, and is in many ways a beginning-of-century play, inaugurating a new poetics: some commentators have seen it as the first of the 'dark comedies', foreshadowing with its representations of actual and feared deaths the later development of tragicomedy. As a result, *Twelfth Night* is an elusive play, as the history of its theatrical and critical reception suggests. It might be useful to turn our attention to that history.

Or what you will: the pleasures and trials of spectatorship

Let us begin at the end. The concluding line of *Twelfth Night* is an implicit appeal to the audience for indulgent applause: 'And we'll strive to please you every day,' promises the clown Feste at the close of his epilogue song. The applause usually arrives, because, however conventional Feste's appeal to the audience may appear, the comedy has in fact received (with a few exceptions) a largely enthusiastic theatrical and critical response – if not 'every day' then certainly over the centuries. The *Twelfth Night* story is on the whole a prolonged success story, and the play's audiences have performed a prominent and active part in the narrative. Indeed, the earliest news that we have of the comedy foregrounds the reactions of a series of conspicuous spectators in the form of personal responses in private diaries.

Twelfth Night is unique among Shakespeare's plays in having received a contemporary review, after a performance by the Lord Chamberlain's Men. The diary of John Manningham, fourth-year law student at the Middle Temple (one of the Inns of Court, or law colleges, in London), has the following entry for 2 February (Candlemas) 1602:

> FEBR. 1601.[1]
> 2. At our feast wee had a play called ~~Mid~~ 'Twelve night, or what you will'; much like the commedy of errores, or Menechmi in Plautus, but most like and neere to that in Italian called Inganni.

1 The year 1601 in the old Julian calendar corresponds to 1602 in the reformed Gregorian calendar introduced in 1582 but not adopted in England until 1752. In Shakespeare's day the New Year began on 25 March.

> A good practise in it to make the steward beleeve his Lady widowe was in Love with him, by counterfayting a letter, as from his Lady, in generall termes, telling him what shee liked best in him, and prescribing his gesture in smiling, his apparraile, &c., and then when he came to practise, making him beleeve they tooke him to be mad.
>
> (Manningham, 48)

Manningham was in many ways an ideal spectator: young and well educated, he brought to the performance an impressive array of precise literary and theatrical knowledge, enabling him to place the comedy culturally. He knew Shakespeare's earlier comedies, as is suggested by his crossing out of 'Mid' – presumably because he had started to write 'Midsummer night's dream' – and the comparison of 'Twelve night' with 'the commedy of errores', which had also been performed at an Inn of Court, Gray's Inn, in 1594. He was also able to compare the play with the Latin source of *The Comedy of Errors*, Plautus's *Menaechmi*, and to identify as the most similar comedy, and thus as another possible source, the *Inganni*, one of the Italian versions of the story. There is one revealing inaccuracy in the account: Manningham mistakenly describes Malvolio's 'Lady' as a widow, an error that may derive from seeing Olivia in the performance dressed in black in mourning for the death of her brother (rather than from his knowledge of Shakespeare's main English source, Riche's story of 'Apolonius and Silla', where the Olivia figure is indeed a widow).

The benevolent tone of Manningham's account of the play, and the particular praise he reserves for the 'good practise in it' of the gulling of the steward, set the tone and the terms for later spectators, who regularly place Malvolio at the centre of their responses. The second mention of the comedy is also a diary entry, again for 2 February and again centred on Malvolio. In 1623 the Master of the Revels, Sir Henry Herbert, records in his diary that 'At Candlemas Malvolio was acted at Court by the King's Servants'

(Winter, 13); on this occasion the most prominent spectator was King James I, who presumably commissioned the performance (the second at his court following an earlier representation given on 6 April 1618). Herbert's reference to a comedy entitled 'Malvolio' may indicate an adaptation or may instead suggest that the court audience, like Manningham, was best pleased with the duping of the steward. This preference is implicitly confirmed by James's successor as the play's most privileged spectator and reader: King Charles I wrote marginal notes to the list of contents in his copy of the 1632 Second Folio indicating the leading – or perhaps his favourite – characters; against the title *Twelfe Night, or what you will*, he wrote 'Malvolio' (Fig. 1). Eight years later

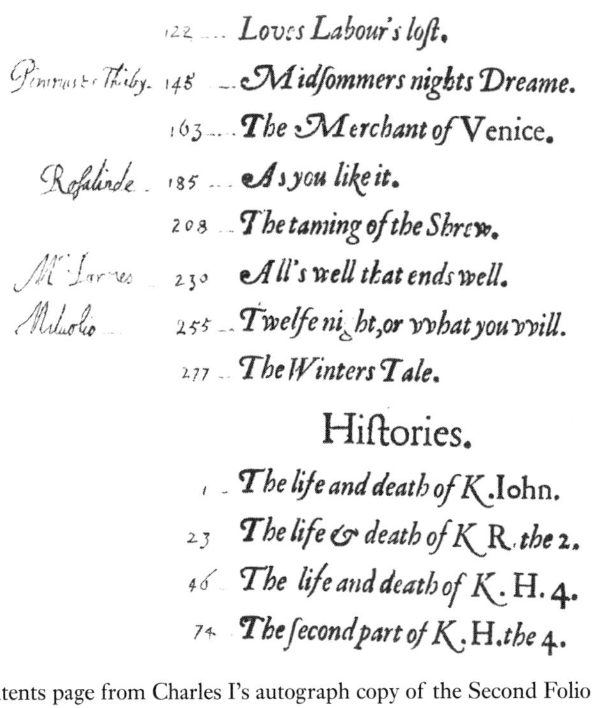
122 … Loves Labour's lost.
Piramus & Thisby. 148 … Midsommers nights Dreame.
163 … The Merchant of Venice.
Rosalinde. 185 … As you like it.
208 … The taming of the Shrew.
Mr Paroles 230 All's well that ends well.
Malvolio 255 … Twelfe night, or what you will.
277 … The Winters Tale.

Histories.

1 … The life and death of K. Iohn.
23 The life & death of K. R. the 2.
46 The life and death of K. H. 4.
74 The second part of K. H. the 4.

1 Contents page from Charles I's autograph copy of the Second Folio

the royal approval of this character was extended into collective audience enthusiasm in the laudatory poem by Leonard Digges appended to the edition of Shakespeare's *Poems* published in 1640, shortly before the closure of the theatres, which reports how 'The Cockpit Galleries, Boxes, all are full / To heare Malvolio that crosse garter'd Gull'.

The *Twelfth Night* story was resumed immediately after the Restoration, and again coincides in large part with the history of its reception, in the guise of three entries in the most celebrated and most 'private' of English diaries. When the comedy was revived for the first time by William Davenant's Company at the Duke of York's on 11 September 1661 the monarch, in this case King Charles II, was again present; we have no news of the king's reaction, but we do have the unsentimental testimony of another conspicuous spectator, the diarist Samuel Pepys, who gave the play its first bad review, although his response seems to have little to do with the actual performance or with the comedy's merits: 'observed at the Opera a new play, "Twelfth Night" was acted there, and the King there; so I, against my own mind and resolution, could not forbear to go in, which did make the play seem a burthen to me, and I took no pleasure at all in it.' Despite this disappointing non-event, Pepys went back for more; the diary entry for 'Twelfth Day' (6 January) 1663 registers a more perfunctory impatience with the comedy, although not with the performance: 'after dinner to the Duke's house, and there saw "Twelfth Night" acted well, though it be but a silly play, and not related at all to the name or day.' Six years later, none the less, he was back for a third attempt; on 20 January 1669, his judgement is still more severe: 'thence to the Duke of York's house, and saw "Twelfth Night", as it is now revived; but, I think, one of the weakest plays that ever I saw on the stage.'

Although the company's prompter, John Downes, defends Davenant's production in his *Roscius Anglicanus*, alleging that it 'had mighty success by its well performance' (Winter, 15), Pepys's judgement was evidently shared by other spectators at the time, probably because the predominant neo-classical taste of the period found the comedy wanting and indeed downright 'silly'. As a result, it disappeared from the London stage repertory – with the exception of an unsuccessful 1703 adaptation (see pp. 96–7) – for over seventy years, until 'rediscovered' by Charles Macklin in 1741. From the middle of the eighteenth century onwards, instead, its theatrical and critical reception has been a more or less uninterrupted success. The most authoritative critical responses of the eighteenth and nineteenth centuries restore Manningham's benevolence, and his emphasis on the pleasurable comic appeal of *Twelfth Night*, especially in performance. 'This play is in the graver part elegant and easy, and in some of the lighter scenes exquisitely humorous,' declared Dr Johnson in 1765. Four decades later William Hazlitt concurred, and attempted to define audience response to the comic action: 'This is justly considered as one of the most delightful of Shakespear's comedies. It is full of sweetness and pleasantry. . . It makes us laugh at the follies of mankind, not despise them.' (Hazlitt, 1.221). The Victorian editor Halliwell in 1853 likewise saw the play as a great comic vehicle, going so far as to elect *Twelfth Night* 'the chief monument of the author's genius for Comedy, and the most perfect composition of the kind in the English or any other language'.

In the case of *Twelfth Night*, the spectator plays the part of co-protagonist. This role is inscribed in the text, beginning with Shakespeare's gesture, in the play's second title, of leaving the responsibility to the audience: the 'you' in *What you will* is addressed directly to us spectators and readers, and can be interpreted either self-referentially as 'find your own title' (compare Olivia's use of the same expression towards Malvolio at 1.5.105, in the sense of 'do whatever you think fit'), or more amply as 'make of the play what you wish'. The comedy goes on to invite an unusual degree of audience complicity with the main action, first in Viola's disguise plot, then in the 'good practice' of the duping of Malvolio, encouraging us to join the company of the plotters hidden in the box tree or sneering in the dark room.

In electing the spectator as co-protagonist of the events, the comedy also interrogates the ethics and psychology of audience participation, obliging us to be acutely and sometimes uncomfortably aware of our own part. Commentators have frequently noted how a shift in spectator sympathies occurs at some point during the tormenting of Malvolio, as a result of a perception of excess in his punishment. Ralph Berry identifies the cross-gartering scene (3.4) as the moment in which the play 'begins to insinuate unease into the audience's consciousness . . . The joke has been taken too far, and we know it' (Berry, 111). In many performances, however, it is the 'dark room' scene (4.2), with its literal imprisoning of the 'mad' steward, that causes the audience to reconsider its complicity in the events and to change its allegiances. In either case, the result, as Mark Van Doren observed in 1939, is that 'Modern audiences have bestowed more sympathy upon Malvolio than Shakespeare perhaps intended, so that the balance is now not what it was. It can scarcely be overthrown, however, whatever changes the whirligig of time brings in' (Van Doren; quoted in Everyman, 211).

The audience's uneasy sense of being caught up in pleasures of a dubious kind is reflected in the unflattering image of spectatorship that the play itself offers, again with reference to the maltreatment of the steward. The recurrent trope used by the plotters in the letter scene (2.5) is that of blood sports: woodcock-trapping (82), trout-tickling (19–20), badger-hunting (102) and above all bear-baiting, the species of violent spectacle that Shakespeare's audience could enjoy at the arenas close to the Globe theatre. When Fabian justifies his unexpected participation in the scene by recalling Malvolio's puritanical disapproval of this sport – 'You know he brought me out o'favour with my lady about a bear-baiting here' (where the adverb 'here' suggests a physically contiguous arena, if not the Globe stage itself) – Sir Toby promises him an appropriate form of retribution, a kind of sporting justice: 'To anger him, we'll have the bear again, and we will fool him black and blue' (2.5.6–9). The play takes on the force of a potentially bloody revenge comedy. The implications of this trope for the audience are not altogether complimentary: if Malvolio is a bear fooled black and blue, his tormentors, us included, are by the same token aggressive hounds. The culmination of this derogatory mirroring of the lookers-on is Malvolio's parting curse in the finale: 'I'll be revenged on the whole pack of you!' (5.1.371), in which the term 'pack' identifies his tormentors precisely as sanguinary dogs and in which the second person pronoun addressed to the assembled company onstage may be extended – as with the 'you' in the play's second title – to the assembled company in the audience.

The pleasures of spectatorship of *Twelfth Night*, therefore, are not quite the straightforward delights, all 'sweetness and pleasantry', applauded by Hazlitt. Nor is the audience's laughter necessarily the benevolent amusement at human foibles detected by the Romantic critic. There seem to be obscurer transactions at play. Not by chance, the comedy's twentieth-century critical history coincides to a considerable degree with reflections precisely on the role of the audience, in the endeavour to define better what is going on in the interaction between stage and auditorium. Thus John Draper's *The 'Twelfth Night' of Shakespeare's Audience* (1950) tries to reconstruct the cultural perspective of the Elizabethan audience, arguing that spectators at the time would have been particularly interested in the play's darker social themes and struggles, such as class relationships. From a more formal perspective, in 1960 Bertrand Evans argues that the dramatist contrives to give the spectator a perceptual advantage over the dramatis personae, not only in the Malvolio scenes but in the twins plot, thereby complicating our response to events: 'The emotional conflict which rises from this unlaughable treatment of a laughable situation' (B. Evans, 128).

Later inquiries deepen and darken the picture. Ralph Berry's 1981 essay, '*Twelfth Night*: the experience of the audience', examines the 'moral responsibility' that the spectator is obliged to assume, and comes to the sobering conclusion that 'the ultimate effect of *Twelfth Night* is to make the audience ashamed of itself' (Berry, 119). Less severe is Stephen Booth's '*Twelfth Night*: I.I: the audience as Malvolio', which identifies the primary delights of spectatorship as intellectual or cognitive: 'I submit that much of our joy in *Twelfth Night* drives from triumphant mental experiences like our modest but godlike achievement in comprehending scene i.' (Booth, '*Twelfth*', 167). Stephen Greenblatt, in his well-known essay 'Fiction and Friction', discerns pleasures of a less cerebral kind, arguing that the 'heat' generated by verbal and corporeal play in the comedy translates into a non-cathartic and decidedly erotic charge for the spectator, especially in his or her post-theatrical experience: 'Shakespeare invested his comedies with a powerful sexual commotion, a collective excitation, an imaginative heat that the plots' promise will be realized offstage, in the marriage beds toward which they gesture' (Greenblatt, 89).

We three: the interpretation compulsion

Watching *Twelfth Night* may be ethically disturbing, intellectually invigorating or erotically arousing, but it is also potentially perilous. In one of his better jokes, Feste offers the audience an implicit warning, a 'caveat spectator'; arriving on the scene in 2.3, in which Sir Toby Belch and Sir Andrew Aguecheek have already begun their serious carousing, the clown opens with a riddle:

SIR ANDREW Here comes the fool, i'faith.
FESTE How now, my hearts? Did you never see the picture of 'we three'?
SIR TOBY Welcome, ass. Now let's have a catch.
(2.3.14–17)

Feste's enigma alludes to a popular painting or inn sign which represented two asses or loggerheads and bore the caption 'We Three' (see Figs 2 and 3), a puzzling tag that inevitably prompted its reader to pose the fatal question: 'Who is the third ass?' To which the reply, of course, was: whoever poses the question. Sir Toby gets the point, identifying Feste as the third member of a company of fools ('Welcome, ass'). His interpretation may not be complete, however. Deciphering the riddle involves a paradox: as Elizabeth Freund observes, 'the interpreter is obliged to take a position both inside the frame and outside it . . . Without conceding asshood, the reader cannot unriddle the picture; but if he fails to read the picture, he is palpably an ass' (Freund, 476). By describing the picture, the clown seems to place himself inside it as participant but outside it as onlooker, leaving the deciphering, or asshood, to others. And not only to Sir Toby: the implication seems to be that the third loggerhead is the audience – us – witnessing and trying to make sense of the joke. Even if Stephen Booth optimistically assures us that 'Audiences of *Twelfth Night* do not, and therefore should not, feel like fools looking at fools, or jackasses looking at jackasses' (Booth, '*Twelfth*', 167), there can be little doubt that Feste's gaze goes out beyond the bounds of the stage.

Feste is the best guide we have to the play's underlying themes, and his visual-verbal riddle is emblematic from various points of view. It is one of a series of enigmas within what is in many ways one of Shakespeare's most enigmatic plays. It foregrounds the spectator not only as interpreter but also as object of inquiry. It makes explicit a question that runs throughout the play: who is the true fool (or, indeed, are we all fools)? And it warns us of the danger of making fools of ourselves through interpretation, including the interpretation of *Twelfth Night* itself, even as, like much else in the play, it irresistibly invites an interpretative response. Among the desires aroused by *Twelfth Night*, perhaps the strongest is cognitive desire, the yearning to know and to understand. A comedy that insistently presents itself as a 'mystery' play, it provokes the temptation – to paraphrase Orsino – to unclasp the book of its secret soul.

One of the play's 'structural' mysteries, a major cause of audience – and especially critical – puzzlement, is its large number of loose ends, whereby plots, events or performances are announced and then abandoned. As William Dodd puts it, 'There is hardly

2 'We Three' (1): 'We Three Loggerheads', portraying the jesters Derry and Archie Armstrong

3 'We Three' (2): The sign of the We Three Loggerheads Inn, Mold, Wales

one initial project which isn't either forgotten or shelved by the characters involved in the tangled love plot, or eased from the centre of the stage by the playwright himself' (Dodd, 147). The most notorious of these 'forgotten' projects is Viola's plan, declared in her first scene, to present herself at Orsino's court 'as an eunuch' (1.2.53). No further (explicit) mention is made of the idea and, when at 2.4.23–6 Viola-as-Cesario alludes obliquely to her love for Orsino, Coleridge is led to affirm: 'And yet Viola was to have been presented to Orsino as a eunuch. Either she forgot this, or Viola had altered her plan' (Coleridge, 1.96). In reality the 'disappearance' of the castrato theme is only apparent (see p. 57–62), but it certainly leaves a 'blank' (2.4.110) at the centre of the main action. In the same announcement, Viola also leads us to expect future musical performances at the duke's court: 'for I can sing / And speak to him in many sorts of music' (1.2.54–5); she fails to perform, and all the singing is left to Feste.

The clown is involved in another of the mysteriously shelved projects. When in 2.3 Maria announces her scheme for the gulling of Malvolio, she includes Feste as participant spectator, telling Sir Toby and Sir Andrew, 'I will plant you two – and let the fool make a third – where he shall find the letter' (2.3.168–9). In the event, however, it is Fabian, introduced for the first time in the scene, who makes the third spectator in the letter episode (2.5), rather than the clown. These loose ends or false starts have been interpreted as signs of authorial revision or as changes dictated by casting problems, but they undoubtedly leave question marks in the text, although whether audiences are really troubled by the missing links, or indeed whether they even notice them, is another matter.

Feste is also the main source of the comedy's more discursive enigmas, riddles and puzzles. His citing, for example, of invented Latin authorities – 'For what says Quinapalus? "Better a witty fool than a foolish wit"' (1.5.33–4) – invites us to search for the deformed 'originals' (Quintilian[us]? Apuleius?; see 33n.). Likewise his 'fooling', reported by the drunken (and not very reliable) Sir Andrew, with its 'Pigrogromitus', 'Vapians' and 'Queubus' (2.3.22–3), has sent commentators into a flurry of hermeneutic inquiry: Furness sees 'Pigrogromitus' as a corruption of 'Tetragrammaton'; Hotson discerns Platonic cosmology in Queubus/Cubus, etc. (see commentary). The clown is the chief exponent of another enigmatic mode that pervades the comedy and that likewise keeps us guessing, namely what John Kerrigan calls 'ontological riddling' (Kerrigan, 109), which consists in pseudo-philosophical affirmations of a tautological kind – 'That that is is'; 'for what is "that" but "that" and "is" but "is"?' (4.2.14–16) – or of a logically self-contradictory variety: 'Nothing that is so is so' (4.1.8). The same riddling mode seems to infect Viola-as-Cesario in her cryptic signals to Olivia, to Orsino or to the audience: 'I am not that I play' (1.5.179); 'I am the man' (2.2.25); 'What I am and what I would are as secret as maidenhead' (1.5.209–10).

Twelfth Night repeatedly professes its own secrecy. As Kerrigan suggests, '*Twelfth Night* pushes one's perception of Renaissance secrecy beyond the usual categories', to include, among other modes of occultation, 'the circulation of secrets as gossip' (Kerrigan, 90). Thus Viola's 'secret as maidenhead', like Orsino's 'secret soul' (1.4.14) or the captain's pledge of silence ('your mute I'll be', 1.2.59), evoke the idea of hidden hermeneutic gems, occult meanings to be uncovered in interpretative treasure hunts. Correspondingly, much of the play's action is taken up with the attempt to decipher impenetrable texts (in the form of letters), bodies (notably Viola's), hearts (Orsino's, Olivia's, Cesario's) and events (such as the shipwreck and its consequences). It is a play 'about' interpretation, as well as a play that has received more than its share of interpretations. The culminating expression of this interpretative compulsion, the desire to disclose illuminating secret meanings, is of course Malvolio's catastrophic attempt to decode 'Olivia's' billet-doux with its notorious conundrums: '*M.O.A.I. doth sway my life.*' . . . what should that alphabetical position portend?' (2.5.106–17). This 'fustian riddle', as Fabian calls it, is a perfect semantic trap for Malvolio, playing on his fatal narcissism. His interpretation is circular; he starts out from the will to 'make that resemble something in me' and ends up finding precisely his own resemblance: '"M." Malvolio. "M" – why, that begins my name!' (2.5.123–4). By discovering his name reflected in the scrambled letters – with perhaps more difficulty than is warranted by the simple enigma itself – the steward elects himself as the object not of Olivia's but of his own interpretative desire, thereby making an ass, or 'a rare turkey-cock', of himself (2.5.28).

Despite the unenviable fate of the steward, and despite the unflattering image of interpretation that the episode presents, the fustian riddle has proved an equally fatal attraction to the comedy's spectators and commentators, who, affected by a sort of mimetic syndrome, are tempted to 'become' Malvolio (Booth) in the endeavour to unscramble the letters. Over the years interpretative speculation on the riddle has reached improbable heights of ingenuity. Hotson (166), for example, sees the letters as the initials of the four elements: Mare (sea), Orbis (earth), Aer (air) and Ignis (fire) – although, as Craik points out (Ard[2], 68), the first two elements should surely be Aqua and Terra. L.S. Cox in 1962 read them as an anagram of 'I am O[livia]' – although they might equally well be taken as a clue to the dubious authorship of the letter: M(aria or) O(livia) A(m) I? Some readings have been based on early modern theories of language. Thus Elam (*Shakespeare's*, 159–64) sees Malvolio's hermeneutic labours as a parody of the earnest anagrammatic endeavours of Renaissance magi to discover the sacred Tetragrammaton, the secret four-letter name of God (in this case Malvolio himself; compare 'Pigrogromitus' above). Peter J. Smith in 1998 also finds a key in the Renaissance conception of meaning as being inherent to language rather than merely conventional, and suggests that the letters, embodying their referent directly in its initials, allude to Sir John Harington's Ovidian parody *The Metamorphosis of Ajax* (*Metamorphosis Of A Iax*), which was at the time the object of scandal; since Harington's 'ajax' plays on 'a jakes', slang for lavatory, the 'inherent meaning' or referent of the acrostic becomes 'toilet' (hence, presumably, the allusion to Olivia urinating in a further letter-riddle: 'thus makes she her great P's', 2.5.87)

There are other insidious enigmas to interpret (or, more wisely, to resist) in the letter, and especially, as it were, in the letters of the letter. On picking up the billet-doux, Malvolio first notices the handwriting, which he attributes to Olivia:

MALVOLIO [*Takes up letter.*] By my life, this is my lady's
hand. These be her very c's, her u's and her t's . . .
SIR ANDREW Her c's, her u's and her t's. Why that?
(2.5.85–9)

Sir Andrew's ingenuous demand for an explanation – he is the only one present not to get the joke – may reflect today the puzzlement of modern audiences, for whom the word 'cut' has lost its Elizabethan slang meaning, having in the meantime gained a letter ('cunt'). But, like Malvolio's own will to knowledge, Aguecheek's desire to understand has also infected critical commentators. Indeed, in recent years c, u and t have attracted even more attention than M.O.A.I. Most of these contemporary readings are surgical or anatomical, from Jonathan Goldberg's association of the letters with the symbolic gelding of the boy actor (Goldberg, 217), to Dympna Callaghan's somewhat analogous discerning of a 'feminized, ridiculed, castrated' Malvolio (Callaghan, 'All', 436; on the theme of castration, see pp. 57–62), to Gail Kern Paster's tracing of a trajectory in Malvolio's voyeuristic desire 'from the genital to the excretory' (Paster, 33). The episode may also point to Malvolio's ambition for social mobility: the idea of watching Olivia pee is not so much an erotic fantasy as a dream of social equality, since only her husband, the 'count' (a title achieved with the addition of another letter: see 2.5.32) has the right to do so. Leah Scragg, instead, offers a socio-historical decoding, suspecting an allusion to the 'cutpurse', the breed of thieves that exercised their skills in the midst of Shakespeare's audience (Scragg, 15–16).

Around Twelfth Night

The impelling need to interpret the play has not been limited to cracking the codes of such local puzzles. There has been a more general interpretative anxiety about what is really going on in

Illyria (itself an enigmatic venue). The main symptom of such anxiety has been the frequently expressed urge to decipher the comedy's main title, despite Pepys's peremptory sentence that it is 'not related at all to the name or day'. A title that is not directly descriptive of the main action (unlike, say, *The Taming of the Shrew*), of the main characters (*The Two Gentlemen of Verona*), of place (*The Merchant of Venice*), of dominant atmosphere (*A Midsummer Night's Dream*) or even overall moral (*Measure for Measure*, *All's Well That Ends Well*), becomes inevitably a happy hermeneutic hunting ground. The meanings given to 'Twelfth Night' tend to reflect the prevailing cultural concerns of the time. Interpretative emphasis has thus shifted over the decades from an early concern with topical and biographical issues, such as the occasion of the 'original' Twelfth Night – the date of the supposed first performance, together with the related identity of Elizabethan personages supposedly alluded to in the dialogue (Hotson; see pp. 93–4) – to a more socio-cultural interest in Twelfth Night as synonym of carnivalesque revelry.

The association of the play with carnival was first suggested in 1867 by the French critic E. Montegut, who observed that 'the title recalls one of those festivals which were most dear to our forebears', in which, as in carnival, 'it was the world turned upside down, a rational hierarchy topsy-turvy, authority created by chance, and the more grotesque the surprise, the merrier the festival' (*SC*, 1.554). This line of interpretation was taken up by Enid Welsford in her 1935 study of the fool: 'Shakespeare transforms into poetry the quintessence of the Saturnalia . . . Illyria is a country permeated with the spirit of the Feast of Fools, where identities are confused, 'uncivil rule' applauded, cakes and ale successfully defended, and no harm done' (Welsford, 572). Such readings culminate in C.L. Barber's seminal 1959 volume, which affirms that '*Twelfth Night* deals with the sort of folly which the title points to, the folly of misrule' (Barber, 248) – that is, the revels associated in early modern England with the last day of the Christmas season, and in particular with the election of a 'Festus' or 'Lord of Misrule' to preside over the maskings, interludes, music, song and other forms of merrymaking. The appointment of a winter festive mock king on 6 January had pagan roots, evoking the anarchic spirit of the ancient Saturnalia or Kalendae (S. Billington; Horner).

Twelfth Night owes a good deal to this saturnalian tradition, most apparently in the scenes of revelry echoing the feasting and especially the communal drinking (traditionally from the wassail bowl) associated with 6 January celebrations. The affinities may run deeper, however. One of the central events of the celebrations was disguising or mumming, later transformed into the court masque, which survived as a Twelfth Night event until the fall of the monarchy in 1642 (see Hutton, *Stations*, 11–22). In this sense, Viola disguised – at the court of Orsino – may be as much a participant in the rites as the noisy revellers. It is also possible to detect in the comedy's frequent acts of donation – Olivia's ring and miniature for Cesario, the repeated tips for Feste, etc. – an allusion to the Twelfth Day custom of bearing gifts (deriving from the presents of the three magi for the infant Christ). The question of which character, if any, represents what the historian John Stow termed the 'master of merry disports' remains an open one. Feste is nominally and professionally closest to the role of Festus (from which his name may derive), but it is Sir Toby who seems to preside over the scenes of 'disports' or misrule. Perhaps we should not exclude the candidacy of Maria, author of the comic revenge plot against Malvolio, especially since there had been a well-known historical winter queen in the person of Mary Fleming, who reigned on Twelfth Day in 1563 (Hutton, *Stations*, 106–7). It may be that misrule in the comedy has a collective master-mistress.

The saturnalian reading of title and play gains force from the oppositional presence of a 'Puritan' steward. Protestant fundamentalists reserved special bile for Christmas misrule as a mode of spectacle, at which, in the words of the Protestant hack Philip Stubbes (whose attitude resembles Malvolio's disdain towards the revellers), 'the foolish people they look, they stare, they laugh, they fleer . . . to see these godly pageants solemnized in this sort' (Barber, 28). The post-Reformation censorship of revelry seems to be re-enacted in Malvolio's interruption of the festivities in 2.3: 'Have you no wit, manners nor honesty but to gabble like tinkers at this time of night? Do ye make an alehouse of my lady's house?' (86–8). Sir Toby's riposte – 'Dost thou think because thou art virtuous there shall be no more cakes and ale?' (2.3.112–13) – may have particular resonance, beyond the generic defence of the right to party. Stubbes directed a violent diatribe against 'Church-ales'. As for 'cakes', the medieval European Twelfth Night cake had been imported into England late in Elizabeth's reign by way of a ritual electoral system, namely the baking of a coin in a cake and awarding the title of 'bean king' (a variant of Festus) to the man who found it in his slice (Hutton, *Rise*, 110). This practice likewise met with disapproval from the nonconformists.

If the censorship of Twelfth Night revelry had historical resonances for Shakespeare's audience in general, the struggle between festivity and sobriety, or misrule and order, may have had specific piquancy for John Manningham and other members of the Middle Temple audience in 1602. Election of a Lord of Misrule had been expressly banned at the Inns of Court since 1580. There had, however, been notorious transgressions against the ban and exemplary punishments, such as the temporary suspension of Richard Martin and others from the Inns of Court for 'making outcries, forcibly breaking open chambers in the night, [and] levying money as the Lord of Misrule's rent' (Hopwood, 1.308). At the same time, the comedy may have recalled for its audience recent and authorized Twelfth Night events at the Middle Temple such as the entertainment of 1597–9, the *Prince d'Amour*, which satirized the folly of lovers (S. Billington, 36). The Middle Temple lawyer Anthony Arlidge goes so far as to argue that *Twelfth Night* was written expressly as a Temple entertainment (see p. 95).

The ideological implications of the saturnalian reading may not be as simple or as neutral as they seem, however. If the comedy is taken to re-enact the century-long struggle between the old 'Merry England', with its vestiges of Christianized pagan ritual, and the reformation of English customs and manners, then the punishment of the 'Puritan' Malvolio looks like revenge comedy of a particular historical and cultural kind. The play's comic plot becomes the expression of nostalgia for a pre-Reformation world, part of a late Elizabethan phenomenon that the social historian Ronald Hutton describes as 'a sentimental reaction in favour of old-style popular merry-making among writers and their patrons' (Hutton, *Rise*, 152).

From a broader – and arguably less conservative – anthropological perspective, the play's festivities and confusions may be seen as part of the movement towards social and individual renewal. This is the 'natural perspective' proposed by Northrop Frye, who detects in *Twelfth Night* and other romantic comedies a tripartite movement from an 'anticomic society' which is 'opposed to the comic drive' (Frye, 73: Orsino's melancholy, Olivia's bereavement, and so on), through a 'second period of confusion and sexual licence' (76: Viola's disguise, the revels), towards the final phase of 'the discovery of identity' (78), which coincides with the renewing force of spring. Here 'Twelfth Night' becomes a seasonal – and specifically 'solstitial' – indicator (121), associated initially with winter and death but looking forward to the later festivities anticipated by Fabian: 'More matter for a May morning' (3.4.138).

Twelfth Night, however, was not exclusively or even primarily the occasion for carnivalesque anarchy or solstitial feasting. It was above all a significant date in the church calendar, the Epiphany, feast of the revelation of Christ. Various commentators have traced the presence of specifically Christian themes. Thus Barbara Lewalski elects Viola and Sebastian as comic types of the incarnate Christ, in the guise of two miraculously delivered outside agents who will help to cure the inhabitants of Illyria. Somewhat analogously, Hassel (77–93) classifies the comedy as part of a specific performance genre, one of a number of early modern epiphany plays (together with Lily's *Campaspe* and *Midas*,

Fletcher's *The Faithful Shepherdess*, and so on). He also argues for the pervasiveness of epiphanic topics, notably that of revelation itself, best expressed in the double recognition (Viola-Sebastian) of the comedy's denouement.

The Epiphany is not the only church festival associated with *Twelfth Night* and its reception history. The two earliest performances mentioned in diaries are dated 2 February, at Candlemas, feast of the purification of Mary. This was a festival of enlightenment, traditionally associated with the bearing of candles in a procession (a tradition again suppressed after the Reformation). Some commentators have seen the comedy's emphasis on the light–dark opposition – and especially the 'purification' of Malvolio in the dark room – as an exploration of the message of the church festival (with the implication that Manningham's Middle Temple performance may have been the first, thereby rendering the play's title deceptive: see Hassel, 94–8). Wishing to stretch what is already an arguable point, the agency of Maria – or 'Marian', as Sir Toby calls her at 2.3.13 – might be linked to the exquisitely Marian devotions of the feast (notably in the form of the 'purifying' of Malvolio).

With regard to the comedy's more explicit religious themes, a long-debated issue has been how seriously – especially in the context of nostalgia for pre-Reformation customs – we are to take Malvolio's supposed Puritanism. Joseph Hunter was the first commentator, in 1845, to see Malvolio as a 'grand attack' on Puritanism, part of 'a systematic design of holding [it] up to ridicule' (397); some later critics have concurred, although in 1884 William Archer objected that 'he is not a Puritan but a Philistine' (Archer, 277). The internal evidence concerning the steward's radical Protestant allegiances is contradictory. Maria first makes the accusation – 'Marry, sir, sometimes he is a kind of Puritan' (2.3.136), provoking in Sir Andrew the impulse to 'beat him like a dog' (137) – and then withdraws it a few lines later (142–3) by denying the steward any ideological coherence: 'The devil a Puritan that he is, or anything constantly but a time-pleaser'. The suspicion remains in the air, however, re-emerging later in Sir Andrew's odd – and uncharacteristically well-informed – allusion to a specific sect of Protestant radicals: 'I had as lief be a Brownist as a politician' (3.2.30).

Some critics have uncovered in the play not merely an opposition between festivity and censorship but what Richard Wilson terms a 'dialectic between Carnival and Lent, Catholic and Protestant, or secrecy and disclosure' (R. Wilson, 251). Wilson finds support in the comedy for his thesis that Shakespeare was a 'secret' Catholic, noting, for example, the presence of pre-Reformation habits such as swearing 'by Saint Anne, and ginger' (*TN* 2.3.114; R. Wilson, 150). Whether or not one subscribes to Wilson's claim that 'Shakespeare's Illyria maps the religious politics of Elizabethan London' (279) – or to such specific historical decodings as Sir Topas being a parodic version of the Jesuit Henry Garnet, or his 'Master Parson' (4.2.15) being an allusion to the Jesuit priest Robert Parsons – it is true that the comedy seems at certain points to evoke the pre-Reformation church calendar, through what Steve Sohmer terms 'calendrical markers' (Sohmer, 199). These include not only Feste's swearing by St Anne but, perhaps more significantly, the number of characters bearing the names of saints, especially of early saints associated with winter feast days, as if by seasonal association with the Epiphany. Thus the play has its Sebastian, named after the saint condemned to death by the emperor Diocletian ('an Illyrian': Sohmer, 206) around AD 288 in Rome, whose feast day is 20 January; its Fabian, from St Fabianus, who died in 250, again in Rome, and who shares the same feast day as Sebastian; its Valentine, from the legendary martyr and patron saint of lovers, who likewise died in Rome in the third century (feast day 14 February); an Antonio, perhaps from Antonios, religious hermit and one of the founders of monasticism, who died in 356 (feast day 17 January); not to mention Andrew, named after one of the Twelve Apostles and the patron saint of Scotland (feast day 30 November), whose name, ironically for the character who bears it, means 'manly' in Greek.

The overall message of these modes of interrogating the text may be that *Twelfth Night* is a play that promises an epiphany – a secret or encoded transcendental signified waiting to be revealed – but strategically withholds it. Hence the search for a semantic key to open up the comedy's supposed mysteries. The danger is the one indicated by Feste and underlined by Montaigne in Florio's 1603 translation, namely over-interpretation: 'There's more adoe to enterprete interpretations, than to interpret things . . . We doe but enter-glose [inter-gloss] ourselves' (Montaigne, 602). But the risk of interpreting interpretations – a risk doubtless incurred in this edition – is one that the comedy itself challenges us to run, and it cannot and should not put an end to speculative hermeneutic readings. Inevitably, and rightly, spectators, critics and even editors continue to find in the play what they will.

A very opal: the play of perspective

In another of his illuminating – or indeed epiphanic – observations, Feste makes fun of the violent mood-changes of Duke Orsino: 'the tailor make thy doublet of changeable taffeta, for thy mind is a very opal' (2.4.73–5). The clown's double metaphor incisively targets Orsino's changeable humours under the pressure of desire: the contrasting tones of the warp and woof of taffeta (shot silk) produce, like the opal stone, an iridescent effect of colour change when viewed from different angles. At the same time, the clown's opalescent image is a powerful trope for the comedy as a whole, demonstrating once again that Feste is the most astute commentator on the play of which he is part. It points to the central question of the arbitrariness of desire and the tyranny of the passions (see pp. 54–5). It introduces the important issue of materiality – of the fabrics, cloths and clothing, jewels and other prestigious objects that make up an important part of the comedy's own texture (see pp. 42–7). But also, and more crucially, it figures what is perhaps the most intriguing characteristic of *Twelfth Night* as a dramatic construct, namely – to coin an oxymoron – its constant mutability under the play of alternative perspectives. Such perspectival iridescence is doubtless one of the main reasons for the multiple interpretations to which the comedy has been subjected, but it is at the same time a vital dramatic principle.

The play of perspective involves in the first instance interpersonal relations between the various characters in the comedy, relations constructed on a series of parallels between the different characters' situations and traits in a prismatic process of multiple mirroring. Such parallels are strongly implied by the extraordinary number of anagrammatic names within the List of Roles, suggesting that the borders between one role and the next are uncertain and unstable, their identities overlapping. 'Viola' and 'Olivia' are virtual anagrams, and this in turn reflects a complex network of parallels and reciprocal identifications between the two female co-protagonists: they have in common a dead father, a 'dead' brother (and hence an initial state of bereavement) and unrequited love (a characteristic they both share with Orsino), as well as such qualities as sexual attractiveness (and attractedness), independence, wit, eloquence, playfulness and a particular partiality towards Feste's fooling. Not by chance is Viola at the outset attracted to the countess through resemblance or identification – 'O that I served that lady' (1.2.38) – just as later Olivia is attracted to her own 'reflection' in Viola-as-Cesario.

The game of the anagrammatic name suggests likewise a negatively specular relationship between the two women and Malvolio, whose own name contains both of theirs but at the same time opposes them through the pejorative combining form 'mal': if he has in common with them a form of frustrated 'desire', he is their negative image on all other fronts, resisting, for example, all forms of playfulness, especially Feste's fooling.

The comedy is characterized by other modes of parallelism and doubling between characters, notably between Feste and others. The clown and Cesario both act as go-betweens, moving between the courts of Olivia and Orsino. Feste, moreover, takes over Viola-as-Cesario's announced role as court singer, while, as we have seen, Feste's part as spectator in the letter scene is taken over by Fabian, appearing from nowhere. In his professional role as truth-sayer, Feste becomes a specular figure, a deforming mirror in which the duke and the countess can see themselves, should they wish to do so. His ventriloquism permits him to double as himself and as 'Sir Topas' in the dark room scene. 'Sir Topas' is another specular figure: his name is in part a deformation of Sir Toby, whose vengeful role in the punishing of Malvolio he takes over, while also acting as a glass reflecting the 'madness' of the imprisoned steward.

The theme of the double finds its fullest expression, of course, in the relationship between Viola and Sebastian. *Twelfth Night* is Shakespeare's second play with twins, his first and only play with opposite-sex twins. If his earlier 'twin' comedy, *Comedy of Errors*, exploited physical similarity almost exclusively for purposes of farce, *Twelfth Night* makes much more of the intersubjective psychological potential of the device. Viola's first thoughts in the play are dedicated to her twin, suggesting the priority of bereavement as a motivating force for her decision to cross-dress. Indeed, one of the primary aims of her disguise must be to keep her 'dead' brother alive, by way of a sort of talismanic magic. As Cesario, she ceases merely to resemble Sebastian, in order to 'become' him; she is not merely his twin but his *doppelgänger*. This process of identification is rendered explicit in one of the comedy's extraordinary moments of psychological awareness; Viola-as-Cesario, on hearing Antonio name her brother, confesses to having created and embodied his literal mirror-image: 'He named Sebastian. I my brother know / Yet living in my glass . . . / For him I imitate' (3.4.376–80). It is her ability to 'imitate' Sebastian's dress and behaviour that explains in part Viola's success in taking on a male role; it also explains the surprising ease with which Sebastian in turn substitutes Cesario in Olivia's affections: he is taking his 'rightful' place, usurped until now by Viola. Cesario is a point of converging identity between Viola and Sebastian.

The doubling of Viola and Sebastian as Cesario is at the centre of the play's criss-cross weave of intersecting desires and interconnecting plots, wreaking havoc among the other characters: Viola-as-Cesario desires Orsino and is desired by Olivia; Olivia in turn is supposedly desired by Orsino, courted at a distance by Sir Andrew and more directly by Malvolio; Sebastian takes the place of his twin Viola-as-Cesario as object of Olivia's desire, which he reciprocates, while Orsino's desire is redirected towards Viola-as-Cesario, and so on. Viola-as-Cesario is a 'blank' (2.4.110), a space into which others project their desires and their own identity anxieties. The result is what the German Romantic critic, August Schlegel, termed 'ideal follies', whereby Cesario is merely the agent rather than the cause of arbitrary and self-deceiving desire, which resides fully in the mind of the beholder: 'the proud Olivia is entangled by the modest and intriguing messenger of the duke, in which she is far from suspecting a disguised rival, and at last, by a second deception, takes the brother for a sister' (Schlegel, 2.175; see also Burwick, 172–3).

The comedy's most slippery conceptual terrain is the definition of gender identity. As Northrop Frye comments, 'In *Twelfth Night* the discovery of sexual identity is combined with the identical-twin theme: Orsino and Olivia are languishing in melancholy until out of the sea comes an ambiguous figure "that can sing both high and low", who eventually becomes male to Olivia and female to Orsino' (Frye, 83). Viola-as-Cesario represents not so much an androgen, half male and half female, as an indeterminate middle ground where the genders of the boy actor playing the role, the female character and the male (or 'eunuch') disguise are superimposed: 'What I am and what I would are as secret as maidenhead' (1.5.209–10), she announces cryptically, alluding to the sexuality that she disguises (as Cesario), that she feigns (as actor) and that she protects (as the virginal Viola).

Viola's cross-dressing and thereby doubling as her own twin have, in Catherine Belsey's words, the effect of disrupting sexual difference: 'Of all Shakespeare's comedies', she affirms, 'it is perhaps *Twelfth Night* which takes the most remarkable risks with the identity of its central figure' (Belsey, 185). She goes on to ask who is speaking in Viola-as-Cesario's dialogue with Orsino in 2.4: 'The answer is neither Viola nor Cesario, but a speaker who at this moment occupies a place which is not precisely masculine or feminine, where the notion of identity itself is disrupted to display a difference within subjectivity, and the singularity which resides in *this* difference' (187). Marjorie Garber goes further, claiming that Viola's cross-dressing 'offers a challenge to easy notions of binarity, putting into question the categories of "female" and "male" whether they are considered essential or constructed, biological or cultural' (Garber, 17). Indeed, Viola's transvestism questions all categorial distinctions and oppositions, creating 'a space of possibility structuring and confounding culture: the disruptive element that intervenes, not just as a category crisis of male and female, but the crisis of category itself' (17). Thus Malvolio's description of Cesario as an unclassifiable liminal figure suggests a category crisis with regard not only to gender but to age: 'Not yet old enough for a man, nor young enough for a boy . . . 'Tis with him in standing water between boy and man' (1.5.152–5).

As a result of these shared problems of perspective, a central cognitive and thematic role in the comedy comes to be played by perception. Observers are led by events to doubt the perceptual and sensorial data they receive, giving rise to a widespread instability regarding the reading of the world of the play. Since the effects of disguise and 'doubling' are mainly optical – and since, in any case, the theatre operates in a primarily visual dimension – the major emphasis throughout is on ocular perception. There are a great number of self-dramatizing or self-doubting references by the play's various perceivers to 'mine eyes', beginning with Orsino's rhapsodic 'O, when mine eyes did see Olivia first', in the opening scene (1.1.18). Olivia herself confesses that Cesario's qualities 'creep in at mine eyes' (1.5.290), and admits her consequent 'fear to find / Mine eye too great a flatterer for my mind' (301–2). The destabilizing impact of the gaze is confirmed by the object of her adoring perception, Cesario, who recounts how 'methought her eyes had lost her tongue' (2.2.20), while Cesario's double, Sebastian, surprised by Olivia's amorous effusions, is led to doubt the reliability of his own perceptual data: 'I am ready to distrust mine eyes' (4.3.13).

This visual discourse reaches its climax in the final scene, with the simultaneous presence of both twins on stage, an event described in terms of optical illusion: 'One face, one voice, one habit and two persons: / A natural perspective, that is and is not' (5.1.212–13). Orsino is alluding to one of the instruments used to create optical 'special effects' (including those employed on the baroque stage, for example in Italy): either anamorphic mirrors or lenses that created distorted or multiple images, or, on the contrary, a perspective glass, namely a tube with faceted lens making multiple images appear as one. There are two complementary conceits involved here: the anamorphic doubling of Cesario into two identical selves, or alternatively the reduction of two separate objects or identities to a single, albeit repeated, image. The choice between the two is a question, precisely, of perspective.

A further variation on the specular and perspectival theme is the issue of self-mirroring, and hence of narcissism. In her celebrated defence of Feste and his verbal fooling in response to Malvolio's severe critique, Olivia puts her steward in his place with a devastating diagnosis of his major vice: 'O, you are sick of self-love, Malvolio' (1.5.86). In the early modern period 'self-love' was primarily a moral malaise consisting in an excess of *amour propre* or self-esteem, but the term could take on a stronger and more literal meaning, namely affective or even erotic self-infatuation. It is the pathology of which the poet accuses the Fair Youth in Sonnet 1 ('But thou, contracted to thine own bright eyes, / Feed'st thy light's flame with self-substantial fuel') and himself in Sonnet 62 ('Sin of self-love possesseth all mine eye / And all my soul, and all my every part'). That Malvolio's self-preoccupation may go beyond the realm of esteem and into the sphere of full-blown narcissism is suggested by other observers. In a play much concerned, as we have seen, with mirror-images, it is significant that he is caught *in flagrante* by Maria in an admiring rapport with his own reflection: 'He has been yonder i'the sun practising behaviour to his own shadow this half-hour' (2.5.14–15). Maria's anatomy of his inability to resist himself and her use of this trait as a trap against him are pitiless: 'the best persuaded of himself, so crammed, as he thinks, with excellencies that it is his grounds of faith that all that look on him love him, and on that vice in him will my revenge find notable cause to work' (2.3.144–8). Malvolio is, in Fabian's words, 'a rare turkey-cock' – by antonomasia a foolishly self-loving beast – who 'jets under his advanced plumes' (2.5.28–9).

If the sin of self-love is a psychopathology in the comedy, it risks becoming an epidemic, as Peter Gill's 1974 RSC production of the play suggested, with its outsize portrait of Narcissus dominating the set (see Fig. 4). D.J. Palmer ('Echo') has shown that Narcissus is the play's governing Ovidian deity (on the play's debt to Ovid, see also Carroll, *Met.*, 80–102, and Bate, 144–51). Other characters are valid potential targets for Olivia's awesome put-down, including, perhaps, Olivia herself, who is not only hermetically self-enclosed in the opening act but becomes infatuated with what is in effect a mirror-image, in the form of the disguised Viola. The leading candidate, however, is without doubt Olivia's supposed admirer, the self-advertising and self-dramatizing Orsino. The duke's (and the play's) opening rhetorical performance is a virtual confession of auto-erotic fixation. Not by chance his effusions on the spirit of love that 'falls into abatement and low price' (1.1.13) recall the complaint of Ovid's Narcissus that 'my plenty makes me poore' (Ovid, *Met.*, 3.587, 38^{r}; see Palmer, 'Echo', 73). Apparently rhapsodizing on his unrequited passion for Olivia, Orsino ends up declaring – by way of an allusion to another myth, that of Acteon, torn to pieces by Diana's hounds – the real object of his desire, namely himself: 'And my desires, like fell and cruel hounds, / E'er since pursue me' (1.1.21–2). In the same scene he imagines himself, in a fantasy of political and sexual imperialism, as absolute monarch of Olivia's body and soul (and, presumably, fortune) on the Malvolio-like grounds of his erotic irresistibility: 'These sovereign thrones, are all supplied, and filled

4 William Dudley's set for Peter Gill's 1974 RSC production

/ Her sweet perfections with one self king!' (1.1.37–8). It might be said that the only characters to save themselves from the condition are Feste and Viola; as Jonathan Bate observes, 'Viola redeems the play because she proves to be selfless, not selfish, in love. She becomes Echo instead of Narcissus' (Bate, 148).

Narcissistic self-concern is one of the forms taken by self-deception in the comedy, and is thus a mode of moral and social blindness. It is also one of the prime causes and effects of foolishness: Malvolio, Orsino and even Olivia make fools of themselves in failing to perceive the illusory nature of their supposed desire, only nominally directed outside of themselves. Each is punished for the 'sin' of self-love: Malvolio through the letter exposing his *amour propre*; Orsino through Olivia's fully justified indifference; Olivia herself through Cesario's caustic resistance to her advances, whereby, in René Girard's words, 'the triumphant narcissism of a woman is overturned by the indifference of another woman in masculine disguise' (p. 106). What is less certain is whether these punishments represent a therapy – even if Maria calls the letter for Malvolio a 'physic' (2.3.155) – and still less a cure, for the pathology, despite Girard's optimistic claim that '*Twelfth Night* suggests the reversibility of all narcissistic configurations' (Girard, 110).

'Tis my picture: deciphering visual images

The problems of perspective and interpretation are particularly acute in one of the comedy's most recurrent visual fields, namely the domain of pictures, paintings and other iconographic images. Feste's 'We three' scene – which is presented as, and actually quotes, a 'picture' – is part of the comedy's insistent concern with forms of visual and graphic representation, including, for example, maps, as in Maria's gibe about Malvolio's face having 'more lines than is in the new map' at 3.2.74–5 (see p. 73). The play also abounds in what we might term optical allusions to Renaissance iconology, particularly emblems, i.e. 'enigmatic' images which (like 'We three') are interpreted through a verbal caption. Emblems were a popular and widely circulating art form, and as such readily recognizable by Shakespeare's audience; they were a model of powerful interaction between word and image, and thus had close affinities with the stage. Several of Shakespeare's Ovidian allusions were illustrated and interpreted in the most prestigious Renaissance emblem book, Andrea Alciato's highly influential *Emblemata* of 1531: Actaeon (Emblem 52), Arion (Emblem 90), Narcissus (Emblem 69, labelled 'Philautia', self-love: see Fig. 5), and so on. The strategic evocation of emblems is most evident in another explicitly pictorial moment in the comedy, Cesario's

5 'Philautia' ('self-love': see 1.5.86), from Andrea Alciato, *Book of Emblems* (1531)

description of his 'sister': 'She sat like Patience on a monument, / Smiling at grief' (2.4.113–14). Cesario appears to be referring to a relatively 'high' public art – an allegorical figure on a memorial or funerary monument – but is probably alluding instead to an emblem from Cesare Ripa's *Iconologia* (1593), which represents Patience as a woman sitting on a stone and bearing a yoke on her shoulders, her feet placed on thorns (see Fig. 6). Cesario takes up Ripa's 'pazienza', but reinterprets it as a sign not of feminine submission but of heroic self-denial, possibly leading to death (hence the funeral monument).

The emblem game may involve a moment of explicitly theatrical iconography. The captain's Ovidian description of Arion on the dolphin's back (1.2.14), was a favourite topic not only of the emblem books but of painted scenery, especially in opera, since Arion was a symbol of the magical and redemptive powers of music. He presided, for example, over the operatic spectacles celebrating the 1589 wedding between Ferdinando de' Medici and Christina of Lorraine at the Pitti Palace in Florence (Fig. 7 shows Buontalenti's set design, where Arion is in the bottom right-hand corner).The allusion may thus be cryptically self-celebratory on the part of one of Shakespeare's most musical plays.

Twelfth Night's most self-conscious iconographic moment involves Olivia's highly theatrical self-revelation to Cesario; playfully but seductively unveiling, she figures the gesture as a sort of vernissage: 'But we will draw the curtain and show you the picture. [*Unveils.*] Look you, sir, such a one I was this present. Is't not well done?' (1.5.226–8). Drawing the curtain has theatrical connotations – evoking, perhaps, the fabric covering the stage doors of the Elizabethan stage – but Olivia's primary reference is to the dust cover protecting a painting. This is something of a standing joke in the comedy, as in Sir Toby's feigned admiration for Sir Andrew's dancing talents: 'Wherefore have these gifts a curtain before 'em? Are they like to take dust, like Mistress Mall's picture?' (1.3.120–2). Like Feste, Olivia figures herself

6 'Patience on a monument' (2.4.114), from Cesare Ripa's *Iconologia* (1593)

overtly as a painting, but here the reference is to a 'high' artistic form – portraiture – which had a somewhat ambiguous status, being a more or less public art representing, at the same time, the private subjectivity of the sitter. Hence the power of Olivia's gesture in revealing or publicizing herself at the moment of greatest intimacy, her private bereavement.

7 Arion and the dolphin: Bernardo Buontalenti's set design for an intermezzo celebrating the 1589 wedding between Ferdinando de' Medici and Christina of Lorraine at the Pitti Palace in Florence

8 'Such a one I was this present' (1.5.227): Salomon Mesdach's portrait of Adriana Van Nesse, with the inscription 'Aetatis suae, 19, Anno 1611' (at the age of 19, in the year 1611)

Olivia goes on to interpret her own portrait: 'such a one I was this present', namely, this is what I looked like at the time the portrait was painted (i.e. this very instant). Here she is rather cryptically evoking the inscription frequently found on Renaissance portraits, *aetatis suae* (of her or his age: see Fig. 8), playing on her double presence as painter and subject of her self-portrait, whereby the time of composing and the time of looking at the picture coincide. There is a certain poignancy to Olivia's speaking and breathing picture, since she is exhibiting precisely the fact that, unlike her mourned brother, she is still alive. She plays on such intimacy later, when she presents Cesario with a literal portrait (''tis my picture', 3.4.203), a miniature set in jewels so that her represented body in the picture can be in close contact with Cesario's 'real' body.

The pictorial qualities of *Twelfth Night* have not gone unnoticed by painters, who have often represented the very 'picture' scenes in question: Olivia's unveiling (Edmund Blair Leighton's painting, Fig. 9) and Viola's monument (Johann Heinrich Füssli's watercolour panels, Fig. 10).

9 'Is't not well done?' (1.5.228): Olivia unveiling, by Edmund Blair Leighton, 1888)

Changeable taffeta: materials and materiality

Orsino's emblematic 'doublet of changeable taffeta' (2.4.74) can be taken literally as part of the comedy's obsessive discourse of materials and material goods. Indeed, although it is traditionally seen as a romantic, even somewhat ethereal comedy, *Twelfth*

10 'Viola' by Johann Heinrich Füssli, *c.* 1777

Night is in many ways the most material of Shakespeare's plays, uniquely concerned with cloth and clothing, dress and dressing, precious and common objects, architecture, furniture, receptacles, tools, and all the practical and physical aspects – or what Olivia calls 'every particle and utensil' (1.5.238) – of everyday life.

Since the action takes place between two households, both indoors and outdoors, there is much concern with domestic architecture, particularly with reference to Olivia's house and estate: from her 'orchard' or garden (3.2.6, 3.4.218) with its gates (1.5.95, 113, 122, 192, 260), 'garden door' (3.1.90), walls and walks (2.5.14), to its interior spaces: the chamber that she waters daily with her tears (1.1.28), the room where Malvolio is enclosed (4.2: the 'dark room' scene) and especially the kitchen (2.3: the 'kitchen' scene). Even erotic fantasies are worked out in terms of domestic structures, as in Maria's joke about bringing Sir Andrew's hand to the buttery-bar or pantry (her breasts, 1.3.68; see Fig. 11). Malvolio's social and sexual reverie, instead, is figured in terms of status furniture: he dreams of lounging in a canopied chair of state (2.5.42) and of getting up from his day-bed, where the sleeping Olivia lies (2.5.45–6). In a more satirical furniture fantasy, Sir Toby imagines Sir Andrew's sheet (of writing paper) fitting the enormous and legendary bed of Ware (3.2.45; see Fig. 12), with a possible allusion to the sexual union with Olivia that Aguecheek, like Malvolio, will never enjoy.

Household implements abound. Within the confines of Olivia's kitchen, Sir Toby's favourite activity introduces a world of drinking receptacles, from his 'unfilled can' or empty tankard (2.3.6) to his 'stoup' of wine (2.3.13). Being the most earthly of the play's characters, his speech is littered with material tropes: he imagines Sir Andrew's hair being curled by tongs (1.3.93–6) and – in another grotesque sexual fantasy – being spun off by a 'housewife' or hussy with a distaff between her legs (1.3.98–100). Elsewhere, the trunk in which, presumably, Viola's maiden weeds are kept (5.1.251) has its own stage history (see 1.2.0.1n.) and reappears in

11 Buttery-bar (1.3.68)

Antonio's metaphor of Sebastian's 'false' virtues as 'empty trunks' (3.4.367).

Other everyday objects fill the play's discursive spaces. In a comedy in which letters play such a prominent part, there is a natural concern with writing materials: sheets of paper, 'gall' (ink coloured with oak-gall dye: 3.2.46), the 'goose-pen' or goose-feather quill (alluding to Sir Andrew's goose-like cowardice: 3.2.47). The comedy's interest in play is reflected in

12 The bed of Ware (3.2.45)

allusions to games and their material parts, from the 'cherry-pit', involving the rolling of cherry stones into a small hole (with probable sexual double entendre: 3.4.113), to the 'philosophers' table' with its double board ('*Primo*, *secundo*, *tertio*', 5.1.33). Such domestic material consciousness extends outwards to familiar community games and objects: the parish whipping-top used as a warming-up exercise (1.3.40; see Fig. 13); the painted 'sheriff's post' on which proclamations were affixed (1.5.144; see Fig. 14), and so on.

The comedy's materiality is best expressed, however, in its intense preoccupation with cloth and clothes. As in no other Shakespeare play, material – the textile, weave and colour of fabric – determines not only distinctions between characters and their

[*Parish Top.*]

13 Parish top (1.3.40)

respective social status but events themselves, as Malvolio discovers to his cost. As Oscar Wilde observes, 'Even small details of dress, such as the colour of a major-domo's stockings, . . . become in Shakespeare's hands points of actual dramatic importance, and by some of them the action of the play in question is conditioned absolutely' (Wilde, 173). There is in consequence a widespread concern with fabrics and textiles, both literal and metaphorical: from the plain, straight and unworked flax of Sir Andrew's hair,

14 Sheriff's posts (1.5.144)

waiting to be broken and spun by spinsters (1.3.98–100), to more sophisticated worked fabrics such as the transparent cypress crepe that 'hides', or fails to hide, Olivia's heart (3.1.119–20), to luxurious cloths like taffeta, damask silk (2.4.112) and velvet (2.5.45).

The comedy's discourse of fabric echoes the language of the sumptuary laws in force in Elizabethan England, designed to prevent excessive luxury and expenditure and especially to regulate dress codes according to social class, with the additional purpose of stemming the increasing affectation and effeminacy of English male fashions. The 1574 sumptuary statute decrees, among other vetoes, that 'None shall wear in his apparel . . . Velvet in gowns, coats, or other uttermost garments . . . except men of the degrees above mentioned, barons' sons, knights and gentlemen.' Thus Malvolio's fantasy of social promotion in which he fancies himself luxuriously garbed in a 'branched velvet gown' (2.5.44–5) represents an imaginary sumptuary transgression, taking him into the forbidden material realms of the gentry.

One of the most exclusive and frequently mentioned materials in the sumptuary laws is silk – together with satin, taffeta or damask – presumably because its glossy sheen bespoke both luxury and dubious masculinity: 'None shall wear satin, damask, silk, camlet, or taffeta . . . except the degrees and persons above mentioned' (*Proclamation*). Here Feste's taffeta metaphor may take on other resonances: Duke Orsino is the play's one male authorized to wear luxury fabrics (and in many productions he is portrayed as showily decked out in silk). The clown's allusion to his silken doublet may, however, imply excess and effeminacy, of dress as of mind, his 'changeable' moods being a traditionally 'feminine' trait. There may in addition be theatrical implications involved. One of the complaints of Protestant reformers against the theatre was the players' wearing of the costumes of their betters, since the companies received clothing from their noble patrons, including silk and velvet gowns. Feste's phrase 'changeable taffeta' (2.4.74) appears twice in the diary of the theatrical impresario Philip Henslowe. From this viewpoint, Orsino is just a dressed-up player like the rest.

The language of cloth also conditions the comedy's discourse of gender. The Elizabethan 'None shall wear' refrain, applied to the ladies; specifies 'any velvet, tufted taffeta, satin . . . except wives of barons, knights of the order, or councillors' ladies, and gentlewomen of the privy chamber and bed chamber, and the maids of honor' (*Proclamation*). In her semi-autobiographical 'Patience on a monument' story in 2.4, Viola-as-Cesario tells Orsino how the young girl 'let concealment . . . Feed on her damask cheek' (2.4.111–12). This material metaphor can be interpreted as an allusion to Viola's 'real' sex, by way of reference to her own silk-like feminine skin, or to her 'real' social class as a member of the damask-wearing gentry. In any case Orsino, as usual, fails to get the point.

It is not surprising that a comedy whose action is dominated by different forms of 'transgressive' dressing-up – Viola's cross-dressing, Malvolio's cross-gartering and yellow hose, Feste's disguising as a priest – is also the Shakespearean play most obsessively preoccupied with dress and with dressing at large. References to modes of dress are legion: to the clown and his 'gaskins' (wide breeches) and their 'points' (laces) in Maria's joke (1.5.21–3); to Antonio and his remembered 'sea-cap' (3.4.327); to Malvolio and his fashion accessories: his pocket watch (2.5.57) and imaginary 'rich jewel' (2.5.58). Even the manly Sebastian is clothes-conscious, apologizing for being 'grossly clad' (as, presumably, is Viola-as-Cesario). It is thanks above all to clothing that Viola is able to imitate and so 'save' her brother: 'he went / Still in this fashion, colour, ornament' (3.4.378–9).

Clothing serves as a means of self-concealment, not only in Viola's 'eunuch' disguise but also in the veil that Olivia uses to hide her face from Cesario (1.5.161) or the transparent 'cypress' silk that she says hides, or fails to hide, her heart, as opposed to a more opaque 'bosom' (the part of the dress covering the breast, 3.1.119). Clothing is a sign of status or professional role, as in Malvolio's steward's garb and chain of office, or Feste's motley. Such livery becomes, however, intimately linked to personal identity. Malvolio in yellow becomes another, a 'madman'. And despite the clown's claim that his costume is merely exterior – '*cucullus non facit monachum*: that's as much to say as I wear not motley in my brain' (1.5.51–3) – it is instead the expression of his whole way of being and of doing in the play, so much so that when he changes identity in acting the role of Sir Topas he changes his attire, despite the total darkness: as Maria points out, 'Thou mightst have done this without thy beard and gown. He sees thee not' (4.2.63–4). But the priest's garb is necessary to the role, and without it Feste cannot do the voices.

Alternatively, clothing is seen – albeit self-deceptively – as a powerful means to social advancement, not only by Malvolio but, for example, by his 'rival' for Olivia's hand, Sir Andrew Aguecheek.

Sir Andrew – an *arriviste* in social drag, a 'carpet' knight who has purchased his knighthood on the titles market (3.4.230) – is an aspiring dandy, displaying false confidence that his leg 'does indifferent well in a flame-coloured stock' (1.3.129–30) and that this will help him to a place in Olivia's house, if not her heart. There is bad news for him and his yellow 'stock', as well as for the steward and his, in Maria's revelation that yellow is 'a colour she [Olivia] abhors' (2.5.193). Onstage Aguecheek often wears yellow, and on Maria's line the other characters look at him tellingly: the destiny he shares with Malvolio – as excluded other – is signalled by their fashion choices.

Dress, therefore, determines personal identity and personal destiny in the play. As Jones and Stallybrass (18) observe, '*Twelfth Night* presents perhaps the most radical vision of the centrality of clothes to the fashioning of a person.' This is nowhere truer, of course, than in the case of Malvolio, who is fooled not only into betraying his personal integrity by dressing up showily against all his puritanical principles, but also into revealing his fatal ignorance of the codes that govern the world he aspires to be part of. Not only does he completely mistake his target by dressing in the yellow that Olivia abhors and by appearing 'cross-gartered – a fashion she detests' (2.5.194), but his chosen form of 'transvestism' is itself a joke, at least for Shakespeare's early audiences. The cross-gartering fashion (see Fig. 15) was tangentially derived from the order of the garter, and thus may appeal to Malvolio's dreams of social promotion, but, as Marie Channing Linthicum pointed out in 1936, by 1600 cross-garters 'were worn chiefly by old men, Puritans, pedants, footmen, and rustic bridegrooms' (Linthicum, 264). This is implicitly confirmed by Maria: 'Most villainously [cross-gartered], like a pedant that keeps a school i'th' church' (3.2.71–2). The joke is thus that Malvolio, aspiring to gentrification and to prestigious marriage, succeeds instead in associating himself with the lower classes from which he desperately wants to distance himself.

15 Cross-gartering, from Abraham de Bruyn, *Omnium pene Europæ, Asiæ, Aphricæ atque Americæ gentium habitus. Habits de diverses nations . . .* (Antwerp, 1581)

Malvolio's mode of 'cross-dressing' – or of would-be cross-class-dressing – is in some ways a negative image of Viola's: it is as disastrous as hers is all too successful, and, while the steward mistakenly believes he is dressing up socially, she has to dress down (her blood being, as she puts it, 'Above my fortunes': 1.5.270). Viola's own transvestism, the comedy's central violation of dress codes, has been the subject of much recent critical debate, particularly with regard to the degree of 'transgressiveness' involved in the figure of the doubly cross-dressed boy actor (dressed as girl dressed as boy). Lisa Jardine believes that in performance the play, in arousing homoerotic passion, went some way towards justifying the accusations of anti-theatrical reformists such as John Rainolds, who attacks plays 'not [only] for making young men come forth in whore's attire, like the lewd woman in the Proverbs; but for teaching them to counterfeit her actions' (Jardine, *Daughters*, 9–36). Laura Levine suggests that it brought to the surface deep-seated fears regarding the stability of gender distinctions and thus of the self (Levine, 10–25). A different point of view is maintained by Kathleen McLuskie,[1] who argues that transvestism was a conventional aspect of the Elizabethan stage that did not challenge gender roles; Jean Howard likewise contests the transgressive force of Viola's cross-dressing: 'Despite her masculine attire and the confusion it causes in Illyria, Viola's is a properly feminine subjectivity; and this fact countervails the threat posed by her clothes and removes any possibility that she might permanently aspire to masculine privilege and prerogatives' (Howard, 432). For Howard it is Olivia, with her social and financial independence, who represents 'the real threat to the hierarchical gender system in this text, Viola being but an *apparent* threat' (432).

It is true that what Viola calls 'this my masculine usurped attire' (5.1.246) paradoxically allows her to express her female identity, and indeed the comedy explores feminine subjectivity

1 Kathleen McLuskie, 'The act, the role, the actor: boy actresses on the Elizabethan stage', *New Theatre Quarterly*, 13 (1987), 120–30

like no earlier dramatic text. Unlike Shakespeare's previous cross-dressed heroines, Viola confesses her discomfort at two points in the play, first when she perceives the effects of her cross-dressed persona on Olivia – 'Disguise, I see thou art a wickedness . . .' (2.2.26ff) – and later in her crisis in the face of the 'phallic' role of sword-wielding duellist, when her confessional aside – 'A little thing would make me tell them how much I lack of a man' (3.4.295–6) – alludes to her 'lack' of manly physical attributes and character. At the same time, to see Viola's disguise as merely a parenthesis that in the end confirms the sexual and gender status quo is misleading. Not only does Viola-as-Cesario arouse bilateral homoerotic passions, in Olivia (since she is a woman) and in Orsino (since she is his male servant), but the play signally, and uniquely, fails to restore the social order of gender differentiation, in that Cesario never gets round to putting on the 'maiden weeds' of which Viola divests herself at the beginning, and remains 'boy' to Orsino till the end (5.1.263); as Phyllis Rackin notes, 'the boy actor cannot put on Viola's clothes, and the play ends on an equivocal note' (Rackin, 127).

The issue of homoeroticism in the comedy concerns equally the bond between Antonio and Sebastian. Their mutual devotion can in part be situated, as some earlier critics argued, within the tradition of friendship literature, in which male bonding often took on quasi-romantic connotations. But the explicit eroticism of Antonio's language – 'I do adore thee so', 2.1.43; 'My desire, / More sharp than filed steel' (3.3.4–5), etc. – goes quite beyond the bounds of such literary conventions. Censored in nineteenth-century stage productions (see p. 98), Antonio's homoeroticism is an open secret in contemporary performances, which have the two friends kissing or even found in bed together (see p. 112).

In what chapter of his bosom?: reading the body

As the clothing and cross-dressing issues suggest, the interpretation compulsion in *Twelfth Night* centres above all on the body, which is subjected to constant scrutiny and anatomy. Indeed, perhaps the major activity in the play is the reading or misreading of the body, turning it into a kind of text. This can be seen at its most literal in Malvolio's self-deceptive deciphering of Olivia's false epistle, which posits her body as a set of alphabetical signifiers (her c's and u's and t's: see p. 17). It also emerges in what we might call the 'blazon' game that Viola and Olivia play with each other and off each other. This game is a literary variation on surgical anatomy, in which the beloved body is as it were dissected into her constituent parts, each of which is then praised hyperbolically (see Sawday). The blazon is very much a male poetic genre, which the supposed 'ladies' have appropriated. Olivia plays the game, for example, in praising Cesario's 'gentle' or gentlemanly qualities: 'Thy tongue, thy face, thy limbs, actions and spirit / Do give thee fivefold blazon,' she exclaims ecstatically at the end of their first encounter (1.5.284–5). And even if her reading is mistaken on the gender plane it is actually quite correct on the social plane, since she rightly interprets Viola's behaviour as a 'blazon' – or armorial sign – of her high-class origins, despite Cesario's servant status. The game also enters into their dialogue itself when Viola launches into her speech in praise of Olivia – ''Tis beauty truly blent, whose red and white . . .' (1.5.231–5)– and Olivia interrupts her with another parody of the anatomical blazon, which she transforms into a catalogue or shopping list: 'as, item, two lips, indifferent red; item, two grey eyes, with lids to them; item, one neck, one chin and so forth' (1.5.238–40).

This idea of the body as text reaches its climax in the same scene with reference to the body of Orsino. Olivia asks Cesario to come to the point of his mission as Orsino's go-between:

OLIVIA Now, sir, what is your text?
VIOLA Most sweet lady –
OLIVIA A comfortable doctrine, and much may be said of
it. Where lies your text?
VIOLA In Orsino's bosom.
OLIVIA In his bosom? In what chapter of his bosom?
(1.5.214–19)

Olivia justifiably questions Orsino's sincerity here, implying that the duke's 'bosom' or heart is an empty text. Olivia claims to be able to 'read' Orsino without hearing the speech, because the enamoured discourse of his languishing body is *déjà vu* or *déjà lu*, full of romantic clichés. Her joke is blasphemous in that what she is actually parodying is a sermon taking as its 'text' (or theme) a passage from the Scriptures. Orsino is not any old text but a sacred text, holy writ.

Immediately afterwards in the same dialogue Olivia and Cesario shift textual genre when the body in question becomes Olivia herself as supposed object of Orsino's desire:

VIOLA . . . Lady, you are the cruell'st she alive
If you will lead these graces to the grave
And leave the world no copy.

OLIVIA O sir, I will not be so hard-hearted. I will give out diverse schedules of my beauty. It shall be inventoried, and every particle and utensil labelled to my will: as, item, two lips, indifferent red; item, two grey eyes, with lids to them; item, one neck, one chin and so forth.

(1.5.233–40)

The textual joke here is on 'copy'. Viola is using a printing metaphor – a copy is literally a printed transcript – for 'child', which Olivia refuses to create by marrying Orsino. There is also a self-ironic allusion here to Cesario himself as a copy or simulacrum, as fake male and as stand-in for Orsino (copy of a copy). Olivia's 'schedules' instead puns on the legal meaning 'copyhold' or transcript of possessions, thereby transforming her into a legal document: she is not holy writ like Orsino but a judicial writ.

The comedy's intensive reading of the body extends to its interior physiological workings and their effect on character, what we might term the psychosomatics of behaviour. The framework available for the exploration of the bodily bases of psychology was the Greek physician Galen's theory of the humours, i.e. psychological dispositions deriving from the dominance of one or other of the internal organs. The first act dedicates particular attention to the dispositions of the moody Orsino, whose position enables him to exercise what Malvolio admiringly terms 'the humour of state', the autocratic temperament befitting the great (2.5.49), as in his rapid mood changes in the opening scene, reflected in Cesario's speculation that Valentine may 'fear his [Orsino's] humour', 1.4.5. Orsino aims to exercise his power by commanding the organs and humours of Olivia: her heart – which, within the Galenic system is, as Cesario puts it, 'the seat / Where love is throned' (2.4.21–2) – and her liver, the seat of passion, and as such the dominant organ within the play's humoural discourse. Rejected by Olivia and her liver, Orsino resentfully decrees that woman's love is 'No motion of the liver, but the palate' (2.4.98). Fabian rightly predicts of Malvolio that the letter 'wins him, liver and all' (2.5.94), and disingenuously assures the lily-livered Sir Andrew that Olivia's indifference towards him is designed 'to put fire in your heart and brimstone in your liver' (3.2.19).

Still in the hepatic realm, the comedy offers a veritable anatomy of the most fashionable of humours, melancholy, caused by an excess of black bile secreted by the liver, but which in the play more often than not turns out to be a behavioural pose. Olivia's initial *malinconia* is justified by her grief, but is impossibly hyperbolic in its effects, especially in her decision to live in seclusion for seven years. The authenticity of her melancholic disposition is immediately placed in doubt by the rapidity with which she abandons it on meeting Cesario, who in turn alludes to the 'green and yellow melancholy' of his 'sister' (2.4.113). Meanwhile, Orsino's pose as melancholic lover ('my woes', 1.4.26) is mocked by Feste: 'Now the melancholy god protect thee' (2.4.73). Malvolio likewise affects 'sadness' as part of his 'Puritan' severity: 'He is sad and civil,' says Olivia approvingly in her melancholy mode, 'And suits well for a servant with my fortunes.' (3.4.5–6). Although Fabian imagines the steward being 'boiled to death with melancholy' (paradoxically, it being the coldest of humours; 2.5.3), his supposedly sad humour is as short-lived as Olivia's grief; upbraided by his mistress for his lover's smile, he reneges his former 'blackness' (the colour of melancholy-provoking bile): 'Not black in my mind, though yellow in my legs' (3.4.25–6). In the end, however, he is literally plunged back into melancholy blackness in the dark room.

The liver, organ of passion, works overtime in *Twelfth Night.* The comedy discloses a wide-ranging discourse of what Thomas Wright termed *The Passions of the Mind* (1601); like the humours, from which they derived, the passions were a fashionable object of inquiry and theorization at the beginning of the seventeenth century. The term 'passion' appears eight times in the play together with a range of synonyms: fire, fervour, will, motion, etc. The prevailing notion in the comedy is of the passion as a mode of affliction or 'perturbation': 'Methought', claims Orsino after Feste's song, 'it did relieve my passion much' (2.4.4). Such is the passionate force of the 'motion of the liver', as Orsino calls it (2.4.98), that it threatens to overwhelm reason. The opposition between passion and reason (or between 'wit' and 'will': 1.5.30) becomes a topos in the comedy. Olivia declares herself intellectually disarmed before the force of her desire for Cesario ('Nor wit nor reason can my passion hide', 3.1.150), thereby losing all control over her behaviour and her discourse, as Cesario testifies: 'methought her eyes had lost her tongue, / For she did speak in starts, distractedly' (2.2.20–1). Olivia's speaking in 'starts' confirms the disruptive effects of the passions, according to theorists such as Thomas Wright, in producing inarticulacy (compare Shakespeare's Richard III on the mimesis of powerful emotion: 'Murder thy breath in middle of a word? / Then again begin, and stop again': *R3* 3.5.2–3).

Olivia's broken speech raises the issue of the representation of the passions in the comedy. The problem, as with melancholy, is one of authenticity, namely the correspondence between the external expression of emotion and the actual inner experience of the subject. The supposedly love-stricken Orsino, unlike Olivia, never loses control over his own eloquence, and indeed delegates the manifestation of his perturbed mind to Cesario: 'O then unfold the passion of my love' (1.4.24). Thus Viola-as-Cesario, obliged to dissimulate her own feelings towards Orsino, is called upon to simulate those of her employer, which she does with excessive emphasis, thereby casting doubt on the sincerity of her source. Olivia is justifiably unimpressed by this performance ('Are you a comedian?') but, invited to reciprocate Orsino's passions ('And let your fervour like my master's be', 1.5.279), she does so, but towards Cesario himself. The result is a passion triangle in which Viola's 'true' feelings (for Orsino) are expressed through her acting out of Orsino's more dubious feelings (towards Olivia) and are reciprocated by Olivia's 'authentic' passion (towards Cesario).

Sicken and so die: disease, contagion and death

The body in *Twelfth Night* is not always an edifying text; it sometimes resembles an epidemiological treatise. The play is replete with references to illness and infection. Sir Andrew's surname, like his gaunt appearance, is a 'symptom' of sickness (*ague*), boding ill for his future; his dull brain and deficient humours have been further debilitated by an excess of roast beef (1.3.82–4), while Sir Toby, in imagining him between the legs of a housewife spinning off his hair, may be wishing him, among other things, a dose of venereal disease, causing his yellow hair to fall out (1.3.98–100). The urine of the 'distempered' Malvolio, meanwhile, is to be analysed for signs of illness (3.4.99). The language of disease becomes general currency for interpersonal relations in the play, above all through the metaphor of contagion: Sebastian warns Antonio that 'the malignancy of my fate might perhaps distemper [i.e. infect] yours' (2.1.4–5); Malvolio has 'taken the infection' of Maria's plot (3.4.125), which in turn might 'take air and taint' or become infected (127–8); the carousing Feste has a 'contagious breath': an infectious singing voice and at the same time a sweet but potentially deadly respiration, 'dulcet in contagion' (2.3.53–5).

Feste's infectious breath reminds us that the most fearful of spectres for Shakespeare's audience, and the most recurrently evoked malaise in the play, was the bubonic plague: the joke on the clown's dulcet contagiousness alludes to the early modern belief that the epidemic was transmitted by means of respiration, making not only singing and carousing but all forms of human intercourse potentially perilous. In this context an idiomatic expression such as Sir Toby's 'What a plague . . .' takes on possible added significance, especially when referring to the death of Olivia's brother – 'What a plague means my niece to take the death of her brother thus?' (1.3.1–2) – just as Olivia's 'Even so quickly may one catch the plague?' (1.5.287) is both a conventional metaphor for falling in love and a stark affirmation of medical fact.

It has not gone unnoticed that this 'happy comedy' is much preoccupied – among other unhappy topics – with death. Frederick Furnivall, for example, noted the 'shadow of death and distress across the sunshine' (*SC*, 1.537), while W.H. Auden observed that in the comedy 'darkness verges on thoughts of death' (*SC*, 1.521–2). The greatest concentration of such deathliness is in the play's triply mortal opening: in the first scene Orsino, musing on both existential and erotic dying, is told by Valentine that Olivia is bewailing 'A brother's dead love' (1.1.30); in the second scene, Viola likewise mourns her lost brother, and the captain mentions not only the death of Olivia's brother but also the earlier demise of her father; the third scene begins with Sir Toby complaining at Olivia's excessive mourning for her brother. This heavy dose of mortality – and specifically of male mortality – is in part the play's version of the 'anticomic' opening typical of Shakespearean comedy (Frye, 73). The shadowy presence of death, however, extends beyond the first act. In the final scene Cesario's proof of his 'true' identity is his knowledge that the twins' father 'died that day when Viola from her birth / Had numbered thirteen years' (5.1.240–1). Elsewhere this presence is marked by recurrent allusion: by Maria's prediction that Sir Andrew 'would quickly have the gift of a grave' (1.3.30–1); by Feste's death-wish song requested by

Orsino (in 'Come away, come away death', 2.4.51ff.); by the supposed threat of the 'intercepter' attending Cesario in his 'mortal arbitrement' with Sir Andrew at 3.4.255; by the priest's measuring of time as movement 'toward my grave' at 5.1.158, and so on. To be male in this comedy is to be in danger of one's life.

Against this insistence on masculine frailty is a powerful lobby on behalf of the affirmation of life; the play's most explicit spokesman against the deadly dictates of the reality principle is Sir Toby, whose opening words are a veritable manifesto on behalf of unrestrained vitality: 'I am sure care's an enemy to life' (1.3.2). He goes on to develop this position in his outraged refusal to 'confine' himself (1.3.9), namely (among other senses) to be shut up in a coffin. The life principle is represented above all, however, by the play's female characters. Viola 'saves' her brother from his putative death by becoming him, just as she saves Orsino from the deadly self-infatuation of the opening scene. Olivia – who likewise contributes to saving Sebastian – is elected as a totem against the plague itself: 'O, when mine eyes did see Olivia first', exclaims Orsino, 'Methought she purged the air of pestilence', thus comparing her to the nosegays or perfumes worn by Shakespeare's contemporaries to ward off the disease (1.1.18–19).

As an eunuch: castration, civility and intertextuality

Still in the domain of the body – and specifically of the mutilated rather than diseased body – the comedy's most conspicuous 'forgotten' project, namely Viola's design to present herself 'as an eunuch' (1.2.53) at the court of Orsino, is often interpreted as the result of Shakespeare's change of plan, or as a sign of mere forgetfulness: 'no further reference', we are told, 'is made to this part of [Viola's] plan' (Ard^2, 10). Viola's second scene, 1.4, is usually taken to indicate her immediate abandoning of her 'eunuch' role, since Orsino addresses her as 'good youth' (15) and 'Dear lad' (29), just as he later calls her 'boy' (2.4.15, etc.), and treats her as a young male servant (although he is hardly likely in any case to address her as 'Dear eunuch').

It is true that no further explicit reference is made to Viola's supposed disguise as castrato, and it is possible to read her single direct allusion in purely metaphorical terms. Her cross-dressing can be seen, for example, as a form of social self-castration, since in becoming a servant she is obliged to deny the 'gentle' blood that Olivia detects in her (1.5.281–5). Alternatively, it might be taken as a mode of sexual self-denial. Stephen Orgel – noting that 'Cesario', the chosen name for Viola, derives from *Caesarius*, 'belonging to Caesar', but also suggests the participle *caesus*, 'cut', and thus castration (Orgel, 53) – observes that 'Viola as eunuch, then, both closes down options for herself and implies possibilities for others – possibilities that were . . . illicit' (56); that is, her denial of her own sexuality proves attractive to both sexes (Orsino and Olivia).

In this respect, the affinities between *Twelfth Night* and the most important Renaissance treatise on civilized behaviour – Castiglione's *Il cortegiano* (*The Book of the Courtier*, 1528) – are instructive. Cesario's celebrated 'Patience on a monument' speech (2.4.110–18), which tells the story of his 'sister', pining perhaps fatally from unspoken love, strikingly resembles Cesare Gonzaga's story in *Il cortegiano* of tragic self-sacrifice by a young woman. In love with a lord who had been forced to marry another, she similarly pined from unexpressed desire until she 'through longe passion verie feint, at the three yeeres ende, died' (Castiglione, Gg3^{v}). Gonzaga tells the story as an example of extreme sexual self-restraint, of the kind exercised by Castiglione's female protagonist, the Countess Elisabetta Gonzaga, who, married to the impotent Duke Guidobaldo, lived 'xv yeeres in companye with her husbande, like a widowe' (Hh3^{r}). Viola-as-Cesario's story is of course autobiographical, describing Viola's own predicament – not 'like a widow' but 'as an eunuch' – of not being able, because of her false gender and her false social class, to tell her love.

Viola's disguise is in this sense a *mise-en-scène* of 'civilized' female decorum, and is not by chance a response to Orsino's misogynistic speech in which he claims that women are biologically and morally inferior because 'they lack retention' (2.4.96) – in the two senses that they lack the capacity for real love and that they lack sexual self-control – since they are dominated by mere animal 'appetite' (97). The duke's tirade again resembles the speech of Gonzaga's interlocutor in *Il cortegiano*, Gaspare Pallavicino, who argues that women are 'unperfect creatures, and consequently of lesse worthinesse than men', that they are incontinent (i.e. promiscuous) and that they are indeed mistakes of nature, mere males *manqués*: 'when a woman is borne, it is a slacknesse or default of nature' (Castiglione, 199–200). At stake here are two opposing versions of female 'castration': Pallavicino's (and Orsino's) vision of woman as an incomplete and uncivilized man, and Gonzaga's (and Viola's) opposing vision of women's capacity for self-castrating virtue. Thus Viola-as-Cesario's enigmatic 'A blank, my lord', in response to Orsino's enquiry into the girl's fate ('And what's her history?': 2.4.109–10), is precisely a confession of her 'castrated' state, deprived as she is of her identity, her social status and her sexuality, just as her admission in the duel scene that 'A little thing would make me tell them how much I lack of a man' (3.4.295–6) discloses the absence of the male 'weapon' that would enable her to combat.

It may be, then, that Viola's eunuch plan does indeed receive 'further reference', even if the reference is somewhat oblique. In another dialogue with his servant, Orsino seems to come close to questioning his messenger's gender; referring, in the first instance, to Cesario's voice, he affirms 'Thy small pipe / Is as the maiden's organ, shrill and sound, / And all is semblative a woman's part' (1.4.32–4). It is hard not to read 'small pipe' as a punning allusion to Cesario's (undeveloped) 'organ' – which in reality is a 'maiden's' organ or 'woman's part' – while the characterization of his voice as 'shrill and sound' alludes at once to its unbroken highness and to its strength. What the duke seems to evoke here is the figure of the castrato singer much in vogue in early seventeenth-century Europe, notably in operas such as Iacopo Peri's *Euridice*, first performed in Florence in 1600 (in the presence, among others, of Duke Orsini of Bracciano, who shortly thereafter set out for the court of Elizabeth I; see p. 93). This may give added meaning to Viola's claim 'for I can sing' (1.2.54), even if her singing is purely discursive: Viola-as-Cesario's vocal performance, with its eloquence and charm, has the same captivating effect as the *evirato* sopranos' voices on the musical stage.

The eunuch trope may not be limited to Viola, since there are strong hints in the play that the same curtailed condition is shared by others. The financial emasculation of Sir Andrew Aguecheek is figured in a series of insinuations regarding his impotence and infertility, from Maria's 'dry jest' and 'now I let go your hand I am barren' (1.3.74, 77), to Sir Toby's description of Sir Andrew's lank hair (which resembles that of Chaucer's eunuch-like Pardoner) in feminine and detumescent terms: 'it hangs like flax on a distaff' (1.3.98). Sir Andrew confirms these innuendoes in his reluctance to use his masculine weapon in the duel with the equally unarmed Cesario (3.4). As for Malvolio, the clues to his 'castrate' status are more cryptic, like the letter in which they are hidden. As John Astington has pointed out, the 'some are born great' passage in the false billet-doux from Olivia (2.5.141–3) is modelled on Christ's discourse on marriage to his disciples: 'For there are some Eunuches, which were so borne from their mothers wombe: and there are some Eunuches, which were made Eunuches of men: and there be Eunuches, which haue made themselues Eunuches for the Kingdome of heauens sake' (Matthew, 19.12, in the King James version). The implicit suggestion is that Malvolio himself belongs to this category, and indeed his public humiliation can be read as 'a displaced gelding' (Astington, 26).

Viola's plan to play the part of an 'unmanned' man has a venerable dramatic genealogy. It signalled, at least to Shakespeare's more learned spectators, the play's debt to the Latin prototype of cross-dressing drama, namely Terence's *Eunuchus* ('The Eunuch'), whose male protagonist, Cherea, disguises himself precisely 'as an eunuch' in order to gain access to the slave girl Pamphila, whom he proceeds, ironically, to rape. Several of the

Italian comedies of cross-dressing and identity confusion, which serve as analogues if not as sources of *Twelfth Night*, draw on the castration theme, as in *Gli inganni* ('Deceptions'), the 1592 version of the 'Twelfth Night' story by the Mantuan nobleman and poet Curzio Gonzaga, in which Leandro falls in love with two twins, one the real Lucrezia, the other her cross-dressed brother, while Lucrezia in turn falls in love with Cesare, who is 'himself' a cross-dressed girl, namely Ginevra (the 'Viola' figure: see Fig. 16). Ginevra-as-Cesare is nearly found out by the maid Filippa, who perceives him/her – in a scene somewhat analogous to *Twelfth Night*'s 'small pipe' exchange – as being either a eunuch or a hermaphrodite:

CESARE (Ginevra) Maybe you thought I was a woman?
FILIPPA Look, Cesare, if I didn't believe you to be a girl, I judged at least from your behaviour that you were double-sexed [*facesti del doppio*], or that you were a meunuch [*megnuco*].
CESARE A eunuch? Ha, ha, you were really crazy, don't you think so now?
FILIPPA I don't know what to think; if you let me touch it with my hand [*se me 'l farai toccar con mano*] I'll know I'm not talking nonsense.

(Gonzaga, 21)

In Barnaby Riche's prose romance 'Of Apollonius and Silla' (1581) – probably the play's most immediate source – the cross-dressed Silla-as-Silvio, accused of getting Julina pregnant, reflects on her lack of the necessary 'implements' for such an act: 'was not this a foule oversight of Julia, that would so precisely sweare so greate an othe that she was gotten with childe by one that was altogether unfurnishte with implements for suche a tourne' (Riche, 361). Silvio's 'unfurnishte' gender status is revealed in a striptease in which he/she 'shewed Julia his breastes and pretie teates' convincing Julia that her lover (whose virility, i.e. that of Silla's twin,

16 Ginevra disguised as Cesare, from Curzio Gonzaga's *Gli inganni* (1592)

she has already verified) is a hermaphrodite (359; for an extended treatment of the castration theme, see Elam, 'Fertile').

As its all-revealing denouement suggests, Riche's romance is a good deal more brutal than Shakespeare's treatment of the same narrative material. Compare, for example, the respective roles of the sea captain in each work: in Riche he endeavours unsuccessfully to rape Silla, while in *Twelfth Night* he offers Viola moral and material aid. There are similarly striking differences between Shakespeare's play and the 'prototype' of the *Twelfth Night* story, *Gl'ingannati* ('The Deceived'), first produced by the Accademia degli Intronati, Siena, in 1533. The Sienese comedy is full of verve, and its female roles, Lelia (Viola) and Isabella (Olivia) have something of the wit and personality of their Shakespearean equivalents (although they were played by women). Indeed, *Gl'ingannati* seems to offer an early version of the rapport between the female protagonist and the audience, as well as a psychological exploration of female subjectivity, notably in Lelia's confession of the difficulty of maintaining her cross-dressed role, apparently analogous to Viola's 'Disguise, I see thou art a wickedness' speech (2.2.27ff.):

'Oh, how I would deserve it [*come mi starebbe bene*] if one of these young rakes took me by force and, dragging me into some house, tried to find out whether I am male or female! That would teach me to go outdoors at this hour . . . Oh what a cruel destiny is mine!' (Intronati, 104). Lelia's reverie of having her real gender 'verified' through rape is in fact far closer to a male erotic fantasy than to feminine introspection. The eroticism of *Gl'ingannati* is cruder and more physical than Shakespeare's: thus the seduction scene between the passionate Isabella and the reluctant Lelia (2.6, roughly equivalent to *TN* 3.1) reaches its climax, in all senses, in the prolonged, passionate kiss between the two girls, accompanied by the obscene comments of two voyeuristic servants, in a *mise-en-scène* of the erotic male gaze.

In addition to the castration theme, *Twelfth Night* inherits from its Italian antecedents – probably through the mediation of Riche's romance – many of its central narrative topics: its combination of the separated twins theme with that of the cross-dressed heroine; its dramatization of intersecting and cross-gender desire; its emphasis on modes of deception (*inganni*) and especially of self-deception, and so on. Whatever its debts to earlier versions of the story, however, *Twelfth Night* seems to enact a 'civilizing' and 'discursivizing' of the often violent sexual and social intercourse of its predecessors. Indeed, from this point of view, the comedy might be said to be more 'Italian' than its Italian models, closer to the courtly ideal of 'civil conversation' as the interplay of ironical and persuasive wit. The affinity of the play's discourse with the conversational and ideological texture of *Il cortegiano* is in many ways more direct than that of *Gl'ingannati* and its offspring. This can be seen in the respective social settings of the plays: the Intronati comedy is set in a bourgeois world of avid *mercanti* (Lelia's merchant father Virginio has promised her in marriage to another old merchant Gherardo), where financial interest is the primary social value. *Gl'ingannati*, moreover, has a precise geographical and historical setting, namely Rome immediately after the traumatic Sack of 1527, whereby the often brutal interpersonal relationships reflect the violence of the political moment. Nothing could be further removed from the Illyrian courts of Orsino and Olivia, dominated by verbal *cortesia*. Not by chance *Twelfth Night* owes a discursive and behavioural debt to Italian courtesy books, not only Castiglione – possibly alluded to at 1.3.41, if we accept Thomas's emendation of *Castiliano vulgo* to 'Castiglione voglio' – but also Stefano Guazzo's influential *Civile conversazione* (*The Civil Conversation*, translated 1586), which Shakespeare sometimes seems to quote or paraphrase, as at 4.1.50 and 4.2.8 (see commentary).

In its more farcical scenes, *Twelfth Night* dramatizes the effects of importing the Italian discourse of civility into Illyrian (or English) culture. In particular, Sir Andrew has difficulty in adapting his behaviour to the polite body languages of dancing and fencing. In 1.3 Sir Toby dazzles his gull with his knowledge of dances, especially the livelier and more sophisticated variety: the courtly coranto or running dance (124), the lively French cinquepace, deformed to 'sink-apace' (125), as well as its English equivalent, the galliard (115); Sir Andrew cannot resist boasting, in reply, of his ability in the 'back-trick', i.e. the *ricacciata* or backward caper that he is obliged to show off (118; see Fig. 17), usually with disastrous consequences in performance.

Worse, and potentially fatal, things happen when the discourse turns to fencing. The aborted duel between Sir Andrew and Cesario in 3.4 evokes and parodies another popular treatise designed to 'civilize' physical combat, the 1595 fencing manual by the immigrant Italian Vincentio Saviolo, which aims to teach the English how to behave, in Sir Toby's phrase 'by the duello' (3.4.301), that is by the Italian rules of duelling. The proper procedure for initiating the duello, according to Saviolo's guide, is by 'giving the lie', challenging the opponent on an unjust accusation. Saviolo, warning of the danger of 'foolish lyes', gives a comic example of how not to challenge 'as he who will giue the lye ere the other speake, saying: if they saye that I am not an honest man, thou lyest in thy throate' (Saviolo, 353). This is a perfect

17 The caper or 'back-trick' (1.3.118), from Thoinot Arbeau, *Orchésographie* (1589) (see List of Ills)

description of the behaviour of Aguecheek, whose altogether unjustified challenge reads, 'But thou liest in thy throat; that is not the matter I challenge thee for' (3.4.151–2). Sir Toby's stylistic advice to Sir Andrew on the writing of the challenge also looks like a parody of Saviolo, who recommends 'the greatest brevity that may be possible, framing the quarrell with certaine, proper, and simple woordes'. Belch's version is more brutal – 'Go, write it in a martial hand, be curst and brief' – but he adds the self-contradictory recommendation, 'It is no matter how witty, so it be eloquent and full of invention' (3.2.41–2), an open invitation to indulge in witless prolixity, as Sir Andrew proceeds to do (see 3.4.143–65). As for actual fencing technique, Sir Toby sadistically overturns Saviolo's rules, warning his crony to avoid responding to his opponent's 'stuck', or *stoccata*, since 'on the answer, he pays you' (3.4.270–1); Saviolo advises the exact opposite, exhorting the fencer to defend himself against the stuck: 'break the stoccata with his left hand, and answer him again with the other' (Saviolo, 17).

There may be a further echo of Saviolo in Sir Toby's description of Cesario as a 'firago', i.e. virago, defined by Florio as 'a manlie or mankynde woman': this description comes close to unmasking Viola, but at the same time recalls Saviolo's praise for various man-like woman combatants, from the Amazons to Joan of Arc, and especially for cross-dressed female warriors such as the 'Portingall gentlewoman that for religions sake about 4. yeeres now past, lefte of the apparell of her sexe' (Saviolo, 484). Viola's own behaviour fails conspicuously to match these heroic models, but Sebastian replaces her in time to justify Sir Toby's description.

Sir Andrew's incompetence in alien bodily arts is matched by his difficulties with foreign languages: despite Sir Toby's claim that his crony 'speaks three or four languages word for word without book' (1.3.24–5), he fails to understand simple French – 'What is 'pourquoi'?' (1.3.89), although he does manage a French greeting at 3.1.69 – and admits, 'I would I had bestowed that time in the tongues that I have in fencing' (1.3.89–91; time ill-bestowed, as we have seen). Not surprisingly, the most evident lexical and cultural presence in the play is Italian, with its particular cultural kudos; Sir Toby, for example, uses Italian as a mode of mystification in promising Sir Andrew to call on him 'at the cubiculo' (i.e. his chamber, with a possible pun on 'culo', arse: 3.2.50). Shakespeare probably derived this term, like 'intercepter' (*intercettore*) (3.4.217) and others, from John Florio's Italian–English dictionary. The following list (taken from Florio, *World*) shows some of the lemmas and definitions that may have influenced the comedy.

Coranta, Corranta, *a kinde of French-dance.*
Cubiculo, *a chamber.*
Culo, *the arse, taile, fundament or bum.*
Duello, *a single combat, a fight between two.*
Festa, *a feast, a holyday a banquet, ioy, pleasure, solace, a shew.*
Intercettore, *a preuenter, a forestaller, an encrocher, an interceptor.*
Maléuolo, *malitious, maleuolent, spitefull, that oweth ill will, that beareth a grudge, enuious.*

Maleuolére, *to hate, to lothe, to detest, to wish euill vnto, to grudge.*
Maluoluto, *hated, lothed, grudged at.*
Orsino, *a young beare whelpe.*
Stoccata, *a foyne, a thrust, a stoccado giuen in fence.*
Vióla, *a flower called a Violet. Also an instrument called a Violl or Violine.*
Vióla di gamba, *a viol* de gamba.
Virago, *a woman of stout and manlie courage, a manlie or mankinde woman.*

With regard to its intertextual debts, however, the comedy's strongest affinities are probably with Shakespeare's own earlier cross-dressing comedies, *Two Gentlemen*, *Merchant of Venice* and *As You Like It*. It revisits many of the earlier plays' themes and topoi: a hostile (or 'anticomic') situation facing the female protagonist, and her consequent decision to cross-dress; bisexual desire resulting from gender ambiguity (in *As You Like It* Rosalind is courted by both Orlando and Phebe); the presence of a truth-telling clown (Touchstone); a finale bringing about the revelation of identities and the announcement or enactment of double weddings, etc. *Twelfth Night*, nevertheless, differs from its predecessors in several important ways. The inclusion of a different-sex twin multiplies the gender confusion exponentially and introduces a new psychological motivation for Viola's transvestism: unlike the earlier heroines, Viola neither cross-dresses for love nor is already in love when she decides to change gender; she disguises from material necessity and in order to keep her brother 'alive'. Her proposed 'eunuch' disguise is unprecedented: Julia in *Two Gentlemen* dresses as a 'well-reputed page' (*TGV* 2.7.43); Portia in *Merchant of Venice* as a 'young doctor' of law (*MV* 4.1.151), Rosalind as a youth in a 'swashing and martial outside' (*AYL* 1.3.114). Viola is the only cross-dressed Shakespearean heroine to experience difficulty in sustaining her male performance. Rosalind – apart from her reported fainting at the sight of Orlando's blood – plays her double gender role with great verve and absolute confidence, while Portia defeats Shylock with supreme dialectical skill. Viola, instead, confesses both her consternation at the effects of her disguise and her inability to handle her phallic weapon. Shakespeare exploits her predicament for some of the most profound moments of feminine introspection in the canon.

Unlike those of the earlier comedies, moreover, the play's denouement fails conspicuously to tie up the loose threads of its various plots. Viola, unlike her predecessors Julia, Portia and Rosalind, remains cross-dressed until the end, with the result that the nuptial celebrations are postponed until she reappears – some time in the post-dramatic future – in her 'maiden's weeds' (5.1.251). The comedy's outsiders, meanwhile, either leave unreconciled (Malvolio) or are left unassimilated (Sir Andrew, Antonio).

Twelfth Night also entertains significant intertextual relations with other Shakespearean plays, not all of them comedies. There are particular narrative and discursive affinities with a near-contemporary tragedy, *Hamlet*, with which it shares dead fathers, a presumed madman, a duel scene (Hamlet 'gives the lie' to Laertes), letters read aloud, and a number of verbal or conceptual constructions (see 2.1.29n., 3.1.41n., 4.2.22n.).

This is Illyria, lady: space and place

Unlike most of its possible dramatic sources or intertexts, *Twelfth Night* distributes its action between two domestic spaces, the twin aristocratic courts of Orsino and Olivia. The cultural model for such courts in the Renaissance was undoubtedly Italian (Castiglione, Guazzo), although by the beginning of the seventeenth century they had spread throughout Europe and England itself, so that the domestic interiors and exteriors of the play are without predetermined national identity. In the first two acts the location alternates between these two poles: 1.1, 1.4 and 2.4 are set in Orsino's court, 1.3, 1.5, 2.3 and 2.5 in Olivia's. The action shifts increasingly, however, towards Olivia's and away from Orsino's court, which is altogether absent from the last three acts. This is significant in terms of the 'power' relations within the comedy, which see a growing predominance of Olivia, not only through her economic independence and her sense of initiative but also because she is at the centre of the play's network of interpersonal exchanges: she is at once object of desire for Orsino, Aguecheek and Malvolio and subject of desire for Cesario/Sebastian, in addition to being the employer of Feste and Maria (and perhaps Fabian) and the long-suffering 'hostess' of Sir Toby and Sir Andrew. Orsino's court is a centrifugal space from which characters (notably Cesario) set out; Olivia's court is a centripetal space which attracts all the play's characters and action; in the end even Orsino comes to Olivia's domain, thereby acknowledging the effective shift in power.

Olivia's court is further articulated into two spatial areas, internal and external. The internal space is the area of domestic intimacy into which only the immediate members of the household (and hangers-on like Sir Andrew) are admitted. The outdoor space is a venue for receiving outsiders – Cesario, Sebastian, Orsino – but becomes also a more or less undifferentiated location for all the later events, from courtship to duels to arrests. The opposition between outside and inside is significant in Olivia's exercise of power and of desire: in 4.3 she invites Cesario/Sebastian into one of the indoor spaces, the chantry, for the pre-marital contract, but not into her 'house' proper (presumably until they are married); Orsino is kept strategically outside, as Olivia herself underlines in promise of future hospitality, again, presumably, when she is fully married: 'Here at my house, and at my proper cost' (5.1.313). Because of its open and inclusive quality, Olivia's outdoor space is the play's primary venue (six scenes) – 1.5, 3.1, 3.4, 4.1, 4.3 and 5.1 – whereas the more exclusive internal area has four scenes: 1.3, 2.3, 3.2 and 4.2.

Within the action and dialogue, Olivia's indoor 'house' is further divided into more specific venues of transgression and of punishment: a convivial space for carousing in 1.3 and 2.3, traditionally represented onstage as the kitchen, and a claustrophobic space for Malvolio's imprisonment in 4.2, referred to as the 'dark room'. The outdoor space in Olivia's court is alluded to alternatively as 'orchard' and 'garden' (the two terms were synonyms). There is a suggestion that this area also has its subdivisions: Olivia's command, 'Let the garden door be shut', at 3.1.90 implies that her conversation with Cesario takes place in a walled garden or *hortus conclusus* – fashionable in the Renaissance as a space for private exchange – whereas more public scenes, especially 5.1, seem to take place in a more open territory.

Beyond the two main poles of the action, there are other locations that act as transitional spaces between the two courts or between scenes or events: the seashore in 1.2 and perhaps in 2.1; the unspecified location (often indicated as the 'street') of the encounters between Sebastian and Antonio; the place (again the 'street'?) where Malvolio catches up with Cesario on his way to Orsino's house in 2.2. There is, however, nothing fixed about these spatial differences, which are often simply functional to the dialogue. Locations are never specified in Folio stage directions and rarely referred to directly in the play. The open and fluid acting area of the Elizabethan stage did not pose many problems of setting, so that the venue could remain unspecified; the problem arose for later directors (and editors). The fluidity of the represented spaces is suggested by certain inconsistencies within the dialogue, as in 3.4: Sir Toby refers to the venue as the 'orchard' (218), whereas later Antonio recalls his 'private brabble' with the officers in the same scene as taking place 'Here in the streets' (5.1.60).

The play's economy of space feeds into its poetics of place. Viola's opening question on finding herself stranded on the shore – 'What country, friends, is this?' – is one that spectators, directors and critics often pose. The play itself does not do much to answer it, especially since the captain's response – 'This is Illyria, lady' – only raises further questions. Even for Shakespeare's early audiences, 'Illyria' probably did not ring distinct geographical bells. Leah Marcus suggests that 'Illyria was scarcely familiar territory, more significant, perhaps, for its evocation of like-sounding exotics – Elysium, delirium – than for concrete geopolitics' (Marcus, 161). The name therefore discouraged the audience from linking the setting with any contemporary geographical or geopolitical reality.

Historically, Illyria was an ancient region of the Balkan peninsula, designating roughly the Adriatic coast north of central Albania and west of the Dinaric Alps. The region was inhabited from the tenth century BC by the Illyrians, an Indo-European people who later became notorious for acts of piracy against Roman shipping. After a series of wars with Rome, it was defeated in 168 BC and established as the Roman province of Illyricum. Occupied by the Slavs from the sixth century, its name eventually changed to Albania. In Shakespeare's time the name Illyria could still be used to refer to part of the Adriatic coast – roughly Dalmatia – at the time under the dominion of the Venetian republic. It was thus historically a hybrid land, geographically Mediterranean, ethnically Slav but politically 'Italian'.

There are few traces in the comedy of this heritage, with the possible exception of the Italian names, perhaps suggesting the contemporary Venetian connection (although the historical Duke Orsini was actually a Roman aristocrat). Antonio's warning to Sebastian that the terrain is 'Rough and unhospitable' (3.3.11) may allude obliquely to the traditionally warlike character of the Illyrians and especially to their notoriety for piracy (compare *2H6* 4.1.108, 'Bargulus, the strong Illyrian pirate'). The latter association is more directly invoked by Orsino when he addresses his former enemy Antonio as 'Notable pirate, thou salt-water thief' (5.1.65), with reference to a somewhat obscure episode of naval hostility not mentioned elsewhere and rarely developed in performance (with the exception of Trevor Nunn's film; see p. 119). Other possible hints of Mediterranean culture are still more tenuous. Viola's decision to disguise herself as a eunuch

(1.2.53) may suggest a southern Mediterranean world, more Turkish than Dalmatian – as indeed does the captain's reply that he will be her 'mute', as in an eastern harem, subject to the harsh laws enforcing the secrecy of the sultan's inner conclave: 'When my tongue blabs then let mine eyes not see' (60).

In many ways, however, the play's principal place-name is more mythical than geopolitical, and its best-known associations were intertextual rather than international: in Ovid's *Metamorphoses*, Cadmus and his wife, like Viola, are shipwrecked 'Upon the c[o]ast of Illirie' (Ovid, *Met*., 4.701). Likewise the birthplace of the twins, 'Messaline', probably owes more to Plautus's *Menaechmi* than to the historical Massilia (Marseille). Back on the beach, Viola punningly associates the place-name with that of another ideal space: 'And what should I do in Illyria? / My brother he is in Elysium' (1.2.2–3). Illyria is a utopia, a no-place that could be any place. As such, it serves Shakespeare as an alibi, an 'elsewhere' not fully identifiable with any well-defined territory. This in turn allows audiences and directors to project their own mental sets onto the space

With respect to Shakespeare's England, Illyria was certainly, if somewhat vaguely, 'eastern'. As Constance C. Relihan notes, however, the dramatist goes out of his way to dilute the orientalism of its main source, Barnaby Riche's story 'Apollonius and Silla' set in Constantinople and Cyprus. Relihan attributes this erasure of the east to Shakespeare's design to explore his main themes of (English) gender and sexuality, without the interference of the 'Turkish' cultural stereotypes of the source. Still, the play recuperates a degree of exoticism – albeit from a strictly western viewpoint – through reference to travel abroad. The comedy's two allusions to the Sophy (or Shah) of Persia – Fabian's 'pension of thousands' (2.5.174–5) and Sir Toby's 'fencer to the Sophy' (3.4.272) – evoke an oriental world of hyperbolic abundance and fearful prowess, or at least imply the English perception of that world. Both references are inspired by the 1599 eastern voyage of Sir Anthony Shirley and his brothers, whose exploits, including the receipt of lavish gifts, had been recently recounted in two pamphlets: an exoticism knowingly filtered through the eyes of western explorers and narrated, with the necessary exaggerations, for English readers hungry for accounts of 'New World' wonders.

Similarly, Maria's conceit of Malvolio's face having 'more lines than is in the new map with the augmentation of the Indies' (3.2.74–6) alludes to strictly western, and more specifically English, representations of the east: in her case, to Edward Wright's 1600 map of the East Indies (Fig. 18), 'augmented' because of its inclusion for the first time of the island of Nova Zembla, a novelty made possible by the disastrous 1596–7 expedition of the Dutch explorer Willem Barentsz, which came to a premature end in the icefields off the island. Barentsz's unhappy expedition gets a second mention, in Fabian's elaborately figurative warning to Malvolio, 'you are now sailed into the north of my lady's opinion, where you will hang like an icicle on a Dutchman's beard' (3.2.24–6), a warning that it is safer and wiser to stay at home (as well as in one's social place) rather than wander into uncharted regions.

The re-importing of eastern colour into a largely deorientalized setting may be related to the issue of sexuality, since the 'east' – notably Turkey – was generically associated with prohibited sexual practices and especially with homoeroticism; as Relihan puts it, 'The play's authorization of male homosexual desire is linked directly to its delicate negotiation between eastern cultures and English values' (Relihan, 91). With reference to same-sex relationships there is a possible final intriguing note to the play's Balkan affiliations. As P. Näcke pointed out in 1908, and as John Boswell has more extensively demonstrated in 1994, in 'Illyria' and particularly in Albania the Catholic and Orthodox churches sanctioned for a period of over a thousand years a ceremony that permitted the lifelong union of same-sex couples. This ceremony, the *adelphopoiia* rite, is described by Mary Shelley as 'the oaths of friendship which it is usual for the Illyrian warriors to take one

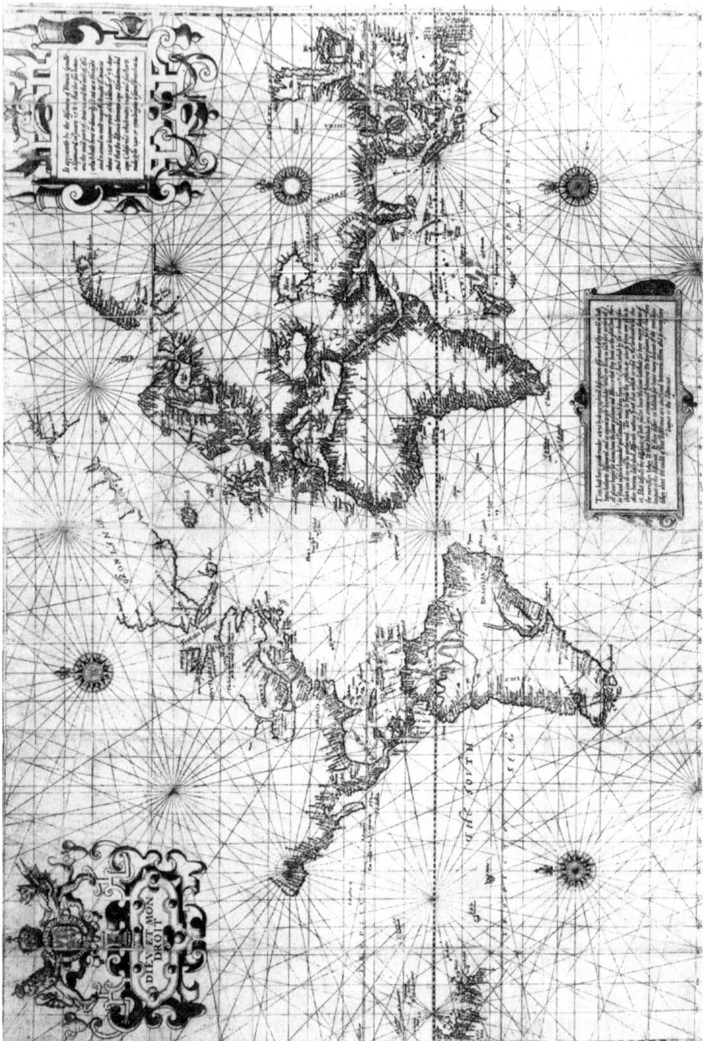

18 'The new map with the augmentation of the Indies' (3.2.75-6), from Edward Wright's *Map of the World*,1600

with the other. Two men thus united are called *Pobratimi*, or half-brothers; they often sacrifice their lives for each other' (Shelley, 73; the text of the ceremony was first published by Jacques Goar in 1647). It is possible that the practice was known to Shakespeare and his contemporaries, as it was to Byron and his. This may cast an oblique light on the unions in *Twelfth Night*: Antonio's passionate attachment to Sebastian, the bond between Orsino and his 'boy', or the 'handfasting' ceremony (see Fig. 19) which supposedly takes place between two women (Olivia and the cross-dressed Viola) but which on the Elizabethan stage was performed by two men.

From many points of view, however, Illyria resembles nothing more than Shakespeare's England. Despite its Italianate names, the comedy presents a gallery of recognizable English social types, from the tankard-wielding knight to the 'Puritan' steward to the professional motley-clad clown or fool (or indeed his alter ego, the ignorant country parson Sir Topas). It also presents evocations of English folklore, such as Sir Toby's comical allusion to the bed of Ware 'in England' (3.2.45), reminding us that we are supposedly abroad. More specifically, there are indications that events are located in the English capital. One of the play's running jokes is a series of allusions, some of them quite overt, to contemporary London. The most explicit of these are Antonio's references in 3.3, where he gives Sebastian money to go sightseeing in what the latter calls 'this city' (24). Antonio's dubious tourist agency advice is to visit 'the south suburbs' (39), the notorious 'liberties' south of the Thames, known not only for their theatres but also, according to a 1596 Privy Council order, for 'stables, ins, alehowses, tavernes, garden howses converted to dwellings, ordinaries, dicying howses, bowling allies and brothell howses' (Browner, 35; see also Mullaney, 20–55). It looks as though Antonio is financing the *ingénu* Sebastian to discover a world of questionable new pleasures. He also has ideas for accommodation: 'at the Elephant, / Is best to lodge'; this continues the joke, since the Elephant Inn on Bankside,

19 'Mutual joinder of your hands' (5.1.153): the handfasting ceremony, from George Wither, *A Collection of Emblems* (1635)

doubtless well known to Shakespeare's audience, was infamous precisely as one of the 'brothell howses' condemned by the Privy Council (Ungerer, 103).

There may be a further, more occult, reference to a London tavern in Feste's 'nonsense' during the nocturnal revels of 2.3: 'the Myrmidons are no bottle-ale houses,' he affirms (2.3.26–7), with a probable punning allusion to the Mermaid Inn in Cheapside, in the City (on the other side of the river from the Elephant). In the same scene Aguecheek's 'I sent thee sixpence for thy leman' (23–4) would have evoked for the audience another East London location, Leman Street, just as the clown's evocation of 'the bells of Saint Bennet' (5.1.35) probably refers to the church of St Bennet Hithe in Paul's Wharf, close to the Mermaid.

In order to get from the City to the south bank with its playhouses and brothels, Londoners crossed the Thames by London Bridge or by boat-taxis; Viola-as-Cesario alludes to this southward and westward river crossing in an exchange with Olivia: 'OLIVIA There lies your way, due west. / VIOLA Then westward ho!' (3.1.132). 'Westward ho!' was precisely the cry of passengers hailing wherrymen to take them across the river: Cesario is ready to set out in the same direction as Sebastian on his sightseeing tour.

The whirligig of time: levels of temporality

Not surprisingly, in a comedy declaredly dedicated to a seasonal occasion, there is a good deal of concern with the passage of time. This is sometimes perceived with anxiety, as in Olivia's 'The clock upbraids me with the waste of time' (3.1.128) and the First Officer's 'The time goes by. Away!' (3.4.361). The play is correspondingly full of references to clocks and watches (2.5.57, 3.1.128, etc.: see Potter, 17) and has its maniacal timekeepers, such as the priest who measures every moment of his mortality: 'Since when, my watch hath told me, toward my grave / I have travelled but two hours' (5.1.158–9). Time, however – and in particular the slow time of personal and social maturation – is also the medium of redemption. Viola twice entrusts her fate to its long-term workings: 'What else may hap to time I will commit' (1.2.57); 'O time, thou must untangle this, not I' (2.2.40). Time is also the object of ideological strife: the play opposes the reality principle of Malvolio's sense of temporal decorum ('to gabble like tinkers at this time of night', 2.3.86–7) to the pleasure principle of Sir Toby's investment in timelessness ('We did keep time, sir, in our catches', 2.3.91).

What this suggests is that there are different perceptions and different levels of time at work in *Twelfth Night*. These differences find expression in the play's notorious 'double' time scheme, whereby on the one hand Valentine congratulates Viola-as-Cesario on becoming the duke's favourite in 'but three days' (1.4.3), while on the other Antonio informs Orsino that he has known Cesario/Sebastian 'for three months', and the duke confirms that 'Three months this youth hath tended upon me' (5.1.95). Such discrepancies do not trouble audiences, and the temporal allusions need not be taken too seriously or too literally, especially as 'three' seems to be the conventional measure of time in the play – Malvolio fantasizes having been married 'three months' to Olivia (2.5.41); the captain calculates the distance of Orsino's court 'Not three hours' travel' from the shore (1.2.21), etc. None the less they do mark differences in the rhythm of events between, on the one hand, the relatively slow development of the overall narrative frame and, on the other, the hectic comings and goings onstage, conducted at a more rapid pace. In the end, these different rhythms converge in the real time of the performance, which alternates episodes of busy stage traffic (3.4, 5.1) with more static scenes of leisurely exchange (1.5, 2.3): 'golden time convents', as Orsino puts it (5.1.375).

Words are very rascals: language and discourse

Everything in a play text is filtered through language, the most important weapon in the dramatist's armoury. In *Twelfth Night* language is both a richly varied expressive means and a significant object of dramatic and comic reflection. The most evident, but not always unproblematic, aspect of the play's linguistic make-up is its division into verse and prose. Malvolio's 'Soft, here follows prose' (2.5.138–9) signals an awareness of the strategic importance of prose and verse distribution within the dialogic economy of the play. In general, verse and prose indicate 'high' and 'low' language respectively, but this distinction is by no means rigid. Verse seems to be set up as the play's 'default' mode in the two opening scenes; Orsino invariably speaks in verse, as does Olivia in her formal moments, and Viola and Sebastian in their more dramatic or 'romantic' scenes. Normally those addressing Orsino adopt his own verse mode – as a sign of decorous respect – with the exception of Feste, licensed to speak prose with everyone. Viola and Sebastian speak verse on their mutual rediscovery (5.1). Verse is also the vehicle of thought in soliloquies.

Prose, the medium of idiomatic realism, is invariably spoken in the 'low' scenes involving Sir Toby and his cronies; it is spoken by Feste (with the exception of his songs) and by Malvolio, as well as by Olivia in informal scenes, for example when she is fooling with Feste, conversing with Sir Toby and, sometimes, with Maria. The verse–prose distinction is not always coherent: Sebastian and Antonio speak prose in their first scene (2.1) and verse in their second (3.3). Other scenes are 'mixed', signalling differences in class and linguistic register: in the dialogues between Olivia and Maria, for example, the former usually speaks verse, the latter prose.

Verse is the medium of Shakespeare's lexical inventiveness. Apart from Feste's playful nonce-words ('impeticos thy gratility', etc.) Shakespeare's apparent neologisms appear especially in verse scenes of particular lyricism, such as 1.4, or dramatic intensity, such as 5.1: for example, 'unprofited' (1.4.22), 'rubious' (1.4.32) and 'semblative' (1.4.34); 'triplex' (5.1.34), 'baubling' (5.1.50), 'unauspicious' (5.1.109), 'joinder' (5.1.153), 'interchangement' (5.1.155) and 'grizzle' (5.1.161). These coinages, a sign of Shakespeare's linguistic creativity in his poetry, contrast with the simpler and more familiar language of the prose, with its mimesis of colloquial conversational discourse. The prose passages make abundant use of 'everyday' idioms, for example so-called discourse markers, namely 'small words and phrases which add emotional tone and colour to what is being said' (Blake, *Grammar*, 290), and which have little direct referential meaning; the master of these typically spoken forms is Sir Toby, with his 'why's, 'what's, 'come come's, 'tut's, 'how now's, 'go to's, 'I say's, and the rest (on the punctuating of discourse markers, see Appendix 1).

Other small but significant words that mark the social and interpersonal dimension of the play's discourse, especially in the prose scenes, are personal pronouns, and in particular the so-called pronouns of power – 'you' and 'thou' – that indicate the degree of familiarity, formality or relative dominance between two speakers. These terms are an important aspect of comedy's representation of social and class relationships. Again it is Sir Toby who displays the greatest degree of skill and self-awareness in deploying these potentially lethal pronominal weapons. He strategically adopts familiar 'thou' with Sir Andrew, while the latter uses a more formal 'you' in their exchanges; such familiarity might be interpreted merely as a sign of equality or of friendly informality, were it not for his advice to his gull to 'thou' Cesario in his letter of challenge, as a sign of contempt (3.2.42–3); this suggests that Sir Toby's own 'thou'-ing of Aguecheek is likewise a calculated put-down. He uses equally dismissive 'thou's towards Malvolio, and even the strategic omission of the pronoun serves to underline the point in his ineffably disdainful 'Art [thou] any more than a steward?' (2.3.112).

The strategic and self-aware deployment of 'thou' and 'you' is part of the play's broader rhetoric of social and class interaction. *Twelfth Night* is perhaps Shakespeare's most class-conscious play, and at its centre is the irresistible drive towards upward social mobility that characterized early seventeenth-century England. The movement towards 'the degree of my betters' (1.3.113) involves all characters who are not already of the gentry, with the exception of Feste, for whom social promotion would entail loss of role and identity. The distribution of social prizes is ironical: those who ardently aspire to gentrification, such as Malvolio and Sir Andrew, fail miserably to achieve it, whereas those on whom it is most generously bestowed, Viola and Sebastian, do not actually desire it. Only Maria manages to pull off the social mobility she tacitly seeks.

The chief domain of *Twelfth Night*'s discursive exploration of social class is the relationship between master/mistress and servant. The comedy presents a veritable catalogue of kinds of domestic staff, including a steward, a 'servingman', a chambermaid and a jester, as well as unspecified servants and attendants. It is, moreover, the only Shakespeare play in which servants (Viola, Malvolio, Maria, Feste, perhaps Fabian) are leading characters, not on behalf of their betters (as with the ingenious servants of the classical tradition, for example in *Comedy of Errors* or *Two Gentlemen of Verona*) but in their own right. Accordingly, it is replete with allusions to service, beginning with Viola's double reference in her first scene, adumbrating her go-between role between two noble houses and two noble rivals for her services: 'O that I served that lady' (1.2.38); 'I'll serve this duke' (1.2.52). Events in the play cause the verb 'serve' to take on the double meaning of 'be a servant to' and 'be romantically devoted to', since both its main and its secondary plots are based on superiors becoming 'servants' (enamoured) of their servants: Olivia and Orsino are both enamoured of Cesario; Olivia is supposedly infatuated with Malvolio (who is 'limed' by the idea of becoming master of the countess – '*She that would alter services with thee*' (2.5.153–4; note the intimate '*thee*'); Sir Toby dotes on and eventually marries Maria (on service and love in the comedy, see Schalkwyk). This overlapping of the domestic and romantic service reaches its climax with Viola-as-Cesario's 'Your servant's servant is your servant, madam' (3.1.100: i.e. Viola, devoted to Orsino, in turn enamoured of Olivia, is at the disposition of the countess as the servant Cesario).

The social rhetoric of *Twelfth Night* is centred precisely on the figure of Viola-as-Cesario, who adopts different discursive strategies, respectively, towards the duke and the countess, even if with both she/he is involved in an asymmetrical relationship (servant–master and messenger–noblewoman respectively), clearly marked by the you–thou dialectic. Cesario respectfully 'you's the duke throughout, even after the latter's proposal of marriage, while the duke 'thou's his servant from the outset. The servant also adopts a systematic strategy of politeness towards his master, both in the observation of conventional deferential forms acknowledging the difference in rank and power between them ('On your attendance, my lord', 'Sure, my noble lord') and in his explicit willingness to subordinate his will to his master's, most notably in his readiness to die in obedience to the duke's violent whim in the final scene ('And I most jocund, apt and willingly / To do you rest a thousand deaths would die', 5.1.128–9; on politeness strategies in Shakespeare, see Magnusson, *Dialogue*, 17–57). Viola-as-Cesario's extreme politeness towards the duke, her/his constant anxiety to be 'very worth his service' (1.2.56), is of course motivated primarily not by social constraints but by interest, since her/his desire 'to serve this noble count' plays on the twin senses of 'serve', the professional and the amorous. Cesario's hyperbolic sense of service at once masks and expresses Viola's love.

Cesario's strategy with Olivia is quite different. While Olivia alternates uneasily between 'you' and 'thou' in their second meeting (3.1), Cesario, as Orsino's reluctant go-between, always duly 'you's his social superior and appears to adopt appropriately deferential modes of address: 'My duty, madam, and most humble service' (3.1.93), etc. In practice, though, he undermines his superficially polite mode through parodic exaggeration – 'Most radiant, exquisite and unmatchable beauty' (1.5.165) – and by blatantly casting doubt on the very identity and social status of the interlocutor: 'The honourable lady of the house, which is she?' (163). This conflict between apparent politeness and actual effrontery is not lost on the countess, who complains, 'Sure you have some hideous matter to deliver when the courtesy of it is so fearful' (201–2). In a play which, as David Schalkwyk observes, 'is as much a study of service and master–servant relations as it is a comedy of romantic love' (Schalkwyk, 86), it is not surprising that politeness should become an overt issue. Viola-as-Cesario's 'fearful' courtesy, or discourtesy, again expresses her/his own interests: Cesario's transgressive flouting of the rules of politeness expresses Viola's desire to sabotage the love mission on the duke's behalf. The irony, of course, is that in practice it only acts to increase the countess's desire – for the servant.

The comedy's social rhetoric is intertwined with its figurative rhetoric. The use of rhetorical figures in the play is selective and strategic, serving specific purposes within given scenes or dialogues. The most rhetorically dense scenes are those in verse, where a figurative flourish may serve to set a 'high' or dramatic tone; here rhetoric becomes a mode of performance, notably in Orsino's self-dramatizing exhibitions, as in the overwrought similes ('like the sweet south', 1.1.5ff.) and elaborately extended metaphors or allegories ('O, when mine eyes', 18ff.) with which he presents his credentials in the opening scene. Rhetorical figures play particular dramatic or comic roles precisely when, as in Orsino's opening performance, they are strategically overdone. This is the case with one of the comedy's most characteristic tropes, the figure of excess *par excellence*, namely hyperbole, which Puttenham baptizes 'the Ouer reacher' and defines as 'when we speake . . . beyond the limites of credit' (Puttenham, 159). Hyperbole, usually in the form of exaggerated metaphor or simile, is at times used in earnest, as in the exchanges of intensely polite and possibly homoerotic compliments between Antonio and Sebastian, 'If you will not murder me for my love, let me be your servant' (2.1.32–3), varied ironically by Maria with reference to Malvolio, 'I have dogged him like his murderer' (3.2.72); or in Olivia's emphatic expressions of amorous effusion towards Cesario: 'I had rather hear you to solicit that / Than music from the spheres' (3.1.107–8). More often than not, however, the hyperbolic mode in the play is pushed towards the verge of parody, as in Cesario's over-emphatic courtesies towards the (hyperbolic) Olivia, designed to make Orsino's courtship look shoddy and to make fun of the countess's own attitude: 'Most radiant, exquisite and unmatchable beauty' (1.5.165). In general, hyperbole becomes so much part of the comedy's linguistic and behavioural texture that Feste, disguised as Sir Topas, attributes the devil's supposed tormenting of Malvolio to it: 'Out, hyperbolical fiend' (4.2.25).

In the same 'dark room' scene, Feste proves himself master of another recurrent figure in the play, namely paradox; indeed it is Sir Topas's disorienting paradoxes, rather than the devil's hyperboles, that torment Malvolio: 'Why,' he says of the dark room, 'it hath bay-windows transparent as barricadoes, and the clerestories toward the south-north are as lustrous as ebony' (4.2.36–8). Being a figure of logical self-contradiction, paradox is one of the main weapons in Feste's armoury as 'artificial' or philosophical fool, allowing him to overturn the conventional wisdom or false politeness of his interlocutors: 'the better for my foes, and the worse for my friends,' he responds to Orsino's 'friendly' but condescending 'How dost thou, my good fellow?' (5.1.9–11). Elsewhere, paradox is the direct verbal expression of stage situations that are in themselves straining with logical self-contradiction, such as the possible simultaneous death and survival of Sebastian, which prompts Viola-as-Cesario to produce the paradoxical conceit, 'Tempests are kind, and salt waves fresh in love' (3.4.381). It is likewise the internal and psychological tensions within the narrative that give rise to a related figure of logical contradiction, oxymoron. Viola-as-Cesario's nautical paradox in the last scene is echoed in her oxymoronic 'happy wreck' (5.1.262), while she also uses oxymoron to express the increasing difficulties of her disguise role after Olivia has fallen in love with her, characterizing it (and her/himself) as the 'proper false' (where 'proper' means both handsome and true; 2.2.29). The dangers inherent in the disguise are similarly condensed in Antonio's 'beauteous evil', used of the treacherous Cesario/Sebastian (3.4.366). Champion of the oxymoron as a mode of ironic put-down, instead, is Sir Toby, while its inevitable victim is Sir Andrew: Toby addresses him as 'dear venom', making fun of his momentary anger (3.2.2), and goes on to mock his 'dormouse valour' as a fighter (3.2.18).

A particularly significant role in this comedy of twins and doubles is played appropriately by syntactic figures of splitting and doubling. Ploce, which Puttenham nicknames 'the doubler' (Puttenham, 168), is a device involving the repetition of a word separated by one or more other words, whereby the meaning of the repeated term changes (or 'doubles'); not by chance it is the figure that Viola and the captain resort to with reference to the former's 'lost' twin, who may or may not have died: 'Perchance [i.e. perhaps] he is not drowned,' suggests Viola hopefully; 'It is perchance that you yourself were saved,' replies the captain, changing the meaning of the word to a less optimistic 'by chance'; 'And so perchance may he be,' she insists (1.2.4–6). A more ironic but perhaps more sinister use of the same device is Maria's reply to Sir Toby's claim that Sir Andrew is blessed with 'the good gifts of nature': she splits the 'gifts' in question into 'the gift [i.e. talent] of a coward' that he possesses and 'the gift [i.e. present] of a grave' that awaits him.

Another prominent splitting or doubling figure in the play is hendiadys, significantly rebaptized by Puttenham as 'the figure of Twynnes', since through it 'ye will seeme to make two of one not thereunto constrained' (Puttenham, 147). It consists in the use of two nouns connected by a conjunction in place of a noun and qualifier: 'that miracle and queen of gems', instead of 'miraculous queen', in Orsino's effusion on Olivia's beauty (2.4.85). Like ploce, this figure of twins is adopted precisely by one of the twins, Sebastian, in a metaphor recalling the storm that separated them: his allusion to Olivia's unexpected passion for him as 'this accident and flood of fortune' (in place of 'accidental flood'; 4.3.11). The opposite process also arises in the comedy, namely a form of ellipsis that we might call hendiadys in reverse; here a phrase comprising two nouns linked by a conjunction is transformed into noun and qualifier: 'I could not with such estimable wonder overfar believe that' (instead of 'esteem and wonder') says Sebastian, with reference to his similarity to Viola (2.1.25–6). These two figures not only mirror each other but mimic the optical mirroring between the twins themselves: the final scene presents the two possibilities of a doubled image (a kind of visual hendiadys) or of two separate images contracted into one (hendiadys in reverse).

The language and metalanguage of the play are marked by a degree of rhetorical self-awareness, often playful or ironical (as in Feste's 'hyperbolical'). In encouraging Sir Andrew to write his challenge, Sir Toby invokes two of the five parts of rhetoric: 'It is no matter how witty, so it be eloquent and full of invention'

(3.2.41–2); the double allusion is to *inventio*, the finding of arguments (for the challenge) and *elocutio*, style. The joke, of course, is that the letter observes neither, proving sublimely witless rather than 'witty'. Sir Andrew none the less endeavours to show off rhetorical knowledge in his disastrous exchange with Maria. Bemused by her semantic acrobatics and suspecting hidden meanings, he is prompted to ask, 'Wherefore, sweetheart? What's your metaphor?' (1.3.69–70). This gives Maria another chance to hint at his impotence ('It's dry, sir'), thereby provoking another semantic crisis: 'SIR ANDREW But what's your jest? / MARIA A dry jest, sir' (73–4). Maria's 'dry jest' may be another rhetorical allusion: the 'drye mock' was Puttenham's term for irony (Puttenham, 157), of the kind Maria adopts against her hapless interlocutor.

Such linguistic self-awareness is part of a broader metalanguage running through the play regarding the very nature of the linguistic sign. The comedy's chief interrogator of the sign is Feste, who repeatedly expresses a radical scepticism concerning the reliability of language as a means of representing the truth: 'words are grown so false I am loath to prove reason with them' (3.1.23–4). Feste's distrust is posited on the arbitrariness of the sign, whereby the relationship between signifier and signified is merely conventional and thus unstable, open to continuous change and easy manipulation: 'A sentence is but a cheverel glove to a good wit: how quickly the wrong side may be turned outward' (3.1.11–13). Such scepticism towards the sign is close to – and may echo – that of Montaigne: 'There is both the name, and the thing . . . the name, is neither part of the thing nor of substance: it is a stranger-piece ioyned to the thing' (Montaigne, 359). The clown's specific accusation, made playfully but at the same time in earnest, is that the arbitrariness of the sign renders it promiscuous, since it is always open to new semantic relationships, especially in the hands or on the tongue of an able word-player: 'They that dally nicely with words may quickly make them wanton' (3.1.14–15). The paradox of this position, of course, is that it is precisely Feste's professional task to exploit the semantic wantonness of words in order to produce the punning and fooling of which he is master: as he admits, 'I am indeed not her fool, but her corrupter of words' (3.1.34–5).

In his encounter with Sebastian, Feste hints at a more radical critique of our pretence to knowledge, affirming drastically that 'Nothing that is so is so' (4.1.8). This suggests a 'Platonic' diffidence not only towards language but to all modes of representation and thus towards all forms of supposed knowledge. The events of the play – in which all visual as well as verbal data are overturned and all representations turn out to be deceptive – go some way to validating his claim, although, lest we take his ontological negation ('Nothing . . . so') too seriously, he states the exact opposite in Sir Topas's parody of logical analysis, namely, 'That that is is' (4.2.14–15: see commentary). This shifting between negation and affirmation feeds into the comedy's dialectic between semiotic scepticism and faith. Feste's critique of the sign runs counter to other moments in the play that affirm emphatically the magical potentialities of verbal and visual representations, from Sebastian's 'wonder that enwraps me thus' before the words and actions of Olivia to the latter's 'Most wonderful!' and Fabian's 'Which I have wondered at', faced with the spectacle of the finale (5.1.221, 352). The last scene brings about a reconciliation between Feste's negation ('Nothing that is so is so') and affirmation ('That that is is') in the duke's 'that is and is not' (213). In *Twelfth Night* the sign is at once itself and its own opposite.

MAKE A GOOD SHOW ON'T: *TWELFTH NIGHT* IN PERFORMANCE

If this were played upon a stage: performances virtual and actual

Twelfth Night is a play unusually aware of its destiny as a script for performance. At several points in the comedy Shakespeare toys with awareness of the *mise-en-scène* in progress: the most explicit of these moments is Fabian's affirmation, in the full flow of the cross-gartering episode, that 'If this were played upon a stage now, I could condemn it as an improbable fiction' (3.4.123–4). This is an 'authenticating' device (Burns), since it presupposes that the scene is *not* being played but is really happening 'now' and here. At the same time it raises a laugh from the real audience, amused by the irony of Fabian's apparent lack of knowledge of where he is (but also by the suspicion that really he does know).

The comedy is replete with the language of performance, hinting at a secret consciousness of what is taking place – or that *it* is taking place – onstage. Viola's début as Cesario, for example, introduces an insistent theatrical vocabulary that goes beyond the simple playing of a disguise role. To Olivia's question 'Are you a comedian?' (1.5.177) – dangerously close to theatrical as well as dramatic truth – Cesario responds, still more dangerously, 'I am not that I play' (179). What gives this metatheatrical language its piquancy is its gendered quality. When Cesario claims that he has taken pains to 'con' his speech, he is not only using actor's parlance but is hinting at the gender complications at work, since 'con' is (French) slang for the female genitals, which Viola conceals and the boy actor feigns to possess. Similarly when, later in the scene, Cesario praises Olivia's charms, but with the proviso 'if God did all' (229), he is alluding in part to the cosmetic transformation of male player into aristocratic female beauty.

Such self-consciousness is linked to a peculiar characteristic of *Twelfth Night*, namely its unusually detailed scripting or inscribing of a virtual performance. Because of its close attention to modes of dress and other forms of behaviour, the play is unusually 'coercive' in specifying the details of what transpires onstage: Malvolio, for example, must have some form of yellow hose and gartering for the joke to work in 3.4, just as Olivia must cover her face in 1.5. There is likewise a strict correspondence between text and performance in the verbal indication of minimal physical actions at the moment they occur onstage, or a moment before or after they occur, from Sir Andrew's capering, to Maria's playing with his hand, to her dropping of the letter, to the men hiding in the box-tree to the innumerable takings of hands and exchanges of objects (Olivia giving a ring and miniature to Viola or a pearl to Sebastian, Orsino and others giving money to Feste, and so on). The text's minimalist implied 'stage directions' in the dialogue even include precise modes of movement such as Sir Toby's 'halting' gait when drunk and injured (5.1.187).

This does not mean, of course, that *Twelfth Night* must always be performed in more or less the same way. What it entails, rather, is an extraordinary interaction between the character's 'virtual' body, appearance and movement and his or her actual representation onstage through the real body of the actor. One of the means of creating this relationship is deictic reference (e.g. through demonstrative pronouns) to the actor's gestures or to props, as in Sebastian's astonished 'This is the air, that is the glorious sun; / This pearl she gave me' (4.3.1–2), which implies an accompanying gesture taking us from the general environment to the particular object in his hand. Such a relationship is one of the causes of intense audience involvement, since the spectator often has the heady impression of witnessing in real time a series of micro-performances planned and commented on by the characters themselves.

A particularly important discursive role in the comedy is played by doors, virtual and (in performance) actual. As Lois Potter notes, '*Twelfth Night* is unusual in the amount of attention that is paid to the business of getting in and out of these doors' (Potter, 25). The two doors of the Middle Temple screen and the two (or possibly three) of the Globe stage become the locus not only of the play's busy onstage traffic but of references, gestures and jokes within the dialogue. Attention to doors is created in part by the difficulty of entering Olivia's household, underlined in Orsino's exhortation to Cesario, 'Be not denied access, stand at her doors' (1.4.16), and in Cesario's obedient obstinacy, 'he says he'll stand at your door like a sheriff's post' (1.5.143–4). Olivia herself later orders, 'Let the garden door be shut' (3.1.90). Olivia's door is varied in the gate to her garden (still represented in performance by a stage door): 'there is at the gate a young gentleman,' Maria informs Olivia (1.5.95). 'What is he at the gate, cousin?' the latter asks anxiously (112–13). The puns on gait/gate (1.4.15, 3.1.81) further foreground the difficulty of entry. The comedy's business with doors includes the split-second timing of simultaneous entrances and exits: Cesario and Malvolio entering at separate doors at 2.2.0.1–2, Sir Toby and his cronies exiting at one door as Sebastian enters at the other at 5.1.204, and so on. Such simultaneity may be exploited in performance for comic effect: for example, the interrupted exits of Orsino and Cesario at 5.1.138ff., both frozen by Olivia's 'husband' (see p. 115), or Malvolio's often exaggerated calling to Maria at the door at 1.5.159–60.

Such onstage comings and goings bring us to the actual business of the play's staging. *Twelfth Night* is fairly long, comprising 2,580 lines (compared, for example, to the 2,299 of *Two Gentlemen* or the 2,222 of *Midsummer Night's Dream*; *As You Like It* is longer at 2,797).[1] It does not, however, make excessive demands in terms of staging or scenery. There is no evident use of balconies or discovery spaces. The only significant item of stage furniture is the box-tree in 2.5, which might be an actual plant or merely a screen or other symbolic representation (in the original staging a property carried or pushed on and off the stage through a door) or may have been purely imaginary: Bernard Beckerman observes that 'the box tree is not really required. No further mention is made of it' (Beckerman, 196). A means of setting apart Malvolio's dark room is needed in 4.2: in modern productions, this requirement can be met by lighting, whereas on the Elizabethan stage the likeliest solution was the trap (as sometimes also in modern productions).

Otherwise, the action can unfold rapidly on a relatively empty stage. As Granville-Barker notes, 'There is much to show that the play was designed for performance upon a bare platform stage

1 These statistics refer to the through-numbering of lines in Charlton Hinman's edition of the First Folio.

without traverses, inner rooms and the like. It has the virtues of this method, swiftness and cleanness of writing and simple directness of arrangement even where the plot is least simple' (Barker, 'Preface', 562). The play is therefore straightforward in its staging demands, although paradoxically it is perhaps the very simplicity of its 'virtual' staging that has provoked some directors and stage-managers to devise elaborate sets: the representation of Orsino's court and Olivia's garden and kitchen, for example, exercised designers' imagination in the nineteenth and twentieth centuries (see pp. 100–1).

Other specific physical requirements are likewise minimalist. Only minor props are called for: letters, tankards, swords, purses, coins, rings, jewels (including a 'miniature'), in addition to Feste's pipe and tabor, although certain extra props, such as trunks and pipes, have become part of the play's stage history. The action and dialogue contain some specification of costume: Viola's male disguise (presumably identical to Sebastian's costume); Feste's motley or some variation of it; his gown and beard as Sir Topas; Malvolio's stockings and garters and chain of office; Olivia's mourning dress and in particular her veil; possibly Sir Andrew's coloured 'stock'. Here too, as with props, certain staging conventions unwarranted by the text have grown up, such as Malvolio's nightshirt (see p. 128).

Certain physical features of the players are also implied, such as Sir Andrew's hair hanging, according to Sir Toby (1.3.98), like flax, and traditionally represented as long, straight and yellow; Sir Toby's other joking reference to him as 'tall' at 1.3.18 is sometimes taken literally, as is his final insult – 'a thin-faced knave' – at 5.1.203; this combination, together with Sir Andrew's own sickly surname, has produced an endless line of lanky and skinny Aguecheeks. Sir Andrew's appearance contrasts strategically, of course, with the corpulence of his exploiter, Sir Toby, implied in the latter's general behaviour and in his specific refusal to 'confine' himself at 1.3.9. Feste's claim at 4.2.6 to be 'not tall enough' to play a priest has also been interpreted perhaps over-literally in some productions, as has the analogous smallness of Maria implied in Cesario's sarcastic allusion to Olivia's 'giant' (1.5.199) and in Sir Toby's affectionate epithet 'wren' (3.2.63). But the greatest 'physical' challenge facing actors and producers is how to achieve a convincing likeness between the twins: a challenge that has more often been failed than met.

One of the issues involved in staging *Twelfth Night* is the choice of rhythm. Some directors have seen the play as divided into roughly two halves: a relatively slow and 'romantic' first half, and a more frenetic and comic second half (see M. Billington, xvii). In reality the play is constructed according to a principle of alternation: the languorous opening scene is followed by the more urgent and dramatic 'shipwreck' scene of 1.2, which in turn gives way to the more static domestic comedy of 1.3, and so on. It is true that from the letter scene (2.5) on there is a crescendo of farce, involving not only the gulling of Malvolio but the simultaneous 'duel' and Sebastian's unwitting involvement in both the fighting and the romance; but the interweaving of rhythms and moods better characterizes the play than any binary splitting into 'romantic' and 'comic' halves.

Problems may arise with the staging of the long and busy final scene, which gathers together all the comedy's various narrative threads and brings onstage most of the main characters. The scene is so full that Granville-Barker, one of the play's most innovative directors, was led to complain: 'From any cause, we certainly have a scandalously ill-arranged and ill-written last scene, the despair of any stage manager' (Barker, 'Preface', 563). The difficulty lies not only in stage-managing the scene's endless series of entries and exits and its various *coups de théâtre* – culminating in the 'natural perspective' of the identical twins, notoriously difficult to stage credibly – but in keeping the audience's attention, in the midst of the comings and goings, focused on the twists and turns of the dramatic narrative.

The success of *Twelfth Night* onstage is in part demonstrated by the sheer number and frequency of productions. The list of

120 productions at the end of this Introduction gives a necessarily selective and incomplete summary of the play's performance history from 1602 to 2004. Each production has been assigned a number (in parentheses) which will be referred to in the subsequent discussion.

First Night

As we have seen (p. 3), the first known staging of *Twelfth Night* bears the date 2 February 1602. If the play's title refers, as is often supposed, to the occasion of its first performance, it was presumably staged on 6 January of the same year, or possibly the year before (an even earlier date is improbable, since Manningham would presumably have known about the comedy). The question of the play's theatrical début clearly influences the issue of the date of composition: a first performance early in January implies composition late in the preceding year (i.e. in 1600 or 1601).

The first plausible hypothesis regarding the comedy's début was advanced by the nineteenth-century German critic Gregor Sarrazin, who linked the play to the presence at Queen Elizabeth's court of Don Virginio Orsini, Duke of Bracciano, on 6 January 1601. Shakespeare, according to Sarrazin, conceived his Duke Orsino as a homage to Duke Orsini in a performance commissioned for the latter's visit. This Italian connection, later taken by J.W. Draper and then elaborated into a full historical narrative by Leslie Hotson in *The First Night of Twelfth Night*, is supported by contemporary documents such as a memorandum of the Lord Chamberlain, Lord Hunsdon (patron of Shakespeare's company), referring to the choice, on the occasion of the Queen's 1601 Twelfth Night festivities, of a play 'that shalbe furnished with rich apparel, have great variety and change of Musicke and daunces, and of a Subiect that may be most pleasing to her Maiestie' (Hotson, 15). It is almost certain that the Lord Chamberlain's Men, Shakespeare's company, performed the chosen play; that it was a comedy is demonstrated by a letter sent by Duke Orsini to his wife, the Duchess Flavia, on 18 January, in which he informs her that 'a comedy was performed, mixed with music and dances', adding, disappointingly, 'but I will save this as well [like other details] to tell you about it in person'[1] (230).

Hotson's 'discovery' has been treated with condescension by later commentators, who have almost unanimously dismissed it. There are, however, a number of striking coincidences, at the least: the presence of Duke Orsini (not Orsino, as Hotson rebaptizes him); the performance of a Twelfth Night comedy by Shakespeare's company; the plausibility of 1601 as a date for first performance, and so on. Some of the arguments against the hypothesis are rather weak. The fact that news of the visit by Orsini – who was passing through London on his way home to Italy after accompanying Maria de' Medici to her wedding in France – arrived only on 25 December, leaving insufficient time to write and rehearse the play (Cam²), does not exclude the possibility that the duke's name in the comedy was simply changed to Orsino for the occasion. Likewise the fact that there is music but no dancing in the play – in contradiction with both quoted documents (Ard²) – means little, since dances could well have been added, for example in the play's finale (as in the 2002 Middle Temple performance). More serious is the objection that the lovesick Orsino is a dubious compliment to the (married) Italian guest, and thus probably not 'most pleasing to her Maiestie' (see Cam²). It might also be added that Orsini fails to note in his letter the extraordinary fact that his namesake is the comedy's male lead (unless he saved this too for his oral account to his wife).

If the Orsino–Orsini hypothesis is, in the end, more suggestive than persuasive, this does not mean that there is no connection at all. It is possible, for example, that Shakespeare, present as an actor at the Whitehall banquet, remembered Duke Orsini when he wrote his comedy, perhaps later in the same year or early in the next. This brings us to the second hypothesis, advanced by John

1 My translation of 'si rappresentò una commedia mescolata con musica e balli, e questa ancora mi riserbo a dire in voce'.

Dover Wilson, namely that the first night was Manningham's night, 2 February 1602. Wilson's belief that the play was written for an Inn of Court audience is based largely on his claim that 'the prose scenes are full of legal jests' (Cam[1], 95; Fabian is sometimes played as a law student: see Potter, 34). Wilson's idea has been revived more recently by the Middle Temple barrister Anthony Arlidge, who suggests that the play was written not only for lawyers but with specific Middle Temple lawyers in mind. Like Dover Wilson, Arlidge adduces by way of internal evidence the comedy's supposed plethora of legal references and 'inn jokes', but also presents external evidence for Shakespeare's Inn connections. The most direct link is the dramatist's (somewhat distant) relative Thomas Greene, a student at the Inn at the time of the performance who later – in addition to becoming treasurer of Middle Temple – lived with the Shakespeares in Stratford, where he became town clerk. Shakespeare's close friend Thomas Russell was also a Middle Templar (Duncan-Jones, 138). Arlidge also reads the play's two allusions to the Shirley brothers' expedition to Persia in 1599 (2.5.175 and 3.4.272: see pp. 72–3) as compliments to the brothers' (again distant) relative John Shurley, treasurer of the Temple in 1602. These connections, however, hardly make up a crushing case for the defence of the Middle Temple theory regarding the play's début.

Twelfth Night, moreover, is not in any obvious way a lawyer's play. It is indeed, like other Shakespearean plays, rich in legal allusions, but when the law is invoked in *Twelfth Night* it is more often than not in the context of legal transgressions, in keeping with the carnivalesque anarchy or 'misrule' that governs much of the comedy (see pp. 18–21). For example, Sir Andrew Aguecheek, in his anger against his supposed rival Cesario, appeals to the contemporary English – officially Illyrian – law on battery, only with a view to overturning it completely: 'I'll have an action of battery against him if there be any law in Illyria. Though I struck him first, yet it's no matter for that' (4.1.33–5). Fabian eggs on Sir Andrew in his altogether unjustified challenge, still supposedly in the name of Illyrian law: 'A good note, that keeps you from the blow of the law' (3.4.148–9; see also 159–60). Rather than a play for lawyers, it often looks like a play that suspends the law.

Manningham himself provides no evidence for or against the Middle Temple first night theory. Certainly, a début on 2 February would have rendered the play's title irrelevant, or at best ironic (it should be something like 'Candlemas'). If the title is indeed referential, the likeliest date of first performance is presumably 6 January 1602, which would have meant that the comedy was still fresh less than a month later at the Candlemas performance, which would thereby become 'second' night. Since there is no record of a Temple performance for that date, it must have been staged elsewhere, probably in another private hall, and may have been commissioned for the festive occasion.

There are, in summary, four possible first nights for *Twelfth Night*: at Whitehall on 6 January 1601; at the Middle Temple on 2 February 1602; at the public theatre – the Globe – rather than a private venue, presumably some time in 1601; or on 6 January 1602 in some other private performance space, prior to its appearance at the Middle Temple, and then on the public stage. This last hypothesis is probably the most plausible, but in the lack of new evidence the jury is likely to be out for a long time to come.

Later Nights: adaptations and rearrangements

As for the second performance for which we have a 'review', the precise contents of the 'silly play' that Samuel Pepys repeatedly and disapprovingly saw in the 1660s (see p. 6) is uncertain: the *Twelfth Night* performed at the Duke of York's may well have been an adaptation by Shakespeare's supposed 'natural son', William D'Avenant. What is certain is that the following production we have precise news of was indeed a radical adaptation, namely William Burnaby's *Love Betray'd: or, the Agreable* [*sic*] *Disapoinment* [*sic*] of 1703 (no. 7), which merges Malvolio and Aguecheek into a single character, Taquilet, who is fooled by Drances (Sir Toby) into believing that Villaretta (Olivia) loves him, while the tangled identity problems are solved through the agency of an invented character, Laura, who had served Cesario in France. The adaptation aroused little interest and survived only for a few nights.

The later performance history of *Twelfth Night* demonstrates that it invited, if not adaptation, at least restless rearrangement, especially on the nineteenth-century stage. The innumerable changes made by producers to the Folio's sequencing of episodes suggest that the structure of the play (in some ways akin to the traditional *commedia dell'arte* scenario, where the order of episodes was likewise highly variable) is modular rather than linear. The three main plots – Viola's, Sebastian's and Malvolio's – intersect and alternate with situations involving parallelism and simultaneity, rather than following a strict narrative order. There are relatively few logical cause-and-effect constraints on the sequencing: the delay in Sebastian's first appearance (2.1), for example, is dictated by dramaturgic rather than chronological motives (i.e. the creation of uncertainty regarding his destiny); the scene in turn delays the presumably simultaneous meeting between Cesario and Malvolio in 2.2, which is logically a continuation of 1.5.

The presiding scene structure is the duologue, namely one-to-one exchanges of a more or less intimate kind, and it is precisely the duologic scenes, especially those involving the twins (1.2, 2.1, 2.2, 3.3, etc.), that were most frequently moved in nineteenth-century productions. Elizabeth Inchbald's 1808 edition – closely related to Kemble's Drury Lane stagings – switches 1.1 and 1.2 and then runs 2.1 into 2.2 without a break. The inversion of the two opening scenes, which became common theatrical practice (see Osborne), was provoked partly by theatrical architecture: the proscenium-arch stage made it more economical to get the seaside scene out of the way in order to concentrate on the alternation between the two houses of Orsino and Olivia. But it was also dictated by a sense of the dramaturgic potency of beginning a play with a tempest rather than a disquisition, and by the opportunity of immediately foregrounding Viola's agency. The transposition of the opening scenes continues today, as in Branagh's 1987 production (no. 102) and Nunn's 1996 film (no. 109). Later acting editions (Oxberry, Cumberland, Lacy, etc.) extend Kemble's gesture by similarly moving the 'twin' duologue scene with the first appearance of Sebastian (2.1) to the end of 2.2. In the Folio text the scene acts as a parenthetic episode, interrupting the narrative sequence that begins with Olivia's sending of her ring to Cesario via Malvolio (1.5) and ends with Cesario's receiving it (2.2). Sebastian's unexpected appearance complicates matters, tying a further knot in the plot; the move turns it, instead, into an 'untying' scene, simplifying matters after Viola's lament, 'It is too hard a knot for me t'untie' (2.2.41).

Kemble's own acting edition also rearranged other scenes: the Malvolio episode in 2.2 (1–16) becomes a separate scene, 1.6, placed after Cesario's interview with Olivia; Antonio's and Sebastian's second meeting, 3.3, is moved forward to follow the gulling of Malvolio (2.5), thus preceding Olivia's declaration of love (3.1) and Sir Andrew's plan for a duel (3.2). Karen Greif suggests that Kemble 'realigned the scene order so that each act comprised a defined block of action, usually with strong opening and closing scenes that centred attention on Viola or Malvolio, the two leads' (Greif, 62). The changes, however, are often modes of censorship, especially on moralistic (sexual) grounds (Osborne, 81–92). Throughout the nineteenth century the two scenes between Antonio and Sebastian were continually cut or moved around, a sign of the embarrassment they caused producers, who systematically omitted Antonio's more ardent effusions in 2.1 and eliminated the parallels between Antonio's declaration of love and those of Viola and Olivia. Equally subject to censorship were Sebastian's 'excessive' thanks to his friend at 3.3.13–16, together with his underlining of Olivia's passion for another woman ('maid and man', 5.1.255–9). Kemble, followed by others, also transforms Viola's 'eunuch' (1.2.53) into the more conventional 'page'.

The scene transposition was varied at the end of the century by Daly, whose 1894 production (no. 37) reduced the play to four acts, cutting around 600 lines (Malvolio appeared only in the dark room scene). It began with 2.1 (Sebastian and Antonio), to which 1.2 was tacked on, while 1.1 (now 1.2) was fused with 1.4 (Cesario as go-between) so as not to change the elaborate set of Orsino's palace. Daly likewise fused 1.3 and 1.5 with 2.2 (Malvolio and the ring; Odell, 406). In the same year, Henry Irving (no. 36) combined 1.1 and 1.4, thereby anticipating Viola's presence at the duke's court; this change was repeated in Nunn's film (no. 109), which has Viola-as-Cesario present as the duke's silent pianist. Beerbohm Tree (no. 41) condensed the comedy into a 'well-made' three-act play whose interminable second scene on Olivia's terrace brought together seven separate Folio scenes in rearranged order (1.2, 1.3, 2.1, part of 3.3, 1.4, 1.5 and 2.2).

Perhaps because of its intense concern with music, the comedy has often been subject to musical adaptation. In 1820 Frederick Reynolds produced a controversial version (no. 23), described by Leigh Hunt in *The Examiner* as being 'interspersed with songs, glees and duetts, taken from the German and English masters' (quoted in Odell, 137). Reynolds drew on a wide range of composers, and imported into *Twelfth Night* extraneous Shakespearean songs and sonnets, together with the masque of Juno and Ceres from *The Tempest*. John Genest complained that 'this was Shakspeare's play degraded to an Opera – it was a wretched piece of business' (Genest, 9.99). Analogously, Augustin Daly's highly successful 1894 adaptation (no. 37), which ran for 111 performances, added a violent opening storm and a moonlit rose garden where Orsino serenaded Olivia in Act 3. Other musical embellishments included 'Come unto these yellow sands', from *The Tempest*, sung by fishermen and peasants before the two shipwreck scenes (1.2 and 2.1), while another group of musicians intoned 'Who is Olivia?' to Schubert's setting of 'Who is Sylvia?' (*TGV*) at the end of Act 3.

A number of modern musicals have taken on this most music-centred of Shakespeare's comedies (in addition to a ballet choreographed in 1943 by Andrée Howard to music by Edvard

Grieg (no. 65)). Hal Hester and Danny Apolinair's 1968 rock musical *Your Own Thing* (no. 86) is set in the city of Manhattan Island, Illyria, where Orson is a theatrical agent and Olivia the operator of a discotheque, while Viola and Sebastian, both rock singers, have lost all their music in a shipwreck. Cheryl L. West's 1997 *Play On!* (no. 111) is instead a jazz version, set to music by Duke Ellington. In 1940s Harlem, Vy, a talented young woman from Mississippi, is determined to succeed as a songwriter. The clown Jester dresses her as a man and introduces her to the great bandleader Duke. Vy-Man, as she's now called, falls in love with Duke, but the latter pines for the singer Lady Liv. Peter Mills's well-received 2002 musical *Illyria*, directed by Cara Reichel (no. 117), is more operetta-like; maintaining characters' names and following Shakespeare's plot fairly faithfully, it incorporates parts of his dialogue into the lyrics (the livelier songs including Feste's 'Silly Little Syllogisms', Sir Toby's drunken 'Cakes and Ale' and Sebastian's 'The Lady Must Be Mad'). Slapstick vaudeville numbers were performed below stairs, while Ames Adamson's farcically snobbish Malvolio expressed himself in Gilbert and Sullivan doggerel.

Our shows are more than will: *Victorian special effects and modernist experiments*

The nineteenth century culminated in productions dominated by stage designers. In 1884 Henry Irving (no. 36) cut most of the music and songs and concentrated on the spectacular scenery of designer Hawes Craven, who provided a giddy succession of sixteen different lavish sets, including a palace for Olivia by a palm-lined blue sea. Herbert Beerbohm Tree's 1901 revival (no. 41) was governed by the set designers Hawes Craven (again) and Joseph Harker. Craven created a hyper-realistic Italianate garden for Olivia, in which the shipwrecked Viola was washed up directly in 1.2; it was based on a picture in *Country Life*, and provoked 'an "Oh!" of surprise and delight' from spectators (*The Sketch*). Dominated by a long grass-covered flight of stairs (down which

Malvolio fell spectacularly), it boasted three box-trees, a marble fountain, a bridge, a griffon-adorned stone bench, green lawns and countless colourful flowers under a hazy painted sky (this was the first in a series of optimistic summer productions), and no fewer than six entrances, put to conspicuous use in the letter scene.

The first reaction against such scenographic excesses came from Germany. In 1881 the Royal Theatre of Saxe-Meiningen, under the direction of Duke George II, visited Drury Lane with a production (no. 34) which restored the (translated) text and offered a simple set and Elizabethan costumes, achieving notable results 'by the excellence of ensemble playing alone' (Koller, 85). Modern directorial readings of the comedy are usually taken to begin, instead, with William Poel, whose productions were again a response to Victorian overindulgence. In order to start afresh, Poel and his Elizabethan Stage Society attempted a return to 'early modern' simplicity, and chose an emblematic theatrical space for the enterprise, namely the Middle Temple Hall, where on 2 February 1897 – 295 years after Manningham's 'first night' – they performed the play before the Prince of Wales (no. 39). The Temple production, advertised as being 'after the manner of the sixteenth century', used a mixed-sex cast (no boy actors) and created a curious architectural hybrid in the use of the hall: instead of employing the 'original' empty performance space, Poel endeavoured paradoxically to achieve sixteenth-century 'authenticity' by erecting within it a mini-Swan theatre inspired by the famous de Witt sketch, consisting of a raised platform with a roof supported by carved columns, and complete with gallery (Speaight, *Poel*, 110). There was no scenery and the only furnishing comprised a table and chair, while the costumes were modelled on those of the Elizabethan court. Renaissance music was played on sixteenth-century Italian instruments (a virginal and lute) and a bass and treble viol. Poel was probably influenced by nineteenth-century musical versions of the play in casting the roles with an ear to the operatic vocal qualities of the actors. The resulting performance, at times inaudible, was dismissed by William Archer as 'staged (more or less) after the manner of the sixteenth century and acted after the manner of the Nineteenth Century Amateur' (quoted in Speaight, *Poel*, 135). Two later productions returned to the primal scene of the Middle Temple Hall. On 2 February 1951 (a year early, because of a misinterpretation of Manningham's diary entry), Donald Wolfit produced a 350th anniversary staging (no. 72), dominated by his hyperbolically pompous Malvolio. On 25 January 2002 (eight days early, but performances continued throughout February) the Globe Theatre Company celebrated the 400th anniversary with a highly successful revival (no. 114).

Poel helped create a fashion for performances in the 'Elizabethan' manner. Ben Greet in his 1904 New York production (no. 43) employed a pseudo-Middle-Temple stage, with raised platform, boxed and panelled set and timbered ceiling. The early years of the century also witnessed the desire for a return to Shakespeare's text after the manipulations of the preceding hundred years. In 1914, also in New York, Margaret Anglin courageously used the unedited Folio text, even if this created some difficulties for the audience (no. 47).

It is in the context of a concerted break with the Victorian tradition that there arose the first modernist staging – and the most influential twentieth-century presentation. Harley Granville-Barker's legendary 1912 Savoy production (no. 46) was described by the poet John Masefield as 'much the most beautiful thing I have ever seen done on the stage' (quoted in Styan, 91), a judgement shared by many commentators. Barker, like Poel and Greet, aimed to achieve simplicity and rapidity of performance through continuous staging, with minimal breaks in the action, on a relatively uncluttered stage, while the text, left virtually uncut, was delivered at a fast pace and with a light 'musical' touch; the *Daily Telegraph* praised 'the long multiplex cadences, the sweet melody, the bewitching variety of Shakespearean rhythm'. Unlike his predecessors, however, Barker went far beyond 'archaeological' reconstruction in his endeavour to invent what he called 'a new hieroglyphic language of scenery' (Styan, 91). Norman Wilkinson's extraordinary non-realist set (see Fig. 20) gave Orsino a palace made up of 'twisted barley-sugar pillars in pink' (Trewin, 55) against a Cubist backdrop of pink and green triangles. Olivia had a formal garden with pale green 'Noah's ark' trees, perhaps in parody of Hawes Craven, while the box-trees in the letter scene were represented by two 'Futurist space needles' (Kennedy, 75–6). Wilkinson's costumes were likewise of bright primitivist colours, notably Orsino's 'decadent' pink, set off against Olivia's severe black.

Two years later another ground-breaking 'avant-garde' staging, much admired by Barker, took place at the Théâtre du Vieux-Colombier in Paris. Jacques Copeau's 1914 version (no. 48), like Barker's, 'immediately became one of those rare productions that assume almost mythical proportions' (Kennedy, 81). Copeau (who also played Malvolio) and his designer, Louis Jouvet (who doubled as Sir Andrew), used an empty forestage with a pink drop, cutting off the rest of the space for Orsino's palace, while Olivia's palace was figured by a single locale comprising a cube, a one-step platform, a central recess, and two artificial shrubs; a yellow drop marked a space for exterior scenes, and the entire set was framed by white curtains. Copeau used groupings to create a series of stunning tableaux marked by harmoniously choreographed movement and speech.

In the 1920s and 1930s the Old Vic became the London 'home' of *Twelfth Night*. Robert Atkins's rather conventional productions (nos 50, 55) were an annual event for many years and employed many of the great names of the London stage. The Vic witnessed two rather more adventurous productions by Tyrone Guthrie; the first, his fast-moving 1933 staging (no. 57), again attempted to recapture something of the openness and fluidity of Elizabethan performance; Wells Coates's austere set, comprising 'two curving staircases [and] two formidable pillars' was 'a scene of the utmost severity, massive, stony, bare . . . not a sprig of nature anywhere, even in a pot, and one dreams in vain of the yew-hedge through

20 Norman Wilkinson's futurist set for Harley Granville-Barker's 1912 production

which the knights were wont to whisper' (*Times*). On this naked stage Guthrie achieved strikingly beautiful groupings. His 1937 staging (no. 58), likewise 'played in a nimble and quick-spirited style', was decidedly downbeat in mood, dominated by the awareness of mortality: 'And over all there hangs, like the shadow cast by a sundial, the knowledge that youth's a stuff will not endure'; even the revels were played against 'an ominous background of darkness' figuring 'the shadow of death' (Stephen Williams, *Evening Standard*). Still at the Vic, Harcourt Williams in 1932 (no. 54) introduced what was to become a recurrent feature in later productions, namely a seventeenth-century setting with Caroline costumes. The production boasted an urban set of the same period, 'with a permanent section of red brick wall, steps, and a verandah that gives something of the flavour of a Dutch picture' (J.G.B., *Evening News*).

In the same year a seventeen-year-old American student directed a highly ingenious staging at the Chicago Drama Festival (no. 56). Orson Welles's all-male Todd Troupers performance, originally produced for his school, won first prize at the festival. It featured a twelve-foot-high 'storybook' set (see Fig. 21), in vivid expressionistic colours, representing a volume whose pages turned with each new scene, symbolizing how dramatic life sprang from the text (Berg & Erskine, 396, France, 38). Welles, who played Malvolio, devised for the production a narrative prologue ('Once upon a time, long, long ago, there was a storm at sea . . .'; compare the prologue to Nunn's 1996 film: see p. 118) and a dialogue between Shakespeare and Burbage. In this, Burbage complains at the size of his part: 'What is offered me, me, Richard Burbage, at the zenith of my own personal career? The Duke! The Duke! In a play about twins!' (Mercury, 8–9). A short 16 mm film version was shot in 1933, while Welles's adapted text was published in his Everybody's Shakespeare series a year later.

Some of the more innovative productions before and after the Second World War were the work of women directors. In 1939 Irene Hentschel became the first woman to direct at the

21 Orson Welles's storybook set for his 1932 production

Stratford Shakespeare Festival (no. 62), and her production, according to one irate reviewer, 'shrieks at the conventions, flouts all the traditions' (*Birmingham Mail*, quoted in Schafer, 216). Particularly irksome to traditionalists was the farcical staging of many scenes. This was, moreover, one of the first Stratford productions to choose a modern historical setting, or rather a strategically changeable period style. Hentschel brought in a team of women designers, known appropriately as 'Motley', to create inconsistent costumes: a Dickensian Malvolio, a Regency Orsino, an Edwardian Sir Toby, and so on. An equally controversial event was Joan Littlewood's Theatre Workshop opening production at the legendary Theatre Royal, Stratford East (London), on 2 February 1953 (no. 74), which, with its ensemble Brechtian acting techniques, set out to involve its audience, who showed their feelings enthusiastically, some of them throwing pennies and toffees at the stage (Goorney, 99).

Seasonal Nights

One can divide many of the stagings of the last fifty years or so into two main directorial camps: 'Twelfth Night' productions and 'Illyrian' productions. The former have a primarily temporal and specifically seasonal emphasis, the latter a more spatial – and especially 'exotic' – take on the play.

Seasonal 'Twelfth Night' productions were effectively inaugurated by Peter Hall's highly successful 1958 staging (no. 81), with its 'mistily russet autumnal sense' (Trewin, 238). The evocative sets by Lila de Nobili (designer for Luchino Visconti at La Scala in Milan) included a gauzy Adriatic coastline complete with cloud-topped towers, which gave way to an English garden, suggesting the mixed geographical allegiances of the comedy. The Caroline historical setting (recalling Harcourt Williams's 1932 staging) underlined the ideological conflict at the heart of the play, pitching a Puritan Malvolio against the others, all in cavalier costumes. Hall's aim was also to deconstruct the binary festivity/melancholy opposition by injecting melancholy into the comic scenes and comedy into the 'serious' ones (see Speaight, *Shakespeare*, 278)

Hall's production created a fashion for seasonal interpretations of the comedy that went on to dominate performances, especially in Stratford, for the next three decades. One of the most celebrated modern versions, John Barton's 1969 RSC staging (no. 87), was also decidedly autumnal in mood (although also brilliantly comic). It was visually dominated by Christopher Morley's set, a 'box tapering in false perspective to a small opening upstage which opens to reveal a garden or a shipwreck' (B.A. Young, *Financial Times*), recalling the illusory 'natural perspectives' of the Renaissance, but at the same time evoking 'a skeletal Riviera of sun-streaked reed lattices, wicker garden furniture and parasols' (Ronald Bryden, *Observer*). Much use was made of the perspective-framed entrance of characters, notably Malvolio 'practising behaviour to his own shadow' (2.5.15) as he moved towards the audience. Barton placed great emphasis on the theme of madness, which infected all the characters in different ways, and put Feste at the perceptual centre of the play, so that events were seen largely from his disenchanted perspective.

Ten years later, still at the RSC, Terry Hands (no. 95) gave a Northrop Frye-like reading of the comedy as a life-renewing seasonal passage from snow-laden and frosty-branched midwinter to daffodilly spring. John Caird, again at Stratford in 1983 (no. 98), took Illyria back to autumn in a version that presented the play unambiguously as a dark comedy; Robin Don's set, inspired by Giorgione's *La Tempesta*, figured a bare rocky promontory accompanied by the sound of the surge of the sea, and dominated by a great gnarled autumnal tree that conditioned the entire performance, not least the movements of the actors. This was very much an 'outdoor' production, as was, four years later, Bill Alexander's summertime RSC staging (no. 100) – returning to the sunny solstitial tradition created by Tree in 1901 (no. 41) – in which Kit Surrey's set of lath and plaster against a blue cyclorama figured a sun-drenched white-walled Greek island (see Fig. 22), its main locale being an open square (in the letter scene the plotters overlooked Malvolio from the windows of surrounding buildings). Alexander took the steward's madness literally, representing him – in Anthony Sher's hyperbolic performance (see p. 126) – as a passion-crazed fanatic in Greek orthodox garb.

In the same year (1987), away from Stratford, Kenneth Branagh's Renaissance Theatre Company touring production (no. 102) was, by contrast, staged at the winter solstice, in keeping with its primarily subdued and at times funereal atmosphere: 'He has taken the title literally and his Edwardian Illyria is locked in the grip of an icy winter,' observed Charles Spencer (*Daily Telegraph*). Bunnie Christy's main set was a snow-covered cemetery littered with 'balustrades, broken masonry, scattered statuary, ivy-twined gates, bare trees' (Martin Hoyle, *Financial Times*). Branagh also made the increasingly popular choice of a Victorian-to-Edwardian Christmas setting, with decorated tree and all. The production was strong on interpersonal mirroring: not only Viola and Sebastian but Orsino and Olivia resembled each other both physically and behaviourally in an intriguing game of multiple reflection. Even more overtly Christmassy, and betraying no fear

22 Malvolio (Anthony Sher) and Olivia (Deborah Findlay) in Bill Alexander's 1987 RSC production

of bad taste, was Ian Judge's 1994 RSC version (no. 107) with its traditional Christmas-card set by John Gunter, featuring a row of snow-roofed, half-timbered Stratford houses against which the characters posed in conventional Elizabethan costumes. Judge affirmed the pure Englishness, indeed Stratfordness, of the play and its setting: 'When I look through the hedges of New Place, or sit in the gardens of Hall's Croft,' he told his cast, 'I understand Illyria' (quoted in Holland, 191). Victorian 'Englishness' had also marked Griff Rhys Jones's 'maritime' production for the RSC in 1991 (no. 104), in which Terence Hillyer's Orsino, in a fancy-dress admiral's uniform and surrounded by a court of naval officers, appeared on a huge ship-deck designed by Ultz out of Gilbert and Sullivan's *HMS Pinafore* (Holland, 83).

Illyrian variations

Because of its 'festive' qualities, *Twelfth Night* has often been used to inaugurate or reopen theatres (see nos 28, 53, 66, 73 and 74). Hugh Hunt's 1950 production (no. 69) reopened the Old Vic, the play's traditional home, and also started off a long line of 'Illyrian' productions, emphasizing the geographical and cultural rather than solstitial setting, and thereby removing the revels from their traditional English habitat. Hunt chose an Italianate picture set portraying 'a small island off the Dalmatian coast' (Hugh Hunt, 1954; in *SC*, 26.233), inhabited by fake *commedia dell'arte* clowns tumbling and striking endless poses, together with a chorus of skipping, clapping and dancing urchins. Despite the local colouring, however, the overall effect was drab post-war British. A more convincing attempt to break with the standard Elizabethan-to-Edwardian English mode was Clifford Williams's athletic, farcical and essential *commedia*-style rendering for the RSC in 1966 (no. 84), decidedly more vigorous and less sentimental than Hunt's picturesque Neapolitanism.

Further away in both fictional and real space, a more radical break with geopolitical tradition was made by Ariane Mnouchkine at the 1982 Avignon Festival (no. 97), in a reading influenced by

Asian theatre and 'adapting an Indian look but not an Indian performance style' (Kennedy, 237). Orientalism, especially Indian culture, has been a recurrent feature of some of the more challenging stagings over the past two decades or so. Michael Kahn's acclaimed 1989 Folger Shakespeare production in Washington (no. 103) had a post-colonial emphasis, being set on an 'eastern' island, somewhere between India, Sri Lanka and Cambodia, at the time of British occupation. Designer Derek McLane drew on a mixture of eastern architectural styles in a set dominated by thousands of movable bamboo slats through which seeped the light of the surrounding jungle. Kahn used the eastern setting to suggest parallels between the rigid social order of Illyria and the regime imposed by the colonialists. Peter Webster's romantic raja Orsino and Kelly McGillis's sexy Viola, splendidly metamorphosing from damp négligé to colonial khaki, clashed with Yusef Bulos's somewhat Chaplinesque Asian clown.

More recently, Stephen Beresford's 2004 Albery production (no. 120) was not generically Asian but unmistakably Indian. The transposition of Illyrian events to modern-day India was posited on a powerful analogy between the early modern class hierarchy and the Indian caste system, above all in the relationship between householders and their servants. Modern India with its maharajas and soothsayers is a workable cultural translation of Renaissance society with its dukes and truth-telling fools, and this interpretation was largely convincing. The production opened spectacularly with a monsoon lashing down on shuttered houses in Jonathan Fensom's set, which was tilted at an angle so as to suggest a world emotionally out of joint. The all-Indian cast (speaking with undisguised Indian accents) included the Bollywood star Neha Dubey and the television celebrity Kulvinder Ghir.

The mettle of your sex: gender and homoeroticism

One of the most important developments in recent productions – parallel to the analogous development within critical studies – has been an increased emphasis on the questions of sexuality and gender dramatized in the comedy. One of the earliest stagings to place the themes of androgyny and sexual ambiguity at the centre of the performance was Peter Gill's 1974 RSC production (no. 93), dedicated primarily to the 'erotic metamorphoses' of the central characters (Irving Wardle, *The Times*), notably Orsino, who, caught 'hugging Cesario to his breast with rapturous abandon' (Michael Billington, *Guardian*), underwent a somewhat dubious conversion to heterosexuality. The overall theme of erotic self-infatuation was emblematically represented by William Dudley's plain box set dominated by the sketch of 'an ambisextrous [*sic*] Narcissus figure gazing into a pool' (Billington, *Guardian*: see Fig. 4).

Lindsay Posner's 2001 RSC version (no. 113) similarly, if less systematically, focused on the play of cross-gender desires, at the centre of which was positioned Cesario, who was alternately kissed vigorously by Olivia and fondled lovingly by Orsino. The production's homoerotic *coup de théâtre*, however, was the discovery of Sebastian and Antonio getting dressed on an unmade double bed on the beach in 2.1 (presumably the bed was washed ashore from the wreck, perhaps with the lovers in it). Even more provocative was Cheek by Jowl's 1986 touring production, directed by Declan Donnellan (no. 99), in which Orsino was caught wholeheartedly petting Cesario, while an unmistakably gay Antonio struck up a liaison with Feste at the end of the dramatic proceedings. Equally controversial in this staging was the mixed-accent crassness of many characters, including a saxophone-playing Maria with a Brooklyn twang and an Aguecheek performed as 'a tumescent jack-rabbit from the boondocks of Middle America' (Michael Ratcliffe, *Observer*).

Adrian Noble's highly inventive, and no less controversial, 1997 RSC staging (no. 110) also began, as one critic put it, 'on a distinctly gay note – with Orsino surrounded by an intimate clutch of young courtiers in crushed velvet suits' (Nicholas de Jongh, *Evening Standard*). Noble's main interests, however, lay in the shifting modes of behaviour and styles of performance to which the play's 'opalescent' mutability lends itself. Like Irene Hentschel's experimental 1939 version (no. 62), Noble's presented shifting periods of costume: Aguecheek sported a 1920s blazer, the women 1940s New Look dresses, and so on. A late-twentieth-century pop-art set, designed by Anthony Ward, featured a lurid sky-blue electric arch and a bright-green cartoon hedge which doubled as topiary in the letter scene. Each scene offered a different stage scenario: in 1.2 Viola was discovered in a hospital bed with intravenous drip, while the captain had his arm in a sling; 1.3 was set in a music hall; in 1.4 Orsino and his court emerged semi-naked from showers; 2.3, the kitchen scene, was dominated by a huge refrigerator full of bottles. The most audacious scene was undoubtedly 4.2, which placed Malvolio literally in the doghouse, a garish pink kennel labelled 'Sowter' (see 2.5.121), through the roof of which Feste fed the steward dog-meal and urine (see Fig. 23).

The most striking and most widely publicized aspect of Tim Carroll's 2002 anniversary production at the Middle Temple (no. 114) was its 'Elizabethan'-style all-male cast. This turned out to be far more than an attention-seeking publicity device. The female parts were performed by adult males, some of them very young (Eddie Redmayne's Viola), others decidedly more mature (Mark Rylance's Olivia and Paul Chahidi's Maria), all of whom achieved a convincing degree of femininity without resorting to falsetto voices or camp gesture. One of the real advantages of this generalized cross-dressing was that it allowed the audience to accept quite happily what often seem improbable fictions, beginning with the mistaken identity between the twins: when Rhys Meredith's Sebastian made his first appearance, his likeness to Eddie Redmayne's Viola/Cesario (see Fig. 24) was so perfect as to send spectators looking at their cast lists, and there were several later moments of justified uncertainty as to which of the two had come on. It also allowed sexual and gender implications to emerge clearly without heavy underlining: Olivia's uncontrollable attraction towards the boy-actor's Viola or

23 Malvolio in the doghouse: Philip Voss (Malvolio) and Stephen Boxer (Feste) in Adrian Noble's 1997 RSC production

passionate kissing of Sebastian were at once innocent, comic and erotically charged. In addition, it made sense of what might have seemed rather forced comedy in the last scene, such as Orsino's kneeling before the wrong twin at 'Boy, thou hast said to me a thousand times' (5.1.263; the 'boy' becomes disturbingly real), or his preparing to go off with Sebastian on 'Your master quits you' (315). Above all, the twins' same-sex likeness produced a genuinely spectacular denouement at their reunion, making the *trompe l'œil* illusion of Shakespeare's 'natural perspective' a moment of true optical magic, and turning Olivia's breathless 'Most wonderful!', at the sight of her doubled lover (221), into a sublime delirium of desire.

Unlike Poel's 1897 Temple performance, there were no mini-Swan theatres in this revival; indeed, one of the main challenges facing the company was to invent staging solutions within a restricted and difficult acting area. Carroll's production was a quest not so much for 'authenticity' as for vitality. Much use was made of the full length of the hall through the invention of a third exit (actually the fire exit) at the opposite end from the screen with its two classical doors, allowing greater liberty of movement, and at the same time imposing a rapid pace on exits, entrances and stage movements in order to counteract the inevitable slowness in negotiating the long vertical axis of the hall. As in Poel's version, Elizabethan musical settings were played on early modern instruments. Carroll's production – probably like the Lord Chamberlain's Men's – later transferred to the Globe, whose stage is notoriously deep; but much of the verticality, as well as the rapidity, of the original staging was saved by exploiting its equally great width, with the action spread out along and across the entire platform. The knowing use of the theatre's plethora of doors (three, plus two curtained openings, making a dizzying total of five, a number that might have astonished Shakespeare's company) allowed rapid simultaneous entrances and exits, and business being conducted at two or more doors at the same time. This gave rise to moments of brilliant physical comedy, as in the final scene when Orsino and Cesario, on the point of exiting together, stop in their tracks and stare at each other, frozen, when Olivia pronounces the fateful word 'husband' (5.1.139).

The second main anniversary performance in 2002, Sam Mendes' otherwise acclaimed Donmar production (no. 116), was

24 'One face, one voice, one habit and two persons' (5.1.212): Eddie Redmayne (Viola) and Rhys Meredith (Sebastian) in Tim Carroll's 2002 Middle Temple production

accused of insensitivity towards the topic of sexuality and gender (suggesting that critics and audiences now expect this issue to be central). Mendes' decidedly heterosexual and overtly Chekhovian reading (the play doubled with his *Uncle Vanya*) placed at the theatrical and iconographic centre of the play, in the award-winning set again designed by Anthony Ward, the theme of the projection of desire, by means of a large gilt picture frame in which the image of a given character's object of affection appeared whenever spoken of: thus Olivia materialized both in 1.1, veiled, during Orsino's speech on love, and in the letter scene, where she turned her back on Malvolio during his reverie. More literally Chekhovian was Declan Donnellan's highly comic 2003 Russian-language International Chekhov Festival production (no. 118), in which 'The vodka-swilling, below-stairs antics' were 'reminiscent of the late-night drinking scenes from Chekhov's *Uncle Vanya*' (Helen Meany, *Irish Times*).

Show you the picture: Twelfth Night *on film*

Twelfth Night offers film directors a variety of outdoor and indoor settings, a fast-moving plot and a number of potential star roles. The first film version of the play – and one of the earliest Shakespeare films ever – is Charles Kent's silent ten-minute Vitagraph production of 1910 (no. 45), with Kent himself as Malvolio and Florence Turner as Viola. Kent creates what was to become a cinematic convention by opening with a narrative 'prologue', here in the 'primitive' form of a caption ('Viola separated from her twin brother Sebastian by a shipwreck'; compare Nunn). The film owes a good deal to nineteenth-century stage productions, especially Tree's 1901 version, whose scenery is recalled in the film's garden set, with its fountain and long flight of steps; and some of its stage business is included, such as Malvolio's placing of the ring on the end of his wand in 2.2. As in various Victorian productions, Viola's arrival on shore (with her brother's trunk) is followed immediately by the rescue of Sebastian. Malvolio becomes a purely comic character, with the omission of the dark room scene, while Antonio is virtually absent. The film's denouement hints at the theme of androgyny by showing a 'feminized' Sebastian, adorned like Viola in long curls and tunic, re-embracing his identical sister.

In the opening of Yakov Fried's Russian-language Lenfilm version of 1955 (no. 78), Sebastian's survival is again shown immediately after Viola's. Combinatory filming (Osborne, 111) allowes Klara Luchko to appear as both twins in the same scene

(5.1), a cinematic possibility exploited in later video versions (see nos 91 and 101). Illyria was 'Russianized', with Feste singing Russian popular songs, while Fried develops the theme of visual and pictorial perception by employing several shots 'quoting' Renaissance art, and by offering 'a first view by Viola of "the coast of Illyria" that looked like a Symbolist painting' (Hattaway, 87).

Ron Wertheim's 1972 film of *Twelfth Night* by *Playboy* Productions (no. 91) – a mixture of sexual-revolution exuberance and soft-porn kitsch – has Orsino as an ageing rock star, while Antonio becomes the black Antonia (thereby eliminating any hint of homosexuality), and Feste, played by Wertheim, the gardener and chauffeur to Olivia, widow of a movie mogul. Nikki Gentile, like Klara Luchko, plays both twins. The film's denouement resolves all gender ambiguities by having Gentile's Viola reveal all, Playmate-fashion (thereby provoking a closing orgy).

Trevor Nunn's ambitious 1996 feature film (no. 109) is notable above all for its long opening sequence dedicated to a realistic account of a *Tempest*-like shipwreck, preceded by an off-screen voice declaiming a bad pseudo-Shakespearean blank-verse prologue: 'Once, upon Twelfth Night – or what you will – / Aboard a ship bound home to Messaline, / The festive company' (evidently this Shakespeare has read his C.L. Barber). The maritime sequence continues with an on-board Victorian party in which the twins, identically disguised in harem-like yashmaks leaving only their eyes visible, perform 'O mistress mine' (2.3.38–43) as a music hall duet; when they reach line 40, 'That can sing both high and low', one voice is indeed high, while the other is baritone: the question is whose voice is which. The piano-playing twin proceeds to pull the yashmak from the concertina-playing sibling's face, revealing a moustache; the other twin in turn peels away the piano player's moustache, whereby the latter is 'fully confirmed as a girl' (Nunn, 4). The climax, as the piano player reaches out, apparently to peel off the other twin's moustache – thereby multiplying the gender confusion exponentially – is interrupted by the storm. All the while Antonio gazes intently from the shadows, 'concentrating on the concertina player' (i.e. Sebastian; Nunn, 3; see Chillington Rutter, 248–50).

This episode elaborately and teasingly anticipates the themes of androgyny and cross-dressing, which are briefly taken up in a later sequence showing Viola's transformation into Cesario, in which she cuts her hair, binds her chest, pads her crotch, attaches a blond moustache (again) and tries out masculine walks. Otherwise, however, the film fails to explore gender issues much further, and indeed it is curious, given these preliminaries, including their masquerade orientalism, that Nunn should have censored Viola's 'eunuch' allusion (as well as the captain's mediation), with awkward and ungrammatical results: 'I shall present me [*sic*] as a boy to him' (Nunn, 12). The film's most original emphasis, instead, is on a background military conflict between Illyria and Messaline, the twins' place of birth, pre-announced in the prologue ('For Messaline with this country is at war') and represented in *Hamlet*-like preparations for war; this makes sense, among other things, of Antonio's and Orsino's past naval skirmishes, referred to at 3.3.26–8 and 5.1.47–72.

Twelfth Night is a point of intertextual reference in another commercially successful end-of-century film, John Madden's *Shakespeare in Love* (1998), written by Marc Norman and Tom Stoppard. Among a myriad of other Shakespearean allusions, the film involves a 'contamination' between *Romeo and Juliet* – which Joseph Fiennes's young Shakespeare is seen writing and rehearsing – and *Twelfth Night*, a version of which he 'lives' by falling in love with Viola de Lesseps (Gwyneth Paltrow), cross-dressed as a male actor. After the triumphant performance of *Romeo and Juliet* – in which Paltrow, like the Cushman sisters combined (no. 26), ends up playing Juliet instead of Romeo – and before Viola leaves for America as Lady Wessex, Judi Dench's Queen Elizabeth commissions a new comedy: 'And tell Master Shakespeare, something more cheerful next time, for Twelfth Night.' The voiceover's closing lines resemble the prologue of Nunn's film in narrating the opening storm of *Twelfth Night*: 'WILLIAM SHAKESPEARE: "My story starts at sea . . . a perilous voyage to an unknown land . . . a shipwreck . . . It will be a love story . . . for she will be my heroine for all time. And her name . . . Viola.'"

Twelfth Night has often been seen as a play particularly suited to the television screen, perhaps because of its 'intimacy' and its domestic interiors, although the results have not always confirmed such suitability. The first television production of the comedy, the 1937 BBC transmission (no. 59), starred Greer Garson as Viola. Two years later the BBC returned to the play in another 'first night', namely the first broadcast of a Shakespeare play (and the second of any stage play) from a theatre, confirming the comedy's vocation as inaugurating event. The programme failed to please the *Times* critic, who complained that the camera's distance made the actors appear too small: 'The impression given was one of extreme restlessness. Viola was now a tiny figure scarcely distinguishable from half-a-dozen others equally diminutive . . . The result was to falsify the fluid grace of the production.' *Twelfth Night* provided the occasion for another 'first' in 1949, the first live stage play broadcast by a major American studio, the NBC (no. 68); the text was much reduced to conform with the studio's timing demands, causing Jack Gould to describe the event as 'A procession of episodes rather than a piece of integrated theatre' (quoted in Rothwell & Henkin, 303).

Later television productions have mostly not been much better received. Harold Clayton's 1950 BBC version, starring Geoffrey Dunn as Malvolio (no. 70), was decidedly melancholic in tone, and was criticized for its lack of comedy. Caspar Wrede's BBC production six years later, with Dilys Hamlett as Viola (no. 79), failed to impress, as did David Greene's stagy 1957 NBC production (no. 80), complete with painted theatrical backcloths, in which Maurice Evans reproduced his 1940 Malvolio (see no. 64), playing him again with a false nose and a strong cockney accent (see p. 126); Sir Toby corrected his pronunciation of 'slough' at 2.5.34, with a glance at Olivier's stage performance two years earlier (no. 77). The most memorable episode was the dark room scene, in which Evans was surrounded by a multitude of mocking masks; at the end of the play the platform from which Malvolio launched his parting curse exploded, to the joy of the assembled company (Rothwell & Melzer, 305).

Somewhat more successful was the 1970 ATV broadcast (no. 88), produced by John Dexter and directed by John Sichel, starring Ralph Richardson as Sir Toby (the role in which he had triumphed in the early thirties: nos 53 and 54), Alec Guinness as Malvolio and Joan Plowright as both twins. This is a distinctly 'televisual' version, full of strategic close-ups (not to mention fadeouts for commercial breaks). As in other video versions, the opening has been reworked, with 1.2 'containing' 1.1, while Sebastian's first and second scenes (2.1 and 3.3) are collapsed into one (see Osborne, 112). John Gorrie's rather dull 1980 production for the BBC Shakespeare series (no. 96) respects the scene order of the Folio text, but is otherwise distinguished only by Alec McCowen's supercilious and somewhat effeminate Malvolio and Trevor Peacock's 'lumbering and loveable mutt' of a Feste (Carr, 5). Perhaps the most convincing of all the television versions is Paul Kafno's rendering of Kenneth Branagh's 1987 Riverside Studios staging (no. 102) for Thames Television, which captures all the stage production's wintry-cemetery and subdued-colour melancholy. Of considerable interest also is Tim Supple's 2003 Channel 4 television film (no. 119), in which Parminder Nagra's Viola and Ronny Jhutti's Sebastian are represented as asylum seekers who have been driven from their native land by a military coup (a 'political' allusion recalling Nunn's film) and washed up in an Illyria that closely resembles contemporary multicultural London, where Feste is a rock star shades of the 1968 musical (no. 86) and the 1972 *Playboy* film (no. 91). The production's many cuts included the 'eunuch' reference, while its additions, as in Nunn's film, included the scene of Viola cross-dressing.

Are you a comedian?: players and parts

Twelfth Night has always been a vehicle for star performers but, unlike those in most plays, the star roles vary. As one would expect, stage productions down the centuries have frequently been memorable for their Malvolios (from Charles Macklin to Richard Bensley, and from Laurence Olivier to Donald Sinden), but equally so for their Violas (Peg Woffington, Dorothy Jordan, Ellen Terry, Suzanne Bing) and their Sir Tobys (Thomas Betterton, John Palmer, Cedric Hardwicke). Historical testimony shows, more surprisingly, that the star performance may occasionally be Sir Andrew, as with James Dodd in the late eighteenth century. Feste has dominated some stagings (especially in recent times, from Emrys James to Mark Hadfield), and Olivia has taken the honours in others (Frances Abington, Geraldine McEwan), while there have even been productions where the star, or at least the co-protagonist, has arguably been Maria (Paul Chahidi). Orsino, despite being the 'romantic' hero, has rarely dominated stage Illyrias, although Alan Howard came close in 1966. It is rare for all the roles to be performed at the same level of skill, but the existence of such a gallery of parts guarantees that at least some scenes will work: an off-day for Belch gives Feste his chance of glory.

One of the features of the performance history of *Twelfth Night* is the way in which actors move across parts, confirming the specularity and interchangeability of the dramatis personae. A notable eighteenth-century case in point is Richard Yates, who started life in the play as Feste in Macklin's 1746 revival (no. 10) and then moved on to become a celebrated Malvolio in 1763 (no. 11). John Palmer was promoted from Sebastian to Sir Toby in 1776 (no. 13); Lily Brayton moved from Viola in 1901 (no. 41) to Olivia a year later; Andrew Leigh from Fabian to Sir Andrew in 1920 (no. 50) to director in 1940 (no. 63); Leon Quartermaine from Sir Andrew in 1912 (no. 46) to Malvolio in 1933 (no. 57); John Laurie from Feste in 1932 (no. 55) to Malvolio in 1939 (no. 62); Laurence Olivier from Belch in 1937 (no. 58) to Malvolio in

1955 (no. 77); Alec Guinness from Sir Andrew in 1937 (no. 58) to director in 1948 (no. 67) to Malvolio in 1970 (no. 88); Judi Dench from Maria in 1958 (no. 81) to Viola in 1969 (no. 87); Emrys James from Feste in 1969 (no. 87) to Malvolio in 1983 (no. 98), and so on. Such role-shifting is not just a matter of career promotion or ageing, but suggests something of the psychological and performative overlapping of the roles, and a characteristic may become a strategic part of a given production: Sybil Thorndike, for example, alternated the roles of Viola and Olivia in the 1916 Old Vic production (no. 49).

The play's performance history has inevitably featured twins or siblings in the parts of Viola and Sebastian: Dorothy Jordan and her brother George Bland (who were more or less of the same height and of similar appearance) in 1790 (no. 18), Mrs Henry Siddons and her brother William Murray in 1815 (no. 22), the Cushman sisters in 1846 (no. 26). In one production, Robert Atkins's 1927 Old Vic version (no. 52), the cast was virtually composed of a single family, the Forbes-Robertson dynasty, perhaps suggesting the almost incestuous quality of relationships in the play. An alternative solution has been for the same actress to play both twins: Madame Meyer Bourke in 1851 (no. 29), Kate Terry in 1865 (no. 32), Jessica Tandy in 1937 (no. 58). Such doubling is decidedly easier in film, a medium that invites optical illusion: Klara Luchko in Yakov Fried's 1955 film (no. 78), Ingrid Adree in the 1962 West German TV production (no. 83), Joan Plowright in the 1970 ATV production (no. 88), and Gillian Jones in Neil Armfield's 1987 film (no. 101) all doubled as the twins.

Individual actors in single parts, however, have naturally dominated the stage history of *Twelfth Night*. Some of the outstanding performances of the play's major roles merit closer attention.

Art any more than a steward?: Malvolio

There is little doubt that in early performances the play's protagonist was the steward. We do not know which actor John Manningham saw and appreciated in 1602: possible candidates are Joseph Taylor and John Shancke. In later seventeenth-century performances Malvolio may have lost his primacy to Sir Toby, but he emphatically reclaimed his place at centre stage in the first significant eighteenth-century production. After the longest interruption in the play's performance history, the great Irish actor Charles Macklin appeared as the steward at Drury Lane in 1741 (no. 8), the same year as his celebrated Shylock (another outsider). Along with Garrick, Macklin was the most revolutionary performer of his age, introducing a naturalistic style of acting; he was famous for the severity of his stage presence, and he gave Malvolio an air of pompous authority.

One of the productions of *Twelfth Night* that have left the strongest traces in theatre history is Robert Bensley's 1785 staging at Drury Lane (no. 16), in which Bensley played Malvolio opposite Dorothy Jordan's celebrated Viola, the gigantic John Palmer's Sir Toby and James Dodd's Sir Andrew. Charles Lamb (not an altogether reliable witness[1]) recalls, thirty years later, Bensley's great dignity and the Hispanic style he lent the part: '[He] threw over the part an air of Spanish loftiness. He looked, spake, and moved like an old Castilian. He was starch, spruce, opinionated, but his superstructure of pride seemed bottomed upon a sense of worth' (C. Lamb, 189). Bensley, a former soldier, first adopted, according to Lamb, a self-important martial gait (although James Boaden recalled that 'his stage walk reminded you of the "one, two, three, hop" of the dancing master': quoted in Winter, 23); then, after reading the letter, 'The man seemed to tread upon air, to taste manna, to walk with his head in the clouds, to mate Hyperion' (C. Lamb, 190).

Under Bensley's influence, 'dignity' became the key word in interpretations of the part. John Liston in 1811 (no. 21) was similarly noteworthy, according to the diarist Henry Crabb Robinson, for his 'inimitable gravity' as well as his 'incomparable smiles, in the Cross-gartered scene' (Winter, 27). Bensley's 'Spanish

1 See Sylvan Barnet, 'Charles Lamb and the tragic Malvolio', *SQ*, 33 (1954), 177–88.

loftiness' likewise became a recurrent topos in later performances. Samuel Phelps in 1848 (no. 27) performed the role as a slow-moving and self-adoring Golden Age *señor*, all grandeur and pride: 'Walled up in his own temple of flesh, he is his own adorer,' observed Henry Morley (139). Henry Irving, in 1884 (no. 36), presented a Quixote-like figure, tall and gaunt, with a pompous walk, wielding his prominent staff of office: 'He looked like some great Spanish hidalgo, a painting of Velasquez',' recalled a later Malvolio, Frank Benson (quoted in Saintsbury & Palmer, 245). Irving's humourless interpretation was much criticized, although Edward Aveling claimed that 'The gradual growth of the great idea in his mind that Olivia loved him was shown as I believe none other could show it' (Salgādo, 116). The 'Spanish' mode survived until relatively recent times: Michael Hordern in 1954 (no. 76) appeared 'dried up, emaciated, elongated . . . like one of those tortured figures in an El Greco' (Harold Hobson, *Sunday Times*).

Not all Malvolios have been aspiring Hispanic grandees, however. Another tradition, beginning at the turn of the century, represented him as a grotesque fantastic entirely lacking in dignity. Following the unpopular austerity of Irving's performance, Beerbohm Tree's altogether more farcical and emphatically over-the-top 1901 interpretation (no. 41) was much better received; his steward was an 'intolerably condescending blue-eyed peacock with a red twirl of beard and a quizzing-glass' (Trewin, 18), and accompanied by four smaller Malvolios who aped his dress and behaviour (as George Bernard Shaw reports, approvingly). Tree gave rise to a line of maniacal Malvolios that has survived into the present. Donald Sinden's universally acclaimed 1969 performance (no. 87), 'a portly soul struggling to get out of an absurdly spindly body' (Hilary Spurling, *Spectator*), had the merit of 'leaving the right bitterness in the mouth when the play's flight from realism might have seemed too precipitate' (Speaight, *Shakespeare*, 439). The grotesque-fantastic tradition continued with John Woodvine's 1979 steward (no. 95), adorned with ringlets and, in the cross-garter scene, an entire yellow body stocking with bulging codpiece.

Another modern Malvolio, Emrys James, a memorable Feste in 1969 (no. 87), performed the role in 1983 (no. 98) as a 'strutting velvet uniformed grotesque' (Irving Wardle, *Times*) and 'a finger-wagging tyrant' (Michael Billington, *Guardian*).

A relatively recent development in the 'grotesque' school of acting has been to transform the maniacal into the psychopathic, making Malvolio literally mad. Alexander's 1987 RSC production (no. 100) was dominated by what one critic called 'Sher madness' (Sheridan Morley, *Punch*), namely Anthony Sher's highly popular but controversial interpretation of the part as 'a mad holy man on the run, a corseted hysteric with gobstopper eyes' (Michael Ratcliffe, *Observer*). Sher's Malvolio, afflicted by an authentic erotic *furor* towards Olivia, became genuinely mad, and was last seen 'still essaying cross-gartered high kicks as if his wits have finally turned' (Michael Billington, *Guardian*). Less overacted, but still disturbingly unhinged, was Richard Briers's steward in the same year (no. 102), 'a frock-coated, wildly ambitious fanatic' (Billington, *Guardian*), with a 'fussy air of primly affronted fastidiousness' (Martin Hoyle, *Financial Times*). Equally fastidious and neurotically driven was Simon Russell Beale's award-winning corpulent 2002 Malvolio (no. 116), who looked as if 'he must have emerged from the womb with that self-important beard and punctilious moustache', while his gait was 'an effeminately officious cross between a march and a scamper' and his tone of voice 'a prissily sibilant sneer' (Paul Taylor, *Independent*).

One of the more interesting lines of interpretation of the role has been in terms of class, whereby the real ambition of Malvolio – of visibly or audibly humble extraction – becomes social promotion rather than erotic satisfaction. In Margaret Webster's 1940 New York production (no. 64) Maurice Evans played him as a 'downstairs' English butler with a distinct cockney accent. The main trait betraying the origins of Laurence Olivier's 1955 steward (no. 77) was 'a rather tortured lisp, as of an aspiring barrow-boy earnestly improving his English at night-school' (Eric Keown, *Punch*). Olivier had comical difficulty in pronouncing the more recherché words in the letter. In 1966 (no. 84) Ian Holm – who physically resembled the Droeshout portrait of Shakespeare (another social climber) – exhibited a 'mongrel' accent composed of 'eccentric gentility and a basis of raw bullying cockney' (*Times*), in representing the steward as an officious and disciplinarian sergeant-major obsessed with his rank.

A variation of the lower-class (usually London cockney) colouring of the character has been a regional, predominantly Welsh, characterization. In 1974 (no. 93) Nicol Williamson's 'immensely tall, bad-tempered, nasal Welshman, stiff-jointed and intolerably haughty' (John Barber, *Daily Telegraph*), made his Welshness a synonym of Puritanism. Another Welsh Malvolio, Desmond Barrit in 1994 (no. 107), used the accent as added colouring for his already farcical music-hall steward, 'a lugubrious man-mountain . . . massively pirouetting in yellow' (Benedict Nightingale, *Times*). A more functional brand of geographical difference marked Paul Bhattacharjee's 2004 Indian Malvolio (no. 120), a bossy white-suited valet with impeccable 'English' manners who is transformed in the cross-gartering scene though his 'extravagant make-up and ghastly, glassy smiles' (Charles Spencer, *Daily Telegraph*).

Being a comedy concerned with the forms, eccentricities and aberrations of behaviour and dress, *Twelfth Night* lends itself to the actor's skill in inventing or varying comic stage business. This is particularly the case with Malvolio: certain lazzi (comic gestures, more or less absurd effects with costume and props, business involving scenery, etc.) introduced by earlier Malvolios have become established over the centuries as conventions, to be transmitted, repeated or modified by their successors. Actors playing him often find themselves, willy-nilly, 'quoting' earlier performances, thereby setting up a kind of intertextual or inter-actorial relationship with their predecessors. Knowledgeable audiences, moreover, have come to expect comic business at certain points in the play, and may even begin to titter in expectation.

The primary source of much traditional stage business was Bensley (no. 16), some of whose lazzi are still present in modern performances. As Boaden notes, Bensley embellished one of the play's great comic moments, Malvolio's cross-gartered entry in 3.4, by introducing a cross-stage movement that mimicked the garters themselves: 'the sliding zig-zag advance and retreat of his figure fixed the attention to his stockings and garters' (Winter, 23). Ever since, the scene has produced funny walks or other forms of conspicuous behaviour: Olivier (no. 77), for example, waved from behind a yew tree, before disappearing suddenly (Brown, 257). Bensley also introduced the convention in the letter scene – an endless opportunity for comic invention – of 'filling in' the pause after 'play with my . . .' at 2.5.57; Lamb describes 'with what ineffable carelessness would he twirl his gold chain; what a dream it was!' (C. Lamb, 190). This has been taken up and varied by almost every actor since: recent examples include Desmond Barrit (no. 107) toying with his genitals and then ordering laughing spectators to leave, and Guy Henry's hand dangling uncertainly in front of his pelvic region (no. 113).

Another potentially grotesque entrance is the steward's interrupting of the kitchen scene at 2.3.84.1. A venerable convention has him come on in his night-shirt; this is usually attributed to another great source of stage business, Beerbohm Tree (no. 41), but actually dates from Kemble's 1811 production (no. 21), whose promptbook specifies that Malvolio enters 'in a Gown and Cap, with a Light'; the idea is still alive today, as at the Middle Temple in 2002 (no. 114). Donald Sinden (no. 87) pompously wore his chain of office over his night-shirt (Potter, 65). Malvolio often sports a night-cap as well, or alternatively – in early twentieth-century productions – curling papers, as if he had been interrupted in the midst of his toilette (Sprague & Trewin, 84). That tradition was parodied by Mendes' 2002 production (no. 116), which had Malvolio in a hairnet. Posner in 2001 (no. 113) had the steward enter in a red dressing-gown and red shoes. Among Beerbohm Tree's contributions to *Twelfth Night*'s performance history is the often repeated business in 2.2 of placing the ring on the tip of the wand and dropping it at Cesario's feet; this was 'quoted' in Kent's 1910 film (no. 45), as well as in later performances.

The letter scene provides a third entrance (at 2.5.20.1) traditionally exploited for slapstick farce. Tree famously had, in the words of Shaw, 'a magnificent flight of stairs on the stage; and when he was descending it majestically, he slipped and fell with a crash sitting . . . Tree, without betraying the smallest discomfiture, raised his eyeglass and surveyed the landscape as if he had sat down on purpose' (Shaw, 249). Tree's show-stopping entry has often been repeated, or otherwise transformed into more sober variations: Emrys James (no. 98), for example, came onstage like Ophelia, bearing a basket of flowers, 'knighting' himself with one of the sprigs before dusting the tree stump and sitting down to read the epistle.

The innumerable micro-episodes making up the letter scene, in which Malvolio is betrayed into 'practising behaviour' on stage, have all given rise to long-lasting lazzi. In many productions Malvolio touches the seal at 'soft' (2.5.91), to discover that the wax is indeed soft; Sher (no. 100) rubbed his chest, repeating the word three times. The steward's pronunciation difficulties with 'M.O.A.I.' (119, 136) and '*slough*' (145), first exploited by Olivier (Pennington, 17), have become common comic stock: Nicol Williamson (no. 93) 'tortures the MOAI conundrum into experimental Welsh words' (Irving Wardle, *Times*), while Desmond Barrit (no. 107) produced a cat-like 'mee-ow'. The letter's invitation '*still smile*' (2.5.171) often prompts Malvolio to practise his smile, as in the case of Mark Hadfield (no. 113); Olivier (no. 77), 'after several wry attempts to smile into a mirror, achieves a satisfied asinine grin' (*Times*, quoted in Brown, 247).

The supreme moment in Malvolio's reading, however – which audiences anticipate with glee – is his reaction to the imperative '*revolve*' (2.5.140). The standard joke is for the steward to misinterpret the verb as 'turn around', which is often what actors do: for example, Emrys James (no. 98) and Philip Voss (no. 110). Fuller Mellish in 1914 (no. 47) 'span round on his heel';

Donald Sinden (no. 87) and John Woodvine (no. 95) turned the letter round; Sher (no. 100) revolved his upper body, and so on. Recently actors have played on spectators' expectations: Barrit (no. 107) looked at the audience, then shook his head; Oliver Cotton in 2002 (no. 114) gazed wonderingly at the expectant spectators and did nothing.

Your drunken cousin: Sir Toby

If the earliest seventeenth-century performances belonged to Malvolio, the star role in the three stagings witnessed by Pepys (nos 4–6) was another: the Duke of York company's male lead, the great Thomas Betterton – usually associated with tragic protagonists such as Hamlet and Macbeth – played Sir Toby. This may be less surprising than it appears, since Belch is the play's longest, if not 'biggest' part (see Appendix 2), and is full of opportunities for both verbal and physical comedy. The Toby seen by Manningham sixty years earlier may have been Thomas Pope – who probably played Buffone in Jonson's *Every Man out of His Humour* – although another candidate is John Heminge, one of the two 'editors' of the Folio and possibly the original Falstaff. Later Belches have often incarnated just such a Falstaffian quality, disenchanted of wit and conspicuous of girth: for example, the great Ralph Richardson in 1931 (no. 53) and 1970 (no. 88), George Devine in 1938 (no. 60) and Bill Fraser, who in 1969 (no. 87) knowingly played Sir Toby as an ageing and somewhat melancholy Sir John. In 1937 (no. 58) a transformed Laurence Olivier – 'a trifle too much bubukled and whelked and knobbed' (*Sunday Times*: see Fig. 25) – was likewise 'a rustic Falstaff whose stupid drunken jollity has its own wretched pathos' (Stephen Williams, *Evening Standard*). Olivier's Falstaffian Belch was malicious and dangerous: '[he] delightedly over-played Sir Toby like a veteran Skye terrier, ears pricked for mischief' (Trewin, 164).

The huge John Palmer, nicknamed 'plausible Jack', in 1776 (no. 13) and 1785 (no. 16), was the most notable Belch of the eighteenth century. One of the most brilliant all-round actors of

25 Laurence Olivier as Sir Toby in Tyrone Guthrie's 1937 Old Vic production

his day, he was instead one of the tallest Tobys in stage history; William Dunlap describes his strategic use of his length: 'Palmer's gigantic limbs outstretched seemed to indicate the enjoyment of the physical superiority which nature had given him, even while debasing it by the lowest of vices' (quoted in Winter, 25).

The kind of comedy produced by the role has varied widely, from the farcical – with emphasis on the corporeal and the alcoholic, as with Barry Stanton in 2001 (no. 113), who at 1.5.116, instead of belching, threw up in front of Olivia – to the aristocratic, as in the 1931 (no. 53) performance of Ralph Richardson's 'ripe, rich and yellow Sir Toby' (W.A. Darlington, *Daily Telegraph*), 'a courtly Sir Toby whose quality was never lost in his cups' (*Times*); and of Cedric Hardwicke's elegant and ironic Belch, undisputed star of Alec Guinness's 1948 production (no. 67): 'Sir Toby was the man in this Illyria . . . Keeping a glazed dignity he led Andrew with drily casual care and a smile that oozed at the corners of his mouth' (Trewin, 211).

An ass-head and a coxcomb and a knave: Sir Andrew

Even Sir Toby's gull has had his day. The importance given in Davenant's Restoration productions to the play's more farcical scenes is confirmed by the presence of the celebrated Henry Harris (Romeo to Betterton's Mercutio) as Sir Andrew (no. 4). The 1771 Drury Lane production (no. 12) was memorable above all for James Dodd's Aguecheek. Lamb vividly re-evokes Dodd's sublime slow-wittedness – what Boaden termed his 'native imbecility' (Winter, 25) – in the later 1785 production (no. 16) in which Dodd reappeared as Aguecheek: 'You could see the first dawn of an idea stealing slowly over his countenance, climbing up little by little, with a painful process, till it cleared up at last to the fulness of a twilight conception – its highest meridian' (C. Lamb, 190–1). The 1771 production inspired a noteworthy portrait by Francis Wheatley of the duel scene (Fig. 26), which captures Dodd's frightened gesture of drawing his sword, 'encouraged' by James Love's Sir Toby; Dodd's expression is mirrored in the equally reluctant leaning pose of Elizabeth Younge's Viola. The costumes are also of interest: including his lank flaxen hair, Dodd's Sir Andrew is emphatically decked out in the colour Olivia detests, cowardly yellow, with the exception of his 'thin legs in scarlet stockings' (Dunlop, quoted in Sprague, 6); while Cesario's pink and blue 'changeable taffeta' suit, plumed turban and red slippers suggest, in addition to effeminacy, an exotic 'Illyrian' or Middle

Eastern flavour (a Turkish eunuch?). A later specialist in slow-wittedness in 1850 (no. 28) was Robert Keeley, who, 'in the expression of semi-idiocy or rustic wonderment . . . had few equals' (Joseph Knight, *DNB*).

Modern Sir Andrews have often accentuated the pathos of the role, best expressed in Aguecheek's most memorable line, 'I was adored once too' (2.3.176). Michael Redgrave in 1938 (no. 60), described by James Agate as 'a giddy, witty maypole', was for W.A. Darlington 'a likeable lunatic' suffering from 'a kind of moonstruck pathos' (*Daily Telegraph*). Richard Johnson in 1958 (no. 81), looking with his long flaxen wig like 'a lachrymose spaniel', played him as a 'paranoid manic-depressive, strongly reminiscent at times of Lucky in *Waiting for Godot*' (*Observer*, 27 April 1958; quoted in Brown, 218). Barrie Ingham represented

26 'He cannot by the duello avoid it' (3.4.301-2): Francis Wheatley's painting of the 1771 production, with Elizabeth Younge as Viola, James Dodd as Sir Andrew, James Love as Sir Toby and Francis Waldron as Fabian

him in 1966 (no. 84) as a hapless and ageing Scottish clown with bagpipes, ever searching for coins in his sporran (and yet capable of a spectacular back-leap), while David Bradley's lugubrious and insecure Sir Andrew behaved in 1987 (no. 100) 'like some irritable newt, muttering all his remarks as though he would rather have snatched them back before releasing them to the sure mockery of the world' (Michael Ratcliffe, *Observer*).

An allowed fool: Feste

The one almost certain presence in the Chamberlain's Men's performance was Robert Armin in the part of the clown, since Armin had joined the company before it left the Curtain and transferred to the Globe in 1599, the year in which his predecessor Will Kemp left (see Wiles, 145). Armin, who had probably already played Touchstone in *As You Like It* and would go on to play the Fool in *King Lear*, was known as a good singer – an essential aspect of the role – and, being also a gifted ventriloquist, specialized in multiple roles (a quality put to good use in 4.2). His intellectual agility and inventiveness are attested to by his work as a comic dramatist in his own right. There is little doubt that Armin lent the role great stage presence, a caustic comic acumen and a beauty of musical performance.

There may be more or less direct traces in the text of Armin's presence in the first production of the play. Olivia's reprimand of the clown's truancy at 1.5.38, after his unauthorized absence at the court of Orsino – 'you grow dishonest' – probably alludes to Armin's 'promiscuity' as comic performer: like Feste on his first entrance in 1.5, Armin first arrived on the Globe stage, and in the company of the Lord Chamberlain's Men, from service for another lord, Lord Chandos, with whose theatrical company he toured the country in 1595–7 and performed at another theatre, the Curtain. Armin alternated – again like Feste – between rival venues, probably continuing, even after joining Shakespeare's company, to appear at the Curtain, as well as in less formal performance spaces such as halls and taverns. Likewise, the clown's doubling of roles as Feste and Sir Topas the curate in 4.2 reflects Armin's well-known ability as a ventriloquist, as in his playing of both the clown Tutch and the fool John i' the Hospital in performances of his own comedy, *The History of the Two Maids of More-clacke*. In the same scene Armin's notorious dwarfishness is directly evoked in Feste's feigned reluctance to play Sir Topas on the grounds that 'I am not tall enough to become the function well' (4.2.6–7). Viola's homage to the clown's art at 3.1.58–64 ('This fellow is wise enough to play the fool . . .') is probably intended as a direct compliment to Armin and may indeed echo his own pamphlet *Quips upon Questions*, published in 1600 ('A merry man is often thought unwise', Armin, *Quips*, sig. C1^{r}; see Mahood), just as Sir Toby's less flattering description of Feste as a 'sot' at 1.5.117 and at 5.1.193 may allude to Armin's pamphlet *Fool upon Fool or, Six Sorts of Sots*, likewise published in 1600.

The most significant trace of the shadow cast by Armin over the play, however, is Feste's abundant singing, one of the actor's main trademarks as a performer. Feste's 'replacement' of Viola as the play's resident singer has been explained precisely with reference to Armin's presence in the company. Since Armin appears to have been a counter-tenor, moreover, his high-pitched voice was an appropriate substitute for the unbroken voice of the boy actor (see Feste's reference to a lover-singer 'That can sing both high and low': 2.3.40). The clown's songs may constitute the comedy's most direct debt to Armin as contributing author: it is at least possible that the words of the final song ('When that I was and a little tiny boy, / With hey, ho, the wind and the rain') are by Armin himself, the more so since an adapted version of Feste's song – 'He that has and a little tiny wit, / With heigh-ho, the wind and the rain' – is sung in *King Lear* (3.2.73–7) by the Fool, likewise played by Armin.

The next Feste we know of is Cave Underhill in the 1660s Duke of York's performances (nos 4–6); Underhill, awkward and ill proportioned, was praised by Colley Cibber for his gift of wooden comic fixity: 'He looked as if it were not in human passions to alter a feature of him' (Winter, 17). Richard Suett produced a similarly celebrated verbal-corporeal performance in 1785 (no. 16): 'a loose and shambling gait, a slippery tongue . . . in words, light as air, venturing truths deep as the centre' (Oxberry, *Dramatic*, 3.226).

Later, the role was marginalized and subject to drastic cuts – already apparent in Bell's 1774 acting edition – and began to regain its original importance only at the beginning of the twentieth century, especially in Beerbohm Tree's 1901 production (no. 41) in which Courtice Pounds's Feste, a presiding and defining presence, was according to Max Beerbohm 'as constant and as indispensable as punctuation' (Greif, 63). This overturning of the eighteenth- and nineteenth-century marginality of the clown, making his the central viewpoint on events (Greif), has been repeated several times since, notably in Barton's 1969 staging (no. 87), in which Emrys James's highly praised clown set the sardonic tone for the whole performance. Equal importance was given to Geoffrey Hutchings's 1979 Feste (no. 95), onstage throughout. Ben Kingsley's clown, in Trevor Nunn's 1996 film (no. 109), likewise provides a defining perspective; as Katherine Eggert observes, 'The film even insinuates that Feste has engineered or at least foreseen the main plot' (Eggert, 84), since at the end of the film Feste returns to Viola a necklace she discarded during her cross-dressing as Cesario.

Another tendency in modern productions has been to make the clown older and more embittered than in the traditional image of the part. Granville-Barker (who restored all Feste's songs) affirmed that he is 'not a young man', and in his staging (no. 46) C. Hayden Coffin, a veteran musical comedy performer then aged fifty, represented him as mature and melancholy. Twenty years later, in Tyrone Guthrie's first production (no. 57), Morland Graham's clown had become a white-haired old man; while in the RSC's 1960 revival (no. 81) Max Adrian's celebrated performance also presented him as elderly and sardonic.

The caustic potential of the role has on occasion turned into raging anger. In conflict with the highly decadent court in Gill's 1974 production (no. 93), Ron Pember's Feste became a Malvolio-like Puritan, described by one critic as 'another life-hater infiltrating the hedonists like a member of Angry Brigade at a coming-out ball . . . angrily banging his drum and baring his teeth on "Come away, death"' (J.W. Lambert, *Sunday Times*). Even more enraged was Anton Lesser's decidedly misanthropic clown in 1987 (no. 102), 'a faintly gypsy-like hobo with a carpet bag, whose smouldering anger and contempt reach a natural climax with the furious baiting of the imprisoned Malvolio' (Martin Hoyle, *Financial Times*).

Feste's ventriloquism, born with Armin, has re-emerged in recent performances. Mark Hadfield's memorable clown in Posner's 2001 RSC production (no. 113), 'a born loner used to corrupting words to grub a living' (Michael Billington, *Guardian*), adopted different voices, shifting from his normal classless southern English to mock-Jewish for the 'Quinapalus' nonsense in 1.5, to homiletic pomposity as Sir Topas. The vocal range was part of his music-hall conception of the role: tiny, sporting a Charlie Chaplin suit and Buster Keaton flat hat and string tie, he moved in a gangling Max Wall fashion and delivered his final song in cabaret style. In Nunn's film (no. 109) the Feste played by the half-Indian actor Ben Kingsley breaks twice into 'mimicry of a colonial-Indian native soldier' (Eggert): first in the 'nonsense' regarding 'Malvolio's nose' (2.3.25), thereby associating the steward with an 'exotic' outsider; and later at 'ginger shall be hot' (114), where the accent perhaps suggests Indian food. Equal 'post-colonial' vocal versatility was put on show by Kulvinder Ghir in 2004 (no. 120), a chameleon-like Indian song-and-dance street artist: 'Now he's a tranny, now he's an untouchable' (Alistair Macaulay, *Financial Times*).

A noble duke: Orsino

Despite being the comedy's 'official' male lead, and ruler of Illyria to boot, Orsino has rarely wielded power onstage. Hotson speculates that the 'original' Orsino may have been Augustine Phillips, but there is no evidence for this. Later dukes tended to fall into a limited range of stereotypes, the most recurrent being the sincerely passionate Petrarchan lover, despite the text's hints at the instability of his desire and the suspicious staginess of his effusions in the opening scene. This characterization prevailed especially in the nineteenth century and occasionally appears today, as in Mark Strong's 2002 performance (no. 116). In the later twentieth century the standard duke became instead a languidly self-indulgent and at times decadent figure, and the play's incipit (Orsino's big scene) served to dramatize his effete sensualism by discovering him in self-pitying prostration, as in the case of the recumbent 'lotus-eating Duke' (Ronald Bryden, *Observer*) in 1969 (no. 87), or Toby Stephens's 'young militarily-dressed man [lying] full-length on a chaise, his left hand covering his eyes, his right arm cradled in a sling' in Nunn's film (Nunn, 13). This tradition found its most extreme expression in Peter Gill's 1974 production (no. 93), in which John Price's Orsino was discovered 'lolling languidly on cushions or homosexually [*sic*] fumbling his page' (John Barber, *Daily Telegraph*; see Fig. 4).

Attempts have been made to overcome this cliché of horizontal preciosity, for example by underlining Orsino's verbal – and potentially physical – violence in 5.1. In 1966 (no. 84) Alan Howard's energetic, angular and anti-romantic duke, like a Petruccio in the wrong play, 'enters the first scene at a run and conducts his campaign against Olivia's affections more in a military than romantic spirit' (*Times*), while Terence Maynard's muscular, shaven-headed and emphatically vertical black Orsino cut a vigorously macho figure in 2002 (no. 114), despite his fancy satin tunic, his lace collar and cuffs and his pearl earring.

Here comes the countess: Olivia

Traditionally conceived as a gracefully mature figure, perhaps because she is a countess – even though the text hardly justifies this, and though her behaviour is anything but aristocratically sedate – the role of Olivia has undergone an evolution over the last century. Little is known of the first 'female' Olivia, Ann Gibbs (the future Mrs Thomas Shadwell) in the 1660s. Later actresses tended to play the role relatively late in their careers: in 1741 (no. 8) 35-year-old Kitty Clive, the liveliest comedienne and best comic singer of her age (she was given an air to music by Thomas Arne), played opposite 26-year-old Peg Woffington's Viola. The former street singer Frances Abington (see Fig. 27), queen of the 'grand coquettes' (Edward Dutton Cook, *DNB*), lent wit and elegance to the part in 1771 (no. 12), at the age of thirty-four, and was likewise given a 'French air' to sing; Charlotte Rusport praised her 'incomparable modulation', claiming that 'her articulation is so exact, that every syllable she utters is conveyed distinctly and even harmoniously' (quoted in *Biographical Dictionary*). Mrs Charles Kemble, née Marie-Thérèse de Camp, known for her French charm, first played the role in 1811 (no. 21), aged thirty-seven, and was described by Leigh Hunt as possessing 'a beautiful figure, fine large dark eyes, and elevated features, fuller of spirit than softness, but still capable of expressing great tenderness' (Hunt, *Autobiography*). The tall and powerful Violet Vanbrugh was also thirty-seven when she appeared in Daly's production in 1894 (no. 37).

The 41-year-old Russian former ballerina, Lydia Lopokova, Lady Keynes, did not break with the 'mature' tradition in Tyrone Guthrie's 1933 production (no. 57), but she was one of the first to depart from the 'graceful countess' commonplace, playing the part with skittish impulsiveness (and with a strong Russian accent), thereby incurring the disapprobation of Virginia Woolf, who found her insufficiently stately, detached and immutable: 'Madame Lopokova loves everybody. She is always changing. Her hands, her face, her feet, the whole of her body, are always quivering in sympathy with the moment' (Woolf, 209). Lesley Brook in Irene Hentschel's 1939 staging (no. 62) similarly disturbed the critics by playing her not as 'the stately and mature lady we are used to but a charming little wilful heiress scarcely out of

27 Mrs Abington as Olivia in 1771

the school-room' (*Daily Telegraph and Morning Post*, quoted by Schafer, 217). In 1947 (no. 66) the traditional age politics were reversed: 19-year-old Daphne Slater contrasted with Beatrix Lehmann's 44-year-old Viola and was 'less the Madonna and grand lady than the impulsive and warm-hearted girl' (*Guardian*). In 1958 (no. 81) Geraldine McEwan, in her mid-twenties, presented Olivia analogously as 'a squeaking flibbertigibbet' (Trewin, 238), 'a pouting, giggling, squealing *poseuse*' (M. Billington, xvii); visibly attracted to Cesario, she threw herself on her knees before him on 'Nor wit nor reason can my passion hide' (3.1.150). In a similar vein, Estelle Kohler, in her early twenties, played her in 1966 (no. 84) as 'a vain and coquettish girl recently released from male protection' (*Times*). Neha Dubey's beautiful Indian aristocrat (2004; no. 120) first appeared deceptively dressed in a solemn black sari, but rapidly metamorphosed into a frivolous young girl sporting a series of colourful, eye-catching saris as a sign of her transformation.

Recent Olivias have given free expression to their sexual impulses: Kate Nicholls in 1979 (no. 95) 'flirtatiously rub[bed] up against Malvolio' and then physically assaulted the disguised Viola, 'leaping at her, cuddling her and pursuing her pell-mell through the garden' (Benedict Nightingale, *New Statesman*); Caroline Langrishe in 1987 (no. 102) was more aristocratic but made it clear that 'she could not wait to get her hands on Orsino's boy-emissary' (M. Billington, xxx). Equally passionate was Mark Rylance – aged forty-two, and male to boot – in the 2002 Middle Temple production (no. 114). His Olivia was in total control of household and stage power; more than a countess, Rylance looked like a perennially embalmed Elizabeth I, complete with white facial mask and coronet, sliding across the stage as if on royal rollers, and delivering his lines with an intriguing mixture of artfulness and ingenuousness. In the Globe revival, Rylance played the part for its comic value, producing moments of outright slapstick under the effect of passion: his Olivia threw a basket at Sir Andrew and a prayer book at Malvolio, wielded an enormous halberd, lost a shoe, had trouble taking off her ring, fainted, fell, screamed and repeatedly stuttered, giving new meaning to Cesario's claim that she 'did speak in starts'. Rylance's Olivia was rivalled in stage presence and comic force by Paul Chahidi's Maria, whose 'flustering and matron-like control is splendidly camp yet convincing' (Lisa Whitbread, *Stage*). If Olivia was a queen (Elizabeth), Chahidi's Maria was 'an actress playing an old queen who plays an old girl ripe for a bit of fun – the actress, in this case, being Edith Evans' (Rhoda Koenig, *Independent*); Evans played the role of Viola in 1932 (no. 54).

I am not that I play: Viola

The play's female protagonist, as we have seen (p. 50), unconventionally underlines her difficulties in acting her disguise role (see 2.2.27–41, 3.4.295–6, etc.), thereby ironically foregrounding the acting of her part by a cross-dressed male actor. In many ways this paradox, written into the text, has conditioned the performances of women (and occasionally men) actors: the degree of their success in reconciling the transition from Viola to Cesario has been one of the benchmarks for critical judgements of their performances.

The first actress to play Viola may have been Mrs Davenport in the 1660s Duke's Theatre productions (nos 4–6). The first certain name that has come down to us is that of Hannah Pritchard, who played opposite Macklin in 1741 (no. 8): a considerable tragic actress, she brought a degree of *gravitas* to the part, unlike her celebrated successor in the 1746 revival (no. 10), the notoriously sensuous Peg Woffington, a popular specialist in breeches roles (male characters *en travestie*) who attracted audiences at least in part by showing off her feminine graces, notably her breeched legs; Woffington's beauty and *savoir-faire* compensated for her 'unpleasant squeaking pipe' of a voice (Tate Wilkinson, quoted in *Biographical Dictionary*). Woffington was probably the first in a long series of unmistakably female Violas whose femininity showed through to greatest effect precisely in the cross-dressed scenes. Similarly, in 1783 (no. 15), Mary Robinson's striking figure was 'seen to great advantage in the masculine dress' (Joseph Knight, *DNB*), captivating, among others, the future George IV, who became her lover. In 1820 (no. 23) Maria Tree was likewise unmistakably female: 'To our taste, indeed, we confess she never looked *so* feminine, as when habited in the costume of the other sex . . . Then her figure was beautifully formed; and her "masculine usurped attire" . . . displayed it to peculiar advantage' (Oxberry, *Dramatic*, 1.205–6); in 1836 (no. 25) her sister Ellen Tree similarly 'puts not off the woman with her attire, but becomes yet more womanly' (*Athenaeum*). Adelaide Neilson's 1877 performance (no. 33) again emphasized delicate femininity, above all as Cesario: she was 'incarnate April sunshine, – an embodiment of exquisitely bright and tender womanhood' (Winter, 42). In 1955 (no. 77) Vivien Leigh's somewhat cold and detached performance worked better in the Cesario scenes, where her beauty was more intriguing: 'As a boy Miss Leigh is charming, as Viola herself curiously unromantic' (Eric Keown, *Punch*).

One of the 'tricks' of actresses wishing to signal their womanliness in the disguise scenes has been to caricature the masculinity of Cesario: a famous example is Ellen Terry (no. 36), who managed to be wittily feminine, even though she had her arm in a sling and had to perform sitting down, playing the part with 'grace, sweetness, and delicate touches of pathos' (Aveling, 117), in spite of, or partly thanks to, her 'charming and laughing assumption of a mannish walk' (*Saturday Review*).

There have been rather fewer attempts to bestow on the Cesario scenes a genuine and non-parodic mimesis of masculinity. Madame Meyer Bourke (1851; no. 29), playing both twins, achieved a form of gender-crossing ventriloquism, prompting the diarist Henry Crabb Robinson to note that 'when personating [Sebastian], she gave a manliness to her voice and step which would have almost deceived us as to her identity' (Robinson, 2.327). Charlotte Cushman, opposite her sister Susan's Olivia in 1846 (no. 26), cut a fine masculine figure in her knee-length skirt and velvet jacket, with a sash and dagger at her waist.[1] Viola Allen likewise attempted a fully fledged male impersonation in 1904

1 Joseph Leach, *Bright Particular Star: The Life and Times of Charlotte Cushman* (New Haven, Conn., 1970), 177.

(no. 42; Winter, 80–1), while in 1947 (no. 66) the 44-year-old Beatrix Lehmann was 'every inch a man' (*Guardian*).

More challenging, but also more difficult to bring off successfully, is a 'middle ground' in which the poles of masculine and feminine are suspended in an indeterminate gender identity. Judi Dench in 1969 (no. 87) went some way in this direction by being attractively ambiguous, 'a dashing cavalier in green velvet, all swagger and girlish trepidation' (Colin Frame, *Evening News*). A more radical attempt at sustained androgyny was made by Jane Lapotaire in Peter Gill's 1974 gender-confusing production (no. 93), although she was criticized for it, for example by Irving Wardle of the *Times*, who complained of her being 'a blank screen on to which others project their fantasies'; this, however, is in many ways precisely what Viola-as-Cesario is: 'blank' (2.4.110). One of the successes of the all-male 2002 Globe theatre revival (no. 114) was the effortless co-existence of biological boyishness and non-camp feminine seductiveness in Michael Brown's 'lovely, willowy Viola' (Kate Kellaway, *Observer*).

A recurrent trait of successful Violas has been their vocal and especially musical quality, as if to justify the character's claim to be able to speak 'in many sorts of music' (1.2.55). Hannah Pritchard's voice (no. 8) was 'deliciously musical' (Winter, 18). In the performance of the great Dora Jordan in 1785 (no. 16) Sir Joshua Reynolds praised 'the music of her melancholy' and 'the music of her laugh' (quoted in Winter, 22), while according to Leigh Hunt, 'Mrs Jordan seems to speak with her soul; her voice, piquant with melody, delights the ear with a peculiar and exquisite fulness' (Hunt, *Criticism*, 163), and for Hazlitt '[her] voice is a cordial to the heart, because it came from it, rich, full, like the luscious juice of the ripe grape; to hear whose laugh was to drink nectar' (quoted in *Biographical Dictionary*). John Hoppner's celebrated portrait of Mrs Jordan (*c.* 1790, Iveagh Bequest) in her Cesario disguise – a hussar costume and hat, with bright red hatband, necktie and belt – in the open against a backdrop of pillars and stormy sky, captures the pathos for which her vocally enchanting performance was known.

Still on a musical note, in Ellen Tree's 1836 performance (no. 25) 'Not a tone of voice but touches the heart' (*Athenaeum*). G.B. Shaw praised 'the true Shakespearian music' of Ada Rehan's performance in Daly's (highly musical) 1894 production (no. 37); Lily Brayton's Viola in Tree's 1901 revival (no. 41) was marked by her 'passionate and satin-voiced' delivery (Trewin, 19), while Julia Marlowe (1905; no. 44) was praised for her 'melodious, sympathetic voice' (Winter, 90). In 1950 (no. 69) Peggy Ashcroft quite dominated Hugh Hunt's staging, not least in the silent music of her rapt stillness in 2.4.

In one memorable interpretation, exquisite musicality was orchestrated with choreographic movement in a richly meaningful dialogue: according to Granville-Barker, Suzanne Bing in Copeau's 1914 version (no. 48) 'spoke very beautifully; she moved with grace. But the movements did not exist apart from their meaning, and every sentence came out conceived as a whole, as a thought and a feeling' (*Observer*; quoted in Speaight, *Shakespeare*, 189). Suzanne Bing is one of the earliest Violas to take full command of the stage. The last century saw an increasing shift – onstage as in critical discourse – away from Malvolio (or Sir Toby) towards Viola as the dramatic and theatrical centre of the play, a shift confirmed in the powerful performances of Peggy Ashcroft, Judi Dench, Jane Lapotaire and – more controversially – Vanessa Redgrave, who played her in 1972 (no. 89) as 'a scrambling, shouting, gawky adolescent' (Michael Billington, *Guardian*). It is quite likely that this centrality of Viola-as-Cesario – more than justified by the text of the comedy – will continue in future.

Performance history: 120 productions of *Twelfth Night*[1]

(1) **1602** (2 Feb.) Middle Temple; Lord Chamberlain's Men
(2) **1618** (6 Apr.) King's Men at court (as *Twelfth Night*)
(3) **1623** (2 Feb.) King's Men at court (as *Malvolio*)
(4) **1661** (11 Sept.) Duke's; AA: Henry Harris; Fe: Cave Underhill; Mal: Thomas Lovell; To: Thomas Betterton; Ol: Ann Gibbs
(5) **1663** (6 Jan.) Duke's; probably same cast as 1661
(6) **1669** (20 Jan.) Duke's; possibly same cast as 1661
(7) **1703** (Mar.) Lincoln's Inn Fields; William Burnaby's adaptation *Love Betrayed*
(8) **1741** (15 Jan.) DL; AA: Henry Woodward; Mal: Charles Macklin; Ol: Kitty Clive; Vio: Hannah Pritchard
(9) **1742** (6 Jan.) Smock Alley, Dublin
(10) **1746** (15 Apr.) DL; Fe: Richard Yates; Mal: Charles Macklin; Ol: Kitty Clive; Vio: Peg Woffington
(11) **1763** (19 Oct.) DL; Mal: Richard Yates; Vio: Miss Plym
(12) **1771** (10 Dec.) DL; AA: James Dodd; Mal: Thomas King; Ol: Frances Abington; Vio: Elizabeth Younge
(13) **1776** (10 Sept.) DL; AA: James Dodd; Mal: Robert Bensley; To: John Palmer
(14) **1777** (17 Mar.) CG; AA: John Quick; To: John Dunstall; Vio: Mrs Barry Spranger
(15) **1783** (7 May) CG; Mal: John Henderson; Vio: Mary Robinson
(16) **1785** (11 Nov.) DL; AA: James Dodd; Fe: Richard Suett; Mal: Robert Bensley; To: John Palmer; Vio: Dorothy Jordan
(17) **1789** (19 Mar.) DL; Mal: John Philip Kemble

1 The abbreviations adopted in this table are as follows: DL: Drury Lane; CG: Covent Garden; SW: Sadler's Wells; Hay: Haymarket; OV: Old Vic; dir: director; des: designer; prod: producer; AA: Sir Andrew; Fe: Feste; Mal: Malvolio; Mar: Maria; Ol: Olivia; Ors: Orsino; Seb: Sebastian; To: Sir Toby; Vio: Viola.

(18) **1790** (10 Feb.) DL; Seb. George Bland; Vio: Dorothy Jordan (his sister)

(19) **1794** (3 Feb.) The Theatre, Boston (first recorded American performance); Mal: Snelling Powell

(20) **1804** (11 June) Park theatre, NY; Mal: John G. Martin

(21) **1811** (5 Jan.) CG; revised J.P. Kemble; Mal: John Liston; Ol: Mrs Charles Kemble

(22) **1815** Theatre Royal, Edinburgh; Seb: William Murray; Vio: Mrs Henry Siddons (his sister)

(23) **1820** (8 Nov.) CG; prod: Frederick Reynolds; AA: John Liston; Mal: William Farren; Vio: Maria Tree

(24) **1824** (10 Aug.) Chatham Garden theatre, NY; Mal: Henry Wallack

(25) **1836** (31 Aug.) Hay; Mal: William Farren; Vio: Ellen Tree

(26) **1846** (25 June) Hay; Ol: Susan Cushman; Vio: Charlotte Cushman

(27) **1848** (26 Jan.) SW; Mal: Samuel Phelps

(28) **1850** (28 Sept.) Princess's (opening prod.); prod: Charles Kean; AA: Robert Keeley; Fe: John Pritt Harley; Vio: Ellen Tree

(29) **1851** (16 June) Court Theatre, Dresden; Vio/Seb: Meyer Bourke

(30) **1852** (29 Mar.) Chambers Street, NY; To: William Evans Burton

(31) **1856** (24 Mar.) Wallack's Lyceum, NY; dir: James Wallack; Mal: John Brougham

(32) **1865** (7 June) Olympic; Vio/Seb: Kate Terry

(33) **1877** (7 May) Fifth Avenue theatre, NY; dir: Augustin Daly; Vio: Adelaide Neilson

(34) **1881** (31 May) DL; *Was Ihr Wollt*, Royal Theatre of Saxe-Meiningen; dir: Duke George II; Fe: Herr Teller; Vio: Fräulein Werner

(35) **1881** (31 Oct.) Fifth Avenue theatre, NY; adapted Charles Webb; AA: Stuart Robson; To: William H. Crane

(36) **1884** (8 July) Lyceum; des: Hawes Craven; prod: Henry Irving; Mal: Irving; Vio: Ellen Terry

(37) **1894** (8 Jan.) Daly's theatre; dir: Augustin Daly; Ol: Violet Vanbrugh; Vio: Ada Rehan

(38) **1895** (21 June) Burlington Hall (Elizabethan Stage Society: first prod.); dir: William Poel

(39) **1897** (10 Feb.) Middle Temple (Elizabethan Stage Society); dir: William Poel

(40) **1900** (23 Mar.) Lyceum; Mal: Frank Benson; Ol: Lily Brayton; Vio: Constance Benson

(41) **1901** (5 Feb.) Her Majesty's; dir: Herbert Beerbohm Tree; des: Hawes Craven & Joseph Harker; Fe: Courtice Pounds; Mal: Tree; Ol: Maud Jeffries; Vio: Lily Brayton

(42) **1904** (8 Feb.) Knickerbocker theatre, NY; dir: Charles Frohman; Vio: Viola Allen

(43) **1904** (22 Feb.) Knickerbocker; dir: Ben Greet; Mal: Greet; Vio: Edith Wynne Matthison

(44) **1905** (16 Oct.) Knickerbocker; dir: E.H. Sothern; Mal: E.H. Sothern; Vio: Julia Marlowe

(45) **1910** (3 Feb.) Silent film (Vitagraph); dir: Charles Kent; scenario: Eugene Mullin; Mal: Charles Kent; Vio: Florence Turner

(46) **1912** (15 Nov.) Savoy; dir: Harley Granville Barker; costume and des: Norman Wilkinson; AA: Leon Quartermaine; Fe: Hayden Coffin; Mal: Henry Ainley; Vio: Lillah McCarthy

(47) **1914** (25 Mar.) Hudson theatre, NY; dir: Margaret Anglin; Mal: Fuller Mellish; Vio: Margaret Anglin

(48) **1914** (15 May) Théâtre du Vieux-Colombier; Paris; dir: Jacques Copeau; des: Louis Jouvet; costume: Duncan Grant; AA: Louis Jouvet; Mal: Jacques Copeau; Vio: Suzanne Bing

(49) **1916** (3 Jan.) OV; dir: Ben Greet; Mal: Ben Greet; To: Robert Atkins; Ol:/Vio: Sybil Thorndike (alternating); Vio: Viola Tree

(50) **1920** (15 Nov.) OV; dir: Robert Atkins; AA: Andrew Leigh

(51) **1923** (28 May) BBC radio; AA: Nigel Playfair; Mal: Herbert Waring

(52) **1927** (17 May) St James's; dir: Robert Atkins; Ol: Maxine Forbes-Robertson; Priest: Johnson Forbes-Robertson; Vio: Jean Forbes-Robertson

(53) **1931** (6 Jan.) SW (reopening prod.); Mal: John Gielgud; To: Ralph Richardson

(54) **1932** (29 Mar.) OV/SW; dir: Harcourt Williams; Mal: Robert Speaight; To: Ralph Richardson; Vio: Edith Evans

(55) **1932** (24 May) New Theatre; dir: Robert Atkins; Fe: John Laurie; Vio: Jean Forbes-Robertson

(56) **1932** Chicago Drama Festival; dir: Orson Welles; Mal: Orson Welles (film version 1933)

(57) **1933** (18 Sept.) OV; dir: Tyrone Guthrie; des: Wells Coates; Fe: Morland Graham; Mal: Leon Quartermaine; Ol: Lydia Lopokova

(58) **1937** (23 Feb.) OV; dir: Tyrone Guthrie; AA: Alec Guinness; To: Laurence Olivier; Vio:/Seb: Jessica Tandy

(59) **1937** (14 May) BBC TV; Ol: Dorothy Black; Vio: Greer Garson

(60) **1938** (1 Dec.) Phoenix; dir: Michel Saint-Denis; AA: Michael Redgrave; To: George Devine; Vio: Peggy Ashcroft (broadcast BBC TV, 2 Jan. 1939)

(61) **1938** (30 Aug.) CBS radio; dir: Orson Welles

(62) **1939** (13 Apr.) Stratford; dir: Irene Hentschel; des: Motley; AA: Alec Clunes; Mal: John Laurie; Ol: Lesley Brook

(63) **1940** (15 Feb.) Kingsway; dir: Andrew Leigh and Donald Wolfit; Mal: Donald Wolfit; Vio: Rosalinde Fuller

(64) **1940** (19 Nov.) St James Theater, NY; dir: Margaret Webster; Mal: Maurice Evans; Vio: Helen Hayes

(65) **1943** (29 June) Lyric (ballet version); music: Edvard Grieg; choreog: Andrée Howard

(66) **1947** (23 Apr.) Stratford (first post-war prod.); dir: Jack Hylton; AA: Paul Scofield; Mal: Walter Hudd; Ol: Daphne Slater; Vio: Beatrix Lehmann

(67) **1948** (21 Sept.) New (OV prod.); dir: Alec Guinness; Mal: Mark Dignam; Seb: Donald Sinden; To: Cedric Hardwicke

(68) **1949** (20 Feb.) NBC TV: live broadcast from Philco Playhouse; dir: Fred Coe; Mal: John Carradine; Vio: Marsha Hunt

(69) **1950** (14 Nov.) OV (reopening); dir: Hugh Hunt; Mal: Michael Horden; Ors: Alec Clunes; Vio: Peggy Ashcroft

(70) **1950** (6 Jan.) BBC TV; dir: Harold Clayton; Mal: Geoffrey Dunn; Ol: Patricia Kneale; Vio: Barbara Lott

(71) **1950** Floridiana, Naples; dir: Orazio Costa; Mal: Salvo Randone; Vio: Anna Proclemer

(72) **1951** (2 Feb.) Middle Temple; dir: Donald Wolfit

(73) **1951** (25 Aug.) Palazzo Grassi (Venice; opening prod.); dir: Giorgio Strehler; Mal: Gianni Santuccio

(74) **1953** (2 Feb.) Theatre Royal, Stratford East, London (opening prod.); dir: Joan Littlewood; AA: Harry H. Corbett; Ors: Gerry Raffles

(75) **1954** Teatro di Via Manoni (Milan); dir: Renato Castellani; Mal: Memo Benassi; To: Glauco Mauri

(76) **1954** (6 Jan.) OV; dir: Denis Carey; Fe: Paul Daneman; Mal: Michael Hordern; Ors: John Neville; To: Richard Burton; Vio: Claire Bloom

(77) **1955** (12 Apr.) Stratford; dir: John Gielgud; Mal: Laurence Olivier; Ol: Maxine Audley; Vio: Vivien Leigh

(78) **1956** Soviet film *Dvenadtsataia noch*; dir: Yakov Fried; Mal: M. Yanshin; Ol: Anna Larionova; Vio:/Seb: Klara Luchko

(79) **1957** (10 Mar.) BBC TV; dir: Caspar Wrede; Mal: John Moffatt; Ors: Robert Hardy; Vio: Dilys Hamlett

(80) **1957** (12 Dec.) NBC TV; dir: David Greene; AA: Max Adrian; Mal: Maurice Evans; Vio: Rosemary Harris

(81) **1958** (22 Apr.) Stratford; dir: Peter Hall; des: Lila de Nobili; AA: Richard Johnson; Ol: Geraldine McEwan; Vio: Dorothy Tutin (revived 1960; Fe: Max Adrian; Mal: Eric Porter)

(82) **1962** (18 Feb.) Royal Court; dir: George Devine; Fe: Albert Finney; Mal: Nicol Williamson; Vio: Lynn Redgrave (prod. without décor)

(83) **1962** West German TV (*Was Ihr Wollt*); dir: Franz Peter Wirth; Vio/Seb: Ingrid Adree

(84) **1966** (16 June) RSC; dir: Clifford Williams; AA: Barrie Ingham; Mal: Ian Holm; Ol: Estelle Kohler; Ors: Alan Howard; Vio: Diana Rigg

(85) **1967** Swedish TV; *Trettondagsafton*; dir: Hans Dahlin; Vio: Bibi Andersson

(86) **1968** (13 Jan.) Orpheum, NY; *Your Own Thing* (musical) by Hal Hester and Danny Apolinair; book by Donald Driver

(87) **1969** (21 Aug.) RSC; dir: John Barton; Fe: Emrys James; Mal: Donald Sinden; To: Bill Fraser; Vio: Judi Dench

(88) **1970** (13 July) ATV; dir: John Sichel; prod: John Dexter; Fe: Tommy Steele; Mal: Alec Guinness; To: Ralph Richardson; Vio:/Seb: Joan Plowright

(89) **1972** (16 May) Shaw theatre; dir: Michael Blakewell; Vio: Vanessa Redgrave

(90) **1972** (19 Apr.) Landestheater, Salzburg (*Was Ihr Wollt*); dir: Otto Schenk; Ors: Klaus Maria Brandauer; Vio: Christine Ostermayer (TV version ORF TV, Austria, 2 Sept. 1973)

(91) **1972** Film (*Playboy* Productions); dir: Ron Wertheim; Fe: Wertheim; Vio:/Seb: Nikki Gentile

(92) **1974** (14 May) BBC TV; dir: David Giles, prod: Cedric Messina; Mal: Charles Gray; Vio: Janet Suzman

(93) **1974** (22 Aug.) RSC; dir: Peter Gill; des: William Dudley; Fe: Ron Pember; Mal: Nicol Williamson; Vio: Jane Lapotaire

(94) **1975** (10 June) Stratford, Ontario: dir: David Jones; Mal: Brian Bedford; Vio: Kathleen Widdoes

(95) **1979** (12 June) RSC; dir: Terry Hands; des: John Napier; Fe: Geoffrey Hutchings; Mal: John Woodvine, Ol: Kate Nicholls; Vio: Cherie Lunghi

(96) **1980** (27 Feb.) BBC TV; dir: John Gorrie; prod: Cedric Messina; Fe: Trevor Peacock; Mal: Alec McCowen; Vio: Felicity Kendall

(97) **1982** (10 July) Palais des Papes, Festival d'Avignon (Théâtre du Soleil); dir: Ariane Mnouchkine

(98) **1983** (20 Apr.) RSC; dir: John Caird; Mal: Emrys James; Vio: Zoë Wanamaker

(99) **1986** Cheek by Jowl touring prod.; dir: Declan Donnellan; des: Nick Ormerod

(100) **1987** (7 July) RSC; dir: Bill Alexander; des: Kit Surrey; AA: David Bradley; Mal: Anthony Sher

(101) **1987** Film (Australia); dir: Neil Armfield; AA: Geoffrey Rush; To: John Wood; Vio:/Seb: Gillian Jones

(102) **1987** (3 Dec.) Riverside Studios (Renaissance Theatre Company); dir: Kenneth Branagh; des: Bunnie Christy; music: Pat Doyle and Paul McCartney; Fe: Anton Lesser; Mal: Richard Briers; Ol: Caroline Langrishe (Thames Television version, 13 Dec. 1988; dir: Paul Kafno)

(103) **1989** (29 Sept.) Shakespeare theatre, Washington, DC; dir: Michael Kahn; des: Derek McLane; Fe: Yusef Bulos; Ors: Peter Webster; Vio: Kelly McGillis

(104) **1991** (6 Apr.) RSC; dir: Griff Rhys Jones; des: Ultz; Mal: Freddie Jones; Ors: Terence Hillyer

(105) **1992** (16 June) Théâtre National de Chaillot (Paris); dir: Jérôme Savary

(106) **1992** *Animated Twelfth Night*, adapted Leon Garfield; dir: Mariya Muat

(107) **1994** (25 May) RSC; dir: Ian Judge; des: John Gunter; Mal: Desmond Barrit

(108) **1995** Deutsches Nationaltheater, Weimar; dir: Katja Paryla; Mal: Bernd Lange; Vio: Cornelia Sikora

(109) **1996** Film; dir: Trevor Nunn; Fe: Ben Kingsley; Mal: Nigel Hawthorne; Ol: Helen Bonham-Carter

(110) **1997** (19 Nov.) RSC; dir: Adrian Noble; des: Anthony Ward; Fe: Stephen Boxer; Mal: Philip Voss

(111) **1997** (20 Mar.) Brooks Atkinson theatre, NY; *Play On!* (musical) by Cheryl L. West; dir: Gary Halvorson; music Duke Ellington; Lady Liv: Tonya Pinkins; Vy: Cheryl Freeman

(112) **1998** (16 July) Lincoln Center, NY; dir: Nicholas Hytner; des: Bob Crowley; Vio: Helen Hunt (broadcast by PBS TV)

(113) **2001** (13 Apr.) RSC; dir: Lindsay Posner; Fe: Mark Hadfield; Mal: Guy Henry; To: Barry Stanton; Vio: Zoë Waites

(114) **2002** (25 Jan.) Middle Temple (Globe Theatre Company); dir: Tim Carroll; Mal: Oliver Cotton; Mar: Paul Chahidi; Ol: Mark Rylance; Ors: Terence Maynard; Vio: Eddie Redmayne (revived Globe theatre, 11 May)

(115) **2002** (21 July) Delacorte, NY; dir: Brian Kluick; Vio: Julia Stiles

(116) **2002** (5 Sept.) Donmar Warehouse; dir: Sam Mendes; Fe: Anthony O'Donnell; Mal: Simon Russell Beale; Ors: Mark Strong; Vio: Emily Watson

(117) **2002** (12 Apr.) Hudson Guild Theater, NY (Prospect Theatre Company); *Illyria* (musical) by Peter Mills; dir: Cara Reichel; Mal: Ames Adamson

(118) **2003** (May) International Chekhov Festival, Moscow (in Russian); dir: Declan Donnellan; des: Nick Ormerod; (revived Olympia, Dublin, Oct. 2004; Vio: Andrei Kuzicher; Ol: Alexei Dadonor; Mal: Dmitri Shcherbina, and Barbican, London, June 2006)

(119) **2003** Film (Channel 4 TV); dir: Tim Supple; Mal: Michael Maloney; To: David Troughton; Vio: Parminder Nagra

(120) **2004** (2 Sept.) Albery; dir: Stephen Beresford; Fe: Kulvinder Ghir; Mal: Paul Bhattacharjee; Ol: Neha Dubey

TWELFTH NIGHT,
OR
WHAT YOU WILL

LIST OF ROLES

VIOLA	*a shipwrecked lady, later disguised as Cesario*
CAPTAIN	*of the wrecked ship, who befriends Viola*
SEBASTIAN	*Viola's twin brother, also shipwrecked*
ANTONIO	*a sea-captain, who befriends Sebastian*
ORSINO	*Duke of Illyria*
CURIO	*gentlemen attending on Orsino*
VALENTINE	*gentlemen attending on Orsino*
Two OFFICERS	
OLIVIA	*a countess*
MARIA	*Olivia's waiting-gentlewoman*
SIR TOBY Belch	*Olivia's kinsman*
SIR ANDREW Aguecheek	*companion to Sir Toby*
MALVOLIO	*Olivia's steward*
FESTE	*clown, Olivia's jester*
FABIAN	*a member of Olivia's household*
PRIEST	
SERVANT	*in Olivia's household*

Musicians, Lords, Sailors, Attendants

LIST OF ROLES The list of characters' names, not present in F, first appears in the Douai MS, while the first printed version is included by Rowe. Rowe's list respects traditional gender and class hierarchy, giving male names first and opening with the duke; Viola's name appears next to last.

1 VIOLA The play's female lead is Shakespeare's fourth cross-dressed heroine – after Jiulia (*TGV*), Portia (*MV*) and Rosalind (*AYL*). Her name is possibly inspired by 'Violetta', the cross-dressed protagonist of Emanuel Forde's romance *Parismus*. In F her first entry SD (TLN 461; 1.5.162.1) has *Enter Violenta* (see Appendix 1). 'Viola', in addition to being a musical instrument, is Italian for 'violet'. The musical connotations of her name are taken up in Sir Toby's 'viol-de-gamboys' (1.3.23–4), while its floral associations are alluded to in Orsino's opening speech ('bank of violets', 1.1.6). The name as such, however, is not mentioned in the dialogue until 5.1.240, where the metre seems to call for the pronunciation ['vaɪələ] (accent on the first syllable). The name of Viola's disguise role, Cesario – deriving from Latin *Caesarius*, 'belonging to Caesar' – may recall Cesare, adopted name of the heroine Ginevra in another version of the story, Curzio Gonzaga's play *Gli inganni* (1592).

3 SEBASTIAN Viola's twin is named after a famous third-century Christian saint (see p. 23), popularized by Renaissance painters, who generally depict him as a beautiful youth pierced by arrows. It may be its association with death that suggested the name (since Sebastian is presumed drowned).

4 ANTONIO another saint's name (see p. 23), common in Shakespeare. It occurs, for example, in *TGV*, *MA* and *Tem*. The homoerotic emphasis of Antonio's attitude towards Sebastian recalls another Antonio, the friend and benefactor of Bassanio in *MV* (see Pequigney). Antonio has a somewhat enigmatic military past, having been involved in naval action against Orsino, who addresses him as 'Notable pirate' (5.1.65). In F the name appears as '*Antonio*' in the entry SD and dialogue in his first scene (2.1), but as '*Anthonio*' in his second scene (3.3) and last scene (5.1), while his third (3.4) has '*Antonio*' in the entry SD and '*Anthonio*' in the dialogue.

5 ORSINO The name of the play's male protagonist (meaning literally 'little bear' in Italian) probably alludes to the Orsini, one of the most ancient and distinguished families of the Roman nobility. At 1.2.22–3 the Captain describes Orsino as being 'A noble duke / In nature, as in name', and Viola has heard her father name him (25). There may be a more specific allusion to Shakespeare's contemporary Virginio Orsini (1572–1615), second Duke of Bracciano. Son of Paolo Giordano Orsini, the notorious first Duke, and of Isabella de' Medici, daughter of the Grand Duke of Tuscany, Virginio had an eventful childhood: in 1576, when he was four, his father probably strangled the duchess in a fit of jealous rage, and later had her lover assassinated. Having fled to Rome, the duke in turn became the lover of Vittoria Accoramboni, wife of Francesco Peretti (nephew of Pope Sisto V); Orsini appears to have had Peretti assassinated in 1583. The couple married shortly before being assassinated themselves in separate incidents in 1585, the year in which Virginio (then aged 13) succeeded to the Duchy of Bracciano. These events inspired Webster's *The White Devil* (1612), in which Virginio becomes 'Giovanni'. Despite the unusual circumstances of his infancy, Orsini became a respected and respectable figure. In 1601 he was sent as envoy to England by his uncle Ferdinand de' Medici; at the court of Elizabeth he witnessed a play, probably performed by Shakespeare's company. It is possible that the character is named after him following this visit: see p. 94. Shakespeare's Orsino is referred to as both duke and count; Duke Virginio

Orsini was also Count of Anguillara.

6 CURIO probably named after Gaius Scribonius Curio, a Roman tribune and ally of Julius Caesar (he is mentioned in Plutarch's *Life of Julius Caesar*, source of *JC*). Curio's is the first name pronounced in the play, at 1.1.16.

7 VALENTINE This, the name of the patron saint of lovers, had become common in romantic comedy: see, for example, *TG*. 'Valentine' is associated with 'Orson' in the French romance *Valentine and Orson* – a story of separated twins – translated into English around 1550, and of a lost anonymous play of the same title, entered in the Stationer's Register on 23 May 1595. Unlike Curio, Valentine is never named in the dialogue.

9 OLIVIA Like 'Viola', 'Olivia' may derive from Forde's *Parismus*, which has a character of the same name. Being a countess, Olivia is inferior in rank to Orsino, as Sir Toby underlines: 'She'll none o'th' count. She'll not match above her degree' (1.3.105–6).

10 MARIA This is the form of the name that appears in all SDs in F, while in the dialogue it alternates with the English equivalent '*Mary*' (four occurrences each, plus a solitary diminutive '*Marian*', TLN 712; 2.3.13); SPs in *F* are abbreviated to *Mar.*, which would allow either version. In textual and stage history the Italian form has always prevailed, partly because there are other Italian names in the play. It is usually given, however, the anglicized pronunciation [mə'raɪə], rhyming with fire, rather than Italian [ma'ri:a]. Sir Toby describes her as 'My niece's chambermaid' (1.3.49), but the term indicated a more elevated rank than it does today: *OED* (giving this example) glosses as 'lady's maid'.

11 SIR TOBY **Belch** Toby is a typical English name, diminutive of the biblical Tobias (the holy man protagonist of the eponymous Old Testament book, whose name in Hebrew means 'God is good'). Unlike Sir Andrew's, his knighthood is apparently hereditary rather than acquired (see 3.4.229–30). The precise degree of Sir Toby's kinship with Olivia is uncertain (see note to 1.3.1, 4), as is his age: Aguecheek's gaffe at 1.3.114, referring to him as an 'old man', need not be taken literally, and he is often played as a relatively young man. His surname speaks, as it were, for itself as a sign of his gastronomic and alcoholic excesses; it is literalized at 1.5.116.

12 SIR ANDREW **Aguecheek** Andrew is the patron saint of Scotland (see p. 23), and Aguecheek is sometimes played as a Scotsman. 'Ague' (pronounced as two syllables) was a generic term in Early Modern English for a fever or fit of shaking; 'cheek' probably has both its modern meanings: facial part (cf. 'Agueface', 1.3.42) and buttock. Sir Andrew's composite surname thus suggests leanness (cf. *JC* 2.2.113: 'that same ague which hath made you lean'), paleness and cowardice (cf. *Cor* 1.4.37–8: 'faces pale / With flight and agued fear'). It may also imply, more literally, a sickly disposition: see Maria's 'he would quickly have the gift of a grave', 1.3.30–1. This is indeed the way Sir Andrew is often portrayed in performance: thin, sickly and highly strung. His nominal cowardice, meanwhile, is confirmed in the 'duelling' episode in 3.4. His fellow knight Sir Toby hints at 3.4.229–30 that Sir Andrew has purchased his title.

13 MALVOLIO In Italian *malvoglio* means literally 'I dislike': the opposite to Benvolio, name of Romeo's cousin in *RJ*. It may have been suggested by the expression 'mala voglia' (ill will), which occurs several times in Bandello's prose version of the 'twelfth night' story (cf. also Florio, *World*, 'Maleuolo, *malitious*', p. 212). He is in turn disliked by others ('Malvoluto, *hated*': Florio, *World*). The morpheme *mal*, moreover, is synonymous with evil or sickness, and indeed Olivia accuses him of being 'sick of self-love' (1.5.86; see p. 29).

14 FESTE The clown's personal name – Italian for 'revels': cf. Florio's 'Festa, *a feast, a holyday*' (Florio, *World*; see

p. 212) – is mentioned only once in the dialogue in F, and never in SDs or SPs, where he is always indicated as *Clo*(*wne*), while the other characters usually refer to him as *fool*. The name may be a casual afterthought on Shakespeare's part, chosen to suggest his role in the revelries within Olivia's household, or perhaps because in Elizabethan pronunciation it rhymed with 'jester' (in the jingle 'Feste the jester', 2.4.11). In 4.2 Feste dresses up as a priest and assumes the name Sir Topas. In literary and theatrical history, this is the name not of a priest but of a knight: first, the protagonist in Chaucer's burlesque romance *The Tale of Sir Thopas* in *The Canterbury Tales* (Chaucer, *Works*, 164–6), and then a braggart knight, Sir Tophas, in Lyly, *Endimion*; both characters act out what is in some ways a false role, like Feste's in 4.2. (On the knight–priest relationship, cf. Cesario's contrasting of 'Sir Priest' and 'Sir Knight' at 3.4.265.) The name, as well as the clerical disguise, may allude to the 'exorcizing' of Malvolio, since according to Scot the topaz stone had therapeutic effects in the treatment of madness: 'a topase healeth the lunatic person of his passion of lunacie' (Scot, 294; see also Burton, 2.4.1.4, 441). The name can also be seen as a deformation of 'Sir Toby', for whom Feste is as it were a representative in this episode (see Sir Toby's 'To him, Sir Topas', 4.2.17). At the same time, the changeable colouring of the gemstone, with its yellow, white or green prismatic crystals, makes it appropriate to Feste's change of dress and identity in this scene (compare his 'very opal' metaphor for Orsino's mind at 2.4.75), while also alluding, perhaps, to the yellow and green of his fool's motley. The spelling *Topas* (rather than 'Topaz') in F may also indicate a pun on top-ass, suggesting that Malvolio is to be made a fool of (by a fool).

15 FABIAN another saint's name (see p. 23). It may have been partly suggested to Shakespeare by 'Fabio', the pseudonym of the cross-dressed Lelia in *Intronati*. A somewhat enigmatic figure, Fabian appears suddenly as a replacement for Feste in the gulling plot in 2.5. He is often played as a servant or member of Olivia's household, or alternatively as a law student, since he refers twice to the law in 3.4 (but also with reference to the play's early performance at the Middle Temple: Shakespeare may have 'brought on' a member of the Inn at the last moment).

TWELFTH NIGHT, OR WHAT YOU WILL

1.1 [*Music.*] *Enter* ORSINO, Duke of Illyria, CURIO *and other Lords.*

ORSINO

If music be the food of love, play on,
Give me excess of it, that surfeiting

TITLE *F's 'Twelfe' is a variant spelling of 'twelfth' (*OED* twelfth *a.* 1a) but may also reflect, in pronunciation, the loss of 't' before 'n' and 'd' (see Kökeritz, 320). The comedy's second title, *What You Will*, is a proverbial catchphrase, not always benevolent (Dent, W280.5): cf. 1.5.105, where Olivia uses it to express her impatience towards Orsino's courtship. John Marston's comedy *What You Will* was probably performed slightly earlier than *TN*.

1.1 The opening scene – often performed as the second scene because of its supposed lack of theatricality (see p. 97) – introduces the important themes of love, death and the powers of music, and presents Orsino in his role as poetic lover. Coleridge observes of Shakespeare's opening scenes that they may 'strike at once the key-note, give the predominant spirit of the play, as in the *Twelfth Night*' (Coleridge, 1.38); this is not altogether true, since this scene is in reality quite unlike much of the rest of the comedy in its intense lyricism. Rowe locates this scene in '*The Palace*', which Capell further specifies as '*A Room in the Duke's Palace*'. The action shifts in the first act between Orsino's palace and Olivia's house, and then (apart from a brief excursion in 3.3) settles in the latter.

0.1 ****Music*** F has no SD in this scene regarding the use of music, but *Enough, no more* (7) suggests that music is playing at the opening of the play. The music might have been provided by a single musician on stage, or by a group, perhaps situated in the gallery.

Illyria On the historical and symbolic implications of the play's setting, see pp. 70–2.

0.2 ***Lords*** The size of Orsino's entourage is unclear and varies in productions.

1 SP *See List of Roles, 5n.

1 **music** It is not by chance that this is the comedy's opening noun. *TN* is one of Shakespeare's most musical plays, and music takes on an important metaphorical as well as literal significance, as a means of expression and persuasion and as a medium for change. See Appendix 3. Cf. *AC* 2.5.1–2, 'music, moody food / Of us that trade in love'.

2 **excess** one of the comedy's key semantic categories (varied in *surfeiting*): cf. e.g. 1.3.7–13, 36–40; 1.5.116–17; 2.3.85–90.

it refers back to *music* but also to *food of love*, which Orsino desires in great quantities

TITLE] *(*Twelfe Night, Or what you will*), Rowe* 1.1] *(Actus Primus, Scaena Prima.)* 0.1 *Music*] *Smock Alley; Musick attending. / Capell after Lords 0.2* 1 SP] *Mahood; Duke. F*

The appetite may sicken and so die.
That strain again, it had a dying fall.
O, it came o'er my ear like the sweet south
That breathes upon a bank of violets,
Stealing and giving odour. Enough, no more,
'Tis not so sweet now as it was before. [*Music ceases.*]
O spirit of love, how quick and fresh art thou
That, notwithstanding thy capacity

2–3 Orsino's conceit is to free himself of desire (*appetite*) by an overabundance causing nausea (*sicken*), i.e. by having too much of a good thing, with the added optimistic aspiration to achieve freedom through sexual release (*die* = end and climax sexually). Shakespeare is possibly mixing and varying the proverbs 'Too much honey cloys the stomach' (Dent, H560) and 'Every surfeit foreruns a fast' (Dent, S1011).

4 **strain . . . fall** refers to a musical cadence (*OED* fall *n.*[1] 10, first occurrence), while continuing the pun on *die* – i.e. the *strain* (= melody and sexual effort) ends with a diminuendo.

5 ***south** Pope's emendation meaning 'south wind' (see *OED* south B 5a), which bears both sound and odour (disproving Furness's prediction that 'Hunter [1870] will prove to be the last editor to adopt Pope's change'). F's 'sound' (as a synonym for *strain*) makes 5 tautological. Cf. Fenner, *Song*, 'com O South, / And on my garden blowe' (sig. C2[r]). On the wind–breath conceit, cf. Sidney, *Arcadia*, 2: 'her breath is more sweete than a gentle Southwest wind, which comes creeping ouer flowrie fieldes and shadowed waters in the extreme heate of sommer.'

6 **violets** a possible 'hidden' and prophetic allusion to Viola, whose name is the original (Latin) form of the flower (see List of Roles, 1n., and cf. 1.3.23–4n.); cf. Lydgate's 'Sweetest viola, that never shall fade' (Lydgate, 300).

7 **Stealing . . . odour** i.e. the wind takes the perfume from the flowers and distributes it. Cf. *Son* 99.1–3, where the 'forward violet' itself, according to the speaking 'I', is the 'Sweet thief' (of his 'love's breath'). A sharp sensory shift from hearing to olfaction.

9–14 ***O . . . minute** F's punctuation renders Orsino's baroque conceit syntactically ambiguous, especially with regard to the subject of *Receiveth* (11): the full stop after *sea* makes the subject the *spirit of love* which, despite (*notwithstanding*) its small size (*capacity*), receives or contains as much as the sea. Adams defends this reading. Rowe emended F's stop after *sea* to a comma, making *thy capacity* the subject of *Receiveth* and therefore equal to that of the *sea*. This simplifies the paradox of Orsino's conceit – that, despite the limitless *capacity* of the *spirit of love*, it rapidly devalues whatever it devours. Orsino thus justifies his own capriciousness.

9 **quick** sharp, lively (*OED* 18c)
fresh hungry (*OED* 11b)

10 **That** in that (Blake, *Grammar*, 5.3.2.1d)
capacity ability to receive or contain (*OED* 1a)

5 south] *Pope;* sound *F;* Wind *Rowe;* south-wind *Keightley* 8 SD] *Collier[3]; after 7 Capell*
9–10 thou / That,] *this edn;* thou, / That *F*

Receiveth as the sea, naught enters there
Of what validity and pitch soe'er
But falls into abatement and low price
Even in a minute. So full of shapes is fancy
That it alone is high fantastical.

CURIO

Will you go hunt, my lord?

ORSINO

What, Curio?

CURIO

The hart.

ORSINO

Why so I do, the noblest that I have.
O, when mine eyes did see Olivia first
Methought she purged the air of pestilence;
That instant was I turned into a hart,

11 **Receiveth . . . sea** can swallow unlimited quantities: proverbial (Dent, S181: 'The sea is never full'). Orsino returns to the idea of the sea-like capaciousness of his love at 2.4.100–1.
there the sea; love's capacity

12 **what . . . soe'er** whatever (split by the interpolation of other words – a form of tmesis); cf. *TNK* 4.3.6.
validity value
pitch height, and thus status: a term from falconry (*OED* $n.^2$ 18a); cf. *R3* 3.7.187, 'Seduc'd the pitch and height of his degree'.

13 **falls . . . price** i.e. depreciates; *abatement* = diminution (*OED* $n.^1$ 2a, giving this example)

14–15 **So . . . fantastical** an allusion to Plato's doctrine of the divine creative frenzy (*Ion*, 533e–534a; Plato, 1.103–17, 107–8) that inspires 'The lunatic, the lover, and the poet', who 'Are of imagination all compact' (*MND* 5.1.7–8). 'The Platonicks', says Puttenham of the poetic variety, 'call it furor' (Puttenham, 1). On the erotic 'furor' or *frenzy*, cf. Olivia at 5.1.277 (see n.); see also 1.5.248n., 2.2.21n., 3.4.14–15n. Cf. *LLL* 2.756–9, 'As love is . . . Full of strange shapes, of habits and of forms'.

14 **shapes** imaginary forms
fancy love (Onions, 2)

15 **alone** exclusively
high fantastical imaginative in the highest degree (*OED* high *adv.* 10b, giving this example)

16–17 The pun on *hart* (stag) and 'heart' is an Elizabethan commonplace. Orsino hunts his own heart, a suggestion of narcissism confirmed at 20–2.

19 **she . . . pestilence** Orsino compares Olivia to one of the air sweeteners used to cleanse the atmosphere, in times of visitation by the plague: 'It is good also', advises Lodge in his *Treatise of the Plague*, 'to weare sweet savors and perfumes about us . . . for such an odour . . . altereth the pestilence of the ayre'(Lodge, sigs $C4^r$–$C4^v$). Cf. 1.3.1n. and 1.5.287n.

20–2 Orsino's allegory alludes to the story of Actaeon, who – having seen Diana naked – was transformed by her into a stag and then hunted to death by his own *hounds* (Ovid, *Met.*, 3.205–304, fols 33^v–34^r; on Diana,

11 sea,] *Rowe*^{3}*;* Sea. *F* naught] *(*Nought*), Kittredge* 16 SP1] *(Cu.), Inchbald*

And my desires, like fell and cruel hounds,
E'er since pursue me.

Enter VALENTINE.

How now, what news from her?

VALENTINE

So please my lord, I might not be admitted,
But from her handmaid do return this answer:
The element itself till seven years' heat
Shall not behold her face at ample view,
But like a cloistress she will veiled walk
And water once a day her chamber round
With eye-offending brine – all this to season
A brother's dead love, which she would keep fresh
And lasting in her sad remembrance.

ORSINO

O, she that hath a heart of that fine frame

see also 1.4.31n.). Ironically, Orsino, refused by Diana–Olivia, ends up hunting, or desiring, himself, suggesting the malady of 'self-love' of which Olivia accuses Malvolio at 1.5.86 (see pp. 29–32). For the conceit of the self-consuming heart, cf. the opening line of the first sonnet in Petrarch's *Canzoniere*, '*quei sospiri ond'io nudriva il core*', 'those sighs on which I fed my heart' (ed.'s translation).

21 **fell** fierce

23 **might not** could not; *might* is here the preterite of 'may', in the sense of 'was [not] permitted' (Blake, *Grammar*, 4.3.7.9a).

25–9 **The . . . brine** Olivia's behaviour is a catalogue of the symptoms of female bereavement; cf. Burton on the melancholy typical of maids, nuns and widows: 'They are apt to loath, dislike, disdain, be weary of every object . . . apt to weep, and tremble' (Burton, 203). Cf. *KL* 4.6.191–3.

25 **element** air – as one of the *four elements* (see 2.3.9n.), i.e. earth, water, air and fire. Cf. also 1.5.267.

till . . . heat for seven summers; *heat* is a metonymy, effect for cause

26 **ample** full

27 **cloistress** cloistered or enclosed nun (*OED*, sole occurrence)

27–9 **walk . . . round** i.e. walk around her room weeping

veiled veilèd

29 **eye-offending brine** salt water (tears) hurting her eyes

season embalm (in *brine*; *OED v.* 3, giving this example)

30 **brother's dead love** love for her dead brother and that brother's love for her, which she has lost (anastrophe or inverted word order)

31 **remembrance** memory (pronounced as four syllables)

32 **of . . . frame** so finely made

22 SD] *Dyce; after 22 F* 23 SP] *(Val.), Cam*[1] 25 years' heat] years hence *Rowe*[3]

To pay this debt of love but to a brother,
How will she love when the rich golden shaft
Hath killed the flock of all affections else
That live in her – when liver, brain and heart,
These sovereign thrones, are all supplied, and filled
Her sweet perfections with one self king!
Away before me to sweet beds of flowers:
Love-thoughts lie rich when canopied with bowers. *Exeunt.*

1.2 *Enter* VIOLA, *a* Captain *and Sailors.*

VIOLA
What country, friends, is this?
CAPTAIN This is Illyria, lady.

34 **golden shaft** In Ovid, *Met.*, 1.565–8, fol. 8^{v}, Cupid's armoury includes a gold-tipped arrow that provokes love.

35 **all affections else** i.e. all other feelings of love (except those for Orsino)

36–7 **liver . . . thrones** According to early modern (essentially Galenic) humour theory, the liver is the seat (*throne*) of passion, the brain that of thought and the heart that of sentiment.

37 **supplied** occupied; cf. *Cor.* 3.3.34–5, 'Keep . . . the chairs of justice / Supplied with worthy men.'

38 **perfections** pronounced as four syllables
one self king one and the same king, namely Orsino (who thereby confirms his high opinion of his own *self*)

1.2 For the theatrical tradition making this the play's opening scene, see p. 97. A brief but intense scene of dramatic exposition, it narrates the storm, establishes the geographical setting and introduces us both to Viola – who conceives her cross-dressing strategy – and (verbally) to her brother, Sebastian. Capell gives as location '*The Sea-coast*', representations of which have varied widely onstage; in Beerbohm Tree's 1901 production, Viola was washed ashore directly on the 'Terrace of Olivia's House' (Tree).

0.1 *Sailors* non-speaking extras, referred to by Viola at 4, their costumes providing a visual clue to the scene's location; often omitted in performance. In some productions (mainly nineteenth century), however, they have been brought on as stage hands to carry a trunk containing Viola's possessions (in Posner's 2001 production a golden trunk was dragged on by the captain himself). This stage tradition may have been prompted by the reference at 5.1.251 to Viola leaving her *maiden weeds* with the captain, but presumably these are the clothes she comes to shore in before she is provided with *man's attire* (see 1.4.0.1–2n.).

37 These] Three *Warburton* 38 perfections] perfection *Capell* self] self same *F2* **1.2**] *(Scena Secunda.)* 0.1 *Sailors*] *Sailors, carrying a Trunk. / Kemble* 1 SP1] *(Vio.), Inchbald*

VIOLA

And what should I do in Illyria?
My brother he is in Elysium.
Perchance he is not drowned. What think you, sailors?

CAPTAIN

It is perchance that you yourself were saved.

VIOLA

O my poor brother! And so perchance may he be.

CAPTAIN

True, madam, and to comfort you with chance,
Assure yourself, after our ship did split,
When you and those poor number saved with you
Hung on our driving boat, I saw your brother,
Most provident in peril, bind himself –
Courage and hope both teaching him the practice –
To a strong mast that lived upon the sea,
Where, like Arion on the dolphin's back,

3 **Elysium** in Greek mythology, the state or abode of the blessed after death: hence, in this context, heaven. Viola plays on the assonance with *Illyria* (rhetorical figure: paronomasia).

4, 5, 6 **Perchance** Viola first uses the adverb in the sense of 'perhaps', willing her brother alive against the odds. The captain's benevolent quibble plays on the etymological meaning of the word, i.e. by chance or fortune, which Viola then optimistically echoes.

7 **chance** The captain continues to play on the multiple meanings of the word: here, possibility (that her brother has survived).

8 **split** break up, because of a storm (*OED v.* 9); cf. *Tem* 1.1.62, 'We split, we split, we split!'

9 **those poor number** The use of a plural demonstrative adjective (*those*) with a singular noun of multitude (*number*) is relatively rare (*OED* II 2c, giving this example).

10 **driving** driven by the wind (*OED ppla.* 2, first occurrence)
boat small open boat (presumably of the kind often pulled by large ships to use as tenders); cf. *CE* 1.1.76–7, 'The sailors sought for safety of our boat, / And left the ship, then sinking-ripe, to us.'

11 **provident** prudent, resourceful; literally, making provision for the future (*OED* 1)

12 **practice** method

13 **lived** remained afloat (a nautical term); cf. Ralegh, 'we . . . brought the Galley as neere as we could, but she had as much adoe to liue as could be' (Ralegh, 89).

14 ***Arion** stressed on second syllable
Arion . . . back semi-legendary Greek poet and musician who, in order to escape being robbed and murdered by sailors, sang, accompanied by his lyre, to charm a dolphin that carried him safely ashore to the island of Corinth (Ovid, *Fasti*, 2.79–118): illustration of

14 Arion] *Pope; Orion F*

I saw him hold acquaintance with the waves
So long as I could see.

VIOLA For saying so, there's gold.
Mine own escape unfoldeth to my hope –
Whereto thy speech serves for authority –
The like of him. Knowst thou this country?

CAPTAIN
Ay, madam, well, for I was bred and born
Not three hours' travel from this very place.

VIOLA
Who governs here?

CAPTAIN A noble duke
In nature as in name.

VIOLA What is his name?

CAPTAIN
Orsino.

VIOLA
Orsino: I have heard my father name him.

the importance and redemptive powers of music in the comedy. Ashore, Arion was helped by his friend Periander, as Sebastian will be by Antonio (2.1). A spectacular water pageant before Elizabeth I at Kenilworth Castle, near Stratford, was reported in 1575, in which '*Arion* that excellent & famous musicien' appeared 'ryding aloft upon his olld friend the Dolphin, (that from hed to tayl was a four & twenty foot long)'; Arion sang 'a delectable ditty of a song' (Laneham, 42–3).

15 **hold acquaintance with** ride, surf

17–19 **Mine . . . him** My own escape leads me to hope – encouraged by your testimony – that he too has escaped.

17 **unfoldeth** makes plain (*OED v.*[1], giving this example)

18 **authority** testimony

19 slightly irregular, possibly explained by a medial pause before *Knowst*, reflecting Viola's change of subject, or by trisyllabic pronunciation of *country* ('countery'), known as anaptyxis (Kökeritz, 292; cf. F's 'Countrey')

22–3 **noble . . . in name** 'Orsino' is noble both because the Orsini were a noble Italian family and because in Italian the word means 'little bear', considered a noble beast (and represented as such in the Orsini family stem). See List of Roles, 5n. Viola's comment at 25 confirms that the name was well known.

25 **my father** a recurrent point of thematic contact between Viola and her brother; the latter, named after him, speaks of 'My father . . . Sebastian of Messaline' at 2.1.16. Viola mentions both father and brother at 2.4.107, 120–1 and, finally, at 5.1.228–41, where knowledge of the year of their father's death is decisive confirmation of the twins' respective identities.

19 country] *(*Countrey*), Rowe* 20 Ay] *(*I*)* 21 travel] *(*trauaile*)* 22–3 A . . . name.] *this edn; one line F*

He was a bachelor then.

CAPTAIN

And so is now, or was so very late,
For but a month ago I went from hence,
And then 'twas fresh in murmur – as you know
What great ones do the less will prattle of –
That he did seek the love of fair Olivia.

VIOLA

What's she?

CAPTAIN

A virtuous maid, the daughter of a count
That died some twelvemonth since, then leaving her
In the protection of his son, her brother,
Who shortly also died, for whose dear love,
They say, she hath abjured the company
And sight of men.

26–7 **a bachelor . . . late** Spedding (cited in Furness) notes that 'if [Orsino] were still a bachelor there would be no female court; therefore no fit place for [Viola]': hence the necessity for her disguise.

27 **late** lately (*OED adv.* 4a)

29 **'twas . . . murmur** there was a new rumour (see *OED* murmur *n.* 3, giving this example)

32 **What's she?** Of what condition and rank is she? (Blake, *Grammar*, 3.2.2.4); 'what' could also mean 'who', permitting comic misunderstanding between the two. Cf. 1.2.50; 1.3.48–9 and n.; 1.5.112–24 and n., 206, 209 and n.; 3.4.228, 310.

33–6 **A . . . died** continues the emphasis on male mortality

34 **some twelvemonth since** about a year ago; for *since* as adverb ('ago'), cf. Blake, *Grammar*, 5.1.3.3 (giving this example).

36 **dear** great (an intensifier); cf. 1.4.25.

37–8 ***company / And sight** Hanmer's inversion of the two nouns in F saves the metre and gives the sentence a stronger climactic structure.

38–41 ***I . . . is** i.e. I might serve that lady and my true identity might not be presented in public (*OED* deliver *v.*[1] 8c, giving this example) until the time is ripe. The syntax is somewhat complex: 'What my estate is' is a redundant object, which qualifies the main object *I* (38), in a passive construction (see Blake, *Grammar*, 3.3.2.1h). Cf. 50 and 1.5.242. Main verb *delivered* (39) and the object *What . . . is* (41); are separated and qualified by the adverbial clause *Till . . . mellow* (40), as indicated by the emended punctuation, which makes *mellow* an adjective, whereas in F it seems to be a transitive verb. Cf. Olivia's equivalent desire 'To keep in darkness what occasion now / Reveals before 'tis ripe' (5.1.149–50).

37 hath] had *F3* 37–8 company / And sight] *Hanmer;* sight / And company *F*

VIOLA O that I served that lady,
And might not be delivered to the world –
Till I had made mine own occasion mellow –
What my estate is.
CAPTAIN That were hard to compass,
Because she will admit no kind of suit,
No, not the duke's.
VIOLA
There is a fair behaviour in thee, captain,
And though that nature with a beauteous wall
Doth oft close in pollution, yet of thee
I will believe thou hast a mind that suits
With this thy fair and outward character.
I pray thee – and I'll pay thee bounteously –
Conceal me what I am, and be my aid
For such disguise as haply shall become
The form of my intent. I'll serve this duke.
Thou shalt present me as an eunuch to him.

40 Cf. *LLL* 4.2.72, 'upon the mellowing of occasion'.
41 **estate** true identity and social status
compass achieve (*OED v.*[1] 11, giving this example)
42 **admit** allow (*OED v.* 2a, giving this example)
suit supplication, courtship
43 **not** not even
46 **close in** enclose (*OED* 17a)
pollution (moral) uncleanness or contamination, alluding to the biblical parable of the whited sepulchres 'which indeed appear beautiful outward, but within full of . . . all filth-iness' (Matthew, 23.27). Cf. 1.3.120n.
47–8 proverbial (Dent, F1)
48 **character** 'The face or features as betokening moral qualities; personal appearance' (*OED n.* 10, giving this example)
49 ***pray thee** F's 'prethee' may be a compositorial substitution: 'Compositor B regularly imposed his preferred form "prethee", a sophistication that would obscure the symmetry of "pray thee" / "pay thee"' (*TxC*, 421).
50 Cf. 1.2.38–41n.
51–2 **haply . . . intent** will perhaps be apt to represent my purpose
51 **become** be fitting to
52 **I'll . . . duke** Johnson observes that 'Viola is an excellent schemer, never at a loss; if she cannot serve the lady, she will serve the duke.' Cf. 26–7n.
53 **eunuch** On the implications of Viola's 'eunuch' disguise, see pp. 57–61.

40 mellow –] *Mahood*; mellow *F* 49 pray thee] *Oxf*; prethee *F*; prithee *Ard*[2] 53 eunuch] page *Inchbald*; boy *Nunn*

It may be worth thy pains, for I can sing
And speak to him in many sorts of music,
That will allow me very worth his service.
What else may hap to time I will commit;
Only shape thou thy silence to my wit.

CAPTAIN
Be you his eunuch, and your mute I'll be.
When my tongue blabs then let mine eyes not see.

VIOLA
I thank thee. Lead me on. *Exeunt.*

1.3 *Enter* SIR TOBY [Belch] *and* MARIA.

SIR TOBY What a plague means my niece to take the death

54 **I can sing** one of the play's loose ends, since Viola gives us no demonstration of her musical talents. All singing is delegated to Feste or his drunken companions. Shakespeare may have changed his mind, because the voice of the boy actor playing Viola had broken, or because the clown Robert Armin, a famously gifted singer, was available to play Feste.

55 **speak . . . music** Viola's choice of verb has two possible, and complementary, implications: that she will use music as a mode of persuasive discourse, or that she will use speech as a charmingly musical means of expression (the second comes closer to describing later events); *many sorts* may indicate either different types of song (or speech), or instrumental as well as vocal performance.

56 **allow me** show me to be
worth worthy of

57 I will entrust my fortunes to the workings of time; cf. 2.2.40–1, where Viola appeals directly to *time* to *untangle* the *knot* that her disguise has created.
hap chance to happen
commit entrust (*OED* 1)

58 **wit** ingenuity

59 **mute** dumb guard. The captain develops Viola's idea at 53, since eunuchs traditionally had mutes as subordinates in eastern courts.

60 **let . . . see** In Turkish harems the guards were supposed to watch over but not look (and still less tell), on pain of being blinded.

1.3 This scene represents virtually a third 'opening' to the play, introducing not only a new environment (Olivia's household) but also a distinct mood, that of the frenetic revelry presided over by Sir Toby.

1–2 Sir Toby's life-affirming attitude shifts the emphasis away from the preoccupation with death in the preceding scenes – the possible drowning of Viola's brother and Olivia's loss of her brother and father.

1 **What a plague** an idiomatic imprecation, frequent in Shakespeare (cf. 1.5.116, 3.4.276), but in this context of multiple (male) deaths it may take on a particular force. Sir Toby makes the play's most resolute stand against death and in favour of the pleasure principle.

1, 4 **niece, cousin** On these kin words, see List of Roles, 11n.

59 eunuch] page *Inchbald* 1.3] *(Scaena Tertia.)* 0.1 Belch] *Malone* 1 SP] *(Sir To.), Cam*[1]

of her brother thus? I am sure care's an enemy to life.

MARIA By my troth, Sir Toby, you must come in earlier o'nights. Your cousin, my lady, takes great exceptions to your ill hours.

SIR TOBY Why, let her except, before excepted.

MARIA Ay, but you must confine yourself within the modest limits of order.

SIR TOBY Confine? I'll confine myself no finer than I am. These clothes are good enough to drink in, and so be these boots too; an they be not, let them hang themselves in their own straps.

MARIA That quaffing and drinking will undo you. I heard my lady talk of it yesterday, and of a foolish knight that you brought in one night here to be her wooer.

SIR TOBY Who, Sir Andrew Aguecheek?

MARIA Ay, he.

SIR TOBY He's as tall a man as any's in Illyria.

MARIA What's that to th' purpose?

SIR TOBY Why, he has three thousand ducats a year.

2 **care's . . . life** proverbial (Dent, C84). Sir Toby's concern for Olivia's state of mind is 'not altogether unselfish' (Furness): he is afraid that it will restrict his own revels.

3 **By my troth** by my faith: a mild oath or discourse marker

4 **o'nights** of nights: at night

6 **let . . . excepted** let her object before being objected to (by me). Sir Toby is quibbling on the legal expression *exceptis excipiendis* (excepting those things that are to be excepted), as if defending himself in court (*OED* except *v.* 2, giving this example).

8 **modest . . . order** bounds of moderate behaviour

9 **confine** dress up; slim down. Sir Toby puns on Maria's sense of 'restrict your behaviour' in 7.

11, 59, 61, 86 **an** if

11–12 **hang . . . straps** a variation on the proverbial expression 'He may go hang himself in his own garters' (Dent, G42)

13 **quaffing** drinking deep

14 **foolish** an epithet frequently applied to Sir Andrew (as he says at 2.5.79, 'many do call me fool'): cf. also 22, 28 and 62–4 and 2.3.82n.

18 **tall** valiant (Onions, 3)

19 Maria responds to *tall* (18) as if its only meaning were 'of great height'.

20 **three thousand ducats** A ducat was a gold coin (originally a silver Italian coin) worth approximately nine shillings (*OED* 1a). Sir Toby thus estimates Sir Andrew's fortune at 27,000 shillings or £1,350 per annum, but this sum is something of a Shakespearean convention (cf. *MV* 1.3.1 and see Elze, 157).

3 SP] *(Mar.), Inchbald*__4 o'nights] (a nights*), Capell*__18 any's] any *Douai MS, Pope*__20, 82 has] (ha's*), F3*

MARIA Ay, but he'll have but a year in all these ducats. He's a very fool and a prodigal.

SIR TOBY Fie that you'll say so! He plays o'th' viol-de-gamboys, and speaks three or four languages word for word without book and hath all the good gifts of nature.

MARIA He hath indeed, almost natural, for, besides that he's a fool, he's a great quarreller, and, but that he hath the gift of a coward to allay the gust he hath in quarrelling, 'tis thought among the prudent he would quickly have the gift of a grave.

SIR TOBY By this hand they are scoundrels and substractors that say so of him. Who are they?

21 **he'll . . . ducats** i.e. he'll lose all his money within a year (precisely Sir Toby's intent: cf. 2.3.177–8n.); *in* = 'to enjoy'

22 **very** true

prodigal spendthrift (either noun, a *prodigal*; or adjective, a *prodigal* fool). For Sir Toby this is Sir Andrew's chief merit.

23 **Fie** Shame on you

23–4 **viol-de-gamboys** a playful corruption of 'viola da gamba' (Italian: 'leg viol'), a bowed, stringed musical instrument, possibly one of those played in the 'music room' during the performance of *TN*, as in Carroll's 2002 Middle Temple production. Florio's gloss – 'because men hold it betweene or upon their legges' (Florio, *New World*, 602) – perhaps hints at a sexual allusion likewise present in Sir Toby's deformation gam*boys*; cf. 99–100n. There is also another possible 'secret' reference to Viola, anticipating the duel in 3.4 (cf. 1.1.6n.).

24 **speaks . . . languages** an ironic claim belied by Andrew's ignorance of French at 89 and by his own confession (89–92) that he has not studied the *tongues*

25 **without book** by heart (*OED* book *n.*15, giving this example); proverbial idiom (Dent, B532). Officially it is a compliment, but it implies that Sir Andrew has never actually opened a book, or that he has learned foreign expressions parrot-fashion.

27 **almost natural** quibble: nearly natural; all most natural, i.e. half-witted (Onions, 4)

28 **fool** a *natural* one, as opposed to an *allowed* professional one such as Feste (see 1.5.90n.)

quarreller wrangler; duellist (looking forward to Sir Andrew's challenge to Viola in 3.4). Maria's epithet, together with *coward* (29), portrays Aguecheek as a kind of *miles gloriosus*, the cowardly braggart of classical comedy.

but that were it not for the fact that

29, 31 **gift** The repetition (rhetorical figure: ploce) plays on two meanings: talent and present.

29 **gust . . . in** taste or relish for

32 **substractors** a (drunken?) deformation of 'detractors' (*OED*, sole occurrence)

27 indeed, almost] indeed all, most *Furness*

MARIA They that add, moreover, he's drunk nightly in your company.

SIR TOBY With drinking healths to my niece. I'll drink to her as long as there is a passage in my throat and drink in Illyria. He's a coward and a coistrel that will not drink to my niece till his brains turn o'th' toe, like a parish top.

Enter SIR ANDREW [Aguecheek].

What, wench, *Castiliano vulgo*, for here comes Sir Andrew Agueface.

SIR ANDREW Sir Toby Belch! How now, Sir Toby Belch?

SIR TOBY Sweet Sir Andrew.

SIR ANDREW [*to Maria*] Bless you, fair shrew.

38 **coistrel** knave, base fellow. Shakespeare may have picked up the insult from Riche's *Farewell*, 'to haue her Chastitie assailed, by suche a simple coisterell' (sig. D2[r]).

39 **brains . . . toe** head spins; 'turn o'th' toe' (*o'th'* = on the) seems to have been used with reference to whipping, as in Nashe, *Traveller*: 'he for his trecherie was turnd on the toe' (sig. C4[r]).

39–40 **like . . . top** proverbial (Dent, P57); in Shakespeare's day a large village whipping-top was frequently kept for use in cold weather as a warming-up exercise (see Fig. 13).

41 ***Castiliano vulgo** The F text may be corrupt here: the meaning of Sir Toby's phrase is obscure, and there is even disagreement as to which language he is using. Accepting F's wording, Mahood takes *Castiliano* as a synonym for 'devil', since Castiliano is the name assumed by a devil in *Grim, the Collier of Croydon* (written *c.* 1600 or earlier, though only printed in 1662); she takes *vulgo* (Latin for 'in the common tongue') as having the force of a Latin or Italian verb meaning roughly 'I talk of'. Sir Toby thus varies the proverbial phrase 'talk of the devil', appropriately enough, as Sir Andrew is entering as he speaks. However, 'castilian' was a variant form of 'castellan', one living in or belonging to a castle (*OED n.*[1]). It is perhaps more likely, therefore, that *Castiliano* is equivalent to the proverbial expression 'lad of the castle', a merry term for a reveller or carouser (Dent, C124.1; cf. *1H4* 1.2.46). Sir Toby is thus characterizing Sir Andrew as a fellow drinking companion using a current colloquial term: 'What, wench, a lad of the castle, as they say.' Cf. Marlowe, *Jew*, sig. H4[r], 'Hey *Riuo Castiliano*, a man's a man.'

45 **shrew** Presumably Sir Andrew intends this as a compliment, meaning 'shrew-mouse', a term of endearment (cf. *mouse* 1.5.59); the colloquial sense of the word, however, was a bad-tempered woman or scold (as in the title of *TS*).

40.1] *this edn; after 42 F* Aguecheek] *Malone* 41 *Castiliano vulgo*] *Castiliano volto / Hanmer; Castiglione voglio (Thomas)* 43 SP] *(And.), Cam[1]* 45 SD] *Oxf*

MARIA And you too, sir.

SIR TOBY Accost, Sir Andrew, accost.

SIR ANDREW What's that?

SIR TOBY My niece's chambermaid.

SIR ANDREW Good Mistress Accost, I desire better acquaintance.

MARIA My name is Mary, sir.

SIR ANDREW Good Mistress Mary Accost.

SIR TOBY You mistake, knight. 'Accost' is front her, board her, woo her, assail her.

SIR ANDREW By my troth I would not undertake her in this company. Is that the meaning of 'accost'?

MARIA Fare you well, gentlemen.

SIR TOBY An thou let part so, Sir Andrew, would thou mightst never draw sword again.

SIR ANDREW An you part so, mistress, I would I might never draw sword again. Fair lady, do you think you have fools in hand?

47 **accost** engage with, assail (*OED v.*6), as Sir Toby defines it at 54–5; originally a naval term meaning 'go alongside' (*OED v.* 3; cf. *board*, 54). As Mahood notes, great play is made with the verb 'accostare' in *Intronati*.

49 Sir Toby pretends to understand 48 as 'Who's that [woman]?' or 'Accost whom?' Cf. 1.2.32n.
chambermaid not in the sense of a woman who cleans bedrooms, but in the socially more elevated (and now obsolete) sense of lady's maid (*OED* 2).

52 **Mary** See List of Roles, 10n.

54–6 **Accost . . . undertake** Sir Toby's definitions of *accost* can be interpreted discursively as 'amorously address' or physically as 'have sex with'. Sir Andrew responds to the second sense.

56 **undertake** take in hand (*OED v.* 5c), in two senses: deal with and have sexual relations with; the second meaning is taken up in the puns on *hand*, 64–77.

56–7 **in this company** in the presence of Sir Toby himself (and the audience: the actor may indicate the spectators, as in Carroll's 2002 Middle Temple production)

59 **An . . . so** i.e. if you let her go without having accosted her

60, 62 **never draw sword** i.e. cease to be a sword-carrying gentleman. Sir Andrew's parroting of the phrase (cf. 25n.) leads him unwittingly to suggest a desire to be impotent (or emasculated). The drawing of swords as a sign of masculinity reappears in 3.4, where both Sir Andrew and Viola are reluctant to unsheathe their weapons. Sebastian has no such problems in 4.1.

62–3 **do . . . hand** 'do you think I am a fool' (*have in hand* = deal with)

50 SP] *F2 (An.); Ma. F* Accost] *Rowe;* accost *F* 53 Mary Accost] *Rowe*[3]*; Mary,* accost *F*
59 let part] let her part *F3*

MARIA Sir, I have not you by th' hand.

SIR ANDREW Marry, but you shall have, and here's my hand.

MARIA [*Takes his hand.*] Now, sir, thought is free. I pray you, bring your hand to th' buttery-bar, and let it drink. [*Brings his hand to her breast.*]

SIR ANDREW Wherefore, sweetheart? What's your metaphor?

MARIA It's dry, sir.

SIR ANDREW Why, I think so. I am not such an ass but I

64 Maria pretends to take *in hand* literally, and by doing so implies that Sir Andrew is indeed a fool (perhaps also insinuating his impotence).

67 **thought is free** 'if you say so'; a proverbial expression (Dent, T244), in answer to the question 'Do you think I am a fool?' (see 62–3), and prompted by Sir Andrew's unwitting admission and demonstration of his folly in giving Maria his hand. Cf. Lyly, *England* (fol. 30[r]), 'why then quoth be, doest thou thinke me a foole, thought is free my Lorde quoth she, I will not take you at your word.'

68 **bring . . . bar** A *buttery* is a room where liquor and provisions are stored: cf. *TS* Induction 1.101–2, 'take them to the buttery, / And give them friendly welcome every one.' The room has a hatch, the ledge of which is the *buttery-bar*, over which drinks and food are served (*OED*, giving this example; see Fig. 11). Maria is still toying with sexual innuendo, presumably inviting Sir Andrew to touch her breasts (where milk or butter is stored), and in some productions the actress helps him do so.

69–73 **What's . . . dry** Sir Andrew takes Maria's metaphorical *dry* (see 71n.) as a literal reference to his *hand*, thus revealing his ignorance of what a *metaphor* really is. Cf. *AW* 5.2.10–13, where the word 'metaphor' itself is literalized: '*Parolles* You need not stop your nose, sir, I spoke but by a metaphor. *Clown* Indeed, sir . . . if your metaphor stink I will stop my nose.'

71 Maria characterizes her *metaphor* of the *buttery-bar* (68) as *dry*, that is witty or ironic (see 74n.), but she also metaphorically rejects Sir Andrew's inept advances by saying that the *bar* is *dry* ('there's no drink there for you'). Paul Chahidi, who played Maria in Carroll's 2002 Middle Temple production, pointed out privately that this may be an ironical allusion to the male actor, whose breast would indeed be *dry* (i.e. without milk).

72–3 **I am . . . dry** An allusion to the proverb 'Fools have wit enough to keep themselves out of the rain' (Dent, F537), with an unintentional quibble on masturbation. Johnson proclaims his bafflement: 'What is the jest of *dry hand*, I know not any better than Sir Andrew.' The 'jest' probably includes a further reference to Sir Andrew's lack of virility: *dry* was a synonym for 'castrated', as in Isaiah, 56.3, 'neither let the eunuch say, Behold I am a dry tree' (see Rubinstein, 83); *dry* hand was correspondingly a sign of impotence, a moist hand proverbially signifying the

67 SD] *Kemble* 68 SD] *this edn*

can keep my hand dry. But what's your jest?

MARIA A dry jest, sir.

SIR ANDREW Are you full of them?

MARIA Ay, sir, I have them at my fingers' ends. [*Lets go of his hand.*] Marry, now I let go your hand I am barren. *Exit.*

SIR TOBY O knight, thou lack'st a cup of canary. When did I see thee so put down?

SIR ANDREW Never in your life, I think, unless you see canary put me down. Methinks sometimes I have no more wit than a Christian or an ordinary man has; but I am a great eater of beef, and I believe that does harm to my wit.

SIR TOBY No question.

SIR ANDREW An I thought that, I'd forswear it. I'll ride home tomorrow, Sir Toby.

SIR TOBY *Pourquoi*, my dear knight?

SIR ANDREW What is 'pourquoi'? Do, or not do? I would

opposite (see Tilley, H86, 'A moist hand argues an amorous'; and cf. *Oth* 3.4.36–8, 'This hand is moist, my lady . . . This argues fruitfulness').

74 **dry jest** arid joke; Maria may also be referring to her own ironical or sarcastic mode of speech: Puttenham (157) rebaptizes irony as 'the drye mock'.

76 **at . . . ends** always ready (proverbial: Dent, F245)

77 **now . . . barren** i.e. I am empty of jests now I have let go of the butt of them; *barren* also because of Sir Andrew's ineffective *hand* (a further insinuation of impotence). The actress often lets go of the hand in question at this point, immediately prior to her exit. As at 71, there may be an allusion to the male actor, who by definition cannot bear children.

78, 81 **canary** a light sweet wine from the Canary Islands (*OED n.* 2, giving this example)

79 **put down** i.e. defeated in repartee; cf. 1.5.80.

81 **put me down** knock me out (as when drunk)

82 **a Christian** an average human being, as distinct from a beast (*OED* 5a); cf. *TGV*, 3.1.267–8, 'She hath more qualities then a water-spaniel, which is much in a bare Christian.'

83–4 **eater . . . wit** According to popular 'medical' lore, beef was supposed to dull the brain; cf. Boorde, *Dyetary*, sig. H3[r], warning that 'olde beef . . . doth ingender melancolye and leprouse humoures'; also *H5* 3.7.150–1, 'And then give [the foolish English] great meals of beef'.

86 **An** if

89 **'pourquoi' . . . do?** suggests a sexual allusion (*OED* doing 1b = copulation) and confirms Sir Andrew's ignorance of foreign languages (hence the adoption here of roman for the French,

76 Ay] *(I)* 76–7 SD] *Kemble subst.; after 77 Cam[1]* 77 SD] *(Exit Maria)* 88 *Pourquoi*] *(Pur-quoy), Collier* 89 'pourquoi'] *(purquoy), Cam*

I had bestowed that time in the tongues that I have in fencing, dancing and bear-baiting. O, had I but followed the arts.

SIR TOBY Then hadst thou had an excellent head of hair.

SIR ANDREW Why, would that have mended my hair?

SIR TOBY Past question, for thou seest it will not curl by nature.

SIR ANDREW But it becomes me well enough, does't not?

SIR TOBY Excellent, it hangs like flax on a distaff, and I hope to see a housewife take thee between her legs and spin it off.

rather than F's italic; cf. 24n.). He suspects *pourquoi* is a verb equivalent to *accost* (47). Perhaps he hears, or repeats, something like 'poke her'.

90 **tongues** languages

91 **fencing** a fashionable pastime among the gentry (to which Sir Andrew aspires) as well as a professional skill of actors; Sir Andrew's claim to have studied it is belied by his evident inability to duel in 3.4, 4.1 and 5.1.
dancing Sir Andrew's claim to be an expert dancer is also highly dubious: his demonstration of his dancing skills usually suggests otherwise in performance (see 136n.).

93–100 These references to Sir Andrew's hair have given rise to a lasting stage tradition that represents him with long and straight yellow locks (see Fig. 26).

93 Sir Toby pretends to understand *tongues* (90) as 'tongs' (for curling hair), pronounced the same way (Kökeritz, 45).

94 **mended** amended, improved

95–6 ***curl by nature** Playing on Sir Andrew's *tongues* (= tongs; 90), and *arts* (92), Sir Toby maliciously suggests that Sir Andrew's appearance could be improved by the 'art' of a hairdresser.

98 **hangs like flax** Long thin strands of flax fibre were used to produce linen, and were characteristically of a soft yellow colour; 'flaxen hair' was idiomatic (*OED* flaxen *a.* 2b). Sir Toby's description of Sir Andrew echoes Chaucer's portrait of the effeminate Pardoner in the General Prologue to the *Canterbury Tales*, 675–6: 'This Pardoner hadde heer as yellow as wex, / But smothe it heeng as dooth a strike of flex' (Chaucer, *Works*, 23): another hint at impotence perhaps (*hangs* implies detumescence). In Dekker's *Blurt*, flaxen-haired men are said to be, like Sir Andrew, 'Chicken-heartes (and yet great quarrellers)' (Dekker, *Blurt*, sig. C4[r]).
distaff forked rod on which fibre was wound for spinning (a symbol of female labour, and thus of femininity). In Sir Andrew's case, it is an ambiguous image, representing both the phallus (with pun on 'staff') and effeminacy.

99 **housewife** pronounced 'hussif' ('huswife' in F); meaning either a woman who keeps house or a hussy or prostitute (Onions)

99–100 **take . . . off** puns on *take thee* (as a *distaff*; sexually) and *spin it off* (spin your hair off the *distaff*; bring to a sexual climax). Underlying the bawdy joke is the comic implication that Sir Toby hopes to see Sir Andrew bald.

99 **between her legs** recalls Sir Toby's earlier equivocal reference to the viola da gamba (see 23–4n.).

93 Then] *fondles him.* Then *Cam[1]* hair.] hair. *curls Andrew's hair with his whip / Tree* 95 curl by] *Theobald;* coole my *F* 97 me] *F2;* we *F* does't] *(*dost*), Rowe* 99 housewife] *(*huswife*)*

SIR ANDREW Faith, I'll home tomorrow, Sir Toby. Your niece will not be seen or, if she be, it's four to one she'll none of me. The count himself here hard by woos her.

SIR TOBY She'll none o'th' count. She'll not match above her degree, neither in estate, years nor wit – I have heard her swear't. Tut, there's life in't, man.

SIR ANDREW I'll stay a month longer. I am a fellow o'th' strangest mind i'th' world. I delight in masques and revels sometimes altogether.

SIR TOBY Art thou good at these kickshawses, knight?

SIR ANDREW As any man in Illyria whatsoever he be, under the degree of my betters; and yet I will not compare with an old man.

SIR TOBY What is thy excellence in a galliard, knight?

102–3 **she'll . . . me** she'll have nothing to do with me

103 **hard by** close

105–6 **She'll . . . degree** confirms the indeterminacy of Orsino's rank (see List of Roles, 5n.): if he is a *count* he is not above the *Countess Olivia* (2.2.1, 5.1.93) in *degree*.

107 **Tut** expression of impatience
there's life in't there's still hope (proverbial: Dent, L265; cf. L269, 'While there's life there's hope'

109–10 **masques and revels** The masque, in which dancing played a prominent role, arrived in England from continental Europe during the sixteenth century, and became a court entertainment for Elizabeth I under the control of the Master of the Revels. Perhaps Sir Andrew fancies himself at court.

110 **altogether** all together: at one and the same time (*OED* 2)

111 **kickshawses** dainty trifles (from French *quelque chose* (*OED* 2, giving this example)); originally a fancy dish, as in *2H4* 5.1.27–8, 'A joint of mutton, and any pretty little tiny kickshaws' (cf. 117n.). In this context of dance discourse, there is probably a pun on 'kicks', and Williams, 1128, suggests a sexual innuendo, as in Fletcher's *The Elder Brother*, where Brisac tells the maid Lilly, 'And th'hast another Kickshaw, I must taste it' (Fletcher, 4.4.53–4, sig. H2^{v}).

112–13 **As . . . betters** i.e. as good as anyone except my social superiors: a characteristically redundant claim

113–14 **I . . . compare** I am not to be compared

114 **an old man** failed attempt at a compliment: Sir Andrew presumably intends 'old hand' or expert (*OED* old *a.* 5), with reference to Sir Toby, but ends up committing a *faux pas* regarding the latter's age. On the age of Sir Toby, see List of Roles, 11n.

115 **thy excellence** aspect in which you excel (*OED* 2, giving this example)
galliard a quick and lively court dance in triple time consisting of five steps, with a *caper* or leap before the fifth (*OED n.*[1] B 2, giving this example);

111 kickshawses] *(*kicke-chawses*), Cam;* kick-shaws *F4*

SIR ANDREW Faith, I can cut a caper.

SIR TOBY And I can cut the mutton to't.

SIR ANDREW And I think I have the back-trick simply as strong as any man in Illyria. [*Dances.*]

SIR TOBY Wherefore are these things hid? Wherefore have these gifts a curtain before 'em? Are they like to take dust, like Mistress Mall's picture? Why dost thou not go to church in a galliard and come home in a coranto? My very walk should be a jig. I would not so much as make water but in a sink-apace. What dost

otherwise known as 'cinquepace' (see 125n.), although Riche (sig. $\mathrm{A3^r}$) considers this a less sophisticated form of *galliard*: 'Our Galliardes . . . are so full of trickes and turnes, that he whiche hath no more but the plaine Sinquepace, is no better accoumpted of then a very bungler'. Elizabeth I is said to have practised galliards as her morning exercise.

116 **cut a caper** dance or leap in a fantastic (literally, goat-like) way (see Fig. 17). In some productions, the actor comically demonstrates the jump here, as at 136 SD.

117 **mutton** a quibble on Sir Andrew's *caper*, in the sense of the pickled bud used to make a sauce for mutton; *mutton* was also slang for 'prostitute' (*OED* 4). Cf. 'The old lecher hath gotton holy mutton to him a Nunne my Lord' (Greene, *Friar*, $\mathrm{H3^r}$).

118 **back-trick** presumably a backward *caper* in a *galliard* (*OED*, giving this example); perhaps an unconscious reference to sexual intercourse, from behind

120 **Wherefore . . . hid?** ironical allusion to the biblical parable of the talents kept hidden beneath a bushel (Matthew, 25.14–30; cf. 1.2.46n. on *pollution* and 1.5.14n.). Cf. Primaudaye, 'hide not this talent, but teach it others, and giue thy selfe an example unto them of well doing, and of profiting euery one' (Primaudaye, 374).

121 **curtain** used to protect a picture from dust and from fading; cf. 1.5.226.

122 **Mistress Mall** This looks like a topical allusion; if so, the most likely candidate is Mary Fitton (*Mall* is a diminutive of 'Mary'), one of Elizabeth I's maids of honour, who fell into disgrace when she bore a child to the Earl of Pembroke in 1601 (Hotson, 103–6). Alternatively, Sir Toby may simply be referring to Maria.

124 **coranto** courtly 'running' dance in 2/4 time (Italian, from French '*courante*'), characterized by a running or gliding step, as distinguished from leaping; cf. *HV* 3.5.32–3, 'They bid us to the English dancing-schools / And teach lavoltas high and swift corantos.' **jig** an improvised northern folk dance performed with rapid footwork and a rigid torso; in Shakespeare's day it became fashionable at the court of Elizabeth I and as a stage dance.

125 **sink-apace** cinquepace (French, literally 'five steps'): another term for the *galliard* (see 115n.). Sir Toby's *make water* suggests a pun on 'sink', i.e. cesspool or sewer (*OED* sink $n.^1$ 1a–b). The pun is varied in *MA* 2.1.69–70, 'and with his bad legs falls into the cinque-pace faster and faster, till he sink into his grave'.

119 SD] *Collier^3 subst.* 124 coranto] *(*Carranto*), Rowe* 125 sink-apace] *(*Sinke-a-pace*), Mahood;* cinque-pace *Hanmer*

thou mean? Is it a world to hide virtues in? I did think by the excellent constitution of thy leg it was formed under the star of a galliard.

SIR ANDREW Ay, 'tis strong, and it does indifferent well in a flame-coloured stock. Shall we set about some revels?

SIR TOBY What shall we do else? Were we not born under Taurus?

SIR ANDREW Taurus? That's sides and heart.

SIR TOBY No, sir, it is legs and thighs – let me see thee caper. [*Sir Andrew capers.*] Ha, higher! Ha, ha, excellent. *Exeunt.*

1.4 *Enter* VALENTINE, *and* VIOLA *in man's attire* [*as Cesario*].

127 **constitution** composition, formation (*OED* 4a, giving this example)

127–8 **formed . . . galliard** made to dance (ironical)

129 **indifferent well** well enough

130 **in . . . stock** On this line in Posner's 2001 RSC production, Sir Andrew raised his trouser legs to show off his (dun-coloured) stockings, anticipating Malvolio in 3.4.

***flame-coloured** F's 'dam'd' (damned) is dubious – since nowhere else in the play does Sir Andrew swear so strongly – and is an odd qualifier for 'coloured stock': a colour word seems more likely. Rowe[3]'s emendation is rejected by Collier[2] in favour of 'dun', and Wilson (114) concurs ('dam'd' being a likelier compositorial misreading of 'dunne' or donne'), but 'dun-coloured' is weak (i.e. colourless): unless this is the point of the joke. Oxf's 'divers-coloured' is interesting in that it suggests a fool's attire, but is somewhat improbable as a misreading. Everett's 'lemon-coloured' has the attraction of anticipating the yellow stockings that Olivia hates and that Malvolio will wear, but then so does Rowe[3]'s emendation, adopted here.

132–5 **born . . . thighs** The signs of the Zodiac were thought to govern different parts of the body. Taurus governed neck and throat, the body parts dearest to drinkers. Sir Andrew gets his signs and organs mixed up. Sir Toby's further misattribution deliberately prompts Sir Andrew into a *caper* (116).

136 SD Sir Andrew shows off the dancing skills he has boasted of, usually with disastrous results in performance, making Sir Toby's praise (*excellent*, 137) ironic. In Posner's 2001 RSC production, Sir Andrew failed to move until Sir Toby tried to 'impale' his feet with his walking stick, forcing him to skip.

1.4 Here Viola appears for the first time disguised as Cesario in the duke's court, and has already had time ('but three days', 3) to gain Orsino's favour and to fall in love with him, complicating her task as go-between on his behalf.

130 flame-coloured] *Rowe*[3]*;* dam'd colour'd *F;* damask-coloured *Knight*; dun-coloured *Collier*[2]*;* lemon-coloured *Everett;* divers-coloured *Oxf* stock] stocken *F3;* stocking *Pope* set] *Rowe*[3]*;* sit *F* 134 That's] *F3;* That *F* 136 SD] *Oxf;* Capers awkwardly *Douai MS; Sir Andrew dances again / Collier*[3] 1.4] *(Scena Quarta.)*

VALENTINE If the duke continue these favours towards you, Cesario, you are like to be much advanced. He hath known you but three days, and already you are no stranger.

VIOLA You either fear his humour or my negligence that you call in question the continuance of his love. Is he inconstant, sir, in his favours?

VALENTINE No, believe me.

Enter ORSINO, CURIO *and Attendants.*

VIOLA I thank you. Here comes the count.

ORSINO
Who saw Cesario, ho?

VIOLA On your attendance, my lord; here.

ORSINO [*to Valentine, Curio and Attendants*]
Stand you awhile aloof. [*to Viola*] Cesario,
Thou knowst no less but all: I have unclasped
To thee the book even of my secret soul.

0.1–2 ***in man's attire*** presumably an outfit identical to that of Sebastian, to permit the subsequent confusions

2 **Cesario** This is the first name that the audience hears with reference to Viola, who is not named in the dialogue by her real name until the final scene (5.1.240). Her adopted name, equally Italian, may derive from 'Cesare', the assumed name of the cross-dressed heroine in Curzio Gonzaga's comedy *Gli inganni*, the version of the 'Twelfth Night' story which comes closest – in both time and tone – to Shakespeare's.
advanced promoted (*OED ppla.* 3)

3 **three days** Temporal references in the comedy are neither precise nor consistent: contrast *three months* at 5.1.90 and 95. Here the emphasis is on the rapidity with which Cesario has entered into Orsino's favour. On the play's multiple time scheme, see pp. 77–8.

5 **humour** disposition or temperament (*OED* 4), with the implication of capriciousness
that in that

6 **continuance** permanence (*OED* 6, giving this example)

8.1 *Attendants* Cf. 1.1.0.2n.

11 **On your attendance** at your service
here i.e. I am here, ready (*OED adv.* 1b)

13–14 **unclasped . . . book** alludes to the often elaborate clasps that fastened the covers of valuable books, especially bibles; the first of a number of references to Orsino's body and mind as a book (cf. 1.5.219)

0.2 *as Cesario*] *Munro subst.* 8.1 ORSINO] *Munro; Duke F* 12 SD1] *this edn* SD2] *Mahood*

Therefore, good youth, address thy gait unto her,
Be not denied access, stand at her doors
And tell them there thy fixed foot shall grow
Till thou have audience.

VIOLA Sure, my noble lord,
If she be so abandoned to her sorrow
As it is spoke, she never will admit me.

ORSINO
Be clamorous and leap all civil bounds
Rather than make unprofited return.

VIOLA
Say I do speak with her, my lord, what then?

ORSINO
O then unfold the passion of my love,
Surprise her with discourse of my dear faith.
It shall become thee well to act my woes.
She will attend it better in thy youth
Than in a nuncio's of more grave aspect.

VIOLA
I think not so, my lord.

15 **address thy gait** direct your steps (*OED* address *v.* 5, giving this example)
16 **access** accèss
17 **fixed** fixèd
grow take root
19 **abandoned** totally given up (*OED v.* 4, giving this example)
21 **civil bounds** limits of courtesy; cf. 1.5.202n., 4.2.33n. On the issue of courtesy, see pp. 58–64.
22 **make unprofited return** come back empty-handed; *unprofited* is the first occurrence in *OED ppla.*
25 **Surprise** capture by force (a military expression; *OED v.* 2b). Cf. *Tit* 1.1.288, 'Treason, my lord – Lavinia is surprised.'
discourse discòurse
dear Cf. 1.2.36n.
28 ***nuncio's** messenger's; the genitive form may be due to the fact that *a nuncio's . . . aspect* is intended to be a parallel with *thy youth* (27): since *thy* is a possessive (genitive), Shakespeare turned the parallel noun into a possessive, thereby producing a double genitive (*-s*, *of*), possible in Early Modern English (NB; cf. Hope, 1.1.4d).
more grave graver. Shakespeare often uses *more* with monosyllabic adjectives in comparative forms (Blake, *Grammar*, 3.2.3.4, giving this example): cf. *more smooth* (32), and 3.1.145, 3.3.5, 3.4.3 and 4.2.47.
aspect aspèct

15 gait] *(*gate*), Capell* 28 nuncio's] *F4 (*Nuncio's*);* Nuntio's *F;* Nuntius *(TxC)*

ORSINO Dear lad, believe it,
For they shall yet belie thy happy years
That say thou art a man. Diana's lip
Is not more smooth and rubious. Thy small pipe
Is as the maiden's organ, shrill and sound,
And all is semblative a woman's part.
I know thy constellation is right apt
For this affair.
[*to Valentine, Curio and Attendants*]
Some four or five attend him –
All, if you will – for I myself am best
When least in company. [*to Viola*] Prosper well in this
And thou shalt live as freely as thy lord,
To call his fortunes thine.

VIOLA I'll do my best
To woo your lady. [*aside*] Yet a barful strife:

30 **belie . . . years** misrepresent your youthful age

31 **thou . . . man** Orsino unwittingly points out the ambiguity of Cesario's gender while apparently alluding to his age. The following passage plays on Viola's position as a boy (actor) disguised as a girl (Viola) disguised as a boy (Cesario) or *eunuch* (1.2.53).

31 **Diana's lip** Diana, already alluded to by Orsino at 1.1.20–2 (see n.) with reference to Olivia, was the Roman moon-goddess, patroness of hunting, fertility and virginity (her *lip* having never been kissed by man). Cesario's face becomes the epitome of feminine beauty.

32 **more smooth** smoother; cf. 28n.
rubious ruby-coloured (*OED n.*[1], first occurrence)
small pipe high treble voice (*OED* pipe *n.*[1] 2a, giving this example); also alluding to the sex of the boy actor who played Viola (cf. Partridge, 160), or to her disguise as a *eunuch* (1.2.53); cf. *Cor* 3.2.113–14, 'a pipe / Small as an eunuch'.

33 **organ** voice (*OED n.*[1] 5b, giving this example); female genitals (cf. 32 n.)
shrill and sound high-pitched and unbroken; cf. *LLL* 5.2.415, 'sound, *sans* crack or flaw'.

34 **semblative** resembling (Onions; *OED*, first occurrence)
woman's part woman's appearance; female dramatic role; female sex

35 **constellation** disposition or character, as determined by the influence of the stars (*OED* 1b, giving this example)

39–40 **live . . . thine** live as independently as your lord, using his fortune as he does: an 'unknowing' glance towards the end of the comedy

41 **a barful strife** i.e. an internal struggle full of bars or impediments (because against her natural inclination); *OED* gives this as sole occurrence of *barful*.

33 shrill and] shrill in *Dyce*[2] 36 SD] *this edn* 38 SD] *Oxf* 41 SD] *Capell subst.*

Whoe'er I woo, myself would be his wife. *Exeunt.*

1.5 *Enter* MARIA *and* FESTE.

MARIA Nay, either tell me where thou hast been or I will not open my lips so wide as a bristle may enter in way of thy excuse. My lady will hang thee for thy absence.

FESTE Let her hang me. He that is well hanged in this world needs to fear no colours.

MARIA Make that good.

FESTE He shall see none to fear.

MARIA A good lenten answer. I can tell thee where that saying was born of 'I fear no colours'.

FESTE Where, good Mistress Mary?

MARIA In the wars, and that may you be bold to say in your foolery.

FESTE Well, God give them wisdom that have it; and

42 There is a probable pun on *would* and wooed, pronounced in the same way (Kökeritz, 155–6).

1.5 This long scene is dominated by the highly ironic duologue in which the disguised Viola, pleading on behalf of Orsino, succeeds instead in winning Olivia's love for herself. Rowe suggests '*Olivia's House*' as the location.

0.1 FESTE This name is mentioned only once in the dialogue, at 2.4.11, and never in stage directions or speech headings in *F*, where Feste is always indicated as *Clown*; see List of Roles, 14n.

1–3 Maria upbraids Feste, Olivia's jester, for his truancy at the court of Orsino, stressing the clown's role as a link between the two houses, a function shared by Viola.

1–2 **I . . . enter** I will keep my mouth firmly closed

2 **bristle** hair (literally, hog hair)
in by

4–5 **He . . . colours** i.e. a hanged man need fear no foes (since he cannot see them: cf. 7); *fear no colours* is proverbial (Dent, C520), the 'colours' being originally those of a regimental flag (*OED* colour *n.*[1] 7a; also 7d, giving this example). In the context of hanging, there is probably a pun on colours/collars (Kökeritz, 99). A sexual quibble may also be present, *well hanged* = 'well hung' (Hotson, 168): a well-endowed man need fear nobody or, possibly, need not fear blushing from embarrassment (*OED* colour *n.*[1] 3b); Cotgrave glosses French *couillatris* as 'well hanged (between the legs)'.

6 **Make that good** prove that

8 **lenten** weak, dismal (literally, pertaining to Lent, the season of fasting: *OED* 2, giving this example)

8–9 **where . . . born** the origin

11 **In the wars** of military origin; in trouble, as Feste is with Olivia for his truancy

13 **God . . . it** a paradox: *have* in place of 'lack'

1.5] *(Scena Quinta.)* 0.1 FESTE] *Munro; Clowne F* 4 SP] *Munro; Clo. F* 8 lenten] *(*lenton*)*

those that are fools, let them use their talents.

MARIA Yet you will be hanged for being so long absent. Or to be turned away – is not that as good as a hanging to you?

FESTE Many a good hanging prevents a bad marriage; and for turning away let summer bear it out.

MARIA You are resolute then?

FESTE Not so neither, but I am resolved on two points.

MARIA That if one break the other will hold; or if both break your gaskins fall.

FESTE Apt in good faith, very apt. Well, go thy way. If Sir Toby would leave drinking, thou wert as witty a piece of Eve's flesh as any in Illyria.

MARIA Peace, you rogue, no more o'that.

Enter Lady OLIVIA *with* MALVOLIO
[*and Attendants*].

14 **let . . . talents** another ironical allusion to the parable of the talents (cf. 1.3.120n.): let all make the most of what they have. There may be a pun here on 'talons' (cf. *LLL* 4.2.65–6), i.e. let those who have no wisdom use their claws.

16 **turned away** dismissed (from Olivia's employment)

18 **Many . . . marriage** proverbial (Tilley, H130, 'Better be half hanged than ill wed'); *good hanging* also retains here its slang sense of virility (cf. 4–5n.), i.e. a generous sexual endowment improves married life.

19 **for turning away** as for dismissal
bear it out make it (i.e. dismissal) bearable, by means of good weather

20 **resolute** determined

21 **resolved** determined: a synonym of *resolute* (20), which Feste pretends to contradict (*Not so neither*).
points matters, particulars (*OED n.*[1] 5a)

22–3 Maria puns on *points* (21) as the tagged laces attaching breeches to a doublet; cf. *1H4* 2.4.207–8, 'Their points [= swords] being broken – / Down fell their hose.'

23 **gaskins** wide breeches

24–6 **If . . . Illyria** This looks forward to the comedy's finale (5.1.356–8), in which we learn that Maria has married Sir Toby.

25–6 **as . . . flesh** as clever a woman. Feste compresses Maria's two potential attractions: her intelligence (*witty*) and her body. Cf. *MA* 4.2.83–4, where Dogberry comically considers himself 'as pretty a piece of flesh as any is in Messina'.

24 apt] apt . . . *she turns to go Cam*[1] 27.1–2] *this edn; after 29 F* 27.2] *Capell subst.*

Here comes my lady; make your excuse wisely you were best. [*Exit.*]

FESTE Wit, an't be thy will, put me into good fooling! Those wits that think they have thee do very oft prove fools, and I that am sure I lack thee may pass for a wise man. For what says Quinapalus? 'Better a witty fool than a foolish wit.' [*to Olivia*] God bless thee, lady.

OLIVIA Take the fool away.

FESTE Do you not hear, fellows? Take away the lady.

OLIVIA Go to, you're a dry fool, I'll no more of you. Besides, you grow dishonest.

FESTE Two faults, madonna, that drink and good counsel will amend: for give the dry fool drink, then is the fool

28 **wisely** ingeniously (*OED* 3, giving this example)

28–9 **you were best** you were best advised to

30 **Wit . . . fooling** i.e. Wit, don't desert me now. Feste is turning the proverbial opposition of *Wit* (= intelligence) and *will* (= desire) on its head, by suggesting that *Wit* has *will*.
an't if it

31–2 **Those . . . fools** Feste alludes to a proverb of biblical origin: 'make the fool answer to his foolishness, lest he be wise in his own conceit' (Proverbs, 26.5; cf. Dent, C582).

33 **Quinapalus** an invented Latin authority, probably inspired – given the context of rhetorical and logical discussion (cf. *syllogism*, 46) – by Quintilian(us), author of the *Institutio Oratoria*, a book much studied in Elizabethan schools and universities. This allusion may be 'contaminated' by another Latin *auctoritas*, Apuleius, author of *The Golden Ass*, and by the name of the Roman coin *quinarius* or quinary, worth five bronze 'asses' and bearing the type of the victoriate, whose 'weight standard had come from Illyria' (*Britannica*, 16.535). Shakespeare seems to be imitating Rabelais's pseudo-pedantic way with invented *auctoritates*. In any case, as Mahood observes, 'this no longer gets a laugh.'

33–4 **Better . . . wit** a variation of the biblical proverb alluded to at 31–2 (see n.).

35–7 **Take . . . you** Olivia's contemptuous dismissal of Feste seems to confirm Maria's prediction regarding her anger at his long absence (3, 15). These lines, however, are often performed in a playful fashion, an interpretation justified by Olivia's jesting with the clown at 55–70 and by her defence of fooling at 89–90.

37 **Go to** come, come: an expression of disapproval (*OED* go *v.* 93b)
dry dull, i.e. barren of jests (as at 1.3.69–70)

38 **dishonest** unreliable (because of his truancy)

39, 133 **madonna** my lady (*OED* 1a: from Italian *mia donna*); used by Shakespeare only for Feste in *TN*. Feste's use of an Italian form of address may help to define Olivia's Mediterranean background. The modern meaning 'Virgin Mary' entered into the language later.

40–1 **give . . . dry** punning on *dry* (37) as 'thirsty'

29 SD] *Pope* 34, 212 SDs] *Oxf* 35 SP] (*Ol.*), *Cam*[1] 37 you're] (y'are)

not dry; bid the dishonest man mend himself – if he mend, he is no longer dishonest, if he cannot, let the botcher mend him. Anything that's mended is but patched: virtue that transgresses is but patched with sin, and sin that amends is but patched with virtue. If that this simple syllogism will serve, so; if it will not, what remedy? As there is no true cuckold but calamity, so beauty's a flower. – The lady bade take away the fool, therefore I say again, take her away.

OLIVIA Sir, I bade them take away you.

FESTE Misprision in the highest degree! Lady, *cucullus non facit monachum* – that's as much to say as I wear not

41, 42 **mend** reform (*OED v.* 1b, giving this example)

43 **botcher** mender of clothes
mend repair; Feste develops the pun on *mend* with *patched* at 44.

44 **patched** 'implying a hasty, clumsy, imperfect, or temporary manner' of repair (*OED* patch *v.* 2, giving this example); falsely equated by Feste with *mended* (43). The point is that a patch is merely a superficial overlay, hence equally applicable to *sin* patching *virtue* (which can hardly be seen as repairing) and vice versa. Malone proposes a further allusion to the patchwork or parti-coloured costume of the fool.

44–5 **virtue . . . virtue** Having reduced virtue and sin to the patches on a garment, Feste sophistically maintains, in his own defence, the superficiality and relativity of transgression and amendment.

45–6 **If that** if (an older form)

46 **syllogism** an argument comprising three propositions (see 43–5). Feste's syllogism parodies logical reasoning in a self-mocking attempt to raise the tone of his defence.

47 **what remedy** it can't be helped (rhetorical question); extending the quibble on *mend* (41–3) and *amends* (45)
no true . . . calamity Only one 'wedded to calamity' (*RJ* 3.3.3) is really faithless, i.e. it is inevitable that Olivia will abandon her mourning in favour of life and love.

48 **beauty's a flower** i.e. it will fade; the classic 'seize the day' topos, Horace's '*carpe diem*' (Horace, *Odes*, 1.11.8). Ard[1] quotes *Summer's Last Will and Testament* (1600), 1588–9: 'Beauty is but a flowre, / Which wrinckles will deuoure.'

51 **Misprision** misunderstanding (*OED n.*[1] 3); wrongful arrest (*OED n.*[1] 2)

51–2 ***cucullus . . . monachum*** the hood does not make the monk; proverbial (Dent, H586). Feste alludes to his fool's attire (see *motley*, 53), and in particular to his cap (possibly also looking forward to his disguise in 4.2). The same tag appears in Latin in *MM* 5.1.261 and in English in *H8* 3.1.23.

52 **as . . . say** as much as to say (a common Early Modern variant); cf. *2H6* 4.2.16.

52–3 **I . . . brain** i.e. I am a fool only by profession, not by nature (contrast Maria's gibe on Sir Andrew as a 'natural' fool at 1.3.27–8).

motley in my brain. Good madonna, give me leave to prove you a fool.

OLIVIA Can you do it?

FESTE Dexteriously, good madonna.

OLIVIA Make your proof.

FESTE I must catechize you for it, madonna. Good my mouse of virtue, answer me.

OLIVIA Well, sir, for want of other idleness I'll bide your proof.

FESTE Good madonna, why mourn'st thou?

OLIVIA Good fool, for my brother's death.

FESTE I think his soul is in hell, madonna.

OLIVIA I know his soul is in heaven, fool.

FESTE The more fool, madonna, to mourn for your brother's soul being in heaven. – Take away the fool, gentlemen.

OLIVIA What think you of this fool, Malvolio, doth he not mend?

MALVOLIO Yes, and shall do till the pangs of death shake

53 **motley** the fool's parti-coloured costume

56 **Dexteriously** dextrously, cleverly (an Early Modern variant)

57 Demonstrate it (continuing the pseudological discourse).

58 **catechize** interrogate systematically, as in a catechism; cf. *Oth* 3.4.16–17, 'I will catechize the world for him, that is, make questions, and by them answer.' Feste proceeds to conduct a mock-religious interrogation of Olivia, perhaps to provoke the upright Malvolio (Oxf[1]).

58–9 **Good . . . virtue** my good virtuous little one. Feste inverts the noun phrase (determiner *my* and modifier *good*), by analogy with expressions like 'Good my lord' (Blake, *Grammar*, 3.3.5a). This may suggest mock deference on the clown's part, since Blake suggests that such inversion often signals a submissive attitude on the part of the speaker to the person spoken to. *Mouse* is a term of endearment for a woman (*OED* 3a): cf. *Ham* 3.4.181.

60 **idleness** pastime
bide wait for; endure

67 ***soul being** F's punctuation ('soule, being') has Olivia mourn her brother's soul, despite the fact that he is in heaven; Rowe, adopted here, makes her mourn the very fact that his soul is in heaven, taking up her statement in 65.

70 **mend** improve (his fooling); cf. 41n., 42n., 43n.

71–2 **Yes . . . him** Malvolio interprets *mend* (70) as 'improve in his folly', and sardonically reinforces this by adding that Feste's folly will increase until he dies.

56 Dexteriously] Dexterously *F4* 66 fool] fool you *F3* 67 soul being] *Rowe;* soule, being *F* 71 SP] *(Mal.), Cam[1]*

him. Infirmity, that decays the wise, doth ever make the better fool.

FESTE God send you, sir, a speedy infirmity, for the better increasing your folly. Sir Toby will be sworn that I am no fox, but he will not pass his word for twopence that you are no fool.

OLIVIA How say you to that, Malvolio?

MALVOLIO I marvel your ladyship takes delight in such a barren rascal. I saw him put down the other day with an ordinary fool that has no more brain than a stone. Look you now, he's out of his guard already. Unless you laugh and minister occasion to him, he is gagged. I protest I take these wise men that crow so at these set kind of fools no better than the fools' zanies.

72–3 **Infirmity . . . fool** i.e. disease or old age (*OED* infirmity 2, giving this example) favours fools by reducing wisdom and increasing foolishness

74 **infirmity** illness

76 **no fox** not clever or crafty (in antithesis with *no fool*, 77). Feste adopts elaborate and quasi-formal balanced clauses (rhetorical figure: isocolon) in making the point that, even if he is the official fool, it is Malvolio who should fear the *infirmity* of true foolishness.
pass pledge (*OED v.* 48a, giving this example)

80 **barren** lacking in wit; possibly sterile. Cf. 1.3.77.
put down . . . with defeated . . . by (in verbal combat); cf. 1.3.79.
with by (*OED prep.* 40a)

81 **ordinary . . . stone** proverbial phrase (Dent, W550: 'He has no more wit than a stone'), probably with a barely disguised allusion to the well-known Elizabethan jester John Stone, referred to in Jonson's *Volpone* as a 'taverne-foole' (2.1; Jonson, *Works*, 465). If this is so, *ordinary* takes on, as noun, the added meaning 'tavern', i.e. where the fool performs (*OED n.* 14b).

82 **out of his guard** defenceless, off his guard (*OED* guard *n.* 5c, first occurrence)

83 **minister occasion** provide an opportunity
gagged speechless (*OED v.*[1], giving this example)

84 **crow** laugh loudly; cf. *AYL* 2.7.30.

84–5 **these . . . fools** The demonstrative adjective *these* agrees, here and elsewhere in Shakespeare, with the main noun (*fools*) rather than the determiner *kind* as in present-day English (Blake, *Grammar*, 6.1.2.3, giving this example).
set contrived, unspontaneous

85 **zanies** stooges, attendants; derives from the Italian *commedia dell'arte* figure of the *zanni* (literally, Giovanni), assistant to the clown, and in its English form came to mean secondary figure or poor imitator, as in *LLL* 5.2.463, 'Some carry-tale, some please-man, some slight zany'. This is rightly taken by Olivia as a discourteous stab at her for laughing uncritically at the 'barren' fool.

81 brain] brains *F4* 84 wise men] *(*Wisemen*), F3*

OLIVIA O, you are sick of self-love, Malvolio, and taste with a distempered appetite. To be generous, guiltless and of free disposition is to take those things for bird-bolts that you deem cannon bullets. There is no slander in an allowed fool though he do nothing but rail; nor no railing in a known discreet man though he do nothing but reprove.

FESTE Now Mercury endue thee with leasing, for thou speak'st well of fools.

Enter MARIA.

MARIA Madam, there is at the gate a young gentleman much desires to speak with you.

OLIVIA From the Count Orsino, is it?

MARIA I know not, madam. 'Tis a fair young man, and well attended.

OLIVIA Who of my people hold him in delay?

MARIA Sir Toby, madam, your kinsman.

86 **sick of self-love** Olivia's *sick* (taken up in *distempered*, 87) suggests that she is accusing Malvolio of something more than an excess of *amour propre* or proud self-centredness, namely morbid self-infatuation or narcissism; cf. *Son* 62.1, 'Sin of self-love possesseth all mine eye.'

87 **distempered** sick

88 **free** magnanimous (Onions, 1)

88–9 **bird-bolts** blunt-headed arrows used for shooting birds (*OED*, giving this example), and as such relatively harmless

89–90 **There . . . rail** Olivia's defence of fooling is less exuberant than Jaques's encomium to the 'motley fool' in *AYL* 2.7.12–43, but it is still noteworthy in a comedy so much concerned with different kinds of 'folly'.

89 **no slander** an allusion to the proverb 'His tongue is no slander' (Dent, T389)

90 **allowed** licensed, permitted by authority to jest without restraint (*OED ppla.* 2, giving this example)
rail use abusive language; jest (*OED v.*[4] 2a)

91 **no railing . . . man** no abuse in someone known to be judicious. This appears to be an attempt by Olivia to mitigate her criticism of Malvolio, although the question remains whether he is *discreet* or *distempered*.

93–4 **Now . . . fools** May Mercury (the god of deception) teach you to lie, since you speak well of fools, i.e. truthfully.

93 **endue** endow
leasing telling lies (*OED v.*[2])

99 **well attended** with several attendants; cf. 1.4.36.

100 **Who** Which
hold . . . delay detains him

OLIVIA Fetch him off, I pray you, he speaks nothing but madman. Fie on him. [*Exit Maria.*]
Go you, Malvolio. If it be a suit from the count, I am sick, or not at home. What you will to dismiss it.
Exit Malvolio.
Now you see, sir, how your fooling grows old and people dislike it.

FESTE Thou hast spoke for us, madonna, as if thy eldest son should be a fool,

Enter SIR TOBY.

whose skull Jove cram with brains, for here comes one of thy kin has a most weak pia mater.

OLIVIA By mine honour, half drunk. [*to Sir Toby*] What is he at the gate, cousin?

102 **Fetch him off** bring him (Sir Toby) away; a hunting term, implying that Sir Toby may be savaging the *fair young man* (98)

103 **madman** madman's talk, with reference to Sir Toby's drunken state (confirmed on his arrival, 116 ff.)

103 SD *Maria does not exit in F, although she comes on again at 160.1; Olivia's order to *fetch off* Sir Toby (102) is surely addressed to her rather than to Malvolio, who is sent off immediately afterwards to take care of the visitor.

105 **What you will** do whatever you think fit (proverbial, echoing the play's second title; cf. Dent, W280.5)

106 **old** stale

110 **Jove** Mahood claims that 'Here and elsewhere this is almost certainly a substitution for "God" in the play's original text', as a result of the 1606 Act prohibiting profane oaths. Since, however, there are 16 occurrences of *God*, as opposed to 9 of *Jove*, this hypothesis is unconvincing. Feste jocularly invokes a pagan deity, as at 93 and 3.1.43. Cf. 2.5.95, 168 and n., 172; 3.4.72, 79; 4.2.11 and n.

***for . . . one** F's punctuation confusingly suggests that Olivia's theoretical *eldest son* and Sir Toby are one and the same. Malone, adopted by most editors, does not resolve the confusion. Rowe[3], by eliminating the pronoun 'he', allows for an easier associative transition from Olivia's unborn child to her present *kin*.

111 **pia mater** brain: literally 'meek mother', the delicate innermost membrane enclosing the brain

112–24 **What . . . devil** Olivia's *What* (112, 123) means 'who' and 'what kind of man'; Sir Toby interprets it first as 'what rank', hence *gentleman* (114), and then as 'what sort of thing', hence *devil* (124). At 206 Olivia gets to ask the *gentleman* himself (see 206–11 and 209n.). Cf. 1.2.32n.

103, 213 SDs] *Capell* 109.1] *this edn; opp.* comes *110 F; after 111 Rowe*[3] 110 for . . . one] *Rowe*[3]*;* for heere he comes. *Enter Sir Toby. /* One *F;* for here he comes, one *Malone*; or – here he comes – one *Cam* 112 SD] *this edn*

SIR TOBY A gentleman.

OLIVIA A gentleman? What gentleman?

SIR TOBY 'Tis a gentleman here. [*Belches.*] A plague o'these pickle herring! [*to Feste*] How now, sot?

FESTE Good Sir Toby.

OLIVIA Cousin, cousin, how have you come so early by this lethargy?

SIR TOBY Lechery? I defy lechery. There's one at the gate.

OLIVIA Ay, marry, what is he?

SIR TOBY Let him be the devil an he will, I care not. Give me faith, say I. Well, it's all one. *Exit.*

OLIVIA What's a drunken man like, fool?

FESTE Like a drowned man, a fool and a madman: one

116, 116 SD *Capell's suggestion that *here* stands for an SD indicating a belch seems improbable (it presumably means 'here at your gate'), but clearly a burp is called for at this point and is not otherwise indicated in F. Sir Toby acts out his surname. In Posner's 2001 RSC production he threw up over the carpet.

116–17 **A plague o'** Cf. 1.3.1n.

117 **pickle herring** i.e. pickled herring, the immediate cause, together with the accompanying wine, of Belch's belching. In *Palladis Tamia*, Francis Meres recalls the tragicomic death of one of Shakespeare's fellow playwrights from the same cause: '*Robert Greene* died of a surfet taken at Pickeld Herrings, & Rhenish wine, as witnesseth *Thomas Nash*, who was at the fatall banquet' (Meres, fol. 286^{v}). The Pickle Herring was a type of clown in the *Englischen Comedien und Tragedien . . . samt dem Pickelhering* ('English comedies and tragedies . . . with Pickle Herring') and the musical *Pickelherings-spiele* ('Pickle Herring plays') performed in early seventeenth-century Germany (*OED*).

sot fool or drunkard (or perhaps, as an insult, drunken fool); Robert Armin, who probably played Feste, was the author of the pamphlet *Foole upon Foole or, Six Sortes of Sottes* (1600). See pp. 34–5.

119 **come . . . by** become possessed . . . by (*OED* come 40b, giving this example)

121 **Lechery** Sir Toby mishears *lethargy* (120), thereby exchanging one vice for another.

one someone

124 **an** if

124–5 **Give me faith** I'm on the side of *faith* (not the *devil*); may allude playfully to the Protestant doctrine whereby man is justified by grace through faith, as opposed to works; cf. 3.2.67n.

125 **it's all one** it makes no difference; cf. 5.1.192, 366–7, 400.

127–9 **one . . . drowns him** one glass too many, warming him above his normal bodily temperature, makes him a fool, two glasses drive him mad, three overwhelm him (another allusion to drowning; cf. 1.2.4)

116 SD] *Theobald* 117 SD] *Mahood; Clown laughs Cam[1]*

draught above heat makes him a fool, the second mads him and a third drowns him.

OLIVIA Go thou and seek the crowner, and let him sit o'my coz, for he's in the third degree of drink – he's drowned. Go look after him.

FESTE He is but mad yet, madonna, and the fool shall look to the madman. [*Exit.*]

Enter MALVOLIO.

MALVOLIO Madam, yon young fellow swears he will speak with you. I told him you were sick. He takes on him to understand so much, and therefore comes to speak with you. I told him you were asleep. He seems to have a foreknowledge of that too, and therefore comes to speak with you. What is to be said to him, lady? He's fortified against any denial.

OLIVIA Tell him he shall not speak with me.

MALVOLIO Has been told so, and he says he'll stand at your door like a sheriff's post and be the supporter to a bench, but he'll speak with you.

OLIVIA What kind o'man is he?

MALVOLIO Why, of mankind.

128–9 **mads him** makes him mad; cf. *R2* 5.5.61, 'This music mads me!'
130 **crowner** coroner
130–1 **sit . . . coz** hold an inquest on my cousin (i.e. relative; see List of Roles, 11n.). Cf. the second clown on the drowned Ophelia, 'The crowner hath sat on her and finds it Christian burial', *Ham* 5.1.4–5.
131 **in . . . degree** at the third (and last) stage (*OED phr.*, first occurrence)
133–4 This anticipates the 'dark room' scene in 4.2, where the disguised Feste will *look to* the 'mad' Malvolio.
134 **look to** look after
137, 139 **and therefore** for which reason
143 ***Has** Omission of personal pronouns (here 'he') was available in Early Modern English (Blake, *Grammar*, 3.3.2.1f); cf. 5.1.171, 192 and 281.
and yet
144 **sheriff's post** Two painted posts – on which proclamations were affixed – were set up at the sheriff's or mayor's door (*OED*; see Fig. 14); thus they (literally) stand for the epitome of firmness.
147 **of mankind** i.e a human being; Malvolio gives a non-answer

130 crowner] Coroner *Rowe* 134 SD] *Rowe* 135 yon] *(*yond*)* 143 Has] *(*Ha's*), Dyce;* He has *Douai MS, Pope;* 'Has *Dyce*[2]*;* He's *Mahood*

OLIVIA What manner of man?

MALVOLIO Of very ill manner: he'll speak with you, will you or no.

OLIVIA Of what personage and years is he?

MALVOLIO Not yet old enough for a man, nor young enough for a boy, as a squash is before 'tis a peascod, or a codling when 'tis almost an apple. 'Tis with him in standing water between boy and man. He is very well favoured, and he speaks very shrewishly. One would think his mother's milk were scarce out of him.

OLIVIA Let him approach. Call in my gentlewoman.

MALVOLIO [*Goes to door.*] Gentlewoman, my lady calls. *Exit.*

Enter MARIA.

OLIVIA

Give me my veil; come throw it o'er my face.

148, 149 **manner** kind, temper (respectively)

149–50 **will . . . no** equivalent to modern 'willy-nilly'; cf. 'Would I or not', 295.

151 **personage** appearance

153 **squash** unripe peapod

peascod synonym of *squash*; Kökeritz, 133, detects a pun on 'codpiece'.

154 **codling** unripe apple (*OED* 1a, giving this example); slang for scrotum and/or testicles (cf. *Witch of Edmonton*, 20, 2.1, 'Has she a minde to codlings already?'; and *AYL* 2.4.49–50, where Touchstone gives 'two cods' from a 'peascod' to his beloved). The irony is that the *codling* Cesario has no codlings.

154–5 **in . . . man** at the turn of the tide, midway between childhood and adulthood; recalls Golding's description of Narcissus, 'he seemde to stande betweene the state of man and Lad, / The hearts of divers trim yong men his beautie gan to move, / And many a Ladie fresh and faire was taken in his love' (Ovid, *Met.*, 3.438–40). The effect of Narcissus' beauty on both sexes resembles the havoc that Cesario's androgynous appeal is about to wreak.

155 **standing** still, i.e. not ebbing or flowing (*OED* 7a, giving this example)

155–6 **well-favoured** good-looking

156 **shrewishly** sharply (*OED* 2b, giving this example); with a shrill (shrew-like) voice

157 **his mother's . . . him** proverbial (Dent, M1204)

161 **Give . . . veil** In theory, since she is in mourning, Olivia should be wearing her veil continuously in public; in practice – since she has to be visible to the audience – she puts it on only in this episode to hide her face from Cesario. Cf. 1.1.27.

149 manner] manners *F3* 159 SD] *Cam*[1] 161 veil;] veil: *Puts Olivia's veil on – then her own. / Powell MS*

We'll once more hear Orsino's embassy.

Enter VIOLA [*as Cesario*].

VIOLA The honourable lady of the house, which is she?

OLIVIA Speak to me, I shall answer for her. Your will?

VIOLA Most radiant, exquisite and unmatchable beauty – I pray you, tell me if this be the lady of the house, for I never saw her. I would be loath to cast away my speech, for, besides that it is excellently well penned, I have taken great pains to con it. Good beauties, let me sustain no scorn: I am very comptible, even to the least sinister usage.

OLIVIA Whence came you, sir?

162.1 *VIOLA F's '*Violenta*' is presumably a compositor's error. The page, sig. Y3^{v}, on which it appears, was the first page of the play to be set in type; Compositor B would therefore not yet have been familiar with the name '*Viola*'. Turner, 130, suggests that he may have expanded an abbreviated manuscript form '*Vio.*' in the SD to '*Violenta*', having last met this name in F when he set sig. X1^{v} in *AW* (though he had set all of *KJ* and some of *R2* in the interim). See Appendix 1.

163 **which is she?** Probably ironical, since Olivia should be recognizable from her veil, although some productions have made Viola's confusion genuine by having Maria and other attendants wear veils as well.

165 **Most . . . beauty** The beginning of Viola's speech, *excellently well penned* (168), is a conventionally complimentary performance delivered in an appropriately 'high' tone. In Sam Mendes's 2002 production, Viola had a written speech that she began to read here – unnecessarily, since she has 'taken great pains to con it' (169; cf. n.).

167–79 **I would . . . play** This passage is full of theatrical jargon (*speech*, *con*, *studied*, *part*, *comedian*, *play*), as Viola plays the role assigned to her by Orsino.

167 **cast away** throw away, waste

168 **excellently well penned** superlatively well written

169 **con** learn by heart (*OED v.*^{1}, 3, giving this example). Viola underlines the studied staginess of her performance. Williams, 289, discerns a sexual pun on French '*con*', which Cotgrave glosses as 'A woman's &c.'; cf. the French princess in *H5* 3.4.47–8, 'De foot, *et* de coun? *O Seigneur Dieu, ils sont les mots de son mauvais*' ('O Lord God, they are words of evil sound').

sustain be subjected to (*OED* 9a, giving this example)

170 **comptible** sensitive (*OED* countable *a.* 1c, sole occurrence)

170–1 **least sinister usage** slightest discourtesy

162.1 VIOLA] *F2; Violenta F* *as Cesario*] *Cam*^{1} 164 will?] *Rann;* will. *F* 165–6 beauty –] *Rowe;* beautie. *F*

VIOLA I can say little more than I have studied, and that question's out of my part. Good gentle one, give me modest assurance if you be the lady of the house, that I may proceed in my speech.

OLIVIA Are you a comedian?

VIOLA No, my profound heart. And yet – by the very fangs of malice, I swear – I am not that I play. Are you the lady of the house?

OLIVIA If I do not usurp myself, I am.

VIOLA Most certain if you are she you do usurp yourself, for what is yours to bestow is not yours to reserve. But this is from my commission. I will on with my speech in your praise, and then show you the heart of my message.

OLIVIA Come to what is important in't – I forgive you the praise.

173 **I can . . . more** Viola refuses to answer Olivia's question about her background and thus identity.
than . . . studied than what I have learnt by heart, i.e. my role

174 **out . . . part** not written in my speech
gentle one lady; *gentle* often signified social status.

175 **modest** moderate, just enough

177 **comedian** professional actor (*OED* 1a, first occurrence); an example of the *sinister usage* feared by Viola at 171 (see 170–1n.), i.e. an impatient (though appropriate) riposte to Viola's insistence on confining herself to her *part*

178 **No . . . heart** absolutely not (*my profound heart* is an intensifier rather than a direct address to Olivia). This emphatic denial reminds the audience of the gender complexity of Viola's role: as a woman she could not be an actor.

179 **fangs of malice** an oath, deriving from the biblical association of evil with the serpent
I am . . . play i.e. I am not equated solely with the part of Orsino's emissary; I am not what I seem: the first of several hints by Viola that she is assuming a disguise

181, 182 **usurp** Olivia playfully means 'supplant' (*OED* 6, giving this example); Viola shifts the sense to an accusatory 'assume improper authority over'.

183 **what . . . reserve** i.e. as 'lady of the house' you shouldn't be concealing yourself by wearing a veil (hence, also, withholding yourself improperly from marriage); *reserve* = withhold

184 **from my commission** outside my commissioned speech (synonymous with 'out of my part', 174); for *from* as 'outside', cf. Blake, *Grammar*, 5.4.2 (giving this example). Cf. 224n.
on continue

187 **I forgive you** I can do without

175 I] *only as catchword on sig.* $Y3^v$ *in F*   179 fangs] (phangs), *Rowe*^{3}; Pangs *Rowe*

VIOLA Alas, I took great pains to study it, and 'tis poetical.

OLIVIA It is the more like to be feigned, I pray you keep it in. I heard you were saucy at my gates, and allowed your approach rather to wonder at you than to hear you. If you be not mad, be gone. If you have reason, be brief. 'Tis not that time of moon with me to make one in so skipping a dialogue.

MARIA Will you hoist sail, sir? Here lies your way.

VIOLA No, good swabber, I am to hull here a little longer. – Some mollification for your giant, sweet lady. Tell me your mind, I am a messenger.

190–1 **poetical . . . feigned** a playful allusion to Renaissance theories of poetry (and of artistic representation in general, especially drama) as a lie, a doctrine derived from Plato (*Republic*, 376d–383c; Plato, 2.1–499, 220–9) and adopted by the Puritans in their attack on literature and the stage; cf. Touchstone's 'the truest poetry is the most feigning', *AYL* 3.3.18–19.

192–3 **allowed . . . approach** let you come in

194–5 **If you be . . . brief** i.e. either have the courtesy to leave or get on with the message. F's 'not mad' has often been unnecessarily emended (see t.n.) because it is synonymous with 'If you have reason' rather than antithetical to it.

195 **'Tis . . . me** I'm not in the mood; I'm not *mad* myself. Changes in the moon were thought to influence the human mind, hence its association with madness (i.e. 'lunacy').

195 **to make one** to participate

196 **skipping** mad (Johnson); incoherent

197 **hoist sail** go away
Here . . . way proverbial (Dent, D556: 'Here is the door and there lies your way')

198 **swabber** deckhand; a gibe at Maria's rank, taking up her own nautical language in 197
hull stay at anchor with furled sails; cf. *R3* 4.4.438–9, 'And there they hull, expecting but the aid / Of Buckingham to welcome them ashore.'

199 **Some . . . giant** Please pacify your protector. In the romance tradition giants acted as guards for ladies (Johnson), but there is probably also an ironical reference here to the diminutive size of the boy actor playing Maria (cf. 2.5.11, 3.2.63).

199–200 **Tell . . . messenger** Many editors, following Hanmer, emend F by attributing 'Tell me your mind' to Olivia as an impatient imperative, 'get on with it'; Viola's 'I am a messenger' becomes a defensive response ('I'm only a go-between'). F, however, makes sense in the context of Viola's irritation both with Olivia's indirectness at 194–5 (see n.) and with Maria's presumptuousness, i.e. as a messenger, I only take orders from the lady of the house (to whom my message is addressed), so you tell me if you want to hear my message or not.

194 not mad] mad *Rann (Mason);* but mad *(Staunton)* 197 way.] way. *she opens the door to thrust her out Cam*[1] 199 Tell] OLIVIA Tell *Hanmer* 200 I] VIOLA I *Hanmer*

OLIVIA Sure you have some hideous matter to deliver when the courtesy of it is so fearful. Speak your office.

VIOLA It alone concerns your ear. I bring no overture of war, no taxation of homage. I hold the olive in my hand: my words are as full of peace as matter.

OLIVIA Yet you began rudely. What are you? What would you?

VIOLA The rudeness that hath appeared in me have I learned from my entertainment. What I am and what I would are as secret as maidenhead: to your ears, divinity; to any other's, profanation.

OLIVIA [*to Maria and Attendants*] Give us the place alone, we will hear this divinity. [*Exeunt Maria and Attendants.*] Now sir, what is your text?

VIOLA Most sweet lady –

OLIVIA A comfortable doctrine, and much may be said of it. Where lies your text?

202 **courtesy** preliminary ceremonies; an important theme word in the play (cf. 4.2.33)
fearful frightening: referring to Viola's bluntness, and perhaps to her obstinacy at the gate (cf. 206n.)
Speak your office deliver your message
203 **alone** only
overture declaration (*OED* 2)
204 **taxation of homage** demand for payment of dues
olive olive branch, as a symbol of peace (punning on *Olivia*)
205 **my . . . matter** all the contents of my message are peaceful
206 **rudely** discourteously: probably referring to Viola's behaviour at the gate
What Cf. 112–24n.
209 **entertainment** reception (by Malvolio and Sir Toby at the gate)
209–11 **What . . . profanation** i.e. my role as messenger and my personal identity are so confidential and intimate that they are strictly for your ears only
209 **What** refers primarily to Viola's function as intimate go-between, but inevitably hints at the question of her true identity ('who') and gender ('of what sex'). Cf. 1.2.32n.
211, 213 **divinity** religious discourse; introduces a dense passage of pseudo-religious terms
214 **text** passage from the Scriptures used as the subject of a sermon (*OED n.*[1] 4a)
215 **Most sweet lady** – often declaimed in production as the beginning of Viola's prepared speech (or *text*), nipped in the rhetorical bud
216 **comfortable** bringing religious comfort; cf. *RJ* 5.3.148, 'O comfortable Friar'.
doctrine lesson. Olivia ironically takes *Most sweet lady* as a statement of the subject matter or *text* (in answer to 214).

204 olive] *(*Olyffe*), Rowe* 206–7] *Pope; F lines* you? / you? / 211 other's] *Rann;* others *F* 212–14] *Pope; F lines* alone, / text? / 215 lady –] *Theobald;* Ladie. *F*

VIOLA In Orsino's bosom.

OLIVIA In his bosom? In what chapter of his bosom?

VIOLA To answer by the method, in the first of his heart.

OLIVIA O, I have read it, it is heresy. Have you no more to say?

VIOLA Good madam, let me see your face.

OLIVIA Have you any commission from your lord to negotiate with my face? You are now out of your text. But we will draw the curtain and show you the picture. [*Unveils.*] Look you, sir, such a one I was this present. Is't not well done?

VIOLA Excellently done, if God did all.

OLIVIA 'Tis in grain, sir, 'twill endure wind and weather.

VIOLA

'Tis beauty truly blent, whose red and white

218 possibly a playful echo of the biblical expression 'in Abraham's bosom' (Luke, 16.22), i.e. heaven, a blessed abode

219 Cf. 1.4.13–14n.
chapter as of the biblical *text* to be quoted

220 **by the method** in the same style
the first the first chapter

221 **heresy** i.e. contrary to the *doctrine* (216) of Olivia's own thoughts and desires

224 **commission** authorization (recalling *my commission*, 184). In connection with the verb *negotiate* (225), there is probably a more specifically financial meaning here, i.e. 'authority given to act as agent . . . for another in the conduct of business or trade' (*OED* 10).

225 **negotiate** do business; cf. *MA* 2.1.163–4, 'Let every eye negotiate for itself, / And trust no agent.'
out . . . text straying from your stated theme

226 Olivia reveals her face as if taking the dust cover off a portrait; cf. 1.3.120–2.

227 **such . . . present** this is what I looked like today. Portraits usually bore the date of composition and the age of the sitter (Cam^2); see Fig. 8. In this case the date of the live portrait is *this present*, the usual form for 'today' when dating letters (*present* is an adjectival noun, stressed on the first syllable). The unveiling ceremony is pronounced by Olivia with mock solemnity.

229 **if . . . all** if it is all natural, i.e. unaided by cosmetics. The actor playing Olivia was made up.

230 **in grain** ingrained: indelible (*OED* grain $n.^1$ 10c, giving this example)

231–5 Viola suddenly changes tone and turns to verse, paying Olivia a Petrarchan compliment typical of love poetry, as in *Son* 20.1 (addressed to the fair youth), 'A woman's face with nature's own hand painted'.

231 **truly blent** naturally blended. Nature and not art has mixed the colours of Olivia's complexion harmoniously (*OED* blend $v.^2$ 4a, giving this example); this atones for the irony of 229.

227 SD] *Craig; after 228 Rowe; after* curtain *226 Capell*

Nature's own sweet and cunning hand laid on.
Lady, you are the cruell'st she alive
If you will lead these graces to the grave
And leave the world no copy.

OLIVIA O sir, I will not be so hard-hearted. I will give out diverse schedules of my beauty. It shall be inventoried, and every particle and utensil labelled to my will, as, item, two lips, indifferent red; item, two grey eyes, with lids to them; item, one neck, one chin and so forth. Were you sent hither to praise me?

VIOLA
I see you what you are, you are too proud;
But if you were the devil you are fair.
My lord and master loves you. O, such love
Could be but recompensed, though you were crowned

232 **cunning** skilful
laid on painted

233 **she** woman; pronoun used as a full noun (Hope, 1.3.2j, giving this example)

234 **graces** beauties, with a possible allusion to the three Graces of Greek mythology, givers of charm and beauty

235 **copy** child; cf. *Son* 11.14, 'Thou shouldst print more, not let that copy die.'

236–7 ^{2}**I . . . beauty** Olivia proposes circulation of a written catalogue of her *graces* (234) as the form of *copy* she will *leave* (235).

237 **divers schedules** various lists; *schedule* is a bureaucratic term referring to 'any tabular or classified statement' (*OED n.* 2, giving this example). Olivia proceeds to give an inventory of her parts, by way of a parody of the 'blazon' or complimentary anatomizing of the woman's body (cf. 281–5 and 285n.).
inventoried listed

238 **particle** atom of my body (literally, minute quantity of matter)
utensil 'part of the human frame serving a special purpose' (*OED* 3a, first occurrence; originally domestic vessel or implement)
labelled . . . will itemized according to my wishes; itemized in a codicil affixed to my last will and testament (punning on Viola's *leave*, 235)
will desire; testament

239, 240 **item** literally 'likewise' (Latin), used to introduce each new article in a list (*OED adv.* A, giving this example)

239 **indifferent** fairly (adverb)

240 **lids** eyelids, with a probable pun on the lids of pots (see 238n. on *utensil*)

241 **praise** commend; appraise, make a valuation of (*item* by *item*)

242–3 'alluding to Lucifer's beauty in heaven, and his fall through pride' (Ard^2); cf. also Dent, L572: 'As proud as Lucifer'.

245 **Could . . . recompensed** would receive no more than its due reward (if you accepted it) (Ard^2)

237 schedules] *(*scedules*), Rowe*

The nonpareil of beauty.
OLIVIA How does he love me?
VIOLA
With adoration's fertile tears,
With groans that thunder love, with sighs of fire.
OLIVIA
Your lord does know my mind: I cannot love him.
Yet I suppose him virtuous, know him noble,
Of great estate, of fresh and stainless youth,
In voices well divulged, free, learn'd and valiant,
And in dimension and the shape of nature
A gracious person; but yet I cannot love him.
He might have took his answer long ago.
VIOLA
If I did love you in my master's flame,
With such a suffering, such a deadly life,
In your denial I would find no sense,
I would not understand it.
OLIVIA Why, what would you?
VIOLA
Make me a willow cabin at your gate

246 **nonpareil** queen (literally, unequalled representative)
247 ***adoration's** Rann's emendation has the advantage of creating three parallel phrases beginning *With*, without resorting to the more radical emendation offered by Pope.
fertile abundant (*OED* 3, giving this example)
248 **thunder** violently manifest
fire passion; a variation on the theme of the amorous furor (see 1.1.14–15n.)
251 **estate** rank; wealth
252 **In . . . divulged** well spoken of; this probably stands alone (as in F), but may govern the adjectives that follow, i.e. 'well spoken of as being'
252 Cf. 1.2.38–41n.
253 **dimension** proportions (*OED* 4, giving this example)
shape of nature natural form
254 **gracious** elegant, attractive
255 **took** taken
256 **in . . . flame** with Orsino's passion
257 **deadly** death-like; cf. *KL* 5.3.288, 'All's cheerless, dark and deadly.'
260 **willow cabin** 'temporary shelter' (*OED* cabin 1a, giving this example), made out of willow branches. In Barton's 1969 RSC production the stage was dominated by a willow-cabin set, anything but temporary (see pp. 107). The willow was the emblem of sorrowful love: cf. *MA* 2.1.172, 199–200, and Desdemona's 'willow' song at *Oth* 4.3.39–56.

247 adoration's] *Rann;* adorations, *F* fertile] with fertile *Pope* 257 suffering] *(*suffring*)*

And call upon my soul within the house;
Write loyal cantons of contemned love
And sing them loud even in the dead of night;
Hallow your name to the reverberate hills
And make the babbling gossip of the air
Cry out 'Olivia!' O, you should not rest
Between the elements of air and earth
But you should pity me.

OLIVIA You might do much.
What is your parentage?

VIOLA
Above my fortunes, yet my state is well:
I am a gentleman.

OLIVIA Get you to your lord.
I cannot love him; let him send no more,
Unless perchance you come to me again
To tell me how he takes it. Fare you well.
I thank you for your pains. [*Offers money.*]
Spend this for me.

261 **call . . . soul** supplicate my beloved (i.e. Olivia)

262 **loyal cantons** songs pledging loyalty (*cantons* is a variant of 'cantos'; cf. *OED* canton *n.*^{2} and loyal *a.* 3, both giving this example)
contemned contemnèd: despised

264 **Hallow** holla, shout; with a pun on *hallow* in the sense of 'bless' (Kökeritz, 111); cf. *2H4* 1.2.188–9.
reverberate reverberating, echoing (*OED ppla.*, giving this example)

265 **babbling . . . air** echo, alluding both materially to the sound of the shouted name being repeated by the hills and mythopoetically to Echo, the mountain nymph who, in Ovid, fades away for love of Narcissus and becomes mere voice; cf. 'A babling Nymph that *Echo* hight' (Ovid, *Met.*, 3.443, fol. 36^r; see Bate, 148). Cf. also Viola's story of her pining *sister* at 2.4.110–21; *babbling* is itself echoed at 3.4.352..

267 **elements . . . earth** Cf. 1.1.25n.

268 **But** unless

270 I am better born than my present circumstances (*fortunes*) indicate; *state* = rank by birth

271 **gentleman** of gentle birth, i.e. not of noble rank but entitled to a coat of arms (see 285n.) and to bear arms. The definition is virtual in respect of Viola's gender but applies fully to Sebastian, whom Olivia will address as *gentle friend* at 4.1.50.

264 Hallow] Hollaw *F2;* Hollow *F3;* Holla *Malone;* Halloo *Collier* 270 fortunes] fortune *Craig* 275 SD] *Collier*^{3}

VIOLA
I am no fee'd post, lady; keep your purse.
My master, not myself, lacks recompense.
Love make his heart of flint that you shall love,
And let your fervour like my master's be
Placed in contempt. Farewell, fair cruelty. *Exit.*

OLIVIA
'What is your parentage?'
'Above my fortunes, yet my state is well:
I am a gentleman.' I'll be sworn thou art –
Thy tongue, thy face, thy limbs, actions and spirit
Do give thee fivefold blazon. Not too fast, soft, soft –
Unless the master were the man. How now?
Even so quickly may one catch the plague?
Methinks I feel this youth's perfections
With an invisible and subtle stealth
To creep in at mine eyes. Well, let it be.
What ho, Malvolio.

276 **fee'd post** hired messenger (*OED* feed *ppla*. 2, giving this example)

278 May Cupid (*Love*) make him that you love have a heart as hard as stone. This recalls the allusion to Cupid's *golden shaft* at 1.1.34: his other arrow was lead-tipped and caused aversion.
that refers back to the possessive *his* rather than the noun *heart* (Hope, 1.4.2f, giving this example)

279 **fervour** passion; cf. 1.1.14–15n.

285 **blazon** coat of arms (here *fivefold*, i.e. having five decorative elements, as listed in 284), which it was the privilege of a *gentleman* (271) to bear (*OED* 2, giving this example); in Cesario's case, it is his own bearing that declares his gentle birth. The term also designated a sixteenth-century poetic mode, 'the detailed enumeration of the parts of the woman's body' (Norbrook, 43; see also Sawday): unwittingly, Olivia has in fact just anatomized Viola's body (284). Cf. 236–40 and 237n.; also *Son* 106.5–6.

285–7 **Not . . . plague** Olivia's incoherence under the effect of passion here bears out Viola's recollection at 2.2.21 of her speaking *in starts*, even if Viola has already left the stage and does not actually witness Olivia's soliloquy.
soft slowly; cf. 2.5.91, 118, 138.

286 **Unless . . . man** i.e. unless the servant Cesario took the place of Orsino; or unless he was actually the *master*, Orsino himself, in disguise

287 **catch the plague** be infected by love; a further metaphorical allusion to the literal and ever-present danger of the plague in the period (*Even so quickly* indeed). Cf. 1.1.19n.

288 **perfections** pronounced as a four-syllable word

289 imperceptibly and insidiously

290 **at mine eyes** Cf. Dent, L501: 'Love comes by looking in at the eyes.'

276 fee'd post] *(*feede poast*), Rowe*

Enter MALVOLIO.

MALVOLIO Here, madam, at your service.

OLIVIA
Run after that same peevish messenger
The county's man. He left this ring behind him,
Would I or not. Tell him I'll none of it.
Desire him not to flatter with his lord,
Nor hold him up with hopes: I am not for him.
If that the youth will come this way tomorrow,
I'll give him reasons for't. Hie thee, Malvolio.

MALVOLIO Madam, I will. *Exit.*

OLIVIA
I do I know not what, and fear to find
Mine eye too great a flatterer for my mind.
Fate, show thy force, ourselves we do not owe.
What is decreed must be – and be this so. [*Exit.*]

2.1 *Enter* ANTONIO *and* SEBASTIAN.

294 ***county's** count's, a common Elizabethan form (from French *conté* or Italian *conte*); cf. *RJ* 4.2.45, 'County Paris'. Capell's emendation restores the metre.
295 **Would . . . not** whether I wanted it or not: cf. 149–50n.
296 **flatter with** fill with false hope (*OED v.*[1] 7a, giving this example)
297 **hold him up** sustain him; delude him
299 **Hie thee** hurry
302 my eye has deceived my mind (into loving Orsino's messenger)
303–4 **Fate . . . so** proverbial: what must be must be (Dent, M1331). Cf. *Faustus*: 'What doctrine call you this, *Che sera, sera* / What will be, shall be?' (Marlowe, *Faustus*, 1.1, A3[r]).
303 **owe** own
2.1 This duologue, in which the audience learns of the survival of Sebastian, befriended by Antonio, parallels 1.2, where the shipwrecked Viola is helped by the captain. Such structural mirroring underlines the bond between the separated twins, even if this scene, unlike 1.2, is in prose. The dialogue explores male friendship in terms that can be read as the language of romantic attachment and desire. Rowe indicates the location as '*The Street*', while Capell suggests '*The Sea-coast*', underscoring the parallel with 1.2. (Kemble specifies '*The Sea-coast. The same as Scene 1 – Act 1*', i.e. 1.2.)

294 county's] *Capell;* Countes *F;* Counts *F2;* count his *Keightley* 304 SD] *Rowe; Finis, Actus primus. F* 2.1] *(Actus Secundus, Scaena prima.)*

ANTONIO Will you stay no longer, nor will you not that I go with you?

SEBASTIAN By your patience, no. My stars shine darkly over me, the malignancy of my fate might perhaps distemper yours. Therefore I shall crave of you your leave that I may bear my evils alone. It were a bad recompense for your love to lay any of them on you.

ANTONIO Let me yet know of you whither you are bound.

SEBASTIAN No, sooth, sir. My determinate voyage is mere extravagancy. But I perceive in you so excellent a touch of modesty that you will not extort from me what I am willing to keep in, therefore it charges me in manners the rather to express myself. You must know of me then, Antonio, my name is Sebastian, which I called Roderigo. My father was that Sebastian of Messaline

1 **nor . . . I** or do you not wish me to; probably a double negative construction ('nor . . . not'), common in Early Modern English (Hope, 2.1.9, Blake, *Grammar*, 6.2.3.3), although *nor* is often used for 'and', as may be the case here (Blake, *Grammar*, 6.2.3.1)

3 **By your patience** by your leave
darkly ominously (*OED adv.* 3, giving this example); an allusion to the shipwreck

4 **malignancy** evil influence: an astrological term (see *stars*, 3)

5 **distemper** infect: another astrological term

5–6 **I shall . . . may** I beg you to let me. Throughout the exchange the two men employ the language of chivalric courtesy (see 32n.).

6 **evils** misfortunes

8 **of** from

10 **sooth** in truth

10–11 **My . . . extravagancy** my only travel plan is to wander aimlessly

10 **determinate** intended (*OED a.* 4, giving this example)

11 **extravagancy** wandering (*OED* 1, first occurrence); cf. *Oth* 1.1.134, 'an extravagant and wheeling stranger' (of Othello).

12 **modesty** courtesy, self-control

12–13 **I am willing** I wish

13 **it charges me** I am obliged
in manners from good manners

14 **express** reveal

15–16 **which . . . Roderigo** Sebastian's reference to his earlier disguise remains unexplained; it may be simply a means of motivating his self-revelation to Antonio, and thus to the audience, and/or a way of 'filling' the time since the shipwreck.

16 **Messaline** perhaps from Massilia, the Latin name for Marseille; Mahood notes that in the *Menaechmi* (a play about twins, and the main source of Shakespeare's *CE*) Plautus mentions the inhabitants of Marseille and Illyria

1 SP] *(Ant.), Cam*[1] 3 SP] *(Seb.), Cam*[1] 16 Roderigo] *(Rodorigo)* Messaline] *Metelin / Hanmer*

whom I know you have heard of. He left behind him myself and a sister, both born in an hour. If the heavens had been pleased, would we had so ended. But you, sir, altered that, for some hour before you took me from the breach of the sea was my sister drowned.

ANTONIO Alas the day!

SEBASTIAN A lady, sir, though it was said she much resembled me, was yet of many accounted beautiful. But though I could not with such estimable wonder over-far believe that, yet thus far I will boldly publish her: she bore a mind that envy could not but call fair. She is drowned already, sir, with salt water, though I seem to drown her remembrance again with more.

ANTONIO Pardon me, sir, your bad entertainment.

together, 'Massiliensis, Hilurios' (Plautus, 2.1.235, sig. B2[v]), translated by Warner as '*Massylia, Ilyria*'. The name also humorously recalls Messalina, notoriously licentious and corrupt wife of the Roman emperor Claudius.

17 **heard of** echoes Viola's 'I have heard my father name him [Orsino]' at 1.2.25. Famous absent fathers are something of a Shakespearean topos: cf., for example, the pedant's 'I have heard of him [Vincentio]' in *TS* 4.2.97.

18–21 **a sister . . . drowned** Sebastian's sorrow for his 'drowned' sister parallels Viola's concern for her lost brother at 1.2.3–4.

18 **in an hour** within one hour of each other (as twins); the article *an* here has the force of 'one' or 'the same' (Hope, 1.1.2a, giving this example).

19 **would . . . ended** I wish we could have died together

20 **some hour** shortly

21 **breach** breaking of waves, surf (*OED n.* 2, first occurrence)

25–6 **But . . . that** although I cannot give too much credit to that (i.e. that she was beautiful); Sebastian continues his somewhat awkward attempt to praise Viola without praising himself.

25 **estimable wonder** esteem and wonder (rhetorical figure: a form of 'hendiadys in reverse'; see p. 85)

26 **over-far** to too great an extent
publish speak of

27 **that . . . fair** that envy itself could not deny was beautiful; *envy* is a personification here, as at 5.1.54.

29 **more** more salt water (i.e. tears). Cf. Laertes on his drowned sister, 'Too much of water hast thou, poor Ophelia, / And therefore I forbid my tears', *Ham* 4.7.183–4.

30 **your bad entertainment** the inadequate hospitality you have received from me

18 an] one *F3*

SEBASTIAN O good Antonio, forgive me your trouble.

ANTONIO If you will not murder me for my love, let me be your servant.

SEBASTIAN If you will not undo what you have done, that is kill him whom you have recovered, desire it not. Fare ye well at once. My bosom is full of kindness, and I am yet so near the manners of my mother that upon the least occasion more mine eyes will tell tales of me. I am bound to the Count Orsino's court. Farewell. *Exit.*

ANTONIO

The gentleness of all the gods go with thee.
I have many enemies in Orsino's court,
Else would I very shortly see thee there.
But come what may I do adore thee so
That danger shall seem sport, and I will go. *Exit.*

2.2 *Enter* VIOLA [*as Cesario*] *and* MALVOLIO *at separate doors.*

31 **your trouble** the trouble I have caused you (possessive adjective *your* in objective sense: Blake, *Grammar*, 3.3.4.5b, giving this example)

32 **If . . . love** if you do not want me to die of a broken heart in losing you. Both Antonio here and Sebastian at 34–5 use the hyperbolic language of courtly love to express their mutual affection.

35 **recovered** restored to life

36 **kindness** tenderness

37 **yet** still

manners . . . mother womanish readiness to weep; cf. *H5* 4.6.31–2, 'And all my mother came into my eyes / And gave me up to tears.'

38 **occasion more** further occasion

tell . . . me betray my feelings (with tears)

40 **gentleness** favour

41 **enemies . . . court** The somewhat mysterious enmity between Antonio and Orsino is referred to at greater length – but still enigmatically – at 5.1.56–72, and leads to Antonio's arrest at 3.4.324–5.

43 **adore thee so** the climax of Antonio's rhetoric of 'religious' worship for Sebastian

2.2 This brief duologue is the sequel to 1.5, with Malvolio obediently but contemptuously 'returning' Olivia's ring, thereby giving Viola the opportunity for her first soliloquy, in which she reflects on the difficulties of her cross-dressed role. Capell locates the scene in '*A Street*'.

0.2 **at separate doors* Their more or less simultaneous entry suggests that Malvolio has been searching for Cesario since their separate exits in

41 many] made *F3* **2.2**] *(Scaena Secunda.)* 0.1 *as Cesario*] *Munro subst.* 0.2 *separate*] *this edn; seuerall F*

MALVOLIO Were not you e'en now with the Countess Olivia?

VIOLA Even now, sir; on a moderate pace I have since arrived but hither.

MALVOLIO She returns this ring to you, sir. [*Shows ring.*] You might have saved me my pains to have taken it away yourself. She adds, moreover, that you should put your lord into a desperate assurance she will none of him. And one thing more: that you be never so hardy to come again in his affairs, unless it be to report your lord's taking of this. [*Offers ring.*] Receive it so.

VIOLA She took the ring of me, I'll none of it.

MALVOLIO Come, sir, you peevishly threw it to her, and her will is it should be so returned. [*Throws down ring.*]

1.5 and has at last caught up with him. In many productions Malvolio rushes onstage, while Cesario walks on at *a moderate pace* (3); in others, Cesario comes on first as Sebastian is exiting, so that for a moment the two twins are simultaneously onstage, without seeing each other.

1 **e'en** (even) just

3 **Even now** Viola's repetition stresses the recentness of her encounter with Olivia in 1.5: barely a moment ago (as the audience can testify).
on at (Blake, *Grammar*, 5.4.2)
since i.e. since I was with Olivia

4 **but hither** this far

6 **to have taken** by taking

7–8 **put . . . assurance** make your lord hopelessly certain

8–9 **will . . . him** will have nothing to do with him

9 **hardy** foolhardy, bold (*OED a.* 2); not used elsewhere by Shakespeare in this sense

10 **in his affairs** on his business

11 **taking of this** i.e. this message (not this ring)
Receive it so Take the ring on these conditions. There is a potentially confusing play of deictic terms here (11, *this* = message; 12, *it* = ring), so much so that Collier glosses the phrase as 'understand it so', still referring to the message. Onstage Malvolio's gesture of offering the ring resolves any ambiguity. On deictics in the comedy, see p. 89.

12 **She . . . me** Dyce[2] is surely mistaken in emending F's 'the ring' to 'no ring' (see t.n.). Cesario goes along with Olivia's invented story (her supposed returning of Orsino's ring), presumably out of politeness and surprised curiosity.
of me from me

13–14 **you . . . returned** Malvolio, recalling Olivia's earlier reference to a *peevish messenger* who 'left this ring behind him' (1.5.293–4), elaborates the invented episode even further as a pretext for throwing the ring contemptuously to the ground.

14 **so** in the same way (as you gave it to her); or, in the following way (see 14 SD): another ambiguous deictic (see 11n.)

5 SD] *this edn* 11 SD] *Cam*[1] 12 the ring] no ring *Dyce*[2] *(Malone* 14 SD] *Douai MS, Kemble*

If it be worth stooping for, there it lies, in your eye; if not, be it his that finds it. *Exit.*

VIOLA [*Picks up ring.*]
I left no ring with her. What means this lady?
Fortune forbid my outside have not charmed her.
She made good view of me, indeed so much
That methought her eyes had lost her tongue,
For she did speak in starts, distractedly.
She loves me sure. The cunning of her passion
Invites me in this churlish messenger.
None of my lord's ring? Why, he sent her none.

14 SD The actor can make comic business out of throwing down the ring; traditionally, Malvolios let it slide down the steward's wand, so as not to have to stoop (Brown, 232).

15 **in your eye** in your sight. In Posner's 2001 RSC production Guy Henry's Malvolio pointed first to Cesario's eye, then to the ground where he had thrown the ring.

17–41 As in her other soliloquies and long asides (see 3.1.58–66; 3.4.370–3, 376–81), Viola speaks in verse, as distinct from the prose she uses in her exchange with Malvolio (unless 12 is taken as verse).

18 **forbid . . . not** a double negative, common in Early Modern English: cf. 2.1.1n.

outside appearance; cf. *AYL* 1.3.117, 'We'll have a swashing and a martial outside.'

charmed enchanted (cf. *the last enchantment*, 3.1.110, referring back to this scene)

20 The proposed emendations (see t.n.) suppose a missing monosyllable after *That*; F2's 'sure' is perhaps suggested by 22. The line as it stands, however, creates no real difficulty for the actor.

her eyes . . . tongue her ogling me had made her lose the power of speech

21 **in starts** in broken phrases (*OED* start *n.*[2] 4e, first occurrence). Broken speech was considered a sign of passion, and indeed 'start' meant a fit of passion (*OED n.*[2] 4d); cf. *1H4* 3.2.125, 'the start of spleen'. In *MND* Theseus defends emotional speakers who 'Make periods in the midst of sentences' (*MND* 5.1.96; on the passions, see p. 54). Olivia actually speaks *in starts* only after Cesario's exit, in her confused and self-interrupting soliloquy at 1.5.281–90 (see 1.5.285–7n.).

distractedly madly (*OED*, giving this example). Olivia, like other characters in this play, is affected by the amorous *furor*; cf. 1.1.14–15, 5.1.277 and notes.

22 **cunning** artfulness

23 **Invites** entices, tries to attract (*OED v.* 1d)

in by means of

24 **None . . . ring** Viola seems to be quoting not from Malvolio's message ('she will none of him', 8–9) but from Olivia's discourse to Malvolio in 1.5 ('I'll none of it', 295), despite the fact that she was not present.

17 SD] *Oxf* 20 That methought] That sure me thought *F2;* That, as methought *Dyce*[2]*;* That straight methought *Oxf (RP)*

I am the man. If it be so, as 'tis,
Poor lady, she were better love a dream.
Disguise, I see thou art a wickedness,
Wherein the pregnant enemy does much.
How easy is it for the proper false
In women's waxen hearts to set their forms.
Alas, our frailty is the cause, not we,
For such as we are made of, such we be.
How will this fadge? My master loves her dearly,
And I, poor monster, fond as much on him,

25 **I . . . man** i.e. that she loves; cf. *AYL* 3.3.2–3, 'And how Audrey, am I the man yet?' This line can be played for laughs; G.H. Lewes disapproved of the way Ellen Tree did so in 1850: 'The look with which she said "I am the man" was perfect; but that little saucy tip of her head, with the playful swagger which followed it, though they "brought down the house", appeared to us to betray a forgetfulness of [the character of] Viola' (Brown, 233).

26 **Poor lady** In Hall's 1958 Stratford production, Dorothy Tutin's Viola pronounced these words in a mischievous drawl, raising a big laugh (M. Billington, xviii).
she were better she had better, i.e. it would be better for her to (Blake, *Grammar*, 3.3.2.1b, giving this example)

27–8 Viola's apostrophe to her disguise is the only instance in Shakespeare where the heroine questions the moral validity of her cross-dressing. Her allusion to the devil in 28 implicitly compares her transvestism to Satan's disguising himself as a serpent in Genesis. For an apparently analogous passage in *Gl'ingannati* (Intronati), see pp. 62–3.

28 **pregnant enemy** the devil, or, as Johnson puts it, 'the dexterous fiend, or enemy of mankind'; *pregnant* here means 'ready', 'receptive' (*OED a.*^{2} 3d): an almost exclusively Shakespearean usage; cf. 3.1.87.

29 **proper false** handsome but deceitful (men): oxymoron. In Viola's case male beauty is literally *false*.

30 to imprint their appearance on women's receptive hearts (like the image impressed in wax by a seal). The 'women are wax' conceit is recurrent in Shakespeare: cf. *MND* 1.1.49–51, *MM* 2.4.128–9, *Luc* 1240–6 (AT).

31–2 *The emendations adopted here (see t.n.) make the overall sense become 'Alas, it is not our [i.e. women's] fault but that of our weakness, because being made of weak flesh we are weak ourselves' – with an evident allusion to the biblical expression 'the flesh is weak' (Matthew, 26.41). Viola's *we* marks a shift from the position of deceptive false man to that of member of the deceived and suffering female sex: she is at once cause and effect.

33 **fadge** turn out

34 **monster** i.e. because she is a hybrid or androgynous creature, half *man* (36) and half *woman* (38). Cf. William Harrison's complaint against his cross-dressed compatriots: 'Thus it is now come to passe, that women are become men, and men transformed into monsters' (W. Harrison, 172).
fond dote (verb: *OED v.* 2, giving this example)

29 proper false] proper-false *Malone* 31 our] *F2;* O *F* 32 made of,] *Rann (Tyrwhitt);* made, if *F;* made, ev'n *Hanmer*

And she, mistaken, seems to dote on me.
What will become of this? As I am man,
My state is desperate for my master's love;
As I am woman, now alas the day,
What thriftless sighs shall poor Olivia breathe?
O time, thou must untangle this, not I.
It is too hard a knot for me t'untie. [*Exit.*]

2.3 *Enter* SIR TOBY *and* SIR ANDREW.

SIR TOBY Approach, Sir Andrew. Not to be abed after midnight is to be up betimes, and *diluculo surgere*, thou knowst.

35 **mistaken** under a misapprehension, i.e. that I am a man (*OED* 3, giving this example)

36 **become** be the outcome (*OED* 4, giving this example)

36, 38 **As** in so far as (Blake, *Grammar*, 5.3.2.2)

36 **man** i.e. as Cesario; also alludes to the gender of the Elizabethan actor

37 **state** condition
desperate hopeless (cf. 8)
for . . . love on account of my love for my master: *master's* is an objective genitive (Blake, *Grammar*, 3.3.1.1b)

39 **thriftless** unprofitable (*OED* 2, giving this example)

41 **knot** probably a reference to the intricate Gordian knot of Greek legend – tied by King Gordius of Phrygia (cf. 3.1.50n.) and virtually impossible to undo – that Alexander the Great cut through with his sword. Cf. *Cym* 2.2.34, 'As slippery as the Gordian knot was hard'. There may also be an allusion here to the maidenhead, as in *Per* 4.2.135, 'Untied I still my virgin knot will keep' (see Carroll, 'Virgin').

2.3 This scene of revelry, parallel to 1.3, is interrupted by the 'Puritan' Malvolio, who presents himself as the play's chief upholder of rule and order. The steward's reproaches set off Maria's plan for revenge. The scene was traditionally set in the kitchen (and sometimes still is, as in Rhys Jones's 1991 RSC production), and thus became known as 'the kitchen scene'. In 1958, instead, Peter Hall placed it in Olivia's garden, even though this setting was incompatible with Maria's threat to have Malvolio 'turn you [Sir Toby] out of doors' at 73.

1 **Approach** perhaps suggesting that Sir Andrew is reluctant to join him onstage

2 **betimes** early in the morning
diluculo surgere part of the Latin proverb '*Diluculo surgere, saluberrimum est*', quoted in Lily's *Grammar* (sig. C4^{r}). Lily's gloss – 'To aryse betyme in the morning is the most wholesome thing in the worlde' – is echoed (*betimes*) by Sir Toby, who ironically turns the proverb into a justification for not going to bed. Since Lily's *Grammar* was used in all Elizabethan schools, Sir Andrew's puzzled response at 4 suggests his lack of education. F spells '*Deliculo*', perhaps indicating Sir Toby's drunken pronunciation. There may also be a pun on Italian *culo*, backside (cf. *cubiculo*, 3.2.50 and n.).

41 SD] *Rowe* 2.3] *(Scoena Tertia.)* 0.1 ANDREW] Andrew discovered *smoking / Powell MS;* ANDREW *discovered, drinking and smoking / Lacy* 2 *diluculo*] *F2 (Diliculo); Deliculo F*

SIR ANDREW Nay, by my troth I know not; but I know to be up late is to be up late.

SIR TOBY A false conclusion. I hate it as an unfilled can. To be up after midnight and to go to bed then is early, so that to go to bed after midnight is to go to bed betimes. Does not our life consist of the four elements?

SIR ANDREW Faith, so they say, but I think it rather consists of eating and drinking.

SIR TOBY Thou'rt a scholar; let us therefore eat and drink. [*Calls.*] Marian, I say, a stoup of wine.

Enter FESTE.

SIR ANDREW Here comes the fool, i'faith.

FESTE How now, my hearts? Did you never see the picture of 'we three'?

SIR TOBY Welcome, ass. Now let's have a catch.

SIR ANDREW By my troth the fool has an excellent breast.

6 **unfilled can** empty tankard

9 **four elements** fire, air, water and earth (see 1.1.25n.). In ancient and medieval science the four elements were believed to exist in every substance and to combine within the human body to form the four humours: choler, blood, phlegm and melancholy. Sir Toby may be implicitly asserting here his own sanguine humour against Sir Andrew's tendency towards melancholy.

13 Sir Toby's call for wine here is frustrated, since it is Feste who comes on, not Maria. He repeats the request at 117, but Malvolio intervenes to reprimand Maria. It may be that Sir Toby's *can* remains comically *unfilled* (6) throughout the scene, although in most productions the wine flows freely.
Marian diminutive of 'Maria'
stoup large tankard

15–16 **picture . . . 'we three'** alludes to a painting or inn sign representing two asses or loggerheads; the caption 'we three' implicated the spectator – here presumably Feste himself – as the third ass or loggerhead (i.e. fool: see pp. 10–11 and Figs 2 and 3). In Carroll's 2002 Middle Temple production, Peter Hamilton Dyer's Feste held up a dead rabbit on either side of his face; in Posner's 2001 RSC production, instead, Mark Hadfield's clown brayed like an ass.

17 **catch** round, i.e. a humorous part-song in which one voice 'catches' or follows on immediately from another; cf. 'like a singing catch, some are beginning when others are ending' (Cornwallis, sig. Ff1[r]).

18 **breast** singing voice (*OED n.* 6, giving this example; rhetorical figure: metonymy)

9 life] *Rowe*[3]; liues *F* 12, 116 Thou'rt] *(*Th'art*)* 13 SD] *Cam*[1] *subst.* Marian] *Maria / Pope* 13.1 FESTE] *Munro; Clowne F*

I had rather than forty shillings I had such a leg, and so sweet a breath to sing, as the fool has. In sooth, thou wast in very gracious fooling last night, when thou spok'st of Pigrogromitus, of the Vapians passing the equinoctial of Queubus. 'Twas very good, i'faith. I sent thee sixpence for thy leman. Hadst it?

FESTE I did impeticos thy gratility – for Malvolio's nose

19 **forty shillings** two pounds, a considerable sum in Shakespeare's day. Here and at 24 (*sixpence*) Sir Andrew counts in English currency, while Sir Toby refers to continental *ducats* at 1.3.20 (see n.).
leg i.e. for dancing (rhetorical figure: metonymy)

21 **gracious** pleasing

22–3 **Pigrogromitus . . . Queubus** Sir Andrew's recollection of the clown's apparently nonsensical fooling may be drunkenly distorted. The general theme seems to concern the heavenly bodies, with possible religious overtones. Furness sees *Pigrogromitus* as a deformation of Tetragrammaton (the ineffable four-letter name for God). Alternatively, it might be the name of an imaginary constellation, formed from *pigro* and *gomito* (Italian for 'lazy' and 'elbow'), with a probable play also on plain English 'pig'. *The Vapians* may recall 'Vesper', the evening star (or plural 'vespers', i.e. evensong), perhaps contaminated by 'vapours' (exhalations damaging to health). The *equinoctial* is presumably the celestial equator (*OED n.* 1), although Hotson suggests that 'the Equinoctial or Equator of Cubus . . . in Plato's cosmology, is the Earth' (Hotson, 157), with *Queubus* being a corruption of Plato's 'Cubus'. Alternatively it may be a deformation of 'quibble' (or of its Latin origin, *quibus*), i.e. the very kind of verbal play Sir Andrew is quoting. It might be noted that in Dutch *kwibus* means 'fool'.

24 **sixpence** in Shakespeare's day a silver coin of some value: it cost sixpence to sit in the galleries of the public theatres such as the Globe (compared to one penny to stand in the yard).
leman sweetheart. In this meaning the word was something of a 'poetic' archaism, and thus incongruous in the present context; cf. Spenser, *FQ*, 3.8.40, 'To be his Leman and his Lady trew' (*FQ*, 165). It became instead synonymous with 'whore', as in Nashe, 'Lemmans this yeere shal be plenty, insomuch that many shall use them to bedward' (Nashe, *Prognostication*, A4^{v}), with a pun on 'lemon', which may also be present here (cf. Kökeritz, 123; Williams, 799–800). In any case, no further reference is made to Feste's supposed girlfriend (but cf. 4.2.71–9n.). As Leman Street is a road in East London (AT), this may also be one of several 'hidden' allusions to the capital (cf. 3.3.39n.).
Hadst it? Did you receive it?

25 **impeticos** pocket (verb): nonce-word compounded from the verb 'impocket' and the noun 'petticoat', i.e. the long coat that fools usually wore, with a possible echo of 'impetigo', an unpleasant pustular skin disease. In other words, Feste put the sixpence for his sweetheart straight into the pocket of his own motley coat.
gratility a deformation of 'gratuity'

16 'we three'] *Cam;* we three *F* 24 leman] *Theobald;* Lemon *F* 25 impeticos] impeticoat *Steevens (Johnson)* gratility] gratuity *Steevens*^{2}

is no whipstock, my lady has a white hand and the Myrmidons are no bottle-ale houses.

SIR ANDREW Excellent! Why, this is the best fooling, when all is done. Now a song.

SIR TOBY [*to Feste*] Come on, there is sixpence for you. Let's have a song.

SIR ANDREW [*to Feste*] There's a testril of me too. If one knight give a –

FESTE Would you have a love-song, or a song of good life?

25–7 **for . . . houses** Feste's obscure explanation of why he impeticosed Sir Andrew's gratility (*for* = because) has usually been taken as pure nonsense. Aguecheek's *best fooling* (28) may suggest, instead, that there is an overall meaning, namely that the clown needs money, and neither Malvolio nor Olivia gives him any.

26 **whipstock** whip handle (*OED* 1a), possibly implying that the mean and puritanical Malvolio is not easily manipulated into giving money (NB); or, whipping-post (*OED* 2), perhaps implying again that money is not going to be easily beaten out of him
my lady i.e. Olivia, not Feste's *leman*
white hand a sign of her nobility; also, perhaps, an indication that she is not going to sully herself by giving filthy lucre to Feste (NB)

27 **Myrmidons** in Homer's *Iliad*, the followers of Achilles at the siege of Troy (the 'mangled Myrmidons' of Shakespeare's *TC* 5.5.33). The term also had the slang sense of 'unscrupulously faithful' followers or hirelings (*OED* 3), the likely meaning here, presumably alluding to Feste himself as faithful servant of the *lady* Olivia. The comparison with *bottle-ale houses* (27) suggests that Feste may also be punning on 'Mermaid Inn', the famous London tavern where Shakespeare supposedly drank with Ben Jonson.
bottle-ale houses low-class taverns; cf. *2H4* 2.4.123, 'you bottle-ale rascal' (of Pistol). Feste is implying that he has expensive tastes in drink, hence his need for another *gratility* from his companions.

30 **there is sixpence** In Carroll's 2002 Middle Temple production, Ian Talbot's Sir Toby got Angus Wright's Sir Andrew to give Feste the tip on his behalf.

32 **testril** sixpence: a corruption of 'tester', slang word for this coin (*OED*, first occurrence). As usual, Sir Andrew imitates Sir Toby's gesture.

33 ***give a –** In F the suspended indefinite article ends a justified line of type, and it is possible that the compositor unwittingly omitted the rest of the sentence in the following line. It is unlikely that Sir Andrew simply comes to a halt. F2 adds a hyphen, probably intended as a dash indicating an interruption. If this is taken as an incomplete line of dialogue, one would expect it to continue with further reference to a sixpence or testril. It may be, rather, that Aguecheek is beginning a song, rapidly quashed by Feste.

34–5 **song . . . life** drinking song. Sir Andrew at 37 seems to understand instead a 'song about virtuous living', which does not appeal to him.

30, 32 SDs] *Oxf* 33 a –] *F2;* a *F*

SIR TOBY A love-song, a love-song.
SIR ANDREW Ay, ay. I care not for good life.
FESTE (*Sings.*)
O mistress mine, where are you roaming?
O stay and hear, your true love's coming,
That can sing both high and low.
Trip no further, pretty sweeting;
Journeys end in lovers meeting,
Every wise man's son doth know.
SIR ANDREW Excellent good, i'faith.
SIR TOBY Good, good.
FESTE [*Sings.*]
What is love? 'Tis not hereafter,
Present mirth hath present laughter.
What's to come is still unsure.
In delay there lies no plenty,
Then come kiss me, sweet and twenty.
Youth's a stuff will not endure.
SIR ANDREW A mellifluous voice, as I am true knight.

38–43 **O . . . know** It is not certain that the words of Feste's song, like his other songs, are by Shakespeare, and it is not known whether the music was that of the instrumental version by Thomas Morley published in 1599; see Appendix 3.

40 **high and low** i.e. in either pitch or volume. Cf. Viola's claim, 'I can sing . . . many sorts of music' (1.2.54n., 55n.); Feste appears to take her place as versatile singer.

41 **Trip** Go
sweeting sweetheart, darling

43 **Every . . . son** every fool; an ironic allusion to the proverb 'A wise man often has foolish children' (Dent, M421)

46–51 For the words and music of this song, see Appendix 3.

48 **still** always

49 **plenty** profit

50 **sweet and twenty** not a literal reference to the beloved's age but a conventional term of endearment; cf. 'his little wanton wagtails: his sweet and twenties . . . as hee himselfe used commonly to call them' (Brewer, sig. C4v).

51 **stuff** material

52 **mellifluous** sweetly flowing. In *Palladis Tamia* Francis Meres praises the 'mellifluous & hony-tongued *Shakespeare*' (Meres, fol. 281v): could this be a self-ironical echo?
am true knight The indefinite article ('a') is often omitted by Shakespeare when the noun acts as a complement (here, of the verb *am*: see Blake, *Grammar*, 3.3.4.3d, giving this example).

38 SP] *Munro; not in F; Clo. / Capell* SD] *(Clowne sings.)* 46 SD] *Cam[1]* 52 true] a true *Douai MS, Rowe*

SIR TOBY A contagious breath.

SIR ANDREW Very sweet and contagious, i'faith.

SIR TOBY To hear by the nose it is dulcet in contagion! But shall we make the welkin dance indeed? Shall we rouse the night-owl in a catch that will draw three souls out of one weaver? Shall we do that?

SIR ANDREW An you love me, let's do't. I am dog at a catch.

FESTE By'r Lady, sir, and some dogs will catch well.

SIR ANDREW Most certain. Let our catch be 'Thou knave'.

FESTE 'Hold thy peace, thou knave', knight? I shall be constrained in't to call thee knave, knight.

SIR ANDREW 'Tis not the first time I have constrained

53 **contagious breath** catching voice. Less poetically, the phrase also implies halitosis (*contagious* = 'foul', *OED* 5c), making contradictory nonsense of Sir Andrew's *sweet and contagious* at 54. There may also be a further reference here to the plague, which was popularly thought to be transmitted through the breath (cf. 1.1.19n.).

55 **To . . . contagion** to judge by hearing and smell, Feste's breath is sweet, because it carries his contagiously sweet voice; alternatively, it is catching only in the sense that it spreads foulness. There is a possible allusion to venereal contagion, particularly syphilis, which could cause the erosion of the nose.
dulcet sweet (especially of sounds, but here extended to smell)

56 **welkin** sky

57 **three souls** a reference to the ancient theory that living beings were made up of three souls or principles (the vital, the sensitive and the rational)

58 **weaver** This may playfully suggest that the *three souls* (57) are 'woven' together. Weavers had specifically musical associations, being reputed to sing as they worked – especially psalms, since many of them were Puritans: cf. *1H4* 2.4.126–7, 'I would I were a weaver; I could sing psalms, or anything.'

59 **An** if
dog at good at (proverbial catchphrase: Dent, D506); cf. Launce talking to his dog Crab in *TGV* 4.4.12–13, 'to be, as it were, a dog at all things'.

61 **By'r lady** by Our Lady (the Virgin Mary): an oath
some . . . well i.e. some dogs will catch a ball or prey well; cf. *MA* 5.2.11–12, 'Thy wit is as quick as the greyhound's mouth, it catches.'

62–4 **Let . . . 'Thou knave'** The round they are about to sing has them comically repeat the phrases *hold thy peace*, telling each other to shut up (cf. Feste's comment at 69), and *thou knave*, insulting each other.

65 **constrained** compelled

66–7 **'Tis . . . knave** Sir Andrew may simply be trying to say that he has often sung this round, but he succeeds in implying that he is a quarrelsome *knave* (cf. 1.3.28).

59 dog] a dog *F3* 64 knight?] *Capell;* knight. *F*

one to call me knave. Begin, fool. It begins 'Hold thy peace'.

FESTE I shall never begin if I hold my peace.

SIR ANDREW Good, i'faith. Come, begin. *They sing the catch.*

Enter MARIA.

MARIA What a caterwauling do you keep here! If my lady have not called up her steward Malvolio and bid him turn you out of doors, never trust me.

SIR TOBY My lady's a Cathayan, we are politicians, Malvolio's a Peg-o'-Ramsey and [*singing*] 'Three merry

69 **hold my peace** Feste pretends to mistake the opening words of the song for the command 'keep quiet'. Rubinstein, 189, suggests a pun on *piece*, Elizabethan slang for 'penis'.

70 SD For the music to the round 'Hold thy peace', see Appendix 3.

71 **caterwauling** a shrill howling or wailing noise made by cats before mating or fighting

74–6 **My . . . 'Three . . . we'** Sir Toby adopts Feste's mode of drunken and apparently nonsensical free association (cf. 25–7).

74 **Cathayan** literally, a person from Cathay, the ancient Mongolian name for China, but which Shakespeare's contemporaries believed to be a separate geographical entity (Billings). Sir Toby appears to use the word in a derogatory sense. Steevens glosses 'thief' or 'sharper', a supposed quality of the Chinese (cf. *OED*'s 'a man of Cathay or China . . . a thief, scoundrel, blackguard', giving this example). It is unlikely, however, that Sir Toby would call Olivia a thief. In *MW* – the only other Shakespearean occurrence – Page's 'I will not believe such a Cataian' (2.1.126) implies the meaning 'liar', possibly deriving from the mendacious accounts of Cathay by Mandeville and other travellers (Billings). The association with *lady* may recall Ariosto's *Orlando furioso*, where Angelica is described as 'the Ladie faire, / That of Cataya was undoubted haire [= heir]' (Ariosto, 147), especially since Angelica is described as being 'Full of deceit' in Boiardo's *Orlando innamorato* (Boiardo, sig. $B4^{r}$). Toby may be implying, more blandly, that Olivia exaggerates, and so her bark is worse than her bite. The first syllable of the word (pronounced 'cat') probably plays on *caterwauling* (71).
politicians deceitful schemers. The word invariably has a derogatory meaning in Shakespeare, connoting self-serving 'Machiavellian' deviousness: cf. Hotspur's 'this vile politician Bolingbroke . . . this king of smiles' (*1H4* 1.3.238–43). There is thus a semantic link between *Cathayan* and *politician*, two kinds of liar. Cf. 2.5.157, 3.2.30.

75 **Peg-o'-Ramsey** There are two ballads to tunes of this title. The first, 'A Merry Jest of John Tomson and Jakaman his Wife . . . to the Tune of Peg of Ramsay', entered into the

70 SD] *(Catch sung)* 74 Cathayan] *(Catayan), Oxf* 75 o'-Ramsey] *Oxf;* a-ramsie *F* 75–111 SDs] Cam^{1}

men be we'. Am not I consanguineous? Am I not of her blood? Tilly-vally, lady! [*Sings.*] 'There dwelt a man in Babylon, lady, lady.'

FESTE Beshrew me, the knight's in admirable fooling.

SIR ANDREW Ay, he does well enough if he be disposed, and so do I too. He does it with a better grace, but I do it more natural.

SIR TOBY [*Sings.*]

O'the twelfth day of December –

MARIA For the love o'God, peace.

Stationers' Register in 1586, narrates the story of a jealous wife who ends up wearing – intriguingly, with reference to this play – 'the yellow hose' (i.e. the trousers), prompting the man's doleful refrain, 'Give me my yellow Hose againe' (cf. 2.5.149, 162, 166, 193; 3.2.68–9; 3.4.15.1, 45–7; 5.1.332). The second ballad, 'Bonny Peggy Ramsey', first published in Playford, 5.139–40, is a bawdy tale of a lusty lass who, in order to make her water-mill work in times of drought, 'Up she pull'd her Petticoats and piss'd into the Dam' (cf. 2.5.86n.; see Ungerer, 98–9). In this case, Malvolio is implicitly compared to another 'loose woman', like *Jezebel* (cf. 2.5.38n.).

76 **consanguineous** related by blood (to Olivia: cf. *of her blood*, 76–7; *OED* 1, first occurrence)

77 **Tilly-vally** nonsense (equivalent to 'fiddlesticks!': *OED*, giving this example); cf. *2H4* 2.4.82.
lady probably addressed scornfully to Maria, rather than being – as many editors assume – a mocking echo of Maria's *my lady* at 71, alluding to Olivia

77–8 **'There . . . lady.'** The opening line and refrain of the popular ballad 'Constant Susan', which tells the story of Susanna and the Elders from the Apocrypha: another tale of a supposedly 'loose' woman (cf. 75n., 2.5.38n.), wrongfully accused of unchasteness by the Elders. Wilson (Cam[1]) argues that Sir Toby implies a parallel with Maria and the men in this scene. The same song is quoted by Sir Hugh Evans in Q1 of *MW*. For the music, see Appendix 3.

79 **Beshrew me** curse me: a mild imprecation (discourse marker)

82 **natural** spontaneously. Sir Andrew unwittingly confesses his stupidity, since *natural* as noun meant 'idiot': cf. 1.3.27n.

83 The opening line of another song, possibly the ballad on the battle of Musselburgh Field, begins 'On the tenth day of December' in Child, 3.378–9, but in a 1665 version it begins as here (Kittredge). Sir Toby may, however, be drunkenly misquoting 'The Twelve Days of Christmas', which – appropriately enough in this play – traditionally begins with 'On the twelfth day of Christmas', i.e. on Twelfth Night. Many modern productions of the play adopt the music for the latter song.

77 Tilly-vally, lady!] *Oxf*[1]; tilly vally. Ladie, *F;* tilly vally. Lady! *F2* 83 O'] *Cam*[1] *(Walker); O F* December –] *Theobald; December. F* 84.1 MALVOLIO] Malvolio *in nightgown (with lighted candle.) / Powell MS*

Enter MALVOLIO.

MALVOLIO My masters, are you mad or what are you? Have you no wit, manners nor honesty but to gabble like tinkers at this time of night? Do ye make an alehouse of my lady's house that ye squeak out your coziers' catches without any mitigation or remorse of voice? Is there no respect of place, persons nor time in you?

SIR TOBY We did keep time, sir, in our catches. Sneck up!

MALVOLIO Sir Toby, I must be round with you. My lady bade me tell you that though she harbours you as her kinsman she's nothing allied to your disorders. If you can separate yourself and your misdemeanours, you are welcome to the house; if not, an it would please you to take leave of her, she is very willing to bid you farewell.

SIR TOBY [*Sings.*]

Farewell, dear heart, since I must needs be gone.

86 **wit** intelligence
honesty decency (*OED* 2)

86–7 **gabble like tinkers** proverbial phrase; itinerant tinkers were held in low repute as a species of noisy vagrant; cf. similar expressions such as 'drunk as a tinker' (equally appropriate to this scene; *OED* tinker *n.* 1a); *gabble* = chatter

88 **squeak out** sing in a squeaky voice (*OED* squeak *v.* 3a, giving this example)
coziers' catches cobblers' songs. Cobblers enjoyed much the same unenviable reputation as tinkers (cf. 86–7n.).

89 **without . . . voice** without any lowering or interruption of your loud singing (*OED* mitigation 1, *OED* remorse 3c, both giving this example)

91–2 **Sneck up!** Go hang (yourself)! (*OED* snick *v.*[1] b, giving this example). Cf. John Taylor the Water-Poet's *Praise of Hempseed*: '*Snickup*, which is in English Gallow-grasse' (J. Taylor, 66).

93 **round** plain, possibly with an unwitting musical pun on Sir Toby's *catches* (91)

94 **harbours** lodges

95 **nothing allied** in no way favourable
disorders irregular behaviour (*OED* disorder *n.* 2b, giving this example)

97 **an** if

100–10 an adapted version of the first two stanzas of a ballad published in Jones (sigs D4^v–E1^r). The original stanzas, together with Jones's music, are given in Appendix 3. The men conflate the two stanzas into one and change the words so as to turn the song into a comic dialogue, in which the protagonist becomes Sir Toby (*I*) rather than the parting beloved (*you*).

97 an] *(*and*)*

MARIA Nay, good Sir Toby.

FESTE [*Sings.*]

His eyes do show his days are almost done.

MALVOLIO Is't even so?

SIR TOBY [*Sings.*]

But I will never die.

FESTE [*Sings.*]

Sir Toby, there you lie.

MALVOLIO This is much credit to you.

SIR TOBY [*Sings.*]

Shall I bid him go?

FESTE [*Sings.*]

What an if you do?

SIR TOBY [*Sings.*]

Shall I bid him go, and spare not?

FESTE [*Sings.*]

O no, no, no, no, you dare not.

SIR TOBY [*to Feste*] Out o'tune, sir – ye lie. [*to Malvolio*] Art any more than a steward? Dost thou think because thou art virtuous there shall be no more cakes and ale?

103 **Is't even so** i.e. is this how you respond to my warning

105 **there you lie** in this you are lying. In the 1789 Drury Lane production, Sir Toby was made to fall drunkenly on *never die* (104) and Feste delivered the line standing over him, thereby equivocating on the meaning of *lie* (see t.n.). In Posner's 2001 RSC production Mark Hadfield's Feste directed *you lie* towards Malvolio.

106 **you** this is presumably plural, addressed to all present

111 **Out o'tune** wrong: a response to Feste's sung accusation *you dare not*

112 **Art . . . steward** Sir Toby rapidly changes target, putting Malvolio in his place, as if in anticipation of the latter's dream of social promotion (2.5.21–69). The omission of the subject pronoun *thou* is quite frequent in Shakespeare, especially in questions (Blake, *Grammar*, 6.3.1.2, giving this example), but here it accentuates the use of the second person singular verb form (*Art*), so as to underline that Sir Toby is addressing an inferior.

113 **cakes and ale** the food and drink traditionally associated with church festivities such as saint's days and holy days (like Twelfth Night), and as such particularly unpalatable to ceremony-hating 'Puritans' like Malvolio (cf. 130–2). In his *Anatomy of Abuses* the Puritan Philip Stubbes

104 die.] die. *Falls down singing / Harrison;* die. *Falls / Powell MS* 105 lie.] lie! *standing over him / Powell MS* 111 tune] time *Theobald*

FESTE Yes, by Saint Anne, and ginger shall be hot i'th' mouth too.

SIR TOBY Thou'rt i'th' right. [*to Malvolio*] Go, sir, rub your chain with crumbs. – A stoup of wine, Maria.

MALVOLIO Mistress Mary, if you prized my lady's favour at anything more than contempt, you would not give means for this uncivil rule. She shall know of it, by this hand. *Exit.*

MARIA Go shake your ears.

SIR ANDREW 'Twere as good a deed as to drink when

attacks 'Church-ales' which result in 'swilling and gulling, night and daye, till [the parishioners] bee as drunke as Rattes and as blockishe as beastes' (Stubbes, sig. 95[r]). The phrase *cakes and ale* – following this play – has become proverbial for 'a good time'.

114 **Saint Anne** the mother of the Virgin Mary: a common oath, perhaps intended here – because it is of Catholic origin – as a provocation to the 'Puritan' Malvolio
ginger used to spice ale and cultivated for its supposed aphrodisiac powers. 'Ginger heateth and drieth in the third degree . . . prouoking Venerie', affirms Gerard, 55; cf. *WT* 4.3.43.

115 Ard[2] and some other editions have Feste exit on this line, on the grounds that he takes no further part in the scene, and that Maria's 'and let the fool make a third' (168–90) implies his absence. The clown's exit at this point, however, is unmotivated, and Maria's phrase could equally well be addressed to the other two in Feste's presence. What to make of his silence is partly a matter of directorial choice: in Hall's 1958 Stratford production he fell asleep.

116–17 **Go . . . crumbs** go and clean your chain of office (as steward): another reminder of Malvolio's lowly status. On this method of cleaning the chain, cf. 'the chippings of the Buttry fly after him, / To scowre his gold Chaine' (Webster, *Malfi*, 3.2, sig. G2[v]).

118 **Mistress Mary** Malvolio is calling Maria to order, reminding her of her role as Olivia's waiting-gentlewoman. In Posner's 2001 RSC production, Guy Henry's Malvolio pointed to the ground, demanding that Alison Fiske's Maria come across stage to him: she obeyed.

119–20 **give . . . rule** provide the drink that encourages this unruly behaviour (*OED* rule *n.* 13a, giving this example)

121 **by this hand** In Gielgud's 1955 Stratford production Laurence Olivier raised his hand on this line, causing his pants to fall down from under his nightshirt (Brown, 237).

122 **Go . . . ears** i.e. like an ass (proverbial: Dent, E16)

123 **as good . . . drink** proverbial phrase (Dent, D183.1); cf. *1H4* 2.1.28, 2.2.21–2; 'Sir Andrew's foolish amplification makes nonsense of it' (Ard[2]).

114 Saint] *(S.), Rowe* 116 SD] *Mahood* 121 SD] *Exit* MALVOLIO, *followed by the Clown, mocking him. / Kemble*

man's a-hungry to challenge him the field and then to break promise with him and make a fool of him.

SIR TOBY Do't, knight. I'll write thee a challenge, or I'll deliver thy indignation to him by word of mouth.

MARIA Sweet Sir Toby, be patient for tonight. Since the youth of the count's was today with my lady, she is much out of quiet. For Monsieur Malvolio, let me alone with him. If I do not gull him into a nayword and make him a common recreation, do not think I have wit enough to lie straight in my bed. I know I can do it.

SIR TOBY Possess us, possess us. Tell us something of him.

MARIA Marry, sir, sometimes he is a kind of Puritan.

SIR ANDREW O, if I thought that, I'd beat him like a dog.

124 **a-hungry** 'the prefix [a-]. . . was probably taken as emphatic' (*OED*, giving this example)
the field to a duel. Sir Andrew considers it the height of wit to break the pledge of a challenge, thus confirming his quarrelsome nature (see note to 66–7) and anticipating his cowardly terror of duelling (in 3.4).

129 **of the count's** double genitive; cf. Blake, *Grammar*, 3.3.2.2; Hope, 1.1.4d

130 **out of quiet** agitated
Monsieur This aping of 'the French custom of prefixing the title to designations of office' (*OED* 1c) mocks Malvolio's self-importance, and especially his pompous sense of *his* office. Cf. 'Monsieur the Nice', *LLL* 5.2.325; 'Mounsieur Cobweb', *MND* 4.1.10.
let leave (*OED v.*[1] 18b, giving this example)

131 ***gull . . . nayword** trick him into making his name a byword for stupidity; cf. 'have a nay-word', *MW* 2.2.118–19, 5.2.5. Rowe's emendation is surely correct, even if some editions, such as Riverside, defend F's 'an ayword'.

132 **a common recreation** an object of sport or entertainment

132–3 **wit . . . bed** This sounds like a proverb (cf. 1.3.72–3) but is not present in Tilley or Dent.

134 **Possess us** let us in on your plan

136 **Puritan** a somewhat ambiguous term of abuse: 'Puritans', as their opponents dubbed them, were reformist Protestants who wished to complete the Reformation with further 'purification' of the church, but the word came to be applied more generally to self-righteous moralists. How literally we are to take Malvolio's supposed 'Puritanism' is a moot point: Maria's gibe at 142 places its seriousness in doubt, but at the same time there are other negative allusions to Puritan ideology in the play, notably Sir Andrew's reference at 3.2.30 to the fanatical Brownists (see pp. 22–3).

131 a nayword] *Rowe;* an ayword *F* 134 SP] *Sir And / Dyce*[2]

SIR TOBY What, for being a Puritan? Thy exquisite reason, dear knight?

SIR ANDREW I have no exquisite reason for't, but I have reason good enough.

MARIA The devil a Puritan that he is, or anything constantly but a time-pleaser; an affectioned ass that cons state without book and utters it by great swathes; the best persuaded of himself, so crammed, as he thinks, with excellencies that it is his grounds of faith that all that look on him love him, and on that vice in him will my revenge find notable cause to work.

SIR TOBY What wilt thou do?

MARIA I will drop in his way some obscure epistles of love, wherein by the colour of his beard, the shape of

138 **exquisite** far-fetched, abstruse (*OED a.* 1a, giving this example). Mahood notes that this word, particularly difficult to pronounce when drunk, is given to the equally drunken Cassio in *Oth* 2.3.18.

140–1 Sir Andrew clearly does not understand Sir Toby's *exquisite*, but in any case finds it self-evident that a Puritan should be beaten like a dog.

142 **The devil . . . is** Maria casts doubt on the seriousness or sincerity of Malvolio's supposed Puritanism, despite the fact that she herself calls him a *Puritan* at 138: his pious severity is just one pose among others, and will be opportunistically abandoned. In doing so, Maria unleashes an appropriately anti-puritanical oath.

***devil** F's 'diu'll' may imply a monosyllabic pronunciation of the word.

constantly consistently (*OED adv.* 3b, giving this example)

143 **time-pleaser** time-server or opportunist; cf. *Cor* 3.1.45.

affectioned affected (*OED* affection *n.* 13)

143–4 **cons . . . book** learns haughty behaviour by heart (*OED* state *n.* 19b); *without book* is a proverbial idiom (Dent, B532): cf. 1.3.25. Malvolio, like Cesario at 1.5.169, is compared to an actor 'conning' his part.

144 **utters . . . swathes** speaks it (his haughty part) in great quantities. *Swathes*, swaths or 'swarths' (F) are literally rows of grass cut down by the mower's scythe (*OED* swath 3a); cf. *TC* 5.5.25, 'Fall down before him, like the mower's swath'.

144–5 **the best . . . himself** thinking very highly of himself

146 **excellencies** excellent qualities (*OED* 2a, first occurrence)

his . . . faith his utter conviction

147 **vice** moral defect. The vice was the representative of evil in the medieval morality play; cf. 4.2.123n.

150, 159 **epistles, letters** The fact that both Maria and Sir Toby refer to letters in the plural suggests that more than one may have been originally intended.

142 devil] *(*diu'll*)* 144 swathes] *(*swarths*), Mahood;* swaths *Collier*

his leg, the manner of his gait, the expressure of his eye, forehead and complexion he shall find himself most feelingly personated. I can write very like my lady your niece. On a forgotten matter we can hardly make distinction of our hands.

SIR TOBY Excellent, I smell a device.

SIR ANDREW I have't in my nose too.

SIR TOBY He shall think by the letters that thou wilt drop that they come from my niece, and that she's in love with him.

MARIA My purpose is indeed a horse of that colour.

SIR ANDREW And your horse now would make him an ass.

MARIA As I doubt not.

SIR ANDREW O, 'twill be admirable.

MARIA Sport royal, I warrant you. I know my physic will work with him. I will plant you two – and let the fool make a third – where he shall find the letter. Observe his construction of it. For this night, to bed and dream on the event. Farewell. *Exit.*

152 **expressure** expression (*OED* b, first occurrence)

154 **feelingly** appropriately, accurately (*OED* 2, giving this example)
personated acted (*OED v.* 4a); like 'cons' (143), a theatrical term

155–6 **On . . . hands** when we no longer remember what it refers to, we can barely tell our handwriting apart

157 **smell a device** suspect a trick (*OED* device 6, giving this example); cf. *AYL* 1.1.144–5, 'entrap thee by some treacherous device'.

162 **a horse . . . colour** one of that nature: a proverbial phrase (Dent, H665)

165 Maria puns on as/ass, thereby slyly insulting Sir Andrew ([you] ass, I doubt not). Cf. *Ham* 5.2.43, 'And many such like "as", sir, of great charge'.

167 **Sport royal** a sport worthy of kings, with reference to hunting
physic medicine

168–9 **let . . . third** Cf. *we three* (15–16 and n.). On this line said in Feste's presence, cf. 115n. There may be a pun here on third/turd; cf. Dr Caius in *MW* 3.3.220, 'I shall make-a the turd'; cf. Kökeritz, 150; Partridge, 207.

170 **construction** interpretation (*OED* 7); from 'construe'

171 **event** outcome (*OED* 3a)

152 gait] *(*gate*), Johnson* 165 As] *this edn;* Asse *F*

SIR TOBY Good night, Penthesilea.

SIR ANDREW Before me, she's a good wench.

SIR TOBY She's a beagle true bred, and one that adores me. What o'that?

SIR ANDREW I was adored once too.

SIR TOBY Let's to bed, knight. Thou hadst need send for more money.

SIR ANDREW If I cannot recover your niece, I am a foul way out.

SIR TOBY Send for money, knight. If thou hast her not i'th' end, call me cut.

SIR ANDREW If I do not, never trust me, take it how you will.

SIR TOBY Come, come, I'll go burn some sack; 'tis too late to go to bed now. Come, knight, come, knight. *Exeunt.*

172 **Penthesilea** Queen of the Amazons, adversary of Achilles in the Trojan wars (Ovid, *Met.*, 12.677, fol. 157[r]): both an admiring reference to Maria's combative spirit and a probable ironical allusion to the boy actor's diminutive size (cf. 1.5.199n.).

173 **Before me** a mild oath in substitution of 'before God'

174 **beagle** small hunting dog: a further allusion to Maria's size and to her spirit in 'pursuing' Malvolio; one of several hunting and blood sports metaphors for the gulling plot (cf. 2.5.6–7, 8–9, 19–20; 3.1.116–17; 3.4.133–4, and notes).

175 **What o'that?** so what of it? – a piece of bravado implying that he is quite used to being adored by women

176 This poignant glimpse into Sir Andrew's sentimental life is rapidly dismissed by Sir Toby, anxious to get back to business (i.e. *money*, 178).

177–8 **Thou . . . money** For Sir Toby 'milking' of Sir Andrew as a source of income, cf. 1.2.21n., 3.2.52–3n. and 3.4.282n.

179 **recover** obtain (*OED v.*[1] 6a)

179–80 **I . . . out** I am in trouble, because out of pocket (literally, I am lost in the mire; cf. *LLL* 5.2.907, 'ways be foul'). Sir Andrew needs to *recover* the money he has invested in his courtship of Olivia: this suggests the nature of his continuing interest in the countess.

182 **cut** short-tailed or gelded horse (*OED n.*[2] 30); an idiomatic term of abuse (Dent, C940). Sir Toby's invitation reintroduces the theme of castration (cf. 1.2.59n.), perhaps with implied reference to Sir Andrew, who will be *cut* or deprived of his money. Malvolio unwittingly spells out the word at 2.5.86.

183–4 **If . . . will** Sir Andrew promises to call Sir Toby a *cut*; 'never trust me' and 'take it how you will' are both proverbial idioms (Dent, T558.1, T27).

185 **burn some sack** warm and spice some white Spanish wine (equivalent to modern sherry)

2.4 *Enter* ORSINO, VIOLA [*as Cesario*], CURIO *and others.*

ORSINO
Give me some music. Now good morrow, friends.
Now good Cesario, but that piece of song,
That old and antic song we heard last night:
Methought it did relieve my passion much,
More than light airs and recollected terms
Of these most brisk and giddy-paced times.
Come, but one verse.

CURIO He is not here, so please your lordship, that should sing it.

ORSINO Who was it?

CURIO Feste the jester, my lord, a fool that the Lady

2.4 This scene is dedicated principally to the long exchange between Orsino and Cesario on the theme of love, and contains the comedy's most extended play on Viola-as-Cesario's androgyny, together with her veiled confession of love to the duke, which he fails to understand. The scene opens with a musical prelude that is also a thematic and stylistic *echo* (21) of 1.1. Rowe locates it in '*The Palace*'.

1–20 Cf. 1.1.1–15.

2 **but** just (i.e. precisely that song)

3 **antic** àntic; strange, fantastic (cf. Hamlet's 'antic disposition', *Ham* 1.5.170), with a possible play on 'antique', synonym for *old* (see t.n.)

4 **passion** suffering, due to unrequited love; cf. 94.

5 **light airs** i.e. sprightly (modern) tunes, in contrast to *old and antic* songs (3); cf. 'these and all other kinds of light music . . . are by a generall name called ayres' (T. Morley, 180). 'Air' was a fashionable term in this period: cf. Dowland (1597) and Jones (1600).
recollected terms affected phrases; for *recollected*, *OED* (recollected *ppl. a.*[1] 1) – giving this as sole occurrence – glosses 'Meaning uncertain', and records hypotheses such as 'refined' and 'studied'. Orsino disdains the artificial lyrics as well as the lively music of the new *airs*.

6 **brisk** quickly passing (*OED a.* 2e, first occurrence)
giddy-paced pacèd: so rapidly changeable as to cause dizziness

11–12 **Feste . . . delight in** the only reference in the play to the name of Feste, perhaps coined to form a rhyming jingle with *jester*. He is described here as an 'old' clown who has been part of Olivia's household for more than a generation, having survived her father (and brother). A dead man's delight in his jester is something of a Shakespearean topos: cf. the countess on the clown in *AW* 4.5.63–6, 'My lord that's gone made himself much sport out of him'; the theme is varied in Hamlet's recollections of Yorick, the dead King's dead jester (*Ham* 5.1.174–84).

2.4] *(Scena Quarta.)* 0.1 ORSINO] *Mahood; Duke F* *as Cesario*] *Munro subst.* 3 antic] *(*Anticke*), Cam*[1]*;* antique *Pope*

Olivia's father took much delight in. He is about the house.

ORSINO

Seek him out, and play the tune the while.

Music plays. [*Exit Curio.*]

[*to Viola*] Come hither, boy. If ever thou shalt love,
In the sweet pangs of it remember me;
For such as I am all true lovers are,
Unstaid and skittish in all motions else
Save in the constant image of the creature
That is beloved. How dost thou like this tune?

VIOLA

It gives a very echo to the seat
Where love is throned.

ORSINO Thou dost speak masterly.

My life upon't, young though thou art, thine eye
Hath stayed upon some favour that it loves.
Hath it not, boy?

VIOLA A little, by your favour.

ORSINO

What kind of woman is't?

VIOLA Of your complexion.

ORSINO

She is not worth thee then. What years, i'faith?

17 **such . . . are** all true lovers are like me

18 **Unstaid and skittish** changeable and fickle: virtually synonyms, by way of emphasis
motions else other emotions

19 **constant** stable (of *image*); faithful (of the lover; *OED a.* 2): in this second, attributive, sense, cf. *MA* 2.3.62–4, 'Men were deceivers ever . . .To one thing constant never.'

21–2 It is a perfect expression of the sentiments of the heart, seat of love.

22 **masterly** with expertise

24 **stayed upon** lingered over
favour face (*OED n.* 9b)

25 **by . . . favour** by your leave; with a pun on *favour* (= face) at 24. Viola's eye has indeed *stayed upon* a face, Orsino's.

26 **complexion** colouring and appearance of the face (as a reflection of temperament; *OED n.* 4a)

14 Seek] Go, seek *Capell* SD *Exit Curio*] *Pope* 15, 67 SDs] *Collier*[3] 18 motions] notions *Warburton*

VIOLA

About your years, my lord.

ORSINO

Too old, by heaven. Let still the woman take
An elder than herself; so wears she to him,
So sways she level in her husband's heart.
For, boy, however we do praise ourselves,
Our fancies are more giddy and unfirm,
More longing wavering, sooner lost and worn
Than women's are.

VIOLA I think it well, my lord.

ORSINO

Then let thy love be younger than thyself,
Or thy affection cannot hold the bent;
For women are as roses, whose fair flower
Being once displayed doth fall that very hour.

29 **still** always

30 **An . . . herself** Coleridge (1.96n.) detects an ironic autobiographical reference here to Shakespeare's own supposedly unhappy marriage to 'an elder', Anne Hathaway; Orsino advises Cesario to do the opposite.
so . . . him so she adapts herself to him, like clothes to the wearer

31 **So . . . level** thus she exerts a consistent influence; with a pun on *sways*: holds sway (cf. 2.5.106), but also swings, like a pendulum, whereby *level* comes to mean 'in perfect balance', implying that a man's heart is *giddy and unfirm* (33) until stabilized by a woman's influence. *Sway* is a recurrent thematic word, suggesting the comedy's concern with interpersonal, and especially inter-gender, 'power relations'; cf. 4.1.51 and 4.3.17.

33 **fancies** inclinations, desires
giddy dizzy: cf. 6.
unfirm unsteady (*OED* 2, sole occurrence)

34 **longing wavering** yearningly indecisive; the phrase is best understood as an intensifier (*longing*) qualifying an adjective (*wavering*); cf. *headstrong potent*, 3.4.199.
worn worn out. Hanmer's emendation 'won' – which presupposes a misreading ('worne' for 'wonne') – has the merit of forming a more obvious couple with *lost*, but the result is a cliché ('lost and won'). F's *worn*, moreover, continues the series of epithets denoting man's fickleness; cf. 'my wonted loue is worne' (Peele, F1^r).

35 **think** believe

37 **Or** otherwise
hold the bent remain strong; literally, stay taut like a drawn bow: a metaphor from archery (*OED* bent *n.*^{2} 9).

38–9 **women . . . hour** women's rose-like beauty and its flower-like brevity are poetic commonplaces; cf. *Son* 1.2, 'that beauty's rose might never die'.

39 **displayed** unfolded, and so put on show

34 longing] *this edn;* longing, *F* worn] won *Hanmer*

VIOLA
And so they are. Alas that they are so,
To die even when they to perfection grow.

Enter CURIO *and* FESTE.

ORSINO [*to Feste*]
O fellow, come, the song we had last night.
Mark it, Cesario, it is old and plain.
The spinsters, and the knitters in the sun
And the free maids that weave their thread with bones
Do use to chant it. It is silly sooth
And dallies with the innocence of love
Like the old age.

FESTE
Are you ready, sir?

ORSINO
I prithee sing.

41 This is Viola's potentially tragic destiny (to die of unrequited love), adumbrated in Cesario's story of his 'sister' at 110–14.

43 Orsino's further description of the song sung *last night* (2, 42) is superfluous if Cesario *heard* it with him (3) and incongruous if he actually sang it, and may thus represent one of the comedy's 'loose ends': see pp. 11–14.

44 **spinsters** women spinning wool or flax (*OED* 1a; cf. 1.3.98–100); unmarried women, the modern meaning given by Minsheu: 'Spinster, *a terme . . . unto* Maids *unmarried*' (Minsheu, 683). Minsheu glosses an established use, and the reference at 45 to *maids* suggests that this derived meaning may already be present here.
knitters women who worked up yarn for clothing (*OED* 2, giving this example)

45 **free** nubile; carefree
bones See Johnson, *Dictionary*, bone *n.* 5: 'A sort of bobbins, made of trotter bones, for weaving bonelace'.

46 **Do use** are accustomed
It . . . sooth The song tells a simple truth (about love); *silly* derives from ME 'seely', i.e. innocent, simple; cf. *R2* 5.5.25, 'like silly beggars'.

47 **dallies with** dwells amorously on

48 **the old age** i.e. the golden age, in which, according to classical pastoral myth, mankind lived in a state of innocence and freedom; cf. *golden time*, 5.1.375 and n. The most authoritative source for this is Ovid, *Met.*, 1.103–5, fol. 2r: 'Then sprang up first the golden age . . . There was no feare of punishment, there was no threatning lawe'; cf. *AYL* 1.1.114–15: '[they] fleet the time carelessly, as they did in the golden world.'

50 **I prithee** I pray thee; please. Theobald reads F's 'I' as an adverb ('Ay' = 'yes'), but this does not change the overall meaning of the phrase.

41.1 FESTE] *Munro; Clowne F* 42 SD] *Oxf* 50 I] Ay, *Theobald* sing.] *this edn;* sing. *Musicke. F*

FESTE (*Sings.*)

Come away, come away death,
And in sad cypress let me be laid.
Fie away, fie away breath,
I am slain by a fair cruel maid.
My shroud of white, stuck all with yew,
O prepare it.
My part of death no one so true
Did share it.

Not a flower, not a flower sweet
On my black coffin let there be strewn.
Not a friend, not a friend greet
My poor corpse, where my bones shall be thrown.
A thousand thousand sighs to save,
Lay me, O where

51–66 No contemporary musical setting survives for this song, whose words may or may not be Shakespeare's, although the 'death-wish' it expresses is in keeping with Orsino's general attitude.

51 **Come away** hurry here (to me)

52 **in sad cypress** in a coffin of black cypress wood; or, in a bier strewn with branches of cypress. It probably alludes to the material of the coffin itself: thus its *sad* funereal colour, characteristic of cypress wood; cf. *my black coffin* (60). The phrase 'sad cypress', however, occurs in *FQ*, 2.1.60, with reference to a branch-strewn grave (see *stuck . . . yew*, 55): 'The great earths wombe they open to the sky, / And with sad Cypresse seemely it embraue' (*FQ*, 65). To complicate matters further, Olivia at 3.1.119 refers to *cypress* in the sense of crepe material, which, since she wears it as a sign of mourning, is again presumably black; cf. *WT* 4.4.221, 'Cypress black as e'er was crow'.

53 **Fie away** be gone (from me). An Early Modern English idiom, in antithesis to 'come away' (51); cf. Florio's gloss for 'O': 'an interiection of . . . reproouing, as . . . figh, away' (Florio, *World*, 242; Oxf^{1}). Rowe's emendation 'Fly away' is unnecessary.

55 **stuck . . . yew** strewn with branches of yew. Like the cypress, the yew tree is traditionally associated with graveyards and mourning; cf. 'under that *Eu*, / As I sat sadly leaning on a graue' (Webster, *Devil*, 1.2, sig. C1^{r}).

57–8 No one as faithful as I ever accepted his lot, namely death.

60 **strewn** pronounced to rhyme with *thrown* (62)

61 **greet** salute; bewail (*OED v.*^{2} 2: cf. *sighs*, 63). As Mahood notes, the transitive use of the verb in this second sense was obsolete in Early Modern English, giving Feste's song 'its antique flavour'.

51 SP] *Munro; not in F; Clo. / Capell* SD] *(The Song.)* 53 Fie . . . fie] Fly . . . fly *Rowe* 55–8] *Pope; F lines it. / it. /* 56, 64 O] *om. Pope* 63–6] *Pope; F lines where / there. /*

Sad true love never find my grave,
To weep there.

ORSINO
There's for thy pains. [*Gives money.*]

FESTE No pains, sir. I take pleasure in singing, sir.

ORSINO
I'll pay thy pleasure then.

FESTE Truly, sir, and pleasure will be paid, one time or another.

ORSINO
Give me now leave to leave thee.

FESTE Now the melancholy god protect thee, and the tailor make thy doublet of changeable taffeta, for thy mind is a very opal. I would have men of such constancy put to sea, that their business might be everything and

65 ***true love** Capell's emendation eliminates the jingle between F's 'louer' and *never*. This would have been an easy error, given the prevalence of *-er* suspensions (RP).

68 **No . . . pleasure** It is unlikely that Feste resents 'Orsino's offhand payment' (Mahood); on the contrary, his *pleasure* at 70 may playfully suggest how content he is to receive the reward.

70 **pleasure . . . paid** Feste is toying with the proverb 'There is no pleasure without pain' (Dent, P420; cf. Tilley, P408, 412, 413, 419), punning on 'pain' and *pains* (67, 68).

72 **Give . . . thee** Orsino dismisses Feste and his wordplay, but in so doing produces his own pun on *leave*: as noun = permission; as verb = depart from.

73 **melancholy god** Saturn, the Roman god of agriculture, identified in astrology with the planet ruling over the melancholy humour, and in alchemy with lead. Feste is making fun of Orsino's habitual 'dark' pose and his current bad mood.

74 **changeable taffeta** shot silk; see pp. 24–25. In Lyly's *Euphues* it is associated with mood changes under the influence of love: 'you haue giuen vnto me a true loues knotte wrought of chaungeable silke' (Lyly, *Euphues*, fol. 24[r]).

75 **opal** See p. 24; cf. Pliny, 'for in the Opall, you shall see the burning fire of the Carbuncle or Rubie, the glorious purple of the Amethyst, the greene sea of the Emeraud, and all glittering together mixed after an incredible maner' (Pliny, 614). Feste allows himself the fool's licence of strongly satirizing the duke's inconstancy, while appearing to pay the compliment of comparing him first with valuable cloth (74) and then with a prized gem.

men . . . constancy i.e. mood-changing lovers: ironic

76 **sea** another traditional symbol of mutability; cf. Ariel's 'suffer a sea-change', *Tem* 1.2.401.

65 true love] *Capell (*true-love*); true louer F*

their intent everywhere, for that's it that always makes
a good voyage of nothing. Farewell. *Exit.*

ORSINO

Let all the rest give place. [*Exeunt all but Orsino and Viola.*]
Once more, Cesario,
Get thee to yon same sovereign cruelty.
Tell her my love, more noble than the world,
Prizes not quantity of dirty lands.
The parts that fortune hath bestowed upon her
Tell her I hold as giddily as fortune;
But 'tis that miracle and queen of gems
That nature pranks her in attracts my soul.

VIOLA

But if she cannot love you, sir?

ORSINO

I cannot be so answered.

VIOLA

Sooth, but you must.

76–8 **their business . . . nothing** i.e. the changeable sea would carry them to and fro on a profitless journey; a sardonic allusion to the proverb 'he is not any where who is every where' (Dent, E194)

77 **that's it** that's the thing; *it* is sometimes used by Shakespeare as a full noun before a relative clause (Hope, 1.3.2c, giving this example)

78 **of** out of; or, consisting of

79 **give place** leave

80 **sovereign cruelty** cruel sovereign (of my heart); supremely cruel lady

81 **the world** society at large, with its materialistic values

82 **dirty** corrupting, because lands and other possessions encourage greed; soiled, because made of earth. Cf. Hamlet's 'spacious in the possession of dirt' (*Ham* 5.2.74–5).

83 **parts** endowments, possessions (*OED n.* 7b)

84 **I . . . fortune** I regard as lightly as fickle fortune does. Orsino plays on two related meanings of *fortune* here and at 83: the capricious goddess personifying chance (84), and the actual riches the goddess has bestowed upon Olivia as heiress (83). The wealthy duke can boast his indifference to the latter.

85 **that . . . gems** Olivia's precious innate qualities, especially her beauty; *miracle and queen* = 'miraculous queen' (rhetorical figure: hendiadys)

86 **pranks her in** adorns her with (*OED v.*[4] 1c). Contrast Coriolanus on the tribunes: 'they do prank them in authority' (*Cor* 3.1.23).
attracts draws forth (*OED v.* 4a, first occurrence)

88 ***I** F's 'It' (= the question) is plausible in itself, but is belied by Cesario's reply, 'you must', which justifies Hanmer's emendation.
Sooth in truth

79 SD] *Capell subst.* 80 yon] *(*yond*)* 88 I] *Hanmer;* It *F*

Say that some lady, as perhaps there is,
Hath for your love as great a pang of heart
As you have for Olivia. You cannot love her;
You tell her so. Must she not then be answered?

ORSINO

There is no woman's sides
Can bide the beating of so strong a passion
As love doth give my heart; no woman's heart
So big to hold so much – they lack retention.
Alas, their love may be called appetite,
No motion of the liver but the palate,
That suffer surfeit, cloyment and revolt.
But mine is all as hungry as the sea,
And can digest as much. Make no compare

90 **pang** sudden sharp pain (*OED n.*[1] 1b, giving this example)

93–103 Orsino's misogynistic speech, in part provoked by his anger at Olivia's indifference, rehearses some of the commonplaces of Renaissance attitudes to women. In particular, it recalls Gasparre Pallavicino's thesis in Castiglione, 'that women are unperfect creatures, and consequently of less woorthinesse then men' (Castiglione, sig. Cc2[v]), and that 'through the weakenes of their kinde, [they] are much more enclined to appetites', as opposed to true passion (sig. Gg1[r]). This contrasts with Orsino's praise of the superior constancy of women at 31–5. It is of course ironical that he should pronounce such a demeaning view of the woman he claims to adore, especially in the presence of Viola, who has already demonstrated – to the audience – her true *passion* for him (94).

94 **bide** bear

96 **retention** the capacity to retain (love): a medical term, referring literally to the body's ability to retain liquid, especially urine; cf. 'Retention of vryne, & costyfnes' (Vigo, fol. cix[r]). Early modern scientific discourse often classified women as incontinent 'leaky vessels' (Paster, 30–4). The incontinence of which women were accused was above all sexual, however: 'I beleave not that men are so incontinent, as women be', affirms Castiglione's Pallavicino (Castiglione, sig. Ff4[r]).

97 **appetite** bodily craving

98 **motion** emotion; inclination (*OED n.* 12a, giving both meanings). Cf. 18.

liver the seat of the passions; cf. 1.1.36–7n.

palate the seat of taste, which is rapidly satisfied

99 **surfeit . . . revolt** i.e. excess (of food or sex) leading to satiety and revulsion; cf. 1.1.2–3n. *OED* gives *cloyment*, satiety, as sole occurrence.

100 **as hungry . . . sea** unlimited in capacity. Ironically, Orsino claims at 1.1.9–13 that the sea causes loss of value.

99 suffer] suffers *Rowe*

Between that love a woman can bear me
And that I owe Olivia.

VIOLA Ay, but I know –

ORSINO
What dost thou know?

VIOLA
Too well what love women to men may owe.
In faith, they are as true of heart as we.
My father had a daughter loved a man,
As it might be, perhaps, were I a woman,
I should your lordship.

ORSINO And what's her history?

VIOLA
A blank, my lord. She never told her love,
But let concealment like a worm i'th' bud

102 **bear** have towards; perhaps pun on 'bearing' sexually and on childbirth; cf. *AYL*, 5.4.207–8, 'O women, for the love you bear to men'.

103, 105 **owe** feel towards

107–15 This *history* of a girl pining stoically from unexpressed love – a barely veiled allusion to Viola's own predicament – recalls the story told by Cesare Gonzaga in Castiglione: significantly, as a reply to Pallavicino's tirade against female incontinency (see 93–103n. and 96n.), just as Cesario is responding to Orsino's misogyny. In Gonzaga's narrative, a young girl, like Viola, refrains from expressing her love for a man she cannot have: 'She thus ferventlye louinge, as a most louing minde coulde loue, continued two yeeres in suche contynencie, that she neuer made anye token to this yonge man of the love that she bore him' (Castiglione, sig. Gg3[r]). The story ends tragically, since the girl dies from unrequited love: a fate that could await Viola herself.

107 **My . . . daughter** a 'hidden' clue to Viola's gender and her love for Orsino, who, as elsewhere, fails to decipher the conundrum

109 **history** story; written historical narrative

110 **blank** plays on both senses of *history* (109): the story is blank (i.e. 'void': *OED n.* 7, first occurrence) because the young woman pined away and thus disappeared; and the page of Cesario's 'historical' narrative is blank because it is yet to be written and acted out: it may end well or tragically, depending on Orsino himself. Cf. 3.1.102.
told revealed (*OED v.* 5a, giving this example). In Bensley's 1785 production, according to Charles Lamb, Dorothy Jordan's Viola paused at the end of this line, 'as if the story had ended – and then the "worm in the bud" came up as a new suggestion – and the heightened image of "Patience" still followed after that . . . thought springing up after thought, I would almost say as they were watered by her tears' (C. Lamb, 185–6).

111 **concealment** the act of hiding (her love)

103 know –] *Rowe;* know. *F*

Feed on her damask cheek. She pined in thought,
And with a green and yellow melancholy
She sat like Patience on a monument,
Smiling at grief. Was not this love indeed?
We men may say more, swear more, but indeed
Our shows are more than will, for still we prove
Much in our vows, but little in our love.

ORSINO

But died thy sister of her love, my boy?

VIOLA

I am all the daughters of my father's house,
And all the brothers too; and yet I know not.
Sir, shall I to this lady?

ORSINO Ay, that's the theme:

112 **damask** pink, like the damask rose (cf. *AYL*, 3.5.123); smooth, like damask silk
thought sadness

113 **green and yellow** pale and sickly, in contrast to pink *damask* (112); an allusion to the green sickness, an anaemic disease (chlorosis) mainly affecting young women, which made the complexion pallid and was often thought to be caused by unrequited desire. Cf. 'His daughter beeing at the age of twentie yeeres, would . . . fall into the greene sicknes for want of a husband' (Greene, *Mamillia*, fol. 8[r]); cf. also *RJ* 3.5.156 (of Juliet), 'Out, you green-sickness carrion!'

114–15 **She sat . . . grief** Cesario's simile evokes an allegorical figure on a memorial or funerary monument, presumably similar to the emblem in Cesare Ripa's *Iconologia* (1593) that represents Patience as a woman sitting on a stone, bearing a yoke on her shoulders, with her feet placed on thorns (see Fig. 6). Chaucer's *Parliament of Fowls*, 242–3, has 'Dame Pacience sitting there . . . / With face pale, upon an hil of sond' (Chaucer, *Works*, 313). Cf. *Per* 5.1.139–40, 'Like Patience gazing on kings' graves, and smiling / Extremity out of act.'

117 **Our . . . will** our outward displays of passion are greater than our actual sentiments
still always

120–1 another of Viola's riddling clues identifying her as the subject of her own *history*; again Orsino fails to take the point (cf. 107). Cf. the conundrum of the cross-dressed Phillida in Lyly's *Gallathea*: 'My Father had but one daughter, and therefore I could haue no sister' (Lyly, *Gallathea*, 3.2, sig. D4[v]). Viola's afterthought *and . . . not* (121) is evidently prompted by her melancholy reflection on Sebastian and his uncertain fate.

122 **theme** idea; literally, the subject of a school exercise (*OED* 3): wooing Olivia is Cesario's homework for the day. Orsino reminds Cesario, and himself, of the main business after their long digression.

To her in haste. Give her this jewel; say
My love can give no place, bide no denay. *Exeunt.*

2.5 *Enter* SIR TOBY, SIR ANDREW *and* FABIAN.

SIR TOBY Come thy ways, Signor Fabian.

FABIAN Nay, I'll come. If I lose a scruple of this sport let me be boiled to death with melancholy.

SIR TOBY Wouldst thou not be glad to have the niggardly, rascally sheep-biter come by some notable shame?

FABIAN I would exult, man. You know he brought me out

123 **jewel** an ornament or piece of jewellery, such as a ring. Cf. 3.4.203.

124 **can . . . denay** can neither yield nor tolerate refusal; *denay* is an alternative spelling for 'deny' (refusal: *OED* deny *n.*[1] 2, giving this example), and is kept here for the sake of the rhyme with *say* (123).

2.5 The gulling of Malvolio through Maria's forged letter – judged by John Manningham in 1602 to be a 'good practise' (see pp. 3–4) – is the play's most celebrated episode, giving actors unrivalled opportunities for both farcical comedy and potential pathos. Pope gives the location as '*Olivia's Garden*'.

1 **Come thy ways** come along (*OED* way *n.*[1] 23b), an exclamation or discourse marker, in which the somewhat archaic adverbial form *thy ways* has fossilized (Blake, *Grammar*, 5.1.2.2ii, giving this example); cf. *othergates*, 5.1.189.
Signor Fabian On Fabian and his sudden appearance in the play, see List of Roles, 15. *Signor* may be one of Sir Toby's jovial terms of address, or may be meant to indicate that Fabian is an Italian visitor to Olivia's house. He is often played, however, as a servant or member of Olivia's household.

2 **Nay** certainly (intensifier)
lose a scruple miss the tiniest part; a *scruple* is a small unit of measurement or weight: cf. 3.4.76n.

3 **boiled . . . melancholy** paradoxical, since melancholy was the cold humour *par excellence*. Kökeritz, 95, suggests a pun on 'boil' and 'bile' (i.e. the cause of *melancholy*).

4 **niggardly** mean

5 **rascally** worthless, wretched
sheep-biter literally, a dog that harasses sheep, thus 'a shifty, sneaking, or thievish fellow' (*OED* 2b, giving this example); colloquially, a whoremonger, from 'sheep' or 'mutton' in the sense of 'prostitute' (*OED* 4). Intriguingly, since the subject is Malvolio, Nashe associates the term with lewd and hypocritical Puritans: 'he must . . . lier like a sheepbiter. If he be halfe a puritan, and haue scripture continually in his mouth, he speeds the better' (Nashe, *Traveller*, sigs G2[v]–G3[r]).
come by suffer

6 **exult** rejoice (*OED* 2, giving this example)

6–7 Fabian's motive for participating in this scene – setting it up in terms of blood sports (cf. 8, 19–20; 2.3.174; 3.1.116–17; 3.4.133–4, and notes) – may confirm Malvolio's supposed

2.5] *(Scena Quinta.)* 2 SP] *(Fab.)*, *Cam*[1] 10.1 *with a letter*] *Oxf*

o'favour with my lady about a bear-baiting here.

SIR TOBY To anger him we'll have the bear again, and we will fool him black and blue, shall we not, Sir Andrew?

SIR ANDREW An we do not, it is pity of our lives.

Enter MARIA [*with a letter*].

SIR TOBY Here comes the little villain. How now, my metal of India?

MARIA Get ye all three into the box-tree. Malvolio's coming down this walk. He has been yonder i'the sun practising behaviour to his own shadow this half-hour. Observe him for the love of mockery, for I know this letter will make a contemplative idiot of him. Close, in the name of jesting! [*The men hide. Maria drops letter.*]

'Puritanism', since, like theatre, *bear-baiting* was the object of reformist Protestant attacks. The *here* at 7 is almost literal, with reference to the Globe playhouse, since bear-baiting took place in arenas close to the theatres.

8 **To . . . again** In this scene it is Malvolio who will play the part of the *bear*, the others that of the dogs baiting him.

9 **fool . . . blue** make a complete fool of him: a variation on the proverbial idiom 'to beat one black and blue' (Dent, B160)

10 **An** if
it . . . lives it is a shame that we should live; proverbial (Dent, P368.1). Cf. *MND* 3.1.40.

12 **metal of India** i.e. gold from India, legendary land of abundance, with a probable pun on 'mettle' (spirit); cf. 3.4.266, 5.1.316. For *of* = 'from', cf. Blake, *Grammar*, 5.4.2.

13 **box-tree** tree or hedge of box (*Buxus sempervirens*), an evergreen that can be clipped into topiary forms. This is one of the few indispensable stage properties required in this play, although the 'tree' need not be literally such: mazes, plants in tubs, and walls (or sliding panels, as in Posner's 2001 RSC production) have been used in production, as well as multiple bushes (one for each eavesdropper).

14 **walk** i.e. a broad garden path, perhaps flanked by trees (*OED n.*[1] 9c, giving this example), an indication developed in some productions (e.g. Tree in 1901) into a full garden set, complete with mazes and the rest

14–15 **He . . . half-hour** another indication of Malvolio's *self-love* (1.5.86)

15 **behaviour** elegant deportment (*OED* 1e)

16 **for . . . mockery** for goodness' sake: discourse marker

17 **contemplative idiot** imbecile staring out vacantly
Close keep close, hide

12 metal] *Malone;* Mettle *F;* Nettle *F2* 18 SD] *Capell subst.; Throws down a Letter / Theobald*

Lie thou there, for here comes the trout that must be caught with tickling. *Exit.*

Enter MALVOLIO.

MALVOLIO 'Tis but fortune, all is fortune. Maria once told me she did affect me, and I have heard herself come thus near, that should she fancy it should be one of my complexion. Besides, she uses me with a more exalted respect than anyone else that follows her. What should I think on't?

SIR TOBY Here's an overweening rogue.

FABIAN O peace. Contemplation makes a rare turkey-cock of him. How he jets under his advanced plumes.

SIR ANDREW 'Slight, I could so beat the rogue!

19–20 **the trout . . . tickling** Catching trout by stroking their gills in shallow water is proverbially easy, although Dent (T537) dates the figurative use of the proverb from this scene. Maria changes the animal metaphor from bears to fish.

20 SD Maria's exit at this point means that she does not witness the success of her plot (although she does see its effects in 3.4). Her unexplained absence turns the episode into an all-male affair.

21 **fortune** chance, i.e. it is mere chance that Olivia is an heiress and Malvolio an underling, and this state of affairs may change. Cf. Orsino's reflections on fickle *fortune* (= chance/riches) at 2.4.83–4; here too the secondary meaning of *fortune* as 'riches' is pertinent to Malvolio's ambitions.

22 **she** Olivia

did affect me was attracted to me (*OED v.*[1] 2, giving this example). Malvolio already imagines himself as object of Olivia's desire before he reads the letter, thanks partly to Maria's skilful preparation of the trap.

22–3 **I . . . near** I have heard her as good as say

23 **fancy** fall in love (*OED v.* 8a, giving this example)

24 **complexion** colouring; temperament. Cf. 2.3.153, 2.4.26.

25 **exalted** high (*OED ppl. a.* 4b, first occurrence)

follows her is in her service

26 **on't** of it

28 **Contemplation** thinking continuously about himself

turkey-cock proverbial symbol of male self-importance, because it puffs itself up and, like the peacock, displays its tail-feathers (Dent, T612); cf. *H5* 5.1.14–15. Another animal metaphor for Malvolio: cf. 5, 6–7, 8, 19–20, 82, 102 and notes.

29 **jets** struts; cf. the description of the vain steward in *Faversham*, '[he] brauely iets it in his silken gowne' (*Faversham*, sig. A2[r]). Rubinstein, 137, detects a pun on 'jet' in the Elizabethan slang sense of 'come sexually', in association with *turkey-cock*.

advanced plumes uplifted feathers. Onstage Malvolio sometimes sported a tall hat with a large feather in this scene.

30 **'Slight** by God's light: a mild oath

SIR TOBY Peace, I say.

MALVOLIO To be count Malvolio.

SIR TOBY Ah, rogue!

SIR ANDREW Pistol him, pistol him!

SIR TOBY Peace, peace.

MALVOLIO There is example for't: the Lady of the Strachy married the yeoman of the wardrobe.

SIR ANDREW Fie on him, Jezebel!

FABIAN O peace, now he's deeply in. Look how imagination blows him.

MALVOLIO Having been three months married to her,

31 **Peace, I say** Cam[1] reattributes this line and *Peace, peace* at 35 to Fabian, who has already cried out *O peace!* at 28 (so that *I say* becomes an emphatic underlining), as he will do so again at 48, 54 and 62. It may be more comical, however, for the men to change roles, restraining each other in turn. Throughout the scene the eavesdroppers run the risk of being found out.

32 **count Malvolio** Malvolio's fantasy of social promotion is not limited by the law: he would not become count even if he were to marry Olivia.

34 **Pistol him** shoot him, or cudgel him with the butt of a pistol; *OED v.*[1] cites as first occurrence *The Famous History of Sir Thomas Wyatt* (1607) by Thomas Dekker and John Webster.

35 **Peace, peace** attributed by Cam[1] to Fabian; see 31n.

36 **example** precedent (*OED n.* 5)

36–7 **the Lady . . . wardrobe** This episode of marriage between a noblewoman and a servant, keeper of her clothes, may be invented, or it may be a theatrical in-joke. Sisson learned of one William Strachey, shareholder in the Children's company at the Blackfriars theatre in 1606, and one David Yeomans, the wardrobe master or 'tireman' of the company. A more probable candidate as *yeoman* is Edward Kirkham, one of Strachey's partners in the Blackfriars company, who was granted a royal patent as 'yeoman or keeper' of 'our Great Wardrobe' in 1586 (Halliwell).

38 **Jezebel** a loose or 'painted' woman: originally, the biblical widow of King Ahab, who decked herself out in order to seduce Jehu and was condemned by the latter to be killed and eaten by dogs (2 Kings, 9.30–7). Sir Andrew is probably unaware of her story and gender, although Malvolio is compared to a loose woman at 2.3.75 and 77–8 (see notes). Malvolio, moreover, like Jezebel, is set upon by 'dogs' in this scene; cf. 8n.

39 **he's . . . in** i.e. he is quite lost in his own reveries

imagination fancy (*OED* 4a, giving this example)

40 **blows him** swells him up. The metaphor probably alludes to flies depositing eggs in rotten flesh (*OED* blow *v.*[1] 28); cf. *LLL* 5.2.408–9, 'these summer flies / Have blown me full of maggot ostentation.'

41–78 Malvolio is *practising behaviour* (15); many actors here 'try out' the grand poses and gestures of Malvolio's future life as 'count'.

31, 35 SPs] *Fabian Cam[1]* 37 Strachy] *(Strachy);* Stracci *Douai MS, Cam (Lloyd);* Stratarch *(Hanmer); Trachy / Warburton;* strachy *Steevens[2];* Strozzi *(Collier);* Strachey *Oxf*

sitting in my state –

SIR TOBY O for a stone-bow to hit him in the eye!

MALVOLIO Calling my officers about me, in my branched velvet gown, having come from a day-bed where I have left Olivia sleeping –

SIR TOBY Fire and brimstone!

FABIAN O peace, peace.

MALVOLIO And then to have the humour of state, and after a demure travail of regard – telling them I know my place, as I would they should do theirs – to ask for my kinsman Toby.

SIR TOBY Bolts and shackles!

FABIAN O peace, peace, peace! Now, now!

MALVOLIO Seven of my people, with an obedient start, make out for him. I frown the while and perchance wind up my watch, or play with my [*touching his chain*] – some rich jewel. Toby approaches, curtsies there to me.

42 **state** canopied chair of state or throne

43 **stone-bow** crossbow used for shooting stones

44 **branched** ornamented with embroidered branches

45 **day-bed** couch for resting in the daytime; contrast *R3* 3.7.72 (Qq), 'He is not lolling on a lewd day bed.' In Posner's 2001 RSC production, Guy Henry's Malvolio acted out his dream by lying on a garden bench.

47 **Fire and brimstone!** Hell!: an oath of biblical origin (Revelations, 19.20)

49 **humour of state** temperament and behaviour of a great authority

50 **demure . . . regard** grave effort of looking at them
travail F's 'trauaile' – as also at 1.2.21 and 5.1.159) – is usually modernized to 'travel', in the sense of moving or casting (eyes); the F spelling, retained here, expresses Malvolio's ineffable reluctance to look at his inferiors.

52 **my kinsman Toby** imagining Belch as his relative and equal, Malvolio familiarly drops the 'Sir' from Toby, who underlines the offence at 65.

53 **Bolts and shackles** fetters (for Malvolio in prison): an imprecation

55 **with . . . start** jumping obediently to attention; *start* = sudden movement

56 **make out** set out (to fetch him) (*OED* make *v.*[1] 93n, giving this example)

57 **watch** pocket watch. Originally a clock, the *watch* in its modern sense was a relatively recent term (*OED n.* 21a gives *LLL* 3.1.187 as first occurrence) and still a luxury item. *OED* (wind *v.*[1] 24e (a)) also gives *wind up* as first occurrence with reference to a watch or clock.

57–8 ***play . . . jewel** Collier's emendation suggests that Malvolio suddenly inter-

42 state –] *Pope;* state. *F* 46 sleeping –] *Collier;* sleeping. *F* 50 travail] Travel *Rowe* 57 my] *om. F3* SD] *Cam[1] subst.* 58 – some] *Collier;* some *F*

SIR TOBY Shall this fellow live?

FABIAN Though our silence be drawn from us with cars, yet peace!

MALVOLIO I extend my hand to him thus, quenching my familiar smile with an austere regard of control –

SIR TOBY And does not Toby take you a blow o'the lips then?

MALVOLIO Saying 'Cousin Toby, my fortunes, having cast me on your niece, give me this prerogative of speech' –

SIR TOBY What, what?

MALVOLIO 'You must amend your drunkenness.'

SIR TOBY Out, scab!

FABIAN Nay, patience, or we break the sinews of our plot.

MALVOLIO 'Besides, you waste the treasure of your time with a foolish knight' –

SIR ANDREW That's me, I warrant you.

MALVOLIO 'One Sir Andrew.'

SIR ANDREW I knew 'twas I, for many do call me fool.

rupts his own train of thought, perhaps because he is about to refer to his steward's chain of office when he realizes that as 'count' he will no longer be wearing it, or because he cannot find a word grand enough to describe the *rich jewel* he imagines playing with. Onstage the actor at this point often toys with his chain; in Posner's 2001 RSC production Guy Henry's hand dangled uncertainly in front of his pelvis, as if he were about to *play with* himself.

61 **with cars** with carts or chariots: an allusion to a method of extorting information (rather than *silence*, as here) from prisoners by tying them to carts pulling in different directions; cf. *TGV* 3.1.264–5, 'a team of horse shall not pluck that from me.'

63 **extend** hold out (*OED* 8, first occurrence)

quenching suppressing

64 **familiar** intimate, friendly

regard of control authoritarian gaze

65 **take . . . lips** give you a punch in the mouth

72 **scab** scoundrel: a common insult in Early Modern English

73 **break the sinews** disable, ruin: the risk of giving the game away

77 **That's me** In performance Sir Andrew usually sticks his head out at this point, running the risk of being discovered as well as named.

61 with cars] with cares *F2;* by th'ears *Hanmer;* with cables *(Tyrwhitt);* with cords *White* 64 control –] *Cam[1];* controll. *F* 69 speech' –] *Rowe;* speech. *F* 76 knight' –] *Rowe*; knight. *F*

MALVOLIO [*Sees letter.*] What employment have we here?

FABIAN Now is the woodcock near the gin.

SIR TOBY O peace, and the spirit of humours intimate reading aloud to him.

MALVOLIO [*Takes up letter.*] By my life, this is my lady's hand. These be her very c's, her u's and her t's, and thus makes she her great P's. It is in contempt of question her hand.

SIR ANDREW Her c's, her u's and her t's. Why that?

MALVOLIO [*Reads.*] *To the unknown beloved, this, and my good wishes.* Her very phrases! By your leave, wax. Soft – and the impressure her Lucrece, with which she uses to seal. 'Tis my lady. To whom should this be? [*Opens letter.*]

80 **employment** business (with reference to the letter)

82 **woodcock** a proverbially stupid bird, easy to snare in a net (cf. 'A springe to catch a woodcock', Dent, S788): a variation on the hunting metaphors used throughout this scene
gin snare

83 **the spirit . . . intimate** may the guiding genius of eccentricity suggest

86–7 **her very . . . P's** Malvolio unwittingly spells out a double innuendo. The first (c-u-t) is a sexual allusion, 'slang for the female genitals', according to Oxf[1], which quotes Webster's Induction to Marston's *The Malcontent*, 'the longest cut stil to draw an Apricoke' (Marston, 25–6, sig. A3^{v}). The second is an allusion to urination ('*P's* = piss', Partridge, 161; *great P's* = abundant urination), perhaps implying social ambition rather than an erotic suggestion, since witnessing the countess's *P's* might symbolize equality and intimacy, reserved for her husband. Steevens noted, disapprovingly, that in the inscription to the letter (90–1) 'there is neither a C, nor a P, to be found', but the absence of literal c's and p's only goes to emphasize Malvolio's state of self-deluding excitement.

87 **great** capital (*OED a.* 6b, giving this example)

87–8 **in . . . question** beyond all doubt (so much so as to make doubt itself absurd)

91 **Soft** gently (cf. 1.5.285), with a probable pun on *wax*; in some productions Malvolio touches the seal and discovers that the *wax* is indeed still *soft*.

92 **impressure** image (of the seal)
Lucrece seal-ring bearing the image of Lucretia, the model of chastity in Roman myth, probably in the act of stabbing herself after being raped by Tarquin. This is the subject of Shakespeare's poem *The Rape of Lucrece*.

92–3 **uses to seal** habitually seals

80 SD] *Collier; after 78 Cam*[1] 85 SD] *Collier; after 81 Rowe* 86, 89 c's . . . u's . . . t's] *(C's . . . V's . . . T's), Cam*[1] *subst.* 90 SD] *Capell; reads the superscription Cam*[1] 93, 95, 103, 140 SDs] *Capell*

FABIAN This wins him, liver and all.
MALVOLIO [*Reads.*]
Jove knows I love,
But who?
Lips, do not move,
No man must know.
'No man must know.' What follows? The numbers altered. 'No man must know.' If this should be thee, Malvolio?
SIR TOBY Marry, hang thee, brock!
MALVOLIO [*Reads.*]
I may command where I adore,
But silence, like a Lucrece knife,
With bloodless stroke my heart doth gore.
M.O.A.I. doth sway my life.
FABIAN A fustian riddle.
SIR TOBY Excellent wench, say I.
MALVOLIO [*Reads.*] *M.O.A.I. doth sway my life.* Nay, but first let me see, let me see, let me see.
FABIAN What dish o'poison has she dressed him!

94 **liver and all** passionately. The liver is the seat of passion; cf. 1.1.36 and 2.4.98.
99–100 **The numbers altered** the metre has been changed
102 **brock** badger, proverbially malodorous (Dent, B679), with the further colloquial sense of 'rogue' (*OED n.*[1] 2, giving this example): another animal metaphor (cf. 5, 6–7, 8, 18–19, 28, 82)
104 ***Lucrece knife*** the 'harmful knife' with which Lucretia killed herself (*Luc* 1724); cf. 92n. *Lucrece* is a proper name used as a modifier (Hope, 1.2.6).
105 [silence] stabs my heart without loss of blood; unlike Lucretia's self-stabbing, after which 'the crimson blood / Circles her body in on every side' (*Luc*, 1738–39); *OED* bloodless 2, first occurrence
106, 109 ***M.O.A.I*** This *fustian riddle* (107) has proved over the decades to be as much a trap for critics as for Malvolio, giving rise to countless 'solutions': see pp. 15–16, for some of the many interpretations.
106 ***sway*** govern
107 **fustian** bombastic, inflated (*OED a.* 2)
111 **dressed him** prepared for him

95–8] *Capell; prose F* 99–101 The . . . Malvolio?] *Theobald; F lines* know, / *Maluolio*? / 103–6] *Capell; F lines knife: / life. /* 109–36 SDs] *this edn* 109 *doth . . . life*] *Capell;* doth sway my life *F* 111 dish o'] *(*dish a*), Cam;* dish of *F3;* a dish of *Rowe*

SIR TOBY And with what wing the staniel checks at it!

MALVOLIO [*Reads.*] *I may command where I adore.* Why, she may command me. I serve her, she is my lady. Why, this is evident to any formal capacity. There is no obstruction in this. And the end – what should that alphabetical position portend? If I could make that resemble something in me! Softly – [*reading*] *M.O.A.I.*

SIR TOBY O ay, make up that! He is now at a cold scent.

FABIAN Sowter will cry upon't for all this, though it be as rank as a fox.

MALVOLIO 'M.' Malvolio. 'M' – why, that begins my name!

FABIAN Did not I say he would work it out? The cur is excellent at faults.

112 ***staniel** kestrel. F's 'stallion' may be, as *OED* (staniel) hypothesizes, a corrupt or dialectal variant of *staniel*. In any case, *wing* indicates a species of bird (cf. *woodcock*, 82), although in this case Malvolio is compared not to a hunted animal but to a bird of prey hovering over its victim.
checks at it turns to fly at it: a term from falconry (*OED* check *v.*[1] 6b, giving this example); cf. 'Checke, is when . . . birds comming in the view of the Hawke, shee forsaketh her natural flight to flie at them' (Latham, paras 1^r–1^v). Cf. 3.1.62.

115 **formal capacity** ordinary intelligence

116 **obstruction** obstacle

117 **alphabetical position** arrangement of letters
portend signify

120 **O ay** oh yes, with a pun on 'O, I', as the spelling in F underlines here and at 131 and 133 (see t.n.)
cold scent the point where the scent of the quarry becomes imperceptible to the hound

121–2 The hound will nevertheless sniff out the *cold scent* and bay at it, as if it stank like a fox's: i.e. Malvolio appears to have missed the clue, but will decipher it eventually and will cry out triumphantly (as indeed he does immediately at 123–4). This passage is often interpreted as meaning that Sowter-Malvolio, an incompetent hound, can only smell the obvious, whereas Fabian's comment in 125–6 suggests the opposite. 'As rank as a fox' was proverbial (Dent, F628). Malvolio becomes a dog again, as at 5.

121 **Sowter** a typical name for a hound (meaning literally 'cobbler'), often used of people as a term of abuse (*OED* souter 1b)
cry upon't yelp at the scent (*OED* cry *v.* 11b, giving this example)
for all this for all that, nevertheless

125–6 **The cur . . . faults** the hound is good at finding lost trails; *fault* is synonymous with *cold scent* (120; *OED* fault *n.* 8a). Cf. *VA* 694, 'The hot scent-snuffing hounds . . . have singled . . . the cold fault cleanly out.'

112 staniel] *Hanmer (*stanyel*)*; stallion *F* 116 this. And] *Collier;* this, and *F;* this – and *Rowe* 120 ay] *(*I*)* 123 Malvolio. 'M' –] *Oxf*[1]*; Maluolio, M. F*

MALVOLIO 'M.' But then there is no consonancy in the sequel. That suffers under probation: 'A' should follow, but 'O' does.

FABIAN And 'O' shall end, I hope.

SIR TOBY Ay, or I'll cudgel him and make him cry 'O!'

MALVOLIO And then 'I' comes behind.

FABIAN Ay, an you had any eye behind you, you might see more detraction at your heels than fortunes before you.

MALVOLIO [*Reads.*] *M.O.A.I.* This simulation is not as the former. And yet to crush this a little it would bow to me, for every one of these letters are in my name. Soft, here follows prose.

[*Reads.*] *If this fall into thy hand, revolve. In my stars*

127–8 ***there . . . probation** there is no logical consistency in what follows; that (i.e. what follows) breaks down when put to the test. Both *consonancy* and *probation* are pseudo-logical or pseudo-legal terms, which help to maintain the self-important tone of Malvolio's monologue. The absence of punctuation in F – possibly due to lack of space, since 'sequel' ends a line – makes *that* govern *consonancy*: i.e. there is no consistency that stands up to investigation; this renders *under* superfluous, while Rowe's emendation restores its meaning.

130 **And . . . end** Johnson is surely right in taking *O* to be the hangman's noose, the *end* Fabian wishes for Malvolio.

133 **Ay . . . behind you** a pun on the expression 'He has an eye behind' (Dent, E236)
an if

134–5 **more . . . you** more disparagement following you than the riches you are pursuing: alluding to the comments being made behind Malvolio's back

136 ***M.O.A.I.*** Actors frequently create comic business out of trying to pronounce the word: in Judge's 1994 RSC production Desmond Barritt's Malvolio emitted a feline 'miaow'.
simulation puzzle

136–7 **as the former** like the previous puzzle (i.e. '*I may command where I adore*', 103 and 113)

137 **crush** force

137–8 **bow to me** bend to form my name; and/or indicate me, yield up its meaning to me

138 **every . . . are** As often in Shakespeare, the verb agrees here with the noun *letters* because it is closer than the subject pronoun *every one* (Blake, *Grammar*, 6.1.1.6b).
Soft gently; cf. 91.

140 ***revolve*** reflect (*OED v.* 10, first occurrence). On the various bits of stage business actors use to accompany this word, see pp. 129–30.

140–55 Malvolio reads the letter without interruption, allowing the audience

128 sequel. That] *Rowe (*Sequel; that*);* sequell that *F* 131, 133 Ay] *(*I*)* 136 *M.O.A.I.*] *F2; M,O,A,I. F* 140 *revolve.*] revolve. *Revolves but doesn't find answer then sits L. / Tree* 140–55 *In . . . Unhappy*] *F3;* In . . . vnhappy *F*

I am above thee, but be not afraid of greatness. Some are born great, some achieve greatness and some have greatness thrust upon them. Thy fates open their hands: let thy blood and spirit embrace them, and, to inure thyself to what thou art like to be, cast thy humble slough and appear fresh. Be opposite with a kinsman, surly with servants. Let thy tongue tang arguments of state; put thyself into the trick of singularity. She thus advises thee that sighs for

to hear it all. *TN* – together with *Ham* – is unusual in having three letters read aloud: cf. 3.4.143–65 and 5.1.297–305.
stars fortune, and hence the social rank that derives from it

141–3 ***Some . . . them*** This passage echoes Christ's speech on chastity and marriage to his disciples in Matthew, 19.12, which distinguishes between three kinds of chastity or celibacy: 'For there are some chaste, which are so borne . . . And there are some chaste, which be made chaste of me: And there be chaste, which haue made themselues chaste' (Bishops' Bible, 1568). The implication may be that Malvolio is doomed to remain chaste or celibate rather than become *great* by marrying Olivia. There may also be a veiled allusion here to the 'eunuch' topos (see 1.2.53n.): as John Astington notes, the Geneva and King James versions of the passage adopt the term 'eunuch' instead of 'chaste' ('For there are some Eunuches, which were so borne . . .'). Malvolio's humiliation by means of the letter can thus be read as 'a displaced gelding' (Astington, 26). See p. 60.

142 ***born*** Rowe's emendation of F's 'become' – an easy misreading of a posited copy form 'borne' (RP) – is clearly right, since the phrase is repeated with *born* at 3.4.39 and again at 5.1.364.

143 ***fates*** This echoes Olivia's actual phraseology: cf. 'Fate, show thy force', 1.5.303.
open their hands make you a generous offer

143–4 ***blood and spirit*** body and soul

144 ***inure*** accustom

145 ***cast . . . slough*** throw off your lowly status like a snake its skin; *slough* (pronounced 'sluff') is the outer or scarf skin shed by snakes and other reptiles (*OED n.*[2] 1): cf. *2H6*, 3.1.228–9, 'as the snake . . . / With shining checkered slough'. In Gielgud's 1955 production Laurence Olivier hesitated over the pronunciation of the word, suggesting Malvolio's social insecurity (Pennington, 17).

146 ***opposite with*** hostile towards (*OED a.* 3a, giving this example)

147 ***tang*** ring out like a bell (*OED v.*[2] 2, giving this example)
arguments of state important political topics (cf. Malvolio's response at 157)

147–8 ***put . . . singularity*** take on the affected mannerisms of eccentricity

148 ***trick*** peculiar habit (*OED n.* 7)
singularity conspicuously unusual behaviour (*OED* 9a). Cf. 'it comes too neare singularitie, and a desire to be noted' (Cornwallis, sig. B4[r]).

142 *born*] *Douai MS, Rowe;* become *F* *achieve*] *F2 (*atcheeve*);* atcheeues *F* 143 *them*] *F4;* em *F*

thee. Remember who commended thy yellow stockings and wished to see thee ever cross-gartered – I say remember. Go to, thou art made if thou desir'st to be so; if not, let me see thee a steward still, the fellow of servants and not worthy to touch Fortune's fingers. Farewell. She that would alter services with thee,

The Fortunate Unhappy.

Daylight and champaign discovers not more. This is open. I will be proud, I will read politic authors, I will

149 ***yellow stockings*** These may have been, as Oxf[1] suggests, 'a garish fashion associated with bachelors' in 1602, but it is more probable that they were hopelessly *out* of fashion: hence the jest. Thomas Overbury in 1615 describes the behaviour of a presumably uncouth country gentleman: 'If he goe to court, it is in yellow stockings' (Overbury, sig. D1^{r}). *Tarlton's News*, sometimes attributed to Robert Armin, in 1590 describes how a husband, wrongly persuaded of his wife's adultery, 'resolues with the crue of the yellow hosde companions, that Mulier . . . is a word of unconstancie' (*Tarlton's News*, 23).

150 ***cross-gartered*** i.e. wearing what Junius in 1585 defines as '*Fasciae crurales* . . . Hose garters going acrosse, or overthwart, both aboue and beneath the knee' (Junius, 168; see Fig. 15); the early date of this gloss makes it probable that they, like *yellow stockings* (149), had become old-fashioned by 1602 (see 149n.). The description of a 'footman' as 'more upright then any gross gartered gentleman-usher' (Overbury, sig. K3^{r}) probably refers back to Malvolio, as does the proverb 'To wear yellow stockings and cross-garters' (Dent, S868), which testifies to the success of this scene and of 3.4 onstage.

150–1 ***Go to*** 'Come on!': a common catchphrase of exhortation or encouragement (*OED* go *v.* 93)

151 ***thou art made*** your fortune is made; cf. *MND* 4.2.17–18, 'we had all been made men'.

152 ***fellow*** equal

153–4 ***alter services*** change places (i.e. between mistress and servant)

155 ***The Fortunate Unhappy*** she who is blessed by wealth but unfulfilled in love

156 **champaign** chàmpaign: open country (from Old French *champaigne*). The *ch* is pronounced as in 'church'.

discovers not more could not make this more plain; the meaning of the letter is as clear as daylight

157 **open** perfectly clear

politic authors writers concerned with political doctrine or *arguments of state* (147). The adjective was particularly associated in early modern England with Machiavelli, taken to be an amoral apologist for the cultivation of power and self-advancement: e.g. 'Secretarie *Machiavell*, a politick not much affected to any Religion' (Nashe, *Pasquill*, sig. B1^{v}). Malvolio appears willing to abandon his 'Puritan' principles in the interests of self-promotion; cf. 1.3.74, 2.3.142 and note.

155–6 *The* . . . Daylight] *Capell;* tht fortunate vnhappy daylight *F; The fortunate and happy.* Daylight / *Hanmer* 156 champaign] *Dyce (*champain*);* champian *F;* champion *F3*

baffle Sir Toby, I will wash off gross acquaintance, I will be point-device the very man. I do not now fool myself to let imagination jade me; for every reason excites to this, that my lady loves me. She did commend my yellow stockings of late, she did praise my leg being cross-gartered, and in this she manifests herself to my love and with a kind of injunction drives me to these habits of her liking. I thank my stars, I am happy. I will be strange, stout, in yellow stockings and cross-gartered even with the swiftness of putting on. Jove and my stars be praised! Here is yet a postscript. [*Reads.*] *Thou canst not choose but know who I am. If thou entertain'st my love, let it appear in thy smiling – thy smiles become thee well. Therefore in my presence still smile, dear my sweet, I prithee.* Jove, I thank thee. I will smile, I will do everything that thou wilt have me. *Exit.*

158 **baffle** treat with contempt (*OED v.* 2); literally, degrade a perjured knight (*OED v.* 1) Malvolio's verb is turned against him at 5.1.363.
wash . . . acquaintance rid myself of vulgar company; *gross* also alludes to Sir Toby's obesity.
159 **point-device . . . man** in every detail the man described in the letter
160 **jade** deceive (like a *jade* or wily old horse that throws its rider)
161 **excites** leads
161–3 **She . . . cross-gartered** This is evidently invented or imagined by Malvolio – unless he is referring to the letter – since at 193–4 Maria notes that Olivia *abhors* yellow and *detests* cross-gartering.
165 **habits** clothes; modes of behaviour (*OED n.* 4)
166 **happy** fortunate in love; contrast *The Fortunate Unhappy* (155).
strange distant, aloof (*OED a.* 6); cf. *RJ* 2.2.102, 'I should have been more strange, I must confess.'
stout proud (from Old French *estout*, fierce); cf. *2H6* 1.1.187, 'As stout and proud as he were Lord of all'.
167 **putting on** (i.e. of the clothes)
168 **Jove** Since Malvolio is determined to become a lover and an unprincipled 'Machiavellian' (157n.), his invocation of the pagan god of erotic conquest is apt enough.
postscript In Carroll's 2002 Middle Temple production Oliver Cotton's Malvolio exited after *praised!*, and then returned to read the *postscript*, by way of an afterthought.
170 ***entertain'st*** accept (*OED v.* 14)
171 ***still*** always
****dear*** *F*'s 'deero' is almost certainly a misprint – presumably due to 'foul case' error – although Daniel, 43, and some editors have justified it as 'dear, O'.
172 **smile** The actor may actually try out his smile, as in Posner's 2001 RSC production.

169 SD] *Collier* 171 *well.*] well; *looking out to audience gives extravagant smirk / Tree* *dear*] *F2; deero F;* dear, O *Cam*[1]

FABIAN I will not give my part of this sport for a pension of thousands to be paid from the Sophy.

SIR TOBY I could marry this wench for this device –

SIR ANDREW So could I too.

SIR TOBY And ask no other dowry with her but such another jest.

Enter MARIA.

SIR ANDREW Nor I neither.

FABIAN Here comes my noble gull-catcher.

SIR TOBY [*to Maria*] Wilt thou set thy foot o'my neck?

SIR ANDREW Or o'mine either?

SIR TOBY Shall I play my freedom at tray-trip and become thy bondslave?

SIR ANDREW I'faith, or I either?

SIR TOBY Why, thou hast put him in such a dream that when the image of it leaves him he must run mad.

MARIA Nay, but say true, does it work upon him?

175 **thousands** i.e. (presumably) of ducats
from by
Sophy the Shah of Persia: a probable allusion to the claim by Sir Anthony Shirley and his brothers to have received rich gifts, including 16,000 pistolets (cf. 'a pension of thousands'), during an embassy to Shah Abbas the Great in 1599, an episode recounted in two pamphlets, *A True Report of Sir Anthony Shirley's Journey*, 1600, and *A New and Large Discourse of the Travels of Sir Anthony Shirley*, 1601. The *Sophy* is mentioned again at 3.4.272.

176 This is virtually a declaration of intent by Sir Toby, who will indeed marry Maria at the end of the play (cf. 5.1.358).

177 Sir Andrew's habit of slavishly echoing Sir Toby creates the interesting prospect of a *ménage à trois* between them and Maria.

181 **gull-catcher** trapper of fools. The expression imitates the more familiar 'cony-catcher'.

182 i.e. I am yours, do what you will with me. Onstage, Sir Toby at this point may bow down (as in Carroll's 2002 Middle Temple production) or even (as in Posner's 2001 RSC production, together with Sir Andrew) throw himself prostrate on the ground.

183, 186 **either** likewise

184 **play** wager
tray-trip a dice game in which one must throw a three (*tray*) to win

188 **when . . . him** when he wakes up from his dream. The same alternative between dreaming and madness is posed by Sebastian at 4.1.60.

176 device –] *Dyce;* deuice. *F* 182 SD] *Oxf*

SIR TOBY Like aqua vitae with a midwife.

MARIA If you will then see the fruits of the sport, mark his first approach before my lady. He will come to her in yellow stockings – and 'tis a colour she abhors – and cross-gartered – a fashion she detests – and he will smile upon her, which will now be so unsuitable to her disposition, being addicted to a melancholy as she is, that it cannot but turn him into a notable contempt. If you will see it, follow me.

SIR TOBY To the gates of Tartar, thou most excellent devil of wit.

SIR ANDREW I'll make one too. *Exeunt.*

3.1

Enter VIOLA [*as Cesario*] *and* FESTE [*playing on pipe and tabor*].

VIOLA Save thee, friend, and thy music. Dost thou live by thy tabor?

190 **acqua . . . midwife** spirits, such as brandy, used by midwives, in theory to revive their patients but in practice to console themselves; cf. *RJ* 3.2.88, 4.5.16.

193 **a . . . abhors** In Barton's 1969 RSC production, everyone turned at this point to look at David Warner's Sir Andrew, dressed from head to toe in yellow (M. Billington, xx).

197 **turn . . . contempt** make him the notorious object of disgrace; *OED* contempt *n.* 3 gives as first occurrence in this sense the 1611 Authorized Bible.

199 **Tartar** hell. In classical mythology Tartarus is the deepest part of the underworld; cf. *H5* 2.2.123, 'He might return to vasty Tartar back.'
devil clever rogue (*OED n.* 4b, first occurrence)

201 I'll be one of the spectators. The joke here may be that Sir Andrew, lost as usual in the repartee, unwittingly undertakes to make a *notable contempt* (197) of himself, a promise he triumphantly fulfils.

3.1 This scene, which sees the disguised Viola continuously present onstage, is structured primarily on her duologues with Feste and Olivia. While the first is devoted to verbal fooling and to the question of the reliability of language, the second is dominated by Olivia's increasingly explicit declaration of love for Cesario. Pope locates the scene in '*Olivia's Garden*'.

0.2 *Collier^2 expanded F's '*Enter Viola and Clowne*' to make sense of Viola's opening reference to Feste's *tabor* (2), a small drum hanging from neck or belt, conventionally played by jesters. Viola's *thy music* (1) may mean that Feste is also playing his pipe, holding it in one hand while beating the drum with the other.

1 **Save thee** God save thee
live by make your living by (playing)

201 SD] *(Exeunt. Finis Actus secundus)* 3.1] *(Actus Tertius, Scaena prima.)* 0.1 *as Cesario*] *Munro subst.* FESTE] *Munro; Clowne F* 0.2] *Powell MS subst., Collier^2; with a tabor / Malone* 2 thy] the *F2*

FESTE No, sir, I live by the church.

VIOLA Art thou a churchman?

FESTE No such matter, sir. I do live by the church, for I do live at my house, and my house doth stand by the church.

VIOLA So thou mayst say the king lies by a beggar if a beggar dwell near him, or the church stands by thy tabor if thy tabor stand by the church.

FESTE You have said, sir. To see this age! A sentence is but a cheverel glove to a good wit: how quickly the wrong side may be turned outward.

VIOLA Nay, that's certain. They that dally nicely with words may quickly make them wanton.

FESTE I would therefore my sister had had no name, sir.

VIOLA Why, man?

3 **live by** live next to

4 **churchman** clergyman. Viola's question is ironically superfluous, since Feste is presumably wearing jester's motley.

5, 6 **do, doth** These are not emphatic forms but parts of normal sentence structure in Early Modern English.

8 **lies by** dwells near

9 **stands by** is maintained by

11 **You . . . sir** I take note (of your ability in punning): a proverbial phrase (Dent, S118.1)

To . . . age! What a time we live in!

11–13 **A sentence . . . outward** Playing on the proverb 'To turn the wrong side out' (Dent, S431.1), Feste introduces the topic, much debated in Shakespeare's day, of the relationship between linguistic sign and referent (or words and things), and thus the reliability of language as a representation of truth (cf. 12n., 14–15n., 18–19n., 19–20n., 23n.; see pp. 86–7).

12 **cheverel** made of kid leather (*OED n.*[1] 2, giving this example), 'noted for its pliancy and capability of being stretched' (*OED n.*[1] 1). Proverbially, this material was associated with lack of moral integrity (Dent, C608), whereas in Feste's version it is language that becomes malleable, being – as this comedy demonstrates – all too readily subverted.

12–13 **the wrong side** the inside (proverbial: Dent, S431.1; see 11–13n.)

14–15 **They . . . wanton** Those who toy daintily with words render their meanings equivocal. Feste's unstable sign–referent relationship (11–13) is turned against him: words may be directly contaminated by their users, especially by punning clowns. Viola equivocates in turn, however: *dally* means idiomatically to indulge in sexual games (as in *R3* 3.7.74: 'Not dallying with a brace of courtesans') and *wanton* = unchaste (*OED a.* 2).

5 sir.] *Munro;* sir, *F* church, for] *Staunton;* Church: For *F* 8 king] *F2;* Kings *F* lies] lives *Collier*[2] *(Capell)* 12 cheverel] *(*cheu'rill*)*

FESTE Why, sir, her name's a word, and to dally with that word might make my sister wanton. But indeed words are very rascals, since bonds disgraced them.

VIOLA Thy reason, man?

FESTE Troth sir, I can yield you none without words, and words are grown so false I am loath to prove reason with them.

VIOLA I warrant thou art a merry fellow, and car'st for nothing.

FESTE Not so, sir, I do care for something; but in my conscience, sir, I do not care for you. If that be to care for nothing, sir, I would it would make you invisible.

VIOLA Art not thou the Lady Olivia's fool?

FESTE No indeed, sir, the Lady Olivia has no folly. She will keep no fool, sir, till she be married, and fools are as like husbands as pilchards are to herrings – the husband's the bigger. I am indeed not her fool, but her corrupter of words.

18–19 **her name's . . . wanton** Feste playfully suggests a direct link between word and thing: unchaste name, unchaste referent (his *sister*). There may be a pun on *wanton* and 'want one'.

19–20 **words . . . them** either, words have lost their honour since legally binding written contracts replaced oral agreements (cf. the proverb 'An honest man's word is as good as his bond': Dent, M458); or, words have been made disreputable by being too often broken (through unfulfilled bonds), with a probable pun on *bonds* in the sense of 'shackles', as if words had been imprisoned following their downfall.

23 **words . . . false** Linguistic scepticism was increasingly prominent in Shakespeare's time, and found its most authoritative expression in Montaigne: 'the name, is neither part of the thing nor of substance: it is a stranger-piece ioyned to the thing, and from it' (Montaigne, 350).

27–9 **I do . . . nothing** The *something* that Feste cares for is money; but he also implies that Cesario is *nothing*, that he is a cypher, a zero: a possible allusion to his ambiguous gender as well as his social status. There may be a degree of hostility in the clown's gibe, since Cesario is his successful 'rival' as go-between between Orsino and Olivia.

29 **make you invisible** an invitation to Cesario to disappear from the scene

31 **folly** foolishness, madness

32–3 **fools . . . herrings** i.e. fools and husbands are akin in their folly, but husbands are the bigger fools. Pilchards and herrings are of the same family, but herrings can grow larger.

35 **corrupter of words** As a sophisticated court fool, Feste's main professional role is precisely that of 'dallier' with language rather than exponent of simpler forms of jesting.

33 pilchards] *(*Pilchers*), Capell*

VIOLA I saw thee late at the Count Orsino's.

FESTE Foolery, sir, does walk about the orb like the sun, it shines everywhere. I would be sorry, sir, but the fool should be as oft with your master as with my mistress. I think I saw your wisdom there.

VIOLA Nay, an thou pass upon me, I'll no more with thee. Hold, there's expenses for thee. [*Gives coin.*]

FESTE Now Jove in his next commodity of hair send thee a beard.

VIOLA By my troth I'll tell thee, I am almost sick for one, though I would not have it grow on my chin. Is thy lady within?

FESTE Would not a pair of these have bred, sir?

36 **late** lately

37–8 **Foolery . . . everywhere** proverbial: 'The sun shines upon all alike' (Dent, S985). Feste is alluding to his own coming and going (like Cesario) between both houses, but is also implying that we are all fools, a thought he expands on at 38–40.

37 **orb** earth (*OED n.*[1] 2a, giving this example)

like the sun a reference to the Ptolemaic theory, still current in the early modern period, according to which the sun revolved around the earth

38–9 **I would . . . mistress** i.e. I ought to apologize, were it not for the fact that it is the duty of the fool (or folly) to be as much with your master as with my mistress, since Orsino is as much a fool as Olivia.

38 **would** should

but were it not that

40 Feste ironically extends his 'all fools' theme (37–8) to Cesario, who, like him, is no more than a hired attendant (cf. 142 and n.), and whose *wisdom* is thus mere foolishness.

41 **an** if

pass upon me make a thrust against me (a fencing metaphor, anticipating the 'duel' scene: cf. 3.4.268n.). In *Ham* 5.2.280–2, *pass* is similarly found in association with *dally* (14, 18) and *wanton* (15, 19): 'you do but dally. / I pray you pass with your best violence. / I am sure you make a wanton of me.' A secondary meaning is 'pass judgement on me'; cf. *MM* 2.1.23, 'thieves do pass on thieves.'

42 **expenses** reimbursement, payment (*OED* 3c, giving this example)

43 **commodity** supply; cf. *1H4* 1.2.82–3.

43–4 **send . . . beard** Feste seems to come close to seeing through Viola's disguise; he may be taunting Cesario for his lack of virility, as well as for his (and the boy actor's) youth.

46 **I would . . . chin** (1) with emphasis on *my*: Viola would like to possess Orsino's beard (and thus him), rather than one of her own; (2) with emphasis on *chin*: Partridge, 63, suggests an allusion to the *beard* of pubic hair.

48 i.e. why not a second coin, which, together with the first, might produce yet another, their 'child'? Feste tries out another line to get Orsino to double his tip at 5.1.26–30.

42 SD] *Hanmer subst.*

VIOLA Yes, being kept together and put to use.

FESTE I would play Lord Pandarus of Phrygia, sir, to bring a Cressida to this Troilus.

VIOLA I understand you, sir, 'tis well begged. [*Gives another coin.*]

FESTE The matter, I hope, is not great, sir, begging but a beggar: Cressida was a beggar. My lady is within, sir. I will conster to them whence you come. Who you are and what you would are out of my welkin. I might say 'element', but the word is overworn. *Exit.*

VIOLA
This fellow is wise enough to play the fool,

49 **put to use** invested in order to produce interest (a form of 'usury'); also, brought together to reproduce.

50–1 **Lord . . . Troilus** Pandarus, Cressida's uncle, acted as go-between in Troilus' wooing of her (see *TC*). Feste is using his learning merely to beg another coin.

50 **Phrygia** an ancient country of Asia Minor, to which Troy supposedly belonged. Cf. 2.2.41n.

53–4 **The . . . [1]beggar** The question/tip, I fear, is of no great importance/amount, since it was begged of a beggar. Feste seems to be implying that there is not much social difference between him and Cesario, since both have to 'beg' for service to their superiors. He may also be alluding to the definition of players – which in reality they both are – as 'beggars' by hostile authorities and by Puritan commentators such as Philip Stubbes: 'for go they never so brave, yet are they counted and taken but for beggars' (Stubbes, 92[v]).

54 **Cressida . . . [1]beggar** In Henryson and other versions of the story, including Dekker and Chettle's lost play *Troilus and Cressida* (1599), the heroine becomes a leper and beggar, a fate spared her in Shakespeare's version. Perhaps another (unwitting?) allusion to Cesario's real gender (see 27–9, 43–4 and notes).

55 **conster to them** explain to those in the house (see *within*, 54); *conster* is a variant of construe (*OED* construe 9, sole occurrence).

56 **welkin** sky (from Old English *weolcen*). By Shakespeare's time the word had become an affected archaism, used only for a rhetorical flourish, as in 'makes the Welkin cracke' (Marlowe, *Tamburlaine*, part 1, 4.2.45, sig. D4[r]). Shakespeare makes fun of it through the pedant Holofernes in *LLL*: '*caelo*, the sky, the welkin, the heaven' (*LLL* 4.2.5).

57 **'element'** sky or air (*OED n.* 10b); a modish literary term that had been over-abused in recent years, as Feste's comment suggests. Sidney uses it with this meaning: 'As soone as the morning had taken a full possession of the Element' (Sidney, *Arcadia*, 446). Dekker pokes fun at it: 'Let the element alone, 'tis out a thy reach' (Dekker, *Satiromastix*, sig. M1[v]). Malvolio uses the word pompously at 3.4.120.

58–66 Viola's praise for Feste's clowning skills unites her with Olivia (see 1.5.69–92): perhaps a compliment to

52 SD] *Collier[2] subst.* 55 conster] construe *Douai MS, Boswell–Malone* come.] *Mahood;* come, *F*

And to do that well craves a kind of wit.
He must observe their mood on whom he jests,
The quality of persons and the time,
And, like the haggard, check at every feather
That comes before his eye. This is a practice
As full of labour as a wise man's art;
For folly that he wisely shows is fit,
But wise men, folly-fallen, quite taint their wit.

Enter SIR TOBY *and* [SIR] ANDREW.

SIR TOBY Save you, gentleman.
VIOLA And you, sir.
SIR ANDREW *Dieu vous garde, monsieur.*

the actor Robert Armin (Cam[1]) that may echo his own pamphlet: 'A merry man is often thought unwise; / Yet mirth in modesty's loude [i.e. loved] of the wise' (Armin, *Quips*, sig. C1[r]; Mahood).

58 **wise . . . fool** The saying 'No man can play the fool so well as the wise man' (Dent, M321) is alluded to by Shakespeare only here.

59 **wit** intelligence

60 **their mood** the mood of those

61 **quality** character

62 **haggard** wild (female) hawk, caught as an adult and thus difficult to train; cf. Hero on Beatrice in *MA* 3.1.36–7, 'Her spirits are as coy and wild, / As haggards of the rock.'

62–3 **check . . . eye** react to (literally, start at) everything he perceives. Like *haggard* (62), *check* is a term from falconry; cf. 2.5.112n.

62 **feather** bird (*OED n.* 4, first occurrence); a rhetorical figure: synecdoche (part for the whole)

63 **practice** profession

64 **As . . . labour** requiring as much skill and effort

65 The foolery that he expresses with discretion is to the point; cf. Armin, *Quips*, quoted in 58–66n.

66 **wise . . . wit** i.e. supposedly sensible men who behave foolishly quite spoil their reputation for intelligence: Malvolio's fate in this play.
taint spoil; literally, contaminate (*OED v.*[1] 4a). This is a thematic word in the play, recurring with various meanings: cf. 3.4.13, 128, 353; 5.1.134, 351 and notes.

69–70 *F's French spelling, since it involves both speakers, is presumably an error of transcription and does not necessarily indicate bad pronunciation. Indeed, despite Sir Andrew's admission that he has not studied *the tongues* (1.3.90), F's '*vou gard*' may be taken as a phonetic rendering of fairly good French, although actors often provide him with an atrocious accent. The fact that Viola responds promptly in French is an indication of her 'gentle' status.

62 And] Not *Rann (Johnson)* 64 wise man's] *(*Wise-mans*)*, *Hanmer* 66 wise . . . taint] *Capell;* wisemens folly falne, quite taint *F;* wise men's folly shewn, quite taints *Hanmer;* wise men's folly, fall'n, quite taints *Malone* 66.1 SIR] *Rowe* 69 *vous garde*] *Rowe; vou guard F*

VIOLA *Et vous aussi; votre serviteur.*

SIR ANDREW I hope, sir, you are, and I am yours.

SIR TOBY Will you encounter the house? My niece is desirous you should enter if your trade be to her.

VIOLA I am bound to your niece, sir – I mean, she is the list of my voyage.

SIR TOBY Taste your legs, sir, put them to motion.

VIOLA My legs do better understand me, sir, than I understand what you mean by bidding me taste my legs.

SIR TOBY I mean to go, sir, to enter.

VIOLA I will answer you with gait and entrance.

Enter OLIVIA and MARIA.

But we are prevented. [*to Olivia*] Most excellent accomplished lady, the heavens rain odours on you.

SIR ANDREW [*aside*] That youth's a rare courtier; 'rain odours' – well!

72 **encounter** 'Bombastically used for: To go to, approach (nonce-use)', *OED v.* 6, sole occurrence

74 **bound to** bound for, with a possible pun on 'obliged to', alluding to Olivia's 'kind' invitation to enter.

75 **list** destination: literally, boundary (*OED n.*[3] 8)

76 **Taste** try (from Middle English *tasten*, to touch, *OED v.* 2). Cf. Hotspur in *1H4* 4.1.119, 'Come, let me taste my horse.'

77–8 **understand . . . understand** support (i.e. stand under), 77; comprehend, 78. The 'under-stand' pun is, as it were, a standing Shakespearean joke: cf. Launce in *TGV* 2.5.31, 'Why, stand under and understand is all one.' Cesario understands (or has learned) the verb *taste* well enough to use it with the same sense of 'try' at 3.4.238.

81 **with . . . entrance** by walking and going in (*OED* entrance 1a, first occurrence): a deliberately affected paraphrase of Sir Toby's *go . . . to enter* (80), with a pun on 'gate' (Kökeritz, 109), through which Viola says she will enter; in the event, the immediate stage *entrance* of Olivia makes it unnecessary for her to move.

82 **prevented** anticipated

83 **the heavens rain** may the heavens rain (subjunctive)

84 **rare** fine, splendid (*OED a.*[1] 6a) **courtier** habitué of Orsino's court (*OED* courtier[1] 1b, giving this example); wooer (*OED* courtier[1] 2)

85 **well!** a good phrase

70 *vous aussi*] *Pope; vouz ousie F; vouz ausie F2* *votre serviteur*] *Capell; vostre seruiture F; vostre serviteur / Rowe*[3] 81 gait] *(*gate*), Capell* 81.1] *Mahood; after* preuented *82 F* MARIA] *Rowe; Gentlewoman F* 82 SD] *Mahood* 84 SD] *Capell subst.*

VIOLA My matter hath no voice, lady, but to your own most pregnant and vouchsafed ear.

SIR ANDREW [*aside*] 'Odours', 'pregnant' and 'vouchsafed' – I'll get 'em all three all ready.

OLIVIA Let the garden door be shut and leave me to my hearing. [*Exeunt Sir Toby, Sir Andrew and Maria.*]
Give me your hand, sir.

VIOLA
My duty, madam, and most humble service.

OLIVIA
What is your name?

VIOLA
Cesario is your servant's name, fair princess.

86 **My . . . voice** what I have to say cannot be spoken
but except

87 **pregnant** receptive, ready: an almost exclusively Shakespearean use (*OED a.*[2] 3d, first occurrence); cf. *Ham* 3.2.57, 'And crook the pregnant hinges of the knee.'
vouchsafed kindly granted, well disposed

89 **I'll . . . ready** I'll learn all three by heart, to use on a suitable occasion

90 **garden door** door in the garden wall. This suggests that Olivia's imminent conversation with Viola takes place in a *hortus conclusus* or walled garden. Originally conceived as a symbol of the soul – 'A garden well locked is my sister, my spouse' (Song of Solomon, 4.12) – the *hortus* was fashionable in the Renaissance as a space for private exchange.

90–1 **leave . . . hearing** let me alone to listen (to Cesario); leave me to my audience. The term *hearing* has legal connotations, as in *MM* 2.1.133–4, 'I'll . . . leave you to the hearing of the cause' – although it is not clear whether it is Cesario or Olivia who is on trial.

91 SD In Posner's 2001 RSC production, Christopher Good's Sir Andrew, before exiting, lingered, looked wistfully at Olivia and tried several times to say something, but failed.

92–5 Olivia's taking of Viola's hand is ambiguous: it is both an act of courtesy and the boldest move so far in her attempted seduction. Viola responds with defensive formality, in some productions kneeling and kissing Olivia's hand.

93 **service** respect (*OED* 9a, first occurrence)

95 **fair princess** Cesario flatteringly exaggerates Olivia's rank, thereby underlining the social gulf separating them.

88 SD] *this edn; to Sir Toby Oxf* 89 three all ready] *Malone;* three already *F;* three ready *F3* ready.] ready. *writing in his table-book. / Collier*[3] 91 SD] *Rowe*

OLIVIA

My servant, sir? 'Twas never mèrry world
Since lowly feigning was called compliment.
You're servant to the Count Orsino, youth.

VIOLA

And he is yours, and his must needs be yours.
Your servant's servant is your servant, madam.

OLIVIA

For him, I think not on him. For his thoughts,
Would they were blanks rather than filled with me.

VIOLA

Madam, I come to whet your gentle thoughts
On his behalf.

OLIVIA O by your leave, I pray you;
I bade you never speak again of him.
But would you undertake another suit,
I had rather hear you to solicit that
Than music from the spheres.

VIOLA Dear lady –

OLIVIA

Give me leave, beseech you. I did send,

96 **'Twas . . . world** things have never been the same; a proverbial expression (Dent, W878.I). The proverb was put to ideological use (pertinent to this comedy) in Throckmorton's 'Martin Marprelate' *Dialogue*, '*Papist* It was neuer merry worlde since there was so many puritans' (Throckmorton, sig. $D2^r$); and to 'class' use (likewise appropriate) in *2H6* 4.2.7–9, 'It was never merry world in England since gentlemen came up.'
97 **lowly feigning** servile hypocrisy
99 **his** what is his
102 **blanks** empty sheets of paper; cf. 2.4.110n.
103 **whet** predispose (literally, sharpen)
104 **by . . . you** Olivia refuses, politely but impatiently, to hear Orsino's suit.
106 **suit** supplication
107 **solicit** petition (*OED v.* 2); seduce (*OED v.* 4b). Cf. *MA* 2.1.60–2, 'if the Prince do solicit you in that kind, you know your answer.'
108 **music . . . spheres** a Platonic concept (*Republic*, 617b–d; Plato, 2.495) widely current in Shakespeare's day. Cf. Cleopatra on Antonio, 'his voice was propertied / As all the tuned spheres' (*AC* 5.2.82–3).

97 compliment] (complement) 98 You're] (y'are) 108 lady –] *Theobald;* Lady. *F* 109 beseech] I beseech *F3*

After the last enchantment you did here,
A ring in chase of you. So did I abuse
Myself, my servant and, I fear me, you.
Under your hard construction must I sit,
To force that on you in a shameful cunning
Which you knew none of yours. What might you
think?
Have you not set mine honour at the stake
And baited it with all th'unmuzzled thoughts
That tyrannous heart can think? To one of your
receiving
Enough is shown: a cypress, not a bosom,
Hides my heart. So let me hear you speak.

VIOLA

I pity you.

110 **enchantment** continues the 'Platonic' compliment to Cesario's eloquence: the music of the spheres supposedly exerted a magical influence. This is possibly an echo of Belleforest's version of the story ('tu *m'as enchantée*'; Ard[2], xlii).

111 **abuse** misuse, wrong

113 **hard construction** severe judgement

114 **To force** for having imposed

115 **none of yours** did not belong to you

116–17 This elaborate bear-baiting metaphor is part of the recurrent discourse on blood sports in the comedy; cf. 2.3.174; 2.5.6–7, 8–9, 19–20; 3.4.133–4 and notes. Here Olivia is the bear-victim, Cesario's cruel thoughts the persecuting hounds.

116 **set . . . stake** tied my honour to a post (like a bear); cf. *JC* 4.1.48–9, 'we are at the stake, / And bayed about with many enemies.'

117 **baited it** attacked it with dogs

unmuzzled unrestrained, free (to attack my heart)

118–20 **To . . . heart** i.e. to someone as perceptive as you, no more need be said, since my feelings are quite transparent

118 **receiving** perceptiveness

119 **cypress** piece of transparent Cyprus gauze – so called because traditionally imported from the island (*OED* cypress[3] 1a) – associated (when black, as presumably here) with mourning. Cf. 2.4.52n.

bosom breast; the part of the dress that covers the breast (*OED n.* 3a). Cf. *MND* 2.2.104, 'That through thy bosom makes me see thy heart'; with a possible allusion to the male actor, who has literally *not a bosom*; cf. 1.3.68n., 71n.

121 **I pity . . . love** proverbial: 'Pity is akin to love' (Dent, P370)

degree step (upwards, as in a staircase)

110 here] *(*heare*), Warburton* 120 my] my poore *F2*

OLIVIA That's a degree to love.

VIOLA

No, not a grize, for 'tis a vulgar proof
That very oft we pity enemies.

OLIVIA

Why then, methinks 'tis time to smile again.
O world, how apt the poor are to be proud!
If one should be a prey, how much the better
To fall before the lion than the wolf! *Clock strikes.*
The clock upbraids me with the waste of time.
Be not afraid, good youth, I will not have you,
And yet when wit and youth is come to harvest,
Your wife is like to reap a proper man.
There lies your way, due west.

VIOLA Then westward ho.

Grace and good disposition attend your ladyship.
You'll nothing, madam, to my lord by me?

122 **grize** step (from Old French *grez*, 'flight of steps, staircase'): a synonym for *degree* (121). The Duke of Venice's gloss in *Oth* 1.3.201 – 'a grise or step' – suggests that it may already have become somewhat obsolete in Early Modern English.
vulgar proof common experience

124 **'tis . . . again** since you reject me, I must show the world a brave face

126–7 **how . . . wolf** It is generally accepted that Olivia 'refers to herself rather than Viola' (Mahood), and that she is proud at least to have fallen for the *lion* Cesario, but she may equally well be referring to his heartlessly patronizing attitude, despite his lowly status: he has, after all, just implied that she is an enemy to be pitied (123). Cesario thereby becomes vicious *wolf* rather than noble *lion*. Olivia, in any case, is casting herself in the role of defenceless lamb, alluding to the proverb 'The lamb is more in dread of the wolf than of the lion' (Dent, L36).

130 **when . . . harvest** when intelligence and youthfulness ripen

131 **like** likely
reap obtain; enjoy sexually
proper good-looking (cf. 2.2.29); real. The second sense is particularly ironical in the circumstances.

132 **There . . . west** i.e. the encounter is over (setting in the *west*). At the same time, she may indicate the exit: in the Elizabethan theatre, one of the stage doors.
westward ho a London expression, namely the Thames watermen's call to passengers from the City going west, for example to the court at Westminster (thus implying, perhaps, the greater social importance of Orsino's house compared to Olivia's). Less flatteringly, the phrase also alluded to imprisonment in Tyburn (*OED* westward *adv.* 2), as in the title of the comedy by Webster and Dekker (1604).

122 grize] grice *F2;* grece *Oxf*

OLIVIA
Stay –
I prithee tell me what thou think'st of me.
VIOLA
That you do think you are not what you are.
OLIVIA
If I think so, I think the same of you.
VIOLA
Then think you right: I am not what I am.
OLIVIA
I would you were as I would have you be.
VIOLA
Would it be better, madam, than I am?
I wish it might, for now I am your fool.
OLIVIA [*aside*]
O, what a deal of scorn looks beautiful
In the contempt and anger of his lip.
A murderous guilt shows not itself more soon

136 **thou** Olivia shifts from formal *you* to familiar *thou*, a pronominal change that ushers in a more intimate exchange, culminating in her declaration of love for Cesario (147–54). On 'thou' and 'you', see pp. 79–80.

137 i.e. you are forgetting yourself in loving one so far beneath your rank (and of the same gender?)

138 [2]**I think . . . you** i.e. I suspect that you are of higher rank than you pretend (cf. her soliloquy on Cesario's *parentage*, 1.5.281–6).

139 **I am . . . am** I am not what I seem; cf. *Oth* 1.1.63. Viola confirms Olivia's insight regarding her gentle blood, and hints at her disguise; cf. 'I am not that I play' (1.5.179). It may echo Corinthians, 15.10, 'I am that I am.'

140 i.e. my husband

142 **might** might be better
I am . . . fool you are making a fool of me; I am a mere attendant, subject to your whims (cf. 38–9n.).

143–4 Cesario's contempt intensifies Olivia's attraction: an Elizabethan commonplace ('disdaine increaseth desire', Lyly, *Met.*, 3.1, sig. C3[v]); cf. Phebe on the cross-dressed Rosalind, 'Sweet youth, I pray you chide a year together' (*AYL* 3.5.64). Cesario's *lip* is the object of fascinated attention from both sexes: cf. Orsino's *Diana's lip* (1.4.31).

143 **deal** quantity, lot

145–62 The final speeches are in rhyming couplets, used elsewhere more parsimoniously, especially as scene closers (1.1.39–40, 1.4.41–2, 2.2.40–1, 2.4.123–4, etc.).

135–6] *Capell; one line F* 143 SD] *Staunton* beautiful] *Pope;* beautifull? *F* 144 lip.] *this edn;* lip, *F;* lip! *Rowe* 145 murderous] *(*murdrous*)*

Than love that would seem hid. Love's night is noon.
– Cesario, by the roses of the spring,
By maidhood, honour, truth and everything,
I love thee so that maugre all thy pride
Nor wit nor reason can my passion hide.
Do not extort thy reasons from this clause:
For that I woo, thou therefore hast no cause.
But rather reason thus with reason fetter:
Love sought is good, but given unsought is better.

VIOLA

By innocence I swear, and by my youth,
I have one heart, one bosom and one truth,
And that no woman has, nor never none
Shall mistress be of it save I alone.
And so adieu, good madam; never more

145–6 **A murderous . . . hid** doubly proverbial: 'Murder will out', 'Love cannot be hid' (Dent, M1315, L500). Rather than 'indulging in wishful thinking' regarding Cesario (Oxf[1]), Olivia is surely referring to her own love for him, which she cannot hide and which she is about to declare openly.

145 **more soon** Cf. 1.4.28n.

146 **Love's . . . noon** a further proverbial variation on 'love cannot be hid' (145–6n.): love shows all the more visibly as we attempt to obscure it (cf. 'Dark night is Cupid's day', Dent, N167)

149 **maugre** in spite of (from Old French *maugré*)
pride haughtiness, arrogance

150 In Hall's 1958 Stratford production, on this line Geraldine McEwan's young Olivia, 'erotically stirred by Cesario, . . . threw herself on her knees in front of him' (M. Billington, xviii).

152–3 do not force a false conclusion from this premise, namely that my wooing you is a good reason for you not to woo me (*OED* extort *v.* 2, first occurrence)

152 **For that** because

153 **reason . . . fetter** restrain that argument with this argument

156 **bosom** the breast as seat of inward thoughts and emotions; cf. *Oth* 3.1.56, 'speak your bosom freely.'

157 **that . . . has** three concurrent meanings: no woman is capable of such integrity; nobody will ever win my heart; I will never love a woman. The first recalls Orsino's misogynistic speech at 2.4.93–103, as if Viola were imitating male discourse. For the ambiguity involving the second meaning (intended for Olivia) and the third (directed towards the audience), cf. the cross-dressed Rosalind's 'And I for no woman' (*AYL* 5.2.86, 91).
no . . . none Viola makes emphatic use of the multiple (here quadruple) negation that was common in Early Modern English (see Blake, *Grammar*, 6.2.3.1, quoting this example).

158 **save I alone** except for me, with the implication that Cesario is *mistress* rather than master: another half-confession

Will I my master's tears to you deplore.

OLIVIA

Yet come again, for thou perhaps mayst move
That heart which now abhors to like his love. *Exeunt.*

3.2 *Enter* SIR TOBY, SIR ANDREW *and* FABIAN.

SIR ANDREW No, faith, I'll not stay a jot longer.

SIR TOBY Thy reason, dear venom, give thy reason.

FABIAN You must needs yield your reason, Sir Andrew.

SIR ANDREW Marry, I saw your niece do more favours to the count's servingman than ever she bestowed upon me. I saw't i'th' orchard.

SIR TOBY Did she see thee the while, old boy? Tell me that.

SIR ANDREW As plain as I see you now.

FABIAN This was a great argument of love in her toward you.

SIR ANDREW 'Slight! Will you make an ass o'me?

160 **deplore** narrate lamentfully (*OED* 1b, sole occurrence)

161–2 **thou . . . love** i.e. you may persuade my heart to like your master's love instead of loathing it

3.2 This brief scene advances the double scheming of Sir Toby and his companions: on the one hand he incites Sir Andrew to challenge Cesario, and on the other Maria reports on the progress of the gulling of Malvolio. Rowe locates this in '*Olivia's House*'; the actor and director Michael Pennington complains, however, that 'the rhythm of [Rowe's location] is feeble on the stage' (Pennington, 155).

1 In Posner's 2001 RSC production, Sir Andrew already had his cases packed.

2–4 **Thy . . . your** Sir Toby, as usual, adopts familiar *thou*, Sir Andrew and Fabian formal *you*, suggesting different degrees of respect.

2 **dear venom** oxymoron, alluding sarcastically to Sir Andrew's supposedly fierce resolution to leave

4 **favours** gestures of goodwill: Sir Andrew saw Olivia take Cesario's hand in the previous scene (3.1.92).

6 **orchard** garden, with which it was originally a synonym (both equivalent to Latin *hortus*: cf. 3.1.90n.); it remains so in Shakespeare: cf. *RJ* 2.2.63, 'The orchard walls are high, and hard to climb.' Shakespeare's contemporaries, though, often made the modern distinction between the two terms.

7 **the while** at the same time

10 **argument** proof

12 **'Slight** by God's light, one of Sir Andrew's preferred oaths (see 2.5.30)

3.2] *(Scoena Secunda.)* 7 thee the] *F3;* the *F*

FABIAN I will prove it legitimate, sir, upon the oaths of judgement and reason.

SIR TOBY And they have been grand-jurymen since before Noah was a sailor.

FABIAN She did show favour to the youth in your sight only to exasperate you, to awake your dormouse valour, to put fire in your heart and brimstone in your liver. You should then have accosted her and, with some excellent jests, fire-new from the mint, you should have banged the youth into dumbness. This was looked for at your hand and this was balked. The double gilt of this opportunity you let time wash off, and you are now sailed into the north of my lady's opinion, where you will hang like an icicle on a Dutchman's beard, unless you do redeem it by some laudable attempt either of valour or policy.

13 **prove it legitimate** make good my case (literally, show it to be authorized by law: *OED* legitimate *a.* 2a)

15 **grand-jurymen** true witnesses (namely *judgement and reason*, 14, with a pun on 'judgement' in the legal sense); literally, members of a grand jury, who decided whether the evidence before them was strong enough to warrant a full trial by judge and jury

15–16 **since . . . sailor** from time immemorial: a deliberately overblown periphrasis.

18 **dormouse valour** sleepy courage: a sarcastic oxymoron. Cf. the proverb 'As dull as a dormouse' (Dent, D568).

19 **brimstone** ardour; literally, sulphur, associated in the Bible with hell-fire (cf. 2.5.47n.)

20 **accosted** boarded; the second time that Sir Andrew fails to *accost*: cf. 1.3.47 and n.

21 **fire-new . . . mint** brand-new, like a freshly minted coin: proverbial (Dent, M985)

22–3 **looked . . . hand** expected of you

23 **balked** missed

double gilt double gilding, as in gold-plated metal; thus a golden opportunity (Mahood), with a pun on 'guilt', i.e. Sir Andrew's fault in missing his opportunity with Olivia

25–6 **into . . . beard** into the cold region of Olivia's disfavour: an allusion to the 1596–7 expedition to the East Indies via the north-east passage by the Dutch explorer Willem Barentsz, who became stranded in icefields off the island of Nova Zembla. The map resulting from this ill-fated voyage is alluded to at 74–6: see 74–6n. and Fig. 18.

28, 30 **policy** shrewd diplomacy (Fabian's positive meaning); 'Machiavellian' political cunning (the pejorative meaning understood by Sir Andrew; cf. 'base and rotten policy', *1H4* 1.3.108). Cf. 2.3.74.

15 grand-jurymen] *(*grand Iurie men*), Dyce*

SIR ANDREW An't be any way, it must be with valour, for policy I hate. I had as lief be a Brownist as a politician.

SIR TOBY Why then, build me thy fortunes upon the basis of valour. Challenge me the count's youth to fight with him. Hurt him in eleven places – my niece shall take note of it. And assure thyself there is no love-broker in the world can more prevail in man's commendation with woman than report of valour.

FABIAN There is no way but this, Sir Andrew.

SIR ANDREW Will either of you bear me a challenge to him?

SIR TOBY Go write it in a martial hand, be curst and brief. It is no matter how witty, so it be eloquent and full of

29 **An't** if it

30 **I . . . lief** I would as willingly
Brownist a follower of the separatist Robert Browne, who in 1581 founded an extremist Puritan sect that later became the Independentists, advocating the separation of church and state. The fact that even the blissfully ignorant Sir Andrew, in reintroducing the topic of Puritanism (see 2.3.136 and 142), appears well informed on nonconformist sects may be an indication of the degree of public interest in the issue.
politician unscrupulous political schemer (as in *1H4* 1.3.238, 'this vile politician Bolingbroke'; cf. 2.3.74). Sir Andrew's association of nonconformism with Machiavellism is probably accidental and ingenuous, but in the context of the comedy may represent a further questioning of Puritan ideology.

31 **build me** This use of *me* is an instance of the 'ethic dative' (literally, 'for me': Blake, *Grammar*, 3.3.2.1a), usually employed primarily for rhetorical emphasis, but here ironical. See also *Challenge me* (32). Sir Andrew's *bear me* (38) may be an attempt at imitation.
basis 'a thing immaterial; a principle' (*OED* 9a, first occurrence)

32 **Challenge me** See 31n.

33 **eleven places** an arbitrary and absurdly exaggerated number, in contrast with Andrew's actual physical cowardice. Cf. Falstaff's boast of having killed 'seven of the eleven' assailants in *1H4* 2.4.234.

34 **love-broker** go-between in love affairs, pander: the role Viola is obliged to play to Olivia on Orsino's behalf

37 Fabian may be facetiously implying that Sir Andrew faces mortal danger, alluding to the proverb 'There is no way but one (i.e. death)' (Dent, W148).

40 **in . . . hand** in an aggressive military style; or, in scrawling soldier-like handwriting. Sir Toby is setting up Sir Andrew as the traditional cowardly braggart soldier of comedy, the *miles gloriosus* (cf. 3.4.175n.); with a possible pun on the Latin satirist Martial (i.e. the letter should be full of invective).
curst bad-tempered
brief curt; a radical version of Saviolo's precept that letters of challenge 'must be written with the greatest breuity that may be possible' (Saviolo, book 2, sig. X1v); see 44n.

41 **witty** clever
so provided that

invention. Taunt him with the licence of ink. If thou thou'st him some thrice, it shall not be amiss; and as many lies as will lie in thy sheet of paper, although the sheet were big enough for the bed of Ware in England, set 'em down. Go, about it. Let there be gall enough in thy ink – though thou write with a goose-pen, no matter. About it.

SIR ANDREW Where shall I find you?

SIR TOBY We'll call thee at the cubiculo. Go. *Exit Sir Andrew.*

FABIAN This is a dear manikin to you, Sir Toby.

SIR TOBY I have been dear to him, lad, some two thousand strong or so.

42 **invention** matter; *eloquent* (41) and *invention* allude to two of the five parts of rhetoric, *elocutio* (style) and *inventio* (subject matter). It is of course impossible for the letter to be stylish and full of matter if it is not at the same time *witty* or intelligent.
with . . . ink with more freedom than you would dare use in speech (i.e. to his face)

42–3 **If . . . him** if you call him 'thou', using a contemptuous sign of superiority, as in the master–servant ('you'/'thou') relationship: the play's most explicit reference to pronouns of 'power' (cf. Hope, 1.3.2b; Blake, *Grammar*, 3.3.2.1.1; and see pp. 79–80). Theobald compares the Attorney-General Edward Cole's scathing remark at the trial of Sir Walter Ralegh (November 1603): 'for I thou thee, thou traitor.' Sir Toby himself calls Sir Andrew 'thou' here, as usual.

44 **lies** accusations of lying. The 'giving of the lie' was the main cause of duels; cf. Saviolo's discussion of 'the giuing and receiuing of the Lie, whereupon the Duello & the Combats in diuers sortes doth insue' (Saviolo, book 2, sig. R3^{v}); cf. 3.4.151n. and Touchstone's parodic discourse on 'a lie seven times removed' (*AYL* 5.4.67–101).
lie fit; tell lies (because the accusations are false)

45 **bed of Ware** a famous Elizabethan bedstead, measuring 3.35 metres (11 feet) square, now in the Victoria and Albert Museum, London: see Fig. 12.

46 **gall** oak-gall, used as dye in the manufacture of ink; bitterness (proverbial: 'As bitter as gall', Dent, G11)

47 **goose-pen** goose-feather quill: an implicit insult, since the goose is a symbol of cowardice

50 **call** call on (*OED v.* 4d)
cubiculo bedroom (Italian), probably borrowed from Florio, *World*, 93, where it is glossed 'a chamber'. Sir Toby uses it to mystify the linguistically innocent Sir Andrew; with a possible pun on Italian *culo*, 'arse' (Florio, *World*, 93). Cf. 2.3.2n.

51 **dear** affectionate (of Sir Andrew)
manikin puppet (literally, little man)

52–3 **I . . . strong** i.e. I have milked him to the tune of two thousand ducats, corresponding, according to Sir Toby's calculations at 1.3.20, to two-thirds of Sir Andrew's annual income.

52 **dear** costly (of Sir Toby)

46 down. Go,] *Capell subst.;* downe, go *F;* down, and go *Hanmer*

FABIAN We shall have a rare letter from him; but you'll not deliver't?

SIR TOBY Never trust me then; and by all means stir on the youth to an answer. I think oxen and wain-ropes cannot hale them together. For Andrew, if he were opened and you find so much blood in his liver as will clog the foot of a flea, I'll eat the rest of th'anatomy.

FABIAN And his opposite, the youth, bears in his visage no great presage of cruelty.

Enter MARIA.

SIR TOBY Look where the youngest wren of nine comes.

MARIA If you desire the spleen, and will laugh yourselves into stitches, follow me. Yon gull Malvolio is turned

54 **rare** exceptional (ironical)

56 **Never . . . then** 'you bet I will': literally, never believe me again (if I fail to deliver the letter). Sir Toby plans to stage-manage an exchange of insults leading to a duel (see *answer*, 57), but changes his mind when he reads Sir Andrew's masterpiece at 3.4.179.
stir on stir up, provoke

57 **oxen and wain-ropes** wagons drawn by oxen; a rhetorical figure: metonymy (*oxen* and *ropes* standing for the *wain* or wagon)

58 **hale** drag

59 **opened** cut open surgically: a reference to anatomy lessons conducted on corpses to display the internal organs. There is considerable violence in Sir Toby's baroque image of dissection and 'cannibalism'; cf. *I'll eat . . .* (60).
blood . . . liver The liver was thought to be the organ that generated blood and was thus the seat of courage; Sir Andrew is bloodless or 'lily-livered'.

60 **clog** weigh down (literally, encumber)
anatomy (dissected) corpse; *OED* 2b cites Ben Jonson's *Every Man in his Humour* (1598), 4.6, 'They must ha' dissected, and made an *Anatomie* o' me' (Jonson, *Works*, 52).

61 **opposite** adversary

62 **presage** promise (literally, omen)

63 ***the youngest . . . nine** i.e. the smallest chick of the smallest bird: an allusion to Maria's diminutive size. Theobald's emendation of F's 'mine' is justified in part by ornithology: wrens do indeed lay a large number of eggs. More to the point, broods of nine are found elsewhere in Shakespeare, as in the witches' '[the sow's] nine farrow' (*Mac* 4.1.65) and Poor Tom's 'the nightmare and her nine foal' (*KL* 3.4.118).

64 **the spleen** a fit of laughter. In early modern popular medicine the spleen was synonymous with sudden passion in general, and was thought to govern uncontrollable laughter as well as anger and melancholy.

65 **gull** dupe

55 deliver't?] *Dyce;* deliuer't. *F* 60 th'] thy *Hanmer* 63 nine] *Theobald;* mine *F* 65 Yon] *(*yond*)*

heathen, a very renegado, for there is no Christian that means to be saved by believing rightly can ever believe such impossible passages of grossness. He's in yellow stockings.

SIR TOBY And cross-gartered?

MARIA Most villainously, like a pedant that keeps a school i'th' church. I have dogged him like his murderer. He does obey every point of the letter that I dropped to betray him. He does smile his face into more lines than is in the new map with the augmentation of the Indies. You have not seen such a thing as 'tis. I can hardly forbear hurling things at him; I know my lady will strike him. If she do, he'll smile and take't for a great favour.

66 **renegado** renegade (Spanish): deserter of the Christian faith, especially a convert to Islam. It was fashionable at this time to give words a Spanish ending, and so Maria may be imitating her 'superiors'.

67 **to . . . believing** a reference to the Protestant doctrine of salvation through faith rather than (as in Catholic doctrine) good works: ironic in view of Malvolio's 'Puritanism'. Cf. 1.5.124–5n.
rightly in an orthodox Christian (here Protestant) manner
can who can

68 **impossible . . . grossness** grossly improbable discourses, i.e. the passages in the letter inviting Malvolio to dress up, which he has credulously obeyed

71 **villainously** abominably

71–2 **a pedant . . . church** a schoolteacher who teaches in church (presumably because of the lack of a schoolhouse). This suggests a rustic or old-fashioned scene, confirming the suspicion that Malvolio's 'fashionable' cross-garters and yellow stockings are in fact hopelessly provincial and out of date: cf. 2.5.149, 150 and notes.

72 **his murderer** Maria's rather sinister simile recalls the violent blood sports metaphors against Malvolio in 2.5.

74 **smile his face** make his face smile. The verb is transitive, suggesting Malvolio's effort to practise expressions he is not used to making, in obedience to the letter (see 2.5.169–72).

74–6 **more . . . Indies** probable allusion to Edward Wright's 1600 map showing the East Indies 'augmented' because it includes the island of Nova Zembla: cf. 25–6n. The wrinkles on Malvolio's smiling face are compared to the rhumb lines on the map: see Fig. 18.

75 **is** The singular form of the verb *to be* with plural subject is frequent in Shakespeare (Blake, *Grammar*, 4.2.2.1, giving this example).

78–9 **strike . . . favour** ironical; it is of course highly unlikely that Olivia would strike Malvolio, but the idea allows Maria to play on three meanings of *favour*: act of kindness; love token; sexual concession.

66 renegado] *(*Renegatho*)*, *Rowe*

SIR TOBY Come, bring us, bring us where he is. *Exeunt.*

3.3 *Enter* SEBASTIAN *and* ANTONIO.

SEBASTIAN
I would not by my will have troubled you,
But since you make your pleasure of your pains
I will no further chide you.

ANTONIO
I could not stay behind you. My desire,
More sharp than filed steel, did spur me forth,
And not all love to see you – though so much
As might have drawn me to a longer voyage –
But jealousy what might befall your travel,
Being skill-less in these parts, which to a stranger,
Unguided and unfriended, often prove
Rough and unhospitable. My willing love,

3.3 In this duologue – the 'continuation' of the somewhat distant 2.1 – Antonio discloses both his past conflicts with Orsino and, again, his passionate attachment to Sebastian, whom he sends off sightseeing in Illyria. Rowe locates it in '*The Street*'.

1 **troubled you** i.e. because Antonio has taken the trouble to follow him, as announced at 2.1.44; cf. 2.1.31.

2 **since . . . pains** since you have willingly gone to this trouble for me; with a pun on *pains* = effort or suffering (in antithesis to 'pleasure')

3 **chide you** i.e. reprimand you for going to such trouble for me

5 **More sharp** Cf. 1.4.28n.
filed filèd: sharpened, like a sword. This is proverbial: 'As sharp as steel' (Dent, S839.1). On the possible homoerotic connotations of Antonio's sharp desire, see p. 50.

6 **not all** not only
love desire
so much so great

7 ***me** Rann's emendation of F's 'one' makes better sense and is in keeping with the other forms in the passage, such as *My* (4) and *me* (5); the misreading of *one/me* is among the easiest in secretary hand (RP).

8 **jealousy** anxiety (*OED* 3)

9 **Being skill-less in** since you are unfamiliar with
stranger foreigner

11 **Rough and unhospitable** Illyria was traditionally associated with pirates; at 5.1.65 Orsino addresses Antonio himself as *Notable pirate* (see note).
willing voluntary, hence spontaneous
love desire (cf. 6): a personification, as subject of *Set forth* (13); i.e. his desire caused him to follow Sebastian

80 SD] *(Exeunt Omnes.)* 3.3] *(Scaena Tertia.)* 7 me] *Rann;* one *F* 8 travel] *(*rrauell*)*

The rather by these arguments of fear,
Set forth in your pursuit.

SEBASTIAN My kind Antonio,
I can no other answer make but thanks,
And thanks, and ever thanks; and oft good turns
Are shuffled off with such uncurrent pay.
But were my worth as is my conscience firm,
You should find better dealing. What's to do?
Shall we go see the relics of this town?

ANTONIO
Tomorrow, sir; best first go see your lodging.

SEBASTIAN
I am not weary, and 'tis long to night.
I pray you, let us satisfy our eyes

12 **The rather** all the more readily (*OED adv.* 4a)
by due to
arguments persuasions (literally, reasons urged, *OED n.* 3a)

13 **Set . . . pursuit** set out to follow you

15–18 **good . . . dealing** This variation on the proverb 'one good turn deserves another' (Dent, T616) introduces, somewhat ironically, the theme of repaying one's debts, which becomes a real issue when Antonio actually lends Sebastian money (38) and Cesario later disclaims all knowledge thereof (3.4.338).

15 ***thanks . . . thanks** This line is two syllables short in F, and is omitted altogether in F2, perhaps because it was considered defective, although Oxf[1] defends it as indicating 'an embarrassed pause' by Sebastian, who cannot reciprocate Antonio's love. It is more likely that something is simply missing, and Theobald's emendation, which continues the emphatic but somewhat awkward reiteration of thanks, is still the best guess to date, since it was relatively easy for the scribe or compositor to miscount the number of repetitions.

16 **shuffled off** shirked, shrugged off. Cf. Hamlet's 'shuffled off this mortal coil' (*Ham* 3.1.66).
uncurrent pay worthless payment, made in coin that is not of legal tender (*OED* uncurrent 1, first occurrence)

17 **worth** wealth
conscience awareness of my debt
firm substantial

18 **What's to do?** What must be done? This construction has lost its Shakespearean sense of obligation (Blake, *Grammar*, 4.4.4d, giving this example).
relics antiquities. Sebastian wants to go sightseeing, to 'gaze upon the buildings' like Antipholus of Syracuse in *CE* 1.2.13.
town The allusions to a supposed Illyrian *town* or *city* (24) are echoed at 5.1.250; in reality the 'urban' references in this scene are to London: cf. 39n.

21 **to** till

15–16] *om. F2* 15 and ever . . . good] *Theobald;* and euer oft good *F;* and ever oft-good *Pope;* and ever. Oft good *Steevens;* still thanks; and very oft good *Collier*[2] 20 lodging.] *F2;* Lodging? *F*

With the memorials and the things of fame
That do renown this city.

ANTONIO Would you'd pardon me.
I do not without danger walk these streets.
Once in a sea-fight 'gainst the count his galleys
I did some service, of such note indeed
That were I ta'en here it would scarce be answered.

SEBASTIAN
Belike you slew great number of his people?

ANTONIO
Th'offence is not of such a bloody nature,
Albeit the quality of the time and quarrel
Might well have given us bloody argument.
It might have since been answered in repaying
What we took from them, which for traffic's sake
Most of our city did. Only myself stood out,

23 **memorials** monuments; cf. *relics* (19).
24 **renown** make famous
city See 19n.
Would you'd please
26 **count his** count's: a frequent form of the genitive in Early Modern English, in particular with proper names (Blake, *Grammar*, 3.2.1.2d; Hope, 1.1.4g, giving this example); the initial *h* of *his* was regularly dropped, producing here the pronunciation 'count iz'.
27 **service** military (naval) operation. The exact nature and occasion of Antonio's *service* against Orsino's fleet are not specified, although it was serious enough to put his life at risk (30–2) and involved the seizing of property (33–5), so much so that Orsino accuses him of piracy (5.1.65).
28 **ta'en** captured; pronounced as one syllable (cf. F's 'tane')
scarce be answered be difficult to defend myself against (in court); or, be difficult to make amends for
29 **Belike** presumably
31 **quality** nature
time occasion
32 **bloody argument** reason for bloodshed
33 **since** in the meantime
answered settled (i.e. the dispute)
in by
34 **for traffic's sake** in the interests of trade: i.e. the other members of Antonio's *city* returned the seized goods in order to restore commerce with Illyria.
35 **our city** members of our community or state. Antonio is presumably referring not to his home town but to the wider community or city-state (the *polis* or *civitas*) to which he belongs, and which is involved in trade wars with Illyria. Cf. *Cor* 3.1.199, 'What is the city, but the people?'
stood out went against the general trend, isolating myself; stood firm. The reason for Antonio's refusal to restore Orsino's property, thereby exposing himself to danger, is again not specified.

26 count his] County's *(Malone)* 28 ta'en] *(*tane*)* 29 people?] *Dyce;* people. *F*

For which if I be lapsed in this place
I shall pay dear.

SEBASTIAN Do not then walk too open.

ANTONIO
It doth not fit me. Hold, sir, here's my purse.
In the south suburbs, at the Elephant,
Is best to lodge. I will bespeak our diet
Whiles you beguile the time and feed your knowledge
With viewing of the town. There shall you have me.

SEBASTIAN
Why I your purse?

ANTONIO
Haply your eye shall light upon some toy
You have desire to purchase; and your store,
I think, is not for idle markets, sir.

36 **lapsed** lapsèd: apprehended. *OED* (lapse *v.* 8) gives this as sole occurrence of the verb in a transitive mode, possibly deriving from the expression 'to fall into the lap(s) of'. More plausibly the verb has its usual meaning in the intransitive mode, i.e. 'fall (into the hands of)', and thus 'be arrested'. Keightley's emendation 'latched', caught, is attractive but does not substantially change F's meaning.

37 **pay dear** pay a high price, i.e. my life
open i.e. to public view (adverb)

38 **fit** suit, behove (*OED v.*[1] 4). This is ambiguous: Antonio may mean either that it is not opportune for him to be seen, or that it does not suit him to go into hiding. In the event, he renders himself visible to all (3.4.307).

39 **south suburbs** an ironic reference to London, and in particular to the Liberties, an area outside the jurisdiction of the City of London, notorious as an area of brothels. Thomas Nashe asks, '*London*, what are thy Suburbes but licensed Stewes?' (Nashe, *Tears*, fol. 77[r]): it is thus a dubious place to *lodge* (40). As it was also the area where the Globe theatre stood, Sebastian does not have to go very far. In the 2002 Middle Temple production Patrick Brennan's Antonio pointed south towards the Thames (and the Globe).
the Elephant a continuation of the *suburbs* joke: there was indeed an Elephant Inn on Bankside, which was in practice 'an inn-cum-brothel' (Ungerer, 103).

40 **Is best** it is best. The omission of the indefinite pronoun (*it*) is quite frequent in Shakespeare (Blake, *Grammar*, 6.3.1.4, giving this example).
bespeak our diet order our meal, 'perhaps in playful antithesis to "feed your knowledge" [41]' (Ard[2])

42 **have me** find me (Schmidt)

44 **Haply** perhaps
toy trifle

45–6 **your . . . markets** the money you possess is not enough to spend on luxuries

36 lapsed] latched *Keightley*

SEBASTIAN
I'll be your purse-bearer, and leave you for an hour.
ANTONIO
To th'Elephant.
SEBASTIAN I do remember. *Exeunt.*

3.4 *Enter* OLIVIA *and* MARIA.

OLIVIA [*aside*]
I have sent after him; he says he'll come.
How shall I feast him? What bestow of him?
For youth is bought more oft than begged or borrowed.
I speak too loud.
[*to Maria*] Where's Malvolio? He is sad and civil,
And suits well for a servant with my fortunes.

3.4 This hectic scene, the second longest in the play, is a *tour de force* of interwoven plots, bringing together nearly all the narrative threads of the comedy: the tormenting of the cross-gartered Malvolio; the farce of the failed duel between the supposed rivals for the hand of Olivia; the latter's continuing courtship of Cesario through the gift of her portrait; and the mistaken intervention and arrest of Antonio – all variations on 'fooling' or (self-)deception. Capell locates this in '*Olivia's Garden*': cf. 218, but see also 304.1n.

1 **he . . . come** This has worried commentators, since Olivia does not learn that Cesario will accept her invitation until 56. Audiences are less troubled by such inconsistencies, and in any case are likely to interpret the phrase as simply a statement of fact.

2 **of** on

3 **bought . . . borrowed** a variation on the proverb that Taverner translates from Erasmus as 'I had leuer [rather] bye, then begge' (Erasmus, *Proverbs*, fol. 13[v]): as Taverner comments, something obtained by begging 'is i dede [indeed] derely bought' (Dent, B783). Olivia is determined not to debase herself by pleading with Cesario, but is willing to buy his love with a gift; in the event she both buys and begs (cf. 203–7).
more oft Cf. 1.4.28n.

4 *This short line is, as it were, an aside within the aside: Olivia comments on her own thinking out (too) loud. F makes this and the following line a single line, playing havoc with the metre. This is the first of a series of prosodic problems in this scene: 8–9, 19–21 and 23–4 are set as verse in F and have been emended by Pope, Capell and later editors to prose. The alternation of verse and prose evidently created difficulties for the compositor.

5 **sad and civil** orderly (*OED* sad *a.* 4a) and well behaved: virtual synonyms here

6 **fortunes** an allusion both to Olivia's bereavement and to her *mad* and *sad* love (14–15)

47] *Boswell–Malone; F lines* you / houre. /; *Theobald lines* for / hour. 48 SD] *they go off in different directions Cam*[1] 3.4] *(Scoena Quarta.)* 1 SD] *Staunton* 4–5] *Pope; one line F* 5, 153 SDs] *Cam*[1]

Where is Malvolio?

MARIA He's coming, madam, but in very strange manner. He is sure possessed, madam.

OLIVIA
Why, what's the matter? Does he rave?

MARIA No, madam, he does nothing but smile. Your ladyship were best to have some guard about you if he come, for sure the man is tainted in's wits.

OLIVIA
Go call him hither. [*Exit Maria.*]
I am as mad as he,
If sad and merry madness equal be.

Enter MALVOLIO[, *in yellow stockings and cross-gartered, with* MARIA].

How now, Malvolio?

MALVOLIO Sweet lady, ho, ho!

OLIVIA Smil'st thou? I sent for thee upon a sad occasion.

MALVOLIO Sad, lady? I could be sad. This does make

9 **possessed** i.e. by the devil, and thus mad. Maria wants to influence Olivia's interpretation of Malvolio's behaviour in advance.

10 The two missing syllables in this line give rise to a heavy caesura after *matter*.

13 **tainted** diseased; cf. 128, 353; 3.1.66; 5.1.134, 351 and notes. Cf. also Antonio's self-portrait in *MV* 4.1.114, 'I am a tainted wether of the flock.'

14–15 **I am . . . be** Olivia's madness – a form of amorous 'furor' (see 1.1.14–15n.) – is melancholy because unrequited, while Malvolio's is *merry* because he smiles all the time.

15.1 *In F Malvolio enters after *hither* at 14, as soon as Olivia tells Maria to call him. This creates comic surprise, but 'upstages' Olivia and makes her comments on her own and Malvolio's 'madness' awkward in his presence. Capell's postponing of the SD thus makes good theatrical sense. In any case, Malvolio's entry in yellow stockings and cross-garters is one of the play's most poignantly comical moments, and actors rarely fail to make the most of it: 'Laurence Olivier waved his fingers from a large yew hedge, and disappeared again as suddenly as he had appeared' (Brown, 257).

18 **Smil'st** Malvolio is smiling conspicuously at Olivia in obedience to the letter.

8–9] *Pope; F lines* Madame: / Madam. / 14] *Capell; F lines* hither. / hee, / SD] *Dyce* 15 merry] *F3;* metry *F;* mercy *F2* 15.1 *Enter* MALVOLIO] *Capell; after* hither *14 F* 15.1–2 *in . . .* MARIA] *Kemble* 17 ho, ho!] ha, ha. *Smile fantastically. / Rowe*

some obstruction in the blood, this cross-gartering, but what of that? If it please the eye of one, it is with me as the very true sonnet is: 'Please one, and please all.'

OLIVIA Why, how dost thou, man? What is the matter with thee?

MALVOLIO Not black in my mind, though yellow in my legs. It did come to his hands, and commands shall be executed. I think we do know the sweet Roman hand.

OLIVIA Wilt thou go to bed, Malvolio?

18,19 **sad, sad** serious (Olivia); melancholy (Malvolio). Malvolio attributes his melancholy – denying his supposed *merry madness* (15) – to the fact that his garters cause an *obstruction* in the flow of blood, slowing it down (19–20). The adjective *sad* occurs five times in fifteen lines here, with a range of meanings: cf. 5n.

18 **occasion** matter

21 **of one** i.e. of Olivia

with for

22 **sonnet** lyric poem, not necessarily of fourteen lines (*OED n.* 2)

'Please . . . all' A bawdy ballad of this title – not a *sonnet*, as Malvolio claims – was published in 1592, signed R.T., probably the clown Richard Tarlton. Its theme is 'Let her doo what she shall', i.e. let women have their way sexually, which is presumably why Malvolio quotes it to Olivia. It is ironic that here, as at 25–6 and 29, the cultural references of the upright Malvolio, designed to impress the countess, should be so dubious. Some Malvolios sing this line.

23 SP *F's attribution of this speech to Malvolio ('*Mal.*') is clearly an error. Collier's emendation '*Mar.*' (Maria) suggests the most plausible compositor's misreading, but it seems unlikely that Maria is speaking here, first because, as Cam[1] puts it, 'Maria nowhere else "thou's" Malvolio', and above all because Malvolio's contemptuous response to her question at 32 indicates that it is Maria's first intervention in the dialogue. F2's attribution is therefore preferable.

25–6 **Not . . . legs** a probable allusion to another popular ballad (cf. 22n.), 'Black and Yellow'. *Not black* also refers to the theory of the humours, and in particular to melancholy, caused by black bile; cf. 2.5.3n. Malvolio contradicts himself (contrast *sad*, 19).

26 **It** the letter

27 **Roman hand** i.e. italic handwriting, as opposed to the English 'secretary' hand. Olivia uses the modish calligraphy imported from Italy, as evidently does Maria.

28 **go to bed** i.e. in order to rest and recover from his 'madness'. Malvolio interprets the invitation as a sexual advance: 'let's go to bed.' Another moment of potential comedy: Malvolios at this point have laughed, cried, jumped, stumbled or simply smiled triumphantly towards Olivia or the audience; in Posner's 2001 RSC production he chased her around the stage, growling.

18] *Capell lines* thou? / occasion. / 19–21 Sad . . . that?] *Pope; F lines* be sad: / blood: / that? / 19 Sad, lady?] *Theobald;* Sad Lady, *F* 22 'Please . . . all.'] *Rowe;* Please . . . all. *F* 23 SP] *F2; Mal. F; Mar. (Collier)* 23–4] *Pope; F lines* man? / thee? /

MALVOLIO To bed? Ay, sweetheart, and I'll come to thee.

OLIVIA God comfort thee. Why dost thou smile so and kiss thy hand so oft?

MARIA How do you, Malvolio?

MALVOLIO At your request? Yes, nightingales answer daws.

MARIA Why appear you with this ridiculous boldness before my lady?

MALVOLIO 'Be not afraid of greatness' – 'twas well writ.

OLIVIA What mean'st thou by that, Malvolio?

MALVOLIO 'Some are born great' –

OLIVIA Ha?

MALVOLIO 'Some achieve greatness' –

OLIVIA What sayst thou?

MALVOLIO 'And some have greatness thrust upon them.'

OLIVIA Heaven restore thee!

MALVOLIO 'Remember who commended thy yellow stockings' –

OLIVIA Thy yellow stockings?

29 This is yet another reference to a bawdy popular ballad (cf. 22n., 25–6n.), quoted in Brome's play *The English Moor*, 1.3: 'Go to bed, sweet heart, I'le come to thee, / Make thy bed fine and soft I'le li[e] with thee' (Brome, 13).

31 **kiss thy hand** Malvolio has been blowing kisses to Olivia from his fingers, in a hopeful gesture of aristocratic courtly love.

33 **At your request?** i.e. How dare you ask me? – with emphasis on *your*. Malvolio questions Maria's right even to address him, now that he is so important.

34 **daws** jackdaws, which croak gracelessly; *daw* also meant 'fool' (*OED n.* 2a): cf. Warwick's 'I am no wiser than a daw' (*1H6* 2.4.18). The contrast with *nightingale* (= Malvolio) does not necessarily imply that he 'has been singing' (Mahood), but refers rather to their supposed difference in class and style.

37–52 Malvolio has learned the letter by heart, and is not put off by Olivia's evident failure to recognize the quotations.

47 Olivia repeats the phrases from the letter in bewilderment. There is no need to emend *Thy* to *My* as in some editions (see t.n.), as if Olivia believed Malvolio to be addressing her directly: she can see that the yellow stockings are his and not hers.

33–4] *Capell; F lines* request: / Dawes. / 33 request?] *Rowe*[3]; request: *F* 39 great' –] *Rowe;* great. *F* 41 greatness' –] *Rowe;* greatnesse. *F* 46 stockings' –] *Rowe;* stockings. *F* 47 Thy] My *Dyce*[2]

MALVOLIO 'And wished to see thee cross-gartered.'
OLIVIA Cross-gartered?
MALVOLIO 'Go to, thou art made if thou desir'st to be so.'
OLIVIA Am I made?
MALVOLIO 'If not, let me see thee a servant still.'
OLIVIA Why, this is very midsummer madness.

Enter Servant.

SERVANT Madam, the young gentleman of the Count Orsino's is returned. I could hardly entreat him back. He attends your ladyship's pleasure.

OLIVIA I'll come to him. [*Exit Servant.*]
Good Maria, let this fellow be looked to. Where's my cousin Toby? Let some of my people have a special care of him; I would not have him miscarry for the half of my dowry. *Exeunt* [*Olivia and Maria*].

MALVOLIO O ho, do you come near me now? No worse man than Sir Toby to look to me! This concurs directly with the letter. She sends him on purpose that I may appear stubborn to him, for she incites me to that in the letter. 'Cast thy humble slough,' says she, 'be opposite with a kinsman, surly with servants. Let thy tongue

51 Olivia's change in pronoun (*thou* to *I*) indicates that she interprets this as direct address to her rather than quotation. She seems to hear either 'thou art maid' or, more probably in the context, 'thou art mad' (and so responds 'Am *I* mad[e]?'). For the triple made/maid/mad pun, cf. Kökeritz, 126.

53 **midsummer madness** proverbial (Dent, M1117): the only occurrence of the expression in Shakespeare, although arguably the whole of *MND* dramatizes it

55 **hardly** with difficulty (*OED* 6)

60 **miscarry** come to harm (*OED* 1)

62–80 This speech is a crescendo of self-deception: Malvolio expresses no sense of defeat at Olivia's failure to respond to his allusions, but on the contrary interprets her concern for his mental health and her involving of Sir Toby as confirmations of the letter's contents.

62 **come near me** begin to understand me: idiomatic (Dent, N56.1); Blake, *Grammar*, 5.4.2 (giving this example), glosses *near* as 'close to what I mean'.

63 **look to** look after

65 **stubborn** fierce (*OED a.* 1a)

57, 295, 305, 316 SDs] *Capell* 61 SD] *Capell; exit F; Exeunt Olivia and Maria different ways / Mahood*

tang with arguments of state; put thyself into the trick of singularity', and consequently sets down the manner how, as a sad face, a reverend carriage, a slow tongue, in the habit of some sir of note and so forth. I have limed her, but it is Jove's doing and Jove make me thankful! And when she went away now, 'Let this fellow be looked to.' 'Fellow', not 'Malvolio', nor after my degree, but 'fellow'! Why, everything adheres together that no dram of a scruple, no scruple of a scruple, no

68 ***tang with** The rare verb *tang* (= ring out) presents no problems to the compositor (or scribe) on its first appearance in the letter (2.5.147) but appears to baffle him here: F's 'langer' is a plausible misreading of secretary initial *t* (uncrossed, or looped) and final *e* (flourished so as to resemble *-er* suspension – as elsewhere in F, e.g. 'lover never' at 2.4.65) (RP). F2 corrects only the verb, while Capell and others go further, eliminating *with* in order to match the letter, and Turner argues that the particle is carried over from the two *with*s in the previous line. This is probably a piece of overcorrecting, since Malvolio, quoting from memory, does not always repeat the letter verbatim – cf. 48, which omits *ever* from the quoted passage (2.5.150) – and the verb phrase makes sense as it stands in F2.

69 **consequently** subsequently (*OED* 1)
sets down puts in writing

70 **as** such as
reverend carriage solemn bearing
slow deliberate

71 **habit** manner (literally, apparel). Cf. the cross-dressed Rosalind in *AYL* 3.2.291–2: 'I will speak to him like a saucy lackey and under that habit play the knave with him.'
sir of note important gentleman

72 **limed** caught; birdlime is sticky resin used to trap small birds, or, metaphorically, the beloved's heart: cf. *TGV* 3.2.68–9, 'You must lay lime, to tangle her desires / By wailful sonnets.' It is, of course, Malvolio who has been *limed* by the letter.

72–3 **it . . . thankful!** probable echo of Psalm 118.23, 'This was the doyng of God: it is marueylous in our eyes' (Ard[1])

72 **Jove** Cf. 1.5.110n. and 2.5.168n.

73, 74, 75 **fellow** Malvolio interprets this optimistically as 'equal' or 'peer', as in *H5* 5.2.238–9, 'fellow with the best king'. Even more promisingly for Malvolio, the term could also signify 'spouse' or 'companion' (*OED n.* 4a), as in *Tem* 3.1.83–4, 'I am your wife, if you will marry me . . . To be your fellow'; but the word was mostly used, as at 58, to address a servant or social inferior.

74–5 **after my degree** according to my rank

75–7 **Why . . . circumstance** In Barton's 1969 RSC production Donald Sinden's Malvolio on these lines famously checked his watch against the garden sundial, and corrected the dial (Sinden, 'Malvolio', 62).

75–6 **adheres together that** coincides to prove that

76 **no . . . [3]scruple** not the slightest impediment or doubt; *dram* and *scruple* are both small apothecaries' weights (respectively 1/8 and 1/24 of an

68 tang with] *F2;* langer with *F;* tang *Capell* 72 Jove's] God's *Halliwell* 72, 79 Jove] God *Halliwell* 76 [2]a scruple] an ounce *Keightley*

obstacle, no incredulous or unsafe circumstance – what can be said? – nothing that can be can come between me and the full prospect of my hopes. Well, Jove, not I, is the doer of this, and he is to be thanked.

Enter [SIR] TOBY, FABIAN *and* MARIA.

SIR TOBY Which way is he, in the name of sanctity? If all the devils of hell be drawn in little, and Legion himself possessed him, yet I'll speak to him.

FABIAN Here he is, here he is. [*to Malvolio*] How is't with you, sir? How is't with you, man?

MALVOLIO Go off, I discard you. Let me enjoy my private. Go off.

MARIA Lo, how hollow the fiend speaks within him. Did

ounce) so that 'scruple of a scruple' is the smallest amount imaginable. Metaphorically, *scruple* also signifies uncertainty: Malvolio has no doubts at all regarding his success. Cf. 2.5.2n.

77 **incredulous** incredible
unsafe unreliable (*OED* 3, giving this example)

79 **prospect** view
hopes i.e. their fulfilment

81 **in . . . sanctity** Sir Toby calls on holy powers as he is about to confront the *possessed* Malvolio.

82 **drawn in little** contracted into a small space (namely that of one body); with a pun on 'painted in miniature' (as in *Ham* 2.2.303, 'his picture in little')
Legion himself i.e. the devil, with confused reference to the episode of possession by a multitude of devils in Mark, 5.9, where the 'foule spirite' tells Jesus 'my name is legion [i.e. innumerable], for we are many'; Sir Toby takes this to mean that *Legion* is literally another name for Satan. There is no evidence to suggest that this was a standing joke, so it is probably a drunken blunder. This is also the first of many possible echoes of the notorious *True Narration* by the Puritan exorcist John Darrell, who affirms that through faith, 'Though Belzabub the prince of Diuelles, and with him Legions had bene in him, yet had you cast them out' (Darrell, 41–2); cf. 4.2.25n., 31n., 32n. and 97n.

86, 87 **Go off** go away

86 **discard** reject: a recent import into English (from Italian *scartare*); *OED v.* 1 gives as first occurrence Florio's gloss, '*o via scartate* . . . goe to, discarde' (Florio, *Second Fruits*, 68–9). Since one of its meanings was 'dismiss from employment' (*OED* 3), Malvolio may be looking forward to when he is in a position to fire Fabian.

87 **private** privacy (*OED n.* 6a, first occurrence)

88 **hollow** with a hollow and echoing voice (adverb). *OED adv.* 1 (first occurrence) suggests 'insincerely'.

80 he] He *Halliwell* 80.1, 212.1, 266.1 SIR] *Rowe* 84, 328, 337, 382 SDs] *Oxf* 84 How] *Sir Toby* How *Cam*[1]

not I tell you? Sir Toby, my lady prays you to have a care of him.

MALVOLIO Aha! Does she so?

SIR TOBY Go to, go to. Peace, peace, we must deal gently with him. Let me alone. How do you, Malvolio? How is't with you? What, man, defy the devil! Consider, he's an enemy to mankind.

MALVOLIO Do you know what you say?

MARIA La you, an you speak ill of the devil, how he takes it at heart. Pray God he be not bewitched.

FABIAN Carry his water to th' wise woman.

MARIA Marry, and it shall be done tomorrow morning, if I live. My lady would not lose him for more than I'll say.

MALVOLIO How now, mistress?

MARIA O Lord!

SIR TOBY Prithee hold thy peace, this is not the way. Do you not see you move him? Let me alone with him.

FABIAN No way but gentleness, gently, gently. The fiend is rough, and will not be roughly used.

91 **Aha . . . so** possibly an aside by Malvolio, who takes Maria's statement as confirming Olivia's love for him. In Carroll's 2002 Middle Temple production, Oliver Cotton's steward started towards Paul Chahidi's Maria on this line, causing him/her to scream.

93 **Let me alone** let me deal with him

94 **defy the devil** Sir Toby pretends to take Malvolio's 'madness' as a sign of possession by the devil; cf. 82n.

96 **Do . . . say?** Do you realize the gravity of what you are saying (i.e. that I of all people should be possessed by the devil)?; or, are you in your right mind (or merely drunk)?

97 **La you** look you
an if

98 **at heart** to heart
bewitched Maria introduces a third possible cause of Malvolio's behaviour, in addition to madness and possession.

99 **water** urine (for diagnosis of disease)
wise woman a benevolent 'witch' or herbalist, expert in charms and remedies against disease and bewitchment (*OED* 1). In *MW* Falstaff is made to cross-dress as 'the wise woman of Brainford' (*MW* 4.5.24–5).

100 **tomorrow morning** i.e. using the urine from Malvolio's overnight chamber-pot

106 **move** excite, upset

93 me] him *Rowe* 106 Let . . . him] *om. F3*

SIR TOBY Why how now, my bawcock? How dost thou, chuck?

MALVOLIO Sir!

SIR TOBY Ay, biddy, come with me. What, man, 'tis not for gravity to play at cherry-pit with Satan. Hang him, foul collier!

MARIA Get him to say his prayers, good Sir Toby, get him to pray.

MALVOLIO My prayers, minx?

MARIA No, I warrant you, he will not hear of godliness.

MALVOLIO Go hang yourselves, all. You are idle shallow things; I am not of your element. You shall know more hereafter. *Exit.*

SIR TOBY Is't possible?

FABIAN If this were played upon a stage now, I could condemn it as an improbable fiction.

109–12 **bawcock . . . biddy** childish terms of endearment, patronizing the 'mad' Malvolio. A *bawcock* (from French *beau coq*) is literally a 'fine cock' or good fellow (cf. *H5* 4.1.44, 'The king's a bawcock, and a heart of gold'); *chuck*, 'chicken', was often used with children, as was *biddy*, likewise 'chicken' (*OED* biddy², first occurrence).

113 **gravity** dignity, reverence. The noun was sometimes used as a title of honour ('your gravity': first use cited in *OED* 1618), and may imply an allegorical personification, as in a morality play, both here and in *1H4* 2.4.285–6: 'What doth Gravity out of his bed at midnight?'
cherry-pit child's game of rolling cherry stones into a small hole: Malvolio is thus on familiar terms with the devil. Ungerer, 99, and Rubinstein, 48, suspect a sexual allusion.

114 **foul collier** dirty coalman, with reference to the devil's blackness. The association is proverbial: 'Like will to like, quoth the devil to the collier' (Dent, L287), which is also the title of a 1568 play by Ulpian Fulwell. In Posner's 2001 RSC production, Sir Toby used his walking stick to make the sign of the cross as he uttered this line.

117 **minx** hussy, impudent girl

119 **idle** foolish, frivolous

120 **of your element** on your low level. At 3.1.56–7 Feste avoids the term because it is *overworn*; Malvolio, however, employs it with pompous solemnity.

123–4 Fabian's ironic metatheatrical comment underlines the almost too perfect success of their plot, but also authenticates the *improbable* scene as *non*-fiction. Fabian's *now* conflates dramatic or fictional time with the 'real' time of the performance; cf. Cassius' and Brutus' reflections on 'this our lofty scene' in *JC* 3.1.111–16.

SIR TOBY His very genius hath taken the infection of the device, man.

MARIA Nay, pursue him now, lest the device take air and taint.

FABIAN Why, we shall make him mad indeed.

MARIA The house will be the quieter.

SIR TOBY Come, we'll have him in a dark room and bound. My niece is already in the belief that he's mad. We may carry it thus for our pleasure and his penance till our very pastime, tired out of breath, prompt us to have mercy on him; at which time we will bring the device to the bar and crown thee for a finder of madmen.

Enter SIR ANDREW [*with a letter*].

But see, but see.

FABIAN More matter for a May morning.

125 **genius** soul (literally, guardian spirit)
hath . . . infection of has been contaminated by: one of numerous references in the play to contagion (e.g. 2.3.53–5)

127 **device** plot, dramatic representation (continuing Fabian's theatrical allusions). Cf. *MND* 5.1.48–50, '*The riot of the tipsy bacchanals* . . . That is an old device.'

127–8 **take . . . taint** be exposed and spoiled (*OED* taint, *v.*[1] C 4b): an allusion either to food going bad by being left in the open, or to the danger of catching a disease through exposure to the air; cf. 13, 353; 3.1.66; 5.1.134, 351 and notes. Maria is afraid the plot might be ruined by becoming public knowledge.

130 **the quieter** i.e. because the 'mad' Malvolio will be put away (see next line)

131 **in . . . bound** the customary treatment at the time for madness (see Reed, 11). Cf. Dr Pinch's proposed cure for Antipholus and Dromio of Ephesus in *CE* 4.4.96, 'They must be bound and laid in some dark room.'

133 **carry it** bring it off (*OED v.* 15b). Cf. *AW* 4.1.26, 'It must be a very plausive invention that carries it.'

133–4 **till . . . breath** until we grow tired from an excess of enjoyment. As in 2.5, the harsh treatment of Malvolio is planned as a form of spectator sport.

135–6 **bring . . . bar** bring our plot into the open (literally, to the prisoner's stand, and thus into open court)

136 **finder of madmen** i.e. member of a jury appointed to decide whether the accused is insane

138 **More . . . morning** more holiday entertainment (i.e. Sir Andrew's challenge). The allusion is to the May games, namely the array of sports and performances associated with May Day festivities, and does not imply the temporal setting of the play.

136.1] *this edn; after 137 F* *with a letter*] *Cam*[1] *subst.*

SIR ANDREW Here's the challenge, read it. I warrant there's vinegar and pepper in't.

FABIAN Is't so saucy?

SIR ANDREW Ay, is't, I warrant him. Do but read.

SIR TOBY Give me. [*Reads.*] *Youth, whatsoever thou art, thou art but a scurvy fellow.*

FABIAN Good, and valiant.

SIR TOBY [*Reads.*] *Wonder not nor admire not in thy mind why I do call thee so, for I will show thee no reason for't.*

FABIAN A good note, that keeps you from the blow of the law.

SIR TOBY [*Reads.*] *Thou com'st to the Lady Olivia, and in my sight she uses thee kindly. But thou liest in thy throat; that is not the matter I challenge thee for.*

FABIAN Very brief, and to exceeding good sense [*aside*] -less.

SIR TOBY [*Reads.*] *I will waylay thee going home, where if it be thy chance to kill me –*

141 **saucy** spicy, insolent

142 **I warrant him** truly. A discourse marker: literally, I stand guarantor for it (the letter); *him* was the dative form of 'it' as well as 'he' (*OED* him 2a).

144 ***thou*** Sir Andrew has accepted Sir Toby's advice to *thou* Cesario (cf. 3.2.42–3).

scurvy worthless

146 ***admire*** marvel (synonymous with *wonder*, and so – typically with Sir Andrew – tautological)

147 ***I will . . . reason*** I am not obliged to explain; I have no motive to produce

148 **A good note** well said

148–9 **keeps . . . law** protects you from the risk of legal action (for breach of the peace)

151 ***thou . . . throat*** you are a complete liar: idiomatic (Dent, T268). Sir Andrew is again following Sir Toby's advice at 3.2.43–4, and closely echoing Saviolo's example of a foolish and low-class challenge: 'euerye daye there riseth from the common sorte new and strange foolishnesses, as he who will giue the lye ere the other speake, saying: if they saye that I am not an honest man, thou lyest in thy throate' (Saviolo, book 2, sig. T2[r]). See 3.2.40n. and 44n. Here the 'lie' is the very idea – never mentioned by Cesario – that Sir Andrew is jealous of him: hence there is no motive, as Fabian points out at 153–4.

142 is't,] *Collier;* ist? *F* 143, 313, 317 SDs] *Rowe* 146, 150, 155, 158, 161 SDs] *Mahood* 156 *me* –] *Rowe; me. F*

FABIAN Good.

SIR TOBY [*Reads.*] *Thou kill'st me like a rogue and a villain.*

FABIAN Still you keep o'th' windy side of the law – good.

SIR TOBY [*Reads.*] *Fare thee well, and God have mercy upon one of our souls. He may have mercy upon mine, but my hope is better, and so look to thyself. Thy friend as thou usest him, and thy sworn enemy,*

Andrew Aguecheek.

If this letter move him not, his legs cannot. I'll give't him.

MARIA You may have very fit occasion for't. He is now in some commerce with my lady, and will by and by depart.

SIR TOBY Go, Sir Andrew. Scout me for him at the corner of the orchard like a bumbaily. So soon as ever thou seest him, draw and, as thou draw'st, swear horrible,

157 **Good** a good line of argument; a good thing if Sir Andrew were to be killed

158 *like . . . villain* This phrase, apart from the tautology, is ambiguous: it could refer back to either *thou* or *me*.

159 **o'th' . . . law** at a safe distance from legal punishment. Mahood takes this to be a hunting metaphor, but it is more probably derived from the nautical expression 'on the windward side', i.e. the law would have to sail against the wind to reach you; cf. *MA* 2.1.296.

163 *my . . . better* i.e. I have a better chance of surviving; Sir Andrew also seems unwittingly to suggest that his soul may not be saved.

163–4 *as . . . him* to the extent that you treat him like one (i.e. not at all). With this self-deconstructing phrase, and the absurd contradiction between *Thy friend* and *thy sworn enemy*, Sir Andrew manages to cancel any residue of meaning from his challenge.

166–7 **I'll give't him** Sir Toby confirms his promise at 3.2.56; in reality, he has no intention of giving Cesario the letter, as he admits at 179 after Sir Andrew exits.

169 **commerce** dealings, exchange (*OED n.* 2a, giving this example)

171 **Scout . . . him** keep an eye open for me (*OED v.* 1a, giving this example); *me* is an 'ethic dative' (= for me: Blake, *Grammar*, 3.3.2.1a); cf. 3.2.31–2n.

172 **bumbaily** bumbailiff, contemptuous term for bailiff, i.e. sheriff's officer, who catches debtors from the rear (hence *bum*; the expression is the equivalent to French *pousse-cul*: *OED*, giving this example)

173 **horrible** horribly (adverb): cf. *KL* 4.6.3, 'Horrible steep'.

166 If] *Hanmer; To.* If *F* 168 You] *F2;* Yon *F* 173 horrible] horribly *F2*

for it comes to pass oft that a terrible oath, with a swaggering accent sharply twanged off, gives manhood more approbation than ever proof itself would have earned him. Away!

SIR ANDREW Nay, let me alone for swearing. *Exit.*

SIR TOBY Now will not I deliver his letter, for the behaviour of the young gentleman gives him out to be of good capacity and breeding. His employment between his lord and my niece confirms no less. Therefore this letter, being so excellently ignorant, will breed no terror in the youth. He will find it comes from a clod-pole. But, sir, I will deliver his challenge by word of mouth, set upon Aguecheek a notable report of valour and drive the gentleman – as I know his youth will aptly receive it – into a most hideous opinion of his rage, skill, fury and impetuosity. This will so fright

174 ***for it** the most likely reading for F's 'for t' (with its wide space between 'for' and 't'); a less probable alternative is 'for't'.

175 **swaggering** insolent, hectoring: another possible allusion to the *miles gloriosus* or cowardly braggart soldier (see 3.2.40n.)
twanged off *OED* glosses *twang* (*v.* 5a) as 'utter with a sharp ringing tone', quoting this example and giving the verb as a variant of 'tang' (cf. 2.5.147). Most early uses of the word, however, suggest the sound of plucking a stringed instrument (*OED* 1–2), which may be closer to the sound being evoked here. Alternatively, the term may already have the more modern meaning, 'spoken with a nasal intonation' (*OED v.* 6, first occurrence 1615). In Jonson's *Poetaster* (1601), 1.2, 'twang' means simply 'speak': 'The tongue of the *oracle* neuer twang'd truer' (Jonson, *Works*, 280).

176 **approbation** credit
proof trial

178 **let . . . swearing** I don't need any help in swearing; cf. 93n. Saying oaths is indeed one of Sir Andrew's few gifts: see, for example, 387; 2.5.30; 3.2.12.

179 **Now . . . letter** Sir Toby changes his mind about delivering the challenge, presumably because of its dubious literary quality: cf. 166–7 and 3.2.56. In Mendes's 2002 Donmar production, Paul Jesson's Toby tore up the letter contemptuously.

181 **of . . . breeding** intelligent and well bred: a further underlining of Cesario's 'gentle' status, despite his servant role; cf. *the gentleman*, 187.

185 **clod-pole** blockhead: literally, having a head (poll) made of a clod of earth (*OED* clod-pate, first occurrence)

186 **set upon** attribute to

187–8 **his . . . receive it** his lack of experience will lead him to react to the challenge

188 **aptly** readily (*OED* 3, giving this example)

174 for it] *Cam[1]*; for't *F*

them both that they will kill one another by the look, like cockatrices.

Enter OLIVIA *and* VIOLA [*as Cesario*].

FABIAN Here he comes with your niece. Give them way till he take leave, and presently after him.

SIR TOBY I will meditate the while upon some horrid message for a challenge.

[*Exeunt Sir Toby, Fabian and Maria.*]

OLIVIA
I have said too much unto a heart of stone
And laid mine honour too unchary on't.
There's something in me that reproves my fault,
But such a headstrong potent fault it is
That it but mocks reproof.

191 **cockatrices** basilisks, mythical monsters able to kill with a glance. Cf. *RJ* 3.2.47, 'the death-darting eye of cockatrice'. 'To kill like a cockatrice' was proverbial (Dent, C496.2), but Sir Toby's ironical conceit of a duel of deadly glances is grotesquely original.

192–3 **Give . . . leave** step aside until he leaves

193 **presently** immediately

194 **horrid** frightening

196 **heart of stone** proverbial (Dent, H311)

197 **laid . . . on't** placed my honour too rashly upon it (i.e. the stone). Most editors have adopted Theobald's emendation 'laid . . . out', in the sense of 'exposed', partly on the grounds that the same 'error' is supposedly made in *WT* 4.4.160 ('look on't' for 'look out') and may be a recurrent vice on the part of compositor B. F's line, however, is surely stronger in developing the 'heart of stone' commonplace. Olivia is probably alluding to the Elizabethan custom of placing money on a stone in church by way of payment of a debt (Sisson, 1.193), with the further 'monetary' implication that she has recklessly wagered her honour on the stone-cold Cesario.

unchary rashly (adverb, from 'chary', cautious: *OED*, first occurrence)

198 **fault** misdeed

199 **headstrong potent** obstinately powerful; *headstrong* is best understood as an intensifier qualifying the adjective *potent*: cf. *longing wavering*, 2.4.34.

fault vice

200 **but** merely

mocks reproof ignores my attempts to correct it

191.1 *as Cesario*] *Munro subst.* 195 SD] *Capell; Exeunt. F2; Exit Maria. Sir Toby and Fabian stand aside / Mahood* 197 on't] out *Theobald*

VIOLA
With the same haviour that your passion bears
Goes on my master's griefs.

OLIVIA
Here, wear this jewel for me: 'tis my picture.
Refuse it not, it hath no tongue to vex you;
And I beseech you come again tomorrow.
What shall you ask of me that I'll deny
That honour saved may upon asking give?

VIOLA
Nothing but this: your true love for my master.

OLIVIA
How with mine honour may I give him that
Which I have given to you?

VIOLA I will acquit you.

OLIVIA
Well, come again tomorrow. Fare thee well.
A fiend like thee might bear my soul to hell. [*Exit.*]

Enter [SIR] TOBY *and* FABIAN.

SIR TOBY Gentleman, God save thee.

201–2 My master's pains of unrequited love continue without end. The *–es* plural ending (*Goes*) is quite frequent in Early Modern English (Hope, 2.1.8).

201 **same . . . bears** same behaviour that your desire provokes in you
haviour behaviour (*OED* 2): not an abbreviation, so no apostrophe required

203 **jewel** miniature set in jewels. The word *jewel* in Shakespeare 'does not properly signify a single gem, but any precious ornament or superfluity' (Johnson).
picture portrait

206–7 *F's punctuation of this somewhat contorted construction does not help to clarify its sense, which is roughly 'How can I deny you anything that I may give you without losing my honour (i.e. my virginity)?'

210 **acquit you** release you from your vows of love for me; take my leave of you (with a pun on 'quit')

211, 212 **thee** Olivia switches, as at 3.1.136, from formal *you* (204–10) to familiar *thou*, which she will continue to adopt with Sebastian at 4.1.50–63. Viola maintains a respectful *you* throughout.

202 Goes] Go *Malone* griefs] Grief *Rowe* 207 honour saved] *Pope;* honour (sau'd) *F;* (honour sav'd) *F3* 212, 381 SDs] *F2*

VIOLA And you, sir.

SIR TOBY That defence thou hast, betake thee to't. Of what nature the wrongs are thou hast done him, I know not, but thy intercepter, full of despite, bloody as the hunter, attends thee at the orchard end. Dismount thy tuck, be yare in thy preparation, for thy assailant is quick, skilful and deadly.

VIOLA You mistake, sir. I am sure no man hath any quarrel to me. My remembrance is very free and clear from any image of offence done to any man.

SIR TOBY You'll find it otherwise, I assure you. Therefore, if you hold your life at any price, betake you to your guard, for your opposite hath in him what youth, strength, skill and wrath can furnish man withal.

VIOLA I pray you, sir, what is he?

215 **That . . . to't** make use of whatever defence you possess; *betake thee to* was commonly followed by 'thy heels' (*OED* betake 4), so that Sir Toby may be implying that Cesario's only hope of survival is to run away.

217 **intercepter** stalker, persecutor: probably borrowed – like *discard* at 86 – from Florio, *World*, 187, where it appears for the first time in English (*OED* 1a). It is glossed in Florio's *New World*, 262, as '*Intercettore*, a preuenter, a forestaller, an encrocher, an interceptor'; there may be a hint that this 'preventer' is a personification of death awaiting his next victim (see *attends thee*, 218).

despite contempt, defiance

217–18 **bloody . . . hunter** a reference to the ritual of smearing the successful huntsman with the blood of his prey (Capell)

218 **attends** awaits

at . . . end outside the garden (cf. 3.2.6); *at the end* here probably means 'just beyond the limit', since it is improbable that Sir Andrew, who enters at 266, is to be imagined as already present in Olivia's estate.

218–19 **Dismount thy tuck** draw thy sword. A *tuck* (*OED n.*[3]) was a small rapier (from Old French *etoc*, Italian *stocco*); cf. *stuck*, 269n. In *Hamlet* Osric calls the straps attaching the sword to the belt 'carriages' (*Ham* 5.2.133), and *dismount* seems to play on the same metaphor.

219 **yare** ready, quick

222 **to me** with me

remembrance recollection

225 **if . . . price** if you value your life at all

225–6 **betake . . . guard** take up a defensive position: a fencing expression. Sir Toby repeats his use of intimidating 'technical' terms with Sir Andrew at 268–70.

226 **opposite** opponent; cf. 3.2.61.

227 **withal** with: an emphatic form (Blake, *Grammar*, 5.4.2)

228 **what** what rank; cf. 1.2.32n.

221 sir . . . no] *Theobald subst.;* sir I am sure, no *F;* sir, I am sure, no *F3*

SIR TOBY He is knight, dubbed with unhatched rapier and on carpet consideration, but he is a devil in private brawl. Souls and bodies hath he divorced three, and his incensement at this moment is so implacable that satisfaction can be none but by pangs of death and sepulchre. 'Hob-nob' is his word: give't or take't.

VIOLA I will return again into the house and desire some conduct of the lady. I am no fighter. I have heard of some kind of men that put quarrels purposely on others to taste their valour. Belike this is a man of that quirk.

SIR TOBY Sir, no. His indignation derives itself out of a very competent injury, therefore get you on and give him his desire. Back you shall not to the house, unless you undertake that with me which with as much safety you might answer him. Therefore on, or strip your

229–30 **dubbed . . . consideration** knighted at court rather than on the battlefield. Sir Andrew is a 'coward carpet knyght' (said of Paris in Ovid, *Met.*, 12.673, fol. 157[r]; 13.123, fol. 159[r]): i.e. he purchased his title, since he was probably of low social origins. Francis Markham affirms disapprovingly, 'these of the vulgar or common sort, are called *Carpet-knights*, because . . . they receiue their honour from the Kings hand, in the Court, and upon Carpets' (Markham, 71; Furness). There is a likely pun on *consideration* meaning sum of money.
unhatched unhacked, i.e. used not for combat but for ceremonial purposes (*OED ppl. a.*[2])

232 **incensement** anger

234 **sepulchre** burial
'Hob-nob' *OED* glosses 'have or have not', but Sir Toby's own gloss (*give't or take't*) suggests a more specific and sinister meaning, i.e. kill or be killed ('it' = death). In Carroll's 2002 Middle Temple production, Sir Andrew emitted the war-cry 'Hob-nob!' offstage.
word motto

236 **conduct** escort (modern 'safe-conduct')

238 **taste** test. Viola claims not to understand the verb when used in this sense by Sir Toby at 3.1.76–8; either she was pretending or she has learned.
Belike probably

239 **quirk** peculiar disposition (*OED n.*[1] 4, first occurrence)

241 ***competent** legally sufficient (to justify the duel) (*OED a.* 6b). F's 'computent' is a variant spelling.
injury offence

243 **undertake** engage in
that i.e. a duel. Sir Toby threatens to fight Cesario himself if he refuses the duel with Sir Andrew.

244 **on** go forward

229 unhatched] unhack'd *Pope;* an hatch'd *Keightley (Malone)* 234 'Hob-nob'] *this edn;* Hob, nob *F;* 'Hob nob' *Oxf[1]* 241 competent] *(*computent*), F4* 244 on, or] on, and *Rann*

sword stark naked, for meddle you must, that's certain, or forswear to wear iron about you.

VIOLA This is as uncivil as strange. I beseech you do me this courteous office as to know of the knight what my offence to him is. It is something of my negligence, nothing of my purpose.

SIR TOBY I will do so. Signor Fabian, stay you by this gentleman till my return. *Exit.*

VIOLA Pray you, sir, do you know of this matter?

FABIAN I know the knight is incensed against you even to a mortal arbitrament, but nothing of the circumstance more.

VIOLA I beseech you, what manner of man is he?

FABIAN Nothing of that wonderful promise to read him by his form as you are like to find him in the proof of his valour. He is indeed, sir, the most skilful, bloody and fatal opposite that you could possibly have found in any part of Illyria. Will you walk towards him, I will make your peace with him – if I can.

VIOLA I shall be much bound to you for't. I am one that had rather go with Sir Priest than Sir Knight. I care not

244–6 **or . . . or** either . . . or. It is just possible, however, that the first *or* (244) is an error: F's 'on, or' might be a dittography (unintentional repetition) on the part of a scribe faced with a deletion (RP).

245 **meddle** fight (*OED v.* 6)

246 **forswear . . . you** give up wearing a sword, and thereby admit to cowardice

247–8 **do . . . of** be so kind as to find out from. This complex construction seems to conflate two idioms: 'be so courteous as to' and 'do me the office to'.

249, 250 **of** due to

255 **mortal arbitrament** trial by combat to the death

258–9 **Nothing . . . form** not as threatening, to judge from his external appearance, as you are likely to find him in the practical demonstration of his courage (i.e. in combat). In Barton's 1969 RSC production Fabian alarmingly rolled bandages during this speech, in preparation for the bloodshed.

261 **fatal opposite** deadly opponent

262 **Will . . . him** F's comma after *him* implies an elided conditional ('If you will . . .'), although actors often turn it into a direct and threatening question to Cesario.

265 **Sir Priest** *Sir*, the English equivalent of Latin *dominus*, was the title given to a graduate in theology, and hence to a clergyman (Johnson). The

248 as to] to *Capell* 252 SD] *(Exit Toby.)*

who knows so much of my mettle. *Exeunt.*

Enter [SIR] TOBY *and* [SIR] ANDREW.

SIR TOBY Why, man, he's a very devil. I have not seen such a firago. I had a pass with him, rapier, scabbard and all, and he gives me the stuck in with such a mortal motion that it is inevitable; and on the answer, he pays

antithesis here with Sir Andrew's 'carpet' knighthood (*Sir Knight*) is ironical, since in reality neither title promises great martial prowess (see 229–30n.).

266 **mettle** temperament: in Early Modern English, a variant spelling of 'metal', used metaphorically; cf. 2.5.12, 5.1.316.

268 **firago** virago; literally, a man-like woman. Sir Toby implicitly questions Cesario's gender. In the Vulgate version of Genesis, 2.23, 'Virago' is Adam's name for Eve, and thus for woman as such. The term was also applicable, however, to a ferocious *male* warrior (*OED* 2b). On these gender ambiguities, cf. John Taylor the Water Poet's *Superbiae Flagellum, or The Whip of Pride* (1621): 'Like shamelesse double sex'd *Hermaphrodites*, / *Virago* Roaring Girles' (J. Taylor, 33). F's spelling probably indicates a colourfully expressive 'error' on Sir Toby's part, suggesting '*fire*, *fury*, *fiend*, *ferociousness*, all combined' (Furness), especially if the first syllable is pronounced as in 'fire'.

pass bout of fencing; literally, a move involving a thrust forward with the sword (from Italian *passata*). Cf. *MW* 2.3.23, 'your passes, stoccadoes, and I know not what'.

scabbard sheath protecting the sword. This implies ironically that Cesario's rapier remained unsheathed during their *pass*. There is a crescendo of phallic references in the scene, leading up to Viola's confession that she has (metaphorically) no sword (295–6).

269 **stuck in** winning thrust: another fencing term (like *tuck*, 219, from Italian *stocco*), consisting in the fencer's 'putting the point of his Rapier under his [opponent's] Rapier, and so giuing him a thrust in the belly' (Saviolo, book 1, fol. 8^{v}). Cf. *Ham* 4.7.159, 'If he by chance escape your venomed stuck'. The particle *in* here has the sense of 'home', i.e. hitting the target, as in the SD in *RJ* 3.1.89, '*Tybalt under Romeo's arm thrusts Mercutio in*.'

269–70 **mortal motion** deadly movement; *motion* is a further fencing term indicating a highly disciplined and regulated stepping movement (*OED n.* 3c).

270 **it is inevitable** ambiguous: either the fencing *motion* cannot be avoided; or death (cf. *mortal*, 269) is the unavoidable consequence of the *stuck*.

270–1 **on . . . you** when you attempt to return his thrust, he puts paid to you. Sir Toby contradicts Saviolo, according to whom the fencer must 'breake the stoccata with his lefte hande, and aunswere againe with an other' (Saviolo, book 1, fol. 17^{r}): this becomes instead a supposedly fatal error against Cesario. For *pay* in the sense of 'kill', cf. *1H4* 2.4.189, 'Two I am sure I have paid.'

268 firago] virago *Rowe*

you as surely as your feet hits the ground they step on. They say he has been fencer to the Sophy.

SIR ANDREW Pox on't, I'll not meddle with him.

SIR TOBY Ay, but he will not now be pacified. Fabian can scarce hold him yonder.

SIR ANDREW Plague on't, an I thought he had been valiant, and so cunning in fence, I'd have seen him damned ere I'd have challenged him. Let him let the matter slip and I'll give him my horse, grey Capulet.

SIR TOBY I'll make the motion. Stand here, make a good show on't. This shall end without the perdition of souls. [*aside*] Marry, I'll ride your horse as well as I ride you.

Enter FABIAN *and* VIOLA [*as Cesario*].

[*aside to Fabian*] I have his horse to take up the quarrel. I have persuaded him the youth's a devil.

FABIAN [*aside to Sir Toby*] He is as horribly conceited of him, and pants and looks pale as if a bear were at his heels.

271 **as . . . on** as certainly as you touch the ground when you walk (but evoking also the image of Sir Andrew's dead body hitting the ground)
hits plural (an example of the 'Northern Personal Pronoun Rule' in Early Modern English: Hope, 2.1.8a)
272 **Sophy** Shah of Persia: cf. 2.5.175.
276 **Plague on't** Cf. 1.3.1n.
an if
277 **cunning** skilful
279 ***Capulet** 'Capul' or 'caple' was a Middle English and dialect word for 'horse' (*OED*), so that the name of Sir Andrew's grey steed may mean simply 'little horse'; also presumably a pretentious reference to the noble Italian name Capulet, Juliet's surname in *RJ*: hence Dyce's emendation.
280 **motion** proposal, offer
281–2 **perdition of souls** loss of life; damnation (due to murder): a pun
282 **ride** have complete control of (*OED v.* 17b). Sir Toby sees another opportunity to 'milk' Sir Andrew, and has no intention of mentioning his offer to Cesario (see 293n.).
284 **take . . . quarrel** settle the dispute; cf. *AYL* 5.4.96–7.
286 **He . . . conceited** he has as terrifying an idea

271 hits] hit *Rowe* 274–5] *Capell; F lines* Pacified, / yonder. / 279 Capulet] *(*Capilet*), Dyce* 282, 390 SDs] *Theobald* 283.1 *as Cesario*] *Munro subst.* 284 SD] *Oxf; to Fab: Douai MS, Rowe* 286 SD] *Oxf; To Sir Toby / Collier*

SIR TOBY [*aside to Viola*] There's no remedy, sir, he will fight with you for's oath' sake. Marry, he hath better bethought him of his quarrel and he finds that now scarce to be worth talking of. Therefore draw for the supportance of his vow. He protests he will not hurt you.

VIOLA [*aside*] Pray God defend me! A little thing would make me tell them how much I lack of a man.

FABIAN [*aside to Sir Andrew*] Give ground if you see him furious.

SIR TOBY [*aside to Sir Andrew*] Come, Sir Andrew, there's no remedy. The gentleman will for his honour's sake have one bout with you; he cannot by the duello avoid it. But he has promised me, as he is a gentleman and a soldier, he will not hurt you. Come on, to't.

SIR ANDREW [*aside*] Pray God he keep his oath!

Enter ANTONIO.

290 **for's oath' sake** for his oath's sake
291 **bethought him** reconsidered
quarrel the grounds for his complaint (against you)
293 **supportance** honouring: Cesario is obliged to fight, according to the code of honour, simply because Sir Andrew has (supposedly) vowed to do so (see 301n.).
295–6 **A little . . . man** It would take little to make me reveal how much I am not a man, i.e. how fearful I am, with a probable innuendo on what Viola lacks in order to be a man: a *thing*, Elizabethan slang for penis (*OED n.*[1] 11c; Partridge, 199). Cf. Portia on her disguise in *MV* 3.4.61–2, 'in such a habit / That they shall think we are accomplished / With that we lack'.
298 **furious** mad with anger
301 **by the duello** by the formal rules governing the code of duelling. In *LLL* Don Armado complains, 'The *passado* he respects not; the *duello* he regards not' (*LLL* 1.2.174–5); by contrast, Mercutio has contempt for his opponent Tybalt as one 'that fights by the book of arithmetic', i.e. by the fencing manual (*RJ* 3.1.103).
304.1 There is some inconsistency regarding the location of this scene, apparently set in Olivia's *orchard* (218). After Antonio's arrest, the officers tell Orsino of a *private brabble* that took place 'Here in the streets' (5.1.60–1). Audiences do not notice such details.

289 SD] *this edn; to Viola. Douai MS, Capell* 290 oath'] *Oxf;* oath *F;* oaths *Douai MS;* oath's *Capell* 297 SD] *this edn; To Sir Andrew Ard*[2] 299 SD] *this edn; crossing to Sir Andrew / Mahood* 304, 322 SDs] *this edn* 304 oath!] oath! *draws. / Capell*

VIOLA [*to Sir Andrew*] I do assure you 'tis against my will. [*Sir Andrew and Viola draw swords.*]

ANTONIO [*Draws sword.*]
[*to Sir Andrew*] Put up your sword. If this young gentleman
Have done offence, I take the fault on me.
If you offend him, I for him defy you.

SIR TOBY You, sir? Why, what are you?

ANTONIO
One, sir, that for his love dares yet do more
Than you have heard him brag to you he will.

SIR TOBY [*Draws sword.*] Nay, if you be an undertaker, I am for you.

Enter Officers.

FABIAN O good Sir Toby, hold. Here come the officers.

SIR TOBY [*to Antonio*] I'll be with you anon.

VIOLA [*to Sir Andrew*] Pray, sir, put your sword up, if you please.

SIR ANDREW Marry, will I, sir. And for that I promised

305–6 **against my will** Viola's resistance to a motiveless duel could be benevolently interpreted as a sign of gentility (James Spedding, in Furness). At the same time, like Sir Andrew, she is admittedly terrified (295–6), and in performance Sir Toby and Fabian usually have to force them together.

307 **Put up** put away

310 **what** who; cf. 1.2.32n.

313 **undertaker** one who takes up a challenge (*OED* 3c, sole occurrence); one who takes on someone else's business, especially a contractor or tax collector (*OED* 5)

314 **for you** i.e. the right person for you

315 **the officers** i.e. officers of justice or of the peace: an early form of police, usually under the command of the sheriff, here directly answerable to Orsino (see 324–5). One of their peace-keeping functions was the suppression of duels and brawls, hence Fabian's concern.

319 **that** i.e. his steed Capulet (see 279). Since Sir Toby has failed to mention Sir Andrew's offer, this adds to Viola's bewilderment. Aguecheek is so relieved not to have to fight that he is prepared to give her his horse anyway.

306 SD] *Ard*[2]*; after 303 Rowe; draws / Capell; Sir Toby and Fabian force them to make a few passes in great fear. / Powell MS; they fight;* VIOLA *very timid, and* SIR ANDREW *tremulously parrying her blows.* SIR TOBY *and* FABIAN *urging them on each other. / Lacy* 307 SD1] *Ard*[1]*; after 309 Rowe* SD2] *Inchbald* 316 anon.] anon. *he hides from the officers behind a tree Cam*[1]*;* anon. *Steps aside to avoid the Officers Riv*

you I'll be as good as my word. He will bear you easily, and reins well.

1 OFFICER [*Indicates Antonio.*] This is the man; do thy office.

2 OFFICER
Antonio, I arrest thee at the suit
Of Count Orsino.

ANTONIO You do mistake me, sir.

1 OFFICER
No, sir, no jot. I know your favour well,
Though now you have no sea-cap on your head.
[*to Second Officer*] Take him away; he knows I know him well.

ANTONIO
I must obey. [*to Viola*] This comes with seeking you.
But there's no remedy; I shall answer it.
What will you do now my necessity
Makes me to ask you for my purse? It grieves me
Much more for what I cannot do for you
Than what befalls myself. You stand amazed,
But be of comfort.

2 OFFICER
Come, sir, away.

ANTONIO [*to Viola*]
I must entreat of you some of that money.

VIOLA
What money, sir?

321 **reins well** responds readily to the rein

326 **favour** face; cf. 378 and 2.4.24–5. The fact that the First Officer knows Antonio suggests that he may have taken part as one of Orsino's sailors in the somewhat mysterious sea battle (cf. *sea-cap*, 327); he is thus also an *officer* in the naval sense (*OED n.* 4a).

327 **sea-cap** sailor's cap

329 **with** as a result of (Blake, *Grammar*, 5.4.2)

330 **answer** pay for; cf. 3.3.28.

334 **amazed** lost in wonder (*OED ppl. a.* 4): more emphatic than in modern English

324–5 Antonio . . . Orsino] *Capell; one line F* 329 SD] *Collier* 331 do now] *Oxf;* do: now *F;* doe? now *F2;* do, now *Dyce* 332 purse?] *Dyce;* purse. *F*

For the fair kindness you have showed me here,
And part being prompted by your present trouble,
Out of my lean and low ability
I'll lend you something. My having is not much.
I'll make division of my present with you.
Hold, [*offering money*] there's half my coffer.

ANTONIO [*Refuses money.*] Will you deny me now?
Is't possible that my deserts to you
Can lack persuasion? Do not tempt my misery,
Lest that it make me so unsound a man
As to upbraid you with those kindnesses
That I have done for you.

VIOLA I know of none,
Nor know I you by voice or any feature.
I hate ingratitude more in a man
Than lying vainness, babbling drunkenness
Or any taint of vice whose strong corruption
Inhabits our frail blood.

339 **fair** pleasing, flattering

340 **part** in part. Cf. *Oth* 5.2.295, 'This wretch hath part confessed his villainy.'

341 **ability** financial means (*OED* 4, giving this example)

342 **My having** what I possess. Cf. *AYL* 3.2.368, 'your having in beard is a younger brother's revenue.'

343 **my present** such money as I have at present

344 **coffer** money (literally chest): an ironic hyperbole, given Viola's limited means

345 **deserts** gestures deserving recompense (*OED n.*[1] 1)

346 **persuasion** the force to move (you)
tempt put to the test

347 **unsound** morally deficient (since *kindnesses*, 348, should not be made in hope of a reward)

349–54 **I know . . . blood** Cesario's list of vices is effectively an expansion of the proverb 'Ingratitude comprehends all faults' (Dent, I66).

352 ***lying . . . drunkenness** F's punctuation has *lying* as a noun, on a par with *vainness*; this, however, creates an asymmetrical relationship with *babbling drunkenness* (adjective + noun), whereas Rowe[3]'s emendation produces two symmetrical phrases.
vainness boastfulness (vainglory). The word is used and glossed by the Chorus in *H5* 5.0.20, 'Being free from vainness, and self-glorious pride'.
babbling incoherent
drunkenness In Posner's 2001 RSC production, Zoë Waites's Viola looked towards Sir Toby.

353 **taint** stain (*OED v.* C 2a, first occurrence); cf. 13, 128; 3.1.66; 5.1.134, 351 and notes.
corruption power of contagion: primarily a medical metaphor, but

344 SDs] *Cam*[1] *subst.* 352 lying vainness, babbling] *Rowe*[3]*;* lying, vainnesse, babling *F*

ANTONIO O heavens themselves!

2 OFFICER
Come, sir, I pray you go.

ANTONIO
Let me speak a little. This youth that you see here
I snatched one half out of the jaws of death,
Relieved him with such sanctity of love,
And to his image, which methought did promise
Most venerable worth, did I devotion.

1 OFFICER
What's that to us? The time goes by. Away!

ANTONIO
But O, how vile an idol proves this god!
Thou hast, Sebastian, done good feature shame.
In nature there's no blemish but the mind:
None can be called deformed but the unkind.
Virtue is beauty, but the beauteous evil
Are empty trunks o'erflourished by the devil.

1 OFFICER
The man grows mad, away with him. Come, come, sir.

'corruption of blood' was also a legal concept, i.e. the effect of an attainder whereby the blood of the culprit was tainted by his crime, causing him and his descendants to lose all rights of rank and title (*OED* 2b). Here the 'crime' is vice in general, which deprives the guilty party of his right to the title of *man* (351) and in particular to that of gentleman.

357 **one . . . death** out of the jaws of death which had half swallowed him

358 **Relieved** aided (*OED v.* 1a, giving this example)
sanctity of love holy love. This and the following passage are couched in the language of religious devotion (cf. 2.1.43), applied to profane love as in the Sonnets, where it is likewise directed towards another man.

359 **image** appearance; religious icon

360 **venerable** worthy of veneration

363 **Sebastian** the first explicit evidence for Viola that her brother is alive: cf. her 'delayed' reaction, 370–3.
feature looks

364 **the mind** in the mind

365 **unkind** hard-hearted; unnatural. Cf. Lear's 'unkind daughters'(*KL* 3.4.73).

366 **beauteous evil** oxymoron. Cf. *proper false*, 2.2.29.

367 **trunks o'er flourished** In prosperous Elizabethan households, trunks, often elaborately ornamented with emblematic and other devices, were an important part of the furniture (Steevens). The trunk plays a conspicuous role in the stage history of this comedy, in part because of this reference: cf. 1.2.01n.

362 vile] *(*vilde*)*, *Pope*

ANTONIO
Lead me on. *Exit* [*with Officers*].

VIOLA [*aside*]
Methinks his words do from such passion fly
That he believes himself. So do not I.
Prove true, imagination, O prove true,
That I, dear brother, be now ta'en for you!

SIR TOBY Come hither, knight; come hither, Fabian. We'll whisper o'er a couplet or two of most sage saws. [*They stand aside.*]

VIOLA
He named Sebastian. I my brother know
Yet living in my glass. Even such and so
In favour was my brother, and he went
Still in this fashion, colour, ornament,
For him I imitate. O, if it prove,
Tempests are kind, and salt waves fresh in love! [*Exit.*]

SIR TOBY [*to Sir Andrew*] A very dishonest, paltry boy, and more a coward than a hare. His dishonesty appears in leaving his friend here in necessity and denying him;

370 **passion** overpowering emotion; with a possible allusion to the *passion* of Christ. On the passions in the comedy, see pp. 54–5.

371 **So . . . I** I do not share his belief; or 'I do not yet believe myself, when . . . I gather hope of my brother's life' (Johnson).

372 **imagination** mental image or representation: the earliest sense of the word (*OED* 1)

375 **saws** wise maxims; Sir Toby may wish to mock Antonio's moralizing (Deighton).

376–7 **I . . . glass** I see my brother's living image when I look at myself in the mirror. Viola cross-dressed is Sebastian's perfect double (hence the vicissitudes of the plot).

378 **favour** appearance; cf. 326.
went appeared

379 **Still** always
fashion way of dressing

380 **For . . . imitate** an interesting insight into one of Viola's motives for cross-dressing, in order as it were to 'reincarnate' her brother (cf. *Yet living*, 377)
prove should prove to be so; for the omitted 'so', cf. Blake, *Grammar*, 5.1.3.5(xxii).

381 **fresh** made of fresh water (in contrast to *salt*). Viola's paradoxes suggest that Sebastian's survival would be a miracle of nature.

383 **a coward** cowardly: proverbial ('As fearful as a hare', Dent, H147)

368] *Dyce; F lines* him: / sir. / 369 SD *with Officers*] *Theobald* 370 SD] *Oxf (Furness)* 371 I.] I? *Cam*[1] 373 ta'en] *(*tane*)* 375 SD] *Capell subst.*

and, for his cowardship, ask Fabian.

FABIAN A coward, a most devout coward, religious in it.

SIR ANDREW 'Slid, I'll after him again and beat him.

SIR TOBY Do, cuff him soundly, but never draw thy sword.

SIR ANDREW An I do not – [*Exit.*]

FABIAN Come, let's see the event.

SIR TOBY I dare lay any money 'twill be nothing yet. *Exeunt.*

4.1 *Enter* SEBASTIAN *and* FESTE.

FESTE Will you make me believe that I am not sent for you?

SEBASTIAN
Go to, go to, thou art a foolish fellow.
Let me be clear of thee.

FESTE Well held out, i'faith! No, I do not know you, nor I am not sent to you by my lady to bid you come speak with her, nor your name is not Master Cesario, nor this

386 **religious in it** i.e. he practises cowardice religiously

387 **'Slid** by God's eyelid (oath)

388 **cuff** beat

390 i.e. if I do not cuff him

391 **event** outcome (*OED n.* 3a)

392 **yet** after all

4.1 This scene involves the unwitting Sebastian in three brief encounters – with Feste, with Sir Toby and Sir Andrew and, finally, with Olivia – all of whom mistake him for Cesario, provoking in him a crescendo of bewilderment. Rowe gives '*The Street*' as location. Sir Toby's threat to throw Sebastian's dagger 'o'er the house' (27–8) suggests such an outdoor setting; an alternative possibility is the 'orchard' or garden mentioned at 3.4.172 and 218 (AT).

1 The scene opens *in medias res*: Feste and Sebastian have apparently been discussing the question of the latter's identity. The clown has evidently been sent by Olivia to fetch Cesario: cf. *come again tomorrow*, 3.4.211.
Will you do you want to

3 **Go to** come, come (expression of disapprobation)

4 **clear** rid (*OED v.* 18b, giving this example)

5 **held out** kept up, insisted: Sebastian continues to deny that he is Cesario.

5–8 **No . . . neither** Feste is playfully exaggerating the use of multiple negatives (Hope, 2.1.9; Blake, *Grammar*, 6.2.3.3): cf. 3.1.157–8n.

390 not –] *Theobald;* not. *F* 392 SD] *Rowe; Exit. F* **4.1**] *(Actus Quartus, Scaena prima.)* 0.1 FESTE] *Munro; Clowne F*

is not my nose neither. Nothing that is so is so.

SEBASTIAN

I prithee vent thy folly somewhere else,
Thou knowst not me.

FESTE Vent my folly! He has heard that word of some great man and now applies it to a fool. Vent my folly! I am afraid this great lubber the world will prove a cockney. I prithee now ungird thy strangeness, and tell me what I shall vent to my lady. Shall I vent to her that thou art coming?

SEBASTIAN

I prithee, foolish Greek, depart from me.

8 **Nothing . . . ²so** This is the general principle of deception or 'fooling' in the play, which Feste adopts as his philosophy. Whether the clown – who may already have seen through Viola's disguise (see 3.1.43–4n.) – recognizes that Sebastian is indeed not *Cesario* is an open question. Contrast Feste's 'That that is is' (4.2.14–15).

9 **vent** give vent to, express (literally blow, from Latin *ventus*, wind); cf. *TS* 1.2.176, ''tis now no time to vent our love.' The verb is taken up by Feste in a more vulgar sense: cf. 15n.

9–10, 17–19 *These lines appear as prose in F; Capell converted them into (incomplete) verse comprising one or two more or less regular pentameter lines followed by one half-line, as here. There is a precedent for this solution at 2–3, given as verse in F. Feste, however, speaks in prose throughout the exchange.

11–12 **He . . . fool** Feste's deriding of Sebastian's phrase, supposedly borrowed from his betters, recalls Moth in *LLL*: 'They have been at a great feast of languages and stolen the scraps' (*LLL* 5.1.35–6).

12 **great** eminent

13–14 **this . . . cockney** this clumsy fool, the world, will turn out to be a milksop: another sarcastic comment on Sebastian's 'affected' language

13 **lubber** clumsy person, lout (etymologically related to Danish *lubbe*, clown: *OED n.* 1a)

14 **cockney** milksop (literally, chicken's egg). *OED* glosses 'effeminate fellow' (*n.* 2a, giving this example): this is ironical in view of Sebastian's – as opposed to Cesario's – virility.

ungird thy strangeness drop your formality: i.e. stop pretending not to know me

ungird release, free (literally by undoing your belt: *OED v.* 2, giving this example)

strangeness aloofness, formality (*OED* 2a)

15 **vent** probably a pun on the colloquial meaning 'excrete' (*OED v.*² 2b), perhaps developing the unbelting metaphor in *ungird*: cf. *Tem* 2.2.105–6, 'Can he vent Trinculos?'

17 **Greek** buffoon. The noun was usually qualified by *merry* (Dent, M901). Matthew Merrygreek is an unruly character in Udall's comedy *Roister Doister*.

9–10, 17–19] *Capell; prose F* 13 lubber the world] lubberly world *Hudson*

There's money for thee. If you tarry longer
I shall give worse payment.

FESTE By my troth thou hast an open hand. These wise men that give fools money get themselves a good report, after fourteen years' purchase.

Enter [SIR] ANDREW, [SIR] TOBY *and* FABIAN.

SIR ANDREW [*to Sebastian*] Now, sir, have I met you again. [*Strikes him.*] There's for you.

SEBASTIAN
Why, [*striking Sir Andrew*] there's for thee,

19 **worse payment** Sebastian, while giving Feste a tip (presumably using Antonio's money), adopts a more 'manly' mode that distinguishes him from the gentler Cesario at 3.1.1–66; this contrast in manners is expressed physically at 25 in his reaction to Sir Andrew, who receives the *worse payment* threatened here.

20 **thou . . . hand** you are generous (perhaps he hopes to receive a second tip, as he did from Viola at 3.1.52); you are ready to give me a beating (implying that Sebastian may have raised his hand in a threatening manner)

21–2 **get . . . purchase** acquire a good reputation at a high price: a reference to the economic laws of the Elizabethan land market in which the purchase value of land was equivalent to twelve years' rent. Sebastian and the others (Viola, Orsino, Sir Toby, Sir Andrew) who have given Feste money have paid more than the market rate for his gratitude.

22 **report** reputation
after at the rate of
purchase payment

23–5 **you . . . thee** Sir Andrew returns incongruously to formal *you* at the very moment he hits Sebastian; Sebastian contemptuously calls him *thee*: cf. 3.2.42–3n.

24 SD Sir Andrew, who did all he could to avoid coming to blows with Cesario in 3.4, ironically finds the courage to hit out only when he meets a 'real' man. In Carroll's 2002 Middle Temple production Angus Wright's Sir Andrew derisively knocked off the hat of Rhys Meredith's Sebastian, who responded likewise.

25 SD *Mahood and Oxf have Sebastian beat Sir Andrew with his dagger, by way of explanation for Sir Toby's threat to throw it away (27–8), but this is surely an exaggerated response to Sir Andrew's (presumably feeble) attack; Sir Toby is belittling Sebastian's prowess rather than referring literally to what he is holding at that moment. In performance, Sebastian usually limits himself to a slap, while in Mendes' 2002 Donmar production he stamped on his opponent's feet.

20–1 wise men] *(*Wise-men*), Rowe* 22.1 SIR] *Rowe* 23 SD] *Oxf* 24 SD] *Rowe subst.* 25–6] *this edn; F lines* there, and there, / mad? / 25 SD] *Douai MS, Rowe subst.; he knocks him down Cam*[1]*; He beats Sir Andrew with the handle of his dagger / Mahood*

And there, and there. Are all the people mad?

SIR TOBY [*Restrains Sebastian.*] Hold, sir, or I'll throw your dagger o'er the house.

FESTE This will I tell my lady straight. I would not be in some of your coats for twopence. [*Exit.*]

SIR TOBY Come on, sir, hold!

SIR ANDREW Nay, let him alone, I'll go another way to work with him. I'll have an action of battery against him if there be any law in Illyria. Though I struck him first, yet it's no matter for that.

SEBASTIAN [*to Sir Toby*]
Let go thy hand.

SIR TOBY Come, sir, I will not let you go. Come, my young

26 **Are . . . mad** Sebastian's bewilderment recalls that of the twin Antipholus of Syracuse in *CE*, mistaken for his brother: 'Am I . . . / Mad or well advised?' (*CE* 2.2.211–12).

28 **dagger** Since Sir Toby later refers to Sebastian's *iron* (i.e. sword, 38), he may be making fun of Sebastian's weapon here (Oxf[1]).
o'er the house Hotson, 140–1, suggests that this refers to an actual roofed structure onstage. It is, however, one of several references to Olivia's *house* (see 2.3.97, 3.1.72, 3.4.235, etc.) and probably does not imply a precise physical space, although it does suggest that the scene takes place outdoors. In performance Sir Toby sometimes gestures backstage or towards the audience.

29 **This . . . straight** Feste is careful to dissociate himself from his erstwhile fellow revellers by acting as 'spy', now that the fooling is degenerating. Yet he remains loyal to the plot against Malvolio, as the following scene demonstrates.
straight straightaway

29–30 **in . . . coats** in some of their shoes (proverbial: Dent, C473; *OED v.* 13, giving this example); with an implied allusion to Feste's own motley 'coat', which gets him out of trouble, since as a fool he – unlike Toby and Andrew – is licensed to be unruly.

30 **twopence** a proverbially modest sum: in Shakespeare's day, a small silver coin. Feste is used to receiving tips of sixpence (see 2.3.30–2). On currency in the play, cf. 1.3.20n. and 2.3.19n.

32–3 **I'll . . . work** I'll deal with him in another fashion: proverbial (Dent, W150)

33 **action of battery** lawsuit claiming an unlawful attack by beating or wounding (*OED* battery 1a, giving this example). As Sir Andrew notes, it is in fact he who committed the offence against Sebastian at 23: 'another joke for the law students' (Mahood).

34 **any . . . Illyria** Sir Andrew is referring to English common law: *Illyria* is as usual a thin disguise.

34–5 **struck him first** Aguecheek continues to disregard the law, as in his challenge at 3.4.143–65.

26 there.] there, and there: *Capell* 27 SD] *Dyce subst.; after 31 Rowe* 30 SD] *Rowe* 34 struck] *F4;* stroke *F;* strook *F3* 36, 49 SDs] *this edn*

soldier, put up your iron. You are well fleshed. Come on.

SEBASTIAN

I will be free from thee. [*Frees himself.*]
What wouldst thou now?
If thou dar'st tempt me further, draw thy sword.
[*Draws sword.*]

SIR TOBY What, what? Nay then, I must have an ounce or two of this malapert blood from you. [*Draws sword.*]

Enter OLIVIA.

OLIVIA

Hold, Toby! On thy life I charge thee hold.

SIR TOBY Madam.

OLIVIA

Will it be ever thus? Ungracious wretch,
Fit for the mountains and the barbarous caves,
Where manners ne'er were preached. Out of my sight!
[*to Sebastian*] Be not offended, dear Cesario.
[*to Sir Toby*] Rudesby, be gone!
[*Exeunt Sir Toby, Sir Andrew and Fabian.*]

38 **iron** sword (metonymy): cf. 3.4.246.
well fleshed hardened, inured to bloodshed (*OED* 2). Since the phrase can also mean 'well furnished with flesh', it is somewhat ironical coming from Sir Toby.
42–3 **ounce . . . blood** Cf. *Cor* 3.1.298–300, 'the blood he hath lost . . . is more than he hath / By many an ounce.'
43 **malapert** impudent (*OED a.*, giving this example)
44 **charge** command (*OED v.* 14a, giving this example)
46 **Will . . . thus** must you always behave in this way
Ungracious rude (*OED* 3a, giving this example)
47 i.e. who should live in distant uncivilized regions
mountains i.e. territory remote from civilization (*OED* 1d, giving this example)
barbarous uncultured, savage (*OED* 3, giving this example)
48 **preached** taught
49 **dear Cesario** Olivia's use of the name underlines the irony of her error. In performance Sebastians often react with surprise at the misnaming, for example by giving the audience a perplexed look.

40, 41 SDs] *Capell subst.* 43 SD] *Capell subst.; They draw and fight. / Rowe*

I prithee, gentle friend,
Let thy fair wisdom, not thy passion, sway
In this uncivil and unjust extent
Against thy peace. Go with me to my house
And hear thou there how many fruitless pranks
This ruffian hath botched up, that thou thereby
Mayst smile at this. Thou shalt not choose but go.
Do not deny. Beshrew his soul for me,
He started one poor heart of mine in thee.

SEBASTIAN

What relish is in this? How runs the stream?
Or I am mad or else this is a dream.
Let fancy still my sense in Lethe steep:

50 **Rudesby** insolent fellow; cf. Guazzo on the lack of manners: 'he which is not [ceremonious] may be taken to be a clowne, a rudesby, or a contemner of others' (Guazzo, fols 77r–77v; *OED*). Shakespeare uses the term only here and in *TS* 3.2.10, 'a mad-brain rudesby full of spleen'.
gentle courteous (a polite term of address, as in the expression 'gentle reader'); gentlemanly: cf. Olivia's meditations on Cesario's social rank at 1.5.283.
friend acquaintance; lover (*OED n.* 4). The latter meaning is optimistic on Olivia's part but will soon be justified.

51 **wisdom . . . passion** Contrary to her advice here, Olivia admits at 3.1.150 that reason cannot hide her own passion.
sway prevail; cf. 2.4.31, 2.5.106, 4.3.17 and notes.

52 **uncivil and unjust** barbarous and lawless
extent attack (*OED n.* 2c, giving this example)

53 **peace** tranquillity

54 **fruitless** idle
pranks mischievous tricks. Cf. Polonius' advice to Gertrude regarding Hamlet: 'Tell him his pranks have been too broad to bear with' (*Ham* 3.4.2).

55 **botched up** stitched clumsily together (*OED v.*[1] 3)
thereby thanks to that

56 **choose but go** choose otherwise than to go

57 **Beshrew** the devil take (mild imprecation)

58 By attacking you, he [Sir Toby] frightened me, since my heart is now yours. Olivia, playing on the heart/hart homophone adopted by Orsino at 1.1.16–22, compares herself to a startled deer during the hunt. Technically, harts are 'roused' from cover rather than *started* (used of hares), 'but "start" is used because of its associations with human demonstrations of fear' (Ard[2]). In Carroll's 2002 Middle Temple production Mark Rylance's *started* Olivia fainted on this line.

59 **relish** sense (literally, taste or flavour)
How . . . stream? what is going on? (proverbial: Dent, S925.1). Sebastian's metaphor anticipates his reference to the Lethe river at 61.

60 **Or . . . or** either . . . or

61 i.e. may my imagination/desire continue to make me forgetful of my senses.

50 SD1] *Oxf* SD2] *Capell; Exeunt Sir Toby and Sir Andrew. / Rowe*

If it be thus to dream, still let me sleep.

OLIVIA

Nay, come, I prithee, would thou'dst be ruled by me.

SEBASTIAN

Madam, I will.

OLIVIA O say so, and so be. *Exeunt.*

4.2 *Enter* MARIA[, *carrying a gown and false beard,*] *and* FESTE.

MARIA Nay, I prithee put on this gown and this beard;

fancy imagination; sexual desire (*OED* 8b; cf. *MV* 3.2.63–4)

sense senses: the noun is probably plural.

Lethe in Greek mythology, the river in Hades whose water caused those who drank it to forget the past; cf. *2H4* 5.2.72, 'May this be wash'd in Lethe and forgotten?'

steep soak

62 **still . . . sleep** let me go on sleeping

63 **would . . . me** if only you would do what I would have you do; cf. Olivia's earlier 'I would you were as I would have you be' (3.1.140).

64 **Madam, I will** Sebastian's readiness to accept Olivia's invitation, despite not knowing her, usually raises a laugh in performance, especially if he gives the impression of taking advantage; but his willingness to go with her can also be seen as part of his surprised surrendering to the *dream* (60).

O . . . be Some Olivias deliver this line as an expression of delight (Brown, 269).

4.2 This is the notorious 'dark room' scene, in which the imprisoned Malvolio is tormented by the disguised Feste, who has the chance here to show off his acting skills. As the opening lines indicate, it is still Maria who directs the practical joke. In performance the 'dark room' has been represented in many different ways: it may be an 'inner stage' or hidden space behind the doors or curtains (see 18 t.n.); or a more claustrophobic space, often – as in Posner's 2001 RSC production – under a stage trapdoor with a grating through which Malvolio speaks and puts his hands. In the 2002 Middle Temple production it was a trunk, which Feste dragged across the stage. Alternatively, the room and its darkness may be shown directly on stage, as in 1884, when Henry Irving was 'seen actually visible, chained as a madman, and recumbent on his pallet' (*Illustrated London News*, quoted by Brown, 76). In Bill Alexander's 1987 RSC production Anthony Sher's Malvolio was likewise visible on stage, tethered to a post like a bear – taking up the 'baiting' metaphors in 2.5 – while the darkness was paradoxically figured by bright light. In Mendes' 2002 Donmar production Simon Russell Beale's Malvolio was simply blindfolded.

1 Feste's dressing up on stage underlines his self-consciously stagy acting of a part, but, as Maria points out at 63–4, his disguise is superfluous: a change of voice would have been sufficient for the 'blind' Malvolio.

4.2] *(Scoena Secunda.)* 0.1 *carrying . . . beard*] *Cam[1] subst.* 0.2 FESTE] *Munro; Clowne F*

make him believe thou art Sir Topas the curate. Do it quickly. I'll call Sir Toby the whilst. [*Exit.*]

FESTE Well, I'll put it on, and I will dissemble myself in't, and I would I were the first that ever dissembled in such a gown. I am not tall enough to become the function well, nor lean enough to be thought a good student, but to be said an honest man and a good housekeeper goes as fairly as to say a careful man and a great scholar.

Enter [SIR] TOBY [*and* MARIA].

The competitors enter.

2 **Sir Topas** On the significance of Feste's adopted name, see List of Roles, 14n.
Sir Cf. 3.4.265n.
curate parish priest (rather than his assistant, as in modern English)

3 **the whilst** in the meantime

4 **dissemble** disguise (*OED v.*[1] 2, giving this example); cf. 5n.

5–6 **I would . . . gown** The hypocrisy and corruption of the clergy are traditional targets of satire, as in the case of Chaucer's Pardoner. There may be an allusion to Puritan clergymen's 'hypocritical' wearing of the Calvinist black gown under their obligatory – but hated – white surplice (Ard[2]), with a glance towards the 'Puritan' Malvolio perhaps.

5 **dissembled** deceived; cf. 4n.

6–9 **I am . . . scholar** i.e. to be a sincere and companionable fellow is as honourable as being a learned man (probably continuing the reference to dissembling priests). Feste's paradoxical 'nonsense' implies the levelling of social differences between men.

6 **not tall enough** i.e. 'to overlook a pulpit' (Steevens). Since there is no evident reason why a priest should be *tall*, this has been interpreted as meaning 'portly', in contrast with *lean* at 7. Other commentators suspect a compositor's error for 'fat' (Farmer) or for 'pale' (Tyrwhitt). It may instead be an allusion to the height of the actor, since Robert Armin was notorious for his dwarfishness (Wiles, 148). The phrase may imply comic stage business involving a gown too long for the clown.
become . . . function fulfil the office (of priest)

7 **lean . . . student** Scholars were traditionally thin, because poor. Feste's supposed plumpness may be confirmed by *good housekeeper* at 8.
student scholar (of divinity)

8 **said** called, reputed
honest honourable (*OED a.* 1a); sincere (*OED a.* 3c). Cf. 'he, which plainly telleth the truth, sheweth himselfe to be an honest man, and of noble condition' (Guazzo, 42).
good housekeeper generous host (literally, one who keeps a good or hospitable house); *OED* 2 cites Holinshed, 2.137, 'a great housekeeper, and of great hospitalitie'.

8–9 **goes as fairly** is as becoming

9 **careful** careworn from study (Onions; cf. *OED* 2)

10 **The competitors** my associates in the gulling of Malvolio. Cf. *R3* 4.4.504–5, 'And every hour more competitors /

3 SD] *Theobald* 5 in] *F2;* in in *F* 6 tall] pale *(Tyrwhitt);* fat *(Farmer)* 7 student] *(*Studient*)* 9 careful] graceful *Hanmer* 9.1] *this edn; after 10 F* SIR] *Rowe* *and* MARIA] *Theobald*

SIR TOBY Jove bless thee, Master Parson.

FESTE [*as Sir Topas*] *Bonos dies*, Sir Toby. For as the old hermit of Prague, that never saw pen and ink, very wittily said to a niece of King Gorboduc, 'That that is is'; so I being Master Parson am Master Parson, for what is 'that' but 'that' and 'is' but 'is'?

SIR TOBY To him, Sir Topas.

FESTE What ho, I say, peace in this prison.

SIR TOBY The knave counterfeits well – a good knave.

Flock to the rebels.' The plural noun indicates that Maria returns onstage with her fellow *competitor* at 9.1, even if she does not speak until 63 and even if F has only '*Enter Toby.*'

11 **Jove** As Feste is not a real *Parson*, the invocation of a pagan deity is comically apt. Cf. 1.5.110n.

12 SD Feste's ventriloquism in this scene reflects the ability of the original actor, since 'the projection of multiple identities is the staple of Armin's clowning' (Wiles, 139; see also Preiss).

12 ***Bonos dies*** Good-day. This may be bad Latin (for *bonus dies*, itself a dubious construction), or bad Spanish (for *buenas días*). In any case, Sir Topas begins with a display of false learning, in keeping with Feste's satirical comment on dissembling priests at 5–6.

12–14 **old . . . Gorboduc** false literary authorities: cf. *Quinapalus*, 1.5.33. The fact that the old hermit of Prague is supposedly illiterate (*never . . . ink*) suggests that he is an extempore (non-literary) invention. Gorboduc, a legendary British king, is the eponymous protagonist of the first English tragedy in blank verse, by Thomas Norton and Thomas Sackville (1565); there is no record, however, of a niece.

14–16 **'That . . .' . . . but 'is'** Feste parodies logical analysis, in particular the self-consistent and self-evident 'axiom of affirming', 'whereby a thing is saide to bee or not to be' (Fenner, *Arts*, C1[r]). This is in direct contrast to Feste's 'Nothing that is so is so' (an 'axiom of denying') at 4.1.8: both are true in this comedy, in which nothing is what it appears to be, but in which 'true' identities are (more or less) re-established at the end.

15 **so . . . [2]Parson** This may be an echo of a celebrated jest in which the clown Richard Tarlton, for the benefit of the Queen, 'got on a Parsons gowne, and . . . repeated these words: a Parson or no Parson?' (*Tarlton's Jests*, A3[r]).

18 **peace . . . prison** This parodies the order for the Visitation of the Sick in the Elizabethan *Book of Common Prayer* (1559, still in use in 1602), which begins: '*The Priest entringe into the sicke persones house, shal saye*, Peace be in this house, and to all that dwel in it' (sig. O3[v]; Ard[2]). The 'priest' Sir Topas is indeed visiting a sick (i.e. 'mad') man, but the house in question is a *prison*.

19 **knave** rogue (said 'jocularly', *OED n.* 3c); cf. King Lear to his Fool: 'How now, my pretty knave, how dost thou?' (*KL* 1.4.95).

counterfeits acts his part

11 Jove] God *Halliwell* 11, 15, 27, 84 Master] *(M.), Steevens;* Mr. *Rowe* 12 SD] *Cam[1] subst.* 14 Gorboduc] *(Gorbodacke), Capell* 14–15 'That . . . is'] *this edn;* that that is, is *F* 15–16 for . . . 'is'?] *Mahood subst.;* for what is that, but that? and is, but is? *F* 18 What] *Opens the door of an inner room.* What *Cumberland*

MALVOLIO (*within*) Who calls there?

FESTE Sir Topas the curate, who comes to visit Malvolio the lunatic.

MALVOLIO Sir Topas, Sir Topas, good Sir Topas, go to my lady.

FESTE Out, hyperbolical fiend, how vexest thou this man! Talkest thou nothing but of ladies?

SIR TOBY Well said, Master Parson.

MALVOLIO Sir Topas, never was man thus wronged. Good Sir Topas, do not think I am mad. They have laid me here in hideous darkness.

20 SD *within* i.e. from inside the 'dark room'. F's stage direction leaves no doubt that in early performances Malvolio was heard but not seen onstage: see 4.2n.

22 **lunatic** This generic term for 'madman' (literally, someone moonstruck: cf. 1.5.195) often occurs in Shakespeare in the context of feigned or imagined madness, as in *CE* 4.3.91, *TS* Induction 1.62 and 2.1.281, *MW* 3.5.97, etc; cf. also 'Hamlet's lunacy' (*Ham* 2.2.49).

25 **Out** 'to hell with you': a common interjection expressing reproach (Blake, *Grammar*, 5.2.2.4, giving this example); cf. *TG* 2.7.54, 'Out, out, Lucetta. That will be ill-favour'd.' At the same time, however, Feste is literally bidding the devil to leave Malvolio's body.

hyperbolical excessive, mendacious. Malvolio's supposedly exaggerated behaviour and language (in his one line so far) betrays the presence of the devil. Hyperbole was condemned by moralists as dishonest, because it strategically departs from truthful description: Guazzo condemns as 'lyers' those who 'craue the Poets priviledge, to use the figure *Hyperbole* at their pleasure' (Guazzo, 43; cf. 8n.). Puttenham, 159, rebaptizes it as the 'loud lyer'. On hyperbole in the comedy, see p. 83.

fiend the devil supposedly possessing Malvolio

vexest thou you torment. The treatment reserved for Malvolio may parody the methods of the Puritan exorcist John Darrell, imprisoned in 1598 and publicly exposed by Harsnett, *Discovery*, which claimed that the 'possessed' were dissemblers and – perhaps significantly, given Feste's performance – that the devils' voices within them were the result of ventriloquism. Darrell describes the 'horrible passions and torments' of the supposed victims, manifested in the 'strong and violente casting up and downe of their bodyes . . . scriking or crying' (Darrell, 34–5); cf. 31n., 32n., 97n. and 3.4.82n. It is ironically appropriate for Malvolio to be cured by 'Puritan' methods of exorcism (on Darrell and this scene, see Schleiner; Hamilton, 86–110; Gibson).

26 **Talkest . . . ladies** Feste pretends to interpret Malvolio's anxiety to see his mistress as a sign of uncontrollable sexual passion, another symptom of diabolical possession. At the same time, he recalls Malvolio's 'mad' ambition to win Olivia.

29 **laid** placed

30 **hideous darkness** Malvolio perceives the dark room as a Dante-like hell (cf. 35), while Sir Topas claims (31–44) that the darkness is caused by Malvolio's possession.

20 SD] *Capell; Maluolio within. F after 19*

FESTE Fie, thou dishonest Satan! I call thee by the most modest terms, for I am one of those gentle ones that will use the devil himself with courtesy. Sayst thou that house is dark?

MALVOLIO As hell, Sir Topas.

FESTE Why, it hath bay-windows transparent as barricadoes, and the clerestories toward the south-north are as lustrous as ebony, and yet complainest thou

31 **Fie** shame on you
dishonest mendacious; lewd (*OED* 2), perhaps still alluding to Malvolio's talk of *ladies* (26)
Satan Darrell, 77, recommends the use of 'proper names of devils' during exorcisms.
I call thee Sir Topas addresses the 'devil' in familiar terms (as 'thou'), suggesting a lack of fear or of undue respect.

32 **modest** moderate; demure (cf. *gentle* and *courtesy*, 32–3). The adjective *dishonest* at 31 is mild compared to the abuse hurled at devils by exorcists, who 'mocke them with reuilinges, Iniuries, and the remembrance of thire saluation' (Darrell, 78).
gentle ones refined people

33 **use . . . courtesy** Feste makes fun of the politeness and gentility that are so central to the play's concerns; see pp. 81–2.

34 **house** room. The two terms are synonymous; cf. Sir Toby's *dark room*, 3.4.131; cf. also Rosalind's claim that love, being 'a madness', 'deserves . . . a dark house' (*AYL* 3.2.389–90). In 'Of Two Brethren and their Wives', the fifth story in Riche – which also contains the prose version of the Twelfth Night story – a man ties his wife 'in a darke house' and pretends that she is a lunatic; she obligingly 'shewed her self . . . to be a right Bedlem, she used no other wordes but Cursynges and Bannynges' (Riche, sig. T2^{r}).

36–9 **Why . . . obstruction** Feste's self-contradictory description plays on the theme 'as clear as mud' and the fact that the two actors perceive different spaces: Feste sees the playhouse, Malvolio a darkened 'inner stage', under-stage or box.

36 **bay-windows** 'These were the rage of the period' (Mahood). They were particularly valued in great houses and halls precisely because they captured light.

37 **barricadoes** barricades, originally made of casks filled with earth and stones (from Spanish *barrica*, cask): thus decidedly untransparent
clerestories rows of windows high up in a wall, letting in daylight (*OED* 1b, giving this example). Sir Topas is probably referring to the windows above the roofs of church aisles, making a spiritual as well as physical contrast with the dark room. High windows are also found in the Middle Temple hall, so that the detail was architecturally accurate, at least in the 1602 performance.

37–8 **south-north** i.e. everywhere or nowhere

38 **lustrous as ebony** luminous as dark wood: another paradox. Ebony was proverbial for its blackness (Dent, E56a): cf. *LLL* 4.3.243, 'thy love is black as ebony.'

31 Satan] *(*sathan*)* 33 that] this *Rann;* that this *Halliwell* 37 clerestories] *Craig;* cleere stores *F;* cleare stones *F2* 37–8 south-north] *(*South north*)*

of obstruction?

MALVOLIO I am not mad, Sir Topas. I say to you this house is dark.

FESTE Madman, thou errest. I say there is no darkness but ignorance, in which thou art more puzzled than the Egyptians in their fog.

MALVOLIO I say this house is as dark as ignorance, though ignorance were as dark as hell; and I say there was never man thus abused. I am no more mad than you are. Make the trial of it in any constant question.

FESTE What is the opinion of Pythagoras concerning wildfowl?

MALVOLIO That the soul of our grandam might haply inhabit a bird.

FESTE What think'st thou of his opinion?

39 **obstruction** shutting out of light (*OED* 2a, first occurrence). Feste may be using one of Malvolio's own more affected terms against him: cf. 2.5.116 and 3.4.20 (Oxf[1]).

42–3 **no . . . ignorance** proverbial (Dent, I16.1)

43 **puzzled** bewildered, lost (*OED v.* 1a, giving this example)

43–4 **the . . . fog** an allusion to the biblical plague of darkness described in Exodus, 10.21: 'and there was a thicke darkenesse upon all the lande of Egypt three dayes long.' It is presumably due to the 'thickness' of the Egyptian darkness that Sir Topas calls it a *fog*.
fog darkness (*OED n.*[2] 3a, first occurrence)

47 **I . . . are** Malvolio repeats this claim to Feste (rather than Sir Topas) at 88, allowing the clown to reply in his own voice, as he cannot here, 'Then you are mad indeed' (89).
more mad Cf. *more grave*, 1.4.28n.

48 **Make . . . question** Test me through any logically consistent question and answer.
constant consistent (*OED a.* 8)

49–50 **Pythagoras . . . wildfowl** The Greek philosopher Pythagoras was renowned for his doctrine of metempsychosis – cf. Dr Faustus' doleful 'Ah Pythagoras *metem su cossis* were that true' (Marlowe, *Faustus*, sig. F2[v]) – which propounded the migration of the soul from one body to another, and especially its reincarnation after death into a new human or animal form (Ovid, *Met.*, 15.183–7, fol. 189[r]). Cf. Rosalind's irreverent 'I was never so berhymed since Pythagoras' time that I was an Irish rat' (*AYL* 3.2.173–4).

51–2 Malvolio gives the correct answer, showing that he can respond aptly to *constant question* (48); what he does not realize is that the question regarding *wildfowl* is a trap, setting up the 'woodcock' joke at 58.

51 **grandam** grandmother (literally, 'grand dame', from French). This was already a somewhat outmoded form: 'grandame words' were precisely obsolete terms (*OED* 5).
haply by chance

51 haply] *Capell;* happily *F*

MALVOLIO I think nobly of the soul, and no way approve his opinion.

FESTE Fare thee well. Remain thou still in darkness. Thou shalt hold th'opinion of Pythagoras ere I will allow of thy wits, and fear to kill a woodcock lest thou dispossess the soul of thy grandam. Fare thee well.

MALVOLIO Sir Topas, Sir Topas!

SIR TOBY My most exquisite Sir Topas.

FESTE Nay, I am for all waters.

MARIA Thou mightst have done this without thy beard and gown. He sees thee not.

SIR TOBY [*to Feste*] To him in thine own voice, and bring me word how thou find'st him. I would we were well rid of this knavery. If he may be conveniently delivered,

54–5 **no . . . opinion** The pagan doctrine of metempsychosis was attacked by early modern Christian writers, including John Donne in *The Progress of the Soul* (1612).

56 **darkness** ignorance; the dark room

56–7 **Thou . . . th'opinion** It is of course absurd that a priest should wish to convert even a 'Puritan' to pagan beliefs: this is an arbitrary pretext for leaving Malvolio in the dark, although it does again raise the question of his religious opinions.

57–8 **allow . . . wits** admit your sanity

58 **woodcock** proverbially stupid bird: cf. Fabian's comparison of Malvolio himself to a 'woodcock near the gin' (2.5.82); Malvolio is now decidedly in the gin.
dispossess drive out (*OED* 3). There is a further allusion here to Malvolio's 'possession' and the (failed) attempt to *dispossess* him.

61 **exquisite** perfect (i.e. in acting his part) (*OED* 4); the third occurrence of the adjective: cf. 1.5.165 and 2.3.140.

62 **Nay** indeed
I . . . waters I can turn my hand to anything (Malone): a variation on the proverb 'to have a cloak for all waters' (Dent, C421). Feste's motley garb – apart from his present disguise – authorizes him to play any role, as does his skill as an actor and ventriloquist in this scene: he is satisfied with his performance. There may also be a play on the topaz-like lustre of *waters*.

63–4 Maria's comment on Feste's superfluous disguise takes up the clothing metaphor implied at 62. It was she who got Feste to dress up in the first place; Mahood suggests that this is an 'afterthought' indicating 'rapid composition', but Maria may simply be trying to put Feste down after his boast. In any case, if the disguise is unnecessary for Malvolio, it certainly helps the audience, who *can* see: cf. the paradoxical SD in *Tem* 3.2.40.1, '*Enter Ariel, invisible.*'

67 **conveniently delivered** set free without too much trouble (Ard[2])

59 soul] house *F2* 62 waters.] waters. *he puts off the disguise Cam[1]* 65 SD] *Oxf* 66 well] all *F2*

I would he were, for I am now so far in offence with my niece that I cannot pursue with any safety this sport to the upshot. Come by and by to my chamber.

Exit [*with Maria*].

FESTE [*As himself; sings.*]

Hey Robin, jolly Robin,
Tell me how thy lady does.

MALVOLIO Fool!

FESTE [*Sings.*]

My lady is unkind, pardie.

MALVOLIO Fool!

FESTE [*Sings.*]

Alas, why is she so?

MALVOLIO Fool, I say!

FESTE [*Sings.*]

She loves another –
Who calls, ha?

MALVOLIO Good fool, as ever thou wilt deserve well at my hand, help me to a candle, and pen, ink and paper.

68–9 **I . . . niece** I have gone so far in provoking my niece's displeasure. Sir Toby attributes great authority to Olivia, fearing her anger.
68 **offence** 'the condition of being regarded with displeasure' (*OED n.* 4a, giving this example)
69 **pursue** proceed with (*OED* 9, giving this example)
70 **upshot** outcome (literally, the final shoot-off to decide the winner of an archery match): cf. *Ham* 5.2.368.
Come . . . chamber Some directors – most influentially, John Barton in his 1969 RSC production – have Sir Toby address this line only to Maria, following Cam[1], who takes it to be an indication 'that the couple are already married'. It is surely more plausible for Sir Toby to tell Feste himself to bring him word how he finds Malvolio, after which he goes off with Maria (whose exit is not marked in F but who fails to speak again), leaving the clown to go about his task.
71–9 Feste signals his presence to Malvolio by singing an old dialogue song which perhaps allows him to alternate two voices (*My lady . . .* and *She loves . . .* being the replies) as he will do later at 94–128. For words and music, see Appendix 3. Feste probably chooses this song as a further means of provoking Malvolio, whose lady likewise *loves another*, namely Cesario.
74 **pardie** by God (from French *par Dieu*)
80–1 **thou … hand** Malvolio, who so far has treated Feste meanly (see especially

69–70 to the] *Rowe;* the *F;* t'the *Riv* 70 SD *with Maria*] *Theobald* 71 SD *as himself*] *this edn* *sings*] *Rowe* 71–2] *Capell; prose F* 74, 76, 78 SDs] *Cam[1]* 74 pardie] *(perdie)*

As I am a gentleman, I will live to be thankful to thee for't.

FESTE Master Malvolio?

MALVOLIO Ay, good fool.

FESTE Alas, sir, how fell you besides your five wits?

MALVOLIO Fool, there was never man so notoriously abused. I am as well in my wits, fool, as thou art.

FESTE But as well? Then you are mad indeed, if you be no better in your wits than a fool.

MALVOLIO They have here propertied me: keep me in darkness, send ministers to me, asses, and do all they can to face me out of my wits.

FESTE Advise you what you say, the minister is here. [*as*

1.5.71–85), promises him a reward for bringing him writing materials: he will repeat the offer at 112–13. Having got into trouble by reading an epistle, he hopes to get himself out of it by writing one, namely the letter read aloud at 5.1.297–305.

82 **gentleman** Malvolio considers himself a gentleman already (as steward), but he may still be alluding to his ever more improbable promotion as Olivia's husband.

84 **Master Malvolio** F's *M.* is probably an abbreviation for *Master*, although it might stand for *Monsieur*: cf. *Monsieur Malvolio* at 2.3.130.

86 **how . . . wits?** how did you come to lose your senses? In the poem *Pastime* Stephen Hawes lists the five wits or mental faculties as common wit, imagination, fantasy, estimation and memory. Five Wits is a personified character in the morality play *Everyman* (*c.* 1495; Ard^2).

87–8 **notoriously abused** disgracefully mistreated. Olivia repeats the phrase, as if quoting Malvolio, at 5.1.372: these are the only uses of the adverb in Shakespeare. *Notorious* is one of Malvolio's theme words, expressing his 'sense of wounded dignity' (Cam^2): cf. 5.1.323 and 372.

89 **But** only

89–90 **Then . . . fool** Feste plays on two meanings of *fool*: jester; idiot.

91 **propertied me** used me like an object (*OED v.* 1). Cf. the equally proud Louis the Dauphin in *KJ*: 'I am too high-born to be propertied' (*KJ* 5.2.79).

92 **ministers** priests (i.e. Sir Topas). Malvolio employs the term adopted by Protestants after the example of Calvinists (*OED n.* 2c): another hint at his 'Puritan' sympathies? Cf. the Puritan Phillip Stubbes: 'Such [names] as at anie hande a Minister of the Gospell ought not to bee called by' (Stubbes, 106^r).

asses Malvolio appears to allude unwittingly to Feste, an *ass* (fool) who played the part of a *minister*.

93 **face . . . wits** bully me out of my senses (*OED* face *v.* 3c, giving this example)

94 **Advise you** consider (*OED* 5, giving this example)

78–9] *Mahood; one line F* 78 another –] *Rowe;* another. *F* 86 besides] beside *Steevens (Capell)* 94–5, 99, 100, 101 SDs] *Hanmer subst.*

Sir Topas] Malvolio, Malvolio, thy wits the heavens restore. Endeavour thyself to sleep and leave thy vain bibble babble.

MALVOLIO Sir Topas!

FESTE [*as Sir Topas*] Maintain no words with him, good fellow. [*as himself*] Who, I, sir? Not I, sir! God b'wi' you, good Sir Topas. [*as Sir Topas*] Marry, amen. [*as himself*] I will, sir, I will.

MALVOLIO Fool, fool, fool, I say!

FESTE Alas, sir, be patient. What say you, sir? I am shent for speaking to you.

MALVOLIO Good fool, help me to some light and some paper. I tell thee I am as well in my wits as any man in Illyria.

FESTE Welladay that you were, sir.

MALVOLIO By this hand, I am. Good fool, some ink,

94–102 The clown's performance as ventriloquist reaches its climax in this direct exchange between his two voices, in which Sir Topas reproaches Feste for having dealings with Malvolio.

95–6 **thy . . . restore** may you come to your senses

96 **Endeavour thyself** try (to get). Shakespeare, here as elsewhere, creates a reflexive verb by adding a reflexive pronoun as object of an intransitive verb (Blake, *Grammar*, 4.4.2).

97 **bibble babble** empty talk. This is the closest of the comedy's possible echoes of Darrell, who recounts that '3. or 4. of [the possessed] gaue themselues to Scoffing and Blasphemy, calling the holy Bible being brought up *bible bable, bible bable*' (Darrell, 9); cf. 25n., 31n., 32n., 3.4.82n. *OED*, however, quoting this example, describes the expression as 'very common in 16th c.'; cf. Fluellen's 'pibble-pabble' in *H5* 4.1.72.

99–100 **good fellow** Feste has Sir Topas address him with respect, not as a 'fool'.

100 **God . . . you** a corruption of 'God be with you', equivalent to modern 'goodbye'

101 **Marry** a mild oath, literally invoking the Virgin Mary (*OED int.* 2a, giving this example)

102 **I will** Since Feste has already responded to *Maintain no words*, 99, he seems to be replying either to something we have not heard 'as if, in the meantime, Sir Topas had whispered' (Johnson), or alternatively to *Marry*, 101, perhaps interpreting it wilfully as 'Get married.'

104 **shent** blamed (past participle of the archaic verb *shend*). Cf. Hamlet of his mother, 'How in my words somever she be shent' (*Ham* 3.2.388).

109 **Welladay** alas. Cf. the Nurse in *RJ*, speaking of Tybalt, 'Ah weraday, he's dead, he's dead, he's dead!' (*RJ* 3.2.37). Feste plays on Malvolio's *well*, 107.

110 **By this hand** truly (mild oath), alluding to giving the (right) hand when making a pledge. Malvolio might offer his hand through the grating or other opening.

100 b'wi'] *Pope;* buy *F*

paper and light, and convey what I will set down to my lady. It shall advantage thee more than ever the bearing of letter did.

FESTE I will help you to't. But tell me true, are you not mad indeed, or do you but counterfeit?

MALVOLIO Believe me, I am not, I tell thee true.

FESTE Nay, I'll ne'er believe a madman till I see his brains. I will fetch you light, and paper, and ink.

MALVOLIO Fool, I'll requite it in the highest degree. I prithee be gone.

FESTE [*Sings.*]

I am gone, sir, and anon, sir,
  I'll be with you again,
In a trice, like to the old Vice,

111 **convey** deliver. Feste does indeed deliver the letter to Olivia, at 5.1.281–2.

112 **advantage** benefit (*OED v.* 4b)

114–15 **are . . . counterfeit?** a trick question: neither possibility (mad or acting mad) places Malvolio in a good light. He responds to *mad* at 116, implying that he *counterfeits*. The question is, of course, the one posed (in earnest) by and of Hamlet: cf. his 'I essentially am not in madness, / But mad in craft' (*Ham* 3.4.185–6).
counterfeit act, pretend (*OED v.* 6, giving this example): cf. 19.

117 **I'll . . . madman** Malvolio is in the 'All Cretans are liars' (or catch-22) trap: as he is 'mad', even his denials confirm his madness.
till . . . brains till I can check whether he has any brains at all (i.e. when he is dead): a variation on the proverb 'you will not believe he is dead till you see his brain' (Dent, B597)

119 **requite** repay

121–8 It is not known whether the words of this song are Shakespeare's. No contemporary music has survived, but Robert Armin as Feste almost certainly sang rather than spoke it. It is an apt conclusion to the scene in so far as it describes both comic acting and the maltreatment of the devil.

121 **anon, sir** at once, sir; the same catchphrase is used repeatedly in *1H4* 2.4.37–95.

123 **In a trice** immediately; synonymous with *anon* (121)
Vice the comic representative of evil in the medieval morality play: apposite, first because the Vice was in some ways the forerunner of the clown/fool, and more specifically because Feste in this scene adopts various Vice-like lazzi or comic stage business: changes in costume and voice (cf. the disguises of the Vice Infidelity in *Magdalene*), wordplay (cf. Richard in *R3*, 'Thus like the formal Vice, Iniquity, / I moralize two meanings in one word', *R3* 3.1.82–3), the display of false Latin, dubious learning, etc.

119–20] *Mahood; F lines* degree: / gone. / 121 SD] *Rowe subst.*

Your need to sustain,
Who with dagger of lath, in his rage and his wrath,
Cries 'Aha!' to the devil,
Like a mad lad, 'Pare thy nails, dad.
Adieu, goodman devil.' *Exit.*

124 ironical: the Vice pretended to befriend his victims, just as Feste and Sir Topas pretend to be concerned for Malvolio's health.

125 **dagger of lath** the wooden weapon worn by the Vice in morality plays and interludes. This prop survived until quite late in the sixteenth century, for example in the moral interlude *Trial of Treasure* (sig. B1[v]). It became synonymous with stagy behaviour: cf. *1H4*, where Falstaff promises Prince Hal to 'beat thee out of thy kingdom with a dagger of lath' (*1H4* 2.4.134–5). There is no extant play in which the Vice beats the devil, but Feste's allusion suggests a specific episode that the audience might recall. This is confirmed by Samuel Harsnett's *Declaration*, which reminisces: 'It was a pretty part in the old Church-playes, when the nimble Vice would skip up nimbly like a Iacke an Apes into the deuils necke, and ride the deuil a course, and belabour him with his wooden dagger, til he made him roare' (Harsnett, *Declaration*, 114–15; on Harsnett, cf. 3.4.25n.).

wrath This may be pronounced comically to rhyme with *lath*.

126 **Cries 'Aha!'** i.e. in defiance: cf. Sir Topas' challenging of the devil at 25 and 31.

127 **mad lad** The Vice is *mad* in his colourful and exuberant behaviour; there may also be a further allusion to Malvolio.

Pare thy nails The devil was supposed to keep his nails long and uncut, so that paring them was an affront (Malone). The phrase was proverbial (Dent, N12). Feste seems to allude again to a specific and recognizable piece of stage business: this is confirmed in *H5* 4.4.68–9, where Pistol is described as 'this roaring devil i'th' old play, that everyone may pare his nails with a wooden dagger.'

dad In some morality plays, such as *Lusty Juventus* (sig. B2[v]), the Vice is the devil's son.

128 **goodman devil** probably addressed to Malvolio rather than to the *devil* supposedly possessing him. Feste's farewell would have been appropriate if Malvolio was under the trapdoor, i.e. in the under-stage space known as 'hell'. Morality play devils often appeared from under the trap, accompanied by smoke and thunder. In some productions, Feste, before exiting, dances triumphantly on the trapdoor (Brown, 273); in Barton's 1969 RSC production he first stamped on Malvolio's hands and then slammed down the trap, causing the screaming steward to fall back into his prison (Sinden, 'Malvolio', 65).

goodman a somewhat condescending title, usually prefixed either to designations of occupation (*OED* 3a), as in 'Goodman Delver' (*Ham* 5.1.14), or to the name of a low-ranking person (*OED* 3b), as in 'goodman Dull' (*LLL* 4.2.37–8). This may be a gibe at Malvolio's servant status.

126 'Aha!'] *this edn;* ah ha, *F;* 'Ah ha!' *Mahood* 127–8 'Pare . . . devil.'] *Mahood;* paire . . . diuell. *F*
128 goodman devil] *Capell;* good man diuell *F;* good Man Drivel *Rowe*[3]

4.3 *Enter* SEBASTIAN.

SEBASTIAN
This is the air, that is the glorious sun;
This pearl she gave me, I do feel't and see't,
And though 'tis wonder that enwraps me thus,
Yet 'tis not madness. Where's Antonio, then?
I could not find him at the Elephant;
Yet there he was, and there I found this credit,
That he did range the town to seek me out.
His counsel now might do me golden service,
For though my soul disputes well with my sense

4.3 In this, the play's briefest scene, Olivia prepares to become betrothed as quickly as possible to the finally co-operative Cesario, while Sebastian accepts his unexpected good fortune with happy disbelief. As in all the comedy's more solemn or romantic episodes, the entire scene is in verse. Sebastian's opening lines indicate that the scene is set outdoors, while Olivia's reference to her *chantry* at 24 suggests a space separate from the main house (the latter was represented on the Elizabethan stage by the door through which they exit).

1–21 Sebastian's sense of bewilderment produces a semantically dense and self-contradictory speech expressing his disbelief at his good luck in the language of logical disputation, as if engaged in an inner debate or psychodrama.

1–2 Sebastian is both celebrating the world, which he now perceives with new enthusiasm, and reassuring himself that his senses are still functioning. His three deictics (*This*, *that*, *This*) take us progressively from the widest and most general (*air*) to the smallest and most particular (*pearl*); on deictics, see p. 89.

2 **pearl** Olivia has given Cesario another jewel: the third, after the ring (1.5, 2.2) and her *picture* (3.4.203).

3 **wonder** amazement
enwraps me absorbs me in contemplation; *OED* 2b, giving this example, suggests that the verb is sometimes confused with the participle 'enrapt' (i.e. carried away).

4 **madness** Sebastian – as at 4.1.60 – fears for his own sanity. This takes on particular piquancy after the 'dark room' episode: in Barton's 1969 RSC production, Malvolio uttered at this point 'a faint sound of nonsensical gibberish' from his prison under the stage (Sinden, 'Malvolio', 65), while in Mendes' 2002 Donmar production Simon Russell Beale's Malvolio, still visible on stage, wept.

5 **Elephant** See 3.3.39n.

6 **was** had been
credit report (literally, something believed; *OED n.* 3, sole occurrence)

7 **range** wander through (*OED v.*[1] 7)

8 His advice would be of inestimable help to me now
golden precious (*OED a.* 4a); cf. 5.1.375n.

9 **disputes . . . sense** argues thoroughly with what I perceive; alluding to formal logical disputations in universities and inns of court. There is a problem

4.3] *(Scaena Tertia.)* 1 SP] *not in F; Rowe subst.* 6 credit] current *Hanmer*

That this may be some error but no madness,
Yet doth this accident and flood of fortune
So far exceed all instance, all discourse,
That I am ready to distrust mine eyes
And wrangle with my reason that persuades me
To any other trust but that I am mad,
Or else the lady's mad. Yet if 'twere so
She could not sway her house, command her followers,
Take and give back affairs and their dispatch
With such a smooth, discreet and stable bearing
As I perceive she does. There's something in't
That is deceivable.

here precisely of logical consistency: Sebastian's *soul* seems to dispute in favour of *error* and his *sense* in favour of *madness*, while at 13–15 he appears to argue with both faculties in favour of someone's being *mad*. But it is probably wrong to look for overall coherence, since at 16–21 he contradicts himself again. He is engaged in a dialectical process: i.e. he changes his mind.

10 **some . . . madness** i.e. a mistake (of identity?) rather than mere folly. This is the main issue in *CE*, which the term *error* seems to recall. Sebastian comes close to realizing that there may be a comedy of errors at work in Illyria but does not take the insight any further.

11 **accident . . . fortune** an overwhelming series of unexpected and fortunate events

accident and flood accidental flood (rhetorical figure: hendiadys)

12 **So far exceed** goes so far beyond

instance precedent: continuing the metaphor of logical and perhaps legal debate

discourse reasoning, understanding; cf. *Ham* 1.2.150, 'a beast that wants discourse of reason'.

14–16 **wrangle . . . mad** i.e. resist any rational argument against the conclusion that one of the two of us is mad. This somewhat baroque construction suggests the convoluted nature of Sebastian's internal dialectic: cf. 9n.

14 **wrangle** argue; synonym of *dispute* (9), likewise signifying a formal public debate at a university or law school (*OED v.* 2)

15 **trust** belief

16–20 **Yet . . . does** Sebastian's testimony to Olivia's skill in governing her household confirms other evidence of her increased authoritativeness, e.g. Sir Toby's fear at 4.2.68–70.

17 **sway** rule; a recurrent thematic word in the comedy: cf. 2.5.106, 4.1.51 and notes.

18 i.e. undertake business and bring it to completion

affairs commercial or professional business (*OED* 2b)

dispatch execution, settlement (*OED n.* 5a)

19 **stable** steadfast (*OED a.* 6a; not found elsewhere in Shakespeare as an adjective)

bearing demeanour, behaviour

21 **deceivable** deceptive (*OED* 1a; Hope, 1.2.2a)

21 SD] *this edn; after 21 F* the lady] she *Pope*

Enter OLIVIA *and* Priest.

But here the lady comes.

OLIVIA

Blame not this haste of mine. If you mean well,
Now go with me and with this holy man
Into the chantry by. There before him,
And underneath that consecrated roof,
Plight me the full assurance of your faith,
That my most jealous and too doubtful soul
May live at peace. He shall conceal it
Whiles you are willing it shall come to note,
What time we will our celebration keep

22 **Blame . . . mine** This is one of the play's ironical perspective games (see pp. 24–32). From Olivia's point of view, her *haste* is due to the fact that Cesario is at last responding to her advances (and may change his mind again); from Sebastian's perspective, her rapidity is so precipitate as to be *mad* (16), but this does not stop him going along. In Mendes' 2002 Donmar production Helen McCrory's Olivia entered draped only in a sheet, giving her *haste* decidedly erotic overtones.

24 **chantry** chapel, dedicated to the singing of daily mass for the souls of the dead (*OED* 3): cf. *H5* 4.1.296–7, 'Two chantries, where the sad and solemn priests / Sing still for Richard's soul'. Olivia's chantry is presumably where the *holy man* (23) sings for the soul of her dead brother (see 1.1.29–30), but it is now transformed into the venue for their marriage vows: a sign of how far Olivia has come from her pledge to shun the world for seven years (1.1.25–7).

by nearby

26 i.e. make a solemn pledge of your true intention to marry me. Olivia proposes a *contract*, as the priest terms it at 5.1.152 (or 'pre-contract' as it is called in *MM* 4.1.72), consisting of an exchange of pre-marital vows. Such a declaration of future intent (*Sponsalia per verba de futuro*) was not absolutely binding but was nevertheless recognized within English common law: hence Olivia's insistence that Cesario is to all intents and purposes her *husband* at 5.1.139–40. The priest describes the betrothal ceremony in detail at 5.1.152–9.

27 **jealous** fearful, apprehensive (*OED* 5)

28–9 **He . . . note** On the priest's concealing of the ceremony he has conducted, cf. Friar Laurence's pledge of silence 'till we can find a time / To blaze your marriage' in *RJ* 3.3.150–1. In the event, Olivia's chaplain is obliged to reveal the pre-marriage on his next appearance at 5.1.152–9.

29 **Whiles** until (*OED* 5, giving this example)

you . . . note you want to make it public

30 **What time** at which time (Blake, *Grammar*, 5.3.2.4e)

celebration wedding, i.e. the full public ceremony which will take place later to ratify their preliminary exchange of vows

keep hold

27 jealous] *(*iealious*)* 28 live] henceforth live *Hanmer* it] it still, *Keightley*

According to my birth. What do you say?

SEBASTIAN

I'll follow this good man and go with you,
And, having sworn truth, ever will be true.

OLIVIA

Then lead the way, good father, and heavens so shine
That they may fairly note this act of mine. *Exeunt.*

5.1 *Enter* FESTE[, *with a letter,*] *and* FABIAN.

FABIAN Now, as thou lov'st me, let me see his letter.

FESTE Good Master Fabian, grant me another request.

FABIAN Anything.

FESTE Do not desire to see this letter.

31 **According . . . birth** in keeping with my rank. Olivia's status as countess makes a secret wedding – as opposed to a 'pre-contract' – unthinkable. This is the only moment in the play in which she explicitly asserts her *birth*: another sign, perhaps, of her increasing authoritativeness (see 16–20n.). **What . . . say?** Do you agree? This often raises a laugh: Sebastian is dumbfounded, and in any case seems to have little *say*, since Olivia has already arranged everything.

34–5 **heavens . . . mine** probable allusion to the proverb 'Happy is the bride the sun shines on' (Dent, B663, sole occurrence in Shakespeare)

35 **fairly note** look favourably upon. Olivia's wish may be extended to the audience as a plea for indulgence towards her *haste* (22).

5.1 This, the last and longest scene in the play, is also the most hectic, bringing onstage nearly all the characters and at the same time pulling together – but not altogether resolving – the separate strands of the various plots. The great number of entrances and exits and the sheer amount of information given make this finale notoriously difficult to stage, so much so that Granville Barker calls it 'a scandalously ill-arranged and ill-written last scene, the despair of any stage manager' (Barker, 'Preface', 28). Particular theatrical problems are created by the 'optical illusion' of the denouement with both twins on stage, although when successful this is one of the play's more memorable episodes. The language of the scene, moreover, is at times extraordinarily dense. Capell's location '*Before Olivia's House*' is suggested by Olivia's offer of hospitality at 310–13.

1 **his** i.e. Malvolio's

4 Feste's request not to request is, as Fabian observes, another of his paradoxical logical games: cf. 4.1.8 and 4.2.14–16 and notes.

35 SD] *(Exeunt. Finis Actus Quartus.)* 5.1] *(Actus Quintus. Scena Prima.)* 0.1, 184.1, 276.1 FESTE] *Munro; Clowne F* 0.1, 320.1 *with a letter*] *this edn* 1 his] this *F2* 2 Master] *(* M.*), Steevens;* Mr. *Rowe*

FABIAN This is to give a dog and, in recompense, desire my dog again.

Enter ORSINO, VIOLA [*as Cesario*], CURIO *and Lords.*

ORSINO
Belong you to the Lady Olivia, friends?

FESTE Ay, sir, we are some of her trappings.

ORSINO
I know thee well. How dost thou, my good fellow?

FESTE Truly, sir, the better for my foes, and the worse for my friends.

ORSINO
Just the contrary: the better for thy friends.

FESTE No, sir, the worse.

ORSINO How can that be?

FESTE Marry, sir, they praise me and make an ass of me. Now my foes tell me plainly I am an ass, so that by my foes, sir, I profit in the knowledge of myself, and by my

5–6 **This . . . again** a probable topical allusion. In his diary entry for 26 March 1602 (= 1603, two days after the death of Queen Elizabeth and a year or so after his description of the Middle Temple performance of *TN*: see pp. 3–4) Manningham records an anecdote about the Queen and her kinsman Dr Boleyn, who 'had a dog which he doted one, soe much that the Q[ueene], understanding of it, requested he would graunt hir one desyre, and he should have whatsoever he would aske. Shee demaunded his dogge; he gave it, and "Nowe, Madame," q[uoth] he, "you promised to give me my desyre." "I will," q[uothe] she. "Then I pray you give me my dog againe"' (Manningham, 210).

6.1 *Lords* Cf. 1.1.0.2n.

7, 9, 25 In this exchange Orsino appears to be speaking verse, while Feste is unambiguously prosaic; cf. 168–84.

7 **Belong you to** are you dependants of; Feste interprets this at 8 as 'are you appendages of' (*OED v.* 4a, giving this example).

8 **trappings** ornaments (literally, the ceremonial harness of a horse)

10–11 **the better . . . friends** Feste's paradox makes fun of Orsino's somewhat patronizing *friends* at 7.

15–18 **Marry . . . abused** The clown's pseudo-logical defence of sincerity plays on the favourite Renaissance moral dictum *nosce teipsum*, 'know thyself': cf. 145n.

5 This] That *Steevens*[2] 6.1 ORSINO] *Mahood; Duke F* as Cesario] *Munro subst.* 9] *Oxf; prose F*

friends I am abused. So that, conclusions to be as kisses, if your four negatives make your two affirmatives, why then, the worse for my friends and the better for my foes.

ORSINO Why, this is excellent.

FESTE By my troth, sir, no, though it please you to be one of my friends.

ORSINO
Thou shalt not be the worse for me: there's gold.
[*Gives coin.*]

FESTE But that it would be double-dealing, sir, I would you could make it another.

ORSINO O, you give me ill counsel.

FESTE Put your grace in your pocket, sir, for this once, and let your flesh and blood obey it.

ORSINO Well, I will be so much a sinner to be a double-dealer. There's another. [*Gives coin.*]

18 **abused** deceived (by flattery)

18–19 **conclusions . . . affirmatives** i.e. since in grammar (especially Latin grammar) two negatives make an affirmative (and four make two), a woman who says 'no, no, no, no' to a kiss is really saying 'yes, yes'. This probably alludes to Sidney, *Astrophel*, sonnet 63, in which Astrophel asks Stella for a kiss and 'Least one should not be heard [she] twice, said no no.' Astrophel interprets this 'grammatically' as a yes: 'For Grammer says (to Grammer who sayes nay) / That in one speech two negatiues affirme' (Sidney, *Astrophel*, 540; Farmer, in Steevens).

19 **your** an indication not of possession but of being 'one of a group' (Wales; Blake, *Grammar*, 3.3.4.5c), and used by Feste for playful emphasis; cf. Lepidus' abuse of the form in *AC* 2.7.26–7: 'Your serpent of Egypt is bred, now, of your mud by the operation of your sun; so is your crocodile'; cf. also *Ham* 4.3.21–4.

22 **this is excellent** Orsino joins Olivia and Viola as one of the admirers of Feste's wit: cf. 1.5.69–92 and 3.1.58–66.

23–4 **though . . . friends** i.e. even if you are so kind as to say so (and possibly reward me)

26 **double-dealing** Feste's usual request to double the tip: cf. 3.1.48–51, 4.1.20.

29 **Put . . . pocket** put away your sense of propriety; put your hand in your pocket (to find money). Feste plays on the expression *your grace* as the proper term of address towards a duke (*OED* grace *n.* 16b); cf. *MM* 4.3.135–6, 'And you shall have . . . / Grace of the Duke.'

30 **let . . . it** i.e. let your instincts follow my *ill counsel* rather than your *grace*

31 **to** as to

18 that . . . kisses] that, Conclusion to be asked, is, *Theobald;* the conclusion to be asked is *Hanmer* 25 SD] *Collier*[2] *subst.*

FESTE *Primo, secundo, tertio* is a good play, and the old saying is 'The third pays for all.' The triplex, sir, is a good tripping measure, as the bells of Saint Bennet, sir, may put you in mind – one, two, three.

ORSINO You can fool no more money out of me at this throw. If you will let your lady know I am here to speak with her, and bring her along with you, it may awake my bounty further.

FESTE Marry, sir, lullaby to your bounty till I come again. I go, sir, but I would not have you to think that

33 ***Primo, secundo, tertio*** first, second, third (Latin). This probably alludes to an elaborate form of mathematical chess, supposedly invented by Pythagoras and known as the philosophers' game or table (*Rythmomachia*). Odd numbers were opposed to even numbers on a double chessboard, and the object was to capture opposing numbers through arithmetical operations such as addition: for example, one and two together could capture three. Lever & Fulwood defend it in their manual of 1563, while Scot refers dismissively to 'a childish and ridiculous toie . . . like unto childrens plaie at *Primus secundus*, or the game called The Philosophers table' (Scot, 198).
play game (cf. Lever & Fulwood's title, '*The Most Noble . . . Play*')

34 **'The third . . . all'** This is, as Feste notes, an *old saying* (Dent, T319), the equivalent of the modern 'third time lucky'. The clown now wants Orsino to triple his tip.
triplex triple time in music (*OED n.* 1a, first occurrence)

35 **tripping** dancing (cf. 'Each one tripping on his toe', *Tem* 4.1.46), with a pun on *triplex*
measure rhythm; *OED* 17a, giving this example, quotes T. Morley, annotation to 29, '*Tripla*. This is the common hackney horse of all the Composers, which is of so manie kindes as there be maners of pricking . . . and yet all one measure.'
Saint Bennet St Benedict. There were several churches in London dedicated to this saint, but Feste could be alluding in particular to St Bennet Hithe across the Thames from the Globe in Paul's Wharf, since its bells may have been audible at the theatre.

36 **one, two, three** i.e. three chimes of the *bells*. Feste varies his earlier *Primo, secundo, tertio* (33) to underline his request for a third coin.

38 **throw** occasion; literally, cast of the dice in gambling (perhaps taking up Feste's *good play*, 33)

40, 41, 44 **bounty** generosity, especially on the part of the wealthy (*OED* 4a)

41 **lullaby** *OED* (*n.* 1b) glosses this as 'farewell'; cf. *PP* 15.15–16. According to Ard^2, the meaning is closer to 'good repose': cf. *take a nap*, 44. It is more probable, however, that the word is used here as a verb (functionally shifted from the noun) meaning 'sing a lullaby (and so send to sleep)': cf. Copley, 59: 'Sweet Sound that all mens sences lullabieth' (Dyce).

32 SD] *Cam^{1}subst.* 34 triplex] triplet *Johnson* 35 as] *Hanmer;* or *F* Saint] *(S.), Capell*

my desire of having is the sin of covetousness. But as you say, sir, let your bounty take a nap, I will awake it anon. *Exit.*

Enter ANTONIO *and* Officers.

VIOLA

Here comes the man, sir, that did rescue me.

ORSINO

That face of his I do remember well,
Yet when I saw it last it was besmeared
As black as Vulcan in the smoke of war.
A baubling vessel was he captain of,
For shallow draught and bulk unprizable,
With which such scatheful grapple did he make
With the most noble bottom of our fleet

43 **of having** to possess
covetousness excessive desire for money or property, considered the deadliest of the seven sins and often personified in morality plays as the principal vice (cf. 4.2.123n.)
44 **take a nap** rest
45 **anon** at once: cf. 4.2.121n.
46 **rescue** Cesario's choice of verb adds to the confusion of identity between the twins: he is referring to Antonio's intervention to stop the duel at 3.4.307, but it is Sebastian that Antonio literally rescues following the shipwreck (see 2.1).
47–55 Orsino's retrospective eulogy of his military enemy is something of a Shakespearean topos (although it is usually reserved for the dead): cf. e.g. Prince Hal's praise for Hotspur in *1H4* 5.4.86–100, or Octavius' for Antony in *AC* 5.1.35–48.
48 **besmeared** dirtied, blackened
49 **Vulcan** the Roman god of fire and metal-working
smoke of war i.e. smoke produced by Vulcan preparing weapons in his foundry, and by the naval battle between Orsino and Antonio
50 **baubling** contemptibly small (literally, like a bauble or child's plaything; *OED*, first occurrence); cf. 'How many shallow bauble boats dare sail' (*TC* 1.3.35).
51 i.e. of little importance in terms of size and depth (and so not worth capturing)
draught depth (literally the amount of water displaced)
unprizable of little worth (*OED* 1, sole occurrence); a 'passivized' adjective (Hope, 1.2.2c)
52 **such . . . make** he engaged in such destructive combat
scatheful harmful, injurious (sole occurrence in Shakespeare)
grapple combat (literally with grappling irons). In Shakespeare the term often retains its nautical connotations: cf. Hamlet on the pirates, 'and in the grapple I boarded them' (*Ham* 4.6.17–18).
53 **bottom** ship; literally, hull (rhetorical figure: synecdoche (part for whole))

45.1] *after 46 Dyce*

That very envy and the tongue of loss
Cried fame and honour on him. – What's the matter?

1 OFFICER

Orsino, this is that Antonio
That took the Phoenix and her fraught from Candy,
And this is he that did the Tiger board,
When your young nephew Titus lost his leg.
Here in the streets, desperate of shame and state,
In private brabble did we apprehend him.

VIOLA

He did me kindness, sir, drew on my side,
But in conclusion put strange speech upon me.
I know not what 'twas but distraction.

ORSINO [*to Antonio*]

Notable pirate, thou salt-water thief,

54–5 **That . . . him** that even envy itself and the voices of those he defeated called for him to be honoured; *envy* is a personification here, as at 2.1.27.
Cried . . . on invoked by outcry (*OED v.* 17, giving this example)

56–61 The officer 'seems to be spurring Orsino to revenge' (Oxf[1]) by giving more information than appears to be called for – e.g. regarding Orsino's nephew – and by characterizing Antonio as a mere street-brawler.

56 **Orsino** It is odd that the officer should omit Orsino's title, as if addressing an equal.

57, 58 **Phoenix, Tiger** ships of Orsino's navy; *Tiger* is also the name of a ship in *Mac* 1.3.7.

57 **fraught** cargo (variant of 'freight')
Candy Crete (from Candia, a town on the island)

59 **Titus . . . leg** The name of Orsino's nephew, together with his loss of limb, evokes *TA*, in which Titus' daughter Lavinia loses her hands and tongue.

60 **desperate . . . state** regardless of personal disgrace and of public order. Some commentators interpret *state* as 'danger to himself', but the context of the conflict between Antonio and the Illyrian authorities suggests public (versus *private*, 61) decorum.

61 **private brabble** personal skirmish; cf. 'this petty brabble' (*TA* 1.1.561).
apprehend arrest

62 **drew . . . side** drew his sword in my defence: cf. 3.4.307.

63 **in conclusion** i.e. in his final speech before his arrest: cf. 3.4.362–7.
put . . . me spoke to me in a strange manner

64 **but distraction** if not madness

65 **Notable** notorious
pirate Illyria was renowned for its dangerous pirates: cf. Suffolk's reference to 'Bargulus, the strong Illyrian pirate' (*2H6* 4.1.108), a paraphrase of 'Bargulus, the Illyrian robber' (Cicero, *De officiis*, fol. 88[v]).
salt-water thief pirate; cf. Shylock's 'water rats, water thieves . . . (I mean pirates)', *MV* 1.3.22–3.

57 fraught] freight *Oxf* 65, 125, 160, 179, 190, 205, 260, 363 SD] *Oxf*

What foolish boldness brought thee to their mercies
Whom thou in terms so bloody and so dear
Hast made thine enemies?

ANTONIO Orsino, noble sir,
Be pleased that I shake off these names you give me.
Antonio never yet was thief or pirate,
Though I confess on base and ground enough
Orsino's enemy. A witchcraft drew me hither:
That most ingrateful boy there by your side
From the rude sea's enraged and foamy mouth
Did I redeem. A wreck past hope he was.
His life I gave him and did thereto add
My love, without retention or restraint,
All his in dedication. For his sake
Did I expose myself – pure for his love –
Into the danger of this adverse town,
Drew to defend him when he was beset,
Where, being apprehended, his false cunning,
Not meaning to partake with me in danger,
Taught him to face me out of his acquaintance,

66 **brought . . . mercies** led you to put yourself at the mercy of those

67 **dear** dire, grievous (*OED a.*[2] 2); cf. 'our dear peril' (*TA* 5.1.228).

69 **Be . . . I** please let me
shake off repudiate; cf. 'these offers . . . he shakes off' (*AC* 3.7.32–3).

70 **thief or pirate** The deletion of the indefinite article (*a*) is common in Shakespeare after *never* (Hope, 1.1.3c, giving this example).

71 **base . . . enough** sufficient grounds: the two nouns are synonyms.

72 **A witchcraft** a spell. Cf. Olivia's 'the last enchantment you [Cesario] did here', 3.1.110.

73 **ingrateful** ungrateful, the first in a crescendo of accusations against the bewildered Cesario in this scene; cf. 99, 142–3 and 175–81.

74 **rude** rough

75 **wreck** ruined person; Sebastian was both literally and morally shipwrecked.

77 **retention** reserve; *OED* 3a, giving this example, glosses as 'keeping to oneself or in one's own hands'. Cf. 2.4.96 and n. for a different use of the same term.

78 **All . . . dedication** devoted entirely to him

79 **pure** purely, only

80 **adverse** hostile

81 **Drew** drew my sword; cf. 62.
beset attacked from all sides

83 **Not . . . partake** not intending to share

84 **face . . . acquaintance** brazenly deny that he knew me

75, 262 wreck] *(*wracke*)*

And grew a twenty years' removed thing
While one would wink, denied me mine own purse,
Which I had recommended to his use
Not half an hour before.

VIOLA How can this be?

ORSINO

When came he to this town?

ANTONIO

Today, my lord, and for three months before,
No interim, not a minute's vacancy,
Both day and night did we keep company.

Enter OLIVIA *and Attendants.*

ORSINO

Here comes the countess; now heaven walks on earth.

85 **grew . . . thing** became as distant as if he had not seen me for twenty years

86 **While . . . wink** in a wink (referring to the rapidity of Cesario's transformation)

87 **recommended** committed (*OED v.*[1] 1c, giving this example)

88 **half an hour** This corresponds more or less to real time in performance: i.e. the brief time-lag between Antonio's giving his purse to Sebastian at 3.3.38 and Cesario's denial of having received it at 3.4.338. Contrast the slow fictional time of *three months* at 90 and 95.

88–9 In performance the first two of these three half-lines (spoken by Antonio and Viola) are usually delivered as making up a metrical and rhetorical unit (statement/rapid response), while Orsino pauses before asking his half-line question.

90, 95 **three months** The length of time that has supposedly passed since the shipwreck – and thus the comedy's opening scene – is more symbolic than descriptive: contrast the *three days* that have elapsed at 1.4.3. Antonio's temporal reference here emphasizes the intensity and intimacy of his bond with Sebastian, while Orsino's repetition of the phrase underlines the fact that his relationship with Cesario has had time to mature. Both point to the quite different temporal patterns of the Sebastian and Cesario plots respectively. On the play's multiple time scheme, cf. pp. 77–8.

91 **interim, vacancy** synonyms for 'interval'

92 **day and night** implying that Antonio and Sebastian slept together. This is not unusual in Shakespeare: cf. e.g. Iago and Cassio (*Oth* 3.3.416).

93 **heaven . . . earth** Orsino returns briefly to the adulatory style of 1.1, in stark contrast with his rough manner towards Olivia at 108–11, thus confirming the rapid changes of mood and attitude suggested in the opening scene (see 1.1.7–8).

91 interim] *(intrim)* 92.1] *after 96 Dyce*

But for thee, fellow – fellow, thy words are madness.
Three months this youth hath tended upon me.
But more of that anon. – Take him aside.

OLIVIA
What would my lord, but that he may not have,
Wherein Olivia may seem serviceable?
Cesario, you do not keep promise with me.

VIOLA
Madam –

ORSINO
Gracious Olivia –

OLIVIA
What do you say, Cesario? Good my lord –

VIOLA
My lord would speak, my duty hushes me.

OLIVIA
If it be aught to the old tune, my lord,

97 **but . . . have** except what I cannot give him (my love)

98 **Olivia** Olivia's self-naming gives her an air of importance just as she is supposedly offering her humble services to the duke (on this rhetorical device, see Viswanathan).
serviceable willing to serve. Olivia defers verbally to Orsino's rank, but – in addition to refusing him – she happily ignores him at 102 (as Cesario points out).

99 Olivia is evidently referring to an appointment made with Sebastian after their exchange of marriage vows, which, the priest tells us at 152–9, took place two hours earlier. Even after the marriage vows, she continues to address her 'husband' as Cesario: Sebastian is named as such in her presence only at 217. Her ignorance of his name serves to keep the mistaken-identity plot alive.

100–1 Viola and Orsino speak simultaneously, the former anxious to defend herself from another 'false' accusation, the latter keen to seize the opportunity to woo Olivia directly: a comic moment in performance.

102–3 Olivia gives precedence to Cesario over his master: indeed, *Good my lord*, while acknowledging Orsino's desire to speak, effectively invites him to shut up. Viola not only re-establishes decorum but implicitly criticizes Olivia for her disregard of hierarchy.

104 **aught** anything
to . . . tune in your usual (amorous) style

94 fellow – fellow] *Dyce subst.;* fellow, fellow *F* 100 Madam –] *Riv;* Madam: *F;* Madam? *Capell* 101 Olivia –] *Theobald subst.; Oliuia. F* 102 lord –] *Rowe subst.;* Lord. *F* 104 aught] *(ought)*

It is as fat and fulsome to mine ear
As howling after music.

ORSINO Still so cruel?

OLIVIA

Still so constant, lord.

ORSINO

What, to perverseness? You uncivil lady,
To whose ingrate and unauspicious altars
My soul the faithfull'st offerings hath breathed out
That e'er devotion tendered – what shall I do?

OLIVIA

Even what it please my lord that shall become him.

ORSINO

Why should I not, had I the heart to do it,

105 **fat** gross
fulsome cloying, nauseating (from excessive repetition; *OED* 3c, giving this example). Olivia expresses outright revulsion at Orsino's courtship: these are strong words, provoking a violent reaction in the duke at 108–27.
106 **howling** i.e. like a dog: another insult; possibly looking back to Orsino's craving for a nauseating excess of music in 1.1.1–3
107 **constant** consistent (in my refusal)
108 **perverseness** obstinacy, waywardness (implying that her rejection of Orsino is altogether unreasonable); cf. the Duke of Milan on his daughter Silvia's refusal of Sir Thurio, 'perversely she persevers so' (*TGV* 3.2.28).
uncivil ill-mannered, barbarous; a recurrent charge in the play, underlining its concern with civility. Malvolio uses it of Sir Toby's festivities (2.3.120), Cesario of Sir Andrew's challenge (3.4.247), and Olivia of Sir Toby's attack on Sebastian (4.1.52).
109 **ingrate** ungrateful
unauspicious inauspicious, unpropitious (*OED*, first occurrence; sole Shakespearean use)
110 **faithfull'st offerings** pledges of absolute fidelity (*OED* faithful 3b, giving this example)
***hath** F's plural 'haue' is probably due to the vicinity of *offerings*.
breathed out expressed
111 **tendered** offered
112 Whatever suits you (a variation on 'What you will'): Olivia patronizes him again. In response, Orsino points out that (as duke) he has indeed the power to do whatever he pleases (113).
113–27 The unexpected violence of this speech – in which Orsino first raises the possibility of killing Olivia, before changing strategy and threatening revenge on Cesario – is often underplayed in performance as one of the duke's passing moods, especially since there are no consequences and Orsino seems rapidly to forget the whole idea. It is none the less a potentially disquieting moment if played straight. The speech also

105 fat] flat *Warburton* 107 lord] my Lord *F3* 110 offerings] *(*offrings*)* hath] *Capell;* haue *F;* has *Pope*

Like to th'Egyptian thief at point of death,
Kill what I love – a savage jealousy
That sometime savours nobly? But hear me this:
Since you to non-regardance cast my faith,
And that I partly know the instrument
That screws me from my true place in your favour,
Live you the marble-breasted tyrant still.
But this your minion, whom I know you love,
And whom, by heaven I swear, I tender dearly,
Him will I tear out of that cruel eye

marks a shift in the object of Orsino's affections, from *what I love* (presumably Olivia) at 115, to whom *I tender dearly* (Cesario) at 122. In some productions, though, Orsino indicates that Cesario may be *what I love* from the beginning of the speech, for example by immediately taking him 'hostage', as in Carroll's 2002 Middle Temple performance.

114 **Egyptian thief** This alludes to Thyamis, an Egyptian robber chief in the Greek romance *Ethiopica* by Heliodorus, who tries but fails to kill his beloved captive Chariclea when his own life is threatened by a rival band. Heliodorus comments, 'And if the barbarous people be once in despaire of their owne safetie, they haue a custome to kill all those by whome they set much, and whose companie they desire after death' (Heliodorus, fols 18^{r}–18^{v}). In response to Olivia's *uncivil* behaviour, Orsino likens himself to the 'barbarous people' (see *savage*, 115), while characterizing his own predicament as that of a desperado ready to defend himself at all costs; the story suggests, however, that Olivia's (or Viola's) life is not really at risk.

116 **savours nobly** exudes or tastes of nobility
hear me ethic dative (i.e. listen to what I say: Blake, *Grammar*, 3.3.2.1a, giving this example); cf. 120 and 3.2.31–2, 3.4.171.

117 **non-regardance** disregard, oblivion (*OED*, sole occurrence)
cast my faith throw my fidelity into oblivion (by disregarding it)

118 **that** since

118–9 **instrument . . . screws** instrument of torture that wrenches

119 **my true place** i.e. Cesario has violently usurped Orsino's rightful position in Olivia's heart: a political metaphor to justify the duke's threatened abuse of power; cf. *tyrant* (120) and *crowned* (124).

120 **Live you** continue to live (ethic dative; cf. *hear me*, 116n.)
marble-breasted a conventional trope of Elizabethan love poetry; cf. Sidney's 'My mistresse Marble-heart' (in 'Ring out your bells', line 28, Sidney, *Arcadia*, 489; Ard^{2}).
tyrant Orsino again justifies his threatened use of absolute power by accusing Olivia of tyranny over him; cf. Olivia's 'tyrannous heart' (of Cesario) at 3.1.118.

121 **minion** sexual favourite (from French *mignon*, pet); cf. the equally derisive 'O thou minion of her pleasure', addressed to the Fair Youth in *Son* 126.9. The term often bore homoerotic connotations: see B. Smith, 189–223.

122 **tender** care for (*OED v.*^{2} 3a); rate: cf. *Ham* 1.3.106, 'Tender yourself more dearly.'

123 i.e. by definitively removing him from your view (through murder)

Where he sits crowned in his master's spite.
[*to Viola*] Come, boy, with me. My thoughts are ripe in mischief.
I'll sacrifice the lamb that I do love
To spite a raven's heart within a dove. [*Goes to door.*]

VIOLA
And I most jocund, apt and willingly
To do you rest a thousand deaths would die.
[*Follows Orsino.*]

OLIVIA
Where goes Cesario?

VIOLA After him I love
More than I love these eyes, more than my life,
More by all mores than e'er I shall love wife.
If I do feign, you witnesses above

124 **crowned** crownèd; cf. Orsino's own fantasy of becoming the *one self king* occupying Olivia's *sovereign thrones*, 1.1.37–8.
in . . . spite to the vexation of his master

125 **ripe in mischief** ready to do harm; cf. *H8* 1.1.160–1, 'as prone to mischief / As able to perform't'.

126 This may have biblical overtones, recalling both Abraham's near-sacrifice of Isaac (Genesis, 22) and Christ as the (sacrificial) lamb of God (John, 1.29).

127 **a raven's . . . dove** ambiguous. It may mean simply 'the cruel heart within Olivia's beautiful form' (Ard[2]; cf. 'Dove-feather'd raven', *RJ* 3.2.76), or it may involve a more complex conceit: a cruel heart (Olivia's) by means of a gentle one (Cesario's). The supposed cruelty of the raven was due mainly to its blackness; in some performances, such as Carroll's 2002 Middle Temple production, Olivia is still dressed in black, lending force to the second interpretation.

128–34 The forthrightness and intensity of Cesario's declaration of love, far beyond the limits of a servant's dedication, is almost as surprising as Orsino's verbal violence at 113–27, and in some performances arouses equal surprise or alarm, especially from Olivia (see 137).

128–9 Cesario's readiness to die for his master recalls his 'Patience on a monument' story (2.4.110–21), in which his 'sister' possibly sacrifices her life for love.

128 **jocund, apt** cheerfully, readily (adjectives used as adverbs)

129 **To . . . rest** to put your mind at rest
die with a possible innuendo on 'come sexually'; cf. 1.1.3n.

130 **After** This suggests that Orsino may already have begun to make his exit; his order to Cesario at 138 may be called from one of the doors, although both actually remain onstage until the end of the scene (see 139n.).

132 **by all mores** by all such comparisons

133 **feign** speak falsely; in another sense, of course, Viola feigns all the time.
above i.e. in heaven, with a possible glance at the privileged spectators in the balcony above the Globe and Middle Temple stages

127, 129 SDs] *Collier[3] subst.*

Punish my life for tainting of my love.

OLIVIA

Ay me detested, how am I beguiled!

VIOLA

Who does beguile you? Who does do you wrong?

OLIVIA

Hast thou forgot thyself? Is it so long?
[*to Attendant*] Call forth the holy father. [*Exit Attendant.*]

ORSINO [*to Viola*] Come, away.

OLIVIA

Whither, my lord? Cesario, husband, stay!

ORSINO

Husband?

OLIVIA Ay, husband. Can he that deny?

ORSINO

Her husband, sirrah?

VIOLA No, my lord, not I.

OLIVIA

Alas, it is the baseness of thy fear
That makes thee strangle thy propriety.
Fear not, Cesario, take thy fortunes up,

134 **tainting of** contaminating (by lying); cf. 351; 3.1.66; 3.4.13, 128, 353 and notes.

135 **Ay me** alas
detested hateful (to Cesario and so, perhaps, to herself)
beguiled deceived, cheated

136 Although it was possible in Early Modern English to use 'semantically empty auxiliary *do* . . . without any implication of contrastive emphasis' (Hope, 2.1.1b), the double use of *does* here is probably emphatic, expressing Viola's incomprehension at Olivia's reaction.

137 **Hast . . . thyself** have you lost all sense of propriety; have you forgotten your own identity

138 **Come, away** Cf. 130n.

139 **husband** In Carroll's 2002 Middle Temple production (Globe revival), Orsino and Viola, exiting at separate doors, stopped dead in their tracks on this word and stared at each other for several seconds in silent disbelief.

142 **baseness** meanness; moral turpitude

143 **strangle thy propriety** deny your true identity (as my husband) (*OED* propriety 3)

144 **take . . . up** accept your good luck/ your new prosperity (as husband of a countess)

138 SD1] *Cam*[1] SD2] *Capell* SD3] *Theobald*

Be that thou knowst thou art, and then thou art
As great as that thou fear'st.

Enter Priest [*and Attendant*].

O welcome, father.
Father, I charge thee by thy reverence
Here to unfold – though lately we intended
To keep in darkness what occasion now
Reveals before 'tis ripe – what thou dost know
Hath newly passed between this youth and me.

PRIEST

A contract of eternal bond of love,
Confirmed by mutual joinder of your hands,
Attested by the holy close of lips,
Strengthened by interchangement of your rings,
And all the ceremony of this compact

145 **Be . . . [1]art** become that which you are, i.e. your true self; this alludes to the proverbial tag *nosce teipsum* ('know thyself'); cf. 15–18n.

145, 146 **that thou** that which you (145); him whom you (146). In both cases *that* represents both the demonstrative and relative pronoun, as commonly at this time (Blake, *Grammar*, 3.3.2.6–7, giving both these examples); cf. *that that* (180n.).

146 of the same rank as him whom you fear (Orsino). This is not actually true: Cesario would not become a count, still less a duke, by marrying a countess; cf. 2.5.32n.

147 **charge** order

148 **unfold** disclose
lately until now

149 **keep in darkness** conceal: as Olivia announced at 4.3.28. She unwittingly reminds us of Malvolio, still kept in the dark room.
occasion the course of events (*OED n.*[1] 6b)

150 **'tis ripe** it is time to disclose it

151 **newly passed** recently taken place

152 **contract** Cf. 4.3.26n. On the morally (as opposed to legally) binding status of the pre-marital contract, cf. *MM* 4.2.72–3, 'He is your husband on a pre-contract: / To bring you thus together 'tis no sin.'

153 An allusion to the ceremony known as handfasting, whereby couples clasped hands and exchanged vows before witnesses; this, like the *contract*, was popularly regarded as a non-canonical form of marriage. See Fig. 19.
joinder joining (from French *joindre*; *OED*, first occurrence)

154 **close** union (*OED* 3, giving this example)

155 **interchangement** exchange (*OED*, first of two occurrences; second 1796)

156 **compact** compàct: agreement

146 SD] *after 146 Capell* *and Attendant*] *Capell subst.* 151, 346, 362 passed] *(*past*)*

Sealed in my function, by my testimony.
Since when, my watch hath told me, toward my grave
I have travelled but two hours.

ORSINO [*to Viola*]

O thou dissembling cub! What wilt thou be
When time hath sowed a grizzle on thy case?
Or will not else thy craft so quickly grow
That thine own trip shall be thine overthrow?
Farewell, and take her, but direct thy feet
Where thou and I henceforth may never meet.

VIOLA

My lord, I do protest –

OLIVIA O do not swear!

Hold little faith, though thou hast too much fear.

157 **Sealed . . . function** ratified by my priestly authority

158 **watch** Cf. 2.5.57n.
toward my grave The priest's measuring of time in terms of movement towards death is a solemn, but also potentially comic, variation on the temporal awareness distinguishing this scene.

159 **but** only
two hours This is the interval of time between the end of the previous scene and the current scene, during which Sebastian has managed not only to stipulate the marriage contract but also to inflict damage on Sir Toby and Sir Andrew (171–2). On time schemes in the play, cf. 88n., 90, 95n. and 1.4.3n.; and see pp. 77–8.

160 **dissembling cub** This may allude to the fox cub, and so to the proverb 'as wily as a fox' (Dent, F629; Oxf[1]), or perhaps to the bear cub, which was supposed to be formless (*OED* cub *n.*[1] 3a), and so able to assume a false appearance. On dissembling, cf. Feste at 4.2.4–6.

161 **sowed** sown
grizzle grey hair (*OED n.*[1] 3, first occurrence)
case skin: literally, animal hide, especially fox-skin (cf. *cub*, 160); cf. 'And if the Lyons skinne doe faile, / Then with the Foxes case assaile' (Florio, *Second Fruits*, 105). Orsino is alluding to Cesario's lack of beard: cf. 3.1.43–4 (AT). There may also be a pun unwittingly alluding to Viola's real sexual identity: Partridge, 76–7, glosses *case* as '[female] pudend . . . because it sheathes a sword'; cf. the play on 'genitive case/ Jenny's case' in *MW* 4.1.50–3.

162–3 Or, on the contrary (*else*), won't your craftiness increase so rapidly that you will bring about your own downfall?

163 **trip** a leg movement in wrestling causing the opponent to fall (*OED n.*[1] 6b, giving this example)

167 **Hold little faith** keep at least a little faith

168–81 While Sir Andrew unmistakably speaks prose in this exchange, the others appear to speak verse, culminating in Viola's unequivocal lines of verse at 182–4.

159 travelled] (trauail'd) 166 protest –] *Rowe;* protest. *F* 167.1 ANDREW] *Andrew with his Head broke. / Rowe*

Enter SIR ANDREW.

SIR ANDREW For the love of God, a surgeon! Send one presently to Sir Toby.

OLIVIA

What's the matter?

SIR ANDREW Has broke my head across, and has given Sir Toby a bloody coxcomb too. For the love of God, your help! I had rather than forty pound I were at home.

OLIVIA

Who has done this, Sir Andrew?

SIR ANDREW The count's gentleman, one Cesario. We took him for a coward, but he's the very devil incardinate.

ORSINO

My gentleman Cesario?

SIR ANDREW 'Od's lifelings, here he is! [*to Viola*] You broke my head for nothing, and that that I did I was set on to do't by Sir Toby.

169 **presently** immediately

171–2 **Has . . . too** Sebastian's beating of Sir Andrew and Sir Toby has taken place offstage at some point between 4.1 and the present scene; cf. 159n.

171 **Has** he has; cf. 1.5.143n.
broke a common form of the past participle in Shakespeare (Blake, *Grammar*, 4.2.5, giving this example)
across from one side to the other, thoroughly

172, 185, 186 **coxcomb** head; the term derives (appropriately) from the cap of a professional fool, shaped like a cock's comb; cf. 202n.

173 **forty pound** Cf. Sir Andrew's earlier 'I had rather than forty shillings I had such a leg' (2.3.19): he is willing to pay twenty times as much for his safety as for his accomplishments (G. Wright). Or does the increased amount suggest that he is running out of money?

177 **incardinate** malapropism for 'incarnate' (i.e. made flesh); as a verb, *incardinate* means raise to the rank of cardinal or principal priest: an incongruous (or unwittingly satirical) association with *devil*. The blunder confirms Sir Andrew's ignorance: cf. the uneducated Launcelot Gobbo's 'the Jew is the very devil incarnation' (*MV* 2.2.25).

179 **'Od's lifelings** by God's little lives: one of Sir Andrew's many mild oaths. Cam[1] notes that he swears like Slender in *MW*: cf. 'Od's heartlings' (*MW* 3.4.56). Possibly both parts were played by the same actor, John Sincler (or Sincklo).

180 **nothing** no reason
and . . . did Sir Andrew immediately contradicts his claim that he did *nothing*.
that that that which; cf. 145, 146n.

171 Has] *(*H'as*), Dyce;* He has *Malone;* 'Has *Dyce*[2] 177 incardinate] incarnate *Rowe*

VIOLA

Why do you speak to me? I never hurt you.
You drew your sword upon me without cause,
But I bespake you fair and hurt you not.

Enter [SIR] TOBY *and* FESTE.

SIR ANDREW If a bloody coxcomb be a hurt, you have hurt me. I think you set nothing by a bloody coxcomb. Here comes Sir Toby halting. You shall hear more; but if he had not been in drink he would have tickled you othergates than he did.

ORSINO [*to Sir Toby*] How now, gentleman? How is't with you?

SIR TOBY That's all one, has hurt me, and there's th'end on't. [*to Feste*] Sot, didst see Dick Surgeon, sot?

FESTE O he's drunk, Sir Toby, an hour agone. His eyes were set at eight i'th' morning.

184 **bespake you fair** addressed you kindly; cf. 'My gentle lord, bespeake these nobles faire' (Marlowe, *Edward II*, sig. C4^{r}).
186 **set nothing by** have no regard for
187 **halting** limping (because of his injuries); this is not always confirmed in performance.
188 **in drink** drunk; the idea of a sober Sir Toby is somewhat improbable.
tickled beaten (euphemism: *OED v.* 6b, giving this example)
189 **othergates** in another way, i.e. more seriously (*gate* = way, road: *OED n.*^{2} 1). This is an archaic adverbial form (Blake, *Grammar*, 5.1.2.2.ii, giving this example).
192 **That's all one** no matter; the phrase recurs in Feste's song at 366–7 and 400.
192–3 **has . . . on't** Sir Toby's clipped style suggests manly indifference, but his elisions may be due to his drunken slur; cf. 171.
192 **has hurt** he has injured
193 **on't** to it
Sot drunkard, fool; cf. 1.5.117n. The drunken Sir Toby asks the supposedly drunken Feste about the drunken doctor.
Surgeon i.e. the surgeon: his profession rather than his surname
194 **agone** ago: the earlier, unabbreviated form of the word, originally past participle of the verb 'to ago', i.e. to pass (of time)
195 **set** fixed (from drunkenness); cf. the clown Stefano on the drunken Caliban, 'Thy eyes are almost set in thy head' (*Tem* 3.2.9).
eight . . . morning i.e. in a squint, and thus pointing, like the hands of a clock, in different directions

184.1 SIR] *Rowe* 189 othergates] *(*other gates*)*, *Capell* 192 has] he has *Douai MS, Pope;* 'has *Dyce*^{2} th'end] an end *F3* 193, 279 SDs] *Mahood* 194 Sir Toby] sir above *F2;* sir, above *F4;* Sir Toby, above *Theobald*

SIR TOBY Then he's a rogue, and a passy-measures pavan. I hate a drunken rogue.

OLIVIA Away with him! Who hath made this havoc with them?

SIR ANDREW I'll help you, Sir Toby, because we'll be dressed together.

SIR TOBY Will you help? An ass-head and a coxcomb and a knave, a thin-faced knave, a gull?

OLIVIA Get him to bed, and let his hurt be looked to.

[*Exeunt Sir Toby, Sir Andrew, Fabian and Feste.*]

Enter SEBASTIAN.

196–7 **passy-measures pavan** Sir Toby's attempt at 'passing-measure pavan', from Italian *passemezzo pavana*, a slow and stately dance in double time: he is presumably alluding to the surgeon's drunken sluggishness. Florio defines '*Passo mezzo*', as 'a cinque-pace, a pace-measure' (Florio, *New World*, 360), making it synonymous with Sir Toby's earlier 'sink-apace' (1.3.125), although in reality it was a decidedly more leisurely dance than the triple-time *galliard*, which Sir Toby mentions approvingly at 1.3.115 and 123. He is an apparent connoisseur of dance, with a preference for lively pace; cf. his references to the *coranto*, *jig* and *caper* (1.3.124–36).

200–1 **be dressed** have our wounds dressed

202 **Will you help** The emphasis is on *you*.

202–3 **An . . . gull** Sir Toby, having milked Sir Andrew dry, can now reveal all his contempt for him. This is a chilling moment in performance, to which Sir Andrews have reacted with a range of responses from open-mouthed shock to feigned indifference. A similar series of scathing epithets is delivered by Fluellen to Gower in *H5* 4.1.79–80, 'an ass and a fool and a prating coxcomb'.

202 **ass-head** blockhead, fool; cf. 2.3.15–16n.

coxcomb fool; cf. 172n.: Sir Andrew both is a *coxcomb* and has a broken one.

203 **thin-faced** an allusion to the physical trait indicated by Sir Andrew's surname; cf. List of Roles, 12n.

gull dupe (i.e. of Sir Toby himself)

204 SD This is the final exit of the two knights, together to the end despite Sir Toby's insults. They (and in some productions Maria) are the only characters not present in the play's denouement.

204.1 This is the first time the twins are onstage together, to the astonishment (first silent, then vocal) of those present. For the audience, the illusionist magic of the episode depends partly on a convincing degree of likeness between the actors. Ben Jonson abandoned the idea of a play about twins 'for that he could never find two so like others that he could persuade the spectators they were one' (reported in Drummond, 37).

196–7 and . . . pavan] *Malone subst.;* and a passy measures panyn *F;* after a passy measures Pavin *F2;* and a past-measure *Painim* / *Pope* 202 help? An] *Malone subst.;* helpe an *F* 204 SD] *Capell subst.; after 203 Rowe*

SEBASTIAN [*to Olivia*]

I am sorry, madam, I have hurt your kinsman,
But had it been the brother of my blood
I must have done no less with wit and safety.
You throw a strange regard upon me, and by that
I do perceive it hath offended you.
Pardon me, sweet one, even for the vows
We made each other but so late ago.

ORSINO

One face, one voice, one habit and two persons:
A natural perspective, that is and is not.

SEBASTIAN

Antonio! O my dear Antonio,
How have the hours racked and tortured me
Since I have lost thee!

206 **the . . . blood** my own brother. This anticipates Sebastian's rediscovery of his cross-dressed sister; cf. 'I never had a brother' (222).

207 **with . . . safety** with sensible concern for my own safety

208 **strange regard** distant look: Sebastian misinterprets Olivia's astonishment as anger. Cf. Antonio's similar complaint at 84–5.

210 **even for** precisely in consideration of

211 **so late ago** so recently

212–54 The denouement, with its revelation of the twins' identities, bears a striking similarity to the equivalent episode in *CE* 5.1.330–89.

212 **One** the same
habit costume. The twins are dressed identically: cf. Viola's 'in this fashion . . . him I imitate' (3.4.379–80).

213 **A natural perspective** an optical illusion produced by nature, rather than by a perspective glass, i.e. an instrument for creating fantastic or distorted images. Cf. Bertram on contempt's 'scornful perspective . . . Which warped the line of every other favour' (*AW* 5.3.48–99). Reginald Scot, making high claims for the illusionist powers of such instruments – 'But the woonderous deuises, and miraculous sights and conceipts made and conteined in glasse, doo farre exceed all other; whereto the art perspective is verie necessarie' – lists sixteen different kinds of perspective, including the variety that produces double or multiple images: 'There be glasses also, wherein one man may see another mans image, and not his owne; others, to make manie similitudes' (Scot, 316).
perspective pèrspective
that . . . not Cf. Feste's 'Nothing that is so is so' (4.1.8).

215 **racked** synonym for *tortured* (*OED* *v.*[3] 1c, first occurrence)

207 safety.] safety. *All stand in amaze. / Theobald*

ANTONIO
Sebastian are you?
SEBASTIAN Fear'st thou that, Antonio?
ANTONIO
How have you made division of yourself?
An apple cleft in two is not more twin
Than these two creatures. Which is Sebastian?
OLIVIA
Most wonderful!
SEBASTIAN [*Sees Viola.*]
Do I stand there? I never had a brother,
Nor can there be that deity in my nature
Of here and everywhere. I had a sister,
Whom the blind waves and surges have devoured.
[*to Viola*] Of charity, what kin are you to me?

217 **Fear'st thou that** do you doubt that
218 **made . . . yourself** split yourself in two
219 **apple . . . two** This recalls Plato's *Symposium*, and in particular Aristophanes' discourse on love, according to which each human being is the male or female half of an original androgynous whole. The primeval human being was a circular-shaped hermaphrodite, until Zeus decided to 'cut men in two, like a sorb-apple which is halved for pickling' (190d–e; Plato, 1.479–555, 522); as a result, each of us is destined to search for his or her lost half. Aristophanes' 'apple' parable also accounts for homoerotic (or 'platonic') love, since some individuals search for their similars and 'embrace that which is like them' (192a; Plato, 1.523). This theory is pertinent to the predicament of the twins in the comedy: not only does each look for the 'lost' other but, in so doing, each finds her or his 'other half' in love, while both attract 'that which is like them' on the way.
twin alike (*OED a.* 4a, giving this example)
221 Olivia's enthusiasm on discovering two Cesarios invariably raises a laugh in performance. Her predicament (but not her enthusiasm) is shared by Adriana in the final scene of *CE*: 'I see two husbands, or mine eyes deceive me' (*CE* 5.1.332).
223–4 **deity . . . everywhere** divine quality of being everywhere. Cf. Hamlet's '*Hic et ubique*?' ('Here and everywhere?') addressed to the ghost (*Ham* 1.5.156). Sebastian suspects a supernatural phenomenon or *witchcraft* (72).
225 **blind** undiscerning (because indifferent to Viola's beauty): possibly an allusion to the recurrent Shakespearean notion of being blind with weeping; cf. *TG* 2.3.13 ('wept herself blind') and *TA* 3.1.270 ('blind with tributary tears') (AT).
surges large waves
226 **Of charity** out of kindness (please tell me)
kin relation

222 SD] *Kemble* 226, 255, 263, 296, 315, 371, 401 SDs] *Rowe*

What countryman? What name? What parentage?

VIOLA

Of Messaline. Sebastian was my father.
Such a Sebastian was my brother too;
So went he suited to his watery tomb.
If spirits can assume both form and suit,
You come to fright us.

SEBASTIAN A spirit I am indeed,
But am in that dimension grossly clad
Which from the womb I did participate.
Were you a woman, as the rest goes even,
I should my tears let fall upon your cheek
And say, 'Thrice welcome, drowned Viola.'

227 **What countryman** from which country
What parentage the question posed by Olivia at 1.5.269

229 **Messaline** Cf. 2.1.16n. In the 1950 Old Vic production, Peggy Ashcroft's Viola produced a long and emotionally charged pause before replying to Sebastian's questions (M. Billington, xvii).

228, 229 **Sebastian** Cf. 2.1.15–16.

229 **Such a** another

230 **So . . . suited** he was dressed in that way, i.e. like you (and me)

231 if ghosts can take on the physical appearance and dress of the living. This is one of Hamlet's dilemmas: 'If it assume my noble father's person' (*Ham* 1.2.242). Cf. also the duke's reaction to the Dromio twins in *CE* 5.1.334–5: 'which is the natural man, / And which the spirit?'

232 **fright us** i.e. being a ghost; cf. Horatio's 'It harrows me with fear and wonder' (*Ham* 1.1.43).
spirit soul; cf. 'My spirit is thine, the better part of me' (*Son* 74.8).

233 **am . . . clad** i.e. I (as soul) am dressed in a corporeal form (*dimension*). There may be a further Platonic echo here (see 219n.): in Plato's *Phaedo* (80e–81e; Plato, 1.388–9), Socrates argues that the soul – which he identifies with the self (cf. 'A spirit I am') – is distinct from the impure body in which it is 'imprisoned'.
grossly materially (*OED* 5, giving this example)

234 **participate** have in common with others (i.e. the human body)

235–7 The logic of these lines (if you were a woman, *I* would cry) appears at first sight somewhat contorted; the point is, of course, that Sebastian would weep for joy (although in most productions he does not) if Cesario turned out to be his lost sister.

235 **as . . . even** as every other circumstance seems to suggest (literally, agrees: *OED* even *adv.* 2, giving this example)

237 **Thrice welcome** a conventional expression of courtesy that also occurs in *1H6* 1.2.47
drowned drownèd
Viola This is the first time that her name is pronounced in the play: it was thus as much a revelation for Shakespeare's audience as it is for the other characters.

228 Messaline] *Metelin / Hanmer*

VIOLA
My father had a mole upon his brow.

SEBASTIAN
And so had mine.

VIOLA
And died that day when Viola from her birth
Had numbered thirteen years.

SEBASTIAN
O, that record is lively in my soul!
He finished indeed his mortal act
That day that made my sister thirteen years.

VIOLA
If nothing lets to make us happy both
But this my masculine usurped attire,
Do not embrace me till each circumstance

238–44 The gradual and indirect mode of the twins' mutual revelation of identity, in addition to maintaining a degree of suspense, underlines their continuing doubt that all may be an optical illusion.

240–4 **when . . . years** Sebastian's *my sister* (244) might seem to imply that it was only Viola's birthday and not his. Since, however, Viola has just volunteered this fact about her father's death as proof of her identity, her brother is merely validating her evidence by repeating it as information applying also to his sister. Without external confirmation, there is still doubt about their identity as brother and sister.

240 **died** As with Olivia's father and brother at 1.2.33–6, the only thing we learn of their father – apart from his mole, his name and his place of residence – is that he is dead; on male mortality in the play, see pp. 56–7.

242 **record** recòrd: memory (*OED n.* 7, giving this example); cf. *AC* 5.2.117, 'The record of what injuries you did us'.
lively vivid

243 **finished** finishèd
mortal act act of dying; life, in the sense that *mortal* means 'pertaining to man as living creature' (cf. Hamlet's 'mortal coil', *Ham* 3.1.66) while *act* signifies a performance or perhaps division of a dramatic work (as in 'Act 5'): cf. Jaques' 'his acts being seven ages' (*AYL* 2.7.143).

244 **made . . . years** i.e. my sister reached her thirteenth birthday

245 **lets** hinders (*OED v.*[2] 1b, giving this example)

246 **But** except
masculine usurped attire false male disguise (*OED masculine* 6, first occurrence with meaning 'relating to the male sex')

247 **Do . . . me** Viola postpones the celebration of their reunion until she can resume her female attire and thus her full feminine identity, i.e. after the end of the play. On the 'inconclusive' aspects of the comedy's finale, see p. 68.

Of place, time, fortune do cohere and jump
That I am Viola – which to confirm
I'll bring you to a captain in this town,
Where lie my maiden weeds, by whose gentle help
I was preserved to serve this noble count.
All the occurrence of my fortune since
Hath been between this lady and this lord.

SEBASTIAN [*to Olivia*]
So comes it, lady, you have been mistook;
But nature to her bias drew in that.
You would have been contracted to a maid,
Nor are you therein, by my life, deceived.

248 **cohere and jump** agree and accord: synonyms (*OED* cohere 4b, first occurrence; jump *v.* 5a); cf. 'Both our inventions meet and jump in one' (*TS* 1.1.189).

249 **That** to prove that

250 **captain** This is the first mention of the captain since his brief appearance in 1.2. In most productions – and probably those of the Lord Chamberlain's Men – the actor playing the part later doubles in another role; see Appendix 2.
this town Cf. 3.3.19n. and 24n.

251 **Where** at whose house
maiden weeds clothes fit for a virgin (cf. 1.2.0.1n.); 'maidenweed' was a popular name for the camomile plant. *Weeds* occurs frequently in Shakespeare: cf. 'Weeds of Athens he doth wear' (*MND* 2.2.70). Such is the importance of the cross-dressed disguise in the play that only Viola's clothes can fully re-establish her 'true' identity. Since she does not change back, however, she remains in a sense Cesario to the end; cf. 259 and 263 and notes.
whose i.e. the captain's

252 **preserved to serve** saved so that I could serve. Theobald emends to 'preferr'd to serve', i.e. helped into the service of (cf. 1.2.52–3). Despite the awkward assonance that this emendation avoids, however, F's reading (with its pun on pre*served*) makes sense as it stands.

253 **the occurrence of** that has happened to (*OED* 1, giving this example). Latin *occurrere* means literally 'run to meet', and in effect Viola's *fortune since* her arrival in Illyria has consisted in running between Orsino and Olivia.

255 **comes it** it turns out
mistook mistaken, misled: a common form of the participle in Early Modern English

256 **to . . . drew** inclined in the right direction: i.e. attracted you indirectly – through Viola's disguise – towards an appropriate (male) object of desire, namely myself. He is 'absolving' Olivia of the (well-founded) suspicion of homoerotic desire. *Bias* is a metaphor from the game of bowls, referring to the lead weight giving the bowl a curving movement, and to this movement itself.

257 **contracted** betrothed; cf. 152.

251 maiden] maids *Theobald* 252 preserved] preferr'd *Theobald* 253–4 occurrence . . . Hath] occurrents . . . Have *Hanmer*

You are betrothed both to a maid and man.
ORSINO [*to Olivia*]
Be not amazed, right noble is his blood.
If this be so, as yet the glass seems true,
I shall have share in this most happy wreck.
[*to Viola*] Boy, thou hast said to me a thousand times
Thou never shouldst love woman like to me.
VIOLA
And all those sayings will I overswear,
And all those swearings keep as true in soul
As doth that orbed continent the fire

259 **maid and man** This brings together three different but interconnected meanings expressing the gender confusions at play: a young woman (Viola) and a man (Sebastian); a man who turns out to be a woman (Viola); a man who is still a virgin (Sebastian). Viola's disguise as Cesario represents all three of these possibilities.
260 **right** most (intensifier)
noble Orsino promotes Sebastian (and so Viola) from the rank of *gentleman* claimed by Cesario at 1.5.271. The grounds for the duke's confident affirmation are not revealed, although both the twins are indeed to become *noble* through marriage.
261 **as . . . true** i.e. since the *natural perspective* glass still appears to provide real and not illusory images; cf. 213n.
262 **share** a part. A financial metaphor: Orsino has part of the investment in – and thus of the dividend deriving (paradoxically) from – the shipwreck (i.e. he has Viola).
happy wreck fortunate shipwreck: oxymoron. Orsino is presumably referring back to Sebastian's brief narrative at 224–5, since he seems to know nothing of Viola's means of arrival in Illyria.
263 **Boy** Orsino continues to address Viola according to the gender he has known her by, often raising an uneasy laugh in performance. He avoids feminine appellatives to the end, while Viola maintains her male disguise.
264 Viola never actually says this onstage: Orsino may be alluding to Cesario's statement that 'perhaps, were I a woman, I should [love] your lordship' (2.4.108–9); Viola's affirmation that 'no woman has [my heart]' is made to Olivia at 3.1.157.
like to as much as
265 **overswear** swear over again: there may be an implication of greater emphasis (Ard[2]).
267 **As doth** i.e. as (the sun) keeps (its fire)
267–8 **orbed . . . night** i.e. the sun (rhetorical figure: periphrasis), or possibly the sphere in which, according to Ptolemaic astronomy, the sun was fixed. Cf. 'my good stars . . . / Have empty left their orbs' (*AC* 3.13.150–1). For *orbed* (pronounced orbèd) as 'spherical', cf. 'th'orbed earth' (*LC* 25). *Continent* has the customary Shakespearean meaning 'container'; cf. *AC* 4.14.41–2.

267 continent the fire] *Rowe;* Continent, the fire, *F*

That severs day from night.

ORSINO Give me thy hand,

And let me see thee in thy woman's weeds.

VIOLA

The captain that did bring me first on shore

Hath my maid's garments. He upon some action

Is now in durance, at Malvolio's suit,

A gentleman and follower of my lady's.

OLIVIA

He shall enlarge him – fetch Malvolio hither.

And yet, alas, now I remember me,

They say, poor gentleman, he's much distract.

Enter FESTE, *with a letter, and* FABIAN.

A most extracting frenzy of mine own

268 **severs** divides: a probable echo of Genesis, 1.14, 'And God sayde: Let there be lyghtes in the firmament of the heauen, that they may deuide the day and the nyght.'

Give . . . hand the first explicit indication of their touching in the play; in most productions Viola is only too eager to oblige. There is further significant touching between them at 319.

269 **thy woman's weeds** your womanly clothes; cf. 251n.

270–1 **The captain . . . garments** Viola repeats the information she gave Sebastian at 250–1.

271–2 **He . . . suit** a curious piece of news, probably introduced to explain the captain's long absence: he has been imprisoned following a lawsuit brought by Malvolio. In addition to underlining the steward's litigious nature, it sets up a parallel with Malvolio himself, still imprisoned in the dark room. We are not informed of the motives for his *action*, but the allusion does suggest that the captain reached Olivia's house as well as (presumably) Orsino's, in order to present Viola.

271 **action** legal charge

272 **in durance** imprisoned

suit lawsuit

273 This description is given for the benefit of Orsino, who does not know Malvolio, mainly because Olivia has always refused the duke entrance to her household. It serves as a pretext for introducing the steward first into the dialogue and then onstage.

274 **He . . . him** It is not altogether clear who is to *enlarge* (= free) whom: in the context of the preceding speech, it ought to be Malvolio who frees the captain, but in the event it is Malvolio who is freed by Fabian at 309, while we learn nothing more of the captain's fate.

275 **remember me** remember (reflexive; *OED v.*[1] 5a)

276 **distract** deranged; cf. 64.

277–8 A distracting madness of my own made me quite forget about his.

277 **extracting** distracting (*OED ppl. a.* 2, sole occurrence); with a punning echo of *distract* (276)

277 extracting] exacting *F2;* distracting *Hanmer*

From my remembrance clearly banished his.
[*to Feste*] How does he, sirrah?

FESTE Truly, madam, he holds Beelzebub at the stave's end as well as a man in his case may do. Has here writ a letter to you. I should have given't you today morning, but, as a madman's epistles are no gospels, so it skills not much when they are delivered.

OLIVIA Open't and read it.

FESTE Look then to be well edified, when the fool delivers the madman. [*Reads madly.*] *By the Lord, madam –*

OLIVIA How now, art thou mad?

FESTE No, madam, I do but read madness. An your

frenzy madness (i.e. her passion for Cesario); cf. 1.1.14–15n. and *MND* 5.1.12.

278 **remembrance** memory
clearly completely (*OED* 8)
his ambiguous: either my memory of him, or his madness

279 **he** As Feste has only just entered, he cannot in theory know who Olivia is referring to, although on entering he may have overheard her mention Malvolio. Since he is carrying the steward's letter, he might naturally interpret *he* as meaning Malvolio. Why Olivia should expect him to know how Malvolio *does* is another matter. Audiences do not have time to pose such problems.

280–1 **holds . . . end** keeps the devil at a distance. The metaphor, from the sport of quarterstaff fighting, is proverbial (Dent, S807). Feste, as if still playing the part of Sir Topas, is again suggesting that Malvolio is, or is about to be, possessed; cf. 4.2.31–3.

281 **case** condition
Has he has; cf. 1.5.143n.

282–3 **today morning** this morning

283 **epistles . . . gospels** multiple wordplay: *epistles* alludes both to Malvolio's letter and to the New Testament Epistles; *gospels* refers both to the first four books of the New Testament and to the proverb 'All is not gospel that cometh out of his mouth' (Dent, A147).

284 **it . . . much** it is of no significance (*OED* skill v^1. 2b): a now obsolete impersonal form (Blake, *Grammar*, 4.4.1a, giving this example)

284, 286 **delivered, delivers** Feste plays on four meanings of the verb: consign to their destination; report (284); set free; perform (286). This last meaning probably alludes to delivery or *actio*, the fifth and last part of rhetoric concerned with the performance of a speech, especially gesture and voice (cf. *vox*, 291).

286 **edified** instructed (*OED v.* 3b, giving this example)

287 SD *Alexander's SD is justified by Olivia's reaction at 288, as well as by performance tradition, in which Feste invariably *delivers* or acts out Malvolio by raving like a madman.

289 **read madness** i.e. in a style appropriate to the author of the letter
An if

281 Has] he has *Douai MS, Malone;* H'as *Rowe;* 'has *Dyce*^{2} 287 SD] *Alexander;* reads. – *Douai MS, Rowe; Reads, very loud. / Collier*^{4}*; he shrieks Cam*^{1}*; He reads frantically / Mahood* madam –] *Mahood; Madam. F*

ladyship will have it as it ought to be, you must allow *vox*.

OLIVIA Prithee read i'thy right wits.

FESTE So I do, madonna, but to read his right wits is to read thus. Therefore, perpend, my princess, and give ear.

OLIVIA [*to Fabian*] Read it you, sirrah.

FABIAN (*Reads.*) *By the Lord, madam, you wrong me, and the world shall know it. Though you have put me into darkness and given your drunken cousin rule over me, yet have I the benefit of my senses as well as your ladyship. I have your own letter that induced me to the semblance I put on, with the which I doubt not but to do myself much right or you much shame. Think of me as you please. I leave my duty a little unthought of, and speak out of my injury.*

The madly used Malvolio.

OLIVIA

Did he write this?

FESTE Ay, madam.

ORSINO

This savours not much of distraction.

290 **allow** permit me to use

291 *vox* (an appropriate) voice or delivery

292 **i'thy . . . wits** according to your true faculties

293 **read . . . wits** perform his true (i.e. mad) state of mind; Johnson detects a playful inversion of 'read his wits right'.

294 **perpend** consider (*OED v.* 1b, giving this example); a knowingly affected term that probably echoes Preston's tragedy *Cambises*: 'My Queen parpend what I pronounce I wil not violate' (*Cambises*, sig. E4r). It may have been a standing theatrical joke: cf. Pistol's pompous 'Perpend my words, O Signieur Dew, and mark' (*H5* 4.4.8).

300 *have . . . well as* I am as sane as

301 *semblance* outward appearance (with reference to the hose and garters) and behaviour

302 *the which* i.e. the letter

but . . . right that I will fully vindicate myself

304 *unthought of* neglected; Malvolio fails to show Olivia his usual respect in speaking out.

injury sense of wrong

305 *madly used* treated like a madman; abused by madmen

308 **savours not** does not give the impression; cf. 116n.

309 SD] *Capell*

OLIVIA

See him delivered, Fabian; bring him hither. [*Exit Fabian.*]
My lord, so please you, these things further thought on,
To think me as well a sister as a wife,
One day shall crown th'alliance on't, so please you,
Here at my house and at my proper cost.

ORSINO

Madam, I am most apt t'embrace your offer.
[*to Viola*] Your master quits you, and for your service
done him –
So much against the mettle of your sex,
So far beneath your soft and tender breeding –
And, since you called me master for so long,
Here is my hand; you shall from this time be
Your master's mistress.

OLIVIA A sister – you are she.

Enter MALVOLIO[, *with a letter, and* FABIAN].

309 **delivered** set free; cf. 284, 286n.

310–11 **so . . . wife** if you please, when you have considered all that has happened, to think as well of me as a sister-in-law as you would have thought of me as a wife: an allusion to her marriage to Sebastian, but also, perhaps, an encouragement to Orsino to marry Viola. Here *thought on* – a 'past participle [forming] a non-finite clause resembling the Latin ablative absolute' (Blake, *Grammar*, 4.3.5, citing this line) – indicates time past.

312 **One . . . on't** this relationship will be sealed on the same (wedding) day
One the same; cf. 212.

313 **at . . . cost** at my own expense

314 **apt** ready (*OED a.* 2b)

315 **quits** acquits, releases from service
your . . . him the service you have done him

316 **mettle** nature, disposition; cf. 2.5.12 (*metal*), 3.4.266.

317 **beneath** unworthy of

320 **master's mistress** Orsino's paradox plays on two meanings of *mistress*: woman with power over him; object of amorous devotion (as in 'O mistress mine', 2.3.38). For the sexual and gender ambiguities of the phrase, cf. *Son* 20.2, 'the Master-Mistress of my passion' (addressed to the Fair Youth).
sister sister-in-law. Olivia's affirmation seems odd, since she is already Viola's *sister* through her marriage to Sebastian, and will not be more so if Viola marries Orsino, who is notoriously unrelated to her. She may simply be expressing wonder at the fact that her own 'master-mistress' Cesario has turned from lover into sister.

312 alliance on't, so] alliance, an't so *Rann;* alliance on's, so *Dyce*[2] 320.1 *and* FABIAN] *Capell subst.*

ORSINO
Is this the madman?
OLIVIA Ay, my lord, this same.
How now, Malvolio?
MALVOLIO Madam, you have done me wrong,
Notorious wrong.
OLIVIA Have I, Malvolio? No.
MALVOLIO
Lady, you have. Pray you peruse that letter.
You must not now deny it is your hand.
Write from it, if you can, in hand or phrase,
Or say 'tis not your seal, not your invention.
You can say none of this. Well, grant it then,
And tell me in the modesty of honour
Why you have given me such clear lights of favour,
Bade me come smiling and cross-gartered to you,
To put on yellow stockings, and to frown
Upon Sir Toby and the lighter people;
And acting this in an obedient hope,
Why have you suffered me to be imprisoned,
Kept in a dark house, visited by the priest,
And made the most notorious geck and gull
That e'er invention played on! Tell me why!

323 **Notorious** disgraceful; cf. 372n. and 4.2.87–8n.
325 **must not** cannot
326 **from it** differently
hand or phrase handwriting or phraseology
327 **invention** composition (*OED* 7, giving this example)
329 **in . . . honour** in the name of decency and propriety (Ard[2])
330 **clear lights** evident signs; this is probably a nautical metaphor, alluding to lighthouse signals (*OED* light *n.* 5d).
333 **lighter** lesser
334 **acting . . . hope** when I carried this out obediently in the hope of my reward
335 **suffered** allowed
337 **geck** dupe, synonym of *gull*; the only other occurrence in Shakespeare is in *Cym* 5.4.67–8: 'to become the geck and scorn / O'th' other's villainy'.
338 **That . . . on** that ever deception toyed with

321–2 Ay . . . Malvolio?] *Capell; one line F* 353 Toby] Sir Toby *Theobald*

OLIVIA
Alas, Malvolio, this is not my writing –
Though I confess much like the character –
But out of question 'tis Maria's hand.
And now I do bethink me, it was she
First told me thou wast mad; then cam'st in smiling
And in such forms which here were presupposed
Upon thee in the letter. Prithee be content;
This practice hath most shrewdly passed upon thee,
But when we know the grounds and authors of it,
Thou shalt be both the plaintiff and the judge
Of thine own cause.

FABIAN Good madam, hear me speak,
And let no quarrel nor no brawl to come
Taint the condition of this present hour,
Which I have wondered at. In hope it shall not,
Most freely I confess myself and Toby
Set this device against Malvolio here,

339, 340, 341 **writing, character, hand** synonyms for 'handwriting'
343 **First . . . mad** Cf. Maria's 'for sure the man is tainted in's wits' at 3.4.13. **cam'st** you came; on the omission of the subject pronoun (*thou*), cf. Blake, *Grammar*, 6.3.1.2 (giving this example), and 2.3.112n.
344 **forms** ways (with reference to his dress and behaviour)
344–5 **presupposed / Upon** suggested beforehand (sole occurrence in Shakespeare)
345 **content** satisfied, calm
346 **practice** trick. Manningham echoes the term in his praise of the play: 'A good practise in it to make the steward beleeve his Lady widowe was in Love with him' (Manningham, 48); see pp. 3–4.
shrewdly mischievously
passed been played
347 **grounds** motives
348–9 an allusion to the proverb 'No man ought to be judge in his own cause' (Dent, M341). In the event, the perpetrators of the *practice* against Malvolio remain unpunished.
350 **quarrel, brawl** synonyms
nor no For the use of multiple negatives, cf. 3.1.157–8n.
to come in future
351 **Taint the condition** spoil the mood; cf. 134; 3.1.66; 3.4.13, 128, 353 and notes. Fabian's plea is of course biased, since he is one of the potential targets of Malvolio's *cause*.
352 **wondered** marvelled
354 **device** plot; cf. 3.4.127n.

356 against] in *Rann (Tyrwhitt)*

Upon some stubborn and uncourteous parts
We had conceived against him. Maria writ
The letter, at Sir Toby's great importance,
In recompense whereof he hath married her.
How with a sportful malice it was followed
May rather pluck on laughter than revenge,
If that the injuries be justly weighed
That have on both sides passed.

OLIVIA [*to Malvolio*]
Alas, poor fool, how have they baffled thee!

FESTE Why, 'Some are born great, some achieve greatness and some have greatness thrown upon them.' I was one, sir, in this interlude, one Sir Topas, sir, but that's all one. 'By the Lord, fool, I am not mad.' But do you

355–6 **Upon . . . him** on account of some obstinate and uncivil qualities that we had discerned and held against him

355 **parts** characteristics (Onions 3); acts (Onions 4), with a possible allusion to the dramatic roles that Malvolio performs (e.g. that of the misanthrope); cf. 1.4.34 and 1.5.174 and notes.

356 **writ** wrote: a common form of the past tense in Early Modern English; cf. *AYL* 5.2.76.

357 **importance** importunity, insistence; cf. *KJ* 2.1.7, 'At our importance hither is he come.' In reality, it is Maria herself who proposes the *device* against Malvolio at 2.3.150–6. Fabian may be endeavouring to protect her from the potential anger of her mistress.

358 **married her** This news is prepared for by Sir Toby at 2.5.176, and Feste also hints at the possibility at 1.5.24–6. Onstage the announcement often provokes surprise among the other characters; it is usually made in the absence of the interested parties, although in some performances, such as Carroll's 2002 Middle Temple production, Maria is present.

359 **sportful** playful (*OED* 1b, first occurrence); *sportful malice* is an oxymoron (Cam^2).

followed carried out

360 **pluck on** induce

361 **injuries** wrongs; cf. 304 and 3.4.241. Fabian's equating of the *injuries* done on both sides may strike audiences as special pleading in view of the 'dark room' scene.

362 **passed** occurred (*OED v.* 13)

363 **poor fool** This phrase recurs frequently in Shakespeare as an expression of pity or compassion, with the sense of 'poor fellow' (Ard^2); cf., for example, *MA* 2.1.295. Malvolio, however, is more literally a *fool* or gull.

baffled gulled. Ironically, Malvolio vows to *baffle Sir Toby* at 2.5.158.

366 **interlude** play, especially a comedy; cf. Prologue to *Roister Doister*, 'Our Comedie or Enterlude which we intende to play' (*Roister Doister*, sig. A2^v).

366–7 **that's all one** it makes no difference; cf. 192n. Feste uses the same expression at the end of his final song (400).

364–5 'Some . . . them.'] *Theobald;* some . . . them. *F* 365 thrown] thrust *Douai MS, Theobald*
367 'By . . . mad.'] *Theobald;* By . . . mad: *F*

remember, 'Madam, why laugh you at such a barren rascal, an you smile not, he's gagged'? And thus the whirligig of time brings in his revenges.

MALVOLIO
I'll be revenged on the whole pack of you! [*Exit.*]

OLIVIA
He hath been most notoriously abused.

ORSINO [*to Fabian*]
Pursue him, and entreat him to a peace. [*Exit Fabian.*]
He hath not told us of the captain yet;
When that is known, and golden time convents,

368–9 **'Madam . . . gagged'** Feste paraphrases, rather than quoting verbatim, Malvolio's venomous gibe at 1.5.79–83, although he recalls precisely the more cutting phrases. The clown's confession of a personal grudge may cast doubt on the apparently detached role he has played until now.

369 **an** if

369–70 **And . . . revenges** Feste is probably parodying the late medieval doctrine of the wheel of fortune leading to the downfall of the great: in Malvolio's case it is a mere spinning top that undoes him. The clown's attribution of events to fate may be designed to lessen the importance of his and his companions' own *revenges* against the steward. The theme of the circular or cyclical movement of time also anticipates the clown's final song (382–401).

370 **whirligig** spinning top or similar whirling toy, hence circular movement (*OED* 3e, giving this example); cf. *parish top*, 1.3.40.

371 **pack** gang. The expression *whole pack* – recalling the hound metaphor at 2.5.8–9 – invariably expressed condemnation or contempt; *OED* (pack *n.*[1] 4a) quotes an anti-Semitic remark in a translation of Erasmus: 'the whole packe of the Jewes' (Erasmus, *Paraphrase*, fol. 40r).

372 **notoriously** disgracefully; Olivia echoes exactly Malvolio's complaint at 4.2.87–8; cf. also 323 and n.

373 SDs *Since F gives no indication of anyone exiting, it is not clear whom Orsino is addressing. Fabian is the likeliest candidate, especially in view of his plea for peace at 350–1, although as a confessed conspirator against Malvolio he has little chance of pacifying him.

375 **that** i.e. the outcome of Malvolio's lawsuit against the captain; cf. 271–3. The fate of the captain, so long forgotten in the play, now appears so important as to delay the concluding double wedding.
golden time This generalized personification of time as propitious agency (*OED* golden *a.* 4b, first occurrence) recalls Ovid's 'golden age' of pastoral innocence (Ovid, *Met.*, 1.103, fol. 2r); cf. *the old age*, 2.4.48 and n.; cf. also 'thy golden time' (*Son* 3.12, referring to the Fair Youth's age).
convents convènts; is fitting (variant of 'convene': *OED* *v.* 5, sole occurrence)

368–9 'Madam . . . gagged'] *Theobald;* Madam . . . gag'd *F* 373 SD1] *this edn* SD2] *this edn; after 374 Ard*[2]

A solemn combination shall be made
Of our dear souls. Meantime, sweet sister,
We will not part from hence. Cesario, come –
For so you shall be while you are a man;
But when in other habits you are seen,
Orsino's mistress and his fancy's queen.
Exeunt [*all but Feste*].

FESTE (*Sings.*)
When that I was and a little tiny boy,
With hey, ho, the wind and the rain,
A foolish thing was but a toy,
For the rain it raineth every day.

376 **combination** alliance, union (*OED* 4c, first occurrence)
377 **dear** loving; precious
378 **We . . . hence** Since Orsino – in most productions and editions, as in this one – is about to exit, his *hence* presumably refers to Olivia's house, into which all except Feste repair: he is accepting her offer of hospitality at 312–13.
378–80 **Cesario . . . seen** Orsino, as at 263–4, seems to go out of his way to underline and even prolong the assumed male identity of the cross-dressed Viola, taking her *habits* (clothes) as a literal impediment to an immediate wedding.
381 **mistress** Cf. 320n..
his fancy's queen ruler of his desire; cf. 1.1.14n.
381 SD *It is not altogether clear whether F's *Exeunt* means that Feste leaves with the others and then returns to sing his song or – as is more likely and as occurs in nearly all productions – remains alone onstage. In *MND* and *AYL* a single character – Puck and Rosalind respectively – remains behind to speak the epilogue, to which the clown's song (especially the closing distich) is in some ways an equivalent.
382–401 On the song (varied in *KL* 3.2.73–7) and its critical reception, see Appendix 3.
382 **and a** probably a metrical makeweight to fit the words to the tune, as in *Oth* 2.3.83, 'King Stephen was and-a worthy peer.'
little tiny catchphrase used twice by Shallow in *2H4* (at 5.1.28 and 5.3.56). Ard[2] considers this to be evidence of 'the (Shakespearean) authenticity of the song'; the expression, however, was relatively common in Early Modern English.
383 This refrain (repeated at 387, 391, 395 and 399) seems to evoke the adversities of life in general: hence *hey, ho*, expressing weariness or disappointment (*OED* heigh-ho *int.*). When adopted by the Fool in *KL* 3.2, the same line comes to evoke more literally the storm in progress.
384 a childish prank was considered merely trivial; with a possible pun on *thing* as phallus (cf. 3.4.295–6n.)
385 **the rain . . . day** i.e. (perhaps) troubles never end

381 SD *all but Feste*] *Dyce subst.* 382 SP] *Munro; not in F; Clo. / Capell* SD] *(Clowne sings.)* tiny] *(tine)*

But when I came to man's estate,
With hey, ho, the wind and the rain,
'Gainst knaves and thieves men shut their gate,
For the rain it raineth every day.

But when I came, alas, to wive,
With hey, ho, the wind and the rain,
By swaggering could I never thrive,
For the rain it raineth every day.

But when I came unto my beds,
With hey, ho, the wind and the rain,
With tosspots still had drunken heads,
For the rain it raineth every day.

386 **when . . . estate** when I grew up to be a man
estate condition, standing
388 implying that the 'I' of the song is a thief or knave, or perhaps, like Feste, an itinerant performer (considered a beggar and knave by the Elizabethan authorities) who failed to find hospitality in a house such as Olivia's; *shut* is in the past tense.
390 **alas** an ironic comment on matrimony
to wive to get married; cf. Petruchio's 'I come to wive it wealthily in Padua' (*TS* 1.2.74).
392 **swaggering** bragging, blustering; cf. Doll Tearsheet on Pistol, 'Hang him, swaggering rascal' (*2H4* 2.4.69). The implication is that the 'I' could not get away with bullying or making empty boasts to his wife, presumably because she saw through the bluster.
394 **when . . . beds** i.e. when I grew old. Hotson, followed by Oxf[1], suggests that *beds* refers to 'the various spots where he happened to fall' (Hotson, 171). The song, however, narrates the different ages of man, rather like Jaques' 'All the world's a stage' speech, which ends with senile 'second childishness' (*AYL* 2.7.165). Cf. Overbury, 'it is beddetime with a man at threescore and ten' (Overbury, sig. G1[v]; Halliwell).
396 *With* may be repeated from the opening of the previous line, and makes no sense; A.W. Pollard's suggested emendation *We* (Cam[1]) is attractive, but identifies the speaking 'I' too directly with the *tosspots* and has not found favour among editors.
tosspots drunkards. There is no necessary connection between the drunkenness and taking *unto my beds*: the sense may simply be that drunkards were still drunkards, no matter how much time had passed.

387, 391, 395, 399 the . . . rain] *Boswell–Malone; &c. F* 389, 393, 397 it . . . day] *Boswell–Malone; &c. F* 390 alas] *at last F3* 394 beds] bed *Hanmer* 396 heads] head *Hanmer*

A great while ago the world begun,
With hey, ho, the wind and the rain,
But that's all one, our play is done,
And we'll strive to please you every day. [*Exit.*]

FINIS

398 At the end of its rapid journey through life, the song seems about to make an important statement about the world, but immediately drops the idea.
begun began

400 **that's all one** it makes no difference; cf. 366–7n..
our Feste is now speaking (or singing) for the company; cf. *we* (401).

401 **strive . . . day** a conventional request for applause, with a possible allusion to the daily performances (in the theatre season) by the Lord Chamberlain's Men; cf. *AW*, 'we will pay / With strife to please you, day exceeding day' (*AW* Epilogue 3–4).

398 begun] *(begon), Rowe* 399 With] *F2; not in F*

APPENDIX 1

THE TEXT AND EDITORIAL PROCEDURES

THE TEXT

Where lies your text?: the publishing of the play

The script of a play is never definitive. It is a metamorphic creature, destined to undergo continuous change. Throughout the history of the theatre, scripts have always been subject to the restless processes of cutting, addition and revision. What appears in print, in the case of published plays, may differ greatly from the playwright's initial manuscript, bearing the signs of the intervention of actors, scribes, printers and others. The printing of Shakespeare's plays, especially in the form of the collected First Folio volume, was the result of a chain of transmission – from author to company, sometimes perhaps via the company's 'bookkeeper', to the publishers to the printers to the booksellers – which did not leave the text unscathed. To begin with, printing entailed a choice of text (by the publishers or by the company): depending partly on availability, the copy-text adopted might be an authorial draft, a transcript of such a draft, a 'prompt' copy marked up for use by the company or a transcript thereof, possibly the transcript of an oral or written version by an actor or actors, or, in the case of republication, an existing printed text; or it might be the result of an 'editorial' mediation between two or more of these. None of these forms of source text – even Shakespeare's manuscript – was pure or unproblematic: to which period of the play's life might an authorial manuscript correspond, for example, and what relationship might it have borne with what the actors performed at the Globe or Blackfriars? Moreover, every mode of mediation had its textual fallout: scribes would have corrected and 'tidied up' the text, normalizing forms, spellings and stage directions, and perhaps misinterpreting the authorial hand. The printers – and especially the workmen who actually set up the text – in turn interpreted, 'corrected' and at times misread or misprinted the copy they had received.

In the pages that follow an account will be given of the publishing of the text of *Twelfth Night*, at least to the extent that we are able to reconstruct it, and the questions that will be addressed are what kind of manuscript the printers used in carrying out their work and how that manuscript fared at their hands. Discussion will then turn to the question of possible revision of the text and of its various inconsistencies and idiosyncrasies.

The only authoritative text that we have of *Twelfth Night* is the one published in the 1623 Folio edition of *Mr William Shakespeare's Comedies, Histories and Tragedies* (see Fig. 28). That this was the first version of the play to appear in print is suggested not only by the lack of known copies or mentions of an earlier quarto edition, but also by the fact that *Twelfth Night* was entered, together with fifteen other hitherto unpublished Shakespeare plays, in the Stationers' Register on 8 November 1623 on behalf of the principal publishers of the Folio, Isaac Jaggard and Edward Blount. Such an optional 'entry of record' served to show that the publishers owned the rights to the work in question (not the same thing as modern 'copyright'). Entering *Twelfth Night* cost the publishers sixpence. They probably paid the Stationers' Company a further fee for a search to establish that no one had previously entered it or the other unpublished plays.

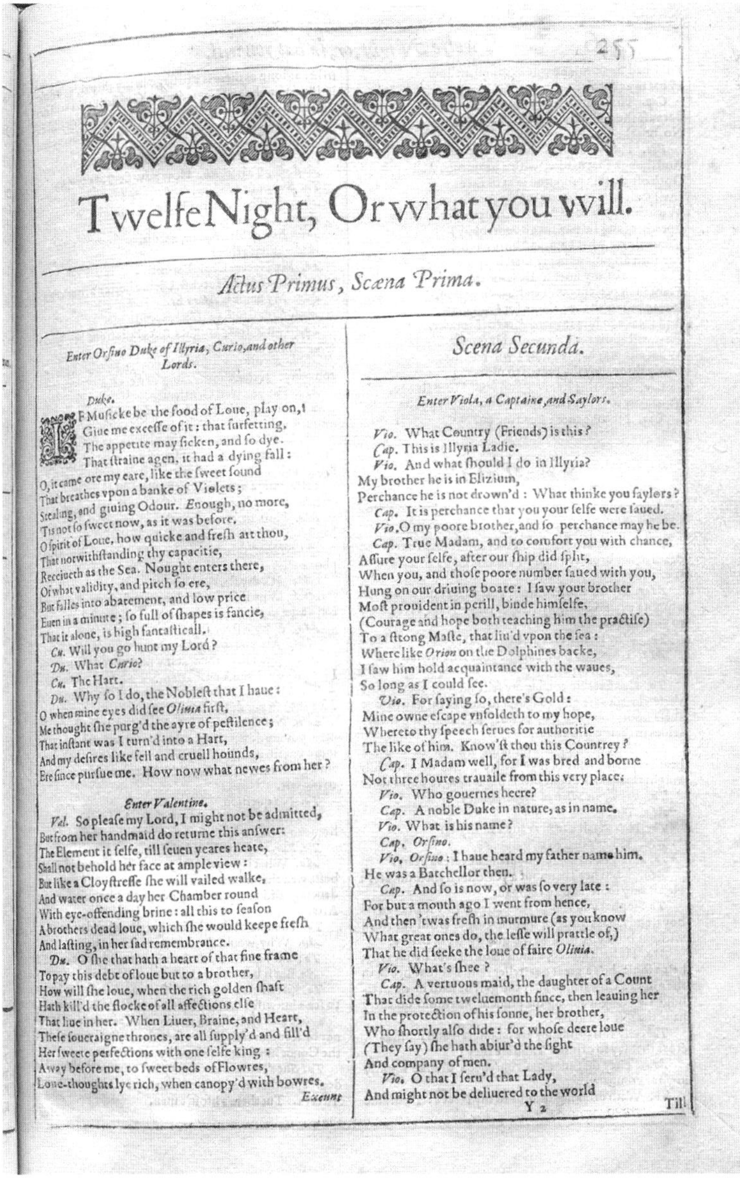

255

TwelfeNight, Or what you will.

Actus Primus, Scæna Prima.

Enter Orſino Duke of Illyria, Curio, and other Lords.

Duke.
If Muſicke be the food of Loue, play on,
Giue me exceſſe of it: that ſurfetting,
The appetite may ſicken, and ſo dye.
That ſtraine agen, it had a dying fall:
O, it came ore my eare, like the ſweet ſound
That breathes vpon a banke of Violets;
Stealing, and giuing Odour. Enough, no more,
Tis not ſo ſweet now, as it was before.
O ſpirit of Loue, how quicke and freſh art thou,
That notwithſtanding thy capacitie,
Receiueth as the Sea. Nought enters there,
Of what validity, and pitch ſo ere,
But falles into abatement, and low price
Euen in a minute; ſo full of ſhapes is fancie,
That it alone, is high fantaſticall.
Cu. Will you go hunt my Lord?
Du. What *Curio*?
Cu. The Hart.
Du. Why ſo I do, the Nobleſt that I haue:
O when mine eyes did ſee *Oliuia* firſt,
Me thought ſhe purg'd the ayre of peſtilence;
That inſtant was I turn'd into a Hart,
And my deſires like fell and cruell hounds,
Ere ſince purſue me. How now what newes from her?

Enter Valentine.

Val. So pleaſe my Lord, I might not be admitted,
But from her handmaid do returne this anſwer:
The Element it ſelfe, till ſeuen yeares heate,
Shall not behold her face at ample view:
But like a Cloyſtreſſe ſhe will vailed walke,
And water once a day her Chamber round
With eye-offending brine: all this to ſeaſon
A brothers dead loue, which ſhe would keepe freſh
And laſting, in her ſad remembrance.
Du. O ſhe that hath a heart of that fine frame
To pay this debt of loue but to a brother,
How will ſhe loue, when the rich golden ſhaft
Hath kill'd the flocke of all affections elſe
That liue in her. When Liuer, Braine, and Heart,
Theſe ſoueraigne thrones, are all ſupply'd and fill'd
Her ſweete perfections with one ſelfe king:
Away before me, to ſweet beds of Flowres,
Loue-thoughts lye rich, when canopy'd with bowres.
Exeunt

Scena Secunda.

Enter Viola, a Captaine, and Saylors.

Vio. What Country (Friends) is this?
Cap. This is Illyria Ladie.
Vio. And what ſhould I do in Illyria?
My brother he is in Elizium,
Perchance he is not drown'd: What thinke you ſaylors?
Cap. It is perchance that you your ſelfe were ſaued.
Vio. O my poore brother, and ſo perchance may he be.
Cap. True Madam, and to comfort you with chance,
Aſſure your ſelfe, after our ſhip did ſplit,
When you, and thoſe poore number ſaued with you,
Hung on our driuing boate: I ſaw your brother
Moſt prouident in perill, binde himſelfe,
(Courage and hope both teaching him the practiſe)
To a ſtrong Maſte, that liu'd vpon the ſea:
Where like *Orion* on the Dolphines backe,
I ſaw him hold acquaintance with the waues,
So long as I could ſee.
Vio. For ſaying ſo, there's Gold:
Mine owne eſcape vnfoldeth to my hope,
Whereto thy ſpeech ſerues for authoritie
The like of him. Know'ſt thou this Countrey?
Cap. I Madam well, for I was bred and borne
Not three houres trauaile from this very place:
Vio. Who gouernes heere?
Cap. A noble Duke in nature, as in name.
Vio. What is his name?
Cap. *Orſino.*
Vio. *Orſino*: I haue heard my father name him.
He was a Batchellor then.
Cap. And ſo is now, or was ſo very late:
For but a month ago I went from hence,
And then 'twas freſh in murmure (as you know
What great ones do, the leſſe will prattle of,)
That he did ſeeke the loue of faire *Oliuia*.
Vio. What's ſhee?
Cap. A vertuous maid, the daughter of a Count
That dide ſome tweluemonth ſince, then leauing her
In the protection of his ſonne, her brother,
Who ſhortly alſo dide: for whoſe deere loue
(They ſay) ſhe hath abiur'd the ſight
And company of men.
Vio. O that I ſeru'd that Lady,
And might not be deliuered to the world

Y 2 Till

28 The opening scene in the First Folio text

In order to proceed with publication, Jaggard and Blount had probably already paid other fees and already sought other, obligatory, forms of permission. In order to be printed legally, a playtext required what was known as authority and licence. Authority, or allowance, was granted by a representative of the church or state. *Twelfth Night* would already have been allowed for performance by the Master of the Revels at the time of its first performance in or around 1601 (at a cost of about 7 shillings), but now required further allowance for publication – either from the Master or from the ecclesiastical authorities – for which the publishers paid another considerable fee (perhaps 10 shillings: Blayney, 'Publication', 2n.). They paid a further, smaller fee (sixpence again) for licence, i.e. permission to publish granted by the Stationers' Company, as opposed to the church or state authorities.

By the time Jaggard and Blount had paid for and obtained their various permissions and had entered their unpublished plays, towards the end of 1623, the actual printing of the Folio was almost complete. The printer, Isaac Jaggard's father William, took nearly two years to set the volume, having begun early in 1622. This was not an unusual length of time for such a substantial volume, and was due in part to the fact that printing was interrupted by problems of publishing rights or the temporary unavailability of manuscripts (as in the case of *Twelfth Night*, as we shall see), but more significantly to the fact that the printer worked concurrently on other texts, in particular Thomas Wilson's *Christian Dictionary*, William Burton's *Description of Leicestershire*, Augustine Vincent's *Discovery of Errors* and a translation from the French of André Favyn's *Theatre of Honour*.

Thanks to Charlton Hinman's full and detailed study, *The Printing and Proof-Reading of the First Folio of Shakespeare* (1963), and further research inspired by it, we know quite a lot about the typesetting of the volume in general and of *Twelfth Night* in particular. Hinman's meticulous comparison of fifty-five copies of the Folio in the Folger Library, in addition to identifying a wide range of variants between different individual copies, enabled him to determine the number of compositors employed by William Jaggard – at least five – and, more importantly, by establishing the spelling habits of each workman, to demonstrate which compositor or compositors worked on a given play. By examining the patterns in the use of type, ornaments and other typographic material in the setting of the Folio and the other volumes prepared in 1622–3, Hinman was able to reconstruct the sequence in which the playtexts and their component pages were set and printed.

Thanks to the relative lack of standardized spelling in Early Modern English, each compositor had his own orthographical idiosyncrasies, which allow us to know who was responsible for the typesetting of each play. It was usual for two compositors to work on a given text, but Hinman shows that *Twelfth Night* was set entirely by the so-called Compositor B, whose preferred spellings of frequently used common words – in particular, 'do', 'go', 'heere' and 'deere', rather than the 'doe', 'goe', 'here' and 'deare' characteristic of Compositor A, the other main workman – appear throughout (see Fig. 29).

B is generally considered to be the less accurate of the two main compositors: 'Both A and B made mistakes, but B made more than A and was especially given to particular kinds of aberration' (Hinman, 1.10). More recently, however, Paul Werstine ('Cases') has shown that, although B sometimes performed poorly, this was not invariable, and indeed, despite the compositor's reputation, the text of *Twelfth Night* is, in W.W. Greg's words, 'unusually clean' (Greg, Folio, 296), i.e. relatively free from major errors such as the wrong attribution of speeches or the mislining of verse, although it is not lacking in misprints, some of them probably due to the compositor's misreading of his copy manuscript (see Appendix 1 p. 364–365; on Compositor B see also Howard-Hill, 'Compositors' and 'Comedies').

In the production of a folio volume, the sheet was folded only once so as to create two large leaves (approximately $8\frac{1}{2} \times 13\frac{3}{8}$ inches), or four printed pages. These were then sewn in sections or quires,

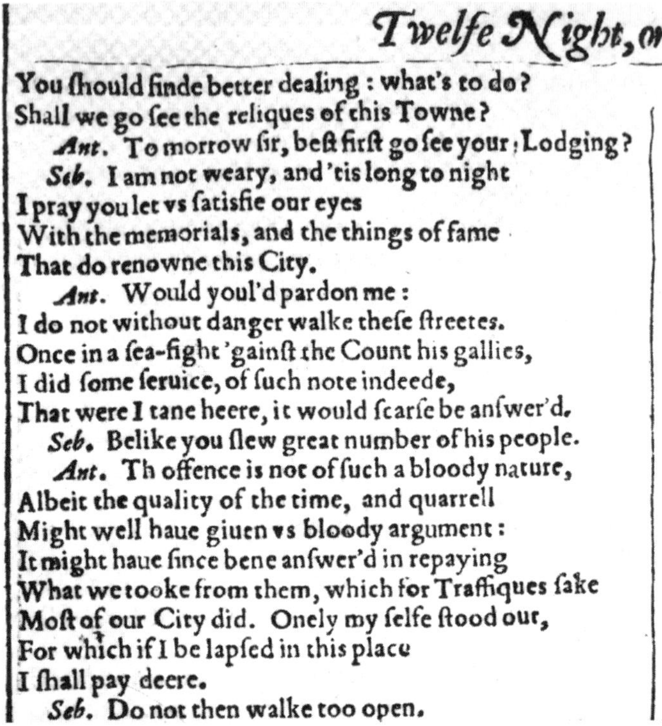

Twelfe Night, or

You ſhould finde better dealing: what's to do?
Shall we go ſee the reliques of this Towne?
Ant. To morrow ſir, beſt firſt go ſee your Lodging?
Seb. I am not weary, and 'tis long to night
I pray you let vs ſatisfie our eyes
With the memorials, and the things of fame
That do renowne this City.
Ant. Would youl'd pardon me:
I do not without danger walke theſe ſtreetes.
Once in a ſea-fight 'gainſt the Count his gallies,
I did ſome ſeruice, of ſuch note indeede,
That were I tane heere, it would ſcarſe be anſwer'd.
Seb. Belike you ſlew great number of his people.
Ant. Th offence is not of ſuch a bloody nature,
Albeit the quality of the time, and quarrell
Might well haue giuen vs bloody argument:
It might haue ſince bene anſwer'd in repaying
What we tooke from them, which for Traffiques ſake
Moſt of our City did. Onely my ſelfe ſtood out,
For which if I be lapſed in this place
I ſhall pay deere.
Seb. Do not then walke too open.

29 A passage from page 267 (Sig. Z2r) of the First Folio (3.3.18-37), showing the preferred spellings of Compositor B: 'do', 'go', 'heere' and 'deere'

normally consisting, with some exceptions, of six leaves (twelve pages). In setting the quires, the master printer or compositors would normally begin by 'casting off' the copy, namely estimating exactly which portion of the text to be printed would fit each of the quire's twelve pages. They then began setting at the middle of the quire with pages 6 and 7 (the first 'forme'), working outwards; pages 5 and 8 came next, followed by 4 and 9, 3 and 10, 2 and 11 and, finally, 1 and 12. If the cast-off had been miscalculated, the affected pages might be too long or too short for the formes, requiring space-saving cuts or increased spacing, for example after scene divisions. In the case of *Twelfth Night* Compositor B seems to have cast off the copy accurately, and the spacing is quite regular. Hinman notes that evidence of proof-reading at press survives for only three pages of the text of *Twelfth Night*, and this proof correction applied only to minor typographical errors and left the text virtually unscathed.

Problems did arise, however, in the printing sequence of the Comedies, and in the composition of *Twelfth Night* in particular. *Twelfth Night* is printed as the penultimate play in the first section of the Folio – the section dedicated to the Comedies – where it follows *All's Well That Ends Well* and precedes *The Winter's Tale*. The text of *Twelfth Night* occupies twenty-one pages, numbered 255–75 and signed Y2 to Z6 (page 265 is misnumbered 273). Sig. Z6^v, following the end of the play, is blank and was originally the end of the Comedies section, *The Winter's Tale* being interpolated after it only at a later stage of the printing of the Folio. In Hinman's reconstruction, the first twenty-one quires of the Folio were printed unproblematically in alphabetical sequence, from the beginning of *The Tempest* (page 1, the start of quire A) to the twenty-third page of *All's Well* (page 252, the end of quire X). At this point, however, the sequence was interrupted for reasons unknown. Instead of proceeding to quires Y and Z (pages 253–75), containing the end of *All's Well* and the whole of *Twelfth Night*, the printers jumped ahead to quires a and b, containing the first twenty-four pages of the Histories section (i.e. the whole of *King John* and the first two pages of *Richard II*). Only then was work resumed on the Comedies.

The probable reason for this interruption was delay in securing the copy of *Twelfth Night* for the compositors. As Hinman puts it, 'From these facts we can only conclude that for some reason the copy for *Twelfth Night* was not readily available when quire X was finished (though it evidently became so soon afterward)' (Hinman, 2.521). Since *Twelfth Night* had never been published, the delay cannot have been due to 'copyright' problems (of the kind that arose, for example, in reprinting *Troilus and Cressida*) but may have concerned physical access to the manuscript, or the need to have a transcript made for the use of the printer.

In addition to this interruption, work on the play was slowed by other, more urgent tasks, since the compositors did not work uninterruptedly on the Folio but moved between this and the other volumes simultaneously in press. There are signs that while working on quire Z of *Twelfth Night* the printers were also completing the typesetting of Vincent's *Discovery of Errors* in particular: the printer William Jaggard prefaced Vincent's text with an angry open letter of his own to the York Herald, Ralph Brooke, responsible for the 'Errors' in question. The final paragraph of this letter, perhaps added or changed at the last minute, contains several types distributed from *Twelfth Night*, suggesting that the two works were set contemporaneously (see Fig. 30).

What is your text?: the question of copy

Much of the debate concerning the printing of *Twelfth Night* – as of other plays in the Folio – has centred on the nature and source of the manuscript used as printer's copy. The copy, namely the manuscript or printed text from which the compositor sets his text, is the starting point for every edition.

Discussion of copy for the Folio plays has been greatly conditioned by W.W. Greg's seminal distinction between the author's so-called 'foul papers' (i.e. 'the text substantially in the form the author intended it to assume though in a shape too untidy to be used by the prompter': Greg, *Editorial*, 31), and the promptbook, namely the authorized manuscript of the text owned by the theatre company and marked up for performance. Each of these manuscripts might in turn have been transcribed, so that, according to Greg's categories, the compositors might have had as their copy-text one of four kinds of manuscript: Shakespeare's foul papers or a scribal transcript of them (a 'fair copy'), or the company's promptbook or a transcript thereof. They might alternatively have used a quarto edition of the play where this existed (as it did for four other comedies, *Love's Labour's Lost*, *The Merchant of Venice*, *A Midsummer Night's Dream* and *Much Ado About Nothing*). In the absence of a quarto edition of *Twelfth Night*, the copy manuscript must have been – in Greg's terms – authorial foul papers or a promptbook (or a transcript of one or other of these). In recent years the terms, and above all the absoluteness, of Greg's distinctions have come under considerable fire (see Werstine, 'Narratives' and 'Plays'). None

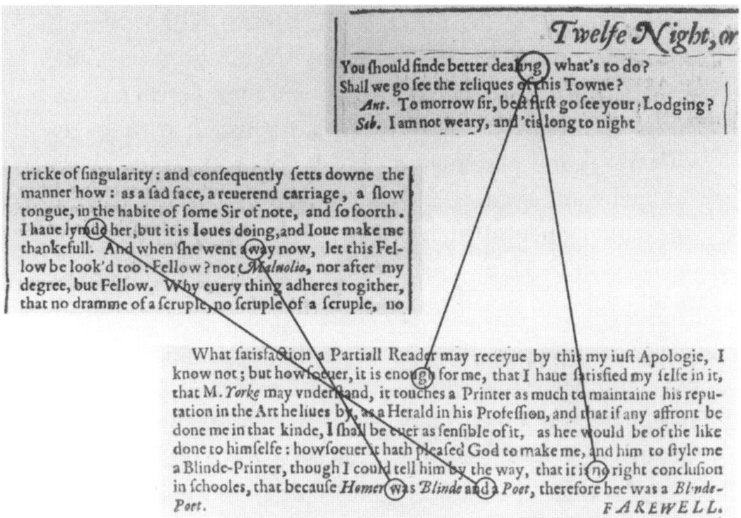

Twelfe Night, or

You ſhould finde better dealing: what's to do?
Shall we go ſee the reliques of this Towne?
Ant. To morrow ſir, beſt firſt go ſee your Lodging?
Seb. I am not weary, and 'tis long to night

tricke of ſingularity: and conſequently ſetts downe the manner how: as a ſad face, a reuerend carriage, a ſlow tongue, in the habite of ſome Sir of note, and ſo foorth. I haue lymde her, but it is Ioues doing, and Ioue make me thankefull. And when ſhe went away now, let this Fellow be look'd too: Fellow? not *Maluolio*, nor after my degree, but Fellow. Why euery thing adheres togither, that no dramme of a ſcruple, no ſcruple of a ſcruple, no

What ſatisfaction a Partiall Reader may receyue by this my iuſt Apologie, I know not; but howſoeuer, it is enough for me, that I haue ſatisfied my ſelfe in it, that M. *Yorke* may vnderſtand, it touches a Printer as much to maintaine his reputation in the Art he liues by, as a Herald in his Profeſſion, and that if any affront be done me in that kinde, I ſhall be euer as ſenſible of it, as hee would be of the like done to himſelfe: howſoeuer it hath pleaſed God to make me, and him to ſtyle me a Blinde-Printer, though I could tell him by the way, that it is no right concluſion in ſchooles, that becauſe *Homer* was *Blinde* and a *Poet*, therefore hee was a *Blinde-Poet*.

FAREWELL.

30 A comparison between the First Folio text of *Twelfth Night* and the open letter to the York Herald, Ralph Brooke, which the printer William Jaggard added to Vincent's *Discovery of Errors*. The two works were set contemporaneously, and the final paragraph of the letter contains several types distributed from *Twelfth Night*. Shown here are two passages from page 267 (sig. Z2^r) of the Folio (3.3.18-21, 3.4.69-76) – each containing two of the types in question - and the final paragraph of Jaggard's letter in which all four types reappear. From Peter W.M. Blayney, *The First Folio of Shakespeare* (1991)

the less, the debate about the provenance of the text of *Twelfth Night* has focused almost exclusively on whether the copy-text was Shakespeare's foul papers or a promptbook.

The relative 'cleanness' of the Folio text of *Twelfth Night*, together with the presence of supposedly 'theatrical' stage directions, led John Dover Wilson to argue that the copy for the play was either a theatrical promptbook or the transcript of a promptbook:

> Stage-directions like 'Enter Viola and Maluolio, at seuerall doores' [2.2.0.1–2] and 'Maluolio within' [4.2.20 SD] suggest that the manuscript from which *Twelfth Night* was printed in 1623 was . . . either itself a theatrical prompt-book or a transcript therefrom. This original, moreover, must have been a fine example of its kind, since the transmitted text contains very few verbal cruxes, most of them long ago solved, is furnished with stage-directions and punctuation which are on the whole both adequate and competent, and gives no serious trouble in the arrangement of its verse or . . . in the distribution of its speeches.
>
> (Cam[1], 89)

Dover Wilson's argument gained cautious but authoritative support from Greg himself: 'There is little here to go upon, but all things considered it seems most likely that it was the prompt-book (or a transcript of it) that served as copy for F' (Greg, *Editorial*, 296).

In reality the evidence for the theatrical provenance of the text is decidedly scant ('There is little here to go upon,' Greg admits). Indeed, the text as printed does not seem to conform to Greg's own specifications regarding the distinctive features of prompt copy: 'characteristic of prompt-copy are the appearance of actors' names duplicating those of (usually minor) characters, possibly the general appearance of directions a few lines too early, and warnings for actors or properties to be in readiness' (Greg,

Editorial, 42). In *Twelfth Night* no actors' names duplicate those of characters. There is no certain instance of an early entrance stage direction. As R.K. Turner notes,

> Maria may be one line ahead of herself at TLN[1] 1188 [2.5.179.1], although the speech which intervenes between the entrance and the cue is so brief as to make the matter inconsequential. Malvolio seems to be brought on two lines early at 1535 [3.4.15.1]. Apart from these trivial instances, however, no entrances are indicated before they are required.
>
> (Turner, 132)

Most of the stage directions are essential and not written in 'technical' theatrical language; Wilson's example of Viola and Malvolio '*at severall doores*' is the only instance of a direct reference to the physical character of the stage. Greg adds examples of directions indicating sound effects ('*Clocke strikes*': TLN 1344, 3.1.127) or music and song ('*Clowne sings*': TLN 2559, 5.1.382; 'Musicke playes': TLN 898, 2.4.14), etc. Cumulatively, these scarcely constitute compelling evidence of theatricality and hardly demonstrate the addition by the company bookkeeper of stage business to the authorial manuscript; in Turner's words, there is 'nothing that an experienced dramatist could not or perhaps would not have provided' (Turner, 132).

On these and other grounds, the promptbook hypothesis was rejected by Turner, who argued that the copy was indeed a scribal transcript – not of a promptbook, however, but of Shakespeare's foul papers. Signs of a 'literary' as opposed to 'theatrical' manuscript include the Latin notations at the end of acts: *Finis Actus Primus*, *Finis Actus secundus*, *Finis Actus Quartus* (the notation is omitted after the third act, presumably through

1 The first line references (TLN) in this section are to the Through Line Numbers of the Norton Facsimile of *The First Folio of Shakespeare*, prepared by Charlton Hinman (New York, 1968; 2nd edn, 1996); the act, scene and line references are to this edition.

oversight by the scribe or compositor); the only other instances in the Folio of such notations are at the end of Act 1 of *Love's Labour's Lost* and of *The Two Gentlemen of Verona*. Since these are, in Turner's words, 'more decorative than functional', they are probably, in his view, to be attributed to a scribe preparing a fair copy. Turner was followed in this opinion by editors such as J.M. Lothian and T.W. Craik: 'The probability is that the printer's copy was a transcript of Shakespeare's foul papers, that these gave the text of the play as it was originally written, and that nothing was added with the exception of what may be called editorial decoration' (Ard^2, xxxv). E.S. Donno asserts even more peremptorily of the Folio text that 'it derives from a transcript, and specifically . . . a transcript of Shakespeare's foul papers' (Cam^2, 156).

These editors' confidence in the origin of the text in Shakespeare's working papers is no less questionable, however, than Dover Wilson's faith in his promptbook theory. Turner arrives at his conclusion primarily through a rejection of Wilson's argument, on the grounds that *Twelfth Night* does not behave as a promptbook-based text should. As Stanley Wells and Gary Taylor point out, however, this presupposes the same kind of confidence regarding what a promptbook should be as Wilson's rejected hypothesis:

> [Turner's] conclusion is based almost entirely upon questionable assumptions about the comprehensive regularity of early prompt-books, combined with an unreasonable expectation that someone preparing a 'literary' transcript of the prompt-book would preserve theatrical annotations such as the names of particular actors, marginal notes about props, or added early 'warning' directions. In the circumstances it seems to us impossible to be confident about the scribe's own copy.
>
> (*TxC*, 421)

The problem with both arguments – the competing promptbook-transcript and foul-papers-transcript hypotheses – is that they depend equally on a rigid binary opposition that has been seriously questioned in recent years, on the grounds that it has more of an ideological than a historical basis (Werstine, 'Plays'). On the one hand, actual existing prompt copies do not behave in quite the way that Greg prescribes, and on the other hand the very term 'foul papers' as the designation of a specific genre of manuscript may be more of an ideal construction by twentieth-century bibliographical scholars than a hard-and-fast, early modern historical category. As a result, Greg's distinction no longer has the ontological clout it once seemed to wield. More generally, it has to be remembered that the copy is a purely virtual object, hypothetically reconstructed by working backwards from the printed play, and we should be cautious in reifying it as an autonomous textual entity that not only preceded and determined the printed play but was indeed more authentic than the latter (because closer to Shakespeare's 'intentions').

Even if we had definite parameters for distinguishing between different kinds or qualities of manuscript, the very 'tidiness' of the text of *Twelfth Night* would in any case render the enterprise problematic. The attempt to establish an absolute difference between a clean 'theatrical' transcript – what Wilson terms a 'fine specimen of good playhouse copy' (Cam^1, 90) – and an accurate 'literary' manuscript seems doomed to failure when the only evidence available is negative evidence (the lack of powerful signs in the printed text of extra-authorial intervention). 'A tidy text', as Wilson himself admits, 'tells us little about its history' (90). Perhaps the most we can say about the manuscript used by the printers is that it was probably a transcript rather than an unmediated authorial draft. Whether it was the transcript of such a draft, originally designed for private use or specially prepared for the printers, or whether it was the transcript of a copy belonging to the theatre company, we cannot know.

Out of your text: misprints, misreadings and other 'mistakes'

Despite the 'cleanness' of the text and the competence of Compositor B, errors inevitably occurred in the printing of the play. These range from banal 'typos' – such as 'tht' for 'the' at TLN 1163, 2.5.155, or 'metry' for 'merry' at 1538, 3.4.15 – to more debatable mistakes, some of which indeed may not be such. The following are the main categories of errors or probable departures from the copy-text (or, through it, from its original).

1 *Misreadings*: substitutions presumably due to the compositor's difficulties in deciphering the scribe's hand. These include 'coole my', probably for 'curle by' (TLN 211, 1.3.95); 'sit' for 'set' (243, 1.3.130); 'made, if' for 'made of' (688, 2.2.32); 'become' for 'borne' (1150, 2.5.142). Some errors may have been caused by the misreading of a final secretary *e* flourished so as to resemble *–er* suspension (RP): 'louer' for 'loue' (952, 2.4.65) and 'langer' for 'tange' (1593, 3.4.68); the latter may also involve a misreading of secretary initial *t* (uncrossed, or looped (RP)). As Turner points out (Turner, 130, n. 7), five Folio readings suggest that a final secretary flourish sometimes appeared to be an 's', or vice versa: 'That' for 'That's' (246, 1.3.134), 'suffer' for 'suffers' (986, 2.4.99), 'atcheeues' for 'atcheeve' (1150, 2.5.142), 'Kings' for 'King' (1221, 3.1.8), 'wisemens' for 'wise men' (1279, 3.1.66). 'Orion' for 'Arion' (65, 1.2.14) may have been a misreading or alternatively an authorial error. Other possible misreadings have given rise to editorial debate and speculation: 'south', possibly for 'sound' (9, 1.1.5); 'dam'd', perhaps for 'flame-' (243, 1.3.130); and 'mine', probably for 'nine' (1446, 3.2.63). For these more dubious cases, see the respective notes in the commentary.

2 *Foul case errors*: errors introduced when the compositor set a piece of type that had been misfiled in a case (i.e. the compositor went to the right box but found the wrong type there). The likeliest instance in *Twelfth Night* is 'deero', presumably for 'deere' (TLN 1179, 2.5.171), although Wilson chooses to read 'dear, O' (Cam[1]).

3 *Homophones*: the substitution of words or phrases with different meanings but identical pronunciation. A probable example is 'an ayword' for 'a nayword' (TLN 829, 2.3.131), although G. Blakemore Evans and Harry Levin (Riv) defend the F reading.

4 *Omissions*: due, for example, to the skipping of a grammatical word, as in '[to] the vppeshot' (TLN 2055, 4.2.69–70); or to the missing of a repeated word or phrase, as in 'And thankes: and euer [thankes: and?] oft' (1482, 3.3.15), or of a near-repetition, '[thee] the' (1389, 3.2.7); or to the jumping of an entire line, as in 'if one knight giue a' (733, 2.3.32–3), where in F the suspended indefinite article ends a justified line of type, so that the compositor may have unwittingly omitted the rest of the sentence in the following line.

5 *Misattribution*: the attribution of a speech to the wrong character. There is one almost certain instance at TLN 1546, 3.4.23, where F has the speech prefix '*Mal.*' (Malvolio, who has just finished speaking), most likely a misreading for '*Ol.*' (Olivia) but just possibly for '*Mar.*' (Maria, who is also present): see the commentary note.

5 *Intertextual contamination*: a compositor's error that has probably been influenced by his recent work on another text. At TLN 461, 1.5.162.1, F has the SD '*Enter Violenta*'; R.K. Turner (130) suggests that Compositor B, who had recently set the page in *All's Well* which has the name Violenta (Shakespeare's original choice of name for 'Diana'), may have expanded 'Vio.' accordingly here.

6 *Compositor B idiosyncrasies*: these are not errors but recurrent orthographic eccentricities of the compositor that may sometimes alter meaning or rhetorical effect. An example is Compositor B's preference for the form 'prethee' for 'prithee' or 'pray thee' – see TLN 939, 2.4.50; 1179, 2.5.172; 1353, 3.1.136; 1631, 3.4.105; 1927, 4.1.9; 1932, 4.1.14; 1935, 4.1.17; 1968, 4.1.50; 1981, 4.1.63; 1986, 4.2.1; 2104, 4.2.120; 2463, 5.1.292; 2521, 5.1.345. At 104, 1.2.49, this produces 'I prethee (and Ile pay thee bounteously)', described by Wells and Taylor as 'a sophistication that would obscure the symmetry of "pray thee"/"pay thee"' (*TxC*, 421; this edition reads 'I pray thee – and I'll pay thee

bounteously –'). The compositor (or his copy) also has a liking for superfluous apostrophes, which may create grammatical ambiguity. In *Twelfth Night* problems arise in particular with B's predilection for the forms 'ha's' or 'h'as' for 'has' in prose passages. These may simply be idiosyncratic spellings of the verb form, especially when preceded by a subject noun or pronoun: 'he ha's' (139, 1.3.20) or 'an ordinary man ha's' (198, 1.3.82). Difficulties arise when there is no subject: 'Ha's beene told so' (441, 1.5.143); 'H'as broke my head a-crosse' (2339, 5.1.171). Editors have usually emended these to 'He has', ''Has' or 'He's', interpreting B's apostrophe, as it were, as the sign of a missing pronoun; in Early Modern English, however, 'has' could stand alone as an elliptical form (= 'he/she has') and in this edition does so ('Has been told so', etc.), thereby interpreting B's apostrophes as mere eccentricities of spelling.

Another orthographic trick is B's use of space-saving abbreviations; in addition to the common *&* and *&c.* (the latter in Feste's closing song, for example), he frequently adopts in prose passages an abbreviated form consisting in *y*, standing for *th* (Old English *þ*), coupled with another character in superscript: y^{u}, for example, stands for 'thou' (rather than 'you'). The following are the occurrences in *Twelfth Night* : 'where y^{t} [that] saying was born' (TLN 304, 1.5.8–9); 'how dost y^{u} [thou] chuck?' (1635, 3.4.109–10); 'blow of y^{e} [the] Law' (1674, 3.4.148–9); 'What wouldst y^{u} [thou] now?' (1957, 4.1.40).

The numbers altered: questions of metre and prosody

Twelfth Night alternates frequently between verse and prose, sometimes within the same dialogical exchange (see pp. 78–9). This caused the compositor understandable problems with the layout of the text, due especially to the occasional indeterminacy of prosodic form; editors have to deal with the same problems of prosody, together with others probably created by the errors of the compositor or scribe.

The question of prosodic indeterminacy arises in the opening exchange of dialogue in 4.1, in which Feste, as usual, speaks prose, while his interlocutor Sebastian speaks what sounds like verse but is metrically defective, so much so that F alternates between verse ('Go too, go too, thou art a foolish fellow, / Let me be cleere of thee': TLN 1921–2, 4.1.3–4) and prose ('I prethee vent thy folly some-where else, thou know'st not me': 1927–8, 4.1.9–10). Modern editors, following Capell, often transform Sebastian's lines to imperfect verse made up of full lines and half-lines. This choice of verse for Sebastian is in part justified by the fact that metrically incomplete lines appear elsewhere in passages printed by F as verse, as at 547, 1.5.247, where the four-foot 'With adorations, fertill tears', among others, is left suspended; at 676, 2.2.20, where 'That me thought her eyes had lost her tongue' is missing a beat; at 2244–6, 5.1.88–9, with its three consecutive half-lines, etc. (see also 132–3, 3.1.104). Editors have sometimes been inspired to perform prodigious feats of prosodic surgery, on the assumption that the scribe or compositor mixed them up, in order to save the metre: a notable case in point is Hanmer's inversion of F's 'the sight / And company' at 90–1, 1.2.37–8.

Such are the vicissitudes of the dramatic text, subject as it is to scribal mediation, to compositorial error and substitution, to editorial inspiration and interpolation. Even in the case of a well-printed Folio play, the answer to Olivia's question 'what is your text?' is not always straightforward.

EDITORIAL PROCEDURES

No consonancy in the sequel: orthographic and lexical forms

This edition is based on the 1623 Folio text. Any substantive departure from the copy-text – i.e. any emendation adopted from later Folios or from subsequent editions, or introduced for the first time in this edition – is indicated in the textual notes and discussed in the commentary. All stage directions in F are retained, sometimes with slightly different wording. Other SDs are borrowed or adapted from later editions, particularly from acting editions, or occasionally from promptbooks, if they provide useful suggestions regarding movement or stage business; a case in point is Kemble's '[*Takes his hand.*]' at 1.3.67. Occasional SDs are introduced for the first time in this edition, particularly with regard to possible stage business that clarifies the sense of the dialogue: examples include '[*Brings his hand to her breast.*]' at 1.3.68 and '[*Shows ring.*]' at 2.2.5. The textual notes record the sources for all these as well as other interesting SDs present especially in acting editions but not adopted in this text (see, for instance, the textual notes to 2.3.104 and 105).

In keeping with Arden's third series practice, speech prefixes are given in full. This is a relatively late editorial phenomenon: in the case of *Twelfth Night* the first editor to give full names or titles – rather than abbreviated forms such as '*Vio.*' or '*Du.*' – was Elizabeth Inchbald in her 1808 acting edition. This edition adopts names rather than titles or roles: thus 'Orsino' rather than 'Duke' (an option first taken up in 1968 by Mahood), and 'Feste' as opposed to 'Clown' (a choice first made in 1958 by Munro). 'Feste' may need some justifying: the name occurs only once in the Folio text and never in SPs or SDs; on the other hand, the clown's name is habitually used by actors and critics alike, and is familiar to audiences and readers, so much so that the speech prefix 'Clown' looks today like a form of strategic distancing or alienation.

As in other Arden Shakespeare editions, the text presented in this edition modernizes the spelling and punctuation of the Folio text, bringing them into line with current English usage. Some of the characteristics of F's spelling are illustrated in the following piece of clowning by Feste:

> *Clo.* Two faults Madona, that drinke & good counsell
> wil amend: for giue the dry foole drink, then is the
> foole not dry: bid the dishonest man mend himself, if

> he mend, he is no longer dishonest; if hee cannot, let the Botcher mend him: any thing that's mended, is but patch'd: vertu that transgresses, is but patcht with sinne, and sin that amends, is but patcht with vertue.
>
> (TLN 335–41, 1.5.39–45)

In addition to Elizabethan orthographic conventions such as medial *u* for *v* (see 'giue', 336; *i* was likewise used medially and initially for *j*), the quoted passage illustrates the relative non-standardization of Early Modern English orthography, whereby the same lexical form may appear in different spellings not only within the same text, but within the same speech or sentence: see 'he' (337) and 'hee' (338); 'patch'd' (339) and 'patcht' (340, 341); 'sinne' (340) and 'sin' (in the same line); 'vertu' (339) and 'vertue' (341). Such variants are standardized and modernized in this edition. This practice is justified by the need to make the play as accessible as possible to contemporary readers. Since, moreover, we do not know precisely whose spelling and punctuation the Folio text represents at a given point – Shakespeare's, the scribe's, the compositor's, a mixture of all three? – modernization, rather than constituting a loss of the authorial 'authenticity' of the copy-text, represents a further stage in the series of mediations to which the script of *Twelfth Night* has been subjected. It may be that certain idiosyncratic orthographic forms, such as 'Olyffe' (503, 1.5.204), reflect Shakespeare's own spelling, but we cannot be sure, and in any case the attempt to retain 'original' Shakespearean forms while modernizing the rest (a practice adopted, for example, by the Riverside edition) would be arbitrary.

A distinction, not always easy to uphold, has been made in this edition between old spellings, which have been modernized, and distinct Early Modern English lexical forms (according to the *OED*), which have been retained. Examples of words retained as autonomous forms include 'crowner' for modern 'coroner' (*OED* crowner[2] 1; TLN 427, 1.5.130), 'comptible' for '(ac)countable' (*OED* countable 1c; 469, 1.5.170), 'conster' for 'construe' (*OED* 9;

1268, 3.1.55) and 'convents' for 'convenes' (*OED* 5; 2552, 5.1.375). Likewise the noun 'grize' (*OED* 1; 133, 3.1.122), sometimes emended to 'grece', has been retained as a recurrent Early Modern (and Shakespearean) lexical rather than orthographic variant. On the other hand, 'computent' is considered an orthographic variant of 'competent' (*OED* 6b; 1765, 3.4.241), 'swarths' a variant spelling of 'swathes' (*OED* 3a; 841, 2.3.144), 'stroke' a variant of 'struck' (*OED* strike 2; 1951, 4.1.34) and 'wrack(e)' a variant of 'wreck' (*OED* 2; 2231, 5.1.75), to give selected examples: all have been modernized. No attempt is made, in general, to retain phonetic variations that may reflect Elizabethan pronunciation – for example 'Countrey' (71, 1.2.19) or 'huswife' (214, 1.3.99). An exception is Sir Toby's 'firago' for 'virago' (1792, 3.4.268), which, in addition to indicating the original pronunciation, may be an attempt to express the fiery ferocity of the referent Sebastian (see commentary note).

Particular problems arise in the relationship between spelling and pronunciation in the case of foreign words. It is often assumed that, when Sir Andrew greets Cesario in French in 3.1, the Folio text's spelling – '*And. Dieu vou guard Monsieur*' (TLN 1283, 3.1.69) – reflects his bad pronunciation, especially since Andrew himself admits his lack of 'the tongues' (1.3.90). Actors often give him a correspondingly atrocious French accent. F's spelling might instead represent a phonetic rendering of contemporary French, in particular because Cesario's reply, even more eccentric according to modern orthographical conventions – '*Vio. Et vouz ousie vostre seruiture*' (1284, 3.1.70) – is unlikely to indicate Viola's linguistic ignorance. In fact it probably consists mainly of an English phonetic version of spoken French, possibly one example of early seventeenth-century French orthography (the old spelling 'vostre') and at least one spelling error ('seruiture') by the author, scribe or compositor. In this edition the exchange has been modernized in correct French, and it is left to the actors to deform the pronunciation if they so choose. Elsewhere editorial problems are created by the difficulty of knowing precisely which language is being attempted. Sir Toby's '*Castiliano vulgo*' (TLN 158, 1.3.41) has been deciphered as Latin, Italian (*volto* or *voglio*) or Spanish. Similarly, Feste's '*Bonos dies*' (1998, 4.2.12) may be bad Latin (standing for the ungrammatical *bonus dies*) or bad Spanish (*buenas días*). In these cases emendation becomes arbitrary, limiting the range of possible interpretations.

Twelfth Night is replete with nonsense words, nonce words and drunken lexical deformations; the editorial task is to decide whether the monstrosities in question are produced by the speaker or by the compositor or scribe. Toby Belch is a particularly rich source of (usually inebriated) solecisms, such as 'substractors' for 'subtractors' (TLN 150–1, 1.3.32), sometimes emended but presumably to be taken as a sort of linguistic alcoholometer. Toby gets into particular trouble with dance terms. 'Sinke-a-pace' for 'cinquepace' (238, 1.3.125) seems to be a deliberate pun on 'sink' and has been left unemended (see commentary). The terpsichorean phrase 'passy measures panyn' (2363, 5.1.196–7) is more problematic and has been the object of much editorial guesswork; here Toby and the compositor may have combined forces to deform something like 'passing-measure pavan' and it is hard to know what degree of emendation, if any, is called for: in this edition a compromise is reached with 'passy-measures pavan'.

Analogous questions arise with Feste's fooling in its more nonsensical moments. The twin neologisms in his 'I did impeticos thy gratility' (TLN 726, 2.3.25) are clearly his own inventions (from the equally invented 'impetticoat' – i.e. to pocket – and from 'gratuity' respectively). Less certain is the much-commented passage at 723–4, 2.3.22–3, with its 'Pigrogromitus' and its 'equinoctial of Queubus'. The problem here is that Feste's clowning is being reported by Sir Andrew, who gives his own possibly garbled version, with or without the help of the compositor. The only reasonable option is to leave the speech gloriously unemended.

On the question of emendation, certain verbal cruces in *Twelfth Night* have a long textual and editorial history, giving the editor a range of options, in addition to the option of leaving the Folio text as it stands. The most notorious of these is Sir Andrew's enigmatic 'dam'd colour'd stocke' (TLN 243, 1.3.130), which has given rise over the centuries to an impressive array of often ingenious alternatives on the plausible assumption that 'dam'd' is a compositor's error (see textual notes and commentary); this edition opts for the 'flame-coloured stock' proposed by the play's first editor Rowe. Similar hermeneutic energy has been exercised on Feste's 'cleere stores' (2022, 4.2.37), variously interpreted by past editors as 'clear stones', 'clear stories', 'clearstores', etc.; the consensus today, followed in this edition, is for the architectonic 'clerestories'. There is less of a general consensus for other emendations adopted here, such as 'youngest wren of nine' for F's '. . . mine' (1446, 3.2.63), an emendation first introduced by Theobald but rejected by many later editors. More controversial still, and indeed decidedly unfashionable, is the emendation – first adopted by Pope and followed here – of 'the sweet south' for 'the sweet sound' (9, 1.1.5). Such editorial interventions will be seen by some as at best unnecessary and at worst arbitrarily invasive; my motives are expounded in the commentary.

Certain orthographical conventions in this edition differ from those adopted in F: 'and' in the sense of 'if' (for example 'and they be not' at TLN 130, 1.3.11) is given as 'an', in the interests of grammatical clarity and in keeping with common Early Modern English practice; 'yond' is given as 'yon', etc. An interesting case is F's 'I' as a space-saving orthographic variant of 'ay' (yes); in most cases 'ay' is an unproblematic substitution, but there is occasional ambiguity: Orsino's 'I prethee sing' (939, 2.4.50), for example, can be interpreted either as 'I prithee sing' (as in this edition) or as 'Ay, prithee sing' (Theobald). The I/ay (and indeed I/eye) homophone is also an easy target for puns, as in the letter scene:

'I, or Ile cudgel him, and make him cry *O*' (1140, 2.5.131); 'I, and you had any eye behinde you' (1142, 2.5.133). Since, however, these are aural rather than visual puns, 'ay' remains the preferred spelling here.

Every point of the letter: punctuation as interpretation

Norman Blake complains that 'It is common for modern editors of Shakespeare to harbour a dismissive attitude to punctuation in early Shakespearean prints', and adds, 'It needs to be taken more seriously than it usually is' (Blake, *Grammar*, 22). One of the problems for the editor is that F's punctuation, like Elizabethan punctuation in general, often has more of a rhetorical than a syntactic function, signalling pauses and emphases for declamation or reading out loud (see Sir Toby's wish in the letter scene: 'the spirit of humours intimate reading aloud to him': TLN 1108–9, 2.5.83–4). Such signs no longer correspond to the principles of modern punctuation, which instead are based primarily on private reading; as a result, certain marks have different values today. The colon, omnipresent in F as a versatile stop – marking a pause, signalling an interruption, adding emphasis to what follows, separating two contrasting clauses, etc. – is less widely used today and its expressive range has been restricted. F's colon may correspond to the modern full stop, comma, semicolon or dash. Other marks, such as inverted commas or exclamation marks, are virtually absent from F, but are often abundantly supplied (especially exclamations) in later editions.

It is not an exaggeration to say that the interpretation and modernization of F's punctuation is one of the more delicate tasks awaiting the editor. Among other things, the choice of punctuation has an important hermeneutic role, privileging one interpretation rather than another and thereby reducing potential ambiguity: as Blake notes (approvingly), 'Punctuation is one of the means used to ensure that, as far as possible, alternative interpretations are reduced to a minimum' (Blake, *Grammar*, 22).

An idea of the problems involved and of the kinds of choices to be made is provided by the false love letter to Malvolio:

> Remember who commended thy yellow stockings, and wish'd to see thee euer crosse garter'd: I say remember, goe too, thou art made if thou desir'st to be so: If not, let me see thee a steward still, the fellow of seruants, and not woorthie to touch Fortunes fingers Farewell, Shee that would alter seruices with thee, tht fortunate vnhappy daylight and champian discouers not more: This is open, I will bee
>
> (1158–64, 2.5.149–57)

The three colons here, for example, have three rather different functions: the first introduces the emphatic 'I say'; the second signals a mild stop after 'so', with the disjunctive 'If not' continuing the argument; the third indicates a more decisive stop after 'not more'. In this edition they are represented by colon, semicolon and full stop respectively. Likewise the commas after 'I say remember' and 'Farewell' – as the capitalized 'Shee' suggests – have a stronger value than the contemporary comma, and are in effect equivalent to the modern full stop. The punctuation is rendered more problematic by the compositor's omission of marks breaking 'tht . . . more' into clauses or sentences, or indeed signalling the end of the letter itself on 'vnhappy' (the lack of italics – in the institutional absence of inverted commas – does not help).

A question that is rarely posed by editors regards the punctuating of discourse markers, namely non-referential idiomatic expressions that indicate the speaker's attitude, adding colour to his or her speech (see p. 79; and Blake, *Grammar*, 290). These markers include single words such as 'why' ('Why so I do, the Noblest that I haue': TLN 23, 1.1.17) or 'fie' ('Fie, that you'l say so': 142, 1.3.23), but also longer idiomatic phrases like 'I warrant' ('I warrant thou art a merry fellow': 1238, 3.1.25), 'by my troth' ('By my troth I would not undertake her': 175, 1.3.56) or 'by this hand' ('By this hand they are scoundrels':

150, 1.3.32). Since such expressions are semantically empty, the question arises how they should be punctuated; in F they are frequently unaccompanied by punctuation marks, whereas in modern editions they are almost invariably separated from what precedes or follows by commas, which often lend them excessive weight, inviting the reader to take them literally. Sir Andrew's 'By my troth I would not undertake her' is not a solemn pledge of loyalty or truthfulness, as a comma after 'troth' might suggest, but a mere idiomatic expansion of 'I would not undertake her'. In this edition discourse markers are not usually set apart by commas, but are signalled in the commentary notes. The question of the choice of punctuation, which might appear the most dryly philological of issues, underlines the fact that every aspect of the editor's task has to do with interpretation.

APPENDIX 2

CASTING

Twelfth Night could be played – so David Bradley estimates – by fourteen actors on the Elizabethan stage (Bradley, 52). (T.J. King's hypothesis of eighteen is probably excessive, partly because it includes walk-on parts (King, 204–5).) Bradley's total is two less than the average number of sixteen required by plays performed between 1580 and 1642 (Bradley, 47). Of the eighteen speaking parts in the play, four minor roles could have been doubled without undue difficulty. The main keys to doubling are the long and crowded scenes 3.4 and 5.1, in which most of the characters are present onstage (eleven and twelve respectively). In 3.4 three minor parts, the servant and the first and second officers, appear for the first and only time; in 5.1 another minor figure, the priest, otherwise present in 4.3 alone, speaks his only lines. Such roles were almost certainly doubled. Two of the likeliest candidates for the doubling are the actors playing Valentine and the captain, missing in both the long scenes: the captain could have doubled, for example, as the servant, while the priest and one officer might have been played by Valentine, and the other officer by his fellow courtier Curio, who is likewise absent from 3.4.

Other combinations are possible. The captain, who appears only in 1.2, might have been played by the actor representing either Fabian – unemployed for the first nine scenes – or Antonio. The Antonio–captain doubling, although potentially confusing, makes some dramatic sense, since it underlines the parallel between the twins and their helpers (Viola–captain/Sebastian–Antonio), and it is a solution adopted in some modern productions (for example, by Branagh in 1987). Alternatively, the actor playing Fabian could have doubled as Valentine. And so on. Whichever combination is adopted, however, the overall number of speaking players remains fourteen.

The following table illustrates the distribution of parts in the play's eighteen scenes, indicating possible doubling solutions. The table also illustrates *Twelfth Night*'s somewhat asymmetrical scene and line economy, whereby some of the characters present in the greatest number of scenes are not those who speak the most or who are generally considered to be the most 'important' roles. It might come as a surprise to find Sir Toby at the head of the list with his presence in nine scenes, although his pre-eminence is confirmed by his 333 lines, compared to the 284 of Viola, who appears in seven scenes. In other cases, the number of scenes in which a character appears does not correspond to speaking time or centrality to the action. For example, Sir Andrew, also present in seven scenes, speaks only 152 lines, whereas Olivia, present in six, has 257. The low number of appearances (four scenes) by Orsino, the comedy's supposed romantic hero, is counterbalanced by his prolixity, which produces 219 lines. Malvolio, who appears in seven scenes, confirms his historically well-founded candidacy as protagonist with a total of seven scenes and 257 lines, six fewer than another central role, Feste, who has 263 lines distributed over the same number of scenes (the totals refer to the number of speaking lines, not including stage directions, etc.).

Roles and scenes	Total	1.1	1.2	1.3	1.4	1.5	2.1	2.2	2.3	2.4	2.5	3.1	3.2	3.3	3.4	4.1	4.2	4.3	5.1	Players	Line nos.
Sir Toby	9			x		x			x		x	x	x		x	x			x	1	333
Viola	8		x		x	x		x		x		x			x				x	2	284
Feste	7					x			x	x		x				x	x		x	3	263
Malvolio	7					x		x	x		x				x		x		x	4	257
Sir Andrew	7			x					x		x	x	x		x				x	5	152
Maria	7			x		x			x		x		x		x		x			6	147
Olivia	6					x						x			x	x		x	x	7	257
Sebastian	5						x							x		x		x	x	8	123
Orsino	4	x			x					x									x	9	219
Fabian	4										x		x		x	x			x	10	113
Antonio	4						x							x	x				x	11	106
Curio	4	x			x					x									x	12	7
1 Officer	1														x					12	18
Valentine	2	x			x															13	13
2 Officer	1														x					13	3
Priest	2																	x	x	14	8
Captain	1		x																	14	32
Servant	1														x					14	3
Lords, attendants																				misc.	
Sailors																				misc.	
	Total	1.1	1.2	1.3	1.4	1.5	2.1	2.2	2.3	2.4	2.5	3.1	3.2	3.3	3.4	4.1	4.2	4.3	5.1		2,286

APPENDIX 3

MUSIC

Many sorts of music

Music is not a decorative addition to *Twelfth Night* but an essential part of the play's dramatic economy. *Twelfth Night* is the only Shakespeare play to begin and end with music. It is also the only play whose opening noun is, precisely, 'music', suggesting immediately the thematic as well as theatrical importance of the topic. This importance is confirmed by the play's later metaphorical or emblematic allusions to music and musicians: for example, the captain's comparison of the shipwrecked Sebastian to the legendary musician Arion, Orpheus-like tamer of animals and nature (1.2.14), introduces music as a magical and benevolent – indeed, literally life-saving – force in the comedy. In the same scene Viola entrusts her own fortunes, if not her life, to her boasted musical skills: 'I can sing / And speak . . . in many sorts of music' (1.2.54–5).

Viola's claim to musical prowess sets up a dialogue or dialectic between music and language ('sing / And speak'): she may intend literally to sing for her supper, or alternatively to achieve Arion-like magical effects through her music-like speech. That she succeeds only too well in this verbal-musical mission is amply confirmed by her unwitting conquest of Olivia, who exclaims hyperbolically: 'But would you undertake another suit, / I had rather hear you to solicit that / Than music from the spheres' (3.1.106–8). The comedy's principal artistic paradigm – perhaps influenced by the presence of the highly musical clown Robert Armin – thus becomes the interaction or co-operation between words and music, best exemplified in the song or ballad.

Part I. ***The Diviſion-Viol.*** 3

Extento ſidenter brachio, *Fides haud procul à ponticulo ſigillatim liquidéque vibrentur, genibus ne fortè offendiculo ſint, cautè reductis.*

Holding the Bow in this poſture, ſtretch out your arm, and draw it firſt over one String and then another; croſſing them in right angle, at the diſtance of two or three Inches from the Bridge. Make each ſeveral String yeild a full and clear ſound; and order your knees ſo, that they be no impediment to the motion of your Bow.

31 'Viol-de-gamboys' (1.3.23-4), from Christopher Simpson, *The Division-Viol, or The Art of Playing Extempore upon a Ground* (1667)

Seven songs are sung in *Twelfth Night*, more than in any other Shakespeare play. Other ballads are begun and then dropped ('O'the twelfth day of December', 2.3.83) or quoted in passing ('Peg-o'-Ramsey', 2.3.75). Singing, moreover, contributes directly to the dramatic action, as in Malvolio's outrage at the revellers' noisy catches in 2.3, which sets off their revenge plot. The play also offers a veritable typology of songs and their singers: weavers' psalms (2.3.58), coziers' catches (2.3.88), the 'old and antic song' sung by Feste (2.4.3) as opposed to modern 'light airs' (2.4.5), which presumably he does not sing, Orsino's imaginary 'lullaby' (5.1.41), and so on.

Twelfth Night is also uniquely preoccupied with another aspect of music, namely tempo, and especially what Feste calls the 'tripping measure' or dance rhythm (5.1.35). The clown himself favours a rapid 'triplex' or triple time (5.1.34), as does Sir Toby, who praises such lively triple-time dances as the galliard (1.3.115), the jig (1.3.124) and the 'sink-apace' (cinquepace, 1.3.125), while scorning statelier rhythms like the 'passy-measures pavan' (5.1.196–7). The play's discourse of music and dance thus sets up an explicit opposition between slow time and fast time. Sir Toby's predilection for rapid rhythms is part of his campaign in favour of the good life, and against the encroachment of death. More in general, the question of musical tempo is closely related to the play's concerns with the passage of time, and the fast–slow opposition reflects the comedy's own double time scheme (see p. 77–8).

Sing both high and low: the songs

1 'O mistress mine' (2.3.38–51)

There is no surviving Elizabethan setting to this song, but two instrumental pieces exist with this title, both based on the same melody, respectively by Thomas Morley (in *The First Book of Consort Lessons*, 1599) and by William Byrd (in the Fitzwilliam Virginal Book, *c.* 1619). (Transcriptions of Morley's setting and of melodies for the other six songs in the play, taken from Ard[2], appear on pp. 339–44.) The tune probably existed prior to Morley's setting, and it is not certain that the words were actually sung to it, although they can be made to fit it. It is likewise unknown whether they are Shakespeare's or are traditional. Opting for Shakespeare, W.H. Auden observes: 'Taken seriously, these lines are the voice of elderly lust, afraid of its own death. Shakespeare forces this awareness on our consciousness by making the audience to the song a couple of seedy old drunks' (Auden, 521–2). The line 'That can sing both high and low', boasting of the lover's musical prowess, recalls Viola's claim to be able to 'sing . . . many sorts of music' at 1.2.54–5.

2 'Hold thy peace' (2.3.70 SD)

The catch 'Hold thy peace', referred to in the SD, was printed in Thomas Ravenscroft's *Deuteromelia* (1609). Another version appeared in a manuscript collection of Elizabethan rounds gathered by Thomas Lant (1580). Ravenscroft's version has been preferred on account of its livelier rhythm. The entire song is a joke where each singer in turn invites the others to keep quiet: a paradox underlined by Feste at 2.3.69.

3 'Three merry men be we' (2.3.75–6)

This is William Lawes's version of the catch, printed in John Hilton's *Catch that Catch Can* (1652). It is given here in the transcription edited by T.W. Craik (Ard[2]) in 3/4 (6/8) tempo (see p. 341). Another version appears in W. Chappell's *Popular Music of the Olden Time* (1855–9), where it is attributed to John Playford (1623–86). The song, a variation on the 'we three' theme, is appropriate to this scene, but it is not known whether the words are Shakespeare's.

4 'There dwelt a man in Babylon' (2.3.77–8)

The music for this song derives from the early sixteenth-century Mulliner Book, a manuscript collection of English keyboard music compiled by the organist Thomas Mulliner (BM MS Add. 30513). Claude M. Simpson claims that a number of ballads sharing the 'Lady, lady' refrain, including this one, were sung to it (Simpson, 410–12). The opening line of the ballad, popularly known as 'Constant Susan', is a biblical quotation: the story of Susanna in the Apocrypha begins, 'There dwelt a man in Babylon, called Joacim, that toke a wife whose name was Susanna, the daughter of Helcia, a very faire woman, and such one as feared God' (Apocrypha, 1–2).

5 'Farewell, dear heart' (2.3.100–10)

This is an adaptation of a song by Robert Jones, published in his *First Book of Songs and Airs* (1600), with the following words:

Farewell dear love, since thou must needs be gone,
Mine eyes do show my life is almost done.
Nay, I will never die,
So long as I can spy,
There may be many mo
Though that she do go.
There be many mo, I fear not,
Why then let her go, I care not.

Farewell, farewell, since this I find is true,
I will not spend more time in wooing you,
But I will seek elsewhere,
If I may find her there.
Shall I bid her go?
What and if I do?
Shall I bid her go and spare not?
Oh no, no, no, no, I dare not.

Shakespeare transforms the song into a comic duet between the two men: see commentary note.

6 'Hey Robin, jolly Robin' (4.2.71–8)

This song has been attributed to Sir Thomas Wyatt (BM MS Egerton 2711, fol. 37^{v}), although it may rework a traditional lyric. The opening stanzas are: 'A Robin, / Joly Robin, / Tell me how thy leman doeth, / And thou shalt know of myn. / My lady is unkynd, perde! / Alack, whi is she so? / She loveth an othre better than me, / And yet she will say no' (for the third line, cf. Sir Andrew's 'thy leman' at 2.3.24). The music, by William Cornish, Wyatt's contemporary at the court of Henry VIII, was originally set as a round for three voices; Feste turns it into a one-man ventriloquist dialogue song.

7 'When that I was and a little tiny boy' (5.1.382–401)

The words of this song may be Shakespeare's or may be traditional – perhaps adapted by Shakespeare, with the addition of the final stanza – or, alternatively, the work of another author, such as Robert Armin. Lines adapted from this song are sung by the Fool in *King Lear*, also played by Armin: 'He that has and a little tiny wit, / With heigh-ho, the wind and the rain, / Must make content with his fortunes fit, / Though the rain it raineth every day' (*KL* 3.2.73–7).

The earliest known setting is Joseph Vernon's, published in *The New Songs in the Pantomime of the Witch . . . composed by J. Vernon* (1772); this is probably an arrangement of a traditional tune, however, that may go back to the Elizabethan era. The version of Vernon's setting given here in E minor (see p.344) first appeared in F.W. Sternfeld's *Music in Shakespearean Tragedy* (1963).

Interpretations of the song and of its relationship to the rest of the play have ranged from its dismissal by early editors as completely irrelevant to the comedy ('to the play it has no relation', Capell), to Knight's defence of it as an appropriate and philosophical reflection on 'the history of a life', to Hotson's reading of it as a bawdy warning against adopting Twelfth Night saturnalia 'as a way of life' (Hotson, 167–72).

Music transcriptions

These transcriptions are taken from Ard[2].

1 'O mistress mine' (2.3.38—51)

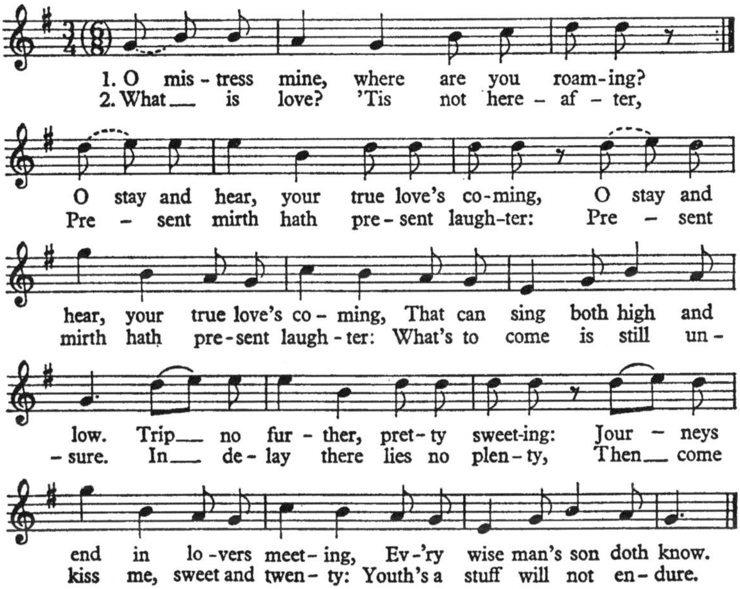

2 'Hold thy peace' (2.3.70 SD)

3 'Three merry men be we' (2.3.75—6)

4 'There dwelt a man in Babylon' (2.3.77—8)

5 'Farewell, dear heart' (2.3.100—10)

6 'Hey Robin, jolly Robin' (4.2.71—8)

7 'When that I was and a little tiny boy' (5.1.382—401)

ABBREVIATIONS AND REFERENCES

Place of publication in references is London unless otherwise stated. Quotations and references to Shakespeare plays other than *Twelfth Night* are from *The Arden Shakespeare Complete Works*, ed. Richard Proudfoot, Ann Thompson and David Scott Kastan, rev. edn (2001). Biblical quotations are from the Geneva Bible unless otherwise indicated.

ABBREVIATIONS

ABBREVIATIONS USED IN NOTES

ed.	edited, editor
edn	edition
fol., fols	folio, folios
n.	(in cross-references) commentary note
n.d.	no date
om.	omitted in
Q	Quarto
RSC	Royal Shakespeare Company
sig., sigs	signature, signatures
SD	stage direction
SP	speech prefix
subst.	substantially
this edn	a reading adopted for the first time in this edition
TLN	through line numbering in *The Norton Facsimile: The First Folio of Shakespeare*, prepared by Charlton Hinman (New York, 1968)
t.n.	textual note
*	precedes commentary notes involving readings altered from the Folio edition on which this edition is based
( )	enclosing a reading in the textual notes, indicates original spelling; enclosing an editor's or scholar's name, indicates a conjectural reading

WORKS BY AND PARTLY BY SHAKESPEARE

AC	*Antony and Cleopatra*
AW	*All's Well That Ends Well*
AYL	*As You Like It*
CE	*Comedy of Errors*
Car	*The History of Cardenio*
Cor	*Coriolanus*
Cym	*Cymbeline*
DF	*Double Falsehood*
E3	*King Edward III*
Ham	*Hamlet*
1H4	*King Henry IV, Part 1*
2H4	*King Henry IV, Part 2*
H5	*King Henry V*
1H6	*King Henry VI, Part 1*
2H6	*King Henry VI, Part 2*
3H6	*King Henry VI, Part 3*
H8	*King Henry VIII*
JC	*Julius Caesar*
KJ	*King John*
KL	*King Lear*
LC	*A Lover's Complaint*
LLL	*Love's Labour's Lost*
Luc	*The Rape of Lucrece*
MA	*Much Ado about Nothing*
Mac	*Macbeth*
MM	*Measure for Measure*
MND	*A Midsummer Night's Dream*
MV	*The Merchant of Venice*
MW	*The Merry Wives of Windsor*
Oth	*Othello*
Per	*Pericles*
PP	*The Passionate Pilgrim*
PT	*The Phoenix and the Turtle*
R2	*King Richard II*
R3	*King Richard III*
RJ	*Romeo and Juliet*
Son	*Sonnets*
STM	*The Book of Sir Thomas More*
TC	*Troilus and Cressida*

Tem	*The Tempest*
TGV	*The Two Gentlemen of Verona*
Tim	*Timon of Athens*
Tit	*Titus Andronicus*
TN	*Twelfth Night*
TNK	*The Two Noble Kinsmen*
TS	*The Taming of the Shrew*
VA	*Venus and Adonis*
WT	*The Winter's Tale*

REFERENCES

EDITIONS OF SHAKESPEARE COLLATED

Alexander	*William Shakespeare: The Complete Works*, ed. Peter Alexander (1951)
Ard[1]	*Twelfth Night: or, What You Will*, ed. Morton Luce, Arden Shakespeare (1906)
Ard[2]	*Twelfth Night: or, What You Will*, ed. J.M. Lothian and T.W. Craik, Arden Shakespeare (1975)
Bantam	*Twelfth Night: or, What You Will*, ed. David Scott Kastan, Robert K. Turner, Jr, and David Bevington, Bantam Shakespeare (New York, 1988)
Barker	*Shakespeare's Comedy of Twelfth Night: An Acting Edition, with a Producer's Preface by Granville-Barker* (1912)
Bell	*Bell's Edition of Shakespeare's Plays, as they are performed at the Theatres Royal*, 9 vols, vol. 5 (1774)
Boswell–Malone	*Plays and Poems*, ed. James Boswell, 21 vols (1821)
Cam	*Works*, ed. W.G. Clark and W.A. Wright, 9 vols (Cambridge, 1863)
Cam[1]	*Twelfth Night or What You Will*, ed. Arthur Quiller-Couch and John Dover Wilson (Cambridge, 1930)
Cam[2]	*Twelfth Night or What You Will*, ed. Elizabeth Story Donno (Cambridge, 1985)
Capell	*Comedies, Histories, and Tragedies*, ed. Edward Capell, 10 vols (1767–8)
Collier	*Works*, ed. John Payne Collier, 8 vols (1842)
Collier[2]	*Plays*, ed. John Payne Collier (1853)
Collier[3]	*Comedies, Histories, Tragedies, and Poems*, ed. John Payne Collier, 6 vols (1858)
Collier[4]	*Plays and Poems*, ed. John Payne Collier, 8 vols (1878)
Craig	*Complete Works*, ed. William James Craig (Oxford, 1892)

Cumberland — *Twelfth Night; or, What You Will . . . as now performed at the Theatres Royal, etc.*, Cumberland's British Theatre, vol. 11 (1830)

Deighton — *Twelfth Night; or, What You will*, ed. K. Deighton (1890)

Douai MS — MS 7.87 in the Douai Public Library (seventeenth-century transcript of *Twelfth Night* and of five other plays by Shakespeare: see G.B. Evans)

Dyce — *Works*, ed. Alexander Dyce, 9 vols (1857)

Dyce[2] — *Works*, ed. Alexander Dyce, 8 vols (1864)

Everyman — *Twelfth Night*, ed. John F. Andrews, Everyman Shakespeare (1994)

F — *Comedies, Histories, and Tragedies*, The First Folio (1623)

F2 — *Comedies, Histories, and Tragedies*, The Second Folio (1632)

F3 — *Comedies, Histories, and Tragedies*, The Third Folio (1663)

F4 — *Comedies, Histories, and Tragedies*, The Fourth Folio (1685)

Folg — *Twelfth Night, or What You Will*, ed. Barbara A. Mowat and Paul Werstine (New York, 1991)

Furness — *Twelfth Night, or What You Will*, ed. Horace Howard Furness (Philadelphia, 1901)

Halliwell — *Works*, ed. James O. Halliwell, 16 vols, vol. 7 (1856)

Hanmer — *Works*, ed. Thomas Hanmer, 6 vols (Hanmer, 1743– 4)

Harrison — *Twelfth Night; or What You Will. A Comedy. As it is Acted in the Theatres-Royal in Drury-Lane and Covent-Garden.* Printed for J. Harrison (1779)

Hudson — *Complete Works*, ed. Henry N. Hudson, 20 vols (Boston, Mass., 1881)

Inchbald — *Twelfth Night, or, What you will . . . as performed at the Theatres Royal . . . with remarks by Mrs Inchbald (1808)*

Johnson — *Plays*, ed. Samuel Johnson, 8 vols (1765)

Keightley — *Plays*, ed. Thomas Keightley, 6 vols (1864)

Kemble — *Twelfth night; or, What you will. A comedy. Revised by J. P. Kemble* (1810)

Kittredge — *Twelfth Night, or What You Will*, ed. George Lyman Kittredge (Boston, Mass., 1941)

Knight — *The Pictorial Edition of the Works of Shakespere*, ed. Charles Knight, 8 vols (1839–42)

Lacy — *Twelfth Night, or What You Will*, Lacy's Acting Edition (1858)

Mahood	*Twelfth Night, or What You Will*, ed. M.M. Mahood, New Penguin Shakespeare (Harmondsworth, England, 1968)
Malone	*Plays and Poems*, ed. Edmond Malone, 10 vols (1790)
Mercury	*The Mercury Shakespeare. Edited for Reading and Arranged for staging by Orson Welles and Roger Hill*, 3 vols (New York, 1939)
Munro	*The London Shakespeare*, ed. John Munro, 2 vols (1958)
Norton	*The Norton Shakespeare: Based on the Oxford Edition*, ed. Stephen Greenblatt, Jean E. Howard and Katharine Eisaman Maus (New York, 1997)
Nunn	Trevor Nunn, *Twelfth Night: A Screenplay* (1996)
Oxberry	*Twelfth Night, or What You Will, . . . Marked with the stage business, and stage directions, as it is performed at the Theatres Royal, by W*[*illiam Henry*] *Oxberry* (1821)
Oxf	*Complete Works*, ed. Stanley Wells and Gary Taylor (Oxford, 1986)
Oxf[1]	*Twelfth Night, or What You Will*, ed. Roger Warren and Stanley Wells (Oxford, 1994)
Pope	*Works*, ed. Alexander Pope, 6 vols (1723–5)
Powell MS	Manuscript notes by William Powell added in 1798 to the British Library copy (shelf mark C.136.bb.10) of *Twelfth Night, or What You Will . . . printed conformable to the representation at the Theatre Royal, Drury Lane under the inspection of James Wrighten, prompter* (1792); the MS hand is represented in the textual notes in italic to differentiate it from the printed text, represented in roman, where appropriate
Quiller-Couch	See Cam[1]
Rann	*The Dramatic Works of Shakespeare*, ed. Joseph Rann, 6 vols (Oxford, 1786–94)
Riv	*The Riverside Shakespeare*, ed. G. Blakemore Evans and Harry Levin (Boston, Mass., 1974; rev. edn 1997)
Rowe	*Works*, ed. Nicholas Rowe, 6 vols (1709)
Rowe[3]	*Works*, ed. Nicholas Rowe, 8 vols (1714)
Sisson	*Complete Works*, ed. C.J. Sisson (1954)
Smith	*Twelfth Night or What You Will: Texts and Contexts*, ed. Bruce R. Smith (Boston, Mass., 2001)
Smock Alley	*Twelfth Night, or What You Will*, Smock Alley prompt-book (*c.* 1685), in *Shakespearean Prompt-books of the Seventeenth Century*, 8 vols, ed. G. Blakemore Evans, vol. 8 (Charlottesville, Va., 1996)

Staunton	*Plays*, ed. Howard Staunton, 3 vols (1858–60)
Steevens	*Plays*, ed. Samuel Johnson and George Steevens, 10 vols (1773)
Steevens[2]	*Plays*, ed. Samuel Johnson and George Steevens, 10 vols, 2nd edn (1778)
Theobald	*Works*, ed. Lewis Theobald, 7 vols (1733)
Theobald[2]	*Works*, ed. Lewis Theobald, 7 vols (Dublin, 1740)
Tree	Herbert Beerbohm Tree, promptbook of *Twelfth Night, or What You Will*, Her Majesty's Theatre, 1901, Enthoven Collection, Theatre Museum, London
Warburton	*Works*, ed. William Warburton, 8 vols (1747)
White	*Works*, ed. Richard Grant White, 12 vols (Boston, Mass., 1857)
Wilson	See Cam[1]

OTHER WORKS CITED

Adams	Barry B. Adams, 'Orsino and the spirit of love', *SQ*, 29 (1978), 52–9
Ariosto	Ludovico Ariosto, *Orlando furioso*, trans. John Harington (1591)
Archer	William Archer, '"Twelfth Night" at the Lyceum', *Macmillan's Magazine*, 50 (1884), 271–9
Arlidge	Anthony Arlidge, *Shakespeare and the Prince of Love: The Feast of Misrule in the Middle Temple* (2000)
Armin, *Fool*	Robert Armin, *Fool upon Fool or, Six Sorts of Sots* (1600)
Armin, *Quips*	Robert Armin, *Quips upon Questions, or, A Clown's Conceit on Occasion Offered* (1600)
Astington	John Astington, 'Malvolio and the eunuchs: texts and revels in *Twelfth Night*', *SS 46* (1993), 23–34
AT	Ann Thompson, private communication
Auden	W.H. Auden, 'Music in Shakespeare', in *The Dyer's Hand and Other Essays* (1963), 500–27
Aveling	Edward Aveling, '"Twelfth Night" at the Lyceum', *Our Corner*, 4 (1884), 115–18
Barber	C.L. Barber, *Shakespeare's Festive Comedy* (Princeton, 1959)
Barker, *Observer*	Harley Granville-Barker, *Observer* review of *Twelfth Night* directed by Jacques Copeau at the Vieux-Colombier, Paris, in Wells, 187–94
Barker, 'Preface'	Harley Granville-Barker, '*Twelfth Night*', *Prefaces to Shakespeare* (1993)

Barton	Anne Barton, '*As You Like It* and *Twelfth Night*: Shakespeare's sense of an ending', in Malcolm Bradbury and David Palmer (eds), *Shakespearian Comedy*, Stratford-upon-Avon Studies 14 (1972), 160–80
Bate	Jonathan Bate, *Shakespeare and Ovid* (Oxford, 1993)
Beckerman	Bernard Beckerman, *Shakespeare at the Globe, 1599–1609* (New York, 1962)
Belleforest	François de Belleforest, *Le Quatrième Tome des histoires tragiques* (1571)
Belsey	Catherine Belsey, 'Disrupting sexual difference: meaning and gender in the comedies', in John Drakakis (ed.), *Alternative Shakespeares* (1985), 166–90
Berg & Erskine	Chuck Berg and Tom Erskine (eds), *The Encyclopedia of Orson Welles* (New York, 2003)
Berry	Ralph Berry, '*Twelfth Night*: the experience of the audience', *SS 34* (1981), 111–19
Billings	Timothy Billings, 'Caterwauling Cataians: the genealogy of a gloss', *SQ*, 54 (2003), 1–28
Billington, M.	Michael Billington (ed.), *Approaches to Twelfth Night* (1990)
Billington, S.	Sandra Billington, *Mock Kings in Medieval Society and Renaissance Drama* (Oxford, 1991)
Biographical Dictionary	*A Biographical Dictionary of Actors, Actresses . . . 1660–1800*, ed. Philip H. Highfill, Jr, Kalman A. Burnim and Edward A. Longhans (Carbondale and Edwardsville, Ill., 1973–91)
Bishops' Bible	*The Holie Bible Conteynyng the Olde Testament and the Newe* (1568)
Blake, 'Editing'	Norman Blake, 'Editing Shakespeare: the role of language studies', *European Journal of English Studies*, 1 (1999), 329–53
Blake, *Grammar*	Norman Blake, *A Grammar of Shakespeare's Language* (Houndmills, England, 2002)
Blake, *Language*	Norman Blake, *Shakespeare's Language: An Introduction* (Basingstoke, 1983)
Blayney, *Folio*	Peter W.M. Blayney, *The First Folio of Shakespeare* (Washington, DC, 1991)
Blayney, 'Publication'	Peter W.M. Blayney, 'The publication of playbooks', in Cox & Kastan, 383–422
Boaden	James Boaden, *Life of Mrs Jordan* (1831)
Boiardo	Matteo Maria Boiardo, *Orlando innamorato*, trans. Robert Tofte (1598)
Boorde, *Dietary*	Andrew Boorde, *Regiment or Dietary of Health* (1542)

Booth, *Nonsense*	Stephen Booth, *Precious Nonsense: The Gettysburg Address, Ben Jonson's Epitaphs on his Children, and 'Twelfth Night'* (Berkeley, Calif., 1998)
Booth, '*Twelfth*'	Stephen Booth, '*Twelfth Night*: 1.1.: The audience as Malvolio', in Peter Erickson and Coppélia Kahn (eds), *Shakespeare's 'Rough Magic'* (Newark, Del., 1985), 149–67
Boswell	John Boswell, *Same-Sex Unions in Premodern Europe* (New York, 1994)
Bradley	David Bradley, *From Text to Performance in the Elizabethan Theatre: Preparing the Play for the Stage* (Cambridge, 1991)
Brewer	Thomas Brewer, *The Life and Death of the Merry Devil of Edmonton* (*c.* 1608; 1631)
Britannica	*Encyclopaedia Britannica*, 15th edn (1998)
Brome	Richard Brome, *The English Moor* (1658)
Brown	John Russell Brown (ed.), *Shakespeare in Performance: An Introduction through Six Major Plays* (New York, 1976)
Brown & Gilman	Roger Brown and Albert Gilman, 'Politeness theory and Shakespeare's four major tragedies,' *Language in Society*, 18 (1989), 159–212
Browner	Jessica A. Browner, 'Wrong side of the river: London's disreputable south bank in the sixteenth and seventeenth century', *Essays in History*, 36 (1994), 35–72
Bullough	Geoffrey Bullough (ed.), *Narrative and Dramatic Sources of Shakespeare*, 8 vols (1957–75)
Burns	Elizabeth Burns, *Theatricality: A Study of Convention in the Theatre and in Social Life* (1972)
Burton	Robert Burton, *The Anatomy of Melancholy* (1652)
Burwick	Frederick Burwick, *Illusion and the Drama: Critical Theory of the Enlightenment and Romantic Era* (University Park, Pa., 1991)
Callaghan, 'All'	Dympna Callaghan, '"And all is semblative a woman's part": body politics and *Twelfth Night*', *Textual Practice*, 7 (1993), 428–52
Callaghan, 'Castrator's'	Dympna Callaghan, 'The castrator's song: female impersonation on the early modern stage', *Journal of Medieval and Renaissance Studies*, 26 (1996), 32–53
Cambises	Thomas Preston, *The Life of Cambises King of Persia* (*c.* 1570)
Carr	Virginia M. Carr, 'The Shakespeare plays on TV: Season One', *Shakespeare on Film Newsletter*, 4.1 (1979), 4–5

Carroll, *Met.* — William C. Carroll, *The Metamorphoses of Shakespearean Comedy* (Princeton, 1985)

Carroll, 'Virgin' — William C. Carroll, 'The virgin not: language and sexuality in Shakespeare', *SS 46* (1994), 107–19

Castiglione — Baldassare Castiglione, *The Courtier*, trans. Thomas Hoby (1561)

Chaucer, *Works* — *The Works of Geoffrey Chaucer*, ed. F.N. Robinson, 2nd edn (Oxford, 1974)

Child — Francis J. Child, *The English and Scottish Popular Ballads*, 3 vols (New York, 1965)

Chillington Rutter — Carol Chillington Rutter, 'Looking at Shakespeare's women on film', in Jackson, 241–60

Cicero, *De officiis* — *Marcus Tullius Cicero's Three Books of Duties to Marcus his Son*, (*De officiis*), trans. Nicolas Grimald (1558)

Coleridge — Samuel Taylor Coleridge, *Shakespearean Criticism*, ed. T.M. Raysor, 2nd edn, 2 vols (1960)

Common Prayer — *The Book of Common Prayer* (1559)

Copley — Anthony Copley, *A Fig for Fortune* (1596)

Cornwallis — William Cornwallis, *Essays* (1601)

Coote — C.H. Coote, *On Shakspere's New Map in 'Twelfth Night'* (1878)

Cotgrave — Randle Cotgrave, *A Dictionary of the French and English Tongues* (1611)

Cox — L.S. Cox, 'The riddle in *Twelfth Night*', *SQ*, 13 (1962), 360

Cox & Kastan — John D. Cox and David Scott Kastan (eds), *New History of Early English Drama* (New York, 1997)

D'Amico — Jack D'Amico, 'The treatment of space in Italian and English Renaissance theater: the example of *Gl'Ingannati* and *Twelfth Night*', *Comparative Drama* 23 (1989), 265–83

Daniel — P.A. Daniel, *Notes and Conjectural Emendations of Certain Doubtful Passages in Shakespeare's Plays* (1870)

Darrell — John Darrell, *A True Narration of the Strange and Grievous Vexation by the Devil, of Seven Persons in Lancashire* (1600)

Davis & Frankforter — J. Madison Davis and A. Daniel Frankforter (eds), *The Shakespeare Name and Place Dictionary* (1995)

Dekker, *Blurt* — Thomas Dekker, *Blurt, Master Constable* (1602)

Dekker, *Satiromastix* — Thomas Dekker, *Satiromastix* (1601)

Dent — R.W. Dent, *Shakespeare's Proverbial Language: An Index* (Berkeley, Calif., 1981)

Dodd	William Dodd, '"So full of shapes is fancy": gender and point of view in *Twelfth Night*', in Robert Clark and Piero Boitani (eds), *English Studies in Transition* (1993), 147–66
DNB	*Dictionary of National Biography* (Oxford, 1997)
Dowland	John Dowland, *The First Book of Songs or Airs* (1597)
Downes	John Downes, *Roscius Anglicanus* (1708)
Draper	John Draper, *The Twelfth Night of Shakespeare's Audience* (Stanford, Calif., 1950)
Drummond	*Ben Jonson's Conversations with William Drummond of Hawthornden*, ed. R.F. Patterson (1923)
Duncan-Jones	Katherine Duncan-Jones, *Ungentle Shakespeare: Scenes from His Life* (2001)
Eggert	Katherine Eggert, 'Sure can sing and dance: minstrelsy, the star system, and the post-coloniality of Kenneth Branagh's *Love's Labour's Lost* and Trevor Nunn's *Twelfth Night*', in Richard Burt and Lynda E. Boose (eds), *Shakespeare, the Movie II: Popularizing the Plays on Film, TV, Video and DVD (*2003), 72–88
Elam, 'Fertile'	Keir Elam, 'The fertile eunuch: *Twelfth Night*, early modern intercourse, and the fruits of castration', *SQ*, 47 (1996), 1–36
Elam, *Shakespeare's*	Keir Elam, *Shakespeare's Universe of Discourse: Language-Games in the Comedies* (Cambridge, 1984)
ELH	*English Literary History*
ELN	*English Language Notes*
Elze	Karl Elze, *Essays on Shakespeare* (1874)
Erasmus, *Paraphrase*	Desiderius Erasmus, *The First Tome or Volume of the Paraphrase of Erasmus upon the New Testament*, trans. Nicholas Udall, Thomas Caius and Mary Tudor (1548)
Erasmus, *Proverbs*	Desiderius Erasmus, *Proverbs or Adages*, trans. Richard Taverner (1539)
Evans, B.	Bertrand Evans, *Shakespeare's Comedies* (Oxford, 1960)
Evans, G.B.	G. Blakemore Evans, 'The Douai Manuscripts: six Shakespearean transcripts (1694–95)', *Philological Quarterly*, 41 (1962), 158–72
Everett	Barbara Everett, 'Or What You Will', *Essays in Criticism*, 35 (1985), 294–314
Farmer	Richard Farmer, contributions to Steevens
Faversham	Anon., *The Lamentable and True Tragedy of Master Arden of Faversham in Kent* (1599)
Fenner, *Arts*	Dudley Fenner, *The Arts of Logic and Rhetoric* (1584)
Fenner, *Song*	Dudley Fenner, *The Song of Songs* (Middleburgh, Netherlands, 1587)

Fletcher	John Fletcher, *The Elder Brother: A Comedy* (*c.* 1625; publ. 1637)
Florio, *World*	John Florio, *A World of Words, or Most Copious and Exact Dictionary in Italian and English* (1598)
Florio, *New World*	John Florio, *Queen Anna's New World of Words, or Dictionary of the Italian and English Tongues* (1611)
Florio, *Second Fruits*	John Florio, *Second Fruits* (1591)
Forde	Emanuel Forde, *Parismus, the Renowned Prince of Bohemia* (1598)
FQ	Edmund Spenser, *Fairie Queene*, 2nd edn (1611)
France	Richard France, *The Theatre of Orson Welles* (Lewisburg, Pa., 1977)
Freund	Elizabeth Freund, '*Twelfth Night* and the tyranny of interpretation', *ELH*, 53 (1986), 471–89
Frye	Northrop Frye, *A Natural Perspective: The Development of Shakespearean Comedy and Romance* (New York, 1965)
Garber	Marjorie Garber, *Vested Interests: Cross-dressing and Cultural Anxiety* (New York, 1992)
Gay	Penny Gay, *As She Likes It: Shakespeare's Unruly Women* (1994)
Genest	John Genest, *Some Account of the English Stage from the Restoration in 1660 to 1830*, 10 vols (Bath, 1832)
Gerard	John Gerard, *The Herbal or General History of Plants* (London, 1597)
Gibson	Marion Gibson, *Possession, Puritanism and Print: Darrell, Harsnett, Shakespeare and the Elizabethan Exorcism Controversy* (2006)
Gillies	John Gillies, *Shakespeare and the Geography of Difference* (Cambridge, 1994)
Gilman	Ernest B. Gilman, *The Curious Perspective: Literary and Pictorial Wit in the Seventeenth Century* (1978)
Girard	René Girard, '"Tis not so sweet now as it was before": Orsino and Olivia in *Twelfth Night*', *Stanford Literature Review*, 7 (1990), 123–32
Goar	Jacques Goar, *Euchologion* (Paris, 1647)
Goldberg	Jonathan Goldberg, 'Textual properties', *SQ*, 37 (1986), 213–17.
Golding	See Ovid, *Met.*
Gonzaga	Curzio Gonzaga, *Gli inganni* (Venice, 1592)
Goorney	Howard Goorney, *The Theatre Workshop Story* (1981)
Greene, *Friar*	Robert Greene, *The Honorable History of Friar Bacon and Friar Bungay* (1594)

Greene, *Mamillia* — Robert Greene, *Mamillia* (1583)

Greenblatt — Stephen Greenblatt, 'Fiction and friction', in *Shakespearean Negotiations: The Circulation of Social Energy in Renaissance England* (Oxford, 1988), 66–91

Greg, *Editorial* — W.W. Greg, *The Editorial Problem in Shakespeare* (Oxford, 1942)

Greg, *Folio* — W.W. Greg, *The Shakespeare First Folio: Its Bibliographical and Textual History* (Oxford, 1955)

Greif — Karen Greif, 'A star is born: Feste on the modern stage', *SQ*, 39 (1988), 61–78

Guazzo — Stefano Guazzo, *The Civil Conversation of M. Steeven Guazzo*, trans. George Pettie (1586)

Halstead — William P. Halstead, *Shakespeare as Spoken* (Ann Arbor, Mich., 1979)

Hamilton — Donna B. Hamilton, *Shakespeare and the Politics of Protestant England* (Lexington, Ky., 1992)

Harrison — William Harrison, *The Description of England*, in Holinshed, 1.131–250

Harsnett, *Discovery* — Samuel Harsnett, *Discovery of the Fraudulent Practices of John Darrel* (1599)

Harsnett, *Declaration* — Samuel Harsnett, *Declaration of Egregious Popish Impostures* (1603)

Hassel — R. Chris Hassel, Jr, *Faith and Folly in Shakespeare's Romantic Comedies* (Athens, Ga., 1980)

Hattaway — Michael Hattaway, 'The comedies on film', in Jackson, 85–98

Hazlitt — William Hazlitt, *Characters of Shakespear's Plays* (1817), in *The Selected Writings of William Hazlitt*, ed. Duncan Wu, 9 vols (1998), 1.83–270

Heliodorus — Heliodorus, *Ethiopica*; trans. *An Ethiopian History*, Thomas Underdown (1587)

Henryson — Robert Henryson, *Testament of Cresseid*, ed. Denton Fox (1968)

Henslowe — Philip Henslowe, *Henslowe's Diary*, ed. R.A. Foakes, 2nd edn (Cambridge, 2002)

Hilman & Mazzio — David Hilman and Carla Mazzio (eds), *The Body in Parts: Fantasies of Corporeality in Early Modern Europe* (1997)

Hinman — Charlton Hinman, *The Printing and Proof-Reading of the First Folio of Shakespeare*, 2 vols (Oxford, 1963)

Hodgdon — Barbara Hodgdon, 'Sexual disguise and the theatre of gender', in Leggatt, 179–97

Hogan — C.B. Hogan, *Shakespeare in the Theatre: A Record of Performances in 1701–1800* (Oxford, 1952)

Holinshed	Raphael Holinshed, *The First and Second Volumes of Chronicles* (1587)
Holland	Peter Holland, *English Shakespeares: Shakespeare on the English Stage in the 1990s* (Cambridge, 1997)
Hope	Jonathan Hope, *Shakespeare's Grammar* (2003)
Hopwood	C.H. Hopwood (ed.), *A Calendar of the Middle Temple Records*, 4 vols (1903)
Horace, *Odes*	*Horace, the Odes*, ed. J.D. McClatchy (Princeton, 2002)
Horner	Olga Horner, 'Christmas at the Inns of Court', in Meg Twycross (ed.), *Festive Drama* (Woodbridge, England, 1996), 41–53
Hotson	Leslie Hotson, *The First Night of Twelfth Night* (1954)
Howard	Jean Howard, 'Crossdressing, the theatre, and gender struggle in early modern England', *SQ*, 39 (1988), 418–40
Howard-Hill, 'Comedies'	T.H. Howard-Hill, 'The compositors of Shakespeare's Folio Comedies', *SB*, 26 (1973), 61–106
Howard-Hill, 'Compositors'	T.H. Howard-Hill, *Compositors B and E in the Shakespeare First Folio, and Some Recent Studies* (Columbia, SC, 1976)
Hunt, *Autobiography*	Leigh Hunt, *The Autobiography of Leigh Hunt: With Reminiscences of Friends and Contemporaries* (1850; repr. New York, 1965)
Hunt, *Criticism*	*Leigh Hunt's Dramatic Criticism, 1808–31*, ed. L.H. and C.W. Houtchens (New York, 1949)
Hunter	Joseph Hunter, *New Illustrations of the Life, Studies and Writings of Shakespeare* (1845)
Hutson	Lorna Hutson, 'On not being deceived: rhetoric and the body in *Twelfth Night*', *Texas Studies in Literature and Language*, 38 (1996), 140–74
Hutton, *Rise*	Ronald Hutton, *The Rise and Fall of Merry England: The Ritual Year, 1400–1700* (Oxford, 1994)
Hutton, *Stations*	Ronald Hutton, *The Stations of the Sun: A History of the Ritual Year in Britain* (Oxford, 1996)
Intronati	Accademia degli Intronati, *Gl'ingannati*, in Guido Davico Bonino (ed.), *Il teatro italiano, II: La commedia del Cinquecento* (Turin, 1977)
Jackson	Russell Jackson (ed.), *The Cambridge Companion to Shakespeare on Film* (Cambridge, 2000)
Jardine, *Daughters*	Lisa Jardine, *Still Harping on Daughters: Women and Drama in the Age of Shakespeare* (Brighton, 1983)
Jardine, 'Twins'	Lisa Jardine, 'Twins and travesties: gender, dependency, and sexual availability in *Twelfth Night*', in Susan Zimmerman (ed.), *Erotic Politics* (1992), 27–38

Johnson, *Dictionary*	Samuel Johnson, *A Dictionary of the English Language*, 2 vols (1755)
Jones	Robert Jones, *The First Book of Songs and Airs* (1600)
Jones & Stallybrass	Ann Rosalind Jones and Peter Stallybrass, *Renaissance Clothing and the Materials of Memory* (Cambridge, 2000)
Jonson, *Works*	Ben Jonson, *Works* (1616)
Junius	Adrianus Junius, *The Nomenclator*, trans. John Higgins (1585)
Kennedy	Dennis Kennedy, *Looking at Shakespeare: A Visual History of Twentieth-Century Performance*, 2nd edn (Cambridge, 2001)
Kerrigan	John Kerrigan, 'Secrecy and gossip in *Twelfth Night*', *SS 50* (1997), 65–80; repr. in John Kerrigan, *On Shakespeare and Early Modern Literature: Essays* (Oxford, 2001), 89–112
King, T.	T.J. King, *Casting Shakespeare's Plays* (Cambridge, 1992)
Kökeritz	Helge Kökeritz, *Shakespeare's Pronunciation* (New Haven, Conn., 1960)
Koller	A.M. Koller, *The Theater Duke: Georg II of Saxe-Meiningen and the German Stage* (Stanford, Calif., 1984)
Lamb, C.	Charles Lamb, 'On some of the old actors' (1822), in *Essays of Elia*, ed. N.L. Hallward and S.C. Hill (1959), 184–97
Lamb, M.	Mary Ellen Lamb, 'Tracing a heterosexual erotics of service in '*Twelfth Night* and the autobiographical writings of Thomas Hythorne and Anne Clifford', *Criticism*, 40 (1998), 1–25
Laneham	Robert Laneham, *A Letter* (1575)
Latham	Simon Latham, *Latham's Falconry* (1615)
Laqueur	Thomas Laqueur, *Making Sex: Body and Gender from the Greeks to Freud* (Cambridge Mass., 1990)
Leggatt	Alexander Leggatt (ed.), *The Cambridge Companion to Shakespearean Comedy* (Cambridge, 2002)
Lever & Fulwood	Ralph Lever and William Fulwood, *The Most Noble, Ancient and Learned Play, called The Philosophers' Game* (1563)
Levine	Laura Levine, *Men in Women's Clothes: Anti-Theatricality and Effeminization 1579–1652* (Cambridge, 1994)
Lewalski	Barbara Lewalski, 'Thematic patterns in *Twelfth Night*', *SSt*, 1 (1965), 168–81

Lewis	Cynthia Lewis, 'A fustian riddle? anagrammatic names in *Twelfth Night*', *ELN*, 22 (1985), 32–7
Lily	William Lily, *A Short Introduction of Grammar*, 2nd edn (1577)
Linthicum	Marie Channing Linthicum, *Costume in the Drama of Shakespeare and his Contemporaries* (Oxford, 1936)
Lloyd	W.W. Lloyd, *The Life of the Poet and Critical Essays on the Plays*, in Singer
Lodge	Thomas Lodge, *Treatise of the Plague* (1603)
London Stage	*The London Stage, 1660–1800* (Carbondale, Ill., 1960–8)
Long	John H. Long, *Shakespeare's Use Of Music: The Study of the Music and its Performance in the Original Production of Seven Comedies*, 3 vols (Gainesville, Fla., 1961–71)
Lusty Juventus	Robert Weaver, *An Interlude Called Lusty Juventus* (1550)
Lydgate	John Lydgate, *The Minor Poems*, ed. H.N. MacCracken (1911)
Lyly, *Endimion*	John Lyly, *Endimion* (1591)
Lyly, *England*	John Lyly, *Euphues and his England* (1580)
Lyly, *Euphues*	John Lyly, *Euphues: The Anatomy of Wit* (1578)
Lyly, *Gallathea*	John Lyly, *Gallathea* (1592)
Lyly, *Met.*	John Lyly, *Love's Metamorphosis* (1601)
Magdalene	Lewis Wager, *A New Interlude . . . Entreating of the Life and Repentance of Mary Magdalene* (1566)
Magnusson, *Dialogue*	Lynne Magnusson, *Shakespeare and Social Dialogue: Dramatic Language and Elizabethan Letters* (Cambridge, 1999)
Magnusson, 'Language'	Lynne Magnusson, 'Language and comedy', in Leggatt, 156–78
Malcolmson	Cristina Malcolmson, '"What You Will": social mobility and gender in *Twelfth Night*', in Valerie Wayne (ed.), *The Matter of Difference: Materialist Feminist Criticism of Shakespeare* (Ithaca, NY, 1991), 29–57
Manningham	John Manningham, *The Diary of John Manningham of the Middle Temple 1602–1603*, ed. Robert Parker Sorlien (Hanover, NH, 1976)
Marcus	Leah Marcus, *The Politics of Mirth* (Chicago, 1978)
Markham	Francis Markham, *The Book of Honour* (1625)
Marlowe, *Edward II*	*The Troublesome Reign and Lamentable Death of Edward the Second, King of England* (1594)
Marlowe, *Faustus*	Christopher Marlowe, *The Tragical History of Dr Faustus* (1604)
Marlowe, *Jew*	Christopher Marlowe, *The Tragedy of the Rich Jew of Malta* (1633)

Marlowe, *Tamburlaine*	Christopher Marlowe, *Tamburlaine the Great* (1590)
Marston	John Marston, *The Malcontent . . . With the Additions . . . by John Webster* (1604)
Meres	Francis Meres, *Palladis Tamia* (1598)
Minsheu	John Minsheu, *Ductoris in Linguas, The Guide into Tongues* (1625)
Montaigne	Michel de Montaigne, *Essays*, trans. John Florio (1613)
Morley, H.	Henry Morley, *The Journal of a London Playgoer, 1851–1866* (1891)
Morley, T.	Thomas Morley, *A Plain and Easy Introduction to Practical Music* (1597)
Mullaney	Steven Mullaney, *The Place of the Stage: Licence, Play and Power in Renaissance England* (Chicago, 1988)
Näcke	Paul Näcke, 'Über Homosexualität in Albanien', *Jahrbuch für sexuelle Zwischenstufen unter besonderer berücksichtigender Homosexualität*, 10 (1908), 313–37
Nashe, *Pasquill*	Thomas Nashe, *The Return of the Renowned Cavaliero Pasquill and his Meeting with Marforius* (1589)
Nashe, *Prognostication*	Thomas Nashe, *A Wonderful, Strange and Miraculous Astrological Prognostication* (1591)
Nashe, *Tears*	Thomas Nashe, *Christ's Tears over Jerusalem* (1593)
Nashe, *Traveller*	Thomas Nashe, *The Unfortunate Traveller* (1594)
NB	Norman Blake, private communication
Norbrook	David Norbrook, *Poetry and Politics in the English Renaissance*, rev. edn (Oxford, 2002)
OED	*Oxford English Dictionary*, 2nd edn (Oxford, 1989)
Odell	G.C.D. Odell, *Shakespeare from Betterton to Irving* (1921)
Onions	C.T. Onions, *A Shakespeare Glossary* (1911), rev. Robert Eagleson (Oxford, 1986)
Orgel	Stephen Orgel, *Impersonations: The Performance of Gender in Shakespeare's England* (Cambridge, 1996)
Osborne	Laurie E. Osborne, *The Trick of Singularity: Twelfth Night and the Performance Editions* (Iowa City, 1996)
Overbury	Sir Thomas Overbury, *New and Choice Characters* (1615)
Ovid, *Fasti*	Ovid, *Fasti*, ed. A.J. Boyle and R.D. Woodard (Harmondsworth, England, 2000)
Ovid, *Met.*	Ovid, *Metamorphoses*, trans. Arthur Golding (1567)
Oxberry, *Dramatic*	*Oxberry's Dramatic Biography and Histrionic Anecdotes*, ed. Catherine E. Oxberry, 5 vols (1825)

Palmer, *Shakespeare* D.J. Palmer (ed.), *Shakespeare: 'Twelfth Night'; A Casebook* (1972)

Palmer, 'Echo' D.J. Palmer, '*Twelfth Night* and the myth of Echo and Narcissus', *SS 32* (1979), 73--8

Partridge Eric Partridge, *Shakespeare's Bawdy* (1968)

Paster Gail Kern Paster, *The Body Embarrassed: Drama and the Disciplines of Shame in Early Modern England* (Ithaca, NY, 1993)

Pastime Stephen Hawes, *The Pastime of Pleasure* (1509), ed. W.E. Mead (1928)

Peele George Peele, *The Love of King David and his Fair Bethsabe* (1623)

Pennington Michael Pennington, *Twelfth Night: A User's Guide* (2000)

Pepys Samuel Pepys, *The Diary of Samuel Pepys*, ed. Robert Latham and William Matthews, 11 vols (1985)

Pequigney Joseph Pequigney, 'The two Antonios and same-sex love in *Twelfth Night* and *The Merchant of Venice*', *English Literary Renaissance*, 22 (1992), 201–21

Petrarch Francesco Petrarca, *Canzoniere*, ed. Rosanna Bettarini (Turin, 2005)

Plato *The Dialogues of Plato*, trans. Benjamin Jowett, ed. D.J. Allan and H.E. Dale, 4 vols (Oxford, 1953)

Plautus Titus Maccius Plautus, *A Pleasant and Fine Conceited Comedy, called Menechmus*, trans. William Warner (1595)

Playford Henry Playford, *Wit and Mirth, or Pills to Purge Melancholy*, 4th edn, 6 vols (1719–20)

Pliny Pliny the Elder, *The History of the World*, trans. Philemon Holland (1601)

PMLA *Publications of the Modern Language Association*

Potter Lois Potter, *Twelfth Night: Text and Performance* (Basingstoke, 1985)

Preiss Richard Preiss, 'Robert Armin do the police in different voices', in Peter Holland and Stephen Orgel (eds), *From Performance to Print in Shakespeare's England* (Houndmills, England, 2006), 208–27

Primaudaye Pierre de la Primaudaye, *The French Academy* (1586)

Proclamation Elizabeth I, [*Proclamation*] *By the Queen . . .* [*against*] *Inordinate Excess in Apparel* (1597)

Puttenham George Puttenham, *The Art of English Poesy* (1589)

Rackin Phyllis Rackin, 'Androgyny, mimesis and the marriage of the boy heroine on the English Renaissance stage', *PMLA*, 102 (1987), 29–41

Ralegh	Walter Ralegh, *The Discovery of the Large, Rich and Beautiful Empire of Guiana* (1596)
Reed	Robert Reed, *Bedlam on the Jacobean Stage* (Cambridge, Mass., 1952)
Relihan	Constance C. Relihan, 'Erasing the east from *Twelfth Night*', in Joyce Green MacDonald (ed.), *Race, Ethnicity, and Power in the Renaissance* (Madison, NJ, 1997), 89–94
Riche	*Barnabe Riche his Farewell to Military Profession* (1583)
Robinson	Henry Crabb Robinson, *Diary, Reminiscences, and Correspondence*, ed. Thomas Sadler, 2 vols (1872)
Roister Doister	Nicholas Udall, *Roister Doister* (1566)
Rothwell & Melzer	Kenneth S. Rothwell and Annabelle Henkin Melzer (eds), *Shakespeare on Screen: An International Filmography and Videography* (1990)
RP	Richard Proudfoot, private communication
R.T.	Richard Tarlton [?], *A Pretty New Ballad, Entitled: The Crow Sits upon the Wall / Please One and Please All* (1592)
Rubinstein	Frankie Rubinstein, *A Dictionary of Shakespeare's Sexual Puns and their Significance*, 2nd edn (Basingstoke, 1984)
Salgādo	Gāmini Salgādo (ed.), *Eyewitnesses of Shakespeare: First Hand Accounts of Performances 1590–1890* (1975)
Saintsbury & Palmer	H.A. Saintsbury and Cecil Palmer (eds), *We Saw Him Act: A Symposium on the Art of Sir Henry Irving* (1939)
Saslow	James Saslow, *The Medici Wedding of 1589* (New Haven, Conn., and London, 1996)
Saviolo	Vincenzo Saviolo, *Vincentio Saviolo's Practice in Two Books* (1595)
Sawday	Jonathan Sawday, *The Body Emblazoned: Dissection and the Human Body in Renaissance Culture* (1995)
SB	*Studies in Bibliography*
SC	*Shakespearean Criticism* (Detroit, 1984–)
Schafer	Elizabeth Schafer, *Ms-Directing Shakespeare: Women Direct Shakespeare* (1998)
Schalkwyk	David Schalkwyk, 'Love and service in *Twelfth Night* and the Sonnets', *SQ*, 56 (2005), 76–100
Schlegel	August Wilhelm von Schlegel, *A Course of Lectures on Dramatic Art and Literature*, trans. John Black, 2 vols (1815)
Schleiner	Winfried Schleiner, 'The Feste–Malvolio scene in *Twelfth Night* against the background of Renaissance ideas about madness and possession', *Deutsche Shakespeare Gesellschaft West: Jahrbuch* (1990), 48–57

Schmidt — Alexander Schmidt, *Shakespeare Lexicon* (New York, 1968)

Scot — Reginald Scot, *Discovery of Witchcraft* (1584)

Scragg — Leah Scragg, '"Her C's, her U's, and her T's: why that?" A new reply for Sir Andrew Aguecheek', *Review of English Studies*, 42 (1991), 1–16

SEL — *Studies in English Literature*

Shattuck, *Shakespeare* — Charles H. Shattuck, *The Shakespeare Promptbooks: A Descriptive Catalogue* (Urbana, Ill., and London, 1965)

Shattuck, *Kemble* — *John Philip Kemble Promptbooks*, ed. Charles H. Shattuck (Charlottesville, Va., 1974)

Shaw — George Bernard Shaw, 'The point of view of a playwright', in Max Beerbohm (ed.), *Herbert Beerbohm Tree: Some Memories of Him and of his Art* (1920), 240–52

Shelley — Mary Shelley, 'Review of Prosper Merimée, *Le Guzla, ou Choix de poésies illyriques*', *Westminster Review*, 10 (1829), 71–81

Shirley — Anthony Shirley, *A True Report of Sir Anthony Shirley's Journey . . . to Casbine in Persia: His Entertainment there by the Great Sophy* (1600)

Sidney, *Arcadia* — Philip Sidney, *The Countess of Pembroke's Arcadia* (1598)

Sidney, *Astrophel* — Philip Sidney, *Astrophel and Stella*, in Sidney, *Arcadia*, 519–69

Simmons — J.L. Simmons, 'A source for Shakespeare's Malvolio: the Elizabethan controversy with the Puritans', *Huntington Library Quarterly*, 36 (1973), 181–201

Simpson — Claude M. Simpson, *The British Broadside Ballad and its Music* (New Brunswick, NJ, 1966)

Sinden, *Laughter* — Donald Sinden, *Laughter in the Second Act* (1985)

Sinden, 'Malvolio' — Donald Sinden, 'Malvolio in *Twelfth Night*', in *Players of Shakespeare*, ed. Philip Brockbank (Cambridge, 1985), 41–66

Sisson — C.J. Sisson, *New Readings in Shakespeare* (Cambridge, 1956)

Smith, B. — Bruce R. Smith, *Homosexual Desire in Shakespeare's England* (Chicago, 1991)

Smith, P. — Peter J. Smith, 'M.O.A.I.: "What should that alphabetical position 'portend?" An answer to the metamorphic Malvolio', *Renaissance Quarterly*, 51 (1998), 1199–224

Sohmer — Steve Sohmer, *Shakespeare's Mystery Play: The Opening of the Globe Theatre 1599* (Manchester, 1999)

Speaight, *Poel*	Robert Speaight, *William Poel and the Elizabethan Revival* (1954)
Speaight, *Shakespeare*	Robert Speaight, *Shakespeare on the Stage: An Illustrated History of Shakespearian Performance* (1973)
Sprague	A.C. Sprague, *Shakespeare and the Actors: The Stage Business in his Plays (1660–1905)* (Cambridge, Mass., 1945)
Sprague & Trewin	A.C Sprague and J.C. Trewin, *Shakespare's Plays Today: Some Customs and Conventions of the Stage* (1970)
SQ	*Shakespeare Quarterly*
SS	*Shakespeare Survey*
SSt	*Shakespeare Studies*
Sternfeld	F.W. Sternfeld, *Music in Shakespearean Tragedy* (1963)
Stubbes	Philip Stubbes, *Anatomy of Abuses* (1583)
Styan	J.L. Styan, *The Shakespeare Revolution: Criticism and Performance in the Twentieth Century* (Cambridge, 1977)
Tarlton's Jests	Richard Tarlton, *Tarlton's Jests* (1613)
Tarlton's News	Richard Tarlton, *Tarlton's News out of Purgatory* (1590)
Taylor, J.	John Taylor, *Works* (1630)
Taylor, G.	Gary Taylor, *Castration: An Abbreviated History of Western Manhood* (New York, 2000)
Thomas	Sir H. Thomas, Letter, *TLS*, 4 June 1933
Throckmorton	Job Throckmorton, *A Dialogue* (1589)
Tilley	Morris P. Tilley, *A Dictionary of the Proverbs in England in the Sixteenth and Seventeenth Centuries* (Ann Arbor, Mich., 1950)
Tree	Herbert Beerbohm-Tree, Promptbook for Her Majesty's Theatre production of *Twelfth Night*, 1901 (Bristol University Drama Library, Tree Collection, Box 138)
Trewin	J.C. Trewin, *Shakespeare on the English Stage, 1900–64* (1964)
Trial of Treasure	*A New and Merry Interlude, Called the Trial of Treasure* (1567)
Turner	Robert K. Turner, Jr, 'The text of *Twelfth Night*', *SQ*, 26 (1975), 128–38
TxC	Stanley Wells and Gary Taylor, with John Jowett and William Montgomery, *William Shakespeare: A Textual Companion* (Oxford, 1987)
Tyrwhitt	Thomas Tyrwhitt, *Observations and Conjectures upon Some Passages of Shakespeare* (Oxford, 1766)
Ungerer	Gustav Ungerer, 'My Lady's a Cathayan', *SS 32* (1979), 85–104

Van Doren — Mark Van Doren, *Shakespeare* (New York, 1939)

Vigo — Giovanni da Vigo, *The Most Excellent Works of Chirurgery*, trans. Bartholomew Traheron (1543)

Viswanathan — S. Viswanathan, '"Illeism with a difference" in certain middle plays of Shakespeare', *SQ*, 20 (1969), 407–15

Wales — Kathleen M. Wales, 'Generic "your" and Jacobean drama: the rise and fall of a pronominal usage', *English Studies*, 66 (1985), 7–24

Walker — W.S. Walker, *A Critical Examination of the Text of Shakespeare*, ed. W.N. Lettsom (1860)

Webster, *Devil* — John Webster *The White Devil* (1612)

Webster, *Malfi* — John Webster, *The Tragedy of the Duchess of Malfi* (1623)

Wells — Stanley Wells (ed.), *Shakespeare in the Theatre: An Anthology of Criticism* (Oxford, 1997)

Welsford — Enid Welsford, *The Fool: His Social and Literary History* (1935)

Werstine, 'Cases' — Paul Werstine, 'Cases and compositors in the Shakespeare First Folio comedies', *SB*, 35 (1982), 206–34

Werstine, 'Narratives' — Paul Werstine, 'Narratives about printed Shakespeare texts: "foulpapers" and "bad" quartos', *SQ*, 41 (1990), 65–86

Werstine, 'Plays' — Paul Werstine, 'Plays in manuscript', in Cox & Kastan, 481–97

Wilde — Oscar Wilde, 'The truth of masks: a note on illusion', in *Intentions* (1891)

Wiles — David Wiles, *Shakespeare's Clown: Actor and Text in the Elizabethan Playhouse* (Cambridge, 1987)

Williams — Gordon Williams, *A Dictionary of Sexual Language and Imagery in Shakespearean and Stuart Literature* (1994)

Wilson, *Happy* — John Dover Wilson, *Shakespeare's Happy Comedies* (1962)

Wilson, R. — Richard Wilson, *Secret Shakespeare: Studies in Theatre, Religion and Resistance* (Manchester, 2004)

Winter — William Winter, *Shakespeare on the Stage* (New York, 1915)

Witch of Edmonton — Thomas Dekker, John Ford and William Rowley, *The Witch of Edmonton* (1658)

Woodbridge — Linda Woodbridge, '"Fire in your heart and brimstone in your liver": towards an unsaturnalian *Twelfth Night*', *Southern Review* (Australia), 17 (1994), 270–91

Woolf — Virginia Woolf, '*Twelfth Night* at the Old Vic' (1933), in Wells, 206–10

Wright, E.	[Edward Wright], *The Map of the World, A.D. 1600, Called by Shakespeare 'The New Map, with the Augmentation of the Indies': To Illustrate the Voyages of John Davis* (1880)
Wright, G.	George T. Wright, *Shakespeare's Metrical Art* (Berkeley, 1988)
Wright, T.	Thomas Wright, *The Passions of the Mind* (1601)

INDEX

Mark Rylance as Richard III in the West End production of *Richard III*

Samuel Barnett as Queen Elizabeth in the Shakespeare's Globe production of *Richard III*

Mark Rylance as Olivia in the West End production of *Twelfth Night*

Stephen Fry as Malvolio in the West End production of *Twelfth Night*

Musicians of *Richard III* in the Shakespeare's Globe production of *Richard III*

☞ Mark Rylance as Richard III in the West End production of *Richard III*

☞ Mark Rylance as Richard III in the Shakespeare's Globe production of *Richard III*

Mark Rylance as Richard III in the West End production of *Richard III*

☞ Jethro Skinner as "A Lord" in the West End production of *Richard III*

☞ Samuel Barnett as Queen Elizabeth in the West End production of *Richard III*

Stephen Fry as Malvolio in the West End production of *Twelfth Night*

John Paul Connolly in the West End Production of *Richard III*

Mark Rylance as Olivia & Stephen Fry
as Malvolio in the West End production of *Twelfth Night*

Paul Chahidi as Maria and Colin Hurley as
Sir Toby Belch in the Shakespeare's Globe production of *Twelfth Night*

Mark Rylance as Olivia in the West End production of *Twelfth Night*

Peter Hamilton Dyer as Feste in the West End production of *Twelfth Night*

☞ Paul Chahidi as Maria in the Shakespeare's Globe production of *Twelfth Night*

Colin Hurley as Sir Toby Belch in the West End production of *Twelfth Night*

☞ Mark Rylance as Olivia in the West End production of *Twelfth Night*

☞ Liam Brennan as Orsino in the West End production of *Twelfth Night*

A unique, limited-edition set of the Arden editions of *Richard III* and *Twelfth Night*, enhanced by a full color collection of sumptuous, vivid images from two UK productions. Each play edition has detailed on-page notes exploring and explaining Shakespeare's rich language with expert introductions to the plays' historical, critical and theatrical contexts.

This limited edition provides both a lasting souvenir of landmark and critically acclaimed productions, and an opportunity to revisit two of Shakespeare's most memorable plays time and again, discovering new insights and delights at every turn.

Photos by Simon Annand

Photos reprinted with permission from Yellow Stockings LP

THE ARDEN SHAKESPEARE

THIRD SERIES

General Editors: Richard Proudfoot, Ann Thompson, David Scott Kastan and H.R. Woudhuysen

KING RICHARD III

THE ARDEN SHAKESPEARE

ALL'S WELL THAT ENDS WELL	edited by G.K. Hunter*
ANTONY AND CLEOPATRA	edited by John Wilders
AS YOU LIKE IT	edited by Juliet Dusinberre
THE COMEDY OF ERRORS	edited by R.A. Foakes*
CORIOLANUS	edited by Philip Brockbank*
CYMBELINE	edited by J.M. Nosworthy*
DOUBLE FALSEHOOD	edited by Brean Hammond
HAMLET	edited by Ann Thompson and Neil Taylor
JULIUS CAESAR	edited by David Daniell
KING HENRY IV Part 1	edited by David Scott Kastan
KING HENRY IV Part 2	edited by A.R. Humphreys*
KING HENRY V	edited by T.W. Craik
KING HENRY VI Part 1	edited by Edward Burns
KING HENRY VI Part 2	edited by Ronald Knowles
KING HENRY VI Part 3	edited by John D. Cox and Eric Rasmussen
KING HENRY VIII	edited by Gordon McMullan
KING JOHN	edited by E.A.J. Honigmann*
KING LEAR	edited by R.A. Foakes
KING RICHARD II	edited by Charles Forker
KING RICHARD III	edited by James R. Siemon
LOVE'S LABOUR'S LOST	edited by H.R. Woudhuysen
MACBETH	edited by Kenneth Muir*
MEASURE FOR MEASURE	edited by J.W. Lever*
THE MERCHANT OF VENICE	edited by John Drakakis
THE MERRY WIVES OF WINDSOR	edited by Giorgio Melchiori
A MIDSUMMER NIGHT'S DREAM	edited by Harold F. Brooks*
MUCH ADO ABOUT NOTHING	edited by Claire McEachern
OTHELLO	edited by E.A.J. Honigmann
PERICLES	edited by Suzanne Gossett
SHAKESPEARE'S POEMS	edited by Katherine Duncan-Jones and H.R. Woudhuysen
ROMEO AND JULIET	edited by Brian Gibbons*
SHAKESPEARE'S SONNETS	edited by Katherine Duncan-Jones
THE TAMING OF THE SHREW	edited by Barbara Hodgdon
THE TEMPEST	edited by Virginia Mason Vaughan and Alden T. Vaughan
TIMON OF ATHENS	edited by Anthony B. Dawson and Gretchen E. Minton
TITUS ANDRONICUS	edited by Jonathan Bate
TROILUS AND CRESSIDA	edited by David Bevington
TWELFTH NIGHT	edited by Keir Elam
THE TWO GENTLEMEN OF VERONA	edited by William C. Carroll
THE TWO NOBLE KINSMEN	edited by Lois Potter
THE WINTER'S TALE	edited by John Pitcher

* Second series

THE ARDEN SHAKESPEARE

RICHARD III

Edited by

JAMES R. SIEMON

BLOOMSBURY

LONDON • NEW DELHI • NEW YORK • SYDNEY

Bloomsbury Arden Shakespeare
An imprint of Bloomsbury Publishing Plc

50 Bedford Square
London
WC1B 3DP
UK

1385 Broadway
New York
NY 10018
USA

www.bloomsbury.com

Bloomsbury is a registered trade mark of Bloomsbury Publishing Plc

This edition of *Richard III* by James R. Siemon, first published 2009
by the Arden Shakespeare
Reprinted by Bloomsbury Arden Shakespeare 2010, 2011 (twice),
2012, 2013 (twice)

British Library Cataloguing-in-Publication Data
A catalogue record for this book is available from the British Library.

ISBN: HB: 978-1-9034-3688-2
PB: 978-1-9034-3689-9

Library of Congress Cataloging-in-Publication Data
A catalog record for this book is available from the Library of Congress.

Printed and bound in the United States of America

The Editor

James R. Siemon is Professor of English at Boston University. He is the author of *Word Against Word: Shakespearean Utterance* (2002) and *Shakespearean Iconoclasm* (1985); he is the editor of Christopher Marlowe's *The Jew of Malta* for the New Mermaids Series (1994).

For Alexandra, Johanna, Rosalie, Anna and Julia

CONTENTS

LIST OF ILLUSTRATIONS

GENERAL EDITORS' PREFACE

The earliest volume in the first Arden series, Edward Dowden's *Hamlet*, was published in 1899. Since then the Arden Shakespeare has been widely acknowledged as the pre-eminent Shakespeare edition, valued by scholars, students, actors and 'the great variety of readers' alike for its clearly presented and reliable texts, its full annotation and its richly informative introductions.

In the third Arden series we seek to maintain these well-established qualities and general characteristics, preserving our predecessors' commitment to presenting the play as it has been shaped in history. Each volume necessarily has its own particular emphasis which reflects the unique possibilities and problems posed by the work in question, and the series as a whole seeks to maintain the highest standards of scholarship, combined with attractive and accessible presentation.

Newly edited from the original Quarto and Folio editions, texts are presented in fully modernized form, with a textual apparatus that records all substantial divergences from those early printings. The notes and introductions focus on the conditions and possibilities of meaning that editors, critics and performers (on stage and screen) have discovered in the play. While building upon the rich history of scholarly activity that has long shaped our understanding of Shakespeare's works, this third series of the Arden Shakespeare is enlivened by a new generation's encounter with Shakespeare.

THE TEXT

On each page of the play itself, readers will find a passage of text supported by commentary and textual notes. Act and scene divisions (seldom present in the early editions and often the product of eighteenth-century or later scholarship) have been retained for ease of reference, but have been given less prominence than in previous series. Editorial indications of location of the action have been removed to the textual notes or commentary.

In the text itself, unfamiliar typographic conventions have been avoided in order to minimize obstacles to the reader. Elided forms in the early texts are spelt out in full in verse lines wherever they indicate a usual late twentieth-century pronunciation that requires no special indication and wherever they occur in prose (except where they indicate non-standard pronunciation). In verse speeches, marks of elision are retained where they are necessary guides to the scansion and pronunciation of the line. Final -ed in past tense and participial forms of verbs is always printed as -ed, without accent, never as -'d, but wherever the required pronunciation diverges from modern usage a note in the commentary draws attention to the fact. Where the final -ed should be given syllabic value contrary to modern usage, e.g.

> Doth Silvia know that I am banished?
> (*TGV* 3.1.214)

the note will take the form

> 214 **banished** banishèd

Conventional lineation of divided verse lines shared by two or more speakers has been reconsidered and sometimes rearranged. Except for the familiar *Exit* and *Exeunt*, Latin forms in stage directions and speech prefixes have been translated into English and the original Latin forms recorded in the textual notes.

COMMENTARY AND TEXTUAL NOTES

Notes in the commentary, for which a major source will be the *Oxford English Dictionary*, offer glossarial and other explication of verbal difficulties; they may also include discussion of points of interpretation and, in relevant cases, substantial extracts from Shakespeare's source material. Editors will not usually offer glossarial notes for words adequately defined in the latest edition of *The Concise Oxford Dictionary* or *Merriam-Webster's Collegiate Dictionary*, but in cases of doubt they will include notes. Attention, however, will be drawn to places where more than one likely interpretation can be proposed and to significant verbal and syntactic complexity. Notes preceded by * discuss editorial emendations or variant readings from the early edition(s) on which the text is based.

Headnotes to acts or scenes discuss, where appropriate, questions of scene location, Shakespeare's handling of his source materials, and major difficulties of staging. The list of roles (so headed to emphasize the play's status as a text for performance) is also considered in the commentary notes. These may include comment on plausible patterns of casting with the resources of an Elizabethan or Jacobean acting company and also on any variation in the description of roles in their speech prefixes in the early editions.

The textual notes are designed to let readers know when the edited text diverges from the early edition(s) or manuscript sources on which it is based. Wherever this happens the note will record the rejected reading of the early edition(s), in original spelling, and the source of the reading adopted in this edition. Other forms from the early edition(s) recorded in these notes will include some spellings of particular interest or significance and original forms of translated stage directions. Where two or more early editions are involved, for instance with *Othello*, the notes also record all important differences between them. The textual notes take a form that has been in use since the nineteenth century. This comprises, first: line reference, reading adopted in the text and closing square bracket; then: abbreviated reference, in italic, to the earliest edition to adopt the accepted reading, italic semicolon and noteworthy alternative reading(s), each with abbreviated italic reference to its source.

Conventions used in these textual notes include the following. The solidus / is used, in notes quoting verse or discussing verse lining, to indicate line endings. Distinctive spellings of the basic text (Q or F) follow the square bracket without indication of source and are enclosed in italic brackets. Names enclosed in italic brackets indicate originators of conjectural emendations when these did not originate in an edition of the text, or when the named edition records a conjecture not accepted into its text. Stage directions (SDs) are referred to by the number of the line within or immediately after which they are placed. Line numbers with a decimal point relate to centred entry SDs not falling within a verse line and to SDs more than one line long, with the number after the point indicating the line within the SD: e.g. 78.4 refers to the fourth line of the SD following line 78. Lines of SDs at the start of a scene are numbered 0.1, 0.2, etc. Where only a line number precedes a square bracket, e.g. 128], the note relates to the whole line; where SD is added to the number, it relates to the whole of a SD within or immediately following the line. Speech prefixes (SPs) follow similar conventions, 203 SP] referring to the speaker's name for line 203. Where a SP reference takes the form e.g. 38+ SP, it relates to all subsequent speeches assigned to that speaker in the scene in question.

Where, as with *King Henry V*, one of the early editions is a so-called 'bad quarto' (that is, a text either heavily adapted, or reconstructed from memory, or both), the divergences from the present edition are too great to be recorded in full in the notes. In these cases, with the exception of *Hamlet*, which prints an edited text of the quarto of 1603, the editions will include a reduced photographic facsimile of the 'bad quarto' in an appendix.

INTRODUCTION

Both the introduction and the commentary are designed to present the plays as texts for performance, and make appropriate reference to stage, film and television versions, as well as introducing the reader to the range of critical approaches to the plays. They discuss the history of the reception of the texts within the theatre and scholarship and beyond, investigating the interdependency of the literary text and the surrounding 'cultural text' both at the time of the original production of Shakespeare's works and during their long and rich afterlife.

PREFACE

While editing any Shakespeare play can and should constitute an educational experience, editing *Richard III* for the Arden series has provided an extended intellectual and emotional challenge beyond anything I could initially have imagined. Although working on this edition sometimes demanded long hours spent far from family and friends, I have never felt lonely. Firstly, there was the extended Arden family of passionately devoted editors and lovers of Shakespeare who stood ready, anywhere, nearly anytime, with support, encouragement and, not least, criticism. Secondly, old friends rose to the occasion, and new friends appeared wherever I went. I may sometimes have bored unsuspecting strangers with discourses on derivative Quarto variants or printing by formes, but friends learned what to expect from me, and hung on nonetheless; over the years I got to know a world of people who cared deeply about Shakespeare. Finally, the challenge made me feel connected with generations of other editors. How they accomplished so much in the years before photocopies, interlibrary loan, microfilm, email, EEBO and JSTOR is beyond me. The list of collated editions in the present volume begins to suggest its indebtedness, but no list sufficiently conveys the feelings of personal relationship that the struggle to edit Shakespeare elicited. I came to look forward to seeing what Theobald had made of an opaque line, what Johnson saw in an obscure reference or what Furness would do with rival interpretations. Whether I agreed or not, I always learned from these encounters.

I am grateful to the extended Arden family, and especially to Richard Proudfoot, who embodies the Arden commitment to scholarly excellence and does so with inspiring graciousness. My heartfelt thanks to David Scott Kastan, who personally talked me through countless revisions, cheering me on (and up) with unfailing humour and gentle reminders that the struggle was worth it. Grateful thanks also go to George Walton Williams for many thoughtful suggestions and corrections. Thank you, as well, to Jessica Hodge, Margaret Bartley and Anna Wormleighton for all manner of aid and encouragement; and to the very helpful proofreader, Jocelyn Stockley, for her acute attention to detail. Finally, and especially, I thank Jane Armstrong, without whose unflagging devotion to clarity, order and accuracy, to, in effect, editing the editor, this edition could never have hoped to aspire to Arden standards.

Then, my thanks go to colleagues from many institutions who shared insights, asked pointed questions, cajoled, challenged and provoked: Leeds Barroll and Susan Zimmerman, Emily Bartels, David Bevington, Peter Blayney, Keir Elam, Ed Gieskes, Andrew Gurr, Andrew Hartley, Diana Henderson, Jeff Henderson, Peter Holland, Jean Howard, Lauren Kehoe, Maydee Lande, Kirk Melnikoff, Cynthia Marshall, Joseph Navitsky, Lena Orlin, Gail Paster, Val Wayne and Robert Weimann. There were those who generously shared their own work and work-in-progress with me: M.C. Aune, Gina Bloom, Clara Calvo, Richard Dutton, Lukas Erne, Andrew Gordon, Andreas Hoefele, Alex Huang, Nina Levine, Barbara Mowat, Patricia Parker, Marie Plasse and Stuart Sillars. I owe special debts as well to those who read, listened to, published, consulted and commented on the work as it grew: especially Bill Carroll, Kent Cartwright, Pete Donaldson, Steve Esposito, Wes Folkerth, Marta Gibińska, Paul Hammer, Mick Hattaway, Jean Howard, Hugo Keiper, Roslyn Knutson, Bob Levine, Bruce Smith, Boika Sokolova, Alden and Ginger Vaughan, Paul Yachnin and Paul Werstine. I thank the Shakespeare Association of America, the International Shakespeare Association, the Shakespeare Theatre of New Jersey and the Shakespeare Theatre Company of Washington, DC, for opportunities to try out my ideas in formal ways. I am grateful for financial assistance from Boston University and its generous Humanities Foundation, the Folger Shakespeare Library and the Arden Bursary. I am delighted to acknowledge the vital aid of librarians at Boston University (particularly Linda Carr), the British Library, the Shakespeare Centre Library, the Bodleian Library, the Public Record Office, the National Archives, the Harvard Theatre Collection, the Library of Congress and, especially, the Folger Shakespeare Library, where Betsy Walsh, Georgianna Ziegler and the dedicated staff make scholarship a joy.

I thank my students from many years of Shakespeare courses and seminars at Boston University for their numberless insights. Finally, and above all, for inspiration and sustenance, emotional and intellectual, I thank Alexandra Siemon, who never lost patience, and the four other brilliant interlocutors named in the dedication and always present in my thoughts. Where would I even begin? Thanks, not least, for the laughter: who would ever have imagined that Anna Siemon, Julia Siemon and Rachel Nolan could transform the rigours of proofreading into raucous competition?

James R. Siemon
Brookline, Massachusetts

INTRODUCTION

THE PLAY

Though it is easily the most performed of Shakespeare's histories, there is no consensus about the rank of *Richard III*, about what sort of play it is or about what to make of its unique 'crook-backed' villain protagonist. The earliest critical response cites the play as support for putting Shakespeare among the best for 'tragedy' (Meres, sig. Oo2^r). With no clear genre of 'history play', Francis Meres accepts the self-designation of the first edition, published in 1597 (Q1): '*The Tragedy of King Richard the third. Containing his treacherous Plots against his brother Clarence: the pittiefull murther of his innocent nephewes: his tyrannicall usurpation: with the whole course of his detested life, and most deserved death*'. The 1623 First Folio (F1) shows less certainty, placing the play as the last of the first eight histories but titling it, uniquely among them, a 'Tragedy'.[1] One thing is clear: it went through a remarkable number of early editions (see p. 423) and has remained a steady theatre favourite.

Subsequent responses debate merit as well as genre. In the early eighteenth century, Charles Gildon pronounced Richard 'shocking' and 'not a fit Character for the Stage', calling the histories failures of 'Tragic Imitation' lacking 'Design' or 'unity' of action and time, and describing them as suggesting a puppet

1 The Folio running title – *The Life and Death of Richard the Third* – suggests biography (Anderson, 111). It is unlikely that the plays were conceived as a group or in Folio order; they were probably never performed before the nineteenth century in chronological order (Mary Thomas Crane, 'The Shakespearean tetralogy', *SQ*, 36 (1985), 291–5; Kastan, *1H4*, 92–3), but some audience members for *Richard III* had probably seen the *Henry VI* plays.

show (Vickers, 2.245, 249). Eighteenth-century editors Lewis Theobald, William Warburton and Samuel Johnson ranked the play 'middling' or 'Class II' (Vickers, 2.459, 3.226). Johnson added 'deservedly', since 'some parts are trifling, others shocking, and some improbable' (Vickers, 5.134). Later sentimentalist and Romantic writers debated Richard's 'character' and his relation to tragic protagonists such as Macbeth (see Donohue). Twentieth-century scholarship placed Richard among his stock theatrical forerunners, the Vice (Spivack, Weimann) or the Machiavel (Charnes, Maus).[1] Genre and relation to Shakespeare's other histories remain debatable: is *Richard III* part of a unified national epic (A.W. Schlegel; Ulrici, 2.283), a moral history and the culmination of the first tetralogy (Tillyard, *History Plays*), a retro-political history imposing providential religious order upon Machiavellian political chaos (Rackin) or a paradoxical comic history treating the values of the earlier plays ironically (Rossiter, 22).[2] Taken by itself, is it melodrama (Wilson, xl; Van Laan, 146–7), tyrant tragedy (W.A. Armstrong), romance (Kastan), a conflicted combination (Brooke, 79; Wilks) or satire, religious or political (Birch, 199; Simpson; Campbell, 321–34)?[3] Finally, after centuries of their omission, truncation or dismissal, what is to be said of the play's prominent, but problematic, female characters?[4]

Over the years, interpretation has assumed neoclassical, sentimentalist, Romantic, Victorian, modernist and post-modern inflections, but attention has consistently returned to the play's unusual protagonist, its highly patterned language and action, its female roles and its religious, historical and political implications.

1 Robert Weimann, *Shakespeare and the Popular Tradition in the Theatre* (Baltimore, 1978).

2 A.W. Schlegel, *Lectures on Dramatic Art and Literature*; trans. John Black (1900), 419; Phyllis Rackin, *Stages of History: Shakespeare's English Chronicles* (Ithaca, NY, 1990), 65.

3 W.A. Armstrong, 'The influence of Seneca and Machiavelli on the Elizabethan tyrant', *RES*, 24 (1948), 19–35; David Scott Kastan, *Shakespeare and the Shapes of Time* (Dover, NH, 1982), 132–3.

4 See Howard & Rackin; Nina S. Levine, *Women's Matters: Politics, Gender, and Nation in Shakespeare's Early History Plays* (Newark, Del., 1998).

Woven through these considerations are different reactions to its pervasive, multiform ironies and comic elements.

In plain sight: Richard

In Jasper Fforde's novel *The Eyre Affair*, *Richard III* appears as an interactive cult ritual modelled on *The Rocky Horror Show*. Performances begin with the audience chanting, '*When* is the winter of our discontent?', to which the stage Richard, chosen nightly from among audience volunteers, responds, 'Now is the winter of our discontent.'[1] Although the premise is that *Richard III* might still resonate with 'our' discontents 'now', Richard's first line is, and always has been, distantly historical. When the play opened in the 1590s, it was about events already over a century past, and 'our discontent' refers to troubles of the York family. Richard's line is only the first of many to invoke grievances that pre-date the play itself. Yet Richard's speech is also about something immediately in our faces. Uniquely for Shakespeare, *Richard III* begins with the protagonist's soliloquy about *his* discontent. Elizabethans thought they already knew about Richard. From the early sixteenth-century narratives of Polydore Vergil and Sir Thomas More, the malformed bogeyman, whose crimes – real, imputed, intended or imagined – included regicide, fratricide, infanticide, uxoricide, incest and ecclesiastical corruption, had appeared not only in Shakespeare's immediate sources (Edward Hall's *Union*, Raphael Holinshed's *Chronicles* and *The Mirror for Magistrates*) but in sermons, ballads, plays, rhetorical exercises, satires, state propaganda and invective. In keeping with early modern clichés about the body expressing the soul, Richard was rendered hunchbacked, lame of arm, crabbed of feature and natally toothed. As far as I know, the limp begins with Shakespeare.[2]

1 Jasper Fforde, *The Eyre Affair: A Novel* (New York, 2002), 183. Lois Potter's 'Shakespeare performed: English and American Richards, Edwards and Henries', *SQ*, 54 (2004), 450–61, called Fforde to my attention.

2 Readers are invited to correct this claim.

No one before had made so much of Richard's bodily challenges: love is out because he is too crippled to dance; dogs bark as he halts by. Everyone else merrily pairs off, making love not war, capering and ambling, while he limps and grumbles:

> But I, that am not shaped for sportive tricks,
> Nor made to court an amorous looking-glass;
> I, that am rudely stamped, and want love's majesty
> To strut before a wanton ambling nymph;
> I, that am curtailed of this fair proportion,
> Cheated of feature by dissembling Nature,
> Deformed, unfinished, sent before my time
> Into this breathing world, scarce half made up,
> And that so lamely and unfashionable
> That dogs bark at me as I halt by them –
> Why, I, in this weak piping time of peace,
> Have no delight to pass away the time,
> Unless to see my shadow in the sun
> And descant on mine own deformity.
> And therefore, since I cannot prove a lover
> To entertain these fair well-spoken days,
> I am determined to prove a villain
> And hate the idle pleasures of these days.
> (1.1.14–31)

He speaks to himself, and also for us, Freud realized, for Richard provides something anyone can identify with.[1] Here, too, we encounter something to resist, interpret or share, an intellectual, kinetic and vocal energy that demands response (Sprague, *Actors*, 136; R. Berry). And he is funny. No Elizabethan would have expected that.

Easily dominating text, performance and criticism, Shakespeare's Richard has prompted extreme responses. There have

1 Freud takes Richard for 'an enormously magnified representation of something we can all discover in ourselves. We all think we have reason to reproach nature and our destiny for congenital and infantile disadvantages; we all demand reparation for early wounds to our narcissism, our self-love' (Freud, 4.322–3; cf. Garber).

been attempts to 'humanize' him on the stage, from Garrick to Branagh, and in sentimentalist commentary from the eighteenth and nineteenth centuries, but other responses downplay 'inwardness' or 'subjective density' (Charnes, 93) to stress personification or monstrosity. He has been taken to embody 'genius' (Charles Lamb, in Bate, *Romantics*, 122), 'intellect' (Coleridge, in Bate, *Romantics*, 145–6), discredited Yorkist rule (Horace Walpole, in Donohue, 198), self-love (Freud, 4.322–3), civil violence (Tillyard, 208), capitalism (Siegel, 80) and masculine discursivity (Sanders, 193). He has been seen as a theatrical property: Punch (G.B. Shaw, in Sprague, *Actors* 135), Vice (Spivack), actor (Rossiter, 16–17), cartoon (H. Bloom, 66), Tudor 'bugaboo' (Budra, 82), or stage Machiavel (Charnes, 47–54).[1] Each designation merits attention; each needs qualification.

In its universality, Freud's figure of wounded 'self-love' that 'we all feel' parallels a relevant theological construct. The spinal curvature Thomas More added to Richard's alleged scapular inequality, whatever its relation to Tudor scapegoating of dynastic competitors, expresses a spiritual deformity that Christians thought 'we all' share as creatures bent and turned from God.[2] Not merely an ugly version of all of us, however, Richard embraces his symptom. Announcing himself 'determined to prove a villain' (1.1.30), he punningly accepts divine predestination to damnation and simultaneously chooses reprobation for himself.[3] Let us descend, as the play does, from pathology and theology, to specifics.

1 Paul N. Siegel, *Shakespeare's English and Roman History Plays: A Marxist Approach* (Rutherford, NJ, 1986); Eve Rachel Sanders, *Gender and Literacy on the Stage in Early Modern England* (Cambridge, 1998); Harold Bloom, *Shakespeare and the Invention of the Human* (New York, 1998).

2 On humanity as 'curvatus', see e.g. Augustine's *Ennarationes* (on Psalm 37) in J.-P. Migne.

3 Richard lacks assurances of God's love, such as those William Perkins urges the Christian to remember: God 'created me a man, when hee might haue made me an vgly Toade' and made me 'of comely bodie, and of discretion whereas he might haue made me vgly, and deformed, franticke, and mad' (Perkins, *Treatise*, 113^{r}). Rejection of brotherhood defines Richard as a reprobate: 'he that loueth not his brother' (Perkins, 'A Case of Conscience', *Works* (1592; STC 19665.5), sig. $B3^{r–v}$).

Deep tragedian or formal Vice

More calls Richard a 'deep dissimuler' and compares public life to playing upon a 'scaffold', but never calls him an 'actor' (*CW2*, 8).[1] *The Mirror for Magistrates* likens existence to a performance before God (*Mirror*, 'Buckingham', 43–9), but does not associate Richard with theatre. In *3 Henry VI*, however, Richard describes himself in terms that recall Elizabethan anti-player polemic – seductive mermaid, gaze-attracting basilisk, orator, deceptive Ulysses, treasonous Sinon, changeable chameleon, shape-shifting Proteus, murderous Machiavel (*3H6* 3.2.186–93).[2] *Richard III* surrounds him with theatrical self-references. Though such vocabulary is not unusual for Shakespeare or for his era, Richard gives these allusions particular resonance when he discusses acting techniques or likens himself to the stage figure polemic had warned theatre-goers they might become: 'you will learne to playe the vice' (Stubbes, L8^{v}).[3]

Richard's self-comparison to 'the formal Vice, Iniquity' and self-announced wordplay – 'Thus . . . I moralize two meanings in one word' (3.1.82–3) – invoke a stock character and his verbal tricks.[4] Besides his exuberantly stagey wit, Richard also shares the Vice's double relationship to the dramatic action, outside as commentator and inside as participant. He introduces the play with commentary on his appearance, plans and nature. He introduces action already under way: 'Plots have I laid, inductions dangerous' (1.1.32), he says; cue victim number one: Enter Clarence.

1 More's Latin *History* comes closer: '[Richard] could assume whatever mask it pleased him to wear and he played the part he had chosen with the utmost diligence' (*CW2*, 8; cf. *CW2*, 168).

2 *The Anatomie of Abuses* claims theatre teaches one 'to play the Hipocrit: to cogge, lye, and falsifie', to 'play ye Sodomits, or worse', to 'become a bawde, vncleane, and to deuerginat Mayds, to deflour honest Wyues . . . to murther, slaie, kill . . . to rebel against Princes, to co[m]mit treasons' (Stubbes, sig. L8^{v}). Henry VI invokes the Roman actor 'Roscius' when confronting Richard in his death 'scene' (*3H6* 5.6.10).

3 On Elizabethan theatrical terminology, see Righter, 89–95.

4 'Iniquity' is the Vice in *Nice Wanton* (1560; STC 25016) and *King Darius* (1565; STC 6277). Cf. Inclination's reversal of sense (*Trial of Treasure*, 1561; STC 24271, sig. D4^{v}).

Such an induction is unparalleled in Shakespeare, but well-anticipated elsewhere. The figure of Dissimulation opens Robert Wilson's *Three Ladies of London* (1584), explaining his disguise as an 'honest' farmer, boasting of his aspiring mind, clever plans and sophisticated amorality, while bragging that everybody, 'men women and children', knows him by his grotesque 'powle [head] and beard painted motley' (sigs A2^{v}–A3^{r}). We share a secret that is no secret: everyone knows Dissimulation to be dishonest, just as everyone, with the possible exception of 'simple, plain' Clarence and his children, knows Richard to be villainous. External signs – motley beard or twisted body – and frequent soliloquies (five in Richard's first three scenes) should keep us focused.[1] We know what he is, and the other characters should too.

The Vice's particoloured head, like the 'notorious identity' blazoned by Richard's bodily disproportions, invites us to 'epistemological self-assurance'.[2] We laugh with these figures as they name, expose and manipulate the weaknesses of others. This makes seduction scenes irresistibly ridiculous. Still wearing his goofy beard, Dissimulation woos Lady Love in the sequel to *Three Ladies*, even though she recognizes him as the 'monster' and 'Deuill' who has caused her 'sorrowes' (R. Wilson, sigs D2^{r}–D3^{v}). No matter, the seducer protests, because 'the griefe / that I thy friend sustaine for thy distresse' is great, and they move straight into wit combat:

> Dis. In thy affections I had once a place:
> loue. These fond affections wrought me foule disgrace,
> Dis. Ile make amends, if ought amisse were done:
> loue. Who once are burn'd, the fire will euer shun.
>
> (sig. D4^{v})

1 On the placement of Richard's early soliloquies and later asides, see MacDonald & MacDonald, 59–60.

2 Concerning audience self-assurance, see Maus, 54; on Richard's 'notorious identity', see Charnes, 20–70.

Sound familiar? The two lengthy wooing scenes in *Richard III* (1.2, 4.4) are wholly invented history but heavily derivative drama (S. Thomas, *Antic*, 30). Richard and Dissimulation share visual stigmata, extra-dramatic commentary, dissembling and witty dialogue. They also share topical functions. Dissimulation mocks contemporary pieties, for example, by calling his evil intentions 'inward zeale' (*Three Ladies*, sig. A3^r), invoking a buzzword associated with hotter Protestants that Buckingham uses in praising Richard's own 'right Christian zeal' (3.7.102). We are far from done with seduction or satiric topicality.

Murderous Machiavel

The Richard of the two early versions of *3 Henry VI* names villains he will outdo: 'murderous *Macheuill*' or 'aspiring *Catalin*'. The Roman Catiline, as Ben Jonson's play *Catiline, his Conspiracy* confirms, conjures up ambition pursued by factional politics. 'Machiavel' derives from Niccolò Machiavelli (1469–1527), notorious for the *realpolitik* analyses of *The Prince* (published 1532) and *Discourses* (published 1531) and object of countless denunciations.[1] The name 'Machiavel' furnished a catch-all for any devious foe, and embodied anxieties about religious and social disorder (Maus, 47).

Richard shares characteristics with this figure of the polemical imagination and the popular stage. Above all, he acts out in *Richard III* the ruthless, self-interested ambition implied in his earlier renunciation (*3H6* 5.6.80–3) of roles ascribed by family and society. A self-professed hypocrite, he mocks authority, holds conscience in contempt, treats religion as a functional tool and delights in strategic manipulation. While some of Richard's attitudes and practices are related to the rationalized power

1 Editions printed in England include John Wolfe's false-imprint Italian printings in the 1580s; Latin and French editions were available. Many Elizabethans acquired their opinions from Innocent Gentillet's *Discours . . . Contre Machiavel* (1576). See Meyer; Catherine Minshull, 'Marlowe's "Sound Machevill"', *Renaissance Drama*, 13 (1982), 35–53; Peter S. Donaldson, *Machiavelli and Mystery of State* (New York, 1982); N.W. Bawcutt, 'The "Myth of Gentillet" reconsidered: an aspect of Elizabethan Machiavellianism', *MLR*, 99 (2004), 863–74.

politics of Machiavelli's works, his more immediate ancestry appears in contemporary polemic and drama.[1] For instance, the Elizabethan divine Henry Smith imagines Machiavel's followers, his 'apes', pervading England with what Katherine Maus calls their 'sinister interiority' (Maus, 40):

> Oh, if Machauil had liued in our countrey, what a Monarch should he be? to what honour, and wealth, and power, and credite, might he haue risen vnto in short time, whether he had been a Lawier, or a Courtier, or a Prelate? me thinkes I see how many fingers woulde poynt at him in the streetes, as they doe at his apes, and say, there goeth a deepe fellowe, he hath more wit in his little finger then the rest in their whole bodie. You talke of Sectaries how fast they growe, and how fast they breed; I warrant you where any Sectary hath one sonne, Machauil hath a score, and those not the brats, but the fatlings of the Land, which if they had but a dram of religion for an ounce of their policie, they might goe like Saints among men.
>
> (Smith, *Sermons*, 420)

Machiavels frequented the stage in the early 1590s: Richard is anticipated in Kyd's Lorenzo (*The Spanish Tragedy*) and Marlowe's Barabas (*The Jew of Malta*).[2] All express the alienation of Richard's 'I am myself alone'. Kyd's Lorenzo proclaims, 'Ile trust my selfe, my selfe shalbe my freend' (*Spanish Tragedy*, 3.2.125).[3] Marlowe's Barabas announces, '*Ego mihimet sum semper*

1 On the figure's Machiavellian roots, see Margaret Scott, 'Machiavelli and the Machiavel', *Renaissance Drama*, 15 (1984), 147–74.

2 Henslowe records performances of *The Spanish Tragedy* in spring 1592 and of *The Jew of Malta* between February and June 1592 (Henslowe, 17, 170). 1591 also saw a play called 'Matchevell' (i.e. *Machiavel*) on Henslowe's stage. Jonathan Bate traces 'a direct line' from Marlowe through Aaron the Moor of *Titus Andronicus* to Richard III (Bate, *Tit*, 87–8).

3 Cf. *R3* 1.4.140–2, where the Second Murderer describes the man who would 'trust to himself'.

proximus' (*Jew of Malta*, 1.1.188).[1] All kill underlings, profess dissembling and boast of their politic strategy (*Jew of Malta*, 5.2.26–46, 110–23; *Spanish Tragedy*, 3.4.46).[2] Despite initial successes, all three come to confusion. However, Barabas and Richard differ from Lorenzo in the religious nature of their hypocrisy, in their revelation of systemic social corruption, in the sheer size of their roles and in their capacity to incite laughter.[3]

Barabas and Richard repeatedly invoke the Bible, lecture others on religious principles and offer 'counterfeit profession' of piety (*Jew of Malta*, 1.2.291–2), while mocking conscience (*Jew of Malta*, 1.1.118–20; *R3* 5.3.309–11) and charity (*Jew of Malta*, 2.3.29; *R3* 1.2.68–9). They also reveal faults in others: the brutality of Christian anti-semitism in *The Jew of Malta* (1.2.106–28) and the self-serving amorality of courtly culture in *Richard III*. Their humour, self-ridicule and ironic detachment differentiate them from truly Senecan villains (S. Thomas, *Antic*, 17). They revel in exaggerated performance, in speeches riddled with audience asides and in antics stretching to grotesque farce, as when Richard plays 'jolly thriving wooer', or Barabas a French musician, complete with lute, silly accent and poisoned flowers.

Deep tragedian

Richard III raises another theatrical option. As Richard and Buckingham plan to deceive the Londoners, they consider playing the 'deep tragedian':

RICHARD

Come, cousin, canst thou quake and change thy colour,
Murder thy breath in middle of a word,
And then again begin, and stop again,

1 Adopted from Terence, *Andria*, 'I am always nearest to myself'. Edward Meyer calls this 'the very pith and gist of all Machiavelli's teachings' (Meyer, 33).

2 Cf. *1H6* 5.3.74, where the phrase 'notorious Machiavel' suggests treachery, and *MW* 3.1.91, where the name denotes being 'politic' or 'subtle'.

3 Kyd's grotesque humour does not centrally involve the Machiavel.

As if thou were distraught and mad with terror?
BUCKINGHAM
Tut, I can counterfeit the deep tragedian,
Speak, and look back, and pry on every side,
Tremble and start at wagging of a straw,
Intending deep suspicion. Ghastly looks
Are at my service, like enforced smiles,
And both are ready in their offices,
At any time to grace my stratagems.
(3.5.1–11)

Does this passage evoke deportment truly appropriate to tragedy, or does it comment on the coarseness of the speakers or the naivety of their intended audience? Does it mock overacting or recommend melodramatic exaggeration?

Contemporary texts mock the overacting 'tragedian' who 'swell[s] / In forcèd passion of affected strains' (Marston, *2 Antonio and Mellida*, 2.3.109–10) or mimics Tamburlaine's 'high-set steps, and princely carriage', filling his 'wide-strained mouth' with 'Big sounding sentences, and words of state' (J. Hall, 8). Hamlet denounces 'overdone' word and action and the player who 'out-Herods Herod', that ranting figure of medieval drama (*Ham* 3.2.1–34). Heywood warns against 'oueracting trickes' (Heywood, *Apology*, sig. C4^{r}). Yet Shakespeare does take emotive signifiers seriously: Clarence's murderer has a 'pale' face and eyes that 'menace' (1.4.169; cf. *AYL* 4.4.168–70). Folio stage directions demand that characters '*start*' at news of Clarence's death (2.1.80 SD). Are Buckingham's prescribed histrionics so different from breast-beating or lip-gnawing (2.2.3, 4.2.27)? Vergil records Richard's lip-gnawing as habitual (227), though More describes him counterfeiting agitation by 'knitting the browes, frowning and froting and knawing on hys lippes' (*CW2*, 47). Othello gnaws his lip and rolls his eyes (*Oth* 5.2.38, 43); Wolsey 'bites his lip, and starts, / Stops on a sudden' (*H8* 3.2.113–14). So in theory Richard and Buckingham advocate suitably 'tragic' action; yet their sheer enjoyment in contemplating the performance suggests the play's oddly close conjoining of tragedy, melodrama and self-irony.

The Mirror for Magistrates articulates a relevant paradox concerning feigned emotions. Rivers should have known Richard false, since 'counterfayte' emotions inevitably overdo the 'naturall mean' to convey 'depe' feeling (*Mirror*, 'Rivers', 410–20). But Richard's performative inventiveness expressed in 'so many a fals device' (*Mirror*, 'Rivers', 424–7) overwhelmed Rivers's scepticism. The victims of Shakespeare's Richard similarly recognize his hostility, duplicity and artificial emotion, but suffer entrapment anyway. Richard's behaviour may be stylized 'performance' and recognized as such, but this does not preclude his successes or mean the play lacks depth, only that depth resides elsewhere than within the 'deep' subjectivity of character.

Some early defenders of the stage claimed that a player could create the convincing illusion of being 'the person personated' (Heywood, *Apology*, sig. C4^{r}). Similarly, some critics have judged *Richard III* 'the drama of consummate *acting*', asserting that 'Except to the audience, [Richard] is invisible' (Rossiter, 17–18), or that his roles are 'completely successful . . . manag[ing] to deceive virtually everyone' (Righter, 97).[1] In fact almost no one is completely fooled (Ornstein, 70–1; D.G. Watson, 102).[2] Consummate performance, however, need not be equated with illusionistic personation. In 1793 George Steevens praised the role of Richard for its dizzying variety, as 'perhaps beyond all others variegated' and comprehending 'a trait of almost every species of character on the stage. The hero, the lover,

1 Van Laan calls Richard a 'magnificent actor', but claims he offers 'melodrama' rather than a convincing portrayal of saintliness (Van Laan, 145, 135, 147).

2 Queen Elizabeth recognizes 'interior hatred' from Richard's 'outward action' (1.3.65–6). Margaret assesses him (1.3.220). His mother discusses his deceptions (2.2.27–32). Hastings recognizes risks in attending him (3.2.27–9). Buckingham wisely deserts (4.2.119–20); the princes scorn him (3.1.120–35); citizens judge him dangerous (2.3.27).

the statesman, the buffoon, the hypocrite, the hardened and repenting sinner &c.' (Vickers, 6.594). Actors have agreed with this assessment, but an early modern account of the historical Richard as 'playing' various roles also deserves attention. Sir Walter Raleigh's *History* defines Richard's 'playing' as ensemble work, enlisting others into his play through manipulation of their 'affection' and self-interest:

> Richard *the Third, the greatest Maister in mischiefe of . . . all that fore-went him: who although, for the necessity of his Tragedie, hee had more parts to play, and more to performe in his owne person, then all the rest; yet hee so well fitted euery affection that played with him, as if each of them had but acted his owne interest. For he wrought so cunningly vpon the affections of* Hastings, *and* Buckingham, *enemies to the Queene and to all her kindred, as hee easily allured them to condiscend, that* Riuers *and* Grey, *the Kings Maternall Vncle and halfe brother, should (for the first) be seuered from him: secondly, hee wrought their consent to haue them imprisoned, and lastly* [*(*] *for the auoyding of future inconvenience) to haue their heads seuered from their bodies.*
>
> (Raleigh, sigs A4^{v}–B1^{r})

Raleigh represents Richard working on desires, circumstances and agencies provided by his social world. This Richard is suggestive for Shakespeare's. Consider the wooing of Anne, a scene often taken as demonstrating either Richard's deceptive 'acting' or Anne's deficient 'character'.

Jolly thriving wooer

Responding in 1779 to neoclassical strictures about the 'vulgarity and even indecency' of the wooing scene, William Richardson defends it as an 'imitation . . . of Nature', given Anne's 'character'. Richard's 'perfect knowledge of her disposition' recognizes her weak principles, and 'vanity' as her 'over-ruling passion' (Vickers, 6.208–9). Such a reading (or its modern variants) focuses on the couple themselves, but in fact, as often, other characters awkwardly share the stage. These others also fall before Richard's onslaught, and not because they are immoral, vain or female.

In a play so dominated by Richard's body, that living symbol of period commonplaces about (mis)proportion and (dis)-order on the social, personal and species levels, the wooing reveals a remarkable disjunction between the body social and the body physical. Fresh from pronouncing himself physically disempowered, Richard proves prodigiously powerful when he – alone, lame, with a withered arm and a single sword – halts a heavily armed procession and disarms a halberdier whose weapon points at his chest:

RICHARD
Villains, set down the corse, or by Saint Paul,
I'll make a corse of him that disobeys.

GENTLEMAN
My lord, stand back and let the coffin pass.

RICHARD
Unmannered dog, stand thou when I command!
Advance thy halberd higher than my breast,
Or by Saint Paul I'll strike thee to my foot
And spurn upon thee, beggar, for thy boldness.
(1.2.36–42)

This is not 'acting' – Richard could hardly convey a physical capacity to strike down and spurn the lot of them – but it is performance. As such it recalls unarmed Talbot suddenly revealing his corporate 'substance' by summoning his hidden troops (*1H6* 2.3); but Richard's strength lies in the power of hierarchy and religion, not in armour or troops.

Richard and the halberdier replay a nightmare version of a scenario moralized in contemporary polemic. To explain why multitudes have 'humbled themselues' before Queen Elizabeth, a 1589 tract adduces her miraculous control over her 'big bodied Holberders'. Any minute, they might 'bende euery man the point of his Holberde at her', but 'the Religion of the land' causes a 'sweet harmonie of peoples harts that remaine faithful and flexible to the shaking of her princely finger' (*2 Pasquill*, sig. B1$^{r–v}$). No simple piety, or not simply piety, disarms Richard's opponents, since they appear initially bound to Anne's own religious undertaking before they give in. But give in to what? Richard is greater in substance than simply his own muscle or an armed company would suggest. Onstage he kills no one, no armed cohort supports him, except dubiously at Bosworth, where mental 'shadows' prove more powerful than the 'substance of ten thousand soldiers' (5.3.216–18). Rather, he manages to enlist, almost magically, the power of the legitimate social order's demands for obedience and deference to hierarchy even while ruthlessly violating such demands himself. The moral 'villain' here shamelessly performs his own status, reducing Anne's troupe to social '[v]illains', 'beggar[s]' (1.2.36, 42) and finally lackeys who try to anticipate his desires (1.2.228–9). Fittingly, Richard invokes Saint Paul, the apostle identified with 'obedience to authority' (*STM*, 2.3.101; cf. *R3* 1.2.36n.).[1] No one need be completely duped to become 'Grossly . . . captive' (4.1.79) to the powers his performances enlist.

'Captivation' provides an approximate term for this process, but the powers Richard wields are not simply matters of hereditary status, religion or faction. Clarity of motive empowers him. When he has the sheer nerve to literalize the hoariest Petrarchan cliché by kneeling and '*lay*[ing] *his breast open*' to his lady's fatal blow (1.2.181 SD), he offers 'revenge' but 'in terms that render it farcically irrelevant' (Neill, 104). Killing would only grant the abject lover his wish. Anne 'falls to Richard precisely because she is *not* deceived, because (as he intends) she

1 Romans, 13.1–5, commanding subjection to authority, is frequently invoked; cf. Perkins, *Works*, 48.

is bowled over by the nerve, the *sprezzatura*, of that performance itself' (Neill, 104). She never takes back her epithets – devil, minister of hell, villain, murderer – and submits with 'Arise, dissembler' (1.2.187). It is not that 'Richard's amorality matters little to her' (D.G. Watson, 104), because in fact, it does matter; it is his *morality* that matters little. Michael Neill's 'ostentatious theatricality' and 'compelling staginess' seem appropriate, but there is more to say, even if Anne never says it, about the social bases for his successes.

Richard '*so well fitted euery affection that playd with him, as if each of them had but acted his owne interest*' (Raleigh, *History*, sig. A4^{v}). Anne never articulates her '*owne interest*', but Queen Elizabeth defines the fearful position of a noble woman without a husband and clarifies the (unremarked) security Richard offers: 'If [Edward] were dead,' Elizabeth demands, 'what would betide on me? . . . The loss of such a lord includes all harms' (1.3.6–8).[1] Systemic female vulnerability surely contributes to Richard's power. So does faction: Richard played upon the '*affections*' of Hastings and Buckingham as '*enemies to the Queene and to all her kindred*', Raleigh writes. Self-alienated from his own family, Richard, himself alone, measures exactly how others intersect and interact as families and groups. Thus his pious rebuff to Margaret – 'God, not we, hath plagued thy bloody deed' (1.3.180) – instantly enlists bitterly divided opponents into a supporting chorus, suddenly united, like Anne's armed entourage, behind him.

Finally, the play develops one other factor in Richard's power: religious hypocrisy. When he lays open his breast, whatever his (unspoken) sense of Anne's (unacknowledged) vulnerability as unprotected female or as disempowered family

1 Cf. Camille Wells Slights, *The Casuistical Tradition in Shakespeare, Donne, Herbert, and Milton* (Princeton, NJ, 1981), 75. Concerning the basis of the historical union, see Kendall, 105–9 (love); C. Ross, *Richard*, 27–8 (status and wealth); the Crowland Continuator (in J.L. Laynesmith, *The Last Medieval Queens: English Queenship 1445–1503* (Oxford, 2004), 70) (property interests). In 1474 the Italian Christofforo di Bollato reports that Richard wed Anne 'by force' (Laynesmith, 70).

member, Richard counts on her having limits and being ignorant of exactly where those limits lie. He routinely flouts eternal damnation by blasphemously invoking Christian virtues and transgressing Christian commandments, while others, to varying degrees, appear subject to limits.[1] Anne can no more kill a disarmed kneeling suitor than, for similarly unspoken reasons of latent principle or repugnance, Buckingham can kill the princes. Lesser agents undertake or subcontract such unspeakable acts, but the warrior elite of the *Henry VI* plays does not furnish their number. Times have changed since the days of bloody Clifford, and ultimately Richard enacts a micro-version of the historical phenomenon known as bastard feudalism, paying clowns, boys and marginal hangers-on to get the dirtier jobs done – offstage. One stabbing (1.4), one severed head (3.5) and one death in battle (5.4) are nothing to the mayhem of earlier histories; instead, this play abounds in complicitous nobles and clerics who are, like Anne, passively compromised. Their motto might be her self-exculpating formula, 'To take is not to give' (1.2.205) – as if acquiescence did not entail volition and, ultimately, accountability. For the smaller fry who take what Richard has on offer – the bishops, the Mayor, clerics like Dr Shaw and others – Brakenbury provides a rationale: 'I will not reason what is meant hereby / Because I will be guiltless from the meaning' (1.4.93–4). So would we all, if life or this play allowed. Here too resides a source of Richard's power.

Richard's performances are highly theatrical, but the nature of their taking power is under-articulated. We are prompted to marvel at his sheer audacity, his clarity of motive, his ruthless exploitation of the factional and ideological limits that constrain others, his watchful alertness among half-conscious sleep-walkers, egotists, blinkered factionalists and time-servers. Richard may halt, but his social command is deft. The Scrivener puts it succinctly: 'Who is

1 With the possible exception of Margaret. For Richard's relation to the forms he flouts, see William C. Carroll, 'Desacralization and succession in *Richard III*', *Deutsche Shakespeare Gesellschaft West*, *Jahrbuch* (1991), 82–96.

so gross / That cannot see this palpable device? / Yet who so bold but says he sees it not?' (3.6.10–12).

Tell-tale women and tender babes

Well, some do speak up. Female characters, including the unhistorical Margaret, speak approximately twenty-two per cent of *Richard III* (Howard & Rackin, 217–18). Prominence does not simply equate with empowerment, of course, but the words 'mother' and 'children' (and cognates) are more numerous than in any other Shakespeare play, and that suggests something important. Sometimes desired, the women are more often resented, mocked, manipulated and marginalized. Janet Adelman finds Shakespeare's first history plays move women 'from positions of power and authority to positions of utter powerlessness, and finally moves them off the stage altogether' (Adelman, 9). Phyllis Rackin observes that the active female characters are negatively depicted, while 'The more sympathetically depicted female characters, such as the victimized women in *Richard III*, never go to war, they play no part in the affairs of state, and they seem to spend most of their limited time on stage in tears' (Rackin, 75–6; cf. Howard & Rackin, 98). These otherwise accurate assessments fail to link female tears to railing, lamentation and cursing, utterances that indeed constitute 'affairs of state'.

The females of *Richard III* appear more choric than active. Margaret, who was boldly erotic, political and military in Shakespeare's *Henry VI* plays, becomes a mouthpiece for passionate exclamations. Margaret Beaufort, who historically furthered both her son's marriage to Elizabeth of York and his English campaign, appears only in references to Richmond's 'mother' or the 'wayward' or sick 'wife' whom Stanley excuses (1.3.20–9) and to whom he must 'look' (4.2.91). The notorious Jane Shore is the unseen object of snide jokes (1.1.93–102) and ridiculous accusations (3.4.67–74). Finally, scenes that could have sympathetically represented female emotion are often treated ironically or omitted (contrast *CW2*, 41), contributing to the play's general avoidance of pathos (A.W. Schlegel, in Bate, *Romantics*, 506). But if 'tenderness of heart' and 'effeminate remorse' are mocked and debased (3.7.209–10), lament, denunciation and curse comprise a powerful female idiom of bitter tears (G. Bloom, 92–4).

Initially, female lamentations, curses and denunciations are isolated, ineffective, even laughable. Anne's laments and curses so quickly change to murmured submission that Richard's delight at female fickleness (1.2.230–2) and her shame at her 'woman's heart' (4.1.78–80) seem validated.[1] It is difficult to resist laughter when Richard's wisecracks cause Margaret to breathe her own 'curse against [herself]' (1.3.230–9). Queen Elizabeth and the Duchess of York become blackly comic as they contest for pre-eminence in grief, only to be rebuffed by Clarence's insolent orphans (2.2.62–5). Yet ultimately, female outbursts convey compelling truths, and the women themselves bond in something larger than self-interest. Even Margaret wins grudging respect.

In a remarkable moment of unity despite factionalism and self-interest, Anne, Queen Elizabeth and the Duchess of York join to denounce Richard, affirm love for the princes and demand their mutual right. Under an expanded definition of 'mother' they oppose Richard's representative:

QUEEN ELIZABETH
. . . I am their mother. Who shall bar me from them?

DUCHESS
I am their father's mother. I will see them.

ANNE
Their aunt I am in law, in love their mother.
Then bring me to their sights. I'll bear thy blame
And take thy office from thee, on my peril.

(4.1.21–5)

1 Though Anne's curse upon any woman who might marry Richard (1.2.26–8) would register prophetically, if not quite accurately in details, with the audience, as it later does with her (4.1.73–84).

Here for the first time motherhood combines rather than divides; being a mother, even if only in feeling ('in love'), trumps self-interest.[1] Affirming this bond empowers an activism that contrasts the women with those who would remain 'guiltless from the meaning' of the wrongs they allow and perpetrate: Brakenbury (1.4.94), the First Murderer (1.4.167), the Cardinal (3.1.57), the witnesses of Hastings's assassination (3.4.78).[2] The women embrace the consequences of doing what is right. Nor is their act of *speaking* negligible.

In this light, Margaret's attainment of one title denied by her mockers acquires particular importance. She never resumes the title 'Queen', but words win her another title. Instead of 'witch' or 'frantic curs[ing]' madwoman (1.3.163, 246), Margaret is ultimately validated as 'prophetess' (1.3.300, 5.1.27) of God's justice (5.1.20). This might appear small consolation, since 'the politically astute Margaret of the early play becomes "poor Margaret . . . prophetess". The curse of the scold is feared . . . as the records of the witch-trials remind us, but it achieves nothing.'[3] Yet the play opens with the deadly effects of 'prophecies, libels and dreams' (1.1.33) and concludes with an armed tyrant shaken by a 'prophet', a dream and a libel (4.2.94–105; 5.3.177–206, 303–5). The roles of 'prophetess' and 'mother' may have power against murderers and tyrants; even dreams may count.[4] A mother's curse could be terrible, as James I warned his son: 'the blessing or curse of the Parents, hath almost euer a Propheticke power ioyned with it' (James I, 44). Nor is it clear that a 'scold' necessarily 'achieves nothing'.

1 Nicole Loraux, *Mothers in Mourning*, trans. Corinne Pache (Ithaca, NY, 1998), 3. See also Doris Märtin, *Shakespeares 'Fiend-like Queens'* (Heidelberg, 1992), 71–82.

2 Cf. Madonne M. Miner, '"Neither mother, wife, nor England's Queen": the roles of women in *Richard III*', in Carolyn Ruth Swift Lenz, Gayle Greene and Carol Thomas Neely (eds), *The Woman's Part* (Urbana, Ill., 1980), 35–55.

3 Lisa Jardine, *Still Harping on Daughters* (Brighton, 1983), 118; cf. Marcus, 94; contrast Kathryn Schwarz, *Tough Love: Amazon Encounters in the English Renaissance* (Durham, NC, 2000), 104.

4 'Dream' (with cognates) also occurs more often in *Richard III* than in any other Shakespeare play; see Marvin Spevack, *A Complete and Systematic Concordance to the Works of Shakespeare* (Hildesheim, 1968–80).

Margaret's authority should not be overstated. True, she resembles Richard in her imposing, extra-dramatic, solo pronouncements: compare her 'induction' and entry prompt 'now' (4.4.1–8) with Richard's opening (1.1.1–40; cf. Hodgdon, *End*, 107–8). Yet despite her eerie appearances and disappearances – manifesting herself invisibly, pronouncing judgement, engaging, then 'withdraw[ing]' (4.4.8, 125) with impunity from a world that others traverse or escape with difficulty – and despite the preponderant accuracy of her predictions, Margaret speaks neither for God nor for Tudor history, at least not entirely. Her prognostications are only absolutely accurate when they concern the violent ends of violent men and the 'course of justice' (4.4.105). Any Elizabethan would have recognized the accurate dooms she pronounces for Richard and his cronies, as well as her general homiletic orthodoxy. But Elizabethans would also have perceived her glaring errors. Above all, Queen Elizabeth will *not* end up childless (1.3.203–8), and her child will wed Richmond, a figure Margaret apparently knows nothing about, to found the Tudor dynasty (Brooks, 'Unhistorical', 727). Margaret also wrongly predicts that Richard's most fearful dream will be (as in the sources) a 'hell of ugly devils' (1.3.226). Her foresight is limited to commonplace notions of divine retributive justice and earthly mutability: the violent shall die violently (5.1.23–4), the mighty shall fall (3.4.95–100), the evil shall torment one another here (2.1.14–15) and be tormented by devils hereafter. She is no mouthpiece for Tudor providentialism, nor does she recognize the power of empathy. Any ethical or political vision transcending feudal clan loyalties and competitive grudges lies beyond her. She may eerily anticipate the new king's words for Richard, 'The bloody dog is dead' (4.4.78, 5.5.2), but she perceives neither the power of hope that Richmond embodies (5.2.23–4, 5.3.173) nor the power of victims who curse, frighten or bless.

Attributing power to victims is not mere sentimentality. More claims that after the princes' deaths Richard 'neuer hadde quiet in his minde, hee neuer thought himself sure' (*CW2*, 87) because the murders caused political insecurity. Killing competitors and claimants was hardly unusual, but 'having Hastings, Rivers, Vaughan and Grey put to death in 1483 was not usual late fifteenth-century violence' (Gillingham, 13; cf. Bellamy, 215).[1] Child murder carried particular stigma.[2] Early chroniclers compared the princes to the innocents slaughtered by Herod, a biblical analogy fraught with peril for perpetrators; rulers apparently postponed judgement and execution of underage pretenders and rebels until they were old enough no longer to be perceived as innocent children (Gillingham, 14; Pollard, 136–8). The treatment of the death of Rutland (historically seventeen years old) as the murder of an 'innocent child' (*3H6* 1.3.8; cf. *R3* 1.2.160–1, 1.3.176–93, 4.4.45) reflects an assessment of violence against children as being so heinous as to cause 'Tyrants themselves' to weep and all men to 'prophe[sy] revenge for it' (1.3.184–5).[3] Richard's crime against the 'little souls' prompts his own mother to regret not having aborted him (4.4.192, 138). Historically, the degree of Richard's guilt mattered less than the political significance of evident facts: 'Because he had deposed his nephew, usurped his throne, shut him and his brother in prison in the Tower and took no steps whatsoever to demonstrate to the world that they were still alive, Richard was believed to have killed them. Because they were innocent children, not adults who had offended, his crime was judged to be even worse' (Pollard, 138). Across multiple lines of alliance and antagonism, continental contemporaries expressed condemnation (Gillingham, 16–17). In London men wept openly (Mancini, 93).

1 John G. Bellamy, *The Law of Treason in England in the Later Middle Ages* (Cambridge, 1970).

2 The princes were eleven and thirteen in 1483; the play accentuates their youthfulness (4.1.97–102); cf. 'tender' George Stanley (5.3.95).

3 Cf. the 'pretie innocents' murdered in Robert Yarington's *Two Lamentable Tragedies* (1601; STC 26076) by hired killers who fall out like the murderers of Clarence (1.4), and the ballad 'The Children in the Wood' (Stationers' Register, 15 October 1595; Var, 611–17). Cf. Wiggins, 116–21.

Such public outbursts were political. They could crystallize opinion, incite violence or prompt powerful figures to capitalize on them. Richard rightly fears that citizens might 'wail [Hastings's] death' (3.5.61), as in other plays rulers fear similar outbursts (*Tit* 4.4.1–26; *Ham* 4.3.4–7; *R2* 1.4.24–36). Without a standing army or professional police, Richard's authority, like that of subsequent Tudor monarchs, depended on a widespread conviction of his sanctity and power.[1] Thus denunciations, prophecies or curses were actionable. If three or more people publicly joined in an outcry, furthermore, the complaint could be construed as riot, a term which, William Lambarde suggested, 'signifieth to braule, or scolde' (Lambarde, 175). Passionate outcries directed at a monarch constituted grounds for prosecution as treason.[2] Although Tudor regimes repeatedly modified fourteenth-century definitions, enactments until the early seventeenth century included 'treason by words', which embraced name-calling – 'calling the king (or his heirs) a heretic, tyrant, schismatic, infidel or usurper' – and 'prophecies foretelling the future, whereby the king's death, deposition or incapacity were predicted'.[3] The name-calling and prophecies of the play's women constitute treasonous acts (4.4.136–96). This is hardly domestic 'scolding', but women who did 'Rail on the Lord's anointed' (4.4.151) were partly shielded by a gendered presumption.[4]

Were they not female, the railing mothers would be risking death alongside those men who balk even slightly at Richard's tyranny. However, his petulant responses to 'tell-tale women',

1 See Carole Levin, '"We shall never have a merry world while the Queene lyveth": gender, monarchy and the power of words', in Julia M. Walker (ed.), *Dissing Elizabeth: Negative Representations of Gloriana* (Durham, NC, 1998), 79.

2 For public outcry and mourning by Londoners, see Archer, 33.

3 See John G. Bellamy, *The Tudor Law of Treason* (1979), 51–2.

4 So, for example, one woman punished for publicly ridiculing a bishop in the Vestiarian controversy of 1566–7 was set upon a cucking-stool, but continued rejoicing in her 'lewd behavior' (Martin Ingram, '"Scolding women cucked or washed": a crisis in gender relations in early modern England?', in Jennifer Kermode and Garthine Walker (eds), *Women, Crime and the Courts in Early Modern England* (Chapel Hill, NC, 1994), 61).

ordering flourishes and drums to drown their 'impatience', bluntly refusing to listen, mocking his mother's emotional 'condition' while urging his own martial affairs, suggest comic trivialization, as if it were all merely female temper, best dealt with by condescension and getting on with more important business (4.4.149–80). This refusal to take women seriously resembles the treatment historically accorded female agency, but presumptions of reduced agency could also lessen criminal culpability. William Lambarde criticizes the legal ambiguity surrounding indictment of women for breach of the peace without a person of 'discretion' – i.e. an adult male – to blame for instigating their actions (Lambarde, 179; Houlbrooke, 182).

The prominence of female 'prophets' and 'petitioners' in public outcries directed at authority from the time of Henry VIII through to the time of the English Civil War suggests a potential strength in presumed weakness. Some action consisted of quietly pursued resolution, as in recusant women's refusal to participate in prescribed worship (Willen, 154); other acts were public and/or collective. Women participated in a range of causes, from confrontation with Anne Boleyn in 1531 (Capp, 138–9) to grain and anti-enclosure riots in the early seventeenth century (Houlbrooke, 176–83).[1] Religious controversy prompted public demonstrations: in assemblies during the Vestiarian controversies of the 1560s (Collinson, *Puritan*, 93; Houlbrooke, 176) or in distributing the Marprelate tracts in the 1580s (Willen, 146). Individuals spoke out, as did Margaret Lawson who confronted Bishop John Aylmer, aided the Hackett conspirators in 1591 (Walsham, 34) and, for 'the immodestie of her tongue' (Cooper, 39), became notorious as the muse of Marprelate's invective (*Almond*, sig. B1^{r}), 'the shrew at Pauls Gate / and enemie to all dumb dogs and tyrannical prelates' (Marprelate, *Epistle*, 9–10). In the 1640s collective female petitioning and prophecy became

1 Bernard Capp, 'Separate domains? Women and authority in early modern England', in Paul Griffiths, Adam Fox and Steve Hindle (eds), *The Experience of Authority in Early Modern England* (New York, 1996).

major political phenomena.[1] Such evidence complicates gendered limits: Phyllis Mack has argued that the socially attributed 'female' qualities of passivity, irrationality and passion which justified exclusion from authority could sometimes confer a power of their own in public outcry or prophecy.[2]

Ever so briefly, female agency in *Richard III* assumes collective form; female public outcry against Richard differs from the actions of the individual women warriors, witches and seductresses in the *Henry VI* plays. Their 'woman's war', directing the 'bitter clamour of . . . eager tongues' (*R2* 1.1.48–9) against Richard, constitutes more open resistance than anyone else manages before Richmond's invasion. In *Richard III*, as Gilles Deleuze says, 'the women do battle for themselves'.[3] Their outburst contrasts with the silence of common Londoners (3.7.3), of clerics (3.4) and of nobles such as Stanley (4.4.491–3). Their 'complaint' adapts the medieval '*ubi sunt*' ('where be?') mutability trope to demand temporal answers. A lyrical form expressing passive loss becomes public indictment.[4] They name names and irritate, even frighten, the killer before his own men (4.4). Nor do their demands for accountability stop at missing relatives: even 'kind Hastings' gets remembered among the disappeared (4.4.148). There is more.

Sustaining the emotional momentum of this joint outcry, Richard's own mother calls down the guilty memories that will vex his ultimate dream, cursing him with a tormenting vision very different from the demons that Margaret or the sources predict (4.4.191–4).[5] Not devils, but innocent victims

1 See Keith Thomas, 'Women and the Civil War sects', *Past & Present*, 13 (1958), 42–57.

2 Phyllis Mack, 'Women as prophets during the English Civil War', *Feminist Studies*, 8 (1982), 19–45.

3 Gilles Deleuze, 'One manifesto less', in Constantin Boundas (ed.), *The Deleuze Reader* (New York, 1993), 205.

4 Cf. the identification of the play's female utterance with Ovidian complaint (Bate, *Ovid*, 66–7).

5 The 'images like terrible diuels, which pulled and haled' Richard, go back to Vergil, and appear in Hall, Grafton and Holinshed (see 5.3.117.1n.); cf. Stephen Batman, *The Doom Warning all Men to the Judgement* (1581; STC 1582), 281.

and 'friends' will haunt him. Furthermore, Queen Elizabeth manages, unlike Anne, to overrule a 'woman's heart' (4.1.78) and, contradicting the sources, says 'not now' to Richard's proposal while meaning 'never', despite his perverse appeals to her as his 'mother' (4.4.315–17).[1] To dismiss these female accusations and negotiations is to underestimate the strength and strategic cunning necessary to resist a tyrant. That Queen Elizabeth accuses and temporizes with the devil himself while avoiding cursing is also revealing. Her resolute critique logically deprives Richard of grounds for oaths and eventually gets him, in frustration, to curse himself (Birney, 36–42; 4.4.399–405n.). Her careful treading marks this scene as different from all other encounters with Richard.

Unlike Shakespeare's Lucrece, whose laments and curses this scene echoes, Elizabeth acknowledges words as means of aggression and self-consolation (4.4.116–17, 130–1) rather than as pointless wind (*Luc* 1027, 1330); she does not curse the tyrant with 'Himself himself' confound (*Luc* 998), but cleverly allows Richard his 'Myself myself confound' (4.4.399). Violated Lucrece, in keeping with the popular genre of female complaint, lyrically expresses the lonely pathos of self-punishment; she submits to the definition of pollution determined by the male order, leaving death her only 'remedy' (*Luc* 1028–9). If political implications are to be drawn from her suicide, men must draw them, or, as nearly happens, not draw them (*Luc* 1730–855).[2]

By contrast with Lucrece, Joan and the Margaret of the *Henry VI* plays, Elizabeth and the Duchess neither kill themselves, lead armies nor direct campaigns. But they turn the stereotypes allotted them – as impatient (1.3.1) 'indirect and peevish' (3.1.31),

1 For reactions to Queen Elizabeth's supposed co-operation with Richard, see 4.4.426–31n.

2 On the political implications of female literary complaint in the 1590s, cf. Hallett Smith, *Elizabethan Poetry* (Cambridge, Mass., 1952), 102–30, with Heather Dubrow, 'A mirror for complaints: Shakespeare's *Lucrece* and generic tradition', in Barbara K. Lewalski (ed.), *Renaissance Genres: Essays on Theory, History and Interpretation* (Cambridge, Mass., 1986), 399–417.

petulant in 'condition' (4.4.158–9), 'lunatic' (1.3.253), 'frantic' (1.3.246), 'wayward' (1.3.29) or 'shallow, changing' (4.4.431) – to use against the tyrant. An analogous use of advantage appears in the right of childish outspokenness that the princes exercise in 'taunt and scorn' described as 'all the mother's' (3.1.153–6). This mother (whom Richard will perversely urge to be his own 'mother'), his biological mother and Margaret Beaufort, Stanley's 'wife' and Richmond's 'mother', do what they can with the licence allowed them, even if, like Stanley, they cannot do what they will (5.3.91). If, unlike Stanley, they openly oppose tyranny, the likelihood of their being 'put to silence' (*JC* 1.2.285) is lessened by gendered attitudes.

Finally, it is important to note an agency falsely attributed to the women. The charge of witchcraft against Queen Elizabeth and Jane Shore is laughable (*R3* 3.4.67–71; More *CW2*, 48). But the historical Richard officially accused Elizabeth of witchcraft, and the earlier histories portrayed 'real' conjurers, spirits, witches and witchcraft (*1H6* 5.3; *2H6* 1.4). Margaret's 'charms' *mostly* come to pass.[1] Does this make her what Richard calls her?

Thomas Cooper puts the positive case: 'When a bad-tongued woman shall curse a party, and death shall shortly follow, this is a shrewd token that she is a witch' (K. Thomas, 512). However, Reginald Scot sceptically dismisses 'witch' as a social slur based on the appearance and characteristic utterance of lonely, enfeebled old women, the guilty consciences of the community and the inevitable misfortunes of earthly circumstance. Those called witches, Scot claims, are 'commonly old, lame, bleare-eied, pale, fowle, and full of wrinkles; poore, sullen, superstitious, and papists' (Scot, sig. C3^{r}). Their 'chief fault', Scot maintains, 'is that they are scolds' (sig. E1^{v}). Responding to abuses and slights real or imagined, the characteristically accusatory utterances of the 'scold', much like Margaret's own, could sound like or

1 For the charge against Elizabeth, see the 1483 Parliamentary text 'Titulus Regius' accusing her of bewitching Edward into marriage (*Rotuli Parliamentorum*, ed. J. Strachey (1776–7), 6.240–1).

become in fact curses. Denied respect, aid and sustenance 'the witch waxeth odious and tedious to hir neighbors' until 'in processe of time they haue all displeased hir, and she hath wished euill lucke unto them all; perhaps with curses and imprecations made in forme. Doubtlesse (at length) some of hir neighbours die, or fall sick' (sig. C4^{v}).[1] It takes a community to make a 'foul, wrinkled witch' – or a tyrant. If ever a community deserved a Margaret or a Richard, it is the England of this play.

CO-TEXTS: INVECTIVE, SATIRE, LIBEL

Along with 'dream', 'mother' and 'children', which appear more frequently in *Richard III* than in any other Shakespeare play, the word 'news' occurs many times – in frequency second only to its appearance in *2 Henry IV*. Understanding of the play can be enhanced by considering not only its pre-history in sources and analogues and post-history in reception and performance, but also its co-history of articulation in the early 1590s. Literary and ideological 'backgrounds', 'sources' or 'origins' (Tillyard; Churchill; Jones, *Origins*) scarcely exhaust the discursive environment of its shaping.

Richard III shares its language and protagonist with a vast tide of contemporary polemic and invective (Simpson; Campbell, 321). The historical Richard provided material for mudslingers of every stripe. The texts involved include the most widely known of the period. *Leicester's Commonwealth* (*The Copy of a Letter Written by a Master of Arts of Cambridge*) (1584), for example, a benchmark character assassination, invokes Richard to denounce the Earl of Leicester. Similarly, the work popularly termed *The Papists' Commonwealth* (*A Treatise of Treasons*) (1572), which troubled the Privy Council for decades, devotes twenty pages to 'infinit resemblances' between Richard's

1 For disputes concerning the 'scapegoat' theory of witchcraft, see *Witchcraft in Early Modern Europe*, ed. Jonathan Barry, Marianne Hester and Gareth Roberts (Cambridge, 1996), 1–45.

England and the 'Machiauellian State' under Elizabeth I's chief counsellor, William Cecil, Lord Burghley, an 'vnknowen Traitour . . . taken for the chiefe and most lawful Gouernour' (*Treatise*, 'Preface', sig. 121r). The incendiary classic *A Conference about the Next Succession* (1595) cites the deposing of Richard to urge Englishmen to determine royal succession (Parsons, pt 1, 61). There is much more.

Anti-Cecil discourse peaked dramatically in 1591–2, the years of the elevation of Burghley's son to the Privy Council, with the text called *Burghley's Commonwealth* (*A Declaration of the True Causes of the Great Troubles*) (1592) and *An Aduertisement Written to a Secretary* (1592). Both attack Burghley for the anti-Catholic Royal Proclamations of October 1591.[1] Furthermore, over the following twenty years, manuscript libels compared Robert Cecil to Richard, demanding: 'Richard, or Robert, wch is the worse? / A Crooktback great in state is Englands curse' (Bod. Tanner MS 299, fol. 13r). Richard's ambition, strategic villainy and bodily configuration suggested comparison with a younger son who rose despite physical limitations to vast power and authority amid factionalized politics.[2]

Richard also appears in anti-Catholic works such as George Whetstone's *The English myrror* (1586), which compares the Pope, 'the Archtyrant of the earth', to 'our arch tyraunt', Richard III, 'manifest monster' and 'sonne of the diuel' (Whetstone, 96, 116–17, 9). Furthermore, just beyond direct reference, various texts levy charges of ambition, factional manipulation, religious hypocrisy and physical deformity in vocabulary and in style

1 *Tudor Royal Proclamations*, ed. Paul L. Hughes and James F. Larkin, 3 vols (New Haven, Conn., 1964–9), 3.86–95. On the affair and on Robert Parsons's Latin *Responsio*, see Victor Houliston, 'The Lord Treasurer and the Jesuit: Robert Persons's satirical *Responsio* to the 1591 Proclamation', *Sixteenth Century Journal*, 32 (2001), 383–401.

2 The most widely known of relevant Cecil materials, Bacon's 'Of Deformity', does not invoke Richard III, but its treatment of the strengths, advantages and strategies incumbent upon disability is revealing (see Bacon, *Works*, 6.480–1; cf. James Siemon, 'Sign, cause or general habit: toward an "historicist ontology" of character on the early modern stage', in Hugo Keiper, Christopher Bode and Richard J. Utz (eds), *Nominalism and Literary Discourse: New Perspectives* (Amsterdam, 1998), 237–50.

shared with the play. Pre-eminent among these are the pro- and anti-Episcopal writings of the Marprelate controversy (1589–90), which in turn shaped the 'prophecies' and 'libells' of the Hackett rebellion (July 1591) on behalf of reformers imprisoned by Archbishop Whitgift, and which ultimately anticipated the Elizabethan satirical vogue.[1] Furthermore, the contemporary 'invention' of the stereotypical 'Puritan' also casts light on aspects of Shakespeare's play and protagonist.

Excellent grand tyrant of the earth or lump of foul deformity

Any Elizabethan would know the 'deformed and ill shaped' Richard III for a 'cruell murtherer, a wretched caitiffe, a moste tragicall tyraunt, and blood succour [sucker], bothe of his nephewes, and brother' (Rainolde, sig. D1[r]). The first theatre-goers might have been surprised by *how* 'ill shaped' Shakespeare's Richard is and by *how much* everyone carries on about it. They might also have been surprised to find that, amid the play's 'violent and vituperative speech' (Chambers, *Shakespeare*, 1.302), Richard himself weeps, sighs, 'play[s] the saint', meekly endures insults and quotes scripture. The violent abuse directed at Richard and his own hypocritical piety and arch foolery carry contemporary polemical resonance.

On the one hand, insults inflate Richard to cosmic dimensions; on the other, they reduce him to subhuman triviality. As 'grand tyrant of the earth' he shares epithets with world-class enemies like the Pope or Philip II of Spain; all three are declared a scourge of God to punish sinful humanity, or even the Antichrist himself – a figure who, it is prophesied, will end creation with 'tyranny and all-embracing persecution, and . . . a mocking and counterfeit religiosity'.[2] Identifying Richard with this

1 For the Hackett rebellion, see Walsham. On the nine figures imprisoned around London, see Collinson, 412–31. The imprisonments were 'so taken to heart; amongst the reforming and zealous brotherhood' as to threaten armed reaction (Bancroft, *Positions*, 146), 338

2 See Stuart Clark, *Thinking with Demons: The Idea of Witchcraft in Early Modern Europe* (Oxford, 1997), 338.

satanic charlatan goes back to John Rous (Hanham, 123–4). But the play's 'devil' (1.2.45), 'cacodemon' (1.3.143) 'hell-hound' (4.4.48), hell's 'minister' (1.2.46), 'son of hell' (1.3. 229), hell's 'factor' (4.4.72), 'hell's black intelligencer' (4.4.71) and 'God's enemy' (5.3.252) is also reductively called 'dog' (1.3.215, 4.4.49, 5.5.2), 'spider' (1.3.241), 'abortive, rooting hog' (1.3.227), 'wolf' (4.4.23), 'toad' (4.4.81), 'Fool' (5.3.192), 'Vice' (3.1.82), 'villain-slave' (4.4.144) and 'lump of foul deformity' (1.2.57). This polarized lexicon has antecedents in treatments of Satan in the Bible or medieval drama, but it also echoes contemporary polemical usage.

Protestants attacked both the Pope and the King of Spain as 'Archtyrant of the earth' (Whetstone, 96; *Declaration*, 76), but also, reductively, compared 'Antichrist' to a 'cocke, w^{t} neuer a feather on her back' or a mouse-like abortive fetus (Whetstone, 121, 123, 159–60). Philip, 'Tyrant of Spayne', father of 'Monsters', 'horrible and hiddious', begetter of 'ignorance, malice, deceit, guile, hypocrisie, robbing, theft, incest, feigned Religion, all kinde of execrations, murder sacrilidge and parracide', is also an 'olde Foxe' with a 'mishapen masse or lumpe' of followers.[1] Catholics attacked Burghley – 'the *Archpolitike*', the 'tyra[n]t *Nero*' and '*Machiauill*', master of 'actors', instigator of 'defamatorie libells' (*Declaration*, 43, 52–3, 33) and a 'Cataline' who has 'diuided [England] into factions' – as merely a spoiled child, 'weeping and whining, like a boye and a babe' (*Treatise*, fols 119^{r}, 166^{v}, sig. i2^{v}). However, for sheer sensationalism nothing exceeds the polarized invective that Protestants hurled at one another in 'the biggest scandal of Elizabeth I's reign'.[2]

Between two bishops

In 1589 Bishop Thomas Cooper complained that since the Armada, English Protestants had turned to warring over the

1 *The Masque of the League and the Spanyard discouered* (1592; STC 7), sigs B1^{r}–B4^{v}, C4^{v}.

2 See *The Collected Essays of Christopher Hill* (Amherst, Mass., 1985), 1.75.

office of bishop (Cooper, 33–5; cf. Bancroft, *Sermon*, 52; *Almond*, sig. A4^{r}). This stage of England's ecclesiastical controversies came to be known for the pseudonymous 'Martin Marprelate', whose name with those of his followers appeared on publications between October 1588 and September 1589 and in counter-attacks by officially sponsored writers.[1] This affair contributed to the factionalizing of Elizabethan politics in the early 1590s (Hammer, 390), to the decade's vogue for satire and to the stereotype of 'the Puritan'.[2] Marprelate's innovation was to mix multi-form humour and burlesque piety with religious critique and bitter invective; the mix would have been inescapably familiar to the first audiences of *Richard III*.

Government spokesmen rightly claimed that the Marprelate authors derived their abusive terms from Presbyterians (Rogers, *Sermon*, 13); this vocabulary also overlapped with anti-papal invective (and the charges aimed at Shakespeare's Richard): satanic ambition, tyrannical usurpation, bestiality, hypocrisy and gross deformity. However, terminology was the least of it. The polarities are familiar: the bishops are 'vsurping Antichristes' (Marprelate, *Epistle*, 8), 'the Lords scourge' (*Theses*, sig. D1^{v}), but also merely 'Hogges, Dogges, Wolues, Foxes' who render the Church a 'deformed bodie' (Bancroft, *Positions*, 63; Rogers, *Sermon*, 8). John Whitgift, Archbishop of Canterbury, 'Pope of Lambeth', 'cruell persecutour' and 'tyrant', bears 'the cursse of God' and is warned to expect 'a fearefull ende' (*Theses*, sig. D3$^{r–v}$).[3] But a new ingredient renders the Marprelate texts 'impudent in the hiest degree' (Rogers, *Sermon*, 13). Whitgift is also jokily represented as bumbling 'nunckle Canterbury' (*Theses*, sig. D3$^{r–v}$)

1 On the main and peripheral Marprelate materials, see Joseph Black, 'The rhetoric of reaction: the Martin Marprelate tracts (1588–89), Anti-Martinism, and the uses of print in early modern England', *Sixteenth Century Journal*, 28 (1997), 707–25.

2 Patrick Collinson, 'Ecclesiastical vitriol: religious satire in the 1590s and the invention of Puritanism', in John Guy (ed.), *The Reign of Elizabeth I: Court and Culture in the Last Decade* (Cambridge, 1995), 150–70; cf. Kristin Poole, 'Facing Puritanism: Falstaff, Martin Marprelate and the grotesque Puritan', in Ronald Knowles (ed.), *Shakespeare and Carnival: After Bakhtin* (Basingstoke, 1998), 97–122.

3 Cf. Lake & Questier, 513, on this rhetoric.

and warned with a story about saucy dogs who might treat a bishop's regalia as disrespectfully as Shakespeare's Richard says they treat his limping gait:

> [T]he B[ishop] did sweat (you must think he labored hard ouer his trencher) The dogg flies at the B. & tooke of his corner capp (he thought belike it had bene a cheese cake) and so away goes the dog with it to his master. Truely my masters of the cleargie / I woulde neuer weare corner cap againe / seeing dogs runne away with them.
>
> (Marprelate, *Epistle*, 43)

Marprelate recasts Antichrist as a sweating trencherman, his idolatrous headgear as cheese cake, his violent rule as pet-wrestling. Similar funny stories abound, such as the one about the preacher who, having once acted the 'vice in a playe', cannot resist running off abruptly mid-service to join passing revellers while mumbling his liturgy.[1] Furthermore, Marprelate narrators mix attack with self-deprecation, adopting the persona of a childlike dunce or 'Plain Percevall', a hunchbacked rustic who admonishes readers, 'thinking belike to ride vpon my Crupshoulders: I am no Ape Carrier'.[2]

Once the bishops stopped huffing, they turned to professional writers to return similar abuse and similar jokes. Of course, Marprelate is Satan's 'intelligencer' or Antichrist, who lamely limps, but leads followers with his name 'on their foreheads' to hell (*Almond*, sigs B2^v^, C2^v^). Or he is a 'Dunce', 'dogge', 'hogge' or 'abhortiue childe' (*Almond*, sigs D3^v^, C2^v^, B1^r^) mouthing '*tinkers termes*' and '*iestes first* Tarleton [put] *on the Stage*' (*Mar-Martine*, sig. A4^v^). Comical images of bishops are countered with comical representations of 'Puritans' as hypocritical cheapskates who quote scripture with sham 'zeal'. One such, for example, when asked by his 'good Ladie' to repay

1 Martin Marprelate, *Hay any Worke for Cooper* ([Coventry,] 1589; STC 17456), 3–4.
2 *Plaine Percevall, the Peace-Maker of England* (1590; STC 12914), 12.

a loan, 'began to storme, and said, he thought her not the child of God, for they must lend, looking for nothing againe; & so to acquite himself of the blot of vsurie, he kept the principall' (*Pappe*, sigs $C4^{v}$–$D2^{r}$). Another, to save funeral costs 'tombled his wife naked into the earth . . . without sheete or shroude to couer her shame, breathing ouer her . . . Naked came I out of my mothers wombe, and naked shall I returne againe' (*Almond*, sig. $B1^{v}$).

A perverse eroticism with a special interest in widows constitutes a significant element in the anti-Marprelate polemic and associated anti-Puritan discourse (cf. Jonson, *Bartholomew Fair*). *Almond* attacks Martin (and his 'puritane perusers') as a 'wretched seducer, that vnder wolues raiment deuourest widowes houses' (*Almond*, sigs $B1^{v}$, $F3^{v}$); compare Richard's attempts on widows Anne and Elizabeth. The paradoxical image of the seducer outwardly wearing a wolf's raiment rather than sheep's clothing may be a misprint, but it suggests oxymoronic qualities in 'Puritan' and Ricardian seduction.

Puritans, though monsters of 'ambition', 'male-con[ten]ted mela[n]choly' and 'seditious discontent' (*Almond*, sig. $D2^{r}$), are also associated with harsh moralism, blasphemous mocking, material self-interest and hyper-seductiveness. Thinking 'to carrie all away with censoricall lookes, with gogling the eye, with lifting vppe the hand, with vehement speeches', the 'Puritane[s]' purvey 'rayling & reuiling Pamphlets' (*2 Pasquill*, sig. $B4^{v}$). But these 'seducers' are like 'mermaides' hiding sinfulness with 'faire speeches' (Bancroft, *Sermon*, 5–6). 'Hypocritically,' they act 'as though all they said proceeded of meere love and Christian charitie', with 'great sighes and grones . . . with a heavy countenance, with casting downe their heads, and with a pittiful voice' (Bancroft, *Sermon*, 92). References to such performance pervades an erotic sub-genre. Puritans may 'seduce' male followers, but '*most labour hath bene bestowed to win and reteine towards this cause them whose iudgements are commonlie weakest by reason of their sex*'; women are '*apter through that naturall inclination vnto pittie*' (Hooker, 17–18). More explicitly, women are positively mad 'to follow men precise', their intense desires making the Puritan woman a '*holy whore*' or '*Pruritane*' (*Mar-Martine*, sig. A2$^{r–v}$). Piety is a special turn-on: praying women scan the room '*The purest man to see. / The purer man, the better grace*' (*Mar-Martine*, sig. A2^{r}). This often obscene polemic presumes 'hote' sexual drives perversely compounded by piety, stern moralizing or sighing meekness.

It was not all funny. The war on dissent led to imprisonment and investigation of prominent reformers between 1589 and 1593, the execution of John Penry (1593), and the only Elizabethan Parliament Act (1593) directed exclusively against Protestant sectaries (Collinson, *Puritan*, 412–31), but the '*laughing libells*' (*Mar-Martine*, sig. A1^{v}) and 'Satyricall immodestie' (Hooker, sig. A5^{r}) even generated stage representations. A July 1589 tract denounces 'stage-players' for serving 'Dick Bancroft' before 'many thousand eie witnesses' (*Theses*, sig. D2^{v}). The nature of such stagings is uncertain, but by autumn 1589 the Star Chamber and the Lord Mayor acted to control representation of 'partes and matters . . . unfytt and undecent to be handled in playes, both for Divinitie and State' (Chambers, *Stage*, 1.295, 4.306–7; cf. *Pappe*, sig. D2^{v}; *2 Pasquill*, sig. C3^{v}; Nashe, 4.465, Lake & Questier, 557–8).[1]

Given this incendiary atmosphere, what to make of the 'never-ending procession of churchmen' (Honigmann, *R3*, 32) who enable Shakespeare's hypocritical tyrant? An archbishop promises sanctuary (2.4), but a compliant cardinal aids Richard in violating it (3.1); the Bishop of Ely hurries to fetch Richard strawberries (3.4). Lesser clerics, including the notorious Shaw, preach on his behalf (3.5.103–5); a chaplain conceals the princes' bodies (4.3.29); bishops appear 'aloft' with him (3.7). How would these ludicrous 'props of virtue' strike Elizabethans who

1 With a character called plain Honesty who denounces 'pure precisians' (344) for 'mocking the divine order of ministry' (1856), *A Knack to Know a Knave* (performed in 1592) is relevant here.

heard bishops defended as 'especiall pillers and ornamentes of [Elizabeth's] state' (*Almond*, sig. C2^{r})? This is all 'history', of course, and Milton assumed Richard's religious hypocrisy to be historical (Milton, 361–2). However, 'historical' parallels served contemporary purposes; just associating Bishop Barlowe with Dr Shaw registered utter contempt.[1]

Bishop Bancroft claimed in 1588, 'a man can scarcelie speake any thing . . . but he shall seeme to pointe at and describe the factions of these daies' (Bancroft, *Sermon*, 14). The depiction of May Day 1517 in *Sir Thomas More* occasioned official warnings about possible analogy with tensions of the 1590s (*STM*, 17–19). The months surrounding the printing of *Richard III* (Stationers' Register 20 October 1597) saw other Shakespearean 'histories' embroiled in disputes about topicality. Sir John Oldcastle was renamed Falstaff for the *1 Henry IV* Quartos of 1598 (Stationers' Register, 25 February 1598).[2] Religion was not the only flashpoint.

Drunken prophecies, libels

Richard employs 'prophecies' and 'libels' (1.1.33), but no known source implicates him for the prophecy about 'G' (cf. Hall, *Edward IV*, fol. ccx^{v}).[3] However, playing on a letter appears prominently in a 1592 attack on Burghley invoking a 'prophecie . . . that one who had two c. c. in his name should be the destruction of Ingland' (*Aduertisement*, 39). Other 1592 polemic accuses Burghley himself of instigating 'prophecies' and 'libells' (*Declaration*, 74–5), as if he were responsible 'for the vain and fond pamphlets and ballads of every idle fellow' (Bacon, *Works*, 8.200). By making Richard the causer of such libels, a lofty intimate of a monarch, a hidden threat and an apparent

1 John Donne, *The Courtier's Library*, ed. Evelyn Mary Simpson (London, 1930), 37, 52.

2 See Kastan, *1H4*, 51–62.

3 Henry Howard's *Defensative against the Poison of Supposed Prophesies* (1583; STC 13858), sigs Hh3^{v}–Hh4^{r}, anticipates Shakespeare in blaming Richard for authoring the prophecy.

ally of his victims, the play parallels his story with anti-Cecil conspiracy polemic.

The Cecils endured smear campaigns until Robert's death in 1612 (Croft, 'Reputation', 46; cf. SPD 12/180/23). Bacon's 1592 defence of Burghley marvels at the sheer variety and 'number of libellous and defamatory books and writings' (Bacon, *Works*, 8.147–8). These libels consistently attack a 'monopolistic figure' who manipulates the monarch, court factions and the nobility.[1] Many, like the 1584 *Copy of a Letter*, employ terms Richard uses to describe himself in *3 Henry VI*: 'Machauel' (*Copy*, 103; *Declaration*, 53), 'Catiline' (*Copy*, 184; *Treatise*, fol. 118^{v}), 'Syren' or Sinon (*Treatise*, fol. 132^{r}). They describe 'hyred murders' (*Treatise*, sig. $i2^{v}$), 'Libelles and Pamphlets' (*Treatise*, fol. 121^{r}), 'Shawes' (*Treatise*, fol. 124^{r}; cf. *Copy*, 124), 'spies and intelligencers' (*Copy*, 79; *Declaration*, 43), all serving Burghley, 'the *primum mobile* in every action' (Bacon, *Works*, 8.198), who 'so cuningly dispos[es] . . . his affaires, into the handes of other principall actors . . . that very ofte[n] tymes, his owne plottes & inuentions have seemed the practizes of others' (*Declaration*, 52). Burghley feigns piety while 'laughing at other mens simplicity' (*Aduertisement*, 61). Physical handicap enters this polemic with Robert Cecil's rise in the early 1590s.

Amid curses calling for 'vengeance of heauen and earth' upon the Cecils, the *Declaration* mentions a work recalled in 1591 for its anti-Burghley implications, Spenser's '*mother Hubberds Tale*', with its 'false fox and his crooked cubbes' (*Declaration*, 68–71). Robert Cecil's body, 'so il shapen and crooked', prompts the *Declaration*'s recourse to the satirical grotesque. After lecturing Queen Elizabeth for having forgotten the 'Philosopher' who warns against 'such so marked by nature, in these woordes: *Caue ab his, quos natura signauit*', the attack shifts into '*Macaronicall* verses' warning 'to beware of such

1 See Simon Adams, 'Favourites and factions at the Elizabethan court', in Ronald G. Asch and Adolf M. Birke (eds), *Princes, Patronage and the Nobility: The Court at the Beginning of the Modern Age, c. 1450–1650* (Oxford, 1991), 273.

deformed creatures, saying in admiration. *O Deus, a[b]guerzis, Zoppis, gobbisq[ue] cauendum est / Nulla fides gobbis, mancum mihi credite Zoppis. / Si . . . guersus bonus est, inter miracula scribam*' ['O God, one must beware of the Guerzi, Zoppi, and Gobbi. There is no trust in Gobbis, believe me, there is something wrong with the Zoppis. If a Guerzo is a good man, I will record that as a miracle.'].[1] After this conjuration of lame, cross-eyed and hump-backed dwarfs come jokes about Cecil's back, birth and function: 'yf her Ma[tie] had bene disposed to prefer him . . . to haue made him a writer vnder some clerck or officier of the courte, had bene very conuenie[n]t for him, because as a courtier told her, he was fittest for such purpose, for that he caried his deske on his back' (*Declaration*, 71). From bitter accusations and passionate curses, the attack descends to grotesque caricature worthy of Nashe. Such tonally volatile combinations characterize the manuscript invective.

Robert Cecil's elevation in May 1591 as the youngest ever Privy Council member occasioned rumours that he would soon fill the powerful post of Secretary, which had been vacant since Walsingham's death in 1590.[2] Speculation also ran high that he would inherit the reversion to the Court of Wards held by his father (SPD 12/239/159). In fact he obtained neither till 1596 and 1599 respectively, but his proximity to such power encouraged comparison with Richard. Manuscripts of various dates call him a 'Dissemblinge smothfacd dwarfe' (Bod. Don c. 54, fol. 20), 'Little Cecil' or 'the Littell one it self', 'his fathers instrument' (SPD 14/71/16). Even Queen Elizabeth addressed him 'under her sporting name of pygmy'.[3] Comparisons with humped beasts abound: like a dolphin and camel, a 'Toad' (Croft, 'Reputation', 47), like a spider, his 'Crookebacks spider shapen' (Bod. Don c. 54, fol. 20) or like an 'Ape / Of crooked fame and

1 *Declaration*, 70; translation thanks to Wolfgang Haase, Steven Esposito and Ron Bogdan.

2 Conyers Read, *Lord Burghley and Queen Elizabeth* (New York, 1960), 465, 477.

3 P.M. Handover, *The Second Cecil* (1959), 57.

crooked shape' (BL Egerton 2230, fol. 33^{r}). Insults infer sexual promiscuity – as, for example, 'Robert Cicil, Compos'd of back and pisle' (BL Add. MS 25348, fol. 9^{r}) – and falsely attribute his death to syphilis:

> Heere lieth Robbin Crooktback unjustly reckond
> A Richard the third, he was Judas the second.
> In their lives they agree, in their deaths somew^{t} alter,
> The more pity the poxe soe cousend the halter.
> Richard, or Robert, wch is the worse?
> A Crooktback great in state is Englands curse.
> (Bod. Tanner MS 299, fol. 13^{r})

The similarities include their 'Machiuillian skill' at 'curb[ing] the Peeres', employing 'faction', 'vile detraction' (Bod. Don c. 54, fol. 20) and pious hypocrisy in 'fained religion, & zealous affection' (Bod. Tanner MS 299, fol. 11^{r}).

PREPOSTEROUS ANTICIPATIONS: THE RICHARDS OF *2* AND *3 HENRY VI*

The protagonist who opens *Richard III* is new to the stage, though aspects of himself and of other, alternative, selves had appeared in the *Henry VI* plays.[1] Some are retained or expanded: bodily shape first. The Quarto version of *2 Henry 6* (*The Contention*) announces his bit-part as 'crook-backe *Richard*' (*Contention*, sig. H1^{v}) and appropriate insults follow: 'foul indigested lump, / As crooked in thy manners as thy shape' (*2H6* 5.1.157–8) or 'Foule Stigmaticke' (*Contention*, sig. H2^{r}; *2H6* 5.1.215). This emphasis remains in the mix, as do religious hypocrisy, bloodthirstiness

1 My analysis is indebted to Pearlman, who refutes claims that Richard's characteristics are implicitly similar (Tillyard, 195; M.M. Reese, *The Cease of Majesty: A Study of Shakespeare's History Plays* (1961), 204) or his character unchanging (Spivack, 388; Larry S. Champion, *Perspective in Shakespeare's English Histories* (Athens, Ga., 1980), 82) in the three plays. Pearlman also complicates arguments about Oedipal change (Pierce, 83). On Richard's metamorphosis, see also David L. Frey, *The First Tetralogy: Shakespeare's Scrutiny of the Tudor Myth* (The Hague, 1976), 42; Smidt, *Unconformities*, 33–4.

and status consciousness, but these elements are modified. Taunting his enemies, early Richard burlesques Christian values by preaching, 'Fie, Charitie for shame, speake it not in spight, / For you shall sup with Iesus Christ to night' (*Contention*, sig. H2^r; *2H6* 5.1.213–14), while to himself he declares, 'heart, be wrathful still: / Priests pray for enemies, but princes kill' (*2H6* 5.2.70–1). Yet the religious hypocrite and ruthless Machiavellian 'prince' are wholly subsumed in the partisan Yorkist warrior; nothing yet suggests the sneaky, ambitious, anti-family, anti-everyone *isolato* who suddenly emerges late in *3 Henry VI*, nor the witty showman who will open *Richard III*.

Richard opens *3 Henry VI* with a grotesque pantomime that wins him the title 'best' son. Holding up a severed head, he bids, 'Speak thou for me, and tell them what I did', and shakes it for emphasis: 'Thus do I hope to shake King Henry's head' (*3H6* 1.1.16, 20). Wit? Subtlety? His subsequent speeches sometimes seem randomly assigned. The taciturn head-shaker channels Senecan rant, lusting, like Richard of *True Tragedy*, for 'lukewarm blood' (*3H6* 1.2.33) or threatening to resurrect an enemy insufficiently railed at: 'If this right hand would buy two hours' life, / That I in all despite might rail at him, / This hand should chop it off, and with the issuing blood / Stifle the villain' (*3H6* 2.6.80–3). 'Revenge' is his theme (*3H6* 2.3.19, 2.4.3). Alternatively, he waxes Marlovian, lyrically enthusing, 'How sweet a thing it is to wear a crown, / Within whose circuit is Elysium / And all that poets feign of bliss and joy' (*3H6* 1.2.28–30; cf. Marlowe, *1 Tamburlaine*, 2.7.28–9). These Richards will not make it to *Richard III*. In Act 3 of *3 Henry VI*, however, the new model Richard, our Richard, 'theatrical, scheming, wicked, ironic' springs to life (Pearlman, 416) in Shakespeare's longest soliloquy (71 lines in F, 28 in Octavo *3H6*). For the first time he expresses an attitude toward his body, and admires himself as if his physical appearance does not matter.

Richard begins by wishing his brother Edward 'wasted, marrow, bones and all', rather than about to marry and put him further from the throne. Frustrated, 'Like one that stands upon a promontory / And spies a far-off shore where he would tread' (*3H6* 3.2.135–6), Richard briefly considers an alternative goal – to 'make my heaven in a lady's lap' (3.2.148). But his body – an arm 'like a withered shrub', 'an envious mountain' on his back, 'unequal' legs and 'disproportion . . . in every part' (3.2.156–60) – rules this out. Turning back to the crown, Richard suddenly reconceives his body 'not as the insignia but the cause of his depravity' (Pearlman, 421). *Because* he cannot be loved, domination offers the only compensation:

> Then, since this earth affords no joy to me
> But to command, to check, to o'erbear such
> As are of better person than myself,
> I'll make my heaven to dream upon the crown
> And whiles I live t'account this world but hell,
> Until my misshaped trunk that bears this head
> Be round impaled with a glorious crown.
> (*3H6* 3.2.165–71)

The hideous image of his 'trunk' somehow rounded with a crown captures the centrality of his body to Richard's logic: the crown becomes a 'heaven' to be entered in compensation for the inaccessible 'heaven' of love. Here is the Richard who will introduce himself as 'I, that am not shaped for sportive tricks' (1.1.14). But how could he possibly get inside the crown?

Frustration returns, compounded, in the image of enveloping thorns enclosing him in a desperate, self-defeating struggle between desire and impossibility, 'like one lost in a thorny wood, / That rents the thorns and is rent with the thorns, / Seeking a way and straying from the way, / Not knowing how to find the open air' (*3H6* 3.2.174–7).[1] Will he 'free' himself, or flail about with a bloody axe? Surprise, again; as it turns out, neither: 'Tut', he announces, he is already free, and on

1 The image develops a commonplace shared with *Mirror*, 'Buckingham', Induction, 512–14.

his way. In a stunning reversal, *3 Henry VI* takes what Elihu Pearlman calls a 'step backward' from psychic 'realism' to an archaic, symbolic or supernatural mode. With no pretence of dramatic preparation or continuity of 'character', a new creature announces himself, claiming a whole bag of hitherto concealed tricks and weapons. And he knows how to use them:

> Why, I can smile, and murder whiles I smile,
> And cry 'Content!' to that which grieves my heart,
> And wet my cheeks with artificial tears,
> And frame my face to all occasions.
> I'll drown more sailors than the mermaid shall,
> I'll slay more gazers than the basilisk,
> I'll play the orator as well as Nestor,
> Deceive more slyly than Ulysses could,
> And, like a Sinon, take another Troy.
> I can add colours to the chameleon,
> Change shapes with Proteus for advantages,
> And set the murderous Machiavel to school.
> Can I do this, and cannot get a crown?
> Tut, were it farther off, I'll pluck it down.
> (*3H6* 3.2.182–95)

Really? Nothing has previously suggested he can do any of these things, but from now on he talks much like this – right into his own play. Here, for the first time, Richard sounds mostly like Richard. No longer dynastic 'Dickie . . . with his grumbling voice' (*3H6* 1.4.76), but a 'creature of indirection, irony and dissembling' (Pearlman, 422) with a link to the Prince of Darkness. The 'historical' or 'tragical' Richard of the sources and analogues appears transfused with the energies and attributes of the morality play Vice.

The new model Richard boldly assumes a multi-abled, supernatural flexibility of identity, like that of the Vice Haphazard, 'a Scholer, or a scholemaister, or els some youth.

/ A Lawier, a student or els a countrie cloune / A Brumman [broom-man], a Baskit maker, or a Baker of Pies'.[1] Consummate dissembling comes from the Vice, too. Richard's pride in multi-tasking, smiling and murdering or crying content while suffering, recalls Skelton's Collusion boasting, 'I can dyssemble, I can bothe laughe and grone'.[2] Weeping at will, while secretly laughing, like Ambidexter in Preston's *Cambises*, he also claims the right to boast about it to us, and also like Ambidexter and others, the possession of a dominant quality, sin or tendency. Here, two-faced 'Machiavel' becomes Richard's true name, but in the final act of *3 Henry VI* he claims an identity of biblical proportions. Stabbing King Henry, Richard invokes hell and renounces love itself:

> Then, since the heavens have shaped my body so,
> Let hell make crook'd my mind to answer it.
> I have no brother; I am like no brother.
> And this word 'love', which greybeards call divine,
> Be resident in men like one another
> And not in me: I am myself alone.
>
> (*3H6* 5.6.78–83)

Affirming the sin of sins by renouncing St Paul's primal '*band of perfection*', Richard adopts the 'cognisance of the diuell', marking the 'Apostata'.[3] He embraces the 'inward war' that Thomas More had ascribed to the historical tyrant: 'For whome trusted he that mistrusted his own brother? whom spared he that killed his own brother? or who could parfitely loue him, if hys owne brother could not?' (More, *CW2*, 71). Rejecting likeness, he refuses the very basis of friendship; and in the Octavo line – 'I have no father, I am like no father' – he further renounces paternity, ascribing to

1 R.B., *A New Tragical Comedie of Apius and Virginia* (1575; STC 1059), sig. B1^{r}.
2 See Wolfgang G. Müller, 'The villain as rhetorician in Shakespeare's *Richard III*', *Anglia*, 102 (1984), 47–8.
3 Smith, *Sermons*, 353–7; cf. William Perkins, 'A Case of Conscience', *Works* (1592; STC 19665.5), sig. B3^{r-v}.

himself Aristotle's definition of monstrosity: 'he who does not resemble his parents'.[1]

3 Henry VI concludes with a Richard anything but the Richard of any previous play and all but the Richard of *Richard III*. Violent, ambitious, cunning and demonically isolated, Richard affirms self-denominations – Proteus, mermaid, chameleon, Sinon, basilisk and Machiavel ('*Catalin*' in O1 *3H6* sig. C8[v]) – fully functional as epithets in any number of early modern invective contexts. However, he has yet to manifest his primary gifts as a performance artist: brazen religious hypocrisy, callous manipulation and bullying seduction. Above all, he is not yet funny or engaging. That surprise awaited playgoers who were probably amazed, at the opening of the next play, to be invited up, at least figuratively, to the scaffold to join in Richard's version of what More calls king's games. We call it *Richard III*.

NOW: DATE OF COMPOSITION, PERFORMANCE AND COMPANY

We know virtually nothing certain about Shakespeare from 1585 until references to him as a London actor and playwright appear in 1592. We do not know which acting company he was with until 1594, when unequivocal evidence connects him with the Chamberlain's Men (George, 305). *Richard III* was written after 1587, when the second edition of Holinshed's *Chronicles* was printed, and before 20 October 1597, when the First Quarto (Q1) was entered in the Stationers' Register (Arber, 3.25). The 1597 title-page announces the play as 'lately Acted by the Right honourable the Lord Chamberlaine his seruants'. Within those ten years, suggested dates of composition range from 1590–1 (Honigmann, *Impact*, 88), 1591 (Hammond, 61), 1592 (Jowett, 7), after June 1592 (Taylor, *TxC*, 115), mid-1592 to 1593 (Lull),

1 Cf. *Coriolanus* 5.2.80, 5.3.36–7. On classical friendship, see Shannon, and Aristotle, *On the Generation of Animals*, 4.4, cited in Marie-Hélène Huet, *Monstrous Imagination* (Cambridge, Mass., 1993), 4.

to 1594 (Bate, *Tit*, 79).[1] Everyone agrees on the early 1590s, and though evidence cannot eliminate either extreme, the dates can be narrowed with probability to 1592–3. Debates about the nature and history of London acting companies during the years 1592–4 preclude certainty about Shakespeare's own affiliation, though features of *Richard III* have suggested possible ties to Pembroke's and Lord Strange's Men.

Richard III builds on the characters, language and action of *3 Henry VI*, later published anonymously 'as . . . acted by . . . the Earle of Pembrooke his seruants' in the 1595 Octavo version (*The True Tragedy of Richard, Duke of York*). Performance of *3 Henry VI/Richard, Duke of York* can be approximately dated by the mockery of one of its lines in *Greene's Groatsworth of Wit* – 'Tiger's heart wrapped in a player's hide' (parodying 'O, tiger's heart wrapped in a woman's hide' (*3H6* 1.4.137). Since *Groatsworth* was entered in the Stationers' Register on 20 September 1592 (Arber, 2.292^{v}), the play that dramatically precedes *Richard III* had been written and probably staged – if the allusion were to be recognizable to readers – before 23 June 1592, after which the London theatres were closed due to unrest and kept shut due to plague until 27 December 1592 (only to be closed again in February 1593).[2] This timing coincides with Philip Henslowe's mention of a '*harey the vj*', marked 'ne' (used to indicate new, newly licensed or otherwise 'marketably new')[3] and performed fifteen times at the Rose theatre between 3 March and 19 June 1592 (Henslowe, 15–19). It is not certain which *Henry VI* play this entry refers to, but Henslowe usually listed initial plays of a sequence without a numerical marker.[4] When

1 Hammond's dating relies on ambiguous influences and shared commonplaces among *Richard III* and Marlowe's *Edward II* and *Faustus* (Hammond, 61); cf. *TxC*, 116. Against Honigmann's 'early start' hypothesis, see Sidney Thomas, 'On the dating of Shakespeare's early plays', *SQ*, 39 (1988), 187–94.

2 For the June 1592 closing, see Chambers, *Stage*, 4.310–11.

3 Knowles, *2H6*, 112; Roslyn Lander Knutson, 'The repertory', in John D. Cox and David Scott Kastan (eds), *A New History of Early English Drama* (New York, 1997), 467.

4 Roslyn Lander Knutson, 'Henslowe's naming of parts', *N&Q*, 228 (1983), 157–60.

coupled with Thomas Nashe's exactly contemporary reference to the onstage death of 'brave Talbot', Henslowe's listing suggests that Part 1 of *Henry VI* was being performed in early 1592, with the likelihood that Parts 2 and 3 had been performed previously (Burns, *1H6*, 5; Knowles, *2H6*, 113, 116).[1]

This evidence does not firmly date *Richard III*, but it would seem likely that composition would have been under way while the Henry VI plays were still being performed, sometime in early 1592. The plays are closely related verbally to *Richard III*, and the close of *3 Henry VI* leads directly into the opening of *Richard III*.[2] When *Richard III* was 'completed' is by definition unclear, since any play would be subject to ongoing modification according to playhouse practice and to the vagaries of performance. It was probably tinkered with right up to printing as Q1 in 1597 (and beyond that, for performance), but my guess would be that a longer substantial draft (FMS) would have dated from the months that followed the closing of the London theatres on 23 June 1592. A second, shorter derivative version (QMS) would have followed sometime before Q1's printing in 1597. This would date some form of *Richard III* as nearly contemporary with *Venus and Adonis* (Stationers' Register 18 April 1593) and *Rape of Lucrece* (Stationers' Register 9 May 1594), *Titus Andronicus* (Stationers' Register 6 February 1594) and *Comedy of Errors* (performed at Gray's Inn in December 1594).[3] Since the two poems alone run to 1194 and 1855 lines (together equivalent to about one and a half plays (George, 320)), it seems likely that Shakespeare did not tour during the intermission of 1592–3, but stayed put and wrote.

1 Arguments that champion sequential composition of the three parts of *Henry VI*, such as those by Hanspeter Born, Emrys Jones (*Origins*, 130–7), Andrew Cairncross and Michael Hattaway (*2H6*, ed. Michael Hattaway (Cambridge, 1991), 2, 61) oppose Kristian Smidt and J.D. Wilson concerning nonconformities among the plays (see Knowles, *2H6*, 113).

2 To be fair, arguing against connection is easy enough; see Smidt, *Unconformities*, for discrepancies.

3 Taylor finds the play's rare vocabulary closest to the *Henry VI* plays, *Titus* and *Comedy of Errors* (*TxC*, 116).

If *Richard III* had not been performed in London by June 1592, then it could not have been staged there before December 1593. This does not rule out performance outside London during the interrupted season of 1592–3. The reasons for thinking it had not been performed in London before the closing of the theatres in June 1592 are derived from Henslowe's relatively complete records for the period and from contemporary polemic.[1] The first responses to any Shakespearean play appear in 1592. *Greene's Groatsworth* attacks an 'vpstart' for penning plays instead of reciting lines written by others. Evidently confronted by those who understood these remarks to attack Shakespeare, Henry Chettle, the editor/author of the book attributed to Robert Greene, apologized.[2] Chettle's *Kind-Harts Dreame* (Stationers' Register 8 December 1592) treats Shakespeare as new on the scene, at least as writer rather than actor. Admitting that he had not been acquainted with Shakespeare before the publication of *Groatsworth* (September 1592), Chettle adds that since then, 'my selfe haue seene' Shakespeare's 'demeanor no lesse ciuill than he exelent in the qualitie he professes', and Chettle's sentence suggests that the 'profess[ion]' to which he refers is acting.[3] Chettle, a stationer and author with a hand in the theatre, thought of Shakespeare as only very recently a writer of plays in 1592.

In August 1592 another book was entered in the Stationers' Register that may also bear on the dating of *Richard III* by failing to mention it explicitly. No one is *au courant* if not Thomas Nashe. *Pierce Penilesse* (Stationers' Register 8 August 1592) defends playing by paying tribute to actors and roles, courts a potential patron associated with theatre and, uncharacteristically, forgoes a wonderful rhetorical opportunity – if Shakespeare's *Richard III*

1 Henslowe records Sussex's Men performing a '*Buckingham*' at the Rose in the December 1593–January 1594 period; no evidence suggests this is *Richard III*.

2 For authorship and allusion, see *Groatsworth*.

3 Chettle adds what he has heard 'reported' about Shakespeare's writing: 'Besides, diuers of worship haue reported, his vprightnes of dealing, which argues his honesty, and his facetious grace in writting, that aprooues his Art' (sig. A4^{r}).

had already been staged. Plays, with their subject matter 'for the most part . . . borrowed out of our English Chronicles', enable 'a rare exercise of vertue', Nashe asserts, and he praises a play that rescues from 'Oblivion' the 'braue *Talbot*', a role recently (and probably exclusively) portrayed in *1 Henry VI* (Nashe, 1.212).[1] Nashe also claims that the stage may dissuade audience members from particular evils:

> In Playes, all coosonages, all cunning drifts ouer-gulyded with outward holinesse, all stratagems of warre, all the cankerwormes that breede on the rust of peace, are most liuely anatomiz'd: they shew the ill successe of treason, the fall of hastie climbers, the wretched end of vsurpers, the miserie of ciuill dissention, and how iust God is euermore in punishing of murther.
>
> (Nashe, 1.213)

With the exception of military 'stratagems', virtually every element Nashe mentions is prominently represented in *Richard III*. An invocation of hypocritical, usurping Richard among hasty climbers and their just deserts would have nicely balanced the tribute to Talbot's virtues.[2] Elsewhere in *Pierce Penilesse* there is a possible glancing allusion to the Richard of *3 Henry VI*, but there is none to *Richard III*, where so many of Nashe's named evils are anatomized.[3]

Pierce Penilesse also appears to miss another rhetorical opportunity – if *Richard III* was already known. Apparently

1 Current estimates support Nashe's claims about large attendance for *Henry VI* at the Rose theatre in spring 1592; cf. Burns, *1H6*, 9. For a compelling argument concerning Nashe's own contribution to Act 1 of *1 Henry VI*, see Brian Vickers, 'Incomplete Shakespeare: or, denying coauthorship in *1 Henry VI*', *SQ*, 58 (2007), 311–52.

2 Hammond assumes that 'cunning drifts ouer-guylded with outward holinesse' refers to Richard (Hammond, 61). *Richard III* and *Pierce Penilesse* share the phrase 'dispaire and die' (*R3* 5.3.120; Nashe, 1.157), but this may reflect shared debt to *Faustus* (see *Doctor Faustus A- and B-texts (1604, 1616)*, ed. David M. Bevington and Eric Rasmussen, Manchester, 1993).

3 Nashe describes an ambitious man without 'comliness' who would swell to a 'mountaine', employing 'stratagems' to resist 'destine' and renouncing 'Father or Brother' (Nashe, 1.176); cf. *3H6* 3.2.124–95.

dedicated to Ferdinando Stanley, Lord Strange, *Pierce Penilesse* praises the star actor of Lord Strange's Men, Edward Alleyn (Nashe, 1.215), while lauding Lord Strange's ancestor Talbot (called 'Lord Strange of Blackmere', *1H6* 4.4.177) (Born, 324). If *Richard III* was then in existence, Nashe missed an opportunity to praise another ancestor of Strange's, since the play gives Thomas, Lord Stanley, later Earl of Derby, special prominence as a victim, defangs possible criticism of him and concludes by having him crown yet another Stanley ancestor, Henry of Richmond, as King Henry VII.

If *Richard III* was not performed in London before 1593, this would make it likely that it was initially staged there – exactly as Q1's 1597 title-page reports – by the Lord Chamberlain's Men, first formed in 1594 and incorporating players from Strange's and Pembroke's Men. After the closure in June 1592, London theatres were open only for five weeks in late December 1592 and January 1593 before plague shut them down again, and Henslowe's records for Strange's Men during this brief period are relatively complete (Rutter, 68–9). The London companies travelled (Strange's Men) or broke up (Pembroke's Men) or both (Queen's Men). Strange's Men are last seen as a company playing at Caludon Castle in Warwickshire on 5 December 1593. Two days later their plays begin to be entered for publication in the Stationers' Register (Arber, 2.303).[1] The theatres re-opened for a brief period on 27 December 1593, but it was not until June 1594 that the newly reorganized London companies began 'a season of unprecedented stability' that ran until March 1595 (Rutter, 84).

A first London performance in 1594 also accords with early references associating Richard's part with Richard Burbage and not with Edward Alleyn, who had probably played 'brave Talbot' in 1592. The twenty-eight-year-old Alleyn, famous as

1 Cf. Lawrence Manley, 'From Strange's Men to Pembroke's Men: *2 Henry VI* and *The First part of the Contention*', *SQ*, 54 (2003), 253–87.

Marlowe's Tamburlaine and Barabas, and since October 1592 son-in-law and business partner of Henslowe, did perform with Strange's Men for an indeterminate time, but by 1594 he was at the Rose with the Lord Admiral's Men; he would exit the stage in late 1597.[1] Burbage, twenty-six in 1594, was an experienced player who, having performed in London since at least 1590 (Chambers, *Stage*, 2.307), rapidly assumed prominence in the Lord Chamberlain's company (continued in the later King's Men), and eventually became one of the three men from his London life who Shakespeare remembered as his 'fellows' in his will.[2] Burbage is the only virtuoso actor of the period besides Alleyn who is known to have undertaken such enormously lengthy and demanding roles as Richard.[3] The play's initial London performances would then probably have been at the Theatre in Shoreditch, which was owned by Burbage's father, James.

Such dating also fits facts of publication. The anonymous Queen's Men play, *The True Tragedy of Richard III*, was entered in the Stationers' Register on 19 June 1594 – the very month that London theatres reopened.[4] *True Tragedy* is by most assessments older, and to be numbered among the Queen's Men plays – *The Troublesome Raigne of King John* (1591), *King Leir* (Stationers' Register 1594) and *The Famous Victories of Henry V* (Stationers' Register 1594) – that inspired Shakespearean versions.[5] Its

1 See S.P. Cerasano, 'Edward Alleyn', *ODNB*, vol. 1, 846–9.

2 Mary Edmond, 'Richard Burbage', *ODNB*, vol. 8, 716–18.

3 In March 1592 Alleyn probably portrayed Barabas in Marlowe's *The Jew of Malta* at Henslowe's Rose theatre. On large roles in Elizabethan public theatre plays, see Scott McMillin, *The Elizabethan Theatre and The Book of Sir Thomas More* (Ithaca, NY, 1987), 62–3.

4 Taylor suggests that this publication was an attempt to exploit the success of Shakespeare's play (*TxC*, 115), but the conjectured timing makes this unlikely (Roslyn Knutson, personal communication). It could have been an attempt at financial survival by the remnants of the Queen's Men. Between December 1593 and May 1595 the initial registrations of public playbooks peaked at twenty-seven publications, compared with three between January and November in 1593 and four from June to December 1595 (Blayney, 'Publication', 385). *The Jew of Malta* was entered on 17 May 1594.

5 For an opposing chronology, see Honigmann, *Impact*.

printing may have encouraged Q1's scrupulous licensing, since the entry for *True Tragedy* enumerates elements that, with the substantial exception of the 'lamentable end of Shores wife', broadly correspond to those of *Richard III*.[1] The financial risks in publishing a work of roughly similar content that might be judged to impact negatively the sale of another were substantial (Blayney, 'Publication', 399).

It has been suggested that *Richard III* was originally staged by Pembroke's Men and that Q1 represents a version staged on provincial tour during the months that the London theatres were closed.[2] John Jowett points to the prominence given both Stanley and Pembroke in Q1 and decides that the play was written 'as if for Strange's Men' but 'given finishing touches towards its close that make it suitable for the new Pembroke company'. This is plausible; however, Jowett adds that there are a good many 'ifs' in any such hypothesis (Jowett, 7–8).[3]

UPON RECORD? MORE'S *HISTORY*: 'PEACE . . . NOT MUCH SURER THEN WAR'

Richard III gets its plot and characters from the same historical compilations that furnished material for the three *Henry VI* plays. *Richard III* differs from them in being based on portions of Edward Hall's *Union* and Raphael Holinshed's *Chronicles* that come from Sir Thomas More's *History of King Richard III* (in slightly

1 '*The Tragedie of RICHARD the THIRD wherein is showen the Death of EDWARD the FFOURTHE with the smotheringe of the twoo princes in the Tower / . with a lamentable end of SHOREs wife / and the Coniunction of the twoo houses of LANCASTER and YORKE*' (Arber, 2.309^{v}).

2 See Andrew S. Cairncross, 'Pembroke's Men and some Shakespearian piracies', *SQ*, 11 (1960), 339–40; Karl Wentersdorf, '*Richard III* (Q1) and the Pembroke "Bad" Quartos', *English Language Notes*, 14 (1977), 257–64; cf. Jowett, 'Derby', 8.

3 Gurr finds positive references to the Stanley family through all the Henry VI plays, but suggests Shakespeare's presence in a Pembroke's company at the Theatre in 1592–3 (Gurr, *Companies*, 262, 271). Some of the staging details Gurr enlists to support Shakespeare's presence in the company could have originated with sources such as *Mirror*.

differing versions). The contrasts between *Richard III* and the earlier history plays in form, characterization and language appear to be related to this difference in origin. *Richard III* follows More in focusing on a single character to whom other characters react. This concentration contributes to the play's claim to be among Shakespeare's first 'tragedies'. Other features of the play also come from More's vituperative, complexly ironic *History*.[1]

Whatever actually happened to bring Richard Plantagenet, later Duke of Gloucester and penultimately Lord Protector, to rule, and whatever occurred during his two-year reign (July 1483 to August 1485), More's usurping tyrant had established himself as 'history' before Shakespeare appropriated him via Hall and Holinshed.[2] Other accounts existed, but Shakespeare is unlikely to have known them, with the possible (insignificant) exception of Robert Fabyan's *Chronicle*.[3] More's *History* – written between 1513 and 1518 in English and Latin, unfinished, and unpublished in his lifetime – shares elements with other accounts, especially that of Polydore Vergil, the Tudors' royal historian.[4] More, supplemented by Vergil's *Anglicae historiae* (Basle, 1534), dominates all subsequent writing about Richard.

1 'More's authorial irony no less clearly anticipates Shakespeare's dramatic departures from the Tudor myth proper than the orthodox line which More's history in its "finished" forms did so much to establish' (Kinney, *Tyrant*, 53).

2 The extreme assessments stress either More's impressive accuracy (Sylvester, in *CW*2, lxxviii–lxxix) or his 'gross inaccuracies . . . willful distortions . . . bias . . . [and] positive virulence' (Kendall, 500).

3 G.B. Churchill's overview remains important. Early accounts of Edward IV had been recorded in a *Historie of the Arrival of Edward IV* by a Yorkist 'servaunt of the Kyngs' (1471) and in John Warkworth's additions to the *Chronicle of Brut* (*c.* 1484). Two Latin *Continuations* of the *History of Croyland Monastery* (1486) describe events up to Richard's deposing and death. Robert Fabyan produced *The new Chronicles of England and of France* (1516; editions in 1533, 1542, 1559), placing Richard within English and French history from the first century. The story to 1486 is recounted by John Rous (d. 1492), whose *Historia Regum Angliae* (published 1716, 1745) originates details of Richard's difficult birth and physiognomy. Other early accounts include the *History of Henry VII* (1500–3), by Bernard André, Henry VII's poet laureate (*Vita Henrici VII*, in James Gairdner (ed.), *Memorials of King Henry the Seventh* (1858)); the *Memoires de Philippe de Commines* (written 1488–1504), by a French counsellor of Charles the Bold and Louis XI; and the notes of Dominic Mancini, which remained in manuscript until 1936.

4 For textual history, see *CW*2, xvii–lix; also *CW*15.

The English *History* was first published when William Rastell, More's nephew, brought out the *Works* in 1557 (the Latin edition was published in Louvain in 1565). However, a version of More, supplemented by Vergil, had already appeared in Richard Grafton's addition to Hardyng's *Chronicle* (1543) and had been incorporated nearly verbatim, along with material from Commines, into Edward Hall's *Union* (1548). Another version of More, incorporating the material added to Hall, went into Holinshed's *Chronicles* (1577, 1587). More's material was invoked by sixteenth-century humanists and inspired literary works such as *The Mirror for Magistrates* (1559–1610), Thomas Legge's Latin university drama *Richardus Tertius* (performed 1579), the anonymous Queen's Men play, *The True Tragedy of Richard the Third* (1594), and at least one (lost) ballad (1586; Arber, 2.210^{v}). Each retelling adds and subtracts, framing Richard's story within different designs.

Roger Ascham lauds More's *History* for avoiding 'flattery and hatred' while providing 'causes cou[n]sels, actes, and issues' along with 'wisedome' for the future. He extols its temporal unity, characterization (providing not only 'the outward shape of the body' but also the 'inward dispositio[n] of the mynde') and linguistic decorum – it varies its language, as had Chaucer, 'higher and lower as matters do ryse and fall' (Ascham, 126). Modern detractors have criticized More for bias against Richard, whom Tudor apologists took to embody the previous dynasty, baronial ambition and factional discord. But More was no simple admirer of Henry VII, Richard's Tudor successor (the play's Richmond), and his claims are often corroborated by others, such as the Italian visitor Mancini.[1] Few would dispute Ascham's other assessments. More's narrative treats its material 'dramatically' and 'only secondarily as a repertory of morals or

1 See Antonia Gransden, *Historical Writing in England*, 2 vols (Ithaca, NY, 1982), 2.300–7; Mancini, 1–26; Hanham, 65–73. Mancini's reliability has been qualified (Horrox, 90–4).

a mere series of events' (Tillyard, 40).[1] Ascham's claims about antecedents also ring true: like Chaucer's *Canterbury Tales* or the mystery plays, the *History* mixes elevated tone, serious matter and noble characters with non-aristocratic figures and language, theology with jokes, 'historical' characters with caricatures. Its form traces the 'ryse and fall' pattern of 'tragedie' that Chaucer derived from Bocaccio as 'The harm of hem that stoode in heigh degree, / And fillen so ther nas no remedie' (Chaucer, 'Monk's Tale', ll. 1991–3).[2]

More provided a tightly focused sequence, with a centre of attention, interrelated characters and an overall shape. Beginning with the death of King Edward, proceeding through Richard's ruthless rise and rapid loss of control, the *History* closes with anticipations of the tyrant's destruction. Unlike Vergil, More does not place Richard's story within all of English history, nor does he embed Richard, as Hall does, in the Wars of the Roses. Richard and his brief tyranny provide dramatic scenes: King Edward's deathbed attempt to reconcile hostile factions (2.1); Buckingham's sleazy sophistry (3.1); Hastings's betrayal (3.4); the commoners' scepticism (3.6); Buckingham's failure to manufacture public support (3.7); Richard's staged reluctance to rule (3.7); his break with Buckingham (4.2); and his commissioning of Tyrrel to murder the princes (4.2). But the *History* also provides more.

More adapts precedents from Tacitus' Tiberian Rome to construct Christian providential interpretations of Richard's England (*CW2*, xci–xcii). Tacitus writes of Tiberius, proud of his 'ability to dissemble' (Tacitus, *Annals*, 4.71; cf. 6.50), More of Richard, 'a deepe dissimuler' (*CW2*, 8). Both stories chart factional politics amid omens, dreams, prognostications and sorcery (cf. *Annals*, 2.43, 6.22, 1.65, 12.22). Both tyrants violate kinship bonds: Tiberius kills 'his daughter-in-law, his brother's

1 Cf. Stuart Gillespie, *Shakespeare's Books: A Study of Shakespeare's Sources* (2001), to which my account is indebted.

2 *The Works of Geoffrey Chaucer*, ed. F.N. Robinson, 2nd edn (Boston, Mass., 1957).

son, his grand-children . . . fill[ing] his whole house with blood' (*Annals*, 6.24); Richard kills brother, nephews, wife and family. Surrounded by mourning widows and orphans (*Annals*, 3.1), they suffer 'anguish of . . . heart' (*Annals*, 6.6) or '*inward troubles*' (*CW*2, 87).

Both Tacitus and More appreciate ironies, but Tacitus' reflections on the 'mockery of human plans in every transaction' (*Annals*, 3.18) are not funny. Contrast More's treatment of Jane Shore's humiliation. More opposes her pathos as a kind-hearted, beautiful adulteress to Richard's repulsiveness as a hard-hearted hypocrite, but her touching story ends with a joke.[1] Unable to convince anyone that she has bewitched him (see *R3* 3.4.66–71), Richard denounces her for lechery, and this prompts More's ridicule. Her lechery was a thing that 'al y[e] world wist', More grants, yet 'euery man laughed . . . to here it then so sodainly so highly taken, y[t] she was nought of her body. And for thys cause (as a goodly continent prince clene & fautles of himself, sent oute of heauen into this vicious world for the amendement of mens maners) he caused the bishop of London to put her to open penance' (*CW*2, 54). This sarcastic caricature of 'highly taken' priggishness anticipates the exaggerated piety of Shakespeare's Richard.

However, More never permits us to laugh *with* Richard. Even when Richard makes sardonic jokes, urging Rivers that he 'should be well inough' just before having him executed, he is always undercut. Rivers tops him by responding that such greetings would be better sent to his nephew since the poor lad is, alas, under Richard's protection (*CW*2, 20). Here is material ripe for dramatic exploitation, but Shakespeare reserves almost

1 Shore might seem, More writes, 'to sleight a thing' to merit inclusion (*CW*2, 56), but she was a popular subject in the 1590s (see Esther Yael Beith-Halahmi, *Angell Fayre or Strumpet Lewd: Jane Shore as an Example of Erring Beauty in 16th Century Literature*, 2 vols (Salzburg, Austria, 1974)). For Shakespeare's failure to write about Shore, see Richard Helgerson, 'Weeping for Jane Shore', *South Atlantic Quarterly*, 98 (1999), 451–76.

all the laughs for Richard while largely denying his victims wit or pathos. Hastings's demise makes a related point.

The downfall of Richard's Lord Chancellor attracted countless moralizers. Even Mancini, who seldom moralizes, reflects on Hastings's destruction 'not by those enemies he had always feared, but by a friend whom he had never doubted. But whom will insane lust for power spare, if it dares violate the ties of kin and friendship?' (Mancini, 90). Vergil emphasizes retributive justice, explaining that 'the law of nature wherof the gospell speaketh (what soever you will that men do unto yow, do you so also unto them) can not be broken without punishment' and reminding us of Hastings's role in killing Prince Edward (Vergil, 181).

Vergil's Hastings appears scarcely more than an embodied gospel moral. More puts him in a chain of circumstances that implicate his character and an entire mode of life. After recounting Stanley's dream about a violent boar on the eve of Hastings's betrayal by Richard, whose insignia is the boar, More's Hastings pronounces himself 'sure of the man' (*CW*2, 50; cf. *R3* 3.2.66–7). This foolhardy confidence persists despite repeated omens. His horse stumbles, 'a token often times notably foregoing some great misfortune' (*CW*2, 51). Then an anonymous figure inquires why Hastings speaks with a priest, having 'no nede of a prist yet', to which More adds, 'as though he would say, ye shal haue sone'; but Hastings 'so little mistrusted, that he was neuer merier nor neuer so full of good hope' (*CW*2, 51). According to the 'blindnes of our mortall nature', such confidence inevitably anticipates downfall, but Hastings was never 'so mery, nor neuer in so great suerty' (*CW*2, 51–2). In sum: 'Thus ended this honorable man, a good knight and a gentle, of gret aucthoritie w^{t} his prince, of liuing somewhat dessolate [dissolute], plaine & open to his enemy, & secret to his frend: eth [easy] to begile, as he that of good hart & corage forestudied no perilles. A louing man & passing wel beloued. Very faithful, & trusty ynough, trusting to much' (*CW*2, 52).

Trusty enough, trusting too much, More's mortal Everyman also embodies martial culture: a 'good knight' is uncalculating, openly hostile to enemies, loyal to friends, sexually dissolute but of 'good hart & corage', easy to beguile since he 'forestudied no perilles'. Hastings is the polar opposite of the strategy-obsessed, dissimulating, priggish Richard, but he also contrasts with More himself, the Christian humanist and political analyst, in embodying a chivalric honour culture that above all prizes loyalty to 'friends' and indifference to calculation.[1]

Thus More's *History* reveals a three-fold perspective: religiously, it portrays the insecurity of 'our mortall nature'; politically, it depicts a particular social order 'vnarmed' by factional 'deuision and discension'; and individually it represents characters whose 'demeanours' enable (Hastings), exploit (Richard) or endure (Jane Shore) this systemic failure. Richard's 'demeanour', his relentless 'desire of suerayntee', constitutes the 'whole matter' of the *History* (*CW*2, 5–6).

Although More does not follow John Rous (d. 1492) in comparing Richard to the Antichrist, he amplifies features from Rous that also appear in Vergil (Hanham, 123; Buck, 286–7). All three represent Richard's body, birth and behaviour as befitting one who breaks 'al the bandes . . . that binden manne and manne together, withoute anye respecte of Godde or the worlde' (*CW*2, 5–6). More inflates his reputed scapular inequality into literal 'croke backed' disability.[2] Richard was:

> little of stature, ill fetured of limmes, croke backed, his left shoulder much higher then his right, hard fauoured of visage, and suche as is in states called

1 On honour culture and calculation, see Mervyn James, *Society, Politics and Culture: Studies in Early Modern England* (Cambridge, 1986), 308–415. For humanist objections that warfare needed calculation, see Steven Marx, 'Shakespeare's pacifism', *RQ*, 45 (1992), 49–95. For the topicality of Erasmus and More, see Dominic Baker-Smith, '"Inglorious glory": 1513 and the humanist attack on chivalry', in Sidney Anglo (ed.), *Chivalry in the Renaissance* (1990), 129–44.

2 See Vergil, 226–7; Buck, 287. Rous's pro-Yorkist Roll extols Richard; his later, post-downfall writings render him the familiar monster (T.D. Kendrick, *British Antiquity* (1950), 21–2).

> warlye, in other menne otherwise. He was malicious, wrathfull, enuious, and from afore his birth, euer frowarde. It is for trouth reported, that the Duches his mother had so muche a doe in her travaile, that shee coulde not bee deliuered of hym vncutte: and that hee came into the worlde with the feete forwarde, as menne bee borne outwarde, and (as the fame runneth) also not vntothed, whither menne of hatred reporte aboue the trouthe, or elles that nature chaunged her course in hys beginninge, whiche in the course of his lyfe many thinges vnnaturallye committed. None euill captaine was hee in the warre, as to whiche his disposicion was more metely then for peace. Sundrye victories hadde hee, and sommetime ouerthrowes, but neuer in defaulte as for his owne parsone, either of hardinesse or polytike order. Free was he called of dyspence, and sommewhat aboue hys power liberall, with large giftes hee get him vnstedfaste frendeshippe, for whiche hee was fain to pil and spoyle in other places, and get him stedfast hatred. Hee was close and secrete, a deepe dissimuler, lowlye of counteynaunce, arrogant of heart, outwardly coumpinable [companiable] where he inwardely hated, not letting [refraining] to kisse whome hee thoughte to kyll: dispitious and cruell, not for euill will alway, but ofter for ambicion, and either for the suretie or encrease of his estate. Frende and foo was muche what indifferent, where his advauntage grew, he spared no mans deathe, whose life withstoode his purpose.
>
> (*CW*2, 7–8)

Even Richard's generosity amounts to bribery, his bravery an estate-specific knightly socio-pathology and his friendly gestures Judas-like. To this monster of calculation, More adds, crucially, that he a 'long time in king Edwardes life, forethought to be king' (*CW*2, 8; cf. Churchill, 122).[1] Shakespeare's Richard will start planning his rise before his play begins, despite multiple claimants ahead of him.[2]

But More's treatment of this 'long forethought' is maddeningly (and typically) elusive. 'Some wise menne' claim Richard helped eliminate Clarence five years before King Edward's death, and 'Menne constantly saye' that Richard 'slewe with his owne handes' King Henry VI, but 'of al this pointe, is there no certaintie, & whoso diuineth vppon coniectures, maye as wel shote to farre as to short' (*CW2*, 8–9).[3] More follows Tacitus in warning against anonymous reports (see *Annals*, 3.16), but More's sceptical rhetoric nevertheless invites readers to follow a chain of tenuous likelihoods. The credence granted More's account, notwithstanding such disclaimers, speaks for itself. Despite isolated resistance, such as George Buck's *History of King Richard the Third* (written before 1623), John Stow's qualifications, Sir William Cornwallis's ironic *Essayes* (1601) or Horace Walpole's *Historic Doubts on the Life and Reign of Richard III* (1768), More's hunchbacked, pre-meditating murderer has passed as history for five centuries.[4] This success in creating the effect of truth, despite or even because of disclaimers, suggests a rhetorical paradox of Shakespeare's play.

Could it have been More's seductive, insinuating narrator who inspired Shakespeare's novel treatment of his protagonist? More the master of rhetorical turns, with his engaging rhetoric of self-disabling admissions, pious admonitions, homely proverbs and lurid revelations, is a character we know far more intimately

1 For More's originality, see *CW*2, lxxix.
2 See *3H6* 3.3.124–195.
3 On the difficulty in tracking the multiple voices More employs, see Annabel M. Patterson, *Reading Holinshed's Chronicles* (Chicago, 1994), 110.
4 For Stow's reservations, see Elizabeth Story Donno, 'Thomas More and *Richard III*', *RQ*, 35 (1982), 445; D.R. Woolf, '"The common voice": history, folklore and oral tradition in early modern England', *Past and Present*, 120 (1988), 37. Stow reprints More in his own history (Buck, cxvii).

than his Richard.[1] The effect of More's entertaining verbal insinuations constitutes a rough analogue for the effect of Shakespeare's master of ceremonies, Richard, on virtually all audiences. Despite moral qualms, we are drawn, at least at first, to Richard's side.

We *ought* to disapprove. Visibly embodying 'vnnaturall' alienation from kin and kind, incarnating primal human evil, Shakespeare's Richard is 'curvatus', as biblical and patristic commonplace says sinful humankind is, bent away from the heavenly Creator.[2] Yet this limping caricature seduces characters and audiences. By contrast, More's Richard is neither attractive nor intimate with us. More invites no sympathy, never presents the world as Richard sees it, gives him no memorable speeches. Furthermore, the *History* omits crucial events. We hear nothing of Elizabeth of York, nor of the battle of Bosworth, nor of Richmond's marriage and coronation. These come to Hall, Holinshed and hence to Shakespeare, largely from Vergil, along with seductions, laments and histrionics.

More hereafter: Holinshed, Hall and The Mirror for Magistrates

By contrast with More's 'vnnaturall' monster of long 'forethought', Vergil's Richard is innocent of Clarence's death and lacks royal designs until Edward IV dies (Vergil, 173, 167–8). However, by the time of Hall's *Union* (1548) and *The Mirror for Magistrates* (1559), his guilt and forethought are presumed. If Shakespeare had only read these two texts he might have missed some of More's self-irony, but Shakespeare also read Holinshed, who retains more of the original's mixture of affirmation and scepticism.

Holinshed offered a combination of More with Hall and minor bits from others. Aside from the crucial factor of its stylistic

1 Shakespeare transfers 'More's alert sense of irony to Richard himself' (David Riggs, *Shakespeare's Heroical Histories: Henry VI and Its Literary Tradition* (Cambridge, Mass., 1971), 144).

2 See e.g. Augustine's *Ennarationes* (on Psalm 37), in Migne.

contributions, his *Chronicles* also provided some specifics: the bleeding of Henry VI's corpse (1.2.56; cf. Churchill, 216; Holinshed, 3.690–1); the punning prophecy of Richard's death (4.2.101–5; only in 1587 Holinshed, 3.746); the rewards promised to Buckingham (from More's Latin version) (3.1.195–6; Holinshed, 3.721), and the mistaken claim that Richmond had been brought up at his 'moothers meanes' (5.3.324; only in 1587 Holinshed, 3.756). Hall, drawing his More from Richard Grafton's 1543 Continuation of Hardyng's *Chronicle*, sometimes curtails More's rhetorical self-qualifications. For example, Hall repeats the claim that Richard acted on his own in murdering Henry VI but omits More's qualifiers concerning hearsay, giving the very words of the murderer.[1] By the 1550s it had become accepted fact that Richard saw to the execution of Clarence after having 'secretly stirr[ed] up Edward's suspicion and wrath against him while publicly pretending to intercede for him'.[2] *The Mirror for Magistrates* agrees (*Mirror*, 'Clarence', 332–47) and presumes his long 'forethought' (*Mirror*, 'Richard of Gloucester', 297).

Hall's *Union* casts Richard as the evil product of the 'vnnatural deuision' between York and Lancaster and as the opponent to its resolution in the marital 'vnion' that produced the Tudor succession. This holy conjunction is compared to the joining of 'Godhed to manhood' in the Incarnation (Hall, *Introduction*, fol. i^{r-v}). This stress on marriage is especially relevant to *Richard III*. Richard's murders are bad, Hall's Richmond admits, but attempting to marry his niece Elizabeth renders Richard 'a tyrau[n]t more then Nero, for he hath not only murdered his nephewe beyng his kyng and souereigne lorde, bastarded his noble brethern and defamed the wombe of his verteous and womanly mother, but also compased all the meanes and waies

1 See Hall, *Edward V*, fol. i^{v}; for Commines, Fabyan, the Great Chronicle and Rous on Henry VI's death, and qualifiers about Richard's involvement, see Buck, 288.

2 A.R. Myers, 'Richard III and historical tradition', *History*, 53 (1968), 183. Rainolde makes Richard the physical perpetrator (Rainolde, fol. xiii^{r}).

y^{t} he coulde inuent how to stuprate and carnally know his awne nece vnder the pretence of a cloked matrimony' (Hall, *Richard III*, fol. lvi^{r}).

This nightmare rape/marriage of a York by a York would have prevented the grand wedding march of Hall's history, and the centrality of marriage to Tudor historical narratives explains other features of his account.[1] Hall exceeds Vergil in denouncing Elizabeth's mother for complying with Richard's desires, and he makes seduction a pervasive metaphor. Queen Elizabeth agrees to the 'vnlawfull and in maner vnnaturall copulacion' of uncle and niece that 'all men and the mayden her selfe' abhorred (Hall, *Richard III*, fol. xlix^{r}). Vergil had denounced her female 'mutability' (Vergil, 210), but Hall fulminates against this surrender to Richard's 'will and pleasure' and her violation of every kinship bond, as if she were a female Richard.[2] Queen Elizabeth 'promised to submyt & yelde her selfe fully and frankely to the kynges will and pleasure. And so she putting in obliuion the murther of her innocente children, the infamy and dishonoure spoken by the kynge her husbande, the lyuynge in auoutrie [adultery] leyed to her charge, the bastardyng of her daughters, forgettyng also ye feithfull promes & open othe made to the countesse of Richmond mother to ye erle Henry, blynded by auaricious affeccion and seduced by flatterynge wordes' delivered her daughters to Richard as lambs to 'the rauenous wolfe' (Hall, *Richard III*, fol. xlviii^{r}; followed by Holinshed, 3.750).

Metaphors of seduction and forgetful 'obliuion' permeate Hall's account of the master dissembler's effects upon often complicitous victims.[3] The imagery of seduction even occurs in

1 Hall's Buckingham acclaims the marriage of Elizabeth and Richmond as inspired by 'the holy ghoste' (Hall, *Richard III*, fol. xxxv^{v}).

2 Holinshed allows that fear may have contributed, but 'women are of a proud disposition' (Holinshed, 3.750).

3 Queen Elizabeth is 'auaricious of affection'; Hastings and Buckingham 'easie to kyndle' with factional hatreds (Hall, *Edward V*, fol. v^{v}); Tyrrel 'nothing straunge' to Richard's manipulations because he is 'kept vnder' (Hall, *Richard III*, fol. xxvii^{r}).

reference to Richard himself. Hall's Richard, like Vergil's and Grafton's (Vergil, 214; Hardyng, *Richard the iii*, fol. xcix^{r}), falls prey to mortal 'security', but Hall describes him as 'seduced and deluded by hys craftie taletellers' into a 'golden slepe' (Hall, *Richard III*, fol. xlix^{v}; as Holinshed, 3.752). Hall's Richard is a seducer seduced, and he is also implicated, unlike More's (or Vergil's or Grafton's) tyrant, in three other themes relevant to Shakespeare's play: confession, self-exculpation and lamentation.

Hall's Richard actually publicly confesses his crimes, lamenting and blaming others for seducing him into seeking the throne. He admits that 'I being seduced & prouoked by sinister cou[n]sail and diabolical temptacio[n] did commyt a facynerous and detestable acte. Yet I haue with strayte penaunce and salt teryes (as I trust) expiated and clerely purged thesame offence, which abhominable cryme I require you of frendship as clerely to forget, as I dayly do remember to deplore and lament thesame' (Hall, *Richard III*, fol. liv^{r-v}; as Holinshed, 3.756). Nothing like this public confession appears in More, nor in Shakespeare's play, but in *Richard III* mock penitence and seduction are enormously elaborated in two wholly invented wooing scenes, while self-exculpation becomes all-pervasive, with virtually every character blaming others for his or her own problems and shortcomings.

Confession, contrition and lamentation permeate another of the play's sources, *The Mirror for Magistrates*. Lamentation constitutes the very substance of the *Mirror*, but Hall anticipates this tonality.[1] Expanding Vergil's account of responses to the deaths of the princes, Hall adds his usual tropes of seduction and obliviousness, but elaborates on the open weeping of 'all the people' in 'euery towne, streate, and place' and the 'lamentable crienge' of Queen Elizabeth herself:

> she was so sodainly amasyd with the greatnes of ye crueltie that for feare she sounded [swooned] and fell

1 For More's single reference to lamentation, see *CW*2, 21.

> doune to the ground, and there lay in a great agonye like to a deade corps. And after that she came to her memory and was reuyued agayne, she wept and sobbyd and with pitefull sighes she repleneshyed the hole mancion, her breste she puncted, her fayre here she tare and pulled in peces & being ouercome with sorowe & penciuenes rather desyred death then life, callyng by name diuers tymes her swete babes, accomptyng her self more then madde that she deluded by wyle and fraudulente promyses delyuered her younger sonne out of the sanctuarie to his enemye to be put to death thinkynge that nexte the othe made to God broke[n] & the dewtie of allegiaunce toward her childre[n] violated, she of all creatures in that poyncte was most seduced and disceaued. After longe lamentacion, when she sawe no hope of reuengynge otherwyse, she knelyd downe and cried on God to take vengeaunce for the disceaytfull periurie, as who saide that she nothyng mystrusted but once he would remember it. What ys he liuyng that if he remember and beholde these .ii. noble enfantes with out deseruing, so shamefully murthered, that wil not abhorre the fact, ye & be moued & tormented with pitie and mercie. And yet the worlde is so frayle and our nature so blynde that fewe be sturred with suche examples, obliuiouslie forgettynge, and littell consyderyng, that oftentimes for the offences by the parentes perpetrate and committed, that synne is punished in there lyne and posterite.
>
> (Hall, *Richard III*, fols xxviii^{v}–xxix^{r}; cf. Vergil, 189–90)

Here is the lamentation and complaint that pervade *Richard III*, but here, too, there is another side to the story.

The object of complaint is not the ultimate cause of the loss that is lamented; Hall's Richard merely represents a cog in the great wheel of divine judgement. Following Vergil, Hall treats the deaths of the princes as transgenerational payback for the sins of their father. Even Richard's means, his 'disceaytfull periurie', replays Edward's own crime: the princes die 'because king Edward . . . promised and sware one thing by his worde thinkyng cleane contrarie in his harte as after dyd appere. And afterward by the death of the duke of Clarence his brother, he incurred (of likelyehod) the great displeasure toward God' (Hall, *Richard III*, fol. xxix^{r}; following Vergil, 189–90).

As the wheels of justice turn, some of Hall's characters foresee the process. Hall invents Margaret the suffering prophet with futile foresight:

> she muche lamented, and bewailed the euill fate and destenie of her husbande, whiche eminently before her iyes, she sawe to approche she accused, reproued, and reuiled, and in conclusion, her senses were so vexed, and she so afflicted, and caste into suche an agony, that she preferred death before life, rather desiryng soner to die, then lenger to liue, and perauenture for this cause, that her interior iye sawe priuily, and gaue to her a secret monicion of the greate calamities and aduersities, whiche then did hang ouer her hed, and were likely incontinent to fall and succede (whiche other persones, neither loked for nor regarded[)]
>
> (Hall, *Edward IV*, fols ccxviii^{v}–ccxix^{r}; not in Holinshed)[1]

Suffering grants an 'interior iye' to see the future, but Margaret's own pains amount to punishments for earlier sins. Mortals take note.

Hall's inevitable divine retribution, accompanied with copious accusation and lamentation, anticipates *The Mirror for*

1 See W. Gordon Zeefeld, 'The influence of Hall on Shakespeare's English historical plays', *English Literary History*, 3 (1936), 317–53. Hall also depicts Margaret mourning the 'losse of Prince Edward her sonne' (Hall, *Edward IV*, fol. ccxxi^{v}).

Magistrates.[1] In minor specifics, the *Mirror* probably provided Shakespeare with the punch-line about Clarence being 'new christened' (1.1.50; see *Mirror*, 'Clarence', 370–1) and Richard's relations with his mother (Jones, *Origins*, 217). No one before Shakespeare says the Duchess reviled Richard (*R3* 4.4.137–96); however, the *Mirror*'s lame 'Claudius' (who married his niece) reports maternal abuse in lines anticipating Richard's opening soliloquy: 'me a monster oft she namde, / Vnperfect all, begun by nature, but begot / Not absolute, not well, nor fully framde. / Sith thus my mother often me defamde' (*Mirror, Additions*, 'Claudius', 8–12; cf. *R3* 1.1.19–21).[2]

More importantly, the *Mirror* anticipates another verbal aspect of *Richard III*. Amid predictable generalities about fickle fortune, the *Mirror* models its world on courtly existence, where the main sins are ambitious scheming and climbing and the likely end a sudden plunge into ruin (Jones, *Origins*, 193). Shakespeare's Hastings, who compares the 'momentary grace of mortal men' to precarious elevation above the deep (3.4.95–100), would be completely at home. But the *Mirror* also provides intensely emotional representations of interiority unparalleled in More, Vergil, Grafton, Hall or Holinshed. Hall leaves Richard's inner workings 'to God whiche knewe his interior cogitations at the hower of his deathe' (Hall, *Richard III*, fol. lix^{r}; cf. Holinshed's expansion, 3.761). The *Mirror*'s Richard merely reports his evil nature and deeds, but other Ricardian figures suggest a greater contribution to Shakespearean characterization.

Thomas Sackville's famous 'Induction' and 'Complaint of Buckingham' turn generic signs of grief – torn hair, rent cloak, broken voice and tear-filled eyes – into dramatic means (*Mirror*, 'Induction', 533–53). Buckingham's language derives from formal complaint, a generic resource exploited in the *Henry*

1 The *Mirror* was first published in 1559 with three relevant complaints; the 1563 edition added six others (Bullough, 3.229). It was further expanded in 1587.

2 Richard's reference to premature birth contradicts Rous's two-year gestation (C. Ross, *Richard*, 139) and the Duchess's claim at 4.4.163–4.

VI plays. Calling down vengeance on his betrayer Banister, Buckingham curses himself, the hour, the time, the place of meeting, the sun, moon and stars, earth and air ('Buckingham', 638–51).[1] But finding invective insufficient, he confronts the question that plagues the victims of Shakespeare's Richard, asking 'Howe shall I curse . . . what shal I say?' (656, 664; cf. *R3* 4.4.117). As the women demand that the earth split (1.2.65, 4.4.75), invoking despair (1.2.84–6) and family destruction (1.2.21–8, 1.3.198–200), so Buckingham wishes the earth 'rent in twaye' (657), urging that Banister 'despayer' (673), that he 'wayle the daye, and wepe the night' (675), that his children die (691–705) while he 'live in death, and dye in lyef' (710).[2] His curses also suggest ironies relevant to Shakespeare's play, as one betrayer curses another with a curse – to 'live in death, and dye in lyef' – that articulates the end that will come home to the curser himself (see 719).

The *Mirror* might also have influenced *Richard III* in another, related matter. No matter how formulaic, Jane's Shore's curses on Richard (*Mirror*, 'Shore's Wife', 330–6) are revealing in a historical sense and significant for a consideration of Shakespeare's railing women. Amid pathetic self-accusations and exculpations, she alone actually curses the tyrant king.[3] Her verbal attack registers a highly relevant gendered asymmetry in the historical treatment of abuse directed against a monarch.

UPON SCAFFOLDS: MORE, HOLINSHED, LEGGE, *TRUE TRAGEDY*

A two-way relationship between Richard's narrative and the stage begins with classical metaphors likening life to a play. Sir Thomas More and the sources dependent on his *History* develop

1 Cf. *3H6* 1.4.111–68; Baldwin, 2.335.
2 The fates he wishes on Banister's children are those Hall says befell Buckingham's own offspring (Churchill, 255).
3 See Mary Steible, 'Jane Shore and the politics of cursing', *SEL*, 43 (2003), 1–17.

this trope. By the early 1590s two dramatic works – in addition to *2* and *3 Henry VI* – had staged Richard: Thomas Legge's Latin drama *Richardus Tertius*, performed at Cambridge in 1579 and widely circulated in manuscript, and the anonymous *True Tragedy of Richard III* (Stationers' Register 19 June 1594), 'playd by the Queenes Maiesties Players'.[1] One other performance, a 1559 London pageant recorded in Holinshed's reprint of Richard Mulcaster's account, deserves attention.

The *theatrum mundi* image comes to More with a history.[2] It appears in its traditional form in *The Mirror for Magistrates*, which compares human existence to a performance played before God and the audience of history (e.g. *Mirror*, 'Buckingham', 43–6). However, More turns cosmic metaphysics to social satire. Calling Richard's Guildhall bid for citizen approval a 'mocckish ellection', More invokes 'Kynges games, as it were stage playes . . . plaied vpon scafoldes', and likens social rituals to stage performance. Social life demands that ordinary people 'forget' mundane identities to sustain assigned public roles and observe their limits – or risk the consequences. More offers an important illustration: 'menne must sommetime for the manner sake not bee a knowen what they knowe. For at the consecracion of a bishop, euery man woteth well by the paying for his bulles, y^{t} he purposeth to be one . . . And yet must he bee twise asked whyther he wil be bishop or no, and he muste twyse say naye, and at the third tyme take it as compelled ther vnto by his owne wyll' (*CW*2, 80–1). While they here exemplify public rituals, kingship and episcopacy were historical institutions of particular concern – for More, and for Shakespeare and his first audiences. Representing a monarch or a bishop on the theatrical scaffold, or posing questions about their social magic, could earn a one-way trip to another scaffold.

Historians have debated the extent of early modern censorship, but sensitivities about potential official reactions were a factor in textual production, in performance and in oral communication

1 See Arber, 2, fol. 309^{v}.
2 More translates Lucian's *Menippus*; see More, *CW*3, 25–43.

in the late 1580s and early 1590s.[1] By November 1589, well into the furious Marprelate exchanges about the office of bishop, the Privy Council fulminated that 'players take vppon them to handle in their plaies certen matters of Divinytie and of State unfit to be suffred' and instructed the Archbishop of Canterbury, the Lord Mayor of London and Edmund Tilney, Master of the Revels, to appoint someone to scrutinize plays performed in London.[2] Michael Hattaway has argued that the *Henry VI* plays show either Tilney's censorship or the players' self-censorship.[3] In March 1591 Spenser's *Complaints* (Stationers' Register 29 December 1590), with its *Mother Hubbard's Tale* suggesting allegorical reference to Lord Burghley and his son Robert Cecil, was called in (Peterson, 10). By the end of the decade, the 1599 Bishops' Ban would insist that 'noe English historyes be printed excepte they bee allowed by somme of her maiesties privie Counsell' and 'noe playes bee printed excepte they bee allowed by such as have aucthorytie' (Arber, 3.316).[4]

Despite official sensitivities, historical persons and events furnished the material for public pageants as well as for the numerous stage representations that make the late sixteenth century the golden age of the history play. Holinshed's *Chronicles* preserves one officially approved staging relevant to *Richard III* in Mulcaster's account of a pageant that had greeted the young Queen Elizabeth on the way to her coronation at Westminster Abbey in 1559:

> Upon the lowest stage was made one seat roiall, wherein were placed two personages, representing king Henrie the seuenth, and Elizabeth his wife, daughter of king Edward the fourth . . . king Henrie the seuenth

1 See *Literature and Censorship in Renaissance England*, ed. Andrew Hadfield (Basingstoke, 2001).

2 *Acts of the Privy Council, 1524–1604*, ed. J.R. Dasent (1890–1907), 18.214–15.

3 Hattaway, *Companion*, 15; cf. Janet Clare, *Art Made Tongue-Tied by Authority: Elizabethan and Jacobean Dramatic Censorship* (Manchester, 1990), 39–43, and Cyndia Clegg, *Press Censorship in Elizabethan England* (Cambridge, 1997).

4 Even the *Mirror* evidences official disapproval (Budra, 22–3).

proceeding out of the house of Lancaster, was inclosed in a red rose, and . . . queen Elizabeth, being heire to the house of Yorke, inclosed with a white rose, each of them roiallie crowned, and decentlie apparelled, as apperteineth to princes, with scepters in their hands, and one vawt surmounting their heads, wherein aptlie were placed two tables, each conteining the title of those two princes. And . . . the one of them joined hands with the other, with the ring of matrimonie perceiued on the finger. Out of the which two roses sprang two branches gathered into one, which were directed vpward to the second stage or degree, wherein was placed one representing . . . king Henrie the eight, which sproong out of the former stocke, crowned with a crowne imperiall, and by him sat one representing the right woorthie ladie queene Anne, wife to the said king Henrie the eight, and mother to our most souereigne ladie queene Elizabeth that now is . . . From their seat also proceeded vpwards one branch, directed to the third and vppermost stage or degree, wherein likewise was planted a seat roiall, in the which was set one representing the queenes most excellent maiestie Elizabeth, now our most dread and souereigne ladie, crowned and apparelled as the other princes were. Out of the fore part of this pageant was made a standing for a child, which at the queens maiesties comming declared vnto hir the whole meaning of the said pageant . . . And all emptie places thereof were furnished with sentences concerning vnitie, and the whole pageant garnished with red roses and white. And in the fore front of the same pageant, in a faire wreath, was written . . . The vniting of the two houses of Lancaster and Yorke. This pageant was grounded vpon the queens maiesties name. For like as the long warres between the two houses of Yorke and Lancaster then ended, when

> Elizabeth daughter to Edward the fourth matched in marriage with Henrie the seuenth, heire to the house of Lancaster: so sith that the queenes maiesties name was Elizabeth, & for somuch as she is the onelie heire of Henrie the eight, which came of both the houses, as the knitting vp of concord: it was deuised, that like as Elizabeth was the first occasion of concord, so she another Elizabeth, might mainteine the same among hir subiects, so that vnitie was the end wereat the whole deuise shot, as the queenes maiesties name moued the first ground.
>
> (Holinshed, 3.1173)

Here history is staged along with current events and future hopes 'concerning vnitie'. Even the location in 'Gracious' (Gracechurch) Street may have borne topical significance, since Elizabeth's mother, Anne Boleyn, had there witnessed a pageant for her own coronation.[1] Men must sometimes forget what they know, More might say, since in 1559 Anne appears represented as an honoured queen and mother of the new Queen Elizabeth and not as disgraced, divorced and doomed. The onstage Elizabeth of York confronts 'another Elizabeth' in the audience, her royal granddaughter, who herself also appears replicated elsewhere on the stage. This 'history' obviously depends on a highly edited past. It omits Yorkist kings, other wives (or heirs) for Henry VIII and other claimants, while implicating an immediate, offstage present.

The warring Houses and the 'chair of estate' for which they contended are woven into a peaceful arbour. The White Rose of York and the Red Rose of Lancaster conjoin in the union of Elizabeth of York with Henry of Richmond, the first Tudor monarch, and grow upwards towards Henry VIII and Anne, who produce Elizabeth I. The conjugal handclasp and 'ring of matrimonie . . . on the finger' of Elizabeth of York must

1 A. Kinney, 20; Mulcaster's pageant appears in the same volume.

have put pressure on the new Elizabeth, who witnessed herself portrayed as the sole uncoupled figure. Perhaps eager to appear the antithesis to her late sister Queen Mary, whose reign (1553–8) had seen persecution of Protestants, marital alliance with Philip of Spain and the loss of Calais (A. Kinney, 20), the new Queen expressed no umbrage at this representation. In a few years, such pointedly topical history would have been very risky. Later Elizabethans would lose their freedoms, limbs and even lives for venturing stage advice about matrimony, succession or Church government.

This highly edited royal flow-chart proclaims from the scaffold that 'ciuill warre, / and shead of bloud did cease, / When these two houses were / vnited into one' (Holinshed, 3.1173); offstage, political life, like family life, proved more complicated. Issues that would trouble the later sixteenth century haunt Mulcaster's mid-century account. The dynastic rose-bush was extensively filiated, giving the authors of polemics such as *Leicester's Commonwealth* (1584) a reason to worry and providing guerilla genealogies, such as Robert Parsons's *Conference* (1595) with a dozen or so budding royal alternatives. Then there is religious division. Just steps beyond the signs urging 'concord', other pageants demanded that 'religion true' should 'break Superstitions head' and quash 'rebellion' (Holinshed, 3.1174). Protestant and Catholic, Protestant and Protestant would continue at odds throughout the century. The years immediately following the Armada of 1588 saw the Marprelate controversy concerning ecclesiastical government, Archbishop Whitgift's vigorous repression of Puritans – and Shakespeare's first plays. Reading about the hopeful pageants of the 1550s might remind Englishmen of the 1590s that Queen and Church would not end divisiveness, even amongst family.

A Londoner of the 1590s might have registered an irony in the 1559 pageant when the gift of an English Bible prompts Elizabeth to turn for assistance to Sir John Perrot, her reputed bastard half-brother. In 1590 Perrot was removed from the

1 Family tree from Edward Hall, *The Union of the Two Noble and Illustre Families of Lancastre and Yorke* (edition of 1550)

Privy Council and sensationally tried for treason. Among other charges, it was alleged that he had protested the ignominy of serving 'a base bastard piss-kitchin woman' (Howell, 1.1321). Perrot's meteoric fall, dramatic trial, notorious imprisonment – first in Burghley's home and then in the Tower – and his death in September 1592 were 'the speache of the Towne' as Shakespeare composed *Richard III*.[1] So much for family unity. Furthermore, though 'treason' provided the official explanation for Perrot's fall, an alternative narrative claimed that he had been betrayed by Burghley, suggesting new levels of brutal factionalism within Elizabeth's government and enlarging public awareness of internal divisions (Hammer, 398). Sound familiar? Dire divisions and subtle deceptions, nasty family infighting and abrupt, contrived downfalls pervade *Richard III*. More's *History* lent itself to such themes, although dramatic treatments could be highly various, as in Legge's Latin *Richardus Tertius* and the anonymous public stage play *The True Tragedy of Richard the Third*.

Richardus Tertius was widely known despite its language, length (some 4,700 lines), single academic performance and its remaining in manuscript until modern times. The 1579 staging at St John's College, Cambridge, constituted 'perhaps the most ambitious dramatic performance ever attempted in England (before or since)'.[2] On successive nights, one Actio of the play's three was performed with the same lead actor and a cast of over one hundred men and boys. It included a coronation scene, battlefield gunfire and a horse to bear Richard's corpse.[3] The text circulated widely in multiple manuscripts. In 1591 Sir John Harington, who may have witnessed the performance, recalled the play's ethical power, saying it 'would moue (I thinke) *Phalaris* the tyraunt, and terrifie all tyranous minded men, fro[m]

1 See Thomas Tresham's letter of March 1591 (Peterson, 22).
2 Nelson, 61.
3 Nelson, 61; citing *REED*, 1.918–19, 944–6; see also 847; cf. *Richardus Tertius*, xiii; 4588.

following their foolish ambitious humors, seeing how [Richard's] ambition made him kill his brother, his nephews, his wife beside infinit others; and last of all after a short and troublesome raigne, to end his miserable life, and to haue his body harried after his death'.[1] Harington's ethical defence is interesting, since the actor who portrayed Legge's Richard was the first to be implicated in the claim that the role negatively affected his offstage existence.[2] Anecdotes connecting scaffold and life would dog stage Richards from Richard Burbage (see p. 83) to John Wilkes Booth (Wood, 164).

Scholars disagree about Legge's influence on *Richard III*.[3] Some shared elements appear coincidental: Norfolk obtains postponement of Lord Strange's execution; Richmond interviews Stanley and citizens react to England's troubles (*Richardus Tertius*, 2649–706; Bullough, 3.235). Other elements might reflect Legge's influence on *True Tragedy*. Strikingly, however, Legge and Shakespeare emphasize female roles and provide two major wooing scenes unparalleled in *True Tragedy*.[4]

Legge twice portrays wooing by Richard or his proxy. As in *Richard III* (1.2, 4.4), only one attempt succeeds. Lovell, at Richard's direction, induces Queen Elizabeth to hand over her daughters so that Richard can bestow 'splendid marriages' on them (*Richardus Tertius*, 3901–4206). Stichomythic exchanges balance her recriminations against Lovell's testimony that Richard's 'face is wet with weeping' for having murdered her two sons and his insinuations of profit and protection for her surviving son; Elizabeth accepts the bargain. The second wooing scene contradicts Legge's sources to represent Richard

1 'An Apologie of Poetrie', in *Orlando Furioso* (1591; STC 746), sig. ¶vi^{r}. Francis Meres includes Legge among 'our best for Tragedy' (Meres, sig. Oo3^{r-v}).

2 Thomas Fuller writes, he 'had his head so possest with a Princelike humor, that ever after, he did what then he acted' (quoted in *REED*, 1.286).

3 Churchill and Bullough find parallel divergence from sources; Brooks and Hammond attribute these to Seneca (Bullough, 3.234–7; Brooks, 'Unhistorical', 721–37; Hammond, 82). Cf. Robert J. Lordi, 'The relationship of *Richardus Tertius* to the main Richard III plays', *Boston University Studies in English*, 5 (1961), 149–53.

4 In *True Tragedy* Lovell reports Richard's suit positively received by Queen Elizabeth and her daughter. Richard woos neither in Heywood's *Edward IV*.

personally wooing Elizabeth of York; this scene draws on Seneca's *Hercules Furens*, and for one detail – Richard's drawn sword – Seneca's *Hippolytus/Phaedra*.[1] A sword will play a pivotal role in Shakespeare's – similarly unprecedented – depiction of Anne's seduction (1.2).

Shakespeare may have been directly influenced by Seneca. Neither Legge nor *True Tragedy* makes female lament as pervasive as does Shakespeare, but Seneca's *Troades* brings together three generations of women, 'each with its own memories and griefs' (Bullough, 3.236). The Duchess of York's claim to be the mother of all 'parcelled' griefs (2.2.80–1) parallels Hecuba's claims: 'Whosesoever woes thou weepest, thou wilt weep mine. Each feels the weight of his own disaster only, but I the disasters of them all' (Seneca, *Troades*, 1060–2). However, *Troades* lacks a central tyrant, and it amply conveys pathos that Shakespeare avoids, including the taking of a child, Astyanax, from the arms of his weeping mother (Seneca, *Troades*, 786–812).

Although generally following chronicle sources, Legge makes Richard neither very deformed nor especially strong. The single reference to his withered arm occurs in the well-known plot against Hastings (*Richardus Tertius*, 1679); otherwise, his body prompts neither self-reflection nor ridicule. Although Richard's lust for power is characterized as disease, madness, murderousness, guile and hypocrisy (*Richardus Tertius*, xviii), he is not More's strong, resourceful character. Instead, he is fearful, declamatory and directed by others (Churchill, 376–9). Catesby appears initially more Ricardian than Richard, with personal reasons for resenting Hastings and a design to dupe Richard into acting at his direction (*Richardus Tertius*, 1425–37, 1533–70).[2]

Legge's dramatic innovations consist of his close adherence to historical record in a drama that incorporates Senecan elements – bloody tyrant, stichomythic dialogue, choric observers, *nuntius* figures and animating supernatural spirits – within a trilogy

1 See Whitaker, 66.
2 Cf. the blame heaped on 'Lawyer Catesby' (*Mirror*, 'Rivers', 456–62).

(*Richardus Tertius*, 269–72; cf. Hodgdon, *End*, 238). Seneca's tyrant and focused action are recast within a format 'vastly larger and more complex in structure and in narrative scope than a Senecan tragedy' (*Richardus Tertius*, xv). Shakespeare need not have read *Richardus Tertius* for its form to have suggested historical tetralogy. There is no doubt he did know – though we are unsure by when – a work indebted to Legge, *The True Tragedy of Richard III*.

True Tragedy and *Richard III* share features that have prompted debate about priority and influence.[1] Their strongest connection is the resemblance between 'A horse, a horse, a fresh horse' (*True Tragedy*, 1984) and 'A horse, a horse, my kingdom for a horse!' (*R3* 5.4.7).[2] Their differences are more revealing.

True Tragedy's prologue describes Richard as 'ill shaped, crooked backed, lame armed, withall, / Valiantly minded, but tyrannous in authoritie' (*True Tragedy*, 57–8), but his physical limitations occasion little comment and provide no motivation. As in Legge, Richard blames Jane Shore for his 'withered arme' (946). The only other reference occurs in a patch of Senecan rant: 'this verie day, I hope with this lame hand of mine, to rake out that hatefull heart of Richmond, and when I haue it, to eate it panting hote with salt, and drinke his blood luke warme' (1978–81). Similar rhetoric, foreign to Shakespeare's play, permeates *True Tragedy*.[3] In their self-direction, the two Richards resemble one another more than Legge's manipulated figure. But the great dissimulation is missing from *True Tragedy*'s Richard, who suffers recurrent

1 Contrast Hammond, 83, with Churchill, 398; see also Bullough, 3.237, and J.D. Wilson, 'Shakespeare's *Richard III* and *The True Tragedy of Richard the Third, 1594*', *SQ*, 3 (1952), 299–306.

2 George Peele's *Battell of Alcazar* (1594; STC 19531, sig. F3^r) has a fleeing character cry, 'A horse, a horse, villaine a horse'. Neither Hall's nor Holinshed's Richard loses a horse, as Shakespeare's does (5.4.4), but both refuse one offered as a means of flight, as do the Richards of *True Tragedy* and *Richard III* (Hall, *Richard III*, fol. lviii^r; Holinshed, 3.759–60). For another similarity see 3.1.84–8. In *Edward III* (Stationers' Register 1595) Prince Edward refuses a horse for flight before battle (*E3* 4.4.88–99).

3 *True Tragedy* includes lines that Hamlet parodies: 'The screeking Raven sits croking for reuenge. / Whole heads of beasts comes bellowing for reuenge' (1879–93).

bouts of conscience (Churchill, 472–3) and is no seducer. He neither woos Anne, nor attempts to win over Queen Elizabeth or her daughter Elizabeth. Nor do female figures have extended laments and accusations, although the treatment of Elizabeth of York is suggestive.

The title of *True Tragedy* promises the 'coniunction' of York and Lancaster, and Elizabeth of York appears at Bosworth to agree to wed Richmond, prompting a messenger to declare: 'Thus Gentles may you heere behold, the ioyning of these Houses' (2164–5). That settled, the play concludes with Tudor genealogy and an encomium to Elizabeth I. Because Elizabeth I's Protestant piety and Tudor family values have 'put proud Antichrist to flight / And bene the meanes that ciuill wars did cease', the audience is enjoined: 'Then England kneele vpon thy hairy knee, / And thanke that God that still prouides for thee' (2206–7).[1] Legge similarly concludes with thanks for 'our mighty sovereign Elizabeth' (*Richardus Tertius*, 4695–6). Both plays express concern about the future.

In 1579 Legge praises the 46-year-old Queen as 'a virgin who overcomes the hoary locks of age', and prays, 'May the thunderer hold His hand over her and make long her life' (*Richardus Tertius*, 4696–701). A decade later, *True Tragedy* proclaims that Elizabeth ought 'to liue for aye', but adds anxiously, 'if her Graces dayes be brought to end, / Your hope is gone, on whom did peace depend' (*True Tragedy*, 2220–3). At the conclusion of Shakespeare's *Richard III*, Richmond invites the audience to consider England's prosperity under his descendants, but this, the play's only straightforward political speech (Campbell, 333–4), neither wishes Elizabeth I eternal life nor denounces ambition and tyranny. Richmond prays for 'peace' and warns against 'treason' and 'traitors':

> That would reduce these bloody days again
> And make poor England weep in streams of blood.

1 RP suggests 'hairy' is a misprint for 'harty'.

Let them not live to taste this land's increase
That would with treason wound this fair land's peace.
Now civil wounds are stopped; peace lives again.
That she may long live here, God say amen.
(5.5.36–41)

Charges of 'treason' against Richard and followers had historical precedent, and *True Tragedy*'s Richmond proclaims 'traytrous Richard' shall be 'drawne through the streets of *Lester*, / Starke naked on a Colliers horse' – 'a traytors due reward' (2153–7).[1] The physical details come from Hall, but not the terms. Hall's Richard concludes a 'caytiue' whose crimes are 'ambicion tyranny and myschiefe' (Hall, *Richard III*, fol. lix^{r}).[2]

Whether seen as a 'history' of the years 1483–5, a timeless 'tragedy' or a mixture of the two, *Richard III* also addresses the 1590s. Its quasi-epilogue warning against treason registers extra-dramatic concerns; its quasi-prologue, uniquely for Shakespeare spoken by the protagonist, conveys others. A misfit soldier without a war, a 'deformed' malcontent younger brother, an ambitious 'villain' sowing faction by 'plots', 'prophecies, libels and dreams', a pious hypocrite, 'seem[ing] a saint' when most he plays the devil, a 'determined' reprobate – this patchwork nightmare limps right out of late Elizabethan anxieties.

UPON STAGES

Since the rich stage history of *Richard III* has been the subject of several books, what follows is a mere sketch.[3] Its worldwide heritage as most popular of the histories in languages other than English lies largely beyond this brief survey.[4]

1 On historical charges of treason against Richard's forces, see Chrimes, 63.
2 Richard is not called traitor in the equivalent passage in Holinshed, 3.760.
3 See Wood, Hankey, Colley, Hassel, Richmond and Day.
4 For popularity, see Hoenselaars, 110–11. For international productions 1949–84, see *Shakespeare Around the Globe*, ed. Samuel L. Leiter (New York, 1986).

Beginnings to 1642

The 1597 First Quarto claims itself 'lately Acted by the / Right honourable the Lord Chamber- / laine his seruants'. The first documented performance is recorded as having been given in 1633 at St James's Palace on Queen Henrietta Maria's birthday (Chambers, *Shakespeare*, 2.352). The play still belonged to company repertory, the King's Men having formed from the Lord Chamberlain's Men in 1603, and evidently remained interesting after nearly forty years. When the theatres reopened after the Civil War, its popularity is briefly unclear. After 1700, it appealed widely, whether in the adaptation by Colley Cibber (from 1700), in translation or eventually as, mostly, itself – in England, in pre-Revolutionary America, black New York in the 1820s, King Kamehameha IV's Honolulu court in the 1850s, Italy in the late nineteenth century, Germany in the 1930s, eastern Europe in the 1970s and France in the 1980s and 1990s.[1]

Richard III also ranks among the most frequently printed Elizabethan plays (Blayney, 'Publication', 388).[2] It is undeniably the first of Shakespeare's very long plays; it appears to have been the longest single stage play ever written in English, and remained so until Q 1604 *Hamlet*. Either it was abbreviated for staging, or its performance took more time than the Elizabethan average.[3] Its later history consists of abbreviations and compromises,

1 *Richard III* was performed in America in 1750 (New York), 1751 (Williamsburg), 1752 (Annapolis) and 1753 (Philadelphia); with *Hamlet* and *Twelfth Night* it was the first American publication as a single play (Boston, 1794) (James G. McManaway, 'Shakespeare in the United States', *PMLA*, 79 (1964), 513–18). It was performed for visiting Cherokee 'chiefs' in 1767 (*New York Journal*, 17 December 1767). On black New York and Nazi Germany, see pp. 95, 104–5; on Edwin Booth's performance for King Kamehameha, see Wood, 159. For Italy, see Tempera, 124–9; for eastern Europe in the 1970s, see Alexander Shurbanov and Boika Sokolova, 'Shakespeare's history plays in Bulgaria', in Hoenselaars, 178–86. On French popularity and adaptations, see Fayard, 137–9.

2 Scholars debate whether plays went into print after losing stage popularity (or when a company had financial trouble), or accompanying revivals or responding to demand created by revivals (see Blayney, 'Publication').

3 See Hart, 147, Hammond, 66. Its length results in reviews with titles like 'The perfidious king dies at 2 a.m.' (Tempera, 129).

but its original length is especially remarkable given its other features.

Many plays of the 1590s, especially 'history' plays, stage parallel plots involving several main characters. Richard, however, like Marlowe's protagonists, dominates even when (briefly) offstage. Onstage for fifteen of twenty-five scenes, Richard speaks more lines (1,145 in F) than any other character in a single Elizabethan play (Barabas in Marlowe's *Jew of Malta* has 1,138) except Hamlet (Wood, 57; Jowett, 73n.). A third of the play's lines are his. Yet his contribution lacks the 'high astounding terms' and fierce declamation of contemporary tragic protagonists. Instead, Richard specializes in puncturing pretension with a suprisingly colloquial tone and a timing 'calculated to bring down the house' (Colley, 6) rather than to convey grandeur or evil machination. The character who in *3 Henry VI* echoed Marlowe's Tamburlaine with 'How sweet a thing it is to wear a crown, / Within whose circuit is Elysium / And all that poets feign of bliss and joy' (*3H6* 1.2.28–30) and vowed on his father's corpse to 'venge thy death / Or die renowned by attempting it' (*3H6* 2.1.87–8), sighs, weeps and simpers 'I thank my God for my humility' (2.1.73), hints at self-deprecation with references to a 'tardy cripple' (2.1.90) and vows to hire 'a score or two of tailors' (1.2.259).

Furthermore, *Richard III* largely eschews combats, processions, ceremonies and the violence of contemporary tragedies or history plays, even Shakespeare's own. A single onstage stabbing and one, silent, combat hardly compare to the mayhem of *Titus Andronicus* or to the eight scenes from five battles in *3 Henry VI*. Nevertheless, the play is hardly decorous by the standards of Horace's Renaissance followers. With a body and demeanour recalling deformed Herods, shifty Vices and ad-libbing clowns, Richard banters with children (3.1.81), mimes a preposterous invasion (3.5.1–30) and snidely mocks a mother's blessing (2.2.109–11).[1] Marlowe's Barabas approximates such outrageousness in looks, speech and action, but Richard is a historical tyrant, not a stage-caricature Jew, so his snarky, self-parodic, shamelessly hypocritical portrayal must have been surprising.

Nevertheless, in 1598 Francis Meres cites *Richard III* to claim Shakespeare 'the most excellent' for 'Tragedy' (Meres, sig. Oo2r). In 1600 Robert Allott's *Englands Parnassus* mines it for poetic utterances. Neither work shows knowledge of performance, but other plays suggest that its subject-matter remained interesting, and in 1606 Barnabe Barnes refers to 'that which is yet fresh in our late Chronicles; and hath been many times represented vnto the vulgar upon our English Theaters, of *Richard Plantagenet*'.[2]

Three other early references may imply performance. An epigram of *c.* 1594–5 (printed sometime between 1595 and 1599) echoes Richard's opening soliloquy:

> I am not fashioned for these amorous times,
> To court thy beutie with lascivious rimes.
> I cannot dally, caper, daunce and sing,
> Oyling my saint with supple sonneting . . .
> Not I by Cock, but shall I tel thee roundly,
> Harke in thine eare, zounds I can (   ) thee soundly.
> (John Davies, 180; cf. Davies & Marlowe, 'Ignoto')[3]

The speaker's combination of self-deprecation, preachy morality and surprising aggression is pure Richard, and becomes strikingly stagey when the poem enlists us to fill in the parentheses. The

1 For Richard Tarleton's joke about parental blessing, see Siemon, 'Power'.

2 C.M. Ingleby, L. Toulmin Smith and F.J. Furnivall (eds), *The Shakespere Allusion Book*, 2 vols (1909), 1.162. Thomas Heywood's *2 King Edward the Fourth* (1599) includes Richard, though less centrally. Ben Jonson was commissioned in 1602 to write a Richard Crookback (R.C. Evans, 'More's *Richard III* and Jonson's *Richard Crookback* and *Sejanus*', *Comparative Drama*, 24 [1990], 97–132); Henslowe records a Buckingham play in 1599; Robert Chamberlain mentions a '*Richard* the third' that can be neither *True Tragedy* nor *Richard III* (*A New Book of Mistakes* (1637; STC 4944), sig. D1v).

3 John Davies, *The Poems of Sir John Davies*, ed. Robert Krueger (Oxford, 1975).

sexual aggression also resonates with an anecdote about the actor who *became* Richard, Richard Burbage.

Years after Burbage's performances, Bishop Richard Corbet records the identification of actor with role, claiming that his guide to Bosworth field 'mistook' the 'Player for a King, / For when he would have said, King *Richard* dy'd, / And call'd a Horse, a Horse, he *Burbage* cry'd'.[1] Similar conflation of actor and role grounds John Manningham's famous 1601 diary entry:

> Vpon a tyme when Burbidge played Rich. 3. there was a citizen greue so farr in liking wth him, that before shee went from the play shee appointed him to come that night vnto hir by the name of Ri: the 3. Shakespeare ouerhearing their conclusion, went before, was intertained, and at his game ere Burbidge came. Then message being brought that Rich. the 3d. was at the dore, Shakespeare caused returne to be made that William the Conquerour was before Rich. the 3. Shakespeares name willm.[2]

There are many interesting things here.[3] Above all, the woman's desire for Burbage 'by the name of' Richard III (and failing to object to someone else taking the part) suggests attraction to the role itself. While the anonymous city female, interchangeable males and final twist recall *fabliaux* or joke books, erotic power is suggestively attributed to Richard elsewhere as well.

John Weever's *Ad Gulielmum Shakespear* (1599) includes '*Richard*' among Shakespearean characters who have heated 'thousands' with 'Their sugred tongues, and power attractiue beuty'.[4] Echoing Richard's boast, Weever praises characters who 'Say they are Saints althogh that Sts they shew not' (cf. 1.3.337).

1 Richard Corbet, *Iter Boreale* (1647), 12.
2 Reproduced in Evans, 1960.
3 The entry suggests physical proximity between audience and actors; Shakespeare's presence at performance; rivalry between actor-playwright and star; Shakespeare's first name specified, as if it were not known; the woman's 'citizen' definition; and the bed-trick format.
4 *Ad Gulielmum Shakespear* in *John Weever*, ed. E.A.J. Honigmann (New York, 1987).

His *Faunus and Melliflora* (1600) depicts Faunus attempting to seduce his 'Sweete Saint' (908) with Richard's question to Anne, 'Are you not then the Autresse of this sinne?' (928; cf. 1.2.120–4).[1] Yet Burbage's Richard must have been ugly. *2 Return from Parnassus* (1601) portrays Burbage and Will Kempe auditioning destitute scholars for stage roles. Kempe spots one for 'a foolish Mayre or a foolish iustice' (1809–11), but Burbage recognizes him for a Richard, telling him, 'I like your face and the proportion of your body for *Richard*, the 3'.[2] Although Burbage also portrayed Romeo, Hamlet, Othello and Lear, the joke depends on his Richard's ugliness of 'face' and 'proportion'.[3]

Burbage's Richard may have influenced offstage behaviour. In 1599 Samuel Rowlands mocks London 'Gallants', who '*like* Richard *the usurper, swagger, / That had his hand continuall on his dagger*'.[4] Dagger-handling appears in sources and other plays, but only Shakespeare's Richard suggests swaggering. Following More, *True Tragedy* interprets Richard's dagger-grabbing to express '*The out & inward troubles of tyrauntes*' (*CW*2, 87), the guilty insecurity that troubles him after murdering the princes.[5] Following Vergil, Hall and Holinshed make it a distracted tic.[6] Only Shakespeare's Richard suggests the Elizabethan 'behavioral genre' of swaggering when he faces down Anne's

1 On the similarity, see *Faunus and Melliflora*, ed. Arnold Davenport (1948), 17n. Citations are from this edition.
2 The scholar starts to recite Richard's opening lines (*Parnassus*, 1835–42).
3 Burbage played the erotically violent Tereus in 'Lechery' from *2 Seven Deadly Sins* (Greg, *Documents*, 2.II); cf. Mark Eccles, 'Elizabethan actors I: A–D', *N&Q*, 236 (1991), 43, and Andrew Gurr, *Playgoing in Shakespeare's London* (Cambridge, 1987), 69.
4 'To the Gentlemen Readers', from *The Letting of Humours Blood in the Head Vaine* (1600), in *The Complete Works of Samuel Rowlands* (Glasgow, 1880), 1.3.
5 See 4.1.84n.
6 Following Vergil (227), Hall writes: 'when [Richard] stode musyng he woulde byte and chaw besely his nether lippe, as who sayd, that hys fyerce nature in his cruell bodye alwaies chafed, sturred and was euer vnquiete: beside that, the dagger that he ware he would when he studied with his hand plucke vpp and downe in the shethe to the middes, neuer drawing it fully out' (Hall, *Richard III*, fol. lix^{r}; cf. Holinshed, 3.760). Even Edwin Booth's restrained, elegant Richard of the 1870s sheathed and unsheathed his dagger (Wood, 160). For an early seventeenth-century image of Richard prominently featuring a dagger, see Fig. 2.

750 King Richard the third.

Another Argument.

Through nights darke shadowes from the house of bale,
The tyrants ghost comes vp to tell his tale.

HOrror purſues the homicides ſad ſoule,
Feare hunts his conſcience with an hue and crie,
That drinkes the blood of men in murders bowle,
Suſpitious thoughts do reſt in life denie,
Hate ſeldome ſuffers him in peace to die,
By heau'ns inuiolate doome it is decreed,
Whoſe hands ſhed blood, his heart in death ſhould bleed.

I was to noble *Yorke* the yongeſt ſonne
Of foure, which he begot in lawfull bed,
Firſt *Edward* was, the next place *Edmund* wonne,
Rutlands yong Earle by *Cliffords* hand ſtrooke dead,
Clarence the third, to death vntimely lead:
I was the laſt; of all the foure the worſt,
By heau'n and nature in my birth accurſt.

When my ſad mother in her fruitfull wombe
Bore me a painfull burthen to and fro,
Then the babes infant bed had been my tombe,
Had not keene raſors to her paine and woe
Cut me a way, vnto the world to goe:
Nature did grudge to think, that from her wombe
A man-like monſter to the world ſhould come.

When

King Richard the third. 751

When firſt I came into this worlds huge vaſt,
My birth was not as others wont to bee;
Firſt did my feet come forth, as if in haſt
The child of diſcord had been then ſet free,
To cauſe the wretched world to diſagree,
Heau'n at that time told b'inauſpitious ſtarres
Nations far off of Englands ciuil warres.

As hunger-ſteru'd to fleſh my iawes in blood
I readie toothed came, as who would ſay,
Nature by ſignes vnto the world hath ſhow'd
How fiercely he ſhall bite another day,
That in his mothers wombe well toothed lay,
And maruaile t'was, ſeeing viper-like he came,
He was not borne by death of his owne damme.

If like a cunning painter on a frame
My ſhape vnto the world I could deſcrie,
And with a curious penſell paint the ſame
In perfect colours, each ſpectatours eie
Would by my lookes into my manners prie:
The bodies ill-ſhapte limbes are oft defin'd
For ſignes of euill manners in the mind.

Little I was, and of a ſmall compact,
My left ſide ſhoulder higher then the right,
Both crooked were, and therewithall contract
Into my backe, ſo that in all mens ſight
I did appeare a moſt miſhapen wight:
And hard it was to iudge, if that my ſoule
Or limbes ill faſhion'd feature were more foule.

The deeds of noble *Yorke* I not recite,
Done in thoſe fatall daies of miſerie,
Nor tell th'euents of euery ſpeciall fight,
As at Saint Albones, Bloreheath, Banburie,
Northhampton, Barnet, Wakefield, Teukesburie,
Seeing they are often ſpoken of before,
By thoſe, that heere their wofull falles deplore.

Th'

2 Richard in armour with a dagger in one hand, from *A Mirror for Magistrates* (1610)

armed entourage (1.2.33–42).[1] Nevertheless, Richard remains among the most widely variegated roles in Shakespeare; there is little opportunity for swagger in later acts.[2]

Pre-Restoration evidence suggests that a child played Richard: Thomas Heywood's Red Bull 'Prologue and Epilogue' (published 1637) are spoken by '*A young witty Lad playing the part of* Richard *the third: at the Red Bull*' who apologizes for being a '*Richard* the

1 For swaggering, see George Chapman, *Achilles Shield* (1598; STC 13635), sig. B2[r], and *2H4* 2.4.70–107. On 'behavioral genre', see V.N. Vološinov, *Marxism and the Philosophy of Language*, trans. Ladislav Matejka and I.R. Titunik (Boston, 1986), 20–1, 91–7.

2 After Richard wins Anne, says Stephen Daedalus, 'the other four acts . . . hang limply from that first' (James Joyce, *Ulysses: A Reproduction of the 1922 Edition* (Mineola, NY, 2002), 203).

third . . . shrunke up like his arm'.[1] Heywood's own Richard play, *2 Edward IV* (1592–9?), echoes *Richard III* but makes no reference to a withered arm. Children eventually played Richard again in the nineteenth century (Wood, 112).

Restoration

The theatres closed in 1642 and remained shut under the Commonwealth and Protectorate. The Restoration of Charles II in 1660 brought reopened theatres, but evidence survives for only two productions before Shakespeare's play became – for a hundred and fifty years – Colley Cibber's.

A 'Prologue' from the 1670s for a Theatre Royal performance survives, as does a cast-list for a production *c.* 1690. Though lack of other evidence suggests scant performance in the Restoration period (Lull, 24), the play's 'Tudor' elements – fickle fortune, blind pride, emulous faction, cunning usurpation, cruel tyranny and restored legitimacy – proved pliable to reinterpretation. The Prologue claims, 'Tyrants . . . / Puft up with pride, still vanish in despair' unlike 'lawfull Monarchs . . . preserv'd by heaven'.[2] Denouncing 'Usurpers' and evoking 'giddy Fortune', it likens Richmond to Charles II and warns audience members against hastily 'joyn[ing]' sympathy with Richard or his contemporary equivalents, because 'liberty' means 'Loyalty'. The 1690s cast-list includes Betterton, who was thought to carry stage traditions from Shakespeare's contemporaries, and Sandford, a type-villain who influenced Cibber's Richard.[3]

1 Thomas Heywood, *Pleasant Dialogues and Drammas* (1637; STC 13358), sig. R4^r. For dating, see George Fullmer Reynolds, *The Staging of Elizabethan Plays at the Red Bull Theater 1605–1625* (New York, 1940), 21. Chambers calls this, 'probably, and certainly if the play was Shakespeare's, some quite exceptional performance' (*Stage*, 2.448).

2 See *Covent Garden Drollery: A Miscellany of 1672*, ed. G. Thorn-Drury (1928), 13–14.

3 See James G. McManaway, '*Richard III* on the stage', *TLS*, 27 June 1935, 416; Montague Summers, *The Playhouse of Pepys* (1935), 223–5; Philip H. Highfill, Jr, Kalman A. Burnim and Edward A. Langhans (eds), *A Biographical Dictionary of Actors, Actresses, Musicians . . . London, 1660–1800*, 16 vols (Carbondale, Ill., 1973–99), 2.75.

Two adaptations reveal a bit about reception.[1] John Caryll's *The English Princess, or the Death of Richard the III* updates the play for 1667 audiences (Wood, 72). Set at Bosworth, the adaptation deprives Richard of humour, but retains his renunciation of conscience and his ghost scene. It moralizes against *popular* tyranny, fearing that Richard may infect the audience.[2] John Crowne's *The Misery of Civil-War* (1680) incorporates elements from *2* and *3 Henry VI* and *Richard III* to admonish against 'Religious Brawls', and brings on the ghost of Richard II to curse Henry VI for his grandfather's role in deposing him, while 'Spirits' reassure Henry of heaven – once he dies for his grandfather's sins.[3] Along with generational payback, Crowne also retains the Shakespearean theme of sexual hypocrisy; his Richard, forced to acknowledge his own 'poor Whore' and 'tawny Bastard', apologizes for censuring royal lust (sigs F4^{v}–G1^{r}). Colley Cibber's *Tragical History of King Richard III* (1700) retains a good deal more Shakespeare.

Cibber

From 1700 to the late nineteenth century the stage play is Cibber's, though after 1741 Richard himself becomes as much Garrick's as Cibber's or Shakespeare's. Despite the appearance of the first scholarly editions, contemporaries acclaimed Cibber's version for its 'compactness', 'plain, simple introduction' and heightened 'spirit' in the final acts.[4] In 1793 the great editor George Steevens acclaimed Cibber's 'reformation', demanding: 'what modern audience would patiently listen to the narrative of Clarence's Dream, his subsequent expostulation with the murderers, the prattle of his children, the soliloquy of the Scrivener, the tedious dialogue of the citizens, the ravings of

1 John Wilson's *Andronicus Commenius* (1663–4) adapts 1.2 but otherwise follows Gibbon.

2 John Caryll, *The English Princess* (1667; Wing C744), fol. 65^{v}.

3 John Crowne, *The Misery of Civil-War* (1680; Wing C7395), sigs K2^{r}–K3^{r}.

4 Francis Gentleman, 1.3–4; cf. his notes to *King Richard III* for Bell's *Shakespeare* (1774), 3.42n. On the play as 'criticism' of Shakespeare, see Sprague, *Histories*, 136.

Margaret, the gross terms thrown out by the Duchess of York on Richard, the repeated progress to execution, the superfluous train of spectres, and other undramatick incumbrances . . . ?' (Vickers, 6.594–5). None of these 'incumbrances' have escaped cutting in modern – 'Shakespearean' – productions (Colley, 19). The stage life of Cibber's text, as itself, as the basis for acting editions and as a continuing influence, registers more than historical oddity.

By 1740 Cibber's *Richard III* had been staged eighty-four times, playing virtually every season, sometimes in two or three houses.[1] The play won praise for clarified exposition and focus, speedier playing time, simplified casting and action that builds to a rousing final battle. For audiences unlikely to know Shakespeare's earlier histories, it provided scenes from *3 Henry VI*, a device still evident in Ian McKellen's 1995 film *Richard III*, which opens with a caption – 'Civil war divides the nation. The King is under attack from the rebel York family, who are fighting to place their eldest son, Edward, on the throne. Edward's army advances, led by his youngest brother, Richard of Gloucester' – followed by Richard killing Prince Edward and Henry VI. Cibber would have approved.

Richard dominates Shakespeare's play, but Cibber cut Margaret, Clarence and his children, the two Murderers, Hastings, King Edward, the Citizens and more, reducing the play by about half and making it 'completely the star's own' (Sprague, *Histories*, 126). Richard gets some seven new soliloquies (editions differ) and speaks 39.9 per cent of the lines (he has 31.2 per cent in F).[2] By pitting Richard against 'a smaller range of innocent victims whose pasts have been wiped clean' (Jowett, 85), Cibber eliminates 'history coming home to roost' but also reduces confusions arising when characters harangue each

1 Colley, 18; Colley Cibber, *The Plays of Colley Cibber*, vol. 1, ed. Timothy J. Viator and William J. Burling (Cranbury, NJ, 2001), 331.

2 Christopher Spencer (ed.), *Five Restoration Adaptations of Shakespeare* (Urbana, Ill., 1965), 27.

other about events that pre-date the play (Hankey, 28; Colley, 4). Remaining characters are helpfully identified in dialogue (see Cibber, *Richard III*, 2.2.14–15). Even today, productions virtually always cut the cast and resort to narrative summaries, genealogy charts or colour-coded clothing to identify factions and families. Margaret is now generally back, but Olivier's film, McKellen's film and Antony Sher's touring *Richard III* did without her. Clarence's children, the Citizens and Queen Elizabeth's extended family still frequently go missing.

Cibber added passages from *3 Henry VI*, *Richard II*, *Henry V* and *2 Henry IV*, hundreds of new lines, new incidents, new pathos and new emphases (Sprague, *Histories*, 123–4). His Richard abuses Lady Anne, fights an extended combat, delivers a rousing death speech and enjoys a eulogy.[1] Ambiguities disappear. Queen Elizabeth explains herself as 'seemingly' complying with Richard's suit (4.4.428–9) 'to let my Child escape' (Cibber, *Richard III*, 4.4.114–16). Richard's obscure mock wager, his 'dukedom to a beggarly denier' (1.2.254), becomes a crude boast, 'My Dukedom to a Widows Chastity' (Cibber, *Richard III*, 2.1.266) – a dumbed-down translation that Laurence Olivier kept. With a curtailed cast, Cibber's Richard can no longer be the game-player who twits the Queen and family, the pious pitier of Margaret or the conniving trapper of Hastings (Hankey, 28). He loses aristocratic haughtiness, trading his brags about high birth (1.3.262–4) for self-pity and worries about being unloved and misunderstood.

Though Cibber read Shakespearean sources and preserved Shakespearean text (printing Shakespeare's lines in italics and paraphrases within inverted commas), his Richard is indebted to the theatre.[2] Samuel Sandford, who had once played Shakespeare's Richard, provided inspiration.[3] His 'low and

1 The princes even die onstage, at least in the first version (Donohue, 227).

2 For sources, see Albert E. Kalson, 'The chronicles in Cibber's *Richard III*', *SEL*, 3 (1963), 253–67.

3 Cibber's apparent ignorance of the performance suggests the play was not well known on the Restoration stage (Lull).

crooked person' and limited range constituted an antithesis to the multi-faceted Burbage.[1] This caricature perhaps inspired Cibber's wooing scene. Where Shakespeare's decisive Richard, proud of 'close' intents (1.1.149–59), pops up abruptly, faces down armed men and bowls Anne over, Cibber's Richard mopes about, commenting and eavesdropping. He screws up enough courage to approach Anne, only to 'retire' and listen in on her laments before – finally – moving towards her, consoling himself that though 'perhaps' his form 'will little move her', his 'Tongue shall wheadle with the Devil' (Cibber, *Richard III*, 2.1.53–66). Initially, he reacts rather than acts, but Cibber's Act 4 is another story, and most thought it better than Shakespeare's.

Cibber remade Richard with Sandford's qualities; but an entirely different order of actor became 'the' Richard (Donohue, 225). In Cibber's earlier acts, David Garrick evinced nuances that still haunt today's Richards who emphasize uncertainty, vulnerability, self-pity and pained self-awareness. From Cibber's final acts, Garrick constructed a hero who dies grandly, and Richards would continue doing so even when translated back into Shakespeare's less supportive play. Cibber's Richard neither forgets himself, strikes his messenger (4.4.440–56, 507–8) nor drinks (5.3.63–74); his 'stern Impatience' permits little time for conscience, pity, love or self-hatred (5.3.177–206).[2] At Bosworth, he 'starts' awake, proclaims, 'O Tyrant Conscience! how dost thou afflict me!', but instantly resolves: 'No, never be it said, / That Fate it self could awe the Soul of *Richard*. / Hence, Babling dreams, you threaten here in vain: / Conscience avant; *Richard's* himself again' (Cibber, *Richard*

1 See Colley Cibber, *An Apology for the Life of Colley Cibber*, ed. B.R.S. Fone (Ann Arbor, Mich., 1968), 77. Sandford was round-shouldered, meagre-faced, spindle-shanked, splay-footed, sour of countenance; Charles II called him 'the best Villain in the World' (Anthony Aston, *A Brief Supplement to Colley Cibber, Esq; His Lives of the late Famous Actors and Actresses* (1748), 11).

2 Only the ghosts of Henry VI, the princes and Anne '*rise*', and only to Richard. The second tent would not reappear until 1845 (Hankey, 59).

III, 5.5.82–5).[1] He dies declaiming: 'let one spirit of the First-born *Cain* / 'Reign in all bosoms', and Richmond laments his 'aspiring Soul' (Cibber, *Richard III*, 5.9.15–17, 21–6; cf. *2H4* 1.1.157–8). Garrick made the pathetic wheedler of Cibber's first acts more sympathetic; his concluding heroics evoked high Romanticism.

Mid-eighteenth to mid-nineteenth centuries: from Garrick to Phelps

On 19 October 1741 Garrick's *Richard III* changed Cibber's play – and Shakespeare's – forever (Colley, 37). This Richard was only the first of over one hundred that Garrick would undertake over thirty-five years. Praised for replacing 'ranting, bombast, and grimace' with 'nature, ease, simplicity, and genuine humour',[2] Garrick's Drury Lane performances doubled normal house totals and made *Richard III* a popular staple; acting texts till the twentieth century derived from his performances (Colley, 39; Donohue, 224). Garrick refused to revive Shakespeare's play (Sprague, *Histories*, 128). His suffering protagonist suited period demands for 'sympathetic imagination' and emphasized 'fluctuation of mind'.[3] Garrick conveyed that 'Kings themselves' by their 'sympathizing Souls . . . were *Men*, and *felt* like the rest of their Species'.[4] His Richard, 'galled and uneasy' about a deformity that 'hurts him',[5] prompted Elizabeth Griffith, who rejected 'chearful' villainy as impossible, to admit that evil might originate with jealousy and to admire the play for arousing 'compassion for

1 William Hogarth's painting portraying Garrick became the most frequently engraved theatrical image of the century (see Jonathan Bate, 'The Shakespeare phenomenon' in Jane Martineau *et al.* (eds), *Shakespeare in Art* (2003), 12). Besides Hogarth, Francis Hayman, Henry Fuseli, Nathaniel Dance, Thomas Bradwell and Philippe de Loutherbourg painted Garrick's Richard (see Stuart Sillars, *Painting Shakespeare: The Artist as Critic, 1720–1820* (Cambridge, 2006)).

2 Thomas Davies, *Memoirs of the Life of David Garrick* (1808; rpt. New York, 1969), vol. 1, 43–5.

3 See Walter Jackson Bate, 'The sympathetic imagination in eighteenth-century English criticism', *ELH*, 12 (1945), 159–60.

4 J.G. Cooper, *Letters Concerning Taste* (1755), 109 (quoted by Donohue, 230).

5 Thomas Wilkes, *A General View of the Stage* (1759), 237.

the misfortune, even while . . . raising an abhorrence for the vice, of the criminal' (Griffith, 317, 312).

Garrick's final scenes, melancholy and grand, foreshadowed the nineteenth century's Byronic Richards (Colley, 41; Donohue, 276). His 'sublimely horrible' tent and death scenes made Fanny Burney shudder, even as she 'glow[ed]' with moral 'indignation'.[1] To convey 'the Terrors of an Imagination distracted by conscious Guilt', Garrick added pauses and gestures: arising from bed, grasping a sword, he boldly began 'Give me another Horse: . . .'; paused midline, coming forward to cry again, with dismay on his face, 'Bind up my wounds!'; then dropped to his knees on 'Have mercy, Heaven'.[2] This is not Cibber's Richard – or Shakespeare's, either – but generations embraced it.

After Garrick, three Richards dominated into the early nineteenth century: John Philip Kemble, George Frederick Cooke and Edmund Kean. All three left legacies. The Covent Garden and Drury Lane theatres, both rebuilt first in the 1790s and again in 1808–9, were much enlarged, rendering subtleties hard to convey. Garrick's Drury Lane had permitted suppressed smiles, passionate glances and whispers, but in 1826 'extravagant gesture' and 'excess of rant' were demanded (Hankey, 43). Cooke and Kean provided excess and extravagance; Kemble their austere opposite.

Kemble's restrained Richard influenced Macready, Phelps and Edwin Booth (Colley, 43), and his scholarly productions promoted period setting and costume. Garrick had engaged the artist Philippe de Loutherbourg, whose Bosworth designs suggest a sublime landscape (Hankey, 36), but typical pre-Kemble sets amounted to 'architecture of no period' (Wood, 111). Kemble

1 See *The Early Diary of Frances Burney; 1768–1778*, ed. Annie Raine Ellis, 2 vols (1913), 1.186.

2 Roger Pickering, *Reflections Upon Theatrical Expression in Tragedy* (1755), 50–1; Sprague, *Actors*, 103–4. Andrew Erskine depicts '*Richard* near his tent': 'He shudd'ring starts, convulsive shakes, / He heaves, he turns, he leaps, he wakes, / Each feature seems with wild amazement hung, / The sudden pray'r to heav'n drops fault'ring / from his tongue' (*Gentleman's Magazine*, 33 (1763), 196).

attempted late medieval costumes and backgrounds (Wood, 111–12; Colley, 46). Until the end of Garrick's era, Richard alone had regularly worn period garb: Hogarth portrays trunks and hose, ruffs at neck and wrists and a short, sleeveless, fur-edged coat revealing the puffed sleeves of a tunic (see Fig. 3; Wood, 108).[1] Richards retained this look up until Olivier.

Kemble's '*gentleman*', with 'ambition' his 'sole impulse' and 'stern valour' his demeanour, downplayed Richard's livelier aspects (Colley, 44; Hankey, 41; Kemble, 167–8). He abandoned traditional clowning in 3.7 (Sprague, *Histories*, 134; Wood, 119), but he tossed aside a prayer-book after the Mayor and men had gone, business that suited Cibber's Richard, left alone onstage, but that survived even when actors returned to Shakespeare's play (Sprague, *Histories*, 134). Critics faulted Kemble's 'uniform' manner.[2] Supporters lauded his 'sublimity' and 'moody defiance', pronouncing it 'impossible not to glory in such a sovereign, by whatever means he gained the title'.[3] Amoral admiration permeates responses in the years that follow.

George Frederick Cooke first appeared as Richard in 1800; he took the role to America in 1810. Cooke, like Kemble, read Shakespeare to prepare for acting Cibber (Hankey, 41; Colley, 55). There the similarities end. In Cooke, Lamb saw 'hypocrisy . . . too glaring'; not wit but 'coarse, taunting humour'; not the 'joy of a defect *conquered*' but '*distaste* and *pain*' (Bate, *Romantics*, 503). Opposing 'musical declamation', Cooke wrote out his lines in prose (Hankey, 42, 45). His energetic Richard, haunted by self-revulsion, influenced Edmund Kean, whose Richard exploded onto the London stage in 1814.

1 On dressing Richard alone in the habit of the times, see Gentleman, 1.10. Remarks of 1801 note Richard's 'fancy cap and feather' (Hankey, 44). The Oxberry 'New English Drama' (1818) describes Kemble and Kean: 'Gloster. 1st dress. Scarlet doublet, trunks, hose, hat, cloak and russet boots. 2nd dress. Black, ditto, ditto, trimmed with gold, crimson velvet robe, white hose, shoes, and plush hat. 3rd dress. Armour body, and hat' (Wood, 119n.).

2 *Remarks on the Character of Richard the Third as Played by Cooke and Kemble* (1801), 24; on Kemble's 'iron and undeviating austerity', see 11.

3 Henry Martin, *Remarks on John Kemble's Performance of Hamlet and Richard III* (1802), 36.

3 William Hogarth's portrayal of Garrick as Richard in his tent, reproduced in an engraving *c.* 1850

The 'quintessential Romantic actor', Kean had writers to appreciate *his* Richard's 'genius, his mounting spirit, which no consideration of his cruelties can depress' (Colley, 61–2; Hankey, 46). Byron enthused: 'He is a soul! . . . Richard is a man, and Kean is Richard' (Wood, 115).[1] In 1814, Thomas Barnes proclaimed that his 'daring and comprehensive intelligence' gave Kean's Richard 'the grasp of a giant', a 'towering superiority' prompting 'awe' as he pursues 'his purpose careless of ordinary duties and ordinary feelings'.[2] Hazlitt called him 'towering and

1 Byron presented a snuff-box with a boar motif to Kean; Kean adopted the boar as his crest (J.F. Molloy, *The Life and Adventures of Edmund Kean Tragedian* (1897), 150). Byron wove Kean's stage business into his portrait of Napoleon (Hankey, 48). On Byron's positive recasting of Richard's disability (and his own) by aligning it with universal forces in his play *The Deformed Transformed*, see Sharon L. Snyder, 'Transforming representation', in Carrie Sandahl and Philip Auslander (eds), *Bodies in Commotion: Disability and Performance* (Ann Arbor, Mich., 2005), 271–83.

2 Reprinted in *Specimens of English Dramatic Criticism, XVII–XX Centuries*, ed. A.C. Ward (1945), 97.

lofty; equally impetuous and commanding; haughty, violent and subtle; bold and treacherous; confident in his strength as well as his cunning' (Hankey, 47). This sublime 'giant' is hardly Cibber's wheedler or Shakespeare's joker. Contemporaries uneasily noted the moral distance separating such adoration from earlier reservations.[1]

Kean triumphed as Richard in America (1820 and 1825) and France (1828); it became his most often performed role and prompted imitation and expansion by, amongst others, two actors very influential in America, J.B. Booth, who transplanted some of Kean's qualities to America in 1821, and the American Edwin Forrest, who played Richard in England and America. Booth performed alternate nights in Kean's style and in his own.[2] Elsewhere in New York that year the African Theatre Company staged *Richard III* for their first production, with James Hewlett as Richard (see Fig. 4). The company included the young Ira Aldridge, who later toured the globe for decades as Richard.[3]

Back to Shakespeare: Macready and Phelps to Irving

In 1821 William Charles Macready tried combining Shakespeare and Cibber. The result was only staged twice. Audiences were confused without passages from *Henry VI*. Macready reintroduced Hastings's entrapment, Clarence's dream and Margaret's curses, much abbreviated since 'the cause of her grief, being so very remote' prevented commiseration (Downer,

1 James Boaden (*c*. 1790–1) notes the 'immoral effect' of Richard's 'triumphant villainy' upon the audience: 'their proper sympathy with his victims is blunted by the *certainty* of his success, and the daring intrepidity with which he hurries them on from one atrocity to another' (*Memoirs of the Life of John Philip Kemble*, 2 vols (1825; rpt. New York, 1969), 2.59).

2 See Arthur Kincaid, 'Junius Brutus Booth' (*ODNB*).

3 See George A. Thompson, *A Documentary History of the African Theatre* (Evanston, Ill., 1998); also Michael Warner *et al.*, 'A soliloquy "Lately Spoken at the African Theatre": race and the public sphere in New York City, 1821', *American Literature*, 73 (2001), 1–46. Cf. Carlyle Brown's play, *The African Company Presents Richard III* (New York, 1998). Aldridge performed *Richard III* in England in the 1830s and around the world for four decades (Errol Hill, *Shakespeare in Sable* (Amherst, Mass., 1984), 17–18).

4 James Hewlett as Richard, a role he played in New York's African Theatre Company production (1821) as well as in later theatrical imitations of famous actors in the role

86). Objecting to the 'bombast' of Cibber's 'Off with his head! so much for Buckingham' and 'Conscience avant!', Macready nevertheless retained them as acting 'points . . . traditional from Garrick' (Macready, 71, 169–70). Such 'points' grounded critical evaluation, and some live still: I heard 'Off with his head' bring down the house in 2006.[1] Macready rejected a 'moody' Richard (Downer, 87); his witty strategist influenced generations of clever plotters (Colley, 82). The popularity of his and Kean's 'Rival Richards' led to competitions; other rivalries followed, not always peacefully (see Fig. 5 and Macready, 145).[2]

In 1845 and 1849 Shakespeare's *Richard III* was performed for the first time in over 150 years, although Samuel Phelps cut radically to allow time for processions and spectacle, while adding lines from *2* and *3 Henry VI* for pre-history. The 'new' role of Margaret won acclaim, but – despite remarkable scenic effects (barges floated the aldermen onto the stage, all the ghosts rose at once, and for the first time since 1700 both Bosworth tents appeared) – Phelps failed to drive Cibber from the stage. Pressure for Shakespeare had grown, but Charles Kean, son of the great Edmund, resisted it (Colley, 93–7). Calling *Richard III* 'less fitted in its integrity for representation on the stage than almost any other generally acted' Shakespeare play, Charles Kean performed Cibber for decades from the 1830s. His spectacular productions anticipated Irving, and even cinematic Shakespeare; in 1854 he employed arches and towers, pillars, painted drops, a functional bridge, showers of arrows and scores of players (72 for the wooing of Anne, 119 for a final tableau) (Colley, 89–92). Still, audiences wanted more Shakespeare; Irving and Edwin Booth

1 I heard laughter, however, rather than the 'tremendous rounds of applause' that halted Vandenhoff's 1837 Covent Garden performance (Charles Rice, *The London Theatre in the Eighteen-Thirties*, ed. Arthur Colby Sprague and Bertram Shuttleworth (1950), 21).

2 For depiction of Kean competing against J.B. Booth, see Colley, 101. The rivalry between Macready's and Forrest's nationalist partisans culminated in the Astor Place Riots of April 1849 (Colley, 104–6; Foulkes, 20–2).

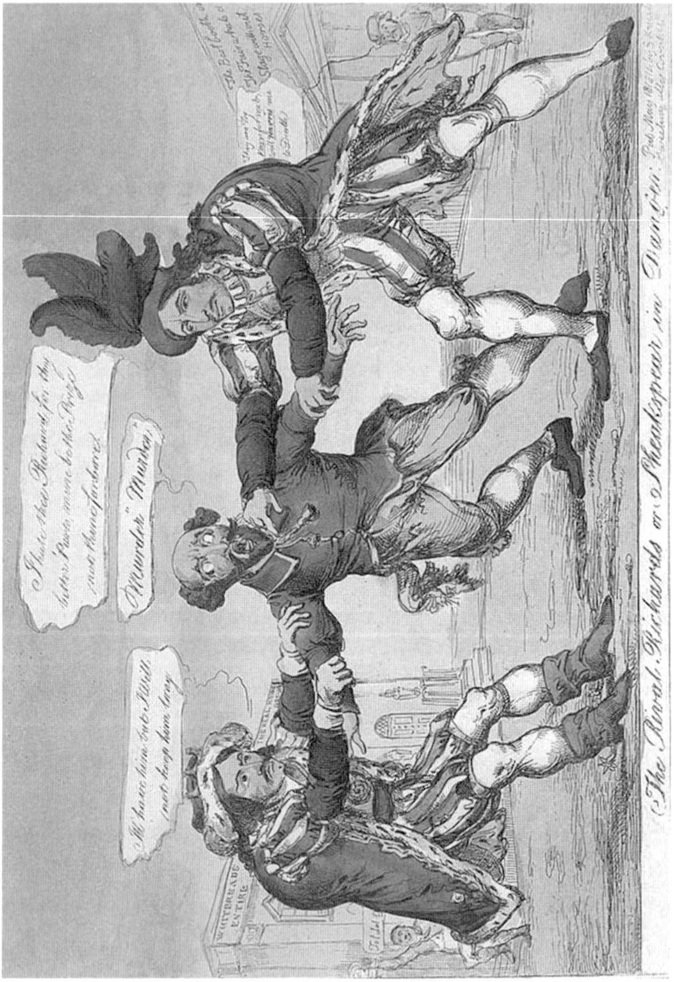

5 'The Rival Richards or Shakespear in Danger'; cartoon (1814) by William Heath, showing Edmund Kean and Charles Mayne Young, one of the Kemble school of actors, tearing Shakespeare between them

responded in the 1870s. Meanwhile, A.W. Schlegel's arguments about the unity of Shakespeare's histories prompted the play's performance within the historical tetralogies; in 1864 Franz Dingelstedt mounted both tetralogies in Weimar (in German) over eight days.[1] English performance of the tetralogies awaited Frank Benson's 1906 Stratford production.[2]

Away from the theatres that featured the dignified Macready, the antiquarian Kean and the melodramatic Forrest and their imitators, popular entertainments provided other perspectives on *Richard III*. Alternative 'Shakespeare' in parodies, burlesques and other strange offerings began another tradition that serves a wide range of popular, topical and frequently comical uses.[3] In 1855 Theodor Fontane witnessed theatricals that featured onstage murder of the princes (played by women) and wife-beating. An equestrian performance in Southwark offered 'Bosworth Field THE BATTLE! And Death of "White Surrey"'.[4] Some burlesques mocked both Cibber and scholarly Shakespearean editions.[5]

Victorian Shakespeare: Irving to Benson

Contemporary performance history of Shakespeare's play begins with Henry Irving in 1877. Cibber remained on London stages up until Barry Sullivan's 1876 production, and would continue

1 See Robert K. Sarlos, 'Dingelstedt's celebration of the tercentenary: Shakespeare's histories as a cycle', *Theatre Survey*, 5 (1964), 117–31. For German productions, see Hortmann, 96–8. *Richard III* was almost continuously in the Vienna Burgtheater repertoire from the 1850s until 1917 in adaptations (Draudt, 196).

2 See Knowles, *2H6*, 5.

3 See, for example, *Monty Python*'s Richard III Ward in the 'Hospital for Overactors' skit (Season 2, episode 25); the *Blackadder* first series, set in the reign of Richard IV; *The Good Bye Girl*'s parody of academic gender analysis; and Julien Temple's documentary *The Filth and the Fury*, in which Johnny Rotten admires Olivier's Richard. Cf. Pierre Pradinas's staging of *La Vie criminelle de Richard III* (1994) with zombies and mechanical dogs (Fayard, 187–8).

4 See Theodore Fontane, *Shakespeare in the London Theatre 1855–58*, trans. Russell Jackson (1999), 10–17; for the playbill, see Foulkes, 56.

5 Cf. Richard A. Schoch, *Not Shakespeare: Bardolatry and Burlesque in the Nineteenth Century* (Cambridge, 2002). F.C. Burnand's 1868 *The Rise and Fall of Richard III; or a New Front to an Old Dickey* jibes at Cibber in a mock footnote justifying interpellated lines from *Macbeth* (n.d., 42).

in America into the twentieth century despite experiments by Jarrett and Palmer (1871) and Edwin Booth (1878) (Sprague, *Histories*, 131; Wood, 161). After 1877, Cibber never returned to London production, at least not entire (Hughes, 151). Irving influenced performers into the twentieth century: Barrymore remembered Irving in his 1920 *Richard III*, and Irving's voice and business influenced Olivier's mid-century portrayals.[1] Irving omitted nearly 1,600 lines: Margaret appeared only in 1.3 in 1877, although she was largely restored in 1896. The deaths of Rivers, Grey and Buckingham (3.3, 5.1) and the Scrivener's soliloquy (3.6) were cut. Clarence lost his discussion with the Murderers (1.4).[2] Irving enhanced his historically appropriate sets and costumes with lowered house lighting, employing the stage pictorially (Colley, 128). In 1877 twenty-two monks and men-at-arms escorted Henry VI's corpse (1.2); in 1896 innumerable extras formed a composition derived from a painting (Hughes, 156–9).[3]

Irving retained Kean's heroics in the later acts – glaring or flinging his gauntlet (Colley, 139) – but he was more character than Titan, and his two Richards (young in 1877, old in 1896) differed substantially. The first he called 'a Plantagenet with the imperious pride of his race, a subtle intellect, a mocking, not a trumpeting duplicity'; his slight deformities prompted him to demonstrate superiority to better-shaped men (Hughes, 153). He expressed pathos in his isolation and in the 'varying changes of his face' (Hughes, 153; Colley, 134). Contemporaries contrasted his 'refined, fascinating' Richard with Barry Sullivan's 'coarse, loud, swaggering bully'

1 For stage business, see Hughes, 154; cf. 3.1.130–2. For Irving's voice, see Colley, 170. Irving's 1888 recording of *R3* 1.1.1–24 survives (*Great Historical Sound Recordings*, Naxos Audiobooks CD, NA 220012, 2000); cf. Wes Folkerth, *The Sound of Shakespeare* (2002), 1–10.

2 Edwin Booth's 1878 Shakespeare revival made similar cuts, eliminating Clarence's children (2.2), the women at the Tower (4.1) and one third of Margaret's lines in 1.3 (Colley, 108–9).

3 Irate viewers of Barrymore's 1920 production expected Anne's entourage to number '70 to 80' (Sprague, *Histories*, 138).

(Sprague, *Histories*, 133). In 1896 Irving made himself up to look even older than his own fifty-eight years, and expressed obvious delight in his own intrigues (Colley, 141). Henry James dismissed both conceptions: faulting the 'pauses and lapses, without a hint of the rapidity, the intensity . . . necessary for carrying off the improbabilities of so explicit and confidential and so melodramatic a hero' in the first (Colley, 130) and condemning the second for attempting 'plausibility' in such 'a loose, violent, straddling romance'.[1]

Under Frank Benson, who kept largely to Shakespeare and avoided many traditional acting points, the Memorial Theatre in Stratford-upon-Avon saw thirteen productions of *Richard III* over thirty years, starting in 1886. Minor roles became important: playgoers were astonished to see the First Murderer acted with 'sincerity and fervour' (Colley, 145–6). Benson's performances survive piecemeal in the first film version of *Richard III*, a 1911 silent produced in the Memorial Theatre.[2] Like half of Benson's productions, the film opens with the battle of Tewkesbury and Henry's murder. Benson, showing little hump or limp, suggests mesmerism by moving his hands behind Anne like a puppet-master. The princes are murdered on camera, and one killer kisses the body he bears to the cellerage. The other very early film rendering is the 1912 James Keane and M.B. Dudley *Richard III*.[3] Shot against painted flats and in outdoor locations, the film is full of action. Frederick B. Warde's mature Richard is not very hunched but grows increasingly stooped in later scenes. Warde, a veteran touring actor, concludes the film in modern dress, bowing to us as if at one of his public lectures.

1 Gamini Salgado, *Eyewitnesses to Shakespeare: First-Hand Accounts of Performance, 1590–1890* (1975), 104–5.

2 See *Silent Shakespeare* (British Film Institute, 1999). On early films, see Robert Hamilton Ball, *Shakespeare on Silent Film: A Strange Eventfull History* (1968); Kenneth Rothwell and Annabelle Henken Melzer, *Shakespeare on Screen: An International Filmography and Videography* (New York, 1990).

3 See *Richard III* (Kino on Video, 2001).

The 1920s: psychology and politics

1920 saw historic productions in America and Germany that anticipated future developments. John Barrymore's Broadway *Richard III* looked far more traditional than Leopold Jessner's Berlin expressionist production. Barrymore, prompted by Arthur Hopkins, one of the first directors influenced by Freud (Morrison, 72), approached Richard through character psychology. Jessner directed Fritz Kortner in a performance that treated 'men and women as rhythmic exponents of driving forces' (Hortmann, 57).

Barrymore's *Richard III* was a great success.[1] To portray Richard's psychological development, a third of the scenes were taken from *3 Henry VI*. Barrymore rejected the 'roaring caricature' of Robert Mantell for Edwin Booth's intellect and introspection.[2] His Richard aged 'from questioning youth to bitter old age' (Colley, 155), an approach indebted to Richard Mansfield. Attributing the difference between the lively joker of the first acts and the later embittered king to the historical passage of fourteen years, Mansfield aged into physical and moral corruption, while indicating remorse far earlier than other Richards ever had (see Fig. 6). Awaiting news about the princes, Mansfield shuddered in dismay at a ray of red light falling on his hand (Colley, 113–17). This stress on internal development anticipated subsequent psychological characterizations.

Sigmund Freud's own brief psychoanalytic interpretation of Richard had appeared in a 1916 essay, but character was of little interest to the 1920 Berlin Staatliches Schauspielhaus production.[3] Leopold Jessner's *Motivtheater* rendered Richard merely one element in a pageant of power and political corruption enacted in stylized movements, spare gestures and abruptly changing vocal rhythms (Kennedy, 88; Hortmann, 61).

1 It ran nearly five hours, and closed after twenty-seven performances because of Barrymore's exhaustion (Colley, 151–2). William Luce's play *Barrymore* (1996) portrays the alcoholic star struggling to recall his stage success as Richard.

2 See Gene Fowler, *Good Night, Sweet Prince: The Life of John Barrymore* (New York, 1944), 194; cf. Colley, 154. On Booth, see Colley, 111; Morrison, 110.

3 Freud's essay referring to *Richard III* first appeared in *Imago* (1916); cf. Garber.

6 Richard Mansfield as Richard, showing him holding a book (1889)

Jessner directly influenced Bertolt Brecht's *The Resistable Rise of Arturo Ui*; his famous stage steps provided Jan Kott with the central metaphor of *Shakespeare Our Contemporary* (published in France in 1963), which, in turn, inspired Peter Hall's *The Wars of the Roses* (1963) (Barton & Hall, xi; Lull, 33). In New York, Barrymore's designer, Robert Edmond Jones, influenced by Edward Gordon Craig and Max Reinhardt, incorporated an ominous 48-foot-high hexagon, complete or in part, into every scene (Morrison, 84). In Berlin, Emil Pirchan (also inspired by Craig and by Adolphe Appia; Kennedy, 83–7) put two stone walls across Jessner's stage, the second rising to a terrace. The walls were transformed into a dungeon, a street, a cloister and a throne room surmounted by a pyramidal flight of red steps that rose from the proscenium to the lower wall. The first three acts kept to horizontal movement within the walls; the last two acts proceeded vertically, up and down the stairs. Richard trod the *Jessnertreppen* in Act 4, descending affably, ascending angrily, as others rose and fell. He descended to die. Red was everywhere: in Richard's scarlet robes, the stairs, a crimson sky and blood-red lighting that cast enormous shadows from the actors (Colley, 159; see Fig. 7).

Germany claimed to stage more Shakespeare than the rest of the world combined (a single year, 1937, saw 320 productions; Strobl, 18–19), and the Nazis, taking Shakespeare as ideologically safer than Lessing, Goethe and Schiller, even adopted Richard as a symbol for the failure of Nordic potential (Strobl, 17–19; Habicht, 115). However, Jürgen Fehling's 1937 *Richard III* dressed Richard's bodyguards as Nazi stormtroopers and in Werner Krauss's Richard suggested a resemblance to the club-footed Josef Goebbels. The Scrivener (3.6) directly addressed the audience, who responded with spontaneous applause or uncanny silence. Richard fell at the mere raising of Richmond's sword, according to Fehling, 'because the divine order claims to be re-established'. House lights went up as Richmond's soldiers knelt to sing a *Te deum*. Shakespeare's histories were officially

7 Richard and his courtiers robed in scarlet, atop the red *Jessnertreppen*, above them a blood-red sky; from the Berlin Staatliches Schauspielhaus production of 1920

suppressed by Goebbels in 1941 (Hortmann, 137–9; Habicht, 117).

Although continental stage innovations influenced Terence Gray's 1928 Cambridge production, with its focused spots and exaggerated shadows, and its cubes, drums and cylinders arranged on a turntable with steps (Kennedy, 115–16), melodrama and character psychology prevailed over expressionism on the English stage. Baliol Holloway, the first Richard to follow Frank Benson's thirty years at Stratford-upon-Avon, was 'a ranting tragedian of the old barn-storming school, playing straight at the audience all the time, and "asking for it" . . . in every gesture'. Foot firmly on the 'loud pedal', Holloway's Richard was 'Punch' (Colley, 160). Psychological approaches produced a first in George Hayes's 1928 insane Richard. Exuding cherubic innocence, he betrayed signs of malignant intellect, keeping his back to others or reading while they spoke. This type anticipated the many 'lunatic-asylum Richards' between 1953 and 1981 (Colley, 162–3).

Elsewhere in Europe, resistance to naturalism continued. In France, Charles Dullin's 1933 presentation of André Obey's version enjoyed great success. Within a set dominated by two massive portals and the dungeon of the Tower, Richard appeared as physically repulsive but sexually exciting, engaging in whirling dances of exultation and ending in a stylized battle beneath a huge lance.[1] Accounts compare Dullin to 'one of Hokusai's warriors'.[2]

Olivier and after

During the 1930s Cibber's *Richard* concluded nearly two centuries as the most popular play in North America (Wood, 134–50). While some of Cibber's spirit lived on in the most notable mid-century *Richard III*, Laurence Olivier's Richard also needs relating to the 1942 portrayal by Donald Wolfit. Although Wolfit followed the blood and thunder of Edwin Forrest and Barry Sullivan (Colley, 167; Sprague, *Histories*, 132), he recognized the play's topical potential as a treatment of despotism (adopting a forehead cowlick to suggest Hitler (Wolfit, 205)), and he grasped the centrality of its female roles.[3] Wolfit deemed 4.4, with the 'women in black whom [Richard] has so grievously wronged', the 'core of the play' (Wolfit, 206) – a point Olivier failed to appreciate.[4]

Olivier first appeared as Richard in 1944, toured in Europe (1945), Australia and New Zealand (1948), and revived the production in London (1949) before starring in the inescapable

1 On the set, see Fortunato Israel, '*Richard III* sur la scène française' in Dominique Goy-Blanquet and Richard Marienstras (eds), *Le Tyran: Shakespeare contre Richard III* (Picardie, 1990), 154.

2 See Robert Speaight, *Shakespeare on the Stage* (Boston, Mass., 1973), 193–4.

3 Irving had omitted the mourning queens from his first production, reinstating them in the second. Mansfield and (sometimes) Benson omitted Margaret (Sprague, *Histories*, 139, 132).

4 Margaret was in 1.3 in Olivier's stage versions (Colley, 176), but disappeared from the film.

1954 film. Cibber provided some lines – including 'Richard's himself again'. Roles disappeared, action was rearranged, traditional points were observed with gestures going back to Kean and vocal echoes of Irving (Richmond, 56–7; Colley, 170), costume and haircut followed the Garrick tradition and the usual pre-Benson focus stayed on Richard. Olivier's film Richard combines unflagging energy, menace, cynicism and caricature. His nose from Disney's Big Bad Wolf, his voice a donnish treble, his soliloquies and asides are shared directly with us in strategic close-ups, and other roles are reduced. We enter the film with him, slyly invited to appreciate the conflict he has exacerbated. Ignoring 'motive and remorse', Olivier's 'sheer theatricality' set a standard (Richmond, 60–5; Hankey, 68–9). Olivier wanted to win the audience to Richard's side with his 'wit, his brilliantly wry sense of humour', with 'acting for acting's sake' (Colley, 177).

Olivier's popularity resulted in other actors being found wanting: Alec Guinness's 1953 Richard was less accomplished in sneering; Marius Goring's 1953 Richard was less dominating (Lull, 32); Christopher Plummer's 1961 Richard lacked Olivier's diction; Ian Holm's 1963 Richard was a 'pocket Olivier' (Colley, 229). No Richard would so dominate until Antony Sher's 1984 portrayal. Even before his film, Olivier's stage presence loomed so large that Stratford-upon-Avon did not see a *Richard III* until the 1953 Goring–Glen Byam Shaw production (Richmond, 64).[1] Goring's Richard was understatedly mad (the first post-war lunatic), with long red hair suggesting vulnerabilities to offset his soldier's demeanour (Day, 101–2). In a variant of Richard's dagger-play, Goring opened with his sword casually across his shoulder, lowered it as a walking-stick at 'Grim-visaged War hath smoothed his wrinkled front' (1.1.9), placed his heavy-booted foot on the forestage to emphasize his being 'rudely stamped' (16),

1 The next would not be for eight years, with Christopher Plummer in William Gaskill's 1961 production.

and then moved the sword to his claw-like left hand on 'Deformed, unfinished' (20) (Day, 101; Richmond, 67). A motif of circulating court documents suggested that war had given way to bureaucracy – no great stretch of imagination for post-Second World War England (Day, 108–9).

Among the most innovative productions with an insane Richard, Peter Hall and John Barton's 1963–4 adaptation set *Richard III* within a half-length first tetralogy, *The Wars of the Roses*. An 1870 commentator had predicted that putting the play in the tetralogy context would expose 'the guile and selfishness, second only to [Richard's] own, by which he was surrounded, and the dreadful circumstances (the consequences of civil war and dynastic ambition) which alone made such a character and such actions possible' (Hankey, 83). To this moral–political mix, Hall and Barton added ingredients from Jan Kott and E.M.W. Tillyard. Hall affirmed Kott's 'staircase' (Kott, 45) as the timeless model of the histories and their 'mechanism of power' (Barton & Hall, xi). Programme notes invoked Stalin, Hitler and Mussolini (Colley, 225). Hall also accepted Tillyard's stress on stable social degree and on the 'curse' upon the House of Lancaster, claiming that 'The bloody totalitarianism of Richard III' was 'the expiation of England' for the deposing of Richard II (Barton & Hall, x, xiii).[1] This conception gave Margaret renewed prominence, though the other women's parts remained reduced (Colley, 228).

Ian Holm's Richard of that year was Kottian but un-Tillyardian. Neither melodramatic nor tragic, Holm portrayed a diminutive, 'likeable juvenile, open-faced and friendly' (Colley, 226). Helmeted, black-clad toughs tramped about in unison with him, as he betrayed madness with blinkings and twitchings, drooling and giggling at secret jokes (Colley, 225, 227). Holm died neither gloriously like Kean, nor desperate like Irving, but gibbering inside a visored helmet through which Richmond stabbed

1 On combining Kott's pessimism with Tillyard's Tudor providentialism, see Hodgdon, *End*, 118.

him (Colley, 229). His reduced size, clownish behaviour and final faceless death ultimately derived via Kott from a 1960 production with Jacek Woszczerowicz (Kott, 46; Hankey, 72), which had made 'superman' a 'super-clown' who is 'smaller than all the other characters . . . a figure of fun' (Kott, 47). The production suggested a paradoxical alliance between 'buffoonery' and tyrannical impersonality imputed to world historical figures. The comedian Richard is ultimately replaced by another one: as 'rows of bars are lowered from above', Richmond 'speaks of peace, forgiveness and justice. And suddenly gives a crowing sound like Richard's, and, for a second, the same sort of grimace twists his face' (Kott, 48–9).

Kott's influence permeated the 1970s, and was compounded by the impact of Peter Weiss's *Marat/Sade* (1964). Weiss's allegory of oppression and revolution, set in a grim asylum where the players are mad and the madmen are players, influenced Barry Kyle's 1975 Stratford production with Ian Richardson (Colley, 204). The actors were attired to suggest mental patients or concentration camp inmates. Margaret served as stage manager, emerging to blow her whistle and curse, to blindfold Richard's victims or to articulate his mother's curses (Colley, 206; Day, 166). Bosworth was a pillow fight. The loose invocation of insanity and the political futility of the gulag and the implied similarities between Richard and Richmond may beg enormous questions (Colley, 207), but also missing were the collusions that tyranny demands and encourages from dupes, time-servers and the oppressed, a theme explored in an adaptation that made a huge impression despite performance in a language largely unknown to English audiences.[1]

The 1979–80 performances of the Rustaveli Company of Tbilisi, Georgia, directed by Robert Sturua, boldly recast text

1 Cf. Lin Zhaohua on his landmark (but financially disastrous) 2001 Beijing production: 'those who lack vigilance against murderous schemes are the conspirator's accomplices' (Li Ruru, *Shashibiya: Staging Shakespeare in China* (Hong Kong, 2003), 228).

and action. Antony Sher recalled Ramaz Chkhikvadze's Richard as a 'giant poisonous toad' (Sher, 28). Evoking Hieronymus Bosch, Miriam Scvelidze's set put a circus tent above a gallows, with a hell gate to either side, peopled by tyrants and subtyrants – even the citizens became oppressors (Tarsitano, 70, 72). Sturua acknowledged Mikhail Bakhtin's concept of the carnivalesque, with its 'gay relativity' and combinations and inversions of high and low characters, physical elements and themes (Stříbrný, 122; Tarsitano, 70). The white-faced Margaret, brandishing the text, prompted the actors, while a jester accompanied Richard, parodying his actions (unseen by Richard), winking and mocking his successes (Tarsitano, 71–3). Richmond provided Richard's primary audience and understudy. In the final moments the jester stared directly at the audience while Richmond gazed at the crown as earlier Richard had looked at it; the jester's motions in removing his hat were mimed by Richmond who, as though copying him, put on the crown (Tarsitano, 74–5).

Julie Hankey argues for Sturua's justice to Shakespeare's non-naturalistic elements, implacable forces and rigid ironies. For example, 'Buckingham taunts the condemned Hastings with the words "we know each other's faces, for our hearts . . ." and is in turn taunted with the same words when his execution falls due. The device of repeating words in a new context is Shakespeare's' (Hankey, 76). Simultaneous staging emphasized the insecure 'security' that pervades Shakespeare's play: Clarence dreams while Richard orders his assassination; Hastings asserts Catesby's loyalty while Buckingham instructs Catesby to double-cross him (Hankey, 76–7). The production made a deep impression on the century's next great Richard.

Antony Sher in the 1984 Bill Alexander RSC production struck many as 'the most impressive Richard since Olivier' (Hassel, 145). Sher combined 'unassuming tones' (Colley, 237) with spectacular physical deformities (see Fig. 8). With draping tunic, Sher resembled a six-legged spider from the front and a vulture from the side; his snake-like tongue flicked in and out

8 Antony Sher's Richard (directed by Bill Alexander, RSC, 1984)

relentlessly. In the first half of the play, despite a grotesque hump and splayed legs, he moved with incredible agility on black elbow-crutches that performed as feelers to rub together when mentioning doing 'naught' with Mistress Shore (1.1), swords to cow the bearers of King Henry's corpse (1.2), a phallic appendage to lift Anne's dress (1.2), a sceptre to 'knight' Buckingham and scissors for Hastings's neck. A world of stylization separates Burbage's swaggering dagger-drawing or Kean's hand-rubbing and peeks beneath Anne's veil from this. From his coronation onwards, Sher abandoned crutches to stagger weakly, to be carried, or to support himself on the sceptre, a sword or a mace (Day, 208; Cerasano, 623).

One further element harked back to Kean – Sher's emphasis on pacing. A distinctive bodily 'rhythm' expressed his inner distortion from the very first moments (Sher, 90, 144; Cerasano, 621): Sher initially appeared rear centre between imposing tomb-like structures, a dark figure seemingly unhobbled, slowly, sweetly evoking 'glorious summer' until 'But I . . . ' (1.1.14), when the crutches flew out into view and he hurtled to the edge of the stage, causing audiences to draw back in alarm (Colley, 239; Hassel, 'Context', 631). Such astonishingly abrupt movement, repeated in gestures and mood swings, put audiences in the position of the courtiers, fascinated, repelled and off balance, unable to anticipate Richard's next move (Colley, 240–1; Hassel, 'Context', 631). Until he was crowned; then Sher's Richard, like Shakespeare's, lost his dominance as things go wrong (Day, 207).

The power of the mourning women became clear in 4.4 where Richard was humiliated and outmanoeuvred by his mother (Yvonne Coulette) and Queen Elizabeth (Frances Tomelty). Sher's progress, on a litter, was interrupted by their verbal attacks which left his bearers unable to escape; his mother seized his hand and forced him to endure her curses (Day, 208). Queen Elizabeth granted him her daughter, but her self-assured seat on the throne and a surprising kiss on his lips as he tried to kiss her hand suggested more ambition than Richard had bargained for (Day, 203). This was not the woman denounced by Shakespeare's sources, but nor was she the desperate, improvising survivor that Shakespeare provides.[1]

Sher's Richard's own breakdown was most powerfully evident in his pre-battle oration (5.3.314–41). Despairing, his voice broke on 'runaways' and 'paltry fellow' (5.3.316, 323), while his followers menaced the audience (Hassel, 'Context', 638). His death enacted a 'sacrificial' elimination (Hammond, 72–3; Hassel, 'Context', 638–40; Day, 216). Kneeling, Richard offered up the crown to God, as the golden, visored Richmond pinned him with a cross-like sword, executing the judgement of providence.

This proved a hard act to follow. Nevertheless, 1988–90 saw an explosion reminiscent of the years of Macready, Kean and J.B. Booth (Colley, 249). Two adaptations appeared within abbreviated trilogies: Adrian Noble's *The Plantagenets* (1988), with Anton Lesser as Richard, and Michael Bogdanov's English Shakespeare Company *The Wars of the Roses* (1988), with Andrew Jarvis as Richard. Stand-alone productions included Derek Jacobi's 1988 *Richard III* at the Phoenix Theatre, directed by Clifford Williams. The year 1990 brought Ian McKellen to the National Theatre, directed by Richard Eyre. Other productions were mounted in New York (Denzel Washington as Richard) and at the Folger Theatre in Washington, DC (Stacy Keach as Richard).[2] Two of these took the play to affective regions it had never before seen.

Despite a prosthetically hooked nose and jet-black, matinee-idol hair, Jacobi went for laughs with a 'roguish effeminacy, pitched half-way between Olivier and Frankie Howerd' (Colley, 250). Richard opened giggling, lying on his back and gleefully

1 At 4.4.206–13 Shakespeare's Elizabeth initially appears to believe that Richard wants to kill, rather than wed, her daughter, and shifts her responses on the spot (see Jones).

2 For Keach's *Richard III*, see a review by Miranda Johnson-Haddad, *SQ*, 42 (1991), 473–6.

kicking his legs in the air while imagining his plots. He closed without a battle, but laughing, laid the crown before Richmond before being neatly dispatched. The jokester emphasis would figure prominently in the Richard of David Troughton. Ian McKellen provided a tight-lipped alternative.

McKellen's stage (1990) and film (1995) performances bracketed the two early 1990s Royal Shakespeare Company productions, Sam Mendes–Simon Russell Beale (1992) and Steven Pimlott–David Troughton (1995). McKellen's National Theatre production evolved into the film (directed by Richard Loncraine). His 'granitic' onstage demeanour was like no other (Jowett, 107). Set in an imaginary England of the 1930s, Richard's rise appeared upon Bob Crowley's spare set as the grim undertaking of a stiffly military figure, killing his way to the top of an order he detested and ending as a black-shirted tyrant (Colley, 260). Any spinal curve was hardly apparent; his arm was unobtrusive, but McKellen performed mechanical wonders with his 'good' arm. Lois Potter describes his opening soliloquy as spoken 'in a dry, old-fashioned, upper-class accent which negates any possibility of making friends with the audience' (Colley, 258). If Sher is the Kean of the recent era, then McKellen's stage Richard is the stately, measured Kemble (Colley, 261).

McKellen's film is another story. The heavy cutting, recast lines and opening recall Cibber. Margaret disappears, and Richard is funnier (and more viscerally repulsive) than he was onstage: his first soliloquy in a men's room is classic. His relationship to his mother (Maggie Smith) provides a subtext. McKellen assesses her 'disgust at his physique', speculating that from her 'Richard learnt how to hate so fiercely' (McKellen, 236, 274). The final moments allude to *White Heat* (1949), in which Jimmy Cagney's gangster, engulfed in flames, shouts, 'Made it, Ma' (Loehlin). As Richard falls into flames, grinning, Richmond 'usurps Richard's privilege and smiles into the camera', to pose 'unsettling' questions about England's future (McKellen, 286). Why there should be questions is unclear, but recent productions generally reject England's purgation and Richmond's innocence.

Richard's capacity to engage the audience with humour, irony and evil, though, is alive and well in Al Pacino's 1996 'home-movie', *Looking for Richard.* Interweaving play scenes with interviews, investigations, exhortations, criticism and brainstorming, the film depicts Pacino struggling with the role (Hodgdon, 'Replicating', 210).[1] Despite its dismissal of scholarship, it is filled with insights. The wooing scene has a demonic intensity that demonstrates how Richard can both repel and project erotic power.

While the Loncraine–McKellen film created a 1930s England that might have been, anachronistic eclecticism prevailed in the 1992–3 Sam Mendes–Simon Russell Beale *Richard III.* In Tim Hatley's spare set, cigars, bowler hats and balloons mixed with armour, ermine-trimmed robes and sweaters. Beale's swollen body and shaven head contrasted with McKellen's austere officer, or any other previous Richard. He indulged in Punch-like 'wide-eyed goggling' in campy disbelief at gullible dupes, or broke into psychotic ruthlessness, his fury only barely restrained as little York jumped onto his back (see Fig. 9). He exuberantly thrust a walking-stick into the brown paper parcel containing Hastings's head (Smallwood, 358–60). Margaret (Cherry Morris) appeared to reiterate the curses of 1.3 as victims met execution (Day, 160–1). She marked the time before Bosworth, tapping as if to the rhythm of the ghosts' curses or the seconds passing (Smallwood, 361; Day, 172–3). Downplaying her derision, she turned revenge to a shared purpose with the other women (Day, 169). There were no tents at Bosworth: Richard and his followers sat at one end of a long table, Richmond and company at the

1 On Pacino and McKellen, see Hodgdon, 'Replicating'; Herbert Coursen, 'Filming Shakespeare's history: three films of *Richard III*', and Barbara Freedman, 'Critical junctures in Shakespeare film history: the case of *Richard III*', both in Russell Jackson (ed.), *The Cambridge Companion to Shakespeare on Film* (Cambridge, 2000), 97–115, 47–71.

other, with the ghosts eerily appearing in between, toasting Richmond and cursing Richard. Countering the Garrick–Kean tradition, Beale's waking soliloquy conveyed little emotion. The intercut battlefield orations either made tyrant and liberator 'interchangeable' (Smallwood, 361–2) or treated Richmond as welcome relief.[1] Richmond's difficult, dirty victory in a peat-filled pit depended on Margaret's grant of dominance; Stanley casually tossed the crown in the dirt for him to pick up and hold aloft, in exhaustion (Smallwood, 362).

This *Richard III* employed a device traceable to Garrick, Edmund Kean and Irving: the micropause – even between syllables. Players have frequently commented on what Hankey calls the play's 'relentlessly iambic' verse. McKellen mentions keeping rhythm with his breath in his gas mask; Troughton remarks on a steady 'de-dum'. Garrick hesitated in order to convey the subtleties of sympathetic imagination, Kean and Irving to express their romantic agonies. This production interpellated pauses to register political struggles as hesitations and resistance.[2]

By contrast, the Steven Pimlott–David Troughton 1995 *Richard III* went for meta-theatre rather than political conflict (Day, 195). Troughton opened by recalling Richard Tarleton, the Elizabethan clown who could bring down the house by protruding his head into view and grimacing. Non-representational clowning continued as Troughton hobbled forward, took a deep breath, mouthed the letter 'N . . .' and froze, interrupted by giggling courtiers on a ledge above him. He scuttled off to return with a jester's cap and bells and bauble, ready to entertain this onstage audience, only to switch back to engaging the theatre audience when he lunged forward on 'But I, that am not shaped for sportive tricks' (1.1.14).

1 Peter Holland, *English Shakespeares: Shakespeare on the English stage in the 1990s* (Cambridge, 1997), 116.

2 See James N. Loehlin, 'Playing politics: *Richard III* in recent performance', *Performing Arts Journal*, 15 (1993), 80–94; Siemon, 'Between'.

9 Simon Russell Beale as Richard, with Kate Duchêne as Prince Edward and Annabelle Apsion as York (directed by Sam Mendes, RSC, 1992–3)

Instead of scaring audiences senseless as Sher had done, Troughton invited them to laugh with him as he deceived the frozen onstage characters (see Fig. 10).[1]

True to Shakespeare in breaking the representational frame, Troughton's jester still endured physical suffering and a troubled maternal relationship. These strands came together in Richard's altered relation to the audience in the second half of the play. From the failed bid for popular adulation (3.7.20–4), when the audience were encouraged to laugh at rather than with him, a rift widened as he displayed ineptitude, conscience (4.2.63–4) and despair. Troughton chose Q1's 'I and I' over the Folio's 'I am I' (5.3.183) for Richard's dream soliloquy to mark this split – the first 'Richard' being the audience and the second the man (Troughton, 95). Beset by censure, Richard despaired and, in effect, killed himself. As the intercut battlefield speeches grew weaker and stronger, Richard laid down sword and crown and walked to the ghosts' side of the stage to applaud – weakly – Richmond's final speech (Day, 218–19), an ironic conclusion perhaps recalling Sturua.

Whatever the uncertain significance of this end, 'the complete absence of any motherly love' was the presumed origin of Richard's suffering (Troughton, 87). Contemporary productions may not trust heroes or providence, but they take mothers seriously. Assessing the crown as a 'substitute' for love, Troughton removed it in 4.4 to curl up in a foetal position with his head in his mother's lap (Troughton, 88). Contemporary productions that ascribe tyranny to thwarted maternal relationships or make Margaret the universal time-keeper certainly contrast with the androcentric hero–villain shows of earlier centuries. Whether or not blaming his mother for Richard or granting Margaret cosmic authority resolves questions about accountability is debatable.

1 Robert Smallwood, '*Richard III* at Stratford', *SQ*, 47 (1996), 327. The bauble had Troughton's face on one side, a death's head on the other (Day, 198; Jowett, 108).

10 David Troughton as Richard with cap, bells and bauble (directed by Steven Pimlott, RSC, 1995)

A similarly logical development of naturalistically conceived character appears in the 2002 Michael Grandage–Kenneth Branagh presentation of a Richard driven by the pain and stigma of disability. On a mostly bare stage, Branagh opened naked except for white underpants, stretched out as if Leonardo's Vitruvian man were forced to fit an apparatus with weights and pulleys. Unable to stand erect without a corset and leg calliper, he collapsed into a heap upon 'But I, that am not shaped for sportive tricks' (1.1.14).[1] Another anti-Sher, but in his evident difficulties also an anti-McKellen; once upright, he could pass for convivial, announcing, like a music hall MC, 'The new-delivered Hastings' (121), but he displayed suddenly changing capacities. He could force a kiss from Anne, but the princes knocked him down, pulled off his brace and clambered onto his back, causing a roar of pain. He hurled Buckingham away at 'I am not in the giving vein' (4.2.114), but laid his head weeping in Queen Elizabeth's lap (4.4).[2] Branagh's Richard conveyed inner misery and self-hatred to portray not the demonic Antichrist, but a trauma victim, a wounded animal, not a 'nice, vulnerable Richard on the inside'.[3]

The next logical step would be actors with disabilities playing Richard, or, conversely, physically imposing actors playing against type. Three New York productions fill these bills. In 2004 Peter DuBois directed Peter Dinklage, standing 4 feet 6 inches, and accepting dwarfism as a strategic asset that kept other characters from taking him seriously.[4] In 3.4 Richard leaped atop the council table to walk to Hastings. In 2007 Heidi Lauren Duke directed Henry Holden, an actor who regularly employs arm-crutches. Richard's role was split between Holden, who spoke Richard's lines when alone, and Andrew Hutcheon, who read Richard's dialogue while Holden mimed his actions. Instead of a 'wink-wink' villain, Holden portrayed 'a normal guy who has had enough', his story that of 'any disabled' person.[5] Finally, the Classic Stage Company's 2007 Richard, Michael Cumpsty (co-directing with Brian Kulick), dominated everyone except the crazed Margaret (Roberta Maxwell) with his tall, handsome,

1 Alastair Macaulay, *Financial Times*, 23 March 2002.
2 Stephen Brown, *TLS*, 5 April 2002; Matt Wolf, *Variety*, 31 March 2002.
3 See Brown; contrast the 1987 Viennese *Richard III*, directed by Claus Peymann, which gave Richard Hitler hair but portrayed him as 'never loved . . . lonely . . . a poor pitiable man, worthy of compassion' (Draudt, 205).
4 Charles McNulty, *Village Voice*, 7 September 2004.
5 *New York Times*, 21 July 2007.

surprisingly able-bodied presence and mordant humour through the third act. Brutal yet charmingly comic ('Chop off his head' was followed by a pause, giggle and 'just joking' tone on 'something we will determine' (3.1.193)), Cumpsty, aided by Buckingham and a laughably corrupt Mayor, enlisted the audience to wave little white boar pennants and to answer Richard's 'Will you enforce me to a world of cares?' (3.7.222) with an enthusiastic 'Yes!' The audience cheered, 'Long live King Richard!'[1]

The early twenty-first century also saw *Richard III* again appear in a cycle. Motifs throughout the tetralogy directed by Michael Boyd emphasized moral failings and political infighting across generations.[2] In 2001 Fiona Bell doubled Margaret and Joan la Pucelle, so the same actor who waved a severed arm at its loser in *1 Henry VI* returned with the bones of her murdered son, tipping them out of their sack and reassembling the skeleton to confront the court (see Fig. 11).[3] Keith Bartlett doubled Talbot (*1H6*) with Stanley, turning him into a virtuous figure working within Richard's inner circle (Day, 186). Aidan McArdle's Richard appeared puckish, capable of saying 'I, as a child, will go by thy direction' (2.2.153) without irony and kissing Buckingham's hand. This gesture returned ironically when promise of the earldom of Hereford (3.1.194–8) prompted Buckingham to attempt shaking hands, only to be given Richard's kingly hand to kiss (Day, 181). Richard died cursed by his mother and father, who together removed his crown. The ghostly blessing of Richmond added lines from *3 Henry VI* commending 'mildness' and 'mercy'. This uplifting conclusion, countering recent ironic

1 For similar cheering, see Michael Dobson's review of the British all-female *Richard III* directed by Barry Kyle at the Globe Theatre ('Shakespeare performances in England 2003', *SS* 57 (2004), 277).

2 The appeal of the tetralogies also registered abroad in Luk Perceval and Tom Lanoye's *Ten Oorlong* (1997), a cycle including a cannibalistic Richard figure; see Ton Hoenselaars, 'Two Flemings at war with Shakespeare', in Hoenselaars, 244–61.

3 Benedict Nightingale, *The Times*, 27 April 2001.

11 Fiona Bell's Margaret spilling out the bones of her son Prince Edward, with Elaine Pyke as Queen Elizabeth (directed by Michael Boyd, RSC, 2001)

tendencies, was complicated by Richard's resurrection, as if he were ready to begin the conflict again (Day, 188–90).

This cycle was revived in 2006–7 with Jonathan Slinger's superbly deranged Richard. Short, scruffy and clumsy, smirking, spitting while speaking, Slinger appeared 'a casualty first, a sadist second – his life story a runt's revenge' among

12 Jonathan Slinger as Richard (directed by Michael Boyd, RSC, 2007–8)

'smooth operators'.[1] Having concluded *3 Henry VI* by addressing the newborn prince in his arms with the single word 'Now . . .' as the stage went black, Slinger, now hairless, opened *Richard III* rocking himself spasmodically while holding what appeared still to be the swaddled prince but turned out to be his empty drool napkin (see Fig. 12). Then, taking his nephew's hand, he began his soliloquy, only to send the boy off before confiding to us his determination to prove a villain.[2]

1 Kate Kellaway, *The Observer*, 28 January 2007.
2 Benedict Nightingale, *The Times*, 25 January 2007.

KING RICHARD III

LIST OF ROLES

KING EDWARD IV	
DUCHESS of York	*mother of King Edward IV*
PRINCE Edward, *later King Edward V* Richard, Duke of YORK	*sons of King Edward IV*
George, Duke of CLARENCE RICHARD, Duke of Gloucester *later* KING RICHARD III	*brothers of King Edward IV*
QUEEN ELIZABETH	*wife of King Edward IV*
Anthony Woodeville, Lord RIVERS	*brother of Queen Elizabeth*
Marquess of DORSET Lord GREY	*sons of Queen Elizabeth*
Sir Thomas VAUGHAN	
GHOST of KING HENRY VI	
QUEEN MARGARET	*widow of King Henry VI*
GHOST of PRINCE EDWARD	*son of King Henry VI*
Lady ANNE	*widow of Prince Edward, son of King Henry VI, and later wife of Richard, Duke of Gloucester*
William, Lord HASTINGS	*Lord Chamberlain*
Lord STANLEY, Earl of Derby	
Henry, Earl of RICHMOND	*stepson of Stanley, later King Henry VII*
Earl of OXFORD Sir James BLUNT Sir Walter HERBERT Sir William Brandon	*Richmond's followers*

Duke of BUCKINGHAM Duke of NORFOLK Sir Richard RATCLIFFE Sir William CATESBY Sir James TYRREL Sir Francis LOVELL Thomas, Earl of SURREY Two MURDERERS PAGE	*Richard, Duke of Gloucester's followers*
CARDINAL Bourchier	*Archbishop of Canterbury*
ARCHBISHOP of York	
Bishop of ELY	
Sir CHRISTOPHER Urswick	*a priest*
John, a PRIEST	
Sir Robert BRAKENBURY	*Lieutenant of the Tower of London*
KEEPER of the Tower	
Lord MAYOR of London	
SCRIVENER	
PURSUIVANT	
SHERIFF	
TRESSEL BERKELEY	*gentlemen attending Lady Anne*
Three CITIZENS	
BOY DAUGHTER	*children of George, Duke of Clarence*

Lords, Bishops, Gentlemen, Aldermen, Citizens, Halberdiers, Soldiers, Attendants, Messengers

LIST OF ROLES not in Qq, F; first provided by Rowe.

1 KING EDWARD IV Edward Plantagenet (1442–83), son of Richard, Duke of York, and Cecily Neville, won the crown during the Wars of the Roses from the Lancastrian Henry VI. He was secretly married in 1464 to Elizabeth, daughter of Richard Woodeville and widow of John Grey, alienating the powerful Earl of Warwick (see *3H6* 3.3). In 1471 he defeated the forces of Warwick and Queen Margaret, capturing Margaret at Tewkesbury after killing her son Edward (see *3H6* 5.5).

2 DUCHESS **of York** Cecily (née Neville, 1415–95), granddaughter of John of Gaunt and Katherine Swynford, mother of Edward IV, Clarence and Richard, grandmother of the play's little princes and their sister, Elizabeth

3 PRINCE **Edward** Edward, Prince of Wales (1470–83), elder son of Edward IV. Taken under the control of Richard of Gloucester while on his way to London after his father's death on 9 April 1483, he never had his scheduled coronation as Edward V and is presumed to have died in the Tower of London. By 22 June 1483 Ralph Shaw had publicized Richard's claim to the throne, and on 26 June Richard III began his reign. By September 1483 Richard's opponents had apparently given up hope of ever seeing Edward alive and transferred their support to Henry, Earl of Richmond.

4 YORK Richard, Duke of York (1473–83), younger son of Edward IV. He is presumed to have been killed along with his brother in the Tower of London, although in the 1490s a figure claiming to be Richard Plantagenet (also identified as Perkin Warbeck) appeared at the centre of a Yorkist rising against Henry VII.

5 CLARENCE George Plantagenet (1449–78), created Duke of Clarence (1461) by his elder brother Edward IV; married to Isabel Neville, elder sister of Lady Anne Neville, Richard's queen. Clarence fought on the Lancastrian side with the Earl of Warwick against his brothers in 1470 but rejoined them in 1471 (see *3H6* 4.1, 5.1). He was later imprisoned by Edward IV in the Tower of London, executed and attainted (see 1.1, 1.4).

6–7 RICHARD . . . KING RICHARD Richard Plantagenet (1452–85), created Duke of Gloucester (1461), later King Richard III; fourth surviving son of Richard, Duke of York, and Cecily, Duchess of York. He was named Lord Protector of his nephew Edward V in 1483, but was himself crowned as Richard III two months later. He was defeated and killed at the battle of Bosworth in August 1485.

8 QUEEN ELIZABETH Elizabeth Grey (née Woodeville, *c.* 1437–92), daughter of Richard Woodeville, 1st Earl of Rivers, and his wife, Jacquetta, dowager Duchess of Bedford. In 1456 she married Sir John Grey, who was killed in 1461 fighting on the Lancastrian side at the second battle of St Albans, leaving her with two sons, Thomas (later Marquess of Dorset) and Richard Grey. Married to Edward IV secretly in 1464 (see *3H6* 3.2), Elizabeth was 'the first subject raised to the throne of England as the wife of the reigning sovereign' (Thomson, 100).

9 RIVERS Anthony Woodeville (or Woodville, Wydeville) (*c.* 1440–83), 2nd Earl Rivers, later Lord Scales, having taken the title by right of his wife, heir of Lord Scales, in 1462; brother of the play's Queen Elizabeth. Having fought for Lancaster in 1460, Rivers later aided Edward IV against Clarence and Warwick and in Edward's victories over the Lancastrians in 1471, and served as mentor to the young Prince Edward. Taken captive by Richard of Gloucester while accompanying Prince Edward to London in April 1483, he was executed at Pontefract for treason on 25 June (see 3.3).

10 DORSET Sir Thomas Grey, Marquess of Dorset (1455–1501), elder son of Queen Elizabeth and her first husband, Sir John Grey. Dorset fought for Edward IV at Tewkesbury and supposedly participated in the murder

of Prince Edward, son of Henry VI (though not in Shakespeare's portrayal; see *3H6* 5.5). He was a bitter opponent of Lord Hastings; historically, he supported Buckingham's abortive rebellion against Richard III in 1483 and joined Richmond in Brittany. He proved an unreliable ally and was left prisoner in France as security for a loan, not participating in the invasion of 1485.

11 GREY Sir Richard Grey (d. 1483), younger son of Queen Elizabeth and Sir John Grey. Arrested by Richard of Gloucester at Ludlow in April 1483, along with his uncle, Anthony, Earl Rivers, he was imprisoned and executed with Rivers and Thomas Vaughan at Pontefract on 25 June (see 3.3).

12 VAUGHAN Sir Thomas Vaughan (d. 1483) was for many years in the service of the Yorkists, rising to become chamberlain and councillor to the young Prince Edward, son of Edward IV. One of those accompanying the prince to London for his coronation in April 1483, Vaughan was intercepted by Richard of Gloucester and the Duke of Buckingham and executed at Pontefract on 25 June (see 3.3).

13 GHOST of KING HENRY VI Henry Plantagenet (1421–71), descended from John of Gaunt, Duke of Lancaster, and only child of Henry V; his troubled reign, beset by rivalries between the houses of York and Lancaster, is the subject of Shakespeare's *1, 2* and *3H6*. Henry's death in the Tower of London in 1471 is portrayed by Shakespeare as a murder by Richard of Gloucester (see *3H6* 5.6).

14 QUEEN MARGARET Margaret of Anjou (1430–82), married to Henry VI (1445). Margaret is prominent in *2* and *3H6* as queen and warrior on Henry's behalf; her son and her husband are murdered in *3H6* by the York brothers (Edward, Richard and Clarence) (see *3H6* 5.5, 5.6). Imprisoned after her defeat by Edward IV at the battle of Tewkesbury in 1471, she was exiled in 1476 to Anjou, where she died the year before Richard III's accession.

15 GHOST of PRINCE EDWARD Edward Plantagenet (1453–71), Prince of Wales, only son of Henry VI and Margaret of Anjou; married to Anne Neville (1470). Shakespeare portrays his death as occurring at the hands of Richard, Clarence and Edward IV before the eyes of Margaret, his mother (see *3H6* 5.5)

16 ANNE Lady Anne Neville (1456–85), younger daughter of the powerful Earl of Warwick (Clarence's wife Isabel was her elder sister). She was first married to the son of Henry VI, Prince Edward, who was killed at the battle of Tewkesbury in 1471 (see *3H6* 5.5). In 1472, at the age of sixteen, she married Richard of Gloucester, and in 1483 was crowned Richard's queen.

17 HASTINGS William, Lord Hastings (*c.* 1430–83), a trusted companion of Edward IV, descended from a family of Yorkist allegiance. Hastings was the most powerful and prominent of the non-royal nobility who owed advancement to the favour of Edward (C. Ross, *Richard*, 39). Made a peer, Knight of the Garter and Lord Chamberlain following the battle of Towton in 1461, as Lord Chamberlain he thereafter controlled access to the king's person. Although he had married King Edward's cousin Katherine Neville in 1462, he was bitterly at odds with the Neville family at the time the play begins. He was notoriously betrayed and then beheaded by Richard in 1483 (see 3.4).

18 STANLEY Thomas, Lord Stanley (d. 1504), later Earl of Derby (1485); councillor and steward of household to Edward IV. In 1482 Stanley married Margaret Beaufort, Countess of Richmond and mother to the play's Richmond by her first marriage. He was imprisoned at the time of Hastings's execution in 1483, but was later named Constable by Richard. He held back on the field at Bosworth, and was subsequently created Earl of Derby (as he is frequently called in Shakespeare's play) (Sutton & Hammond, 399).

19 **RICHMOND** Henry Tudor (1457–1509), Earl of Richmond, afterwards King Henry VII. Richmond was the posthumous son of Henry VI's half-brother Edmund Tudor and his wife, Margaret Beaufort, great-great-granddaughter of Edward III through John of Gaunt and his mistress and (later) third wife, Katherine Swynford. He is the stepson of the play's Lord Stanley. Supposedly prophesied to become king by Henry VI in 1470 (see *3H6* 4.6), he fled to Brittany the following year with his uncle Jasper Tudor, Earl of Pembroke, and lived at the Breton court from 1476. He was proclaimed king during Buckingham's abortive revolt of 1483, but his invasion fleet was scattered by storms and he returned to Brittany, vowing to marry Elizabeth of York. In 1485 he invaded England with the support of France, landing in Wales on 7 August; he gathered forces from around England and defeated Richard on 22 August at Bosworth, where he was crowned on the field (see 5.3–5).

20 **OXFORD** John de Vere (1442–1513), Earl of Oxford, a Lancastrian partisan, escaped imprisonment in Calais in 1484 to join Richmond and commanded Richmond's vanguard at the battle of Bosworth.

21 **BLUNT** Sir James Blunt (d. 1492), a soldier, having been an esquire of the body to Richard III, left England for France to join Richmond in November 1484. He was knighted by Richmond in 1485 at his landing at Milford Haven, and subsequently rewarded with land forfeited by Richard's allies.

22 **HERBERT** Sir Walter Herbert, second son of Sir William Herbert, a Yorkist supporter (see *3H6* 4.1.129). Hall and Holinshed report that Richard III initially trusted Walter Herbert to halt Richmond's progress towards Bosworth. He appears prominently among the supporters of Richmond in 5.2 and 5.3.

23 **Brandon** Sir William Brandon (d. 1485), Richmond's standard-bearer at Bosworth (see 5.3), killed there by Richard III according to Polydore Vergil

24 **BUCKINGHAM** Henry Stafford, 2nd Duke of Buckingham (1455–83); married (1466) Katherine, sister of Elizabeth Woodeville (the play's Queen Elizabeth, wife of Edward IV). A member of the royal family by right of his illegitimate Beaufort descent from John of Gaunt (shared with Richmond), and of direct descent from Thomas of Lancaster, second youngest son of Edward III, Buckingham was head of one of the wealthiest and longest-established of English magnate families. Appointed Lord High Steward of England under Edward IV (1478), he was subsequently excluded from offices and responsibilities. Under Richard III he held the offices of Constable of England and Lord Great Chamberlain. He led an unsuccessful rebellion against Richard in 1483 and was executed on 2 November 1483 (see 4.4, 5.1).

25 **NORFOLK** John Howard (*c.* 1430–85), created 1st Duke of Norfolk (28 June 1483), was loyal to Edward IV and later to Richard III (C. Ross, *Richard*, 38). He carried Richard's crown at his coronation, and was presented with one of Richard's former titles, Lord High Admiral, and with nearly as many manors as Buckingham (Seward, 138–9). He died leading Richard's vanguard at Bosworth.

26 **RATCLIFFE** Sir Richard Ratcliffe (d. 1485), younger son of a family from the minor gentry, served Richard of Gloucester from 1475; he was created knight and banneret by Richard on the Scottish campaigns of 1480–2. Ratcliffe, the 'Rat' in William Collingbourne's famous rhyme (see 27n.), was one of Richard's most trusted confidants, and presided over the execution of Rivers, Vaughan and Grey in 1483 (see 3.3). He appears to have died at Bosworth, fighting for Richard.

27 **CATESBY** Sir William Catesby (d. 1485), councillor under Edward IV, knighted by Richard III and named Chancellor of the Exchequer in 1483, replacing William, Lord Hastings, his

close associate. He became Speaker in Richard's parliament in 1484, and was executed after the battle of Bosworth (1485). Catesby is notoriously remembered as the 'Cat' in William Collingbourne's couplet: 'The Cat, the Rat and Lovell our Dog / Rule all England under the Hog' (Horrox, 222).

28 **TYRREL** Sir James Tyrrel (d. 1502). Tyrrel is associated with the murder of the children of Edward IV in Polydore Vergil. Thomas More characterizes him as a man of 'right goodlye p[e]r-sonage' led astray by Richard III, who exploited his high ambition. He served Richard as Master of the Horse and Master of the Henchmen (Seward, 140). Historically, Tyrrel prospered under Henry VII until his execution in 1502 for favouring Edmund de la Pole (Sutton & Hammond, 407).

29 **LOVELL** Francis Lovell (*c.* 1457–*c.* 1488) was one of Richard of Gloucester's closest friends, and with wide estates in Lincolnshire and Yorkshire was one of the wealthiest barons beneath the rank of earl. He served under Richard in the Scottish military campaigns of 1480–2, was knighted by Richard (1481), made viscount (1483) and two days after Richard's assumption of the throne became the king's chamberlain, an office implying constant personal contact with the king. He is 'our Dog' in William Collingbourne's rhyme (see 27n.). Sent to guard the south coast against Richmond's invasion in 1485, he may not have been at Bosworth. He participated in later rebellions after Richmond's victory.

30 **SURREY** Thomas Howard (1443–1524), a supporter of Edward IV and of Richard of Gloucester. He helped arrest Lord Hastings at the Tower of London on 13 June 1483, and was created Earl of Surrey fifteen days later. He remained close to Richard III, helping to suppress Buckingham's rebellion, and was wounded and captured fighting for Richard at Bosworth. After three years' imprisonment in the Tower of London he served Henry VII and was restored as Earl of Surrey in 1489.

33 **CARDINAL** Thomas Bourchier (*c.* 1411–86), Archbishop of Canterbury (1454), Lord Chancellor under Henry VI (1455), and Cardinal (invested 1472). He crowned three kings, Edward IV, Richard III and Henry VII, and married Henry VII to Elizabeth of York (1486). He was involved in persuading Queen Elizabeth to surrender her younger son to Richard of Gloucester (see 3.1).

34 **ARCHBISHOP** Thomas Rotherham (1423–1500), Archbishop of York, Keeper of the Privy Seal for Edward IV; arrested along with Hastings (and John Morton, Bishop of Ely) in the Tower in June 1483 (C. Ross, *Richard*, 42)

35 **ELY** John Morton (d. 1500), Bishop of Ely and later (1486) Archbishop of Canterbury. Morton's early and close association with Margaret of Anjou and the Lancastrian court led to his imprisonment after Edward IV seized the crown. He escaped and joined Queen Margaret in France, serving as Keeper of the Privy Seal to Henry VI. Pardoned by Edward IV in 1471, he eventually became one of his counsellors. He was arrested by Richard on 13 June 1483 at the same council meeting that led to Hastings's execution, and placed in the custody of the Duke of Buckingham. Morton eventually aided Buckingham's abortive rebellion and escaped to Flanders to serve Richmond, first as a diplomat and later as a member of the king's council and Chancellor. A patron of Sir Thomas More, he may be one source of More's account of Richard III.

36 **CHRISTOPHER** Sir Christopher Urswick (*c.* 1448–1522), a priest and supporter of the Stanleys, was chaplain to Lady Margaret Beaufort and involved in negotiating the marriage of her son, Richmond, to Elizabeth of York (see 4.5). He joined Richmond in France and accompanied him to Bosworth in 1485.

38 **BRAKENBURY** Sir Robert Brakenbury (d. 1485), appointed Lieutenant of the

Tower of London by Richard III in 1483 (i.e. years after the imprisonment and death in 1478 of George, Duke of Clarence, depicted in 1.1 and 1.4), died fighting on Richard's side at Bosworth.

40 **MAYOR** Historically, the Lord Mayor of London depicted in the play was Edmund Shaa (or Shaw) (in office 1482–3; d. 1488). He served on a commission to inquire into treasons within the City in December 1483 (Sutton & Hammond, 394). His brother Raffe (or Ralph) delivered a notorious sermon claiming the bastardy of Edward IV's children (see 3.5).

47 **BOY** Edward Plantagenet, Earl of Warwick (1475–99), the only surviving son of George, Duke of Clarence, and Isabel Neville (d. 1476), orphaned in 1478; he was imprisoned in the Tower by Henry VII, found guilty of conspiring against Henry with Perkin Warbeck (see 4n.) and executed in 1499 (Hammond & Sutton, 385).

48 **DAUGHTER** Margaret Plantagenet (1473–1541), daughter of George, Duke of Clarence, and Isabel Neville, married to Sir Richard Pole by Henry VII (not by Richard as claimed in 4.3) in 1487; she was executed by Henry VIII on charges of treason.

KING RICHARD III

1.1 *Enter* RICHARD, Duke of Gloucester, *alone.*

RICHARD
Now is the winter of our discontent
Made glorious summer by this son of York,

1.1 location: '*The* COURT' (Pope) or 'London: *A Street*' (Capell); references suggest proximity to the Tower of London. After Irving, a street scene became the norm. The play's earliest texts seldom name specific locations for scenes (but see 3.3.0.3), usually allowing the dialogue to establish location whenever specificity is required. Editors have generally tried to aid readers by suggesting locations for the action.

0.1 ***Enter*** Richard is the only character to open a Shakespeare play with a soliloquy; Cibber's version opened with the imprisoned Henry VI and discussed the struggles between York and Lancaster. Kemble and Cooke entered majestically, Edmund Kean 'hastily – head low – arms folded' (Colley, 66–7). Junius Brutus Booth used delay to enormous effect (Matthews & Hutton, 111). Simon Russell Beale's cane tapped his way onto the dark stage (de Jongh).
alone Cf. Queen Margaret's entry at 4.4.0.1 ('*sola*' Qq).

1 SP *Richard's first speech lacks a SP in F, Qq. Richard is usually '*Glo.*' in Qq SPs – until his crowned entrance in 4.2; thereafter he is '*Ki.*', '*King.*' or '*King Ri.*' In F he is '*Rich.*', '*Ric.*' or '*Ri.*' until 3.1.63–180, where he is '*Glo.*' He then becomes Richard again until 5.3. From 5.3.49 on, he is usually '*King.*' but otherwise '*Rich.*'

1 **Now** Dramatic rather than historical chronology: Holinshed has Edward IV enter London on 21 May 1471, victorious over the house of Lancaster; Henry VI was killed that day (by Richard, according to Holinshed) or died soon after (from melancholy displeasure, according to writers 'fauoring . . . the house of Yorke'), in the Tower of London. Clarence was killed in February 1478 and Edward IV died in April 1483. The first two acts span 12 years.

1–2 **winter . . . summer** Metaphors of seasonal transformation are ubiquitous in Tudor poetry (e.g. Sidney, *Astrophil and Stella*, 69), but Richard reverses the famous opening of Kyd's *Spanish Tragedy*, wherein the 'sommer joyes' of love are aborted by 'Deaths winter' (1.1.12–13). By 1601 Shakespeare's lines were famous enough to be quoted in mockery (*Parnassus*, 343).

2 **son** Edward IV, Richard's brother, son of the Duke of York killed in *3H6*, but possibly a punning reference to the sun that Edward assumed as his emblem after three suns appeared during his victorious battle with the Lancastrians (*3H6* 2.1.21–40; cf. C. Ross, *Wars*, 53); cf. 1.3.265–6. GWW suggests that *son* refers to the infant prince (later Edward V) introduced in *3H6* as the future hope of his father and kissed by Richard, who informs the audience of his evil intentions toward this child who stands between him and the throne.

1.1] *F (Actus Primus. Scœna Prima.); not in Qq, which lack act and scene divisions throughout* 0.1 Gloucester, *alone*] *F, Qq (Gloster, solus subst.)* 1 SP] *Capell (Ric.); not in Qq, F* of our] *F, Q1–2;* of *Q3–6* 2 son] *F (*Son*);* sonne *Qq*

And all the clouds that loured upon our house
In the deep bosom of the ocean buried.
Now are our brows bound with victorious wreaths,
Our bruised arms hung up for monuments,
Our stern alarums changed to merry meetings,
Our dreadful marches to delightful measures.
Grim-visaged War hath smoothed his wrinkled front;
And now, instead of mounting barbed steeds
To fright the souls of fearful adversaries,
He capers nimbly in a lady's chamber
To the lascivious pleasing of a lute.

3 **loured** frowned
house the York family

6 **bruised** bruisèd
bruised arms . . . monuments war-battered weapons displayed as memorials; cf. *Luc* 110.

7 **alarums** calls summoning to arms (*OED sb.* 4a) made with drums (4.4.149) or trumpets (*2H6* 5.2.3); or sudden or unexpected attacks (*OED sb.* 11)
meetings encounters, possibly playing on encountering in arms, battles (*OED sb.* 2a)

8–13 Lyly's *Campaspe* opposes dancing 'measurs' to a military 'march' (4.3.32–4). Cf. Venus' boasts to have converted Mars from 'drum and ensign red' and taught him to 'sport and dance, / To toy, to wanton, dally, smile, and jest' (*VA* 97–108). Edward III rejects the drum for the amorous lute (*E3* 2.2.56). Opposition of weaponry to music and dance is conventional in soldierly admonition (cf. de Somogyi, 44). Richard was successful militarily, especially against the Scots in 1481–2 (Mancini, 65).

8 **measures** tunes or melodies (*OED sb.* 17); with possible senses of grave or stately dances (*OED sb.* 20a) or the boundaries of a fencer's reach (*OED sb.* 2e)

9 **Grim-visaged War** Cf. 'Warre . . . With visage grym' (*Mirror*, 'Induction', 386–7).
wrinkled front frowning brow

10–13 Cf. 'Is the warlike sou[n]d of drumme and trumpe turned to the soft noyse of lire and lute? the neighing of barbed steeds . . . to dilicate tunes and amorous glaunces?' (Lyly, *Campaspe*, 2.2.35–9).

10 **barbed** barbèd; prepared for combat with an armoured covering for the breast and flanks

11 **fearful** either dreadful, terrifying, or frightened, timorous (*OED a.* 1a, 3a)

12–13 **capers . . . lute** Cf. 'they are too dainty for the wars. / Their fingers made to quaver on a Lute, / Their armes to hang about a Ladies necke: / Their legs to dance and caper in the aire' (Marlowe, *Works*, *2 Tamburlaine*, 1.3.28–31); also 'Ignoto' in Davies and Marlowe (see p. 82). Near *mounting*, *lascivious*, *sportive*, *tricks* and *amorous*, capering 'in a lady's chamber' carries clear sexual connotations.

13 **pleasing** pleasure

7 alarums] *F, Q2–6; Q1* (alarmes) 8 measures] *F, Q1–3;* pleasures *Q4–6* 10 instead] *F, Q2–6 subst.;* in steed *Q1* 13 lute] *F;* loue *Qq*

But I, that am not shaped for sportive tricks,
Nor made to court an amorous looking-glass;
I, that am rudely stamped, and want love's majesty
To strut before a wanton ambling nymph;
I, that am curtailed of this fair proportion,
Cheated of feature by dissembling Nature,
Deformed, unfinished, sent before my time
Into this breathing world, scarce half made up,
And that so lamely and unfashionable
That dogs bark at me as I halt by them –
Why, I, in this weak piping time of peace,

14 **But I** Since Irving, it has been customary to mark this transition to personal assessment. Irving's production halted its festive bells (Hankey, 89); Sher lurched forward spectacularly (Colley, 239).
sportive amorous or wanton
tricks games, ways
15 **amorous** pertaining to paraphernalia commonly associated with lovers
16 **rudely stamped** roughly fashioned, as in a crudely pressed coin
want lack
17 **wanton ambling nymph** woman who walks in a sexually provocative manner; Hamlet calls Ophelia 'nymph' and claims 'you jig and amble and you lisp' (*Ham* 3.1.88, 143).
18–23 **I . . . halt** Richard's claim to have been born unfinished parallels the self-characterization of the lame Emperor Claudius in *Mirror*, *Additions*, 'Claudius', 11–12. See p. 66 and Jones, *Origins*, 217–18.
18 **curtailed . . . proportion** shortened, cut off in respect of proper dimensions
curtailed cùrtailed
19 **feature** outward appearance
dissembling Nature another personification, here oddly depicting Nature as being – as Richard proclaims himself to be – a dissembler, a cheating hypocrite. Richard earlier claims that Love bribed 'frail' Nature to deform him (*3H6* 3.2.153–5; cf. *VA* 729–44). Sixteenth-century interpreters typically treated birth abnormalities as witnessing divine power and wrath (Cressy, *Travesties*, 39).
20 In *3H6* Richard is called 'an undigested and deformed lump' (5.6.51); stories about his birth and body go back to Rous, who claims he was 'retained within his mother's womb for two years' (Hanham, 120; cf. p. 52n.). Sources suggest that his mother's difficult labour was lengthy (cf. 4.4.163–4).
21 **breathing** i.e. mortal (cf. *Son* 81)
22 **lamely and unfashionable** grammatically, a double adverb with single adverbial termination; Richard represents himself as only partially finished, *lamely* created by nature, as well as *unfashionable* – i.e. not stylish – in the new time of love and peace.
23 **halt** limp
24 **piping** musical, or specifically referring to music of the pastoral pipe (as distinguished from the martial fife or trumpet) (*OED ppl. a.* 1b); cf. *MA* 2.3.13–15.

14 shaped for] *F (*shap'd for*), Q1–3 (*shapte for*);* sharpe for *Q4–5;* sharpe of *Q6* 15 Nor] *F, Q1, 3–6;* Not *Q2* 21 scarce] *F, Q1–2; om. Q3–6*

Have no delight to pass away the time,
Unless to see my shadow in the sun
And descant on mine own deformity.
And therefore, since I cannot prove a lover
To entertain these fair well-spoken days,
I am determined to prove a villain
And hate the idle pleasures of these days.
Plots have I laid, inductions dangerous,
By drunken prophecies, libels and dreams,
To set my brother Clarence and the King
In deadly hate, the one against the other;
And if King Edward be as true and just
As I am subtle, false and treacherous,
This day should Clarence closely be mewed up
About a prophecy, which says that 'G'
Of Edward's heirs the murderer shall be.

27 **descant on** comment upon or, in musical terms, sing or play a melodious accompaniment to a theme
28 **prove** become, turn out to be
29 **entertain** occupy, while away (cf. *Son* 39); used with two other senses in this act: to employ (1.2.259) and to permit oneself (1.3.4).
30 **determined** determinèd; Richard may mean that he is personally resolved or that his role has been determined by birth, a sense supported by his self-designation as 'ordained' to kill Henry VI (*3H6* 5.6.58); cf. *3H6* 2.2.137 and 5.7.23 on his physical features as destined and ordained.
32 **inductions** initial steps (*1H4* 3.1.2), suggesting literary or theatrical prefaces or preambles (*OED* 3c, 3b) as at 4.4.5–7, which connects inductions with the generically 'tragical'; *Plots* reinforces theatrical association. Richard provides an 'induction' to *Richard III* as a Prologue figure might (cf. *2H4*).
33 **libels** accusatory or defamatory bills or pamphlets, publicly posted or circulated; libels were frequent in the 1580s and 1590s, with prominent figures often accused of being their hidden instigators; cf. pp. 36–7.
38 **closely** securely
mewed up caged, often referring to hawks or poultry (*OED* *v.*[2]); cf. 132 and 1.3.138.
40 **Edward's heirs** King Edward's children; sources record this prediction, but not that Richard originated it. Holinshed reports that this 'foolish prophesie, which was, that, after K. Edward one should reigne, whose first letter of his name should be a G', was later taken to refer to Richard (Holinshed, 3.703); see pp. 36–7.

26 see] *F;* spie *Qq* 32 inductions] *F, Q3–6;* inductious *Q1–2;* inductious, *Oxf*[1] 39 a prophecy] *F, Q1–3, 6;* adrohesie *Q4–5* 40 murderer] *F, Q3–6 (*murtherer*);* murtherers *Q1–2*

Dive, thoughts, down to my soul; here Clarence comes.

Enter CLARENCE, *guarded, and* BRAKENBURY

Brother, good day. What means this armed guard
That waits upon your grace?

CLARENCE His majesty,
Tendering my person's safety, hath appointed
This conduct to convey me to the Tower.

RICHARD
Upon what cause?

CLARENCE Because my name is George.

RICHARD
Alack, my lord, that fault is none of yours;
He should for that commit your godfathers.
O, belike his majesty hath some intent
That you should be new christened in the Tower.
But what's the matter, Clarence, may I know?

41 **Dive, thoughts** Honigmann notes this unusual admission that a soliloquy is spoken aloud; cf. 1.3.338n.

41.1 *guarded* surrounded by guards
BRAKENBURY Other accounts do not give Sir Robert Brakenbury a role in imprisoning Clarence, since he only became Constable of the Tower five years after Clarence's death; cf. 1.4.75.1n.

42 **armed** armèd

43 **waits upon** attends; ironic, given Clarence's constraint by armed guards

44 **Tendering** caring for; cf. 2.4.73.
safety Clarence plays upon the meaning 'confinement or close custody' (*OED* 2; cf. *KJ* 4.2.158).

45 **conduct** escort
the Tower the Tower of London; the first of some 25 references

48 **commit your godfathers** i.e. because Clarence was given his name in the baptismal ceremony; *commit* = consign to imprisonment (also at 61)

49 **belike** probably

50 **new christened** Cf. 1.4. In *The Mirror for Magistrates* Clarence describes his murder by drowning in a wine barrel as a baptism (*Mirror*, 'Clarence', 370–1). New christening would award him a new name and thus enable him to evade the accusations against him.

51 **the matter** i.e. the real cause at issue (between King Edward and himself)

41] *F; Qq line* soule, / comes, / 41.1] *F; opp. 41 Qq (lined with / men. /)* *guarded, and* BRAKENBURY] *Rowe*[3]*; and Brakenbury, guarded F; with / a gard of men Qq subst.* 42 day] *F;* dayes *Qq subst.* 43–5] *Pope (43 one line Steevens); F lines* Grace? / safety, / Tower / ; *Qq line* grace? / ap- / pointed *(*ap- / p nted *Q1 BL, Hn)* / tower. / 44 Tendering] *F (*tendring*), Qq* 45 the Tower] *Qq;* th'Tower *F* 46+ SP] *F (Rich.); Glo. Qq* 46] *Steevens; F, Qq line* cause? / *George.* / 48 godfathers] *F, Q1–3;* good fathers *Q4–6* 50 should be] *F;* shalbe *Q1;* shall be *Q2–6* christened] *F, Q2–5 (*Christned*), Q1, 6* 51 what's] *F, Q1–2 subst.;* what is *Q3–6*

CLARENCE

Yea, Richard, when I know; but I protest
As yet I do not. But, as I can learn,
He hearkens after prophecies and dreams,
And from the crossrow plucks the letter G;
And says a wizard told him that by 'G'
His issue disinherited should be.
And for my name of George begins with G,
It follows in his thought that I am he.
These, as I learn, and such like toys as these,
Hath moved his highness to commit me now.

RICHARD

Why, this it is, when men are ruled by women:
'Tis not the King that sends you to the Tower;
My Lady Grey his wife, Clarence, 'tis she

52 ***but** Some editors prefer Qq's 'for', presuming compositorial or scribal anticipation; however, F's repeated 'but' could suggest Clarence's excited emotional state.

54 **hearkens after** pays attention to

55 **crossrow** the alphabet, called the Christ-crossrow for the cross printed with it in the hornbook from which children learned their letters

58 **for** because

60 **toys** trifles

61 **Hath** singular form used with a plural subject, frequent in Shakespeare (Abbott, 334)

62–116 This sequence replays a passage in *3H6* that begins with Richard prompting Clarence's animosity against Queen Elizabeth by glancing at her humble origins and then referring to Edward's uncontrollable lust before being warned by a third party to 'forbear this talk' (*3H6* 4.1.1–6).

62 Cf. Richard's insult wishing that Queen Margaret 'might still have worn the petticoat / And ne'er have stol'n the breech from Lancaster' (*3H6* 5.5.23–4).

63–5 Although the charge that the Queen sends Clarence to prison appears clearly fabricated, Dominic Mancini (unlike others) maintains that the Queen 'concluded that her offspring by the king would never come to the throne, unless the duke of Clarence were removed; and of this she easily persuaded the king.' Mancini reports that Richard swore vengeance for Clarence's death (Mancini, 63).

64 **My Lady Grey** Richard demeans the Queen by invoking the name of her deceased first husband, Sir John Grey; in part, Richard's hostility arises from her lower social rank. In *3H6* she rightly says she is 'not ignoble of descent' (*3H6* 4.1.70). Hall calls her marriage to Edward 'ioyous to the quene & profitable to her bloud, which were so highly exalted,

52 I know] *F, Q1–5;* I doe know *Q6* but] *F;* for *Qq* 59 follows] *F, Q1–4, 6;* fellowes *Q5* 61 Hath] *F;* Haue *Qq*

That tempers him to this extremity.
Was it not she and that good man of worship,
Anthony Woodeville, her brother there,
That made him send Lord Hastings to the Tower,
From whence this present day he is delivered?
We are not safe, Clarence; we are not safe.

CLARENCE

By heaven, I think there is no man secure
But the Queen's kindred and night-walking heralds

yea, & so sodainly promoted, that all the nobilitie more maruayled then allowed this sodayne risyng and swift eleuacion' (*Edward IV*, fol. cxcv[r]).

65 **tempers** governs, overrules, often with a sense of moulding or shaping (cf. *2H4* 4.3.127–8); Q2's 'tempts' could have prompted F's addition of 'harsh' for metrical reasons; but cf. *TxC*, 232–3. 'Tempts' appears frequently in association with Richard's interactions with others (1.4.12; 4.2.35, 39; 4.4.418, 419); *tempers* continues a theme from *Mirror for Magistrates*: 'This made [Richard] plye the while the waxe was soft ('Clarence', 341).

66 **good . . . worship** sarcastic, since 'goodman' was for persons under the rank of gentlemen and could be used ironically (*OED* 3b; cf. 'goodman Dull', *LLL* 4.2.36); a 'man of worship' was a person of good reputation, but the phrase could imply non-noble standing. Stow (1.327) differentiates between persons of 'worship' and those of 'honour' (i.e. belonging to the nobility). See also 3.7.137n. Richard shows lack of respect in employing Woodeville's family name rather than his new title, Earl Rivers. Social prejudices against the Woodevilles as upstart nobility are widely reported, but Mancini (67–9) records that his moral goodness won Earl Rivers exemption from 'hatred' and 'jealousy' (cf. More, *CW2*, 14).

67 ***Woodeville** F's '*Woodeulle*' allows trisyllabic pronunciation; Steevens claims that it was so pronounced by a contemporary of his. In *1H6* the name is disyllabic, and F spells it 'Wooduile' (*1H6* 1.3.22).
there probably conveying denigration (*OED adv.* 3b), but taken in some productions to indicate presence within sight of the speaker

72 **Queen's kindred** The association of the Queen's family members with the nocturnal go-betweens employed by King Edward suggests participation in sexual debauchery. The Queen's sons, Dorset and Grey, and her brother, Edward Woodeville, were reputed 'promoters and companions of [Edward's] vices' (Mancini, 67–9). Richard twice proclaimed such charges against Elizabeth's male kin (Mancini, 113n; *Paston Letters*, 6.81).
night-walking heralds i.e. secret messengers between the King and his mistress; 'night-walker' could suggest criminal intent.

65 tempers] *Q1;* tempts *F, Q2, 4–6;* temps *Q3* extremity] *Qq;* harsh Extremity *F* 67 Woodeville] *Capell; Woodeulle F;* Wooduile *Qq* 71 secure] *F;* is securde *Q1–3;* securde *Q4–6 subst.*

That trudge betwixt the King and Mistress Shore.
Heard you not what an humble suppliant
Lord Hastings was [Q]to her[Q] for his delivery?

RICHARD

Humbly complaining to her deity
Got my Lord Chamberlain his liberty.
I'll tell you what: I think it is our way,
If we will keep in favour with the King,
To be her men and wear her livery.
The jealous o'erworn widow and herself,
Since that our brother dubbed them gentlewomen,
Are mighty gossips in our monarchy.

73 **trudge** Clarence's term carries ironic connotations; 'trudging' meant walking laboriously, wearily or without spirit, or was 'an undignified equivalent' for walking (*OED v.*[1] 1).
Mistress Shore Jane (historically Elizabeth) Shore, notorious mistress of Edward IV and later of Hastings (see pp. 55–6 and 3.1.185). 'Mistress' was a title of respect for a female ruler and a title for a woman, married or unmarried (as 'Ms': *OED sb.* 5a, 14a–b), so here it conveys superficial, minimal respect, ironic hyperbole (see 76) and awareness of Shore's illicit relations with Edward (*OED sb.* 11).

75 ***was . . . his** Qq's wording makes more sense than F's 'was, for her'. GWW suggests that Qq's line might have an unaccented 11th syllable elided as 'de-liv- | -ry'.

76 **her deity** mock title attributing godlike status to Mistress Shore

77 **Lord Chamberlain** Hastings; the Lord Chamberlain was a chief officer with shared oversight of all officers of the Royal Household.

78 **way** i.e. most advisable course of action, best hope of success (*OED sb.*[1] III 12b)

80 **her men . . . livery** the uniformed servants or badged retainers of Mistress Shore; in fact she has neither livery nor retainers.

81 **o'erworn widow** i.e. Queen Elizabeth (see 64n.); *o'erworn* conveys advanced age (see *Son* 63), but coupling it with *widow* insinuates being worn out from much use by men (cf. *AC* 1.2.166–75). *o'erworn* also continues the clothing metaphor from *livery* (80), contrasting the two women in King Edward's life (Jowett).

82 **Since that** since
dubbed a parodic usage, in that only knights were dubbed
gentlewomen sarcastically inaccurate: Queen Elizabeth was born to gentle status and had claim to noble standing when her father was made Baron (later Earl) Rivers, before she met Edward IV. Jane Shore was neither gentle nor noble, and never would be. Typically, Richard elides differences to evoke a grouping that his interlocutor would find socially distasteful.

83 **gossips** either female friends, insinuating their light or trifling character, or godparents, perhaps covertly alluding to the impending

74 you] *F;* ye *Qq* 75 was . . . his] *Qq;* was, for her *F;* was, for his *F2* 76 Humbly] *F, Q1–4;* Humble *Q5–6* 83 our] *F;* this *Qq*

BRAKENBURY

I beseech your graces both to pardon me.
His majesty hath straitly given in charge
That no man shall have private conference,
Of what degree soever, with your brother.

RICHARD

Even so; an't please your worship, Brakenbury,
You may partake of any thing we say.
We speak no treason, man; we say the King
Is wise and virtuous, and his noble Queen
Well struck in years, fair and not jealous.
We say that Shore's wife hath a pretty foot,
A cherry lip, a bonny eye, a passing pleasing tongue,
And that the Queen's kindred are made gentlefolks.
How say you, sir? Can you deny all this?

'christening' of Clarence in 1.4. Gossips could be men or women. Richard's joke about dubbing foregrounds gender as well as social baseness; hence his oxymoronic assessment of them as *mighty gossips* threatening the patriarchal order. Given the importance of the play's female voices, the sense of gossips as women who delight in 'idle talk' (*OED sb.* 3) carries unintended irony. No evidence supports Richard's assertions concerning alliance between Elizabeth and Jane Shore (cf. 3.4.69–71).

85 **straitly . . . charge** strictly ordered

87 **Of . . . soever** no matter how high in rank (referring to *man* in 86)

88 **an't please** if it please; 'and' in such constructions is generally regularized to conditional 'an' (*OED* an' 2; cf. *LLL* 5.2.575).

92 **Well struck** perhaps euphemistic, suggesting 'well preserved' (Jowett); the basic meaning is 'advanced in age' (*OED* struck *ppl. a.*).

***jealous** F's 'iealious' may record trisyllabic pronunciation. Perhaps a typical Compositor B spelling even where metre requires a disyllable (*TxC*, 233), but at 81, where a disyllable is required, the spelling is 'iealous' (Lull). Cf. 'iealious' in F's *Oth* 3.4.157–61.

93–4 **foot . . . tongue** More concentrates on Jane Shore's discursive skills: she 'delited not men so much in her bewty, as in her plesant behauiour' (*CW*2, 56).

94 *Editors since Pope have abbreviated or modified this extra-syllabic line. Thompson suggests that it might be a snatch from an old song in 'fourteen' metre (cf. *MND* 5.1.324–6: 'Must cover thy sweet eyes. / These lily lips, / This cherry nose').

passing exceptionally

84+ SP] *F (Bra.); Bro. Qq* 87 your] *F;* his *Qq* 88 an't] *F, Qq (*and*), Pope* 88, 105 Brakenbury] *F;* Brokenbury *Qq* 92 jealous] *F (*iealious*), Qq (*iealous*)*

BRAKENBURY

With this, my lord, myself have nought to do.

RICHARD

Naught to do with Mistress Shore? I tell thee, fellow,
He that doth naught with her, excepting one,
Were best to do it secretly, alone.

BRAKENBURY

What one, my lord?

RICHARD

Her husband, knave. Wouldst thou betray me?

BRAKENBURY

I do beseech your grace to pardon me, and withal
Forbear your conference with the noble Duke.

CLARENCE

We know thy charge, Brakenbury, and will obey.

RICHARD

We are the Queen's abjects, and must obey.

97–8 ***nought . . . Naught** F's spelling suggests a pun which distinguishes between 'nought' (nothing) and 'naught' (mischief, evil: *OED sb.* A 2, citing this line). Jane Shore was 'naught of her body' (Hall, *Edward V*, fol. xvi[r]); to 'be naught with' had sexual connotation (*OED* naught *sb.* B 2c)

98–104 *These frequently unmetrical lines have prompted emendation. Richard may approach prose as he becomes sexually suggestive (Hammond).

98 **thee, fellow** Richard descends from mock formality (*your worship* and *you, sir*) to nearly contemptuous intimacy (*OED* fellow *sb.* 10a; Abbott, 231); see 1.2.263n., 3.2.104.

101–2 *These two lines first appear in Q2, which is otherwise merely derivative from Q1, and are reprinted in all subsequent early editions, including F. They may be a stop-press correction, a change introduced into some copies of a text (in this case Q1) in the course of printing. For a change in Q2 that appears to be such a correction, see 1.3.120. See pp. 433–4.

102 **betray me** i.e. prompt me to reveal what I think concerning this delicate and potentially dangerous subject of royal infidelity

103 **withal** in addition, besides, likewise

104 **conference** conversation

106 **Queen's abjects** (abjècts) i.e. instead of being the King's subjects; Richard combines two meanings of 'abject' – one who is rejected and one who is degraded – to suggest that they have been not only rejected by the Queen but degraded by

97 nought] *F, Q1, 6;* naught *Q2–5* 98–100] *Qq; F lines Shore?* / her / alone. / 100 to] *F;* he *Qq* 101–2] *F, Q2–6; not in Q1* 103–4] *Capell; F lines* Grace / forbeare / Duke. / ; *Qq line* forbeare / Duke. / 103 do] *F; not in Qq*

Brother, farewell. I will unto the King,
And whatsoe'er you will employ me in,
Were it to call King Edward's widow 'sister',
I will perform it to enfranchise you.
Meantime, this deep disgrace in brotherhood
Touches me deeper than you can imagine.

CLARENCE
I know it pleaseth neither of us well.

RICHARD
Well, your imprisonment shall not be long;
I will deliver you, or else lie for you.
Meantime, have patience.

CLARENCE I must perforce. Farewell.

Exeunt Clarence [, *Brakenbury and guard*].

RICHARD
Go, tread the path that thou shalt ne'er return;

their submission. 'Abject' is used theologically for the reprobate cast out of God's favour (*OED ppl. a., sb.*). Lyly suggests difference between proper subjection and objectionable abjection: 'I accompt all those abiects, that be not hir [Elizabeth's] subiectes' (2.208).

109 **widow** i.e. the widow whom King Edward has made his wife

110 **enfranchise** release from confinement (*OED v.* 2)

112 Some editors (following Marshall) direct that Richard tearfully embraces Clarence. This seems clumsy (cf. 1.4.243–4). Simon Russell Beale's Richard did embrace Clarence, burying his head in his brother's chest, but this unexpected intimacy awakened obvious amazement in Clarence (Day, 167).

113 **I know** The misplaced assurance of Richard's first victim–associate concerning Richard's thoughts and feelings anticipates the presumption of the second victim, Hastings, also present in this scene; see 3.2.70, 3.4.14.

114 equivocal, since Richard does not expect Clarence to live long in any case

115 **lie for you** take your place; Richard equivocates, reminding the audience of his self-announced capacity for lying and deceiving. For a similar play on 'lie', see *Oth* 3.4.1–13. In *Othello* the jokes on 'lie' belong to a Clown, suggesting Richard's genealogy in such stock theatrical figures (cf. 3.1.82 and pp. 6–8).

116 **patience . . . perforce** proverbial (Dent, P111); see *RJ* 1.5.89, Kyd, *Spanish Tragedy*, 3.9.12–13.
perforce of necessity

108 whatsoe'er] *F; Qq (*whatsoeuer*)* 112 deeper] *F, Qq;* dearer *Oxf;* nearer *Cam*[1] 115 else] *F; not in Qq* 116] *Steevens; F, Qq line* patience. / Farewell. / SD] *Capell; Exit Clar. F, Qq; Ex.* Brak. Clar. *Rowe* 117 ne'er] *F, Q1, 3–6 subst.;* neare *Q2*

Simple, plain Clarence, I do love thee so
That I will shortly send thy soul to heaven,
If heaven will take the present at our hands.
But who comes here? The new-delivered Hastings?

Enter Lord HASTINGS.

HASTINGS
Good time of day unto my gracious lord.

RICHARD
As much unto my good Lord Chamberlain.
Well are you welcome to this open air.
How hath your lordship brooked imprisonment?

HASTINGS
With patience, noble lord, as prisoners must;
But I shall live, my lord, to give them thanks
That were the cause of my imprisonment.

RICHARD
No doubt, no doubt; and so shall Clarence too,
For they that were your enemies are his
And have prevailed as much on him as you.

HASTINGS
More pity that the eagles should be mewed,

118 **thee** Richard uses 'you' to Clarence while he is present; cf. Cassius' contemptuous shift in pronominal usage (*JC* 1.2.307; cf. Abbott, 233).

120 Richard parodies the idea of sacrifice in which the supplicants render a tribute that they hope will be acceptable to God. Richard's plural *our* follows the communal language in the communion service of the *Book of Common Prayer* (Jowett). Richard's parodic invocations of religious language and sentiment in early soliloquies (cf. 151) allow the audience to appreciate the irony attending his expressions of piety to onstage characters.

122 **Good . . . day** conventional salutation (*OED* good *a.* III 10c); cf. 2.1.48.

125 **brooked** endured

127 **give them thanks** pay them back, vengefully; another perversion of religious idiom, but, as with Hastings's wordplay (135n.), the irony is less pointedly deployed by characters other than Richard.

132–3 **eagles . . . buzzards** In many Renaissance accounts, the proper order of nature resembled a hierarchi-

121 new-delivered] *F, Qq (*new deliuered*), hyphen Pope* 124 this] *F, Q3–6;* the *Q1–2* 132 eagles] *F;* Eagle *Qq*

Whiles kites and buzzards play at liberty.

RICHARD

What news abroad?

HASTINGS

No news so bad abroad as this at home:
The King is sickly, weak and melancholy,
And his physicians fear him mightily.

RICHARD

Now by Saint John, that news is bad indeed.
O, he hath kept an evil diet long,

cal human society: eagles, as the most royal of birds, would stand in freedom and dignity above the lower ranks, amongst which kites and buzzards, as scavengers, would be inferior (cf. 1.3.69–70 and *Cym* 1.2.70–1).

134 An odd question to ask a man just released from prison (Jowett). Richard prompts others to reveal what they feel and think – the strategy imputed to Brakenbury at 102. However, Richard's reactions at 145 suggest that he has genuinely learned an important fact about King Edward's illness.

news This word occurs more frequently in *Richard III* than in any other of Shakespeare's works except *2H4*; characters repeatedly discuss the *news*, often asking versions of Richard's question: the citizens (2.3.3), the Archbishop (2.4.38), the Duchess of York (2.4.42), Hastings (3.2.36) and, above all, Richard (4.2.46; 4.3.24, 45; 4.4.432, 456, 462).

abroad at large, circulating generally

135 **abroad . . . home** Hastings's response superficially mimics one of Richard's characteristic verbal modes, taking a term from his interlocutor and twisting its sense: so, instead of taking *abroad* to mean 'at large', Hastings playfully turns it to mean 'in foreign regions' by opposing it to *at home* (i.e. domestically). Hastings's witticism is pointless, suggesting clumsy jocularity and ease in Richard's presence, while Richard's playing on the words of others (as at 98 or 1.2.123–4) is almost invariably pointed, even sinister.

137 **fear him** fear for him (cf. *1H4* 4.1.24 and Abbott, 200)

138–42 Richard here first plays the deceptively pious moralist; this effect is heightened by his oath, his exclamatory *O* as he disapproves of Edward's *evil* diet, and his pained references to the *grievous* torments he has suffered at his brother's sinful behaviour. For the most egregious instance of such posturing, see 3.7.103–246. This element does not characterize Richard in *2H6* and *3H6*.

138 ***Saint John** Qq give Richard his typical oath, 'by Saint Paul' (cf. 1.2.36n.).

139 **evil** unwholesome (*OED a.* 7b) and morally wicked (*OED a.* 1)

diet way of life (*OED sb.*[1] 1); from More (*CW*2, 8), used to refer to sexual overindulgence (cf. *surfeit*, 1.3.196), but also with a play on overeating (cf. *consumed*, 140). Mancini (67) reports that Edward grew fat from overeating and taking emetics.

133 Whiles] *F;* While *Qq* play] *F;* prey *Qq* 138 Saint John] *F* (S. Iohn)*;* Saint Paul *Qq* that] *F;* this *Qq*

And over-much consumed his royal person.
'Tis very grievous to be thought upon.
Where is he, in his bed?

HASTINGS He is.

RICHARD
Go you before, and I will follow you. *Exit Hastings.*
He cannot live, I hope, and must not die
Till George be packed with post-horse up to heaven.
I'll in to urge his hatred more to Clarence
With lies well steeled with weighty arguments,
And if I fail not in my deep intent,
Clarence hath not another day to live;
Which done, God take King Edward to His mercy,
And leave the world for me to bustle in.
For then, I'll marry Warwick's youngest daughter.

141 **grievous** painful

142 ***Where** Qq's 'What' renders the line an (unpunctuated) exclamation, i.e. 'What! is he in his bed?' This sense is supported by a comma in Q4–6 ('What, is he . . . ?'). On F arising from 'incorrect conjectural emendation' of Q3 copy, see Walton, *Copy*, 83–4. However, Richard's prosaic question about the royal bed may rhetorically reiterate his disgust at the inevitability of finding the King, yet again, *in his bed* – now in illness as earlier in the lust that Richard implies to have been the cause of that illness.

146 **with post-horse** i.e. by the swiftest means possible; a post-horse was kept at a post-house or inn for post-riders or travellers (*OED*). Richard's echo of 2 Kings, 2.11, describing Elijah borne into heaven by horses of fire, is 'characteristic . . . blasphemy' (Wilson).

147 **his** i.e. King Edward's

148 **steeled** hardened, as a warrior armed or protected with steel (*OED ppl. a.* 2, *a.* 5)

149 **deep** profound in craft and subtlety (*OED a.* 17); cf. 2.1.38; the word is used variously throughout the play, occurring more often than in any other work by Shakespeare.

151 **God . . . mercy** Cf. 120n.

152 **bustle** bestir oneself or display activity with noise or agitation, usually implying excessive or obtrusive show of energy (*OED v.* 2a); or scuffle, contend, and elbow one's way (*v.* 3)

153 **Warwick's youngest daughter** Lady Anne Neville, daughter of the Earl of Warwick (the 'King-maker'; cf. *3H6* 2.3.37), widow of Prince Edward, son of Henry VI. Anne is erroneously taken to be Warwick's elder daughter in *3H6* (3.3.242, 4.1.118).

142 Where] *F;* What *Qq* 144 ²you] *F, Q1–2, 4–6;* yon *Q3*

What though I killed her husband and her father?
The readiest way to make the wench amends
Is to become her husband and her father;
The which will I, not all so much for love
As for another secret close intent
By marrying her which I must reach unto.
But yet I run before my horse to market:
Clarence still breathes; Edward still lives and reigns.
When they are gone, then must I count my gains. *Exit.*

154 **What though** i.e. what if? what does it matter that?
husband . . . father husband and her father-in-law; Shakespeare's earlier plays follow Hall and Holinshed in making Richard the accomplice of his brothers Edward and Clarence in the killing of Prince Edward (*3H6* 5.5). See 1.4.200–6.

155 **wench** insulting for an aristocrat, but in keeping with Richard's general social reduction of women (cf. *gossips*, 83)

156 **husband . . . father** Richard proposes to marry Anne and care for her in a fatherly way, replacing the men he has taken from her, but this confusion of kinship relations and marital relations has wider historical resonance. Richard was denounced vehemently by Hall and Holinshed for attempting to wed his niece Elizabeth, and tyrants are traditionally associated with unnatural crimes such as incest (McCabe, 156–9).

157–8 Richard's intention is left unstated, though the historical figures wed and had a son (nowhere mentioned in this play). In *3H6* the marriages of Anne to Prince Edward and her sister Isabel to Clarence signify alliance with their father, the Earl of Warwick (3.3.240–50, 4.1.120–2). Hall describes hopes for alliance between Warwick and Margaret's forces in the conjunction of Anne and Prince Edward in 1470, suggesting that power politics motivated the 'straunge' marriages of one daughter to the Yorkist Clarence and the other to the princely descendant of the Lancastrian Henry VI (*Edward IV*, fols ccvi^{v}–ccvii^{r}). By contrast, Shakespeare represents Richard's marital plans as obscure of motive, manifest in villainy and prompting witty self-congratulation – a combination recalling the dramatic tradition of the Vice (see pp. 6–8). Anne's substantial property and standing in the northern region suggest compelling historical explanations for Richard's desire. Richard, the youngest son, was largely dependent on the favour of his royal brother; the 16-year-old Anne and her elder sister Isabel, married to Clarence, were joint heiresses of the substantial Warwick inheritance. Although the historical Anne and Richard appear to have been acquainted in childhood, there is no evidence of an extended relationship before their marriage. Cibber (*Richard III*, 2.1.24–35) invents a prehistory for Richard's encounter with Anne.

160 **run . . . market** proverbial for over-hasty behaviour (Dent, M649). Although Richard often invokes familiar proverbs, this tendency is more pronounced in *3H6*, where he is compared to Aesop (5.5.25).

1.2 *Enter the corse of Henry the Sixth with Halberds to guard it,* Lady ANNE *being the mourner* [, *attended by* TRESSEL, BERKELEY *and other* Gentlemen].

ANNE

Set down, set down your honourable load,
If honour may be shrouded in a hearse,
Whilst I awhile obsequiously lament
Th'untimely fall of virtuous Lancaster.
Poor key-cold figure of a holy king,
Pale ashes of the house of Lancaster,
Thou bloodless remnant of that royal blood,
Be it lawful that I invocate thy ghost

1.2 location: '*a Street*' (Theobald)

0.1–3 This is not a vast stately procession (as it has often been staged) but an act of personal and familial grief. Henry VI's funeral took place in May 1471, and Anne was not part of it. Holinshed records that Henry's corpse bled before spectators. The body was subsequently taken to Chertsey by boat, 'without priest or clerke, torch or taper, singing or saieng', for burial (Holinshed, 3.690–1; see 243).

0.1 *corse* corpse (*OED sb.* 2b)
Halberds men armed with halberds, weapons with points like spears and blades like battle-axes on handles five to seven feet long; Henry's corpse was 'conveied with billes and glaues pompouslie (if you will call that a funerall pompe)' (Holinshed, 3.690–1), suggesting that glaives – halberds – were hardly pompous.

0.2 **mourner** It is likely that Anne is dressed in black (cf. Dessen & Thomson, 145).

1 **Set down, set down** Cf. 'Set downe, set downe the load not worth your pain' (*TRKJ*, Pt 2, xiii.1, sig. D2^v); see 5.3.177–206n. To 'set down' the corpse was a ritual feature of funeral processions (*Lancaster, 1590*, 5–6).
***load** Folger and Huntington Q1 have 'l', but Bodleian and British Library Huth have 'lo:' and 'lo', possible abbreviations for 'lord', the word found in subsequent quartos (including Q7–8); cf. *holy load* (29).

2 **hearse** either a wooden framework supporting a funeral pall, the cloth itself covering the body, or a coffin (*OED sb.* 3, 4, 5)

3 **obsequiously** mournfully, as in performance of funeral obsequies; cf. *Tit* 5.3.151.

4 **virtuous Lancaster** Henry VI, depicted in *3H6* and elsewhere as especially pious, here addressed by his family name, embodying the family displaced by the *son of York* (1.1.2)

5 **key-cold** very cold, as a key; cf. *Luc* 1774 and Tilley, K23.
figure image, likeness (*OED sb.* 9)

6 **Pale ashes** mortal remains (Dent, A339; cf. *RJ* 3.2.55)

8 **Be it** i.e. let it be (Abbott, 365)
lawful Anne unhistorically alludes to

1.2] *F (Scena Secunda.); not in Qq* 0.1–3] *Enter the Coarse of Henrie the sixt with Halberds to guard it, / Lady Anne being the Mourner. F; Enter Lady Anne with the hearse of Harry the 6. Qq* 0.2–3 *attended* . . . Gentlemen] *Ard*[2] 1 SP] *F; Lady An[.]ne Qq* Set . . . set] *F, Q1, 3–6;* Sit . . . sit *Q2* load,] *F;* l *(Fo, Hn),* lo *(BL),* lo: *(Bod) Q1;* lord *Q2;* Lord, *Q3–6* 4 Th'untimely] *F;* The vntimely *Qq*

To hear the lamentations of poor Anne,
Wife to thy Edward, to thy slaughtered son,
Stabbed by the selfsame hand that made these wounds.
Lo, in these windows that let forth thy life
I pour the helpless balm of my poor eyes.
O, cursed be the hand that made these holes;
Cursed the heart that had the heart to do it;
Cursed the blood that let this blood from hence.
More direful hap betide that hated wretch
That makes us wretched by the death of thee
Than I can wish to wolves, to spiders, toads
Or any creeping venomed thing that lives.

Protestant objections to the invocation of saints in prayer (Whitaker, 80; Goodland, 144); see *Homilies*, 115–17; cf. 4.4.75, 5.3.241. Henry VI was widely venerated into the reign of Henry VIII (Knox, 3–7).

invocate invoke, as in prayer (*OED v.* 1), but suggesting 'conjure' (*OED* invoke *v.* 2a); cf. *H5* 1.2.103–5, where Henry V is urged to 'invoke' the spirits of his ancestors, with no nervousness about the lawfulness of such prayer.

10 **Wife** Anne was betrothed and then married to Henry's son, Prince Edward, in 1470.

11 ***hand** F's sense of a single murderer (see 14), is contradicted by *3H6* 5.5.38–40, where all three York brothers stab Prince Edward.

12 **windows** i.e. wounds

13 **helpless** useless, unavailing (*OED a.* 3)

balm figuratively, a healing or restorative agency (*OED sb.* 6); literally an aromatic ointment for soothing pain or healing wounds (*OED sb.* 5)

14 **cursed** cursèd; F's dissyllabic pronunciation is suggested by Qq's use of 'fatall' to complete the line opening with monosyllabic 'Curst'.

15, 16 **Cursed** cursèd

16 *Alice Walker (32) suggests that this line 'possibly' belongs before the previous one, connecting *blood* to *holes*; Walton agrees (*Quarto*, 143); as does Wilson. Hammond judges insufficient warrant for changing F's order.

17 **direful hap betide** terrible consequence befall

19 **wolves, spiders, toads** Richard's connection with these animals (see 1.3.241–5, 4.4.23) goes back to Rous (Hanham, 118, 120) and recurs in *Mirror* ('Richard, Duke of Gloucester', 124, 'Rivers', 480). Richard's father denounces Margaret as a 'she-wolf' with a poisonous tongue (*3H6* 1.4.111–12). The repeated preposition *to* appears to cut the connection between wolves and creeping things; Richard's anti-Lancastrian violence has been a wolflike open attack rather than secret treachery.

11 hand . . . wounds] *F;* hands . . . holes *Qq* 12 these] *F;* those *Qq* 14 O, cursed . . . these] *F;* Curst . . . these fatall *Q1–2;* Curst . . . the fatall *Q3–6* 15 Cursed] *F;* Curst be *Qq* 16] *F (*Cnrsed*); not in Qq* 19 wolves, to spiders] *F;* adders, spiders *Qq*

If ever he have child, abortive be it,
Prodigious, and untimely brought to light,
Whose ugly and unnatural aspect
May fright the hopeful mother at the view,
And that be heir to his unhappiness.
If ever he have wife, let her be made
More miserable by the death of him
Than I am made by my young lord and thee.
– Come now towards Chertsey with your holy load,
Taken from Paul's to be interred there;
And still, as you are weary of this weight,
Rest you, whiles I lament King Henry's corse.

Enter RICHARD, Duke of Gloucester.

RICHARD

Stay, you that bear the corse, and set it down.

ANNE

What black magician conjures up this fiend

21–8 Anne echoes and outdoes Margaret's curses upon Richard and his brothers for murdering her son (*3H6* 5.5.65–7).
21 **abortive** born prematurely; also useless, unsuccessful (*OED a.* A 1a, 2)
22 **Prodigious** monstrous in appearance (cf. *KJ* 2.2.46); unnatural and ominous (*OED a.* 1, 2, 3)
untimely prematurely
23 **aspect** aspèct (on shifting accents generally, see Abbott, 490); appearance, countenance
25 **that** i.e. the child
unhappiness evil, misfortune; with an active quality: the 'unhappy' person can work evil, an association missing in the current sense of 'unhappiness' as an emotional state.
27–8 *F is clear enough (Anne prays that Richard's hypothetical wife may feel even sorrier when Richard dies than she does now), cf. Walton, *Quarto*, 143–4. Cibber simplifies to 'More miserable by the Life of him, / Than I am now by *Edward's* death and thine' (*Richard III*, 2.1.78–9); cf. 4.1.74–6.
28 **by . . . thee** i.e. by the deaths of Prince Edward and his father, Henry VI
29 **Chertsey** monastery in Surrey, west of London, south of the River Thames near Staines
30 **Paul's** St Paul's Cathedral in London
interred interrèd
31 **still** ever, whenever
34 **black magician** a specifically malevolent agent who *conjures* for evil intent

25] *F; not in Qq* 26 made] *F, Q1–5;* mad: *Q6* 27 More] *F;* As *Qq* 28 Than . . . young] *F;* As . . . poore *Qq* 31 weary] *F, Q1–2;* awearie *Q3–6 subst.* this] *F;* the *Qq* 32.1] *F; Enter Glocester. Qq* 33+ SP] *F (Rich.); Glo. Qq* 34+ SP] *F (An[ne].); La[d[y]]. Qq*

To stop devoted charitable deeds?

RICHARD

Villains, set down the corse, or by Saint Paul,
I'll make a corse of him that disobeys.

GENTLEMAN

My lord, stand back and let the coffin pass.

RICHARD

Unmannered dog, stand thou when I command!
Advance thy halberd higher than my breast,
Or by Saint Paul, I'll strike thee to my foot
And spurn upon thee, beggar, for thy boldness.

ANNE

What, do you tremble? Are you all afraid?

35 **devoted** vowed, dedicated, consecrated

36 ***Villains** F/Qq frequently disagree when a noun is followed by a word beginning with *s*; see 'lip'/'lips' (174) and 'eagles'/'eagle' (1.1.132) (cf. Var, 50).
by Saint Paul Richard's favourite oath (see 41, 1.1.138n., 3.4.75–6n., 5.3.216) derives from a single instance in More. Here the oath may reflect Richard's assertion of dominance, since Saint Paul was associated with demands for deference to authority (cf. p. 15). The Hand D portion of *Sir Thomas More* has More warn that 'th'apostle' urges 'obedience to authority' (*STM* 2.3.99–101). This refers to Romans, 13.1–2: 'Let euerie soule be subiect vnto the higher powers: for there is no power but of God: & the powers that be, are ordeined of God . . . and they that resist, shal receiue them selues iudgement' (Geneva). The reference to conjuring in 34 may allude to Paul's struggles with the exorcists of Ephesus (Acts, 19.17–19) (Jowett).

38 **coffin** either a coffin or the bier on which the body rests (*OED sb.* 3b)

39–40 *There is debate about Richard's addressee(s). A gentleman could be a halberdier (Davison). If 36–7 address the attendants generally or the corpse-bearers as *Villains*, then 39 may respond to the Gentleman who speaks 38. At 40 Richard could command another individual, an eager halberdier, to cease threatening him.

39 **Unmannered** unmannerly
stand halt; F's 'Stand'st' could be a demand in the form of a question: i.e. are you going to stand still or not when I issue the order?
thou Richard's pronoun, depending on its addressee, could either be an unmarked form of address to a social inferior or a strong signal of anger or contempt to a gentle stranger (Abbott, 233); cf. 46.

40 i.e. return your halberd to an upright, non-aggressive position.

42 **spurn** trample contemptuously (*OED v.*[1] II 5)

43 **What** interjection expressing surprise or indignation

36 Villains] *F;* Villaine *Qq* 38 SP] *F, Q3–6 (Gen.), Q1–2 (Gent.); Halberdier Ard*[2] My lord] *F, Q1–5 (*My L. *Q3); om. Q6* 39] *Qq; F lines* Dogge, / commaund: / stand] *Qq;* Stand'st *F*

Alas, I blame you not, for you are mortal,
And mortal eyes cannot endure the devil.
– Avaunt, thou dreadful minister of hell!
Thou hadst but power over his mortal body;
His soul thou canst not have. Therefore begone.

RICHARD

Sweet saint, for charity, be not so curst.

ANNE

Foul devil, for God's sake hence, and trouble us not,
For thou hast made the happy earth thy hell,
Filled it with cursing cries and deep exclaims.
If thou delight to view thy heinous deeds,
Behold this pattern of thy butcheries.
– O gentlemen, see, see dead Henry's wounds
Open their congealed mouths, and bleed afresh.

46 **Avaunt** begone; Shaheen relates to Jesus's rejection of the devil: 'Auoyde Sathan' (Matthew, 4.10). Cf. 4.4.418–19n. and *2H6* 1.4.40.
thou Anne's pronoun signals contempt for a social equal for whom she feels no affection (Abbott, 233; cf. Buckingham at 3.2.120–1). Use of *thou* might mark her speech as directed to a supernatural being, here to a 'minister of hell'; cf. Horatio and Hamlet to the Ghost from heaven or hell (*Ham* 1.1.45–50, 1.4.40–56).
minister agent (*OED sb.* 2a); cf. 1.4.219 and *2H6* 5.2.33–4.

47–8 Anne draws on familiar Christian distinctions (Matthew, 10.28: 'And feare ye not them, which kyll the body, but are not able to kyll the soule. But rather feare hym, which is able to destroy both soule and body in hell').

49 **saint, charity** Adopting Anne's language concerning *charitable deeds* (35), Richard hypocritically recalls Gospel demands for the 'charitie' that is a 'fulfyllyng of the lawe' (Romans, 12.10). Richard invokes Christian charity to taunt Young Clifford (*2H6* 5.1.213).
curst ill-tempered (*OED ppl. a.* 4a)

50–2 **Foul devil . . . cursing** Anne continues Richard's form and vocabulary: *Sweet saint* is countered with *Foul devil*; admonition about *curst* behaviour is echoed in references to the *cursing* that his deeds have occasioned.

50 **hence** go hence, depart

51 **made . . . hell** Cf. the Duchess of York on Richard's making 'the earth my hell' (4.4.167).

52 **exclaims** exclamations; cf. 4.4.135.

54 **pattern** prime example, epitome (*OED sb.* 1a, 6)

56 **bleed afresh** referring to the belief that a victim's body would bleed in the presence of the murderer (cf. *Arden*, 16.4–6). Holinshed (but not Hall) mentions that King Henry's body bled (3.691), but does not connect this legend to Richard.

46 dreadful] *F, Q1–5;* fearefull *Q6*   50] *Qq; F lines* Diuell, / not, /

– Blush, blush, thou lump of foul deformity,
For 'tis thy presence that exhales this blood
From cold and empty veins where no blood dwells.
Thy deeds, inhuman and unnatural,
Provokes this deluge most unnatural.
– O God! which this blood mad'st, revenge his death.
O earth! which this blood drink'st, revenge his death.
Either heaven with lightning strike the murderer dead,
Or earth gape open wide and eat him quick,
As thou dost swallow up this good king's blood,
Which his hell-governed arm hath butchered.

RICHARD

Lady, you know no rules of charity,
Which renders good for bad, blessings for curses.

ANNE

Villain, thou knowst nor law of God nor man.

57 **lump . . . deformity** King Henry calls Richard 'an undigested and deformed lump' (*3H6* 5.6.51).

58 **exhales** causes to flow, draws forth (*OED v.*[2] 1b, citing this line)

60–1 **deeds . . . Provokes** Plural subjects (perhaps singular in thought) paired with verbs ending in *-s* are 'extremely common' in F (Abbott, 333); cf. 2.3.35.

60 **inhuman** 'human' and 'humane' were interchangeable (*OED* inhuman).

62 *F's exclamation marks (also at 63, 73) are unusual for this play.

63 The image of the earth drinking blood is derived from the story of Cain and Abel: 'the voyce of thy brothers blood crieth vnto me out of the grounde' (Genesis, 4.10–11; cf. *1H4* 1.1.5–6, *R2* 1.1.104–5). While Richard's crime is not fratricide, Henry was Richard's cousin. See also 4.4.29–30.

65 Noble (131) notes biblical parallels, including Numbers, 16.30, which describes the destruction of the men of Korah: God makes 'the earth open her mouth, and swallowe them vp . . . and they go downe quicke into the pit'. There is a possible classical intersection with Seneca's *topos* '*Dehisce tellus*' ('Yawn, *or* Gape, earth': *Hippolytus*, 1238–9; cf. *Oedipus*, 868, *Troades*, 519). See also 4.4.75 and *3H6* 1.1.161.
quick alive

67 **butchered** butcherèd

68–9 A favourite Christian precept: 'loue your enemies, blesse them that curse you, do good to them that hate you, pray for the[m] which hurt you and persecute you' (Matthew, 5.43–4); cf. Romans, 12.14.

70 **nor . . . nor** i.e. neither . . . nor

60 deeds] *F;* deed *Qq* inhuman] *F, Q1–5 (*inhumane*), Rowe;* inhumaine *Q6* 62 mad'st] *F; Qq (*madest*)* 64 heaven] *F (*Heau'n*), Qq* murderer] *F (*murth'rer*), Qq (*murtherer*)* 66 dost] *F;* doest *Q1–5;* didst *Q6* 70 knowst nor] *F;* knowest *(*knowst *Q3–6)* no *Qq*

No beast so fierce but knows some touch of pity.

RICHARD

But I know none, and therefore am no beast.

ANNE

O wonderful, when devils tell the truth!

RICHARD

More wonderful, when angels are so angry.
Vouchsafe, divine perfection of a woman,
Of these supposed crimes, to give me leave
By circumstance, but to acquit myself.

ANNE

Vouchsafe, diffused infection of [Q]a[Q] man,
Of these known evils, but to give me leave
By circumstance, to curse thy cursed self.

RICHARD

Fairer than tongue can name thee, let me have
Some patient leisure to excuse myself.

71–3 A notoriously lame non-argument: Anne implies that Richard is not only inhuman but less than a beast since even beasts feel pity. Richard replies that since he feels none, he is not a beast. Anne deduces Richard to be a devil.

71 **but knows** i.e. but it knows (Abbott, 123)
touch feeling, sensation (*OED sb.* III 13b; as *TGV* 2.7.18: 'the inly touch of love') or slight amount or trace (*OED sb.* 19a; as 4.4.158)

73 **devils . . . truth** Cf. Dent, D266: 'The Devil sometimes speaks the truth.'

75 **Vouchsafe** grant

76 **supposed** supposèd

77 **circumstance** fact which makes an action more or less criminal, or an accusation more or less probable (*OED sb.* I 3)

78 **diffused** confused, disordered, obscure or spread abroad, dispersed (*OED ppl. a.* I 1, II 2); F, Qq spell 'defus[e]d'. Richard appears either compounded of a diseased disorder or the source of spreading pestilence. The sense of 'disordered' appears in *H5* 5.2.61. Given its close echo of 75, the formula *diffused . . . man* may be 'more for sound than sense' (Holland).

80 **cursed** cursèd

81 Cibber's Richard offers rapturous praises: 'But see, my Love appears: Look where she shines, / Darting pale Lustre, like the Silver Moon' (*Richard III*, 2.1.54–5).

82 **leisure** opportunity (*OED sb.* 1b)

73 truth] *F, Q2–6;* troth *Q1*   75 Vouchsafe] *F, Q3–6; Q1 (*Voutsafe*), Q2 (*Vouchafe*)*   76 crimes] *F;* euils *Qq*   78 diffused] *F, Qq (*defused *subst.)*   79 Of] *F;* For *Qq*   80 curse] *F, Qq;* accuse *Cam[1] (Spedding)*

ANNE
Fouler than heart can think thee, thou canst make
No excuse current but to hang thyself.
RICHARD
By such despair I should accuse myself.
ANNE
And by despairing shalt thou stand excused
For doing worthy vengeance on thyself
That didst unworthy slaughter upon others.
RICHARD
Say that I slew them not.
ANNE
Then say they were not slain.
But dead they are, and, devilish slave, by thee.
RICHARD
I did not kill your husband.
ANNE
Why then he is alive.
RICHARD
Nay, he is dead, and slain by Edward's hands.
ANNE
In thy foul throat thou liest; Queen Margaret saw
Thy murderous falchion smoking in his blood,

84 **current** with the quality of current coin; sterling, genuine: opposed to counterfeit (*OED a.* 5)

85–7 **despair . . . vengeance** Anne recommends that Richard kill himself in despair to avenge those he has killed; neither despair nor taking vengeance on a malefactor, in this case himself, could palliate eternal judgement. Richard echoes this exchange at 5.3.185–6; see also 5.3.200n.

89–90, 92–3 For other trimeter couplets in dialogue exchange, see 195–205 and Abbott, 500.

94 **by Edward's hands** a partial truth: Edward, Richard and Clarence stab Prince Edward in turn (*3H6* 5.5.38–40); cf. 1.1.154n. on *husband . . . father*.

95 **In . . . liest** 'to lie in one's throat' meant lying outrageously (Dent, T268; cf. *LLL* 4.3.10–11).

96 **falchion** curved broad sword
smoking giving off a vapour, steaming

83–4] *Qq; F lines* thee, / currant, / selfe. / 86 shalt] *F;* shouldst *Qq* 88 That] *F;* Which *Qq* 89 not.] *F, Q1, 3–6;* not? *Q2* 90] *F;* Why then they are not dead, *Qq* 94 hands] *F;* hand *Qq* 95–6] *Qq; F lines* Ly'st, / saw / blood: / 95 Margaret] *F, Qq (*Margret *Q3–6)* 96 murderous] *F (*murd'rous*);* bloudy *Q1–2;* bloodly *Q3–6*

The which thou once didst bend against her breast,
But that thy brothers beat aside the point.

RICHARD
I was provoked by her slanderous tongue,
That laid their guilt upon my guiltless shoulders.

ANNE
Thou wast provoked by thy bloody mind,
That never dream'st on aught but butcheries.
Didst thou not kill this king?

RICHARD I grant ye.

ANNE
Dost grant me, hedgehog? Then God grant me too
Thou mayst be damned for that wicked deed.
O, he was gentle, mild and virtuous.

RICHARD
The better for the King of Heaven that hath him.

ANNE
He is in heaven, where thou shalt never come.

RICHARD
Let him thank me that holp to send him thither,
For he was fitter for that place than earth.

ANNE
And thou unfit for any place but hell.

97 **bend** aim or direct
99, 101 **provoked** provokèd
102 **aught** anything
103 Richard 'slewe with his owne handes king Henry the sixt', More writes (*CW*2, 8), surrounding the claim with typical hedging (see pp. 59–60); cf. *3H6* 5.6.
***ye** Q1–2's 'yea' is one spelling of 'ye' (*TxC*, 233); on 'ye' in F, see Honigmann, 'Variants', 193–4.
104 **hedgehog** referring to the hump-backed animal, bristled like the boar, Richard's heraldic emblem (see 1.3.227, 3.2.10, 5.2.7–10).
105 **damned** damnèd
107–8 Cf. *Leir* ('You are fitter for the King of heauen', sig. F3[r], 1604; 'to send vs both to heauen / Where, as I thinke, you neuer mean to come', sig. I4[r], 2596–7).
109 **holp** helped

98 brothers] *F, Q1–2;* brother *Q3–6* 99 slanderous] *F (*sland'rous*), Qq (*slaunderous*)* 100 That] *F;* Which *Qq* guilt] *F, Q1–5;* guift *Q6* 102 That . . . dream'st] *F;* Which . . . dreamt *Qq* 103] *Qq; F lines* King? / ye. / ye] *F;* yea *Q1–2;* yee *Q3–6* 104] *Qq; F lines* Hedge-hogge, / too / 105 mayst] *F;* maiest *Qq* damned] *F, Q3–6;* damnd *Q1–2* 107 better] *F;* fitter *Qq*

RICHARD
Yes, one place else, if you will hear me name it.
ANNE Some dungeon.
RICHARD Your bedchamber.
ANNE
Ill rest betide the chamber where thou liest.
RICHARD
So will it, madam, till I lie with you.
ANNE
I hope so.
RICHARD I know so. But, gentle Lady Anne,
To leave this keen encounter of our wits
And fall something into a slower method:
Is not the causer of the timeless deaths
Of these Plantagenets, Henry and Edward,
As blameful as the executioner?
ANNE
Thou wast the cause, and most accurst effect.

114 McKellen's film renders this as an aside, whispered in confidence to the camera; thus Anne (Kristin Scott Thomas) is shocked by Richard's subsequent direct approaches and surprised into spitting at him (McKellen, 76).
115 **betide** befall
115–16 **chamber . . . lie** recalling double meanings at 1.1.12, 15
117 **I hope so** Anne presumes that she will never lie with him.
119 **something** somewhat
method In the context of lines concerning cause and effect, the term carries associations with logical investigation, and may suggest the ordered procedure specific to rhetorical exposition and literary composition (*OED sb.* II 4, 6a).
120 **timeless** out of its proper time, premature (*OED a.* 1a), but suggesting the unparalleled nature of the crime and the loss it has occasioned
122 **executioner** the agent who enacts a design or perpetrates an evil deed (*OED* 1) and the one who puts another to death (*OED* 4, citing 188)
123 **accurst** execrable, damnable (*OED ppl. a.* 2)
effect perhaps meaning 'effecter', i.e. agent; alternatively, Anne may say that everything is entirely Richard's fault since he begins and ends (as cause and effect) the entire murderous sequence. In 124 Richard reduces *effect* to mean 'result'.

112 you] *F, Q1–2, 6;* ye *Q3–5* 113–14] *F; one line Qq* 117] *Steevens; F, Qq line* so. / *Anne*, / 118 keen] *F, Q1;* kinde *Q2–6* 119 something] *F;* somewhat *Qq* 120 timeless] *F, Q1–3, 5–6;* teem-lesse *Q4* 123 wast] *F (*was't*);* art *Qq* and most] *F, Qq;* of that *Cam*[1] *(Walker);* of most *Oxf*[1]

RICHARD

Your beauty was the cause of that effect:
Your beauty, that did haunt me in my sleep
To undertake the death of all the world,
So I might live one hour in your sweet bosom.

ANNE

If I thought that, I tell thee, homicide,
These nails should rend that beauty from my cheeks.

RICHARD

These eyes could not endure that beauty's wrack;
You should not blemish it, if I stood by.
As all the world is cheered by the sun,
So I by that. It is my day, my life.

ANNE

Black night o'ershade thy day, and death thy life.

RICHARD

Curse not thyself, fair creature; thou art both.

ANNE

I would I were, to be revenged on thee.

RICHARD

It is a quarrel most unnatural,
To be revenged on him that loveth thee.

ANNE

It is a quarrel just and reasonable,
To be revenged on him that killed my husband.

RICHARD

He that bereft thee, lady, of thy husband,

128 **homicide** murderer
129 **nails . . . beauty** Cf. *2H6* 1.3.141–3, *Luc* 1472.
130 **wrack** destruction (*OED sb.*[1] 2)
132–3 Hammond points to sonneteers' clichés (with examples from Sidney).
132 **cheered** cheerèd

125 that] *F;* which *Qq* 127 live one] *F;* rest one *Q1–4;* rest that *Q5–6* 129 rend] *Qq;* rent *F* my] *F, Q1–5;* their *Q6* 130 not endure that] *F;* neuer indure sweet *Qq* 131 it] *F;* them *Qq* 132 sun] *F, Q3–6 (*Sunne*);* sonne *Q1–2* 134 o'ershade] *F (*ore-shade*);* ouershade *Qq* 135] *Qq; F lines* Creature, / both. / 136 were,] *F;* were *Qq* 138 thee] *F;* you *Qq* 140 killed] *F;* slew *Qq* 141 thee] *F (*the*), Qq*

Did it to help thee to a better husband.

ANNE
His better doth not breathe upon the earth.

RICHARD
He lives that loves thee better than he could.

ANNE
Name him.

RICHARD Plantagenet.

ANNE Why, that was he.

RICHARD
The selfsame name, but one of better nature.

ANNE
Where is he?

RICHARD Here. *[Q]She[Q] spits at him.*
Why dost thou spit at me?

ANNE
Would it were mortal poison, for thy sake.

RICHARD
Never came poison from so sweet a place.

ANNE
Never hung poison on a fouler toad.
Out of my sight! Thou dost infect mine eyes.

145 **Plantagenet** family name dating back to the nickname of Geoffrey of Anjou, father of Henry II of England. Although technically belonging to both sides in the Wars of the Roses (as Anne notes), the name was apparently first affirmed by the Duke of York, Richard's father, for himself, in hopes of strengthening his royal claim (see *1H6* 2.4). Richard will be the last monarch to claim the name, his demise bringing in the Tudor dynasty.

146 **nature** inherent disposition, character

147–8 **spit . . . poison** Cf. Dent, V28: 'He has spit his venom.'

150 **toad** thought to be poisonous (cf. 1.3.245 and *3H6* 2.2.138)

151–2 That the eyes of the beloved could infect the lover with love was a poetic commonplace (cf. *LLL* 5.2.421); proverbially, a person with an eye disease could impart it to a sound person by looking at him or her (Dent, E246).

151 ***mine** For the use of 'mine' instead of 'my' before a vowel, see 1.4.22–3, 3.7.20, 4.1.80, 81.

144 He] *F;* Go to, he *Qq* 145] *Steevens; F lines* him. / *Plantagenet.* / he. / ; *Qq line* Plantagenet. / hee. / that was he] *F, Q1–2;* what was he? *Q3–6* 147] *Steevens; F, Qq line* he? / Heere: / me. / SD] *F, Q2–5; after* he *Q1* *spits*] *F; spitteth Qq* 151 mine] *F;* my *Qq*

RICHARD

Thine eyes, sweet lady, have infected mine.

ANNE

Would they were basilisks, to strike thee dead.

RICHARD

I would they were, that I might die at once;
For now they kill me with a living death.
Those eyes of thine from mine have drawn salt tears,
Shamed their aspects with store of childish drops;
These eyes, which never shed remorseful tear –
No, when my father York and Edward wept
To hear the piteous moan that Rutland made
When black-faced Clifford shook his sword at him;

153 **basilisks** mythical serpentlike creatures (sometimes identified with cockatrices), named for a spot resembling a crown on their heads (*OED* 1) and supposed to kill by gazing; cf. 1.3.224 and 4.1.54–5 and Richard's threat to 'slay more gazers than the basilisk' (*3H6* 3.2.187).

155 **living death** sonnet usage; cf. Thomas Watson's 'Loue is a sowr delight; a sugred greefe, / A liuinge death' (*Hekatompathia*, Sonnet xviii) and *VA* 413.

156–7 Richard refused to weep at his father's murder, choosing revenge instead (*3H6* 2.1.79–88). His readiness to appear to weep in this play is noteworthy: he claims he will shed *repentant tears* (1.2.218) and *beweep* the fate of Clarence (1.3.327); Clarence claims Richard parted weeping from him (1.4.243–5); Richard protests readiness to weep for the loss of Hastings's loyalty (3.5.24). Of course, he mocks tears as the recourse of *fools* (1.3.352) and asserts that 'Tear-falling pity dwells not in this eye' (4.2.65). Richard does not weep in More, but he employs grossly hypocritical tears in *Mirror* ('Rivers', 400–2).

157 **aspects** aspècts; looks, glances (*OED sb.* 1b)
store abundance (*OED sb.* 4a)

158–69 *This passage appears only in F. It has been argued that it was cut to accelerate the scene (Patrick, 124–5), or to remove historical inaccuracies (Smidt, *King Richard*, 123–4) or obscure references (Hammond, 333). Conversely, Grace Ioppolo (130) argues that it was 'added by the author' to provide 'dramatic and theatrical unity and continuity' in the first tetralogy; against this claim, see 160–1n. Speed seems the most likely motivation for omission.

158 **remorseful** compassionate, full of pity (*OED* 2)

159 **Edward** Richard's eldest brother, now Edward IV

160–1 **Rutland . . . Clifford** For the death of Rutland, second son of Richard, Duke of York, at Clifford's hands, see *3H6* 1.3. Neither York nor Edward was present, a fact which perhaps tells against the notion that the tetralogy was conceived as a unified construction. Cf. 162.

161 **black-faced** ominous looking

155 they] *F, Q1–4, 6;* thy *Q5*   157 aspects] *F;* aspect *Qq*   158–69] *F; not in Qq*

Nor when thy warlike father, like a child,
Told the sad story of my father's death
And twenty times made pause to sob and weep,
That all the standers-by had wet their cheeks
Like trees bedashed with rain – in that sad time
My manly eyes did scorn an humble tear;
And what these sorrows could not thence exhale,
Thy beauty hath, and made them blind with weeping.
I never sued to friend, nor enemy;
My tongue could never learn sweet smoothing word.
But now thy beauty is proposed my fee,
My proud heart sues, and prompts my tongue to speak.
She looks scornfully at him.
Teach not thy lip such scorn, for it was made
For kissing, lady, not for such contempt.
If thy revengeful heart cannot forgive,
Lo, here I lend thee this sharp-pointed sword,

162 **thy warlike father** the Earl of Warwick; a messenger, not Warwick, announces the death of Richard's father (*3H6* 2.1).
165 **That** i.e. so that (Abbott, 283)
166 **bedashed** injured or spoiled as the wind dashes flowers (*OED* dash *sb.*[1] 1a)
168 **exhale** See 58.
170 **sued to** petitioned
171 **smoothing** flattering (*OED* smooth *a.* 7b). Qq's 'soothing' has a similar sense; cf. 1.3.297.
172 **proposed my fee** offered to me as a reward; legal vocabulary (as *sues* in 173)
177–81 Cf. Seneca, *Hercules Oetaeus*, 1000–1, 1015. John Studley's translation for Newton's volume reads, 'My breast lies bare unto thy hand. Stryke, I thy gylt forgeve . . . Th' offence I did was ment in loue' (2.228). Cf. Phaedra to Hippolytus: 'I would not hesitate to offer my breast to naked swords' (*Hippolytus*, 616), and her offer in the presence of his corpse: 'in my wicked heart will I thrust the sword' (*Hippolytus*, 1176–7). Shakespeare quotes elsewhere from *Hippolytus* (*Tit* 4.1.81–2). Legge's Richard similarly attempts to woo young Elizabeth in a passage laced with physical threats (*Richardus Tertius*, 4190–204). The offer to *lay . . . naked* his *breast* if she may be *please*[*d*] *to hide* the blade in it constitutes a remarkable verbal regendering of the sexual dynamic (cf. 4.4.229n.). For staging, see Hankey; for Olivier's film, see Hassel, 13–14.

170 friend] *F, Q1–5;* friends *Q6* 171 smoothing word] *F;* soothing words *Qq* 173 SD] *F; not in Qq* 174 lip . . . it was] *F;* lips . . . they were *Qq*

Which if thou please to hide in this true breast
And let the soul forth that adoreth thee,
I lay it naked to the deadly stroke
And humbly beg the death upon my knee.
He [kneels and] lays his breast open, she offers at [it] with his sword.
Nay, do not pause; for I did kill King Henry,
But 'twas thy beauty that provoked me.
Nay, now dispatch; 'twas I that stabbed young Edward,
But 'twas thy heavenly face that set me on.
She falls the sword.
Take up the sword again, or take up me.

ANNE
Arise, dissembler; though I wish thy death,

178 ***this true** The curious inversion of Q3 ('true this') is the first of several striking F/Qq reversals (194, 198, 202). F shows careful correction (e.g. 194, where F corrects 'thou shalt' from Q2–6), but also remarkable oversights (e.g. omission of 205) and discrepancies (228).
180 **lay it naked** bare my breast
181 **the death** death, execution in a judicial context
181 SD The dialogue directs that Richard be kneeling here. Capell plausibly had him kneel at 176. He might rise when ordered in 187 (since he would presumably, but not certainly, be upright when offering to kill himself in 189). The sequence probably derives from Phaedra's confession of her passion while 'grovel[ing]' before Hippolytus with his drawn sword (Whitaker, 66; Seneca, *Hippolytus*, 710–14).
offers at makes an attempt or show of intention towards
182–4 *Qq preserve the chronological sequence of Richard's crimes, but F gains rhetorical force by naming last the loss that nearest concerns Anne. Arguments about order and correction based on chronology also enter into editorial considerations of discrepancies between Q1–2 and Q3–F at 5.3.145.1–158.
183 **provoked** provokèd
185 SD *falls* lets fall (cf. 5.3.163)
186 These are hardly the only alternatives, but the arch manipulator drives Anne into a corner, knowing her incapable of using the sword. For phrasing, cf. *The First Part of Hieronimo* (1591?, printed 1605): 'Take up thy pen, or I'll take up thee' (Kyd, *Hieronimo*, 6.28).
187 ***Arise** Richard may rise during or immediately after this line; but he might remain kneeling until the offer of the ring in 204.

178 this true] *F, Q1–2, 4–6;* true this *Q3* breast] *F;* bosome *Qq* 180 the] *F, Q1–5;* thy *Q6* 181 SD] *F; not in Qq* *kneels and*] *Capell after 176* *it*] *Rowe* 182 for . . . Henry] *F;* twas I that kild your husband *Qq* 184 stabbed young Edward] *F;* kild King Henry *Qq* 185 SD] *F; Here she lets fall / the sword. Qq opp. 185–6*

I will not be thy executioner.

RICHARD

Then bid me kill myself, and I will do it.

ANNE

I have already.

RICHARD That was in thy rage.

Speak it again and, even with the word,
This hand, which for thy love did kill thy love,
Shall for thy love kill a far truer love;
To both their deaths shalt thou be accessary.

ANNE

I would I knew thy heart.

RICHARD

'Tis figured in my tongue.

ANNE

I fear me both are false.

RICHARD

Then never man was true.

ANNE

Well, well, put up your sword.

188 Cf. Phoebe's remark to Silvius (*AYL* 3.5.8).

194 ***shalt thou** Cf. 178.
accessary trisyllabic (àc-cess-ry); participating in a crime (*OED a.* 1)

195–205 Such clear stichomythia is unusual in Shakespeare, but see Edward's wooing of Lady Grey (*3H6* 3.2). Abbott uses this passage to illustrate trimeter couplets in brief dialogue exchanges (Abbott, 500). Jowett's sense that Anne has the initiative is complicated by the fact that the sequence starts with the highly compromised lovers' diction of 195; the dynamic changes at 200 when Richard takes the lead, posing demands to which Anne must respond or offer resistance.

195 familiar lovers' discourse (cf. 'I would I knew his mind', *TGV* 1.2.33), marking a development in the interaction

196 **figured** displayed

197 **fear me** fear

198 ***man was** F agrees with Q3, but offers a more metrical (and more unusual) word-order than Q1–2 (*TxC*, 234); cf. 178, 194.

199 **your** Anne's respectful 'you' may register surrender (Davison, 154; cf. Abbott, 231).

188 thy] *F;* the *Qq* 190] *Steevens; F, Qq line* already. / rage: / That] *F;* Tush that *Qq* thy] *F, Q1–2;* the *Q3–6* 192 This] *F;* That *Qq* 194 shalt thou] *F, Q1;* thou shalt *Q2–6* be] *F, Q1–5;* by *Q6* 198 man was] *F, Q3–6;* was man *Q1–2*

RICHARD
Say then my peace is made.

ANNE
That shalt thou know hereafter.

RICHARD
But shall I live in hope?

ANNE
All men I hope live so.

^Q^RICHARD^Q^
Vouchsafe to wear this ring.

^Q^ANNE
To take is not to give.^Q^

RICHARD
Look how my ring encompasseth thy finger;
Even so thy breast encloseth my poor heart.
Wear both of them, for both of them are thine.
And if thy poor devoted servant may
But beg one favour at thy gracious hand,
Thou dost confirm his happiness forever.

ANNE What is it?

RICHARD
That it may please you leave these sad designs

203 Anne's Christian commonplace – all humanity hopes for heaven – characteristically evades responsibility for its implied assent to Richard's specific erotic request, which is that he may *hope* for her assent (cf. Siemon, 'Power').

204–5 *F omits 204 SP and all of 205, indenting 204 and setting it at the same distance from the edge of the page as SPs elsewhere.

204 **Vouchsafe** grant

205 Wilson detects parody of the marriage service: a pledge of troth is given and a ring is taken. Qq's line neatly encapsulates Anne's complicity while seeming to deny her own agency (and guilt); cf. 203 and pp. 15–17.

206 **Look how** just as (*OED* look *v.* 4b)

207 **breast . . . heart** a familiar conceit: 'My true love hath my hart and I have his' (Sidney, 75), 'My heart is in thy breast' (*LLL* 5.2.810); cf. *Son* 22 and Dent, L565.

213 **leave** i.e. to leave; 'to' omitted in infinitive (Abbott, 349)

201 shalt thou] *F;* shall you *Qq* 202 shall I] *F, Q1;* I shall *Q2–6* 204 SP] *Qq (Glo.)* Vouchsafe] *F, Q2–6; Q1 (*Voutsafe*)* 205 SP] *Qq (La.)* 206 my] *F;* this *Qq* 207 my] *F, Q1–4;* me *Q5–6* 208 Wear] *F, Q1–3;* Were *Q4–6* 209 devoted] *F, Q1; om. Q2–6* servant] *F;* suppliant *Qq* 213 may please you] *F;* would please thee *Qq*

To him that hath most cause to be a mourner,
And presently repair to Crosby House,
Where, after I have solemnly interred
At Chertsey Monastery this noble king
And wet his grave with my repentant tears,
I will with all expedient duty see you.
For diverse unknown reasons, I beseech you,
Grant me this boon.

ANNE
With all my heart, and much it joys me too
To see you are become so penitent.
– Tressel and Berkeley, go along with me.

RICHARD
Bid me farewell.

ANNE 'Tis more than you deserve;
But since you teach me how to flatter you,
Imagine I have said farewell already.

Exeunt two with Anne.

GENTLEMAN Towards Chertsey, noble lord?

215 **presently** at once, immediately (*OED adv.* 3)
repair go, proceed (*OED v.*[1] 1)
Crosby House one of Richard's London residences, also called Crosby Place (cf. 1.3.344, 3.1.190)

219 **expedient** quick, expeditious

220 **diverse unknown** i.e. various secret, such as must not be told; although what requires secrecy remains unclear, the point may be Richard's demonstration of dominance in making such a demand. In any case, how remarkable to direct a single gentlewoman to go and wait at the house of an unmarried man (GWW), abandoning the body of a relative to the disposing of his slayer.

227 SD The '*two*' are Tressel and Berkeley (see 224).

228 *Qq include Richard's command – 'Sirs take vp the corse' – and 228 is spoken by a servant. F's sequence also makes sense, since F's '*Gent.*' would be merely doing what other characters routinely do in anticipating – sometimes mistakenly – Richard's wishes.

214 most] *F;* more *Qq* 215 House] *F;* place *Qq* 217 Monastery] *F (*Monast'ry*)*, *Qq* 224 Berkeley] *F, Q1–2 (*Barkley*);* Bartley *Q3–6* 225] *Steevens; F, Qq line* farwell. / deserue: / 227 SD] *F (Exit . . . Anne), Rowe; Exit. Qq* 228] *F; Glo.* Sirs take vp the corse. / *Ser.* Towards . . . Lord. / *Qq subst.* SP] *F (Gent.)*

RICHARD

No, to Whitefriars; there attend my coming.

Exeunt [the rest with the] corse.

Was ever woman in this humour wooed?
Was ever woman in this humour won?
I'll have her, but I will not keep her long.
What? I that killed her husband and his father,
To take her in her heart's extremest hate,
With curses in her mouth, tears in her eyes,
The bleeding witness of my hatred by,
Having God, her conscience and these bars against me,
And I, no friends to back my suit withal
But the plain devil and dissembling looks?
And yet to win her? All the world to nothing!
Ha!
Hath she forgot already that brave prince,

229 **Whitefriars** Carmelite priory in London; Holinshed follows More in saying that the body went to Blackfriars (Hall does not specify) and thence by water to Chertsey (Holinshed, 3.690–1). Specifics may be less significant than the peremptoriness of Richard's redirection of the cortège, behaviour repeated throughout the play.

230–40 Cf. Berowne's surprise and consternation at the absurdity of his falling in love (*LLL* 3.1.169–200).

230, 231 **humour** temporary mood (*OED sb.* II 5), as in 4.1.64; the meaning should be contrasted with the more settled disposition implied at 4.4.269. Cf. *JC* 2.2.56.

230–1 **wooed . . . won** Cf. 'All women may be won' (Dent, W681), 'She is a woman, therefore may be wooed; / She is a woman, therefore may be won' (*Tit* 2.1.83–4).

236 **by** near

237 **Having** Abbott suggests an elided or softened *v* rendering the word monosyllabic (Abbott, 466); cf. *VA* 828, *1H4* 3.1.33.

bars impediments

238 **friends . . . suit** relatives (*OED sb.* 3) to support my wooing; *friends* were important to the corporate process of wedding (cf. *MND* 1.1.139). A possible legal connotation to *suit* could continue the metaphor begun with *bars* (237).

withal *Although *withal* first appears here in Q3 for Q1–2's 'at all', it is frequent in this play (e.g. 3.7.56, 3.7.196, 5.3.315, 5.5.6). Here it means 'in addition' or 'besides' (cf. *R2* 4.1.18 and Abbott, 196).

240 **All . . . nothing** against enormous odds; cf. *RJ* 3.5.213.

229 SD] *Capell; Exit Coarse. F; Exeunt. manet Gl. Qq opp. 230* 233 his] *F, Q1–2;* her *Q3–6* 234 hate] *F, Q1;* heate *Q2–6* 236 my] *F;* her *Qq* 238 no friends] *F;* nothing *Qq* withal] *F, Q3–6 subst.;* at all *Q1–2* 240–1] *F; one line Qq*

Edward, her lord, whom I, some three months since,
Stabbed in my angry mood at Tewkesbury?
A sweeter and a lovelier gentleman,
Framed in the prodigality of Nature,
Young, valiant, wise and, no doubt, right royal,
The spacious world cannot again afford;
And will she yet abase her eyes on me,
That cropped the golden prime of this sweet prince
And made her widow to a woeful bed?
On me, whose all not equals Edward's moiety?
On me, that halts and am misshapen thus?
My dukedom to a beggarly denier,
I do mistake my person all this while!

243 **her lord** i.e. her husband
three months since This marks the date as August 1471 (Malone), while Act 2 dramatizes King Edward's death (April 1483). Richard's dating is off in any case: the battle of Tewkesbury was fought on 4 May 1471, and King Henry's body was taken to Chertsey that same month.

244 **Tewkesbury** site of Henry VI's defeat by Edward IV

245–8 Syntax becomes confused as the comparative opening shifts to a claim that the world cannot *again* produce a *sweeter* gentleman.

246 **Framed . . . Nature** gifted, fashioned from Nature's most generous creative force. Cf. Boyet's praise of the Princess of France as endowed with graces by 'Nature . . . When she did starve the general world beside / And prodigally gave them all to you' (*LLL* 2.1.9–12).

247 **no doubt** apparently an ironic qualifier, since there were no doubts about Edward's royal descent or princely character; Fabyan dismisses slanders concerning his paternity (2.456).
royal noble, majestic, generous, munificent (*OED sb.* 9a, citing this line); but *OED* observes that the term's force is 'not always clear' in Shakespeare. Here there is a possible joke (a likelihood heightened by *no doubt*) based on the simple meaning 'of kingly blood', whereby Richard enjoys a laugh at the expense of hereditary royalty: this prince never got a chance to prove *royal*. The financial terms in subsequent lines reinforce an economic sense ('generous, munificent').

249 **abase** lower, with a possible economic sense of depreciating or debasing (cf. Qq 'debase') coinage (*OED v.* 1, 3)

250 **cropped . . . prime** cut short the springtime of early manhood (*OED* crop *v.* 4)
golden flourishing (*OED a.* 7), also playing on a metallurgical sense conveyed by *abase* in 249

252 **not equals** i.e. does not equal (Abbott, 305; cf. *2H4* 4.1.98)
moiety half

253 **halts** limps

254 **denier** the twelfth of the sou; a copper coin used as the type of a very small sum

249 abase] *F;* debase *Qq* 253 halts] *F;* halt *Qq* misshapen] *F;* vnshapen *Qq* 254 to] *F, Q1–4;* to be *Q5–6*

Upon my life, she finds, although I cannot,
Myself to be a marvellous proper man.
I'll be at charges for a looking-glass
And entertain a score or two of tailors
To study fashions to adorn my body;
Since I am crept in favour with myself,
I will maintain it with some little cost.
But first I'll turn yon fellow in his grave
And then return lamenting to my love.
Shine out, fair sun, till I have bought a glass,
That I may see my shadow as I pass. *Exit.*

1.3 *Enter* QUEEN ELIZABETH, Lord RIVERS, [*the* Marquess of DORSET] *and* Lord GREY.

257 **proper** well-made, handsome
258 **be . . . for** i.e. pay for
259 As Ian McKellen says, 'Forty tailors indeed!' (McKellen, 88).
entertain employ
261–5 The immediate sense of 261 is 'since I have crept into my own good graces', but Abbott suggests: 'since I have crept into (Lady Anne's) favour *with the aid of* my personal appearance, I will pay some attention to my person' (Abbott, 193). The self-reflexivity (and the vocabulary of sun, shadow and love) recalls Richard's earlier meditations on his own image (1.1.14–27) and anticipates his later division of self and conscience (5.3.179–206); *crept* echoes *creeping* things (20).
262 **some little** i.e. considerable? But contrast 2.2.120.
263 **fellow** The term is insulting when used for a king, but it appears in other ways that implicate social difference. Lords may properly address a messenger, a pursuivant or a sheriff as *fellow* (3.2.18, 104; 5.1.10), but Richard abruptly terminates his display of mock respect to Brakenbury by calling him *fellow* (1.1.98), the term Brakenbury uses for a murderer (1.4.85). Richard calls Richmond *a paltry fellow* (5.3.323).
in into (Abbott, 159)
265–6 Cf. 1.1.24–7.
265 **Shine . . . sun** The elation and newly-won self-confidence of David Troughton's Richard took visible form, as the lighting responded to his cue (Troughton, 90).
glass mirror
1.3 location: '*the Palace*' (Theobald)
0.1 QUEEN ELIZABETH F prematurely calls Elizabeth '*Queene Mother*' (as Qq 4.1.0.1). In 4.1 she is queen mother to young King Edward, but here she is '*Queene*', i.e. Edward IV's queen consort.
0.2 DORSET Dorset does not speak until 185, but the entry often given him (41.1) brings him on with his enemy, Richard.

257 marvellous] *F (*maru'llous*), Qq (*merueilous *subst.)* 258 looking-glass] *F; Qq (*looking glass*)* 259 a] *F;* some *Qq* 260 adorn] *F, Q1–2;* adore *Q3–6* 262 some] *F, Q1–2;* a *Q3–6* 263 yon] *F, Q1–3;* you *Q4–6* 265 out] *F, Q1–5;* our *Q6* 1.3] *F (Scena Tertia.); not in Qq* 0.1–2] *F; Enter Queene, Lord Riuers, Gray. Qq subst.* 0.1 ELIZABETH] *Malone; the Queene Mother F* 0.2 *the . . .* DORSET] *Hanmer subst.*

RIVERS
Have patience, madam. There's no doubt his majesty
Will soon recover his accustomed health.

GREY
In that you brook it ill, it makes him worse;
Therefore for God's sake entertain good comfort
And cheer his grace with quick and merry eyes.

QUEEN ELIZABETH
If he were dead, what would betide on me?

GREY
No other harm but loss of such a lord.

QUEEN ELIZABETH
The loss of such a lord includes all harms.

GREY
The heavens have blessed you with a goodly son
To be your comforter when he is gone.

QUEEN ELIZABETH
Ah, he is young, and his minority
Is put unto the trust of Richard Gloucester,
A man that loves not me, nor none of you.

RIVERS
Is it concluded he shall be Protector?

3 **brook it ill** endure or tolerate it badly (*OED* brook *v.* 3)

4 **entertain good comfort** accept cheer or consolation

5 ***with** Q2 corrects Q1's omission.
quick lively, alert, vigorous (*OED a.* III 20a)
quick . . . eyes Qq's 'quick . . . words' is attractive, but 'quick eyes' are vital for courtiers; cf. 47–9 and 'let thine eye look like a friend on Denmark' (*Ham* 1.2.69).

6 *Repeated in F perhaps as the result of its position at the foot of one page and the head of the next. The F catchword '*Gray*.' indicates that he has the first line of the next page (sig. r1^{r}). If the repetition were intended, Queen Elizabeth would be more distraught than her subsequent speeches suggest.
betide on become of (*OED v.* 2)

11 **minority** condition of being under-age, too young to rule

14 **Protector** regent, in charge of the kingdom during the minority, absence or incapacity of the sovereign (*OED sb.* 2a); Edward IV's will 'commyttyd [his sons] to the tuytion of Rycherd his brother' (Vergil, 171). For issues and dates, see Hanham, 5–6.

3 it ill,] *F, Q2–6;* it, ill *Q1*   5 with quick] *F, Q2–6;* quick *Q1*   eyes] *F;* words *Qq*   6+ SP] *F, Qq (Qu.), Malone subst.*   6 on] *F;* of *Qq*   *F repeats last line from sig. q6^{v} on sig. r1^{r}; F sig. q6^{v} c.w. Gray.*   7 SP] *F (Gray.); Ry. Q1; Ri. Q2–6*   8 harms] *F;* harme *Qq*   11 Ah] *F;* Oh *Qq*   12 Richard] *F;* Rich. *Qq*   14 Is it] *F, Q1–5;* It is *Q6*

QUEEN ELIZABETH
It is determined, not concluded yet;
But so it must be, if the King miscarry.

Enter BUCKINGHAM *and* [STANLEY, Earl of] Derby.

GREY
Here come the lords of Buckingham and Derby.
BUCKINGHAM
Good time of day unto your royal grace.
STANLEY
God make your majesty joyful, as you have been.
QUEEN ELIZABETH
The Countess Richmond, good my lord of Derby,
To your good prayer will scarcely say amen.
Yet Derby, not withstanding she's your wife
And loves not me, be you, good lord, assured
I hate not you for her proud arrogance.
STANLEY
I do beseech you, either not believe

15 **determined, not concluded** resolved, but not yet officially instituted
16 **miscarry** die (*OED v.* 1); given the frequent references to abortive or malformed birth, associations with premature or unviable foetuses (*OED v.* 4; cf. *2H4* 5.4.10) are perhaps relevant.
16.1 ***Derby** Thomas, Lord Stanley, only became Earl of Derby in 1485. Qq, F call him 'Derby' (or 'Darby') in this scene's SDs, SPs and dialogue, but use 'Stanley' in dialogue after this scene. Names in later SDs and SPs vary (see pp. 450–1).
17 ***come the lords** Q3 changes 'come' to 'comes', but F has 'Lord', thereby either making two lords appear one person ('Lord of Buckingham & Derby') or reducing Derby to an afterthought; 'comes' could be plural (Abbott, 333).
20 **Countess Richmond** Stanley's wife, Margaret Beaufort, whose first marriage (1455) had been to Edmund Tudor, Earl of Richmond and half-brother to Henry VI. By her first marriage she is mother of the play's Richmond. Stanley was her third husband. Historically, she formed a 'conspiracie' against Richard with Queen Elizabeth in an 'enterprise betweene the two mothers' to wed Richmond to Queen Elizabeth's daughter, Elizabeth of York (Holinshed, 3.742).
21 **say amen** i.e. concur with, ratify (a wish or prayer) (*OED sb.* 2a); cf. 3.7.240, 5.5.41.

16.1] *F; Enter Buck. Darby Qq opp. 16* STANLEY, Earl of] *Theobald subst.* 17 come the lords] *Q1–2;* comes the Lord *F;* comes the Lords *Q3–6* 19+ SP] *Theobald; Der. F; Dar. Qq* 21 prayer] *F;* praiers *Qq* 24 arrogance] *F, Q1–2;* arrogancie *Q3–6* 25 do] *F, Q1–2; om. Q3–6*

The envious slanders of her false accusers,
Or, if she be accused on true report,
Bear with her weakness, which I think proceeds
From wayward sickness, and no grounded malice.

QUEEN ELIZABETH
Saw you the King today, my lord of Derby?

STANLEY
But now the Duke of Buckingham and I
Are come from visiting his majesty.

QUEEN ELIZABETH
What likelihood of his amendment, lords?

BUCKINGHAM
Madam, good hope. His grace speaks cheerfully.

QUEEN ELIZABETH
God grant him health. Did you confer with him?

BUCKINGHAM
Ay, madam; he desires to make atonement
Between the Duke of Gloucester and your brothers,

26 **envious** malicious, spiteful, emulous (*OED a.* 2, 3); her descent from Edward III might have occasioned envy. This lineal distinction will provide one source of Richmond's claim and perhaps explains remarks about her *proud arrogance* (24).

28–9 **weakness . . . sickness** The sources suggest concern for the Countess's health (Holinshed, 3.741; Vergil, 195), but Stanley's exculpations – either she is innocent or she is impaired, perhaps sick, perhaps wilful (see 29n.) – employ (rhetorically useful) misogynist stereotypes to excuse her as a weak or *wayward* woman rather than fear her as the political force that Margaret Beaufort was historically, if not in this play (see p. 18).

29 **wayward** not yielding readily to treatment, obstinate (*OED* 1e); suggesting 'erratic' or 'perverse' in judgement (*OED a.* 1c, 2a) as opposed to *grounded*
grounded immovable, firmly fixed (*OED ppl. a.*[1] 1)

30 SP *Qq give this line to Rivers.

31 **But** just

33 **amendment** recovery from illness (*OED* 4)

36 **atonement** reconciliation

37 **brothers** Only one of Queen Elizabeth's historical brothers (Lord Rivers) appears in the play, but the F, Qq plural here (also 67, F only) is echoed at 4.4.92 (F, Qq), 4.4.380 (F only) and 3.1.6, 12 (F, Qq). Shakespeare may mistake Elizabeth's son by a previous marriage, Lord Grey, for one of her brothers (Furness). F mistakes Anthony Woodeville's name and two titles (Earl Rivers and Lord Scales) as referring to three individuals (cf. Hall,

26 false] *F, Q1–2; om. Q3–6* 27 on] *F;* in *Qq* 30 SP] *F; Ry. Qq subst.* of] *F, Q1–5; om. Q6* 32 Are come] *F;* Came *Qq;* Came forth *Oxf*[1] 33 What] *F, Q3–6;* With *Q1–2* 34 speaks] *F, Q1–2, 4–6;* speaketh *Q3* 36 Ay, madam] *F;* Madame we did *Qq* to make] *F, Q1–3, 5–6;* make *Q4* 37 Between] *F;* Betwixt *Qq*

And between them and my Lord Chamberlain,
And sent to warn them to his royal presence.

QUEEN ELIZABETH
Would all were well, but that will never be;
I fear our happiness is at the height.

Enter RICHARD [*and* HASTINGS].

RICHARD
They do me wrong, and I will not endure it!
Who is it that complains unto the King
That I, forsooth, am stern and love them not?
By holy Paul, they love his grace but lightly
That fill his ears with such dissentious rumours.
Because I cannot flatter, and look fair,
Smile in men's faces, smooth, deceive and cog,
Duck with French nods and apish courtesy,
I must be held a rancorous enemy.
Cannot a plain man live and think no harm

Edward V, fol. v[r]: 'lord Antony Wooduile erle Ryuers and lorde Scales, brother to the quene'). Qq avoid confusion: see 67, 2.1.0.2, 2.1.67–8 and pp. 458–9.

38 **Lord Chamberlain** i.e. Hastings

39 **warn** summon

41 **at the height** i.e. as elevated as it will ever be

41.1 Although Richard's theatrical repertoire includes unaccompanied entry (1.2.32.1, 3.4.20.1), Hastings has no entry elsewhere in F or Qq, so he may enter here. He seems to be absent at 38; at 182 he takes the lead, perhaps significantly, given the conjectural entry with Richard, in supporting Richard's Yorkist perception of past events.

44 **forsooth** a mild oath ('in truth'), often laughable (cf. Jonson, *Poetaster*, 4.1.33–4). Pious Henry VI used no oath but 'forsooth' (Holinshed, 3.691).

45 **holy Paul** Saint Paul

46 **dissentious** quarrelsome

47 **cannot . . . fair** Cf. Richard's looks at 3.4.48–53.

48 **smooth** flatter (cf. 1.2.171)
cog employ feigned flattery, fawn, wheedle (*OED v.* 5); senses include cheating and sleight of hand (*OED v.* 3).

49 **Duck** bow or stoop quickly, often connoting cringing servility (*OED v.* 2a); cf. Marlowe, *Jew of Malta*, 3.3.53.
French . . . courtesy affected gestures of foolish or imitative courtliness; see *RJ* 2.4.28–45, and Thomas Dekker's denunciation of '*Apishnesse*' (58).

50 **held** considered, taken for

51–2 **plain . . . simple** terms typical of authorial personae in contemporary

38 between] *F;* betwixt *Qq* 41 height] *F;* highest *Qq* 41.1 RICHARD] *F; Glocester Qq and* HASTINGS] *Hanmer* 43 is it] *F;* are they *Qq* 44 That] *Qq;* Thar *F* and] *F, Q1–5; om. Q6* 47 look] *F;* speake *Qq*

But thus his simple truth must be abused
With silken, sly, insinuating jacks?

GREY
To who in all this presence speaks your grace?

RICHARD
To thee, that hast nor honesty nor grace.
When have I injured thee? When done thee wrong?
– Or thee? – Or thee? – Or any of your faction?
A plague upon you all! His royal grace,
Whom God preserve better than you would wish,
Cannot be quiet scarce a breathing while
But you must trouble him with lewd complaints.

QUEEN ELIZABETH
Brother of Gloucester, you mistake the matter:
The King, on his own royal disposition
And not provoked by any suitor else,
Aiming, belike, at your interior hatred,

complaint and satire; Richard uses these adjectives pejoratively to characterize Clarence (1.1.118).

52 **truth** veracity, sincerity

53 **With** by
silken elegant; ingratiating, flattering (*OED* II 7b)
jacks contemptuous term for commoners (*OED sb.*[1] 2a; cf. *TS* 2.1.285); Shakespeare elsewhere uses the term (mistakenly) for the keys on virginals (*OED sb.*[1] 14), suggesting flattery and courtly insinuation (*Son* 128); cf. 71–2. Such an association would continue Richard's musical vocabulary (e.g. 1.1.8–13, 27). For 'jack' as a mechanical figure on a clock, see 4.2.112.

54, 55 **grace** Richard evokes the theological and courteous senses of the honorific title, maintaining that Grey lacks divine favour and courtly gracefulness (cf. 320, 2.1.120–33, 2.4.20–4). As a duke, Richard may be addressed as *your grace*; Grey, as son of a knight, is not so entitled. Richard reminds Grey of their differences in birth. Cf. *True Tragedy*, 809–10.

55 **thee** an insulting pronoun; cf. 1.2.46. Richard's *your* at 57 is plural.
nor . . . nor neither . . . nor (cf. 1.2.70)

60 **breathing while** short time, the time of a breath

61 **lewd** foolish, ill-mannered, suggesting social denigration, as *jacks* (53) (*OED* 3, 4)

62 **Brother** i.e. her brother-in-law

63–8 **King . . . send** i.e. the fact that the King guesses your hatred makes him send (Abbott, 376)

63 **disposition** inclination

65 **Aiming, belike** guessing, perhaps

52 his] *F, Q1–4;* in *Q5–6* 53 With] *F;* By *Qq* 54 SP] *F; Ry. Qq subst.* who] *F;* whom *Q1–5;* home *Q6* all] *F, Q1–5; om. Q6* 55 [2]nor] *F, Q1–3, 5–6;* not *Q4* 58 grace] *F;* person *Qq* 63 on] *F;* of *Qq*

That in your outward action shows itself
Against my children, brothers and myself,
Makes him to send, that he may learn the ground.

RICHARD
I cannot tell; the world is grown so bad
That wrens make prey where eagles dare not perch.
Since every Jack became a gentleman,
There's many a gentle person made a jack.

QUEEN ELIZABETH
Come, come, we know your meaning, brother
Gloucester.
You envy my advancement, and my friends'.
God grant we never may have need of you.

RICHARD
Meantime, God grants that I have need of you.
Our brother is imprisoned by your means,
Myself disgraced, and the nobility
Held in contempt, while great promotions

67 **children, brothers** See 37n.
68 *F, Qq appear difficult or garbled. Many editors follow Pope ('Makes him to send, that he may learn the ground / Of your ill will, and thereby to remove it').
Makes causes
ground i.e. the basis (of your ill will)
69 **I cannot tell** I have no idea.
70 Cf. 1.1.132–3. For tiny wrens to dominate mighty eagles, one familiar early modern hierarchical order would have to be inverted; however, Richard's insults go further: the lowly insectivorous wren appears as an audacious bird of prey, daring to hunt where eagles fear to perch. Cf. *Mac* 2.4.12–13.
71, 72 **Jack, jack** Cf. 53n.
71 **Jack . . . gentleman** proverbial for social climbing: 'Jack would be a gentleman' (Dent, J3).
72 **gentle** well-born, belonging to a family of position; originally synonymous with 'noble', but afterwards distinguished, either as a wider term, or as designating a lower degree. Also heraldic: having the rank or status of 'gentleman', distinguished by the right to bear arms (*OED a.* 1a).
74 **advancement** social elevation; cf. 4.4.242.
friends' kinsmens' (*OED* 3)
76 **you** Richard appears to switch from 'thou' to 'you' forms (see 55), but his *you* may be a plural directed toward the Queen and her *friends* (74); his *you* to Queen Elizabeth (89) certainly employs the respectful form.
77 See 1.1.63–5.

66 That] *F;* Which *Qq* action] *F;* actions *Qq* 67 children, brothers] *F;* kindred, brother *Qq* 68] *F;* Makes him to send that thereby he may gather / The ground *(*grounds *Q6)* of your ill will and to remoue it. / *Qq* 70 make prey] *F, Q2;* make pray *Q1;* may prey *Q3–6* 71 Jack] *Qq (*Iacke*);* Iacke *F* 74 my advancement] *F, Q1;* mine aduancement *Q2–6* 76 grants] *F, Q1–2;* grant *Q3–6* I] *F;* we *Qq* 79 while great] *F;* whilst many faire *Qq*

Are daily given to ennoble those
That scarce some two days since were worth a noble.

QUEEN ELIZABETH
By Him that raised me to this careful height
From that contented hap which I enjoyed,
I never did incense his majesty
Against the Duke of Clarence, but have been
An earnest advocate to plead for him.
My lord, you do me shameful injury
Falsely to draw me in these vile suspects.

RICHARD
You may deny that you were not the mean
Of my Lord Hastings' late imprisonment.

RIVERS
She may, my lord, for –

RICHARD
She may, Lord Rivers; why, who knows not so?
She may do more, sir, than denying that:
She may help you to many fair preferments,
And then deny her aiding hand therein
And lay those honours on your high desert.
What may she not? She may, ay, marry, may she.

81 **noble** gold coin worth one third of a pound in the mid-16th century
82 **careful height** elevated position full of cares
83 **hap** condition, fortune (*OED sb.*[1] 1)
86 **advocate to plead** attorney to argue his case
88 **in** into
suspects suspicions
89 **deny . . . not** double negative used as an intensifier (Abbott, 406)
mean means, cause (*OED sb.*[2] II 10a)
91 **for –** This truncated utterance (not in Qq) makes Richard's verbal dominance especially apparent.
92 On Richard's play with *may* as 'virtuoso performance', see McDonald.
94 **preferments** advancements or promotions
96 **lay . . . on** attribute those honours to
high desert great merit
97 ***ay** F, Qq differ frequently (including 120, 125, 135, 262) over 'ay' (meaning 'yes' and written as 'I') and 'yea'; on F's preference as authorial, and Q1's 'yea' as attributable to Valentine Simmes, see *TxC*, 234. However, two variants occur in the portion of Q1 printed by Short (4.4.249, 282). On F's prejudice against 'yea', see Honigmann, 'Variants', 192–3.
marry indeed, to be sure; derived from invocation of the Virgin Mary

89 mean] *F;* cause *Qq* 91 lord, for –] *F;* Lord. *Qq* 96 desert] *F;* deserts *Qq* 97 ay] *F (I);* yea *Qq*

RIVERS

What, marry, may she?

RICHARD

What, marry, may she? Marry with a king,
A bachelor, and a handsome stripling too;
Iwis your grandam had a worser match.

QUEEN ELIZABETH

My lord of Gloucester, I have too long borne
Your blunt upbraidings and your bitter scoffs.
By heaven, I will acquaint his majesty
Of those gross taunts that oft I have endured.
I had rather be a country servant maid
Than a great queen with this condition,
To be so baited, scorned and stormed at.

Enter old QUEEN MARGARET.

Small joy have I in being England's queen.

QUEEN MARGARET [*aside*]

And lessened be that small, God I beseech Him.

100 **stripling** youth, just passing from boyhood to manhood (*OED* 1)

101 **Iwis** certainly; 'I wis' (F, Q4–5, 7–8) suggests confusion of the adverb (resembling German *gewiß*) with the subject–verb form, 'I know'.
grandam Richard's insult attacking the grandmother of Rivers and Queen Elizabeth instead of their mother, who had notoriously married beneath her (Hall, *Henry VI*, fol. cxxxiv^{r}), has been much discussed (see Var). Jowett suggests the play's uncertainty about Elizabeth's male relatives ('Pre-editorial', 129–30).
worser worse, a double comparative (Abbott, 11)

106–7 Similar contrasts between queen and maid appear in Elizabeth I's 1576 parliament speech and in anecdotes about her (Shannon, 151n.).

107 **condition** stipulation, limitation

108 **baited** persecuted or harassed (*OED* *v.* 4)
stormed stormèd

108.1 ***old*** **QUEEN MARGARET** Margaret (born 1429), widow of Henry VI; following the battle of Tewkesbury (1471) she was imprisoned until exiled to France (1476), where she died (1482) at the age of 53. This scene occurs in 1483, and F flaunts its fictionalized chronology at 166–7.

110 SP *For Qq's SPs, see Walton, *Copy*, 74–6.

100 and a] *F;* a *Qq* 101 Iwis] *Q1–3, 6;* I wis *F, Q4–5* a worser] *F, Q1–4, 6 subst.;* worser *Q5* 105 Of] *F;* With *Qq* that oft I] *F;* I often *Qq* 108 so . . . stormed] *F (*scorn'd*);* thus taunted, scorned, and baited *Qq* 108.1] *F after 109; Qq opp. 108–9 old*] *F; not in Qq* 110+ SP] *Qq (Q[u]. M[ar]. except 279); Mar., Margaret., Q.M. F* 110, 117, 125, 133, 136, 142, 154 SD] *Marshall* 110 lessened] *F, Qq (*lesned*), Bevington^{4}* Him] *F;* thee *Qq*

Thy honour, state and seat is due to me.

RICHARD

What? Threat you me with telling of the King?
[Q]Tell him and spare not. Look what I have said[Q]
I will avouch't in presence of the King.
I dare adventure to be sent to th' Tower.
'Tis time to speak; my pains are quite forgot.

QUEEN MARGARET [*aside*]

Out, devil! I do remember them too well:
Thou killed'st my husband Henry in the Tower,
And Edward, my poor son, at Tewkesbury.

RICHARD

Ere you were queen, ay, or your husband king,
I was a packhorse in his great affairs,
A weeder-out of his proud adversaries,
A liberal rewarder of his friends.
To royalize his blood, I spent mine own.

QUEEN MARGARET [*aside*]

Ay, and much better blood than his, or thine.

RICHARD

In all which time, you and your husband Grey

111 **Thy** Margaret uses 'thee/thou' forms to everyone.
state condition, prosperity (*OED sb.* 1)
seat throne
112 **Threat** threaten
with telling of i.e. with the act of telling (Abbott, 178)
113 *Absent from F for no clear reason. It would not be absolutely necessary for sense, given F's 'avouch't' in 114 instead of Qq's 'auouch'.
Look what whatever
114 **avouch't** acknowledge it as one's own
115 **adventure** risk
116 **pains** efforts (on King Edward's behalf)
117 **Out** exclamation expressing abhorrence or indignant reproach
them Margaret twists Richard's *pains* to mean both his 'efforts' and the sufferings that he inflicted on her family.
121 **packhorse** beast of burden; possibly referring to Richard's shape (see 148n.)

112 of] *F, Q1, 3–5;* or *Q2; om. Q6* 113 have] *Q1–2; om. Q3–6* 114 avouch't] *F;* auouch *Qq* 115] *F; not in Qq* 116] *Qq; F lines* speake, / forgot. / my] *F, Q1–5;* when *Q6* 117] *Qq; F lines* Diuell, / well: / do] *F; not in Qq* 118 killed'st] *F (*killd'st*);* slewest *Qq* 120] *Qq; F lines* Queene, / King: / ay] *F (*I*);* yea *Qq* or] *F, Qq;* of *Q2 Tn* 122 weeder-out] *F, Qq (*weeder out*), hyphen Capell* 124 spent] *F;* spilt *Qq* 125] *Qq; F lines* blood / thine. / Ay] *F;* Yea *Qq*

Were factious for the house of Lancaster.
– And Rivers, so were you. – Was not your husband
In Margaret's battle at Saint Albans slain?
– Let me put in your minds, if you forget,
What you have been ere this, and what you are;
Withal, what I have been, and what I am.

QUEEN MARGARET [*aside*]
A murderous villain, and so still thou art.

RICHARD
Poor Clarence did forsake his father Warwick,
Ay, and forswore himself – which Jesu pardon –

QUEEN MARGARET [*aside*] Which God revenge.

RICHARD
To fight on Edward's party for the crown,
And for his meed, poor lord, he is mewed up.
I would to God my heart were flint, like Edward's,
Or Edward's soft and pitiful, like mine.
I am too childish-foolish for this world.

QUEEN MARGARET [*aside*]
Hie thee to hell for shame, and leave this world,
Thou cacodemon. There thy kingdom is.

127 **factious for** i.e. promoting dissension in the special interest of

128 **your husband** Sir John Grey, Queen Elizabeth's first husband, was slain fighting for the Lancastrians at St Albans (1461), although Holinshed leaves his allegiance doubtful (Holinshed, 3.668). This passage corrects *3H6* 3.2.1–7, where 'Richard Grey' is a Yorkist.

129 **Margaret's battle** 'Battle' may mean a body of troops (*OED sb.* II 8a), so Richard says Grey died among Margaret's supporters. Alternatively, *Margaret's battle* may be so-called to distinguish the second battle of St Albans from an earlier conflict in 1455.

132 **Withal** besides

134–7 Clarence first deserted his brothers to marry Isabel Neville, Warwick's elder daughter and Lady Anne's sister. Subsequently he betrayed his oath to Warwick to fight on Edward's side (*3H6* 4.1, 5.1; Hall, *Edward IV*, fols cc[r], ccvii[r], ccxvi[r]); cf. 1.4.49–51.

134 **father** father-in-law

138 **meed** reward
mewed up caged (cf. 1.1.38)

139 **heart were flint** Cf. Dent, H311.

142 **Hie** hasten
leave this world Margaret ironically echoes Richard's words at 1.1.152 (RP).

143 **cacodemon** evil spirit

130 minds] *F, Q1–4 subst.;* minde *Q5;* mind *Q6* you] *F;* yours *Qq* 131 this] *F;* now *Qq* 133 murderous] *F (*murth'rous*), Qq (*murtherous*)* 135 Ay] *F;* Yea *Qq* 141 childish-foolish] *F, Q3–6 (*childish foolish*), hyphen Theobald;* childish, foolish *Q1–2* 142 this] *F;* the *Qq*

RIVERS
My lord of Gloucester, in those busy days
Which here you urge to prove us enemies,
We followed then our lord, our sovereign king.
So should we you, if you should be our king.

RICHARD
If I should be? I had rather be a pedlar.
Far be it from my heart, the thought thereof.

QUEEN ELIZABETH
As little joy, my lord, as you suppose
You should enjoy, were you this country's king,
As little joy you may suppose in me
That I enjoy, being the queen thereof.

QUEEN MARGARET [*aside*]
As little joy enjoys the queen thereof,
For I am she, and altogether joyless.
I can no longer hold me patient. [*Comes forward.*]
Hear me, you wrangling pirates, that fall out
In sharing that which you have pilled from me:
Which of you trembles not, that looks on me?
If not, that I am queen, you bow like subjects,
Yet that, by you deposed, you quake like rebels.

145 **urge** refer to
148 **pedlar** Honigmann suggests reference to Richard's back, which makes him resemble a pedlar bearing a sack.
154 ***As** F, Qq agree on 'A', but Margaret would be saying she has 'a little joy' before calling herself 'altogether joyless' (*TxC*, 234). 'As' echoes 152. Alternatives are: 'Ah' (Bevington, Wells & Taylor, Jowett), 'Ay' (Hammond), 'As' (Dyce (following Heath, 292), Wilson, Mowat & Werstine), 'And' (White). 'Ah' is spelled 'A' at Qq 3.7.23, but F, Qq print 'Ah' as 'Ah' in 4.4.9.
157–8 ironically echoing the Duke of York (*2H6* 1.1.219–28); now a Lancastrian watches Yorkists squabble over spoils (Tillyard, *History Plays*, 200).
158 **pilled** plundered (*OED* $v.^1$ 1a)
160–1 i.e. if you do not bow to your queen, you nevertheless quake like rebels before me, the monarch you have deposed (cf. Abbott, 378).

146 sovereign] *F;* lawfull *Qq* 147 you, if] *F, Q1–5 subst.;* now, if *Q6* 148 If I] *F, Q1–5;* If *Q6* 149 thereof] *F;* of it *Qq* 150 SP] *F, Q1–2 (Qu.), Q3–4 (Q.M.), Q5–6 (Qu. Mar. subst.)* 152 you may] *F;* may you *Qq* 154 As] *Dyce (Heath);* A *F, Qq;* And *White;* Ay, *Ard*^{2}*;* Ah, *Oxf* 156 SD] *Capell (advancing.)* 158 sharing] *F, Q1;* sharing out *Q2–6* 159 of] *F* (off), *Qq* looks] *F, Q1–4;* looke *Q5–6* 160 am] *F;* being *Qq* 161 by you] *F, Q1–2, 5–6;* byou *Q3;* by on *Q4*

– Ah, gentle villain, do not turn away.

RICHARD

Foul wrinkled witch, what mak'st thou in my sight?

QUEEN MARGARET

But repetition of what thou hast marred;
That will I make before I let thee go.

RICHARD

Wert thou not banished on pain of death?

QUEEN MARGARET

I was, but I do find more pain in banishment
Than death can yield me here by my abode.
A husband and a son thou ow'st to me;
– And thou a kingdom; – all of you, allegiance.
This sorrow that I have, by right is yours,
And all the pleasures you usurp are mine.

RICHARD

The curse my noble father laid on thee
When thou didst crown his warlike brows with paper,
And with thy scorns drew'st rivers from his eyes,
And then to dry them, gav'st the Duke a clout
Steeped in the faultless blood of pretty Rutland –

162 **gentle** well-born; combining *gentle* with *villain* invokes the social and moral senses of *villain*.
163 **what . . . sight?** What are you doing here?
164 Margaret first takes Richard's question literally before playing upon a commonplace – 'to make and/or mar' – meaning 'to do and undo' (Dent, M48; cf. *LLL* 4.3.187–8).
repetition recital (*OED* I 3)
166–8 *Patrick (108) ascribes absence from Qq to actorial omission, but Malone and Smidt (*Impostors*, 107) note the odd question of *banishment* with Margaret apparently remaining free. Hammond observes her non-naturalistic treatment including her mysteriously untrammelled movement.
166 **banished** banishèd
168 **here . . . abode** by my living here
169 **thou** i.e. Richard
170 **thou** i.e. Queen Elizabeth
171 **by right** rightfully
173 **curse** See *3H6* 1.4.
175 **scorns** scoffs
176 **clout** cloth
177–93 For Rutland's death, see 1.2.160–1n.

162 Ah] *F;* O *Qq* 166–8] *F; not in Qq* 169 ow'st] *F; Qq* (owest) to] *F, Q1–5;* vnto *Q6* 171 This] *F;* The *Qq* 172 are] *F, Q1–2;* is *Q3–6* 173 my] *F, Q1–5;* me *Q6* 175 scorns] *F;* scorne *Qq* 177 faultless] *F, Q1–2; om. Q3–6*

His curses then, from bitterness of soul
Denounced against thee, are all fall'n upon thee;
And God, not we, hath plagued thy bloody deed.

QUEEN ELIZABETH
So just is God, to right the innocent.

HASTINGS
O, 'twas the foulest deed to slay that babe,
And the most merciless, that e'er was heard of.

RIVERS
Tyrants themselves wept when it was reported.

DORSET
No man but prophesied revenge for it.

BUCKINGHAM
Northumberland, then present, wept to see it.

QUEEN MARGARET
What? Were you snarling all before I came,
Ready to catch each other by the throat,
And turn you all your hatred now on me?
Did York's dread curse prevail so much with heaven
That Henry's death, my lovely Edward's death,
Their kingdom's loss, my woeful banishment,
Should all but answer for that peevish brat?

178 **bitterness of soul** See Job, 10.1, 21.25.

180–2 The phrasing creates a strong impression that *thy bloody deed* is the murder of Rutland by Margaret herself, a sense supported by Hastings's lines about the *deed*, but contrary to fact (Adelman, 240–1).

181 a familiar sentiment; cf. *Thomas Lord Cromwell* (1602): 'How iust is God to right the innocent' (2.3.63).

182 **babe** Hall says Edmund, Earl of Rutland, was 12 when he died (*Henry VI*, fol. clxxxiii[r]). The two princes, also in early adolescence, are called *babes* (4.3.9; cf. 2.2.84). If *babe* is intended to exaggerate Rutland's youth, this usage would anticipate Queen Margaret's rhetorical advice to Queen Elizabeth to 'Think that thy babes were sweeter than they were' (4.4.120).

185 **No . . . prophesied** i.e. there was no one who did not prophesy

186 Cf. *3H6* 1.4.150–1.

187–9 For the canine pack dynamic, see Dent, C917.1.

193 **but** merely
peevish foolish, silly (*OED* 1)

179 all] *F, Q1–2; om. Q3–6* fall'n] *F (*falne*), Qq (*fallen*)* 183 e'er] *F; Qq (*euer*)* 189 all . . . now] *F, Q1;* now . . . all *Q2–6* 193 Should] *F;* Could *Qq*

Can curses pierce the clouds and enter heaven?
Why then give way, dull clouds, to my quick curses.
Though not by war, by surfeit die your king,
As ours by murder, to make him a king.
– Edward thy son, that now is Prince of Wales,
For Edward our son, that was Prince of Wales,
Die in his youth, by like untimely violence.
Thyself a queen, for me that was a queen,
Outlive thy glory, like my wretched self.
Long mayst thou live to wail thy children's death
And see another, as I see thee now,
Decked in thy rights, as thou art stalled in mine.
Long die thy happy days before thy death,
And, after many lengthened hours of grief,
Die neither mother, wife, nor England's queen.
– Rivers and Dorset, you were standers-by,
And so wast thou, Lord Hastings, when my son
Was stabbed with bloody daggers. God, I pray Him,
That none of you may live his natural age,

194 **pierce the clouds** Shaheen detects an echo of the Homilies: 'For the prayer of them that humble themselues, shall pearce through the clouds' (*Homilies*, 142). Cf. Marlowe, *Jew of Malta*, 3.2.33.

195 **dull** gloomy, overcast (*OED* 7), but antithesis with *quick* suggests 'insensible, obtuse, senseless' (*OED* 2).
quick keen, strongly felt (*OED a.* A II 17)

196 **surfeit** overindulgence; cf. King Edward's *diet* (1.1.139); also *Mirror*, 'Clarence', 337–8.

197 as our king was murdered to make yours king

203–8 Most of Margaret's curses come to pass, but this one is not entirely fulfilled, as any Elizabethan would have known (see p. 21; cf. Brooks, 727).

205 **stalled** installed, enthroned

206 **Long . . . days** i.e. long may your happy days be dead (Abbott, 365).

209–10 **Rivers . . . Dorset . . . Hastings** Richard, Clarence and King Edward were present at Tewkesbury when Prince Edward was slain before Margaret's eyes (*3H6* 5.5). Hall blames those who 'stode about' – Richard, Clarence, Dorset and Hastings – for the killing: 'The bitternesse of which murder, some of the actors, after in their latter dayes tasted and assayed by the very rod of Iustice and punishment of God' (*Edward IV*, fol. ccxxi^{v}). See also 3.3.14–16n.

211 **God . . . Him** I pray God

196 Though] *F;* If *Qq* 197 ours] *F, Q1–2;* our *Q3, 5–6;* out *Q4* 198 that] *F;* which *Qq* 199 our son, that] *F;* my sonne which *Qq* 200 violence] *F, Q1–5;* violences *Q6* 203 death] *F;* losse *Qq* 205 rights] *F, Q1;* glorie *Q2–6* 210 wast] *F, Q1–2;* was *Q3–6* 212 his] *F;* your *Qq*

But by some unlooked accident cut off.

RICHARD

Have done thy charm, thou hateful withered hag.

QUEEN MARGARET

And leave out thee? Stay, dog, for thou shalt hear me.
If heaven have any grievous plague in store
Exceeding those that I can wish upon thee,
O, let them keep it till thy sins be ripe,
And then hurl down their indignation
On thee, the troubler of the poor world's peace.
The worm of conscience still begnaw thy soul;
Thy friends suspect for traitors while thou liv'st,
And take deep traitors for thy dearest friends;
No sleep close up that deadly eye of thine,
Unless it be while some tormenting dream
Affrights thee with a hell of ugly devils.
Thou elvish-marked, abortive, rooting hog,

213 **But . . . unlooked** but be by an unanticipated

214 **charm** curse, associating Margaret's prayer with demonic magic as Anne associates Richard's appearance with *conjur*[*ing*] (1.2.34)
hag evil spirit or demon in female form (*OED sb.*[1] 1a), or a woman supposed to have dealings with infernal powers, a witch (*OED sb.*[1] 2); cf. *1H6* 3.2.51.

215 **Stay** Margaret's command that Richard stop speaking and/or stand still repeats Richard's command at 1.2.33.

218 **them** i.e. the heavens (for a similar plural, see 5.5.21).

221–3 **worm . . . begnaw . . . deep traitors** biblical vocabulary (see 221n.); Henry Smith describes the 'gnawing conscience' that will afflict the sinner unable to resist Satan, 'this wretched traytor. His subtilties are wel called the depth of Sathan: for he is so deepe, that few can sou[n]d him' (*Sermons*, 901).

221 **worm of conscience** a pain of hell (*OED* 6); cf. the Geneva Bible gloss for 'their worm shall not die': 'a continuall torment of conscience, whiche shall euer gnawe them and neuer suffer them to be at rest' (Isaiah, 66.24).
still ever

224 **deadly eye** alluding to the power of the mythical basilisk (see 1.2.153)

227 **elvish-marked** birth-marked by elves, who were thought to be spiteful
abortive prematurely born, but also useless (see 1.2.21)
rooting hog alluding to Richard's heraldic emblem, the white boar (see 1.2.104n.); *rooting* connects with the metaphors of lineage and vegetation (see 2.2.41–2): Richard attacks lineal succession as a hog uproots plants. Cf. the title-page of Hall's *Union* (1550), depicting Yorkist and Lancastrian branches (Fig. 1), and pp. 69–72.

215 thee?] *F, Q3–6;* the *Q1–2* 222 while] *F, Q1–5;* whilst *Q6* liv'st] *F;* liuest *Qq* 223 for thy] *F, Q1–3, 5–6;* forth *Q4* 225 while] *F;* whilest *Q1–5;* whilst *Q6* 227 elvish-marked] *F, Qq (*eluish mark'd *subst.), hyphen Rowe*

Thou that wast sealed in thy nativity
The slave of nature and the son of hell;
Thou slander of thy heavy mother's womb,
Thou loathed issue of thy father's loins,
Thou rag of honour, thou detested –

RICHARD Margaret.

QUEEN MARGARET Richard!

RICHARD
Ha?

QUEEN MARGARET I call thee not.

RICHARD
I cry thee mercy then, for I did think

228 **sealed** stamped

229 **slave of nature** i.e. nature has marked Richard for its own through birthmarks. In a theological sense he remains enslaved to sinful nature rather than being in a state of redemption; cf. *Thirty-Nine Articles*, Article 9, concerning Original Sin, the 'corruption of the nature of euery man'.
son of hell i.e. demon

230 **slander** source of discredit, disgrace (*OED sb.* 3d)
***heavy mother's womb** *heavy* may be a displaced modifier of *womb* (as Qq), meaning 'heavy with child', or it might mean 'sorrowful' and so modify *mother*.

231 **loathed** loathèd

232 **rag** small, worthless fragment or shred (*OED sb.*[1] I 1a)
***detested** – Qq's 'detested, &c.' might indicate actors should ad lib (Davison, 21), but the dramatic point is Richard's rapid verbal intervention, which turns Margaret's curse upon herself and is not an opportunity for further discussion.
Margaret Richard's interjection resembles Barabas's comic deflection of an accusation – 'Thou hast committed' – when he interjects, 'Fornication? / But that was in another country: / And besides, the wench is dead' (Marlowe, *Jew of Malta*, 4.1.40–2). Stage Vices were sometimes empowered to improvise verbal counter-turns, as *All for Money* has it: 'Here the vyce shal turne the proclamation to some contrarie sence everie time all for money hath read it' (S. Thomas, 32). In *True Tragedy* Richard finishes Buckingham's 'God saue the King' by interjecting 'Richard' (785–6). In *3H6* Richard breaks into Henry VI's line with 'I'll hear no more! Die, prophet, in thy speech' and a dagger thrust (5.6.56–7; cf. *R2* 2.1.115).

232–3 ***QUEEN MARGARET . . . Ha?** F follows Qq in printing this exchange as a single shared line. This unusual typographical practice argues for the reliance of F printers on annotated Q copy (Walker, 14).

233–5 **call . . . called** a play on 'call' as summoning by name (to which Richard's *Ha?* responds) and as calling someone insulting names

234 **I . . . mercy** I beg your pardon (cf. 4.4.513, 5.3.224).

230 heavy mother's] *F;* mothers heauy *Qq* 232–3] *this edn (RP); F, Qq line* detested – / *Margaret.* / Ha. / not. / *subst.* 232 detested –] *F;* detested, &c. *Qq* 233 Ha?] *Q8;* Ha. *F, Q1–7* thee] *F, Q1–5;* the *Q6* 234] *F;* Then I crie thee mercy, for I had thought *Qq*

That thou hadst called me all these bitter names.

QUEEN MARGARET

Why, so I did, but looked for no reply.
O, let me make the period to my curse.

RICHARD

'Tis done by me and ends in 'Margaret'.

QUEEN ELIZABETH [*to Queen Margaret*]

Thus have you breathed your curse against yourself.

QUEEN MARGARET

Poor painted queen, vain flourish of my fortune,
Why strew'st thou sugar on that bottled spider,
Whose deadly web ensnareth thee about?
Fool, fool, thou whet'st a knife to kill thyself.
The day will come that thou shalt wish for me
To help thee curse this poisonous bunch-backed toad.

HASTINGS

False-boding woman, end thy frantic curse,
Lest to thy harm thou move our patience.

QUEEN MARGARET

Foul shame upon you, you have all moved mine.

RIVERS

Were you well served, you would be taught your duty.

237 **period** conclusion, but also with the sense of completing a rhetorically constructed sentence of several clauses

240 **painted** artificial, feigned, unreal
vain . . . fortune worthless and ostentatious embellishment of my own substance – i.e. the throne and office. The first of F's 12 mentions of *fortune*.

241 **strew'st thou sugar** do you flatter, attempt to ingratiate; cf. *Ham* 3.1.47–8.
bottled swollen, protuberant

243 **whet'st . . . thyself** Cf. Dent, K157.2: 'To whet a knife for one's own throat'.

245 ***poisonous** 'poisoned' (Q2–8) may represent metrical adjustment and meant 'venomous' (*OED ppl. a.* 3).
bunch-backed hump-backed (*OED* bunch *sb.*[1] 1a)

246 **False-boding** falsely prophesying
frantic lunatic, insane

247 **move** disturb

249 **Were . . . served** i.e. if you were treated as you deserve
duty deference, obedience

235 That] *F, Q1; om. Q2–6* 236 looked] *F (*look'd*), Q1–5 (*lookt*);* looke *Q6* 238 in] *F, Q1–5;* by *Q6* 239 SD] *Oxf subst.* 244 day] *F;* time *Qq* that] *F, Q1;* when *Q2–6* 245 this] *F;* that *Qq* poisonous] *F, Q1;* poisoned *Q2–6* 246 False-boding] *F, Qq (*False boding*), hyphen Theobald*

QUEEN MARGARET

To serve me well, you all should do me duty:
Teach me to be your queen, and you my subjects.
O, serve me well, and teach yourselves that duty.

DORSET

Dispute not with her; she is lunatic.

QUEEN MARGARET

Peace, master Marquess, you are malapert.
Your fire-new stamp of honour is scarce current.
O, that your young nobility could judge
What 'twere to lose it and be miserable.
They that stand high have many blasts to shake them,
And if they fall, they dash themselves to pieces.

RICHARD

Good counsel, marry. Learn it, learn it, Marquess.

DORSET

It touches you, my lord, as much as me.

RICHARD

Ay, and much more; but I was born so high.
Our aerie buildeth in the cedar's top,

250–2 Margaret again appropriates the discourse of others for her own ends, adapting Rivers's vocabulary to demand the service and homage appropriate to one who ought to be queen.

254 **master Marquess** Margaret couples the exalted title *Marquess* (a degree between Duke and Earl) with the reductive *master*, a (minimal) title of respect for ordinary learned or gentle folk or for holders of minor office (e.g. 'Master Parson', *MW* 3.1.42). King Edward properly refers to Dorset as *Lord Marquess* (2.1.25).
malapert impudent, presumptuous

255 **fire-new stamp . . . current** Margaret employs terminology derived from coinage (as does Richard at 81), telling Dorset that his title is so recent (he became Marquess in 1475; Holinshed, 3.702) that it is now just barely accepted (cf. Dent, M985: 'New out of the mint', *TN* 3.2.21).
current having the quality of current coin; genuine

258–9, 262–5 The equation of physical elevation and social standing is frequent in admonitions against the desire to be raised above the station allotted by birth (cf. Dent, T509, W450).

259 Cf. Dent, S823: 'The higher standing (up), the lower (greater) fall.'

263 **aerie . . . cedar** An aerie is the nest of a bird of prey, often the eagle (cf. *KJ* 5.2.149), and also, figuratively, the brood in the nest (*OED* 1, 2). The eagle

251 you] *F, Q1, 3–6;* yon *Q2* 258 blasts] *F, Q2–6;* blast *Q1* 261 touches] *F;* toucheth *Qq* 262 Ay] *F (I);* Yea *Qq*

And dallies with the wind, and scorns the sun.

QUEEN MARGARET

And turns the sun to shade. Alas, alas,
Witness my son, now in the shade of death,
Whose bright out-shining beams thy cloudy wrath
Hath in eternal darkness folded up.
Your aerie buildeth in our aerie's nest.
O God, that seest it, do not suffer it;
As it is won with blood, lost be it so.

BUCKINGHAM

Peace, peace, for shame, if not for charity.

QUEEN MARGARET

Urge neither charity nor shame to me.
[*to the others*] Uncharitably with me have you dealt,
And shamefully my hopes by you are butchered.
My charity is outrage, life my shame,

was thought the monarch of birds and the cedar the highest-ranking among evergreen trees (cf. Ezekiel, 17.3).

264 **scorns the sun** Eagles were thought uniquely able to gaze directly into the sun (cf. *LLL* 4.3.222–4, Dent, E3).

265 **turns** converts, transforms. 'Turning' occurs with various senses: in Richard's clouds changed to sunshine and war to love; in his 'turn[ing]' King Henry's corpse into the earth and 'return[ing]' to his love (1.2.263–4); in Margaret's complaint about those who have 'turn[ed]' their hatred toward her (1.3.189); in Buckingham's protestations that he will not *turn* against King Edward (2.1.32) and his recognition that his prayers and sword have 'turn[ed]' against himself (5.1.21, 24); in Herbert's speculations that allies will *turn* from Richard (5.2.19); and in Richmond's mercy to soldiers who will *return* to accept him as king (5.5.17).

265–6 **sun . . . son** Cf. 1.1.2.

270 **suffer** permit

271 **is** i.e. was, is and will be; in the context of her prayer for the future, occasioned by memory of past sufferings and by knowledge of present trends, Margaret's pan-temporal verbal construction makes sense.

272 **charity** Once again, the principal Gospel command occurs in an admonition that could be construed to be, as at 1.2.68, self-interested. Buckingham's twisted usage suggests the alliance that becomes overt at 1.3.295.

274 SD *Mowat and Werstine's SD answers objections concerning F, Qq attribution of 272 to Buckingham; *you* in 274 is plural (contrast *thee* in 280).

276 **My . . . outrage** i.e. the only charity I have received is the outrage you have done me; or, the nearest thing to charity I feel is my outraged anger.
life my shame i.e. my whole life is a shame; or, continuing to live is shameful for me.

266 son] *F, Q1–4 (*sonne *F, Q2–4);* sunne *Q5–6* 271 is] *F;* was *Qq* 272 SP] *F, Qq; Gloucester Cam[1] (Walker)* Peace, peace] *F;* Haue done *Qq* 274 SD] *Folg* 275 my . . . you] *F (*my hopes (by you)*);* by you my hopes *Qq*

And in that shame, still live my sorrow's rage.

BUCKINGHAM

Have done, have done.

QUEEN MARGARET

O princely Buckingham, I'll kiss thy hand
In sign of league and amity with thee.
Now fair befall thee and thy noble house.
Thy garments are not spotted with our blood,
Nor thou within the compass of my curse.

BUCKINGHAM

Nor no one here, for curses never pass
The lips of those that breathe them in the air.

QUEEN MARGARET

I will not think but they ascend the sky,
And there awake God's gentle sleeping peace.
O Buckingham, take heed of yonder dog.
Look when he fawns, he bites; and when he bites,
His venom tooth will rankle to the death.

277 **in . . . rage** i.e. while I continue to live in shame may the rage born of my treatment live too.

279 **princely** This epithet appears 15 times in F (13 in Q1); Buckingham's royal blood came by direct descent from Thomas of Woodstock, next-to-youngest son of Edward III, and by Beaufort descent from John of Gaunt, an ancestry he shared with Henry Tudor (Hanham, 4).
thy Margaret appears to single out Buckingham as worthy of intimacy in this, for her, rare non-vituperative speech (Jowett); cf. Edward to *princely Buckingham* (2.1.29–30).

280 **league** alliance

281 **fair befall** may good fortune come to; cf. 3.5.47.

283 **compass** scope

284–5 **curses . . . air** i.e. curses never affect anyone but the one who curses; ironically recalling Margaret's warning to Suffolk (*2H6* 3.2.330–2).

286 **think but** think otherwise than that

287 **awake . . . peace** For the image of God awakened from sleep, see Psalms, 44.23.

288 **yonder** Richard is now evidently some distance from Margaret (cf. 294).

289 Cf. 'We Jews can fawn like spaniels when we please; / And when we grin we bite' (Marlowe, *Jew of Malta*, 2.3.20–1); also Tilley, D445.
Look when whenever

290 **venom** venomous (*OED a.*)
rankle fester

277 that] *F;* my *Qq* still] *F, Q1–5;* shall *Q6* 278] *F;* Haue done. *Qq* 279 SP] *F, Q1–4; Q. Mary Q5–6* princely] *F, Q1–3, 5–6;* pricely *Q4* I'll] *F;* I will *Qq* 281 noble] *F;* Princely *Qq* 285 those] *F, Q1–5;* them *Q6* 286 I . . . think] *F;* Ile not beleeue *Qq* 288 take heed] *F;* beware *Qq* 290 rankle] *F, Q2–6;* rackle *Q1* to the] *F;* thee to *Qq*

Have not to do with him, beware of him;
Sin, death and hell have set their marks on him,
And all their ministers attend on him.

RICHARD
What doth she say, my lord of Buckingham?

BUCKINGHAM
Nothing that I respect, my gracious lord.

QUEEN MARGARET
What, dost thou scorn me for my gentle counsel,
And soothe the devil that I warn thee from?
O, but remember this another day,
When he shall split thy very heart with sorrow,
And say poor Margaret was a prophetess.
– Live each of you, the subjects to his hate,
And he to yours, and all of you to God's. *Exit.*

BUCKINGHAM
My hair doth stand on end to hear her curses.

RIVERS
And so doth mine. I muse why she's at liberty.

RICHARD
I cannot blame her; by God's Holy Mother,
She hath had too much wrong, and I repent
My part thereof that I have done to her.

QUEEN ELIZABETH
I never did her any to my knowledge.

292 **marks** Cf. 227.
293 **attend on** wait upon, serve
295 **respect** heed, pay attention to
297 **soothe** support, humour, flatter (*OED v.* 3, 5)
303 SP *Either Buckingham's hair stood on end (F) or Hastings's did (Qq). Buckingham has claimed not to *respect* Margaret's utterances (295), but his speeches may be rhetorical, seeking to downplay the effect of Margaret's speeches in the earlier remark and to associate himself with Richard's expressions of shock and horror at her freedom in the later (Hammond).
303 **on** F, Qq spellings are interchangeable (*OED* on).
304 **muse** wonder
308 SP *Walton explains F's confusion concerning the speaker by the hypothesis that F was set throughout from Q3 (*Copy*, 74–7).

296] *Qq; F lines* me / counsell? / 297 soothe] *F, Q1–5 subst.;* soothd *Q6* 301 to] *F;* of *Qq* 302 yours] *F;* your *Q1–2;* you *Q3–6* 303 SP] *F; Hast. Qq* on] *F (*an*), Qq* 304 muse why] *F;* wonder *Qq* 307 to her] *F; not in Qq* 308 SP] *Q1–5 (Qu.); Mar. F; Hast. Q6*

RICHARD

Yet you have all the vantage of her wrong.
I was too hot to do somebody good
That is too cold in thinking of it now.
Marry, as for Clarence, he is well repaid:
He is franked up to fatting for his pains.
God pardon them that are the cause thereof.

RIVERS

A virtuous and a Christian-like conclusion,
To pray for them that have done scathe to us.

RICHARD

So do I ever – (*Speaks to himself.*) being well advised,
For had I cursed now, I had cursed myself.

Enter CATESBY.

CATESBY

Madam, his majesty doth call for you,
– And for your grace, – and yours, my gracious lord.

QUEEN ELIZABETH

Catesby, I come. – Lords, will you go with me?

309 **vantage** advantage
310 **hot** eager, zealous
somebody i.e. King Edward
313 **franked . . . fatting** penned up as an animal in a sty to be fattened
pains efforts
315–16 These lines convey Jesus's commands – 'loue your enemies, blesse them that curse you, do good to them that hate you, pray for the[m] which hurt you, and persecute you' (Matthew, 5.44) – but typically turn Christian sentiments to aggressive uses as Rivers derides Richard for hypocrisy.
316 **scathe** injury (*OED sb.* 2)
317 **well advised** judicious
320 *The final word has provoked debate as to whether it should be singular or plural, although the sense of F and Q1–2 is not especially obscure. After summoning the Queen in 319, Catesby addresses the two onstage dukes – Richard and Buckingham – in turn as 'your grace, and yours' ('your grace', once exclusively used to kings and queens, came to be used for dukes and archbishops, *OED sb.* II 16b). Subsequently, Rivers speaks for the attending lords beneath ducal rank, reminding everyone that his faction has a *grace* – Queen Elizabeth – on its side (Paul Werstine, private communication).
321 *F avoids the royal plurals of Qq (Davison).

309 Yet . . . her] *F;* But . . . this *Qq* 314 thereof] *F;* of it *Qq* 317 SD] *F after* aduis'd*; not in Qq* 318.1] *F; not in Qq* 320 grace] *F, Q1–2;* noble Grace *Q3–6* yours] *F;* you *Qq* gracious lord.] *F;* noble Lo: *Q1–2;* noble Lord. *Q3–6;* noble lords. *Capell;* gracious lords. *Alexander* 321 I . . . me] *F;* we . . . vs *Qq*

RIVERS

We wait upon your grace.

Exeunt all but [Q]*Richard*[Q] [, *Duke of*] *Gloucester.*

RICHARD

I do the wrong, and first begin to brawl.
The secret mischiefs that I set abroach
I lay unto the grievous charge of others.
Clarence, who I indeed have cast in darkness,
I do beweep to many simple gulls,
Namely to Derby, Hastings, Buckingham,
And tell them 'tis the Queen and her allies
That stir the King against the Duke my brother.
Now they believe it, and withal whet me
To be revenged on Rivers, Dorset, Grey.
But then I sigh, and, with a piece of scripture,
Tell them that God bids us do good for evil;
And thus I clothe my naked villainy
With odd old ends, stol'n forth of Holy Writ,

323 Cf. Dent, C579 and *CE* 4.1.50–1. **brawl** raise a clamour, make a disturbance (*OED v.* 2)
324 **abroach** afoot
325 **lay . . . others** blame others
326 **cast in darkness** biblical diction, as in Matthew, 8.12 ('the chyldren of the kyngdome shalbe caste out, into vtter darcknesse'); *cast in darkness* could mean 'put in prison', but *shade of death* and *eternal darkness* (266, 268) provide ominous resonances.
327 **beweep** weep for **gulls** simpletons, credulous dupes
328 **Derby, Hastings, Buckingham** Richard's list of *simple gulls* should be remembered as we discover their reservations and resistance. Given the familiarity of stories about Richard, audiences might register his overconfidence.
329 **allies** allìes
331 **withal** furthermore **whet** urge, incite
332 ***Dorset** Vaughan, not Dorset, is executed in 3.3; however, Dorset is more prominent in the play and more important as Richard's enemy.
333–7 On Richard as Shakespeare's 'fullest portrayal of explicitly religious hypocrisy', see Frye, 185.
334 **do . . . evil** a biblical commonplace: see 315–16n.
335–7 Cf. Dent, D230: 'The devil can cite scripture for his own purpose.'
336 **odd old ends** variation on 'odds and ends'

322 We wait upon] *F;* Madame we will attend *Qq subst.* SD] *F (Gloster); Exeunt man. Ri. (Clo. Q3, 5, 6; Glo. Q4) Qq Duke of*] *Eccles* 323 the] *F, Q1–3;* thee *Q4–6* begin] *F;* began *Qq* 324 mischiefs] *F, Q1–2;* mischiefe *Q3–6* 326 who . . . cast] *F;* whom . . . laid *Qq* 328 Derby, Hastings] *F;* Hastings, Darby *Qq* 329 tell them 'tis] *F;* say it is *Qq* 331 it] *F;* me *Qq* 332 Dorset] *F;* Vaughan *Qq* 333 I sigh] *F, Q1–2, 4;* sigh *Q3, 5–6* 334 do] *F, Q1–4;* to do *Q5–6* 336 odd old . . . forth] *F;* old odde . . . out *Qq*

And seem a saint when most I play the devil.

Enter two Murderers.

But soft, here come my executioners.
– How now, my hardy, stout, resolved mates;
Are you now going to dispatch this thing?

1 MURDERER
We are, my lord, and come to have the warrant,
That we may be admitted where he is.

RICHARD
Well thought upon. I have it here about me.
When you have done, repair to Crosby Place;
But sirs, be sudden in the execution,
Withal obdurate; do not hear him plead,
For Clarence is well-spoken and perhaps
May move your hearts to pity, if you mark him.

1 MURDERER
Tut, tut, my lord, we will not stand to prate.
Talkers are no good doers; be assured

337 **play** A strikingly theatrical verb, given Richard's resolution to 'prove a villain' (1.1.30). Since the proverb is 'To seem a saint but be a devil' (Tilley, S30), in what sense could Richard mean to *play* rather than to 'be' satanic?

338 **soft** an imperative exclamation, enjoining silence or urging restraint (*OED* soft *adv.* 8a; cf. *Ham* 3.1.87); thus, Richard either acknowledges that a soliloquy has been spoken aloud (as 1.1.41) or anticipates his next tricky move.

339 **hardy, stout, resolved** This triple adjectival sequence without a conjunction is unusual for Shakespeare (Var). The point may be the exaggerated nature of the attributes projected upon the killers. Richard and his helpers have difficulty maintaining resolution (see 1.4.104–277, 5.3.177–206); the Murderers will have to reassure themselves about their own stoutness (1.4.148–9).
resolved resolvèd; determined, firm of purpose

341 SP *Neither F nor Qq differentiates the assassins here (although they do in 1.4), awarding 341–2 and 349–51 to '*Vil.*' (F) or to '*Execu.*' and '*Exec.*' (Q1).

344 **repair** go (*OED v.* 1)

348 **mark** pay attention to

349 **prate** chatter, talk idly

350 **Talkers . . . doers** Cf. *H8* 2.2.77–8 and Dent, T64: 'Greatest talkers are the least doers.'

337.1] *F (murtherers); Enter Executioners. Qq opp. 338* 338 come] *F, Q1;* comes *Q2–6* 340 you] *F, Q1–2;* ye *Q3–6* now] *F, Q1–5;* not *Q6* thing] *F;* deede *Qq* 341+ SP] *Capell subst.; Vil. F; Execu. Qq* 343 Well] *F;* It was well *Qq* 347 well-spoken] *F, Qq (*well spoken*), hyphen F3* 349 Tut, tut] *F;* Tush feare not *Qq* 350 doers; be assured] *F4 (*doers; be assur'd,*);* doers, be assured: *Q2, F;* doers be assured: *Q1, 3–6*

We go to use our hands and not our tongues.

RICHARD

Your eyes drop millstones when fools' eyes fall tears.
I like you lads. About your business straight.
Go, go, dispatch.

1 MURDERER We will, my noble lord. [Q]*Exeunt.*[Q]

1.4 *Enter* CLARENCE *and* Keeper.

KEEPER

Why looks your grace so heavily today?

CLARENCE

O, I have passed a miserable night,
So full of fearful dreams, of ugly sights,
That, as I am a Christian faithful man,
I would not spend another such a night
Though 'twere to buy a world of happy days,
So full of dismal terror was the time.

KEEPER

What was your dream, my lord? I pray you tell me.

CLARENCE

Methoughts that I had broken from the Tower,

352 **eyes drop millstones** Cf. Dent, M967: 'He weeps millstones'; the cliché connotes hard-heartedness.
fall drop, shed (*OED v.* IX 49a)
353 **straight** immediately (*OED adv.* 2)
354 SD Given the conspiratorial enterprise, Richard probably departs separately.
1.4 location: the Tower of London
0.1 ***Keeper** Qq have Brakenbury ('Brokenbury') for *Keeper*.
Keeper jailer
1 **heavily** with sorrow, grief or displeasure (*OED* 3)
4 **as . . . man** an expression attesting to a statement (*OED* as *adv.* 14), here on the basis of Christian faith; use of *faithful* in this religious sense appears to be unique in Shakespeare (Var). It might mean 'true to one's word' – which would be ironic when employed by a character prominently accused of breaking his word (see 1.3.134–5, 1.4.50, 55, 200–7).
5 **a** used redundantly (Abbott, 85)
6 **world** age or (long) period of time (*OED* I 5a)
9, 24, 58 **Methoughts, methought** it seemed to me; cf. *MV* 1.3.67, *WT* 1.2.154.
9 ***had . . . Tower** See 13n. on **There*.

351 go] *F;* come *Qq* 352 fall] *F;* drop *Qq* 353 straight] *F; not in Qq* 354] *F; not in Qq Steevens; F lines* dispatch. / Lord. / SP] *Capell subst.; Vil. F; Both. Ard*[2] SD] *Qq opp. 353* 1.4] *F (Scena Quarta.); not in Qq* 0.1] *F; Enter Clarence, Brokenbury Qq* 1+ SP] *F (Keep.); Brok. Qq subst.* 3 fearful . . . sights] *F;* vgly sights, of gastly dreames *Qq* 8 my . . . me] *F;* I long to heare you tell it *Qq* 9–10] *F;* Me thoughts I was imbarkt for Burgundy, *Qq subst.* 9 Methoughts] *F, Q1–3 (*Me thoughts*);* Me thought *Q4–6*

And was embarked to cross to Burgundy;
And in my company my brother Gloucester,
Who from my cabin tempted me to walk
Upon the hatches. There we looked toward England,
And cited up a thousand heavy times,
During the wars of York and Lancaster,
That had befall'n us. As we paced along
Upon the giddy footing of the hatches,
Methought that Gloucester stumbled, and in falling
Struck me (that thought to stay him) overboard
Into the tumbling billows of the main.
O Lord, methought what pain it was to drown,
What dreadful noise of water in mine ears,
What sights of ugly death within mine eyes.
Methoughts I saw a thousand fearful wracks,

10 **embarked . . . Burgundy** Clarence and Richard had made the voyage before when, in danger from Margaret's troops, they were sent in 1461 to Utrecht to the care of Duke Philip the Good of Burgundy (C. Ross, *Richard*, 5), their sister's husband (see 5.3.324n.).

13 **hatches** deck (*OED* 3)

***There** As elsewhere in this scene, F sometimes sides with Q6 or other derivative Qq against Q1, sometimes agrees with earlier Qq against Q6 or agrees with Q1 against Q3–6, and sometimes offers alternatives varying slightly from readings in all Qq. Q1–5's 'thence' is more precise in meaning 'from that place' (*OED* 1) than Q6, F's 'There', so F hardly constitutes considered 'correction', but the effect is relatively inconsequential. By contrast, at 9, Qq lack the irony of Clarence's failure to connect Richard with his imprisonment; cf. 36–7, where Qq lack Clarence's suicidal wishes.

14 **cited up** called to mind, referred to (*OED* 5)

17 **giddy** causing or apt to produce dizziness

19 **thought to stay** intended to support (*OED* stay *v.*[2] 1)

20 **main** open ocean

22 ***water** The many nearby plurals make it easy to imagine Q1–5's 'waters' as a mistake by a compositor, copyist or corrector (Walton, *Copy*, 25).

22, 23 ***mine** This first person possessive pronoun (Q2–6, F) is more typically used in Shakespeare than Q1's 'my' before vowels when the possessive form is unemphatic (Abbott, 237); cf. 1.2.151, 3.7.20, 4.1.80, 81.

24–33 The *thousand heavy times* during the 'wars of York and Lancaster' (14–15) produce a vision of *a thousand fearful wracks* and *a thousand men*, their

13 There] *F, Q6;* thence *Q1–5* toward] *F, Q1–5;* towards *Q6* 14 heavy] *F;* fearefull *Qq* 16 befall'n] *F (*befalne*), Qq (*befallen*)* paced] *F (*pac't*), Q1 (*pact*);* past *Q2–6* 18 falling] *F;* stumbling *Qq* 21 O Lord] *F;* Lord, Lord *Qq* 22 water] *F, Q6;* waters *Q1–5* mine] *F, Q2–6;* my *Q1* 23 sights of ugly] *F;* vgly sights of *Qq* mine] *F, Q2–6;* my *Q1* 24 Methoughts] *F (*Me thoughts*);* Me thought *Qq*

A thousand men that fishes gnawed upon,
Wedges of gold, great anchors, heaps of pearl,
Inestimable stones, unvalued jewels,
All scattered in the bottom of the sea.
Some lay in dead men's skulls, and in the holes
Where eyes did once inhabit, there were crept –
As 'twere in scorn of eyes – reflecting gems,
That wooed the slimy bottom of the deep
And mocked the dead bones that lay scattered by.

KEEPER

Had you such leisure in the time of death
To gaze upon these secrets of the deep?

CLARENCE

Methought I had, and often did I strive
To yield the ghost, but still the envious flood
Stopped in my soul and would not let it forth
To find the empty, vast and wandering air,

lifeless *skulls* anticipating the Bishop of Carlisle's prophecy (*R2* 4.1.144–5). Cf. *H5* 1.2.164–5 for the 'bottom of the sea / With sunken wrack and sumless treasuries'; and Spenser's Cave of Mammon for 'heapes of Gold' including 'great Ingowes and . . . wedges square' where 'all the grownd with sculs was scattered / And dead mens bones' (*Faerie Queene*, 2.7.5, 7; Brooks, 'Antecedents', 149).

24 **wracks** wrecked ships (*OED sb.* 2)

27 **Inestimable, unvalued** too valuable to be measured (*OED* unvalued 1), but also 'unvalued' in being lost beyond recovery (*OED* 2)
jewels Cf. *Son* 21: 'sea's rich gems'.

28 *Many editors since Pope follow Qq in omitting this line (cf. Smidt, *Impostors*, 70).

30–3 **crept . . . scorn . . . reflecting . . . wooed . . . mocked** These terms link the death's head with Richard; cf. creeping (1.2.20, 1.2.261, 4.4.47), scorn (1.2.167, 1.3.108), reflection in a mirror (1.1.15, 1.2.258), wooing (1.2.230, 4.3.43) and abundant mockery of others throughout.

30–1 Cf. the pearls that replace the eyes of the drowned in *Tem* 1.2.399.

31 **scorn** mockery, derision

36–7 ***and . . . ghost*** See 13n. on **There*.

37 **yield the ghost** give up, release the spirit or soul; cf. Matthew, 27.50: 'Jesus . . . yeelded up y[e] ghost'.
envious malicious, spiteful (*OED* 2)

38 **Stopped in** closed in, shut up in a vessel with a cover, plug or other stopper (*OED* stop *v.* 7a)

39 **wandering** The air's freedom to wander is biblical. See John, 3.8, likening it to the motions of the spirit; also *AYL* 2.7.47–9.

25 A] *F;* Ten *Qq* 28] *F; not in Qq* 29 lay in] *F, Q1–3, 5–6;* lay *Q4* dead men's] *F (*dead-mens*), Q1–3, 5–6; Q4 (*deadmens*)* the] *F;* those *Qq* 32 That] *F;* Which *Qq* wooed] *F, Q1–4;* wade *Q5–6* 35 these] *F;* the *Qq* 36–7 and . . . ghost,] *F; not in Qq* 37 but] *F;* for *Qq* 38 Stopped] *F;* Kept *Qq* 39 find] *F;* seeke *Q1–2;* keepe *Q3–6* wandering] *F, Q3–6 (*wand'ring*), Q1–2*

But smothered it within my panting bulk,
Who almost burst to belch it in the sea.

KEEPER

Awaked you not in this sore agony?

CLARENCE

No, no, my dream was lengthened after life.
O, then began the tempest to my soul.
I passed, methought, the melancholy flood,
With that sour ferryman which poets write of,
Unto the kingdom of perpetual night.
The first that there did greet my stranger-soul
Was my great father-in-law, renowned Warwick,
Who spake aloud: 'What scourge for perjury
Can this dark monarchy afford false Clarence?'
And so he vanished. Then came wandering by
A shadow like an angel, with bright hair
Dabbled in blood, and he shrieked out aloud:

40 **bulk** physical body; the belly or trunk (*OED sb.*[1] 2a)

41 **Who** which
belch vent with vehemence or violence; sometimes compared to the action of a volcano or cannon (*OED v.* 2)

42 **agony** intense distress, also specifically the throes or pangs of death

44 **tempest . . . soul** Cf. Marlowe, *Works*, *1 Tamburlaine*, 3.2.86: 'tempest to my daunted thoughts'.

45 **melancholy flood** the river Styx, over which the souls of the dead were ferried by the boatman Charon to the classical underworld

46 **sour ferryman . . . of** For Charon's foreboding appearance, see Seneca, *Hercules Furens*, 764–71.

47 **perpetual night** Cf. Marlowe, *Works*, *Faustus* [2.1.]445, where Lucifer is 'Chiefe Lord and Regent of perpetuall night'; Seneca, *Hippolytus*, 221 ('*nocte perpetua*' (perpetual night)); see also 2.2.46n.

49 **renowned** renownèd

49–50 **Warwick . . . perjury** See 1.3.134–7. Hall describes Clarence's 'condigne punishment, for violatyng and brekyng hys othe . . . to the erle of Warwycke, for God not many yeres after, suffered hym lyke a periured person to dye a cruell & a stra[n]ge death' (*Edward IV*, fol. ccxvi[r]).

50 **scourge** punishment (literally a whip or lash)

53 **shadow** ghost (of Prince Edward, Henry VI's murdered son); 'shadow like an angel' combines classical and Christian elements (Clemen, 72).

54 **Dabbled** spattered, sprinkled
shrieked Ghosts were often said to have shrill, squeaking or shrieking voices (*Ham* 1.1.115; *JC* 2.2.24); Qq's 'squeakt' (or 'squakt') is possible.

41 Who] *F;* Which *Qq* 42 in] *F;* with *Qq* 43 No, no] *F;* O no *Qq* 44 to] *F, Q1–5;* of *Q6* 45 I] *F;* Who *Qq* 46 sour] *F;* grim *Qq* 50 spake] *F;* cried *Qq* 52 wandering] *F, Qq (*wand'ring*)* 53 with] *F;* in *Qq* 54 shrieked] *F;* squakt *Q1;* squeakt *Q2–6 subst.*

'Clarence is come, false, fleeting, perjured Clarence,
That stabbed me in the field by Tewkesbury.
Seize on him, furies! Take him unto torment!'
With that, methought, a legion of foul fiends
Environed me, and howled in mine ears
Such hideous cries, that with the very noise
I, trembling, waked, and for a season after
Could not believe but that I was in hell,
Such terrible impression made my dream.

KEEPER

No marvel, lord, though it affrighted you;
I am afraid, methinks, to hear you tell it.

CLARENCE

Ah keeper, keeper, I have done these things,
That now give evidence against my soul,
For Edward's sake; and see how he requites me.
– O God! If my deep prayers cannot appease Thee,

55 **fleeting** fickle, inconstant, vacillating (*OED ppl. a.* 2)

57 Famously, *The Spanish Tragedy* evokes hell's regions and the threat of the 'deepest hell, / Where bloudie furies shakes their whips of steele' (Kyd, 1.1.64–5). The furies were classical deities with snakes twined in their hair, sent from the underworld to avenge wrong and punish crime.

58 **legion** vast multitude, frequently referring to spirits or angels (*OED* 3a); cf. *Mac* 4.3.55–6 and Mark, 5.9.

59 **Environed** surrounded with hostile intention (*OED v.* 2b)
howled howlèd

61 **for a season** for some time

64 **No marvel . . . though** i.e. it is not strange that (cf. *VA* 390)
affrighted frightened

68 **Edward's** i.e. Edward IV's
requites repays

69 **deep** solemn, weighty, important (*OED* II 7a, b)

69–72 *Hammond (333) conjectures that incompatibility between Christian terminology and the classical imagery of Clarence's dream led to Qq omission, but Clarence's self-assessment as a *Christian faithful man* (4) remains. Smidt suggests that historical inaccuracy is the issue, since Clarence's wife had died before the time of the scene (*Impostors*, 124), but this presumes unduly stringent standards. Divine vengeance 'in the thirde and fourth generations' is biblical (Numbers, 14.18), and Richard's reign provides examples of condign punishment for the 'offence of the parentes' (Hall, *Edward IV*, fol. ccxv[r]); but Clarence's children were actually executed under Henry VII

57 unto torment] *F;* to your torments *Qq* 58 methought] *F, Q2–6 (*me thought*);* me thoughts *Q1* 59 me] *F;* me about *Qq* 63 my] *F;* the *Qq* 64 lord] *F;* my Lo: *Qq subst.* 65 am afraid, methinks,] *F;* promise you, I am afraid *Qq* 66 Ah keeper, keeper . . . these] *F;* O Brokenbury . . . those *Qq* 67 That . . . give] *F;* Which . . . beare *Qq* 69–72] *F; not in Qq* 69 prayers] *F (*prayres*)*

But Thou wilt be avenged on my misdeeds,
Yet execute Thy wrath in me alone;
O, spare my guiltless wife and my poor children.
– Keeper, I prithee sit by me awhile;
My soul is heavy, and I fain would sleep.

KEEPER
I will, my lord. God give your grace good rest.

Enter BRAKENBURY, *the Lieutenant.*

BRAKENBURY
Sorrow breaks seasons and reposing hours,

(the play's Richmond) and Henry VIII, not under Richard, so Campbell (314) cites awareness of this Tudor violence as a possible explanation for Qq omission. Clarence's daughter is absent from Qq 4.1.1–2. For Clarence's speech in relation to arguments about divine providence, see Kelly, 278–9 and Prior, 52.

70 **But** except, unless, on the other hand (Abbott, 121)

72 **wife** Historically, Clarence's wife Isabel was dead in 1476, before the time in which this scene is set.

73, 82 ***prithee, between** Honigmann argues that F's 'prithee' (cf. 117, 2.1.97, 2.4.26, 31) represents a general F 'prejudice' ('Variants', 194). Jackson suggests that it goes against Shakespeare's own pre-1600 preference for 'pray thee' but reflects his post-1600 orthography ('Copy', 354). Jackson also maintains that Qq's 'atypical' preference for 'betwixt' over 'between' suggests their 'lesser authority' ('Two', 189).

74 **My . . . heavy** Shaheen compares Jesus's pronouncement – 'My soule is heauy' – as he watches and prays, aware that betrayal and death are at hand, and rebukes his disciples for falling asleep (Matthew, 26.38, 40–6).

heavy sorrowful, grieved, despondent
fain gladly

75.1 **BRAKENBURY** On the play's ahistorical association of Brakenbury with Clarence's death, see 1.1.41n. Brakenbury does appear (with his keys) as a figure whose resistance must be overcome in the murder of the princes as depicted by More, Hall, Holinshed, *Mirror* and *True Tragedy*.

76–83 *Hammond finds it 'odd' that Brakenbury should speak this monologue with the Keeper present. Marshall suggests Brakenbury pauses at some distance from Clarence to contemplate his plight. Perhaps the Keeper has already moved to *sit by* Clarence as he has been asked to do (73). Brakenbury's meditation on princes and outward ceremony echoes Henry VI's laments about the oppressive life and troubled sleep of monarchs (*3H6* 2.5.41–54) and anticipates Henry V's similar utterance (*H5* 4.1.234–82); all three stand at odds with the perspective of the ordinary sentinel of *1H6* 2.1.5–7. On the monologue's disconnection from its dramatic occasion, see Clemen (78); on its eight-line *strambotto* form and its subject shared with Wyatt's 'Stand whoso list upon the slipper toppe', see

73] *F;* I pray thee gentle keeper stay by me *Qq* 75.1] *F; not in Qq* 76 SP] *F; not in Qq* breaks] *F, Q2–6;* breake *Q1*

Makes the night morning, and the noontide night.
Princes have but their titles for their glories,
An outward honour for an inward toil;
And for unfelt imaginations
They often feel a world of restless cares,
So that between their titles and low name
There's nothing differs but the outward fame.

Enter two Murderers.

1 MURDERER Ho, who's here?

Jones (*Origins*, 194). Clarence evokes the 'careful crowne' in *Mirror*. This speech furnishes two of the play's five entries in *Englands Parnassus* (Allott, 1401, 1551).

76–7 See Job, 17.11–12: 'My dayes are past, and my counsailes and thoughtes of my heart are vanished away, Chaunging the night into day, and the light approching into darkenesse.'

76 **breaks** interrupts
seasons right, proper, due or appointed times (*OED sb.* II 14)
reposing hours proper time for resting

78 **but** only

79 an external reward that is the only consolation for mental labour and care

80 **unfelt imaginations** i.e. non-existent pleasures that others (wrongly) imagine princes to enjoy

82–3 Cf. 1.3.82–3, 106–9.

82 **low name** the undistinguished reputation of the common person

84–end *There is more difference between Qq and F from here to the end of 1.4 than in most of the rest of the text. Aside from possible revision of F to avoid prosecution for profanity under the Statute of 1606 (e.g. the deletion of 'In God's name' from 85 or 'Zounds' from 125, and the omissions at 188–9; see p. 457), the reasons for divergence are unclear; nor are such excisions consistent, since 'In God's name' appears in Qq and F at 162. Clemen (79–80) argues that the contrast between the Murderers as 'clownish ruffians' (in their prose dialogue) and as 'eloquent accusers . . . using language and scriptural references quite out of character' suggests that the two parts were not conceived as a unit. However, the gravity of their undertaking – signalled by reference to *thunder* (166) and the claim, 'My voice is now the King's' (167) – renders their role awful in its seriousness for early modern political theology. The dramatic rhythm of this extended delay, in which the audience knows what is going to happen, or thinks that it knows, but must endure a protracted verbal exchange, is typical of the play (cf. Richard and Anne in 1.2, Richard and Queen Elizabeth in 4.4).

84+ SP MURDERER The designations 'murderers' (F) and 'executioners' (Qq) are discussed in *3H6* when Richard comes to slay Henry VI. To Richard's question – 'Think'st thou I am an executioner?' – King Henry replies: 'If murdering innocents be executing, / Why then, thou art an executioner' (5.6.30–3).

80 imaginations] *F;* imagination *Qq* 82 between] *F;* betwixt *Qq* their] *F, Q1–2;* your *Q3–6* name] *F;* names *Qq* 83.1] *F; The murtherers enter. Qq* 84] *F; not in Qq* 85 SP] *F; not in Qq* What . . . fellow?] *F;* In Gods name what are you, *Qq* cam'st thou] *F;* came you *Qq*

BRAKENBURY
What wouldst thou, fellow? And how cam'st thou hither?
2 MURDERER I would speak with Clarence, and I came hither on my legs.
BRAKENBURY What, so brief?
1 MURDERER 'Tis better, sir, than to be tedious. – Let him see our commission, and talk no more.
[*Brakenbury*] *reads.*
BRAKENBURY
I am in this commanded to deliver
The noble Duke of Clarence to your hands.
I will not reason what is meant hereby
Because I will be guiltless from the meaning.
There lies the Duke asleep, and there the keys.

85–7 Cf. Dent, L191.
85 *Qq anticipate Qq, F 162 (Greg, *Problem*, 83). Cf. *R2* 5.5.69, where the imprisoned King Richard quizzes the groom: 'What art thou, and how comest thou hither . . . ?'
how i.e. by whose permission
86 SP *Many editors since Malone allocate this speech to 1 Murderer and 89 to 2 Murderer. This might make sense, since the speaker of 84 is 1 Murderer. However, the passage could be choric, and its speakers interchangeable (Hammond); alternatively, the entrance sequence may be either physically confusing, with the Second Murderer actually first to approach Brakenbury, and/or vocally clamorous. Some claim the First Murderer's greater ferocity (Clarke, *Characters*, 464; Smidt, *Impostors*, 49; Lull), but the Second Murderer assumes an active, leading role at 145–51.
93–5 Cf. 'The keyes he rendered, but partaker would not be / Of that flagitious facte' (*Mirror*, 'Richard, Duke of Gloucester', 85–6).
93 **reason** question, discuss, consider (*OED v.* 4a)
94 **will be** desire to be (Abbott, 319)
guiltless from innocent of; attempting to remain *guiltless* by refusing to interpret would be futile, for 'not only he is a murtherer & a Homicide before God who slayeth or killeth, a Man with materiall sword, but he also who may preuent the same, and will not. And not onely, he is guiltie of haynous transgression that committeth any euill really, but also he who consenteth to it as he doth, who holdeth his peace, or he who by any means might auoid it, and either for negligence wil not, or for feare of the world dare not' (Stubbes, sig. ¶3r).
95 **there the keys** The keys are possibly left lying or now tossed at the feet of the intruders. Such a transfer, which removes Brakenbury even further

86 SP] *F (2. Mur.); Execu. Qq* 88 What] *F;* Yea, are you *(*ye *Q3–6) Qq* 89 SP] *F (*1.*); 2 Exe. Qq* 'Tis better, sir] *F;* O sir, it is better *Qq* than to be] *F;* to be briefe then *Q1–2;* be briefe then *Q3–6* 89–90 Let him see] *F;* Shew him *Qq* 90 and] *F; not in Qq* SD] *F (Reads); He readeth it. Qq* 93 hereby] *F, Q1–2;* thereby *Q3–6* 94 from] *F;* of *Qq* 95] *F;* Here are the keies, there sits the Duke a sleepe *Qq*

I'll to the King, and signify to him
That thus I have resigned to you my charge.

1 MURDERER You may, sir; 'tis a point of wisdom. Fare you well. *Exeunt* [*Brakenbury and Keeper*].

2 MURDERER What, shall we stab him as he sleeps?

1 MURDERER No. He'll say 'twas done cowardly, when he wakes.

2 MURDERER Why, he shall never wake until the great Judgement Day.

1 MURDERER Why, then he'll say we stabbed him sleeping.

2 MURDERER The urging of that word 'Judgement' hath bred a kind of remorse in me.

1 MURDERER What? Art thou afraid?

2 MURDERER Not to kill him, having a warrant, but to be damned for killing him, from the which no warrant can defend me.

1 MURDERER I thought thou hadst been resolute.

from appearance of agency, would be in keeping with the general displacement of guilt that characters strive for (see 2.1.57n. and pp. 17, 63). Qq's 'here' implies handing over the keys; cf. 'here with teares I deliuer you the keyes, and so farwell maister Terrell' (*True Tragedy*, 1204).

100 ***we** Many editors follow Q1–2 and make this line a personal expression of individual misgiving; however, F, Q3–6's 'we' plausibly expresses hesitation about a collective enterprise.

103–4 **great Judgement Day** referring to the Christian belief in a final reckoning when all souls will be judged by God; see Jude, 6 ('the iudgement of the great Day') and cf. 3.1.78, 5.1.12. The exchange that follows may be a comic version of contemporary theological dialogue (Rozett, 255); cf. Perkins, *Treatise*, fols 107^{r}–114^{v}.

107 **urging** prompting, strong incitement

108 **remorse** either pity for the victim or a more precise theological term meaning deep regret and repentance for a sinful undertaking (*OED* 2a, 3a)

113–14 *Smidt believes Qq omission is deliberate, and 114 out of 'character' (*Impostors*, 108). For similar wavering

96] *F;* Ile to his Maiesty, and certifie his Grace *Qq* 97 to . . . charge] *F;* my charge *(*place *Q3–6)* to you *Qq* 98–159] *prose Pope; Qq line as verse; F lines 98–9, 110–12, 117–19, 133–6 as verse, otherwise prose* 98+ SP] *F (*1 *until 278); Exe. Qq* 98–9] *F lines* wisedome: / well. / 98 You . . . 'tis] *F;* Doe so, it is *Qq* 98–9 Fare you well.] *F; not in Qq* 99 SD] *Evans (subst.); Exit. after 97 F; not in Qq* 100+ SP] *F (2 until 275), Qq (2)* 100 we] *F, Q3–6;* I *Q1–2* 101 He'll] *F;* then he will *Qq* 103 Why] *F;* When he wakes, / Why foole *Qq* until the great] *F;* till the *Qq* 105 he'll] *F;* he will *Qq* 110–12] *prose Pope; F lines* Warrant, / which / me. / ; *Qq line* dãnd / vs. / 110 warrant] *F;* warrant for it *Qq* 111–12 the which . . . me] *F;* which . . . vs *Qq* 113–14] *F; not in Qq*

2 MURDERER So I am, to let him live.

1 MURDERER I'll back to the Duke of Gloucester and tell him so.

2 MURDERER Nay, I prithee stay a little. I hope this passionate humour of mine will change. It was wont to hold me but while one tells twenty.

1 MURDERER How dost thou feel thyself now?

2 MURDERER [Q]Faith,[Q] some certain dregs of conscience are yet within me.

1 MURDERER Remember our reward when the deed's done.

2 MURDERER Zounds, he dies! I had forgot the reward.

1 MURDERER Where's thy conscience now?

2 MURDERER O, in the Duke of Gloucester's purse.

1 MURDERER When he opens his purse to give us our reward, thy conscience flies out.

2 MURDERER 'Tis no matter; let it go. There's few or none will entertain it.

and invocation of 'resolution', see *True Tragedy*, 1294–1301; cf. 1211. For resolution see also 1.3.339n.

118 **passionate humour** compassionate (*OED* 5b, citing this line) mood
wont accustomed

119 **tells** counts (*OED v.* B II 21a); Wells and Taylor, Davison and Jowett add indications that the Murderers pause. However, one can imagine effects that involve virtually no pause at all. It might seem unlikely that the two would actually observe Wells and Taylor's '*He counts to twenty*', but Terry Hands's 1970 production had the count run to twenty and resume with 'twenty-one, twenty-two, twenty-three' after 122 (Hankey, 126).

121 ***Faith** 'Faith' may have been excised from F along with 'Zounds' (125, 143), but 'Faith' was a much milder oath. Bishop Cooper claims '*by my faith* signifieth no more, but *in very trueth, bona fide, in trueth, assuredly*' (Cooper, 62). 'In faith' occurs throughout More's account (e.g. *CW*2, 19, 30, 35). F leaves variants of 'faith' or 'in/by/on my faith' or 'good faith' intact elsewhere (e.g. 2.4.16, 23; 3.2.114; 4.4.176), but correction for oaths is uneven (see 84–end n.), and other offensive phrasing in 1.4 may have prompted cuts here.
dregs small remnant, residue

125, 143 **Zounds** contraction of 'God's wounds!', referring to Christ's bodily sufferings during the crucifixion; a strong oath, definitely covered by the prohibition of 1606 (see 84–end n.).

131 **entertain** receive, show hospitality to, as a guest (*OED v.* 13); or employ (cf. 1.2.259)

115 I'll] *F; not in Qq* and] *F; not in Qq* 117–19] *prose Pope; F lines* little: / change, / twenty. / ; *Qq line* will / xx. / 117 Nay, I prithee . . . little] *F;* I pray thee . . . while *Qq* 117–18 this . . . mine] *F;* my holy humor *Qq* 118–19 It was . . . tells twenty] *F;* twas . . . would tel xx *Qq* 123 deed's] *F;* deede is *Qq* 125 Zounds] *Qq;* Come *F* 126 Where's] *F;* Where is *Qq* 127 O,] *F; not in Qq* 128 When] *F;* So when *Qq* 130 'Tis no matter] *F; not in Qq* let it] *F, Q1, 3–6;* Let vs *Q2*

1 MURDERER What if it come to thee again?

2 MURDERER I'll not meddle with it; it makes a man a coward: a man cannot steal but it accuseth him; a man cannot swear but it checks him; a man cannot lie with his neighbour's wife but it detects him. 'Tis a blushing, shamefaced spirit that mutinies in a man's bosom. It fills a man full of obstacles. It made me once restore a purse of gold that by chance I found. It beggars any man that keeps it. It is turned out of towns and cities for a dangerous thing, and every man that means to live well endeavours to trust to himself, and live without it.

1 MURDERER [Q]Zounds,[Q] 'tis even now at my elbow, persuading me not to kill the Duke.

2 MURDERER Take the devil in thy mind, and believe

133–4 **it makes . . . coward** Cf. Richard's lonely panic at his affliction by *coward conscience* (5.3.179) and his hollow boast, 'Conscience is but a word that cowards use' (5.3.309).

134–6 Relevant Commandments forbid stealing, taking the name of the Lord in vain and adultery; see Exodus, 20.3–17.

135–6 **lie . . . wife** Possibly derived from the *BCP* Commination: 'Cursed is he that lieth with his neighbour's wife' (Noble, 133); cf. 196n.

137 ***shamefaced** F's word arose as an 'etymological misinterpretation' of Qq's term 'shamefast', meaning 'restrained by shame', abashed or ashamed (*OED* shamefast). Henry VI is called 'shamefac'd' in F's *3H6* (4.8.52; cf. 'shamefast' in its octavo form, *The Tragedy of Richard, Duke of York*). The obvious facial reference in *blushing* prompts Jowett's Q-based edition to accept F's term.

139 **beggars** reduces to beggary

140 **keeps** either retains for employment (*OED v.* 20; cf. *MW* 1.2.256), a sense which continues the personification of *entertain* (131); or cares for, regards (*OED v.* 9c). Langland writes of conscience as a counsellor to be kept, i.e. regarded (*Piers Plowman: The A Version*, ed. George Kane (1988), *Passus* iv, 156).

140–1 **turned out . . . for** thrown out . . . as

143 **at my elbow** i.e. close by (*OED* elbow *sb.* 4a); cf. Dent, D243.1: 'The devil is at one's elbow.'

145–6 **Take . . . not** A difficult phrase: either, apprehend (*OED* take *v.* B II 2a) or attack (see 152) the devil (who appears diabolical from the Murderer's inverted perspective because he counsels mercy) and do not credit his advice; or, conversely, mentally accept the devil (who is, because diabolical, against mercy) and, following the

132 What] *F;* How *Qq* 133–6 I'll . . . him;] *prose Pope; F lines* Coward: / cannot / his / *; Qq line* thing, / steale, / him: / detects / 133 it; it] *F;* it, it is a dangerous thing, / It *Qq* 134–5 a man cannot swear] *F;* he cannot sweare *Q1–2;* he cannot steale *Q3–6* 135 a man cannot lie] *F;* He cannot lie *Qq* 136 'Tis] *F;* It is *Qq* 137 shamefaced] *F (*shamefac'd*), Q1, 3, 6 (*shamefast*), Q2, 4–5 (*shamfast*)* 138 a man] *F;* one *Qq* 139 purse] *F, Q1–2;* piece *Q3–6* by chance] *F; not in Qq* 140 of] *F;* of all *Qq* 142 trust to] *F, Q2–6;* trust to / To *Q1* live] *F;* to liue *Qq* 143 'tis] *F;* it is *Qq*

him not. He would insinuate with thee but to make thee sigh.

1 MURDERER I am strong-framed; he cannot prevail with me.

2 MURDERER Spoke like a tall man that respects thy reputation. Come, shall we fall to work?

1 MURDERER Take him on the costard with the hilts of thy sword, and then throw him into the malmsey butt in the next room.

2 MURDERER O excellent device! And make a sop of him.

1 MURDERER Soft, he wakes.

devil, reject the advice of *conscience* (i.e. *him*) which pleads for mercy. For a case resembling the confusion of values in the first reading, cf. Launcelot Gobbo's internal debate (*MV* 2.2).

146 **insinuate** ingratiate himself

146–7 **make thee sigh** i.e. with unhappiness

148 **strong-framed** Qq's 'strong in fraud' sounds like a perversion of biblical 'strong in fayth' (Romans, 4.20). Although both versions suggest misplaced confidence, they carry different implications. F's speaker suggests misplaced faith in physical resources when spiritual resources are required; Qq's speaker presumes that he is experienced enough in cunning practices to outwit the devil. F's speaker seems marginally less intelligent, since no material strength can claim superiority in its own right to demonic powers, let alone to those of the prince of demons, but stories about outwitting the devil are many.

150 **tall** brave, stout (*OED* I 3); 'like a tall man' carries unsophisticated, possibly oafish or rustic overtones (cf. *RJ* 2.4.31).

152 **Take** strike (*OED v.* B II 5a)
costard head (applied humorously: *OED sb.* 2a); literally, a large apple
hilts hilt

153–4 ***throw . . . room** Cf. *3H6* 5.6.92, where Richard contemptuously addresses the murdered Henry VI: 'I'll throw thy body in another room'. Qq's 'chop' (also at 269) meaning 'to thrust with sudden force' (*OED v.*[1] 7a) occurs nowhere else in Shakespeare with this sense.

153 **malmsey butt** barrel of strong, sweet wine; More has Clarence 'attainted . . . by parliament and iudged to the death, and therupon hastely drouned in a Butte of Malmesey' (*CW*2, 7). Similar details appear in Mancini (63, 111n.) and others.

155 **device** project, scheme (*OED* 6)
sop cake or bread soaked in wine (*OED sb.*[1] 1; see 2d, citing this line)

157 **Soft** Cf. 1.3.338n.

146 but] *F; not in Qq* 148 I am strong-framed] *F (*strong fram'd*), hyphen Capell;* Tut, I am strong in fraud *Qq* 149 me.] *F;* me, / I warrant thee. *Qq* 150 Spoke] *F, Q1–3;* Soode *Q4;* Stood *Q5–6* man . . . thy] *F;* fellow . . . his *Qq* 151 fall to work?] *F;* to this geere. *Qq* 152 on] *F;* ouer *Qq* 153 thy] *F, Q1–2;* my *Q3–6* throw him into] *F;* we wil chop him in *Qq* malmsey butt] *F (*Malmesy-Butte*), Q1–2 (*malmsey But*), Q3–6 (*Malmesy-but*);* Malmesy, but *Q7–8* 155 And make] *F;* make *Qq* sop] *F, Q1–2; Q4–6 (*soppe*);* scoope *Q3* 157] *F;* Harke he stirs, shall I strike. *Qq*

2 MURDERER Strike!

1 MURDERER No, we'll reason with him.

CLARENCE
Where art thou, keeper? Give me a cup of wine.

2 MURDERER
You shall have wine enough, my lord, anon.

CLARENCE
In God's name, what art thou?

1 MURDERER A man, as you are.

CLARENCE But not as I am, royal.

1 MURDERER Nor you as we are, loyal.

CLARENCE
Thy voice is thunder, but thy looks are humble.

1 MURDERER
My voice is now the King's, my looks mine own.

CLARENCE
How darkly, and how deadly dost thou speak!
Your eyes do menace me. Why look you pale?
Who sent you hither? Wherefore do you come?

2 MURDERER To, to, to –

CLARENCE To murder me?

159 Contrast the Murderer's thrice-iterated rejection of talking at 1.3.349–51.

160, 161 **thou, You** As a social superior, Clarence consistently employs 'thou' to inferiors. His *you* (169) is a plural. As the scene continues, the Murderers change from the respectful 'you' to forms of 'thou' expressing condemnation (see 200). At 231 they shift back to 'you' forms (Abbott, 232); cf. 196, 231.

161 **anon** soon

166–9 *humble* looks and *pale* complexion seem at odds with menacing eyes (169), since *pale* often denotes feebleness, fearfulness (*OED a.* 3; cf. *H5* 2.0.14), as in *LLL* 1.2.97: 'fears by pale white shown'. But *humble* could mean low in status, and the Murderers might exhibit bold authority, by virtue of their regal commission, along with a socially appropriate timorousness that sits uneasily with that authority.

168 **darkly** in a gloomy, frowning, ominous manner

170 **Wherefore** why

158] *F; not in Qq* 159 SP] *F;* 2 *Qq* we'll] *F;* first lets *Qq* him.] *F, Q1–2;* him. *Cla. awaketh. Q3–6* 161 SP] *F;* 1 *Qq* 163 SP] *F;* 2 *Qq* 165 SP] *F, Q5–6;* 2 *Q1–4* 167 SP] *F;* 2 *Qq* 168 speak] *F, Q1–2, 5–6;* spake *Q3–4* 169] *F; not in Qq* 170] *F;* Tell me who are you, wherefore come you hither? *Qq* 171 SP] *F; Am. Qq*

BOTH Ay, ay.

CLARENCE

You scarcely have the hearts to tell me so,
And therefore cannot have the hearts to do it.
Wherein, my friends, have I offended you?

1 MURDERER

Offended us you have not, but the King.

CLARENCE

I shall be reconciled to him again.

2 MURDERER

Never, my lord; therefore prepare to die.

CLARENCE

Are you drawn forth among a world of men
To slay the innocent? What is my offence?
Where is the evidence that doth accuse me?
What lawful quest have given their verdict up
Unto the frowning judge? Or who pronounced
The bitter sentence of poor Clarence' death?
Before I be convict by course of law,
To threaten me with death is most unlawful.
I charge you, as you hope to have redemption,
[Q]By Christ's dear blood, shed for our grievous sins,[Q]

180–7 This passage shares a general point with *Mirror*'s Clarence, who claims to have been 'Imprisoned first, accused without cause, / And doen to death, no proces had by lawes' ('Clarence', 167–8). *Mirror* also shares many legal terms: offence, accuse, quest, verdict and pronounced ('Clarence', 350–6).

180 **drawn forth** singled out, chosen **world** vast quantity (*OED sb.* IV 19a); cf. *LLL* 5.2.353.

183 **quest** inquiry, body of jurors (*OED sb.*[1] 1, 2); *Mirror*'s Clarence is subjected to a covert 'quest' just before being murdered ('Clarence', 351–7).

186 **convict** convicted; cf. Abbott, 342.

188 **charge** order

188–9 ***to . . . sins** Qq's references to Christ might fall under the 1606 statute (see 84–end n. and p. 457). A similar reference to Christian redemption is left untouched in *MM* 2.2.78–82, but censorship was inconsistent. The generally ironic treatment of religion in *Richard III* may have occasioned particularly close scrutiny (Birch, 199–200).

173 SP] *F, Qq (Am.)* Ay, ay.] *F;* I. *Qq* 174 hearts] *F, Q1–5;* heart *Q6* 180 drawn . . . among] *F;* cald . . . from out *Qq* 182 is . . . that doth] *F;* are . . . that doe *Q1–2;* are . . . to *Q3–6* 185–6 death? . . . law,] *F2;* death, . . . law? *F, Qq* 188 to have redemption] *Qq;* for any goodnesse *F*

That you depart and lay no hands on me.
The deed you undertake is damnable.

1 MURDERER
What we will do, we do upon command.

2 MURDERER
And he that hath commanded is our king.

CLARENCE
Erroneous vassals, the great King of kings
Hath in the table of His law commanded
That thou shalt do no murder. Will you then
Spurn at His edict, and fulfil a man's?
Take heed, for He holds vengeance in His hand,
To hurl upon their heads that break His law.

2 MURDERER
And that same vengeance doth He hurl on thee
For false forswearing and for murder too.
Thou didst receive the sacrament to fight
In quarrel of the house of Lancaster.

194–9 The *Sermon on Obedience* maintains that 'we may not obey kings, Magistrates, or any other (though they bee our owne fathers) if they would commande vs to doe any thing contrary to Gods commandements' (*Homilies*, 74).

194 **vassals** underlings, servants, but with an insulting sense, as abject persons or slaves (*OED sb.* 2b, 3); the Murderers err in considering themselves primarily as subjects to King Edward (rather than to God).
King of kings God or Christ; the phrasing is biblical (Revelation, 17.14), see Noble, 133–4.

195 **table . . . law** the Ten Commandments, divinely engraved upon tables or tablets of stone (Exodus, 20.3–17, 32.15–16)

196 **thou . . . you** Clarence shifts from the biblical diction of the Commandments ('Thou shalt not . . . ') to the plural *you* in directly addressing the Murderers. Qq do not register the shift from allusion to direct address. The phrase *do no murder* (for the biblical 'kill' of the Commandment) follows *BCP*: 'Thou shalt do no murder' (Noble, 133).

197 **Spurn at** reject with contempt or disdain (*OED v.*[1] II 6)

201 **false forswearing** perjury, breaking of a sworn promise

202–3 **receive . . . Lancaster** i.e. take an oath upon partaking of the holy Eucharist to fight for the cause of Henry VI; cf. 5.5.18.

193 our] *F;* the *Qq* 194 vassals] *F;* Vassaile *Qq* 195 the] *F, Q1–2;* his *Q3–6* table] *F;* tables *Qq* 196 murder] *F, Q3–6 (*murther*), Q1–2* Will you] *F;* and wilt thou *Qq* 198 hand] *F;* hands *Qq* 200 hurl] *F;* throw *Qq* 201 murder] *F, Q6 (*murther*), Q1–5* 202–3 sacrament . . . In] *F;* holy sacrament, / To fight in *Qq*

1 MURDERER
And like a traitor to the name of God
Didst break that vow, and with thy treacherous blade
Unrip'st the bowels of thy sovereign's son.

2 MURDERER
Whom thou wast sworn to cherish and defend.

1 MURDERER
How canst thou urge God's dreadful law to us
When thou hast broke it in such dear degree?

CLARENCE
Alas! For whose sake did I that ill deed?
For Edward, for my brother, for his sake.
He sends you not to murder me for this,
For in that sin he is as deep as I.
If God will be avenged for the deed,
O, know you yet, He doth it publicly;
Take not the quarrel from His powerful arm.
He needs no indirect or lawless course

206 **son** Prince Edward, son of Henry VI

208–9 Cf. Romans, 2.23: 'Thou that makest thy boast of the lawe, through breakyng the lawe dishonorest God' (Noble). This verse, together with Romans, 2.21, strongly denounces the hypocrisy (prominent throughout this play) of lecturing others about their wrongs while remaining guilty oneself.

209 **in . . . degree** to such dire extent

214–18 This passage recounts the Christian objection to personal vengeance. For God's exclusive right of vengeance, see Deuteronomy, 32.15–43 and Romans, 12.19: 'auenge not your selues, but rather geue place vnto Wrath: for it is written, Vengeaunce is myne, I wyll repay sayth the Lorde.' Calvin explains: 'it belongs not to us to revenge, except we would assume to ourselves the office of God' (*Commentaries*, 475; cf. *Homilies*, 69–71). Campbell (310–12) calls this 'Shakespeare's most detailed statement of the whole Elizabethan philosophy of vengeance', with its three related concerns: God's vengeance for sin, public vengeance, executed by the ruler or his representatives as agents of God's justice and punishment, and private vengeance, which usurps divine authority and is therefore forbidden.

216 **quarrel** i.e. settlement of the issue, punishment of the deed
His powerful arm For God's actions characterized in terms of strength of hand and arm, see Jeremiah, 21.5; Ezekiel, 20.33.

217 **indirect** devious, underhanded

207 wast] *F;* wert *Qq* 209 such] *F;* so *Qq* 212 He] *F;* Why sirs, he *Qq* you] *F;* ye *Qq* murder] *F (*murther*), Qq* 213 that] *F;* this *Qq* 214 avenged for the] *F;* reuenged for this *Qq* 215] *F; not in Qq* 217 or] *F;* nor *Qq* lawless] *F, Q1;* lawfull *Q2–6*

To cut off those that have offended Him.

1 MURDERER

Who made thee then a bloody minister,
When gallant-springing, brave Plantagenet,
That princely novice, was struck dead by thee?

CLARENCE

My brother's love, the devil and my rage.

1 MURDERER

Thy brother's love, our duty and thy faults
Provoke us hither now to slaughter thee.

CLARENCE

If you do love my brother, hate not me.
I am his brother, and I love him well.
If you are hired for meed, go back again,
And I will send you to my brother Gloucester,
Who shall reward you better for my life
Than Edward will for tidings of my death.

218 **cut off** bring to an end or put to death (suddenly or prematurely) (*OED* cut *v.* 56c, d)

219 **minister** agent (*OED sb.* 2a); cf. 1.2.46 and 5.3.113, which cast Richard and Richmond as, respectively, 'ministers' of hell and heaven. Shaheen (83) maintains a contrast between a self-appointed *bloody minister* and a duly appointed 'minister' of God. The Murderers may be now, as Clarence was in the past, agents of providential justice (Prior, 47). In a well-known passage concerning subjection to earthly authorities, Saint Paul characterizes the ruler as a minister for aid and a scourge for punishment: 'For he is the minister of God for thy wealth. But yf thou do euyll, feare; for he beareth not the sworde in vayne, for he is the minister of God, reuenger of wrath on hym that doth euyll' (Romans, 13.4).

220 **gallant-springing** filled with admirable youthful vigour like a new seedling; cf. youthful Rutland as a tender branch that did 'sweetly spring' (*3H6* 2.6.46–50).

Plantagenet Prince Edward

221 **novice** beginner; Prince Edward is knighted by Henry VI in *3H6* 2.2.58–66.

223 ***our duty** F continues the Murderers' strain of self-righteousness. If Qq's 'the diuell' is not merely taken over by a compositor from the previous line, it could constitute a sarcastic echo.

227 **meed** profit, reward (*OED sb.* 1) or specifically corrupt gain or bribe (*OED sb.* 2)

220 gallant-springing] *F, Q1 (*gallant springing*), hyphen Pope;* gallant spring *Q2–6* 221 That] *F, Q1–5;* The *Q6* struck] *F;* stroke *Q1;* strooke *Q2–6* 223 our duty . . . faults] *F;* the diuell . . . fault *Qq* 224 Provoke . . . slaughter] *F;* Haue brought . . . murder *(*murther *Q3–6) Qq* 225 If . . . my] *F;* Oh if you loue my *Q1–3;* Oh, if you loue *Q4–6* 227 are] *F;* be *Qq* meed] *F, Q1;* neede *Q2–6 subst.* 229 shall] *F;* will *Qq*

2 MURDERER
You are deceived; your brother Gloucester hates you.

CLARENCE
O no, he loves me, and he holds me dear.
Go you to him from me.

1 MURDERER
Ay, so we will.

CLARENCE
Tell him, when that our princely father York
Blessed his three sons with his victorious arm,
[Q]And charged us from his soul to love each other,[Q]
He little thought of this divided friendship.
Bid Gloucester think on this, and he will weep.

1 MURDERER
Ay, millstones, as he lessoned us to weep.

CLARENCE
O, do not slander him, for he is kind.

1 MURDERER
Right, as snow in harvest. Come, you deceive yourself.
'Tis he that sends us to destroy you here.

CLARENCE
It cannot be, for he bewept my fortune,

231–69 ***you** F's Murderers shift their pronouns for the balance of these exchanges, again employing 'you' as in 161–77. Qq's Murderers continue to use 'thee' forms consistently to Clarence.

236 *Most editors include this Qq line as essential to the meaning of the line which follows in F. The stress on love accords with the extended argument (222–52) concerning brotherly love and kindness. The likely explanation for absence from F would be compositorial omission. The fatherly blessing does not appear in *3H6*.

239 **millstones** See 1.3.352n.
lessoned instructed

240 **kind** kindly, good-natured; the First Murderer takes the word to mean 'natural'.

241 **as . . . harvest** i.e. as unnatural (and destructive) as snow at harvest season (cf. Dent, S590)

241, 242 **you** On the pronominal shift here, see 231–69n.

243–4 **bewept . . . hugged** Hammond, following Marshall, takes these lines to direct the staging of 1.1.112, but Furness suggests Clarence seeks

231] *Qq; F lines* deceiu'd / you. / 233] *Steevens; F, Qq line* me. / will. / SP] *F; Am. Qq* 238 on] *F, Q6;* of *Q1–5* 239 SP] *F; Am. Qq* 241] *Qq; F lines* Haruest: / selfe, / Right,] *F, Q3–6;* Right *Q1–2* Come . . . yourself] *F;* thou deceiu'st thy selfe *Qq* 242 that sends] *F;* hath sent *Q1;* that sent *Q2–6* to . . . here] *F;* hither now to slaughter thee *Q1;* hither now to murder *(*murther *Q6)* thee *Q2–6* 243 he . . . fortune] *F;* when I parted with him *Qq*

And hugged me in his arms, and swore with sobs
That he would labour my delivery.

1 MURDERER
Why so he doth, when he delivers you
From this earth's thraldom to the joys of heaven.

2 MURDERER
Make peace with God, for you must die, my lord.

CLARENCE
Have you that holy feeling in your souls
To counsel me to make my peace with God,
And are you yet to your own souls so blind
That you will war with God by murdering me?
O sirs, consider: they that set you on
To do this deed will hate you for the deed.

2 MURDERER
What shall we do?

CLARENCE Relent, and save your souls.

through desperate overstatement to convince the Murderers of a bond between his brother and himself.

245 **labour my delivery** The same phrase appears in *The Spanish Tragedy* (Kyd, 3.7.33).

246–7 Cf. Richard's joking intention to benefit Clarence by sending him to heaven in the first scene (1.1.118–19) and that scene's various uses of 'deliver'.

247 **thraldom** bondage, servitude

249–55 **Have . . . do?** This is Clarence's first clear-cut appeal to conscience, and though it appears to have an effect, it ironically eventuates in a death blow (Wiggins, 119).

253 ***O** For another variation between Qq's 'Ah' and F's 'O', see 4.4.31, but cf. 66, 1.3.11, 2.1.134, 2.2.27 for a few of the many changes in the opposite direction; Honigmann notes the play's reversal of general F usage ('Variants', 197).

253–4 **they . . . deed** Cf. Dent, K64: 'A King (prince) loves the treason but hates the traitor,' and *R2* 5.6.38.

255–61 *The discrepancy between F and Qq, along with F's apparent digressiveness, has elicited editorial comment since Johnson's edition and Thomas Tyrwhitt's suggested re-arrangement in *Observations and Conjectures upon Some Passages of Shakespeare* (1766) (Var; Walton, *Quarto*, 147; Wilson). This edition retains Clarence's extended plea for sympathy in F's seemingly awkward position – i.e. between his injunction ('Relent, and save your souls') and First Murderer's response ('Relent? No. 'Tis cowardly and womanish.').

244 And] *F;* He *Qq* 246 SP] *F;* 2 *Qq* when . . . you] *F;* now . . . thee *Qq* 247 earth's] *F;* worlds *Qq* 248 SP] *F;* 1 *Qq* Make] *F, Q2–6;* Makes *Q1* 249 Have you . . . your souls] *F;* Hast thou . . . thy soule *Qq* 251 are you . . . your own souls] *F;* art thou . . . thy owne soule *Qq* 252 you will] *F;* thou wilt *Qq* by] *F, Q1–2;* for *Q3–6* murdering] *F, Q1 (*murd'ring*), Q2–5 (*murdering*), Q6 (*murthering*)* 253 O] *F;* Ah *Qq* they] *F;* he *Qq* 254 the] *F;* this *Qq* 255] *Steevens; F, Qq line* do? / soules: /

Which of you, if you were a prince's son,
Being pent from liberty, as I am now,
If two such murderers as yourselves came to you,
Would not entreat for life? Ay, you would beg,
Were you in my distress.

1 MURDERER
Relent? No. 'Tis cowardly and womanish.

CLARENCE
Not to relent is beastly, savage, devilish.
[*to 2 Murderer*] My friend, I spy some pity in thy looks.
O, if thine eye be not a flatterer,
Come thou on my side, and entreat for me;
A begging prince, what beggar pities not.

2 MURDERER Look behind you, my lord.

1 MURDERER
Take that, and that! (*Stabs him.*)
If all this will not do,

Marshall has argued for F's sequence: Clarence's 'rapid and passionate appeal' prevents immediate reply and awakens the Murderers' further reflections, so that the First Murderer's response is a hesitant question ('Relent?') followed by a negative decision ('No.'), while the Second Murderer shows – at least to Clarence's eye – outward signs of relenting (Marshall, 108). Thus, Clarence directs 263–6 to the Second Murderer, hoping to build on his display of pity.

255 **Relent** Perhaps a weak substitute for the Christian formula, 'Repent and save your souls' (Rozett, 257).

259 ***Ay** Many editors have thought that F's line requires emendation for grammatical reasons. Theobald offered 'ah!' for 'as'; Wells and Taylor retain 'As', leaving Clarence's sentence incomplete ('As you would beg / Were you in my distress – ').

261 **womanish** For a similar conjunction of *relent*[*ing*] with a gendered (mis)conception, see 4.4.431; cf. Dent, W724.1: 'To fear is womanish.'

264 **flatterer** i.e. one who encourages hope on false or insufficient grounds (*OED* flatter *v.*^{1} 7a)

265 **Come . . . side** Clarence may be asking the Second Murderer to stand next to him in beseeching mercy from the First Murderer, or perhaps simply requesting that he plead on Clarence's behalf.

267 *This highly dramatic line, in which the Second Murderer attempts to warn Clarence, is not in Qq. The last line on Q1's D3^{r} is 266, and the catchword is '1 I' (i.e. 1 MURDERER Ay), which begins the first line on Q1's D3^{v}.

268 *Although 'thus' is an all-purpose marker for staged action (see 4.3.9–10), Qq's 'I thus, and thus' repeats the line which accompanies the murder of

256–60] *F; not in Qq* 259 Ay] *Ard*^{2}*;* as *F;* ah! *Theobald* 261 No] *F; not in Qq* 262 devilish] *F, Q1;* and diuelish *Q2–6* 263 SD] *Sisson* thy] *F, Q1–5;* your *Q6* 264 thine] *F;* thy *Qq* 267] *F; not in Qq* 268] *F;* I thus, and thus: if this wil not serue *Qq* SD] *F after* do; *He stabs him. Qq opp.* serue

I'll drown you in the malmsey butt within. *Exit [with body].*

2 MURDERER

A bloody deed, and desperately dispatched.
How fain, like Pilate, would I wash my hands
Of this most grievous murder.

Enter First Murderer.

1 MURDERER

How now? What mean'st thou that thou help'st me not?
By heaven, the Duke shall know how slack you have been.

2 MURDERER

I would he knew that I had saved his brother.
Take thou the fee, and tell him what I say,
For I repent me that the Duke is slain. *Exit.*

1 MURDERER

So do not I. Go, coward as thou art.
Well, I'll go hide the body in some hole
Till that the Duke give order for his burial.
And when I have my meed, I will away,
For this will out, and then I must not stay. *Exit.*

Horatio in *The Spanish Tragedy* (Kyd, 2.4.56).
If . . . do i.e. if these wounds have not been sufficient to cause death

269 *Q's line is a nearly exact repetition of 153–4.

270 **desperately** recklessly, with utter disregard of risks or consequences (*OED* 4); possibly referring to despair, the spiritual state accompanying rejection of God and usually associated with suicide or a death-wish (see 1.2.84–7, 2.2.36–7, 5.3.120)

271 **fain** gladly
like Pilate see Matthew, 27.24 and Dent, H122; Pontius Pilate's public washing to cleanse himself symbolically of guilt at the sentencing of Jesus was a notorious example of hypocrisy (cf. *R2* 3.1.5–6).

274, 277, 280 **the Duke** As this title shifts its reference from Richard to Clarence and back to Richard, the play anticipates the confusion that accompanies rapid interchanges among proper names elsewhere (see e.g. 4.4.40–6).

275 **would** wish

282 **this will out** This will be discovered (Dent, M1315: 'Murder will out').

269 drown you . . . within] *F;* chop thee . . . in the next roome *Qq* malmsey butt] *F (*Malmesey-But*), Qq (*malmesey But*)* SD] *Malone subst.; Exit. F; not in Qq* 270 dispatched] *F;* performd *Qq* 271 hands] *F;* hand *Qq* 272 murder] *F;* guilty murder done *Qq* 272.1] *F; not in Qq* 273–4] *verse Rowe; prose F;* Why doest thou not helpe me, / By heauens the Duke shall know how slacke thou art *Qq subst.* 274 heaven] *F, Q6;* heauens *Q1–5* 279 Well . . . the] *F;* Now must I hide his *Qq* 280 Till that . . . give] *F;* Vntill . . . take *Qq* 281 will] *F;* must *Qq* 282 then] *F;* here *Qq* SD] *F; Exeunt. Qq*

2.1 *Flourish. Enter* KING [EDWARD] *sick,* QUEEN [ELIZABETH], Lord Marquess DORSET, RIVERS, HASTINGS, CATESBY, BUCKINGHAM.

KING EDWARD

Why, so. Now have I done a good day's work.
You peers, continue this united league.
I every day expect an embassage
From my Redeemer to redeem me hence,
And more in peace my soul shall part to heaven,
Since I have made my friends at peace on earth.
– Hastings and Rivers, take each other's hand;
Dissemble not your hatred. Swear your love.

2.1 location: '*The* COURT' (Pope)

0.1 ***Flourish*** fanfare of horns announcing a person of distinction

sick to '*Enter sick*' frequently entails being led onto the stage (Dessen & Thomson, 198); Edward leaves with 'help' (134).

0.2 *The play names the Queen's brother Anthony Woodeville (1.1.67), but F here creates a second character who is called by his title, Lord Rivers (1.3.37n.), and later a third (2.1.67); see pp. 458–9.

0.3 CATESBY Catesby remains silent in this scene; F includes him here, perhaps as the messenger who has summoned the others to King Edward's presence (1.3.319–20).

3 **embassage** ambassador, messenger, or the message itself

4 **redeem** deliver, liberate from sin and its consequences

5 ***more in** F's 'more to peace' does not sound right, especially with King Edward's promised departure *to heaven*; Qq's 'now in peace' is possible, but editors often follow Rowe's 'more in' or Capell's 'more at'.

***to** Q1–2's 'from' is clearly wrong; corrected copies of Q1 substitute 'to'.

7 ***Hastings and Rivers** Qq correctly name Edward's addressees, given that Dorset makes no reply in the following exchanges and has no evident quarrel with his uncle Rivers. More names Dorset and Hastings as representing the groups needing reconciliation (*CW*2, 10–11).

take . . . hand Edward's gesture ironically recalls Henry VI's similarly futile attempt to unite the factious Warwick and Clarence (*3H6* 4.6.38–9).

8 **Dissemble not** Do not disguise (your hatred) by feigned appearance (of affection).

2.1] *F (Actus Secundus. Scæna Prima.); not in Qq* 0.1–3] *F (Flourish. / Enter the King sicke, the Queene, Lord Marquesse Dorset, Riuers, Hastings, Catesby, Buckingham, Wooduill.); Enter King, Queene, Hastings, Ryuers, Dorcet, &c. Q1–2; Enter King, Queene, Hastings, Riuers, &c. Q3–6* 0.1 EDWARD] *Rowe* 0.2 ELIZABETH] *Malone* 1+ SP] *King. F, Q3–6; Kin. Q1–2* 1 Why . . . I] *F;* So, now I haue *Qq* 5 more in] *Rowe;* now in *Qq;* more to *F;* more at *Capell* to] *F, Q1c (Fo, Bod, Y), Q3–6;* from *Q1u (BL (Huth), Hn), Q2* 6 made] *F;* set *Qq* friends] *F, Q1–5;* friend *Q6* 7 Hastings and Rivers] *Rowe;* Riuers and Hastings *Qq; Dorset* and *Riuers F*

RIVERS

By heaven, my soul is purged from grudging hate,
And with my hand I seal my true heart's love.

HASTINGS

So thrive I, as I truly swear the like.

KING EDWARD

Take heed you dally not before your king,
Lest He that is the supreme King of kings
Confound your hidden falsehood, and award
Either of you to be the other's end.

HASTINGS

So prosper I, as I swear perfect love.

RIVERS

And I, as I love Hastings with my heart.

KING EDWARD

Madam, yourself is not exempt from this;
– Nor you, son Dorset; – Buckingham, nor you.
You have been factious one against the other.
– Wife, love Lord Hastings. Let him kiss your hand,
And what you do, do it unfeignedly.

QUEEN ELIZABETH

There, Hastings, I will never more remember
Our former hatred, so thrive I and mine.
[*Hastings kisses her hand.*]

10 **seal** ratify an agreement by a ceremonial act (*OED v.*[1] I 1c)

11, 16, 24 **So, so** 'on condition of my speaking the truth' (Abbott, 133)

12 **dally** trifle under the guise of serious action; play with mockingly (*OED* 3)

13 **King of kings** See 1.4.194n.

14 **Confound** defeat utterly, destroy, rout (*OED* 1)

14–15 **award . . . end** destine you to destroy one another; 'Euen so doth God punish the wicked one by another' (Mornay, 209), cf. *Ham* 3.4.171–3.

19 ***you, son** Since Dorset is present, and since King Edward speaks by turns to the various nobles, F's 'you, son' appears more likely than Qq's 'your son'.
son i.e. stepson

20 **factious** inclined to form parties, or act for party purposes; seditious (cf. 1.3.127)

9 soul] *F;* heart *Qq* 10 heart's] *F, Q1–5;* hears *Q6* 11 truly] *F, Q1–2; om. Q3–6* 13 Lest] *F;* Least *Qq* 18 is] *F;* are *Qq* from] *F;* in *Qq* 19 you, son] *F subst.;* your son *Qq* 23 There] *F;* Here *Qq* 24 SD] *Bevington*[3]*; Capell (after* There *23)*

KING EDWARD

Dorset, embrace him. – Hastings, love Lord Marquess.

DORSET

This interchange of love, I here protest,
Upon my part shall be inviolable.

HASTINGS

And so swear I. [*They embrace.*]

KING EDWARD

Now, princely Buckingham, seal thou this league
With thy embracements to my wife's allies,
And make me happy in your unity.

BUCKINGHAM

Whenever Buckingham doth turn his hate
Upon your grace, but with all duteous love
Doth cherish you and yours, God punish me
With hate in those where I expect most love.
When I have most need to employ a friend,
And most assured that he is a friend,
Deep, hollow, treacherous and full of guile
Be he unto me. This do I beg of God,
When I am cold in love to you or yours.

[*They*] *embrace.*

KING EDWARD

A pleasing cordial, princely Buckingham,

25 **Lord Marquess** i.e. Dorset

29, 41 **princely Buckingham** Cf. 1.3.279n.

30 **to** of

32–5 *Lines constituting one of Wilson's 'tangles' (see also 1.3.68, 2.2.7, 3.7.132–5). The difficulty may arise from combining two strong, but opposed, asseverations in one sentence (Thompson).

33–4 **but . . . Doth cherish** i.e. instead of . . . cherishing (Abbott, 125)

36 **employ** i.e. use for some purpose

37 **most** i.e. I am most
assured assurèd

38 **Deep** skilled in craft or subtlety (*OED a.* II 17)

39 ***God** F's 'heauen' possibly reflects the Statute of 1606; cf. 1.4.84–end n. For inconsistency of F's changes, see 34.

41 **cordial** medicine, food or beverage which invigorates the heart (*OED sb.* 2)

25] *Rowe*[3]*; F lines* him: / Marquesse. / *; not in Qq* 26 This] *F, Q1;* Thus *Q2–6* 27 inviolable] *F;* vnuiolable *Qq* 28 I] *F;* I my Lord *Qq* SD] *Capell* 30 embracements] *F, Q1–5;* embracement *Q6* 33 Upon your grace] *F;* On you or yours *Qq* 39 God] *Qq;* heauen *F* 40 love] *F;* zeale *Qq* SD] *F; not in Qq* *They*] *Capell*

Is this thy vow unto my sickly heart.
There wanteth now our brother Gloucester here
To make the blessed period of this peace.

Enter RATCLIFFE *and* [RICHARD, Duke of] Gloucester.

BUCKINGHAM
And in good time,
Here comes Sir Richard Ratcliffe and the Duke.

RICHARD
Good morrow to my sovereign King and Queen,
And princely peers, a happy time of day.

KING EDWARD
Happy indeed, as we have spent the day.
Gloucester, we have done deeds of charity,
Made peace of enmity, fair love of hate,
Between these swelling, wrong-incensed peers.

RICHARD
A blessed labour, my most sovereign lord.

43 **wanteth** is needed (Abbott, 293)
44 **blessed** blessèd
period conclusion (*OED* II 5b); cf. Richard's surprise *period* (1.3.237–8).
44.1 *RATCLIFFE Ratcliffe has not been introduced, has no lines here and will not figure in the action until 3.3, so Qq omission here makes sense. However, his prominence among Richard's *bloodsuckers* (3.3.5) makes it difficult to ignore F's inclusion here. More describes him as one of Richard's closest associates: in 'counsel and in thexecucion of such lawles enterprises [i.e. the beheading of Rivers and other lords], as a man y^t had ben long secret w^t him, hauing experience of ye world & a shrewde wit, short & rude in speche, rough & boustiouse of behauiour, bold in mischief, as far from pite as from al fere of god' (*CW2*, 57).
45 'And just at the right moment'; this stagey entry is appropriate for Richard, but Hastings, young York and Brakenbury all enter *in good time* (3.1.24, 95, 4.1.12). The formula is characteristic of Latin New Comedy (RP).
48 **happy . . . day** a simple greeting, like 'Good time of day' (1.1.122)
52 **swelling** inflated with anger (*R2* 1.1.201), pride (*Oth* 2.3.52) or hatred (see 2.2.117)
wrong-incensed incensed by wrongs; mistakenly incensed; incensèd
53 **blessed** blessèd

44 blessed] *F;* perfect *Qq* 44.1] *F (Gloster) after 46; Enter Glocest. Qq opp. 44* 45–6] *F;* And in good time here comes the noble Duke. *Qq* 50 Gloucester] *F;* Brother *Qq* 52 wrong-incensed] *F, Qq (*wrong incensed *subst.), hyphen Rowe*[3] 53 my] *F, Q1–2; om. Q3–6* lord] *F;* liege *Qq*

Among this princely heap, if any here
By false intelligence or wrong surmise
Hold me a foe;
If I unwittingly, or in my rage,
Have aught committed that is hardly borne,
By any in this presence, I desire
To reconcile me to his friendly peace.
'Tis death to me to be at enmity;
I hate it, and desire all good men's love.
– First, madam, I entreat true peace of you,
Which I will purchase with my duteous service;
– Of you, my noble cousin Buckingham,
If ever any grudge were lodged between us;
– Of you and you, Lord Rivers and of Dorset,
That all without desert have frowned on me;
– Dukes, earls, lords, gentlemen; indeed, of all.
I do not know that Englishman alive

54 **heap** multitude (*OED sb.* 3); possibly oxymoronic when modified by *princely*. Simon Russell Beale delivered Richard's line 'with a split second of hesitation before choosing the appropriate collective noun and then hitting its final plosive with just sufficient excess force to draw attention to the brilliant precision of the epithet's implications for Woodville pretensions to royalty' (Smallwood, 359).

55 **false intelligence** misinformation

57 ***unwittingly** Qq give a more easily comprehended sense; however, characters throughout the play (and this scene) shirk blame for decisions and actions, so 'unwillingly' is possible.

58 **hardly borne** i.e. taken amiss, resented (*OED* bear *v.*[1] II 16)

59 **presence** company; cf. 79, 85.

60 **me** myself

64 **purchase** obtain

66 **lodged** harboured, entertained (feelings, thoughts); figuratively, as in the reception of a guest (*OED v.* 2c)

67 *In the light of the confusion about historical identities (see 0.2n.), Qq's phrasing looks like correction; it might also serve Qq's reduction of parts. Qq's 'Gray' is not specifically mentioned in an entry direction. Jowett argues that alternative designations (the title *Dorset* and the family name *Grey*) are used for the same figure in 2.1 and 1.3.

68 **all without desert** altogether without my deserving it

70–3 Citing these lines, Milton's *Eikonoklastes* accuses Charles I of modelling himself on Richard's hypocrisy in affection and religion (Milton, 361).

54 Among] *F;* Amongst *Qq* 56–7] *Malone; one line F, Qq* 57 unwittingly] *Qq;* vnwillingly *F* 59 By] *Qq;* To *F* 60 his] *F, Q1, 3–6;* this *Q2* 63 true] *F, Q1–2; om. Q3–6* 64 will] *F, Q1–5; om. Q6* 67] *F;* Of you Lo: Riuers, and Lord Gray of you, *Q1–4;* Of you my Lord Riuers, and Lord Gray of you *Q5–6* 68 me;] *Qq subst.;* me: / Of you Lord *Wooduill*, and Lord *Scales* of you, *F*

With whom my soul is any jot at odds
More than the infant that is born tonight.
I thank my God for my humility.

QUEEN ELIZABETH

A holy day shall this be kept hereafter.
I would to God all strifes were well compounded.
My sovereign lord, I do beseech your highness
To take our brother Clarence to your grace.

RICHARD

Why, madam, have I offered love for this,
To be so flouted in this royal presence?
Who knows not that the gentle Duke is dead?

They all start.

You do him injury to scorn his corse.

KING EDWARD

Who knows not he is dead? Who knows he is?

QUEEN ELIZABETH

All-seeing heaven, what a world is this?

BUCKINGHAM

Look I so pale, Lord Dorset, as the rest?

DORSET

Ay, my good lord, and no man in the presence
But his red colour hath forsook his cheeks.

70–2 For ironies in Richard's protestations, see R. Watson, 22.

71 **jot** least bit

75 **compounded** settled (*OED v.* II 6a); cf. *TS* 1.2.26.

77 **to your grace** i.e. into your favour

79 **flouted** mocked, insulted (*OED* flout *v.* 1)

81 **scorn his corse** show disrespect to his corpse

82 *Hammond follows Qq, opposing F's attribution to King Edward on the grounds that the line is inconsistent with his being the speaker of 87, but the initial shock expressed here could be consistent with Edward's later, more subdued recognition of his own complicity in the death.

83 **what . . . this?** Cf. *AYL* 2.3.14 and Dent, W899.1.

84 **pale** Cf. 136–7.

85 **the presence** i.e. the King's presence (*OED* 1)

76 lord] *F;* liege *Qq* your] *F, Q1–5;* you *Q6* highness] *F;* Maiesty *Qq* 79 so flouted] *F;* thus scorned *Qq* 80 gentle] *F;* noble *Qq* SD] *F; not in Qq* 82 SP] *F (King.); Ryu. Q1; Riu. Q2; Ri. Q3–6* 82] *Qq; F lines* dead? / is? / 85 man] *F;* one *Qq* the] *F;* this *Qq*

KING EDWARD
Is Clarence dead? The order was reversed.

RICHARD
But he, poor man, by your first order died,
And that a winged Mercury did bear;
Some tardy cripple bare the countermand,
That came too lag to see him buried.
God grant that some, less noble and less loyal,
Nearer in bloody thoughts, and not in blood,
Deserve not worse than wretched Clarence did,
And yet go current from suspicion.

Enter [STANLEY,] Earl of Derby.

STANLEY
[*Kneels.*] A boon, my sovereign, for my service done.

87 **order** More's Edward 'bewailed and sorowfully repented' the death of Clarence (after Parliamentary judgement and at his own command), but did not attempt to rescind the order (*CW2*, 7). The close conjunction of Clarence's death and Edward's (given by Holinshed as 1477 and 1483 respectively), is Shakespeare's invention.

89 **winged Mercury** wingèd; messenger of the gods, often depicted with wings on helmet and feet (cf. 4.3.55)

90 **tardy cripple** perhaps brazenly referring to Richard himself

91 **lag** belatedly (*OED a.* B 1a, citing this line)
buried burièd

92 **some** i.e. the Queen and her relatives

93 i.e. more 'near', more intimate, with violent intentions, and less near than Clarence in blood relationship to King Edward. There is ambiguity about who has *bloody thoughts* here, since Richard could be both accusing the Queen's family of such thoughts and also admitting to his own violent thoughts; they are 'near' to him as a focus of his antagonism and 'near' to him physically at this moment. Cf. *Mac* 2.3.140–1: 'the near in blood, / The nearer bloody'.

95 **go . . . suspicion** are received as genuine (*OED a.* 8), passing as current coin, not counterfeit (*OED a.* 5)
from free from

96–134 When asked for clemency, Hall's King Edward exclaims, 'O infortunate brother, for whose lyfe not one creature woulde make intercession, openly spekyng, and apparauntly meanyng that by the meanes of some of the nobilitie, he was circumuented, and brought to hys confusion' (*Edward IV*, fols l^v–li^r).

96 **boon** favour
service Stanley's request for a *quid pro quo* – a *boon* for *service* rendered – evokes feudal relationships: a tenant

88 man] *F;* soule *Qq* 89 winged] *F, Q2–6;* wingled *Q1* 90 bare] *F;* bore *Qq* 93 and] *F;* but *Qq* 95.1] *F; Enter Darby. Qq subst.* STANLEY] *Theobald subst.* 96+ SP] *Theobald subst.; Der. F; Dar. Qq* 96 SD] *Oxf subst.*

KING EDWARD
I prithee, peace. My soul is full of sorrow.
STANLEY
I will not rise, unless your highness hear me.
KING EDWARD
Then say at once what is it thou requests.
STANLEY
The forfeit, sovereign, of my servant's life,
Who slew today a riotous gentleman
Lately attendant on the Duke of Norfolk.
KING EDWARD
Have I a tongue to doom my brother's death,
And shall that tongue give pardon to a slave?
My brother killed no man; his fault was thought,
And yet his punishment was bitter death.
Who sued to me for him? Who, in my wrath,
Kneeled at my feet and bid me be advised?
Who spoke of brotherhood? Who spoke of love?
Who told me how the poor soul did forsake

or knight would render 'service' in exchange for his lord's favour.

96, 126 SD *Kneels . . . rises* Stanley's lines and the royal responses require that he kneel between his entry and 98. He may rise at 126 when the King appears to grant his demand (*OED* hear *v.* 7a: 'accede to, grant [a request or prayer]').

100 i.e. the cancellation of the death penalty upon my servant

101 **riotous** given to wantonness, revelry or dissolute life (*OED a.* 2)

102 **Lately attendant on** recently in the service of

103 **doom . . . death** condemn my brother to death

104 **slave** servant, but here used contemptuously

105 **killed no man** Clarence did kill, and on King Edward's behalf (1.4.199–204). King Edward here (as at 122–3) overstates his innocence; cf. Margaret on the exaggerations necessary for effective curses (4.4.119–23).
fault was thought i.e. he may have thought about wrongs but did not commit them.

107 **sued . . . him** pleaded his case with me

108 ***at . . . bid** Qq's 'at' is certainly correct, and *bid* may serve as a past tense.
be advised i.e. consider, be judicious

110–11 Cf. 1.3.134–7.

97 prithee] *F (*prethee*), Qq (*pray thee*)* 98 hear me] *F;* grant *Qq* 99 say] *F;* speake *Qq* requests] *F;* demaundst *Qq* 100 SP] *F, Q1–2, 4–6; om. Q3* 104 that tongue] *F;* the same *Qq* 105 killed] *F;* slew *Qq* 106 bitter] *F;* cruell *Qq* 107 wrath] *F;* rage *Qq* 108 at] *Qq;* and *F* bid] *F;* bad *Qq* 109 spoke of . . . spoke of] *F;* spake of . . . of *Qq*

The mighty Warwick and did fight for me?
Who told me in the field at Tewkesbury,
When Oxford had me down, he rescued me
And said, 'Dear brother, live, and be a king'?
Who told me, when we both lay in the field,
Frozen almost to death, how he did lap me
Even in his garments, and did give himself,
All thin and naked, to the numb-cold night?
All this from my remembrance brutish wrath
Sinfully plucked, and not a man of you
Had so much grace to put it in my mind.
But when your carters or your waiting vassals
Have done a drunken slaughter and defaced
The precious image of our dear Redeemer,
You straight are on your knees for pardon, pardon;

113 The historical sources do not place Oxford at Tewkesbury; however, Shakespeare includes him among the forces that war with King Edward at Tewkesbury in *3H6* 5.4 and 5.5.

116 **lap** enfold in a wrap or wraps, swathe (*OED v.*[2] 3)

118 **thin** i.e. thinly clad (*OED adv.* C 1a)

120–33 This passage is particularly dense with religious vocabulary and allusion. God's grace has been freely offered to pardon sinful mankind. King Edward measures his own *ungracious* failure to pardon Clarence and the failure of his followers to beg for that pardon against the supreme sacrifice by the *dear Redeemer*. Having failed to grant or seek *pardon* for Clarence, he fears that he and his court will be judged undeserving of mercy and suffer divine *justice* rather than attain mercy by means of divine *grace*. 'Like many of Richard's victims, [Shakespeare's] Edward finally accepts his guilt but soothes his conscience with the perverse consolation that he will not suffer alone' (E. Berry, 87).

122 **carters** literally, drivers of carts, but also stock figures of rough demeanour and low birth; in reference to Stanley's *servant* (100) this constitutes rhetorical exaggeration (cf. *slave*, 104).
waiting vassals servants acting as attendants (*OED* waiting *ppl. a.* 1)

123 **drunken slaughter** Stanley refers to a 'riotous gentleman', saying nothing about the sobriety of his slayer; King Edward again denigrates the figure for whom Stanley pleads and, hence, the merit of his plea.

123–4 **defaced . . . Redeemer** referring to the idea that humanity is made in the image and likeness of God (Genesis, 1.26–7); cf. Calvin, 2.8.40: 'If we do not wish to violate the image of God, we ought to hold our neighbour sacred.'

125 **straight** immediately

112 at] *F;* by *Qq* 117 garments] *F;* owne garments *Q1–5;* owne armes *Q6* did give] *F;* gaue *Qq* 118 numb-cold] *F, Q3–6 (*numbe cold*), Q1–2 (*numbcold*), hyphen Capell* 120 plucked] *F, Q2–6;* puckt *Q1*

And I, unjustly too, must grant it you. [*Stanley rises.*]
But for my brother, not a man would speak,
Nor I, ungracious, speak unto myself
For him, poor soul. The proudest of you all
Have been beholding to him in his life,
Yet none of you would once beg for his life.
O God! I fear Thy justice will take hold
On me, and you, and mine and yours for this.
– Come, Hastings, help me to my closet. – Ah, poor
Clarence. *Exeunt some with King and Queen.* [*Richard, Buckingham, Stanley and Ratcliffe remain.*]

RICHARD

This is the fruits of rashness: marked you not
How that the guilty kindred of the Queen
Looked pale when they did hear of Clarence' death?
O! They did urge it still unto the King.
God will revenge it. Come, lords, will you go
To comfort Edward with our company?

BUCKINGHAM

We wait upon your grace. *Exeunt.*

127 Cf. 96–134n.
130 **beholding** obliged, indebted
in his life while he lived
134 **Hastings** As Lord Chamberlain, Hastings's duties included attendance on the sovereign in private chambers.
closet private room, inner chamber
134 SD Minimally, King Edward, Queen Elizabeth and Hastings leave while Buckingham and Richard remain, but Richard invites *lords* to depart (139) in F. Richard's accusations against the Queen's *kindred* (136) dictate that Dorset and Rivers be no longer onstage. This leaves Stanley and Ratcliffe probably present. Although Catesby is at some point *sworn* to Richard's faction (3.1.158–60), the fact that his alliance needs explicit mention may argue against his remaining here; so he probably departs among '*some*' (134 SD).
135 **This . . . rashness** Cf. Iago's self-righteous rhetoric: 'This is the fruits of whoring' (*Oth* 5.1.116).
136–7 There are two obvious problems with Richard's imputation of guilt: first, everyone looks *pale* at the news of Clarence's death (84–6); secondly, paleness could be caused by other strong emotions, especially fear (*LLL* 1.2.97); cf. 3.5.1n.
138 **still** continually
139 **God . . . it** Cf. 1.4.214–18, 2.2.14.

126 SD] *Cam*[1] *(Furnivall)* 127 man] *F, Q1–2, 6;* mast *Q3–5* 130 beholding] *F, Q1–3;* beholden *Q4–6* 131 beg] *F;* pleade *Qq* 133 yours] *F, Q1–5;* your *Q6* 134] *Qq; F lines* Closset. / *Clarence.* / Ah] *F;* oh *Qq* SD *Exeunt . . . Queen.*] *F; Exit. Qq* *Richard . . . remain.*] *Oxf*[1] 135 fruits] *F;* fruit *Qq* rashness] *F, Q1–2;* rawnes *Q3–6* 139 Come . . . go] *F;* But come lets in *Qq* 141] *F; not in Qq* SD] *F; opp. 140 Qq*

2.2 *Enter the old* DUCHESS of York, *with the two* Children *of Clarence.*

BOY
Good grandam, tell us, is our father dead?

DUCHESS No, boy.

DAUGHTER
Why do [Q]you[Q] weep so oft, and beat your breast?
And cry, 'O Clarence, my unhappy son'?

BOY
Why do you look on us, and shake your head,
And call us orphans, wretches, castaways,
If that our noble father were alive?

DUCHESS
My pretty cousins, you mistake me both;
I do lament the sickness of the King,
As loath to lose him, not your father's death.

2.2 location: '*a Room in the Palace*' (Capell)

0.2 **Children** Margaret (b. 1473) and Edward (b. 1475) Plantagenet. Clarence's children are more directly in the line of succession than Richard (see *3H6* 4.6.57 and Hall, *Edward IV*, fol. ccx[v]). The play does not invoke their dynastic claims, but Richard takes steps against them (4.2.53–5, 4.3.36–7). Historically, Edward was attainted for treason and executed by Henry VII in 1499, and Margaret, later Countess of Salisbury, was attainted and executed by Henry VIII in 1541 (Holinshed, 3.703, 787). Holinshed notes their 'like misfortune' within the same precincts of the Tower where their father's murder took place; with Margaret 'died the verie surname of Plantagenet' (3.703).

1 SP *F names Edward only here. The F annotator may have intended the name to be used throughout the scene (*TxC*, 236), but with so many Edwards inhabiting and haunting the play, retaining '*Boy*' might assist the reader.

1 ***grandam** grandmother; Qq's 'grannam' may be a colloquial form.

4 **unhappy** unfortunate (*OED a.* 2)

6 **castaways** literally, ones who are cast away or rejected, but also conveying a theological sense of being numbered among the reprobate, rejected by God (*OED sb.* B, citing this line); cf. *Homilies*, 128.

7 **If that . . . were** For the conditional form and 'that' as a conjunctional affix, see Abbott, 287, 371. One of Wilson's linguistic 'tangles'.

8 **cousins** relatives (*OED sb.* 1)

2.2] *F (Scena Secunda.); not in Qq* 0.1–2] *F; Enter Dutches of Yorke, with Clarence Children. Qq* 1 SP] *Qq; Edw. F* Good . . . us] *F;* Tell me good Granam *Qq* 3 SP] *F (Daugh.); Boy. Qq* weep so oft] *F;* wring your hands *Qq* 5 SP] *F; Gerl. Qq* 6 orphans, wretches] *F;* wretches, Orphanes *Qq* 7 were] *F;* be *Qq* 8 both] *F;* much *Qq* 10 not . . . death] *F, Q1–5;* now . . . dead *Q6*

It were lost sorrow to wail one that's lost.

BOY

Then you conclude, my grandam, he is dead.
The King mine uncle is to blame for it.
God will revenge it, whom I will importune
With earnest prayers, all to that effect.

DAUGHTER

And so will I.

DUCHESS

Peace, children, peace. The King doth love you well.
Incapable and shallow innocents,
You cannot guess who caused your father's death.

BOY

Grandam, we can, for my good uncle Gloucester
Told me the King, provoked to it by the Queen,
Devised impeachments to imprison him;
And when my uncle told me so, he wept,
And pitied me, and kindly kissed my cheek,

11 A remarkable objection, given the copious wailing for the lost in this play; cf. Dent, T127: 'For a lost thing care not.'

12 **conclude** reach the conclusion, demonstrate, prove (*OED v.* 9)

13 ***to blame** F, Qq have 'too', perhaps meaning 'too blameworthy, culpable'; see *OED* blame *v.* 6, citing this line, and Abbott, 73 (cf. *1H4* 3.1.173; *Oth* 3.3.214).

14 **God . . . it** Cf. 2.1.139 and also Clarence's more tentative, but self-serving, invocation of divine vengeance (1.4.214–18).
importune beg (*OED v.* 4)

15 **all** entirely

18 **Incapable and shallow** unable to take in (*OED a.* I 2) and deficient in ordinary capacity (*OED a.* I 5); for *shallow* referring to inadequacy, see 3.2.24, 4.4.361, 4.4.431, 5.3.219. Contrast the many uses of *deep* (e.g. 2.1.38, 4.2.42).

20 **good** Richard will be called *good* by allies and those seeking favour, but this is the first time that he has been so called since Henry VI rejected the epithet as 'preposterous' (*3H6* 5.6.2–5).

22 **impeachments** charges

23 **wept** On Richard's tears and the theatrical Vice, see Spivack, 399.

24 **kindly** affectionately, lovingly, with sympathy (*OED adv.* 2), but, given subsequent references to family relationships, with a sense of that which is natural, especially among kin (*OED a.* 1, 2); cf. 1.4.233–41 and More's ironic reference to Richard as a 'kindly king' (*CW2*, 83).

11 sorrow to wail] *F;* labour to weepe for *Qq* 12 you . . . grandam] *F;* Granam you conclude that *Qq* 13 mine . . . it] *F;* my . . . this *Qq* to] *F, Qq (*too*), F2* 15 earnest] *F;* daily *Qq* 16] *F; not in Qq* 21 to it] *F; not in Qq* 23 my uncle] *F;* he *Qq* 24 pitied me] *F;* hugd me in his arme *Qq* cheek] *F, Q2–5;* checke *Q1;* cheekes *Q6*

Bade me rely on him as on my father,
And he would love me dearly as a child.

DUCHESS

Ah! That deceit should steal such gentle shape,
And with a virtuous visor hide deep vice.
He is my son, ay, and therein my shame,
Yet from my dugs he drew not this deceit.

BOY

Think you my uncle did dissemble, grandam?

DUCHESS Ay, boy.

BOY

I cannot think it. Hark, what noise is this?

Enter QUEEN [ELIZABETH] *with her hair about her ears,* RIVERS *and* DORSET *after her.*

QUEEN ELIZABETH

Ah! Who shall hinder me to wail and weep,
To chide my fortune, and torment myself?
I'll join with black despair against my soul
And to myself become an enemy.

26 ***a** Qq's 'his' is attractive, given the blandness of 'love me dearly as a child'.

27 ***Ah!** F frequently follows introductory exclamations with exclamation marks (e.g. 34, 62, 80, 86). Q1 has no such exclamatory punctuation in this scene.

shape guise, disguise (*OED sb.*[1] 7); by 1604 the term occurs with a theatrically specific sense, meaning make-up and costume suited to a part (*OED sb.*[1] 8).

28 **visor** mask to conceal the face (*OED sb.* 2), used figuratively for an outward appearance concealing something (*OED sb.* 3a)

30 **dugs** breasts; cf. Dent, E198: 'He sucked evil from the dug.'

33.1 ***with . . . ears*** Dishevelled hair signalled emotional extremity, especially grief (cf. *TC* 2.2.96 SD; Dessen & Thomson, 107).

33.2 *On Qq absence of Rivers and Dorset here and abbreviation elsewhere, see pp. 451–4.

37 The divided self is an image for despair, desperation (cf. 5.3.185–90) or civil dissension (2.4.63–4); warring upon oneself is a metaphor for self-destructiveness (cf. 1.2.83–8).

25 Bade] *F (*Bad*);* And bad *Qq* [2]on] *F, Q2–6;* in *Q1* 26 a] *F;* his *Qq* 27 Ah!] *F;* Oh *Qq* shape] *F;* shapes *Qq* 28 visor . . . vice] *F;* visard hide foule guile *Qq* 29 ay,] *F (*I,*);* yea, *Q1–3;* yea *Q5–6; om. Q4* 33.1–2] *F (the Queene); Enter the / Quee. Qq (subst. opp. 33–4)* 33.1 ELIZABETH] *Malone* 34 Ah! Who] *F;* Oh who *Q1–2, 4;* Wh who *Q3;* Whoy *Q5 (Edin., Hn, Fo 1);* Who *Q5–6* 36 soul] *F, Q1–4;* selfe *Q5–6*

DUCHESS

What means this scene of rude impatience?

QUEEN ELIZABETH

To make an act of tragic violence.
Edward, my lord, thy son, our king, is dead.
Why grow the branches, when the root is gone?
Why wither not the leaves that want their sap?
If you will live, lament; if die, be brief,
That our swift-winged souls may catch the King's,
Or like obedient subjects follow him
To his new kingdom of ne'er-changing night.

DUCHESS

Ah, so much interest have [Q]I[Q] in thy sorrow

38–9 **scene . . . act . . . tragic** As elsewhere (3.5.1–11), the play employs common theatrical discourse, building on *shape* and *visor* (27, 28); see p. 6.

38 **rude** violent, harsh (*OED a.* A I 5) **impatience** failure to bear suffering with equanimity (*OED* 1), here conveying emotional distress; cf. *JC* 4.3.150.

39 i.e. to enact a violent action and emotion proper to tragic narrative; *make* may mean 'make up' or 'complete', as in *Cym* 1.4.9 (Thompson).

40 **Edward** King Edward actually died in 1483; Clarence had been dead since 1478.
lord i.e. husband

41–2 probably proverbial, roughly paralleled in *E3* 2.1.419–20. Shaheen detects an echo of John, 15.4–6: 'As the braunche can not beare fruite of it self, except it byde in the vine . . . he is cast foorth as a braunch, and withereth.' Given another nearby echo possibly from Kyd's *Spanish Tragedy* (see 46n.), the invocation of vegetative nature might recall Isabella's laments for her murdered son, proclaiming, 'I will not leave a root, a stalke, a tree, / A bowe, a branch, a blossome, nor a leaf' (Kyd, *Spanish Tragedy*, 4.2.10–11).

41 ***gone** Hammond, following Patrick, argues that Qq's 'witherd' confuses what is clear and apt in F, which has King Edward, the root, gone and not merely withered.

42 **want** lack

43 **brief** expeditious or hasty (*OED a.* 1b)

44 **swift-winged** swift-wingèd

46 ***ne'er-changing night** This phrase and its Qq alternative ('perpetuall rest') have occasioned debate about relative merits, especially since Qq approximate 1.4.47 ('the kingdom of perpetual night'). F recalls *The Spanish Tragedy* ('Through dreadfull shades of ever glooming night', Kyd, 1.1.56); Qq resemble *Doctor Faustus* (see 1.4.47n.).

47–8 **interest . . . title** legal metaphors: to have 'interest' is to possess a right to a share in something (*OED sb.* I 1c); 'title' is the right to the possession of property (*OED sb.* 7a).

39 make] *F, Qq;* mark *Cam[1] (Maxwell)* 40 thy] *F;* your *Qq* 41 when . . . gone] *F;* now . . . witherd *Qq* 42 that . . . sap] *F;* the sap being gone *Qq* 46 ne'er-changing night] *F;* perpetuall rest *Qq*

As I had title in thy noble husband.
I have bewept a worthy husband's death
And lived with looking on his images;
But now two mirrors of his princely semblance
Are cracked in pieces by malignant death,
And I, for comfort, have but one false glass
That grieves me when I see my shame in him.
Thou art a widow, yet thou art a mother,
And hast the comfort of thy children left;
But death hath snatched my husband from mine arms
And plucked two crutches from my feeble hands,
Clarence and Edward. O, what cause have I,
Thine being but a moiety of my moan,
To overgo thy woes and drown thy cries!

BOY

Ah, aunt! You wept not for our father's death.
How can we aid you with our kindred tears?

DAUGHTER

Our fatherless distress was left unmoaned;
Your widow-dolour likewise be unwept.

50 **with** i.e. by

50–1 **images . . . mirrors** i.e. children; oddly, given the Yorkists' repeated recollections of Rutland's death (1.2.160–1, 1.3.177–93), the Duchess fails to invoke his memory, thinking only of King Edward and Clarence as her husband's *images*.

51–3 **mirrors . . . semblance . . . glass** Cf. Lucretius' lament for his dead daughter: 'Poor broken glass, I often did behold / In thy sweet semblance my old age new born; / But now that fair fresh mirror dim and old, / Shows me a bare-boned death by time outworn' (*Luc* 1758–61).

51 **semblance** the likeness of someone or something (*OED* 2)

60 **moiety** half (see 1.2.252)

61 **overgo thy woes** surpass your lamentations

62–5 The children address Queen Elizabeth.

63 **kindred** showing resemblance (*OED* A 1b); belonging to family, relatives (*OED* B 1b); allied in nature (*OED* B 2); cf. 24n.

65 i.e. may (or let) your grief as a widow similarly be unbewept (Abbott, 365; cf. 1.3.206).

50 with] *F;* by *Qq* 54 That] *F;* Which *Qq* 56 left] *F;* left thee *Qq* 57 husband] *F;* children *Qq* 58 hands] *F;* limmes *Qq* 59 Clarence and Edward] *F;* Edward and Clarence *Qq* 60 Thine . . . a moiety] *F;* Then, . . . moity *Qq subst.* moan] *F;* griefe *Q1–5;* selfe *Q6* 61 woes] *F;* plaints *Qq* (plants *Q2*) [2]thy] *F, Q1–4;* the *Q5–6* 62 Ah] *F;* Good *Qq* 63 kindred] *F;* kindreds *Qq* 64 SP] *F; Gerl. Qq* 65 widow-dolour] *F;* widdowes dolours *Qq*

QUEEN ELIZABETH

Give me no help in lamentation,
I am not barren to bring forth complaints:
All springs reduce their currents to mine eyes,
That I, being governed by the watery moon,
May send forth plenteous tears to drown the world.
Ah, for my husband, for my dear lord Edward!

CHILDREN

Ah, for our father, for our dear lord Clarence!

DUCHESS

Alas for both, both mine, Edward and Clarence!

QUEEN ELIZABETH

What stay had I but Edward? And he's gone.

CHILDREN

What stay had we but Clarence? And he's gone.

DUCHESS

What stays had I but they? And they are gone.

QUEEN ELIZABETH

Was never widow had so dear a loss.

66 **Give me** i.e. even if you give me (though possibly a command)

67 **barren . . . forth** i.e. unable to give birth to

68–70 apocalyptic rhetoric demonstrating Queen Elizabeth's capacity for lamentation; she asks that the earth's sources of water all return their liquid to her eyes so that her tears may drown the world.

68 **reduce** i.e. be brought back (*OED* I 3); cf. 5.5.36 and Abbott, 365.

69 **governed . . . moon** The moon's connection to tides is familiar in Shakespeare: Falstaff refers to his fortune's 'being governed, as the sea is, by . . . the moon' (*1H4* 1.2.27–8); thus the moon is the 'watery moon' (*MND* 2.1.162).

71 ***dear** Qq's 'eire' or 'heire' would be possible if the second half of Queen Elizabeth's line were taken to refer to the anticipated plight of her son Edward rather than to the death of her husband King Edward (but *both* in 73 makes this unlikely, DSK).

74–9 *Variants in phrasing subsequent to Q1 incline progressively towards rhetorical questions rather than exclamations (as in Q1 and F).

74 **stay** support (*OED sb.*^{2} 1b)

77–9 **Was never . . . Were never** i.e. there was/were never (Abbott, 414). Wilson detects 'Spenserism' ('Was neuer Prince so faithfull and so faire, / Was neuer Prince so meeke and debonair', Spenser, *Faerie Queene*, 1.2.23, ll. 4–5).

77 **dear** grievous, severe (*OED a.*^{2} 2)

67 complaints] *F;* laments *Qq* 69 watery moon] *F;* watry moane *Qq* 71 Ah, for] *F;* Oh for *Qq* dear] *F;* eire *Q1–2;* heire *Q3–6* 72, 75, 78 SP] *F (Chil.); Am[bo][.] Qq* 72 Ah] *F;* Oh *Qq* 74, 75 he's] *F;* he is *Q1–5;* is he *Q6* 76 stays] *F, Q1–5;* stay *Q6* 77 never] *F, Q1–3, 5–6;* euer *Q4*

CHILDREN

Were never orphans had so dear a loss.

DUCHESS

Was never mother had so dear a loss.
Alas! I am the mother of these griefs.
Their woes are parcelled; mine is general.
She for an Edward weeps, and so do I.
I for a Clarence weep, so doth not she.
These babes for Clarence weep, [Q]and so do I;
I for an Edward weep,[Q] so do not they.
Alas! You three, on me, threefold distressed,
Pour all your tears. I am your sorrow's nurse,
And I will pamper it with lamentation.

DORSET [*to Queen Elizabeth*]

Comfort, dear mother. God is much displeased
That you take with unthankfulness His doing.
In common worldly things, 'tis called ungrateful
With dull unwillingness to repay a debt
Which with a bounteous hand was kindly lent;
Much more to be thus opposite with heaven,
For it requires the royal debt it lent you.

RIVERS

Madam, bethink you, like a careful mother,

80–1 Cf. Hecuba's claim to all 'woes' (Seneca, *Troades*, 1060–2); see p. 76.

80 **mother** i.e. as the eldest authority figure of the house of York

81 **parcelled** divided up into small portions (*OED ppl. a.*)

84–5 *Hammond suggests compositor 'eye-skip' to explain F's abbreviation. Confusions here may result in part from a position spanning a page-break in F at sig. r4$^{r–v}$.

87 **nurse** one who suckles or cares for an infant (*OED sb.*[1] 1a)

89–100 *Absence of these lines from Qq, combined with other omissions, eliminates Rivers and Dorset from the scene.

92 **dull** insensible, obtuse (*OED a.* 1, 2)

94 **opposite** hostile, antagonistic, adverse (*OED a.* A 4a); cf. *TN* 2.5.144.

95 **For** because
royal debt cf. Dent, G237: 'I owe God a death.' For the debt/death pun see *1H4* 5.1.126.

96 **bethink you** i.e. think

78 Were] *F;* Was *Qq* 78, 79 never] *F, Q1;* euer *Q2–6* 78, 79 so dear a] *F;* a dearer *Qq* 80 griefs] *F;* mones *Qq* 81 is] *F;* are *Qq* 82 an] *F; not in Qq* 83 weep] *Qq;* weepes *F* 84–5] *Qq; one line F* 85 weep] *Q1–3, 5–6; om. Q4* so do not] *F, Q1;* and so do *Q2–6* 87 Pour] *F (*Power*), Q1 (*Poure*), Q3–6 (*Powre*);* Proue *Q2* 88 lamentation] *F;* lamentations *Qq* 89–100] *F; not in Qq* 89 SD] *Bevington*[3]

Of the young prince your son: send straight for him;
Let him be crowned. In him your comfort lives.
Drown desperate sorrow in dead Edward's grave
And plant your joys in living Edward's throne.

Enter RICHARD, BUCKINGHAM, [STANLEY, Earl of] Derby, HASTINGS *and* RATCLIFFE.

RICHARD
Sister, have comfort. All of us have cause
To wail the dimming of our shining star,
But none can help our harms by wailing them.
– Madam my mother, I do cry you mercy;
I did not see your grace. Humbly on my knee
I crave your blessing. [*Kneels.*]

DUCHESS
God bless thee and put meekness in thy breast,
Love, charity, obedience and true duty.

RICHARD
Amen, [*rising; aside*] and make me die a good old man.

100 **plant** Lull suggests a play on the royal family name, Plantagenet; cf. 3.7.215.

100.1 *Enter* RICHARD Cibber entered weeping and commenting on his own performance in an aside; Kean took out a white handkerchief before coming forward (Hankey, 141). On the group that enters with Richard here, see 2.1.134 SDn.

100.2 RATCLIFFE For the second time F has Ratcliffe enter with Richard (see 2.1.44.1) only to remain silent; in Qq he does not appear until 3.3.

101 ***Sister** F (unlike Qq) has Richard here fulfil his sarcastic promise to address the Queen by a title he finds distasteful (1.1.109); cf. 2.2.143.

104 **I . . . mercy** i.e. I beg your pardon.

105–6 **on . . . blessing** For children asking a blessing upon greeting their parents and often kneeling while doing so, see *Tit* 1.1.164–6, *KL* 4.7.57–9 and *Cor* 2.1.169–73; for the historical practice, see Young. This is the second time Richard begs a female figure *humbly* – and hypocritically – upon his knee (see 1.2.181).

109–11 The solemn blessing often constituted an opportunity for early modern stage clowning; cf. *MV* 2.2.72–94; for Tarleton's blessing joke, see Peacham, 102–5 and Siemon, 'Power'.

109 SD *rising* Richard's rise here differentiates his *Amen* from his subsequent words, which are clearly not directed

100.1–2] *F; Enter Glocest. / with others. / Qq opp. 88, 101* 100.1 STANLEY, Earl of] *Theobald subst.* 101+ SP] *F (Rich.); Gl[o]. Qq* Sister] *F;* Madame *Qq* 103 help our] *F;* cure their *Qq* 106 your] *F, Q1–5;* you *Q6* SD] *Cam[1] after* grace *105* 107 breast] *F;* minde *Qq* 109 SD *rising*] *Ard[2] subst.* *aside*] *Collier; after 111 Hanmer* and] *F, Q1–5; om. Q6*

That is the butt-end of a mother's blessing;
I marvel that her grace did leave it out.

BUCKINGHAM

You cloudy princes and heart-sorrowing peers
That bear this heavy mutual load of moan,
Now cheer each other in each other's love.
Though we have spent our harvest of this king,
We are to reap the harvest of his son.
The broken rancour of your high-swoll'n hates,
But lately splintered, knit and joined together,
Must gently be preserved, cherished and kept.
Meseemeth good that with some little train
Forthwith from Ludlow the young Prince be fet
Hither to London, to be crowned our king.

RIVERS

Why with some little train, my lord of Buckingham?

to at least some onstage audience members.
**aside* Most recent editors follow Collier in taking *Amen* as spoken aloud, with subsequent lines uttered aside.

110 **butt-end** mere concluding part (*OED sb.* 1b, citing this line); Jowett suggests *butt* as in cask (*OED sb.*[2]), a sardonic pun given the copious lamentation for Clarence's death in this scene.

112 **cloudy** gloomy, sullen, troubled (*OED a.* 6b); cf. *Luc* 1084.

113 **moan** grief; cf. 'mass of moan' (*TC* 2.2.107).

117–19 Buckingham's images urge that limbs, previously broken by factional division and still swollen, be gently handled to permit continuation of a healing process that was recently begun when they were splinted by King Edward's attempts at reconciliation. Cf. 'To show the rancour of their high-swoll'n hearts' (*E3* 3.1.131).

118 **splintered** splinted (*OED v.* 2, citing this line); cf. *Oth* 2.3.317–18.

120 **Meseemeth** it seems to me
train retinue, body of attendants (*OED sb.*[1] III 9a); Buckingham also suggests removing the Prince from his allies in *True Tragedy* (409–13), but More's Richard persuades the Queen to this action without Buckingham's input (*CW2*, 16–17).

121 **Ludlow** castle in Shropshire near the Welsh border, 150 miles from London
fet fetched (an obsolete form: *OED* fet)

123–40 *On the possible theatrical economy that might explain Qq omission, see 89–100n. The lines explain the strategic decision to greet the Prince with a reduced train. The decision is described as treachery in *Mirror* ('Rivers', 365–92,

110 That is] *F;* Thats *Qq* a] *F, Q1;* my *Q2–6* 111 that] *F;* why *Qq* 113 heavy mutual] *F;* mutuall heauy *Qq* 115 of] *F, Q1;* for *Q2–6* 116 son] *F, Q1–5* (sonne)*;* soone *Q6* 117 high-swoll'n] *F* (high-swolne), *Qq* (high swolne) hates] *F;* hearts *Qq* 118 splintered] *F, Q1* (splinter'd)*;* splinted *Q2–6* 119 gently] *F, Q1;* greatly *Q2–6* 121 fet] *F;* fetcht *Qq* 123–40] *F; not in Qq* 123] *Pope; F lines* Traine, / Buckingham? /

BUCKINGHAM

Marry, my lord, lest by a multitude
The new-healed wound of malice should break out,
Which would be so much the more dangerous
By how much the estate is green and yet ungoverned.
Where every horse bears his commanding rein
And may direct his course as please himself,
As well the fear of harm as harm apparent,
In my opinion, ought to be prevented.

RICHARD

I hope the King made peace with all of us,
And the compact is firm and true in me.

RIVERS

And so in me, and so, I think, in all.
Yet since it is but green, it should be put
To no apparent likelihood of breach,
Which haply by much company might be urged;
Therefore I say with noble Buckingham
That it is meet so few should fetch the Prince.

HASTINGS

And so say I.

RICHARD

Then be it so, and go we to determine

519–53). More represents the logic here articulated by Buckingham as Richard's own. The parts have sometimes been editorially redistributed, often by exchanging the attribution of the speeches of Richard and Rivers at 132 and 134, but Richard may appear strategically lukewarm to allow Rivers the opportunity to talk himself into the proposed arrangement (Hammond).

124 **Marry** indeed

127 **By . . . green** to the extent that the condition of the state is immature; *green* refers to the newness of the peace brokered by King Edward.

128 **bears . . . rein** commands himself according to his own will (rather than submitting to a master)

129 **as please himself** i.e. as it should please him (the horse)

132 **with** i.e. among

134 The agreement of Rivers with Buckingham's devious recommendation is remarkable, but perhaps the play here represents the helpless confusion or deluded shortsightedness of the characters who surround Richard. Lull suggests intimidation by Buckingham at 123–4.

135 **green** See 127n.

137 **haply** perhaps
urged incited, impelled (*OED* urge *v.* II 3)

139 **meet** appropriate

Who they shall be that straight shall post to Ludlow.
– Madam, and you my sister, will you go
To give your censures in this business?

[Q] QUEEN ELIZABETH, DUCHESS
With all our hearts.[Q]

Exeunt all but Buckingham and Richard.

BUCKINGHAM
My lord, whoever journeys to the Prince,
For God's sake let not us two stay at home;
For by the way I'll sort occasion,
As index to the story we late talked of,
To part the Queen's proud kindred from the Prince.

RICHARD
My other self, my counsel's consistory,

142 **post** hasten, as on post-horses (*OED sb.*[2] III 8i)

143 **sister** Cf. 101n.; Thompson favours Qq's wording, which puts the queen-dowager first, since Richard would appropriately address the ranking person before addressing his mother. Dyce argues that F's version, which has Richard first addressing his mother, allows him a subtle insult to Elizabeth; however, Marshall counters that first addressing his own mother, who is after all Elizabeth's elder, implies no disrespect for the Queen, who is not herself a queen regnant (see Var).

144 **censures** judgements, opinions (*OED sb.* 3)

145 *Most recent editors include this Qq line. It provides an opportunity for actors to register degrees of compliance and/or reluctance on the part of Queen Elizabeth and the Duchess of York in this matter. Qq's SP '*Ans.*' may be a corruption of '*Amb*' for '*Ambo*' ('both') (Marshall; cf. 2.2.72, 75, 78); '*Ans.*' might stand for 'Answer' (Jowett; cf. Perkins, 1.162). Line 144 occupies the last line of the first column of F sig. r4^{v}; that position and the SDs which surround it – '*Exeunt.*' at the end of column a and, at the top of column b, '*Manet Buckingham, and Richard*' – may have resulted in confusion and F's omission of 145.

148 **sort occasion** i.e. choose an opportunity

149 **index** preface, introduction (*OED sb.* 5a); cf. 4.4.85. Buckingham will take the first step in the plot to separate Queen Elizabeth's family and followers from Prince Edward.

150 **Prince** Qq title Edward 'King', but he was never crowned and is referred to throughout the play as 'Prince'. Hall and Holinshed give '*Kyng Edwarde the fyft*' a chapter, but Hall's 1550 frontispiece shows the crown hovering above Edward's head. See Fig. 1.

151 **My other self** i.e. my close confidant (see Dent, F696: 'A friend is one's second self'); the idea appears in Aristotle, and Erasmus invokes it (31.31).

142 Ludlow] *Qq;* London *F* 143 sister] *F;* mother *Qq* 144 business] *F;* waighty busines *Qq* 145 SP] *Qq (Ans.)* SD] *F (Exeunt. Manet Buckingham, and Richard.); Exeunt man. Glo. Buck. Qq* 146 whoever] *F, Q1–3, 5–6;* who *Q4* 147 God's] *Qq;* God *F* stay] *F, Q1;* be *Q2–6* at home] *F;* behinde *Qq* 149 late] *F, Q1;* lately *Q2–6* of] *F, Q1–2;* off *Q3–6* 150 Prince] *F;* King *Qq*

My oracle, my prophet, my dear cousin,
I, as a child, will go by thy direction:
Toward Ludlow then, for we'll not stay behind. *Exeunt.*

2.3 *Enter one* Citizen *at one door, and* Another *at the other.*

1 CITIZEN
Good morrow, neighbour; whither away so fast?

2 CITIZEN
I promise you, I scarcely know myself.
Hear you the news abroad?

1 CITIZEN
Yes, that the King is dead.

2 CITIZEN
Ill news, by'r Lady. Seldom comes the better.

consistory council chamber; thus Buckingham would be figuratively the meeting room in which Richard's counsels may be articulated to himself. The notion of Buckingham as an echo-chamber is apt, at least at this point in the play. Richard's own secret 'counsels' with himself and his yes-man also stand in punning place of the learned 'councils' demanded by humanist notions of right rule. Of course we, as audience members, also share Richard's confidences.

152 **oracle** person of great wisdom or knowledge; cf. *H8* 3.2.104.
prophet given the importance of prophecy and curse in the play, a striking term to make light of here.

153 **as a child** Compare this sinister remark from the notorious child-slayer with other invocations of childish vulnerability at 26, 1.2.162 and 4.3.8.

2.3 location: '*a Street near the* Court' (Theobald). This scene was usually cut, from Cibber until the mid-20th century, but it has been important to later productions (Hankey, 144). More mentions 'muttering amonge the people, as though al should not long be wel' (*CW*2, 44) in response to the several councils of June 1483 (see 3.1.179).

0.1 **Citizen** inhabitant of a city or town, especially one possessing civic rights and privileges, as a burgess or freeman (*OED* 1)

1 **neighbour** anyone who lives nearby, but, with *masters* (9) and *friends* (18), suggesting the idiom of an urban middling sort; cf. Menenius to Rome's 'Citizens' as 'masters, my good friends, mine honest neighbours' (*Cor* 1.1.61).

3 **abroad** i.e. currently circulating

4 **by'r Lady** by Our Lady (an oath by the Virgin Mary)
Seldom . . . better See Dent, B332; accepting what one has rather than hoping for something better. Cf. the political ballad (appending a picture of Elizabeth I) 'Seldome comes the better: Or, An admonition to all sorts of people . . . to auoid mutability, and to fix their minds on what they possesse' (pr. 1629; STC 22179).

153 as] *F;* like *Qq* 154 Toward] *F;* Towards *Qq* Ludlow] *Qq;* London *F* we'll] *F;* we will *Qq* SD] *F; Exit. Q3–6; not in Q1–2* **2.3**] *F (Scena Tertia.); not in Qq* 0.1] *F; Enter two Cittizens. Qq subst.* 1, 2, 6 SP] *F, Qq (*1. *Cit.,* 2. *Cit.,* 3. *subst.;* I, 2, 3 *throughout)* 1 Good morrow, neighbour] *F;* Neighbour well met *Qq* whither] *F (*whether*), Qq* 3] *Steevens; F, Qq line* abroad? / dead. / Hear] *F;* I *(SP)* Heare *Qq* SP] *F (*1.*); 2 Qq* Yes] *F;* I *Qq* 4 SP] *F (2.); 1 Qq* Ill] *F;* Bad *Qq*

I fear, I fear, 'twill prove a giddy world.

Enter another Citizen.

3 CITIZEN
Neighbours, God speed.

1 CITIZEN
Give you good morrow, sir.

3 CITIZEN
Doth the news hold of good King Edward's death?

2 CITIZEN
Ay sir, it is too true, God help the while.

3 CITIZEN
Then, masters, look to see a troublous world.

1 CITIZEN
No, no, by God's good grace, his son shall reign.

3 CITIZEN
Woe to that land that's governed by a child.

2 CITIZEN
In him there is a hope of government,
Which in his nonage, council under him,

5 **giddy** mad, insane, foolish (*OED a.* 1)

6 **God speed** i.e. may God cause you to prosper.

7 **Doth . . . hold** i.e. is the news confirmed?

8 **God . . . while** i.e. may God help us in the meanwhile; an expression of grief.

9 **masters** title of compliment, used vocatively like 'sirs' (*OED sb.*[1] 20); here an address appropriate to male heads of household (*OED sb.*[1] 5a) or guild members (*OED sb.*[1] 15a); see 1n.
troublous causing trouble or grief; troubled, disordered

11 From Ecclesiastes, 10.15–16; cf. More (*CW*2, 74); Hall ('woo to that realme whose king is a child', *Edward V*, fol. xxii[r]); and Dent, W600. In *1H6* anxieties about infant rulers and dangerous *emulation* (25) are accompanied by the claim that even a 'simple man' can predict ill events in a 'factious' court (4.1.187–91).

12–15 i.e. he shows promise that he may govern well, first with a good *council* governing in his name, and then in his own right when he comes of age; this difficult passage prompted Johnson and Malone to conjecture a missing line. The emphasis on proper counsel for the child contrasts with the inside joke about *counsel* made by the factiously childlike Richard (2.2.151–3).

13 **nonage** condition of being under age; the period of legal infancy (*OED* 1)

5 giddy] *F; troublous Q1;* troublesome *Q2–6* 5.1] *F; Ent. ano- / ther Citt. Qq opp. 5–6* 6] *Steevens; F lines* speed. / sir. / ; *Qq differ* Neighbours, God speed.] *F;* Good morrow neighbours. *Qq* 1 CITIZEN . . . sir.] *F; not in Qq* 7 the] *F;* this *Qq* King] *F, Q1–2, 4, 6;* Kings *Q3, 5* 8 2 CITIZEN Ay . . . while.] *F;* I *(SP)* It doth. *Qq* 10 good] *F, Q1; om. Q2–6* 13 Which] *F;* That *Qq*

And in his full and ripened years, himself,
No doubt shall then, and till then, govern well.

1 CITIZEN
So stood the state when Henry the Sixth
Was crowned in Paris but at nine months old.

3 CITIZEN
Stood the state so? No, no, good friends, God wot,
For then this land was famously enriched
With politic grave counsel; then the King
Had virtuous uncles to protect his grace.

1 CITIZEN
Why, so hath this, both by his father and mother.

3 CITIZEN
Better it were they all came by his father,
Or by his father there were none at all,
For emulation who shall now be nearest
Will touch us all too near, if God prevent not.
O, full of danger is the Duke of Gloucester,
And the Queen's sons and brothers haught and proud;
And were they to be ruled, and not to rule,

16 **Henry the Sixth** Henry became king at nine months of age in 1422; see *2H6* 4.9.4. During his minority, England was governed by royal council under the direction of the Bishop of Winchester and the dukes of Bedford and Gloucester.

18 **wot** knows

19 **famously** probably conveying a sense of 'excellently' (cf. *Cor* 1.1.35)

20 **politic** judicious, expedient (*OED a.* A 2a)
grave respected, dignified (*OED a.* 1, 3a)

21 **virtuous uncles** the Bishop of Winchester (actually a great-uncle) and the dukes of Bedford and Gloucester, elsewhere called 'wurthy' (*Mirror*, 'Salisbury', 104–5), though *1H6* and *2H6* depict their violent, often selfish contentions

25 **emulation** ambitious rivalry for power or honours; contention between rivals
nearest i.e. to the Prince in trust

26 **touch . . . near** i.e. concern us all too seriously

27 More reports popular opinion that Gloucester would be likely to take the throne on Edward's death (*CW*2, 9).

28 **haught** haughty, high in their own estimation; cf. *3H6* 2.1.168.

29 **And . . . ruled** i.e. if indeed they were to be ruled by others

16 Henry] *F;* Harry *Qq* 17 in] *F;* at *Qq* nine] *F, Q1, 3–6 subst.;* xi. *Q2* 18 No . . . wot] *F;* no good my friend not so *Qq* 22 SP] *F;* 2 *Qq* Why, so . . . his] *F;* So . . . the *Qq* 23, 24 his] *F;* the *Qq* 25 who shall now] *F;* now, who shall *Qq* 26 Will] *F, Q1;* Which *Q2–6* 28 sons . . . haught] *F;* kindred hauty *Qq* 29 [2]to] *F, Q1–5; om. Q6*

This sickly land might solace as before.

1 CITIZEN
Come, come, we fear the worst; all will be well.

3 CITIZEN
When clouds are seen, wise men put on their cloaks;
When great leaves fall, then winter is at hand;
When the sun sets, who doth not look for night?
Untimely storms makes men expect a dearth.
All may be well; but if God sort it so,
'Tis more than we deserve, or I expect.

2 CITIZEN
Truly, the hearts of men are full of fear.
You cannot reason almost with a man
That looks not heavily and full of dread.

3 CITIZEN
Before the days of change, still is it so.
By a divine instinct, men's minds mistrust
Ensuing danger, as by proof we see
The water swell before a boisterous storm.
But leave it all to God. Whither away?

30 **solace** take comfort or consolation; cf. *RJ* 4.5.47.
31 Cf. Dent, W912: 'It is good to fear the worst.'
35 **Untimely** unseasonal
36 **sort** dispose, ordain (*OED v.*^{1} I 1b); cf. *MV* 5.1.132.
39 **cannot . . . with** can scarcely talk with (*OED* reason *v.* 2; cf. 1.4.93, 159); on 'almost' in negative sentences, see Abbott, 29.
40 **heavily** with sorrow, grief, displeasure (*OED adv.* 2)
41–4 More writes: 'before such great thinges, mens hartes of a secret instinct of nature misgiueth them. As ye sea w^{t}out wind swelleth of himself somtime before a tempest' (*CW2*, 44); rendered almost verbatim in Hall and Holinshed. For the Senecan original, see *Thyestes*, 961–4.
41 **still** always
42 **instinct** instínct (Abbott, 490)
mistrust suspect the existence of or anticipate the occurrence of (something evil) (*OED v.* 3)
43 ***Ensuing** F prints 'Pursuing', but the catchword on the previous page is 'Ensuing'.
proof experience (*OED sb.* II 5)

31 SP] *F;* 2 *Qq* will be] *F;* shalbe *Qq* 32 are seen] *F;* appeare *Qq* 33 then] *F;* the *Qq* 35 makes] *F;* make *Qq* 36 may] *F, Q1–5;* men *Q6* 38 SP] *F;* I *Qq* hearts] *F;* soules *Qq* fear] *F;* bread *Q1–2;* dread *Q3–6* 39 You] *F;* Yee *Qq* reason almost] *F (*reason (almost)*);* almost reason *Qq* 40 dread] *F;* feare *Qq* 41 days] *F;* times *Qq* 43 Ensuing] *F (sig. r4*^{v} *c.w.), Qq;* Pursuing *F (sig. r5*^{r}*)* danger] *F;* dangers *Qq* see] *F;* see. *Q1–2;* see, *Q3–6* 44 water] *F;* waters *Qq* boisterous] *F (*boyst'rous*), Q1–2 (*boistrous*), Q3–6 (*boystrous*)*

2 CITIZEN

Marry, we were sent for to the justices.

3 CITIZEN

And so was I. I'll bear you company. *Exeunt.*

2.4 *Enter* ARCHBISHOP [of York], *young* [Duke of] YORK, QUEEN [ELIZABETH] *and the* DUCHESS ^{Q}of York^{Q}.

ARCHBISHOP

Last night, I hear, they lay at Stony Stratford,
And at Northampton they do rest tonight.
Tomorrow, or next day, they will be here.

46 **justices** It is unclear why and to whom the citizens have been summoned; perhaps to a sessions of the Justices of Assize to give evidence or serve on a jury (Wilson). Honigmann notes apparent contradiction with line 2.

2.4 location: '*the* Court' (Theobald); '*A Room in the Palace*' (Capell)

0.1 ARCHBISHOP Qq call the Archbishop 'Cardinall', the title of the Archbishop of Canterbury, Thomas Bourchier, who appears in 3.1 (where Qq call him 'Cardinall' and F closely follows Q3). There he urges delivering the young Duke of York from sanctuary. The prelate in the present scene who supports the flight to sanctuary is Thomas Rotherham, Archbishop of York. Rotherham was Lord Chancellor, his office providing him the Great Seal he promises (71–2); however, evidence suggests confusion about whether Rotherham or Bourchier actually held the Seal at this point (Mancini, 119n., 121n.). More's English version (followed by Holinshed, 3.716–17) confuses the two figures, making York the priest of 3.1 (*CW2*, 27); Hall distinguishes them, having Rotherham advocate sanctuary in the events of 2.4 (*Edward V*, fols vii^{r}, ix^{r}). Cf. 3.1.0.

1 ***hear** Many editors since Capell have favoured Q1–2 to prevent the ambiguity concerning the time they lay at Stony Stratford that is created by the past tense in Q3–6, F.

1, 2, 3 **they** the Prince and those thought to accompany him (see 43–4, 2.2.120–54)

1–2 **Stony Stratford . . . Northampton** F follows sources which have Prince Edward's travel from Ludlow towards London interrupted by Richard at Stony Stratford, where the Prince spent one night. After the arrest of Rivers, Grey and Vaughan, the Prince was taken away from London to Northampton, where he spent the next night (Hall, *Edward V*, fol. vi^{r-v}). Qq reverse the names of Northampton and Stony Stratford, showing geographical insight but not historical knowledge.

46 Marry, we were] *F;* We are *Qq* justices] *F;* Iustice *Qq* 2.4] *F (Scena Quarta.); not in Qq* 0.1–3] *F (the Queene); Enter Cardinall, Dutches of Yorke, Quee. young Yorke. Qq subst.* 0.1 of York] *Rowe* Duke of] *Rowe* 0.2 ELIZABETH] *Malone* 1+ SP] *F (Arch.); Car. Qq* 1 hear] *Q1–2;* heard *F, Q3–6* Stony Stratford] *F;* Northhampton *Qq* 2 And . . . rest] *F;* At Stonistratford will they be *Qq*

DUCHESS
I long with all my heart to see the Prince.
I hope he is much grown since last I saw him.

QUEEN ELIZABETH
But I hear no. They say my son of York
Has almost overta'en him in his growth.

YORK
Ay, mother, but I would not have it so.

DUCHESS
Why, my good cousin, it is good to grow.

YORK
Grandam, one night as we did sit at supper,
My uncle Rivers talked how I did grow
More than my brother. 'Ay,' quoth my uncle
Gloucester,
'Small herbs have grace; great weeds do grow apace.'
And since, methinks I would not grow so fast
Because sweet flowers are slow and weeds make haste.

DUCHESS
Good faith, good faith, the saying did not hold
In him that did object the same to thee.
He was the wretched'st thing when he was young,
So long a-growing, and so leisurely,
That if his rule were true, he should be gracious.

9 **cousin** kinsman, relative (see 2.2.8n.)
12 ***uncle** Q1's 'Nnckle' is possibly an attempt to render 'nuncle' (cf. *KL* 1.4.170).
13 **grace** virtue or efficacy (*OED sb.* 13); cf. *RJ* 2.3.11–14.
great . . . apace proverbial: 'An ill weed grows apace' (Dent, W238); cf. 3.1.103.
apace rapidly
14 **since** i.e. since then (Abbott, 62)
16 **Good faith** i.e. in fact, truth to say (*OED sb.* 12b); cf. 23, 1.4.121n.
hold prove true (*OED v.* II 23c, citing this line)
17 **object** apply, adduce
18 **wretched'st** most lacking in ability, capacity or character (*OED* wretched 5)
20, 21 **gracious** echoing the titular address ('your grace') appropriate to dukes, duchesses and archbishops and playing on the discussion of actual *grace*

6+ SP] *F, Qq (Qu.), Malone* 7 Has] *F (*Ha's*);* Hath *Qq* almost] *F, Q1–5; om. Q6* 9 [1]good] *F;* young *Qq* 10 Grandam] *F, Q1–2;* Granam *Q3–6* 12 uncle] *F, Q2–6;* Nnckle *Q1* Gloucester] *F, Q1–2, 4;* Clo. *Q3, 5;* Glo. *Q6* 13 do] *F; not in Qq* 15 flowers] *F (*Flowres*), Qq* 20 his . . . true] *F;* this were a true rule *Q1–2;* this were a rule *Q3–6*

ARCHBISHOP

And so no doubt he is, my gracious madam.

DUCHESS

I hope he is, but yet let mothers doubt.

YORK

Now by my troth, if I had been remembered,
I could have given my uncle's grace a flout
To touch his growth nearer than he touched mine.

DUCHESS

How, my young York? I prithee let me hear it.

YORK

Marry, they say my uncle grew so fast
That he could gnaw a crust at two hours old;
'Twas full two years ere I could get a tooth.
Grandam, this would have been a biting jest.

DUCHESS

I prithee, pretty York, who told thee this?

YORK

Grandam, his nurse.

DUCHESS

His nurse? Why, she was dead ere thou wast born.

21 SP *Most editors assign this line to the Archbishop, despite F's '*Yor.*' Little York does not address his *grandam* as *gracious madam*. Since the Archbishop is Archbishop of York, the three onstage Yorks create ample opportunity for confusion. Qq assign to '*Car.*'; cf. 37.

23 **by my troth** by my faith (a mild oath); see 1.4.121n.
been remembered remembered (Abbott, 295)

24 **uncle's grace** York puns on the title *grace* and the attribute of *grace*. See also 13, 20, 21; cf. 2.1.120–33, 1.3.320.
flout mocking speech, jeer

25 i.e. to tease him about his size more tellingly than he mocked mine

27–8 Following Rous, More writes: 'It is for trouth reported, that the Duches his mother had so muche a doe in her trauaile, that shee coulde not bee deliuered of hym vncutte: and that hee came into the world with the feete forwarde . . . and (as the fame runneth) also not vntothed' (*CW*2, 8, 167n.) Cf. 4.4.49.

30 ***biting** Q2 misses the pun on *biting* as 'sharp', and later Qq follow.

21 SP] *Capell; Car. Qq; Yor. F* And] *F;* Why Madame, *Qq* is . . . madam] *F;* is *Qq* 22 he is] *F;* so too *Qq* 25] *F;* That should haue neerer toucht his growth then he did mine. *Qq* 26] *Qq; F lines* Yorke, / it. / young] *F;* prety *Qq* 26, 31 prithee] *F; Qq (*pray thee*)* 27 say] *F, Q1;* say that *Q2–6* 28 old] *F, Q1–2, 4, 6;* hold *Q3, 5* 30, 32 Grandam] *F;* Granam *Qq* 30 biting] *F, Q1;* pretie *Q2–6* 31 this] *F;* so *Qq* 33 His nurse] *F, Q1; om. Q2–6* wast] *F;* wert *Qq*

YORK

If 'twere not she, I cannot tell who told me.

QUEEN ELIZABETH

A parlous boy; go to, you are too shrewd.

DUCHESS

Good madam, be not angry with the child.

QUEEN ELIZABETH Pitchers have ears.

Enter a Messenger.

ARCHBISHOP

Here comes a messenger. – What news?

MESSENGER

Such news, my lord, as grieves me to report.

QUEEN ELIZABETH

How doth the Prince?

MESSENGER

Well, madam, and in health.

DUCHESS

What is thy news?

MESSENGER

Lord Rivers and Lord Grey are sent to Pomfret,
And with them Sir Thomas Vaughan, prisoners.

DUCHESS

Who hath committed them?

35 **parlous** dangerously cunning, clever, mischievous (*OED a.* 2, citing this line); cf. 3.1.154–6.
shrewd naughty (*OED* 1a), but also cunning, artful (*OED* 13)
36 SP *Qq assign to '*Car.*' (cf. 21).
37 **Pitchers . . . ears** proverbial: 'Small pitchers have wide ears' (Dent, P363); cf. *TS* 4.4.52.
37.1 ***Messenger** Patrick (21) argued that Qq's '*Dorset*' here makes little dramatic sense because the Queen would greet her son; Urkowitz (450–2) suggests 'coldness between mother and son'. Variants suggest Qq revision to accommodate the replacement of 'Messenger' by Dorset. See 49n. and pp. 454–6.
43–4 See 1–2n.
43 **Pomfret** the castle at Pontefract, in Yorkshire; see 3.3.9n.

35 parlous] *F;* perilous *Qq* 36 SP] *F; Car. Qq* 37.1] *F; Enter Dorset. Qq (after 38 Q2)* 38] *F;* Here comes your sonne, Lo: M. Dorset. / What newes Lo: Marques? / *Qq subst.* 39+ SP] *F (Mes.); Dor. Qq* 39 report] *F;* vnfolde *Qq* 40 doth] *F;* fares *Qq* 42 thy] *F, Q1;* the *Q2–6* news] *F;* newes then *Qq* 43–4] *Qq; F lines Grey, / them, / Prisoners. /* 44 And with] *F;* With *Qq*

MESSENGER The mighty Dukes,
Gloucester and Buckingham.

ARCHBISHOP For what offence?

MESSENGER
The sum of all I can, I have disclosed.
Why, or for what, the nobles were committed
Is all unknown to me, my gracious lord.

QUEEN ELIZABETH
Ay me! I see the ruin of my house:
The tiger now hath seized the gentle hind;
Insulting tyranny begins to jut
Upon the innocent and aweless throne.
Welcome destruction, blood and massacre.
I see, as in a map, the end of all.

DUCHESS
Accursed and unquiet wrangling days,
How many of you have mine eyes beheld?
My husband lost his life to get the crown,

45 **committed** imprisoned

47 **can** i.e. have knowledge of (Abbott, 307); the Messenger says he has disclosed all that he knows.

48 **Why . . . what** *Why* may perhaps refer to the past cause for which they were imprisoned and *what* to the future object of that imprisonment (Abbott, 75); cf. *CE* 2.2.43–4: 'they say every why hath a wherefore'.

49 ***lord** Qq's 'Lady' suggests an adaptation of this speech to the character of Dorset, who could be addressing his mother rather than his questioner (Var; cf. Davison, 168).

50 ***my** F's 'my' is more appropriate for Queen Elizabeth speaking to an anonymous messenger; Qq's 'our' better fits mother speaking to son (Delius in Var; cf. *TxC*, 237).

51 **hind** female deer

52 **Insulting** scornfully triumphant (*OED ppl. a.*); cf. Death's 'insulting tyranny' (*1H6* 4.7.19).
jut encroach; the same word as Qq's 'iet' (*OED* jet *v.*[2] I 1b); cf. *Tit* 1.2.64. Given Richard's lameness, there may be an association with the sense of 'jet' meaning to walk or move in an ostentatious manner, to strut or swagger (*OED v.*[1] 1a); thus 'Insulting tyranny' would be deporting itself offensively while seizing the throne.

53 **aweless** inspiring no awe (*OED* 3, citing this line)

55 **map** metaphorically, an outline or projection of the future
end outcome; destruction

56 **Accursed** accursèd

45–6 The . . . Buckingham] *Steevens; one line F, Qq* 48 or for] *F, Q1, Q3–6;* or *Q2* the] *F;* these *Qq* 49 lord] *F;* Lady *Qq* 50 ruin of my] *F;* downfall of our *Qq* 52 jut] *F;* iet *Qq* 53 aweless] *F;* lawlesse *Qq* 54 blood] *F;* death *Qq*

And often up and down my sons were tossed
For me to joy and weep their gain and loss.
And being seated, and domestic broils
Clean overblown, themselves the conquerors
Make war upon themselves, brother to brother,
Blood to blood, self against self. O preposterous
And frantic outrage, end thy damned spleen,
Or let me die, to look on earth no more.

QUEEN ELIZABETH
Come, come my boy, we will to sanctuary.
Madam, farewell.

DUCHESS Stay, I will go with you.

QUEEN ELIZABETH
You have no cause.

ARCHBISHOP [*to Queen Elizabeth*] My gracious lady, go,
And thither bear your treasure and your goods.
For my part, I'll resign unto your grace

61 **seated** i.e. on the throne
broils conflicts (cf. *1H4* 1.1.3)

62 **Clean overblown** completely finished; cf. *TS* 5.2.3.

63–4 **Make . . . self** Cf. representations of civil contention elsewhere in Shakespeare ('this house against this house', *R2* 4.1.146; 'rebellious arm 'gainst arm', *Mac* 1.2.57) and at 5.5.23–4. Cf. images of self-division at 2.2.37, 5.3.186.

64 **preposterous** monstrous, contrary to natural order, to reason or to common sense (*OED* 2). King Henry claims 'Good Gloucester' or 'good devil' would be 'preposterous' (*3H6* 5.6.4–5). On preposterousness in wider senses, see Parker.

65 **frantic** lunatic, insane; also used of diseases, attended with delirium (*OED a.* 1, 3a)
damned damnèd
spleen violent ill-nature or ill-humour (*OED sb.* 6a)

66 ***earth** Qq's 'death' has in its favour the fact that the Duchess has just been talking about the violence of civil conflict.

67 **sanctuary** a church or other place in which a fugitive from justice, or a debtor, was entitled to immunity from arrest (*OED sb.*[1] II 5a). Here the reference is to the precinct of Westminster Abbey, a legal refuge for criminals and persons in danger until the dissolution of the monastery, and for debtors until 1602. Queen Elizabeth took 'her yonger sonne and her doughters oute of the Palyce of westminster in whiche shee then laye, into the Sainctuarye' (More, *CW2*, 20–1).

63 brother to brother] *F; not in Qq* 64 Blood to blood] *F;* bloud against bloud *Qq after* themselues *63* 66 earth] *F;* death *Qq* 68] *Steevens; F lines* farwell. / you. / ; *one line Qq* Madam, farewell] *F; not in Qq* Stay . . . go] *F;* Ile go along *Qq* 69] *Steevens; F, Qq line* cause. / go, / SD] *Malone subst.*

The seal I keep; and so betide to me
As well I tender you and all of yours.
Go, I'll conduct you to the sanctuary. *Exeunt.*

3.1 *The Trumpets sound. Enter young* PRINCE [Edward], *the* Dukes of Gloucester *and* BUCKINGHAM, [F]Lord[F] CARDINAL, [CATESBY,] *with others.*

BUCKINGHAM
Welcome, sweet Prince, to London, to your chamber.

RICHARD
Welcome, dear cousin, my thoughts' sovereign.

72 **seal** the Great Seal of England; for the Archbishop's gift of the Seal to Elizabeth, his second thoughts and subsequent secret recovery of it, fearing charges of 'ouermuch lightnesse' and departure from precedent, see Holinshed, 3.716; see also Hall, *Edward V*, fol. vii[r].

72–3 **so . . . yours** So may my fortune turn out as well as I take care of you and your family.

Note: The basic text for 3.1.1–166 is Q1. Thus the order of texts collated is different in this portion of the textual apparatus. See p. 435.

3.1 location: '*A Street*' (Capell)

0.1 ***young*** **PRINCE** Until Cibber, the Prince and his brother were played by boys (Tommy Kent and 'a little boy' in 1689–90). Cibber's 1700 cast includes Mrs Allison and Miss Chock in these parts; young women played them into the 20th century (Hankey, 150).

0.3 **Lord CARDINAL** Thomas Bourchier, Cardinal Archbishop of Canterbury; the identity of this figure suggests indebtedness to Hall (contrast 195–6, where Holinshed is the source; cf. 164n., 165n.). Holinshed follows More's English version (*History*), which has, through a mistake not in the Latin, the Archbishop of York, Thomas Rotherham (*CW*2, 27, 28, 194n.). If Shakespeare had followed Holinshed, the same figure who aids the Queen in 2.4 (called 'Cardinal' in Qq) would now be coming round to work for Richard; he would also have re-entered immediately after speaking at the close of the previous scene, an unusual violation of early modern theatrical norms. For another interpretation of the Cardinal's apparent cooperation with Richard, see 57n. The churchmen may be, like the nobility, divided. Historically, the Archbishop of 2.4, Thomas Rotherham, was a member of the Woodeville party, and the Cardinal of 3.1, Thomas Bourchier, among 'neutral councillors' (Hanham, 4–5). In *True Tragedy* a 'Cardinal' persuades the Queen to abandon sanctuary (840–90).

1 **chamber** capital or metropolis (*OED sb.* I 6); Hall and Holinshed repeat More's terms for London – 'the kings especiall chamber' (Holinshed, 3.729; Hall, *Edward V*, fol. xx[r]).

2 **my thoughts' sovereign** The Prince is Richard's actual sovereign, but Richard turns regal address toward sonneting usage; see *Son* 57.

74 Go] *F;* Come *Qq* **3.1**] *F (Actus Tertius. Scœna Prima.); not in Qq* 0.1–166] *text is that of Q1* 0.2 Dukes] *Q1–5, F; Duke Q6* 0.3 CATESBY] *Capell* *with others*] *F; &c. Qq* 1] *Qq; F lines* London, / Chamber. / 2, 7, 17, 181, 188, 190, 193, 198 SP] *F (Rich.); Glo. Qq*

The weary way hath made you melancholy.

PRINCE

No, uncle, but our crosses on the way
Have made it tedious, wearisome and heavy.
I want more uncles here to welcome me.

RICHARD

Sweet Prince, the untainted virtue of your years
Hath not yet dived into the world's deceit,
Nor more can you distinguish of a man
Than of his outward show, which, God He knows,
Seldom or never jumpeth with the heart.
Those uncles which you want were dangerous;
Your grace attended to their sugared words
But looked not on the poison of their hearts.
God keep you from them, and from such false friends.

PRINCE

God keep me from false friends, but they were none.

RICHARD

My lord, the Mayor of London comes to greet you.

Enter Lord MAYOR [*with others*].

MAYOR

God bless your grace with health and happy days.

4 **crosses** troubles, adversities (*OED* cross *sb*. B I 10b), i.e. the arrests of the Queen's relatives, referred to obliquely in 6; cf. 126 for a possible biblical echo.

5 **heavy** hard to perform or accomplish; laborious (*OED a*. VI 24a)

6, 12 **want** desire or lack (*OED v*. 2) **uncles** Earl Rivers was the Prince's uncle, but Grey was his half-brother – continuing the apparent confusion about Grey (cf. 1.3.37n.).

9–11 i.e. you can tell no more about someone than you can glean from outward appearances, which, God knows, seldom or never coincide with inner reality (Abbott, 174); cf. 1 Samuel, 16.7: 'man loketh on the outward appearaunce, but the Lorde beholdeth the heart'; also Luke, 16.15.

10 **God He knows** i.e. God knows; see Abbott, 243.

11 **jumpeth** agrees completely, coincides (*OED* jump *v*. I 5)

17.1 ***with others*** The Prince's thanks to *you all* (19) reveal that the Mayor is accompanied.

8 Hath] *Q1–5, F;* Haue *Q6* 9 Nor] *Qq;* No *F* 16] *Qq; F lines* Friends, / none. / from] *Q1–3, 5–6, F;* frō such *Q4* 17.1 *with others*] *Folg; and his train. / Capell* 18 SP] *Qq (Lo: M.), F (Lo. Maior.)*

PRINCE
I thank you, good my lord, and thank you all.
I thought my mother and my brother York
Would long ere this have met us on the way.
Fie, what a slug is Hastings, that he comes not
To tell us whether they will come or no.

Enter Lord HASTINGS.

BUCKINGHAM
And in good time, here comes the sweating lord.

PRINCE
Welcome, my lord. What, will our mother come?

HASTINGS
On what occasion God He knows, not I,
The Queen your mother and your brother York
Have taken sanctuary. The tender Prince
Would fain have come with me to meet your grace,
But by his mother was perforce withheld.

BUCKINGHAM
Fie, what an indirect and peevish course
Is this of hers! – Lord Cardinal, will your grace
Persuade the Queen to send the Duke of York
Unto his princely brother presently?
– If she deny, Lord Hastings, go with him,

22 **slug** slow, lazy fellow, sluggard
24 **in good time** See 2.1.45n.
25 **What** interjection introducing an expression of surprise, exclamation or question (*OED adv.* 21, *int.* 1–2)
26 **On what occasion** for what reason
God . . . I See Dent, G189.1; cf. *Oth* 3.3.302, where 'Heaven knows, not I' may imply that Emilia does not *want* to know the reasons for what is happening.
29 **fain** gladly
30 **perforce** forcibly (*OED adv.* 1); see 36.
31 **indirect** devious
peevish foolish (cf. 1.3.193), but also perverse, headstrong, obstinate, capricious (*OED* 4)
course way of action, manner of proceeding
34 **presently** at once

23.1] *F; opp. 23 Qq (Enter* L. *Ha[st].)* 29 have come] *Q1–2, 4, F;* come *Q3, 5–6* 33 to send] *Q1–2, 4, 6, F;* thesend *Q3;* they send *Q5* 35 him] *Q1–4, F;* them *Q5–6*

And from her jealous arms pluck him perforce.

CARDINAL

My lord of Buckingham, if my weak oratory
Can from his mother win the Duke of York,
Anon expect him here; but if she be obdurate
To mild entreaties, God in heaven forbid
We should infringe the holy privilege
Of blessed sanctuary. Not for all this land,
Would I be guilty of so deep a sin.

BUCKINGHAM

You are too senseless-obstinate, my lord,
Too ceremonious and traditional.
Weigh it but with the grossness of this age,
You break not sanctuary in seizing him.

36 **jealous** suspicious, apprehensive of evil (*OED* 5)
perforce Implications of moral or physical force (30) here become distinctly physical and violent.

39 **Anon** shortly, instantly

40–2 **God . . . sanctuary** Cf. the Cardinal's scruples: 'God forbyd that any manne shoulde, for any yearthely, enterprise to breake the immunyte and libertie of that sacred sanctuary' (Hall, *Edward V*, fols viii^{v}–ix^{r}).

42 **blessed** blessèd

44 **senseless-obstinate** unreasonably obstinate (*OED* senseless 3b), one of a number of unusual verbal compounds in the play (cf. 4.2.42, 4.4.55)

45 **ceremonious** punctilious in observing formalities (*OED* 5), but when coupled with accusations of being too *traditional*, a powerful charge to levy in the 1590s against a prelate. The *Book of Common Prayer* (1559) proclaims the long-standing Protestant rejection of 'ceremonial' emphases in worship (*BCP*, 19). Such strictures were balanced by fears of 'innovations and newfangleness' and an emphasis on retaining those ceremonies that were in keeping with 'order' and 'quiet discipline in the Church' (*BCP*, 20).

46–7 *Frequently emended: how can the 'grossness of this age' – a phrase often taken to mean the 'lack of refinement' in habits, ideas or morality of the times – justify an argument asserting legal technicalities rather than indicting current mores? It has been argued that 46 should refer to the previous remarks about being too ceremonious and traditional. Dr Johnson suggested that the sense of the lines is that if one compare the act of seizure with the gross practices of these times it will not be considered wrong, for the act may be defended with the kind of coarse reasons men have grown accustomed to accepting (Var). Buckingham's self-serving pronouncements are frequently sophistic and may not sustain scrutiny for logical coherence.

47–56 A concise excerpt from an extended argument (*CW*2, 28–33, repeated

38 the] *Q1–2, 4–6, F;* to *Q3* 40 in heaven] *Q1–2; om. Q3–6, F* 43 deep] *Q1–2;* great *Q3–6, F* 44 senseless-obstinate] *Qq, F (*sencelesse obstinate*), hyphen Theobald* 46 grossness] *Q1–5, F;* greatnesse *Q6*

The benefit thereof is always granted
To those whose dealings have deserved the place
And those who have the wit to claim the place.
This prince hath neither claimed it nor deserved it
And therefore, in mine opinion, cannot have it.
Then taking him from thence that is not there
You break no privilege nor charter there.
Oft have I heard of sanctuary men,
But sanctuary children, never till now.

CARDINAL
My lord, you shall o'errule my mind for once.
– Come on, Lord Hastings, will you go with me?

HASTINGS
I go, my lord.

PRINCE
Good lords, make all the speedy haste you may.
Exeunt Cardinal and Hastings.
Say, uncle Gloucester, if our brother come,
Where shall we sojourn till our coronation?

in Hall, and Holinshed, 3.718). Cf. Richard's similarly specious reasoning concerning an oath to Henry VI (*3H6* 1.2.22–7).

50 **wit** intelligence

54 **charter** privilege, immunity (*OED sb.*[1] 3)
there in that respect

55–6 **sanctuary men . . . children** This claim from More (Holinshed, 3.718) is not necessarily true for Shakespeare's day (Machyn, 121).

56 ***never** Qq's 'neuer' is closer to Holinshed than is F's 'ne're' (Honigmann, 'Text', 50).

57 Motivation for the Cardinal's co-operation is unclear. Mancini (89) claims, 'the cardinal was suspecting no guile, and had persuaded the queen to do this, seeking as much to prevent a violation of the sanctuary as to mitigate by his good services the fierce resolve of the duke'.

60 **speedy haste** Does this redundancy pun on Hastings's name? *Leicester's Commonwealth* (1584) plays on the Hastings family name of the Earl of Huntingdon, calling him 'the Hastie Earle' (*Copy*, 106); cf. 'Hastynges I am, whose hastned death, whoe knewe' (*Mirror*, 'Hastings', 1).

61–2 **our . . . we** i.e. my . . . I; the Prince's first unambiguous royal plural (cf. 4, 21, 23). He is now King Edward V although not yet crowned. See 96.

53 taking] *Q1–5, F;* take *Q6* 56 never] *Qq;* ne're *F* 57 o'errule] *F* (o're-rule*), Qq (*ouerrule*)* 60 SD] *Q3–6, F opp. 59; not in Q1–2 Exeunt*] *Rowe; Exit Q3–6, F*

RICHARD

Where it seems best unto your royal self.
If I may counsel you, some day or two
Your highness shall repose you at the Tower;
Then where you please and shall be thought most fit
For your best health and recreation.

PRINCE

I do not like the Tower, of any place.
– Did Julius Caesar build that place, my lord?

BUCKINGHAM

He did, my gracious lord, begin that place,
Which since succeeding ages have re-edified.

PRINCE

Is it upon record, or else reported
Successively from age to age, he built it?

BUCKINGHAM

Upon record, my gracious lord.

PRINCE

But say, my lord, it were not registered,
Methinks the truth should live from age to age,

63–7 Beginning with an apparent offer of self-determination to the Prince, Richard's show of deference and tentative advice becomes insistence with his *shall*, only to morph again in his final ambiguous offer. The 'Machiavel who delights in manipulating others to do his bidding revealingly qualifies the ascription of choice to the prince in a line that could refer to himself but elides subject and agency: "shall be thought most fit"' (Dubrow, 357).

64 **some** On 'some' used with numeral adjectives qualifying nouns of time, see Abbott, 21.

65 **the Tower** The Tower had been used as a royal residence, even by Edward IV. According to Vergil 'this [lodging] causyd no suspytion' (178); but by Shakespeare's time it had acquired a sinister reputation, in part through the events depicted in this play. The murders of Henry VI and Clarence (cf. 144–5) would account for the Prince's reluctance.

68 **of any place** i.e. of all places; cf. Abbott, 409.

69–74 Buckingham affirms a legend; the oldest parts of the Tower, built close inside the city's Roman walls, date only to the 11th century (see Stow, 1.48).

71 **re-edified** rebuilt; cf. *Tit* 1.1.356.

72 **upon record** i.e. written down

75 **registered** set down in writing

63–154 SP] *Capell (Ric.); Glo. Qq, F* 63 seems] *Q1–2;* thinkst *Q3–6, F*

As 'twere retailed to all posterity,
Even to the general all-ending day.

RICHARD [*aside*]

So wise so young, they say, do never live long.

PRINCE

What say you, uncle?

RICHARD

I say, without characters fame lives long.
[*aside*] Thus, like the formal Vice, Iniquity,
I moralize two meanings in one word.

PRINCE

That Julius Caesar was a famous man,
With what his valour did enrich his wit,

77 **retailed** recounted, repeated to others (*OED v.* 2); cf. 4.4.335. See also 86.

78 **the . . . day** Judgement Day, the biblical end of the world (see 1.4.103–4). On its 'general trumpet' summoning all humanity, see *2H6* 5.2.40–3.

79 See Dent, L384: 'Too soon wise to live long'; but also presumed medical fact (see Bright, 54). Mancini, who knew the Prince's physician, John Argentine, writes that 'he gave . . . many proofs of his liberal education, of polite, nay rather scholarly, attainments far beyond his age' (93; cf. C. Ross, *Richard*, 71).

81 **characters** charàcters; writing (cf. *Son* 59), literally, written letters of the alphabet. Contrast written 'characters' as a defence against time in *MM* 5.1.10–13.

82 **formal Vice, Iniquity** the 'unmistakable' or 'precise' (*OED* formal 3, 6) stage figure of the Vice named Iniquity; cf. *1H4* 2.4.441. Vices often equivocate and invite audience appreciation for 'dexterity in deceit' (Spivack, 394–5). See pp. 6–8.

83 **moralize** interpret morally or symbolically (*OED* 1, citing this line); cf. *AYL* 2.1.44.
one word a single sentence, utterance (*OED* 1) or, perhaps, a single word. Cf. Speed's punning observation: 'your old vice still: mistake the word' (*TGV* 3.1.278). In *3H6* Richard uses 'word' to mean utterance (*3H6* 5.5.27). It is difficult to single out a word from Richard's lines for special notice; suggestions include *characters*, *say* or *lives long*.

84–8 A notoriously difficult speech, despite the apparent clarity of 87–8. For similarly idealistic (and ill-fated) pronouncements, see *LLL* 1.1.1–7; cf. *Son* 55, 63–5. For a counter-perspective on Caesar as an ambitious, bloody monster difficult to reconcile with his writings, see *Fennes Frutes* (1590; STC 10763), fol. 9^{r-v}. In *True Tragedy* Richard's simple formula – 'Valour brings fame, and fame conquers death' (397–8) – leaves 'wit' out of the equation.

85 **what** i.e. that with which (Abbott, 252)

78 all-ending] *Q1;* ending *Q2–6, F* 79 SD] *Johnson* 82 SD] *F2* Thus] *Q1–5, F;* That *Q6*

His wit set down to make his valure live.
Death makes no conquest of this conqueror,
For now he lives in fame, though not in life.
I'll tell you what, my cousin Buckingham.

BUCKINGHAM
What, my gracious lord?

PRINCE
An if I live until I be a man,
I'll win our ancient right in France again
Or die a soldier as I lived a king.

RICHARD [*aside*]
Short summers lightly have a forward spring.

Enter young [Duke of] YORK, HASTINGS ^{F}*and*^{F} CARDINAL.

BUCKINGHAM
Now in good time here comes the Duke of York.

86 **set down** put into writing (*OED* set *v.*[1] 143a; cf. *Ham* 1.5.107), but given the proximity of *valure* and *conqueror*, possibly hinting at 'set down' meaning to besiege, to encamp an army (*OED* 143b), as *Cor* 5.3.1–2. 'Set down' also signified establishing a price for something (*OED* 143e), a meaning apparently irrelevant here except for the proximity of *enrich* and *valure* and the troublesome obscurity of the phrasing.
***valure** This term (Q1–2) has the same triple meaning as 'valour' (Q3–6, F), but *valure* reminds one of its polysemousness. Both terms could mean worthiness, courage and monetary or material value (*OED* valour 1a, 1c, 2, 3). The material sense is reinforced by reference to enrichment and by *retailed* in 77. *The Mirror of Friendship* (1584; STC 17979.7) uses 'valure' in all three senses (sigs Aiii^{r}, B6^{v}–B7^{r}, C1^{r}).

88 **lives in fame** Cf. *Tit* 1.1.161.
91 **An if** i.e. if
92 **ancient . . . France** the claim dating at least to Edward II's marriage in 1308 to Isabella, daughter of Philip IV of France, repeatedly asserted by English invasions during the Hundred Years' War (1337–1453). Henry V was named 'King of England and Heir of France' in 1420, but by 1453 his son, Henry VI, had lost what Henry V had gained in battle (see *1H6*, *2H6*). For Elizabethan invocation of Caesar's conquests and the English 'right' in France, see the *Preface* to *The Eight Books of Caius Julius Caesar* (1590; STC 4336).
94 proverbial (Tilley, F774: 'Sharp frosts bite forward springs'); Dent excludes.
lightly probably, commonly (*OED* 6)
forward early (*OED a.* 5b; cf. *TGV* 1.1.45), playing on 'forward' as presumptuous, pert (*OED a.* 8); see 155.
95 **in good time** i.e. just at the right moment

86 valure] *Q1–2;* valour *Q3–6, F* 87 this] *Q1;* his *Q2–6, F* 91 An] *Qq, F* (And), *Theobald*
94 SD] *Johnson* 94.1 Duke of] *Ard*^{2}

PRINCE
Richard of York, how fares our loving brother?

YORK
Well, my dread lord – so must I call you now.

PRINCE
Ay, brother, to our grief, as it is yours.
Too late he died that might have kept that title,
Which by his death hath lost much majesty.

RICHARD
How fares our cousin, noble lord of York?

YORK
I thank you, gentle uncle. O my lord,
You said that idle weeds are fast in growth.
The Prince my brother hath outgrown me far.

RICHARD
He hath, my lord.

YORK
And therefore is he idle?

RICHARD
O my fair cousin, I must not say so.

YORK
Then he is more beholding to you than I.

RICHARD
He may command me as my sovereign,
But you have power in me as in a kinsman.

96 **our** The Prince's royal plurals signal his difference in rank from his brother (see 61–2n.).
97 **dread** held in awe, revered (*OED ppl. a.* 2); appropriate to his now kingly brother, but probably with playful exaggeration as in York's subsequent lines.
99 **late** lately, recently
he Edward IV, their father
that might i.e. who we wish would (Abbott, 313)
101 **cousin** kinsman
103 **idle** useless (*OED* 3); cf. 2.4.13n.
106 **must** Richard denies that the Prince is idle, but his utterance leaves open the possibility that he might say such a thing if it were not forbidden by deference.
107 **beholding** obliged (see 2.1.130)
109 **power . . . kinsman** For the range of interpersonal claims that could be empowered by early modern kinship relations, see Cressy, 'Kinship'.
in . . . in over me in that I am

96 Richard] *Q6, F;* Rich. *Q1–5* loving] *Q1–2;* noble *Q3–6, F* 97 dread] *Q1–2;* deare *Q3–6, F* 105] *Steevens; Qq, F line* Lo: / idle? /

YORK

I pray you, uncle, give me this dagger.

RICHARD

My dagger, little cousin? With all my heart.

PRINCE

A beggar, brother?

YORK

Of my kind uncle, that I know will give,
And being but a toy, which is no grief to give.

RICHARD

A greater gift than that I'll give my cousin.

YORK

A greater gift? O, that's the sword to it.

RICHARD

Ay, gentle cousin, were it light enough.

YORK

O, then I see you will part but with light gifts;
In weightier things you'll say a beggar nay.

RICHARD

It is too heavy for your grace to wear.

110–31 The 1970 Terry Hands promptbook registers the tensions generated by young York's insults and petulance and Richard's barely concealed resentment and menace: Richard offered a toy, which York threw down, demanding the dagger, only to throw it down at *greater gift* (116). At *light gifts* (118) he stamped on the toy; the Prince cried out York's name ('Richard!') and picked up the toy, while York went for Richard's sword. When his uncle bent down for the dagger, York jumped on his back at 'bear me on your shoulders' (131), to be shaken off and fall to the floor (Hankey, 155).

110–11 **dagger** The prominence of Richard's dagger in the sources and, possibly, in early performances is suggested only here. See p. 84; cf. 4.1.84n.

111 **With . . . heart** Richard's superficially eager generosity suggests that he would give the Prince his dagger by stabbing him with it.

112 **A beggar** Are you now a beggar?

114 **toy** trifle (*OED sb.* II 5)
grief trouble

116 **to it** that goes along with it (i.e. the dagger)

117–18 **light . . . light** light in weight . . . trivial, inconsequential

119 **weightier** more valuable or consequential
say . . . nay deny one who begs

111 With all] *Q3–6, F;* withall *Q1–2* 114 grief] *Q1–5, F;* gift *Q6* 120 heavy] *Q1;* waightie *Q2–6, F* your] *Q1–5, F;* you *Q6*

YORK
I weigh it lightly, were it heavier.
RICHARD
What, would you have my weapon, little lord?
YORK
I would, that I might thank you as you call me.
RICHARD How?
YORK Little.
PRINCE
My lord of York will still be cross in talk.
Uncle, your grace knows how to bear with him.
YORK
You mean to bear me, not to bear with me.
– Uncle, my brother mocks both you and me.
Because that I am little, like an ape,
He thinks that you should bear me on your shoulders.

121 Literally, 'I consider it light even if it were heavier'; figuratively, 'I consider it merely a trivial gift even if it were of more value or consequence'. On the inappropriateness of such a statement from someone who has just requested the dagger and on the oddity of Richard's response, see *TxC*, 239. Richard's *What* may signal surprise or incomprehension, and his line might mean 'What, do you want it or not?' Richard may resent the challenge to his verbal dominance.

122 **weapon** i.e. Richard's sword

123 ***as** F's retention of Q3's mistaken 'as as' constitutes crucial evidence for Q3 as the basic text for F 3.1. See p. 435.

125 **Little** i.e. York would give him small thanks, just as Richard gives him little respect by terming him paltry, contemptible (*OED* little *a.* I 9).

126 **still** always
cross perverse, inclined to quarrel (*OED a.* 5a); possibly introducing a play in 127 on Jesus's reference to one who does not 'beare his crosse' (Luke, 14.27); cf. 4.

130–1 **ape . . . shoulders** In popular entertainments a bear might carry a monkey on its shoulders, so York's insults suggest Richard's ungainliness and his shape recalling the burdened bear. Fools, too, carried apes (as does Will Somers in the anonymous Hampton Court painting of Henry VIII's family, *c.* 1545). For late Elizabethan association of ape-bearing and hunchbacks, see p. 33. As a little ape on Richard's shoulders, York recalls the image of the scolding jackanapes (*Almond*, sig. E4[r]). York's triple play on *bear* – to endure, to carry and the animal – outpuns Touchstone (*AYL* 2.4.10–12). Richard's failure to respond verbally may suggest 'vulnerability' to 'contempt that he neither initiates nor directs' (Anderson, 115),

123 would,] *Q1;* would *Q2–6, F* as] *Q1–2, 4–6;* as as *Q3;* as, as, *F* 124–5] *F; one line Qq* 130 ape,] *Q1–4, F;* Ape. *Q5–6*

BUCKINGHAM [*aside*]
With what a sharp-provided wit he reasons:
To mitigate the scorn he gives his uncle,
He prettily and aptly taunts himself.
So cunning and so young is wonderful.

RICHARD [*to the Prince*]
My lord, will't please you pass along?
Myself and my good cousin Buckingham
Will to your mother to entreat of her
To meet you at the Tower and welcome you.

YORK [*to the Prince*]
What, will you go unto the Tower, my lord?

PRINCE
My Lord Protector needs will have it so.

YORK
I shall not sleep in quiet at the Tower.

RICHARD Why, what should you fear?

YORK
Marry, my uncle Clarence' angry ghost.
My grandam told me he was murdered there.

PRINCE
I fear no uncles dead.

but strong stage reactions date back to Irving's 1896 production, which gave Richard a 'look of concentrated rage and hatred'. A related stage tradition (see e.g. Olivier's film and Sam Mendes's 1992 production) has York leap upon Richard's shoulders (see p. 115 and Fig. 9).

132 SD *aside* Capell suggested direction to Hastings, but perhaps an observation shared with the audience.

132 **sharp-provided** agile, pointed, ready for any occasion (here, with witticisms) (*OED* provided *ppl. a.* 2); Richard's own *sharp* wit goes back to Vergil (227).

133 **scorn** taunt; cf. *1H4* 3.2.64.

134 **prettily** cleverly, skilfully (*OED* 1, citing this line)

135 **cunning** clever, skilful and/or crafty, guileful (*OED a.* 2, 5)

136 **pass along** continue on your way

140 **What,** The comma might be omitted, making the line less exclamatory (Jowett) and taking *What* as 'Why' (Abbott, 253; cf. *Tit* 1.1.192).

141 **needs** Q1 provides the syllable missing from Q2–6, F (Thompson).

132 SD] *Capell (to* Hastings.*)* sharp-provided] *Qq, F (*sharpe prouided*), hyphen Theobald* 133 gives] *Q1–2, 4, F;* giue *Q3, 5–6* 136, 140 SD] *Folg, Bevington*[4] 141 needs] *Q1; om. Q2–6, F* 145 grandam] *F;* Granam *Qq* murdered] *Qq (*murdred*), F (*murther'd*)*

RICHARD

Nor none that live, I hope.

PRINCE

An if they live, I hope I need not fear.
But come, my lord. With a heavy heart,
Thinking on them, go I unto the Tower. [F]*A sennet.*[F]

Exeunt [*all but*] *Richard, Buckingham* [F]*and Catesby*[F].

BUCKINGHAM

Think you, my lord, this little prating York
Was not incensed by his subtle mother
To taunt and scorn you thus opprobriously?

RICHARD

No doubt, no doubt. O, 'tis a perilous boy,
Bold, quick, ingenious, forward, capable.
He is all the mother's, from the top to toe.

BUCKINGHAM

Well, let them rest. – Come hither, Catesby.

148 **An if** if; the Prince does not directly answer Richard's question, but suggests concern about his recently arrested relatives (see 2.4.43–6).

148–50 **they . . . them** referring to Rivers and Grey; Grey was the Prince's half-brother (see 6n., 1.3.37n.).

150 SD 1 ***sennet*** set of notes on a trumpet or cornet, signalling a ceremonial entrance or exit

152 **incensed** incensèd; incited to action (*OED* *v.*^{2} 4)

153 **opprobriously** abusively (*OED* 1)

154 ***perilous** Qq and F agree on 'perilous', but F employs the alternative 'parlous' at 2.4.35 (set by Compositor B). Both forms could convey danger as well as cunning. Q7–8 have 'perlous'.

155 **quick** full of vigour, energy or activity (*OED a.* III 19a)
forward precocious, pert (*OED a.* 7, 8); when Richard and his brothers coerce him into entailing the crown upon the Yorkist line, Henry VI calls them York's 'forward sons' (*3H6* 1.1.203).
capable intelligent, competent; contrast the Duchess's *Incapable* grandchildren (2.2.18).

156 **mother's** In *3H6* Richard makes a similar claim about young Prince Edward of Lancaster: 'Whoever got thee, there thy mother stands, / For well I wot thou hast thy mother's tongue' (*3H6* 2.2.133–4).
from . . . toe proverbial (Dent, T436)

157 Once again, as in 31–56 and 2.2.120–50, Buckingham appears to take charge. His prominence at such moments prompted 18th- and 19th-century cuts to effect a 'neutralization' of his part (Hankey, 151, 158).
let them rest i.e. let them be

148 An] *Qq, F (*And*), Theobald* 149 With] *Qq;* and with *F* 150 SD2 *Exeunt . . . Buckingham*] *Qq, F subst. (Exeunt Prin. Yor. Hast. (Hast. Hast. Q3) Dors. manet, Rich. Buc[k]. Q1–4; Exeunt Prin. Yor. Hast. Dors manet. Bich. Buc. Q5; Exeunt Prin. Yor. Hast. Dors manet. Bish. Buc. Q6; Exeunt Prince, Yorke, Hastings, and Dorset. / Manet Richard, Buckingham, F)*

Thou art sworn as deeply to effect what we intend
As closely to conceal what we impart.
Thou knowst our reasons, urged upon the way.
What think'st thou? Is it not an easy matter
To make William, Lord Hastings, of our mind
For the instalment of this noble Duke
In the seat royal of this famous isle?

CATESBY

He for his father's sake so loves the Prince
That he will not be won to aught against him.

BUCKINGHAM

What think'st thou then of Stanley? Will not he?

CATESBY

He will do all in all as Hastings doth.

BUCKINGHAM

Well then, no more but this: go, gentle Catesby,
And as it were far off, sound thou Lord Hastings
How he doth stand affected to our purpose

160 **urged . . . way** discussed on the journey (from Ludlow to London)

163 **instalment** installation (*OED* 1, citing this line)

164 **seat royal** Richard 'sate in the seate roial' after being proclaimed king (Hall, *Richard III*, fol. xxv^{r}; Hardyng, *Richard III*, fol. lxxvii^{v}); More and Holinshed do not use the phrase. See evidence for Hall as source at 0.3n.; for Holinshed as source, see 195–6n.

165 **for . . . sake** i.e. for the sake of King Edward, the Prince's father; Hastings is Edward's 'chiefest friend' (*3H6* 4.3.11). Queen Elizabeth disliked Hastings 'for the great fauour the king bare him: and also for that she thought him secretlie familiar with the king in wanton companie' (Holinshed, 3.713).

167 *At this point F resumes full textual authority, no longer reprinting Q3 verbatim. This line is the last on sig. F2^{r} in Q3, 6.

170–7 Catesby's actions in 3.2 differ from his orders in 172–3 (Smidt, *Impostors*, 112), thus providing a possible explanation for absence of these lines from Qq. More characterizes Buckingham as speaking 'wyth some words cast out a farre of' (*CW2*, 46; cf. Holinshed, 3.722). Cf. 'It is better to sound a person with whom one deals, afar off, than to fall upon the point at first' (Bacon, *Works*, 6.493).

170 **far off** i.e. elliptically (cf. 3.5.93)
sound discover by conversational means; cf. 3.4.16n.

171 **doth stand affected** i.e. is disposed

160 knowst] *F (*know'st*), Qq (*knowest*)*   161 think'st] *F; Qq (*thinkest*)*   167] *F resumes as text until 5.3.49*   think'st] *F; Qq (*thinkest*)*   Will not] *F;* what will *Qq*   169–71] *Pope; F lines* this: / off, / *Hastings*, / purpose, / ; *Qq line* this: / off, / affected / willing, /   170 far] *F;* a farre *Qq*   thou] *F, Q1–2; om. Q3–6*   171 doth stand . . . to] *F;* stands . . . Vnto *Qq*   our] *F, Q1–3, 5–6;* your *Q4*

And summon him tomorrow to the Tower
To sit about the coronation.
If thou dost find him tractable to us,
Encourage him, and tell him all our reasons.
If he be leaden, icy, cold, unwilling,
Be thou so too, and so break off the talk,
And give us notice of his inclination;
For we tomorrow hold divided councils,
Wherein thyself shalt highly be employed.

RICHARD

Commend me to Lord William. Tell him, Catesby,
His ancient knot of dangerous adversaries
Tomorrow are let blood at Pomfret Castle,
And bid my lord, for joy of this good news,
Give Mistress Shore one gentle kiss the more.

BUCKINGHAM

Good Catesby, go effect this business soundly.

CATESBY

My good lords both, with all the heed I can.

173 **sit about** discuss in council
179 **divided councils** separate meetings – one concerning the coronation, one in private consultation with Richard (at Crosby House according to Hall) about making him king. More says Richard and Buckingham 'set the lord Cardinall, the Archebishoppe of Yorke than lorde Chauncellor, the Bishoppe of Ely, the lord Stanley & the lord Hastinges than lord chamberleine, w[t] many other noble men to commune & deuise about the coronacion in one place: as fast were they in an other place contryuyng the contrary, & to make the protectour kyng'. These proceedings occasioned 'muttering amonge the people' (*CW*2, 44).
181 SP *With this line the SPs for Richard in Qq and F, '*Glo.*' and '*Rich.*', stabilize until 3.7.245.
181 **Lord William** i.e. Hastings
182 **ancient knot** long-standing group (*OED* knot *sb.*[1] III 18); cf. *JC* 3.1.117.
183 **are let blood** i.e. will bleed; surgical bleeding here used euphemistically for execution
185 **Mistress Shore** More says Jane Shore became Hastings's mistress after King Edward's death (*CW*2, 53).
186 **soundly** thoroughly (*OED* 3)
187 **heed** care, attention (*OED sb.* 1a)

172–3] *F; not in Qq* 174] *F;* if he be willing, *Qq* 175 tell] *F;* shew *Qq* 177 the] *F;* your *Qq* 181+ SP] *F (Rich.); Glo. Qq* 184 lord] *F;* friend *Q1–5;* friends *Q2 (Hn 69352), Q6* 185 Mistress] *F, Q1–2;* gentle Mistresse *Q3–6* 186 go] *F; not in Qq* 187 can] *F;* may *Qq*

RICHARD
Shall we hear from you, Catesby, ere we sleep?
CATESBY
You shall, my lord.
RICHARD
At Crosby House, there shall you find us both. *Exit Catesby.*
BUCKINGHAM
Now, my lord, what shall we do if we perceive
Lord Hastings will not yield to our complots?
RICHARD
Chop off his head; something we will determine.
And look when I am king, claim thou of me
The earldom of Hereford and all the moveables

188–9 *A version of these lines occurs again at Qq 4.2.81. Catesby does not carry out this commission until the next morning; therefore Daniel (xix) reasons that the lines were transposed in revision of F to a place in Qq where they better fit the situation but were never struck out here. Jowett (381) argues that Qq's repetition is 'purposefully echoic, drawing attention to the compulsively repetitive nature of Richard's crimes'.

192 **yield . . . complots** assent to our conspiracies
complots complòts (còmplots in 200)

193 *Hammond argues for Qq, with its familiar 'man' expressing Richard's 'hail-fellow-well-met tone'; White (290) appreciates F's pun on *determine* as 'bring to an end'. F's sequence has a characteristic feel: immediate decision ('Chop off his head') followed by teasing reference to *something* later to be *determine*[*d*] to justify the precipitous execution (cf. Richard's unspecified *secret intent* at 1.1.56–8 and vague *complots* at 3.1.200).

194 **look when** as soon as

195–6 Holinshed, closely following More (*CW2*, 44), records that Richard agreed to Buckingham's 'quiet possession of the earldome of Hereford', and 'of his owne mind promised [Buckingham] a great quantitie of the kings treasure, and of his household stuffe' (3.721). Buckingham could claim the earldom of Hereford by descent from Thomas of Woodstock, who had been married to Eleanor, daughter and co-heiress of Humphrey de Bohun, Earl of Hereford, Essex and Northampton. Buckingham's claim to the Earldom of Hereford was a claim to the moiety of the Bohun possessions which, by the marriage of a younger co-heiress, had passed to an elder branch of the royal family (Thompson; cf. Horrox, 133; More, *CW2*, 267n.; Vergil, 192–3). See also 4.2.87–120. Hall does not include this material.

195 **moveables** moveable personal property (as opposed to real estate) (*OED* B *sb.* 2)

190 House] *F;* place *Qq* SD] *F; opp. 189 Q3–6; not in Q1–2* 191] *Qq; F lines* Lord, / perceiue / 192 Lord] *F;* William Lo: *Qq* 193] *Qq; F lines* Head: / determine: / head; something . . . determine] *F;* head man, somewhat . . . doe *Qq* 195 Hereford] *F, Q1–2;* Herford *Q3–5; Hertford Q6* all] *F; not in Qq*

Whereof the King my brother was possessed.

BUCKINGHAM

I'll claim that promise at your grace's hand.

RICHARD

And look to have it yielded with all kindness.
Come, let us sup betimes, that afterwards
We may digest our complots in some form. *Exeunt.*

3.2 *Enter a* Messenger *to the door of Hastings.*

MESSENGER My lord, my lord. [*Knocks.*]

HASTINGS [*within*] Who knocks?

MESSENGER One from the Lord Stanley.

HASTINGS [*within*]

What is't o'clock?

MESSENGER Upon the stroke of four.

Enter Lord HASTINGS.

HASTINGS

Cannot my Lord Stanley sleep these tedious nights?

199 **betimes** soon
200 **digest** ponder, settle and arrange methodically (*OED v.* 3), but, given *sup* (199), also playing on physical digestion **complots** See 192n.
3.2 location: '*before Lord* Hastings's *House*' (Theobald)
0.1 *door* Elizabethan staging dictates the Messenger's entry at one rear door to knock at the other, with subsequent entries and exits through the first door. *Mirror* mentions Jane Shore in Hastings's arms at this moment ('Hastings', 393–4); many productions bring her on with him (Hankey, 160). The knock at his door ironically connects Hastings's guilty past and doomed future: in *3H6* he knocks at the city door of York for King Edward, who falsely swears his innocence of any plot against Henry VI (*3H6* 4.7.16). Hall excoriates this perjury as meriting punishments extending into the reign of Richard III (*Edward IV*, fols ccxiv^{v}–ccxv^{r}).
1–4 *Qq dialogue conveys that the speaker is a 'messenger' who knocks 'at the door'. F's SDs typically specify such details (Greg, *Problem*, 172).

196 was] *F;* stood *Qq* 197 hand] *F;* hands *Qq* 198 all kindness] *F;* all willingnes *Q1;* willingnesse *Q2–6* 3.2] *F (Scena Secunda.); not in Qq* 0.1 *the door of*] *F; Lo: Qq* 1] *F;* What ho my Lord. *Qq* SD] *Capell subst.* 2 SD] *Theobald* knocks?] *F;* Who knockes at the dore. *(*dore? *Q2–5;* coore? *Q6) Qq* 3 One] *F;* A messenger *Qq* 4] *Steevens; F, Qq line* Clocke? / foure. / SD] *Steevens; not in F, Qq* What is't o'clock] *F (*a Clocke*);* Whats a clocke *Qq* 4.1] *F; opp. 3 Qq* 5 my Lord Stanley] *F;* thy Master *Qq* these] *F, Q1;* the *Q2–6* tedious] *F, Q1–2, 4, 6;* teditous *Q3, 5*

MESSENGER
So it appears by that I have to say.
First, he commends him to your noble self.
HASTINGS What then?
MESSENGER
Then certifies your lordship that this night
He dreamt the boar had razed off his helm.
Besides, he says there are two councils kept,
And that may be determined at the one
Which may make you and him to rue at th'other.
Therefore he sends to know your lordship's pleasure,
If you will presently take horse with him
And with all speed post with him toward the north,
To shun the danger that his soul divines.
HASTINGS
Go, fellow, go. Return unto thy lord.
Bid him not fear the separated council:
His honour and myself are at the one,

9 **certifies** informs

10 **boar** Richard's heraldic animal (1.3.227); Q1's 'beare' persists until Q6 changes to 'Boare', a remarkable persistence since Hastings's next Qq speech has 'boare' four times.
razed . . . helm slashed, torn off his helmet, suggesting erasing (razing) the heraldic family crest (see *Son* 25 for 'rased/razed' as erasure). More's Stanley dreamed 'that a bore with his tuskes so raced [Hastings and himself] bi the heddes, that the blood ranne aboute both their shoulders' (*CW2*, 50; cf. Hall, *Edward V*, fol. xiv[v]; Holinshed, 3.722).

11 **two councils** See 3.1.179.
***kept** held (*OED v.* 34); since to 'keep counsel' means to keep something secret (*OED v.* 31; cf. *RJ* 2.4.195), F's 'kept' may carry more sinister associations than Qq's 'held'.

12 **that** i.e. something

13 **rue** repent, regret

15 **presently** immediately

16 **post** ride quickly, see 1.1.146.
north perhaps towards Stanley's holdings in Lancashire or Hastings's in Leicestershire and Northampton (Hall, *Edward V*, fol. xiii[v]). Holinshed has Stanley advising escape 'so farre the same night, that they should be out of danger' by day (Holinshed, 3.723); *Mirror* has him suggest riding 'strayght homewarde' ('Hastings', 389).

17 **divines** predicts or prophesies (*OED v.* I 3, citing this line)

20 **His honour** i.e. Stanley

6 appears] *F;* should seeme *Qq* 7 self] *F;* Lordship *Qq* 8–9] *F; one line Qq* 8 What] *F;* And *Qq* 9] *F;* And then he sends you word. *Qq* 10 dreamt] *F;* dreamt to night *Qq* boar] *F, Q6;* beare *Q1–5* razed off] *F (*rased off*);* raste *Q1–4;* caste *Q5;* cast *Q6* 11 kept] *F;* held *Qq* 13 th'other] *F;* the other *Qq* 15 you will presently] *F;* presently you will *Qq* 16 with him toward] *F;* into *Qq* 18 Go, fellow] *F, Q1–2;* Good fellow *Q3–6* 19 council] *F (*Councell*);* counsels *Qq subst.*

And at the other is my good friend Catesby,
Where nothing can proceed that toucheth us
Whereof I shall not have intelligence.
Tell him his fears are shallow, without instance;
And for his dreams, I wonder he's so simple
To trust the mockery of unquiet slumbers.
To fly the boar before the boar pursues
Were to incense the boar to follow us
And make pursuit where he did mean no chase.
Go, bid thy master rise and come to me,
And we will both together to the Tower,
Where he shall see the boar will use us kindly.

MESSENGER

I'll go, my lord, and tell him what you say. *Exit.*

Enter CATESBY.

CATESBY

Many good morrows to my noble lord.

HASTINGS

Good morrow, Catesby. You are early stirring.
What news, what news, in this our tottering state?

21 ***good friend** F follows More, Hall and Holinshed in having Hastings designate Catesby a trusted associate (Holinshed, 3.722); *Mirror*'s Hastings calls him 'the apple of myne eye' ('Hastings', 319–28). Qq's 'seruant' need not imply a menial position (see *OED sb.* 2e, 4a; cf. 1.2.209, Qq 3.7.57).
22 **toucheth** concerns
24 **instance** cause, motive (*OED sb.* I 2); sign, token or mark (*OED sb.* III 7; cf. *Luc* 1511)
26 **mockery** unreal appearance (*OED* 2); cf. *Mac* 3.4.106: 'Unreal mock'ry, hence!'
32 **kindly** Hastings means that Richard will treat them with kindness, but 16th-century audiences would have been aware that Hastings will be notoriously dealt with in a manner that is in kind with Richard's violent, boarish nature; cf. 2.2.24n. and Hamlet's pun on 'kind' (*Ham* 1.2.65).
33 *Cf. Qq here and at 3.7.69 ('Ile tell him what you say my Lord.'); cf. 3.1.188–9n. for similar Qq repetition. For F repetition, see 110n.

21 good friend] *F;* seruant *Qq* 24 without] *F;* wanting *Qq* instance] *F, Q1;* instancie *Q2–6* 25 he's] *F;* he is *Qq* so simple] *F;* so fond *Q1–3, 5–6;* fond *Q4* 26 mockery] *F (*mock'ry*), Qq* 27 pursues] *F;* pursues vs *Q1–2;* pursue vs *Q3–6* 29 no chase] *F, Q1–3, 5–6;* to chase *Q4* 33 I'll . . . and] *F;* My gratious Lo: Ile *Qq* SD] *F, Q3–6; not in Q1–2* 33.1] *F; Enter / (Cates. Q1–2 opp. 33–4; Enter Catesby to L. Hastings. Q3–6* 36 tottering] *F (*tott'ring*), Qq*

CATESBY
It is a reeling world indeed, my lord,
And I believe will never stand upright
Till Richard wear the garland of the realm.

HASTINGS
How? Wear the garland? Dost thou mean the crown?

CATESBY Ay, my good lord.

HASTINGS
I'll have this crown of mine cut from my shoulders
Before I'll see the crown so foul misplaced.
But canst thou guess that he doth aim at it?

CATESBY
Ay, on my life, and hopes to find you forward
Upon his party for the gain thereof;
And thereupon he sends you this good news,
That this same very day your enemies,
The kindred of the Queen, must die at Pomfret.

HASTINGS
Indeed, I am no mourner for that news,
Because they have been still my adversaries.
But that I'll give my voice on Richard's side
To bar my master's heirs in true descent,
God knows I will not do it, to the death.

CATESBY
God keep your lordship in that gracious mind.

39 **garland** The term appears in More, Hall (*Edward V*, fol. xxi^{r}) and *Mirror* ('Richard', 262).
42 **crown** i.e. head; cf. Stanley's dream (10) and Hastings's later beheading.
44 **canst thou guess** i.e. do you imagine
45 **forward** ready, eager (*OED a.* 6a)
46 **Upon his party** on his side (cf. 1.3.137)
51 **still** always
53, 57 **my master's** Edward IV's; cf. Richard's mocking use of *master's* at 3.4.39.
53 i.e. to prevent King Edward's heirs from inheriting the throne
54 **to the death** i.e. even though it cost my life (which it will)

38 will] *F;* it will *Q1–2;* twill *Q3–6* 40] *Qq; F lines* Garland? / Crowne? / How] *F, Q1–2;* Who *Q3–6* 43 Before I'll] *F;* Ere I will *Qq* 45 Ay . . . life] *F;* Vpon my life my Lo: *Qq* 50 that] *F, Q1–3, 5;* this *Q4, 6* 51 my adversaries] *F;* mine enemies *Qq*

HASTINGS
But I shall laugh at this a twelve-month hence,
That they which brought me in my master's hate,
I live to look upon their tragedy.
Well, Catesby, ere a fortnight make me older,
I'll send some packing that yet think not on't.

CATESBY
'Tis a vile thing to die, my gracious lord,
When men are unprepared and look not for it.

HASTINGS
O monstrous, monstrous! And so falls it out
With Rivers, Vaughan, Grey; and so 'twill do
With some men else that think themselves as safe
As thou and I, who, as thou knowst, are dear
To princely Richard and to Buckingham.

CATESBY
The princes both make high account of you –
[*aside*] For they account his head upon the Bridge.

HASTINGS
I know they do, and I have well deserved it.

Enter Lord STANLEY.

Come on, come on. Where is your boar-spear, man?
Fear you the boar and go so unprovided?

57–8 i.e. that I will see those who brought me into King Edward's disfavour suffer downfall and death

59 *Qq's line with Catesby breaking into Hastings's speech resembles similar interruptions in Qq's 3.4.30–1 (Davison).

60 **packing** Cf. 1.1.146.

68 **make . . . of** i.e. have high regard for; *high* is ironic in such contexts, where advancing, rising or mounting are routinely associated with ascending to the gallows (cf. 4.4.242–3; Kyd, *Spanish Tragedy*, 3.2.98; *1H4* 1.2.37).

69 **account** expect, reckon or count on (*OED v.* I 2a)
upon the Bridge on London Bridge, where traitors' heads were displayed on poles

56 twelve-month] *F; Q1–5* (tweluemonth), *Q6* (twelmonth) 57 which] *F;* who *Qq* 59 Well, Catesby] *F;* I tell thee Catesby. *Cat.* What my Lord? *Qq* older] *F;* elder *Qq* 60 on't] *F;* on it *Qq* 65 that] *F;* who *Qq* 66 knowst] *F, Q3–6; Q1–2* (knowest) 69 SD] *F4* 70 deserved it.] *F, Q1–2, 4, 6;* deserued i. *Q3, 5* 71 Come on, come on] *F;* What my Lo: *Qq* 72 go] *F, Q1–5;* goe you *Q6*

STANLEY

My lord, good morrow. – Good morrow, Catesby.
– You may jest on, but, by the Holy Rood,
I do not like these several councils, I.

HASTINGS

My lord, I hold my life as dear as [Q]you do[Q] yours,
And never in my days, I do protest,
Was it so precious to me as 'tis now.
Think you, but that I know our state secure,
I would be so triumphant as I am?

STANLEY

The lords at Pomfret, when they rode from London,
Were jocund, and supposed their states were sure,
And they indeed had no cause to mistrust;
But yet you see how soon the day o'ercast.
This sudden stab of rancour I misdoubt.
Pray God, I say, I prove a needless coward.
What, shall we toward the Tower? The day is spent.

HASTINGS

Come, come, have with you. Wot you what, my lord?

74 **Holy Rood** the cross of Christ
75 For emphatic repetition of 'I', see *TGV* 5.4.130: 'I care not for her, I.'
several separate
76 *The meaning of Qq and F appears clear – Hastings values his own life as dearly as Stanley values his – but the lines have frequently prompted editorial intervention.
79 **but that I** i.e. if I did not
state condition
80 **triumphant** exultant (*OED* 4)
84 **o'ercast** became overcast
85 **stab of rancour** unclear, probably referring to Richard's move against the Queen's faction
misdoubt suspect (*OED v.* 3); cf. *LLL* 4.3.191.
86 **needless coward** i.e. fearful for no reason
87 ***spent** F's statement that day is 'spent' appears to contradict line 4. However, Marshall claims that Adonis' 'The night is spent' (*VA* 717) means that night has arrived and is well under way.
88 **have with you** i.e. I will accompany you.
Wot know

75 councils, I] *F (*Councels, I*);* councels I *Qq* 77 days] *F;* life *Qq* 78 so . . . as 'tis] *F;* more . . . then it is *Qq* 81 at] *F, Q1–5;* of *Q6* 82 were] *F;* was *Qq* 83 they] *F, Q1–2; om. Q3–6* 84 o'ercast] *F (*o're-cast*), Q3–6 (*orecast*);* ouercast *Q1–2* 85 stab] *F;* scab *Qq* 86 I say] *F, Q1–3, 5–6; om. Q4* 87] *F;* But come my Lo: shall we to the tower? *Qq* 88] *Pope; F lines* you: / Lord, / ; I go: but stay, heare you not the newes, *Qq*

Today the lords you talked of are beheaded.

STANLEY

They, for their truth, might better wear their heads
Than some that have accused them wear their hats.
But come, my lord, let's away.

Enter a Pursuivant.

HASTINGS

Go on before. I'll talk with this good fellow.
Exeunt Lord Stanley and Catesby.
How now, sirrah? How goes the world with thee?

PURSUIVANT

The better that your lordship please to ask.

HASTINGS

I tell thee, man, 'tis better with me now
Than when thou met'st me last where now we meet.
Then was I going prisoner to the Tower
By the suggestion of the Queen's allies;
But now I tell thee – keep it to thyself –

90 **truth** honesty

91 **wear their hats** Fran Teague (private communication) agrees with Evans (1959) that this probably refers to Richard and Buckingham, who might wear the ducal cap in the presence of the monarch, no hat-like head-covering being allowed to any below the rank of duke.

92.1 *Qq follow More, Hall and Holinshed in naming this pursuivant 'Hastings'; see p. 457.
Pursuivant royal or state messenger empowered to execute warrants; a junior heraldic officer attendant on the heralds (*OED* 1, 2)

94 **sirrah** address used to men or boys, usually expressing contempt, reprimand or assumption of authority by the speaker

97 ***when . . . last** Qq's 'when I met thee' repeats Holinshed (3.723) and Hall (*Edward V*, fol. xv^{r}) (Honigmann, 'Text', 49).

99 **suggestion** instigation
allies kindred, relatives (*OED* II 3); Rivers was a chief instigator of Hastings's fall into disgrace with King Edward (More, *CW*2, 51); cf. 1.1.66–8.

89 Today the lords] *F;* This day those men *Qq* talked] *Q1–2 (*talkt*);* talke *F, Q3–6* 91 hats] *F, Q1, 6;* hat *Q2–5* 92 let's] *F;* let vs *Qq* 92.1] *F; Enter Hastin. / (a Purssuant. / opp. 92–3 Q1–2, after 93 Q3–6* 93 on] *F;* you *Qq* talk . . . fellow] *F;* follow presently *Qq* SD] *F; opp. 92 Q3–6; not in Q1–2 Exeunt*] *Rowe; Exit F, Q3–6* 94 How now, sirrah] *F; Hast.* Well met Hastings *Qq* 95 your lordship please] *F;* it please your Lo: *Q1–2;* it please your good Lordship *Q3–6* 96 man] *F;* fellow *Qq* 97 thou met'st me] *F;* I met thee *Qq*

This day those enemies are put to death,
And I in better state than e'er I was.

PURSUIVANT
God hold it to your honour's good content.

HASTINGS
Gramercy, fellow. There, drink that for me.
Throws him his purse.

PURSUIVANT I thank your honour. *Exit.*

Enter a Priest.

PRIEST
Well met, my lord. I am glad to see your honour.

HASTINGS
I thank thee, good Sir John, with all my heart.
I am in your debt for your last exercise.
Come the next sabbath, and I will content you.
[Q]*He whispers in his ear.*[Q]

PRIEST
I'll wait upon your lordship.

103 **hold it** i.e. preserve your condition as it is

104 **Gramercy** thank you
drink that i.e. enjoy this

106, 110 *Qq omissions eliminate a speaking part, but references to the priest remain (Smidt, *Impostors*, 112). David Troughton's Richard doubled as this priest (Day, 210).

107 **Sir** title of respect given to a priest (*OED sb.* II 11); cf. Sir Christopher Urswick in 4.5. 'Sir John' was itself a generic name for a priest (*OED* John 3).

108 **exercise** i.e. religious observance (*OED sb.* 10a; cf. *Oth* 3.4.41), probably the rite of confession, *shriving work* (113), which was remunerated by the penitent in pre-Reformation England (Lea, 1.404–11). Sermon, preaching or prophesying (*OED sb.* 10c, citing this line) are possible meanings; however, a stage Puritan refers to 'exercise of prayer' as apparently differing from sermonizing or 'godly exhortation on Sunday' (*Knack*, 1650–60).

109 **content** compensate to your satisfaction (*OED v.* 4)

110 *i.e. I am at your service. F repeats the phrase at 121, perhaps reinforcing the sense in which Hastings occupies a structurally similar position

102 e'er] *F (*ere*);* euer *Qq* 104 fellow] *F;* Hastings *Qq* There . . . me] *F;* hold spend thou that *Qq* SD] *F; He giues / (him his purse. Qq opp. 104–5* 105] *F;* God saue your Lordship *Qq* SD] *F, Q3–6 (Exit Pursuiuaunt. (Pur. Q3–6)); not in Q1–2* 105.1] *F; opp.* What Sir Iohn, you are wel met, *which follows 105 Q1–2; opp. 105 Q3–6* 106] *F; not in Qq* 107] *F;* What Sir Iohn, you are wel met, *Qq* 108 in your debt] *F;* beholding to you *Qq* exercise] *F;* daies exercise *Qq* 109 SD] *opp. 109–110.1 Qq* 110] *F; not in Qq*

Enter BUCKINGHAM.

BUCKINGHAM
What, talking with a priest, Lord Chamberlain?
Your friends at Pomfret, they do need the priest;
Your honour hath no shriving work in hand.

HASTINGS
Good faith, and when I met this holy man
The men you talk of came into my mind.
What, go you toward the Tower?

BUCKINGHAM
I do, my lord, but long I cannot stay there.
I shall return before your lordship thence.

HASTINGS
Nay, like enough, for I stay dinner there.

BUCKINGHAM [*aside*]
And supper too, although thou knowst it not.
– Come, will you go?

HASTINGS I'll wait upon your lordship. *Exeunt.*

vis-à-vis Buckingham to that which the priest occupies in his attendant relation to Hastings. F, Qq provide the priest no exit direction; *this holy man* (114) suggests his presence (but see 5.5.0.2–3n.). He may withdraw from Hastings's immediate proximity upon Buckingham's appearance (*TxC*, 240).

111 SP Holinshed, following More, has Sir Thomas Howard 'merilie' ask Hastings about his 'need of a priest' (3.723; *CW2*, 51; cf. p. 56).

113 **shriving work** confession and absolution; rites appropriate for those about to die (cf. *Ham* 5.2.47, 'shriving time').
in hand in process (*OED sb.* 29f)

114 **and** used emphatically in statements after ejaculations (Abbott, 98)

119 **like** i.e. likely
stay i.e. stay for

120 **supper** Shaheen suggests the heavenly supper promised in Revelation, 19.9. Cf. Richard's threat: 'you shall sup with Jesu Christ tonight' (*2H6* 5.1.214).
thou perhaps signifying secret contempt (Abbott, 233)

121 See 110.

111] *F;* How now Lo: Chamberlaine, what talking with a priest, *Qq* 115 The] *F;* Those *Qq* 116 toward] *F;* to *Qq* Tower] *F;* tower my Lord *Qq* 117 do, my lord . . . cannot stay there] *F;* doe, . . . shall not stay *Qq* 119 Nay] *F;* Tis *Qq* 120 SD] *Rowe* knowst] *F, Q3–5; Q1–2 (*knowest*);* knowh *Q6* 121] *Steevens; F lines* goe? / Lordship. / ; Come . . . along? *Qq* will you go] *F;* shall we go along *Qq* I'll . . . lordship] *F; not in Qq*

3.3 *Enter* Sir Richard RATCLIFFE, *with Halberds, carrying the nobles* [Q]RIVERS, GREY *and* VAUGHAN[Q] *to death at Pomfret.*

RIVERS
Sir Richard Ratcliffe, let me tell thee this:
Today shalt thou behold a subject die
For truth, for duty and for loyalty.

GREY
God bless the Prince from all the pack of you.
A knot you are of damned bloodsuckers.

VAUGHAN
You live, that shall cry woe for this hereafter.

RATCLIFFE
Dispatch. The limit of your lives is out.

RIVERS
O Pomfret, Pomfret! O thou bloody prison,

3.3 location: 'Pomfret-*Castle*' (Theobald), i.e. Pontefract Castle in West Yorkshire. This is the only scene in the first four acts set outside London and Westminster.

0.1 ***Halberds*** guards bearing halberds; see 1.2.0.1n.

0.2 ***carrying*** leading as prisoners (Dessen & Thompson, 43)

2 **Today** More has this scene's events occurring as Hastings is beheaded in the Tower (*CW*2, 57); the play sandwiches 3.3 between Buckingham's ominous remark concerning Hastings (3.2.120) and his arrest and condemnation to immediate death (3.4.75).

4 **bless** protect, guard (*OED v.* I 3; cf. *KL* 3.4.56)
pack set of persons, implying low character, evil purpose, or the speaker's contempt (*OED sb.*[1] 3a); here and in *Tim* 5.1.112, 115 suggesting dogs in violent pursuit (Bate, *Ovid*, 147n.).

5 **knot** small group; cf. 3.1.182.
damned damnèd

6 *Qq's omission of 6 appears deliberate, since 7 is virtually transferred to 23 (Thompson). This might save a speaking part here, but Vaughan remains in Qq's entry SD, is addressed in 24 and retains lines as a ghost (5.3.142–3). Cf. the Priest (Qq 3.2.106, 110).
cry woe Cf. 'Woe, woe for England' (3.4.79).

7 **Dispatch** hurry
The limit . . . out i.e. your lives have run their course.

3.3] *F (Scena Tertia.); not in Qq* 0.1 Richard RATCLIFFE] *F; Rickard Ratliffe Q1; Richard Ratliffe Q2–5; Richad Ratliffe Q6* 0.1–2 *Halberds, carrying the nobles*] *F; the Lo: Q1; the Lord Q2–6* 0.3 *to . . . Pomfret*] *F; prisoners Qq* 1] *F; Ratl. (Rat. Q3–6)* Come bring foorth the prisoners. / *Ryu.* Sir . . . this: *Qq* 4 bless] *F;* keepe *Qq* 6] *F; not in Qq* 7 Dispatch . . . lives] *F;* Come come dispatch, . . . linea *(*lines *Q2;* liues *Q3–6) Qq after 22*

Fatal and ominous to noble peers!
Within the guilty closure of thy walls,
Richard the Second here was hacked to death;
And for more slander to thy dismal seat,
We give to thee our guiltless blood to drink.

GREY

Now Margaret's curse is fall'n upon our heads,
When she exclaimed on Hastings, you and I,
For standing by when Richard stabbed her son.

RIVERS

Then cursed she Richard; then cursed she Buckingham;
Then cursed she Hastings. O, remember, God,
To hear her prayer for them, as now for us.
And for my sister and her princely sons,
Be satisfied, dear God, with our true blood,

9 **Fatal and ominous** Before the time of the play's action, Pontefract Castle saw the execution of Thomas, Earl of Lancaster, for rebelling against Edward II (1322), the murder of Richard II (1400), the pre-execution imprisonment of Archbishop Scrope (1405) and the murder of Richard Neville, Earl of Salisbury (1460).

10 **closure** bound or limit

11 **Richard the Second** See *R2* 5.5.

12 **slander** discredit, disgrace, shame (*OED sb.* 3)
dismal boding or bringing misfortune; unlucky, sinister (*OED a.* 2)
seat residence, abode

14–16 *Margaret does not curse Grey but exclaims against Dorset (1.3.209–13). Daniel suggests that absence of 15 from Qq may represent an attempt to avoid the discrepancy; but Buckingham is not cursed by Margaret, as is said in Qq 17 (Daniel, xviii). Buckingham regards himself as falling under Margaret's prophecies (5.1.25–7). Historically, Rivers, Grey and Vaughan had no connection with the killing of Margaret's son (More, *CW2*, 57–8). The play's modifications emphasize a 'symmetrical pattern of retribution' (E. Berry, 90–1).

14 **Margaret's curse** Cf. 3.4.91, 4.1.45, 5.1.25; this scene marks the first recollection and partial fulfilment of curses from 1.3. The listing of those cursed and of further potential victims (17–20) prepares for Richard's subsequent crimes and downfall (Clemen, 137).

18–22 **O . . . spilt** Hall's Vaughan appeals to God, recalls the prophecy about Edward's heirs, identifies 'G' as Richard and proclaims his own innocence (*Edward V*, fol. xvii^{r-v}); cf. *Mirror* ('Rivers', 562–3). Holinshed has Ratcliffe prevent the men from speaking (3.725).

20–2 Cf. 1.4.69–72.

9 ominous] *F, Q1, 6;* dominious *Q2–3;* ominious *Q4–5* 12 seat] *F;* soule *Qq* 13 to thee] *F;* thee vp *Qq* blood] *F;* blouds *Qq* 14 Margaret's] *F, Q1–5;* Margarts *Q6* is] *F, Q1–5;* if *Q6* 15] *F; not in Qq* 17] *Qq; F lines Richard, / Buckingham, /* 17–18 Richard . . . Hastings] *F;* Hastings . . . Richard *Qq* 19 prayer] *F;* praiers *Qq* 20 sons] *F;* sonne *Qq* 21 blood] *F;* blouds *Qq*

Which, as thou knowst, unjustly must be spilt.

RATCLIFFE

Make haste. The hour of death is expiate.

RIVERS

Come, Grey, come, Vaughan. Let us here embrace.
Farewell, until we meet again in heaven. *Exeunt.*

3.4 *Enter* BUCKINGHAM, [STANLEY, Earl of] Derby, HASTINGS, Bishop of ELY, NORFOLK, RATCLIFFE, LOVELL, *with others, at a table.*

HASTINGS

Now, noble peers, the cause why we are met
Is to determine of the coronation.
In God's name speak: when is the royal day?

BUCKINGHAM

Is all things ready for the royal time?

23 **expiate** fully come (*OED ppl. a.*, citing this line); 'expiate' could mean 'end' (cf. *Son* 22). Here it may play on the idea of propitiation, echoing Rivers's prayer that God might be *satisfied* with their blood.

24–5 The embrace and anticipation of heavenly reunion ironically recall Warwick, Edward and Richard at the battle of Towton (*3H6* 2.3.42–5).

3.4 location: '*The Tower*' (Pope)

0.1–3 Qq's cast is abbreviated: Lovell is not here (nor anywhere in Qq); Norfolk (mute in F's 3.4) is not named; Qq do not mention F's '*others*'. Catesby replaces F's Ratcliffe (as in Qq 3.5), possibly because 3.3 depicts Ratcliffe in Yorkshire on the same day (but see 6 SPn.). This obvious contradiction in F is compounded by F's deviation from early modern theatrical practice, which normally precluded re-entry in subsequent scenes (see p. 459 and Qq 'Cardinal' in 2.4, 3.1).

0.2 **Bishop of** ELY John Morton, later Archbishop of Canterbury (1486), Chancellor (1487) and Cardinal (1493); he was Thomas More's patron and perhaps his informant.

0.3 ***at a table*** '*to Councell*' (Qq) probably implies F's '*at a table*' (Dessen & Thomson, 58).

1–3 Hastings assumes control as Lord Chamberlain; cf. 1.1.77.

2 **determine of** decide about
coronation i.e. of Prince Edward as King Edward V

4 ***Is** F's verb form is consistent with Stanley's response (*It is*); cf. 'Is all things well?' (*2H6* 3.2.11).

22 knowst] *F; Qq (*knowest*)* 23] *F; see above at 7 Qq* 24 here] *F;* all *Qq* 25 Farewell] *F;* And take our leaue *(*leaues *Q6) Qq* again] *F; not in Qq* **3.4**] *F (Scæna Quarta); not in Qq* 0.1–3] *F; Enter the Lords to Councell. Qq* 0.1 STANLEY, Earl of] *Theobald subst.* 1 Now, noble peers] *F;* My Lords at once *Qq* 3 speak] *F;* say *Qq* the] *F;* this *Qq* 4 Is . . . ready for the] *F;* Are . . . fitting for that *Qq*

STANLEY
It is, and wants but nomination.

ELY
Tomorrow, then, I judge a happy day.

BUCKINGHAM
Who knows the Lord Protector's mind herein?
Who is most inward with the noble Duke?

ELY
Your grace, we think, should soonest know his mind.

BUCKINGHAM
We know each other's faces; for our hearts,
He knows no more of mine than I of yours,
Or I of his, my lord, than you of mine.
– Lord Hastings, you and he are near in love.

HASTINGS
I thank his grace, I know he loves me well;
But for his purpose in the coronation,
I have not sounded him, nor he delivered
His gracious pleasure any way therein.
But you, my honourable lords, may name the time,
And in the Duke's behalf I'll give my voice,

5 **wants but nomination** lacks only the naming of a date
6 SP *Q1's '*Ryu.*' (Rivers) is corrected by Q3 to '*Bish.*' Rivers has just been led to execution in 3.3. Perhaps Q1's compositor misread '*By.*' (Bishop) as '*Ry.*' (Hammond).
6 **happy** fortunate, favourable (*OED a.* 3)
8 **inward** intimate (*OED* A *a.* I 3)
10–12 Discussion of Richard's 'heart' recalls Anne's 'I would I knew thy heart' (1.2.195) and Richard's lecture to the Prince about discrepancy between *outward show* and *the heart* (3.1.9–11), and anticipates 53–5. (Cf. Dent, F1.)
10 **for** as for
15 **purpose in** intention concerning
16 **sounded him** i.e. examined him in conversation; cf. 3.1.170n. on *sound*.
19 **give my voice** As Lord Chamberlain, Hastings would serve as the monarch's official mouthpiece (Chambers, *Stage*, 1.38).

5+ SP] *Theobald; Darb. F; Dar. Qq* 5 wants] *F, Q1–2;* let *Q3, 5–6;* lack *Q4* 6 SP] *F; Ryu. Q1; Riu. Q2; Bish. Q3–6* judge . . . day] *F;* guesse . . . time *Qq* 9+ SP] *F; Bi./By./Bish. Qq* 9 Your . . . think,] *F;* Why you my Lo: me thinks you *Qq* 10–12] *F;* Who I my Lo? we know each others faces: / But for our harts, he knowes no more of mine, / Then I of yours: nor I no more of his, then you of mine: / *Qq* 17 gracious] *F;* Graces *Qq* 18 honourable lords] *F;* noble Lo: *Q1–2;* L. *Q3–6*

Which I presume he'll take in gentle part.

Enter [RICHARD, Duke of] Gloucester.

ELY

In happy time, here comes the Duke himself.

RICHARD

My noble lords and cousins all, good morrow.
I have been long a sleeper, but I trust
My absence doth neglect no great design
Which by my presence might have been concluded.

BUCKINGHAM

Had you not come upon your cue, my lord,
William, Lord Hastings, had pronounced your part –
I mean your voice for crowning of the King.

RICHARD

Than my Lord Hastings, no man might be bolder;
His lordship knows me well, and loves me well.
– My Lord of Ely, when I was last in Holborn
I saw good strawberries in your garden there;

20 **in gentle part** graciously (as 'in good part': *OED* part *sb.* 26b)

22 **lords and cousins** Richard speaks to Buckingham and other relations; Qq's 'L.' could be singular or plural, so in Qq he might be singling out one addressee before turning to the others. 'Cousin' was also 'used by a sovereign in addressing or formally naming another sovereign, or a nobleman of the same country' (*OED sb.* 5a).

23 **been . . . sleeper** Richard attempts to appear uninterested in the proceedings; the claim is found in More. Cf. *True Tragedy* (925–6).

24 **neglect** cause to be neglected (*OED v.* 5)

26–7 **cue . . . part** Buckingham employs theatrical discourse (cf. 3.5.5–11).

28 **voice** i.e. opinion or vote; cf. 19.

32 **strawberries** This bizarre episode appears in More with no explanation for its motivation. Perhaps More records an anecdote (maybe from Morton himself) with no larger purpose; however, strawberries have emblematic connections to unseen treachery (cf. L.J. Ross). The episode conveys Richard's 'careless ease, in the midst of all his crimes' (Griffith,

20 he'll] *F;* he will *Qq* gentle] *F, Q1–5;* good *Q6* 20.1] *F; Ent. Glo. Q1–2 turned down below 21; Enter Gloster. Q3–6 after 21* RICHARD, Duke of] *Evans 1959* 21 In happy] *F;* Now in good *Qq* 22 lords] *F;* L. *Qq* 23 a sleeper] *F, Q1–5;* a sleepe *Q6* but] *F, Q1;* but now *Q2–6* trust] *F;* hope *Qq* 24 design] *F;* designes *Qq* 26 you not] *F;* not you *Qq* cue] *F* (Q), *Qq* (kew), *Rowe* 27 had] *F;* had now *Qq* your] *F, Q1–5;* you *Q6* 30 well.] *F;* well. / *Hast.* I thanke your Grace. / *Qq* 31 Ely, when] *F;* Elie, *Bish.* My Lo: / *Glo.* When *Qq*

I do beseech you, send for some of them.

ELY

Marry and will, my lord, with all my heart.

Exit Bishop [*of Ely*].

RICHARD

Cousin of Buckingham, a word with you.
[*They talk apart.*] Catesby hath sounded Hastings in our business,
And finds the testy gentleman so hot
That he will lose his head ere give consent
His master's child, as worshipfully he terms it,
Shall lose the royalty of England's throne.

BUCKINGHAM

Withdraw yourself awhile. I'll go with you.

Exeunt [*Richard and Buckingham*].

STANLEY

We have not yet set down this day of triumph.
Tomorrow, in my judgement, is too sudden,
For I myself am not so well provided
As else I would be, were the day prolonged.

Enter the Bishop of ELY.

317). Relaxed improvisation amid otherwise tense circumstances is characteristic of Richard until he gets the crown.

34 **Marry and will** i.e. indeed I will (cf. 'Marry, and shall', *3H6* 5.5.42).

37 **testy** Jowett detects sardonic allusion to the (early modern) French *teste*, 'head'.

39 **worshipfully . . . it** with due honour he puts it

41 ***go with** Qq omit Buckingham from the exit SD here and the re-entry at 57.1 (see p. 427).

42 **set down** established
triumph public festivity (*OED sb.* 4)

44 **provided** prepared

45 **prolonged** postponed (*OED v.* 3)

33 do] *F, Q1–3, 5–6;* now *Q4* 34] *F;* I go my Lord. *Qq* SD] *F; not in Qq of Ely*] *Rowe subst.* 35 of] *F; not in Qq* 36 SD] *Capell subst.* 37 testy] *F, Q1–3, 5–6;* resty *Q4* 38 That] *F;* As *Qq* ere] *F, Q2–4, 6; Q1, 2 (BL, Hn 69352) (*eare*);* are *Q5* 39 child] *F;* sonne *Qq* worshipfully] *F;* worshipfull *Qq* 41 yourself awhile] *F;* you hence my Lo: *Qq* go with] *F;* follow *Qq* SD *Exeunt*] *F; Ex. Gl. Qq subst. Richard and Buckingham*] *Pope* 43 my judgement] *F;* mine opinion *Qq* sudden] *F, Q1;* soone *Q2–6* 45.1] *F, Q3–6; Enter B. / of Ely. Q1–2 opp. 44–5*

ELY

Where is my lord the Duke of Gloucester?
I have sent for these strawberries.

HASTINGS

His grace looks cheerfully and smooth this morning.
There's some conceit or other likes him well
When that he bids good morrow with such spirit.
I think there's never a man in Christendom
Can lesser hide his love or hate than he,
For by his face straight shall you know his heart.

STANLEY

What of his heart perceive you in his face
By any livelihood he showed today?

HASTINGS

Marry, that with no man here he is offended,
For were he, he had shown it in his looks.

Enter RICHARD *and* BUCKINGHAM.

RICHARD

I pray you all, tell me what they deserve

48 **smooth** i.e. smoothly, pleasantly (adverbial ellipsis; cf. 'lamely and unfashionable', 1.1.22); *looks* = directs the eyes (*OED v.* 1)

49 **conceit** idea, conception (*OED sb.* I 1)
likes him well pleases him (cf. *Ham* 5.2.242)

53 **straight** immediately

55 **livelihood** i.e. liveliness, animation (cf. *AW* 1.1.49–50); Qq's 'likelihood' is possible, meaning 'a ground of probable inference' (*OED* likelihood 3).

57 *Qq follow with an unmetrical line for Stanley.

57.1 *Enter* RICHARD More's Richard returns 'al changed with a wonderful soure angrye countenaunce, knitting the browes, frowning and froting and knawing on hys lippes' (*CW*2, 47).

46–7] *F; one line Qq* 46 lord . . . Gloucester] *F;* L. protector *Qq* 48 this morning] *F;* to day *Qq* 49 well] *F, Q1–3, 5–6 (*well,*);* well. *Q4* 50 that he bids] *F;* he doth bid *Qq* such] *F;* such a *Qq* spirit.] *F, Q1–4;* spirit, *Q5–6* 51 there's] *F;* there is *Qq* 52 Can] *F;* That can *Qq* 55 livelihood] *F;* likelihood *Qq* 57 were he] *F;* if he were *Qq* had shown] *F (*had shewne*);* would haue shewen *(*shewne *Q6) Qq* looks.] *F;* lookes. *(*face. *Q2–6) / Dar.* I pray God he be not, I say. */ Qq* 57.1] *F; Enter Glocester. Qq* 58 tell me what] *F;* what doe *Qq*

That do conspire my death with devilish plots
Of damned witchcraft, and that have prevailed
Upon my body with their hellish charms?

HASTINGS

The tender love I bear your grace, my lord,
Makes me most forward in this princely presence
To doom th'offenders, whosoe'er they be.
I say, my lord, they have deserved death.

RICHARD

Then be your eyes the witness of their evil.
Look how I am bewitched! Behold, mine arm
Is like a blasted sapling withered up;
And this is Edward's wife, that monstrous witch,
Consorted with that harlot, strumpet Shore,
That by their witchcraft thus have marked me.

HASTINGS

If they have done this deed, my noble lord –

59 **conspire** conspire for

59–65 **devilish . . . hellish . . . death** Charges of 'sorcery & witchcraft' come from More (*CW2*, 48), but not the stress on demonic association. Sixteenth-century English religious, legal and popular understandings of witchcraft did not stress devil worship or make supposed non-lethal bodily injury a capital offence (K. Thomas, 442). More's Richard advocates the special appropriateness of the death penalty on the basis of his royal blood (*CW2*, 48). For parallels in attitude and vocabulary see *Newes*. Peter Hall's 1963–4 production directs 'they all clap' at 65 (Hankey, 170).

60 **damned** damnèd

63 **forward** ready, prompt, eager in a cause **presence** company

64 **doom** condemn

65 **deserved** deservèd

67–71 Sources agree that 'no man was there present, but wel knew that his harme [i.e. arm] was euer such since his birth' (*CW2*, 48; cf. *Mirror*, 'Hastings', 574–6). More originates the charge of collaboration with Mistress Shore (Hanham, 169; contrast Vergil, 180–1), noting its preposterousness, since the Queen would hardly collaborate with her late husband's lover, 'whom of all women she most hated' (*CW2*, 48).

68 **blasted** blighted; stricken by supernatural agency (*OED ppl. a.* 1)

70 **Consorted** associated (*OED v.* 4)

71 **marked** markèd

63 princely] *F;* noble *Qq* 64 th'offenders] *F; Qq (*the offenders*)* whosoe'er] *F;* whatsoeuer *Qq* 66 their evil] *F;* this ill *Qq* 67 Look] *F;* See *Qq* 69 And this is] *F;* This is that *Qq* 71 witchcraft] *F, Q1;* witchcrafts *Q2–6* 72 deed . . . lord –] *Rowe;* deed . . . Lord. *F;* thing my gratious Lo: *Qq*

RICHARD

If? Thou protector of this damned strumpet,
Talk'st thou to me of ifs? Thou art a traitor.
– Off with his head! Now by Saint Paul I swear
I will not dine until I see the same.
– Lovell and Ratcliffe, look that it be done.
– The rest that love me, rise and follow me.

Exeunt. Lovell and Ratcliffe remain with the Lord Hastings.

HASTINGS

Woe, woe for England, not a whit for me,
For I, too fond, might have prevented this.
Stanley did dream the boar did raze his helm,

73 **protector** wonderfully ironic, given the recent reiteration of Richard's official title as 'Lord Protector' (7)
damned damnèd

74 **ifs** More's Richard berates Hastings for using 'iffes' and 'andes' (*CW*2, 48; cf. Hall, *Edward V*, fol. xiv[r–v]; Holinshed, 3.722); see also Dent, I16. The *ifs* have elicited stage business: Charles Macready in 1821 struck a table for emphasis; Edwin Booth in the 1870s stamped his foot on the word to accompany his blows upon the table (Colley, 84, 110). In More, Richard's blow to the table signals entry of his armed men (cf. *Mirror*, 'Hastings', 583–4). Armed entry has been staged here since Phelps and Irving in the 1840s and 1870s (Hankey, 170).

75–6 **Saint Paul . . . same** Execution before dinner is familiar in Tudor drama (cf. *Jack Straw*, 933–4), but this line comes from More ('by saynt Poule (quod he) I wil not to dinner til I se thy hed of', *CW*2, 49) and appears in Hall, Holinshed and *True Tragedy*. More's 'by saynt Poule' constitutes the sole warrant for the habitual oath of Shakespeare's Richard (see 1.2.36n.). There is possibly an allusion to Acts, 23.12–14 in which 'certayne of the Iews' vow 'we wyll eate nothyng untyll we haue slayne Paul'.

77 ***Ratcliffe** F's glaring inconsistency (see 0.1–3n.) is probably preferable to Qq's awkward and inconsistent substitutions of Catesby for Ratcliffe and Lovell; see pp. 452–3.

78 Cf. Clarence's exit demanding, 'You that love me and Warwick, follow me,' leaving Richard and Hastings behind among King Edward's allies (*3H6* 4.1.123). Consistent loyalty to Edward IV and his line results in Hastings's victimization here. By omitting Richard's troops from Hastings's downfall, Shakespeare portrays Richard (once again) exercising his performative power to force others – Stanley and Ely, as before Anne – into demonstrating 'love' for him.

80 **fond** foolish

81–90 More originates these omens (*dream, horse, priest, pursuivant*), but laces them with scepticism (Hanham, 172–3); see 83n. on *stumble* and p. 56.

81 ***raze** Qq 'race' is a form of 'raze'; cf. 3.2.10.

74 Talk'st thou to] *F;* Telst thou *Qq* 75 I swear] *F; not in Qq* 76–7] *F;* I will not dine to day I sweare, / Vntill I see the same, some see it done, / *Qq* 78 rise] *F;* come *Qq* SD *Exeunt.*] *Qq, opp. 77 F Lovell . . . Hastings.*] *F (Manet Louell and Ratcliffe, with the / Lord Hastings.); manet / Cat. with Ha. Qq opp. 78–9* 81 raze his helm] *Qq (*race*);* rowse our Helmes *F*

And I did scorn it and disdain to fly.
Three times today my foot-cloth horse did stumble,
And started when he looked upon the Tower,
As loath to bear me to the slaughterhouse.
O, now I need the priest that spake to me.
I now repent I told the pursuivant,
As too triumphing, how mine enemies
Today at Pomfret bloodily were butchered,
And I myself secure in grace and favour.
O Margaret, Margaret, now thy heavy curse
Is lighted on poor Hastings' wretched head.

RATCLIFFE

Come, come, dispatch. The Duke would be at dinner.
Make a short shrift. He longs to see your head.

HASTINGS

O momentary grace of mortal men,
Which we more hunt for than the grace of God!

83 **foot-cloth** large, richly ornamented cloth laid over the back of a horse; a mark of dignity and state (*OED*); cf. *2H6* 4.1.54, 4.7.43.
stumble Horses stumble naturally, More notes, 'yet hath it ben of an olde rite & custome, obserued as a token often times notably foregoing some great misfortune' (*CW2*, 50).
84 **started** moved suddenly, involuntarily
85 **As** as if
86–7 **priest . . . pursuivant** Cf. 3.2.92.1–122.
88 **too triumphing** i.e. too much exulting
90 **secure** often conveying culpable carelessness (*OED* security 3); cf. *Mac* 3.5.32–3. A 17th-century reader records: 'hastings securest confidence . . . of constant / successe when he wes going to put his head in his / ennemies hand to be cut off' (Yamada, 157). On the perils of spiritual 'security', see Perkins, 488–9.
93–4 **dispatch . . . head** Cf. *The Wounds of Civil War* (1594): 'Dispatch . . . For sore I long to see the traitor's head' (Lodge, 2050–5).
94 **short shrift** hasty confession (from More, *CW2*, 49)
95–6 ***grace . . . grace** F opposes worldly to divine 'grace'; Qq miss this point.
96 ***God** F and Qq reverse their normal terms for the Deity (see 1.4.84n. and p. 457). Cf. 2.1.39: 'heauen' (F) and 'God' (Qq).

82 And . . . disdain] *F;* But I disdaind it, and *(*disdained, and *Q4)* did scorne *Qq* 83 foot-cloth horse] *F (*Foot-Cloth-Horse*), Qq (*footecloth horse*)* 84 started] *F;* startled *Qq* 86 need] *F;* want *Qq* 88 too triumphing, how] *F;* twere triumphing at *Qq* 89 Today] *F;* How they *Qq* 92 lighted] *F, Q1–5;* lightened *Q6* 93 SP] *F (Ra.); Cat. Qq* Come, come, dispatch] *F;* Dispatch my Lo: *Qq* 95 grace of mortal] *F;* state of worldly *Qq* 96 than] *F, Q1–2 (*then*);* then for *Q3–6* God!] *F;* heauen: *Qq*

Who builds his hope in air of your good looks
Lives like a drunken sailor on a mast,
Ready with every nod to tumble down
Into the fatal bowels of the deep.

LOVELL

Come, come, dispatch. 'Tis bootless to exclaim.

HASTINGS

O bloody Richard! Miserable England,
I prophesy the fearfull'st time to thee
That ever wretched age hath looked upon.
– Come, lead me to the block; bear him my head.
They smile at me who shortly shall be dead. *Exeunt.*

[3.5] *Enter* RICHARD *and* BUCKINGHAM *in rotten armour, marvellous ill-favoured.*

RICHARD

Come, cousin, canst thou quake and change thy colour,

97 **air** manner, outward appearance (*OED sb.*[1] III 13); cf. 'the air of the court' (*WT* 4.4.734). 'Building in air' means trusting in the unsubstantial or conjectural (*OED* air *sb.*[1] 3).
your good looks approving glances granted by the imaginary figure who personifies the 'grace of mortal men'

97–100 The fall into the sea recalls Clarence's dream (1.4); cf. Proverbs, 23.31–4 on drunkenness as resembling sleep 'vppon the top of the maste of a ship' (also *Homilies*, 99). *Mirror* reflects on the 'slyppery state wherein aloft we swymme' ('Hastings', 634).

101 **bootless** pointless, unprofitable
exclaim cry out

106 **They** Hastings's enemies in general, but perhaps specifically referring to the present (smirking?) insolence of Lovell and Ratcliffe

3.5 location: '*the* Tower-*walls*' (Theobald). Cibber, all 19th-century and many later productions cut this scene, often inserting 72ff. into 3.1 (Hankey, 172).

0.1–2 More describes Richard and Buckingham wearing 'old il faring briginders' as if 'some sodaine necessitie had constrained them' (*CW*2, 52; 'briginders' or 'briganders' are body-armour for foot-soldiers) to 'set some color upon' the execution of Hastings. Cf. 'In rousty armure as in extreame shyft, / They cladd them selues, to cloake theyr diuelysh dryft' (*Mirror*, 'Hastings', 689–90).

0.1 ***rotten*** unsound, in decay and disorder (*OED* 2b, 8a)

0.2 ***marvellous ill-favoured*** i.e. remarkably ugly-looking

1–11 On this passage and acting, see pp. 10–12.

1 **change thy colour** i.e. change your

97 hope] *F;* hopes *Qq* good] *F;* faire *Qq* looks] *F, Q1–3, 5–6;* looke *Q4* 98 a drunken sailor] *F, Q1–3, 5–6;* drunken Saylers *Q4* 100 the fatal] *F, Q1–5;* fatall *Q6* 101–4] *F; not in Qq* 106 who] *F;* that *Qq* 3.5] *Capell* 0.1–2] *F; Enter Duke of Glocester and Buckingham in armour. Qq* 1+ SP] *F; Glo. Qq* 1] *Qq; F lines* Cousin, / colour, /

Murder thy breath in middle of a word,
And then again begin, and stop again,
As if thou were distraught and mad with terror?

BUCKINGHAM

Tut, I can counterfeit the deep tragedian,
Speak, and look back, and pry on every side,
Tremble and start at wagging of a straw,
Intending deep suspicion. Ghastly looks
Are at my service, like enforced smiles,
And both are ready in their offices,
At any time to grace my stratagems.
But what, is Catesby gone?

RICHARD

He is, and see, he brings the Mayor along.

Enter the [Lord] MAYOR *and* CATESBY.

appearance; flush with emotion or grow pale with fear are possible. For pallor related to shock or guilt, see 2.1.84–6, 136–8.

2 **Murder** i.e. choke off, extinguish, possibly suggesting 'to spoil by bad execution or pronunciation' (*OED v.* 2); cf. 34n.

4 **were** *thou were* is subjunctive (*OED* be A III 7), but Shakespeare nowhere else employs F's form (Wilson).
distraught driven to madness; cf. Juliet's images of living entombment (*RJ* 4.3.49) for melodramatic connotations.

5 **counterfeit** imitate, frequently used for playing a role (e.g. *1H4* 5.4.113–18; *AYL* 4.3.165–81; *KL* 3.6.60).
deep tragedian tragic actor of grave, serious aspect (*OED* deep II 7b)

6 **look . . . side** i.e. glance over one's shoulder and peer around apprehensively; cf. 19.

7 **wagging** slight movement; cf. Dent, W5.

8 **Intending** asserting, pretending (*OED* 22, citing this line); cf. 3.7.44.

9 **like** i.e. as well as
enforced enforcèd

10 **offices** functions, uses

11 **grace** embellish (*OED v.* 4a), but in proximity with *offices* playing on the meaning 'countenance' (*OED v.* 2a) as an official might 'grace' a subordinate; cf. 3.4.95–6.

12 *Qq omit because Catesby is the executioner of Hastings in the previous scene in Qq, and in Qq enters with Hastings's head at 20.1; for the problem with 17 in Qq, see p. 453 and 20.1n.

13 **Mayor** More describes enlisting the Lord Mayor, Edmund Shaa (Shaw), that he 'vpon trust of his own aduauncement, whereof he was of a proud hart highly desirouse, shold frame the cite [i.e. city] to their appetite' (*CW2*, 58).

2 Murder] *F, Qq (*Murther*), Q8* 3 again begin] *F;* beginne againe *Qq* 4 were] *F;* wert *Qq* 5 Tut, I] *F;* Tut feare not me. / I *Qq* 7] *F; not in Qq* 7–8 straw, . . . suspicion.] *Pope (*straw, . . . suspicion:*);* Straw: . . . suspition, *F* 8 deep] *F, Q1–3, 5–6;* deere *Q4* 11 At any time] *F; not in Qq* 12] *F; not in Qq* 13] *F;* Here comes the Maior. *Qq* 13.1] *F; Enter Maior. Qq opp. 11* Lord] *Rowe*

BUCKINGHAM
Lord Mayor –

RICHARD
Look to the draw-bridge there!

BUCKINGHAM Hark, a drum!

RICHARD
Catesby, o'erlook the walls! [*Exit Catesby.*]

BUCKINGHAM
Lord Mayor, the reason we have sent –

RICHARD
Look back! Defend thee! Here are enemies.

BUCKINGHAM
God and our innocency defend and guard us.

Enter LOVELL *and* RATCLIFFE, *with Hastings's head.*

RICHARD
Be patient. They are friends: Ratcliffe and Lovell.

LOVELL
Here is the head of that ignoble traitor,
The dangerous and unsuspected Hastings.

16, 18 *Qq reverse. Qq's order might allow Buckingham to go on pretending to converse with the Mayor before shouting with Richard (Smidt, *Impostors*, 45).

16 **drum** probably imaginary, which would suit an exchange exhorting the Mayor to *imagine* a non-existent plot (35–9)

17 **o'erlook** look over the top of

19 **Look back** i.e. look behind you (cf. 6).

20 **innocency** innocence (as *KJ* 4.3.110)

20.1 *Qq have Catesby enter here with Hastings's head, but this leaves Qq 17 without an onstage addressee. Perhaps 'Catesby' in Qq 17 is 'as imaginary as the unnamed figure [Richard] calls to "Looke to the drawbridge"' (*TxC*, 241).

head Hastings's head has occasioned grotesque stage business: Donald Wolfit's Richard ate strawberries while gloating over the head in a bag; José Ferrer's Richard waved his bloody sack at the Mayor, driving him from the stage; Terry Hands's 1970 promptbook calls for tossing the head to the Mayor, who faints (Hankey, 173).

14] *F;* Let me alone to entertaine him. Lo: Maior, *Qq* 16] *F;* The reason we haue sent for you. *Qq* 17 o'erlook] *F* (o're-looke), *Qq* (ouerlooke) SD] *Ard*^{2} 18] *F;* Harke, I heare a drumme. *Qq* 20 innocency] *F, Q2–6* (Innocencie); innocence *Q1* and guard] *F; not in Qq* 20.1] *F; Enter Catesby / with Hast. head. Qq (opp. 20–1 Q1–2; after 21 Q3–6)* 21] *F;* O, O, be quiet, it is Catesby. *Qq* 22 SP] *F; Cat. Qq*

RICHARD
So dear I loved the man that I must weep.
I took him for the plainest harmless creature
That breathed upon the earth a Christian;
Made him my book, wherein my soul recorded
The history of all her secret thoughts.
So smooth he daubed his vice with show of virtue
That, his apparent open guilt omitted –
I mean his conversation with Shore's wife –
He lived from all attainder of suspects.

BUCKINGHAM
Well, well, he was the covert'st sheltered traitor
That ever lived.
Would you imagine, or almost believe,

24 **weep** Cf. 1.2.156–7n.
25 **plainest harmless** i.e. plainest, (most) harmless; or perhaps a compound word, 'plainest-harmless' (Abbott, 398)
27 **book** i.e. commonplace book, or diary where Richard recorded his thoughts
29 A 'typical act of cunning displacement' (Maus, 52), but also ascribing to Hastings a term that permeates Richard's verbal environment: *smooth* has been repeatedly employed to characterize others from whom Richard differentiates himself as *plain* (cf. 25) – War's *smoothed* front (1.1.9), the *smoothing* words of others (1.2.171), his flattering enemies' ability to *smooth* (1.3.48) – and it occurs ominously in Hastings's misapprehension of Richard's *smooth* appearance (3.4.48).
daubed covered with a specious exterior; whitewashed (*OED v.* 7)
30 **apparent** manifest, obvious
31 **conversation** sexual intimacy (*OED* 3)
32 **from** free from
attainder stain of dishonour (*OED* 2b, citing this line); cf. *LLL* 1.1.155.
suspects suspicion
33 **Well, well** Cf. Dent, W269 ('Well, well is a word of malice') and *R2* 3.3.170.
covert'st sheltered most deceitful (*OED* covert *a.* 1, 3), protected from punishment (*OED* shelter *v.* 1c); perhaps retorting to *plainest harmless* (25).
34 *Qq attach this half-line to a version of the next line. Some editors omit it; others add a half-line from Qq's 26, 'Look ye, my Lord Mayor'. This edition joins Mowat and Werstine, Lull and Jowett in retaining F's half-line. Could this short line possibly represent Buckingham following Richard's suggestions about histrionic pauses and hesitations (2–4)?
35 **almost** hardly, nearly; 'Would you suppose without evidence, or (I may *almost* say) believe upon evidence?' (Abbott, 29).

25 creature] *F;* man *Qq* 26 the] *F, Q4;* this *Q1–3, 5–6* Christian;] *F* (Christian.*);* christian, / Looke ye my Lo: Maior. / *Qq* 27 Made] *F, Q1–4;* I made *Q5–6* 32 lived . . . suspects] *F;* laid . . . suspect *Qq* 34–6] *F; Qq line* imagined, / preseruation / 34] *F; om. Pope;* That ever liv'd. – Look you, my lord mayor, *Capell* 35 imagine] *F;* haue imagined *Qq*

Were't not that by great preservation
We live to tell it, that the subtle traitor
This day had plotted in the council house
To murder me and my good lord of Gloucester?

MAYOR

Had he done so?

RICHARD

What? Think you we are Turks or infidels?
Or that we would, against the form of law,
Proceed thus rashly in the villain's death,
But that the extreme peril of the case,
The peace of England, and our persons' safety,
Enforced us to this execution?

MAYOR

Now fair befall you! He deserved his death,
And your good graces both have well proceeded
To warn false traitors from the like attempts.

BUCKINGHAM

I never looked for better at his hands
After he once fell in with Mistress Shore.

36 **great preservation** protection by Providence; Richard has been protected by divine intervention.
41 **Turks or infidels** The third collect for Good Friday prays: 'Have mercy upon all Jews, Turks, infidels, and heretics' (*BCP*, 144).
43 **rashly** speedily
44 **But** except
47 **fair befall you** i.e. may it be well with you (Abbott, 297); cf. 1.3.281.
49 **the like** similar
50–2 *Q1–2 assign 50–1 to the Mayor and give a SP at 52 ('*Dut.*') that apparently misreads Buckingham ('*Buc.*'). Q3 assigns it to someone who is at least onstage, but misspells the prefix ('*Clo.*'); Q4 corrects to '*Glo.*' Thompson suggests that Buckingham attempts to work on the Mayor's prejudices by underlining the charge mentioned at 31. Wells and Taylor note that the chief problem with F's attribution to Buckingham is the shift in first-person pronouns to what look like regal plurals (except in 56), but see 56n.
50 **at his hands** i.e. from him

36 Were't] *F, Q1–5 (*Wert*);* were *Q6* that] *F; not in Qq* 37 it, that the] *F;* it you? The *Qq* 38 This day had] *F;* Had this day *Qq* 39 murder] *F (*murther*), Qq* 40] *F;* What, had he so? *Qq* 41 you] *F, Q1–2;* ye *Q3–6* 42 form] *F, Q1–2;* course *Q3–6* 43 in] *F;* to *Qq* 44 extreme] *F, Q1–3, 5–6;* very extreame *Q4* 46 this] *F, Q1–3, 5–6;* that *Q4* 48 your good graces] *F;* you my good Lords *Qq* 50 SP] *F; not in Qq*

Yet had we not determined he should die
Until your lordship came to see his end –
Which now the loving haste of these our friends,
Something against our meanings, have prevented –
Because, my lord, I would have had you heard
The traitor speak and timorously confess
The manner and the purpose of his treasons,
That you might well have signified the same
Unto the citizens, who haply may
Misconster us in him and wail his death.

MAYOR

But, my good lord, your graces' words shall serve
As well as I had seen and heard him speak;
And do not doubt, right noble princes both,
But I'll acquaint our duteous citizens
With all your just proceedings in this case.

52 **had . . . die** ambiguous: either 'we had not determined he should die' or 'we would not have determined that he should die'

54 **friends** Lovell and Ratcliffe; Qq retain this plural, despite Catesby's replacement of Lovell and Ratcliffe in Qq. See p. 453.

55 **Something . . . meanings** somewhat contrary to our intentions
have prevented has anticipated (*OED* prevent *v.* I 1); *have* may be a plural due to *friends* in 54.

56 **I** Buckingham possibly changes back to first person singular (as in 50) to express his individual reasoning.
had you heard i.e. have wished you to have heard (cf. Abbott, 491)

58 ***treasons** Hall and Holinshed three times use the singular (as do Qq) in this context (Smidt, *Memorial*, 40).

59 **signified** communicated

60 **haply** perhaps

61 **Misconster . . . him** i.e. misconstrue our treatment of him; the Elizabethan written forms 'conster' and 'construe' were both pronounced 'cònster' (*OED* construe *v.*).

62 ***graces'** Hammond argues for the plural possessive, referring to the words of both Buckingham and Richard, but 'my good lord' prompts many editors to adopt the singular form ('grace's').

63 **as** as if (Abbott, 107)

65 **But** i.e. but that

66 ***case** F's 'case' may arise from a Q6 misprint ('ease'), but 'case' and 'cause' could carry the same meaning (*OED* case *sb.*[1] 6; cause *sb.* II 8).

52 Yet] *F; Dut.* Yet *Q1–2; Clo.* Yet *Q3, 5; Glo.* Yet *Q4, 6* we not] *F;* not we *Qq* 53 end] *F;* death *Qq* 54 loving] *F;* longing *Qq* 55 Something . . . meanings] *F;* Somewhat . . . meaning *Qq* 56 I] *F;* we *Qq* 58 treasons] *F;* treason *Qq* 60 haply] *F;* happily *Qq* 61 Misconster] *F, Q1–5;* Misconstrue *Q6* 62 But, my] *F, Q1–2 subst.;* My *Q3–6* words] *F;* word *Qq* 63 and] *F;* or *Qq* 64 do not doubt] *F;* doubt you not *Qq* 65 our] *F;* your *Qq* 66 case] *F;* cause *Q1–5;* ease *Q6*

RICHARD

And to that end we wished your lordship here,
T'avoid the censures of the carping world.

BUCKINGHAM

Which, since you come too late of our intent,
Yet witness what you hear we did intend.
And so, my good Lord Mayor, we bid farewell.

Exit [*Lord*] *Mayor.*

RICHARD

Go after, after, cousin Buckingham.
The Mayor towards Guildhall hies him in all post.
There, at your meetest vantage of the time,
Infer the bastardy of Edward's children.
Tell them how Edward put to death a citizen
Only for saying he would make his son
Heir to the crown, meaning indeed his house,
Which, by the sign thereof, was termed so.

68 **carping** censorious
69 **Which** i.e. as to which (Abbott, 272)
of our intent i.e. to help our plan
70 **witness** i.e. bear witness to
71 *F's farewell is less abrupt than Qq's.
73 **Guildhall** meeting hall of the Corporation of the City of London
hies . . . post i.e. goes with great haste
74 ***meetest vantage** i.e. most appropriate moment; Qq/F variants have been important to debates about the roles of Q3 and Q6 in constituting F's text. See p. 440.
75 **Infer** allege; cf. 3.7.12.
bastardy See 3.7.4–6n. for the complicated basis of this charge.
76 **put . . . citizen** Probably the notorious story of Walker, a citizen from Cheapside, whom Hall calls Burdet: this merchant, who dwelled at the sign of the Crown, told his son that he would inherit the Crown 'meaning his awne house: but these wordes kyng Edward made to be mysconstrued, & interpreted that Burdet meante the croune of the realme: wherfore within lesse space then iiii. houres, he was apprehended, iudged, drawen and quartered' (*Edward V*, fol xxi^{r}). Holinshed tells an analogous story concerning Thomas Burdet of Warwickshire (3.703). Richard's *citizen* suggests indebtedness to Hall.
78 **house** tavern
79 **termed** termèd

67 wished] *F, Q1–5 subst.;* wish *Q6* 68 T'avoid] *F; Qq (*To auoyde*) subst.* censures . . . world] *F;* carping censures of the world *(*word *Q3) Qq* 69 Which] *F;* But *Qq* come] *F, Q1–2;* came *Q3–6* intent] *F;* intents *Qq* 70 you hear] *F; not in Qq* intend.] *F;* intend, and so my Lord adue. *Qq* 71] *F; not in Qq* SD] *F; opp. 72 Qq* 72 Go] *F; not in Qq* 74 meetest vantage] *F;* meetst *(*meetest *Q6)* aduantage *Qq*

Moreover, urge his hateful luxury
And bestial appetite in change of lust,
Which stretched unto their servants, daughters, wives,
Even where his raging eye or savage heart,
Without control, lusted to make a prey.
Nay, for a need, thus far come near my person:
Tell them, when that my mother went with child
Of that insatiate Edward, noble York
My princely father then had wars in France,
And by true computation of the time
Found that the issue was not his begot,
Which well appeared in his lineaments,
Being nothing like the noble duke, my father.
Yet touch this sparingly, as 'twere far off,
Because, my lord, you know my mother lives.

BUCKINGHAM

Doubt not, my lord; I'll play the orator

80–4 Accusations concerning Edward's promiscuous desires are prominent in the speeches More gives Buckingham (*CW2*, 71–2; Holinshed, 3.729); they also appear in Mancini (67); cf. 3.7.8.

80 **urge** assert, present forcefully
luxury lechery; cf. *Ham* 1.5.83.

81 **change of lust** i.e. pursuit of sexual variety

83 **Even where** wherever
raging violent, passionate with sexual desire (*OED* rage *sb.* 6a, b); cf. 'His rage of lust' (*Luc* 424).

85 **for a need** i.e. if necessary

86–90 Hall's and Holinshed's Dr Shaw asserts the bastardy of Edward IV and Clarence based on their dissimilarity to the Duke of York and their physical resemblance to other men (Hall, *Edward V*, fol. xx[r]; Holinshed, 3.727). Mancini (95) writes that Richard 'so corrupted preachers of the divine word' that they preached that Edward 'was conceived in adultery and in every way was unlike the late duke of York, whose son he was falsely said to be, but Richard, duke of Gloucester, who altogether resembled his father, was come to the throne as the legitimate successor'; cf. 3.7.9–14.

86–7 **went . . . Edward** i.e. was pregnant with the child that would become the insatiable Edward

90 **issue . . . begot** i.e. child was not fathered by him

93 **as . . . off** i.e. elliptically, by hints; cf. 3.1.170 and *H5* 1.2.240.

95 **Doubt** i.e. fear
play the orator i.e. assume the role of an accomplished rhetorician; cf. Dent, O74.1. Richard boasts, 'I'll play the orator as well as Nestor' (*3H6* 3.2.188),

81 bestial] *F, Q6 (*beastiall*), Q1–5* 82 unto] *F;* to *Qq* 83 raging] *F;* lustfull *Qq* 84 lusted . . . a] *F;* listed . . . his *Qq* 85 come] *F, Q1–3, 5–6;* comes *Q4* 87 insatiate] *F;* vnsatiate *Qq* 89 true] *F;* iust *Qq* 93 Yet . . . 'twere] *F;* But . . . it were *Qq* far] *F, Q1–3, 5–6;* a farre *Q4* 94 my . . . know] *F;* you know, my Lord *Qq* my mother] *F, Q1–4;* my *(*me *Q6)* brother *Q5–6* 95 Doubt] *F;* Feare *Qq*

As if the golden fee for which I plead
Were for myself. And so, my lord, adieu.

RICHARD
If you thrive well, bring them to Baynard's Castle,
Where you shall find me well accompanied
With reverend fathers and well-learned bishops.

BUCKINGHAM
I go, and towards three or four o'clock
Look for the news that the Guildhall affords.
Exit Buckingham.

RICHARD
Go, Lovell, with all speed to Doctor Shaw.
[*to Ratcliffe*] Go thou to Friar Penker. Bid them both

so Buckingham might be modelling himself on Richard, but elsewhere Edward also claims to 'play the orator' (*3H6* 1.2.2), and Henry VI similarly describes Clifford's rhetoric (*3H6* 2.2.43). Even King Henry is mocked for attempting to 'play the orator' (*1H6* 4.1.175).

96 **golden fee** i.e. the crown; 'fee' could refer to a prize or a monetary reward, or to goods or a heritable estate (*OED* *sb.*[1], *sb.*[2]).

98 **Baynard's Castle** Richard's London residence on the north bank of the Thames, between London Bridge and Blackfriars. After belonging to Henry VI it became a possession of the York family until Richard's death. In 1483 it was the residence of the Duchess of York. In Shakespeare's day it was in the possession of William Herbert, Earl of Pembroke.

103–5 *These lines are not in Qq, presumably because of Lovell's absence from Qq. Smidt claims on the basis of 98–100 that Richard has already had the idea of appearing with the clerics at Baynard's Castle, so that Qq's omission of 103–5 may represent an (incompletely executed) authorial decision to let Buckingham later claim Richard's appearance with the clerics as his own idea (*Impostors*, 165–6). But Richard may be vaguely suggesting an idea and subsequently arranging its implementation before allowing Buckingham the (mistaken) illusion of his own originality in 3.7.

103–4 **Doctor Shaw . . . Friar Penker** both notorious for preaching in support of Richard's claim. More discusses Shaw's sermon (see 86–90n.) and characterizes both as having 'no scrupilouse consience' (*CW2*, 58).

104 SD *Addressing this line to Catesby (following Capell) leaves Ratcliffe idle; if Catesby exits at 17, however, then Ratcliffe is the only choice for Richard's errand here. This makes F's stage direction at 105 ('*Exit.*') a false singular and 109 a false plural, but they may have been transposed in transcription.

97 And . . . adieu] *F; not in Qq, but see 102* 101–2] *F;* About three or foure a clocke look to heare / What news Guildhall affordeth, and so my Lord farewell. / *Qq* 102 SD] *F; Exit Buc. Qq opp. 106* 103–5] *F; not in Qq* 104 SD] *Rowe* Penker] *Capell; Peuker F*

Meet me within this hour at Baynard's Castle.
Exeunt [*Ratcliffe and Lovell*].
Now will I go to take some privy order
To draw the brats of Clarence out of sight,
And to give order that no manner person
Have any time recourse unto the princes. *Exit.*

[**3.6**] *Enter a* Scrivener [Q]*with a paper in his hand*[Q].

SCRIVENER
Here is the indictment of the good Lord Hastings,
Which in a set hand fairly is engrossed,
That it may be today read o'er in Paul's.
And mark how well the sequel hangs together:
Eleven hours I have spent to write it over,
For yesternight by Catesby was it sent me;

106 **take . . . order** i.e. make secret arrangements
107 **brats of Clarence** On Clarence's children, see 2.2.0.2n.
108 ***manner person** An elliptical form (abbreviating 'manner of person') shared by F, Q3–4 and not by Q1–2, 5–6 and thus supporting the argument that Q3 furnished copy for F throughout the play (see p. 439).
109 **recourse** access
3.6 location: '*A Street*' (Capell); omitted by Cibber
0.1 **Scrivener** professional copyist, notary. Any child might have perceived problems with the proclamation against Hastings, More writes, and bystanders joked about its being written by 'prophesie' (Holinshed, 3.724–5; More, *CW*2, 54; Hall, *Edward V*, fol. xvi[r]); Mancini (91) says 'the real truth was on the lips of many'. Here, an ordinary person pursuing his occupation realizes that he aids Richard's injustice. For an Elizabethan case in which time factors involved in prosecution were interpreted as implicating higher, even royal, involvement, see Sir John Perrot's treason trial of April 1592 (Howell, 1.1329).
2 **set hand** formal, ceremonious handwriting (*OED* set *ppl. a.* I 5a)
engrossed written out large
3 **read . . . Paul's** read aloud in St Paul's churchyard at Paul's Cross where there were 'sermons . . . euery Sundaye in the forenoone' (Stow, 1.331).
4 **sequel** sequence (of events)
4–11 **hangs together . . . palpable** terminology (*res cohaerens, manifestaque est*) derived from classical rhetorical *confirmatio* (Baldwin, 2.326–8)

105 SD] *Rowe subst.; Exit. F; not in Qq* 106 go] *F;* in *Qq* 108 order] *F;* notice *Qq* manner] *F, Q3–4;* maner of *Q1–2, 5–6* 109 Have any time] *F;* At any tyme haue *Qq* SD] *Qq; Exeunt. F* **3.6**] *Capell* 1 SP] *F (Scr.); not in Qq* Here] *F;* This *Qq* 3 today] *F;* this day *Qq* o'er] *F; Qq (*ouer*)* 5 have] *F; not in Qq* 6 sent] *F;* brought *Qq*

The precedent was full as long a-doing;
And yet within these five hours Hastings lived,
Untainted, unexamined, free, at liberty.
Here's a good world the while. Who is so gross
That cannot see this palpable device?
Yet who so bold but says he sees it not?
Bad is the world, and all will come to nought
When such ill dealing must be seen in thought. *Exit.*

[3.7] *Enter* RICHARD *and* BUCKINGHAM *at several doors.*

RICHARD
How now, how now, what say the citizens?

BUCKINGHAM
Now by the Holy Mother of our Lord,
The citizens are mum, say not a word.

7 **precedent** the original document from which a copy is made
a-doing i.e. in writing out
8 **within . . . hours** i.e. five hours ago
9 **Untainted** not accused (see 3.5.32)
10 **Here's . . . while** Cf. *KJ* 4.2.100: 'bad world the while'.
gross lacking discernment, stupid (*OED a.* A IV 13a)
11 **palpable device** obvious trick
13 **nought** nothing (*OED sb.*1); used interchangeably with Q1–2's 'naught' = evil (*OED* A *sb.* 2) (cf. 1.1.97–8).
14 **seen in thought** i.e. perceived but not spoken about (cf. *TGV* 4.4.170); 'thought' could mean anxiety, distress of mind (*OED* 5a).
3.7 location: 'Baynard's *Castle*' (Theobald); cf. 3.5.98–105.
0.1 *several* separate
1 Richard Simpson (436–7) suggests that Richard's quest for acclamation from the *citizens* represents a new historical understanding of a power-base more important to future politics than the barons of the earlier plays. The role of the commons here resembles that implied by the attempt of Richard's father to use the Cade rebellion to 'perceive the commons' mind, / How they affect the house and claim of York' (*2H6* 3.1.373–4).
How now i.e. how is it now? (*OED* how *adv.* 4)
citizens inhabitants of a city or town, often specifically those possessing rights and privileges as freemen (*OED* 1); see 200.
3 **mum** silent, possibly suggesting an inarticulate sound signifying inability or unwillingness to speak (*OED sb.*[1] 1); cf. *KL* 1.4.185–7 and Dent, W767: 'No word but mum'.

8 Hastings lived] *F;* liued Lord Hastings *Qq* 10–11] *Qq; F lines* while. / deuice? / 10 Who is] *F;* Why whoes *Qq* 11 cannot see] *F;* sees not *Qq* 12 who] *F, Q3–6;* whoes *Q1–2* bold] *F;* blinde *Qq* 13 nought] *F, Q3–6;* naught *Q1–2* 14 ill] *F;* bad *Qq* dealing] *F, Q1–3, 5–6;* dealings *Q4* **3.7**] *Pope* 0.1] *F; Enter Glocester at one doore, Buckingham at another. Qq* 1 How . . . [2]now] *F;* How now my Lord *Qq* 3 say] *F;* and speake *Qq*

RICHARD
Touched you the bastardy of Edward's children?
BUCKINGHAM
I did, with his contract with Lady Lucy
And his contract by deputy in France;
Th'unsatiate greediness of his desire
And his enforcement of the city wives;
His tyranny for trifles; his own bastardy,
As being got your father then in France,
And his resemblance being not like the Duke.
Withal, I did infer your lineaments,
Being the right idea of your father,
Both in your form and nobleness of mind;

4 **Touched you** i.e. did you bring up

4–6 **bastardy . . . France** According to More, Edward IV had a child by Elizabeth Lucy, without formally contracting marriage; this relationship was publicly brought against him by his mother, the Duchess of York, when he sought to wed Elizabeth Grey. His marriage to Elizabeth Grey alienated the Earl of Warwick, who had been in France as Edward's deputy contracting a dynastic union with the Lady Bona of Savoy (*CW2*, 64–5; cf. *3H6* 3.3.49–265). More says the 'pretext' supporting the charge of bastardy against Edward's children rests on the claim that his earlier commitments made his relationship with Lady Grey bigamous (*CW2*, 59).

5–6, 8, 11 *Absence from Qq has been explained as motivated by a desire to avoid offending Elizabeth I, since some of the charges roughly resemble those brought against her father, Henry VIII (Marshall). Smidt suggests Q1 cut to avoid repetitiveness (of 3.5.75–92 and 178–90) (*Impostors*, 114–15).

5 **contract** betrothal

7 **unsatiate** insatiable; F and Qq reverse their former usage (see 3.5.87).

8 **enforcement** sexual compulsion

9 **tyranny for trifles** i.e. excessive punishment for minor infractions. More's Buckingham says that Edward IV inflated all charges 'aboue the mesure' (*CW2*, 70).

9–14 **bastardy . . . form** Cf. 3.5.86–92.

10 **got** begotten, conceived

11 **resemblance** appearance, characteristic features; see 3.5.86–90n.
Duke the Duke of York, Richard's and Edward's father

12 **Withal** in addition

13 **idea** image, likeness, figure (*OED sb.* II 7a); the *right idea* suggests the closest approximation to an original. How egregious is Buckingham's flattery supposed to be when he likens Richard 'in form' to the Duke of York despite his limp, arm and back (cf. *TxC*, 242)? The flattering portrait of Richard by More's Dr Shaw (*CW2*, 67–8) emphasizes facial likeness (cf. Hall, *Edward V*, fol. xx[r]; Holinshed, 3.727). Vergil's Shaw claims discrepancy in body and face between the Duke of York and King Edward (184).

5–6 his . . . France] *F; not in Qq* 7 Th'unsatiate] *F;* the insatiate *Qq* desire] *F;* desires *Qq* 8] *F; not in Qq* 11] *F; not in Qq* 14 your] *F, Q1–2;* one *Q3–6*

Laid open all your victories in Scotland,
Your discipline in war, wisdom in peace,
Your bounty, virtue, fair humility;
Indeed, left nothing fitting for your purpose
Untouched or slightly handled in discourse.
And when mine oratory drew toward end,
I bid them that did love their country's good
Cry, 'God save Richard, England's royal King!'

RICHARD
And did they so?

BUCKINGHAM
No, so God help me, they spake not a word,
But like dumb statues or breathing stones
Stared each on other and looked deadly pale;
Which when I saw, I reprehended them

15 **Laid open** i.e. brought up
victories in Scotland Richard commanded the English invasion of Scotland in 1482, captured Berwick and advanced as far as Edinburgh; his warlike prowess is prominent in *3H6*.

16 **discipline** training or skill in military affairs (*OED sb.* 3b)

17 **bounty** generosity
fair spotless, unblemished (*OED a.* III 9); or possibly, plainly to be seen (*OED a.* IV 17). The second meaning would underline the outrageousness of Richard's inherently self-contradictory claims to *humility*, which Buckingham here echoes (cf. 2.1.73).

19 **slightly handled** i.e. passed lightly over

20–41 closely following Hall (*Edward V*, fol. xxii[v]) and Holinshed (3.730–1), though they have Buckingham twice attempting to move the assembly; contrast Fabyan's emphasis (2.515) on Buckingham's eloquence, which moves even 'wise men' with his 'sugred wordes' and their 'good ordering'.

20 ***mine . . . toward** F agrees with Q3–6, preferring 'my' to Q1–2's 'mine'; however, F's 'drew toward' may allow for the same syllable count as Q1–2, 4 ('grew to an') and thus both may differ from 'grew to' in Q3, 5–6. Abbott (237) claims 'mine' and 'my' to be generally interchangeable, but when Shakespeare uses 'my' as the possessive before a noun beginning with a vowel, as in F, usually the effect is emphatic. Thus F's 'my' might stress Buckingham's claim to his own oratory while Q1–2's 'mine' would be unemphasized, with the stress falling on *oratory*; cf. 1.4.22, 23n., 4.1.81n.

23 *Qq's 'A' might represent 'Ah!' (cf. 1.3.154n.).

25 **statues** trisyllabic, as *JC* 2.2.76

26 **each on other** i.e. at one another

15 open] *F, Q1–5;* vpon *Q6* victories] *F, Q1–3, 5–6;* victorie *Q4* 18 your] *F;* the *Qq* 20 mine] *Q1–2;* my *F, Q3–6* drew toward] *F;* grew to an *Q1–2, 4;* grew to *Q3, 5–6* 21 bid] *F, Q1–4;* bad *Q5–6* did love] *F, Q1–2;* loues *Q3–6* 23 And] *F;* A and *Q1;* A, and *Q2–6;* Ah! and *Cam* 24 they . . . word] *F; not in Qq* 25 statues] *F, Qq;* statuas *Steevens* breathing] *F, Q1–2;* breathlesse *Q3–6* 26 Stared] *F;* Gazde *Qq*

And asked the Mayor what meant this wilful silence?
His answer was, the people were not used
To be spoke to but by the Recorder.
Then he was urged to tell my tale again:
'Thus saith the Duke; thus hath the Duke inferred' –
But nothing spoke in warrant from himself.
When he had done, some followers of mine own
At lower end of the hall hurled up their caps,
And some ten voices cried, 'God save King Richard!'
And thus I took the vantage of those few:
'Thanks, gentle citizens and friends,' quoth I;
'This general applause and cheerful shout
Argues your wisdom and your love to Richard:'
And even here brake off and came away.

RICHARD

What tongueless blocks were they! Would they not
  speak?
Will not the Mayor then, and his brethren, come?

30 **Recorder** rècorder; legal official appointed to 'record' the proceedings of the courts and the customs of the city. Holinshed terms him 'the mouth of the citie' (3.730).

32 **inferred** asserted, alleged (*OED v.* 2)

33 **in . . . himself** on his own authority

35 **lower end** the end of the hall opposite the raised upper end, with its dais
hall Guildhall's great hall, approximately 150 by 50 feet (45 by 15 metres), capable of holding a large assembly and central to city government

37 **vantage of** i.e. the opportunity provided by (cf. 3.5.74)

38–40 ***gentle . . . cheerful . . . love** F's progression from 'gentle', flattering the common (i.e. not gentle) citizens, to 'cheerful', with its interpretation of their approbation, to the culminating claim of 'love' suggests a developing argument (Hammond). Qq's 'louing', 'louing' and 'loue' show no rhetorical development.

40 **Argues** proves, indicates (*OED* I 1)

41 **brake** broke

43 **brethren** i.e. fellow-citizens, perhaps carrying civic or religious connotations, since guild or corporation members (*OED* brother *sb.* 4) or co-religionists among Elizabethan Puritans (*OED sb.* 3) could be so called. The religious sense is, of course, inappropriate to the time of the play, but religious divisions were hotly discussed, debated and satirized by the 1590s. See pp. 31–6. In *3H6* 'brethren' are identified with aldermen (*3H6* 4.7.16.1–2, 34.1).

28 meant] *F, Q1–5;* meanes *Q6* 29 used] *F;* wont *Qq* 33 spoke] *F;* spake *Q1–5;* speake *Q6* 35 lower] *F;* the lower *Qq* 37] *F; not in Qq* 38 gentle] *F;* louing *Qq* 39 cheerful] *F;* louing *Qq* 40 wisdom] *F, Q3–6;* wisedomes *Q1–2* love] *F, Q1–2;* loues *Q3–6* 41 even here] *F;* so *Qq* 42] *Qq; F lines* they, / speake? / speak?] *F;* speake? / *Buc.* No by my troth my Lo: / *Qq*

BUCKINGHAM

The Mayor is here at hand. Intend some fear.
Be not you spoke with but by mighty suit;
And look you get a prayer book in your hand,
And stand between two churchmen, good my lord,
For on that ground I'll make a holy descant.
And be not easily won to our requests;
Play the maid's part: still answer nay, and take it.

RICHARD

I go, and if you plead as well for them
As I can say nay to thee for myself,
No doubt we bring it to a happy issue.

BUCKINGHAM

Go, go up to the leads, the Lord Mayor knocks.

[Q]*Exit*[Q] [*Richard*].

Enter the [Lord] MAYOR *and* Citizens.

44 **Intend** pretend (*OED* 22) (cf. 3.5.8)

45 **but . . . suit** i.e. unless they entreat you urgently

48 **ground** melody upon which the descant or melodious variation is raised (cf. 1.1.27); Richard perhaps anticipates Buckingham's scenario (cf. 3.5.98–100). ***make** Qq's 'build' plays on the musical and architectural senses of *ground*.

49 ***And** Buckingham's speech in F appears as an additive series of recommendations, as if each were occurring to him at the moment; in contrast to F's four uses of *and* in this speech, Qq have only two instances of the word.

50 i.e. say no, but do it anyway (see Dent, M 34); cf. *TGV* 1.2.55–6. Richard exploits a 'feminine' position. **still** always

51–2 **you . . . thee** Explaining F's pronouns, Abbott asserts that 'thou' may be used in statements and requests while 'you' is employed in conditional and other sentences in which there is no direct appeal to the person addressed (Abbott, 234; contrast *TxC*, 242).

51 **for them** i.e. to me on their behalf

52 i.e. as I am able to pretend plausibly, in my own person, to refuse your offers

53 *This line begins the portion of Q1 printed by Peter Short (see Hammond, 21–4; cf. pp. 425–31). **it** i.e. the entire transaction **issue** conclusion

54 **leads** the roof, covered with sheets or strips of lead (*OED sb.*[1] I 7a)

54.1 **MAYOR** Since the 18th century the Mayor has frequently been played as a buffoon (see Hankey, 179–80 for horseplay).

44 SP] *F, Q3–6 subst.; Glo. Q1–2* at hand] *F, Q1–2; om. Q3–6* Intend] *F;* and intend *Qq* 45 you spoke with] *F;* spoken withall *Qq* by] *F;* with *Qq* 47 between] *F;* betwixt *Qq* 48 make] *F;* build *Qq* 49 And] *F; not in Qq* easily] *F, Q1;* easie *Q2–6* requests] *F;* request *Qq* 50 still . . . and] *F;* say no, but *Qq* 51 I . . . you] *F;* Feare not me, if thou canst *Qq* 53 we] *F;* weele *Qq* 54] *F;* You shal see what I can do, get you vp to the leads. *Qq* 54.1] *F; not in Qq* Lord] *Rowe*

Welcome, my lord; I dance attendance here.
I think the Duke will not be spoke withal.

Enter CATESBY.

BUCKINGHAM

Now, Catesby, what says your lord to my request?

CATESBY

He doth entreat your grace, my noble lord,
To visit him tomorrow, or next day.
He is within, with two right reverend fathers,
Divinely bent to meditation;
And in no worldly suits would he be moved
To draw him from his holy exercise.

BUCKINGHAM

Return, good Catesby, to the gracious Duke;
Tell him myself, the Mayor and aldermen,
In deep designs, in matter of great moment,
No less importing than our general good,

55 **dance attendance** wait upon a person with assiduous attention (*OED* dance *v.* 5). Cf. *2H6* 1.3.172, *H8* 5.2.30; also Dent, A392.

56 **withal** with

57 *Cf. Qq's announcement of Catesby's entrance with 81 F; Qq again employ the term 'seruant' for Catesby (cf. 3.2.21).

60–3 Shakespeare develops Richard's 'pious exercises' from a single phrase in Hall describing his appearance between two bishops (see 93.1n.); otherwise, the sources have him acting as if anxious about the uncertain purposes of such a large assembly (Hall, *Edward V*, fol. xxiii[r]; Holinshed, 3.731).

60 **right reverend** title properly belonging to bishops (*OED* reverend 2)

61 **bent** mentally inclined, disposed (*OED v.* 16), here perhaps implying a physical sense

62 **worldly suits** i.e. secular concerns

63 **exercise** act of devotion, religious observation; cf. 3.2.108.

65 **aldermen** originally, officials or wardens of guilds, but later, magistrates next in dignity to the mayor (*OED* 2, 3). Qq's 'Cittizens' might spare the expense of aldermen's robes (Patrick, 27).

66 **deep** serious, weighty (*OED a.* II 7b), but when coupled with *designs* also conveying a sense of being profound in craft or subtlety, as at 2.1.38

67 **No less importing** i.e. concerned with nothing less

55 Welcome, my lord] *F;* Now my L. Maior *Qq* 56 spoke] *F, Q1–2;* spoken *Q3–6* 57] *F;* Here coms his seruant: how now *Catesby* what saies he. *Qq* 58 He . . . grace, my noble lord] *F;* My Lord, he . . . grace *Qq* 60 right] *F, Q1–2; om. Q3–6* 62 suits] *F;* suite *Qq* 64 the gracious Duke] *F;* thy Lord againe *Qq* 65 aldermen] *F;* Cittizens *Qq* 66 in matter] *F;* and matters *Qq* 67 than] *F, Q1–5 (*then*);* them then *Q6*

Are come to have some conference with his grace.

CATESBY

I'll signify so much unto him straight. *Exit.*

BUCKINGHAM

Ah ha, my lord, this prince is not an Edward.
He is not lulling on a lewd love-bed,
But on his knees at meditation;
Not dallying with a brace of courtesans,
But meditating with two deep divines;
Not sleeping, to engross his idle body,
But praying, to enrich his watchful soul.
Happy were England, would this virtuous prince
Take on his grace the sovereignty thereof.
But sure I fear we shall not win him to it.

MAYOR

Marry, God defend his grace should say us nay.

BUCKINGHAM

I fear he will. Here Catesby comes again.

Enter CATESBY.

Now, Catesby, what says his grace?

CATESBY

He wonders to what end you have assembled

71 **lulling** leaning idly, reclining in a relaxed attitude (*OED* loll *v.* 1 4) **love-bed** perhaps a Shakespearean coinage (*OED* love *sb.*[1] 15a, citing this line) carrying, like Qq's 'day-bed' (*OED* day-bed, citing this line), sexual associations (*TN* 2.5.46–7)

73 **brace** pair, originally of dogs, also of game (*OED sb.*[2] III 15a); cf. *3H6* 2.5.129.

74 **deep** learned

75 **engross** fatten, make gross (*OED v.* III 9); associations with sexuality occur in *RJ* 2.4.165, *Ham* 1.2.136 and *Oth* 1.1.132.

76 **watchful** wakeful, accustomed to keeping awake; cf. 5.3.115. Jesus repeatedly admonishes his followers to 'watch' or to 'watch and pray' (Mark, 13.33–8, Matthew, 26.38–44).

80 **God defend** God forbid

69] *F;* Ile tell him *(*Ile him *Q6)* what you say my Lord *Qq* 71 love-bed] *F;* day bed *Qq* 77 virtuous] *F;* gracious *Qq* 78 his grace . . . thereof] *F;* himselfe . . . thereon *Qq* 79 not] *F;* neuer *Qq* 80 defend] *F;* forbid *Qq* 81 Here . . . again] *F;* how now Catesby *Qq* 81.1] *F, Q1–2; after 80 Q3–6* 82] *F;* What saies your Lord? *Qq* 83 He] *F;* My Lo. he *Qq*

Such troops of citizens to come to him,
His grace not being warned thereof before.
He fears, my lord, you mean no good to him.

BUCKINGHAM

Sorry I am my noble cousin should
Suspect me that I mean no good to him.
By heaven, we come to him in perfect love;
And so once more return and tell his grace. *Exit* ^{Q}*Catesby*^{Q}.
When holy and devout religious men
Are at their beads, 'tis much to draw them thence,
So sweet is zealous contemplation.

Enter RICHARD *aloft, between two Bishops.*
[*Enter* CATESBY.]

84 **troops** This potentially inflated claim for the number of citizens has often been played for laughs (Hankey, 180).

92 **beads** prayers, by Shakespeare's time usually implying reference to the rosary (*OED sb.* 1a, b)
much a great matter, difficult

93 **zealous** intensely earnest (*OED* 1d); by the early 1590s a potentially divisive term when employed to characterize religious attitudes, practices and factions. In attacking Puritanism, Richard Hooker refers to 'this present age, wherein zeal hath drowned charity, and skill meekness' (*Laws*, 170). By contrast, Henry Smith laments that religious 'zeale is counted no vertue' and the zealous 'are counted curious, factious, precise, phantasticall', adding 'some giddy spirites thinke now, that they which are zelouser than the[m] selues know not what they say nor doe' (*Sermons*, 935–6, 921).

93.1 ***aloft . . . Bishops*** More describes Richard's appearance 'aboue in a galarye' (*CW2*, 77); '*aloft*' is the usual Shakespearean term for the playing space above the main stage platform (Dessen & Thomson, 4). Richard plays the rest of the scene from this elevated location. No clerics appear here in More (*CW2*, 77) or Holinshed (3.731); in Grafton's edition of Hardyng and in Hall, Richard appears 'with a bishop on euery hande of hym' (Hall, *Edward V*, fol. xxiii^{v}; Hardyng, *Edward V*, fol. lxxv^{r}). Two clerics flank the royal person in coronation pageantry (Lyons, 23); cf. Richard's historical coronation between two bishops (Sutton & Hammond, 216).

93.2 CATESBY Since Catesby left at 90 to fetch Richard and has lines at 202ff., this seems like a good time for his re-entry; F and Qq provide no indications. He enters to the main playing stage rather than above.

84 come to] *F;* speake with *Qq* 86 He . . . lord] *F;* My Lord, he feares *Qq* 89 we . . . love] *F (*perfit*);* I come in perfect loue to him *Qq* 92 much] *F;* hard *Qq* thence] *F, Q1–4;* hence *Q5–6* 93.1] *F; Enter Rich. with (and Q3–6) two bishops a loste (aloft Q2–6). Qq* 93.2] *Theobald (*Catesby *returns.)*

MAYOR

See where his grace stands, 'tween two clergymen.

BUCKINGHAM

Two props of virtue for a Christian prince,
To stay him from the fall of vanity;
And see a book of prayer in his hand,
True ornaments to know a holy man.
– Famous Plantagenet, most gracious prince,
Lend favourable ear to our requests,
And pardon us the interruption
Of thy devotion and right Christian zeal.

RICHARD

My lord, there needs no such apology.
I do beseech your grace to pardon me,
Who, earnest in the service of my God,
Deferred the visitation of my friends.
But leaving this, what is your grace's pleasure?

BUCKINGHAM

Even that, I hope, which pleaseth God above
And all good men of this ungoverned isle.

95–8 **props, ornaments** Richard's public exploitation of bishops in his tyrannical usurpation suggests contentious issues for the early 1590s (see pp. 31–6). The word *props* means 'supports'; the sense of stage requisites is not recorded before the 19th century (*OED* property *sb.* 3), though Quince speaks of a 'bill of properties' (*MND* 1.2.98–9; cf. *MW* 4.4.77).

96 **stay** prevent, restrain (*OED v.*[1] III 23) **fall of vanity** i.e. succumbing to worthless worldly temptations and falling into sin

97 **book of prayer** Qq lack 97–8, but the prayer-book seems made for the moment. A similar devotional book is employed hypocritically in *Ham* 3.1.43–5. Henry VI's piety is registered by his entry 'with a prayer book' (*3H6* 3.1.12.1), and by his reading of a devotional 'book' just before his murder by Richard (*3H6* 5.6.1). For 'book' as *Book of Common Prayer*, see *OED* book *sb.* 5b.

98 **ornaments** the bishops and the prayer-book (cf. 95–8n.) **to know** i.e. by which to recognize

102 **right** true, proper (*OED a.* II 7a) **zeal** see 93n.

109 **ungoverned** i.e. lacking a supreme ruler

94 his grace . . . 'tween] *F;* he . . . between *Qq* 97–8] *F; not in Qq* 100 ear] *F;* eares *Qq* our] *F, Q1;* my *Q2–6* requests] *F;* request *Qq* 104 I . . . to] *F;* I rather do beseech you *Qq* 106 Deferred] *F;* Neglect *Qq*

RICHARD

I do suspect I have done some offence
That seems disgracious in the City's eye,
And that you come to reprehend my ignorance.

BUCKINGHAM

You have, my lord. Would it might please your grace,
On our entreaties, to amend your fault.

RICHARD

Else wherefore breathe I in a Christian land?

BUCKINGHAM

Know then, it is your fault that you resign
The supreme seat, the throne majestical,
The sceptered office of your ancestors,
Your state of fortune, and your due of birth,
The lineal glory of your royal house,
To the corruption of a blemished stock;
Whiles in the mildness of your sleepy thoughts,
Which here we waken to our country's good,

111 **disgracious** displeasing, out of favour (*OED* 2); cf. 4.4.178.

112 **ignorance** offence or sin caused by ignorance (*OED* 2); cf. the Litany: 'That it may please thee to give us true repentance, to forgive us all our sins, negligences, and ignorances' (*BCP*, 71).

115 **Else wherefore** i.e. otherwise why **breathe** live; cf. 1.1.21.

116 **resign** relinquish, surrender (*OED v.*[1] 1); cf. *VA* 1039–40.

119, 126 *Absence from Qq may represent an effort at tightening up this speech (Jowett), but reference to Richard's *state of fortune* (119) contributes an element of *realpolitik* in urging him to make good on the opportunity that fortune has provided, and reference to grafting (126) recalls plant imagery in other early plays by Shakespeare (see 126n.). Richard later expounds upon Buckingham's themes (166–7, 171).

119 **state of fortune** i.e. the status and power that fortune has granted you

120 **house** i.e. family, house of York

121 **corruption . . . stock** The metaphor is horticultural: Edward is a bastard; the York family is corrupted by his effect upon their lineal stem. See 126, 166, 215 for development of the metaphor. Cf. the text of Dr Shaw's Paul's Cross sermon: 'Bastard slippes shall neuer take deepe root' (Holinshed, 3.727). For visual embodiments of the metaphor, see pp. 69–72 and the frontispiece to Hall's 1550 edition (Fig. 1).

111 seems] *F, Q1–4;* seeme *Q5–6* eye] *F;* eies *Qq* 113] *Qq; F lines* Lord: / Grace, / might] *F; not in Qq* 114 On . . . your] *F;* At . . . that *Qq* 116 Know then] *F;* Then know *Qq* 119] *F; not in Qq* 122 Whiles] *F;* Whilst *Q1;* Whilest *Q2–6* your] *F, Q1, 3–6;* you *Q2* 123 our] *F, Q1–4;* your *Q5–6*

The noble isle doth want her proper limbs;
Her face defaced with scars of infamy,
Her royal stock graft with ignoble plants,
And almost shouldered in the swallowing gulf
Of dark forgetfulness and deep oblivion;
Which to recure, we heartily solicit
Your gracious self to take on you the charge
And kingly government of this your land,
Not as protector, steward, substitute,
Or lowly factor for another's gain,
But as successively from blood to blood,
Your right of birth, your empery, your own.

124 **want** lack

124, 125, 126 **her, Her** For England personified as female in a passage that echoes *Richard III* 1.4.24–33, see *H5* 1.2.155–73. Thompson argues that the F repetition of 'his' and its occurrence in a line peculiar to F (126) suggest that it is not an error (cf. Smidt, *Memorial*, 53). The alternative argument is that 'his' first appeared in 124 as a Q3 error, went uncorrected in F and influenced F's 'His' in 125, so that F's added 126, although derived from FMS, was altered in print to agree with the mistaken pronouns in 124–5 (Hammond). This edition somewhat uneasily accepts this argument. The gendering here is interesting in a play where one crippled male character 'want[s] his proper limbs' and another promiscuous male figure is said to have had his 'stock graft with ignoble plants'.

124 **proper** rightful, own (*OED a.* I 1), but also, given Richard's limbs, ironically implying 'well-made, handsome' (*OED a.* II 9)

126 **graft** engrafted; cf. *2H6* 3.2.212–14.

127 **shouldered in** pushed roughly into with the shoulder, jostled (*OED v.* 1); cf. *1H6* 4.1.189–90, where 'factious' nobles engage in 'shouldering' each other.

swallowing gulf A *gulf* might be an abyss or chasm, but *swallowing* determines the sense as 'whirlpool' (*OED sb.* 3; cf. *H5* 2.4.10). For destruction and death associated with falling into water, see 1.4.18–62, 3.4.97–100. Cf. Henry VI to Richard for having murdered his son: 'thyself, the sea / Whose envious gulf did swallow up his life' (*3H6* 5.6.24–5).

129 **recure** remedy, redress (*OED v.* 2b)

130 **charge** responsibility of taking care of (*OED sb.* 13)

132–5 another of Wilson's linguistic 'tangles'

133 **factor** one who acts for another as agent (*OED sb.* 3); cf. 4.4.72.

134 **successively . . . to blood** i.e. by succession of descent from generation to generation

135 **empery** absolute dominion or territory of an absolute ruler

124 The] *F;* This *Qq* her] *Q1–2;* his *F, Q3–6* 125 Her] *Qq;* His *F* scars] *F, Q1, 5–6;* stars *Q2–4* 126] *F; not in Qq* Her] *Pope;* His *F* 127 the] *F, Q1–2;* this *Q3–6* 128 dark . . . deep] *F;* blind . . . darke *Qq* 129 recure] *F, Q1–5;* recouer *Q6* 130–1 charge . . . land] *F;* soueraingtie thereof *Qq* 133 Or] *F, Q1–2;* Nor *Q3–6*

For this, consorted with the citizens,
Your very worshipful and loving friends,
And by their vehement instigation,
In this just cause come I to move your grace.

RICHARD

I cannot tell if to depart in silence
Or bitterly to speak in your reproof
Best fitteth my degree or your condition.
If not to answer, you might haply think
Tongue-tied ambition, not replying, yielded
To bear the golden yoke of sovereignty,
Which fondly you would here impose on me.
If to reprove you for this suit of yours,
So seasoned with your faithful love to me,
Then on the other side I checked my friends.
Therefore, to speak, and to avoid the first,

136 **consorted** associated (*OED v.* 4); cf. 3.4.70.

137 **worshipful** honourable; while the term could mean distinguished in rank or importance (see 3.4.39), it had begun to evolve in Shakespeare's day towards more restricted application to members of livery companies (*OED* 2, 3); see also 1.1.66–7. In passages from Hall that Shakespeare drew upon for *3H6*, Edward addresses the aldermen of York as 'worshipfull' (*Edward IV*, fol. ccxiv[v]).

142 **degree** position in the scale of dignity or rank (*OED* 4)
condition state in regard to wealth or circumstances (*OED sb.* 10); or character, moral disposition (*OED sb.* 11). Condition and degree appear nearly synonymous in *2H4* 4.3.1–8, but here Richard differentiates them, asking whether it better befits his exalted degree and the citizens' lower social or moral condition to leave without responding or to reprove them for their inappropriate solicitations.

143–52 *Absence of these lines from Qq abbreviates Richard's lengthy remarks, but results in omission of the carefully crafted development they give to 140–2; Patrick (127) suggests inexact parallelism between 140–2 and 153.

143–5 Cf. Dent, S446: 'Silence is (gives) consent.'

143 **haply** perhaps

144 **yielded** i.e. yielded to your entreaties

146 **fondly** foolishly

148 **seasoned** qualified by a beneficial admixture (*OED v.* 1d)

149 **on . . . side** i.e. going to the other extreme
checked rebuked, reprimanded; 'you might haply think' is implied from 143.

137 very] *F, Q1–2; om. Q3–6* loving] *F, Q1–2;* very louing *Q3–6* 139 cause] *F;* suite *Qq* 140 cannot tell if] *F;* know not whether *(*whither *Q5–6) Qq* 143–52] *F; not in Qq*

And then, in speaking, not to incur the last,
Definitively thus I answer you:
Your love deserves my thanks, but my desert
Unmeritable shuns your high request.
First, if all obstacles were cut away,
And that my path were even to the crown
As the ripe revenue and due of birth,
Yet so much is my poverty of spirit,
So mighty and so many my defects,
That I would rather hide me from my greatness,
Being a bark to brook no mighty sea,
Than in my greatness covet to be hid
And in the vapour of my glory smothered.
But, God be thanked, there is no need of me,
And much I need to help you, were there need.
The royal tree hath left us royal fruit,
Which, mellowed by the stealing hours of time,
Will well become the seat of majesty,
And make, no doubt, us happy by his reign.

153–4 **desert / Unmeritable** i.e. unworthiness, undeserving merit

155–6 **cut . . . crown** Cf. Richard's image of hewing through thorny woods to the crown (*3H6* 3.2.174–81); see also 121n., 126n.

156 **that** if

even smooth, unimpeded

157 **ripe revenue** rèvenue (as *R2* 2.1.226); benefit or return that is ready to be inherited (*OED* revenue 3); there may be an anticipated (but implicit) contrast between Richard's ripeness in age and the immaturity of the Prince, the *fruit* that needs further mellowing (166–7).

158 **poverty of spirit** biblical (Matthew, 5.3: 'Blessed are the poore in spirite: for theirs is the kyngdome of heauen.')

160 **my greatness** i.e. my royal title

161 **bark** small ship

brook endure

162 **covet** i.e. desire

163 **vapour** exhalation of the nature of steam, here denoting something unsubstantial or worthless (*OED sb.* 2a, 2c)

165 **much I need** i.e. I am lacking in the quality necessary (to help you, if help were needed).

167 **stealing** i.e. slipping away imperceptibly; cf. 5.3.85.

168 **well become** i.e. be well suited to

169 **no doubt** Denying doubt rhetorically raises the possibility of doubt; cf. Mark Antony's damning asseveration: 'And sure he is an honourable man' (*JC* 3.2.100).

157 the ripe] *F;* my ripe *Q1;* my right *Q2–6* of] *F;* by *Qq* 160 That I would] *F;* As I had *Qq* 164 thanked, there is] *F (*thank'd, there is*);* thanked there's *Qq* of] *F, Q1–2;* for *Q3–6* 165 were there need] *F;* if need were *Qq*

On him I lay that you would lay on me:
The right and fortune of his happy stars,
Which God defend that I should wring from him.

BUCKINGHAM

My lord, this argues conscience in your grace,
But the respects thereof are nice and trivial,
All circumstances well considered.
You say that Edward is your brother's son;
So say we too, but not by Edward's wife.
For first was he contract to Lady Lucy –
Your mother lives a witness to his vow –
And afterward by substitute betrothed
To Bona, sister to the King of France.
These both put off, a poor petitioner,
A care-crazed mother to a many sons,

171 **happy stars** i.e. fortunate destiny; cf. 119n.

172 **defend** forbid
wring wrest or wrench, acquire by exaction or extortion (*OED v.* 7); cf. *3H6* 2.1.153, *JC* 4.3.73.

173 **this argues conscience** i.e. this speech evidences scrupulous conscience.

174 **respects thereof** considerations (*OED sb.* 14) that support your argument
nice unimportant (*OED* 10b), suggesting overly subtle (*OED* 7); cf. *3H6* 4.7.58, where Richard urges Edward to seize the crown, 'Why, brother, wherefore stand you on nice points?' Richard's blunt demand that his brother take forceful action in spite of (Edward's own) principled objections provides an ironic contrast to Buckingham's tortuously constructed rhetorical justifications for usurpation.

175 **considered** considerèd

176 **Edward** i.e. Prince Edward

177–81 See 4–6.

178 **contract** contràct; i.e. contracted (Abbott, 342); cf. 5.

181 **sister** sister-in-law; Lady Bona's eldest sister was King Louis's second wife; cf. *3H6* 3.3.0.1.

182 **put off** i.e. thrust aside
a poor petitioner For Elizabeth Grey's petitions to Edward IV and his lustful response, see *3H6* 3.2.

183 **care-crazed** shattered by care; cf. woe-wearied (4.4.18).
a many 'a' is frequently inserted before 'many' to indicate that the objects enumerated are thought of collectively as one (Abbott, 87).
sons Before marrying Edward IV, Elizabeth had three children, a daughter and two sons, by her first husband, Sir John Grey; the two sons in this play are the Marquess of Dorset and Lord Grey.

170 that] *F;* what *Qq* 178 was he] *F;* he was *Qq* contract] *F, Q1–5;* contracted *Q6* 179 his] *F;* that *Qq* 180 afterward] *F, Q1–5;* afterwards *Q6* 182 off] *F;* by *Qq* 183 to a . . . sons] *F;* of a . . . children *Q1;* of . . . children *Q2–6*

A beauty-waning and distressed widow,
Even in the afternoon of her best days,
Made prize and purchase of his wanton eye,
Seduced the pitch and height of his degree
To base declension and loathed bigamy.
By her, in his unlawful bed, he got
This Edward, whom our manners call the Prince.
More bitterly could I expostulate,
Save that, for reverence to some alive,
I give a sparing limit to my tongue.
Then, good my lord, take to your royal self
This proffered benefit of dignity,
If not to bless us and the land withal,
Yet to draw forth your noble ancestry
From the corruption of abusing times
Unto a lineal, true-derived course.

186 **prize and purchase** gains, winnings; especially that which is taken in the hunt, in pillage, robbery or in war (*OED* purchase *sb.* 8)

187 **pitch** height to which a falcon or other bird of prey soars before swooping down on its prey (*OED sb.*[2] 18a); cf. *1H6* 2.4.11. The line continues the play's social commentary by means of references to birds (see e.g. 1.1.132–3).

188 **declension** decline from a standard, here the standard of Edward's royal rank (*OED* 2); cf. *Ham* 2.2.146.
bigamy Not only was Edward IV bound by previous 'contract' to Lady Lucy (see 4–6n.), but according to ecclesiastical law remarriage after death of a first wife or husband and marriage of, or with, a widow or widower also constituted bigamy (*OED* 2, citing this line). Edward's own mother raised the accusation of adultery against him to dissuade him from his marriage (Holinshed, 3.726). The charge is remarkable, given Richard's own marriage to Anne, the widow of Prince Edward (Furness).

190 **our manners** i.e. our sense of politeness

191 **expostulate** expound the matter

192 **some alive** i.e. the Duchess of York, Richard and Edward IV's mother (see 3.5.93–4)

193 **give . . . to** i.e. restrain

195 **benefit of dignity** benefaction, gift (*OED sb.* 2c) of high estate

197 **draw forth** rescue

198 **of abusing times** arising from the abuses of Edward IV's reign

199 **true-derived** true-derivèd; lawfully descended

186 wanton] *F;* lustfull *Qq* 187 Seduced] *F, Q1–5 subst.;* Seduce *Q6* his degree] *F;* al his thoughts *Qq* 189 his] *F, Q1–5;* this *Q6* 190 call] *F;* terme *Qq* 191 I] *F, Q1–5; om. Q6* 197 forth . . . ancestry] *F;* out your royall stocke *Qq* 198 times] *F;* time *Qq* 199 true-derived] *F, Qq (*true deriued*), hyphen Theobald*

MAYOR
Do, good my lord. Your citizens entreat you.

BUCKINGHAM
Refuse not, mighty lord, this proffered love.

CATESBY
O, make them joyful. Grant their lawful suit.

RICHARD
Alas, why would you heap this care on me?
I am unfit for state and majesty.
I do beseech you, take it not amiss;
I cannot, nor I will not, yield to you.

BUCKINGHAM
If you refuse it, as in love and zeal
Loath to depose the child, your brother's son –
As well we know your tenderness of heart
And gentle, kind, effeminate remorse,
Which we have noted in you to your kindred,
And equally indeed to all estates –
Yet know, whe'er you accept our suit or no,
Your brother's son shall never reign our king,
But we will plant some other in the throne
To the disgrace and downfall of your house.

200 **Your citizens** Perhaps strategically ambiguous: in a loose sense the phrase suggests popular partisanship (i.e. the citizens that are on your side), but its strict sense was reserved for the sovereign (i.e. the citizens that belong to you by virtue of your sovereignty); cf. 1n.

207 **as** being

210 **effeminate** gentle, tender, compassionate (*OED a.* 1c, citing this line); Tawney notes this as the only non-pejorative use in Shakespeare (Var). Cf. *womanish* compassion (1.4.261). Hall speaks positively of Prince Edward, son of Henry VI, as 'a goodly femenine & a well feautered yonge gentelman' (*Edward IV*, fol. ccxxi^{r}).
remorse pity, compassion (*OED sb.* 3); cf. 1.2.158 and *Mac* 1.5.43.

211 **to** toward

212 **estates** orders, ranks, sorts of people (*OED sb.* 5)

213 **whe'er** whether (see also 228)

215 Cf. 2.2.100.

200 Do,] *F4;* Do *F, Qq*   201] *F; not in Qq*   203 this care] *F;* those *(*these *Q1)* cares *Qq*   204 majesty] *F;* dignitie *Qq*   211 kindred] *F;* kin *Qq*   212 equally] *F, Q3–6 (*egally*), Q1–2 (*egallie*)*   213 know, whe'er] *Theobald;* know, where *F;* whether *Qq*   accept] *F, Q1–5;* except *Q6*

And in this resolution here we leave you.
– Come, citizens. Zounds, I'll entreat no more.

[Q]RICHARD

O, do not swear, my lord of Buckingham![Q]

Exeunt [Buckingham and some others].

CATESBY

Call him again, sweet prince; accept their suit.
If you deny them, all the land will rue it.

RICHARD

Will you enforce me to a world of cares?
Call them again. *[Exit Catesby.]*
I am not made of stones,
But penetrable to your kind entreaties,
Albeit against my conscience and my soul.

Enter BUCKINGHAM *and the rest.*

Cousin of Buckingham, and sage, grave men,

218–19 *F's omission of Richard's memorable line would be difficult to understand if not for the need to excise Buckingham's 'Zounds' – i.e. by His (Christ's) wounds – in keeping with the Statute of 1606 (see 1.4.84–end n.). Richard's pious admonition contributes a puritanical emphasis to his hypocrisy; the deceitful priest in *Knack* proclaims, 'Fie, not an oath we sweare', taking this principle as definitive for those who would be 'tearmed pure Precisians' (338–44).

219 SD *Since Catesby in F speaks of calling 'him back' (220) but also refers to 'them' (221), and since F also has a re-entry for '*Buckingham, and the rest*' (225), F's '*Exeunt*' includes Buckingham and others. Not everyone exits, since 223–5 are addressed to someone as Catesby goes to summon Buckingham and the others. Richard's reference in both F and Qq to 'Buckingham, and [you Qq] sage graue men' (226) suggests that the leaders – the Mayor and certain aldermen – depart with Buckingham.

221 *Qq have an anonymous speaker ('*Ano.*'), which potentially makes the sentiments of the crowd seem less obviously the product of manipulation.

222 **enforce me to** i.e. force upon me

223 SD There is not much time for Catesby to exit and summon the group that re-enters two lines later, which makes an incomplete exit by Buckingham and the others and a summoning gesture from Catesby staging possibilities (Hammond).

218 Zounds, I'll] *Qq;* we will *F*   219 SD *Exeunt*] *F; not in Qq*   *Buckingham . . . others*] *Oxf*   220 him . . . prince;] *F;* them again, my lord, and *Qq*   221] *F; Ano.* Doe, good my lord, least all the land do rew it. *Qq*   222 Will . . . cares] *F;* Would . . . care *Qq*   223 Call] *F;* Well, call *Qq*   SD] *Theobald subst.*   224 entreaties] *F;* intreates *Qq subst.*   225.1] *F; not in Qq*   226 sage] *F;* you sage *Qq*

Since you will buckle fortune on my back,
To bear her burden, whe'er I will or no,
I must have patience to endure the load;
But if black scandal or foul-faced reproach
Attend the sequel of your imposition,
Your mere enforcement shall acquittance me
From all the impure blots and stains thereof,
For God doth know, and you may partly see,
How far I am from the desire of this.

MAYOR

God bless your grace; we see it and will say it.

RICHARD

In saying so, you shall but say the truth.

BUCKINGHAM

Then I salute you with this royal title:
Long live King Richard, England's worthy king!

227 **buckle . . . back** An odd image, calling attention to Richard's spinal configuration; Lyons (23) suggests emblems representing Hope as a man walking doubled over, burdened by Fortune's wheel strapped to his back; cf. *bent* (61).

231 **Attend** follow, accompany
sequel . . . imposition i.e. the aftermath of the duty you impose on me

232 **mere** unassisted, sole (*OED a.* 2)
acquittance acquit

239 Cf. the proclamation of Richard's father, the Duke of York, as king: 'Long live our sovereign Richard, England's king!' (*2H6* 2.2.63). In the 2001 Michael Boyd–Aiden McArdle RSC production, Buckingham (Richard Cordery) encouraged the audience (who had been introduced to Richard as 'these good friends' in a modified 3.7.65 and included in the action by raised house lights) to join in acclaiming 'King Richard the Third'; he then responded to the silence (or laughter) of the house by quickly turning to question Richard about the date of the coronation (Day, 184).
***King Richard** Many editors drop Richard's title, recognizing the Q3 origin of *King* and perhaps prompted by a sense of redundancy. However, Buckingham's lines frequently indulge in repetitiveness and rhetorical overkill. Furthermore, 238 is clearly intended to introduce a 'salute' to Richard with 'this royal (F)/kingly (Qq) title' – i.e. with the exact phrase that names his new pre-eminence, 'King Richard', at this juncture in More. In sum, it seems inadvisable to alter F here when the hard-sell tactics employed in peddling

227 you] *F, Q1–2, 4–6;* your *Q3* 228 her] *F, Q1–2;* the *Q3–6* whe'er] *Rann;* where *F;* whether *Qq* 230 foul-faced] *F;* soule-fac't *Q1–2;* so foule fac't *Q3–5;* so foulefac't *Q6* 234 doth know] *F;* he knowes *Qq* 235 of this] *F;* thereof *Qq* 238 this royal] *F;* this kingly *Q1–3, 5–6;* the kingly *Q4* 239 King Richard] *F, Q3–6;* Richard *Q1–2* worthy] *F;* royall *Qq*

ALL Amen.

BUCKINGHAM
Tomorrow may it please you to be crowned?

RICHARD
Even when you please, for you will have it so.

BUCKINGHAM
Tomorrow, then, we will attend your grace,
And so most joyfully we take our leave.

RICHARD
Come, let us to our holy work again.
– Farewell, my cousin, farewell gentle friends. *Exeunt.*

4.1 *Enter* QUEEN [ELIZABETH], *the* DUCHESS of York *and* Marquess [of] DORSET [Q]*at one door*[Q]; ANNE, Duchess of Gloucester [, *with Clarence's* Daughter,] [Q]*at another door*[Q].

Richard's kingship are so evident and when the speaker has already demonstrated linguistic limitations. Peele's *Edward I* (1593) has a line resembling Q3, F's phrasing: 'God saue king *Baliol* the Scottish king' (742; sig. C4^{r}).

240 SP *Qq have the Mayor speak for everyone.

242 Richard's denial of his own agency echoes, yet again, his rhetorical stance throughout the scene.

243 **Tomorrow** According to Shakespeare's sources, the interview with the Mayor and citizens took place on 25 June 1483; Richard was crowned on 6 July (More, *CW*2, 82), but his accession was dated from 26 June, when he went publicly to Westminster Hall to assume rule.

246 ***cousin** F has Richard address everyone familiarly as 'Cousins', a plural form he elsewhere uses to a group that includes non-relatives (3.4.22), but then Richard speaks with nobles and peers as well as family. It seems improbable that he would be so familiar with mere citizens, since he has expressly distinguished his own *degree* from their *condition* (142).

246 SD Cibber has Richard send everyone off while he gloats in soliloquy. Garrick added a touch that has had a long theatrical afterlife by flinging away his prayer-book (Hankey, 187).

4.1 location: '*before the* Tower' (Theobald). Cibber sets in the Tower.

240 SP] *F; M yor. Q1; Mai. Q2–4; May. Q5–6* 241 may] *F;* will *Qq* 242 please, for] *F;* will, since *Qq* 244] *F; not in Qq* 245 work] *F;* taske *Qq* 246 my] *F;* good *Qq* cousin] *Qq;* Cousins *F* SD] *F, Q1, 3–6; om. Q2* 4.1] *F (Actus Quartus. Scena Prima.); not in Qq* 0.1–4] *Enter the Queene, Anne Duchesse of Gloucester, the / Duchesse of Yorke, and Marquesse Dorset. F; Enter Quee. mother, Duchesse of Yorke, Marques Dorset, at / one doore, Duchesse of Glocest. at another doore. Qq* 0.3 *with Clarence's* Daughter] *Eccles; leading Clarence's young Daughter. / Theobald*

DUCHESS

Who meets us here? My niece Plantagenet,
Led in the hand of her kind aunt of Gloucester?
Now, for my life, she's wandering to the Tower,
On pure heart's love, to greet the tender Prince.
– Daughter, well met.

ANNE God give your graces both
A happy and a joyful time of day.

QUEEN ELIZABETH

As much to you, good sister. Whither away?

ANNE

No farther than the Tower, and, as I guess,
Upon the like devotion as yourselves,
To gratulate the gentle Princes there.

QUEEN ELIZABETH

Kind sister, thanks. We'll enter all together.

Enter [BRAKENBURY,] *the Lieutenant.*

1 **My niece Plantagenet** Theobald recognized that this referred to Clarence's daughter, the Duchess's granddaughter (*OED* niece 1a). Qq lack the second line, so Qq's Duchess may refer to Anne, her 'niece' ('female relative' *OED*) by marriage, losing the touching detail of Anne's caring for Clarence's daughter, a demonstration of humanity remarkable for this play.

2 **in** by (cf. *Tit* 5.3.138)
aunt of Gloucester i.e. Lady Anne

3 **for my life** i.e. upon my life (Abbott, 150); a mild oath
wandering Since the Duchess (correctly) guesses that Anne and Clarence's daughter travel to the Tower, perhaps they proceed 'by uncertain and devious routes' (*OED* wandering *ppl. a*).

4 **On** i.e. out of; cf. Abbott, 180 and *AC* 3.6.58: 'On my free will'.
tender having the delicacy of youth, immature (*OED a.* 4) and perhaps also the object of tender feeling, precious (*OED a.* 8b); cf. 98.
Prince See 14–16n.

5 **Daughter** i.e. daughter-in-law

7 **sister** i.e. sister-in-law

9 **Upon . . . devotion** i.e. with the same devoted purpose (*OED sb.* II 7)

10 **gratulate** greet, salute (*OED v.* 1); cf. *Tit* 1.1.225.

1+ SP] *Rowe subst.; Duch. Yorke. F; Du[ch].[yor.] Qq subst.* 1] *Qq; F lines* heere? / *Plantagenet,* / 2–4] *F; not in Qq* 3 wandering] *F (*wandring*)* 5 Daughter, well met.] *F; Qu.* Sister well met, *Qq* 5–6 ANNE . . . day.] *F (lines* happie / day. / *), Pope; not in Qq* 7 As . . . sister] *F; not in Qq* Whither away] *F;* whether awaie so fast *Qq subst.* 8 SP] *F; Duch. Q1; Du. Q2; Dut. Glo. Q3–6* 10 gentle] *F;* tender *Qq* 11.1] *F; Enter / Lieutenant. Q1–2 opp. 11–12; Enter the Lieutenant of the Tower. Q3–6* BRAKENBURY] *Capell*

And in good time, here the Lieutenant comes.
Master Lieutenant, pray you, by your leave,
How doth the Prince and my young son of York?

BRAKENBURY
Right well, dear madam. By your patience,
I may not suffer you to visit them.
The King hath strictly charged the contrary.

QUEEN ELIZABETH
The King? Who's that?

BRAKENBURY I mean the Lord Protector.

QUEEN ELIZABETH
The Lord protect him from that kingly title.
Hath he set bounds between their love and me?
I am their mother. Who shall bar me from them?

DUCHESS
I am their father's mother. I will see them.

ANNE
Their aunt I am in law, in love their mother.
Then bring me to their sights. I'll bear thy blame

14–16 ***Prince . . . them** In F the object of the visitors first appears to be singular (4) and then ultimately to be plural (10). Qq initially refer to 'Princes' (10) but later to 'the Prince' (14) and to 'him' (16).

15 **By your patience** with your permission, indulgence (*OED* patience *sb.* 3); cf. *Tem* 3.3.3.

16 **suffer** allow

17–18 **King . . . Lord Protector** His clumsy self-correction (*I mean*) makes it clear that Brakenbury's slip is designed to be noticed; yet its significance for a non-aligned speaker is uncertain. Without the Vice's wit or deceptive purpose, Brakenbury's verbal substitution suggests self-betraying utterance (see e.g. King Edward's verbal slip in *E3*, 2.2.34–42). In Hall and Holinshed the Prince learns that Richard has taken the title of King and deduces his danger from this (Hall, *Richard III*, fol. xxvii[v]). In *True Tragedy* the Prince hears Myles Forest refer to Richard as King (1271).

20 **bounds** limits, boundaries

23 **in law** by marriage

24 **their sights** i.e. the sight of them; cf. *Tim* 1.1.250.

14] *F;* How fares *(*feares *Q6)* the Prince? *Qq* 15, 18, 26 SP] *Capell; Lieu. F, Qq* 15] *F;* Wel Madam, and in health, but by your leaue, *Qq* 16 them] *F;* him *Qq* 17 strictly] *F;* straightlie *Qq* 18] *Steevens; F, Qq line* that? / Protector. / Who's] *F;* whie, whose *(*who's *Q3–6) Qq* I mean] *F;* I crie you mercie, I meane *Qq* 20 between] *F;* betwixt *Qq* 21 shall bar] *F;* should keepe *Qq* 22 SP] *F, Q1; om. Q2–6* their . . . I] *F (*Fathers*);* their Fathers, Mother, I *Q1;* their father, Mother, and *Q2–3, 5–6;* theirs father mother, and *Q4* 23+ SP] *F; Duch.[glo]. Qq* 24 bring . . . sights] *F;* feare not thou *Qq*

And take thy office from thee, on my peril.

BRAKENBURY

No, madam, no. I may not leave it so.
I am bound by oath, and therefore pardon me. *Exit.*

Enter STANLEY.

STANLEY

Let me but meet you ladies one hour hence,
And I'll salute your grace of York as mother
And reverend looker-on of two fair queens.
[*to Anne*] Come, madam, you must straight to
  Westminster,
There to be crowned Richard's royal queen.

QUEEN ELIZABETH

Ah, cut my lace asunder
That my pent heart may have some scope to beat,
Or else I swoon with this dead-killing news.

ANNE

Despiteful tidings. O, unpleasing news.

25 **office** duty, assigned charge
26 *Hammond (5–6) adduces the similarity between Brakenbury's Q1 26, Q1, F 1.1.84 ('I beseech your Graces both to pardon me') and Q1, F 1.1.103 ('I do beseech your Grace / To pardon me' (F); 'I beseech your Grace to pardon me' (Q1)) to argue for memorial construction of Q1.
leave it i.e. abdicate my obligation
29–30 **mother . . . queens** mother-in-law of Elizabeth, widow of King Edward, and of Anne, wife of King Richard
31 **straight** go immediately
Westminster i.e. Westminster Abbey
32 **crowned** crownèd
33 **lace** cord or string drawing together the opposite edges of a bodice
34 **scope** room (*OED sb.*^{2} 8)
35 **dead-killing** deadly; cf. Tarquin's 'dead-killing eye' (*Luc* 540).
36 **Despiteful** cruel, malignant (*OED* 2)

26] *F;* I doe beseech your graces all to pardon me: *Qq* 27 and . . . me] *F;* I may not doe it. *Qq* SD] *F (Exit Lieutenant.); not in Qq* 27.1 STANLEY] *F; L. Stanlie Q1–2; Lord Standly (Stanley Q4) Q3–6* 28 you ladies one] *F;* you Ladies an *Q1–4;* you Ladies at an *Q5;* your Ladies at an *Q6* 30 reverend] *F;* reuerente *Qq* 31 SD] *Johnson subst.* straight] *F;* go with me *Qq* 33–5] *F; Qq line* heart, / sound, / newes. / 33 Ah] *F;* O *Qq* asunder] *F;* in sunder *Qq* 35 else I] *F, Q1, Q3 (all but Hn), Q5–6;* else *Q2, Q3 (Hn), Q4* swoon] *F;* sound *Qq* dead-killing] *F; Q1–4 (*dead killing*);* dead liking *Q5–6* 36] *F; not in Qq*

DORSET

Be of good cheer, mother. How fares your grace?

QUEEN ELIZABETH

O Dorset, speak not to me. Get thee gone.
Death and destruction dogs thee at thy heels.
Thy mother's name is ominous to children.
If thou wilt outstrip death, go, cross the seas
And live with Richmond, from the reach of hell.
Go hie thee, hie thee from this slaughterhouse,
Lest thou increase the number of the dead
And make me die the thrall of Margaret's curse,
Nor mother, wife, nor England's counted queen.

STANLEY

Full of wise care is this your counsel, madam.
[*to Dorset*] Take all the swift advantage of the hours.
You shall have letters from me to my son
In your behalf, to meet you on the way.
Be not ta'en tardy by unwise delay.

DUCHESS

O ill-dispersing wind of misery.

39 **dogs** Death and destruction are taken as a collective singular.

41 **outstrip** outrun (*OED v.*[1] 1), continuing the image of *dogs* (39)

42 **with Richmond** i.e. with Henry Tudor, Earl of Richmond, and later Henry VII, who had taken refuge in Brittany after the battle of Tewkesbury in 1471 (*3H6* 4.6.89–102). Since Shakespeare's early history plays often spell out historical details, this brief reference, the play's first mention of Richmond, presumes audience familiarity. Richmond's name will be spoken another 16 times before he finally appears in 5.2.0.1. **from** beyond

43 **hie** hasten (*OED v.* 2)

45 **thrall** subject, slave, captive (*OED sb.*[1] 1)

45–6 **Margaret's curse . . . queen** See 1.3.208.

46 **Nor . . . nor** neither . . . nor **counted** accepted

49 **son** Richmond, Stanley's stepson (see 5.3.82) by marriage to Richmond's mother, Lady Margaret Beaufort, *c.* 1482

51 **ta'en** taken, caught

52 **ill-dispersing** i.e. scattering evil abroad

37 Be . . . mother.] *F (*Be of good cheare: Mother,*);* Madam, haue comfort, *Qq* 38 gone] *F;* hence *Qq* 39 dogs . . . thy] *F;* dogge . . . the *Qq* 40 ominous] *F, Q1–4, 6;* ominious *Q5* 41 outstrip] *F, Q1–5;* ouerstrip *Q6* 42 reach] *F, Q1–5;* race *Q6* 48 SD] *Marshall* hours] *F;* time *Qq* 49 my] *F, Q1–5;* me *Q6* 50] *F;* To meete you on the way, and welcome you, *Qq* 51 ta'en] *F, Q1 subst.;* taken *Q2–6* 52 ill-dispersing] *F, Qq (*ill dispersing*), hyphen Theobald*

O my accursed womb, the bed of death.
A cockatrice hast thou hatched to the world,
Whose unavoided eye is murderous.

STANLEY

Come, madam, come. I in all haste was sent.

ANNE

And I with all unwillingness will go.
O, would to God that the inclusive verge
Of golden metal that must round my brow
Were red-hot steel to sear me to the brains.
Anointed let me be with deadly venom,
And die ere men can say 'God save the Queen'.

QUEEN ELIZABETH

Go, go, poor soul; I envy not thy glory.
To feed my humour wish thyself no harm.

ANNE

No? Why? When he that is my husband now
Came to me as I followed Henry's corse,
When scarce the blood was well washed from his hands

53 **accursed** accursèd
bed i.e. place of procreation and of birth

54 **cockatrice** serpent, identified with the basilisk (*OED* 1) (see 35n., 1.2.153n., 1.3.224); for hatching a cockatrice's egg as bringing evil into the world, see Dent, C496.1.

55 **unavoided** not avoided or escaped (*OED* 1); contrast 4.4.218, where the word means 'unavoidable'.

58 **inclusive** enclosing (*OED a.* 1)
verge circle or rim (*OED sb.*[1] 13); i.e. the crown (cf. *R2* 2.1.102). 'Verge' also meant the bounds or limits of a jurisdiction (*OED sb.*[1] 11, 12), and the 12-mile radius surrounding the king's court.

59 **round** encircle (*OED v.* 11a); cf. *R2* 3.2.160–1: 'the hollow crown / That rounds the mortal temples of a king'.

60–1 possibly alluding to the murder of Creusa by Medea (Seneca, *Medea*, 573-4, 817–39), or possibly suggesting punishment by placing a heated crown upon the criminal or regicide

61 a grotesque parody of the use of holy oil in the coronation ceremony

64 **feed my humour** please my mood (cf. 1.2.230, 1.4.118)

66 **corse** corpse (cf. 1.2.0); Qq's 'course' could also mean route or progress in a path (*OED sb.* 11, 2).

67 **scarce** scarcely

54 hatched] *F, Q2–6 (*hatcht*);* hatch *Q1*   56 madam, come] *F;* Madam, *Qq*   sent] *F, Q1–2;* sent for *Q3–6*   57 with] *F;* in *Qq*   58 O] *F;* I *Qq*   60 red-hot] *F, Qq (*red hot*), hyphen Pope*   brains] *F;* braine *Qq*   61 me be] *F, Q1–2, 4, 6;* me *Q3, 5*   venom] *F;* poyson *Qq*   63 Go, go] *F;* Alas *Qq*   thy] *F, Q1, 3–6;* the *Q2*   65 Why?] *F; not in Qq*   66 as I] *F, Q1–5;* I *Q6*   corse] *F;* course *Qq*

Which issued from my other angel husband
And that dear saint which then I weeping followed;
O when, I say, I looked on Richard's face,
This was my wish: 'Be thou', quoth I, 'accursed
For making me, so young, so old a widow;
And when thou wed'st, let sorrow haunt thy bed;
And be thy wife, if any be so mad,
More miserable by the life of thee
Than thou hast made me by my dear lord's death.'
Lo, ere I can repeat this curse again,
Within so small a time, my woman's heart
Grossly grew captive to his honey words
And proved the subject of mine own soul's curse,
Which hitherto hath held mine eyes from rest;
For never yet one hour in his bed

68–9 **angel husband . . . dear saint** i.e. the deceased Prince Edward and his father, Henry VI; cf. Edward as an angel (1.4.53).

72 **so young, so old** i.e. so young in age but made so old by suffering and sorrow, or perhaps so young but doomed to so long a life of widowhood

74–6 *F recalls but alters 1.2.26–8, changing a curse asking that any wife of Richard's be *made* more miserable by his *death* into a wish that anyone so 'mad' as to marry him may be made even more miserable by continued 'life'. The Qq 1.2, 4.1 passages are closer to one another, both wishing Richard's 'death' might cause misery in anyone who might marry him. Hammond accepts F, presuming Anne's 'growth': by 4.1 it is clear that life with Richard would mean more suffering to a wife than his death (cf. Lull). Jowett accepts F's 'Life', presuming Anne lacked 'foreknowledge' in 1.2.

79 **Grossly** stupidly (*OED* 6; see 3.6.10); Q2–8's 'Crosselie' could mean 'adversely', perhaps suggesting 'perversely' (*OED* 3, 4). Either would suggest historically available misogynist discourse. For sexual insinuations, see 3.7.75n.

honey i.e. honied; cf. *venom tooth* (1.3.290).

81 **hitherto** until now

***mine** Although F's possessive form may have originated with Q6, or from a compositor's eye-skip, or from the compositors' preference for 'mine' over 'my' before vowels (Walker, 25), Abbott's point concerning the unemphatic nature of 'mine' (Abbott, 237) argues for retaining the Q6, F reading here (Walton, *Copy*, 26); cf. 1.4.22–3n., 3.7.20n.

69 dear] *F;* dead *Qq* 74 mad] *F; Q1–2 (*madde*);* badde *Q3–6* 75 More] *F;* As *Qq* life] *F;* death *Qq* 76 Than] *F (*Then*);* As *Qq* 77 ere] *F; Q1 (*eare*);* euen *Q2–6* 78 Within . . . time] *F;* Euen in so short a space *Qq* 79 Grossly] *F, Q1;* Crosselie *Q2;* Crosly *Q3–6* 80 subject] *F, Q1;* subiectes *Q2, 4–6 subst.;* subsects *Q3* mine] *F;* my *Qq* 81 hitherto . . . held mine] *F;* euer since . . . kept my *(*mine *Q6) Qq* rest] *F;* sleepe *Qq*

Did I enjoy the golden dew of sleep,
But with his timorous dreams was still awaked.
Besides, he hates me for my father Warwick,
And will, no doubt, shortly be rid of me.

QUEEN ELIZABETH
Poor heart, adieu. I pity thy complaining.

ANNE
No more than with my soul I mourn for yours.

DORSET
Farewell, thou woeful welcomer of glory.

ANNE
Adieu, poor soul, that tak'st thy leave of it.

DUCHESS [*to Dorset*]
Go thou to Richmond, and good fortune guide thee,

83 **golden . . . sleep** For Richard's brief overconfidence as 'golden sleepe', see Holinshed, 3.752 and Hall, *Richard III*, fol. xlix[v]; cf. the 'golden sleep' that Hotspur has lost through care (*1H4* 2.3.40) and the 'honey-heavy dew of slumber' that Brutus forgoes (*JC* 2.1.229). Although *gold* and *golden* appear frequently in the play, this line, 1.2.250 and 5.3.19, where the associations are respectively with sleep, youth and the sun, are the only places in which the words appear outside a context of contention, ambition and greed.

84 **timorous** fearful; Richard's (offstage) wakefulness and nightmares are here treated as characteristic rather than specifically occasioned by the murder of the princes, as in the sources. Hall, closely following More, writes: 'after this abhominable deed done, [Richard] neuer was quiet in his mynde, he neuer thought himselfe sure where he wente abroade, his body prively feinted, his eyen wherled aboute, his hande euer on his dagger, his countenaunce and maner lyke alwaies to stricke againe, he toke euill reste on nightes, laye long wakyng and musying, forweried with care and watche, rather slombred then slept, troubled with fearefull dreames' (*Richard III*, fol. xxviii[r]; cf. Holinshed, 3.735).
still continually

85 Warwick changed allegiances, invaded England on behalf of Lancastrian interests and forced Richard to flee to the continent with Edward IV; Richard led the opposing forces when Warwick fell at Barnet (see *3H6*).

87 **complaining** lamentation

89 SP *Q2's '*Qu.*' (for F, Q1's Dorset) appears thoughtful given the ongoing exchange between the two women and Anne's response at 90, contrasting her interlocutor as taking leave of glory to herself as its *welcomer*. Q2 offers another correction at 1.1.101–2.

89 **welcomer of glory** so-called because she is about to be crowned

83 Did I enjoy] *F;* Haue I enioyed *Qq* 84] *F;* But haue bene waked by his timerous dreames, *Qq* 86 no doubt] *F, Q1; om. Q2–6* 87 Poor heart, adieu] *F;* Alas poore soule *Qq* complaining] *F;* complaints *Qq* 88 with] *F;* from *Qq* 89 SP] *F, Q1; Qu. Q2–6* 90 that] *F;* thou *Qq* 91, 92, 93 SD] *F2 subst.*

[*to Anne*] Go thou to Richard, and good angels tend
thee.
[*to Queen Elizabeth*] Go thou to sanctuary, and good
thoughts possess thee.
I to my grave, where peace and rest lie with me.
Eighty-odd years of sorrow have I seen,
And each hour's joy wracked with a week of teen.

QUEEN ELIZABETH
Stay, yet look back with me unto the Tower.
– Pity, you ancient stones, those tender babes
Whom envy hath immured within your walls,
Rough cradle for such little pretty ones;
Rude ragged nurse, old sullen playfellow
For tender princes, use my babies well.
So foolish sorrows bids your stones farewell. *Exeunt.*

93 **sanctuary** perhaps disyllabic (cf. 3.1.42)

95 **Eighty-odd** The Duchess was actually 68 at Richard's accession in 1483.

96 **wracked** destroyed (*OED ppl. a.*), or tortured, racked (*OED* racked *erron. ppl. a.* 3)
teen misery, grief (*OED sb.*[1] 3); cf. *LLL* 4.3.161.

97–103 *F's 'sentimental apostrophe' follows an apparent exit couplet (Patrick, 127); however, Margaret has a similar couplet at 4.4.114–15, but stays onstage. Here the Duchess is called upon to *Stay*. Queen Elizabeth's reference to her *foolish sorrows* (103) suggests self-awareness at her extreme personification of the Tower as a nurse or playmate; compare Titus' address to the stones of Rome (*Tit* 3.1.35–47). Qq's 4.4.385 echoes this passage (Hammond, Appendix 1).

99 **immured** imprisoned, shut up within walls (*OED v.* 2)

100 **little pretty** Cf. Dent, T188: 'Little things are pretty'; cf. Jonson, *Volpone*, 3.3.10 and *LLL* 1.2.21–2.

101 **ragged** rough, irregular, having a jagged outline (*OED a.*[1] 2); cf. *2H4* Ind.35.

103 SD With their goals defined by the Duchess (91–6), characters may leave by both doors as they entered. Wells and Taylor give characters individual exits during her lines; such departure makes more sense in Qq, which omit Queen Elizabeth's final speech.

92 tend] *F;* garde *Qq* 93 and] *F; not in Qq* 95 Eighty-odd] *F, Q1–4 (*Eightie odde*), hyphen Bevington*[4]*;* Eightie olde *Q5–6 subst.* 96 of teen] *F;* ofteene *Qq* 97–103] *F; not in Qq* 103 SD] *F; not in Qq*

4.2 [Q]*The trumpets*[Q] *sound a sennet. Enter* RICHARD *in pomp*, BUCKINGHAM, CATESBY, RATCLIFFE, LOVELL [Q]*with other Nobles*[Q] [*and a* Page].

KING RICHARD
Stand all apart. – Cousin of Buckingham.

BUCKINGHAM
My gracious sovereign.

KING RICHARD
Give me thy hand.
[Q]*Here he ascendeth the throne.*[Q] *Sound* [*trumpets*].
Thus high, by thy advice
And thy assistance is King Richard seated.
But shall we wear these glories for a day?

4.2 location: '*The Court*' (Pope); '*A Room of State*' (Capell)

0.1 ***sennet*** set of notes on the trumpet to signal ceremonial entrance or exit (*OED* 1)

0.1–2 ***in pomp*** in splendour, perhaps in formal procession (*OED sb.*[1] 1, 2); Qq's '*crownd*' and SP '*King*' or '*King Ri.*' (see 1 SPn.) register regality. On public wearing of the crown by Richard and by Edward IV, see C.A.J. Armstrong.

0.2–3 ***RATCLIFFE, LOVELL** not included in Qq's scene

1 SP *Although Qq refer to '*Rich.*' or '*Glocester*' in SDs, until this scene Richard's speeches are headed '*Glo.*' (once '*Gl.*'). Here the designation changes to '*King*', and with occasional exceptions (e.g. '*King Ri.*' at 8) remains so to the end of the play. Up to this point, F generally has '*Rich.*' (or variations) for SPs, except for a portion of that part of 3.1 (63–180) set directly from Q3, where Richard is '*Glo.*' After 4.2, F sometimes agrees with Qq in SDs, sporadically calling him '*King Richard*', and F, Qq SPs also sometimes agree on '*King*'. This form becomes dominant in the final portion of the play set directly from Q3 (5.3.49–end of play), with exceptions, such as 5.3.53–78 and all of 5.4, where F employs '*Rich.*' as SP.

1 **apart** aside

3 SD ***ascendeth*** perhaps onto a raised platform (Dessen & Thomson, 15).

3–4 **Thus . . . seated** The use of *Thus* (with accompanying trumpets in F) indicates Richard's movement to the throne, as Qq's SD demands, assisted by Buckingham's hand. The metaphor of being seated *high* in fortune is commonplace (see 5n.). The hypocritical ruler seating himself in glory before lesser figures who seek reward recalls the Chester *Coming of Antichrist* (Lumiansky & Mills, 1.408–38).

5–17 This exchange, in which a usurper attempts to commission assassination by indirect insinuation, resembles – until Richard's direct statement at 18

4.2] *F (Scena Secunda.); not in Qq* 0.1 *a sennet*] *F; not in Qq* 0.1–2 *in pomp*] *F; crownd Qq* 0.2–3 RATCLIFFE, LOVELL] *F; not in Qq* 0.3 *and a* Page] *Capell* 1+ SP] *Qq (King[.] [Ri.]); Rich. F* 2] *F; not in Qq* 3–4] *Rowe; F lines* hand. / assistance, / seated: / ; *Qq line* hand: / aduice / seated: / 3 SD *Here . . . throne.*] *Qq (Here he ascendeth / the (his Q4–6, om. Q3) throne. opp.* hand: *and* aduice*)* *Sound*] *F; not in Qq* *trumpets*] *after 2 White* 5 glories] *F;* honours *Qq*

Or shall they last, and we rejoice in them?

BUCKINGHAM
Still live they, and forever let them last.

KING RICHARD
Ah, Buckingham, now do I play the touch
To try if thou be current gold indeed:
Young Edward lives; think now what I would speak.

BUCKINGHAM
Say on, my loving lord.

KING RICHARD
Why, Buckingham, I say I would be king.

BUCKINGHAM
Why so you are, my thrice-renowned lord.

KING RICHARD
Ha! Am I king? 'Tis so – but Edward lives.

BUCKINGHAM
True, noble prince.

KING RICHARD O bitter consequence
That Edward still should live 'true noble prince'!

– the reported conversation between the newly-crowned Henry IV and Sir Piers Exton (*R2* 5.4). King John's attempt to enlist Hubert in murdering young Arthur (*KJ* 3.2) similarly progresses from insinuation to direct statement.

5 The question is rhetorical, but from this moment on, Richard's difficulties recall a passage in Hall: 'from thence forth not onely all his counsailles, doynges and procedynges, sodainlye decayed and sorted to none effecte: But also fortune beganne to froune and turne her whele douneward from him' (*Richard III*, fol. xxx^{r}; cf. Churchill, 334).

7 **Still live they** i.e. may they long continue

8 **play the touch** i.e. test (Buckingham's) genuineness, as a touchstone rubbed against a metal allowed differentiation of true gold

9 **current gold** genuine coin, as opposed to counterfeit (*OED* current *a.* 5)

13 **thrice-renowned** thrice-renownèd
***lord** Many editors since Pope have accepted 'liege' from Qq, though 'Q is generally unreliable with respect to such formulae' (*TxC*, 243).

15 **consequence** i.e. conclusion from what has been said

16 **true noble prince** Richard again moralizes two meanings in one word, turning Buckingham's designation of him as a *noble prince* (i.e. king) into a bitter rejoinder that young Edward remains the *true* 'noble prince'; cf. 4.4.471–2n.

7 forever] *Q7;* for euer *F, Q1, 3–6;* for for euer *Q2* let them] *F;* may they *Qq* 8 Ah] *F;* O *Qq* do I] *F, Q1–2;* I do *Q3–6* 10 speak] *F;* say *Qq* 11 loving lord] *F;* gracious soueraigne *Qq* 13 lord] *F;* liege *Qq* 15] *Steevens; F, Qq line* Prince. / consequence! /

Cousin, thou wast not wont to be so dull.
Shall I be plain? I wish the bastards dead,
And I would have it suddenly performed.
What sayst thou now? Speak suddenly. Be brief.

BUCKINGHAM
Your grace may do your pleasure.

KING RICHARD
Tut, tut, thou art all ice; thy kindness freezes.
Say, have I thy consent that they shall die?

BUCKINGHAM
Give me some little breath, some pause, dear lord,
Before I positively speak in this.
I will resolve you herein presently. *Exit.*

CATESBY [*aside to others*]
The King is angry. See, he gnaws his lip.

KING RICHARD [*aside*]
I will converse with iron-witted fools

17 **wont** accustomed
dull obtuse, wanting intelligence or, possibly, hard of hearing (*OED a.* 1, 2a)
19, 20 **suddenly** immediately (*OED* 2)
23–31 Shakespeare invents this falling out over Buckingham's refusal to murder the princes, although Hall's Buckingham tells Morton he 'neuer agreed nor condiscended' to their deaths (*Richard III*, fol. xxxiv[v]). The figure who refuses Richard's commission is Sir Robert Brakenbury, who 'plainly answered' Richard's emissary 'that he woulde neuer put them to deathe' (fol. xxvii[r]).
24 **breath** i.e. breathing space (*OED* 8); cf. *H5* 2.4.145.
25 **positively** definitely
26 **resolve you** i.e. give you an answer to your question; cf. *3H6* 3.2.19.
herein i.e. in this matter
27 It is not clear to whom Catesby speaks.
gnaws his lip Vergil (227) and More (*CW*2, 47) mention Richard's lip-gnawing as, respectively, habitual or feigned; cf. 3.4.57.1n. Here it appears to be one of the first signs of his genuine anger, fear and uncertainty; More's Richard only becomes subject to anxious fears, torments of conscience and uncertainty *after* the murder of the princes (Ornstein, 72; More *CW*2, 87). Cf. 4.1.84 and p. 11. Nineteenth-century Richards emphasized nervous tics: Cooke resorted to 'fiddling with his sword, the quivering of his lip and under jaw, the convulsive starting of his muscles, the clawing with his fingers' (Colley, 56)
28–9 **iron-witted . . . boys** Contrast the ideal royal counsellor: an adult between the ages of 30 and 60 with 'a quicke and liuely wytte', never 'dull

17 wast] *F;* wert *Qq* 20 sayst thou now] *F;* saist *(*saiest *Q6)* thou *Qq* 22 freezes] *F;* freezeth *Qq* 24 little . . . dear] *F;* breath, some little pause my *Qq* 25 in this] *F;* herein *Qq* 26 you herein presently] *F;* your grace immediatlie *Qq* 26 SD] *F (Exit Buck.); Exit. Q1; om. Q2–6* 27 SD] *after Capell (to a Stander-by.; after Hanmer [Aside.])* gnaws his] *F;* bites the *Qq* 28 SD] *Ard*[2]

And unrespective boys. None are for me
That look into me with considerate eyes.
High-reaching Buckingham grows circumspect.
– Boy!

PAGE My lord?

KING RICHARD
Knowst thou not any whom corrupting gold
Will tempt unto a close exploit of death?

PAGE
I know a discontented gentleman
Whose humble means match not his haughty spirit.
Gold were as good as twenty orators,
And will, no doubt, tempt him to anything.

KING RICHARD
What is his name?

PAGE His name, my lord, is Tyrrel.

KING RICHARD
I partly know the man. Go, call him hither, boy. *Exit* [*Page*].
[*aside*] The deep-revolving, witty Buckingham

and gross wytted' (Blundeville, sigs L2^{v}–L3^{r}, E1^{r}–E2^{r}).

28 **iron-witted** dull-witted, stupid (*OED* iron *a.* 3d, 4)

29 **unrespective** inattentive, heedless (*OED* 1); contrast *considerate* (30) and 'respective' (*RJ* 3.1.126).
for me i.e. appropriate to be among my associates (cf. 'these are not men for me', Marlowe, *Works*, *Edward II*, 1.1.50); on my side

30 **considerate** thoughtful, careful (*OED* 1, 2)

31 **High-reaching** aspiring, ambitious (*OED*); as a possible rival
circumspect attentive, cautious (*OED a.* 2)

34–41 More's Richard converses with a 'secrete page' (*CW*2, 83–4; Holinshed, 3.734); cf. *True Tragedy*, 973–1017.

35 **close** secret
exploit explòit; an act or deed, a feat (*OED sb.* 3)

38 Cf. Dent, G285a: 'Gold speaks.'

41 **partly** partially, imperfectly (cf. *TC* 3.1.17)

42 **deep-revolving** profoundly meditating, seriously turning things over (*OED* revolve *v.* 4b); cf. *Cym* 3.3.14. Given Buckingham's earlier inclusion among *simple gulls* (1.3.327), Richard may be sneering at his pretensions to cunning (cf. 4.4.332). Following More, Hall reports both Buckingham

31 High-reaching] *F;* Boy, high reaching *Q1–5; Boy,* high reaching *Q6* 32] *F; not in Qq* 33+ SP] *F; Boy. Qq* 33 My lord] *F, Q1–2;* Lord *Q3–6* 34 Knowst] *F, Q1, 3–6; Q2 (*Knowest*)* 35 Will] *F;* Would *Qq* 36 I] *F;* My lord, I *Qq* 37 spirit] *F;* mind *Qq* 40] *Steevens; F, Qq line* Name. / *Tirrell.* / 41 I . . . man] *F; not in Qq* hither, boy] *F (*hither, / Boy.*);* hither presentlie *Qq* SD] *Pope subst.; Exit. F; not in Qq* 42 SD] *Ard*^{2} deep-revolving] *F, Qq (*deep reuoluing*), hyphen Pope*

No more shall be the neighbour to my counsels.
Hath he so long held out with me, untired,
And stops he now for breath? Well, be it so.

Enter STANLEY.

How now, Lord Stanley, what's the news?

STANLEY
Know my loving lord,
The Marquess Dorset, as I hear, is fled
To Richmond, in the parts where he abides.

KING RICHARD
Come hither, Catesby. Rumour it abroad
That Anne my wife is very grievous sick.
I will take order for her keeping close.

and Richard as having a 'deepe dissymulyng nature' (*Richard III*, fol. xxx[v]).
witty cunning, crafty (*OED* 2b); cf. *MA* 4.2.25.

43 **neighbour to** i.e. close associate of (*OED sb.* 2b)

44 **held out** continued, endured

47–9 *These lines have been frequently emended in attempts to regularize them metrically. Pope deletes both *Know* and *loving*. Rann (here followed) retains F with minimal relineation.

48–9 Dorset did not flee to Richmond until after Buckingham's ill-fated expedition, in which he played a leading role (Hall, *Richard III*, fol. xxxix[v]); cf. 4.4.311–14.

50–65 Although Richard's change of subjects makes it seem that he fails to register Stanley's news, his later remark (84) reveals that he has heard what he has been told; his plans for Anne and the children of Clarence provide the first of his panic reactions (Honigmann, 229n.).

51, 57 **sick, die** Anne's illness is treated here as if it were merely a false rumour to be spread about. The sources speculate about whether Richard effected Anne's death by aggravated mental stress or by poison (Hall, *Richard III*, fol. xlviii[v]; Holinshed, 3.751). Sixteenth-century polemic invokes Richard's rumours 'secretlie . . . giuen abroode that his own wyfe was dead' in accusing the Earl of Leicester of murdering his wife (*Copy*, 105). Qq print Richard's 'That Anne my wife is sicke and like to die' at both 51 and 57.

52 **take order** i.e. make secret arrangements; cf. 3.5.106.
keeping close secluded confinement

43 counsels] *F;* counsell *Qq* 45 Well . . . so] *F; not in Qq* 45.1 STANLEY] *F; Darby Qq* 46 Lord . . . news] *F;* what neewes vvith you *(*yon *Q3) Qq* 47+ SP] *F; Darby. Qq subst.* 47–9] *Rann; F lines Dorset / Richmond,* / abides. / ; My Lord, I heare the Marques Dorset / Is fled to Richmond, in those partes beyond the seas where he / abides. / *Qq subst.* 50 Come hither] *F; not in Qq* Catesby.] *F (Catesby,);* Catesby. *Cat.* My Lord. *Qq* Rumour] *F; King.* Rumor *Qq* 51 very grievous sick] *F;* sicke and like to die *Qq*

Inquire me out some mean poor gentleman,
Whom I will marry straight to Clarence' daughter.
The boy is foolish, and I fear not him.
Look how thou dream'st! I say again, give out
That Anne my queen is sick and like to die.
About it, for it stands me much upon
To stop all hopes whose growth may damage me.
[*Exit Catesby.*]
I must be married to my brother's daughter,
Or else my kingdom stands on brittle glass.
Murder her brothers, and then marry her –
Uncertain way of gain. But I am in
So far in blood that sin will pluck on sin.

53 **Inquire me out** find for me
mean inferior in rank or quality (*OED a.*[1] 2), thus *mean poor* is not redundant. In fact, she will marry Sir Richard Pole and give birth to the famous Cardinal Pole. Holinshed relates Richard's plan to marry off Lady Cecily Plantagent (with whom Shakespeare confuses Clarence's daughter) to 'a man . . . of an vnknowne linage and familie' (3.752).

54 **straight** immediately

55 **boy** Clarence's son Edward
foolish Clarence's son is not depicted as particularly *foolish* unless belief in Richard's sincerity (2.2.20–33) signifies lack of intelligence. Holinshed and Hall (following Vergil) do describe him later in life at the time of his execution by Henry VII (1499) as a dazed victim of prolonged imprisonment who 'coulde not decerne a Goose from a Capon' (Hall, *Henry VII*, fol. l[r]).

56 **dream'st . . . again** For the second time in this scene, Richard, formerly master of effective communication, appears unable to get his message across. Perhaps Catesby is 'taken aback by Richard's murderous intentions' (Lull).
give out let it be known

58 **About** i.e. set about
stands . . . upon is imperative upon me (Abbott, 204). Cf. *Ham* 5.2.62.

59 **hopes** i.e. the possible claimants to the throne as well as the feelings that they might elicit in those subjects who look to them for the future

60 **brother's daughter** i.e. Elizabeth of York (1465–1503), daughter of Edward IV and Queen Elizabeth, later wife of Henry Tudor (this play's Richmond and Henry VII) and grandmother of Elizabeth I (see pp. 71–8).

61 **brittle glass** common image for the fragility of power and office; e.g. *Mirror*, 'Wolsey', 466–7; *R2* 4.1.287–8; Dent, G134

63 **of gain** i.e. to prosper

63–4 **But . . . sin** While suggesting the notorious Senecan code of Elizabethan stage revengers: '*per scelera semper sceleribus tutum est iter*' ('through crime ever is the safe way for crime', Seneca, *Agamemnon*, 115; cf. Kyd, *Spanish Tragedy*, 3.13.6), this line remarks the *Uncertain way* that Richard must pursue, anticipating Macbeth's realization that he is self-

53 poor] *F;* borne *Qq*   57 queen] *F;* wife *Qq*   59 SD] *Johnson*   64 will pluck] *F, Q1;* plucke *Q2–5;* plucks *Q6*

Tear-falling pity dwells not in this eye.

Enter TYRREL.

Is thy name Tyrrel?

TYRREL

James Tyrrel, and your most obedient subject.

KING RICHARD

Art thou indeed?

TYRREL Prove me, my gracious lord.

KING RICHARD

Dar'st thou resolve to kill a friend of mine?

TYRREL

Please you. But I had rather kill two enemies.

KING RICHARD

Why then thou hast it. Two deep enemies,
Foes to my rest, and my sweet sleep's disturbers,
Are they that I would have thee deal upon.
Tyrrel, I mean those bastards in the Tower.

entrapped 'in blood' (3.4.137–9). 'So far in blood' recalls Buckingham's 'So diepe in blud' (*Mirror*, 'Buckingham', 348), rhetorically heightening the entrapment that More suggests (*CW2*, 43).

64 **pluck on** drag, pull along (*OED* pluck *v.* 2a); cf. *MM* 2.4.146.

65 **Tear-falling pity** i.e. pity that prompts tears to fall (cf. 1.3.352)

68 **Prove** test

70 *Q2 appears to anticipate the next line in its 'two deepe enemies'; Q3–8 follow.

Please you i.e. if it please you

71 **deep** great, profound (*OED a.* 18); strikingly hyperbolic in imputing threatening agency to the victimized children – a rhetorical trend continued when Richard blames them for his disturbed sleep (72). The word *deep* appears elsewhere in the play with other senses – 'cunning' (2.1.38) and 'profoundly learned' (3.7.74); cf. Drakakis, 32.

72 ***disturbers** Thompson compares Qq's substantive – 'disturbs' – to Qq 'intreates' (3.7.224).

73 **deal upon** set to work upon (*OED v.* 2. 18)

74 Richard's self-explication appears remarkably unmotivated given Tyrrel's anticipations and compliance in 70. Why would he feel the need to be so specific to someone who clearly knows the score?

65 Tear-falling] *F; Q1–5 (*Teare falling*);* Teares falling *Q6* 65.1 TYRREL] *F; Tirrel Qq* 68] *Steevens; F lines* indeed? / Lord. / ; *Qq line* indeed? / soueraigne, / lord] *F;* soueraigne *Qq* 70] *Qq; F lines* you: / enemies. / Please you] *F;* I my Lord *Qq* enemies] *F, Q1;* deepe enemies *Q2–6* 71 then] *F;* there *Qq* 72 disturbers] *F;* disturbs *Qq*

TYRREL

Let me have open means to come to them,
And soon I'll rid you from the fear of them.

KING RICHARD

Thou sing'st sweet music. Hark, come hither, Tyrrel.
Go by this token. Rise, and lend thine ear,
[Q]*He*[Q] *whispers* [Q]*in his ear*[Q].
There is no more but so. Say it is done,
And I will love thee and prefer thee for it.

TYRREL

I will dispatch it straight. *Exit.*

Enter BUCKINGHAM.

BUCKINGHAM

My lord, I have considered in my mind
The late request that you did sound me in.

KING RICHARD

Well, let that rest. Dorset is fled to Richmond.

BUCKINGHAM

I hear the news, my lord.

KING RICHARD

Stanley, he is your wife's son. Well, look unto it.

75 **open . . . come** i.e. unimpeded access
78 **by this token** Richard apparently hands Tyrrel some symbol, perhaps a ring, that will allow access to the prisoners on Richard's authority.
79 **There . . . so** i.e. there's nothing more to say (than what Richard has whispered); cf. 'No more but so?' (*Ham* 1.3.10). Cf. Abbott, 411; Dent, M1158.1.
*__it is__ The interrogative word order ('is it') of Q1–2, 6–8 is obviously wrong; Q3–5 agree with F.
80 **prefer** promote, advance
81 *Qq's exchange between Richard and Tyrrel recalls F at 3.1.188–9.
83 **sound me in** ask me about
86 **he** i.e. Richmond (see 1.3.20)

77] *Qq; F lines* Musique: / *Tyrrel,* / Hark] *F; not in Qq* 78 this] *F;* that *Qq* 79 There is] *F;* Tis *Qq* it is] *F, Q3–5;* is it *Q1–2, 6* 80 for it] *F;* too *Qq* 81] *F;* Tis done my gracious lord. / *King* Shal we heare from thee *Tirrel* ere we sleep? *Enter Buc.* / *Tir.* Ye shall my lord, *(Tir.* Yea my good Lord. *Q6) Qq* SD] *F; not in Qq* 83 request] *F;* demand *Qq* 84 rest] *F;* passe *Qq* 85 the] *F;* that *Qq* 86 wife's] *F, Q2–6 (*Wiues*), Q1 (*wifes*)* son] *F, Q4–6;* sonnes *Q1–3* unto] *F;* to *Qq*

BUCKINGHAM

My lord, I claim the gift, my due by promise,
For which your honour and your faith is pawned:
Th'earldom of Hereford and the moveables
Which you have promised I shall possess.

KING RICHARD

Stanley, look to your wife; if she convey
Letters to Richmond, you shall answer it.

BUCKINGHAM

What says your highness to my just request?

KING RICHARD

I do remember me, Henry the Sixth
Did prophesy that Richmond should be king,
When Richmond was a little peevish boy.
A king perhaps –

87–90 Richard's refusal to grant the earldom of Hereford has political contexts. More calls the title 'enterlaced with the title to the crowne', and says Richard's 'spiteful' rejection of Buckingham's claim aroused hatred, mistrust and fear in him (*CW*2, 89; cf. Holinshed, 3.736). Vergil's Richard compares Buckingham to the usurper Henry IV and accuses him of trying to open a way to the crown for himself (193). On Buckingham's claim to the throne and Richard's promises, see More, *CW*2, 267; for the Hereford inheritance, cf. 3.1.194–8.

88 **pawned** pledged

89 **moveables** goods belonging to the earldom but not attached to the soil (see 3.1.195). Lands would be entailed and go with the title; portable possessions required specific mention.

91 The accounts of Richard's concern about Margaret Beaufort's correspondence with Richmond comment on gender politics. Holinshed writes: 'forsomuch as the enterprise of a woman was of [Richard] reputed of no regard or estimation; and that the lord Thomas hir husband had purged himselfe sufficientlie to be innocent of all dooings and attempts by hir perpetrated and committed: it was giuen [Stanley] in charge to keepe hir in some secret place at home, without hauing anie seruaunt or companie' (3.746).

92 **answer** i.e. answer for

94 **remember me** i.e. recollect

94–6 See *3H6* 4.6.68–76.

96 **peevish** foolish or fretful (cf. 1.3.193)

97–114 *The longest passage exclusive to Qq in the play; most commentators agree that it is Shakespearean. Explanations for its Qq presence and F absence differ widely. Hammond surveys the critical positions laid out in Var, 300–1. The main alternative lines of argument are that the passage was:

87 the] *F;* your *Qq* 89 Th'earldom] *F;* The Earledome *Qq* Hereford] *Q1–3, 5–6 (*Herford*);* Hertford *F;* Herfort *Q4* 90 Which] *F;* The which *Qq* you have] *F;* you *Q1, 3–6;* your *Q2* shall] *F;* should *Qq* 93 request] *F;* demand *Qq* 94 I . . . me] *F;* As I remember *Qq* 97 perhaps –] *Pope;* perhaps. *F;* perhaps, perhaps. *Q1–3, 5–6;* perhaps, *Q4*

[Q]BUCKINGHAM My lord.

KING RICHARD

How chance the prophet could not at that time
Have told me, I being by, that I should kill him?

BUCKINGHAM

My lord, your promise for the earldom –

KING RICHARD

Richmond! When last I was at Exeter,
The Mayor in courtesy showed me the castle
And called it Rougemont, at which name I started,
Because a bard of Ireland told me once
I should not live long after I saw Richmond.

BUCKINGHAM

My lord –

KING RICHARD

Ay, what's o'clock?

BUCKINGHAM

I am thus bold to put your grace in mind
Of what you promised me.

originally part of the play, but subsequently cut by Shakespeare (Spedding in Var); omitted by a corrector when printing F for its metrical irregularities (Pickersgill, 94); originally part of the play but lost due to a defective manuscript (Patrick); a playhouse addition for the benefit of the actor playing Richard, later 'deliberately struck out' of Q copy by the printers of F (Daniel, ix); a revision added to the first version of the play by the author (Hammond). One line of argument proposes that F cut to avoid offending the Jacobean Duke of Buckingham and his patron, James I, who had a palace at Richmond (Griffin). For an argument concerning Jacobean political implications attending the abbreviation of the role of the Duke of Buckingham in F's *2H6*, see Hodgdon, *End*, 62. Both Hall (*Richard III*, fol. xxxiv^{r-v}) and Holinshed (3.739) have Buckingham describe a prolonged ordeal rather than F's tyrannically curt exchange.

98 **How chance** i.e. how was it that (*OED v.* 5)
prophet Henry VI; Richard murders Henry with the taunt, 'Die, prophet' (*3H6* 5.6.57).

99 **by** nearby; Richard was not onstage when Henry VI uttered his prophecy in *3H6* 4.6.

101–5 This incident during Richard's 1483 visit to Exeter appears only in the second edition of Holinshed: Richard 'came to the castell; and when he vnderstood that it was called Rugemont, suddenlie he fell into a dumpe, and (as one astonied) said; Well, I see my daies be not long. He spake this of a prophesie told him, that when he came once to Richmond, he should not long liue after' (3.746).

103 **Rougemont** pronounced like 'Richmond'

KING RICHARD Well, but what's o'clock?

BUCKINGHAM

Upon the stroke of ten.

KING RICHARD Well, let it strike.

BUCKINGHAM

Why let it strike?

KING RICHARD

Because that, like a jack, thou keep'st the stroke
Betwixt thy begging and my meditation.
I am not in the giving vein today.[Q]

BUCKINGHAM

May it please you to resolve me in my suit?

KING RICHARD

Thou troublest me; I am not in the vein.

Exit [*followed by all but Buckingham*].

BUCKINGHAM

And is it thus? Repays he my deep service
With such contempt? Made I him king for this?
O, let me think on Hastings and be gone
To Brecknock while my fearful head is on. *Exit.*

112 **jack** the figure who struck the hours on clocks (*OED sb.*[1] I 6, citing this line), but also meaning a commoner or an ill-mannered person (*OED sb.*[1] I 2), as at 1.3.53. The deposed Richard II expresses his own futile inconsequence by comparing himself to a 'jack o' the clock' (*R2* 5.5.60).
keep'st the stroke continue to strike

114 **vein** mood (*OED sb.* 14)

115 *F reiterates a question that has repeatedly been raised, despite the insults in the immediately previous passage as it appears in Qq; contrast Qq's forceful alternative – 'Whie then resolue me whether you wil or no?' (*TxC*, 244). F's line could be inflected many different ways, expressing frustration, despair, incredulity or any combination of these emotions mixed with a desire not to offend.

116 Edmund Kean expressed 'sarcastic petulance', but Hazlitt claimed the line should have conveyed 'stifled hatred, and cold contempt' (5.183). J.B. Booth portrayed 'fretful anger' rather than a 'cool and kingly slight' (Gould, 44).

117 **deep** serious, weighty

120 **Brecknock** Buckingham's family estate of Brecon in south-east Wales

109] *Cam*[1]*; Qq line* me. / clocke? / 110] *Cam*[1]*; Qq line* ten. / strike. / 112 keep'st] *Q1, 3, 5–6;* keepest *Q2, 4* 115] *F;* Whie then resolue me whether you wil or no? *Qq* 116 Thou] *F;* Tut, tut, thou *Qq* SD *followed . . . Buckingham*] *Cam subst.* 117] *F;* Is it euen so, rewardst *(*rewards *Q2–6)* he my true seruice *Qq* 118 contempt] *F;* deepe contempt *Qq*

[4.3] *Enter* TYRREL.

TYRREL

The tyrannous and bloody act is done,
The most arch deed of piteous massacre
That ever yet this land was guilty of.
Dighton and Forrest, who I did suborn
To do this piece of ruthful butchery,
Albeit they were fleshed villains, bloody dogs,
Melted with tenderness and mild compassion,
Wept like to children in their deaths' sad story.

4.3 location: '*The same*' (Capell). F lacks a new scene here, but the stage has been cleared with Buckingham's exit, and time has advanced from 10 a.m. (4.2.110) to evening (4.3.31).

1–22 Holinshed, following More, says Tyrrel 'shewed [Richard] all the manner of the murther; who gaue him great thanks' (3.735; cf. Hall, *Richard III*, fol. xxvii[v]). Charles Lamb found it difficult to reconcile Shakespeare's pathos-laden speech with its speaker; however, the royal infanticide evoked strong emotional reaction (More, *CW*2, 85–7; Hall, *Richard III*, fol. xxxii[v]). Cf. Heywood's melodramatic rendering in *2Ed4*, 3.5 and Mancini's claim (93) that 'many men burst forth into tears and lamentations' after Edward's disappearance. This soliloquy changes audience relation to Richard by describing his most heinous act without allowing him to shape our responses as he had in previous soliloquies (Van Laan, 142).

2 **arch** pre-eminent (*OED a.* 1)

3 *With this line, which begins a new page in F, Compositor B begins setting F until deep into 4.4. On the large number of Qq/F variants in this scene, see Hammond.

4 **Dighton, Forrest** More names Miles Forest, 'a felowe fleshed in murther', and Iohn Dighton, Tyrrel's 'horsekeper, a big brode square strong knaue', as the murderers and recounts their fittingly horrible futures (*CW*2, 85–7).
suborn bribe or procure by underhand means to commit a misdeed (*OED* 1)

5 ***ruthful** Most editors since Pope have preferred F's word-order while also preferring Qq's term 'ruthles' to F's 'ruthfull' (compassionate: see *OED* 1), which first appears in Q3. However, 'ruthful' could mean 'lamentable' (*OED* 2), as in 'villainies / Ruthful to hear' (*Tit* 5.1.65–6).

6 **fleshed** inured to bloodshed, hardened (*OED* fleshed *ppl.* 2); appropriate to the subsequent image of *bloody dogs* since a hawk or hound might be rewarded with flesh of the game in order to whet its appetite for hunting (*OED* flesh *v.* 1); cf. 4n. for More's use.

8 ***to** Qq's 'two' has been preferred by many editors since Pope, but weeping

4.3] *Pope* 0.1] *F; Enter Sir Francis Tirrell. Qq* 1 act] *F;* deed *Qq* 2 arch deed] *F;* arch-act *(*arch act *Q4) Qq* 4 who] *F;* whom *Qq* 5 piece of ruthful] *F;* ruthles peece of *Q1–2;* ruthfull peece of *Q3–6;* piece of ruthless *Pope* 6 Albeit] *F;* Although *Qq* 7 Melted] *F;* Melting *Qq* mild] *F;* kind *Q1–5; om. Q6* 8 to] *F;* two *Qq* deaths'] *F, Q1–3, 5–6 (*deaths*);* death *Q4* story] *F;* stories *Qq*

'O thus', quoth Dighton, 'lay the gentle babes'.
'Thus, thus', quoth Forrest, 'girdling one another
Within their alabaster innocent arms.
Their lips were four red roses on a stalk,
And in their summer beauty kissed each other.
A book of prayers on their pillow lay,
Which once', quoth Forrest, 'almost changed my mind.
But, O, the Devil – ' There the villain stopped;
When Dighton thus told on: 'We smothered
The most replenished sweet work of nature,
That from the prime creation e'er she framed.'
Hence both are gone with conscience and remorse;
They could not speak, and so I left them both
To bear this tidings to the bloody King.

like to children makes sense; for two/too/to spelling variants, see 4.4.385n.
in . . . story i.e. in the telling of the sad story of their deaths

9–10 **thus** implying action; in this case, a mimicry of the postures of the princes

11 **alabaster** Shakespeare often likens the skin of sleeping victims to alabaster (cf. *Luc* 419), which, as Othello's simile 'smooth as monumental alabaster' (*Oth* 5.2.5) suggests, was frequently employed in statuary figures recumbent upon tombs. 'Alablaster' is an alternative spelling.

14 **book of prayers** Mancini (93) records Edward's attending physician's report that 'the young king, like a victim prepared for sacrifice, sought remission of his sins by daily confession and penance, because he believed that death was facing him'. Contrast the treatment of a *book of prayer* at 3.7.97.

17 **smothered** smotherèd

18–19 Contrast Richard as 'Cheated of feature by dissembling Nature' (1.1.19).

18 **replenished** replenishèd; full, perfect (*OED*), here modifying *sweet*

19 **prime** first
***she** F, Qq disagree on gender again; cf. England's personification (3.7.124–6).
framed created, fashioned

20 **gone with** overcome by; cf. 'too far gone with grief' (*R2* 2.1.184).

22 **To** in order to
tidings construed as singular (cf. *KJ* 4.2.115)

9 O] *F;* Lo *Qq* the gentle] *F;* those *(*these *Q6)* tender *Qq* 10 one] *F, Q3–6;* on *Q1–2* 11 alabaster innocent] *F (*Alablaster*);* innocent alablaster *Qq* 12 were] *F, Q1;* like *Q3–6; om. Q2* 13 And] *F;* Which *Q1–5;* When *Q6* 15 once] *Qq;* one *F* 16 But . . . There] *Theobald (after Rowe);* But oh the Diuell, there *F;* But ô the Diuell their *Q1;* But ô the diuel: their *Q2;* But O the diuel: there *Q3–4;* But O the diuel! there *Q5–6* 17 When] *F;* Whilst *Qq* 19 e'er she] *F;* euer he *Qq* 20] *F, Q1–2; om. Q3–6* Hence] *F;* Thus *Q1–2* 22 bear] *F;* bring *Qq* this] *F, Q1–5;* these *Q6*

Enter ^Q^KING^Q^ RICHARD.

And here he comes. All health, my sovereign lord.

KING RICHARD
Kind Tyrrel, am I happy in thy news?

TYRREL
If to have done the thing you gave in charge
Beget your happiness, be happy then,
For it is done.

KING RICHARD But didst thou see them dead?

TYRREL
I did, my lord.

KING RICHARD And buried, gentle Tyrrel?

TYRREL
The chaplain of the Tower hath buried them,
But where, to say the truth, I do not know.

KING RICHARD
Come to me, Tyrrel, soon at after-supper,
When thou shalt tell the process of their death.
Meantime, but think how I may do thee good,
And be inheritor of thy desire.
Farewell till then.

TYRREL I humbly take my leave. ^Q^*Exit.*^Q^

25 **gave in charge** i.e. ordered
29–30 Combining two stages of More's account: Tyrell had the bodies buried 'at the stayre foote . . . vnder a great heape of stones'; subsequently Richard had 'a prieste of syr Robert Brakenbury' rebury them 'secretely' (*CW*2, 86).
31 **after-supper** dessert; cf. *MND* 5.1.33–4 concerning the three hours 'Between our after-supper and bed-time'. F's Richard requests to be spoken to after he has eaten.
32 **process** narration (*OED sb.* 4a)
34 **inheritor** possessor; cf. 'inherit', *R2* 1.1.85.

22.1 KING] *Qq (Ki[.][ng])* 23 comes] *F, Q1–5;* come *Q6* health . . . lord] *F;* haile . . . leige *Qq* 24+ SP] *F (Ric[h].), Qq (King.)* 24 am] *F, Q1–5;* and *Q6* 25 gave] *F, Q3–6;* giue *Q1–2* 27] *Steevens; F lines* done. / dead. / ; *Qq line* Lord. / dead? / done] *F;* done my Lord *Qq* 28] *Steevens; F, Qq line* Lord. / *Tirrell.* / 30 where . . . truth] *F;* how or in what place *Qq* 31 SP] *F (Rich.), Q3–6 (King.); Tir. Q1–2* at] *Qq;* and *F* 32 When] *F;* And *Qq* 33 thee] *F (*the*), Qq* 35] *Steevens; F lines* then / leaue. / ; *Qq different* then] *F;* soone *Qq* TYRREL I . . . leave.] *F; not in Qq* SD] *Qq (Exit Tirrel.) opp. 34*

KING RICHARD

The son of Clarence have I pent up close,
His daughter meanly have I matched in marriage,
The sons of Edward sleep in Abraham's bosom,
And Anne my wife hath bid this world good night.
Now, for I know the Breton Richmond aims
At young Elizabeth, my brother's daughter,
And by that knot looks proudly on the crown,
To her go I, a jolly thriving wooer.

Enter RATCLIFFE.

RATCLIFFE My lord.

KING RICHARD

Good or bad news, that thou com'st in so bluntly?

36–43 Even without the culminating bravado of 43, Cibber's triumphant speech furnished Macready an opportunity to elicit a sustained ovation in his first performance as Richard (Macready, 141).

36–9 References to the accomplishment of plots only just articulated, as if in panic, in the previous scene emphasize Richard's speed and efficiency. Actions here occurring within a day transpired over three years, from the murder of the princes after Richard's coronation (1483) to Anne's death (1485), 'either by inwarde thought and pensyuenes of hearte, or by intoxicacion of poyson' (Hall, *Richard III*, fol. xlix^{r}; cf. Vergil, 211). The temporal compression here resembles that in *Richard II* (2.1) when news of Bolingbroke's armed expedition comes in the same scene that depicts the action precipitating it. For the historical accounts and the play's depiction of Richard's actions against Clarence's children, see 4.2.53n., 55n.

38 **sleep . . . bosom** Cf. Luke, 16.22; also *R2* 4.1.104–5 and Dent, A8.

40 **for** because (Abbott, 151)
Breton Richmond had been in Brittany, and Richard elsewhere uses the term as abuse (cf. 5.3.333); Jowett suggests denigration of Richmond's Welsh identity (cf. 4.4.476) since 'Briton' could mean 'Welshman' (*OED* Briton *sb.* 1b). For spellings, see *OED* Britain sb^2 and *a*.

42 **knot** i.e. marriage
looks . . . crown i.e. arrogantly expects to possess the crown

43 **jolly** lively, gallant (*OED a.* 1, 5), suggesting showy (*OED* 8a) or handsome (*OED* 10) appearance
thriving flourishing, prosperous

43.1 *RATCLIFFE There have been problems with Ratcliffe and Catesby since 3.4 and 3.5, where the roles are interchanged in Qq. See pp. 452–4.

39 this] *F;* the *Qq* good night] *F; Q1–2 (*godnight*), Q3–6 (*goodnight*)* 40 Breton] *F (*Britaine*), Qq (*Brittaine*), Capell* 41 At] *F, Q1–5;* And *Q6* 42 on] *F;* ore *Qq* 43 go I] *F;* I go *Qq* 43.1 RATCLIFFE] *F; Catesby Qq* 44+ SP] *F (Rat.); Cat[es]. Qq* 45 or bad news] *F;* newes or bad *Qq* com'st] *F, Q1; Q2–6 (*comest*)*

RATCLIFFE

Bad news, my lord. Morton is fled to Richmond,
And Buckingham, backed with the hardy Welshmen,
Is in the field, and still his power increaseth.

KING RICHARD

Ely with Richmond troubles me more near
Than Buckingham and his rash-levied strength.
Come, I have learned that fearful commenting
Is leaden servitor to dull delay.
Delay leads impotent and snail-paced beggary;
Then fiery expedition be my wing,
Jove's Mercury, and herald for a king.
Go muster men. My counsel is my shield.
We must be brief when traitors brave the field. *Exeunt.*

46 **Morton** John Morton, Bishop of Ely (see 3.4.0.2n.); More reports him imprisoned for plotting against Richard, and later drawing on his 'depe insighte in politike worldli driftes' to encourage Buckingham to revolt (*CW2*, 90–3). Morton fled to Flanders 'secretlie disguysed' (Hall, *Richard III*, fol. xxxvi[v]); cf. 4.4.467n. Qq have 'Ely' for F's 'Morton' at 4.4.467.

47–8 Time is again foreshortened: the disillusioned Buckingham (4.2) has already fielded an army.

48 **in the field** i.e. on the march

49 **near** closely, directly

50 **rash-levied** hastily raised; but perhaps suggesting instability. Holinshed describes the 'wild Welshmen' as 'falshearted' (3.743). Cf. *R2* 2.4.

51 **fearful commenting** anxious discussion

52 **leaden servitor** slow servant

53 **leads** leads to
snail-paced beggary Cf. Dent, S579: 'As slow as a snail'.

54 **expedition** haste, speed (*OED* 5)
wing i.e. figuratively, power or means of flight, or of action figured as flight (*OED sb.* 3b); *fiery expedition* may also be invoked here as a prosthetic substitute for Richard's impaired arm. 'Wing' could refer to either of the two divisions (right and left) on each side of the main body of an army in battle array (*OED sb.* 7a).

55 **Jove's Mercury** Mercury was the speedy messenger of the king of the gods, Jove; Richard invokes the haste (*expedition*) of Mercury to serve as his own royal herald and messenger in his undertaking.

56 **My counsel . . . shield** i.e. my only concerns will be deeds of arms rather than deliberations with councillors (cf. 51–2).

57 **brief** expeditious, hasty (*OED a.* A 1b)
brave challenge; cf. *KJ* 4.2.243.

57 SD 'Go' in F 56 suggests departure 'severally'; Qq's 'Come' suggests leaving together.

46 Morton] *F; Ely Qq* 50 rash-levied] *F, Qq (*rash leuied*), hyphen Pope* strength] *F;* armie *Qq* 51 learned] *F;* heard *Qq* 54 wing] *F, Q1–2;* wings *Q3–6* 55 Jove's] *F, Q1–2 (*Ioues*);* Ioue, *Q3, 5–6;* Loue, *Q4* 56 Go] *F;* Come *Qq*

[4.4] *Enter old* QUEEN MARGARET.

QUEEN MARGARET
So now prosperity begins to mellow
And drop into the rotten mouth of death.
Here in these confines slyly have I lurked
To watch the waning of mine enemies.
A dire induction am I witness to,
And will to France, hoping the consequence
Will prove as bitter, black and tragical.
Withdraw thee, wretched Margaret. Who comes
here? [*Stands aside.*]

Enter DUCHESS [Q]of York[Q] *and* QUEEN [ELIZABETH].

QUEEN ELIZABETH
Ah, my poor princes! Ah, my tender babes,

4.4 location: '*Before the Palace*' (Capell)

1–2 Contrast *glorious summer* (1.1.2); cf. the prophetic 'fall like mellowed fruit with shakes of death' (Marlowe, *Works*, *1 Tamburlaine*, 2.1.47). As Richard begins the play with a soliloquy, so Margaret's *induction* (5) launches its final action, Richard's downfall – and then she leaves (6, 125); cf. Furor's opening of Actio 3 of Legge's *Richardus Tertius* and subsequent departure, with the declaration: 'I, Madness, shall spare England here-after, and seek for myself a new home' (2772–4).

1 **mellow** ripen (*OED v.* 1b)

3 **confines** region, territory (*OED* confine *sb.*^{2} 2)

5 **induction** introductory part of a work; cf. 1.1.32n.; *tragical* (7) continues the literary vocabulary.

6 **will to France** Historically, Margaret had been in France since 1476, nine years before the time of this scene, and dead since 1482. While most of the play's characters suffer confinement, Margaret moves unimpeded through space and time, lurking *slyly* (3), commenting or cursing, exiting when she pleases, provoking wonder at her *liberty* (1.3.304).

consequence outcome, result

7 **black and tragical** Black trappings were associated with Elizabethan stage tragedy; see *1H6* 1.1.1, *Luc* 766 and Marston's *Insatiate Countess* (4.5.4–5).

8 **Withdraw thee** i.e. step aside (implicit SD); since she declares her intention to withdraw before questioning who *comes here*, Margaret may hear the approaching characters before seeing them. The women may wear mourning veils (Jowett), which might explain Richard's apparent failure to recognize his mother (136).

9, 10 **my, My** In the Sher–Alexander production, Frances Tomelty's Elizabeth emphasized self-reference by accenting these possessive pronouns (Day, 201).

4.4] *Pope; Scena Tertia. F; not in Qq* 0.1] *F; Enter Queene Margaret sola. Qq* 1+ SP] *Qq (Q[u]. Mar.); Mar. F* 4 enemies] *F;* aduersaries *Qq* 8 SD] *Collier (Retiring.)* 8.1] *F (Enter Dutchesse and Queene.); Enter the Qu. and the Dutchesse of Yorke. Qq* ELIZABETH] *Malone* 9 poor] *F;* young *Qq*

My unblowed flowers, new-appearing sweets!
If yet your gentle souls fly in the air
And be not fixed in doom perpetual,
Hover about me with your airy wings
And hear your mother's lamentation.

QUEEN MARGARET [*aside*]

Hover about her; say that right for right
Hath dimmed your infant morn to aged night.

DUCHESS

So many miseries have crazed my voice
That my woe-wearied tongue is still and mute.
Edward Plantagenet, why art thou dead?

QUEEN MARGARET [*aside*]

Plantagenet doth quit Plantagenet;
Edward for Edward pays a dying debt.

QUEEN ELIZABETH

Wilt thou, O God, fly from such gentle lambs

10 **unblowed** unopened, still in the bud; form of Qq's 'unblown' (*OED ppl. a.* 2)
sweets fragrant flowers or herbs (*OED sb.* 7); cf. *Ham* 5.1.232.
12 **doom** judgement, not necessarily negative (*OED sb.* 2)
13 **airy** ethereal (*OED a.* 3)
15 **right for right** 'justice answering to the claims of justice' (Johnson)
15–16 **right . . . night** These rhymes may signal an aside (Abbott, 515), but rhymes elsewhere (e.g. 166–71) do not necessarily indicate asides.
16 **aged** agèd
17 **crazed** cracked (*OED ppl. a.* 1)
19 **Edward Plantagenet** her grandson Edward V or her son Edward IV (though Clarence's son is also Edward Plantagenet)
20 **Plantagenet** the name they all, whether York or Lancaster, share; see 1.2.145n.
quit balance, be an equivalent for (*OED v.* 11c); cf. Dent, M800: 'Measure for measure'.
21 **Edward for Edward** probably Edward V, Elizabeth's son, for Edward, Prince of Wales, son of Margaret and Henry VI
dying debt i.e. a debt paid by a death; with proverbial echoes (Dent, D148: 'Death pays all debts') frequent in Shakespeare (e.g. *Tem* 3.2.131; *Cym* 5.4.157). Here the specific reference is to the *debt* of reciprocated vengeance; cf. *royal debt* (2.2.95) and Hal to Falstaff: 'Thou owest God a death' (*1H4* 5.1.126).
22–3 The lines echo John, 10.12–13, in which Christ, the good shepherd who gives his life for the sheep, is contrasted with the hireling who 'seeth the wolf commyng, and leaueth the sheepe, and fleeth, and the

10 unblowed] *F;* vnblowne *Qq* flowers] *F, Q1–5;* flower *Q6* new-appearing] *F, Qq (*new appearing*), hyphen Pope* 13 about] *F, Q1–5;* aboue *Q6* 15, 20, 25 SD] *Collier subst.* 17–19] *F; after 34 Qq* 18 still and mute] *F;* mute and dumbe *Qq* 20–1] *F; not in Qq*

And throw them in the entrails of the wolf?
When didst thou sleep when such a deed was done?

QUEEN MARGARET [*aside*]

When holy Harry died, and my sweet son.

DUCHESS

Dead life, blind sight, poor mortal living ghost,
Woe's scene, world's shame, grave's due by life usurped,
Brief abstract and record of tedious days,
Rest thy unrest on England's lawful earth, [*She sits.*]
Unlawfully made drunk with innocent blood.

QUEEN ELIZABETH

Ah, that thou wouldst as soon afford a grave,

wolfe catcheth them, & scattereth the sheepe'. Cf. 229, Rous's *Historia* (Churchill, 47) and *3H6* 5.6.7. More characterizes Prince Edward as 'the lamb . . . betaken to the wolfe to kepe' (*CW*2, 24–5).

22 **fly from** abandon

23 **throw** probably to twist about, wreathe (*OED* v^1 1); or perhaps to cast abruptly into some relation (32a)
entrails *OED* cites as meaning 'intestines' (entrail $sb.^1$ II 1b) as *Tit* 1.1.147, but *throw* suggests 'coils' (*OED* $sb.^2$) as in 'folds . . . stretcht now forth at length without entraile' (Spenser, *Faerie Queene*, 1.1.16).

24 **sleep** Cf. 1.3.287n.; this image begins a series of echoes of Kyd's *Spanish Tragedy*, which has Revenge asleep onstage while evil proceeds apparently unchecked.

25 **holy Harry** Henry VI (called 'holy' by Hall) is associated with exceptional piety throughout the Henry VI plays (cf. *2H6* 1.1.244).

26 These extreme oxymorons, used to convey emotional intensity, suggest other Shakespearean passages which treat oxymoronic rhetoric ironically (e.g. *RJ* 1.1.176–81).

27 **grave's due** i.e. that which rightfully belongs to death

28 **abstract** epitome, summary (*OED sb.* 2)
record recòrd; account preserved in writing or otherwise, here in a person (*OED sb.* 5, citing this line)

29 **Rest thy unrest** also found in *Tit* 4.2.31, but here perhaps recalling Kyd's grieving Viceroy (Kyd, *Spanish Tragedy*, 1.3.5; cf. 3.13.29). The Duchess may seat herself to be joined subsequently by Queen Elizabeth; grief is frequently associated with sitting or lying on the ground (cf. *R2* 3.2.155, 178). In *The Three Lords and Three Ladies of London* (1590) three female figures sit and bemoan their miseries; each is then, as Queen Elizabeth will be, wooed by a Vice-like character (Wilson, *Three Lords*, sigs $D1^v$–$E1^r$); cf. pp. 7–8. Margaret earlier laments that mischance has 'laid me on the ground, / Where I must take like seat unto my fortune' (*3H6* 3.3.9–10).
lawful i.e. law-abiding

29–30 **earth . . . drunk** Cf. the image of civil conflict in *1H4* 1.1.5–6.

31 **thou** i.e. the earth
soon readily (*OED* soon 8)
afford grant, yield

25 Harry] *F, Q1–2; Mary Q3–6* 26 Dead . . . sight] *F;* Blind sight, dead life *Qq* 27 due by] *Qq;* due, by *F* 28] *F; not in Qq* 29 thy] *F, Q1–4;* they *Q5;* their *Q6* SD] *Capell subst.* 30 Unlawfully] *F, Q1–5;* Vnlawfull *Q6* innocent] *F;* innocents *Qq* 31 Ah] *F;* O *Qq* as soon] *F* (assoone); aswel *Qq*

As thou canst yield a melancholy seat,
Then would I hide my bones, not rest them here.
Ah, who hath any cause to mourn but we? [*She sits.*]

QUEEN MARGARET [*Comes forward.*]
If ancient sorrow be most reverend,
Give mine the benefit of seniory,
And let my griefs frown on the upper hand.
If sorrow can admit society,
[Q]Tell over your woes again by viewing mine.[Q]
I had an Edward, till a Richard killed him;
I had a husband, till a Richard killed him.
Thou hadst an Edward, till a Richard killed him.

32 **melancholy seat** i.e. a place fitting to the expression of melancholy

34 ***we** Qq's 'I' accords with the play's pervasive self-centredness, but this moment is about as close as the speakers come to genuine sympathy (ironically counterpointed by Margaret's asides). For the female bonding here as opposed to more constrictive notions of family and place, see Willis, 102–3 and pp. 19–20.

35–7 Cf. the competing mourners for Lucrece; Collatine even 'bids Lucretius give his sorrow place' (*Luc* 1773). This contestatory element creates a contrast with the otherwise similar scene in which Henry VI comments on his distress while empathetically witnessing the lamentations of feuding partisans (*3H6* 2.5.55–124); it should also qualify comparisons with the medieval staging of the three Marys who lament the death of Jesus (Clemen, 186). Contrast the sympathy uniting the three female lamenters in R. Wilson (see 29n.).

36 **seniory** seniority (*OED* signeurie, citing this line); possibly seigniory (lordship, domination, sovereignty: *OED sb.* 1). Given reference to 'frown[ing] on the upper hand' (37) there may be a sense of 'authority or supremacy expressed in looks or bearing' (*OED* signory 1b).

37–8 *Theobald's punctuation corrects for F's omission of 39.

37 **on . . . hand** i.e. from a position of superiority; cf. Dent, H95: 'To get the upper hand'. Margaret may remain standing, above the mourners.

38 **admit society** allow fellowship

39 **Tell over** narrate (*OED v.* 2a) or enumerate (*OED v.* 22b)

40 **Edward** Prince Edward, son of Henry VI and Margaret, killed at the battle of Tewkesbury by Richard and his brothers (*3H6* 5.3)

41 **husband** Henry VI, killed by Richard in the Tower (*3H6* 5.6); F's 'husband' interrupts a sequence of proper nouns (Thompson), but Qq's 'Richard' is clearly wrong.

42 **Edward** young Edward V, Elizabeth's son, just murdered in the Tower at Richard's instigation

34 Ah] *F;* O *Qq* we] *F; I Qq* SD] *Steevens subst.* 35 SD] *Collier subst. after 35* reverend] *Cam;* reuerent *F, Qq* 36 seniory] *F (*signeurie*);* signorie *Q1–5;* signiorie *Q6;* seigneury *Rowe;* seniority *Pope* 37 griefs] *F;* woes *Qq* 37–8 hand. . . . society,] *Theobald;* hand . . . Society. *F;* hand, . . . societie, *Qq* 41 husband] *F;* Richard *Qq;* Henry *Rann (Capell)*

Thou hadst a Richard, till a Richard killed him.

DUCHESS

I had a Richard too, and thou didst kill him;
I had a Rutland too; thou holp'st to kill him.

QUEEN MARGARET

Thou hadst a Clarence too, and Richard killed him.
From forth the kennel of thy womb hath crept
A hell-hound that doth hunt us all to death:
That dog, that had his teeth before his eyes,
To worry lambs and lap their gentle blood;
That excellent grand tyrant of the earth,
That reigns in galled eyes of weeping souls;
That foul defacer of God's handiwork
Thy womb let loose to chase us to our graves.
O upright, just, and true-disposing God,

43 [1]**Richard** Richard, Duke of York, the younger of Elizabeth's sons, also murdered by Richard's assassins

44 **Richard** Richard, the late Duke of York, the Duchess's husband and King Richard's father, killed by Margaret's army at Wakefield in 1460 (*3H6* 1.4)

45 **Rutland** the Duchess's second son, Edmund, Earl of Rutland, killed by Clifford (*3H6* 1.3)
holp'st helped

47–9 **kennel . . . eyes** Richard's alleged birth with teeth, which 'plainly signified' that he should 'snarl and bite and play the dog' (*3H6* 5.6.77), is elaborated to claim that, also like a dog, he was born unable to see. Milton may have recalled this passage in depicting Sin in *Paradise Lost* (Martin).

50 **worry** seize by the throat, tear or lacerate by biting and shaking, said of dogs or wolves attacking sheep (*OED v.* 3)

51–3 *F apparently reverses 51 and 52: *tyrant* should be the subject of *reigns*, putting 51 before 52. However, 53 could come after 50, as it does in F, Qq, without spoiling the sense.

51 **excellent** pre-eminent, supreme (in a neutral or negative sense) (*OED a.* B 1b); cf. 'a very excellent piece of villainy' (*Tit* 2.2.[2.3.]7).
grand pre-eminent, chief; resembling uses of 'arch' in transferring the sense of an official title, as in 'Grand Turk' (*OED a.* 3a, citing this line). Cf. 'The grand conspirator' (*R2* 5.6.19). See pp. 29–31.

52 **galled** gallèd; sore from chafing (*OED ppl. a.*[2] 1b); cf. *Ham* 1.2.155.

53 **defacer** disfigurer, mutilator; cf. 3.7.125.
God's handiwork i.e. humanity, created in God's image (Genesis, 1.26–7); cf. 2.1.123–4.

55 **true-disposing** i.e. rightly ordering (*OED* dispose *v.* 2)

45 too; thou holp'st] *F2 (*too, thou holp'st*); * too, thou hop'st *F, Q1–2;* too, and thou holpst *Q3–6* 46] *Qq; F lines* too, / him. / and] *F, Q1;* till *Q2–6* 50 blood] *F;* blouds *Qq* 51–3] *Ard*[2]*; in sequence 53, 52, 51 F; 53, 51, 52 Capell* 51–2] *F; not in Qq*

How do I thank thee that this carnal cur
Preys on the issue of his mother's body
And makes her pew-fellow with others' moan.

DUCHESS

O Harry's wife, triumph not in my woes!
God witness with me, I have wept for thine.

QUEEN MARGARET

Bear with me. I am hungry for revenge,
And now I cloy me with beholding it.
Thy Edward he is dead, that killed my Edward,
Thy other Edward dead, to quit my Edward.
Young York, he is but boot, because both they
Matched not the high perfection of my loss.
Thy Clarence he is dead that stabbed my Edward,
And the beholders of this frantic play,
Th'adulterate Hastings, Rivers, Vaughan, Grey,
Untimely smothered in their dusky graves.

56 **carnal** carnivorous, bloody, murderous (*OED a.* 6, citing this line); possibly suggesting 'related in blood' (*OED a.* 2), with the Duchess as Richard's mother

58 **pew-fellow** one who shares a pew in church, a fellow-worshipper (*OED*)
moan lamentation

60 **God . . . me** i.e. may God witness my claim

61 **Bear with me** i.e. be patient

62 **cloy** surfeit or satiate (*OED v.* 7); cf. *R2* 1.3.296.

63 **Thy Edward . . . my Edward** Edward IV . . . Prince Edward, Margaret's son

64 ***Thy other Edward** The Duchess's grandson, Edward V. F's 'The' injects further ambiguity into a confusing litany, but might interchangeability have been the playwright's point? Margaret's 'hunger' for revenge expresses itself in the devaluation of her interlocutor's family: the Duchess's two Edwards fail to even the balance.
quit Cf. 20.

65 **boot** compensation, thrown in to make up a deficiency of value (*OED sb.*[1] 2)

68–9 This exceptional rhyme renders the victims mere parts of a 'generalized accumulation of death' (Brooke, 51).

68 **this frantic play** i.e. the murder of Prince Edward; earlier Margaret mentions Dorset instead of his brother Grey as a witness (1.3.209–10n.).
frantic lunatic, violently mad (*OED a.* 1; cf. 1.3.246); Qq's 'tragicke' accords with Margaret's theatrical references.

69 **adulterate** i.e. adulterous (for his relationship with Mistress Shore)

70 **Untimely smothered** i.e. prematurely extinguished in burial; Janet Adelman notes the odd emphasis on

59 wife] *F, Q2–6;* wifes *Q1* 60 thine] *F, Q1;* thee *Q2–6* 63 killed] *F;* stabd *Qq* 64 Thy] *Qq;* The *F* quit] *F, Q1–5 subst.;* quite *Q6* 66 Matched] *F;* Match *Qq* 67 stabbed] *F;* kild *Qq* 68 frantic] *F;* tragicke *Qq* 69 Th'] *F; Qq (*The*)*

Richard yet lives, hell's black intelligencer,
Only reserved their factor to buy souls
And send them thither. But at hand, at hand
Ensues his piteous and unpitied end.
Earth gapes, hell burns, fiends roar, saints pray,
To have him suddenly conveyed from hence.

smothering and suggests a change from stabbing in the earlier history plays, citing 1.4.40, 4.3.17, 4.4.134 and Clarence's drowning (Adelman, 241). See also *strangling* in the womb (4.4.138).

71 **intelligencer** agent, one who obtains secret information or conveys intelligence (*OED sb.* a; cf. *2H4* 4.2.20), but perhaps working two ways: while Richard spies for Satan, everything about him also conveys information to humanity about hell's nature and designs (Torrey, 142). For official fears about intelligencers during the late 1580s and 1590s, see Fox, 340–50.

72 **Only reserved** i.e. preserved alive solely in order to be
their hell's
factor mercantile agent (*OED sb.* 4a) or someone who works for another (*OED sb.* 3); cf. 3.7.133. 'Satans chiefest drift & maine point . . . is the inlargement of his owne kingdome' by acquiring more damned souls (Mason, 55), but *buy* lends this line a quality of understatement (contrast the melodrama of 75). The mundane commercial sense of *factor* here differs from that in *Mirror* passages concerning disguised fiends who walk the earth as 'factours for all evylls' ('Hastings', 246), but it does connect with Elizabethan religious discourse. Henry Smith acknowledges Satan's title as '*The God of this World*', but, more humbly, he is 'a factor between the Merchant and the Mercer, and the Gentleman and the tenant' or a master artisan: 'there is a craft of compassing, and Satan is the craftesmaster, and the rest are prentises, or factors vnder him' (*Sermons*, 987, 994–6).

73 **at hand** near in time, rapidly approaching (*OED sb.* II 25b)

74 **piteous and unpitied** A wonderfully expressive formula for this play, in which the most deplorable (*OED* piteous 3) suffering frequently fails to elicit pity from onstage observers.

75 **gapes** i.e. opens wide, like a mouth, with an association of the opening and the mouth of hell (*OED v.* 1b); cf. 1.2.65n.
fiends . . . saints Both hell and heaven have a stake in Richard's actions and their consequences. The conjunction of otherwise opposing forces accurately suits Richard's complicated role as an unwitting instrument of heavenly purposes, even as he pursues the goals of hell on earth. This is the second reference to the practice – strongly denounced by Protestants – of prayer to or by the saints (see 1.2.8n., 5.3.241n.). Hammond detects 'Faustian overtones' in 71–6, but Richard's roles include that of the tyrannical scourge who, with divine allowance, inflicts punishment upon sinners, while Marlowe's Faustus fulfils no such function.

76 **conveyed** carried away forcibly (*OED v.* 3)

73 thither] *F, Q2–6; Q1 (*thether*)* hand, at hand] *F, Q2–6;* hand at handes *Q1* 75 hell] *F, Q1–5;* hels *Q6* 76 from hence] *F;* away *Qq*

Cancel his bond of life, dear God I pray,
That I may live and say, 'The dog is dead.'

QUEEN ELIZABETH

O, thou didst prophesy the time would come
That I should wish for thee to help me curse
That bottled spider, that foul bunch-backed toad.

QUEEN MARGARET

I called thee then vain flourish of my fortune;
I called thee then, poor shadow, painted queen,
The presentation of but what I was,
The flattering index of a direful pageant,
One heaved a-high, to be hurled down below,
A mother only mocked with two fair babes,
A dream of what thou wast, a garish flag
To be the aim of every dangerous shot,
A sign of dignity, a breath, a bubble,

77 **bond of life** covenant or agreement, respecting the term of his life; cf. *Mac* 3.2.49. While Richard's life has been preserved that he might function as hell's spy and agent, God is capable of terminating the bond that sets the terms of his life.
I pray Margaret joins the *saints* who *pray* (75); cf. 1.3.211.

79–80 See 1.3.244–5.

81 **bottled . . . toad** See 1.3.241–5.

82–115 On the figure of anaphora, or repetition, prominent in this speech, see 153n.

82–3 **flourish . . . painted** See 1.3.240.

83 **shadow** image; elsewhere used to characterize actors (*MND* 5.3.209–10, 417)

84 **presentation of but** representation, likeness only of (*OED* presentation III 5b). See Abbott, 129 on placement of 'but'.

85 **flattering index** prologue, preface (*OED sb.* 5a; cf. 2.2.149), *flattering* because, although pleasing to the imagination, ultimately unreal (cf. *TS* Ind.1.43: 'a flatt'ring dream')
direful dreadful, terrible (*OED*)
pageant scene acted upon the stage (*OED sb.* 1a)

86 suggesting the rolling of Fortune's wheel
a-high aloft, on high

87 **only mocked with** i.e. merely deceived in thinking that she truly had (the children); cf. 'mock'd . . . with a husband' (*MM* 5.1.415).

88–9 **garish . . . shot** gaudy military standard that attracts the shots of enemy marksmen

90 **sign** badge, emblem (*OED sb.* 5a, b) or vestige (here, of lost *dignity*) (*OED sb.* 8a); either sense emphasizes the insubstantiality of the signifier – *breath, a bubble* – as opposed to the substance signified (cf. 'honour' as 'mere scutcheon', *1H4* 5.1.139–40).
breath Cf. Falstaff's 'What is in that

78 and] *F;* to *Qq* 81 bunch-backed] *F, Q1;* hunch-backt *Q2–6* 86 a-high] *F, Qq (*a high*), hyphen Dyce* 87 fair] *F;* sweete *Qq* 88–90] *F;* A dreame of which thou wert a breath, a bubble, / A signe of dignitie, a garish flagge, / To be the aime of euerie dangerous shot, / *Qq subst.*

A queen in jest, only to fill the scene.
Where is thy husband now? Where be thy brothers?
Where be thy two sons? Wherein dost thou joy?
Who sues, and kneels, and says, 'God save the Queen'?
Where be the bending peers that flattered thee?
Where be the thronging troops that followed thee?
Decline all this, and see what now thou art:
For happy wife, a most distressed widow;
For joyful mother, one that wails the name;
For one being sued to, one that humbly sues;
For queen, a very caitiff crowned with care;
For she that scorned at me, now scorned of me;
For she being feared of all, now fearing one;

word "honour"? What is that "honour"? Air' (*1H4* 1.1.134–5).
bubble Cf. Dent, M246: 'Man is but a bubble.'

91 **in jest** without serious intention, the opposite of 'in earnest' (*OED sb.* 6a; cf. *R2* 5.3.99–100), but also with a theatrical connotation: *jest*, meaning pageant or masque (*OED sb.* 8; cf. Kyd, *Spanish Tragedy*, 1.4.137 or *Ham* 3.2.228, where both meanings appear present), supported by reference to filling a *scene*.

92–6 **Where is . . . Where be** Cf. the medieval *ubi sunt* formula, lamenting the mutability of the world, its people and goods by demanding where they may have gone; cf. 144–8.

92 **be** On 'be' used to refer to a number of persons and for 'euphony and variety', see Abbott, 300.

94 **sues** petitions

95 **bending** bowing
peers nobles of the degrees of duke, marquess, earl, viscount or baron (*OED sb.* 4a)

96 **troops** retinue, attendants

97 **Decline** say or recite in formal order (*OED v.* 20b, citing this line), but the exhaustiveness and formulaic nature of what follows suggests the grammatical exercise of declining a word through different cases (*OED v.* 20a). Cf. Thersites' attempt to 'decline the whole question' of Patroclus (*TC* 2.3.50–65).

98 **For** instead of (Abbott, 148)

99 **wails the name** bewails, laments at the very title (of mother)

100–4 *F preserves the sequence of categories in 92–5 – questions about spouse, children, suitors and queenly office (Patrick, 42; Greg, *Problem*, 82) – more nearly constituting a 'declension' than Qq (Hammond).

100 ***to** Q2–6, F appear to disagree with Q1, but see 385n. on *too*.

101 **very caitiff** truly poor wretch, absolutely miserable person (*OED* 2)

102 **scorned at . . . scorned of** mocked, derided . . . mocked by

103 **feared . . . fearing** playing on *feared* = respected (by all) and *fearing* = being afraid of (Richard)

93 be . . . sons] *F;* are *(*be *Q3–6)* thy children *Qq*   94 [1]and . . . says] *F;* to thee, and cries *Qq*   100–4] *F; in sequence 101, 100, 104, 102 Qq*   100 to] *F, Q2–6 (*too*), Q1*   102 she] *F;* one *Qq*   103] *F; not in Qq*

For she commanding all, obeyed of none.
Thus hath the course of justice whirled about
And left thee but a very prey to time,
Having no more but thought of what thou wast
To torture thee the more, being what thou art.
Thou didst usurp my place, and dost thou not
Usurp the just proportion of my sorrow?
Now thy proud neck bears half my burdened yoke,
From which, even here I slip my wearied head
And leave the burden of it all on thee.
Farewell, York's wife, and queen of sad mischance.
These English woes shall make me smile in France.

QUEEN ELIZABETH

O thou, well skilled in curses, stay awhile
And teach me how to curse mine enemies.

QUEEN MARGARET

Forbear to sleep the night, and fast the day;
Compare dead happiness with living woe;

105 **course** onward path (*OED sb.* 2a) or, given *prey* (106), the action of pursuing game with dogs (*OED sb.* 7a) **whirled about** turned about an axis like a wheel (Qq 'whe'eld'), possibly referring to Fortune's wheel (cf. 86); cf. 'justice always whirls in equal measure' (*LLL* 4.3.358).

106 **very** in the fullest, most emphatic sense (*OED a.* A 3a) **prey to time** Cf. 'cormorant devouring time' (*LLL* 1.1.4), 'Devouring time' (*Son* 19) and Dent, T326: 'Time devours all things.'

107 **thought** memory

110 **just proportion** i.e. the amount (of sorrow) allotted (to me) by right (of my woes)

111–12 See Dent, N69: 'To slip one's neck out of the collar'. F's 'wearied head' emphasizes the mental nature of the sufferings bequeathed to Elizabeth as *crowned with care* (101) and permits a remark on the (false) pride embodied in her *proud neck*.

117–23 Seneca's Chorus seeks instruction in grieving from Hecuba, who complies by detailing how to lament (Seneca, *Troades*, 79–98); cf. Lucrece's demand: 'Teach me to curse him that thou taught'st this ill' (*Luc* 996).

118 ***night . . . day** F agrees with Q3–6's singular forms; cf. *TS* 5.2.151 ('To watch the night in storms, the day in cold') and *Mirror*, 'Buckingham', 675 ('To wayle the daye, and wepe the weary night').

104 she] *F;* one *Qq* 105 whirled] *F;* whe'eld *Q1;* wheel'd *Q2–6* 107–8 wast . . . art.] *F4 (*wast, . . . art.*);* wast. . . . art, *F;* wert, . . . art, *Q1–2;* art, . . . art. *Q3–6* 112 wearied] *F, Q6;* wearie *Q1–2;* weary *Q3–5* head] *F;* necke *Qq* 115 woes] *F, Q1–3, 5–6;* wars *Q4* shall] *F;* will *Qq* 118 night . . . day] *F, Q3–6;* nights . . . daies *Q1–2*

Think that thy babes were sweeter than they were,
And he that slew them fouler than he is.
Bettering thy loss makes the bad causer worse.
Revolving this will teach thee how to curse.

QUEEN ELIZABETH

My words are dull. O, quicken them with thine.

QUEEN MARGARET

Thy woes will make them sharp and pierce like mine. *Exit.*

DUCHESS

Why should calamity be full of words?

QUEEN ELIZABETH

Windy attorneys to their clients' woes,
Airy succeeders of intestate joys,
Poor breathing orators of miseries,
Let them have scope, though what they will impart
Help nothing else, yet do they ease the heart.

DUCHESS

If so, then be not tongue-tied. Go with me,

120–3 On Margaret's methods of cursing, see p. 21.

120 ***sweeter** Qq's 'fairer' provides an antithesis with *fouler* (121); cf. 'sweete' (Qq) and 'faire' (F) in 87.

122 **Bettering** exaggerating, amplifying, as in rhetorical hyperbole
causer Cf. 1.2.120.

123 **Revolving** pondering (cf. 4.2.42)

124–5 **dull . . . sharp** Following an antithesis of *dead* and *living* (119), Margaret recasts Elizabeth's opposition of *dull* to *quick*[*en*] (124) by taking *dull* to mean 'blunt' rather than 'slow', thereby, characteristically, heightening the verbal aggression.

124 **quicken** animate, enliven

125 SD And just like that, Margaret simply goes – for good (see 6).

127–31 In effect, words are insubstantial representatives for substantial griefs that are their motivating *clients*, or words are fruitless inheritors of joys that have died leaving no inheritance to their successors, or they are merely empty speakers who give speeches about unfelt miseries. Cf. *Luc* 1016–27. See p. 23.

128 ***intestate** not having made a will (*OED a.* 1); F's 'intestine' would render *airy* succession alimentary (Lull).

130 **scope** liberty, room for exercise (*OED sb.*^{2} 7a)

130–3 **impart . . . smother** Cf. Dent, G447: 'Grief is lessened when imparted to others.' The Duchess renders 'imparting' – i.e. sharing with other sufferers – as violence, to *smother* Richard with what they have to impart (communicate) to him (see G. Bloom, 92–3).

120 thy] *F, Q1–3, 5–6; om. Q4* sweeter] *F;* fairer *Qq* 122 Bettering] *F, Qq (*Bett'ring*)* causer] *F, Q1–3, 5–6;* causes *Q4* 125] *Qq; F lines* sharpe, / mine. / SD] *F (Exit Margaret.); Exit. Mar. Qq opp. 126* 127 their] *F;* your *Qq* clients'] *F, Q4 (*Clients*);* Client *Q1–3, 5–6* 128 intestate] *Qq;* intestine *F* 130 will] *F;* do *Qq* 131 nothing else] *F;* not at al *Qq* 132 If so, then] *Qq;* If so then, *F*

And in the breath of bitter words let's smother
My damnèd son, that thy two sweet sons smothered.
[*Trumpet sounds.*]
The trumpet sounds. Be copious in exclaims.

Enter KING RICHARD *and his Train* [*including* CATESBY],
[Q]*marching with drums and trumpets*[Q].

KING RICHARD
Who intercepts me in my expedition?

DUCHESS
O, she that might have intercepted thee,
By strangling thee in her accursed womb,
From all the slaughters, wretch, that thou hast done.

QUEEN ELIZABETH
Hid'st thou that forehead with a golden crown
Where should be branded, if that right were right,
The slaughter of the prince that owed that crown

135 **exclaims** exclamations (cf. 1.2.52)

135.1–2 Catesby needs to enter before 442. Richard needs the drums and trumpets (mentioned only in Qq SD) at 149.

136 **Who** Richard's seeming lack of recognition admits at least three interpretations. Socially, Richard's question might rhetorically express the offended dignity of a monarch who finds himself interrupted – even by his mother – in an important undertaking. Physically, entry in military order may insulate him from immediate contact with onlookers; or perhaps the women wear mourning veils (see 8n.).
expedition warlike enterprise (*OED* 2), possibly conveying 'haste' (*OED* 5) as at 4.3.54.

137–9 **might have . . . From** i.e. could have . . . from committing

138 **accursed** accursèd

140–1 **forehead . . . branded** Shaheen suggests allusion to God's mark upon Cain for his fratricide, but Cain's mark is meant to preserve him from violent retribution (Genesis, 4.15) while Richard's brand should manifest guilt, as in the case of Shore's wife, who protests, 'If thy faults were so written in thy forehead as mine is, it would be as wrong with thee' (*True Tragedy*, 1175–6). Cf. Isaiah, 3.9: '[God] shall finde marke of their impietie in their forehead' (Geneva). Addressing the mark on the forehead of the biblical Whore of Babylon, an Elizabethan sermon invokes a commonplace: 'Wee vse

134 that] *F;* which *Qq*   sweet] *F, Q1–2; om. Q3–6*   SD] *Collier subst.*   135 The trumpet sounds] *F; I* heare his drum *Qq*   135.1 *and his Train*] *F; not in Qq*   *including* CATESBY] *Ard*^{2} 136+ SP] *King[.] Qq; Rich. F*   136 me in] *F; not in Qq*   137 O] *F;* A *Qq*   141 Where] *Qq;* Where't *F*   should] *F, Q1–3, 5–6;* would *Q4*   branded] *F;* grauen *Qq*   right,] *Qq;* right? *F*

And the dire death of my poor sons and brothers?
Tell me, thou villain-slave, where are my children?

DUCHESS

Thou toad, thou toad, where is thy brother Clarence,
And little Ned Plantagenet his son?

QUEEN ELIZABETH

Where is the gentle Rivers, Vaughan, Grey?

DUCHESS

Where is kind Hastings?

KING RICHARD

A flourish, trumpets! Strike alarum, drums!
Let not the heavens hear these tell-tale women
Rail on the Lord's anointed. Strike, I say! *Flourish. Alarums.*

to say if euerie mans faults were written in their foreheads, some would pull down their hats very low' (Gifford, 328; cf. Dent, F120).

142 **owed** owned (*OED v.* B 1)

143 **brothers** See 1.3.37n.

144–8 Here the *ubi sunt* formulae (see 92–6n.) are woven into interactive dialogue, as actual demands rather than as a generalized lyrical lament. See also p. 25.

147 *Qq's 'kind Hastings' is unlikely from Queen Elizabeth, given her antagonism towards him.

149–430 On the strange 'temporal loop' in this scene, the odder for keeping Richard's forces onstage during the prolonged verbal struggle between Richard and Queen Elizabeth, see Jones, *Origins*, 221–6.

149–54 The opposing of drums to voices resembles *KJ* 5.2.159–80.

149 **flourish** A flourish is a fanfare announcing the approach of a person of distinction (*OED sb.* 7a), as at 2.1.0.1 and 5.5.0.4, so perhaps ironically Richard has to command his own flourish – after he has already arrived on the scene and while he attempts to assert his legitimacy to his own mother!

alarum Cf. 1.1.7n.

150 **tell-tale** tale-telling, or in the present case, those who are 'tell-tales' (*OED a.* 3a, citing this line); a 'tell-tale' idly or maliciously discloses private or secret matters (*OED sb.* 1a). Richard typically condescends to the women as idle gossips who trade in mere tales, but in fact they threaten his authority by public accusation (see pp. 23–5).

151 **Rail . . . anointed** referring to the practice of anointing the newly crowned monarch with oil, based on biblical precedent: in 1 Samuel, 16 God summons Samuel to render David 'the Lordes annoynted', recognizing him, the Bishops' Bible explains, as 'appoynted of God to be made king'. Richard's biblical language shares terms with official attempts to silence critics of the Elizabethan ecclesiastical authorities. Bishop Bancroft quotes Exodus, 22.28 and 1 Samuel, 24.10: 'Thou shalt not rayle vpon the *Iudges*, neyther speake euill of the Ruler of

143 poor] *F;* two *Qq* 145] *Qq; F lines* Toade, / *Clarence?* / 146 Plantagenet] *F, Q1–2, 6; Q3–5 (*Plantaget*)* 147 the gentle] *F;* kind *Hastings Qq* 148] *F; not in Qq* 151 SD] *F; The trumpets Q1; The trumpets sound. (sounds. Q3–6) Q2–6*

Either be patient and entreat me fair,
Or with the clamorous report of war
Thus will I drown your exclamations.

DUCHESS

Art thou my son?

KING RICHARD

Ay, I thank God, my father and yourself.

DUCHESS

Then patiently hear my impatience.

KING RICHARD

Madam, I have a touch of your condition,
That cannot brook the accent of reproof.

DUCHESS

O, let me speak.

KING RICHARD Do then, but I'll not hear.

DUCHESS

I will be mild and gentle in my words.

KING RICHARD

And brief, good mother, for I am in haste.

the people. The Lord keepe me from laying my hand on him. For he is the Lordes annointed' (Bancroft, *Positions*, sig. A3v). See p. 23.

Rail complain vehemently

151 SD Plutarch's Lepidus, fearful that Antony, wearing 'a mourning gowne' for Caesar, will win his troops' allegiance from him, commands 'all the trompetts to sownd together to stoppe the souldiers eares' (Plutarch, 978; Honigmann, 232).

152 **patient** composed, calm in suffering (*OED a.* 1)

entreat me fair treat (*OED* entreat *v.* 1) or beseech (*OED v.* 9) me politely (cf. *3H6* 1.1.271)

153 **report** resounding noise (*OED sb.* 7a), but possibly conveying a specific response, especially a musical note answering to or repeating another (*OED sb.* 6a). Puttenham (108) uses 'report' for anaphora or 'Repetition in the first degree', a verbal device relevant to this highly repetitious scene and also to the sense in which Richard's noises answer in the masculine register of *Grim-visaged War* (1.1.9) the lamenting accusations of the female characters.

155 Cf. Lear's weighty reproof, 'Are you our daughter?' (*KL* 1.4.209; Pierce, 123n.) and Leontes to Mamillius, 'Art thou my boy?' (*WT* 1.2.120).

158 **condition** temperament, disposition (cf. *Oth* 2.1.248)

159 **brook** endure (*OED v.* 3a)

accent tone (*OED sb.* 5)

153 clamorous] *F, Q1–3, 5–6;* clamour *Q4* 159 That] *F;* Which *Qq* 160] *Steevens; F lines* speake. / heare. / ; *not in Qq* 161 words] *F;* speach *Qq*

DUCHESS

Art thou so hasty? I have stayed for thee,
God knows, in torment and in agony.

KING RICHARD

And came I not at last to comfort you?

DUCHESS

No, by the Holy Rood, thou knowst it well:
Thou cam'st on earth to make the earth my hell.
A grievous burden was thy birth to me;
Tetchy and wayward was thy infancy.
Thy school days frightful, desperate, wild and furious;
Thy prime of manhood daring, bold and venturous;
Thy age confirmed proud, subtle, sly and bloody,
More mild, but yet more harmful, kind in hatred.
What comfortable hour canst thou name
That ever graced me with thy company?

KING RICHARD

Faith, none but Humfrey Hower, that called your grace

163 **stayed for** awaited the coming of (*OED v.*[1] 14), here referring to the labour of childbirth
166 **Holy Rood** cross of Christ (see 3.2.74)
169 **Tetchy** peevish, testy (*OED a.* 1; cf. *RJ* 1.3.32)
wayward refractory, disobedient (*OED a.* 1)
170 **frightful** alarming
desperate reckless or violent (*OED a.* II 4a); F elides (desp'rate).
171 *This line appears in Q1–2 and F, and is absent from Q3–6, suggesting the close relationship of FMS and QMS. See p. 446.
prime first age in time, perfection or vigour (*OED sb.*[1] 6, 9); cf. 1.2.250.
172 **age confirmed** i.e. maturity; the historical Richard lived only to 33.
173 **kind in hatred** possibly alluding to Richard's behaviour toward Clarence in 1.1 (Thompson)
174 **comfortable** pleasant (*OED a.* 5a)
176 **Humfrey Hower** never satisfactorily explained (Var); certainly punning on (and an alternative spelling for) *hour* (174). To 'dine with Duke Humphrey' meant to go dinnerless (*OED* dine *v.* 1b), and there was an association with walking in St Paul's church or sitting there in 'the chair of Duke Humphrey' while others were elsewhere eating (Harvey, 1.206; J. Hall, *Satire* III, vii.6–7; Dent, D637). Richard perhaps personifies hunger as Humphrey Hower who summoned his mother to breakfast by 'gracing' her (i.e. calling her *your grace*), leaving Richard alone and thereby providing him a *comfortable* time with her no longer around.

164 torment and in] *F;* anguish, paine and *Qq* 170 desperate] *F (*desp'rate*), Qq* 171] *F, Q1–2; om. Q3–6* 172 sly and bloody] *F;* bloudie, trecherous *Qq* 173] *F; not in Qq* 175 with] *F;* in *Qq* 176] *Qq; F lines Hower*, / Grace /

To breakfast once, forth of my company.
If I be so disgracious in your eye,
Let me march on and not offend you, madam.
Strike up the drum.

DUCHESS I prithee, hear me speak.

KING RICHARD
You speak too bitterly.

DUCHESS Hear me a word,
For I shall never speak to thee again.

KING RICHARD So.

DUCHESS
Either thou wilt die by God's just ordinance
Ere from this war thou turn a conqueror,
Or I with grief and extreme age shall perish
And nevermore behold thy face again.
Therefore take with thee my most grievous curse,

177 **forth of** away from

178 **disgracious** unpleasing

181 David Troughton (88–9) cried out 'desperately' here, deprived of motherly love.

183 **So** George Bernard Shaw observed, 'I would sacrifice anything else in the play sooner than that monosyllable "So"; which tells more of Richard than a dozen stabbings and baby smotherings' (Pierce, 123–4n.); Pierce (115) suggests Richard's 'irony is reduced to a petulant "So" by her measured tones'.

184 **ordinance** divine ordering or dispensation (*OED sb.* 5b), possibly punning on 'implements of war' (*OED* ordnance)

185 **turn** return

188–96 Cf. Richard's mockery of his mother's blessing at 2.2.107–11 (E. Berry, 97). On the early modern dread of the parental curse, see K. Thomas, 505–6. John Barrymore's Richard nervously crossed himself and cowered (Colley, 156); David Troughton's Richard, who curled up with his head in his mother's lap, was shocked by the betrayal of his desire for maternal comfort (88).

188 **grievous** burdensome, pressing heavily (*OED a.* 1a), synonymous with 'heauy' (Qq); appropriate to the curse of fatigue which follows
curse Willis (102) suggests the (relatively) positive nature of cursing here and its ultimately beneficial effect in the ghostly visitations of 5.3.

177 my] *F, Q1–3, 5–6; om. Q4* 178 I] *F, Q1;* it *Q2–3, 5–6; om. Q4* disgracious] *F, Q1–2;* gratious *Q3–6* eye] *F;* sight *Qq* 179 you, madam] *F;* your grace *Qq* 180] *Steevens; F lines* Drumme. / speake. / *; not in Qq, but see 181–2 t.n.* 181] *Steevens; F lines* bitterly. / word: / You . . . bitterly] *F; not in Qq, but see 183 t.n.* 181–2 Hear . . . again] *F;* O heare me speake for I shal neuer see thee *(*the *Q2–4)* more. *Qq* 183] *F;* Come, come, you art *(*are *Q2–6)* too bitter. *Qq* 187 nevermore behold] *F (*neuer more behold*);* neuer looke vpon *Qq* 188 grievous] *F;* heauy *Qq*

Which in the day of battle tire thee more
Than all the complete armour that thou wear'st.
My prayers on the adverse party fight,
And there the little souls of Edward's children
Whisper the spirits of thine enemies
And promise them success and victory.
Bloody thou art; bloody will be thy end.
Shame serves thy life and doth thy death attend. *Exit.*

QUEEN ELIZABETH

Though far more cause, yet much less spirit to curse
Abides in me. I say amen to her.

KING RICHARD

Stay, madam, I must talk a word with you.

QUEEN ELIZABETH

I have no more sons of the royal blood
For thee to slaughter. For my daughters, Richard,
They shall be praying nuns, not weeping queens,
And therefore level not to hit their lives.

KING RICHARD

You have a daughter called Elizabeth,
Virtuous and fair, royal and gracious.

QUEEN ELIZABETH

And must she die for this? O, let her live,
And I'll corrupt her manners, stain her beauty,

189 **tire** i.e. let it tire; perhaps a pun on 'attire' continued in 190 (Lull).

190 **complete armour** còmplete armour; contrasted with the foot-soldier's partial armour or brigander (cf. 3.5.0.1–2n.)

192–4 See 5.3.146–53.

193 **Whisper** whisper to (subjunctive)

196 Shame is personified as an attendant who *serves* Richard during his life and who anticipates (*OED* attend *v.* III 15) 'attending' him in death.

202 **nuns** Elizabeth's third daughter, Bridget, was a nun (Holinshed, 3.711).

203 **level** aim (*OED* *v.*[1] II 6, 7a), with a weapon

205 ***gracious.** F's '?' could serve for either an exclamation mark or a question mark. RP suggests the comic potential of an interrogatory tone here. Qq's full stop is more neutral.

193 spirits] *F, Q1–3, 5–6;* spirit *Q4* 195 art] *F, Q1–5;* art, and *Q6* be] *F, Q1–4, 6;* by *Q5* 198 her] *F;* all *Qq* 199 talk] *F;* speake *Qq* 200 more] *F, Q2–6;* moe *Q1* 201 slaughter.] *F;* murther *Q1;* murther, *Q2–6* 205 gracious.] *Qq;* Gracious? *F*

Slander myself as false to Edward's bed,
Throw over her the veil of infamy.
So she may live unscarred of bleeding slaughter,
I will confess she was not Edward's daughter.

KING RICHARD
Wrong not her birth. She is a royal princess.

QUEEN ELIZABETH
To save her life, I'll say she is not so.

KING RICHARD
Her life is safest only in her birth.

QUEEN ELIZABETH
And only in that safety died her brothers.

KING RICHARD
Lo, at their birth good stars were opposite.

QUEEN ELIZABETH
No, to their lives ill friends were contrary.

KING RICHARD
All unavoided is the doom of destiny.

209 **veil of infamy** Queen Elizabeth suggests protecting her daughter by making her 'shame or disgrace' (*OED* infamy) visible and repulsive; such an outward *veil of infamy* reverses the familiar sense of the veil as concealing shame, disgrace or ugliness (e.g. 'Where beauty's veil doth cover every blot', *Son* 95; *MV* 3.2.98–9). A similar reversal occurs in the description of the young Henry V as having 'obscured his contemplation / Under the veil of wildness' (*H5* 1.1.63–4). See also 8n.

210 **So** i.e. provided that (Abbott, 133)
of i.e. by

211 **confess** A nice irony that false confession may protect rather than destroy one of Richard's victims; contrast the defamation of Hastings (3.5.56–61).

214 **safest only in** i.e. only protected by

215 **only . . . safety** i.e. merely as a result of that protection

216 **Lo** interjection directing attention to what is about to be said (*OED int.*[1])
opposite hostile, opposed; when good stars are opposed, their beneficent effects are neutralized. For astrological 'opposition' among 'evil aspects', see Lilly, 24; cf. 402.

218 Cf. Dent, F83: 'It is impossible to avoid Fate.'
unavoided inevitable (*OED*, citing this line); contrast 4.1.55.

208–9 bed, . . . infamy.] *Pope;* bed: . . . Infamy, *F;* bed . . . infamie, *Q1;* bed, . . . infamie, *Q2–6* 210 of] *F;* from *Qq* 212 a royal princess] *F;* of roiall bloud *Qq* 214 safest only] *F;* onlie safest *Qq* 216 birth] *F;* births *Qq* 217 ill] *F;* bad *Qq*

QUEEN ELIZABETH
True, when avoided grace makes destiny.
My babes were destined to a fairer death,
If grace had blessed thee with a fairer life.
KING RICHARD
You speak as if that I had slain my cousins.
QUEEN ELIZABETH
Cousins indeed, and by their uncle cozened
Of comfort, kingdom, kindred, freedom, life.
Whose hand soever lanched their tender hearts,
Thy head, all indirectly, gave direction.

219–21 Referring to the controversial idea that one might reject God's grace and make one's own damnable destiny, Queen Elizabeth counters both the emphasis on divine predestination in contemporary Calvinism and Richard's assertion of irrefutable destiny by positing the importance of the individual human will in accepting or rejecting God's grace. However, she also reactivates a sense of overriding divine direction by invoking the lives the princes were denied because God's 'grace' had not 'blessed [Richard] with a fairer life'. These complicated lines suggest the compromises of the Elizabethan Church in these matters.

219 **avoided** probably, given the context of 219–21, with an active sense, as in refuted or made to no effect (*OED* avoid 2), rather than merely evaded (as at 3.5.68)

220 **were** i.e. would have been

222–35 *This F only passage displays more melodramatic emotional intensity than Queen Elizabeth's other exchanges with Richard (Hammond, Appendix I). Otherwise cooler and more controlled, she here employs elaborately vituperative rhetorical figures recalling the *Henry VI* plays (see Hodgdon, *End*, 269n.). However, there is verbal consistency in her references to *lambs* and *entrails* (229; see 22–3), so perhaps here she erupts with a *wild grief* implied in her earlier lines. The metaphor of 'Lambes' surrendered to 'the rauenous wolfe' is in the sources (Hall, *Richard III*, fol. xlviii[r]); the play on *indirectly . . . direction*, the analogy equating desperation with a boat out of control and the idea of whetting a knife on one's heart are Shakespearean (see *2H4* 4.5.106–7, *MV* 4.1.123–4). Absence from Qq may represent abbreviation.

222 **that** used as a conjunctional affix (Abbott, 287)

223 **cozened** cheated (*OED* *v.* 1b); cf. Dent, C739.

225 **Whose hand soever** i.e. whosoever's hand
lanched lanced, pierced (*OED* launch 1; lanch); cf. Edmund's 'lancht' arm (*KL* 2.1.51). Lull suggests discrepancy with claims that the princes were smothered (4.3.17, 4.4.134).

226 **all** altogether
indirectly by suggestion rather than in express terms (*OED* 2b), or wrongfully (*OED* 1b)
indirectly . . . direction Cf. 'By indirections find directions out' (*Ham* 2.1.63) and 'Yet indirection thereby grows direct' (*KJ* 3.1.202).

222–35] *F; not in Qq*

No doubt the murderous knife was dull and blunt
Till it was whetted on thy stone-hard heart,
To revel in the entrails of my lambs.
But that still use of grief makes wild grief tame,
My tongue should to thy ears not name my boys
Till that my nails were anchored in thine eyes,
And I in such a desperate bay of death,
Like a poor bark of sails and tackling reft,
Rush all to pieces on thy rocky bosom.

KING RICHARD

Madam, so thrive I in my enterprise
And dangerous success of bloody wars,
As I intend more good to you and yours
Than ever you and yours by me were harmed.

QUEEN ELIZABETH

What good is covered with the face of heaven,

227 **murderous** F elides to 'murd'rous'.

227–8 **knife . . . heart** Cf. 'Thou hid'st a thousand daggers in thy thoughts, / Which thou hast whetted on thy stony heart' (*2H4* 4.5.106–7; cf. *MV* 4.1.123–4) and Dent, H311.

229 **revel** Richard's knife first *dull and blunt*, then whetted to an edge by his hard heart to *revel* (i.e. make merry, *OED v.*[1] 1) in the entrails of the children renders infanticide grotesquely sexual. Cf. 1.2.177–81n., male arousal as a keen edge (*Ham* 3.2.242–3) and *Cym* 3.4.93.

230 **still** constant (Abbott, 69)

232 For threats to use finger nails, see *2H6* 1.3.141–2, *MND* 3.2.298.

233–5 The ship bereft of tackling and wildly tossed toward destruction is a common Petrarchan image for love's desperation; see Petrarch, *Rime* 189, Thomas Wyatt's 'My galley charged with forgetfulness' and the suicidal Romeo (*RJ* 5.3.117–18).

233 **desperate** F elides ('desp'rate').
bay inlet of water (*OED sb.*[2] 1), as in the following image of the ship; or the final extremity of a hunted animal turned at bay to face the pursuing hounds (*OED sb.*[4] 3)

234 **bark** boat
reft bereft, robbed (*OED* reave *v.*[1])

236–8 **so thrive I . . . As I intend** i.e. may I prevail . . . to the extent that I intend; cf. 397-8.

237 **dangerous success** hazardous result (*OED* success *sb.* 1a)

239 ***and** Many editors prefer 'or' (Q1–5); 'and' (Q6, F) maintains parallelism with 238 (*you and yours*) in a play 'where one line is often exactly balanced against another' (Walton, *Copy*, 25). Alternatively, compositors of Q6 and of F may have assimilated 239 to 238 (RP).

240 **covered . . . heaven** i.e. is to be found anywhere under heaven

227 murderous] *F (*murd'rous*)* 233 desperate] *F (*desp'rate*)* 236–7] *F;* Madam, so thriue *I* in my dangerous attempt of hostile armes *Qq* 238 I intend] *F, Q1–5;* Intend *Q6* 239 and] *F, Q6;* or *Q1–5* by . . . harmed] *F;* were by me wrongd *Qq*

To be discovered, that can do me good?

KING RICHARD

Th'advancement of your children, gentle lady.

QUEEN ELIZABETH

Up to some scaffold, there to lose their heads.

KING RICHARD

Unto the dignity and height of fortune,
The high imperial type of this earth's glory.

QUEEN ELIZABETH

Flatter my sorrow with report of it:
Tell me what state, what dignity, what honour,
Canst thou demise to any child of mine?

KING RICHARD

Even all I have – ay, and myself and all –
Will I withal endow a child of thine;
So in the Lethe of thy angry soul
Thou drown the sad remembrance of those wrongs
Which thou supposest I have done to thee.

241 **discovered** i.e. uncovered, revealed

242 **advancement** Richard echoes Queen Elizabeth's attack upon him (1.3.74).

243 reminiscent of Richard's own brand of humour, as in offering to *deliver* Clarence or *lie for* him (1.1.115)

245 **imperial** having the rank or authority of a supreme ruler (*OED a.* 4)
type symbol, emblem (*OED sb.*[1] 1a) and/or summit (*OED* tipe *sb.*[1] 2; literally, cupola or dome: *sb.*[1] 1). Cf. 'high tipe [type, Holinshed] of his honor' (Hall, *Edward IV*, fol. cxcix[r]). The royal position is both emblem and acme of earthly glory.

246 **Flatter** falsely indulge

247 **state** high status, exalted position (*OED sb.* II 16)

248 **demise** convey, transmit (*OED v.* 2, citing this line); perhaps the conveying or transferring of a title, as by the death or abdication of a sovereign (Jones, *Origins*, 223)

250 **withal** On placement of 'withal', see Abbott, 196.
thine Richard shifts pronouns as he begins his earnest appeal (Abbott, 231).

251 **So** provided that
Lethe river of the classical underworld whose waters produced forgetfulness (Virgil, *Aeneid*, 6.713–15)

242 Th'advancement] *F; Qq (*The aduancement*)* gentle] *F;* mightie *Qq* 244 Unto] *F;* No to *Qq* fortune] *F;* honor *Qq* 245 high] *F, Q1;* height *Q2–6* 246 sorrow] *F;* sorrowes *Qq* 249 ay] *F (*I*);* yea *Qq*

QUEEN ELIZABETH
Be brief, lest that the process of thy kindness
Last longer telling than thy kindness' date.

KING RICHARD
Then know that from my soul I love thy daughter.

QUEEN ELIZABETH
My daughter's mother thinks it with her soul.

KING RICHARD What do you think?

QUEEN ELIZABETH
That thou dost love my daughter from thy soul;
So from thy soul's love didst thou love her brothers,
And from my heart's love I do thank thee for it.

KING RICHARD
Be not so hasty to confound my meaning:
I mean that with my soul I love thy daughter
And do intend to make her queen of England.

QUEEN ELIZABETH
Well then, who dost thou mean shall be her king?

KING RICHARD
Even he that makes her queen. Who else should be?

254–5 **process . . . date** *process* may mean 'narration' (see 4.3.32), but 'the proceedings in any action at law' (*OED sb.* 7a) seems likely, given surrounding legal discourse, from *demise* (248) to *date*. Compare 'date', 'term', 'forfeit' and 'suit' together in *RJ* 1.4.108–13.

255 **date** duration (*OED sb.* 4)

258 Richard's need to have a stichomythic response explained to him should be related to various changes, including diminished verbal acuity, that have come over him since his enthronement in 4.2; cf. his need to self-explicate at 263.

259–61 **from . . . from . . . from** Elizabeth plays on Richard's 'from my soul I love thy daughter', taking his *from* to mean 'apart from' (Abbott, 158). Her verbal capacity matches Richard in aggressiveness, if not deviousness. On her amphibology, see Kehler, 118–20.

263 **I mean** For the third time since his crowning, Richard appears compelled to explain his own utterances; cf. 4.2.18, 74.

255 date] *F;* doe *Qq* 256] *Qq; F lines* know, / Daughter. / 259 soul;] *F4 subst.;* soule *F;* soule, *Qq* 260 soul's love] *F, Q1–5;* soule *Q6* thou love] *F, Q1, 6;* thou *Q2–5* 264 do intend] *F;* meane *Qq* 265 Well] *F;* Saie *Qq* 266] *Qq; F lines* Queene: / bee? / Who . . . be] *F;* who should be else *Q1;* who should else *Q2–4, 6;* how should else *Q5*

QUEEN ELIZABETH
What, thou?
KING RICHARD Even so. How think you of it?
QUEEN ELIZABETH
How canst thou woo her?
KING RICHARD That would I learn of you,
As one being best acquainted with her humour.
QUEEN ELIZABETH
And wilt thou learn of me?
KING RICHARD Madam, with all my heart.
QUEEN ELIZABETH
Send to her, by the man that slew her brothers,
A pair of bleeding hearts; thereon engrave
'Edward' and 'York'. Then haply will she weep.
Therefore present to her – as sometime Margaret
Did to thy father, steeped in Rutland's blood –
A handkerchief, which say to her did drain
The purple sap from her sweet brother's body,
And bid her wipe her weeping eyes withal.
If this inducement move her not to love,
Send her a letter of thy noble deeds:
Tell her thou mad'st away her uncle Clarence,

268 ***would I** Most recent editors prefer 'would I' (Q1–2) to 'I would' (Q3–6, F).
269 **humour** disposition (*OED sb.* II 5b); here with more the sense of a settled and characteristic temperament than in 1.2.230–1 or 4.1.64
270 **And** used to suggest emphatic interrogation; i.e. 'Do you indeed wish to learn of me?' (Abbott, 99).
273 **haply** perhaps
274 **sometime** once (*OED adv.* 2b); 'sometime' (Q3–6, F) seems preferable to Q1–2, 7–8's 'sometimes' since the remark concerns a single action; however, 'sometimes' could have this meaning (*OED adv.* 2a).
275–7 *See pp. 446–7.
275 **Rutland's blood** See 1.3.176–7 and *3H6* 1.4.78–83.

267–8] *Steevens; F lines* thou? / it? / her? / you, / ; *Qq line* thou? / Maddame? / her? / you. / 267 Even so] *F;* I euen I *Qq* How] *F;* what *Qq* it] *F;* it Maddame *Qq* 268 would I] *Q1–2;* I would *Q3–6, F* 269 being] *F;* that are *Q1–2;* that were *Q3–6* 270] *Steevens; F, Qq line* me? / heart. / 273 haply will she] *F;* happelie she wil *Qq* 274 sometime] *F, Q3–6;* sometimes *Q1–2, 7–8* 275–7] *F;* Did to thy father, a handkercher steept in Rutlands bloud, *Qq subst.* 278 wipe . . . withal] *F;* drie . . . therewith *Qq* 279 move] *F;* force *Qq* 280 letter . . . deeds] *F;* storie . . . acts *Qq* 281 mad'st] *F, Q3–6; Q1 (*madst*); Q2 (*madest*)*

Her uncle Rivers, ay, and for her sake
Mad'st quick conveyance with her good aunt Anne.

KING RICHARD

You mock me, madam. This [Q]is[Q] not the way
To win your daughter.

QUEEN ELIZABETH There is no other way,
Unless thou couldst put on some other shape
And not be Richard, that hath done all this.

KING RICHARD

Say that I did all this for love of her.

QUEEN ELIZABETH

Nay, then indeed she cannot choose but hate thee,
Having bought love with such a bloody spoil.

KING RICHARD

Look what is done cannot be now amended.
Men shall deal unadvisedly sometimes,
Which after-hours gives leisure to repent.
If I did take the kingdom from your sons,
To make amends, I'll give it to your daughter.
If I have killed the issue of your womb,
To quicken your increase I will beget

283 **conveyance** removal (*OED sb.*[1] 3, citing this line); often with a sense of contrivance and trickery (cf. *1H6* 1.3.2)

288–342 *In this F only passage, Richard briefly revisits his verbal strategies of 1.2: he offers the excuse of doing everything for love, and then rapidly returns to wooing.

289–90 These lines cast intense disapproval on Anne's acquiescence in 1.2 (cf. 4.1.65–9).

289 **cannot choose but** i.e. must, of necessity (cf. *MW* 5.3.17)

290 **spoil** damage, plunder (*OED sb.* 7, 3)

291 Cf. Dent, T200 ('Things done cannot be undone') and *Mac* 5.1.69.
Look what i.e. whatever (*OED* look *v.* 4b), an indefinite relative rather than an imperative

292 **Men shall** expressing necessity, i.e. men must (Abbott, 315)
deal unadvisedly act imprudently – quite a euphemism, given the magnitude of the crimes to which it refers

293 **Which** i.e. which dealing

297 **quicken your increase** i.e. bring your offspring to life (*OED* increase *sb.* 2b)

282 ay] *F (I); yea Qq* 283 Mad'st] *F; Q1 (*Madst*), Q2–6 (*Madest*)* 284 You] *F;* Come, come, you *(*ye *Q3–6) Qq* me, madam] *F;* me *Qq* 285] *Steevens; F, Qq line* daughter. / way, / 288–342] *F; not in Qq*

Mine issue of your blood upon your daughter.
A grandam's name is little less in love
Than is the doting title of a mother.
They are as children but one step below,
Even of your metal, of your very blood,
Of all one pain, save for a night of groans
Endured of her for whom you bid like sorrow.
Your children were vexation to your youth,
But mine shall be a comfort to your age.
The loss you have is but a son being king,
And by that loss your daughter is made queen.
I cannot make you what amends I would;
Therefore accept such kindness as I can.
Dorset your son, that with a fearful soul
Leads discontented steps in foreign soil,
This fair alliance quickly shall call home
To high promotions and great dignity.
The king that calls your beauteous daughter wife
Familiarly shall call thy Dorset brother.
Again shall you be mother to a king,

301 **one step below** one grade or degree (*OED* step *sb.*[1] 8a) removed genealogically from being your own children

302 **metal** substance, character (*OED sb.* 1f)

303–4 Her grandchildren, Richard claims, will demand the same trouble and efforts from her as they would from their mother, excepting only the night of labour pains their mother will suffer, but Queen Elizabeth herself underwent similar painful labour for her own daughter's birth.

303 **pain** trouble, effort (*OED sb.*[1] 5, 6)

304 **bid** underwent, suffered (past tense of bide, *OED* 9)

307 **son being king** i.e. son's occupation of the office of king

309 **would** i.e. would wish

310 **can** am able to provide

311–14 The promise to advance Dorset appears in Richard's offers (Hall, *Richard III*, fol. xlviii[r]). However, after leaving sanctuary, Dorset did not go directly to Richmond (as in 4.1.38–51, 91; 4.2.48–9), but gathered forces in Yorkshire to help Buckingham (Hall, *Richard III*, fol. xxxviii[v]). After Buckingham's rebellion failed, Dorset fled to Richmond (see 518).

312 **foreign soil** i.e. Brittany (cf. 4.1.42)

316 **Familiarly** i.e. in the manner of an intimate acquaintance, but suggesting pertaining to one's family (*OED* familiar *a.* 1a)
brother Richard eases himself, rhetorically at least, from the generation of Dorset's mother, to that of her son (and daughter) (Lull); cf. his *mother* at 317, 325, 412.

317 **Again** Elizabeth had already been mother to one king, the uncrowned Edward V.

And all the ruins of distressful times
Repaired with double riches of content.
What! We have many goodly days to see.
The liquid drops of tears that you have shed
Shall come again, transformed to orient pearl,
Advantaging their love with interest
Of ten times double gain of happiness.
Go then, my mother; to thy daughter go.
Make bold her bashful years with your experience;
Prepare her ears to hear a wooer's tale;
Put in her tender heart th'aspiring flame
Of golden sovereignty; acquaint the princess
With the sweet silent hours of marriage joys;
And when this arm of mine hath chastised
The petty rebel, dull-brained Buckingham,
Bound with triumphant garlands will I come
And lead thy daughter to a conqueror's bed;
To whom I will retail my conquest won,
And she shall be sole victoress, Caesar's Caesar.

QUEEN ELIZABETH

What were I best to say? Her father's brother

318–22 **ruins . . . times . . . riches . . . pearl** Perhaps ironically recalling the *wracks*, *times*, *stones* and *heaps of pearl* from Clarence's dream (1.4.14–26).

320 **What!** interjection introducing an exclamation or question (*OED* B I 1)

322 **orient** lustrous, shining

323 i.e. increasing the value of the love that inspired them; the 'advantage' is a name for the favourable terms received by a lender (cf. *MV* 1.3.68). Theobald conjectured that F's 'Loue' should be 'Lone' (i.e. loan).

330 **silent** i.e. either performed in silence (*OED* 3a), or perhaps not to be spoken of because the *joys* are sexual? Either way, the insinuation is sexual, as Richard urges making 'bold her bashful years' (326) and invokes the *conqueror's bed* (334).

331 **chastised** chastisèd

332 **dull-brained Buckingham** Cf. Buckingham's place among 'simple gulls' (1.3.327–8); but Richard's other (sarcastic?) references to 'deep-revolving, witty Buckingham' are less securely dismissive (4.2.31, 42).

335 **retail** recount; but for a commercial sense cf. 3.1.77n. and 3.1.86n. on *valure*

336 **Caesar's Caesar** Cf. 'our great captain's captain' (*Oth* 2.1.74) and 'Our general's wife is now the general' (*Oth* 2.3.309–10).

337–8 The nomenclatural problem underlines the violation of incest taboos; see

324 Of ten times] *Theobald;* Often-times *F*

Would be her lord? Or shall I say her uncle?
Or he that slew her brothers and her uncles?
Under what title shall I woo for thee,
That God, the law, my honour and her love
Can make seem pleasing to her tender years?

KING RICHARD
Infer fair England's peace by this alliance.

QUEEN ELIZABETH
Which she shall purchase with still lasting war.

KING RICHARD
Tell her the King, that may command, entreats.

QUEEN ELIZABETH
That at her hands, which the King's King forbids.

KING RICHARD
Say she shall be a high and mighty queen.

QUEEN ELIZABETH
To vail the title, as her mother doth.

KING RICHARD
Say I will love her everlastingly.

QUEEN ELIZABETH
But how long shall that title 'ever' last?

KING RICHARD
Sweetly in force, unto her fair life's end.

McCabe, 158 (cf. 1.1.156n.). Richard's historical advisers (Catesby and Ratcliffe) were uneasy about public reaction to such a marriage (C. Ross, *Richard*, 145–6).

343 **Infer** adduce (*OED v.* 2); cf. 3.5.75.

344 **still lasting** eternal

345 Cf. 'I entreat where I may command; commaunde thou, where thou shouldest entreate' (Lyly, *Sapho*, 4.2.23–5).

346 **King's King forbids** The marriage would be forbidden by God as violating prohibitions on marriage between uncle and niece (see Leviticus, 18.16–17). The *Book of Common Prayer* prohibited marriage to a 'Brother's Daughter' (Noble, 137). The phrase recalls 1.4.194–9.

348 **vail** abase, lower (*OED v.*[2] 4a); perhaps abandon; *vail* (F) preserves the play on *high* (347), unlike Qq's 'waile'.

349–50 Cf. Orlando's professions of love 'forever and a day' and Rosalind's searching responses (*AYL* 4.2.135–9).

351 **in force** operative

351, 352 **fair, fairly** happy, happily

343 this] *F, Q1–3, 5;* tuis *Q4;* his *Q6* 345 Tell her] *F;* Saie that *Qq* that] *F;* which *Qq* 346 forbids] *F, Q1;* forbid *Q2–6* 348 vail] *F;* waile *Qq* 350 'ever'] *Dyce, after Theobald (*, ever,*);* euer *F, Q1–4, 6; om. Q5*

QUEEN ELIZABETH
But how long fairly shall her sweet life last?
KING RICHARD
As long as heaven and nature lengthens it.
QUEEN ELIZABETH
As long as hell and Richard likes of it.
KING RICHARD
Say I, her sovereign, am her subject low.
QUEEN ELIZABETH
But she, your subject, loathes such sovereignty.
KING RICHARD
Be eloquent in my behalf to her.
QUEEN ELIZABETH
An honest tale speeds best being plainly told.
KING RICHARD
Then plainly to her tell my loving tale.
QUEEN ELIZABETH
Plain and not honest is too harsh a style.
KING RICHARD
Your reasons are too shallow and too quick.
QUEEN ELIZABETH
O no, my reasons are too deep and dead,
Too deep and dead, poor infants, in their graves.
KING RICHARD
Harp not on that string, madam; that is past.

353–4 **lengthens . . . likes** a singular verb used with a compound subject; cf. 4.1.39.
354 **likes of** likes; on 'of' after 'like', see Abbott, 177.
358 Cf. 'Truth's tale is simple' (Dent, T593).
speeds succeeds (*OED v.* 2a)
361 **shallow** trivial, superficial; cf. 431n.
361–2 **quick . . . dead** taking Richard's *quick* as if it meant 'living' instead of 'hasty'
364 *This line appears after 365 in F and is omitted from Q2–8. F's misplaced insertion of a line exclusive to Q1 constitutes strong evidence that F was set from quarto copy collated against a manuscript. See pp. 445–6.

352 her sweet life] *F, Q1–2;* that title *Q3–6* 353, 354 As] *F;* So *Qq* 355 low] *F;* loue *Qq* 359 plainly . . . tell] *F;* in plaine termes tell her *Qq* 361 Your] *F;* Madame your *Qq* 363 graves] *F;* graue *Qq* 364] *Q1; after 365 F; om. Q2–6* on] *F;* one *Q1*

QUEEN ELIZABETH
Harp on it still shall I, till heart-strings break.

KING RICHARD
Now by my George, my Garter and my crown –

QUEEN ELIZABETH
Profaned, dishonoured and the third usurped.

KING RICHARD
I swear –

QUEEN ELIZABETH By nothing, for this is no oath:
Thy George, profaned, hath lost his lordly honour;
Thy Garter, blemished, pawned his knightly virtue;
Thy crown, usurped, disgraced his kingly glory.
If something thou wouldst swear to be believed,
Swear then by something that thou hast not wronged.

KING RICHARD
Then by myself –

QUEEN ELIZABETH Thyself is self-misused.

KING RICHARD
Now by the world –

Harp . . . string proverbial (Dent, S934); used by More (*CW*2, 36; cf. Hall, *Edward V*, fol. xi^{r-v}).

365 **heart-strings** nerves supposed to sustain the heart (*OED sb. pl.* 1); thus figuratively referring to intense feelings, frequently with allusion to stringed instruments (*OED* 2b, 2c).

366–77 Wilson compares *Leir*, in which reiterated offers of 'I sweare' are rebuffed with 'Sweare not by heauen', 'earth', 'hell' etc. (*Leir*, 1625–33; cf. *RJ* 2.2.107–16).

366 **George . . . Garter** worn by members of the Order of the Garter: the George was a pendant depicting Saint George and the dragon, and the Garter was a blue ribbon worn beneath the left knee. The George did not come in until the Tudor era.

369–71 **his** its; on 'his' as the original possessive or genitive neuter and the rise of 'its' in the 16th and 17th centuries, see *OED* its.

374–7 *Steevens's shared lines emphasize Queen Elizabeth's power to interrupt Richard with negations. Hammond asserts the 'rhetorical hierarchy' of Qq's failed oaths (by world, father's death, self, God), but F's oaths by self, world, father's death and heaven enforce a clear progress in the

365 SP] *F, Q1 (Qu.); King Q2; om. Q3–6* 366 crown –] *Rowe;* Crowne. *F, Qq* 368] *Steevens; F lines* sweare. / Oath: / swear –] *Collier, after Capell (*swear:*); sweare. F;* sweare by nothing. *Qq* 369, 370, 371 Thy] *F;* The *Qq* 369 lordly] *F;* holie *Qq* 371 glory] *F;* dignitie *Qq* 372 wouldst] *F;* wilt *Qq* 374–7] *in 4 lines as Steevens; F lines* Selfe. / selfe-misvs'd. / World. / wrongs. / death. / dishonor'd. / Heauen. / all: / ; *Qq line* world. / wrongs. / death. / dishonord. / selfe. / misusest. / God. / all, / 374] *F; King.* Then by my selfe. / *Qu.* Thy selfe, thy selfe misusest. *Qq after 376*

QUEEN ELIZABETH 'Tis full of thy foul wrongs.
KING RICHARD
My father's death –
QUEEN ELIZABETH Thy life hath it dishonoured.
KING RICHARD
Why then, by God.
QUEEN ELIZABETH God's wrong is most of all.
If thou didst fear to break an oath with Him,
The unity the King my husband made
Thou hadst not broken, nor my brothers died.
If thou hadst feared to break an oath by Him,
Th'imperial metal circling now thy head
Had graced the tender temples of my child,
And both the princes had been breathing here,
Which now, too tender bed-fellows for dust,
Thy broken faith hath made the prey for worms.

spiritualization of Richard's references. Richard could conceivably imagine never having wronged himself (as he asserts in F) but not to have left the world unwronged as he claims in Qq (Smidt, *Memorial*, 21).

375 **by the world** a mild oath (see *LLL* 4.3.16)

377 ***God, God's** F prints 'Heaven[s]', according to the directives of 1606; cf. 3.7.218n.

379 **unity** i.e. the reconciliation of contending factions attempted in 2.1

380 **brothers** Earl Rivers is Queen Elizabeth's only brother in this play (cf. 1.3.37n.).

382 **metal** gold (*OED sb.* 1d)

385–6 Cf. Job, 21.26: 'They shal slepe bothe in the dust, & the wormes shal couer them' (Geneva). Cf. Tilley, Dent, M253. Qq's 'plaie-fellowes' plays on the sound of *prey* (386), but makes little sense in relation to dust; however, it does echo a line omitted from Qq at 4.1.101 describing the Tower as 'old sullen playfellow' (Delius, 150).

385 ***too** Qq, F have 'two'; Roderick (223) suggested *too*. McKerrow (*Prolegomena*, 9) considers 'too'/'two' as possibly variant spellings, adducing 'two much credit' (Nashe, 1.134) and 'two liberall' (Nashe, 3.172). *A most straunge, rare, and horrible murther committed by a Frenchman of the age of too or three and twentie yeares* (1586; STC 11377) repeats 'too' for 'two' on its second page, answering McKerrow's worries about mere typographical errors. See Q1/F variants at 100.

375] *F; after 373 Qq* 376 life] *F, Q1–2;* selfe *Q3–6* it] *F;* that *Qq* 377 God] *Qq;* Heauen *F* God's] *Qq;* Heanens *F* 378 didst fear] *F;* hadst feard *Qq* with] *F;* by *Qq* 379 my husband] *F;* my brother *Q1–5, 6u (BL C34 k.51; Bod, Tn, Hn copies);* thy brother *Q6c (other copies)* 380 Thou hadst not] *F;* Had not bene *Qq* brothers died] *F;* brother slaine *Qq* 382 Th'imperial] *F;* The emperiall *Qq* head] *F;* brow *Qq* 385 too] *F, Qq (*two*), Capell (Roderick)* bed-fellows] *F;* plaie-fellowes *Qq* 386 the] *F;* a *Qq* worms] *F, Q1–5;* worme *Q6*

What canst thou swear by now?

KING RICHARD The time to come.

QUEEN ELIZABETH

That thou hast wronged in the time o'erpast;
For I myself have many tears to wash
Hereafter time, for time past wronged by thee.
The children live whose fathers thou hast slaughtered,
Ungoverned youth, to wail it in their age;
The parents live whose children thou hast butchered,
Old barren plants, to wail it with their age.
Swear not by time to come, for that thou hast
Misused ere used, by times ill-used o'erpast.

KING RICHARD

As I intend to prosper and repent,
So thrive I in my dangerous affairs

388 **wronged** wrongèd
o'erpast i.e. already past

390 **Hereafter time** i.e. in the future

391 ***fathers** Queen Elizabeth's list of victims does mention Anne's *conveyance* (283), but since the play makes Anne childless, she would not be included under Qq's 'parents'; therefore F's 'fathers' makes more sense, especially in the light of references to Richard's male victims (339).

392 ***in** Since F's 'with' appears in Q5 and looks half-corrected in Q6 (in the incorrect 'with her'), editors since Pope have generally accepted Q1's 'in', though 'with' would maintain parallels between 392 and 394.

394 ***barren** Qq's 'withered' makes sense, but F's 'barren' maintains the stress on violence to generational continuity while suggesting the female suffering occluded by *fathers* (391). In *LLL* (4.2.28) 'barren plants' refers to a lack of mental capacity.

395–6 Richard cannot swear by the future because he has already compromised it by past wrongs that will continue to have effects in time to come.

396 ***o'erpast** F's 'repast' may be a missetting of 'orepast'.

397–9 **As . . . arms** i.e. 'may I succeed in my dangerous military ventures only insofar as I intend to repent', a parallel to 236–7, but here Richard promises to *repent*. In the light of his subsequent failure to repent, which assures his damnation despite recognition of his sins (5.3.177–206), the irony is obvious. This is the last appearance of the word 'repent'; previously employed hypocritically by Richard (1.2.218, 1.3.306, 4.4.293) and sincerely by the Second Murderer (1.4.277) and Hastings (3.4.87).

387] *Steevens; F lines* now? / come. / What . . . now?] *F; not in Qq* The] *F;* By the *Qq* 388 the] *F; not in Qq* 390 past . . . thee] *F;* by the *(*thee *Q5–6)* past wrongd *Qq* 391 fathers] *F;* parents *Qq* 392 in their] *Q1–4;* with their *F, Q5;* with her *Q6* 394 barren] *F;* withered *Qq* plants] *F, Q1–5;* plaints *Q6* 396 ere] *F, Q6; Q1–3, 5 (*eare*);* nere *Q4* times ill-used] *F;* time misused *Qq* o'erpast] *Qq (*orepast*);* repast *F* 398 affairs] *F;* attempt *Qq*

Of hostile arms. Myself myself confound!
Heaven and fortune bar me happy hours.
Day, yield me not thy light; nor, night, thy rest.
Be opposite all planets of good luck
To my proceeding, if with dear heart's love,
Immaculate devotion, holy thoughts,
I tender not thy beauteous, princely daughter.
In her consists my happiness and thine;
Without her follows to myself and thee,
Herself, the land and many a Christian soul,
Death, desolation, ruin and decay.
It cannot be avoided but by this;
It will not be avoided but by this.
Therefore, dear mother – I must call you so –
Be the attorney of my love to her:
Plead what I will be, not what I have been;
Not my deserts, but what I will deserve.

399–405 **Myself . . . daughter**. Richard details ill-effects that should be visited upon him if he should fail dearly to love Queen Elizabeth's daughter. Once again, a curse will prove accurate. Holland notes that this curse-filled scene gives Richard's self-curse a concluding prominence. Birney (36–42) traces the steps to Richard's self-cursing: Margaret weaves together the women's objections and advises how to curse, and then the Duchess of York echoes Margaret's curses from 1.3 in cursing Richard (184–96); but Queen Elizabeth avoids the cursing mode and traps Richard into cursing himself by depriving him of things to swear by.

399 **Myself myself confound** *confound* = bring to ruin. Cf. 'he himself himself confounds' (*Luc* 160) and Lucrece's curse on Tarquin: 'Himself himself seek every hour to kill!' (998); cf. 5.3.186–7.

400 **bar** prohibit, prevent (*OED v.* 7)

402 **opposite** opposed, hostile; see 216.

404 Richard's religious language recalls his hypocritical portrayal as *holy and devout*, engaged in *holy exercise* of *meditation* (3.7.91, 61–3).

Immaculate unsullied, pure

405 **tender** treat with tenderness (*OED v.*^{2} 3a)

princely royal (*OED a.* 1a)

406 **consists** i.e. exists, is comprised (*OED* consist *v.* 6a)

412 **dear mother** Richard attempts to 're-mother' himself after being cursed (188–96) by his own mother (Hodgdon, *End*, 108).

413 **attorney** i.e. advocate; cf. 5.3.83. *Plead* (414) continues the legal language.

400] *F; not in Qq* 403 proceeding] *F;* proceedings *Qq* dear] *F;* pure *Qq* 404 Immaculate] *F, Q1;* Immaculatd *Q2;* Immaculated *Q3–6* 405 tender] *F, Q1, 2, 4;* render *Q3, 5–6* 407 myself and thee] *F;* this land and me *Qq* 408 Herself, the land] *F;* To thee her selfe *Qq* 409 Death,] *F;* Sad *Qq* 411 by this] *F, Q2–6;* this *Q1* 412 dear] *F;* good *Qq* 415 my] *F;* by *Qq*

Urge the necessity and state of times,
And be not peevish found in great designs.

QUEEN ELIZABETH

Shall I be tempted of the devil thus?

KING RICHARD

Ay, if the devil tempt you to do good.

QUEEN ELIZABETH

Shall I forget myself to be myself?

KING RICHARD

Ay, if your self's remembrance wrong yourself.

QUEEN ELIZABETH

Yet thou didst kill my children.

KING RICHARD

But in your daughter's womb I bury them,
Where, in that nest of spicery, they will breed

416 **state of times** present conditions

417 i.e. do not be found to be merely foolish when great plans demand more. Cf. 'have great care / I be not found a talker' (*H8* 2.3.76–7); 'peevish-fond' (Malone) could mean wilfully silly. **great designs** important undertakings

418–19 Citing Christ's temptation in the wilderness (Matthew, 4.1–10, Luke, 4.1–13), Hammond notes that Satan can urge things not necessarily evil, but can only tempt one to 'do good' if, to his limited perception, evil will result. Satan's efforts are, according to Calvin, part of the divine plan (Calvin, *Institutes*, 1.18.1–2, 2.4.2–7). Richard remarkably, if hypothetically, admits his satanic nature (Hammond).

418 **tempted . . . devil** Shaheen refers to Jesus 'tempted of the deuyll' (Matthew, 4.1; cf. Luke, 4.2). For another possible echo of this biblical passage, see 1.2.46n.

420–1 Queen Elizabeth asks if she should forget who she is (by succumbing to Richard's temptations); Richard replies that she should, if remembering her identity causes her harm.

423 Cf. Richard's attack on his brother's marriage to Elizabeth: 'But in your bride you bury brotherhood' (*3H6* 4.1.55). ***bury** Q1–2's past tense ('buried') is an obvious error; Q3 'burie' (F 'bury') uses the present tense for the future (as Q4–8's 'Ile burie'). The unusual agreement of Q3 and F against all other Qq argues for Q3 copy for the whole of F (Walton, *Copy*, 39; but contrast Hammond, 37).

424 **nest of spicery** Steevens suggests allusion to the nest of the phoenix, built of aromatic boughs and from which the new bird arises out of the ashes of the old one (Ovid, *Metamorphoses*, 15.391–407). While the scarcely euphemized anatomical specificity of Richard's words

417 peevish found] *F;* pieuish, fond *Q1–2;* peeuish fond *Q3–6* 419 you] *F;* thee *Qq* 422 Yet] *F;* But *Qq* 423 I bury] *F, Q3;* I buried *Q1–2;* Ile burie *Q4–6* them,] *Qq;* them. *F* 424 they will] *F;* they shall *Q1–2;* there shall *Q3–6*

Selves of themselves, to your recomforture.

QUEEN ELIZABETH

Shall I go win my daughter to thy will?

KING RICHARD

And be a happy mother by the deed.

QUEEN ELIZABETH

I go, write to me very shortly,
And you shall understand from me her mind.

KING RICHARD

Bear her my true love's kiss; and so farewell.

Exit Queen [*Elizabeth*].

to the girl's mother is grotesque in itself, a further irony is that his dying father predicted Richard himself as a hideous phoenix: 'My ashes, as the phoenix, may bring forth / A bird that will revenge upon you all' (*3H6* 1.4.35–6).

425 **recomforture** consolation, comfort (*OED*, citing this line)

426–31 The reaction of the play's Queen Elizabeth has prompted different interpretations, although the historical sources all have her accept Richard's offers (exchanged by messengers), thereby demonstrating female 'inconstancie', since 'women of the verie bonde of nature will folowe their awne kynde' (Hall, *Richard III*, fol. xlviii^r; cf. Holinshed, 3.750). A 17th-century Folio reader judges her 'ouercome at last' (Yamada, 159). Tillyard credits Richard's assessment of Elizabeth as a *Relenting fool* (431), assuming that she again changes her mind once offstage (*History Plays*, 214). Thompson adduces '*varium et mutabile semper femina*' ('woman is always various and changeable', Virgil, *Aeneid*, 4.569–70). But Richard rapidly changes his own mind at 456 (Johnson), and Shakespeare may '[displace] those attributes the chronicler ascribes to the Queen onto Richard' (Hodgdon, *End*, 109–10). Richard also misjudges the Messenger (Sprague, *Histories*, 139; cf. *True Tragedy*, 1425–60). Cibber's Elizabeth explains herself to the audience as only 'seemingly comply[ing]' (*Richard III*, 4.4.114–16). See pp. 62, 89, and 430n.

426–7 **will . . . deed** These lines hinge on 'daughter'/'mother' and 'will'/'deed' oppositions; the *deed* of winning her daughter over to his *will* recalls her opposition of *hand* to *head* (225–6), accusing Richard of planning and fomenting deeds physically perpetrated by others.

429 **you** Despite Richard's repeated, sometimes rapid, alternations between 'you' and 'thee' in addressing Queen Elizabeth (e.g. 316–17, 325–6), this is her first use of the more respectful 'you' form, as if to assure him of her acquiescence (Brown, 113).

430 **kiss** Richard may actually kiss Queen Elizabeth, or he may simply wish her to convey a sentiment. The entire exchange takes place while the army stands waiting for its leader. The Sher–Alexander production made Elizabeth (Frances Tomelty) the physical aggressor and left Richard surprised (Colley, 243; Day, 203). Susan

425 recomforture] *F; Qq (*recomfiture*)* 429] *F; not in Qq* 430 and so] *F; not in Qq* SD] *Exit Qu. Q3–6; Exit Q. opp. 429 F; Exit. Q1–2*

Relenting fool, and shallow, changing woman.

Enter RATCLIFFE.

How now, what news?

RATCLIFFE

Most mighty sovereign, on the western coast
Rideth a puissant navy. To our shores
Throng many doubtful hollow-hearted friends,
Unarmed and unresolved to beat them back.
'Tis thought that Richmond is their admiral,
And there they hull, expecting but the aid
Of Buckingham to welcome them ashore.

KING RICHARD

Some light-foot friend post to the Duke of Norfolk:
Ratcliffe, thyself – or Catesby. Where is he?

CATESBY

Here, my good lord.

KING RICHARD Catesby, fly to the Duke.

Brown's Elizabeth in the Pimlott production was surprised by Richard's kiss on her lips rather than upon the hand she had offered, and once out of his vision wiped the kiss from her lips (Brown, 113).

430 SD *F prints Queen Elizabeth's exit at the end of 429, which might indicate her beginning to leave before Richard's offer of a kiss, but F's 430 runs nearly to the margin, leaving no space even for '*Exit Q.*' F's 431 is the final line on the page, with a catchword immediately below it; thus, the SD at 429 appears to be a turn-up from 430.

431 **shallow** cf. 361; used with similar irony when Hastings trivializes Stanley's premonitions (3.2.24) and Richard dismisses the threat of Richmond (5.3.219). Elizabeth perhaps performs 'shallowness' as Brutus enacts a 'shallow habit' of affability (*Luc* 1814) – an outer show concealing inner resistance. Simon Russell Beale hesitated on 'sh-shallow' as if betraying Richard's disbelief in this judgement (Day, 171).

434 **Rideth** lies at anchor (*OED v.* II 7a) **puissant** powerful

435 **doubtful** untrustworthy or apprehensive

438 **hull** drift with furled sails (*OED v.*[2] 1)

440 **light-foot** nimble, light-footed (*OED* 1)

431.1] *after 432 F; opp. 431 Qq (Enter Rat.)* 432] *F; not in Qq* 433 Most mighty] *F;* My gracious *Qq* 434 our shores] *F;* the shore *Qq* 438 they] *F, Q1, 3–6;* thy *Q2* 442] *Steevens; F lines* Lord. / Duke. / ; *Qq line* Lord. / Salisburie. / good] *F; not in Qq* Catesby] *F; not in Qq*

CATESBY
I will, my lord, with all convenient haste.

KING RICHARD
Ratcliffe, come hither. Post to Salisbury.
When thou com'st thither –
[*to Catesby*] Dull unmindful villain,
Why stay'st thou here, and go'st not to the Duke?

CATESBY
First, mighty liege, tell me your highness' pleasure,
What from your grace I shall deliver to him.

KING RICHARD
O true, good Catesby. Bid him levy straight
The greatest strength and power that he can make
And meet me suddenly at Salisbury.

CATESBY I go. *Exit.*

RATCLIFFE
What, may it please you, shall I do at Salisbury?

KING RICHARD
Why, what wouldst thou do there before I go?

RATCLIFFE
Your highness told me I should post before.

KING RICHARD
My mind is changed.

443 **convenient** suitable to the conditions (*OED a.* 4b)
449 **levy straight** raise immediately
451 **Salisbury** city south-west of London in Wiltshire; since Richmond is off the south-western coast, Richard hastens to Salisbury to prevent the junction of Richmond with Buckingham's forces from Wales. On the temporal compression in the play, see 531–3n.
456 *Qq's repetition is unusual, especially in close proximity to another instance (466). Editors have often attributed these features to stage practice.

443–4 CATESBY . . . hither.] *F; not in Qq* 444 Ratcliffe] *Rowe; Catesby F* Post] *F;* post thou *Qq* 445 com'st thither] *F;* comst (comest *Q2–6)* there *Qq* SD] *Rowe* villain] *F, Q1–5;* villanie *Q6* 446 stay'st] *F;* standst *Q1–3, 5–6;* stands *Q4* here] *F;* still *Qq* 447 liege . . . pleasure] *F;* Soueraigne, let me know your minde *Qq* 448 to him] *F;* them *Q1–2;* him *Q3–6* 450 that] *F; not in Qq* 451 suddenly] *F;* presentlie *Qq* 452, 452 SD] *F; not in Qq* 453 may . . . I] *F;* is it your highnes pleasure, I shall *Q1–4;* it is your highnes pleasure I shal *Q5;* is your highnesse pleasure, I shal *Q6* 454 wouldst] *F, Q1–3, 5–6;* woulds *Q4* 456] *Capell; F, Qq line* changd: / you? / changed] *F;* changd sir, my minde is changd. *Qq* SD] *F; Enter Darbie. Q1–2 after 456; Enter Darby. Q3–6 opp. 456* Stanley] *F;* How now *Qq*

Enter Lord STANLEY.

Stanley, what news with you?

STANLEY
None good, my liege, to please you with the hearing,
Nor none so bad but well may be reported.

KING RICHARD
Hoyday, a riddle! Neither good nor bad.
What need'st thou run so many miles about
When thou mayst tell thy tale the nearest way?
Once more, what news?

STANLEY Richmond is on the seas.

KING RICHARD
There let him sink, and be the seas on him,
White-livered runagate. What doth he there?

STANLEY
I know not, mighty sovereign, but by guess.

KING RICHARD
Well, as you guess?

STANLEY
Stirred up by Dorset, Buckingham and Morton,
He makes for England, here to claim the crown.

457 *F4's punctuation supplies an antithesis for *none so bad* in the following line.

457–62 This, Stanley's only circumlocution, may suggest influence of *True Tragedy* (Maguire, 192–3, 374).

459 **Hoyday** hey-day, an exclamation of surprise or gaiety (*OED*), but here conveying irritated impatience

461 **the nearest way** i.e. directly

464 **White-livered** cowardly; cf. *Mac* 5.3.15 and Dent, F180.
runagate renegade, vagabond (*OED* 1)

466 *The repetition in Qq's line does not appear in F or in Q7–8; cf. 456.

467 After the council meeting (3.4), John Morton, Bishop of Ely, was confined (see 4.3.46n.) at Buckingham's castle at Brecon (4.2.120), where he encouraged Buckingham's rebellion (More, *CW2*, 90–3) before fleeing to Flanders to render Richmond 'good seruice' (Hall, *Richard III*, fols xxx[r]–xxxvi[v]; Holinshed, 3.737–41).

457+ SP] *F (Sta[n].); Dar. Qq* 457 None good,] *F4;* None, good *F;* None good *Qq* liege] *F;* Lord *Qq* 458 well . . . reported] *F;* it may well be told *Qq* 460 What need'st] *F;* Why doest *Qq* miles] *F;* mile *Qq* 461 the nearest] *F;* a neerer *Qq* 462] *Steevens; F, Qq line* newes? / Seas. / 466] *F;* Well sir, as you guesse, as you guesse. *Q1–6;* Well sir, as you guesse. *Q7–8* 467 Morton] *F;* Elie *Qq* 468 here] *F;* there *Qq*

KING RICHARD
Is the chair empty? Is the sword unswayed?
Is the King dead? The empire unpossessed?
What heir of York is there alive but we?
And who is England's king but great York's heir?
Then tell me, what makes he upon the seas?

STANLEY
Unless for that, my liege, I cannot guess.

KING RICHARD
Unless for that he comes to be your liege,
You cannot guess wherefore the Welshman comes.
Thou wilt revolt and fly to him, I fear.

STANLEY
No, my good lord; therefore mistrust me not.

KING RICHARD
Where is thy power, then, to beat him back?
Where be thy tenants and thy followers?

469 **chair . . . sword** throne and sword of state
unswayed unruled
470 **empire** i.e. supreme government of the state (*OED sb.* 1)
471–2 'little Ned Plantagenet' (146) is the male heir of the house of York; other heirs include his sister. Stanley's non-response suggests the importance of self-silencing in the play's depiction of tyranny. It might also suggest the fence-sitting and self-preservation attributed to the historical Stanley family (M. Jones, 32–3). Cf. 477n. and pp. 25–7.
472 **great York** the third Duke of York (d. 1460), father of Richard, Clarence and Edward IV
473 **makes he** is he doing
474, 475 **Unless for that** Stanley means that unless Richmond comes for *that* reason – i.e. 'to claim the crown' – he cannot imagine why he comes. Richard takes *Unless for that* and turns it around to mean 'unless Richmond comes in order to be Stanley's lord'; cf. Richard's echo of Buckingham at 4.2.15–16.
476 **Welshman** Richmond's grandparents were the Welsh Owen Tudor and Katherine of Valois, widow of Henry V. Richard's dismissive treatment of Welsh identity contradicts Tudor affirmation of this heritage.
477 On Stanley's secret 'intent to be in a perfect readinesse to recieue the earle of Richmond at his first arriuall in England', see Holinshed, 3.751.
478 **therefore** i.e. with respect to that
479 **power** forces
480 **tenants** those who held land by title of a lord (in this case Stanley) (*OED*), and who were obliged to render feudal military service

473 makes] *F;* doeth *Qq* seas] *F;* sea *Qq* 476 Welshman] *F, Q1–3, 5–6 subst.;* Welchmen *Q4* 478 my good lord] *F;* mightie liege *Qq* 480 be] *F;* are *Qq*

Are they not now upon the western shore,
Safe-conducting the rebels from their ships?

STANLEY
No, my good lord, my friends are in the north.

KING RICHARD
Cold friends to me. What do they in the north
When they should serve their sovereign in the west?

STANLEY
They have not been commanded, mighty King.
Pleaseth your majesty to give me leave,
I'll muster up my friends and meet your grace
Where and what time your majesty shall please.

KING RICHARD
Ay, thou wouldst be gone to join with Richmond,
But I'll not trust thee.

STANLEY Most mighty sovereign,
You have no cause to hold my friendship doubtful;
I never was, nor never will be, false.

KING RICHARD
Go then, and muster men, but leave behind
Your son George Stanley. Look your heart be firm,

483 **in the north** Stanley's lands were in Cheshire and Lancashire, and he had power in North Wales.

484–5 Edmund Kean made this speech a major acting point (Pickersgill, 101).

484 **Cold** i.e. unenthusiastic, but also with a sense of the cold northern climate

487 **Pleaseth** if it please

495 **George Stanley** Thomas Stanley was one whom Richard 'moost mystrusted', and when Stanley pretended to visit his family in order secretly to prepare for Richmond, Richard kept George Stanley 'as an hostage' (Hall, *Richard III*, fol. xlix[r]; Holinshed, 3.751). George Stanley's prominence (see 4.5.3; 5.3.61, 95, 344–6; 5.5.9–10) may compliment the 5th Earl of Derby, Ferdinando, Lord Strange, who succeeded to the earldom in 1592, and who from 1588 to his death in 1594 was patron of the acting company that may first have performed *Richard III*. George Stanley was the great-great-grandfather of the 5th Earl. Other evidence suggests the play may have been written or adapted for the Earl of Pembroke's Men (see 5.3.28–32n. and p. 51).
Look i.e. take care that

484 me] *F;* Richard *Qq* 486 King] *F;* soueraigne *Qq* 487 Pleaseth] *F;* Please it *Qq* 490 Ay] *F (I);* I, I *Qq* wouldst] *F, Q2–6; Q1 (*wouldest*)* 491] *Steevens; F lines* thee. / Soueraigne. / ; *Qq line* Sir. / Soueraigne, / But . . . thee] *F; I* will not trust you Sir *Qq* 494 Go then, and] *F;* Well, go *Qq* but] *F;* but heare you *Qq* 495 heart] *F;* faith *Qq*

Or else his head's assurance is but frail.

STANLEY

So deal with him as I prove true to you. *Exit Stanley.*

Enter a Messenger.

MESSENGER

My gracious sovereign, now in Devonshire,
As I by friends am well advertised
Sir Edward Courtney and the haughty prelate,
Bishop of Exeter, his elder brother,
With many more confederates are in arms.

Enter another Messenger.

2 MESSENGER

In Kent, my liege, the Guilfords are in arms,
And every hour more competitors
Flock to the rebels, and their power grows strong.

Enter another Messenger.

3 MESSENGER

My lord, the army of great Buckingham –

496 **assurance** security (*OED* 7)
498 **Devonshire** county in the south-west of England
499 **advertised** advertisèd; warned (*OED* 4)
500–1 Hall says, 'Sir Edwarde Courtney and Peter his brother bishop of Exsetter, reised another army in deuonshire and cornewall' (*Richard III*, fol. xxxix^{r}), but the bishop was actually Edward's cousin. Hall and Holinshed say nothing about either being the *elder* or about haughtiness, but *haughty prelate* sounds Shakespearean (see *1H6* 1.3.23); cf. 'proud prelate' (*2H6* 1.1.139).
500 ***Edward** Hall and Holinshed call him both Edward and Edmund (or Edmonde) (Hall, fol. xxxix^{r-v}; Holinshed, 3.743).
503 **Kent** county south-east of London **Guilfords** (or Guildfords) Sir Richard Guilford and his father, Sir John, had long supported Richmond.
504 **competitors** associates, seeking a common goal (*OED* 2, citing this line)

497 So] *F, Q1–3, 5–6; om. Q4* SD] *F; Exit Dar. Q3–5; Exit. Q6; not in Q1–2* 500 Edward] *F;* William *Qq* 501 elder brother] *F;* brother there *Qq* 502 more] *F, Q1–6 (*mo*[*e*]), Q7* 503 SP] *Capell subst.; Mess. F, Qq* In . . . liege] *F;* My Liege, in Kent *Qq* 505 the . . . strong] *F;* their aide, and still their power increaseth *Qq* 506, 509, 517 SP] *Capell subst.; Mess. F, Qq* 506 My] *F, Q1–3, 5–6; om. Q4* great] *F;* the Duke of *Qq* Buckingham –] *Rowe; Buckingham. F, Qq*

KING RICHARD
Out on you, owls! Nothing but songs of death.
He striketh him.
There, take thou that, till thou bring better news.
3 MESSENGER
The news I have to tell your majesty
Is that by sudden floods and fall of waters
Buckingham's army is dispersed and scattered,
And he himself wandered away alone,
No man knows whither.
KING RICHARD I cry thee mercy.
There is my purse to cure that blow of thine.
Hath any well-advised friend proclaimed
Reward to him that brings the traitor in?
3 MESSENGER
Such proclamation hath been made, my lord.

Enter another Messenger.

507 **Out on you** an expression of impatience
owls . . . death The owl's cry was supposed to be ominous, accompanying death and disaster; cf. Dent, R33: 'The croaking raven (screeching owl) bodes misfortune.' Henry VI tells Richard, 'The owl shrieked at thy birth' (*3H6* 5.6.44), marking the conjunction in him of birth and death.
510–12 On the terrible weather and floods that thwarted Buckingham's forces and the events that led to his ultimate isolation, see Hall, *Richard III*, fol. xxxix[r] and Holinshed, 3.743.
510 **fall of waters** i.e. rainfall
513 **I . . . mercy** I beg your pardon; cf. 1.3.234.
514 **my purse** Davison argues on behalf of Qq that a king would not normally carry a purse, citing *H5* 4.8.58–60.
515 **well-advised** well-advisèd; i.e. prudent, thoughtful (cf. 2.1.108) or provided with satisfactory information (cf. *H5* 2.0.12: 'advised by good intelligence')

507 you] *Q1–5;* ye *F, Q6* SD] *F; after 506 Qq* 508 There . . . bring] *F;* Take that vntill thou *(*you *Q6)* bring me *Qq* 509] *F;* Your grace mistakes, the newes *I* bring is good, *Qq* 510 Is] *F;* My newes is *Qq* floods] *F;* floud *Qq* waters] *F, Q7–8;* water *Q1–6* 511 Buckingham's] *F;* The Duke of Buckinghams *Qq* 512 wandered away alone] *F;* fled *Qq* 513] *Steevens; F lines* whither. / mercie: / No . . . whither] *F; in 512 Qq (*whether *Q1)* I . . . mercy] *F;* O I crie you mercie, I did mistake *Qq* 514] *F;* Ratcliffe reward him, for the blow I gaue him *Qq* 515 proclaimed] *F;* giuen out *Qq* 516 Reward to] *F;* Rewardes for *Qq* the traitor in] *F;* in Buckingham *Qq* 517 lord] *F;* liege *Qq*

4 MESSENGER

Sir Thomas Lovell and Lord Marquess Dorset,
'Tis said, my liege, in Yorkshire are in arms;
But this good comfort bring I to your highness:
The Breton navy is dispersed by tempest.
Richmond in Dorsetshire sent out a boat
Unto the shore to ask those on the banks
If they were his assistants, yea or no?
Who answered him they came from Buckingham,
Upon his party. He, mistrusting them,
Hoised sail and made his course again for Brittany.

KING RICHARD

March on, march on, since we are up in arms,
If not to fight with foreign enemies,
Yet to beat down these rebels here at home.

Enter CATESBY.

CATESBY

My liege, the Duke of Buckingham is taken.
That is the best news. That the Earl of Richmond
Is with a mighty power landed at Milford

518 **Lovell** Sir Thomas Lovell would become Chancellor of the Exchequer under Henry VII and appears prominently in *H8*. He should not be confused with Lord Francis Lovell, who appears in 3.4.
Dorset Cf. 311–14n.
519 **Yorkshire** county in the north-east of England
521 **Breton** Cf. 4.3.40.
522 **in Dorsetshire** i.e. on the south-west coast of England
524 **assistants** supporters
526 **Upon his party** on his behalf, cf. 1.3.137.
527 **Hoised** hoisted (*OED v.* 1)
531 Cibber follows with a famous (and long-lived) flourish: '*Off with his head. So much for* Buckingham.'
531–3 These lines compress Richmond's (failed) attempt to join with Buckingham's forces (October 1483) with the successful expedition here recounted (August 1485).
533 **Milford** Milford Haven, in south-west Wales

518 SP] *Capell; Mess. F, Qq* 519 in Yorkshire are] *F;* are vp *Qq* 520 But] *F;* Yet *Qq* highness] *F;* grace *Qq* 521–3] *F; Qq line* Dorshire / shore, / 521 Breton] *F, Qq (*Brittaine*), Capell* by tempest] *F; not in Qq* 522 Dorsetshire] *F, Q6;* Dorshire *Q1–5* 523 Unto the shore] *F; not in Qq* those . . . banks] *F;* them . . . shore *Qq* 527 Hoised] *F (*Hoys'd*);* Hoist *Qq* his course again] *F;* away *Qq* Brittany] *F, Qq (*Brittaine*), Cam* 532 That is] *F;* Thats *Qq*

Is colder tidings, yet they must be told.

KING RICHARD

Away towards Salisbury! While we reason here
A royal battle might be won and lost.
Someone take order Buckingham be brought
To Salisbury. The rest march on with me. *Flourish. Exeunt.*

[**4.5**] *Enter* [STANLEY, Earl of] Derby *and* Sir CHRISTOPHER [Urswick].

STANLEY

Sir Christopher, tell Richmond this from me:
That in the sty of the most deadly boar
My son George Stanley is franked up in hold;
If I revolt, off goes young George's head.
The fear of that holds off my present aid.

534 **colder** more discouraging (*OED a.* cold 10a, citing this line)
***tidings, yet** Many editors since Dyce have favoured Q1–5's phrasing over F's 'news, but yet'. F suggests an attempt to pad Q6 to create a metrical line. See pp. 440–1.

535, 538 ***Salisbury** F's 'Salsbury' differs from 444, 451 and 453 where it agrees with Qq's 'Salisburie' or 'Salisbury'. The pronunciation would most likely be the same, but the contracted form might register elision.

535 **reason** debate, discuss

536 **royal** in military uses denoting grand scale, great size or strength (*OED* royal 10a, citing this line)
won and lost One of many verbal and thematic links to *Macbeth* (1.1.4); however, the sense here is clearly proverbial (Dent, M337: 'No man loses but another wins') rather than enigmatic.

537 **take order** i.e. direct that

4.5 location: '*Lord* Stanley's *House*' (Theobald). Stanley's family residence is in north-west England.

0.2 **Sir CHRISTOPHER** Christopher Urswick, chaplain to the Countess of Richmond, was commissioned to go to Brittany by her (not by Stanley) in 1483, but recalled in favour of a messenger of more consequence (Holinshed, 3.742). He would later serve as chaplain to Henry VII. 'Sir' is a courtesy title for a priest (cf. 3.2.107).

2 **boar** i.e. Richard

3 **franked . . . hold** shut up in a pen (cf. 1.3.313)

5 **present** immediate

534 tidings, yet] *Q1–5;* newes, yet *Q6;* news, but yet *F* 535, 538 Salisbury] *F (*Salsbury*), Qq* 538 SD *Flourish*] *F; not in Qq Exeunt*] *F, Q1; om. Q2–6* **4.5**] *Capell; Scena Quarta. F; not in Qq* 0.1] *F; Entee (Enter Q2–6) Darbie, Sir Christopher. Qq* STANLEY, Earl of] *Pope subst.* 0.2 Urswick] *Theobald* 1+ SP] *Pope subst; Der. F; Dar. Qq* 2 the most deadly] *F;* this most bloudie *Qq* 5 holds off] *F;* with holdes *Qq*

So get thee gone. Commend me to thy lord.
Withal, say that the Queen hath heartily consented
He should espouse Elizabeth her daughter.
But tell me, where is princely Richmond now?

CHRISTOPHER
At Pembroke or at Ha'rfordwest in Wales.

STANLEY
What men of name resort to him?

CHRISTOPHER
Sir Walter Herbert, a renowned soldier,
Sir Gilbert Talbot, Sir William Stanley,
Oxford, redoubted Pembroke, Sir James Blunt,
And Rice ap Thomas, with a valiant crew,

6–8 *Qq's arrangement may give the most important news 'a more emphatic position' and avoid a 'double dispatch and commendation' (*TxC*, 246), but Marshall's commentary is decisive for F: 'Urswick wants Stanley to declare for Richmond. Stanley answers that he cannot do so openly at present, and then, before sending him off, communicates the important news of Elizabeth's consent to the proposed marriage of her daughter to Richmond. This announcement comes much more properly at the beginning of the scene than thrust in, as a mere afterthought, at the end.'

7 **Withal** in addition

10 **Pembroke** in Wales, near Milford Haven
Ha'rfordwest Haverfordwest, in Pembrokeshire, Wales, north-east of Milford Haven

11 **name** title
resort make their way (*OED v.*[1] 5a)

12–14 **Herbert . . . Pembroke** See 5.3.28–32n.

12 **Herbert** family name of the earls of Pembroke
renowned renownèd

13 **Talbot** ancestor of the Stanley family in Shakespeare's time
Sir William Stanley Stanley's brother

14 **redoubted** feared, respected (*OED ppl. a.*)
Pembroke Jasper Tudor, Earl of Pembroke, a son of Owen Tudor and thus Richmond's uncle
Blunt Blunt's descendants owned land in Stratford-upon-Avon and were related to the Combe family there (Hammond). The Blunts were not knighted until 1588 (Sidney Shanker, 'Shakespeare pays some Compliments', *Modern Language Notes*, 63 (1948), 540–1).

15 **Rice ap Thomas** Rhys ap Thomas, the leader of a Welsh contingent that fought for Richmond, and Sir Walter Herbert 'ruled Wales with egall powre and lyke aucthoritee' (Hall, *Richard III*, fol. lii^{v}; Holinshed, 3.754). Hall

6 So . . . gone] *F; not in Qq* 6–8 Commend . . . daughter] *F;* commend me to him, / Tell him, the Queene hath hartelie consented, / He shall espouse Elizabeth her daughter *(after* lord *in 19) Qq* 10 Pembroke] *Q1–2; F (*Penbroke*), Q3–6 (*Pembrooke *subst.)* Ha'rfordwest] *Q1 (*Harford-west*), Capell;* Herford-west *Q2, 5;* Hertford-west *Q3–4; Hertford* west *Q6;* Hertford West *F* 12 SP] *F (Chri.); S. Christ. Qq* 14 redoubted] *F, Q1–3, 5–6;* doubted *Q4* 15 And] *F; not in Qq* ap] *F, Q6;* vp *Q1–5*

And many other of great name and worth;
And towards London do they bend their power,
If by the way they be not fought withal.

STANLEY

Well, hie thee to thy lord. I kiss his hand.
My letter will resolve him of my mind.
Farewell. *Exeunt.*

5.1 *Enter* BUCKINGHAM *with* [Sheriff *and*] *Halberds, led to execution.*

BUCKINGHAM

Will not King Richard let me speak with him?

SHERIFF

No, my good lord; therefore be patient.

BUCKINGHAM

Hastings, and Edward's children, Grey and Rivers,
Holy King Henry, and thy fair son Edward,
Vaughan and all that have miscarried
By underhand, corrupted, foul injustice,
If that your moody, discontented souls
Do through the clouds behold this present hour,

and Holinshed report that Richard had 'trusted' in their forces.
crew band or company of soldiers (*OED sb.*[1] 1)
16 **name** reputation
17 **bend their power** i.e. turn their forces
19 **hie** hasten
20 **resolve . . . mind** inform him of my thinking
5.1 location: 'SALISBURY' (Pope)
0.1 ***Sheriff** Ratcliffe has the Sheriff's lines in Qq. See p. 451.
Halberds i.e. halberdiers, armed with halberds (*OED sb.* 2); cf. 1.2.0.1. Serving under the Sheriff, they constitute with him the *officers* (28, 29 SD).
1 **speak with him** Elsewhere mention is made of Buckingham's intended assassination of Richard; see *H8* 1.2.193–9 and Holinshed, 3.864; cf. 3.744.
4 **thy** i.e. Henry VI's
5 **miscarried** miscarrièd; perished, came to harm
7 **moody** angry, wrathful

16 And] *F;* With *Qq* other . . . name] *F;* moe of noble fame *Qq* 17 do they] *F;* they doe *Qq* power] *F;* course *Qq* 19 Well . . . to] *F;* Retourne vnto *Qq* thy] *F, Q1;* my *Q2–6* I . . . hand] *F;* commend me to him *Qq* 20 My letter] *F;* These letters *Qq* **5.1**] *F (Actus Quintus. Scena Prima.); not in Qq* 0.1 Sheriff *and*] *Rowe* 0.1–2 *with Halberds, led*] *F; not in Qq* 2, 11 SP] *F (Sher.); Rat. Qq* 2 good] *F; not in Qq* 3 Grey and Rivers] *F;* Riuers, Gray *Qq*

Even for revenge mock my destruction.
– This is All Souls' Day, fellow, is it not?

SHERIFF It is.

BUCKINGHAM
Why then, All Souls' Day is my body's doomsday.
This is the day which, in King Edward's time,
I wished might fall on me when I was found
False to his children and his wife's allies.
This is the day wherein I wished to fall
By the false faith of him whom most I trusted.
This, this All Souls' Day to my fearful soul
Is the determined respite of my wrongs:
That high All-seer which I dallied with
Hath turned my feigned prayer on my head

9 **revenge** Henry VI and his son would have no personal cause to feel vengeful toward Buckingham. 'Revenge' is broadly invoked and sometimes means merely punishment or chastisement (*OED sb.* 5). However, Buckingham's utterance may signify a recognition of guilt for joining with Richard against Henry's descendants and family.
mock It is difficult to imagine 'Holy King Henry' jeering. Does Buckingham project one of Richard's (and the play's) own most prominent verbal modes onto Henry, imagining him responding to the misfortunes of others as does everyone else in the play?

10 **All Souls' Day** 2 November; in the Roman Catholic Church, a day to commemorate those Christians whose souls are believed to be in purgatory. Buckingham was executed in 1483; the Battle of Bosworth occurred in August of 1485. Displacing its closing scenes to November, the play maintains the sense of the seasonal year that opens the action. References to All Souls' Day and to the hosts of victim/spectators (3–5) prepares for Richard's ghostly visitants in 5.3; on this anticipation and the medieval belief that 'souls in purgatory could appear on this day . . . to persons who had wronged them during their life', see Jones, *Origins*, 226–32.

11 A curt response, omitting Buckingham's title; does the Sheriff take offence at being addressed as *fellow* (Marshall)?

12 **my body's doomsday** The day associated with divine judgement upon departed souls in general (doomsday) is anticipated by the earthly sentence executed upon Buckingham's body (cf. 1.4.103–4).

13–17 See 2.1.32–40.

16 **wherein** on which

19 **determined respite** ordained time to which punishment has been deferred (*OED* respite *sb.* 5)
wrongs i.e. Buckingham's ill deeds

20 **dallied** trifled

21 **feigned** feignèd; simulated, sham

10 fellow] *F;* fellowes *Qq* 11] *F;* It is my Lord. *Qq* 13 which] *F;* that *Qq* 15 and] *F;* or *Qq* 17 whom . . . trusted] *F;* I trusted most *Qq* 20 That] *F, Q1, 3–6;* What *Q2* which] *F;* that *Qq*

And given in earnest what I begged in jest.
Thus doth he force the swords of wicked men
To turn their own points in their masters' bosoms.
Thus Margaret's curse falls heavy on my neck:
'When he', quoth she, 'shall split thy heart with sorrow,
Remember Margaret was a prophetess.'
– Come, lead me, officers, to the block of shame.
Wrong hath but wrong, and blame the due of blame.
Exeunt Buckingham with Officers.

5.2

Enter RICHMOND, OXFORD, BLUNT, HERBERT *and others, with Drum and Colours.*

RICHMOND
Fellows in arms, and my most loving friends,
Bruised underneath the yoke of tyranny,
Thus far into the bowels of the land
Have we marched on without impediment;
And here receive we from our father Stanley

22 **in earnest** in all seriousness
23–4 Psalm 37 promises that 'the meeke spirited shall possesse the earth: and shalbe delighted in the aboundaunce of peace' (11), but that the swords of the wicked 'shall go thorow their owne heart: & their bow shalbe broken' (15).
25–7 See 1.3.298–300.
26 **he** Richard
29 **blame . . . blame** i.e. censure and reproach are the appropriate rewards of blameworthiness or culpability (*OED* blame *sb.* 1, 3)
29 SD *Officers* the Sheriff and his men (see 0.1n.)
5.2 location: '*The Camp*' (Pope), '*near Tamworth*' (Hanmer), i.e. near Bosworth in central England
0.2 ***Drum and Colours*** drummers and standard-bearers
2 **yoke of tyranny** Contrast *yoke of sovereignty* (3.7.145).
3–10 **bowels . . . embowelled** 'bowels' means interior (*OED sb.*[1] 4); the land of England, being penetrated to its heart by Richmond, is related to the bodies of individuals, threatened with evisceration (embowelment) by Richard.
5 **our** Richmond appears to adopt the royal plural.
father stepfather

23 swords] *F, Q1–2;* sword *Q3–6* 24 own points in] *F;* owne pointes, on *Q1–2;* points on *Q3–6* bosoms] *F;* bosome *Qq* 25 Thus] *F;* Now *Qq* falls . . . neck] *F;* is fallen vpon my head *Qq* 28 lead me, officers] *F;* sirs, conuey me *Qq* 29 SD] *F; not in Qq* **5.2**] *F (Scena Secunda.); not in Qq* 0.1–2] *F; Enter Richmond with drums and trumpets. Qq* 1, 22 SP] *F (Richm[.]), Qq (Rich.)* 1 Fellows] *F, Q1–4, 6;* Fellowe *Q5*

Lines of fair comfort and encouragement.
The wretched, bloody and usurping boar,
That spoiled your summer fields and fruitful vines,
Swills your warm blood like wash, and makes his
  trough
In your embowelled bosoms, this foul swine
Is now even in the centre of this isle,
Near to the town of Leicester, as we learn.
From Tamworth thither is but one day's march.
In God's name, cheerly on, courageous friends,
To reap the harvest of perpetual peace
By this one bloody trial of sharp war.

OXFORD

Every man's conscience is a thousand men
To fight against this guilty homicide.

HERBERT

I doubt not but his friends will turn to us.

7 **wretched** reprehensible, hateful (*OED a.* 4)

7–8 See Psalm 80 on the vine: 'The wyld bore out of the wood rooteth it up: and the wyld beast of the fielde deuoureth it' (13). Cf. 15 and 2.2.115–16.

9 **Swills** eats freely or greedily, as a pig (*OED v.* 3)
wash swill or refuse used as food for swine (*OED sb.* 11a)

10 **embowelled** disembowelled (*OED* 1); cf. *1H4* 5.4.109.

11–12 ***centre . . . Near** F's 'centry' is synonymous with 'centre' (*OED* centry 1, citing this line) and hardly evidence of 'uneven correction' (Hammond). Qq/F variation of 'Near' recalls 1.1.117, where a contextually preferable reading (F's 'Ne'er') differs from similar alternatives. F was here set by Compositor B, who usually spelled 'near' as 'neere'; Walton (*Copy*, 84–5) posits 'incorrect sophistication' in which B misread Q3's 'Neare', but 'Neare' is an alternative spelling of 'Ne'er' (*OED* ne'er).

12, 13 **Leicester, Tamworth** towns in central England

14 **cheerly on** i.e. go forward eagerly

16 **sharp** fierce, keen (*OED a.* 4c)

17 Cf. 5.3.193 and Dent, C601: 'Conscience is a thousand witnesses'; contrast 5.3.309–11.

18 **guilty** Richard's conscience will concur (5.3.199).

19 **doubt not but** i.e. believe (Abbott, 122); cf. 1.3.286.
friends allies, but Richard will lament that 'no creature loves me' (5.3.200).

8 summer fields] *F; Q1–2 (*somer-fieldes*);* sommer-field *Q3–8* 10 embowelled] *F (*embowel'd*);* inboweld *Q1–5;* imboweld *Q6* 11 Is] *F;* Lies *Qq* centre] *F (*Centry*), Qq* 12 Near] *Q1–5 (*Neare*);* Neere *Q6;* Ne're *F* 13 thither] *F, Q2–6; Q1 (*thether*)* 14 cheerly] *F, Q1;* cheere *Q2–6* 17 SP] *F (Oxf.);* 1 *Lo. Qq* men] *F;* swordes *Qq* 18 this guilty] *F;* that bloudie *Qq* 19 SP] *F (Her.);* 2 *Lo. Qq* turn] *F;* flie *Qq*

BLUNT

He hath no friends but what are friends for fear,
Which in his dearest need will fly from him.

RICHMOND

All for our vantage. Then in God's name, march.
True hope is swift and flies with swallow's wings;
Kings it makes gods, and meaner creatures kings. *Exeunt all.*

[5.3] *Enter* KING RICHARD *in arms, with* NORFOLK, RATCLIFFE *and the* Earl of SURREY, ^{Q}*with others*^{Q}.

KING RICHARD

Here pitch our tent, even here in Bosworth field.
– My lord of Surrey, why look you so sad?

20–1 Some of Richard's forces served 'more for dread than loue' and 'kissed them openlie, whome they inwardlie hated. Other sware outwardlie to take part with such, whose death they secretlie compassed, and inwardlie imagined. Other promised to inuade the kings enimies, which fled and fought with fierce courage against the king. Other stood still and looked on, intending to take part with the victors and ouercommers. So was his people to him vnsure and vnfaithfull at his end, as he was to his nephues vntrue and vnnaturall in his beginning' (Holinshed, 3.757; Hall, *Richard III*, fol. lv^{r}). Cf. Macbeth's forces (*Mac* 5.2.19–20, 5.4.13–14).

21 **dearest** most urgent

23–4 A remarkable statement, since the desire to be *gods* is the fundamental error of tyrants and the aspiration of *meaner creatures* to be kings motivates countless Elizabethan tragedies. These lines appear in *Englands Parnassus* (Allott); Cibber's Richmond claims that '*True hope*' actually '*mounts with Eagles wings*' (*Richard III*, 5.1.28). See Siemon, 'Power'.

23 Cf. Dent, S1023: 'As swift as a swallow'.

24 **meaner creatures** i.e. those lesser in rank

5.3 location: 'Bosworth *Field*' (Pope)

0.2 ***SURREY** Qq have Catesby instead of Surrey throughout 5.3. 5.3.3 is Surrey's only line in the play.

1 ***tent** Qq have 'tentes'; Richard could refer here to the tents of his forces, and later to his own tent (7, 14). For a similar scene *c.* 1590–1 with a sleeping king (Henry VI) and human and allegorical visitants, see the plot of *2 Seven Deadly Sins* (Greg, *Documents*, 2). *3H6* 4.3 is set outside a king's battlefield tent.

Bosworth The battle of Bosworth Field occurred on 22 August 1485.

2 **sad** serious

20 SP] *F; 3 Lo. Qq* what] *F;* who *Qq* 21 dearest] *F;* greatest *Qq* fly] *F;* shrinke *Qq* 24 makes] *F, Q6;* make *Q1–5* SD] *F; Exit. Q1; om. Q2–6 all*] *F (Omnes)* 5.3] *Pope* 0.1 *in arms, with*] *F; not in Qq* 0.2 *and . . .* SURREY] *F; Catesbie Qq* 1–48 SP] *Qq (King.); Rich. F* 1 tent] *F;* tentes *Qq subst.* 2 My . . . Surrey] *F;* Whie, how now Catesbie *Qq* look you] *F;* lookst *(*lookest *Q2–6)* thou *Qq* sad] *F, Q2–6;* bad *Q1*

SURREY

My heart is ten times lighter than my looks.

KING RICHARD

My lord of Norfolk.

NORFOLK Here, most gracious liege.

KING RICHARD

Norfolk, we must have knocks, ha, must we not?

NORFOLK

We must both give and take, my loving lord.

KING RICHARD

Up with my tent. Here will I lie tonight,

[*Soldiers begin to set up Richard's tent.*]

But where tomorrow? Well, all's one for that.
Who hath descried the number of the traitors?

NORFOLK

Six or seven thousand is their utmost power.

KING RICHARD

Why, our battalia trebles that account.
Besides, the King's name is a tower of strength
Which they upon the adverse faction want.

5 **knocks** blows (cf. *H5* 3.2.3–8)
6 Cf. 'Give and take' (Dent, G121).
8 possibly an aside (Thompson)
all's . . . that i.e. be that as it may
9 **descried** discovered by observation, found out (*OED v.*[1] III 7)
10 ***utmost** F's agreement with corrected Q1 argues that Q1 was 'partly set, or set in some partial way, from a sound manuscript . . . linked by unbroken written transmission' with FMS (Smidt, *Memorial*, 36). See pp. 430–1.
10–11 Richmond and 'Standley' discuss the relative strength of the opposing forces in *True Tragedy*. Richmond encourages himself by saying, 'thou fightest in right, to defende thy countrey from the tyrannie of an vsurping tyrant' (1867–8). The sources do not mention the odds affecting the spirits of the leaders (Churchill, 515).
11 **battalia** large body of men in battle array (*OED* 2); cf. *battle* (88, 134).
12 Cf. Proverbs, 18.10: 'The Name of the Lord *is* a strong towre' (Geneva; 'strong castell' in the Bishops' Bible). Cf. 'Strong as a tower in hope' (*R2* 1.3.102).
13 **adverse** opposing
want lack

3 SP] *F; Cat, Qq* 4] *Steevens; F lines* Norfolke. / Liege. / My . . . Norfolk] *F;* Norffolke, come hether *(*hither *Q2–6) Qq* Here . . . liege.] *F; not in Qq* 5] *Qq; F lines* knockes: / not? / 6 loving] *F;* gracious *Qq* 7 tent] *F;* tent there *Qq* SD] *after Capell (Tent set up.)* 8 all's] *F;* all is *Qq* 9 traitors] *F;* foe *Qq* 10 utmost] *F, Q1c (BL, Bod, Fo);* greatest *Q1u (Hn), Q2–6* power] *F;* number *Qq* 11 battalia] *F;* battalion *Q1, 4, 6;* battailon *Q2–3, 5* 13 faction] *F;* partie *Qq*

– Up with the tent! – Come, noble gentlemen,
Let us survey the vantage of the ground.
Call for some men of sound direction.
Let's lack no discipline, make no delay,
For lords, tomorrow is a busy day. [*Richard's tent is ready.*]
Exeunt.

Enter RICHMOND, *Sir William Brandon,* OXFORD *and* DORSET [, *with* BLUNT, HERBERT *and others who set up Richmond's tent*].

RICHMOND
The weary sun hath made a golden set,
And by the bright track of his fiery car
Gives token of a goodly day tomorrow.
– Sir William Brandon, you shall bear my standard.
– Give me some ink and paper in my tent;
I'll draw the form and model of our battle,

15 **vantage . . . ground** military opportunity offered by the topography of the land
16 **sound direction** administrative capacity (*OED* direction 2); cf. 302 and 'directions' (*H5* 3.2.71–80).
18.2 DORSET Dorset neither speaks nor is addressed in the scene; sources have him left behind by Richmond in France (Holinshed, 3.752; Hall, *Richard III*, fol. 1^v). The play earlier has him *in arms* against Richard in England (4.4.518–19).
20 ***track** F's 'tract' could also mean 'track' (*OED* tract $sb.^3$ IV 8).
car chariot
21 Cf. 'A red sky in the evening is a sign of a fair day' (Dent, S515); contrast 277–87.
22 **standard** flag
23–6 *Since Pope these lines have been sometimes moved, typically approximating Qq by placement after *Blunt* in 44 or after 44, but F suggests Richmond reacting to evolving plans and events: ordering that supplies be brought (23), issuing preliminary assignments (22, 27–9) and remembering the need for further communications (29–34); cf. York's confusion (*R2* 2.2.87–122). Cf. Richard's camp (49–75) and the demand for *ink and paper* (49).
24 **form and model** i.e. sketch of the plan

14 the . . . noble] *F (*the Tent: Come Noble*);* my tent there, valiant *Qq* 15 ground] *F;* field *Qq* 17 lack] *F;* want *Qq* 18 SD *Richard's . . . ready.*] *Ard^2 subst.* 18.1–2 *Sir . . .* DORSET] *F; with the Lordes, &c. Q1–2; with the Lords. Q3–6* 18.2–3 *with . . . tent*] *this edn after Capell* 19 sun] *F, Q2–6 (*Sunne*);* sonne *Q1* set] *F;* sete *Q1;* seate *Q2–5;* seat *Q6* 20 track] *Qq;* Tract *F* 21 token] *F;* signall *Qq* 22] *F;* Where is Sir William Brandon, he shall beare my standerd, *Qq* 23–6] *F; after* Blunt *44 Qq*

Limit each leader to his several charge,
And part in just proportion our small power.
– My lord of Oxford, you, Sir William Brandon,
And you, Sir Walter Herbert, stay with me.
The Earl of Pembroke keeps his regiment;
– Good Captain Blunt, bear my goodnight to him,
And by the second hour in the morning
Desire the Earl to see me in my tent.
Yet one thing more, good captain, do for me:
Where is Lord Stanley quartered, do you know?

BLUNT

Unless I have mista'en his colours much,
Which well I am assured I have not done,
His regiment lies half a mile at least
South from the mighty power of the King.

RICHMOND

If without peril it be possible,
Sweet Blunt, make some good means to speak with him,
And give him from me this most needful note.

BLUNT

Upon my life, my lord, I'll undertake it,
And so God give you quiet rest tonight.

25 appoint the leaders to their particular assignments

26 **part** divide
just exact

28–32 **Herbert . . . Earl** The prominence of Sir Walter Herbert and the Earl of Pembroke here (cf. 4.5.12–14) may compliment their Elizabethan descendant, Henry Herbert, 2nd Earl of Pembroke and patron of Pembroke's Men (Jowett, 5–7). The anticipated interview with Pembroke, though apparently of extreme importance, is not staged. Gurr argues that Shakespeare was with Pembroke's Men in 1592–3 (*Companies*, 271).

29 **keeps** stays or remains with (*OED v.* 33)

35 **colours** battle flag or ensign (*OED sb.*[1] 7a)

40 *Qq repeat 30.
make . . . means take the right steps (*OED* mean *sb.*[2] 10d)

41 **needful** necessary

26 power] *F;* strength *Qq* 27–8] *F; not in Qq* 28 you] *F2;* your *F* 29 keeps] *F;* keepe *Qq* 33 captain . . . me] *F;* Blunt before thou goest *Qq* 34 do you] *F;* doest thou *Qq* 37 lies] *F, Q1–2;* liet *Q3, 5;* lieth *Q4, 6* 40] *F;* Good captaine Blunt beare my good night to him, *Qq* 41 note] *F;* scrowle *Qq* 43] *F; not in Qq*

RICHMOND

Good night, good Captain Blunt. [*Exit Blunt.*]
Come, gentlemen,
Let us consult upon tomorrow's business.
Into my tent; the dew is raw and cold.
[*Richmond, Brandon, Dorset, Herbert and Oxford*]
withdraw into the tent. [*The others exeunt.*]

Enter [*to his tent*] [Q]KING[Q] RICHARD, RATCLIFFE,
NORFOLK, CATESBY [Q]*and others*[Q].

KING RICHARD

What is't o'clock?

CATESBY

It's supper time, my lord; it's nine o'clock.

KING RICHARD

I will not sup tonight. Give me some ink and paper.
What, is my beaver easier than it was,
And all my armour laid into my tent?

46.2 ******and others*** Given the number and kinds of orders issued in the lines that follow (49–75), some, but surely not all, directed to Ratcliffe, Q1–2 appropriately allow for attending figures.

48 ***It's . . . it's** ''Tis' was the standard contraction (*OED* it *pron.* A 1a 2–3) employed in the 1590s (Jowett).
nine Harrison claims, 'the nobility, gentry, and students do ordinarily go to dinner at eleven before noon and to supper at five, or between five and six' (144). Thus 'supper time' ordinarily would more likely be 6 p.m., as Qq; however, the sun sets in 19, suggesting a later hour for August. Copyists could easily confuse 'nine' and 'six' ('it is six' (Qq) could resemble 'its ix'); *nine* is printed as 'ix.' in Qq 2.3.17.

49–end of play *From 49 on, F evidences very little correction of Q3 copy; thus Q1, the authoritative Quarto, furnishes the basic text for the rest of the play (see p. 419). The order of editions in the text notes is adjusted accordingly (cf. 3.1.1–166).

50 **beaver** lower portion of the face-guard of a helmet, when worn with a visor (*OED sb.*[2] 1)
easier looser, better fitting

44] *Capell; F lines Blunt:* / Gentlemen, / Good night] *F;* Farewell *Qq* Captain Blunt] *F;* Blunt *Qq* SD] *Capell* Come, gentlemen] *F; not in Qq* 45 Let] *F;* Come, let *Qq* 46 Into] *F, Q6;* In to *Q1–5* my] *F;* our *Qq* dew] *F;* aire *Qq* 46 SD *Richmond . . . Oxford*] *Ard*[2]*; They F; not in Qq* *withdraw . . . tent*] *F; not in Qq* *The others exeunt*] *Ard*[2] 46.1 *to his tent*] *Capell* 46.2 CATESBY *and others*] *Q1–2 (Catesbie, &c.); Catesby. Q3–6; & Catesby. F* 47 is't o'clock] *F (* is't a Clocke*);* is a clocke *Qq* 48] *F (*a clocke*);* It is sixe of clocke *(*the clocke *Q3–6)*, full supper time. *Qq* 49–end of play] *Basic text is Q1; order of collated editions adjusted. See p. 419.* 49 SP] *Qq, F (King.)* 49] *Qq; F lines* night, / Paper: /

CATESBY

It is, my liege, and all things are in readiness.

KING RICHARD

Good Norfolk, hie thee to thy charge,
Use careful watch, choose trusty sentinels.

NORFOLK

I go, my lord.

KING RICHARD

Stir with the lark tomorrow, gentle Norfolk.

NORFOLK

I warrant you, my lord. F*Exit.*F

KING RICHARD

Catesby.

CATESBY

My lord.

KING RICHARD Send out a pursuivant-at-arms
To Stanley's regiment. Bid him bring his power
Before sun-rising, lest his son George fall
Into the blind cave of eternal night. [*Exit Catesby.*]
Fill me a bowl of wine. Give me a watch.

53 **hie** hasten (*OED v.*[1] 3)
charge commission

54 **Use careful watch** guard carefully
***sentinels** F's plural (correcting Qq 'centinell') makes sense.

56 Cf. 'Go to bed with the lamb and rise with the lark' (Dent, B186).

58 *F's 'Ratcliffe' appears to represent an attempt to reconcile the inconsistency between 58 and 59 in Qq. Richard addresses Catesby in Qq 58, but '*Rat.*' responds, suggesting confusion of 'C' and 'R' in the SP. Surely Richard's order to find a pursuivant would be immediately acted upon, but Ratcliffe has no exit in F or Qq until 78.

59 **pursuivant-at-arms** junior officer attendant on the heralds (*OED* pursuivant *sb.* 1)

62 Cf. 1.4.47 and 2.2.46.
blind dark, obscure (*OED a.* III 6a)

63–5 On the addressee(s), see 46.2n.; cf. 72–5.

63 **bowl** drinking vessel (*OED sb.*[1] 1b)
Give . . . watch Richard may ask that a sentinel guard him, or perhaps he requests a watch-candle, marked to register elapsed time as it melts (*OED* watch *sb.* VII 26). Both are plausible (see 76 and 180). Jowett suggests a time-piece; cf. 276.

53+ SP] *Qq (*Kin*[g][.]), exc. 177 (K[ing][.] Ri[c].); Rich. F, exc. 72, 208–347 (K[ing].)* 54 sentinels] *F (*Centinels*);* centinell *Qq* 58 Catesby] *Qq; Ratcliffe F* 59] *Steevens; Qq, F line* lord. / armes / 59 SP] *Pope; Rat. Qq, F* 61 sun-rising] *Q1–5 (*sun rising*), hyphen Q6, F* 62 SD] *Cam*

Saddle white Surrey for the field tomorrow.
Look that my staves be sound and not too heavy.
– Ratcliffe.

RATCLIFFE My lord.

KING RICHARD
Sawst thou the melancholy Lord Northumberland?

RATCLIFFE
Thomas the Earl of Surrey and himself,
Much about cock-shut time, from troop to troop
Went through the army, cheering up the soldiers.

KING RICHARD
So, I am satisfied. Give me a bowl of wine.
I have not that alacrity of spirit
Nor cheer of mind that I was wont to have.
[*Wine is brought.*]

64 **white Surrey** Richard rode a 'greate whyte courser' into Leicester (Hall, *Richard III*, fol. lii^{v}; Holinshed, 3.754). His horses apparently included one 'White Surrey' (Kendall, 492). Given other references to Revelation and the ironic reversal of dragon and saint at 349–50, it may be significant that Richard requests a white horse, the Son of God's mount in the final victory over evil in Revelation, 19, the reading appointed for All Saints' Day, 1 November (Shaheen, *History Plays*, 19), i.e. yesterday, according to the play's fictional calendar (see 5.1.10).

65 **staves** shafts of lances (*OED* staff *sb.*[1] 3a); combatants could be armed with several lances (Holinshed, 3.834).

68 **melancholy Lord Northumberland** Northumberland's 'melancholy' has never been clearly explained. Holinshed observes, 'whether it was by the commandement of king Richard, putting diffidence into him; or he did it for the loue and fauour that he bare' for Richmond, Northumberland 'stood still with a great companie, and intermitted not in the battell', which won him 'fauour' of Richmond (3.759). Northumberland's melancholy, like Surrey's *sad* appearance (5.3.2), may suggest reluctance. Richard himself is described as 'Melancolye' at news of Richmond's unopposed approach (Hall, *Richard III*, fol. lii^{v}), and the play elsewhere transfers attributes from one character to another (see 4.4.426–31n.). Kemble relates Richard to Macbeth: 'Each of the tyrants alike, in his concern about the feelings of others, clearly reveals the agitation of his own breast' (116–17).

70 **cock-shut time** i.e. twilight; when poultry are shut up for rest or when woodcocks fly or 'shoot' (*OED*)

72–5 See 46.2n.

73 **alacrity** liveliness (*OED*); Richard 'prognosticated before the doubtfull chance of the battell to come; not vsing the alacritie and mirth of mind and countenance as he was accustomed to doe' (Holinshed, 3.755).

74 **wont** accustomed

65–6] *Rowe*[3]*; one line Qq, F* 66 Ratcliffe] *Q6, F;* Ratliffe *Q1–5* 68 Sawst] *Q1, F; Q2–6 (*Sawest*)* thou] *Qq; om. F* 70 about] *Q1–5, F;* like *Q6* 74 SD] *Capell*

Set it down. Is ink and paper ready?

RATCLIFFE

It is, my lord.

KING RICHARD Bid my guard watch. Leave me.
Ratcliffe, about the mid of night come to my tent
And help to arm me. Leave me, I say.

Exit Ratcliffe [*with others*].

[*Richard goes into his tent to sleep.*]

Enter [STANLEY, Earl of] Derby *to Richmond* [*and Lords*] *in his tent.*

STANLEY

Fortune and Victory sit on thy helm.

RICHMOND

All comfort that the dark night can afford
Be to thy person, noble father-in-law.
Tell me, how fares our loving mother?

STANLEY

I, by attorney, bless thee from thy mother,
Who prays continually for Richmond's good.

76 **watch** stand watch

78 SD2 From 51 and 77 – in which Richard respectively asks if his armour has been brought 'into my tent' and then orders Ratcliffe to 'come to my tent' – it appears Richard is not yet *in* his tent at 77. He insists Ratcliffe *Leave* in 78 and enters the tent where he must be asleep by 118.

78.1–2 ***Richmond . . . tent*** Some characters appear to have remained in Richmond's tent with him; see *lords* (103) and *lords and gentlemen* (107).

79 ***sit** Q1's 'set' could mean 'sit' (Q2–6, F), but it risks confusion by conveying a directly opposed sense (cf. 351; also 'Fortune her selfe dooth sit upon our Crests', Marlowe, *Works*, *1 Tamburlaine*, 2.2.73). From subsequent curses employing *Let me sit* (118, 131, 139), Stanley's utterance appears to be a blessing (i.e. *Let* Fortune and Victory sit on thy helm); cf. Richard's hollow declaration that 'Victory sits on our helms' (351).

81 **father-in-law** i.e. stepfather (*OED* 2)

82–4 Contrast Richard's abuse of family ties and mockery of his mother's blessing and prayers (2.2.105–11).

83 **by attorney** i.e. by proxy, as a deputy

76] *Steevens; Qq, F line* lord. / me. / 77 Ratcliffe] *Q3, 5–6, F;* Ratliffe *Q1–2, 4* mid] *Q1–5, F;* midst *Q6* 78 SD1 *Ratcliffe*] *Q6, F; Ratliffe Q1–5* *with others*] *Cam subst.* SD2 *Richard . . . tent*] *after Malone* 78.1 STANLEY, Earl of] *Pope subst.* Derby] *F; Qq (Darby)* 78.2 *and Lords*] *Theobald subst.* 79+ SP] *Pope; Dar. Qq subst.; Der. F* 79 sit] *Q2–6, F;* set *Q1* 82 loving] *Q1–2;* noble *Q3–6, F*

So much for that. The silent hours steal on,
And flaky darkness breaks within the east.
In brief, for so the season bids us be,
Prepare thy battle early in the morning
And put thy fortune to the arbitrament
Of bloody strokes and mortal-staring war.
I, as I may – that which I would, I cannot –
With best advantage will deceive the time
And aid thee in this doubtful shock of arms.
But on thy side I may not be too forward,
Lest, being seen, thy brother, tender George,
Be executed in his father's sight.
Farewell. The leisure and the fearful time

85 **So . . . that** i.e. enough about that **steal on** go by unobserved (*OED* steal *v.*[1] II 11a); cf. 'The hour steals on' (*CE* 4.1.52).

86 **flaky darkness breaks** Shakespeare frequently describes darkness broken into cloudy fragments with the arrival of daylight; e.g. 'fleckled darkness' (*RJ* 2.2.190). Temporal references are symbolic: in Richmond's camp dawn approaches, but it is *dead midnight* in Richard's camp (180).

87 **season** time

88 **battle** body of troops in battle array (*OED sb.* II 8a)

90 **mortal-staring** both deathly and glaring; cf. the fatal gaze of the basilisk (1.2.153) and the *wrinkled front* of *Grim-visaged War* (1.1.9).

91 **that . . . cannot** perhaps echoing in a political sense the spiritual dilemma described in Romans, 7.15: 'for that which I do I alowe not. For what I woulde, that do I not: but what I hate, that do I.' Cf. Dent, M554: 'Men must do as they may, not as they would.' Erasmus (32.146) quotes a phrase from Terence's *Andria* in which a streetwalker modestly confesses her occupation.

92 i.e. [I] will conceal my true intentions in order to take advantage of the best opportunity that the present circumstances offer; cf. *Mac* 1.5.63–4. Holinshed characterizes Stanley as a 'wilie fox' in this deceit (3.754).

93 **doubtful** uncertain **shock** encounter of opposing armed forces in a charge or onset (*OED sb.*[3] 1a)

95 **being seen** i.e. I being seen (Abbott, 378) **brother** i.e. half-brother **tender George** George Stanley was an adult by 1485. Hall and Holinshed describe him as 'the child' (Hall, *Richard III*, fol. lviii[v]), but 'child' may mean 'young nobleman' (Thompson; cf. *KL* 3.4.178). Richard's very young victims are called *tender* (4.4.328, 383, 385), and he once berated the 'cruel child-killer' Clifford for slaying 'tender' Rutland (*3H6* 2.2.112, 115).

97 **leisure** duration of opportunity, time remaining before it is too late (*OED sb.* 2b); thus, in fact, the lack of leisure (cf. *R2* 1.1.5)

85 that.] *F;* that *Q1–2;* that: *Q3, 5–6;* that, *Q4* 89 the arbitrament] *Qq; F (*th'Arbitrement*)* 90 mortal-staring] *Qq, F (*mortal staring*), hyphen Steevens* 95 brother, tender] *Q1–5, F subst.;* tender brother *Q6* 96 his father's sight] *Q1–3, 5–6, F;* thy fathers fight *Q4*

Cuts off the ceremonious vows of love
And ample interchange of sweet discourse,
Which so-long-sundered friends should dwell upon.
God give us leisure for these rites of love.
Once more, adieu; be valiant and speed well.

RICHMOND

Good lords, conduct him to his regiment.
I'll strive with troubled thoughts to take a nap,
Lest leaden slumber peise me down tomorrow
When I should mount with wings of victory.
Once more, good night, kind lords and gentlemen.

Exeunt [F]*all but Richmond*[F].

O Thou, whose captain I account myself,
Look on my forces with a gracious eye;
Put in their hands Thy bruising irons of wrath,

100 ***sundered** Q5 offers the modern spelling. 'Sundry' could mean 'separate' or 'apart', but *OED* does not record Q1–2's 'sundried'.

101 ***rites** F's spelling provides the modern form of the word, which Shakespeare sometimes spells as it appears in Qq (cf. *MND* 4.1.132); see also *OED* right *sb.*[2].

102 **speed well** i.e. prosper

103 Given Stanley's need for secrecy, perhaps this command responds to the theatrical need to get the attendant lords out of Richmond's tent (Hammond). Lines 103–7 allow the lords to come out of the tent, assemble with Stanley and exit.

104 **with** i.e. against
***thoughts** R.G. White argues for F's 'noise', since struggling with troubled *thoughts* lessens Richmond's contrast with Richard (Var). Richmond is addressed as *Quiet, untroubled soul* (157), but he mentions his *watchful soul* (115), and both Holinshed (3.754) and Hall (*Richard III*, fol. liii[r]) emphasize his initial fears and uncertainties.

105 **leaden** heavy, dull; cf. slumber's 'leaden mace' (*JC* 4.3.266) and Dent, L136.1.
peise burden, oppress (*OED v.* 4a)

107 SD Richard may remain visible, sleeping in his tent as Richmond speaks his prayer in front of his own tent before retiring to sleep in 117.

108 **captain** in serving God as a captain Richmond takes an intermediary role, since the general was the head of a country's forces and normally the monarch (see Burns, 323–5; Cruikshank, 42, 50–5).

110 **bruising irons** i.e. maces; Shakespeare typically uses 'iron' to refer to a sword, but *bruising* contradicts that meaning and suggests the prophecy hailing the Lord's anointed in Psalms, 2.9: 'Thou shalt bruise them with a rod of iron: and breake them in peeces like a potters vessell.' Cf. 112.

100 so-long-sundered] *Qq, F (*so long sundried*), hyphens Theobald* sundered] *Q5–6;* sundried *Q1–2;* sundired *Q3–4;* sundred *F* 101 rites] *F;* rights *Qq* 103 lords] *Q1–3, 5–6, F;* Lord *Q4* 104 thoughts] *Qq;* noise *F* 107 SD *all but Richmond*] *F (Manet Richmond.)*

That they may crush down with a heavy fall
The usurping helmets of our adversaries;
Make us Thy ministers of chastisement,
That we may praise Thee in the victory.
To Thee I do commend my watchful soul,
Ere I let fall the windows of mine eyes:
Sleeping and waking, O, defend me still! [F]*Sleeps.*[F]

Enter the GHOST *of young* PRINCE EDWARD,
son [F]*to*[F] *Harry the Sixth.*

111 **fall** downward stroke (of a sword, etc.) (*OED sb.*[1] 1h); cf. *Oth* 2.3.230.

112 ***The** F's elided form ('Th'') may signal an abbreviation for the sake of rhythm that would be automatic (if difficult to pronounce) (Hammond); *adversaries* is probably trisyllabic.
usurping helmets an odd metonymy displacing the opprobrium for Richard's individual political usurpation onto the collective military capacity of his forces (Mowat & Werstine). In effect, support for a reigning monarch against an invading army is equated with the original crime(s) of usurpation, a problematic equation since some maintained that continuance in office could render even a violent usurper a 'lawfull prince' (Perkins, 918). Given the echo of Psalms, 2.9 in 110, the crushing of the helmets may recall the Geneva phrasing: 'Thou shalt krush them with a sceptre of yron'.

113 **ministers of chastisement** Richmond appropriates the function of the ruler as defined in Romans, 13.4: 'For he is the minister of God for thy wealth. But yf thou do euyll, feare: for he beareth not the sworde in vayne, for he is the minister of God, reuenger of wrath on hym that doth euyll.' Similar phrasing appears frequently in the Homilies and elsewhere (cf. *KJ* 2.1.87–8). Hall's Richmond exhorts his troops as 'trew men against traytors, pitifull persones against murtherers, trew inheritors against vsurpers, y[e] skorges of God against tirau[n]tes' (*Richard III*, fol. lvi[v]).

115 **commend . . . soul** perhaps echoing Jesus's last words: 'Father, into thy handes I commende my spirite' (Luke, 23.46)
commend entrust for keeping (*OED v.* 1b)
watchful wakeful

116 ***Ere** Q1's 'Eare' is a variant spelling.
windows Shakespeare uses *windows* for eyelids (as here and in *RJ* 4.1.100) and for the eyes themselves (*LLL* 5.2.826); cf. *OED sb.* 4a.

117.1 Vergil's account of Richard's demonic visions (not ghosts) is echoed by Grafton, Hall and Holinshed: 'it seemed to him being asleepe, that he did see diuerse images like terrible diuels, which pulled and haled him, not suffering him to take anie quiet or rest' (Holinshed, 3.755; Vergil, 221; Hall, *Richard III*, fol. liii[v]; Hardyng, *Richard III*, fol. civ[r]). However, in *True Tragedy* Richard proclaims that 'nightly dreames' terrorize his 'wounded conscience' as 'their ghoasts comes gaping for reuenge, / Whom I haue

112 The usurping] *Qq; F (*Th'vsurping*)* helmets] *Q1–4, F;* helmet *Q5–6* 114 the] *Q1–2, 6;* thy *Q3–5, F* 116 Ere] *Q1 (*Eare*), Q2–6, F* 117.1 *young*] *Q1–2; om. Q3–6, F* 117.2 *to*] *Q2–6, F; not in Q1* *Harry*] *Q1;* Henry *Q2–6, F* *Sixth.*] *Q3–6, F (sixt.); sixt, to Ri. Q1–2*

GHOST [of PRINCE EDWARD] (*to Richard*)
Let me sit heavy on thy soul tomorrow.
Think how thou stab'st me in my prime of youth
At Tewkesbury. Despair therefore, and die.
(*to Richmond*) Be cheerful, Richmond, for the wronged souls
Of butchered princes fight in thy behalf.
King Henry's issue, Richmond, comforts thee. [*Exit.*]

Enter the GHOST *of* HENRY THE SIXTH.

GHOST [of HENRY VI] (*to Richard*)
When I was mortal, my anointed body
By thee was punched full of deadly holes.

slaine in reaching for a Crowne . . . And euery one cries, let the tyrant die' (1875–85). The ghostly visitants differ from the 'tormenting dream' of 'a hell of ugly devils' (1.3.225–6) that Margaret wishes for Richard (Greenblatt, 177). Early modern stage ghosts usually dressed like the characters when alive, but were sometimes dressed and/or made up in white (Dessen & Thomson, 100). In 1622 Drayton evokes ghostly victims threatening Richard with their 'pale hands', a detail possibly derived from early make-up (*Poly-Olbion*, Song XXII, 1424–5).

118 **sit heavy on** i.e. oppress; for spiritual heaviness wished upon the guilty, cf. 'Be Mowbray's sins so heavy in his bosom' (*R2* 1.2.50).

119 **prime of youth** Cf. 1.2.250.

120 **Tewkesbury** Cf. 1.2.244.
Despair . . . die as Faustus to himself: 'Damned art thou *Faustus*, damned, despaire and die' (Marlowe, *Works*, *Faustus*, [5.1.]1725). The phrase was bandied back and forth in the Nashe–Harvey exchanges of 1592 (Nashe, 1.157; Harvey, 1.196).
therefore on that account

121 **wronged** wrongèd

123 **issue** offspring

123–76 SDs ***Exit*, *Exeunt*** Nothing except the limited size of an early modern acting company demands that the ghosts exit singly rather than remaining and vanishing collectively at 176 (as Rowe).

124 **When . . . mortal** echoing the famous opening of *The Spanish Tragedy*, 'When this eternall substance of my soule, / Did live imprisond in my wanton flesh' (Kyd, *Spanish Tragedy*, 1.1.1–2).
anointed See 4.4.151.

125 Marshall nominates this as one of the worst lines in all of Shakespeare.
punched punchèd
***deadly** Without Q1's 'deadlie' the line is a foot short, a fact used to argue the setting of F from a derivative Quarto (Var).

118 SP GHOST] *Qq; Gh. F* SD] *Q1–2, F (to Ri.); to K. Ri[c]. Q3–6* 121] *Qq; F lines* Richmond, / Soules / 121 SD] *Qq (To Rich.); Ghost to Richm. F* 123, 130, 138, 145, 153, 158, 166 SD] *Cam[1] subst.* 124 SD] *Q1–2 (to Ri.); to K. Ri. Q3–6; om. F* 125 deadly] *Q1; om. Q2–6, F*

Think on the Tower and me. Despair and die.
Harry the Sixth bids thee despair and die.
(*to Richmond*) Virtuous and holy, be thou conqueror.
Harry, that prophesied thou shouldst be king,
Doth comfort thee in thy sleep. Live and flourish. [*Exit.*]

Enter the GHOST of CLARENCE.

GHOST [of CLARENCE (*to Richard*)]
Let me sit heavy in thy soul tomorrow,
I, that was washed to death with fulsome wine,
Poor Clarence, by thy guile betrayed to death.
Tomorrow in the battle think on me,
And fall thy edgeless sword. Despair and die.
(*to Richmond*) Thou offspring of the house of
Lancaster,
The wronged heirs of York do pray for thee.
Good angels guard thy battle. Live and flourish. [*Exit.*]

Enter the GHOSTS of RIVERS, GREY [F]*and*[F] VAUGHAN.

[GHOST of RIVERS (*to Richard*)]
Let me sit heavy in thy soul tomorrow,
Rivers that died at Pomfret. Despair and die.
[GHOST of] GREY [(*to Richard*)]
Think upon Grey, and let thy soul despair.

126 **Tower** the site of Henry VI's death at Richard's hand (*3H6* 5.6)
129 See *3H6* 4.6.68–74.
132 **fulsome** cloying, satiating (*OED* 3)
135 **fall** imperative, i.e. drop, let fall (cf. 1.2.185 SD and Abbott, 291). This line is repeated at 163 (cf. 143).
edgeless blunt
136 Richmond descended from the Lancastrians by his mother, Margaret Beaufort, great-granddaughter of John of Gaunt (although the matter is not as simple as here presented: see 5.5.30n.). The support here posthumously offered by the York family foreshadows the symbolic merger of the two houses (Lull).
137 **wronged** wrongèd
138 **battle** troops (cf. 11, 88)

128, 136 SD] *Qq (To Rich.), F (To Richm.)* 130 thy] *Qq; om. F* 131, 139, 141, 142, 154 SD] *Rowe (To K. Rich.)* 131 sit] *Q2–6, F;* set *Q1* in] *Q1–4, F;* on *Q5–6* 138.1 GHOSTS] *Q1–2, 6, F; Ghoast Q3–5* 139 SP] *Dyce; Riu. Q3–6, F; King Q1–2* 139 in] *Q1–4, F;* on *Q5–6* 141, 142 SP GHOST of] *Dyce*

[GHOST of] VAUGHAN [(*to Richard*)]
Think upon Vaughan, and with guilty fear
Let fall thy lance. Despair and die.

ALL (*to Richmond*)
Awake, and think our wrongs in Richard's bosom
Will conquer him. Awake, and win the day. [*Exeunt.*]

Enter the GHOSTS *of the two young* PRINCES.

GHOSTS [of PRINCES] (*to Richard*)
Dream on thy cousins smothered in the Tower.
Let us be lead within thy bosom, Richard,
And weigh thee down to ruin, shame and death.
Thy nephews' souls bid thee despair and die.
(*to Richmond*) Sleep, Richmond, sleep in peace and wake in joy;
Good angels guard thee from the boar's annoy.
Live, and beget a happy race of kings;
Edward's unhappy sons do bid thee flourish. [*Exeunt.*]

143 *The Variorum account provides a history of editorial interventions from the adding of an epithet to modify lance – e.g. 'hurtless' (Capell) or 'pointless' (Collier) – to the presumption of physical gesture or verbal repetition (Marshall). The assumed parallelism with 135 also encourages such emendations.

145.1–158 SD *Q3 changes the Q1–2 order, moving the princes to follow Hastings; thus Q3–F follow the sequence of the other ghosts, who appear in order of their deaths. Q3 has no textual authority in this portion of the play (but see 183n.). See also pp. 437–9.

146 **cousins** nephews (cf. 2.2.8)

147 ***lead** Q1's 'lead' better agrees with 148 (and with *heavy* in 139) than does Q2–8, F's 'laid' (Theobald); cf. *leaden slumber* (105).

150 **sleep in peace** Psalms, 4.8 has 'I wil laye me downe, & also slepe in peace' (Geneva), noting that peace comes from the Lord (either God or King David) and that the speaker 'shulde dwel as ioyfully alone as if he had manie about him, because the Lord is with him'.

151 **annoy** that which causes discomfort, annoyance (*OED sb.* 2)

144 SD] *Qq (to Ri[ch].), F (to Richm.)* 144] *Qq; F lines* Awake, / Bosome, / Richard's] *Q1, F;* Ri. *Q2–5; Ric. Q6* 145 Will] *Q2–6, F;* Wel *Q1* 145.1–153 *Enter . . .* flourish.] *Q1–2; after 158 Q3–6, F* 145.1 *the two*] *Q1–5, F; two Q6* 146 SP GHOSTS] *F; Ghost Q1–2, 6; Gho. Q3–5* SD] *Q1–2 (to Ri.); to K.R. Q 3–6; om. F* 146] *Qq; F lines* Cousins / Tower: / 147 lead] *Q1;* laid *Q2–6, F* 149 souls bid] *Qq;* soule bids *F* 150] *Qq; F lines* Richmond, / Ioy, / 150 SD] *Qq (To Ri[ch].), F (Ghosts to Richm.)*

Enter the GHOST of HASTINGS.

GHOST [of HASTINGS (*to Richard*)]
Bloody and guilty, guiltily awake,
And in a bloody battle end thy days.
Think on Lord Hastings. Despair and die.
(*to Richmond*) Quiet, untroubled soul, awake, awake.
Arm, fight and conquer for fair England's sake. [*Exit.*]

Enter the GHOST of Lady ANNE, *his wife.*

[F]GHOST [of ANNE] (*to Richard*)[F]
Richard, thy wife, that wretched Anne, thy wife,
That never slept a quiet hour with thee,
Now fills thy sleep with perturbations.
Tomorrow in the battle think on me,
And fall thy edgeless sword. Despair and die.
(*to Richmond*) Thou quiet soul, sleep thou a quiet sleep.
Dream of success and happy victory.
Thy adversary's wife doth pray for thee. [*Exit.*]

Enter the GHOST of BUCKINGHAM.

[F]GHOST [of BUCKINGHAM] (*to Richard*)[F]
The first was I that helped thee to the crown;
The last was I that felt thy tyranny.
O, in the battle think on Buckingham,
And die in terror of thy guiltiness.
Dream on, dream on, of bloody deeds and death.
Fainting, despair; despairing, yield thy breath.

160 Cf. 4.1.82–4.
163 See 135.
172 **Fainting** growing faint of heart (*OED*)

153.1 HASTINGS] *Q1–2; L. Hastings Q3–6; Lord Hastings F* 154 SP GHOST] *Q1–2, 6; Gho. Q3–5, F* 157 SD] *Qq (To Ri[ch].), F (Hast. to Rich.)* 157] *Qq; F lines* soule, / awake: / 158.1 Lady] *Q1–2; Queene Q3–6; om. F* 159] *Qq; F lines* Wife, / Wife, / 161 perturbations] *Q2–6, F;* preturbations *Q1* 164] *Qq; F lines* soule, / sleepe: / 164 SD] *Qq (To Rich.), F (Ghost to Richm.)* 167] *Qq; F lines* I / Crowne: /

(*to Richmond*) I died for hope ere I could lend thee aid;
But cheer thy heart, and be thou not dismayed.
God and good angels fight on Richmond's side,
And Richard fall in height of all his pride. [*Exit.*]

Richard starteth up out of a dream.

KING RICHARD

Give me another horse! Bind up my wounds!
Have mercy, Jesu. – Soft, I did but dream.
O coward conscience, how dost thou afflict me!
The lights burn blue. It is now dead midnight.

173 ***hope** Frequently emended, but *hope* makes sense if 'for' means 'for want of' or 'as regards' (cf. *Mac* 1.5.36: 'almost dead for breath'). Thus Buckingham may say: 'I languished for lack of hope before I had opportunity to aid you.' Richard's proposal 'To stop all hopes whose growth may damage me' (4.2.59) is countered by Richmond's affirmation of *True hope* at 5.2.23–4.

176 **Richard fall** i.e. let Richard fall (cf. 163 and Dent, P581: 'Pride will have a fall.')

177–206 Richard's 'strange vision not so suddenlie strake his heart with a sudden feare, but it stuffed his head and troubled his mind with manie busie and dreadfull imaginations' (Holinshed, 3.755). Richard's refusal to repent contrasts with Clarence's response to his dream in 1.4; cf. the Second Murderer's repentance (1.4.270–7) and Dighton and Forrest's *conscience and remorse* (4.3.20). Grafton summarizes Richard's spiritually 'desperate' state: 'I thynke that this was not a dreame, but rather his conscience pricked with the sharpe styng of his mischeuous offences, whiche although they do not pricke alway, yet moost com[m]only they wyll byte moost towarde the latter daye, representyng vnto vs not onely them selfe, but also the terrible punishement that is ordeyned for the same, as the sight of the deuill tearyng and halyng vs, so that thereby (if we haue grace) we may take an occasyon to be penitent, or else for lacke of the same dye in desperacion' (Hardyng, *Richard III*, fol. civ^{r-v}). A 17th-century Folio reader annotates: 'Richard affrighted by fearefull visions . . . dispaire of conscience and memorie of abominable cruelties and periuries make Richard madde' (Yamada, 160). This passage shows similarities with a speech from *Troublesome Raigne* already echoed at 1.2.1 (*TRKJ*, Pt 2, xiii.1–13, sigs D2^{v}–D3^{r}).

177–8 For Garrick's influential delivery of Cibber's lines, see p. 92.

177 **Give . . . horse** A dream again anticipates the future (see 5.4.13; cf. Toole, 31).

178 **Soft** i.e. wait a moment

179 **coward conscience** Richard blames his conscience for making him cowardly by besieging him with moral accusations and visions of disaster (cf. 193). See also Dent, C606.

180 **lights burn blue** Candles were thought to register the presence of spir-

173 SD] *Qq (To Ri[ch].), F (Ghost to Richm.)* 173] *Qq; F lines* hope / Ayde; / 176 fall] *F;* fals *Qq* 176 SD] *Cam^{1} (vanishes.); The ghosts vanish. / Rowe* 176.1 *Richard starteth up*] *Q1–2; K. Richard starteth Q3–6; Richard starts F* a] *Qq; his F* 177 SP] *Qq (King Ri[ch].); Rich. F* 180 now] *Q1;* not *Q2–6, F*

Cold fearful drops stand on my trembling flesh.
What do I fear? Myself? There's none else by.
Richard loves Richard, that is, I am I.
Is there a murderer here? No. Yes, I am.
Then fly! What, from myself? Great reason why?
Lest I revenge. What, myself upon myself?
Alack, I love myself. Wherefore? For any good
That I myself have done unto myself?
O, no. Alas, I rather hate myself,
For hateful deeds committed by myself.
I am a villain. Yet I lie; I am not.

its by burning low (cf. *JC* 4.3.273) and blue (cf. Lyly's *Galathea*, 2.3.62–5).
***now** F's nonsensical 'not', originating with Q2's mistake and continued in all subsequent quartos, argues that this portion of F was set from a derivative quarto with only the most minimal correction (but see changes to *eaves-dropper*, 221).
dead midnight Cf. dawn approaching in 86; time, like the weather (contrast 86 with 277–8), is differently remarked in the two camps.

182–203 **fear . . . love . . . pity** Richard, murdering Henry VI, characterizes himself as 'I that have neither pity, love nor fear' (*3H6* 5.6.68).

183 ***am** Hammond and Jowett prefer 'I and I' (Q1) over 'I am I' (Q2–8, F). Malone wondered if Q1 might be right (Var); Evans has argued that eye-skip involving *I am* (184) could account for 'am' ('Restored', 46). Q2 shows only minimal correction in this scene (e.g. at 2, 147, 180, 282, 320, 321), but 'am' anticipates Richard's self-definition ('I am a villain. Yet I lie; I am not', 191), echoes his claim to singularity ('I am myself alone', *3H6* 5.6.83) and mocks his confident definition of 'what I am' (1.3.132). It parallels the Bastard's claim to stable self-identity ('I am I, howe'er I was begot', *KJ* 1.1.175). It would also express Richard's resistance to such 'conversion' as represented by Oliver's renunciation of his villainous past (''Twas I, but 'tis not I') to become 'the thing I am' (*AYL* 4.3.134–6). 'I am I' adapts that divine identity statement ('I am that I am') which is deployed strategically by Viola (*TN* 3.1.142), treated cavalierly in *Son* 121 and perverted by Iago's 'I am not what I am' (*Oth* 1.1.64). Cf. Exodus, 3.14: 'God aunswered Moyses, I am that I am. And he said: This shalt thou say vnto the chyldren of Israel, I am, hath sent me'.

186 **myself upon myself** Richard threatens to make good upon his oath at 4.4.399 ('Myself myself confound'); cf. 2.4.64, 4.4.420. Richard's reference to *despair* (200) recalls Queen Elizabeth's threat to join with 'despair . . . And to myself become an enemy' (2.2.36–7).

187 **I love myself** Self-love contradicts the soldier's creed announced by Young Clifford: 'He that is truly dedicate to war / Hath no self-love' (*2H6* 5.2.37–8).

191, 195 **villain** Cf. 1.1.30; Richard has fulfilled his determination 'to prove a villain' (MacDonald & MacDonald, 59).

181 stand] *Q1–4, 6, F;* stands *Q5* 182 What . . . Myself?] *Q1;* What do I feare my selfe? *Q2–6;* What? do I feare my Selfe? *F* 183 am] *Q2–6, F;* and *Q1* 185 reason why?] *Q1–2;* reason why, *Q3–6;* reason: why? *F* 188 I] *Q1–5, F; om. Q6*

Fool, of thyself speak well. Fool, do not flatter.
My conscience hath a thousand several tongues,
And every tongue brings in a several tale,
And every tale condemns me for a villain.
Perjury, perjury, in the highest degree;
Murder, stern murder, in the direst degree;
All several sins, all used in each degree,
Throng to the bar, crying all, 'Guilty, guilty!'
I shall despair. There is no creature loves me,
And if I die, no soul will pity me.

193 Cf. 5.2.17 and Dent, C601; 'Conscience is a thousand witnesses' (Erasmus, 32.277).
several individually separate, different (*OED a.* 2a)

194 **brings in** adduces as evidence

196–7 **Perjury . . . Murder** The two lines represent opposed roles in Richard's imaginary courtroom: the first voice (196) cries *Perjury*, rejecting the charge that he is a *villain* which has been brought by the 'tales' (195); the second voice responds by reiterating the charge against him: 'Murder . . . in the dir'st degree' (197). This internal debate replicates formal features of Faustus's soliloquies (Marlowe, *Works*, *Faustus*, [2.1.]389–402) and recalls the hybrid morality play; Apius, for example, represents the voices within himself: 'Conscience saith crueltye sure will detest me: / And Iustice saith, death in thende will molest me' (*Apius*, *sig.* C1[r]; cf. Spivack, 271).

198 **used . . . degree** i.e. committed in every stage of intensity or amount (*OED* degree *sb.* 6a)

199 **Throng . . . bar** crowd to the barrier or wooden rail marking the precinct of the judge's seat, at which prisoners were stationed for arraignment, trial or sentence; here evoking the tribunal of conscience (*OED* bar *sb.*[1] III 22a, b, citing this line). 'Conscience', Perkins writes, 'is like to a Iudge that holdeth an assize and take notice of inditements, and causeth the most notorious malefactour that is to hold up his hand at the barre of his iudgement. Nay it is (as it were) a little god sitting in the middle of mens hearts arraigning them in this life as they shall be arraigned for their offences at the tribunall seate of the euerliuing god in the day of iudgement. Wherefore the temporary iudgement that is giuen by the conscience is nothing els but a beginning or a fore-runner of the last iudgement' (*Discourse*, 10). See also Wilks, 97.

200 **shall despair** Observing the iambic stress on *shall*, Troughton (96) emphasizes the degree to which Richard commits himself to despair and its inevitable extension in self-destruction, ironically recalling Richard's witty trifling about hanging himself in 'despair' at 1.2.85.

200–3 **There . . . myself** Objecting to Henry Irving's 1896 omission of 201–3, George Bernard Shaw imagines Richard should catch the 'sentimental cadence' in his voice in 200 and awaken 'the mocker' in himself in 201 (Colley, 139).

196 perjury,] *Q1–2; om. Q3–6, F* highest] *Qq; F (*high'st*)* 197 Murder . . . murder] *Q1–5, F (*Murther . . . murther*), Q6* direst] *Qq; F (*dyr'st*)* 199 Throng] *Q1–2;* Throng all *Q3–6, F* to the bar] *Qq; F (*to'th'Barre*)* 201 will] *Q1–2;* shall *Q3–6, F*

And wherefore should they, since that I myself
Find in myself no pity to myself?
Methought the souls of all that I had murdered
Came to my tent, and every one did threat
Tomorrow's vengeance on the head of Richard.

Enter RATCLIFFE.

RATCLIFFE My lord.

KING RICHARD Zounds, who is there?

RATCLIFFE
Ratcliffe, my lord, 'tis I. The early village cock
Hath twice done salutation to the morn;
Your friends are up and buckle on their armour.

KING RICHARD
O Ratcliffe, I have dreamed a fearful dream!
What think'st thou, will our friends prove all true?

RATCLIFFE
No doubt, my lord.

KING RICHARD O Ratcliffe, I fear, I fear.

RATCLIFFE
Nay, good my lord, be not afraid of shadows.

203 **pity** The last instance of this word in the play comes appropriately and ironically from Richard, who rejects pity (4.2.65; see also *3H6* 5.6.68), invokes it in witty mockery (1.2.71), professes it hypocritically (1.3.140) and performs its outward semblance (2.2.24).

204–5 *Walton (*Copy*, 117–18) argues for F's collation of MS here (and at 202 to produce 'Nay').

208 William Winter describes Richard Mansfield mistaking the entering character 'for yet another apparition' (Colley, 117).

*Zounds deleted from F in accord with the Jacobean reform (cf. 1.4.84n., 1.4.120, 3.7.218).

212–14 *Compositor's eye-skip from *O Ratcliffe* (212) to Richard's next *O Ratcliffe* (214) plausibly explains F's omission. Ratcliffe's *shadows* (215) refers to the dream mentioned in the omitted lines (Smidt, *Memorial*, 19–20).

212–13 **fearful . . . true** ironic, given Richard's admonishment concerning the futility of *fearful commenting* at 4.3.51–2 (Churchill, 380–1).

202 And] *Qq;* Nay *F* 204 had] *Q1, F; om. Q2–6* murdered] *Qq, F (*murtherd*), Johnson (*murder'd*)* 205 Came] *Q1–2, F;* Came all *Q3–6* 206.1 RATCLIFFE] *Q1–2, 4–6, F; Ratliffe Q3* 208 Zounds, who is] *Qq;* Who's *F* there] *Q1–3, 5–6, F;* heare *Q4* 209 Ratcliffe] *Q1–2, 5–6, F;* Ratliffe *Q3–4* 212–14 KING . . . lord.] *Qq; om. F* 214] *Steevens; Qq line* Lord. / feare. /

KING RICHARD

By the Apostle Paul, shadows tonight
Have struck more terror to the soul of Richard
Than can the substance of ten thousand soldiers
Armed in proof, and led by shallow Richmond.
'Tis not yet near day. Come, go with me.
Under our tents I'll play the eavesdropper,
To see if any mean to shrink from me.

Exeunt [F]*Richard and Ratcliffe*[F].

Enter the Lords *to Richmond* [F]*sitting in his tent*[F].

LORDS

Good morrow, Richmond.

RICHMOND

Cry mercy, lords and watchful gentlemen,

216 **Apostle Paul** Cf. 1.2.36, 41, 3.4.75.

216–18 **shadows . . . substance** Talbot claims that alone he constitutes but 'a shadow of himself', while his true self is corporately embodied in the 'substance' of his soldiers (*1H6* 2.3.61–2). Here, *shadows* of individual conscience appear stronger than armed forces.

218 **ten thousand** Cf. 'six or seven thousand' (10).

219 **Armed** armèd
proof impenetrable armour, proof armour (*OED sb.* B II 10)
shallow wanting in depth of mind or character (*OED a.* 6c)

221 **Under** The 'eavesdrop' is the space outside a house overhung by the roof (*OED sb.*); perhaps Richard speaks of standing beneath overhanging portions of tents, as in the tent 'fly'.
eavesdropper F and Q1 share the same spelling; Q2–6 show remarkable variance: 'ease', 'euse' and 'eaues' are equivalents (*OED* eaves 1a). The image of a king sneaking about and listening outside tents to ascertain the loyalty of his troops resembles but significantly differs from that of the disguised Henry V engaging his soldiers in discussion (*H5* 4.1). On parallels and contrasts between the two, see Potter. This skulking Richard contrasts with the bold master of circumstances of Act 1 (Ornstein, 73).

222.1 *sitting . . . tent* F makes it clear that Richmond sits in his tent when the lords enter; he will rise to greet them and proceed outside to deliver his oration.

223 SP *F is clearly wrong, and Q1–2 SPs are ambiguous; Q3–6's decisive plural seems preferable (see 226, 235). Richmond could be greeted with a collective *Good morrow* (*TxC*, 248).

224 **Cry mercy** i.e. I'm sorry (omitting pronouns; cf. 1.3.234.
watchful wakeful (cf. 115)

220 day. Come] *F;* day come *Q1;* day, come *Q2–6* 221 eavesdropper] *F4;* ease dropper *Q1;* ewse dropper *Q2;* ewse-dropper *Q3;* eawse-dropper *Q4;* ewese-dropper *Q5–6;* Ease-dropper *F* 222 see] *Q1–2;* heare *Q3–6, F* mean] *Q1–3, 5–6, F;* means *Q4* SD *Ratcliffe*] *F (Ratliffe)* 223 SP] *Q1–2 (Lo[r].), 3–6; Richm. F*

That you have ta'en a tardy sluggard here.

LORD

How have you slept, my lord?

RICHMOND

The sweetest sleep and fairest-boding dreams
That ever entered in a drowsy head
Have I since your departure had, my lords.
Methought their souls whose bodies Richard murdered
Came to my tent and cried on victory.
I promise you my soul is very jocund
In the remembrance of so fair a dream.
How far into the morning is it, lords?

LORD

Upon the stroke of four.

RICHMOND

Why, then 'tis time to arm and give direction.

His oration to his soldiers.

More than I have said, loving countrymen,

225 **ta'en . . . sluggard** i.e. caught a dilatory, lazy person; Richmond's apparent ease contrasts with Richard's terrors and with his pretence of nonchalance at 3.4.23.

226 SP *Unlike the case of 223, Qq are consistently ambiguous here. Any lord from the group will do for the speaker.

227–34 Thompson finds no chronicle precedents for Richmond's dreams.

227 **fairest-boding** most auspicious

231 **cried on** invoked by outcry (*OED* cry *v.* II 17); cf. *Ham* 5.2.348.

235 SP *See 223, 226; Q1–2's '*Lo.*' remains ambiguous in Q3–6, F's '*Lor.*' F4 first registers a clearly plural '*Lords.*'

236 SD Holinshed heads Richmond's speech with 'The oration of King Henrie the sea*uenth to his armie*' (3.757) and also gives a heading to Richard's battlefield speech (cf. 313 SD). The play's SDs appear uniquely (for Shakespeare) aimed at the reader; Legge similarly follows the sources (*Richardus Tertius*, 4460, 4526); see p. 450. In *3H6*, Margaret and Edward have similarly contrasting battlefield speeches (5.4.67–82). Hall implies Richmond's oratorical manner: 'mounted on a lyttel hyll' before all his troops, 'he pawsed a while, and after with a lowde voyce and bolde spirite spake to his compaignions these or lyke wordes folowyng' (*Richard III*, fol. lv[r–v]).

225 a] *Q1–3, 5–6, F; om. Q4* 226 SP] *Qq (Lo[r].); Lords. F* 227] *Qq; F lines* sleepe, / Dreames, / fairest-boding] *Qq, F (*fairest boding*), hyphen Theobald* 229 departure] *Q2–6, F; Q1 (*depature*)* 230 murdered] *Qq, F (*murtherd*), Johnson (*murder'd*)* 232 soul] *Qq;* Heart *F* 235 SP] *Qq, F (Lo[r].)*

The leisure and enforcement of the time
Forbids to dwell upon. Yet remember this:
God, and our good cause, fight upon our side.
The prayers of holy saints and wronged souls,
Like high-reared bulwarks, stand before our faces.
Richard except, those whom we fight against
Had rather have us win than him they follow.
For, what is he they follow? Truly, gentlemen,
A bloody tyrant and a homicide;
One raised in blood, and one in blood established;
One that made means to come by what he hath,
And slaughtered those that were the means to help him;
A base foul stone, made precious by the foil
Of England's chair, where he is falsely set;
One that hath ever been God's enemy.
Then if you fight against God's enemy,
God will, in justice, ward you as His soldiers;
If you do sweat to put a tyrant down,

238 **leisure** i.e. lack of leisure (cf. 97)

241 **prayers . . . saints** This phrase is not from Hall or Holinshed, and the idea is controversial, since, according to mainstream Protestants, the only saints that could pray would be the living, not the departed (see 1.2.8n. on *lawful*, 4.4.75n. on *fiends . . . saints* and the Second Homily 'concerning Prayer', *Homilies*, 116–17). Shaheen cites Revelation, 5.8, describing the adoration of the Lamb of God, worshipped with 'the prayers of saintes', and 6.9–10, in which the martyrs cry out 'with a loude voyce, saying: howe long taryest thou Lorde, holy and true, to iudge and to auenge our blood'.
wronged wrongèd

243 **except** excluded

247 **raised** i.e. elevated in status

248 **made means** cf. 40; here the meaning is sinister.

250 **foil** a thin layer of metal placed under a precious stone to increase its brilliancy or under some transparent substance to give it the appearance of a precious stone (*OED sb.*[1] 5a); cf. *R2* 1.3.265–7; *1H4* 1.2.204–5.

251 **chair** throne
set i.e. as a jewel is set

252, 253 **God's enemy** perhaps suggesting Satan as 'the Enemy' (*OED sb.* 1b)

254 **ward** protect

255 **sweat** labour; Hall and Holinshed agree on 'sweat': 'labour for your gayne, and swet for your right' (Hall, *Richard III*, fol. lxvi[v]); 'sweare' (Q3) misprints Q1–2's 'sweate'.

242 high-reared] *Qq, F* (high reard), *hyphen Pope* reared] *Q1–3, 5–6, F;* read *Q4* 243 Richard except,] *Q3–6;* (*Richard* except) *F;* Richard, except *Q1–2* 249 slaughtered] *Q1–3, 5–6, F;* slandered *Q4* 250 foil] *Q1–2;* soile *Q3–5;* soyle *Q6, F* 255 do sweat] *Q1–2;* do sweare *Q3–5, F;* sweare *Q6*

You sleep in peace, the tyrant being slain;
If you do fight against your country's foes,
Your country's fat shall pay your pains the hire.
If you do fight in safeguard of your wives,
Your wives shall welcome home the conquerors.
If you do free your children from the sword,
Your children's children quits it in your age.
Then in the name of God and all these rights,
Advance your standards, draw your willing swords.
For me, the ransom of my bold attempt
Shall be this cold corpse on the earth's cold face;
But if I thrive, the gain of my attempt
The least of you shall share his part thereof.
Sound drums and trumpets boldly and cheerfully.
God, and Saint George, Richmond, and victory! [*Exeunt.*]

Enter KING RICHARD, RATCLIFFE *and Soldiers.*

258 **fat** wealth, surplus goods (cf. Genesis, 45.18: 'and ye shall eate the fat of the lande'). This biblical language euphemizes Richmond's promises of 'aboundance of riches and copie of profit' (Holinshed, 3.758) and avoids any hint of the greed that tarnished his later reputation as one who 'coveted to accumulate treasure' (Bacon, *Henry VII*, 262; cf. Chrimes, 207–18).
pay . . . hire pay you the salary for your efforts

262 **quits** requites, repays (*OED v.* II 10; cf. 4.4.20, 64)

264 **Advance** raise, lift up (*OED v.* III 9; cf. 348 and *LLL* 4.3.341)

265-6 i.e. if defeated the only ransom I expect the enemy to be paid is my dead body; cf. Hall's account (with a verbal similarity to 1.1.12): 'you shall fynde me this daye, rather a dead carion vppon the coold grounde, then a fre prisoner on a carpet in a laydes chamber' (*Richard III*, fol. lvi^{v}).

265 **ransom** fee paid for release of a prisoner (*OED sb.* 2a), referring to the medieval practice of setting a pre-battle ransom price to be paid for oneself if captured (Mowat & Werstine; see *H5* 4.7.68)

267 Cf. Abbott, 417 for redundant noun clauses.

270 **Saint George** England's patron saint: 'all souldiers, entring into battaile . . . shall haue for their common crie and word, *S. George, S. George*, forward, or vpon them, *S. George*, whereby the souldier is much comforted, and the enemy dismaied' (Garrard, 47); cf. 349–50 and *H5* 3.1.34.

270.1 *F's addition of Catesby perhaps suggests influence (unusual in this portion of the play) of FMS, since Catesby neither speaks nor is spoken or referred to in the remainder of the scene (Walton, *Quarto*, 261).

270 SD] *Capell* 270.1 *and Soldiers*] *Ard*^{2}*; Attendants, and Forces with them / Capell; &c. Qq; and Catesby F*

KING RICHARD
What said Northumberland, as touching Richmond?
RATCLIFFE
That he was never trained up in arms.
KING RICHARD
He said the truth. And what said Surrey then?
RATCLIFFE
He smiled and said, 'The better for our purpose.'
KING RICHARD
He was in the right, and so indeed it is. *The clock striketh.*
Tell the clock there. Give me a calendar.
Who saw the sun today?
RATCLIFFE Not I, my lord.
KING RICHARD
Then he disdains to shine, for by the book
He should have braved the east an hour ago.
A black day will it be to somebody.
Ratcliffe!
RATCLIFFE
My lord.
KING RICHARD The sun will not be seen today.

271–5 This passage represents the meagre fruit of Richard's spying (see 220–2).
271 **Northumberland** cf. 68–71; Richard keeps a close eye on Northumberland, despite his going about *cheering up* the soldiers.
as touching concerning
272 **trained** trainèd
276 **Tell the clock** count the strokes of the clock (cf. 1.4.119)
calendar almanac (*OED sb.* 2)
278–87 The sun's absence seems to be Shakespeare's invention (possibly contradicting 86). Richmond 'had the sonne at his backe and in the faces of his enemies' (Hall, *Richard III*, fol. lvi^{v}). The dying Richard of *True Tragedy* invokes tragic meteorology: 'you watry heauens rowle on my gloomy day, and darksome cloudes close vp my cheerful sownde, downe is thy sunne Richard, neuer to shine againe' (1989–91; Churchill, 521).
278 **book** i.e. the almanac requested in 276
279 **braved** adorned, made splendid (*OED v.* 5)
280 Cf. Dent, D88: 'To be a black day to somebody'.

275 so indeed] *Qq (*so in deede *Q1c (Hn, Fo),* soin deede *Q1u (BL)), F* SD] *Qq opp.* there. *276; Clocke strikes. F opp.* there. *276* 276] *Pope; Qq, F line* there. / to day? / 277] *Steevens; Qq, F line* day? / Lord. / 280–1 A . . . Ratcliffe] *Johnson; one line Qq, F* 280 somebody.] *F;* some bodie *Qq* 281 Ratcliffe!] Rat. *Q1–5; Rat. Q6; Ratcliffe. F* 282] *Steevens; Qq, F line* Lord. / day, / not] *Q2–6, F;* nor *Q1*

The sky doth frown and lour upon our army.
I would these dewy tears were from the ground.
Not shine today? Why, what is that to me
More than to Richmond? For the selfsame heaven
That frowns on me looks sadly upon him.

Enter NORFOLK.

NORFOLK
Arm, arm, my lord! The foe vaunts in the field.

KING RICHARD
Come, bustle, bustle. Caparison my horse.
– Call up Lord Stanley; bid him bring his power.
– I will lead forth my soldiers to the plain,
And thus my battle shall be ordered:
My foreward shall be drawn out all in length,

283 **lour** The 'clouds that loured upon our house' (1.1.3) have returned.

284 **from** away from (cf. 3.5.32)

286–7 **selfsame . . . him** a perverse echo of the Sermon on the Mount, where Jesus spells out God's general providence: 'he maketh his sonne to aryse on the euyll, and on the good, and sendeth rayne on the iust, and on the vniust' (Matthew, 5.45). Contrast Henry IV concerning an ill-omened sky before battle: 'with the losers let it sympathize, / For nothing can seem foul to those that win' (*1H4* 5.1.7–8). Cf. Dent, S985: 'The sun shines upon all alike.'

288 **vaunts** boasts (*OED v.* 1)

289 **bustle, bustle** Cf. 1.1.152.

Caparison put trappings on, deck, harness (*OED v.*); a caparison was a cloth or covering spread over the saddle or harness of a horse, often gaily ornamented (*OED sb.*).

291–300 Richard, 'bringing all his men out of their campe into the plaine, ordered his fore-ward in a maruellous length, in which he appointed both horsemen and footmen . . . and in the fore-front he placed the archers like a strong fortristed trench or bulworke. Ouer this battell was capteine, John duke of Norfolke, with whome was Thomas earle of Surrie, his sonne. After this long vant-gard, followed king Richard himselfe with a strong companie of chosen and approued men of warre, hauing horssemen for wings on both sides of his battell' (Holinshed, 3.755; Hall, *Richard III*, fols liii^{v}–liv^{r}).

291 **to the plain** i.e. into the field of battle (*OED* plain *sb.*^{1} 2, citing this line), thus not necessarily describing the topography of the battle site

292 **ordered** orderèd

293 **foreward** vanguard

drawn . . . length i.e. stretched out along a line; Richard attempted to frighten the enemy by creating the appearance of a great multitude of soldiers (Hall, *Richard III*, fols liii^{v}–liv^{r}; Holinshed, 3.755).

287 looks] *Q1–5, F;* looke *Q6* 287.1 NORFOLK.] *Qq (Norffolke. Q1c (Hn, Fo), Norffolke Q1u (BL)), F* 293 out all] *Q1; om. Q2–6, F*

Consisting equally of horse and foot;
Our archers shall be placed in the midst.
John, Duke of Norfolk, Thomas, Earl of Surrey,
Shall have the leading of this foot and horse.
They thus directed, we will follow
In the main battle, whose puissance on either side
Shall be well winged with our chiefest horse.
This, and Saint George to boot. What think'st thou,
Norfolk?

NORFOLK

A good direction, warlike sovereign.
He sheweth him a paper.
This found I on my tent this morning:
'Jockey of Norfolk, be not so bold,
For Dickon thy master is bought and sold.'

294 **horse and foot** cavalry and infantry
295 **placed** placèd
298 **we** i.e. Richard
299–300 i.e. the main body of troops will be supported on either side by the best cavalry.
299 **battle** troop formation
puissance power
300 **winged** wingèd; flanked with forces on the wings (*OED v.* II 9a)
301 **to boot** in addition, besides (*OED sb.* I 1); *OED* also cites this line as meaning 'Saint George to our help' (*OED sb.* II 7c).
302 **direction** battle plan (cf. 16)
304–5 *Since Capell many editors have had Richard read these lines; Wilson reasons that Norfolk would be incapable of reading such an insult aloud to his king. Cibber's Richard does the reading, providing Kemble with an opportunity to demonstrate calm contempt (actually only assumed for his troops) before striking the paper aside with his sword (Colley, 49). Edmund Kean eyed Norfolk 'suspiciously for a moment, then reads it – strikes it to the ground scornfully with the blade of his sword' (Colley, 75).
304 **Jockey** diminutive of John, Norfolk's Christian name; Hall has 'Iack' (*Richard III*, fol. lvii^{v}); Holinshed has 'Iacke'.
***so** Capell's emendation 'too' (cf. Q6's '*to*') follows Hall and Holinshed.
305 **Dickon** diminutive of 'Dick' for Richard
bought and sold perhaps 'betrayed for a bribe' (*OED* buy II 11b, citing this line), but 'tricked, deceived' is possible (Dent, B787: 'To be bought and sold'); cf. *1H6* 4.4.13 ('bought and sold Lord Talbot') and the insult to Ajax in *TC* 2.1.45–6 ('thou art bought and sold among those of any wit'), which implies being held in contempt. On Henry VII's later reputation and corruption, see 258n.

297 this] *Q1–2;* the *Q3–6, F* 299 main] *Q2–6, F;* matne *Q1* 301] *Qq; F lines* boote. / Norfolke. / boot] *Q3–6, F;* bootes *Q1–2* think'st] *Q1 (*thinkst*), F; Q2–6 (*thinkest*)* Norfolk?] *Q1, F;* Nor. *Q2–5;* not. *Q6* 302 SD] *Qq (opp. 302–3); om. F* 304] *Qq, F; Ric.* Jockey . . . *bold; [reads. / Capell* so] *Q1–5, F; to Q6*

KING RICHARD

A thing devised by the enemy.
– Go, gentlemen, every man unto his charge.
Let not our babbling dreams affright our souls.
Conscience is but a word that cowards use,
Devised at first to keep the strong in awe.
Our strong arms be our conscience, swords our law.
March on, join bravely, let us to it pell-mell,
If not to heaven, then hand in hand to hell.

His oration to his army.

What shall I say more than I have inferred?

306 **devised** devisèd

308 **our . . . dreams . . . our souls** Richard's plurals suggest displacement of his personal dreams and anxieties onto his companions; cf. his plurals when speaking to Clarence (1.1.70). This rhetoric may be meant to appear inauspicious or even desperate, since he offers nothing more on behalf of communal purpose than the amoral precepts of 309–10. These cynical lines could hardly appeal to any but his most compromised followers, and he needs all the *gentlemen* on his side.

309–10 Richard's pronouncements derive from a discourse associated with the Machiavel; cf. Marlowe, *Jew of Malta* (Prol.14–27, 1.1.118–19) and pp. 8–10. This bold amorality contradicts Richard's 'oration' in the sources, which have him admitting his 'abhominable cryme', blaming others for his seduction and proclaiming his tearful penitence (Hall, *Richard III*, fol. liv^{r-v}; Holinshed, 3.756; and p. 63). Trust in the *strong arms* of human forces directly opposes the *powerful arm* of the Lord (1.4.216).

312 **join** meet in conflict (*OED* II 12)
pell-mell without keeping ranks, at close quarters, hand to hand (*OED* 1c), but suggesting headlong disorder and hurry, recklessly (*OED* 3)

313 Cf. Richard's threat to Young Clifford: 'If not in heaven, you'll surely sup in hell' (*2H6* 5.1.216).

314–41 Wilson notes an abrupt change from Richard's lines urging *pell-mell* combat to the deliberate form of his oration; though *inferred* suggests continuity of utterance. Richmond, by contrast, progresses by orderly degrees from sweet dreams to an oration expanding upon the *prayers* from *wronged souls* heard in those dreams (227–42). If 309–13 are addressed to *gentlemen* (307) and this oration is directed *to his army*, Richard may again be differentiating values assumed to appeal to one audience or another; Richmond's utterances, by contrast, are more generally of a piece (but see 5.2.23–4n.). Richard's oration, like that of Richmond, is sometimes directed to the theatre audience. The SD derives from Hall and Holinshed, but both record the oration as directed '*to the chiefteins of his armie*' (Holinshed, 3.755).

Along with his silence concerning his sins (see 309–10), Shakespeare's

306 SP] *Qq, F (King[.]); Richard continues, Capell* 307 unto] *Qq;* to *F* 309 Conscience] *Qq;* For conscience *F* but] *Q1–2; om. Q3–6, F* 310 at] *Q1–4, F;* as *Q5–6* 312 to it] *Q1–2; Q3–6 (*too it*), F (*too't*)* 313 SD] *Qq; om. F*

Remember whom you are to cope withal,
A sort of vagabonds, rascals and runaways,
A scum of Bretons and base lackey peasants,
Whom their o'ercloyed country vomits forth
To desperate adventures and assured destruction.
You sleeping safe, they bring to you unrest;
You having lands and blessed with beauteous wives,
They would restrain the one, distain the other.
And who doth lead them but a paltry fellow?
Long kept in Bretagne at our mother's cost,

Richard also fails to mention his years of good rule, omitting a prominent element in Hall and Holinshed's versions of this speech (cf. Courtenay, 2.114).

314 **inferred** alleged or reported (*OED* 2), carrying specific associations with oratory (see 3.5.75, 3.7.12, 3.7.32, 4.4.343); cf. *3H6* 2.2.43–4: 'Clifford played the orator, / Inferring arguments of mighty force.'

315 **cope** encounter, contend, fight (*OED v.*[2] II 2)

316 **sort** band, company, group, or set of persons (*OED sb.*[2] II 17a); given the class-based references to *vagabonds* and *base lackey peasants* (which lack precise equivalents in Hall or Holinshed), also suggesting a group distinguished by social stratum (cf. 'the vulgar sort', *1H6* 3.2.4).

vagabonds vagrants who wander without fixed abodes, but also referring to those lacking regular occupation or obvious means of support and so assumed to be idle loafers (*OED sb.* B 1a); cf. the punishment described in 327–9. Hall and Holinshed have Richard call his enemies 'traytors, thefes, outlawes and ronnegates of our awne nacion' and 'beggerly Britons & faynt harted Frenchmen' (Hall, *Richard III*, fol. liv[v]). Richard's assessment may have some historical validity (Chrimes, 40).

317 **scum of Bretons** Richard's rhetorical xenophobia might appeal to what Ian Archer (30–1) calls 'the most basic element of the political consciousness of Londoners . . . a hatred of "all sorts of strangers"'; such discourse was especially incendiary in the volatile years 1586–93. Hall's Richard characterizes the enemy as 'effeminate & lasciuious' (Hall, *Richard III*, fol. lv[r]; Holinshed, 3.756).

lackey camp follower, hanger-on (*OED sb.* 2), also one who is servilely obsequious (*OED sb.* 1a)

318 **o'ercloyed** o'ercloyèd; oversatiated (*OED*)

322 **restrain** withhold, keep back (*OED v.*[1] 4a)

distain defile, dishonour (*OED v.* 2)

324 **mother's** Shakespeare follows Holinshed's 1587 edition which mistakenly prints 'brought up by my moothers meanes' instead of the correct reading – 'my brothers meanes' – which appears in Hall and in Holinshed's first edition and refers to Richmond's support by Charles, Duke of Burgundy, Richard's brother-in-law (see 1.4.10n.). On the felicity of the misprint for Shakespeare's conception of Richard, see Willis, *Nurture*, 204; cf. p. 459.

317 Bretons] *Qq, F (*Brittain*[*e*]*s*), Capell* lackey] *Q1–5, F;* Iackey *Q6* 320 to you] *Q1;* you to *Q2–6, F* 321 blessed] *Qq, F (*blest*)* wives] *Q2–6, F;* wifes *Q1* 324 Bretagne] *Qq, F (*Brit[t]aine*), Theobald*

A milksop, one that never in his life
Felt so much cold as over shoes in snow.
Let's whip these stragglers o'er the seas again,
Lash hence these overweening rags of France,
These famished beggars, weary of their lives,
Who, but for dreaming on this fond exploit,
For want of means, poor rats, had hanged themselves.
If we be conquered, let men conquer us,
And not these bastard Bretons, whom our fathers
Have in their own land beaten, bobbed and thumped,
And in record left them the heirs of shame.
Shall these enjoy our lands? Lie with our wives?
Ravish our daughters? ^F^*Drum afar off.*^F^
Hark, I hear their drum.
Fight, gentlemen of England! – Fight, bold yeomen!

325 **milksop** from Hall and Holinshed; cf. *1H4* 2.3.31.

326 **over shoes** i.e. the cold felt when snow comes in over one's shoes; proverbial for 'to be deeply immersed in something' (Tilley, Dent, S380), cf. *TGV* 1.1.24. The point is to evoke a minor discomfort.

327–9 The punishment prescribed by the Elizabethan statutes against vagabonds is whipping and return to their place of origin (see Carroll).

328 **overweening rags** Richard's metonymic figure (reminiscent of *usurping helmets* in 112), displaces the self-assertive ambition and financial dependency of Richmond onto tattered garments which stand for the men who allegedly wear them; cf. *rag of honour* (1.3.232).

330 **but . . . on** i.e. if they had not had the consolation of their fantasies about
fond foolish

331 **want of means** lack of the means for survival

333–5 Richard alludes to victories over the French by Edward III, the Black Prince and Henry V during the Hundred Years' War.

333 **bastard** not in Hall or Holinshed's accounts

334 **bobbed** beaten with a fist (*OED* *v.*^{2} 1)

335 **record** recòrd; i.e. historical account (cf. 3.1.72, 4.4.28)

336–7 **Lie with . . . Ravish** This play and *H5* are the only Shakespearean history plays to associate rape with military invasion and to represent marriage as a desired conclusion of the action (Howard & Rackin, 198). *E3* 3.2 (not always attributed to Shakespeare) makes the same association.

338 **yeomen** freeholders under the rank of gentlemen (*OED* II 4a), usually taken to form the bulk of English foot-soldiers (*OED* II 5a)

325 milksop] *Q6, F;* milkesopt *Q1–5* 333 Bretons] *Qq, F (*Brit*[*t*]*ain*[*e*]*s*), Capell* 335 in] *Q1–2;* on *Q3–6, F* 336 lands?] *F;* lands, *Q1–3, 5–6;* land? *Q4* 337] *Qq; F lines* daughters? / Drumme, / 338 Fight, gentlemen] *Q1–2 (*Fight gentlemen*);* Right Gentlemen *Q3–6, F* bold] *Q1;* boldly *Q2–6, F*

– Draw, archers, draw your arrows to the head!
– Spur your proud horses hard and ride in blood.
Amaze the welkin with your broken staves.

F*Enter a* Messenger.F

– What says Lord Stanley? Will he bring his power?

MESSENGER
My lord, he doth deny to come.

KING RICHARD Off with his son George's head!

NORFOLK
My lord, the enemy is past the marsh:
After the battle let George Stanley die.

KING RICHARD
A thousand hearts are great within my bosom.
Advance our standards! Set upon our foes!
Our ancient word of courage, fair Saint George,
Inspire us with the spleen of fiery dragons.
Upon them! Victory sits on our helms. *Exeunt.*

339 **draw . . . head** i.e. pull your bowstring till the arrow's head touches the bow (*OED* draw *v.* 9)

340 **in blood** in full vigour of pursuit, as dogs after game in a hunt (*OED* blood *sb.* 7), and literally through the blood shed on the field of battle

341 perhaps recalling 'shivered Launces darke the troubled aire' (Kyd, *Spanish Tragedy*, 1.2.54); cf. *KJ* 5.2.172; *Cor* 4.5.111–12.
welkin sky
staves lance shafts (see 65)

341.1 **Messenger** At 59–60 Richard orders that a *pursuivant-at-arms* be sent by Catesby to check on Stanley; this SD appears only in F, but F, Qq agree on the SP for 343.

343 **deny** refuse

344 This abrupt order might have suggested Cibber's famous addition after 4.4.531: '*Off with his head. So much for* Buckingham' (Thompson).

345 **marsh** 'Betweene both armies was a great marish' (Holinshed, 3.758).

349 **word of courage** phrase, utterance (*OED sb.* 10) urging courage (cf. 270)

349–50 **Saint George . . . dragons** Richard asks that his troops be inspired with the fury of the beast that was vanquished by the saint; contrast 270 (Clemen, 230). On the apocalyptic overtones throughout this act, and the dragon to be overcome in the end of days, see E. Berry, 101; cf. Revelation, 12, 19.

350 **spleen** courage, resolute mind (*OED sb.* 5 a); cf. *KJ* 2.1.68: 'fierce dragons' spleens'.

351 Cf. 79.

351 them! Victory] *Pope;* them victorie *Q1;* them, victorie *Q2–6, F* helms] *Q1–2, 4;* helpes *Q3, 5–6, F* SD] *Q1–2; om. Q3–6, F*

[**5.4**] *Alarum, excursions. Enter* [NORFOLK *with Soldiers, and*] CATESBY.

CATESBY

Rescue, my lord of Norfolk. Rescue, rescue!
The King enacts more wonders than a man,
Daring an opposite to every danger.
His horse is slain, and all on foot he fights,
Seeking for Richmond in the throat of death.
Rescue, fair lord, or else the day is lost.

[*Exeunt Norfolk and Soldiers.*]

[F]*Alarums.*[F] *Enter* [KING] RICHARD.

KING RICHARD

A horse, a horse, my kingdom for a horse!

CATESBY

Withdraw, my lord. I'll help you to a horse.

KING RICHARD

Slave, I have set my life upon a cast,
And I will stand the hazard of the die.

5.4 Location: the action continues at Bosworth Field.

0.1 ***Alarum*** call to arms (cf. 1.1.7)
excursions sorties (*OED sb.* 3; cf. alarm *sb.* 4)
NORFOLK *with Soldiers* Norfolk is urged to provide rescue, a demand necessitating forces to assist him. Catesby could call to Norfolk and men offstage; however, 2–5 appear to be addressed to someone, unless, as Jowett suggests, they are soliloquy.

2–4 Hall and Holinshed follow Vergil, who describes Richard fighting fiercely and charging directly at Richmond (Vergil, 224; Hall, *Richard III*, fol. lvii[r]), but not as losing his horse; cf. 7n.

2 **than a man** i.e. than are humanly possible

3 i.e. challenging any adversary who presents himself to face every risk of mortal combat
opposite opponent, adversary (*OED sb.* B 3; cf. *TN* 3.4.266)

7 Frequently echoed and parodied (Var) and still an acting 'point' (Hankey, 246n.). For relation to *True Tragedy*, Hall and Holinshed, see p. 77.

9 **cast** throw of the dice (*OED sb.* 3a)

10 **stand . . . die** endure the risk entailed in the roll of the die

5.4] *Capell* 0.1–2 NORFOLK . . . *and*] *Capell subst.* 1] *Qq; F lines* Norfolke, / Rescue, Rescue: / 3 an] *Q1–7, F;* and *Q8* 6 SD] *Ard*[2] 6.1 KING] *Rowe* 7+ SP] *Qq (King[.]); Rich. F* 10 die] *Q1–2, 7–8;* dye *Q3, 5–6, F;* day *Q4*

I think there be six Richmonds in the field;
Five have I slain today instead of him.
A horse, a horse, my kingdom for a horse! [*Exeunt.*]

[**5.5**] *Alarum, Enter* [KING] RICHARD *and* RICHMOND*; they fight. Richard is slain. Then retreat being sounded,* [*exit Richmond, and Richard's body is removed.*] [F]*Flourish.*[F] *Enter Richmond,* [STANLEY, Earl of] Derby, *bearing the crown, with other Lords and Soldiers.*

RICHMOND
God and your arms be praised, victorious friends:
The day is ours; the bloody dog is dead.

11–12 The sources mention no doubles and claim that Richard instantly recognized Richmond (Hall, *Richard III*, fol. lvii[r], following Vergil, 224). The doubling may come from Henry IV (Holinshed, 3.523); cf. *1H4* 5.3.1–28.

5.5 Location: the action continues at Bosworth Field. On scene divisions in battle sequences involving flourishes, see G. Williams.

0.2 ***Richard is slain*** The only onstage death occurs silently. Vergil reports that Richard died 'fyghting manfully in the thickkest presse of his enemyes', and John Rous claims that he 'defended himself as a noble knight with great courage to his last breath' (Vergil, 224; cf. Michael Jones, 'Richard III as a soldier', in Gillingham, 112). Hall describes Richard overthrowing Richmond's standard and slaying its bearer, Sir William Brandon, overthrowing Sir John Cheyney, 'a man of great force & strength', and proceeding 'by dent of swerde' to Richmond, who 'kept hym at the swerdes poincte without auantage' a long time until 'sodainly' Stanley and his three thousand 'tall men' entered the fray, causing Richard's men to flee 'and he him selfe manfully fyghtynge in the mydell of his enemies' to be slain (*Richard III*, fol. lvii[r–v]; Holinshed, 3.759). Cibber's Richard gets a stirring final speech. Kean's Richard 'fought like one drunk with wounds . . . as if his will could not be disarmed' (Hazlitt, 5.182). Irving's 1896 Richard, by contrast, died from repeated stabbings by Richmond while surrounded by Richmond's soldiers. More recent productions have often emphasized similarities in the two combatants rather than heroism in either (Colley, 5).

0.3–4 ***exit . . . removed*** Since Richmond re-enters with Stanley, who bears Richard's crown from the site of his death, they enter to a different fictional location than that of the killing (Dyce); Richard's corpse would therefore have been removed. The phrase *this bloody wretch* (5) does not demand presence (cf. 5.2.10, 18).

2 **bloody . . . dead** Richmond's phrase fulfils Margaret's and the Duchess of York's curses (4.4.78, 195); cf. Willis, *Nurture*, 202.

13 SD] *Theobald* 5.5] *Dyce* 0.1 KING] *Rowe* 0.2–3 *Then . . . sounded*] *Qq; Retreat, and Flourish. F* 0.3–4 *exit . . . removed*] *Ard*[2] *subst.* 0.4–5 STANLEY, Earl of] *Pope subst.* 0.5 Derby] *Qq (Darby), F* *other*] *Qq; diuers other F* 0.6 *and Soldiers*] *Ard*[2]*; &c. Q1–2; om. Q3–6, F* 1] *Qq; F lines* Armes / Friends; /

STANLEY

Courageous Richmond, well hast thou acquit thee.
[*Presents the crown.*] Lo, here this long-usurped royalty
From the dead temples of this bloody wretch
Have I plucked off to grace thy brows withal.
Wear it, enjoy it and make much of it.

RICHMOND

Great God of heaven, say amen to all.
But tell me, is young George Stanley living?

STANLEY

He is, my lord, and safe in Leicester town,
Whither, if it please you, we may now withdraw us.

RICHMOND

What men of name are slain on either side?

^{F}STANLEY^{F}

John, Duke of Norfolk, Walter, Lord Ferrers,
Sir Robert Brakenbury and Sir William Brandon.

3 **acquit** i.e. acquitted (cf. Abbott, 342); discharged the duties of your position (*OED v.* II 13)

4 SD Sources have Stanley crown Richmond in response to the cry 'King Henry', 'as though' being 'elected' through acclamation 'by the voyce of the people' (Hall, *Richard III*, fol. lviii^{v}; Holinshed, 3.760; following Vergil, 226). *True Tragedy* has Stanley tell Richmond 'the Peeres by full consent, in that thou hast freed them from a tyrants yoke, haue by election chosen thee as King' (2087–9). Shakespeare avoids such 'election' by putting Henry to God's approval (8, 41), not that of 'the people' (but see 22). On Stanley as political subject, see Gurr, 'Democratic'.

4 **royalty** the crown (*OED* 5b; cf. *1H4* 4.3.57); Bacon calls it 'a crown of ornament' (*Henry VII*, 70). Carrying the crown into battle was taken by some as signifying leadership (C.A.J. Armstrong, 72), but Vergil interprets it as symbolizing Richard's having staked everything on the battle (Vergil, 225).

6 **withal** with

12 **name** rank or reputation (*OED sb.* 7a, b)

13 **Norfolk** For the irony of Norfolk's death despite his warning, see 5.3.304–5 (cf. Hall, *Richard III*, fol. lvii^{v}; Holinshed 3.759). Hall and Holinshed praise Norfolk's loyalty as a subject and his faithfulness to his oath of allegiance, but Holinshed reflects on the questionable value of service rendered to a tyrant.

3+ SP] *Pope; Dar. Qq; Der. F* 3–4] *Qq; F lines* Richmond, / Loe, / Royalties, / 4 SD] *Ard^{2} subst.* this] *Qq;* these *F* royalty] *Q1;* roialties *Q2–6, F* 7 enjoy it] *Q1–2; om. Q3–6, F* 11 Whither] *Q1 (*Whether*), Q2–6, F* if . . . you] *Qq;* if you please *F* now] *Qq; om. F* 13–14] *F; Q1 lines sir / Brandon. / ; Q2–6 line Robert / Brandon. /* 13 SP] *F (Der.)* Walter] *Q1–5 (Water), Q6, F* Ferrers] *Qq, F (Ferris), Capell* 14 Brakenbury] *Qq, F (Bro[o]kenbury), F4*

RICHMOND

Inter their bodies as become their births.
Proclaim a pardon to the soldiers fled
That in submission will return to us;
And then, as we have ta'en the sacrament,
We will unite the white rose and the red.
Smile heaven upon this fair conjunction,
That long have frowned upon their enmity.
What traitor hears me and says not amen?
England hath long been mad and scarred herself:
The brother blindly shed the brother's blood;
The father rashly slaughtered his own son;
The son, compelled, been butcher to the sire.
All this divided York and Lancaster,
Divided in their dire division.
O, now let Richmond and Elizabeth,

15 **as . . . births** i.e. according to their ranks

18 **we** unambiguous royal plural
ta'en the sacrament promised upon an oath sealed with the Eucharist (cf. 1.4.202–3 and Hall, *Richard III*, fol. xli^{v}).

19 **white . . . red** the houses of York and Lancaster

20 **Smile heaven** i.e. may heaven smile
conjunction union (with marital and astrological senses)

22 Cf. the coerced *Amen* at 3.7.240; the soldiers may respond. One wonders about early theatre audiences, since failing to say 'Amen' to this announcement of the Tudor regime could mark one as a *traitor* by Richmond's formula.

22, 35, 39 **traitor, traitors, treason** Historically, Richard and a few supporters were convicted and attainted as traitors for high treason – as of the day of this battle – against the 'rightful king'. This proceeding caused some parliament members to wonder what kind of loyalty this precedent would inspire in future subjects on the day of battle (Chrimes, 63).

23–4 Cf. 2.4.63–4.

25–6 Cf. *3H6* 2.5.

27–8 Much discussed (see Var): Wells and Taylor substitute 'United' for *Divided*; Jowett proposes 'Deformèd'. However, 23–6 evoke the ways that England has been *Divided* (faction against faction, brother against brother, generation against generation) by the two 'divided houses'. All divisions are blamed on the effect and example of the two warring houses. This recalls Hall's Introduction, though the play has largely concentrated on Richard's violence against his own house and faction.

15 Inter] *Q1–4, F;* Enter *Q5–6* 17 to] *Q1–5, F; om. Q6* 21 have] *Q1–5, F;* hath *Q6*

The true succeeders of each royal house,
By God's fair ordinance conjoin together;
And let their heirs, God, if Thy will be so,
Enrich the time to come with smooth-faced peace,
With smiling plenty and fair prosperous days.
Abate the edge of traitors, gracious Lord,
That would reduce these bloody days again
And make poor England weep in streams of blood.
Let them not live to taste this land's increase

30 **true succeeders** rightful heirs; a Tudor commonplace, but hardly self-evident. For all the complex, inter-related claims and claimants, see M. Levine, 15–16. Chrimes (50) argues that 'There is no evidence of much if any overt discussion at the time. It was taken for granted that Henry was the male heir of the house of Lancaster through his mother Margaret Beaufort, whose own claims as heiress were ignored. The God of battles had confirmed such hereditary right as existed, and acclamation on the field itself rounded off the traditional procedure for attainment of the throne'. The genealogical issues remained interesting in Shakespeare's day; cf. Bacon's discussion of the inconveniences resulting from Henry's opportunism and limited foresight in these matters, as well as his determination to 'depress' the line of York (*Henry VII*, 69–71). Even before leaving for London following the battle, Richmond ordered Clarence's son detained in the Tower, where he remained until his execution in 1499 for supposed involvement in the Perkin Warbeck plot. Among those eliminated by Henry as king would also be William Stanley, who some identified as the presenter of the crown at Bosworth (Bacon, *Henry VII*, 70). Henry Peacham (65) reflects how William Stanley 'was shortly after beheaded for treason, albeit he set the Crowne (found throwne in a hawthorne bush) upon the kings head in the field'.

31 **ordinance** that which is ordained or decreed by God (*OED sb.* 5b); cf. 4.4.184.

32 ***their** Q3–F's 'thy', addressing God, emphasizes divine approval. *True Tragedy* and *Richardus Tertius* specify Elizabeth I (granddaughter of Richmond and Elizabeth) as the heir anticipated. By contrast, when James I invokes divine favour in a March 1603 speech to Parliament, both Elizabeths virtually disappear from his patrilineal account of England 'first setled and vnited in [Richmond] . . . now reunited and confirmed in me, being iustly and lineally descended, not onely of that happie coniunction, but of both the Branches thereof many times before' (James I, 271; Hodgdon, *End*, 103).

33 **smooth-faced peace** contrast *Grim-visaged War* attempting to [*smooth*] *his wrinkled front* (1.1.9).

35 **Abate . . . edge** literally to turn back or blunt the swords (of traitors) (*OED* abate *v.*[1] III 8), but figuratively to take away the aggressive *edge* of their tongues (*OED* edge *sb.* 2a, citing this line) and dulling their ardour (*OED* edge *sb.* 2b); see 4.4.229n.

36 **reduce** bring back (cf. 2.2.68)

38 **increase** prosperity, especially that which grows from the earth (*OED sb.* II 7a; cf. *Son* 97)

32 their] *Q1–2;* thy *Q3–6, F* Thy] *Q1–4, F;* they *Q5–6*

That would with treason wound this fair land's peace.
Now civil wounds are stopped; peace lives again.
That she may long live here, God say amen. [F]*Exeunt.*[F]

FINIS

40 **stopped** stanched, as in preventing the bleeding of a wound (*OED* *v.* 6)

41 **God say** may God say

41 here] *Q1–3, 5–6 (*heare*), Q4, F*

APPENDIX 1

THE TEXTS OF *RICHARD III*

Richard III exists in two substantive texts: the First Quarto (Q1), printed in 1597, and the First Folio (F), printed in 1623. If either version had survived only by itself, there would be no doubt about its being, as the Second Quarto (Q2, 1598) claims, '*By* William Shake-speare'. Even if Q1 and F were completely independent of one another, there might be questions about which to prefer. However, the two texts are materially and temporally interrelated in complex ways. Q1 was printed from a high-quality manuscript (QMS) of uncertain nature provided by Shakespeare's acting company, the Lord Chamberlain's Men. Twenty-six years later, F was printed from copy that incorporated at least one (Q3, 1602) and probably more than one of the quartos derived from Q1 (Q3, and Q6, 1622), along with accumulated reprinting errors, while also referring to another, different but highly authoritative manuscript (FMS). Furthermore, FMS, employed in the 1623 Folio, appears to represent an earlier state than QMS, the source for 1597 Q1. The hypothetical stemma is:

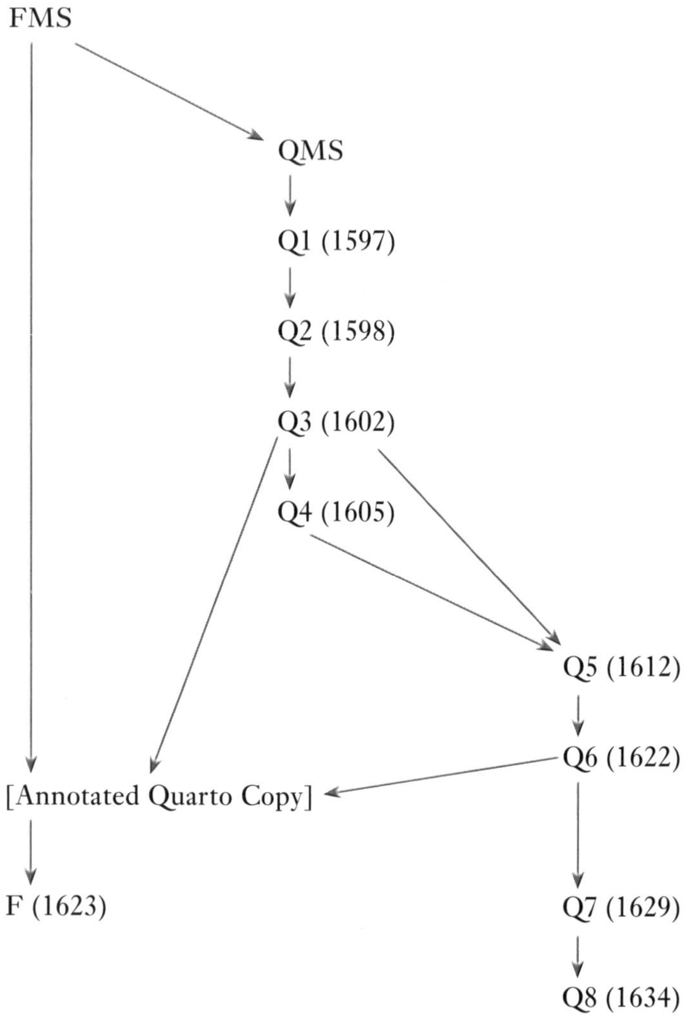

In sum, 'the versions of *Richard III* crisscross: the first printed version, almost all scholars agree, provides a second state of the play, and later printings of this second state, in turn, influenced the printing of the play in the first state' (Mowat &

Werstine, xlvii–xlviii; cf. *TxC*, 230). Neither manuscript (QMS or FMS) has survived, but the two substantive printed texts (Q1 and F) are of very high quality and are, depending on one's angle of vision, either very much alike or strikingly different.[1]

Quarto and Folio *Richard III* are identical for a sixth of the play. From 3.1.1 to 3.1.166 and from 5.3.49 to the end of the play, F simply reprints Q3.[2] For the other five-sixths of the play, the degree of difference varies according to the standard of measurement applied. Statistically, F is about 180 lines longer than Q1, while Q1 contains just under forty lines not in F, including one extended passage of some twenty lines (Smidt, *King Richard*, 7–8). Nevertheless, so much remains roughly the same that E.K. Chambers could claim, with only slight exaggeration, that 'in the main the texts agree in arrangement, speech for speech, and even line for line' (Chambers, *Shakespeare*, 1.297). Theatrically, Peter Davison claims that modern audiences would be unlikely to detect which version had provided the basis for a production (Davison, 5). Nonetheless, differences in word choices, stage directions, lineation, punctuation, spelling and roles are pervasive and serious, so that, for the editor (or the actor), discrepancies run into very high numbers (Hammond, 2).

Since both Q1 and F are by all recent accounts 'Shakespearean' in language, dramatic form and origin, and since they are at times identical word for word while elsewhere closely related but different, several narratives have been constructed to account for the differences. These narratives advance or limit the claims of either text's 'authority'. The vast majority of editions have accepted F; this preference is understandable. F is more regular metrically; many accounts judge Q1's linguistic variants to lack

1 Q1 *Richard III* has never been entirely relegated to 'bad' quarto status, even W.W. Greg finding it 'doubtful' (Kathleen O. Irace, *Reforming the 'Bad' Quartos: Performance and Provenance of Six Shakespearean First Editions* (Newark, Del., 1998), 17, citing Greg, *Problem*, 76–87). Gary Taylor calls it 'far and away the best – that is, the most accurate and most complete – of the bad quartos' (Gary Taylor, 'Copy-text and collation (with special reference to *Richard III*)', *The Library*, series 6, 3 (1981), 33–42, 34n.).

2 R. Koppel first pointed this out in 1877 (Walton, *Copy*, 11).

the precision, force or design of F's alternatives. Almost all agree that Q1 confuses or misallocates roles that F assigns correctly.[1] Q1 has had modern champions: the Cambridge Shakespeare (1864) accepted Q1 as its basis, as did the Eversley (1900) and New Temple (1935) editions. However, the Oxford Shakespeare (1904) and the Arden first series (1907) were based on F, and with the rise of the new bibliography opinion ran against Q1. Building on W.W. Greg, E.K. Chambers and Peter Alexander, D.L. Patrick argued that the manuscript behind Q1 amounted to a 'memorial reconstruction' by the play's first performers. Some designated Q1 a 'bad' quarto, though it was admittedly awfully 'good' to be called 'bad'.[2]

Such assessment of Q1 determined the editorial procedures of the New Cambridge (1954), Riverside (1974), Scott Foresman (1980) and Arden second series (1981) editions. More recently, questions about new bibliographic assumptions and about 'bad quartos' and 'memorial reconstructions' have had positive effects.[3] *Richard III* has appeared in two series of Shakespeare's quartos – Peter Davison's New Cambridge (1996) and John Drakakis's Harvester/Wheatsheaf (1996) editions – and Q1 provides the basic text for the Oxford Shakespeare single-volume *Richard III*, edited by John Jowett (2000). Jowett argues Q1's authority on the basis of its 'theatrical' nature (Jowett, 127), usefully reversing previous denigration of Q1 for 'contamination' by stage practice. However, such arguments also support a traditional critical binary between the 'authorial' (F being closer to Shakespeare's holograph) and the 'theatrical' (Q1 closer to a playbook, exhibiting effects originating with 'the actors').[4] A variant of this narrative claims that Q1 incorporates 'revision',

1 On metre, see Hammond, 3; 'loss of force', Davison, 7; 'higher literary quality', Lull, 210–11; 'more compact, more metrical, more meaningful, more crafted', *TxC*, 229; role misallocation, Mowat & Werstine, xlix.

2 See Patrick; Chambers, *Shakespeare*; W.W. Greg, *Two Elizabethan Stage Abridgements* (Oxford, 1922); Peter Alexander, *Shakespeare's Henry VI and Richard III* (Cambridge, 1929).

3 For critique of new bibliographic assumptions, see Maguire.

4 Q1 is 'based on a memorial reconstruction of a lost prompt-book' (Davison, 49); Q1 is based on a 'communal reconstruction' (*TxC*, 229).

and represents Shakespeare's alternative draft (Urkowitz), the work of an 'adapting theatrical scribe, with some contribution from Shakespeare as reviser' (Jowett, 127), or 'revision by a playwright' (Holland, xliii).

Each claim deserves consideration, but given the limits of what we know, no argument for superior 'authority' can be entirely consistent. Too many factors pull in different directions. The five-sixths of F not simply reprinted from Q3 appears to be based on a manuscript that precedes Q1 and from which Q1 is derivative. Q1 is shorter, and certain roles suggest adaptation for performance economy; however, F omits one extended passage and shows cutting elsewhere (Smidt, *Impostors*, 25). Q1 has more non-metrical lines, but F contains verses that are as padded, jumbled and repetitious as some of those in the earlier text (Smidt, *Memorial*, 20; Lull, 212). Sometimes F more closely follows the sources; at other times Q1 can claim closer proximity to them.

In theory, there could be warrant for distinct 'Folio-based' and 'Quarto-based' editions. In practice, recent editions have demonstrated the practical necessity for employing elements from *both* early texts. Even in an age suspicious of 'conflated' editions, the interdependence of Q and F *Richard III* makes its own case. The two New Cambridge editions, based on Q1 (Davison) and F (Lull), include words and entire lines from their alternative texts, as does the Oxford edition based on Q1 (Jowett). Purists may argue that any emendation from an alternative basic text constitutes 'conflation', but instead of textual purity perhaps we need a richer sense of early playtexts in their various manifestations as raw material for acting companies, or even as 'literary' works potentially imagined for readers.

No single theory efficiently accounts for everything about the two early texts or their relationships, nor does any available justification provide sufficient grounds for ignoring the other version when difficulties arise in the basic text. This edition incorporates substantive variants from both Q and F, while joining the overwhelming editorial majority in generally deferring to

F as its basic text for portions of the play where F does not simply reprint uncorrected quarto copy. Where F directly reprints Q3 – mistakes and all – then Q1, the only authoritative quarto, becomes the basic text. Furthermore, since F itself appears to be, even when not simply reprinting quarto copy, already a composite text, based on the printer's consultation of manuscript (FMS) and printed copy from Q3 and Q6, and therefore subject to printers' mistakes and interventions in any and all of six quartos, efforts have been made to trace all substantial variants that might have influenced F.[1] This has meant tracking variants in *any* of the six quartos that precede F. Each page records textual variations so readers may evaluate editorial decisions. Superscript markings (^{FF} and ^{QQ}) appear whenever a reading is adopted that has no equivalent in the basic text. The goal is a *Richard III* that is both readable and easy to evaluate. You should enjoy Shakespeare, the range of Shakespeare that the various texts provide, but know when you are reading 'Shakespeare' of 1597, 'Shakespeare' of 1623, Pope's 'Shakespeare' of 1725, that of Steevens in 1793 or Siemon in 2009.

THE FIRST QUARTO (Q1), 1597

On 20 October 1597 the Stationers recorded the relevant legal data for what would become the first printed version of *Richard III*: 'Andrewe wise / Entred for his copie vnder th[e h]andes of master BARLOWE, and master warden man. / *The tragedie of kinge RICHARD the THIRD with the death of the Duke of CLARENCE.*' (Arber, 3.25). Andrew Wise, the would-be publisher, fulfilled several legal requirements, each involving a fee. The playtext had been examined by the ecclesiastical authorities (ultimately the Bishop of London or the Archbishop of Canterbury, here represented by Archbishop John Whitgift's Chaplain, William Barlow),

1 Turned or dropped letters, fount and case changes, non-syllabic contracted spellings without metric implication and inconsequential spelling variants are uncollated, except in special cases.

who oversaw 'allowance' of any printed book, at least in theory, and probably of any potentially controversial publication, such as works dealing with English history (Blayney, 'Publication', 397). The text was 'licensed' by the Stationers' Company, under its Warden, Thomas Man, giving Wise rights of 'copy'. Thereafter, no one might publish any work – for instance a different version of this or a similar play based on Richard's reign – that might be judged to infringe upon Wise's ability to dispose of his printed copies for sale (Blayney, 'Publication', 399). Licensing also meant that the Stationers did not believe that *Richard III* might negatively affect sales of recently printed similar works, such as *The True Tragedy of Richard III* (entered and licensed on 19 June 1594 and published by Thomas Creede).[1] Finally, the play was 'entered' in Company records, giving the publisher the best protection against infringement and probably indicating optimism about sales prospects (Blayney, 'Publication', 404).

Although, by contrast with verse or devotional works, plays were not particularly hot literary property, *Richard III* and two other Shakespeare history plays – *Richard II* and *1 Henry IV*, also entered for Wise between 29 August 1597 (*R2*) and 25 February 1598 (*1H4*) – proved popular playbooks. The three were among the ten most popular plays of the era, judging by the number of reprints in the twenty-five years following initial publication (they all transferred to Matthew Law in June 1603) (Blayney, 'Publication', 388).[2] By the late seventeenth century, *Richard III* had appeared in eight quartos (Q1–8: 1597, 1598, 1602, 1605, 1612, 1622, 1629 and 1634) and four folios (F–F4: 1623, 1632, 1663 and 1685). Perhaps as remarkably, the reprints of these three plays are the first to carry Shakespeare's name, and they do so in a way unique among dramatic publications of the period.

1 *Henry V* offers a revealing parallel, since the publishers had to get consent from Thomas Creede, who published *The Famous Victories of Henry the Fifth* in 1598 (Blayney, 'Publication', 399).

2 Apart from the three Shakespeare history plays and *Much Ado*, to which he also had rights, Wise published only two sermons before the end of 1600; he disappears from the records after transferring rights in 1603 (Erne, 88).

Before 1598, a few title-pages of printed plays had included the playwright's name; most name only the relevant acting company. Q1 *Richard III* announces itself 'As it hath been lately Acted by the / Right honourable the Lord Chamber- / laine his seruants.'[1] The first reprints of *Richard III* and *Richard II* in 1598 are unusual because they add '*By* William Shake-speare' to their anonymous 1597 title-pages; the anonymous 1598 First Quarto of *1 Henry IV* was similarly reprinted in 1599, with the addition: 'Newly corrected by *W. Shake-speare*'.[2] Not only was it extremely rare to add an author's name to the reprint of a play first published anonymously, but according to Lukas Erne it would remain unrepeated for any other playwright during Shakespeare's lifetime (Erne, 58).

There is one other striking feature of Q1 *Richard III* besides its popularity and the attribution of its reprints – its length. At about 3,480 lines, Q1 *Richard III* is roughly 1,000 lines longer than the period average of 2,400–500 (Hart, 147–9; cf. Smidt, *Impostors*, 26–35).[3] In 1597 it was probably the longest single play ever printed in English.[4] The 1623 Folio text is even longer, running to just under 3,600 lines. This unprecedented length should be remembered when we examine the early printed texts; both Q1 and F show evidence of cutting, though either text would probably have been cut further to be played. Sometime between some version of what Shakespeare wrote and what found its way into print as Q1, someone – perhaps Shakespeare, the acting company, a theatrical scribe, the printers or their

1 By the 1590s first editions of some plays name authors – Marlowe's *Massacre at Paris*, *Edward II* and *Dido, Queen of Carthage* (1594); George Peele's *Edward I* (1593) and *David and Bethsabe* (1599); Lyly's *The Woman in the Moon* (1597) – though each playwright had other plays published anonymously (Erne, 63).

2 The claim of authorial 'correction' is supported by no evidence in Q2 *1 Henry 4*, which shows the number and kind of obvious corrections (and new errors) ordinary in reprinting without authorial contribution (Kastan, *1H4*, 111). The 1598 Q1 of *Love's Labour's Lost*, which may be based on a non-extant Q0, also titles itself, 'Newly corrected and augmented / *By W. Shakespere*'.

3 Line numbers differ according to methods of counting, but the proportional relations between Q1 and F and their contemporary plays are generally agreed upon; on Hart's numeration, see Smidt, *Impostors*, 28–35. Erne tabulates from Hart (Erne, 141).

4 It would soon be surpassed by Ben Jonson's *Every Man Out* of 1599 (4,400 lines) (Smidt, *Impostors*, 34) and by *Hamlet* of 1604–5 (3,668) (Erne, 141). These plays were exceptions.

employees – shortened the text. He, they, any or all of them appear to have done other things to it as well.

Sometime after entry into the Stationers' Register, Q1 *Richard III* was printed by Valentine Simmes (see Fig. 13).[1] Simmes shared printing responsibilities for Q1 with the press of Peter Short (*True Tragedy*, v; cf. Jackson, 'Two', 175);[2] such work-sharing was widely practised.[3] Simmes printed the first seven sheets (gatherings A–G, from the opening as far as 3.7.52) of the twelve included in Q1. Short printed the remaining sheets (gatherings H–M, omitting J (a letter then usually undifferentiated from 'I'), from 3.7.53 to the end). The large number of wrong-fount letters in Short's well-produced portion suggests paucity of type. Setting by formes allowed for recycling available type within a single gathering; it suggests working copy legible enough to be precisely cast off and marked up for the compositor before being set (Hammond, 22). Q1 shows little stretching to fill up space, but betrays abundant evidence of compression.

Simmes's pages are far more cramped than Short's, and both printers virtually forgo one common strategy for managing space; neither employs variable numbers of blank lines before and after stage directions (there are exceptions at 1.1.1, sig. A1^{r}, and 5.3.206, sig. M1^{r}). The estimation of space works out so well that there is just room to conclude the final page (sig. M3^{v}) with '*FINIS*' and a small ornament.[4] Both printers occasionally run together short lines; this space-saving device, like relegation

1 Five copies of Q1 survive: British Library (Huth, 47), Bodleian (Malone 37, Arch. G. d. 44, with missing leaves supplied from Q2), Folger, Huntington and Yale (Elizabethan Club, sheets C and D only). For details, see Smidt, *King Richard*. On Simmes, see W. Craig Ferguson, *Valentine Simmes* (Charlottesville, Va., 1968).

2 The type used by Simmes had been employed for *Richard II*, and Short would re-use his type in printing *1 Henry IV* early in 1598 (Hammond, 21).

3 On shared printing, see Chiaki Hanabusa, 'Shared printing in Robert Wilson's *The Cobbler's Prophecy*', *PBSA*, 97 (2003), 333–49. Blayney includes Short among printers with 'fairly high standards of craftsmanship' (Blayney, 'Publication', 405).

4 The neat fit of M3^{v} matches that of G4^{v}, the last page of Simmes's stint (RP). Q1 pages normally run to 38 lines, but 39 lines appear on sigs A2^{v}, D3^{v}, E1^{v} and I2^{v}; the catchword line contains text at sigs D3^{v} and E1^{v} (Smidt, *King Richard*, 16).

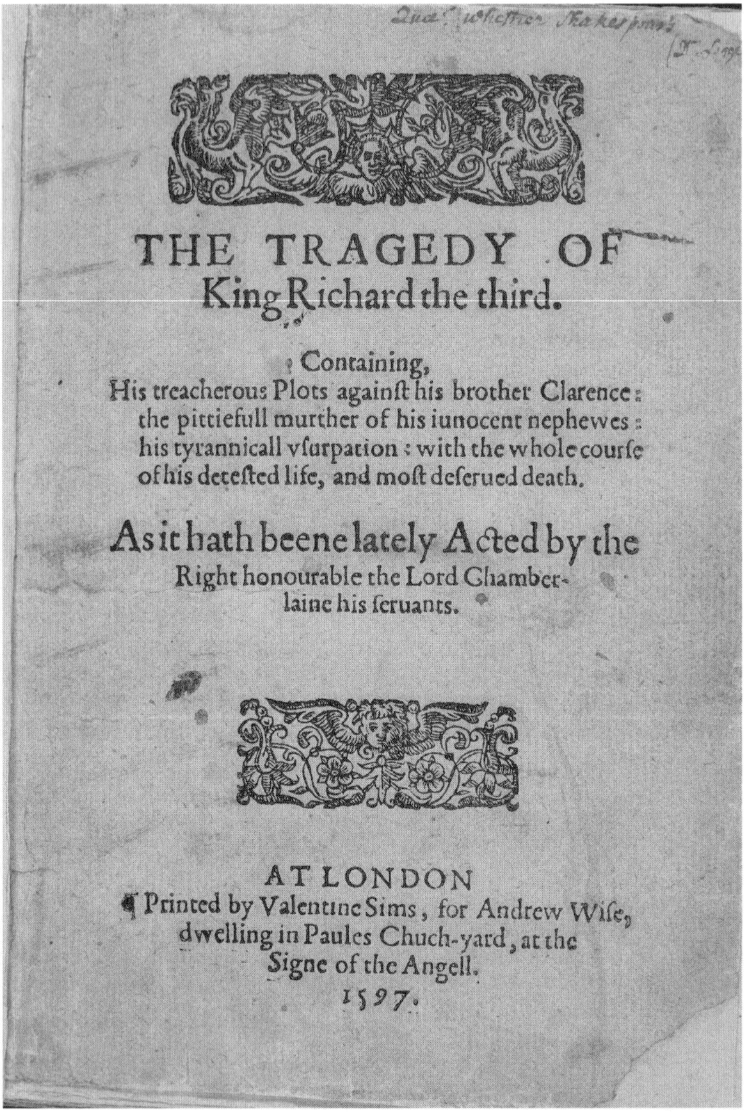

THE TRAGEDY OF
King Richard the third.

Containing,
His treacherous Plots againſt his brother Clarence:
the pittiefull murther of his iunocent nephewes:
his tyrannicall vſurpation: with the whole courſe
of his deteſted life, and moſt deſerued death.

As it hath beene lately Acted by the
Right honourable the Lord Chamber-
laine his ſeruants.

AT LONDON
¶ Printed by Valentine Sims, for Andrew Wiſe,
dwelling in Paules Chuch-yard, at the
Signe of the Angell.
1597.

13 Title-page of the 1597 First Quarto (Q1) of *Richard III*

of mid-scene entry directions to the right margin and splitting of directions over two lines, is more frequent in Simmes's portion. Spatial considerations had textual effects. Sig. E3^{r} (2.3.7–8) shows line-sharing that employs every single space and omits final punctuation.[1] Although possibly reflecting authorial lack of specificity, stage directions are frequently abbreviated, sometimes radically: Q1 3.4 opens with '*Enter the Lords to Councell.*' (sig. G1^{r}); F reads, '*Enter Buckingham, Darby, Hastings, Bishop of Ely, / Norfolke, Ratcliffe, Louell, with others, / at a Table.*' Limits of space may occasionally have determined the representation of action. Richard's exit with Buckingham at 3.4.41 – clearly indicated in F ('Withdraw your selfe a while, Ile goe with you. / *Exeunt.*') – is suggested by Q1's dialogue, but only Richard gets an exit ('*Buc.* Withdraw you hence my Lo: Ile follow you. *Ex. Gl.*' (sig. G1^{v})). Q1's line is full measure, and the next line nearly so, precluding further stage direction.[2] The need for compression may have led to a character's absence from an entry direction: despite his substantial speaking part, Buckingham's entries go unspecified at the head of 2.1 (perhaps among '*&c.*', sig. D3^{v}) and at 2.2.100 (perhaps among '*others*', sig. E2^{v}).

Throughout Simmes's portion, lines are frequently turned up or down. Short's portion contains only two such resorts (4.4.398–9 (sig. K1^{v}) and 4.4.453 (sig. K4^{r})). It is unclear why there is such difference in the treatment of space. Perhaps Short's printers relaxed, having realized that there was sufficient room to conclude at the bottom of sig. M3^{v} (Hammond, 23; cf. Jowett, 115). Alternatively, Jackson has suggested a variation in manuscript copy, arguing that placement of stage directions in Simmes's portion reveals that whoever prepared the manuscript copy (QMS) appears 'to have been fully conscious of scene divisions' and to have distinguished between entries which

1 This line is repeated unpointed in Q2. For lines shared between speakers, see sigs F2^{r} (3.1.124–5), G1^{v} (3.4.31–4), I1^{v} (4.2.97) and I1^{r} (4.2.50). For directions split over two lines, see sigs A2^{v} (1.1.41), E1^{v} (2.2.33–4), F3^{v} (3.2.33–4), F4^{v} (3.2.92–3), G2^{r} (3.4.78), G3^{r} (3.5.20–1) and M2^{v} (5.3.302–3).

2 For other complete-measure lines with abbreviated stage directions in Short's portion of Q1, see sigs H1^{r} (3.7.54) and I1^{v} (4.2.81).

head scenes (mostly centred) and entries within scenes (mostly set right). This changes in Short's portion at sig. I3[r] with the relaxation of space requirements (Jackson, 'Two', 178).

Q1 printing involved at least two and perhaps three compositors. It appears likely that one compositor worked on Simmes's portion, but Short's portion has occasioned dispute.[1] Given how little is known about Short's compositor(s), it is not clear that compositorial involvement in sheets H–M (3.7.53 to the end of the play) bears editorial implications. However, a good deal has been suggested about changes and errors that Simmes's Compositor A might have contributed. Alan Craven has claimed to identify Compositor A's work in gatherings A–G of Q1 *Richard III* and in Q2 *Richard II* (1598). Comparing Q2 *Richard II* with Q1 *Richard II*, from which it was set, Craven finds A abbreviating names and titles and introducing numerous changes. A's portion of Q2 *Richard II* shows 146 substantive dialogue variants and 9 in the stage directions, about one change in seventeen lines. Only five of these result in obviously unsatisfactory readings (Craven, 'Simmes', 55). Whether or not one accepts this particular compositor for Q1 *Richard III*, these findings suggest interventions that could be virtually impossible to detect. A introduces into *Richard II* 63 substitutions ('what I speake, my' (*R2* Q1) becomes 'what I sayd my' (*R2* Q2)); 30 omissions ('the death or fall of Kings' becomes 'the death of Kings'); 14 interpolations ('our slavish' becomes 'our countries slavish'); 25 literals ('whose taste the' becomes 'whose state the'); 8 transpositions ('But then more why?' becomes 'But more than why?'); 9 sophistications ('to my owne' becomes 'to mine owne'); 6 corrections ('Canst thou' becomes 'Camst thou'). This list includes few additions, omissions or transpositions of letters and many changes and omissions of words, suggesting not misreading of copy-text but 'memorial' errors that 'almost

1 See Jackson, 'Two'; Susan Zimmerman, 'The uses of headlines: Peter Short's Shakespearian quartos *1 Henry IV* and *Richard III*', *The Library*, 6.7 (1985), 218–55.

always make tolerably good sense' (Craven, 'Simmes', 56). Thus, so-called 'memorial' errors in Q1 *Richard III* 'may originate with the compositor' (Hammond, 26).[1]

Regarding Short's portion of Q1 *Richard III* (sheets H–M; 3.7.53 to the end of the play), less has been asserted about personnel, but printing by formes requires setting all pages for one side of a sheet and printing them before setting the pages for the other side of the sheet. This meant that 'the two series of pages for the two sides of a sheet were not consecutive but had to interlock with each other' (Gaskell, 41), and do so precisely, without gaps or overrun. The procedure increases the likelihood that compositors will have to adjust copy to demands of space. If the manuscript is confusing or ambiguous, making estimation difficult, then condensation, even omission, becomes likely.[2]

The other process requiring mention is correction. Early modern printers did not discard printed sheets on which errors had been detected but bound them in their uncorrected state. Even the few surviving copies of Q1 differ in minor details. Typically, some obvious flaws like missing and turned letters are corrected. Craven characterizes the correction of sheets A–G in Simmes's shop as 'minimal', none appearing to have demanded consultation of QMS (Craven, 'Proofreading', 363, 369). However, two bits of evidence suggest manuscript consultation in correcting Q1: an addition appears in the otherwise highly accurate Q2 reprint, and a word change occurs in Short's portion of Q1 itself.

Although Q1 has many minor compositorial errors, it corrects some obvious misprints, while leaving other errors – wrong

1 Craven has been challenged (see Peter Davison, 'The selection and presentation of bibliographic evidence', *AEB* 1 (1977), 101–36). Paul Werstine (private communication) suggests scepticism about constructed compositors (cf. McKenzie). Charles Forker finds Craven's evidence relevant to A's effects on *Richard II*: 'widespread interpolation, omission and substitution' (Forker, 539).

2 And expansion, 'stretching', is possible, as can be seen in the First Folio (see p. 443n.), which was also set by formes, and left a large blank space after *Richard III* – a luxury perhaps not to be indulged in the much less expensive quarto editions.

letters, turned letters, repeated speech prefixes, misattributed speeches – uncorrected.[1] The missing 'i' in 'appointed' at 1.1.44 in the British Library and Huntington copies (sig. A2^{v}) appears in the Bodleian and Folger copies; 'soin deede' (at 5.3.275) in the British Library copy (sig. M2^{r}) is rendered 'so in deede' in the Huntington and Folger copies. A full stop missing after '*Norffolke*' (5.3.287.1) in the British Library copy appears in the Huntington and Folger copies (sig. M2^{r}). A colon in 1.2.1 of the Bodleian copy reveals the 'l' or 'lo' of other copies as 'lo:' – an abbreviation for 'Lord(s)'. One of the few substantive Q1 press variants corrects 2.1.5 'from heauen' (sig. D3^{v}; British Library, Huntington) to 'to heauen' (Folger, Bodleian, Elizabethan Club). Such changes do not refute claims that Elizabethan proofreading largely confined itself to correcting superficial blemishes rather than seeking accuracy of copy.[2]

Manuscript copy does appear to have been consulted at 5.3.10, where 'greatest' (Huntington) is corrected to 'vtmost' (Folger, Bodleian, British Library). Unmotivated by grammar, metre or sense, this correction agrees uniquely with F, against all derivative Qq, and thus against any of the printed copies from which scholars have ever claimed F to have been set.[3] This agreement of corrected Q1 with F in a non-essential change argues that F is related to Q1 independently of the derivative quartos. The logical inference is that the copy for F included a manuscript (FMS) closely related to the manuscript behind Q1 (QMS). Ironically, the same line raises questions about the proximity of QMS and FMS.

Corrected Q1 reads 'vtmost number'; F has 'vtmost power'. Since it is difficult to imagine Short's corrector breaking down an otherwise suitable line to adjust a single, perfectly acceptable, word to match manuscript copy without also correcting the word

1 For a partial list, see Davison, 8. Davison notes the rash of errors in 4.1.

2 Against Hinman's dismissal of early modern correction, see McKenzie, 40–9; Gaskell, 110–16.

3 This correction occurs on the same side of sheet L (L2^{r}) that shows 'lordsc onduct' (L3^{v} Huntington) corrected to 'lords conduct' (Folger, Bodleian, British Library).

next to it, the Q1/F variance suggests difference in underlying manuscripts. Furthermore, in context, Q1's 'number', which may be inferred to have been present in QMS since it is left uncorrected, seems likely to have been carried over from the preceding line:

> *King*. . . .Who hath discried the number of the foe.
> *Norff.* Sixe or seuen thousand is their vtmost number.
> (Q1c, sig. L2r)

Since two different speakers are involved, any 'memorial' error here seems most likely a simple, and common, compositorial mistake and evidently not present in FMS. 'Memorial' errors bedevil necessary functionaries such as scribes or compositors (or editors!) every bit as much as any hypothetical actor-recounters (Hammond, 29; Maguire, 155; cf. McKerrow, *Bibliography*, 254).[1]

Such differences in early printed texts constitute clues to the nature and relation of QMS and FMS. The many exclusive agreements that may be inferred between them argue for close relationship, but their differences suggest that QMS derived from FMS.[2] Further claims about these absent but conceptually useful entities demand first considering the reprinting of Q1 and the printing of F.

THE DERIVATIVE QUARTOS (Q2–8)

Q1 (1597) begins a remarkable print history with seven subsequent quarto editions, of which five (Q2–6) pre-date the First Folio of 1623 and two (Q7–8) follow it in 1629 and 1634. Although Q3 (1602) announces itself 'Newly augmented, / By *William Shakespeare*', it contains no new dialogue; its minimal adjustments

1 According to Joseph Moxon, the compositor 'first reads so much of his *Copy* as he thinks he can retain in his memory till he have *Composed* it, as commonly is five or six words, or sometimes a longer Sentence' (Joseph Moxon, *Mechanick Exercises on the whole art of printing, 1683–4*, ed. Herbert Davis and Harry Carter (1958), 204).

2 Alice Walker numbers some three hundred occasions when a substantive variant exclusive to Q1 is restored to F dialogue (Walker, 24; Hammond, 31).

to stage directions and speaking order do not require authorial intervention. The derivative quartos are widely, but not universally, acknowledged to merely reprint one another, with no generally accepted evidence of consultation of manuscript copy and with plentiful incidental error.[1] The inertia involved in reprinting is evident from the fact that the claim to be 'Newly augmented' is simply passed along by five editions (Q3–7) from 1602 to 1629, before being dropped after thirty-two years in Q8 (1634). One two-line passage first appearing in Q2 is an exceptional case that may arguably support the general rule. Nevertheless, the reprinted quartos deserve attention.

There is no doubt that Q3 provided a sixth of the F text, and it has been long accepted that Q3 and/or Q6 furnished printed copy that Folio collators annotated with reference to a manuscript (FMS) for the other five-sixths. Since Q3 and Q6 incorporate or reject variants from earlier quartos, all six quartos preceding F require scrutiny in a Folio-based edition. That the derivative quartos frequently differ from Q1, sometimes obviously erring, other times usefully 'correcting' it, is not in doubt; nor is it to be doubted that F incorporates readings which agree with the derivative quartos against Q1.[2] Such readings common to F and the derivative quartos may sometimes be coincidence, a matter of quarto printers independently getting something right that happens to differ from Q1 and to agree with FMS, but Mowat and Werstine rightly note that 'no editors . . . have been able to eliminate the possibility that F may have picked up these readings from the derivative quartos' (liii). Thus, attention to Q2–6 variants is crucial to the editorial process, and a process it must be, even when an edition accepts F as its basic text.

Q2 (1598) to Q5 (1612) were printed by Thomas Creede; on 25 June 1603 the profitable title was acquired from Andrew Wise,

1 Q5 provides the single deviation from the practice of reprinting each quarto from its immediate predecessor, with sheets C and E–M being printed from Q3 (W.W. Greg, '*Richard III* – Q5 (1612)', *The Library*, 4th series, 17 [1936], 88–97).

2 Smidt finds approximately 80 substantive F agreements with Q3–6 against Q1 in portions of F not directly reproduced from Q3 (Smidt, *Impostors*, 179–90).

along with *Richard II* and *1 Henry IV*, by Matthew Law. Q6 (1622) was printed for Law by Thomas Purfoot. The two quartos that came after F, Q7 (1629) and Q8 (1634), were printed by John Norton. These late reprints testify to the play's continuing popularity in an inexpensive, easily readable format.[1] From this unusually long run, two reprints – Q3 (1602) and Q6 (1622) – are particularly important. F prints Q3 text virtually unaltered from 3.1.1 to 3.1.166 and from 5.3.49 to the end of the play, and many have argued for the role of Q6 in constituting the rest of F's text.

No scholar has asserted such importance for other quartos in determining copy for F, but Q2 (1598) introduces two new lines (1.1.101–2) that are accepted in all subsequent quartos and into F. It is easy to imagine how two lines could be lost in printing; but how could they come to be added to an otherwise careful reprint of Q1? Two opposing theories offer to explain this addition.[2]

In Q1 Richard's joke about Mistress Shore doing 'naught' (with King Edward) (1.1.98–100) elicits only the jailer's reiterated demand that Richard cease conversing with Clarence:

> *Glo.* Naught to do with Mistris Shore, I tell thee fellow,
> He that doth naught with her, excepting one
> Were best he doe it secretly alone.
> *Bro.* I beseech your Grace to pardon me, and withal
> for- (beare
> Your conference with the noble Duke.
> (Q1, sig. A3r)

Q2 reprints Richard's speech, but adds a query and Richard's response:

> *Bro.* What one my Lord?
> *Glo.* Her husband knaue, wouldst thou betray me?
> (Q2, sig. A3r)

1 Q7 and Q8 may sometimes suggest printers' efforts to grapple with textual issues raised by Q6, issues that F's printers might also have had to face (Walton, *Copy*, 27–35).

2 Mowat and Werstine suggest spurious printing-house addition (305).

With minor relineation, F repeats this Q2 exchange.

One argument attributes the new lines to the Q2 printer's use of a press-corrected copy of Q1 for which no exemplar survives. The strongest support for this hypothesis is the absence of conclusive evidence that printers ever consulted manuscript copy in printing any of the derivative quartos. In fact, recognizable patterns of error have enabled scholars to determine exactly which printed quarto served for copy in each case (Hammond, 29; Mowat & Werstine, lii). The convenient hypothesis of a no longer extant Q1 that included this press correction has been countered by claims that in this passage alone the printers working for Thomas Creede, the legal owner of the manuscript copy for Q1, consulted QMS rather than, as elsewhere, following Q1 (Smidt, *Memorial*, 52–3; Jowett, 115–16). This assertion is no more, or less, verifiable than its alternative. The added lines require Q2's printers to modify the preceding page (sig. A2ᵛ) from its form in surviving copies of Q1 by introducing a turn-up and by printing on the catchword line (Jowett, 115). But Q1 and Q2 print elsewhere on a catchword line (sig. E1ᵛ) and begin and end every other page at exactly the same words, so it does not follow that it is less likely that Q1 was press-corrected than that Q2 involved a single instance of manuscript consultation. In sum, Q2 probably reprints a corrected version of Q1 that does not survive among the five extant copies. No instance of 'correction' in subsequent quartos demands the printer's having consulted QMS, though variants introduced by Q2–6 sometimes appear arguably preferable to Q1 alternatives.[1]

The most extensive recent arguments for manuscript consultation concern Q3, printed in 1602 by Andrew Wise, who retained legal rights to QMS. No real change in dialogue justifies Q3's claim to be 'newly augmented', but there is editing of some stage directions and speech prefixes, a correction of fact and

1 Q2, for example, changes 5.3.183 'I and I' (Q1) to 'I am I' (Q2–8, F); cf. Wilson, 143–4. See also 1.3.5n. and 5.3.183n. Q2 contributes its share of errors, later corrected (e.g. 1.3.245; 1.4.16; 4.1.35).

an intelligent inversion of two speeches. Some knowledgeable reader in the printing-house closely examined at least portions of Q3. Smidt and Jowett argue for manuscript consultation (Smidt, *Memorial*, 54; Jowett, 116), but intelligent reading – by whom is unclear – could explain Q3's modifications of Q2.

Since Q3 is the direct source for a sixth of F, anything casting light on Q3 may carry considerable textual implications. The play's first two acts exhibit hundreds of substantial verbal differences between Q1 and F. Part-way through the first 166 lines of dialogue in 3.1 such differences decline almost to zero. F even begins to reproduce the distinctive Qq speech prefix for Richard, designating him *Glo.* rather than *Rich.*, which is invariable in F until this point (3.1.63) and to which F returns (3.1.181). These 166 dialogue lines contain only thirteen substantive verbal differences (excluding contractions) between F and Q1. Ten of these are found variously in the derivative quartos (Q2–6) that could theoretically have furnished text for F, but Q3 alone has all ten. At 3.1.123 F repeats a misprint exclusive to Q3. As printed in Q1–2 and substantially repeated in Q4–7, the line reads: 'I would, that I might thanke you as you call me.' Q3 and F print: 'I would that I might thanke you as as you call me.' (Q3) and 'I would that I might thanke you as, as, you / call me.' (F; TLN 1706–7). F repunctuates Q3's dittography to suggest stammering ('as, as,').[1] The fact that Q4 and F2 both correct this Q3/F error indicates its glaring nature. No smoking gun appears elsewhere, but comparable statistical similarities from 5.3.49 to the end of the play again reveal Q3 as the direct basis for F (Mowat & Werstine, liii).

Elsewhere in F *Richard III* the situation is less certain, but scholars have long argued that Q3 and/or Q6 furnished copy that was annotated by F's printers. Neither quarto has been conclusively demonstrated to be *the* one to furnish copy. Since Q3

1 Cf. F's apparent attempt at 5.3.199 to compensate for Q3's interpolation of 'all' (found twice in the previous line and once more in the line itself) with elision marks ('to'th'Barre').

literally furnished part of F, and since Q3 and/or Q6 probably influenced what the printers set elsewhere, both are important for their possible effects in determining, supplementing, supporting, clarifying, substituting for or overriding what may have survived to 1623 of FMS. Yet each mostly reprints its preceding reprint, itself already distant from Q1, the only quarto certainly set from manuscript, while introducing new errors (Hammond, 30). What, then, is the evidence that Q3 was printed with consultation of QMS?

Discerning corrections appear scattered throughout Q3 stage directions, but the instances that might be said to be 'newly augmented' merely reveal attention to the previous quarto (Q2). For example, at 1.4.159 Q3 adds '*Cla. awaketh.*' just after dialogue mentions that 'he stirs' in his sleep and just before Clarence speaks.[1] Similarly, at 3.1.59 Q3 adds '*Exit. Car. & Hast.*' after the Cardinal asks Hastings 'will you go with me?' and Hastings replies 'I go my Lord'. Similarly obvious, stage directions are added at 3.2.33.1, 3.2.92, 3.2.105 SD and 4.4.497 SD and in identification of the '*Lieutenant*' at 4.1.11.1 (Q2, sig. H3^{r}) as '*Lieutenant of the Tower*' (Q3–6; not in F).

The same assessment – correct but obvious – applies to Q3's augmentations and changes to other stage directions. The Ghosts explicitly address Richard rather than Richmond at 5.3.118, 124 and 146, because Q3 puts '*to K. Ri.*' or '*to K.R.*' (Q3–6) in place of '*to Ri.*' (Q1–2). '*K.*' (for 'King') may seem useful here, but Q3 inserts titles where there can be no confusion: '*K. Richard starteth out of a dreame.*' (Q3–6) replaces '*Richard starteth vp out of a dreame.*' (Q1–2; 5.3.176 SD2); the ghost of '*Ladie Anne*' (Q2, sig. L4^{r}) becomes that of '*Queene Anne*' (Q3–6; '*Anne*' in F 5.3.158.1); the ghost of '*Hastings*' (Q2, sig. L4^{r}) becomes that of '*L. Hastings*' (Q3–6; '*Lord Hastings*' in F 5.3.153.1). Q3

1 Oddly, despite F's close relation to Q3 and Q6, this stage direction is omitted from F. This fact might lend weight to the argument that the direction was *not* in FMS.

stage directions hardly reveal special alertness to 'ambiguity' of address, let alone consultation of QMS (Jowett, 116).

True, certain other Q3 corrections might appear 'authoritative', but, with two possible exceptions, these are roughly equivalent to Q3's additions to stage directions. Obvious mistakes are corrected: a false plural (1.1.40); a mistaken tense (4.4.423); misallocated speeches (3.4.6; 3.5.52; 5.3.139). Elsewhere, Q3 introduces variants that may arguably represent improvements (e.g. 1.3.33; 4.1.35), along with misprints (2.2.34; 2.2.149; 3.1.123; 5.3.250), obvious mistakes (2.1.135; 3.2.83; 3.7.14, 21; 4.4.107–8, 352; 5.3.338, 351), abbreviated entries (5.3.18.2–3, 46.2), and omitted speech headings (2.1.100). Some new corrections, some new mistakes – like *all* the quarto reprints. The exceptions require explanation.

At 2.3.17 Q3 corrects Q2 in historical fact, accurately revising Henry VI's age at coronation from 'xi' (Q2) to 'nine' months (as Q1 'ix'). But this fact is not obscure (see *Mirror*, 'Nicholas Burdet', 78; *2H6* 4.9.4; *3H6* 1.1.112). A much more substantial Q3 variant appears in the altered speaking order of the Ghosts. In Q1–2 all the Ghosts except for Hastings and the princes address Richard according to the chronological sequence of their deaths. Q3 inverts the speaking order of their Q1–2 passages (5.3.146–58) to follow chronological death order. Hammond takes Q1–2's order as arising from misreporting and accepts Q3's reordering as 'inspired correction'. Jowett also invokes theatrical explanations, claiming that the Q1–2 order 'probably reflect[s] actual stage practice' because putting the princes on before Hastings would have allowed for one boy actor to exit and return as Anne (Jowett, 116). Perhaps so, but why would a printer care enough to intervene substantially and uniquely here? Jowett offers multiple hypothetical agents for the change: if the Q3 printers consulted manuscript, they might have seen ambiguous markings; Wise or Shakespeare might have intervened. But without substantial change or manuscript consultation anywhere else and with no obvious reason for Wise or Shakespeare to intervene here and nowhere else with a large-scale change, these alternatives hardly exhaust possible explanations.[1]

Uncertainties might have arisen from Q3's new pagination. To conserve paper, the printer's second most costly expense after labour, Q3 normally prints 39 lines per page, rather than the 38 typical of Q1–2, and often crowds in 40 lines, printing on the catchword line of verso pages, to save one full leaf (ending on sig. M2[v]). It could not have been easy to mark up so many repaginations, and since reversing the two speeches provides no obvious spatial advantage, it might be no more than random happenstance. Yet someone examined this portion of Q3 carefully enough to correct an erroneous speech prefix (5.3.139); perhaps this same press reader – who nowhere else betrays independent authority or innovation beyond mere close reading – simply read the final ghostly utterance and drew a conclusion about order from it:

Enter the Goast of Buckingham.
The first was I that helpt thee to the Crowne,
The last was I that felt thy tyrannie.
(Q2, sig. L4[v])

One could hardly ask for a clearer suggestion of sequence for the Ghosts; accordingly, Q3's corrector puts them in order of their deaths at Richard's hand.

We do not know why Q3 here differs from Q2, but editions have to make choices. Q3's rearrangement may look like a good one, especially to an editor basing his or her work on the Folio which follows it; nevertheless, the present edition rejects it. What we do know about this portion of 5.3 is that, for the most part, F simply follows Q3, even when Q3 is clearly wrong. It would be ironic, but no surprise, given the unknowns (and unknowables) surrounding the early texts of Shakespeare, to learn that an Elizabethan reader in 1602 correctly deduced a formal aspect

1 For 'access to authoritative manuscript which was completely ignored throughout the rest of the text' as the least plausible explanation for Q3's reordering, see *TxC*, 248.

of the play that would otherwise have remained obscure until the Folio printers consulted FMS in 1623. That would be one interesting narrative, and 'coincidental corrections' by quarto printers sometimes hit upon readings eventually proved right by what we can deduce about FMS.[1] However, in this portion of 5.3 there may have been no FMS for Folio printers to consult, since F reproduces Q3 virtually unaltered (but see 5.3.204–5n.). Thus, F might here simply reprint a printer's earlier mistake, a chance error or 'wrong' deduction of 1602 that scholars have since largely accepted as 'By *William Shakespeare*'. I like that story, too. Its ironies implicating authority, purpose, chance, error, individuality, anonymity and scholarship point to issues that surround the Folio itself. Before dealing with F, it is worth briefly considering the remaining derivative quartos, including Q6, the quarto that enjoys with Q3 the most advocates in debates about printed copy for F.

Since P.A. Daniel in 1886, the extent and nature of quarto copy for the five-sixths of F *Richard III* not set from Q3 continues in dispute. The possibility that an annotated copy of Q6 was used for those portions has been rejected by Walton, who judged Daniel's twelve exclusive F/Q6 agreements insufficient to rule out annotated Q3 copy (Walton, *Copy*, 34). Although W.W. Greg, J.D. Wilson and Fredson Bowers also came to agree that Q3 furnished copy throughout, Hammond judges the relative importance of Q3/Q6 impossible to determine beyond the Q3 portions of F (Hammond, 32–41). Bowers changed his mind, admitting possible contributions by Q6 to F (Walton, *Quarto*, 61–2). Taylor has argued that pages from Q6 and Q3 were interleaved with pages from FMS throughout F (*TxC*, 229–30); Jowett concurs.

1 For similarly effective correction see 3.2.91, where Q2 introduces a mistake ('hat'), corrected by Q6 ('hats'), which agrees with Q1 and F; 4.4.260, where Q2 reduces Q1's 'thou love' to 'thou' until corrected by Q6, which agrees with Q1 and F; 3.5.26, where Q4 alone agrees with F on 'the' (cf. Hammond, 39).

The principal evidence supporting the use of Q6 in printing F is of two sorts. Firstly, a dozen or so F readings substantively agree with Q6 against all other quartos (Hammond, 35–7). Secondly, two passages suggest F attempting to 'correct' a reading unique to Q6. The first passage occurs at 3.5.74:

Q1–5 There at your meetst aduantage of the time,

Q6 There at your meetest aduantage of the time,

F There, at your meetest vantage of the time,

Walton argues that Q6 only coincidentally agrees with FMS on 'meetest'. Hammond counters that the F collator could have looked at Q6 copy and emended to make the line metrical (Hammond, 36). But the metre could be easily corrected by eliding 'meetest', the kind of change that appears frequently throughout F (*TxC*, 242). This instance seems inconclusive to me.

A more convincing case for influence of Q6 copy appears at 4.4.534. Q6 replaces Q1–5's 'tidings' with the unmetrical 'news', perhaps because the compositor carries the word over from two lines earlier: 'Thats the best newes, that the *E*arle of Richmond' (Q1–5). F retains Q6's erroneous 'news', but adds a word that renders the line metrical:

Q1–5 *I*s colder tidings, yet they must be told.

Q6 Is colder news, yet they must be told.

F Is colder Newes, but yet they must be told.
(4.4.534, TLN 3342)

In this case, Q6 might by chance have come up with the very word found in FMS, correctly but accidentally substituting 'news' for 'tidings'. Alternatively, both F and Q6 might share the same mistake, simply and independently, carrying over 'news'. However, both these hypotheses are rendered doubtful by F's addition of 'but', which would not fit metrically with 'tidings'.

This addition suggests F's *post facto* regularization of Q6 rather than consideration of FMS, since attention to FMS might have revealed the mistaken entry of 'news' caught by Q6 from the earlier line and have prompted reinstatement of Q1–5's 'tidings'. This case suggests direct influence of Q6 on F. The force of such evidence has prompted the present edition, in full awareness of its own seeming inconsistency, to follow F in 3.5.74 and Q1 in 4.4.534. Further reasons for such apparent self-contradiction will emerge in considering the strengths and limitations of F itself.

Finally, the later quartos demonstrate that the play, along with two other histories also first published by Wise and later by Law, *Richard II* and *1 Henry IV*, remained popular, outdistancing Shakespeare's comedies and even such popular tragedies as *Hamlet* in reprints (Erne, 50). Their print history suggests that these three plays taken together, as Jowett notes, probably dominated the seventeenth-century perception of Shakespeare's histories before the 1623 Folio, since Law followed Wise's precedent of bringing them out in tandem: Q4 *Richard III* and Q3 *1 Henry IV* (1604–5), Q4 *Richard II* and Q4 *1 Henry IV* (1608), Q5 *Richard III*, Q5 *Richard II* and Q5 *1 Henry IV* (1612–15). In 1619 Thomas Pavier brought out reprints of some other histories – Q3 *2 Henry VI*, Q3 *3 Henry VI* and Q3 *Henry V* – but the Folio put the history plays into their historical order. Q5 *Richard III* (1612) is notable for finally updating the acting company on the title-page, to the King's Majesty's Servants, although Q4 (1605) could have done so seven years earlier. After the Folio, two further quartos (Q7, 1629, and Q8, 1634) appear with little evident awareness of F. Considering the importance of the First Folio for subsequent editions and scholarship, the independent production and marketing of Q7 (with bookseller Matthew Law retaining rights he had held since 1603) and Q8 (printed by John Norton) remind us of the many lives of this play – for readers as well as playgoers.

THE FIRST FOLIO (F)

By any measure, the 1623 Folio edition of *Mr William / Shakespeares / Comedies, Histories, & Tragedies. / Published according to the True Originall Copies* constitutes a major historical event in dramatic publication. It must have been conceived and perceived as such. Produced posthumously with the aid of John Heminge and Henry Condell, two of Shakespeare's former colleagues in the King's Men, the Folio is an expensive and carefully printed volume that represented an economic risk. Costing approximately 15s unbound or £1 in plain calf, the Folio was, as Peter Blayney terms it, 'by far the most expensive playbook that had ever been offered to the English public'. It would be followed after a brief nine years by a second edition.[1] The publishers were the relative newcomer Isaac Jaggard and the well-established Edward Blount; the printer was Jaggard's father, William Jaggard (Blayney, 'Intro', xxviii).

Folio *Richard III* is remarkable for changing a play that had been more or less constantly in print for twenty-six years. Intrinsically, there are several new passages, a few substantial cuts and thousands of small changes. Extrinsically, the Folio puts the play within a chronological sequence, making it appear part of a grand 'national' narrative. Beginning with the externally threatened and internally troubled reign of King John (events of 1199–1218), the sequence runs through seven plays depicting troubled rule and disputed dynasty, briefly interrupted by a play that represents Henry V effecting a precarious national unity while waging a successful campaign in France. The whole ends with Henry VIII and the promise-filled birth of Queen Elizabeth (events of 1520–36). This sequence follows neither the order of composition nor that of performance, but has its own logic. The Folio order provides patterns of ideology and

1 Blayney, 'Intro', xviii; Ben Jonson's *Workes* (1616) included non-dramatic works, cost less, and would not be reprinted for twenty-four years. Blayney estimates the initial First Folio print-run at something like 750 copies (xxxiii).

outcome that can be paralleled in the primary historical sources; it is unlikely that Shakespeare anticipated anyone encountering these plays in such order, but some early readers did read them in sequence and expected continuity.[1]

Richard III follows *3 Henry VI* and precedes *Henry VIII* in the Folio quires devoted to the histories. 'The Tragedy of Richard the Third: / with the Landing of Earle Richmond, and the / Battell at Bosworth Field' also employs a running title – '*The Life and Death of Richard the Third*' – following a biographical formula also found in *King John* and *Richard II*. F provides numbered acts and scenes, generally conforming, at least through the first four acts, to units adopted by later editions. *Richard III* fills thirty-two double-columned pages (sigs q5^{r}–t2^{v}). Like the rest of the Folio, the play was set by formes. Copy was cast-off in advance in units estimated to fill one folio page, with the printing of each twelve-page quire beginning with the middle pages (6 and 7) and working outwards successively through 5 and 8, then 4 and 9 and so on to pages 1 and 12 (Blayney, 'Intro', xxxii). The casting-off of copy for *Richard III* was not always precise. The printers sometimes divide perfectly suitable (and printable) verse lines in two in order to fill up the page.[2] Confused lineation implicates the nature of the copy involved, and argues against passive deference to F lineation.

Richard III was set by compositors known as A and B. Charlton Hinman established their shares of labour (Hinman, 2.113–27; 220–5):

B set 1.1 through line 1.3.125 (sigs q5^{r} through r1^{r})
A set 1.3.126 through 1.3.255 (sig. r1^{v})
B set 1.3.256 through 3.1.19 (sigs r2^{r} through r5^{r})

1 Marcus, 95; cf. Samuel Schoenbaum, *William Shakespeare: A Documentary Life* (New York, 1975), 144. Contrast Ioppolo's suggestion that Shakespeare may have reworked passages from the history plays to create continuities for a revival (Ioppolo, 130).

2 See 1.2.39, 50, 83–4, 95–6, 104 and 135. This page is the last of the inner forme of gathering q, and Compositor B appears to have stretched copy to prevent a gap at the end of the quire (Hammond, 45). B also expands lines on sig. r1^{r} at 1.3.116, 117, 120 and 125.

A set 3.1.20 through 4.3.2 (sigs r5^{v} through s3^{v})
B set 4.3.3 through 4.4.431 (sigs s4^{r} through s5^{v})
A set 4.4.432 through 4.4.532 (sig. s6^{r})
B set 4.4.533 through end of play (sigs s6^{v} through t2^{v})
(Hinman, 2.113–27; 220–5)

The effects are sometimes obvious: contrast speech prefixes set by B on sig. r1^{r} (1.3.110–25) and sig. r2^{r} (1.3.265–96), where Margaret is '*Mar.*' or '*Margaret.*', with those set by A on sig. r1^{v} (1.3.134–254), where she is '*Q.M.*' Typical spelling preferences are 'heere', 'do', 'go' (B) and 'here', 'doe', 'goe' (A). There was an interruption in setting, with a major break occurring at the end of sig. s6^{v} (5.3.16) while work was undertaken on the tragedies and on *H8* (Blayney, 'Intro', xxxvi).

Proof corrections are evident in six pages (sigs q6^{r-v}, r2^{r}, s5^{v}, s6^{v}, t1^{v}), most of them amounting to elimination of technical errors such as inking spaces and letter inversions (Hammond, 44). The few true corrections are: 'and' replaces 'end' (sig. s5^{v}; 4.4.354); 'off' replaces 'oft' and 'want' replaces 'went' (sig. s6^{v}; 4.5.4 and 5.3.13). Obvious misprints (for example, 'necke' replaces 'neeke') are corrected on the same page. None of these demands reference to copy, nor do two substantial corrections on sig. r2^{r} – the obviously mistaken speech prefix '*Riu.*' (Rivers) becomes '*Ric.*' (Richard) at 1.3.343, and the stage direction opening 1.4 ('*Enter Clarence and Keeper.*') is added.[1]

THE FOLIO MANUSCRIPT (FMS)

New dialogue, amounting to over two hundred lines not in Qq and including several extended passages, makes it clear that manuscript (FMS), which has not survived, contributed to F

1 For F variants, see Hinman, 1.276–8.

Richard III.[1] We need to consider the nature of that manuscript, its relation to the manuscript that formed the basis for Q1 (QMS), which itself contains just under forty lines not found in F, including one lengthy passage (4.2.97–114), and the means by which FMS was incorporated into F.

Outside the portions of F comprising completely new passages from manuscript and those portions reprinting Q3, evidence suggests that F was set from printed quarto copy annotated with reference to FMS. At 4.4.362–6, for instance, F inserts a line that exists only in Q1 and no other quarto (Greg, *Problem*, 86). This line, which must have come to F from FMS, appears set one line too soon, a dislocation arguing that F's printers inserted lines from FMS into printed quarto copy.

Q1 prints the passage from 4.4 in the following order:

> *Qu.* O no my reasons are to deepe and dead.
> *T*oo deepe and dead poore infants in their graue.
> *King* Harpe not one that string Madam that is past.
> *Qu.* Harpe on it still shall I till hartstrings breake.
> *King* Now by my George, my Garter and my crown.
> (Q1, sig. K2v)

Subsequent quartos make a hash of it, omitting Richard's command that Elizabeth drop the subject of her dead children and nonsensically giving Richard himself the rejoinder in which she insists on the right to dwell upon her losses. This confusion is obvious in its initial printed instance because Q2 speech prefixes make Richard answer himself:

> *Qu.* O no my reasons are too deepe and dead.
> Too deepe and dead poore infants in their graue.
> *King*. Harpe on it still shal I, till hartstrings breake.
> *King*. Now by my George, my Garter and my Crowne.
> (Q2, sig. K2v)

1 Passages present in F but not (or not entirely) in Qq include 1.2.158–69; 1.4.69–72, 256–60; 2.2.89–100, 123–40; 3.4.101–4; 3.5.103–5; 3.7.143–52; 4.1.2–4, 97–103; 4.4.222–35 and 288–342.

Q3–8 drop the final speech prefix, but retain Q2's misordered form.

F prints this passage with the line missing since 1597 – Richard's 'Harpe not on that string Madam, that is past' – one of approximately three hundred instances in which F dialogue agrees substantively with Q1 against all subsequent quartos. These unique agreements bespeak a close relationship between FMS and QMS. However, F retains Q2's order, putting Richard's newly restored line in the wrong place:

> *Qu.* O no, my Reasons are too deepe and dead,
> Too deepe and dead (poore Infants) in their graues,
> Harpe on it still shall I, till heart-strings breake.
> *Rich.* Harpe not on that string Madam, that is past.
> Now by my George, my Garter, and my Crowne.
> (F 4.4.362–6; TLN 3147–51)

Apparently 'the line was written in the margin of one of the derivative quartos used as Folio copy and . . . either the collator failed to make clear where it was to be inserted or . . . the compositor was careless in incorporating it in the Folio text' (Walker, 15; cf. Hammond, 31; Smidt, *Memorial*, 54). Walker points to other anomalies in F lineation (such as an unusual shared line at 1.3.232–3; disorder at 1.4.255–61) that argue for quarto copy for F (Smidt, *Memorial*, 54). But more can be deduced about FMS and its relation to QMS.

Folio manuscript (FMS) comes first and the manuscript behind Q1 (QMS) is derived from it. The clearest evidence takes two forms. Q1 prints apparently garbled versions of passages that appear competently rendered in F; Q1 portrays characters engaging in actions and delivering speeches that appear inappropriate for them but that are appropriately allocated by F.

D.L. Patrick notes the confusion of Q1's version of 4.4.271–8, with its transposed (and more colloquial) order, its unmetrical line, synonym substitution and missing text (Hammond, 7–8).

Q1's Queen Elizabeth asks Richard to send a handkerchief steeped in Rutland's blood to her daughter Elizabeth; this gesture would make no difference to her, since Richard's murdered brother means nothing to either Elizabeth:

> *Qu.* Send to her by the man that slew her brothers,
> A paire of bleeding harts thereon ingraue,
> Edward and Yorke, then happelie she wil weepe,
> Therefore present to her as sometimes Margaret
> Did to thy father, a handkercher steept in Rutlands bloud,
> And bid her drie her weeping eies therewith
> (Q1, sig. K2^r)

By contrast, F makes sense: Queen Elizabeth invites Richard to send her daughter a handkerchief steeped in her brothers' blood, as Margaret had once given a bloody handkerchief soaked in his own son's blood to York, father of Rutland and Richard:

> *Qu.* Send to her by the man that slew her Brothers,
> A paire of bleeding hearts: thereon ingraue
> *Edward* and *Yorke*, then haply will she weepe:
> Therefore present to her, as sometime *Margaret*
> Did to thy Father, steept in Rutlands blood,
> A hand-kercheefe, which say to her did dreyne
> The purple sappe from her sweet Brothers body,
> And bid her wipe her weeping eyes withall.
> (F 4.4.271–8; TLN 3055–62)

Q1 appears to be a distorted rendering of FMS. For their number and nature, Q1's multiple condensations and confusions seem to derive neither from scribal or compositorial error, nor from specifically authorial revision. This is not to claim that F does not occasionally garble passages that appear coherently rendered in Q1, nor that Q1 does not sometimes get details right where F makes mistakes.

F has its own weak spots: lines necessary to sense are omitted though present in Q1; lines that occur singly in Q1 are simply repeated; lines and passages that Q1 renders clearly are misplaced and confused. For the most part, these weaknesses are readily attributable to composing or printing processes rather than to failings in FMS. For example, by contrast with Q1's confusions about the handkerchief, F's problems at 2.2.83–5 suggest compositorial error rather than bungled derivation. Q1 correctly and clearly reads:

> She for Edward weepes, and so doe I:
> I for a Clarence weep, so doth not she:
> These babes for Clarence weepe, and so do I:
> I for an Edward weep, so do not they.
> (Q1, sig. $E2^{v}$)

Q2 mistakenly drops 'not' from the final line, an error repeated by all subsequent quartos. F uniquely agrees with Q1 on 'not', while making the first line metrical, but adds new confusions:

> She for an *Edward* weepes, and so do I:
> I for a *Clarence* weepes, so doth not shee:
> These Babes for *Clarence* weepe, so do not they.
> (F, sig. $r4^{r-v}$; TLN 1356–8; cf. 2.2.82–5)

Here, as in other passages spanning a page or column, F's printers drop the ball (see 1.3.6, 2.2.145). 'I' beginning the second line is the first word on sig. $r4^{v}$, and the printer apparently interprets it as an interjection ('Ay') rather than a personal pronoun, and substitutes a third-person verb form ('weepes'), while eyeskip leads directly from the third to fourth lines, neatly and nonsensically excising 'and so do I: / I for an Edward weep'. Such mistakes underline the necessity for editorial vigilance, even if F's text is generally more coherent and based on a manuscript closer to Shakespearean holograph.

MANUSCRIPTS FOR F (FMS) AND Q (QMS)

No manuscript for *Richard III* survives, but both printed versions clearly depend on manuscript copy. The many times when F restores a reading shared exclusively with Q1 testify to the proximity of the two manuscripts and to the thoroughness of F's annotation of its derivative-quarto copy.[1] The evidence of the printed versions strongly supports their basis in manuscripts that were closely related to one another and to Shakespeare's holograph, but that nonetheless differed substantially. Neither manuscript conforms easily to labels like 'foul papers', 'promptbook' or 'playbook' (Jowett, 120).[2] The evidence reveals FMS to be a more originary, 'literary' version of the play's 'raw material' and QMS to be derivative from FMS, possibly registering incomplete adaptation for ostensibly 'theatrical' purposes.[3] The occasion and nature of this partial adaptation is difficult to characterize, and the identity of its agent(s) probably unknowable.[4]

Various stories have been constructed to account for such different yet closely related manuscripts. One narrative maintains that for some reason – loss, damage, exigencies of travel, etc. – Shakespeare's company found themselves compelled to recreate the play from memory and produced QMS from collaborative recall.[5] Such accounts usually rely on instances in which Q1 has been judged to provide a vague, often briefer or less pointed approximation of verbal formulations appearing in F (Davison, 7). Obvious problems haunt such arguments: some Q1 lines are arguably 'better' than F equivalents (e.g. 1.1.133, 2.4.66; cf.

1 F restores just under twenty Act 1 readings that agree with Q1 exclusively against all derivative quartos. If one adds instances when F agrees with Q1–2, but with neither quarto (Q3 and Q6) thought to have provided F with copy, the number is larger (see Jowett, 366–8 (Appendix B)).

2 On FMS as prompt copy, see Hammond, 42–3. Inconsistencies weigh against it. As for foul papers: 'F is relatively regular in its speech-prefixes and thorough in its stage directions, far more so than the recognized foul-paper texts' (*TxC*, 230). On 'foul papers' generally, see Paul Werstine, 'Narratives about printed Shakespeare texts: "foul papers" and "bad quartos"', *SQ*, 41 (1990), 65–86.

3 For 'raw material', see Blayney, 'Intro', xxx; Dutton, 174.

4 On FMS as a transcript for a patron, see *TxC*, 230; Jowett offers Henry Herbert, 2nd Earl of Pembroke, patron of Pembroke's Men, and father to dedicatees of the Folio (Jowett, 122). For argument based on the number of supernumeraries mentioned in stage directions that FMS was autograph, see Walton, *Quarto*, 261.

5 For 'memorial transmission' including 'memorial lapses', see Smidt, *Memorial*, 25; for 'not memorial', see Smidt, *Impostors*; concerning 'memories of individual actors' on 'provincial tour', see *TxC*, 228; or for 'reported text' incorporating cuts 'probably by Shakespeare himself' for 'a smaller or touring company', see Ioppolo, 129. The memorial hypothesis often adduces a decline in F/Q1 similarity in the speeches of Clarence's murderers, anonymous messengers and Buckingham (*TxC*, 228; contrast Smidt, *Impostors*, 140).

Walker, 30; Hammond, 338); Q1 alone contains the clearly Shakespearean jack of the clock passage (4.2.97–114); and Q1 is sometimes closer to historical sources (Smidt, *Memorial*, 42).

Perhaps most difficult to reconcile with oral reconstruction are certain non-dialogue features that Q1 shares with F. For example, Q1 includes notations for two battlefield speeches – '*His oration to his souldiers*' (Q1, sig. M1^{v}; 5.3.236 SD) and '*His oration to his army*' (Q1, sig. M2^{v}; 5.3.313 SD) – that closely replicate marginal notations in the sources – 'The oration of King Henrie the sea*uenth to his armie*' and 'The oration of king Richard the third *to the chiefteins of his armie*' (Holinshed, 3.757, 755). It is easy to imagine how F could omit one of these markers, but more difficult to explain how or why an actor or theatre professional would 'remember' such a purely textual feature in recreating QMS from memory. Of course, the 'actor' doing the recollecting could have been Shakespeare, but other non-dialogue elements of Q1 and F show a similarly remarkable consistency that confounds the idea of even authorial 'recollection' as a sufficient, non-textual basis for QMS.

In line with the 'detailed and relatively efficient' correction of quarto copy by F's annotators outside the portions set uncorrected from Q3 (Jowett, 'Derby', 76), F's speech headings are relatively consistent, with one notable exception: the non-dialogue designations for Stanley/Derby/Darby/Darbie are consistent within scenes, but vary among them, and even clash with dialogue. The textual significance of this oddity has been debated. Hammond dismisses it, since 'Derby' – although anachronistic for the action – is Stanley's eventual title. Smidt, by contrast, takes the parallel patterns in Q1 and F non-dialogue names to reveal that 'the manuscript underlying F had an inconsistency similar to that of the manuscript used by Q' (Smidt, *Memorial*, 31; cf. Jowett, 'Derby', 75).

This pattern has been thoroughly examined by Jowett (375). In dialogue, the character begins as Derby/Darby (F/Q1) in 1.3; from 3.1 onwards, he is consistently 'Stanley' or 'Stanlie' in both texts. Non-dialogue identifiers also run parallel in Q1 and F (except for two scenes):

Non-dialogue identifiers Stanley/Derby

F	Derby in 1.3, 2.1 and 2.2 Stanley in 3.2, 4.1 Derby in 3.4 (conflicts with dialogue) Stanley in 4.2 and 4.4 Derby in 4.5 to end (conflicts with dialogue)
Q1	Derby in 1.3, 2.1 (not named in Q1 2.2) Stanley in 3.2, 4.1 Derby in 3.4 (conflicts with dialogue) Derby in 4.2 and 4.4 (conflicts with dialogue) Derby in 4.5 to end (conflicts with dialogue)

This similarity in an unspoken inconsistency appears too extensive, unmotivated and uncorrected to be coincidental, and it argues that QMS and FMS are linked by textual transmission. The handling of dramatic roles in the two texts reveals the direction of that transmission: QMS is derivative from FMS.

Q1 has fewer speaking parts than F, and speeches and actions are often differently attributed: in Q1 Brokenbury absorbs the Keeper's lines (1.4); the Cardinal replaces the Archbishop (2.4); Dorset speaks the Messenger's lines (2.4); Catesby takes over the roles of Lovell and Ratcliffe (3.4, 3.5); Catesby replaces Ratcliffe (4.3); Ratcliffe replaces the Sheriff (5.1); Catesby replaces Surrey (5.3). Dorset and Rivers are absent from 2.2; the Priest loses his speeches in 3.2; Clarence's silent daughter vanishes from 4.1; silent Norfolk disappears from 3.4; silent Brandon, Oxford and Herbert disappear from 5.3. Because such Q1 differences eliminate speaking parts (Keeper, Archbishop, Messenger, Sheriff, Surrey, Priest and Lovell), locally abbreviate others (Ratcliffe in 4.3, Vaughan in 3.3, Dorset and Rivers in 2.2), reduce the number of boy actors required simultaneously in 4.1 and ease doubling in 5.3, they have been taken to reflect – inconsistently realized – attempts at theatrical economy.[1]

Some changes are deft: Richmond's address to Brandon (5.3.22) becomes a reference to an offstage character in Q1 – 'Where is Sir William Brandon, he shall beare my standard' (L2^{v}).[2] Others are awkward: Catesby, Ratcliffe and Dorset provide useful examples that support the conclusion that Q1 is 'the later version than F' (Mowat & Werstine, xlix).

In Q1 Catesby performs the actions of F's Lovell and Ratcliffe in leading Hastings to execution, while retaining one speech of F's Ratcliffe. This conforms to Q1's omission of Lovell and abbreviation of Ratcliffe's part. In F 3.4 Richard orders Hastings's death, singling out his agents from those who sit '*at a Table*' till Richard bids them 'rise':

> I will not dine, vntill I see the same.
> *Louell* and *Ratcliffe*, looke that it be done: *Exeunt.*
> The rest that loue me, rise, and follow me.
> *Manet Louell and Ratcliffe, with the Lord Hastings.*
> (F 3.4.76–8; TLN 2048–52)

No one else aids the designated executioners, and it seems unlikely that anyone but Richard's intimates would risk remaining, given his demand that everyone register affection by leaving. The corresponding Q1 passage reads:

> I will not di[n]e to day I sweare,
> Vntill I see the same, some see it done,
> The rest that loue me, come and follow me *Exeunt. manet Cat. with Ha.*
> (Q1, sig. G2^{r})

Vaguely, 'some' are told to execute the order, but only one stays. Conceivably, Richard's invocation of 'some' to help could be

1 And perhaps literal economy; Q1 avoided Archbishop's robes, as Patrick notes.
2 Cf. Clarence's daughter at 4.1.1–5.

rhetorical pressure on the lords: either they stay, aiding contrived murder, or leave, showing their 'loue'. However, this difference between Richard's order and its result resembles other discrepancies where Q1's Catesby stands for F's Lovell and Ratcliffe.

Richard's order to Catesby to overlook the walls appears in 3.5 in both Q1 and F. Two lines later Q1's Catesby – rather than F's '*Louell and Ratcliffe*' – enters bearing the head of Hastings. This entry is preceded by Richard's contrived warning against approaching 'enemies':

> *Glo.* Looke backe, defend thee, here are enemies.
> *Buc.* God and our innocence defend vs. *Enter Catesby*
> *Glo.* O, O, be quiet, it is Catesby. *with Hast.head.*
> (Q1 sig. G3[r])

Even if this plural ('enemies') were rhetorical, meant to evoke imaginary offstage forces rather than the single entering character (cf. Urkowitz, 455), similar disagreements vex the following lines. In Q1 and F Buckingham refers to Hastings's executioner(s) as 'these our friends' (3.5.54); 'these' better suits F's Lovell and Ratcliffe than Q1's solitary Catesby.

True, numerical agreement is frequently uncertain in Shakespeare (see 3.5.55n.).[1] 'This' and 'these' may refer to offstage characters (e.g. 1.1.2, 5.5.0.3–4n.). Characters may lack entry directions (e.g. Q1's Catesby at 3.5.13.1 or Ratcliffe at 5.1.0) or exit unremarked (e.g. Q1's Buckingham at 3.4.41). Thus, Richard's 'friends' (3.5.54) might enter with whoever bears Hastings's head and leave similarly without notice. Ultimately, though, a question remains about motivation for the differences, since Q1 elsewhere awkwardly retains Ratcliffe.[2]

Ratcliffe serves as Buckingham's executioner in Q1 5.1, but Buckingham addresses his former ally as if undistinguished

1 For 'variants in number' that compromise 'automatic preference' for F, see Honigmann, 'Text', 54.

2 Rivers and Dorset are similarly retained despite local omission from Q1 2.2.

among anonymous 'fellowes' or 'sirs' (Q1), which would be more appropriate for F's Sheriff (whom Buckingham calls 'Fellow') (see 5.1.0.1n.).[1] This impersonality contrasts with the vehemently personal denunciation of Ratcliffe by Rivers and Grey (3.3.1–5), but parallels the surprising lack of emotion Hastings displays towards his own Q1 executioner(s) in 3.4. F's Hastings is led to death by Ratcliffe and Lovell. While they know one another (appearing jointly in 2.1 and 2.2) nothing suggests the intimacy that obtains between Hastings and his Q1 executioner, Catesby. In both texts Hastings earlier shares with Catesby his ill-founded confidences, staking his life on 'my good friend *Catesby*' (F) or 'my seruant Catesby' (Q1) (3.2.21). However, in 3.4.79–106 Hastings and his executioner(s) speak impersonally. In a play filled with ironies of over-confidence and betrayal, it is difficult to explain Hastings's failure to remark Catesby's treachery. Mowat and Werstine judge that this evidence argues Q1 is 'a version derivative from the F version' (li).

Differences concerning Dorset support a similar conclusion. His interaction with his mother in Q1 2.4.40–68 is oddly impersonal, especially when contrasted with their exchanges at 4.1.37–46. At 2.4.39–49 a speaker whom Q1 calls 'Dorset' and F calls 'Messenger' announces the imprisonment of Rivers, Grey and Vaughan, dire news prompting passionate reactions from those onstage, including Queen Elizabeth, Dorset's mother. Dorset reveals Richard's violent onslaught against their family, but mother and son express no concern for one another. However, two tiny variants suggest Q1's 'improvised attempt to make Dorset react to Elizabeth's presence' and vice versa (Hammond, 15–16). Q1 has Dorset address a 'Lady' instead of F's 'Lord' at 2.4.49, and has Queen Elizabeth invoke 'the downfall of our house' instead of

1 Buckingham and Ratcliffe are together in 2.1, 2.2, 3.3, 3.4, 3.5 and 4.2, but never directly address one another (Urkowitz, 458).

F's 'ruine of my House' in response. Not much change, and 'Lady' possibly addresses the Duchess. In any case, Queen Elizabeth summons only her youngest son to accompany her in flight, as if no other son were present – true in F but at odds with Q1's inclusion of Dorset.

By contrast, in Q1 4.1 Queen Elizabeth and Dorset express mutual concern at the 'dead killing newes' of Richard's sequestration of Prince Edward. Dorset urges, 'Madam, haue comfort, how fares your grace?' and she responds:

> O Dorset speake not to me, get thee hence,
> Death and destruction dogge thee at the heeles,
> Thy Mothers name is ominous to children,
> If thou wilt outstrip death, go crosse the seas,
> And liue with Richmond, from the reach of hell
> (Q1, sig. H3^{v}; 4.1.38–42)

These different renderings of the Q1 mother/son relationship support the Cambridge editors: 'The change [from F's Messenger to Q1's Dorset in 2.4] must have been deliberate, and as the Queen does not greet the person who brings the intelligence, and expresses no anxiety for his safety when she herself is going to sanctuary, it seems more proper that the messenger should be one of inferior rank . . . His ignorance of the cause of the arrest of the nobles and the terms in which he speaks of them are in keeping with the character of a messenger' (Cam, 642n.). Some have dissented about details (*TxC*, 237) or attempted refutation.

Steven Urkowitz proposes that Q1 could represent an 'early state' of a work which, in revised form, constitutes the 'later state' of F (Urkowitz, 466). Seconding Kristian Smidt's attacks on faulty arguments for F's priority (cf. Hammond, 16; Maguire, 169), Urkowitz suggests that Shakespeare might have written a draft of QMS and then noticed 'the apparent coldness' of mother and son and revised 'to develop this coldness' while re-assigning Dorset's lines 'to an anonymous messenger' (Urkowitz, 451). Authorial revision is possible, even probable, in both FMS and QMS, but 'coldness' demands more support than the texts provide.[1] On balance, the majority opinion, that FMS precedes QMS, appears credible, but Urkowitz correctly imagines precedence as subject to exceptions and qualifications (cf. Ioppolo, 129). There is no reason to think that a reviser, revisers or an author might not return to a manuscript or manuscripts and change them before one or both reached print. In fact this seems the most likely hypothesis.[2]

VERBAL VARIANTS Q1/F: THEORY AND PRACTICE

If the discrepancies in roles between Q1 and F suggest incomplete attempts at theatrical economy, then the dialogue line totals permit similar inference. The differences add up to over two hundred lines that appear in F but not in Qq, not a great number, but they are sometimes locally purposeful in appearance. Absence from Q1 of two lengthy passages amounting to 69 lines of F 4.4 (4.4.222–35, 288–342) contributes to an approximately 84-line difference between that scene's versions. It is easy to imagine Q1 shortening for theatrical economy but difficult to conceive of F intentionally expanding the scene – at least for the theatre. But Q1 uniquely contains the brilliant jack of the clock passage (4.2.97–114), which is dependent on Holinshed (see 4.2.101–5n.; Churchill, 222) and evidently Shakespearean. This challenging counter-instance may represent the pressures of censorship or self-censorship weighing upon the author, compilers or printers of F, but it remains possible that it was added to QMS rather than subtracted (or omitted) from FMS.[3]

1 Taking Dorset's advice in F 2.2 as 'insensitive' ignores early modern admonitions against excessive grieving (see Pigman).

2 For recent views that quartos may provide alternative, abbreviated drafts, incorporating revision and redaction of the longer texts of Shakespeare's plays, see *The First Quarto of King Henry V*, ed. Andrew Gurr (Cambridge, 2000), ix; Halio, 137; Blayney, 'Publication', 394; Erne, 219.

3 For arguments about the passage, see 4.2.97–114n. The missing lines occur very near the end of Compositor A's stint (end of s3^{v}), and similar locations occasion problems and result in omissions elsewhere (see Forker, 540).

While 'in general, F in its verbal variants is closer than Q to the play's acknowledged sources' (*TxC*, 230), the evidence is not uniform. Historical details constitute some of the strongest evidence for the 'authority' of QMS. Q1 gets some things right that F gets wrong. For example, Q1 follows More, Hall and Holinshed (3.723) in naming the Pursuivant in 3.2 'Hastings', while F vaguely calls him '*a Pursuiuant*' and Hastings calls him 'sirrah' and 'fellow'. Here, one might debate whether Q1 more probably reflects revision of FMS by someone with source in hand or mind, or whether F reflects someone else editing FMS for some other reason. After all, someone edited FMS to remove oaths offensive under an Act of 1606, leaving particularly evident effects of removal in F 1.4 (see notes to 1.4.84–end, 121, 125 and 143, 188–9). The 'Acte to Restrain Abuses of Players' (1606) was aimed not at published texts like Folio *Richard III* but at performers who might 'jestingly or prophanely speake or use the holy Name of God or of Christ Jesus, or of the Holy Ghoste or of the Trinitie . . . in any Stage play, Interlude, Shewe, Maygame, or Pageant' (Chambers, *Stage*, 4.338–9). Thus, F's evident (and imperfect) removal of such materials may represent the efforts of someone interested in constructing a performance text from FMS.[1] Removal of the Pursuivant's name might represent an attempt, possibly but by no means necessarily authoritative, to remove an apparent confusion of identities from Qq.

Ultimately, Q1 is closer than F to the sources here; even in phrasing (Honigmann, 'Text', 49). It is difficult to imagine Q1's printers adding the name or phrasing, so one possible deduction is that QMS contained accurately recorded historical details that FMS lacked.[2] That would make QMS here a revision by a very authoritative reviser. An alternative is that FMS also had these details, but that they were omitted or purposely edited

1 On expurgation or substitution of secular for religious oaths in F texts of other plays with quarto editions, see Ioppolo, 79; cf. 1.4.84–end.n., 121n., 188–9n.

2 For Q1 agreements with Holinshed and Hall, see Honigmann, who argues that despite 'memorial corruption, [Q1] is partly based' on a 'very badly damaged' manuscript (Honigmann, 'Text', 52). Smidt offers a similarly complex assessment (Smidt, *Memorial*, 42).

out by someone before or during the production of F. Similarly accurate details occur at Q1 2.2.142 and 154, where the Prince's location is 'Ludlow', rather than F's 'London'. Here, however, F itself is locally inconsistent, because earlier he is said to need fetching 'from Ludlow . . . / Hither to London' (2.2.121–2). This appears to be a production mistake in F rather than a proof of superior authority for QMS. For simple mistakes, Q1's misuse of the 'beare' as a metaphor for Richard at 3.2.10, uncorrected until Q6 despite references to Richard as the boar (3.2.27–32), is strikingly wrong. Q1 gives Tyrrel different names: he is historically 'Iames *T*irrell' at 4.2.67, but enters 4.3 as '*Sir Francis Tirrell*'. This discrepancy remains through Q8 but is not present in F. These sorts of errors appear in both texts. Other factual disagreements are more instructive.

F has Richard's party proceed from Stony Stratford to London via Northampton (2.4.1–2); this makes no geographical sense, but follows the sources which describe the Prince being taken to Northampton after the arrest of Rivers, Grey and Vaughan. Q1 corrects this 'mistake' on the basis of geography, an incorrect correction unlikely to originate with the author. F does make a historical error involving Lord Rivers that Q1 avoids. F mistakes 'lord Antony Woouduile erle Ryuers and lorde Scales, brother to the quene' (Hall, *Edward V*, fol. v[r]) for two characters or even three (see 2.1.0.2n.). By contrast, Q1's entry direction names only '*Ryuers*', and its dialogue lacks F's line, 'Of you lord *Wooduill*, and Lord *Scales* of you'. This seems to be correction, but determining its agent and authority is complicated, because Q1's choices could merely amount to another of its inconsistent attempts at theatrical economy, while F's proximity to Hall marks FMS as closer to the written sources and hence, perhaps, to authorial draft.

Why, then, does this edition allow F's geography in 2.4 but accept Q1's roles in 2.1? It seems less probable that a printing-house corrector would have to hand the relevant facts of genealogy rather than those of geography (*TxC*, 229). Thus, the case of Q1's Rivers could support a relatively 'authoritative' correction by some knowledgeable person(s) (Jowett, 121). Practically speaking, there seems little to gain in following F's historical error – no matter how 'authoritative' – to add a single appearance by yet another silent character, or even two, in a densely populated play. So the present edition defers to Q1 in this case.

This is not an affirmation of historical 'fact' as determinative in editorial decision-making. Choosing to follow Q1 instead of F regarding Rivers should be balanced against the choice to accept a mistake concerning 'mother's cost' at 5.3.324. Q1 and F both follow a misprint; Holinshed's second edition has 'moothers' instead of the first edition's 'brothers' (as in Hall). Since the line occurs in the portion of F set directly from uncorrected Q3, one cannot argue that F validates Q1. However, Q1's agreement with Holinshed's error argues for the playwright as its likely origin, and this play provides strong thematic relevance for 'mother's' (Willis, *Nurture*, 204). In this case, only a questionable notion of editorial authority might justify setting the author's history straight.

In many cases the decisions are difficult. Q1 follows the historical sources in omitting Ratcliffe from the council scene (3.4). F not only includes him, but has him in Yorkshire executing Rivers, Grey and Vaughan in 3.3 before immediately re-entering in 3.4 for the same day's London meeting. Here Q1 seemingly offers the better choice: historically authoritative, and observant of probability and stage convention; however, choosing is complicated by Q1's other confused and incomplete attempts to remove Ratcliffe. As argued above, Hastings's 3.4 speeches are more appropriate in the presence of Ratcliffe and Lovell (F). Furthermore, even if QMS may have 'corrected' FMS about Ratcliffe's bi-location, it is problematic to invoke concern for theatrical principle or probability, since Q1 has the Cardinal re-enter (3.1.0) and has Rivers in London *after* his Yorkshire execution (see 3.4.6 SPn.).

Small matters, tough editorial decisions, but this edition, following its general tendency, sides with F; you may see it differently. I hope the apparatus will make the editorial choices involved both evident and (appropriately) arguable. This edition attempts to provide as much as it can of the 'raw material' from which actors and readers have constructed and continue to construct *Richard III*.[1] Ultimately, they will make it their own anyway. Shakespeare's plays probably never achieved final form, but existed in multiple, sometimes inconsistent, versions (McKerrow, *Prolegomena*, 6). This multiplicity may have been the case in Shakespeare's lifetime; it has been overwhelmingly so since. 'The' play amounts to the many 'plays' that texts and traditions make of it. Some are probably better than others, but even Cibber's version has its charms; it all depends on how one judges and on who does the judging. I do not think Shakespeare (or 'Shakespeare'), the Lord Chamberlain's Men or the King's Men would mind at all.

1 Cf. Blayney, 'Intro', xxx; Dutton, 174.

APPENDIX 2

CASTING

We do not know with certainty how many actors performed *Richard III* in Shakespeare's time, and changing circumstances of performance would obviously have affected casting, doubling and, in all likelihood, cutting. Leaving room for some approximation, T.J. King suggests that 11 adults and 6 boys could have performed the principal parts in the Q1 version of the play as well as in the longer F version (T.J. King, *Casting Shakespeare's Plays: London Actors and their Roles* (Cambridge, 1992), 80); however, David Bradley suggests 12 adults and 8 boys for performing Q1 and 15 to 16 adults and 8 boys for performing F (David Bradley, *From Text to Performance in the Elizabethan Theatre: Preparing the Play for the Stage* (Cambridge, 1992), 52, 233). The difference between such informed estimates conveys the wide range of possibilities. In any case, the play's many minor parts could easily have been covered in various ways by the company's principal adult and child actors. To take one example, in modern productions the actor playing Richard sometimes acts as one of the Citizens in 2.3. The chart which follows offers one suggestion for performing *Richard III* as the play appears in this edition; it does not attempt to distribute the play's many minor and silent parts.

DOUBLING CHART

Actor	Role	1.1	1.2	1.3	1.4	2.1	2.2	2.3	2.4	3.1	3.2	3.3	3.4	3.5	3.6	3.7	4.1	4.2	4.3	4.4	4.5	5.1	5.2	5.3	5.4	5.5	Total
1	Richard	x	x	x		x	x			x			x	x		x		x	x	x				x	x	x	15
2	Buckingham			x		x	x			x	x		x	x		x		x				x		x			11
3	Clarence	x			x																			x			3
4	Hastings	x		x		x	x			x	x		x											x			8
5	Richmond																						x	x		x	3
	King Edward					x																					1
6	Stanley			x		x	x				x		x				x	x		x	x			x		x	11
	Scrivener														x												1
7	1 Murderer			x	x																						2
	Ratcliffe					x	x					x	x	x				x	x	x				x			9
8	2 Murderer			x	x																						2
	Lord Mayor									x				x		x											3
9	Catesby			x		x				x	x			x		x		x		x				x	x		10
	3 Citizen							x																			1
10	Rivers			x		x	x					x												x			5
	Tyrrel																	x	x								2

Actor	Role	1.1	1.2	1.3	1.4	2.1	2.2	2.3	2.4	3.1	3.2	3.3	3.4	3.5	3.6	3.7	4.1	4.2	4.3	4.4	4.5	5.1	5.2	5.3	5.4	5.5	Total
11	Brakenbury	x			x												x										3
	Archbishop								x																		1
12	Dorset			x		x	x										x							x			5
	Messenger										x																1
Boy actor																											
1	Queen Elizabeth			x		x	x		x								x			x							6
2	Queen Margaret			x																x							2
3	Anne		x														x							x			3
4	Duchess of York						x		x								x			x							4
5	Prince Edward									x														x			2
	Daughter of Clarence						x																				1
6	York								x	x														x			3
	Son of Clarence						x										x										2

APPENDIX 3

GENEALOGICAL TABLE

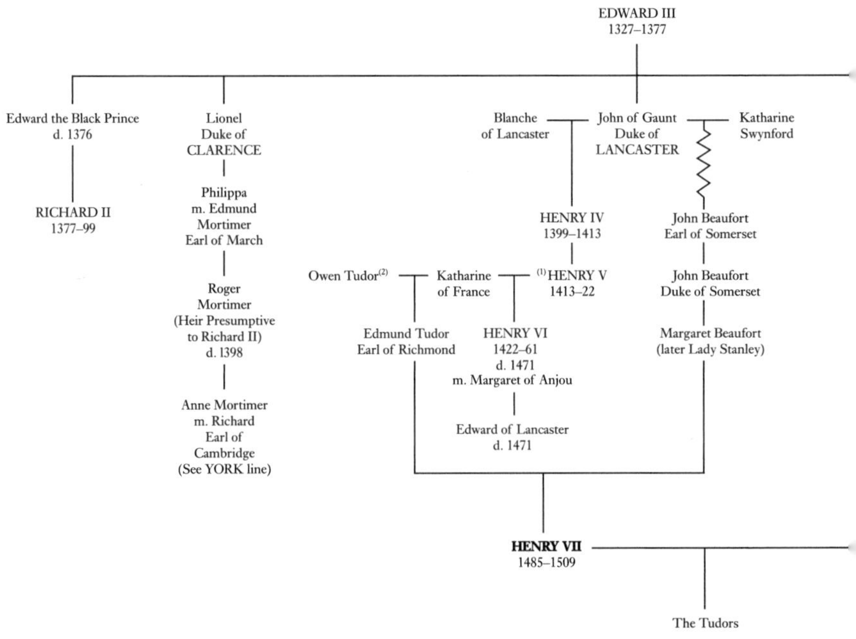

Genealogical table, from *Richard III and the Princes in the Tower*, by A.J. Pollard (New York, 1991), showing the marriages linking families and individuals (by permission of A.J. Pollard and recreated by DC Graphic Design Ltd)

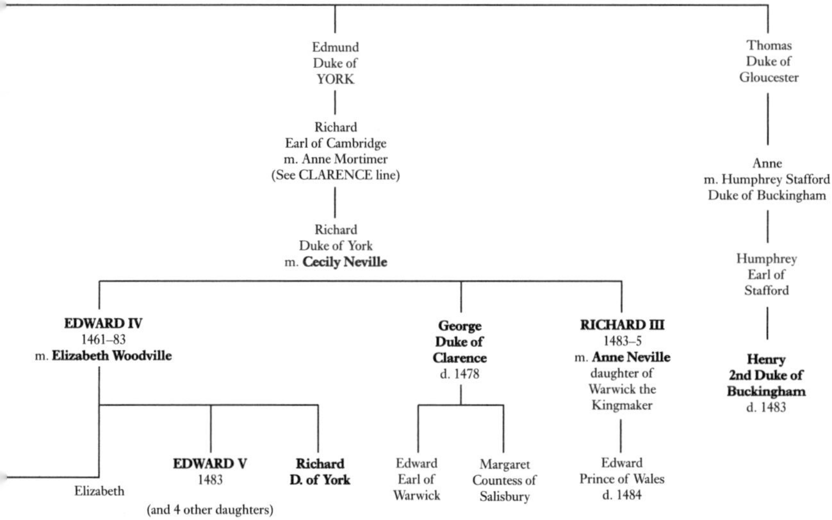

ABBREVIATIONS AND REFERENCES

References to Shakespeare's works are to Arden 3 editions published at the time of writing, and otherwise to Arden 2 editions. Biblical references are taken from the Bishops' Bible (*The holie Bible conteynyg the olde Testament and the newe* (1568; STC 2099)) or from the Geneva Bible (*The Bible and Holy Scriptures conteyned in the Olde and Newe Testament* (Geneva, 1561; STC 2095)); where the source is Geneva, this is indicated in the text. Place of publication is London unless otherwise noted.

ABBREVIATIONS

ABBREVIATIONS USED IN NOTES

*	precedes commentary notes involving textual issues, especially variations and inconsistencies in readings among the primary texts on which this edition is based
BL	British Library
Bod.	Bodleian Library
c.	corrected state
conj.	conjectured by
c.w.	catchword
Edin.	Edinburgh University Library
F	Folio
FMS	Folio manuscript
Fo	Folger Library
Hn	Huntington Library
n.	commentary note
n.d.	no date
O	Octavo
Q	Quarto
QMS	Quarto manuscript
om.	omitted
opp.	opposite
RSC	Royal Shakespeare Company
SD	stage direction
SP	speech prefix

subst.	substantially
this edn	a reading adopted for the first time in this edition
TLN	through line numbering in *The First Folio of Shakespeare, prepared by Charlton Hinman*, Norton Facsimile (New York, 1996)
Tn	Trinity College Library
t.n.	textual note
u.	uncorrected state
Y	Yale University Library

WORKS BY AND PARTLY BY SHAKESPEARE

AC	*Antony and Cleopatra*
AW	*All's Well That Ends Well*
AYL	*As You Like It*
CE	*Comedy of Errors*
Car	*The History of Cardenio*
Cor	*Coriolanus*
Cym	*Cymbeline*
DF	*Double Falsehood*
E3	*King Edward III*
Ham	*Hamlet*
1H4	*King Henry IV, Part 1*
2H4	*King Henry IV, Part 2*
H5	*King Henry V*
1H6	*King Henry VI, Part 1*
2H6	*King Henry VI, Part 2*
3H6	*King Henry VI, Part 3*
H8	*King Henry VIII*
JC	*Julius Caesar*
KJ	*King John*
KL	*King Lear*
LC	*A Lover's Complaint*
LLL	*Love's Labour's Lost*
Luc	*The Rape of Lucrece*
MA	*Much Ado about Nothing*
Mac	*Macbeth*
MM	*Measure for Measure*
MND	*A Midsummer Night's Dream*
MV	*The Merchant of Venice*
MW	*The Merry Wives of Windsor*
Oth	*Othello*
Per	*Pericles*

PP	*The Passionate Pilgrim*
PT	*The Phoenix and Turtle*
R2	*King Richard II*
R3	*King Richard III*
RJ	*Romeo and Juliet*
Son	*Sonnets*
STM	*The Book of Sir Thomas More*
TC	*Troilus and Cressida*
Tem	*The Tempest*
TGV	*The Two Gentlemen of Verona*
Tim	*Timon of Athens*
Tit	*Titus Andronicus*
TN	*Twelfth Night*
TNK	*The Two Noble Kinsmen*
TS	*The Taming of the Shrew*
VA	*Venus and Adonis*
WT	*The Winter's Tale*

REFERENCES

EDITIONS OF SHAKESPEARE COLLATED

Alexander	*William Shakespeare: The Complete Works*, ed. Peter Alexander (1951)
Ard^1	*The Tragedy of King Richard the Third*, ed. A. Hamilton Thompson, Arden Shakespeare (1909)
Ard^2	*King Richard III*, ed. Antony Hammond, Arden Shakespeare (1981)
Bevington	See Bevington^4
Bevington^3	*The Complete Works of Shakespeare*, ed. David Bevington, 3rd edn (Glenview, Ill., 1980)
Bevington^4	*The Complete Works of Shakespeare*, ed. David Bevington, 4th edn (New York, 1992)
Cam	*Works*, ed. William George Clark and William Aldis Wright, 9 vols (Cambridge and London, 1863–6)
Cam^1	*Richard III*, ed. John Dover Wilson (Cambridge, 1954)
Cam^2	*King Richard III*, ed. Janis Lull (Cambridge, 1999)
Capell	*Mr. William Shakespeare His Comedies, Histories and Tragedies*, ed. Edward Capell, 10 vols (1767–8)
Collier	*The Works of William Shakespeare*, ed. John Payne Collier, 8 vols (1842–4)

Dyce	*The Works of William Shakespeare*, ed. Alexander Dyce, 6 vols (1857)
Eccles	*The Tragedy of Richard the Third*, ed. Marc Eccles (New York, 1964)
Evans	*The Riverside Shakespeare*, ed. G. Blakemore Evans (Boston, 1974)
Evans, 1959	*The Tragedy of Richard the Third*, ed. G. Blakemore Evans (Baltimore, Md, 1959)
F	*Comedies, Histories and Tragedies*, The First Folio (1623)
F2	*Comedies, Histories and Tragedies*, The Second Folio (1632)
F3	*Comedies, Histories and Tragedies*, The Third Folio (1663)
F4	*Comedies, Histories and Tragedies*, The Fourth Folio (1685)
Folger	*The Tragedy of Richard III*, ed. Barbara A. Mowat and Paul Werstine, New Folger Library Shakespeare (New York, 1996)
Furness	See Var
Hammond	See Ard^2
Hanmer	*The Works of Shakespear*, ed. Thomas Hanmer, 6 vols (1743–4)
Holland	*The Tragedy of King Richard the Third*, ed. Peter Holland (2000)
Honigmann	*King Richard the Third*, ed. E.A.J. Honigmann (Harmondsworth, 1968)
Johnson	*The Plays of William Shakespeare*, ed. Samuel Johnson, 8 vols (1765)
Jowett	See Oxf^1
Keightley	*The Plays and Poems of William Shakespeare*, ed. Thomas Keightley, 6 vols (1864)
Knight	*The Pictorial Edition of the Works of Shakespere*, ed. Charles Knight, 8 vols (1838–43)
Lull	See Cam^2
Malone	*The Plays and Poems of William Shakespeare*, ed. Edmond Malone, 10 vols (1790)
Marshall	*The Henry Irving Shakespeare: The Works of William Shakespeare*, ed. Henry Irving and F.A. Marshall, 8 vols (1887–90)
Mowat & Werstine	See Folger
Oxf	*The Complete Works*, ed. Stanley Wells and Gary Taylor (Oxford, 1986)
Oxf^1	*Richard III*, ed. John Jowett, Oxford Shakespeare (Oxford, 2000)
Pope	*The Works of Shakespear*, ed. Alexander Pope, 6 vols (1723–5)

Q1	*The Tragedy of King Richard the Third* (1597)
Q2	*The Tragedy of King Richard the Third* (1598)
Q3	*The Tragedy of King Richard the Third* (1602)
Q4	*The Tragedy of King Richard the Third* (1605)
Q5	*The Tragedy of King Richard the Third* (1612)
Q6	*The Tragedy of King Richard the Third* (1622)
Q7	*The Tragedy of King Richard the Third* (1629)
Q8	*The Tragedy of King Richard the Third* (1634)
Rann	*The Dramatic Works of Shakespeare*, ed. Joseph Rann, 6 vols (1786–91)
Rowe	*The Works of Mr. William Shakespear*, ed. Nicholas Rowe, 6 vols (1709)
Rowe^{2}	*The Works of Mr. William Shakespear*, ed. Nicholas Rowe, 2nd edn, 6 vols (1709)
Rowe^{3}	*The Works of Mr. William Shakespear*, ed. Nicholas Rowe, 3rd edn, 8 vols (1714)
Singer	*The Dramatic Works of William Shakespeare*, ed. Samuel Weller Singer, 10 vols (1826)
Sisson	*The Complete Works*, ed. Charles Jasper Sisson (1954)
Steevens	*The Plays of William Shakespeare*, ed. George Steevens and Isaac Reed, 4th edn, 15 vols (1793)
Theobald	*The Works of Shakespeare*, ed. Lewis Theobald, 7 vols (1733)
Thompson	See Ard^{1}
Var	*The Tragedy of Richard the Third*, ed. Horace Howard Furness, New Variorum Shakespeare (Philadelphia, 1908)
Warburton	*The Works of Shakespeare*, ed. William Warburton, 8 vols (1747)
Wells & Taylor	See Oxf
White	*The Works of William Shakespeare*, ed. Richard Grant White, 12 vols (1857–66)
Wilson	See Cam^{1}

OTHER WORKS CITED

Abbott	E.A. Abbott, *A Shakespearian Grammar*, 2nd edn (1870)
Adelman	Janet Adelman, *Suffocating Mothers: Fantasies of Maternal Origin in Shakespeare's Plays* (New York, 1992)
Aduertisement	*An Aduertisement Written to a Secretary* (Antwerp, 1592; STC 19885)
Allott	*Englands Parnassus, compiled by Robert Allott, 1600*, ed. Charles Crawford (Oxford, 1913)

Almond — *An Almond for a Parrat* (London?, 1589; STC 534)

Anderson — Judith H. Anderson, *Biographical Truth: The Representation of Historical Persons in Tudor–Stuart Writing* (New Haven, Conn., 1984)

Apius — R.B., *A new tragicall comedie of Apius and Virginia* (1575; STC 1059)

Arber — Edward Arber (ed.), *Transcript of the Registers of the Company of Stationers of London*, 5 vols (1874–94)

Archer — Ian W. Archer, 'Popular politics in the sixteenth and early seventeenth centuries', in Paul Griffiths and Mark S.R. Jenner (eds), *Londinopolis: Essays in the Cultural and Social History of Early Modern London* (Manchester, 2000)

Arden — *The Tragedy of Master Arden of Faversham*, ed. M.L. Wine, Revels Plays (1973)

Armstrong, C.A.J. — C.A.J. Armstrong, 'The inauguration ceremonies of the Yorkist kings and their title to the throne', *TRHS*, 4th series, 30 (1948), 51–73

Ascham — Roger Ascham, *English Works*, ed. W.A. Wright (Cambridge, 1904)

Bacon, *Henry VII* — Francis Bacon, *The History of the Reign of King Henry the Seventh*, ed. F.J. Levy (Indianapolis, 1972)

Bacon, *Works* — Francis Bacon, *The Works of Francis Bacon*, ed. James Spedding, Robert Leslie Ellis and Douglas Denon Heath, 14 vols (1861–79)

Baldwin — T.W. Baldwin, *William Shakespere's Small Latine and Lesse Greeke*, 2 vols (Urbana, Ill., 1944)

Bancroft, *Positions* — Richard Bancroft, *Daungerous positions and proceedings* (1593; STC 1344)

Bancroft, *Sermon* — Richard Bancroft, *A Sermon Preached at Paules Crosse, 1588* (1589; STC 1346)

Barton & Hall — John Barton and Peter Hall, *The Wars of the Roses* (1970)

Bate, *Ovid* — Jonathan Bate, *Shakespeare and Ovid* (Oxford, 1993)

Bate, *Romantics* — Jonathan Bate (ed.), *The Romantics on Shakespeare* (1992)

Bate, *Tit* — *Titus Andronicus*, ed. Jonathan Bate, Arden Shakespeare (1995)

BCP — *The Book of Common Prayer 1559*, ed. John E. Booty (Charlottesville, 1976)

Berry, E. — Edward I. Berry, *Patterns of Decay: Shakespeare's Early Histories* (Charlottesville, 1975)

Berry, R. — Ralph Berry, 'Richard III: bonding the audience', in J.C. Gray (ed.), *Mirror up to Shakespeare* (1984), 114–27

Bible — *The holie Bible conteynyg the olde Testament and the newe*, 'The Bishops' Bible' (1568; STC 2099)

Birch — W.J. Birch, *An Inquiry into the Philosophy and Religion of Shakespere* (1848)

Birney — Alice Lotvin Birney, *Satiric Catharsis in Shakespeare: A Theory of Dramatic Structure* (Berkeley, Calif., 1973)

Blayney, 'Intro' — Peter Blayney, 'Introduction to the second edition', *The First Folio of Shakespeare, prepared by Charlton Hinman*, Norton Facsimile (New York, 1996)

Blayney, 'Publication' — Peter Blayney, 'The publication of playbooks', in Cox & Kastan, 383–422

Bloom, G. — Gina Bloom, *Voice in Motion: Staging Gender, Shaping Sound in Early Modern England* (Philadelphia, 2007)

Blundeville — Thomas Blundeville, *A Very Briefe and Profitable Treatise . . . of Counselers* (facsimile reprint, *Of Councils and Counselors*, 1570; STC 11488), ed. Karl-Ludwig Selig (Gainesville, Fla., 1963)

Booth — Edwin Booth, *Edwin Booth's Prompt-book of Richard III*, ed. William Winter (New York, 1878)

Born — Hanspeter Born, 'The date of *2, 3, Henry VI*', *SQ*, 25 (1974), 323–34

Bright — Timothie Bright, *A Treatise of Melancholie* (1586), intro. by Hardin Craig (New York, 1940)

Brooke — Nicholas Brooke, *Shakespeare's Early Tragedies* (1968)

Brooks, 'Antecedents' — Harold F. Brooks, '*Richard III*: antecedents of Clarence's dream', *SS* 32 (1979), 145–50

Brooks, 'Unhistorical' — Harold F. Brooks, '*Richard III*: unhistorical amplifictions: the women's scenes and Seneca', *MLR*, 75 (1980), 721–37

Brown — Susan Brown, 'Queen Elizabeth in Richard III', in Robert Smallwood (ed.), *Players of Shakespeare 4* (Cambridge, 1998), 101–13

Buck — Sir George Buck, *The History of King Richard III*, ed. Arthur Noel Kincaid (Gloucester, 1982)

Budra — Paul Budra, *A Mirror for Magistrates and the de casibus Tradition* (Toronto, 2000)

Bullough — Geoffrey Bullough (ed.), *Narrative and Dramatic Sources of Shakespeare*, 8 vols (London and New York, 1957–75)

Burns — *King Henry VI, Part 1*, ed. Edward Burns, Arden Shakespeare (2000)

Calvin, *Commentaries* — John Calvin, *Commentaries on the Epistle of Paul the Apostle to the Romans*, ed. John Owen, vol. 38 (1948; rpt. Grand Rapids, Mich., 1959)

Calvin, *Institutes*	John Calvin, *Institutes of the Christian Religion*, ed. John T. McNeill, trans. Ford Lewis Battles, 2 vols (Philadelphia, 1960)
Campbell	Lily B. Campbell, *Shakespeare's Histories: Mirrors of Elizabethan Policy* (San Marino, Calif., 1947)
Carroll	William C. Carroll, *Fat King, Lean Beggar: Representations of Poverty in the Age of Shakespeare* (Ithaca, NY, 1996)
Cerasano	S.P. Cerasano, 'Churls just wanna have fun: reviewing *Richard III*', *SQ*, 36 (1985), 618–29
Chambers, *Shakespeare*	E.K. Chambers, *William Shakespeare: A Study of Facts and Problems* (Oxford, 1930)
Chambers, *Stage*	E.K. Chambers, *The Elizabethan Stage*, 4 vols (1923; corrected edn Oxford, 1967)
Charnes	Linda Charnes, *Notorious Identity: Materializing the Subject in Shakespeare* (Cambridge, Mass., 1993)
Chettle	Henry Chettle, *Kind-Harts Dreame* (1593?; STC 5123)
Chrimes	S.B. Chrimes, *Henry VII* (1972; rev. edn New Haven, Conn., 1999)
Churchill	George B. Churchill, *Richard the Third up to Shakespeare* (1900; rpt. Totowa, NJ, 1976)
Cibber, *Richard III*	Colley Cibber, *The Tragical History of King Richard III*, in Christopher Spencer (ed.), *Five Restoration Adaptations of Shakespeare* (Urbana, Ill., 1965)
Clarke, *Characters*	Charles Cowden Clarke, *Shakespeare-Characters* (1863)
Clemen	Wolfgang Clemen, *A Commentary on Shakespeare's Richard III*, trans. Jean Bonheim (1968)
Colley	Scott Colley, *Richard's Himself Again: A Stage History of Richard III* (New York, 1992)
Collinson, *Puritan*	Patrick Collinson, *The Elizabethan Puritan Movement* (Berkeley, Calif., 1967)
Cooper	Thomas Cooper, *An Admonition to the People of London* (1589; STC 5683a)
Copy	*The Copie of a leter, vvryten by a Master of Arte of Cambrige* ([Paris,] 1584; STC 5742.9)
Courtenay	Thomas Peregrine Courtenay, *Commentaries on the Historical Plays of Shakespeare*, 2 vols (1840; rpt. New York, 1972)
Cox & Kastan	John D. Cox and David Scott Kastan (eds), *A New History of Early English Drama* (New York, 1997)
Craven, 'Proofreading'	Alan E. Craven, 'Proofreading in the shop of Valentine Simmes', *PBSA*, 68 (1974), 361–72
Craven, 'Simmes'	Alan E. Craven, 'Simmes' Compositor A and five Shakespeare quartos', *SB*, 26 (1973), 37–60

Cressy, 'Kinship'	David Cressy, 'Kinship and kin interaction in early modern England', *Past and Present*, 113 (1986), 38–69
Cressy, *Travesties*	David Cressy, *Travesties and Transgressions in Tudor and Stuart England: Tales of Discord and Dissension* (Oxford, 2000)
Croft, 'Reputation'	Pauline Croft, 'The reputation of Robert Cecil: libels, political opinion and popular awareness in the early seventeenth century', *TRHS*, 6th series (1991), 43–69
Cruikshank	C.G. Cruikshank, *Elizabeth's Army* (Oxford, 1966)
*CW*2, 3, 15	See More
Daniel	P.A. Daniel, Introduction to William Griggs's facsimile of *Richard the Third, The First Quarto* (1886)
Davies & Marlowe	John Davies and Christopher Marlowe, *Epigrammes and Elegies* (*c.* 1596; STC 6350)
Davison	*The First Quarto of King Richard III*, ed. Peter Davison (Cambridge, 1996)
Day	Gillian Day, *King Richard III* (2002)
Declaration	[Richard Verstegan,] *A Declaration of the true causes of the great troubles* (Antwerp, 1592; STC 10005)
de Jongh	Nicholas de Jongh, *Evening Standard*, 12 August 1992, Shakespeare Centre Clipping Book
de Somogyi	Nick de Somogyi, *Shakespeare's Theatre of War* (Aldershot, 1998)
Dekker	Thomas Dekker, *Seven Deadly Sinnes of London*, in A.B. Grosart (ed.), *The Non-dramatic Works of Thomas Dekker*, 5 vols (1885; rpt. New York, 1963)
Delius	N. Delius, 'Ueber den ursprünglichen Text des *Richard III*', *Shakespeare Jahrbuch*, 7 (1872), 124–69
Dent	R.W. Dent, *Shakespeare's Proverbial Language: An Index* (Berkeley, Calif., 1981)
Dessen & Thomson	Alan C. Dessen and Leslie Thomson, *A Dictionary of Stage Directions in English Drama 1580–1642* (Cambridge, 1999)
Donohue	Joseph Donohue, *Dramatic Character in the English Romantic Age* (Princeton, NJ, 1970)
Downer	Alan S. Downer, *The Eminent Tragedian William Charles Macready* (Cambridge, Mass., 1966)
Drakakis	*King Richard the Third*, ed. John Drakakis, Shakespearean Originals: First Editions (London, 1996)
Draudt	Manfred Draudt, 'Shakespeare's histories at the Vienna Burgtheater', in Hoenselaars, 196–212
Drayton	Michael Drayton, *Works*, ed. J. William Hebel, 5 vols (Oxford, 1933)

DSK	David Scott Kastan, private communication
Dubrow	Heather Dubrow, '"I fear there will a worse come in his place": surrogate parents and Shakespeare's *Richard III*', in Naomi J. Miller and Naomi Yavneh (eds), *Maternal Measures: Figuring Caregiving in the Early Modern Period* (Aldershot, 2000), 348–62
Dutton	Richard Dutton, 'The birth of the author', in Cedric C. Brown and Arthur F. Marotti (eds), *Texts and Cultural Change in Early Modern England* (1997), 153–78
E3	*King Edward III*, ed. Giorgio Melchiori, New Cambridge Shakespeare (Cambridge, 1998)
ELH	*English Literary History*
ELR	*English Literary Renaissance*
Erasmus	Desiderius Erasmus, *Adages*, trans. Margaret Mann Phillips, ann. R.A.B. Mynors, *The Collected Works of Erasmus* (Toronto, 1974–)
Erne	Lukas Erne, *Shakespeare as Literary Dramatist* (Cambridge, 2002)
Evans, 'Restored'	G. Blakemore Evans, '*Shakespeare Restored* – once again!', in Anne Lancashire (ed.), *Editing Renaissance Dramatic Texts* (New York, 1976), 139–56
Fabyan	Robert Fabyan, *The Chronicle of Fabian . . . continued . . . to thende of Queene Mary* (1559; STC 10664)
Fayard	Nicole Fayard, *The Performance of Shakespeare in France since the Second World War* (Lewiston, NY, 2006)
Forker	*King Richard II*, ed. Charles Forker, Arden Shakespeare (2002)
Foulkes	Richard Foulkes, *Performing Shakespeare in the Age of Empire* (Cambridge, 2002)
Fox	Adam Fox, *Oral and Literate Culture in England 1500–1700* (Oxford, 2000)
Freud	Sigmund Freud, 'Some character-types met with in psycho-analytic work', trans. E. Colburn Mayne, in *Collected Papers*, ed. Joan Riviere, 5 vols (1950), vol. 4, 318–44
Frye	Roland Mushat Frye, *Shakespeare and Christian Doctrine* (Princeton, NJ, 1963)
Garber	Marjorie Garber, 'Descanting on deformity: Richard III and the shape of history', in Heather Dubrow and Richard Strier (eds), *The Historical Renaissance* (Chicago, 1988), 79–103
Garrard	William Garrard, *The Arte of Warre* (1591; STC 11623)
Gaskell	Philip Gaskell, *A New Introduction to Bibliography* (Oxford, 1972)

Geneva	*The Bible and Holy Scriptures conteyned in the Olde and Newe Testament* (Geneva, 1561; STC 2095)
Gentleman	[Francis Gentleman,] *The Dramatic Censor*, 2 vols (1770; rpt. New York, 1972)
George	David George, 'Shakespeare and Pembroke's Men', *SQ*, 32 (1981), 305–23
Gifford	George Gifford, *Sermons vpon the Whole Booke of the Revelation* (1596; STC 11866)
Gillingham	John Gillingham (ed.), *Richard III: A Medieval Kingship*, (New York, 1993)
Goodland	Katharine Goodland, *Female Mourning in Medieval and Renaissance English Drama* (Aldershot, 2005)
Gould	Thomas R. Gould, *The Tragedian: an Essay on the Histrionic Genius of Junius Brutus Booth* (New York, 1868)
Grafton	Richard Grafton, *A Chronicle at Large of the History of the Affairs of England*, 2 vols (1569; rpt. 1809)
Greenblatt	Stephen Greenblatt, *Hamlet in Purgatory* (Princeton, NJ, 2001)
Greg, *Documents*	W.W. Greg, *Dramatic Documents from the Elizabethan Playhouses* (Oxford, 1931)
Greg, *Problem*	W.W. Greg, *The Editorial Problem in Shakespeare* (1942; 2nd edn Oxford, 1951)
Griffin	William J. Griffin, 'An omission in the Folio text of *Richard III*', *RES*, 13 (1937), 329–32
Griffith	Mrs [Elizabeth] Griffith, *The Morality of Shakespeare's Drama* (1775)
Groatsworth	*Greene's Groatsworth of Wit*, ed. D. Allen Carroll (Binghamton, NY, 1994)
Gurr, *Companies*	Andrew Gurr, *The Shakespearian Playing Companies* (Oxford, 1996)
Gurr, 'Democratic'	Andrew Gurr, '*Richard III* and the democratic process', *Essays in Criticism*, 24 (1974), 39–47
GWW	George Walton Williams, private communication
Habicht	Werner Habicht, 'Shakespeare and theatre politics in the Third Reich', in Hanna Scolnicov and Peter Holland (eds), *The Play out of Context: Transferring Plays from Culture to Culture* (Cambridge, 1989), 110–20
Halio	Jay L. Halio, 'Handy-dandy: Q1/Q2 *Romeo and Juliet*', in Jay L. Halio (ed.), *Shakespeare's Romeo and Juliet': Texts, Contexts, and Interpretation* (Newark, Del., 1995), 123–50

Hall — Edward Hall, *The Union of the Two Noble and Illustre Families of Lancastre & Yorke* (1548, STC 12721)

Hall, J. — Joseph Hall, *The Collected Poems of Joseph Hall*, ed. A. Davenport (Liverpool, 1949)

Hammer — Paul E.J. Hammer, *The Polarisation of Elizabethan Politics: The Political Career of Robert Devereux, 2nd Earl of Essex, 1585–1597* (Cambridge, 1999)

Hanham — Alison Hanham, *Richard III and His Early Historians 1483–1535* (Oxford, 1975)

Hankey — *Richard III*, ed. Julie Hankey (1981)

Hardyng — John Hardyng, *The Chronicle of Ihon Hardyng* (1543; STC 12767), with a *Continuation* by Richard Grafton

Harrison — William Harrison, *The Description of England*, ed. Georges Edelen, Folger Documents of Tudor and Stuart Civilization (Ithaca, 1968)

Hart — Alfred Hart, 'The length of Elizabethan and Jacobean plays', *RES*, 8 (1932), 139–54

Harvey — Gabriel Harvey, *The Works of Gabriel Harvey*, ed. A.B. Grosart, 3 vols (1884; rpt. New York, 1966)

Hassel, 'Context' — R. Chris Hassel, Jr, 'Context and charisma: the Sher–Alexander *Richard III* and its reviewers', *SQ*, 36 (1985), 630–43

Hassel, *Performance* — R. Chris Hassel, Jr, *Songs of Death: Performance, Interpretation, and the Text of Richard III* (Lincoln, Nebr., 1987)

Hattaway, *Companion* — Michael Hattaway (ed.), *Cambridge Companion to Shakespeare's History Plays* (Cambridge, 2002)

Hazlitt — William Hazlitt, *The Complete Works of William Hazlitt*, ed. P.P. Howe, 21 vols (1930)

Heath — Benjamin Heath, *A Revisal of Shakespear's Text* (1765)

Henslowe — *Henslowe's Diary*, ed. R.A. Foakes and R.T. Rickert (Cambridge, 1961)

Heywood, *Apology* — Thomas Heywood, *An Apology for Actors* (1612; STC 13309)

Heywood, *Edward IV* — Thomas Heywood, *The First and Second Partes of King Edward the Fourth* (1600; STC 13342)

Hinman — Charlton Hinman, *The Printing and Proof-Reading of the First Folio of Shakespeare*, 2 vols (Oxford, 1963)

Hodgdon, *End* — Barbara Hodgdon, *The End Crowns All: Closure and Contradiction in Shakespeare's History* (Princeton, NJ, 1991)

Hodgdon, 'Replicating'	Barbara Hodgdon, 'Replicating Richard: body doubles, body politics', *Theatre Journal*, 50 (1998), 207–25
Hoenselaars	Ton Hoenselaars (ed.), *Shakespeare's History Plays: Performance, Translation and Adaptation in Britain and Abroad* (Cambridge, 2004)
Holinshed	Raphael Holinshed, *The Chronicles of England, Scotland and Ireland*, 2nd edn (1587; STC 13569)
Homilies	Mary Ellen Rickey and Thomas B. Stroup (eds), *Certaine Sermons or Homilies (1547–1571)*, facsimile of 1623 edition (Gainesville, Fla., 1968)
Honigmann, *Impact*	E.A.J. Honigmann, *Shakespeare's Impact on His Contemporaries* (1982)
Honigmann, 'Text'	E.A.J. Honigmann, 'The text of Richard III', *Theatre Research*, 7 (1965), 48–55
Honigmann, 'Variants'	E.A.J. Honigmann, 'On the indifferent and one-way variants in Shakespeare', *The Library*, 5th series, 22 (1967), 189–204
Hooker, *Laws*	Richard Hooker, *Of the Lawes of Ecclesiasticall Politie* (1593; STC 13712)
Horrox	Rosemary Horrox, *Richard III: A Study of Service* (Cambridge, 1989)
Hortmann	Wilhelm Hortmann, *Shakespeare on the German Stage: The Twentieth Century* (Cambridge, 1998)
Houlbrooke	R.A. Houlbrooke, 'Women's social life and common action in England from the fifteenth century to the eve of the Civil War', *Continuity and Change*, 1 (1986), 171–89
Howard & Rackin	Jean E. Howard and Phyllis Rackin, *Engendering a Nation: A Feminist Account of Shakespeare's Histories* (1997)
Howell	T.B. Howell (ed.), *A Complete Collection of State Trials*, 21 vols (1816)
Hughes	Alan Hughes, *Henry Irving, Shakespearean* (Cambridge, 1981)
Ioppolo	Grace Ioppolo, *Revising Shakespeare* (Cambridge, Mass., 1991)
Jackson, 'Copy'	MacD.P. Jackson, 'The manuscript copy of the quarto (1598) of Shakespeare's *1 Henry IV*', *N&Q*, ser. 7, 33 (1986), 353–4
Jackson, 'Two'	MacD.P. Jackson, 'Two Shakespeare quartos: *Richard III* (1597) and *1 Henry IV* (1598)', *SB*, 35 (1982), 173–91
Jack Straw	*The Life and Death of Jack Straw* [1594], ed. Kenneth Muir and F.P. Wilson (Oxford, 1957)

James I — King James I, *The Political Works of James I*, ed. Charles Howard McIlwain (Cambridge, Mass., 1918)

Jones, M. — Michael Jones, 'Richard III and the Stanleys', in Rosemary Horrox (ed.), *Richard III and the North*, Studies in Regional and Local History, no. 6 (Hull, 1986), 27–50

Jones, *Origins* — Emrys Jones, *The Origins of Shakespeare* (Oxford, 1977)

Jonson — *Ben Jonson*, ed. C.H. Herford and Percy and Evelyn Simpson, 11 vols (Oxford, 1925–52)

Jowett, 'Derby' — John Jowett, '"Derby", "Stanley", and memorial reconstruction in Quarto *Richard III*', *N&Q*, 245 (2000), 75–9

Jowett, 'Pre-editorial' — John Jowett, 'Pre-editorial criticism and the space for editing: examples from *Richard III* and *Your Five Gallants*', in Christa Jansohn (ed.), *Problems of Editing* (Tübingen, 1999), 127–49

Kastan, *1H4* — *King Henry IV, Part 1*, ed. David Scott Kastan, Arden Shakespeare (2002)

Kehler — Dorothea Kehler, 'Shakespeare's *Richard III*', *Explicator*, 56 (1997–8), 118–20

Kelly — Henry Ansgar Kelly, *Divine Providence in the England of Shakespeare's Histories* (Cambridge, Mass., 1970)

Kemble — John Philip Kemble, *Macbeth and King Richard the Third* (2nd edn, 1817; rpt. 1970)

Kendall — Paul Murray Kendall, *Richard the Third* (1955)

Kennedy — Dennis Kennedy, *Looking at Shakespeare: A Visual History of Twentieth-Century Performance*, 2nd edn (Cambridge, 2001)

Kinney, A. — Arthur F. Kinney (ed.), *Renaissance Drama: An Anthology of Plays and Entertainments* (Oxford, 1999)

Kinney, 'Tyrant' — Daniel Kinney, 'The tyrant being slain: afterlives of More's *History of King Richard III*', in Neil Rhodes (ed.), *English Renaissance Prose* (Tempe, Ariz., 1997), 35–56

Knack — *A Knack to Know a Knave, 1594*, ed. G.R Proudfoot (Oxford, 1964)

Knowles, *2H6* — *King Henry VI, Part 2*, ed. Ronald Knowles, Arden Shakespeare (1999)

Knox — Father Ronald Knox and Shane Leslie, *The Miracles of King Henry VI* (Cambridge, 1923)

Kott — Jan Kott, *Shakespeare Our Contemporary*, trans. Boleslaw Taborski (New York, 1964)

Kyd, *Hieronimo* — Thomas Kyd, *The First Part of Jeronimo*, in *The First Part of Hieronimo and The Spanish Tragedy*, ed. Andrew S. Cairncross (Lincoln, Nebr., 1967)

Kyd, *Spanish Tragedy*	Thomas Kyd, *The Spanish Tragedy*, ed. T.W. Ross (Berkeley, Calif., 1968)
Lake & Questier	Peter Lake and Michael Questier, *The Antichrist's Lewd Hat: Protestants, Papists and Players in Post-Reformation England* (New Haven, Conn., 2002)
Lambarde	William Lambarde, *Eirenarcha or the Office of Justices of Peace 1581/82*, ed. P.R. Glazebrook (Abingdon, Oxon, 1972)
Lancaster, 1590	'A Description . . . of the County of Lancaster, about the Year 1590', ed. F.R. Raines, in *Remains Historical & Literary . . . of Lancaster and Chester*, 96 (1875), 1–48
Lea	Henry Charles Lea, *A History of Auricular Confession and Indulgences in the Latin Church*, 4 vols (Philadelphia, 1896)
Leir	*The True Chronicle History of King Leir, 1605*, ed. W.W. Greg, Malone Society Reprints (Oxford, 1907)
Levine, M.	Mortimer Levine, *Tudor Dynastic Problems 1460–1571* (1973)
Lilly	William Lilly, *An Introduction to Astrology* (1647; rpt. 1939)
Lodge	Thomas Lodge, *The Wounds of Civil War* (1594), ed. John Dover Wilson, Malone Society Reprints (Oxford, 1910)
Loehlin	James N. Loehlin, '"Top of the world, Ma": *Richard III* and cinematic convention', in Lynda E. Boose and Richard Burt (eds), *Shakespeare the Movie* (London, 1997), 67–79
Lumiansky & Mills	*The Chester Mystery Cycle*, ed R.M. Lumiansky and David Mills (1974)
Lyly	*The Complete Works of John Lyly*, ed. R. Warwick Bond, 3 vols (1902; rpt. Oxford, 1967)
Lyons	Bridget Gellert Lyons, '"Kings games": stage imagery and political symbolism in *Richard III*', *Criticism*, 20 (1978), 17–30
McCabe	Richard A. McCabe, *Incest, Drama and Nature's Law 1550–1700* (Cambridge, 1993)
MacDonald & MacDonald	Andrew and Gina MacDonald, 'The necessity of evil: Shakespeare's rhetorical strategy in *Richard III*', *SSt* [Japan], 19 (1980–1), 55–69
McDonald	Russ McDonald, '*Richard III* and the tropes of tragedy', *Philological Quarterly*, 68 (1989), 465–83
Machyn	Henry Machyn, *The Diary of Henry Machyn*, ed. John Gough Nichols, Camden Society, vol. 42 (1848)

McKellen — Ian McKellen, *William Shakespeare's Richard III: A Screenplay written by Ian McKellen and Richard Loncraine* (Woodstock, NY, 1996)

McKenzie — D.F. McKenzie, 'Printers of the mind: some notes on bibliographical theories and printing-house practices', *SB*, 22 (1969), 1–75

McKerrow, *Bibliography* — R.B. McKerrow, *An Introduction to Bibliography for Literary Students* (Oxford, 1927)

McKerrow, *Prolegomena* — R.B. McKerrow, *Prolegomena for the Oxford Shakespeare* (1939; Oxford, 1969)

Macready — William Macready, *Macready's Reminiscences*, ed. Frederick Pollock (New York, 1875)

Maguire — Laurie E. Maguire, *Shakespearean Suspect Texts: The 'Bad' Quartos and their Contexts* (Cambridge, 1996)

Mancini — Dominic Mancini, *The Usurpation of Richard III*, trans. C.A.J. Armstrong (Oxford, 1969)

Marcus — Leah S. Marcus, *Puzzling Shakespeare: Local Reading and Its Discontents* (Berkeley, Calif., 1988)

Marienstras — Richard Marienstras, 'Of a Monstrous Body', in *French Essays on Shakespeare and His Contemporaries*, ed. Jean-Marie Maguin and Michèle Willems (Newark, Del., 1995), 153–74

Marlowe, *Works* — *The Complete Works of Christopher Marlowe*, ed. Fredson Bowers, 2nd edn, 4 vols (Cambridge, 1981)

Marlowe, *Jew of Malta* — Christopher Marlowe, *The Jew of Malta*, ed. James R. Siemon (1994)

Mar-Martine — *Mar-Martine* (London?, 1589; STC 17461)

Marprelate, *Epistle* — Martin Marprelate, *Oh Read Ouer* ([East Molesey, Surrey], 1588; STC 17453)

Marston — *The Complete Works of John Marston*, ed. A.H. Bullen, 3 vols (1887)

Martin — R.F. Martin, 'Milton's hell-hounds', *N&Q*, 36 (1989), 31–2

Mason — James Mason, *The Anatomie of Sorcerie* (1612; STC 17615)

Matthews & Hutton — Brander Matthews and Laurence Hutton (eds), *Kean and Booth and Their Contemporaries* (New York, 1886)

Maus — Katherine Eisaman Maus, *Inwardness and Theater in the English Renaissance* (Chicago, 1995)

Meres — Francis Meres, *Palladis Tamia* (1598; STC 17834)

Meyer — Edward Meyer, *Machiavelli and the Elizabethan Drama* (1897; rpt. New York, 1969)

Migne	J.-P. Migne (ed.), *Patriologia Latina* (Paris, 1844–55), vol. 36
Milton	*The Complete Prose Works of John Milton*, ed. Merritt Y. Hughes, vol. 3 (New Haven, Conn., 1962)
Mirror	William Baldwin, *The Mirror for Magistrates*, ed. Lily B. Campbell (1938; rpt. New York, 1960)
Mirror, Additions	John Higgins and Thomas Blenerhasset, *Parts Added to The Mirror for Magistrates*, ed. Lily B. Campbell (Cambridge, 1946)
MLR	*Modern Language Review*
More, *CW*2	Sir Thomas More, *The History of King Richard III*, ed. Richard Sylvester, in *The Complete Works of St Thomas More*, 21 vols, vol. 2 (New Haven, Conn., 1963)
More, *CW*3	*The Complete Works of St Thomas More*, vol. 3, part 1, ed. Craig R. Thompson (New Haven, Conn., 1974), 25–43
More, *CW*15	Sir Thomas More, *Historia Richardi Tertii: Text and Translation*, ed. Daniel Kinney, in *The Complete Works of St Thomas More*, 21 vols, vol. 15 (New Haven, Conn., 1986), 313–633
Mornay	Philippe de Mornay, *Concerning the Trewnesse of the Christian Religion*, trans. Philip Sidney and Arthur Golding (1587; STC 18149)
Morrison	Michael A. Morrison, *John Barrymore: Shakespearean Actor* (Cambridge, 1997)
N&Q	*Notes and Queries*
Nashe	Thomas Nashe, *The Works of Thomas Nashe*, ed. Ronald B. McKerrow, 5 vols (1958; rpt. New York, 1965, ed. F.P. Wilson)
Neill	Michael Neill, 'Shakespeare's halle of mirrors: play, politics, and psychology in *Richard III*', *SSt*, 8 (1975), 99–129
Nelson	Alan H. Nelson, *Early Cambridge Theatres* (Cambridge, 1994)
Newes	*Newes from Scotland* (1592; STC 10841a)
Noble	Richmond Noble, *Shakespeare's Biblical Knowledge and Use of the Book of Common Prayer* (1935; rpt. Folcroft, Pa., 1969)
ODNB	H.C.G. Matthew and Brian Harrison (eds), *Oxford Dictionary of National Biography* (Oxford, 2004)
OED	*The Oxford English Dictionary*, 2nd edn (Oxford, 1989)
Ornstein	Robert Ornstein, *A Kingdom for a Stage: The Achievement of Shakespeare's History Plays* (Cambridge, Mass., 1972)

Ovid — Publius Ovidius Naso, *Metamorphoses*, trans. Frank Justus Miller, rev. G.P. Goold, 3rd edn, 2 vols (Cambridge, Mass., 1984)

Pappe — *Pappe with an Hatchett* (1589; STC 17463)

Parker — Patricia Parker, 'Preposterous events', *SQ*, 43 (1992), 186–213

Parnassus — *The Three Parnassus Plays*, ed. J.B. Leishman (1949)

Parsons — Robert Parsons, *A Conference about the Next Succession* (1595; STC 19398)

2 Pasquill — *The Returne of the renowned Caualiero Pasquill of England* (1589; STC 19547)

Paston Letters — *The Paston Letters*, ed. James Gairdner, 6 vols (1904)

Patrick — David Lyall Patrick, *The Textual History of Richard III* (Stanford, Calif., 1936)

PBSA — *Papers of the Bibliographical Society of America*

Peacham — Henry Peacham, *The Truth of Our Times* (1638; STC 19517)

Pearlman — E. Pearlman, 'The invention of Richard of Gloucester', *SQ*, 43 (1992), 410–29

Peele, *Edward I* — George Peele, *King Edward I* [1593], ed. W.W. Greg (Oxford, 1911)

Perkins, *Discourse* — William Perkins, *A Discourse of Conscience* (Cambridge, 1596; STC 19696)

Perkins, *Treatise* — *A Treatise tending vnto a Demonstration, whether a man bee in the state of damnation* (1591; STC 19753)

Perkins, *Works* — William Perkins, *Works* (Cambridge, 1603; STC 19647)

Peterson — Richard S. Peterson, 'Laurel crown and ape's tail: new light on Spenser's career from Sir Thomas Tresham', *Spenser Studies*, 12 (1991), 1–31

Pickersgill — Edward H. Pickersgill, 'On the Quarto and Folio of Richard III', *New Shakespere Society's Transactions*, series 1, 3–4 (1875), 77–124

Pierce — Robert B. Pierce, *Shakespeare's History Plays: The Family and the State* (Columbus, Ohio, 1971)

Pigman — G.W. Pigman III, *Grief and English Renaissance Elegy* (Cambridge, 1985)

Plutarch — Plutarch, *The Lives of the Noble Grecians and Romanes*, trans. Thomas North (1579; STC 20065)

Pollard — A.J. Pollard, *Richard III and the Princes in the Tower* (New York, 1991)

Potter — Lois Potter, 'Bad and good authority figures: *Richard III* and *Henry V* since 1945', *Shakespeare Jahrbuch* (1992), 39–54

Prior — Moody Prior, *The Drama of Power: Studies in Shakespeare's History Plays* (Evanston, Ill., 1973)

Puttenham — George Puttenham, *The Arte of English Poesie*, ed. Gladys Doidge Willcock and Alice Walker (1936; rpt. Cambridge, 1970)

Rackin — Phyllis Rackin, 'Women's roles in the Elizabethan history plays', in Hattaway, *Companion*, 71–88

Rainolde — Richard Rainolde, *Foundacion of Rhetorike* (Cambridge, 1563; STC 20925a.5)

Raleigh, *History* — Sir Walter Raleigh, *The History of the World* (1617; STC 20638)

REED — *Records of Early English Drama: Cambridge*, ed. Alan H. Nelson, ongoing series (Toronto, 1989)

RES — *Review of English Studies*

Richardus Tertius — Thomas Legge, *Richardus Tertius*, in *Thomas Legge: The Complete Plays*, ed. and trans. Dana F. Sutton, 2 vols (New York, 1993)

Richmond — Hugh M. Richmond, *King Richard III* (Manchester, 1989)

Righter — Anne Righter (Barton), *Shakespeare and the Idea of the Play* (1964)

Roderick — Richard Roderick, 'Remarks', in Thomas Edwards, *The Canons of Criticism*, 6th edn (1758), 212–38

Rogers, *Sermon* — Thomas Rogers, *A Sermon vpon the 6. 7. and 8. Verses of the 12. Chapter of S. Pauls Epistle vnto the Romanes* (1590; STC 21240)

Ross, C., *Richard* — Charles Ross, *Richard III* (Berkeley, Calif., 1981)

Ross, C., *Wars* — Charles Ross, *The Wars of the Roses: A Concise History* (1976)

Ross, L.J. — Lawrence J. Ross, 'The meaning of strawberries in Shakespeare', *Studies in the Renaissance*, 7 (1960), 225–40

Rossiter — A.P. Rossiter, *Angel with Horns and Other Shakespeare Lectures*, ed. Graham Storey (New York, 1961)

Rous — John Rous, *Historia Regum Angliae*, ed. Thomas Hearne, 2nd edn (Oxford, 1745)

Rozett — Martha Tuck Rozett, *The Doctrine of Election and the Emergence of Elizabethan Tragedy* (Princeton, NJ, 1984)

RP — Richard Proudfoot, private communication

RQ — *Renaissance Quarterly*

Rutter — Carol Chillington Rutter, *Documents of the Rose Playhouse*, rev. edn (Manchester, 1999)

SB — *Studies in Bibliography*

Scot	Reginald Scot, *The Discouerie of Witchcraft* (1584; STC 21864)
SEL	*Studies in English Literature*
Seneca	Lucius Annaeus Seneca, *Seneca's Tragedies*, trans. Frank Justus Miller, 2 vols (1917; rpt. Cambridge, Mass., 1929)
Seneca, *Tragedies*	Lucius Annaeus Seneca, *Seneca, His Tenne Tragedies* (1581), ed. Thomas Newton, 2 vols (1927)
Seward	Desmond Seward, *Richard III: England's Black Legend* (1982; rpt. 1997)
Shaheen, *Biblical*	Naseeb Shaheen, *Biblical References in Shakespeare's Plays* (Newark, Del., 1999)
Shaheen, *History Plays*	Naseeb Shaheen, *Biblical References in Shakespeare's History Plays* (Newark, Del., 1989)
Shannon	Laurie Shannon, *Sovereign Amity: Figures of Friendship in Shakespearean Contexts* (Chicago, 2002)
Sher	Antony Sher, *The Year of the King* (1985)
Sidney	Sir Philip Sidney, *The Poems of Sir Philip Sidney*, ed. William A. Ringler (Oxford, 1962)
Siemon, 'Between'	James R. Siemon, 'Between the lines: bodies/languages/times', *SSt*, 29 (2001), 36–43
Siemon, 'Power'	James R. Siemon, 'The power of hope? An early modern reader of *Richard III*', in Jean Howard and Richard Dutton (eds), *A Companion to Shakespeare's History Plays* (Oxford, 2003), 361–78
Simpson	Richard Simpson, 'The political use of the stage in Shakespere's time' and 'The politics of Shakespere's historical plays', *New Shakespere Society's Transactions*, series 1, 1–2 (1874; rpt. 1965), 371–95, 396–441
Smallwood	Robert Smallwood, 'Shakespeare at Stratford-upon-Avon, 1992', *SQ*, 44 (1993), 343–62
Smidt, *Impostors*	Kristian Smidt, *Iniurious Impostors* (Oslo, 1964)
Smidt, *King Richard*	*The Tragedy of King Richard III, Parallel Texts of the First Quarto and First Folio with Variants of the Early Quartos*, ed. Kristian Smidt (Oslo, 1969)
Smidt, *Memorial*	Kristian Smidt, *Memorial Transmission and Quarto Copy in Richard III: A Reassessment* (Oslo, 1970)
Smidt, *Unconformities*	Kristian Smidt, *Unconformities in Shakespeare's History Plays* (Atlantic Highlands, NJ, 1982)
Smith, *Sermons*	Henry Smith, *The Sermons of Master Henrie Smith* (1592; STC 22718)
SPD	*State Papers Domestic*
Speaight	Robert Speaight, *Shakespeare on the Stage* (Boston, Mass., 1973)

Spedding — James Spedding, 'On the corrected edition of *Richard III*'. *New Shakespere Society's Transactions*, series 1, 3–4 (1875), 1–76

Spenser — Edmund Spenser, *The Faerie Queene*, in *The Works of Edmund Spenser*, ed. Edwin Greenlaw, Charles Grosvenor Osgood and Frederick Morgan Padelford (Baltimore, Md., 1932)

Spivack — Bernard Spivack, *Shakespeare and the Allegory of Evil* (New York, 1958)

Sprague, *Actors* — Arthur Colby Sprague, *Shakespeare and the Actors* (Cambridge, Mass., 1948)

Sprague, *Histories* — Arthur Colby Sprague, *Shakespeare's Histories: Plays for the Stage* (1964)

SQ — *Shakespeare Quarterly*

SS — *Shakespeare Survey*

SSt — *Shakespeare Studies*

STC — *A Short-title Catalogue of Books Printed in England, Scotland, and Ireland: and of English Books Printed Abroad 1475–1640*, A.W. Pollard and G.R. Redgrave, ed. W.A. Jackson, F.S. Ferguson and Katharine F. Pantzer, 3 vols (2nd rev. and enlarged edn, 1976–91)

STM — *Sir Thomas More*, ed. Vittorio Gabrieli and Georgio Melchiori (Manchester, 1990)

Stow — John Stow, *A Survey of London*, ed. C.L. Kingsford, 2 vols (Oxford, 1908)

Stříbrný — Zdenek Stříbrný, *Shakespeare and Eastern Europe* (Oxford, 2000)

Strobl — Gerwin Strobl, 'Shakespeare and the Third Reich', *History Today*, 47 (1997), 16–21

Stubbes — Philip Stubbes, *The Anatomie of Abuses* (1583; STC 23376)

Sutton & Hammond — Anne F. Sutton and P.W. Hammond (eds), *The Coronation of Richard III the Extant Documents* (Gloucester, 1983)

Tacitus, *Annals* — Cornelius Tacitus, *Complete Works of Tacitus*, trans. Alfred John Church, William Jackson Brodribb and Sara Bryant (New York, rpt. 1942)

Tarsitano — Marie Tarsitano, 'Sturua's Georgian *Richard III*', *Theatre History Studies*, 9 (1989), 69–76

Tempera — Mariangela Tempera, 'Italian responses to Shakespeare's histories', in Hoenselaars, 115–32

Theses — *Theses Martinianae* ([1589], STC 17457)

Thirty-Nine Articles	*Articles whereupon it was agreed in the . . . yeere of our Lorde God 1562 . . . for the auoyding of the diuersities of opinions, and for the stablishing of consent touching true religion* (1590)
Thomas, K.	Keith Thomas, *Religion and the Decline of Magic: Studies in Popular Beliefs in Sixteenth and Seventeenth Century England* (1971; rpt. New York, 1997)
Thomas, S., *Antic*	Sidney Thomas, *The Antic Hamlet and Richard III* (New York, 1943)
Thomas Lord Cromwell	*Thomas Lord Cromwell* [1602], in C.F. Tucker Brooke (ed.), *The Shakespeare Apocrypha* (Oxford, 1908)
Thomson	W.H. Thomson, *Shakespeare's Characters: A Historical Dictionary* (New York, 1951)
Tilley	Morris Palmer Tilley, *A Dictionary of the Proverbs in England in the Sixteenth and Seventeenth Centuries* (Ann Arbor, Mich., 1951)
Tillyard	E.M.W. Tillyard, *Shakespeare's History Plays* (1944; rpt. New York, 1946)
Toole	William B. Toole, 'The motif of psychic division in *Richard III*', *SS*, 27 (1974), 21–32
Torrey	Michael Torrey, '"The plain devil and dissembling looks": ambivalent physiognomy and Shakespeare's Richard III', *ELR*, 30 (2000), 123–53
Treatise	*A Treatise of Treasons Against Q. Elizabeth, and the Croune of England* ([Louvain], 1572, STC 7601)
TRHS	*Transactions of the Royal Historical Society*
TRKJ	*The Troublesome Raigne of John, King of England* (1591), ed. J.W. Sider (New York, 1979)
Troughton	David Troughton, 'Richard III', in Robert Smallwood (ed.), *Players of Shakespeare 4* (Cambridge, 1998), 71–100
True Tragedy	*The True Tragedy of Richard the Third, 1594*, ed. W.W. Greg (Oxford, 1929)
TxC	Stanley Wells and Gary Taylor, with John Jowett and William Montgomery, *William Shakespeare: A Textual Companion* (Oxford, 1987)
Ulrici	Hermann Ulrici, *Shakespeare's Dramatic Art*, trans. L. Dora Schmitz, 2 vols (1891; German edn 1839)
Union	Edward Hall, *The Union of the Two Noble and Illustre Families of Lancastre & Yorke* (1548; STC 12721)
Urkowitz	Steven Urkowitz, 'Reconsidering the relationship of Quarto and Folio texts of *Richard III*', *ELR*, 16 (1986), 442–66

Van Laan — Thomas F. Van Laan, *Role-playing in Shakespeare* (Toronto, 1978)

Vergil — Polydore Vergil, *Three Books of Polydore Vergil's History of England*, ed. Henry Ellis, Camden Society, vol. 29 (1844)

Vickers — Brian Vickers (ed.), *Shakespeare: The Critical Heritage*, 6 vols (London and Boston, 1974–80)

Virgil — Virgil, *The Aeneid*, ed. and trans. H. Rushton Fairclough, Loeb Classical Library, 2 vols (Cambridge, Mass., 1860)

Walker — Alice Walker, *Textual Problems of the First Folio* (Cambridge, 1953)

Walsham — Alexandra Walsham, '"Frantick Hacket": prophecy, sorcery, insanity, and the Elizabethan Puritan movement', *Historical Journal*, 41 (1998), 27–66

Walton, *Copy* — J.K. Walton, *The Copy for the Folio Text of Richard III* (Auckland, NZ, 1955)

Walton, *Quarto* — J.K. Walton, *The Quarto Copy for the First Folio of Shakespeare* (Dublin, 1971)

Watson, D.G. — Donald G. Watson, *Shakespeare's Early History Plays: Politics at Play on the Elizabethan Stage* (Athens, Ga., 1990)

Watson, R. — Robert N. Watson, *Shakespeare and the Hazards of Ambition* (Cambridge, Mass., 1984)

Watson, Thomas — Thomas Watson, *The Hekatompathia* (1582), facsimile edn, S.K. Heninger, Jr (Gainesville, Fla., 1964)

Whetstone — George Whetstone, *The English myrror* (1586; STC 25336)

Whitaker — Virgil K. Whitaker, *Shakespeare's Use of Learning: An Inquiry into the Growth of His Mind and Art* (San Marino, Calif., 1953)

Wiggins — Martin Wiggins, *Journeymen in Murder: The Assassin in English Renaissance Drama* (Oxford, 1991)

Wilks — John S. Wilks, *The Idea of Conscience in Renaissance Tragedy* (1990)

Willen — Diane Willen, 'Women and religion in early modern England', in Sherrin Marshall (ed.), *Women in Reformation and Counter-Reformation Europe* (Bloomington, Ind.,1989), 140–65

Williams — George Walton Williams, 'Scene indivisible: the battle of Birnam Wood', *Shakespeare Newsletter*, 55 (2005), 33, 36

Willis, *Nurture* — Deborah Willis, *Malevolent Nurture: Witch-Hunting and Maternal Power in Early Modern England* (Ithaca, NY, 1995)

Willis, 'Witch-hunts'	Deborah Willis, 'Shakespeare and the English witch-hunts: enclosing the maternal body', in Richard Burt and John Michael Archer (eds), *Enclosure Acts: Sexuality, Property, and Culture in Early Modern England* (Ithaca, NY, 1994), 96–120
Wilson, *2H6*	William Shakespeare, *2 Henry VI*, ed. John Dover Wilson (1952)
Wilson, *Three Ladies*	R[obert] W[ilson], *The Three Ladies of London* (1584; STC 25784)
Wilson, *Three Lords*	R[obert] W[ilson], *The Three Lords and Three Ladies of London* (1590; STC 25783)
Wing	Donald Wing (ed.), *A Short-Title Catalogue of Books Printed in England, Scotland, Ireland, Wales and British America and of English Books Printed in Other Countries 1641-1700*, 3 vols (New York, 1945–51)
Wolfit	Donald Wolfit, *First Interval* (1954)
Wood	Alice I. Perry Wood, *The Stage History of Shakespeare's King Richard the Third* (New York, 1909)
Yamada	Akihiro Yamada (ed.), *The First Folio of Shakespeare: A Transcript of Contemporary Marginalia in a Copy of the Kodama Memorial Library of Meisei University* (Tokyo, 1998)
Young	Bruce Young, 'Parental blessing in Shakespeare's plays', *Studies in Philology*, 89 (1992), 179–210

INDEX

The index covers the Introduction, the commentary notes and the Appendices; it excludes references in the textual notes and references to the OED. Page numbers in italics refer to figures. The abbreviation 'n.' is only used for footnotes in the Introduction and Appendices; it is not used for commentary notes.